THE YEAR'S WORK
IN ENGLISH STUDIES 1993

The Year's Work in English Studies

Volume 74 • 1993

Edited by

PETER J. KITSON
ELAINE TREHARNE

and

MACDONALD DALY
LIONEL KELLY
R. E. PRITCHARD
(associate editors)

Published for
THE ENGLISH ASSOCIATION

© The English Association 1996

First published 1996

Blackwell Publishers Ltd
108 Cowley Road
Oxford OX4 1JF

Blackwell Publishers Inc.
238 Main Street
Cambridge, Massachusetts 02142
USA

British Library Cataloguing in Publication Data

A CIP catalogue record for this book is
available from the British Library.

Library of Congress Cataloging-in-Publication data
has been applied for.

ISSN 0084 – 4144
ISBN 0–631–20010 X

**Typeset by Hodgson Williams Associates,
Tunbridge Wells and Cambridge**

**Printed and bound in Great Britain by
Hartnolls Limited, Bodmin, Cornwall**

This book is printed on acid-free paper

Preface

The Year's Work in English Studies is a narrative bibliography that records and evaluates scholarly writing on English language and on literature written in English. It is published by Blackwell Publishers on behalf of the English Association.

The Editors and the English Association are pleased to announce that this year's Beatrice White Prize has been awarded to Seth Lerer, for *Chaucer and His Readers: Imagining the Author in Late Medieval England* (PrincetonUP).

The authors of *YWES* attempt to cover all significant contributions to English studies. Writers of articles can assist this process by sending offprints to the journal, and editors of journals that are not readily available in the UK are urged to join the many who send us complete sets. These should be addressed to The Editor, *YWES*, The English Association, The University of Leicester, Floor 18, Attenborough Building, University Road, Leicester LE1 7RH.

Our coverage of articles and books is greatly assisted by the Modern Language Association of America, who supply proofs of their annual *International Bibliography* in advance of publication. We should like to record our gratitude for their generous co-operation.

The Editors

The English Association

This bibliography is an English Association publication. It is available through membership of the Association; non-members can purchase it through any good bookshop.

The object of the English Association is to promote the knowledge and appreciation of English language and literature.

The Association pursues these aims by creating opportunities of co-operation among all those interested in English; by furthering the recognition of English as essential in education; by discussing methods of English teaching; by holding lectures, conferences, and other meetings; by publishing a journal, books, and leaflets; and by forming local branches overseas and at home.

Publications

The Year's Work in English Studies. An annual bibliography. Published by Blackwell Publishers, Oxford and Cambridge, MA.

The Year's Work in Critical and Cultural Theory. The first issue of this new critical theory volume appeared in 1994. Published by Blackwell Publishers, Oxford and Cambridge, MA.

Essays and Studies. An annual volume of essays by various scholars assembled by the collector covering usually a wide range of subjects and authors from the medieval to the modern. Published by Boydell and Brewer, Woodbridge, Suffolk.

English. The journal of the Association, *English*, is published three times a year by the English Association.

Use of English. This journal is published three times a year by the English Association.

Primary English. This journal is published three times a year.

Benefits of Membership

Institutional Membership

Full members receive copies of *The Year's Work in English Studies, Essays and Studies, English* (three issues), and three *News-Letters*.

Ordinary Membership covers *English* (three issues) and three *News-Letters*.

Schools Membership covers one copy of each issue of *English*, one copy of *The Use of English*, one copy of *Essays and Studies*, three *News-Letters*, and preferential booking for Sixth Form Conference places.

Individual Membership

Individuals take out basic membership, which entitles them to buy all regular publications of the English Association at a discounted price and three *News-Letters*.

For further details write to The Secretary, The English Association, The University of Leicester, Floor 18, Attenborough Building, University Road, Leicester LE1 7RH.

Contents

Abbreviations

1. Journals, Series, and Reference Works

A&D	Art and Design
A&E	Anglistik und Englishunterricht
AAR	African American Review
ABäG	Amsterdamer Beiträge zur Älteren Germanistik
ABC	American Book Collector
ABELL	Annual Bibliography of English Language and Literature
ABMR	Antiquarian Book Monthly Review
ABQ	American Baptist Quarterly
ABR	American Benedictine Review
AC	Archeologia Classica
Academy Forum	Academy Forum
ACar	Analecta Cartusiana
ACH	Australian Cultural History
ACLALSB	ACLALS Bulletin
ACM	The Aligarh Critical Miscellany
ACS	Australian-Canadian Studies: A Journal for the Humanities and Social Sciences
Acta	Acta (Binghamton, N.Y.)
ADS	Australasian Drama Studies
AEB	Analytical and Enumerative Bibliography
Æstel	Æstel
AF	Anglistische Forschungen
AfricanA	African Affairs
AfrSR	The African Studies Review
AgeJ	The Age of Johnson: A Scholarly Annual
Agenda	Agenda
Agni	Agni Review
AH	Art History
AHR	The American Historical Review
AHS	Australian Historical Studies
AI	American Imago
AJ	Art Journal
AJES	The Aligarh Journal of English Studies (now The Aligarh Critical Miscellany)
AJL	Australian Journal of Linguistics
AJS	American Journal of Semiotics
AKML	Abhandlungen zur Kunst-, Musik- and Literaturwissenschaft

AL	*American Literature*
ALA	African Literature Association Annuals
ALASH	*Acta Linguistica Academiae Scientiarum Hungaricae*
AlexS	Alexander Shakespeare
ALH	*Acta Linguistica Hafniensia: International Journal of Linguistics*
ALitASH	*Acta Litteraria Academiae Scientiarum Hungaricae*
ALLCJ	*Association for Literary and Linguistic Computing Journal*
Allegorica	*Allegorica*
ALR	*American Literary Realism, 1870–1910*
ALS	*Australian Literary Studies*
ALT	*African Literature Today*
Alternatives	*Alternatives*
AmDram	*American Drama*
AmerP	*American Poetry*
AmerS	*American Studies*
AmLH	*American Literary History*
AmLS	*American Literary Scholarship: An Annual*
AMon	*The Atlantic Monthly*
AmRev	*The Americas Review: A Review of Hispanic Literature and Art of the USA*
Amst	*Amerikastudien/American Studies*
AN	*Acta Neophilologica*
Anais	*Anais*
AnBol	*Analecta Bollandiana*
ANF	*Arkiv för Nordisk Filologi*
Anglia	*Anglia: Zeitschrift für Englische Philologie*
Anglistica	Anglistica
AnH	Analecta Husserliana
AnL	*Anthropological Linguistics*
AnM	*Annuale Mediaevale*
Ann	*Annales: Economies, Sociétés, Civilisations*
ANQ	*ANQ: A Quarterly Journal of Short Articles, Notes, and Reviews* (formerly *American Notes and Queries*)
AntColl	*The Antique Collector*
AntigR	*Antigonish Review*
Antipodes	*Antipodes*
ANZSC	*Australian and New Zealand Studies in Canada*
ANZTR	*Australian and New Zealand Theatre Record*
APBR	*Atlantic Provinces Book Review*
AppLing	*Applied Linguistics*
APR	*The American Poetry Review*
AQ	*American Quarterly*
Aquarius	*Aquarius*
AR	*The Antioch Review*
ArAA	*Arbeiten aus Anglistik und Amerikanistik*
Arcadia	*Arcadia*
Archiv	*Archiv für das Studium der Neueren Sprachen und Literaturen*

ARCS	*The American Review of Canadian Studies*
ArdenS	Arden Shakespeare
ArielE	*Ariel: A Review of International English Literature*
ArQ	*Arizona Quarterly*
ARS	Augustan Reprint Society
ArtB	*Art Bulletin*
ArthI	*Arthurian Interpretations*
ArthL	*Arthurian Literature*
AS	*American Speech*
ASch	*The American Scholar*
ASE	*Anglo-Saxon England*
ASInt	*American Studies International*
ASoc	*Arts in Society*
Aspects	*Aspects: Journal of the Language Society of the University of Essex*
AspectsAF	*Aspects of Australian Fiction*
ASPR	*Anglo-Saxon Poetic Records*
ASSAH	*Anglo-Saxon Studies in Archaeology and History*
Assaph	*Assaph: Studies in the Arts (Theatre Studies)*
Assays	*Assays: Critical Approaches to Medieval and Renaissance Texts*
ASUI	*Analele Stiintifice ale Universitatii 'Al.I. Cuza' din Iasi (Serie Noua), e. Lingvistica*
ATQ	*American Transcendental Quarterly: A Journal of New England Writers*
AuBR	*Australian Book Review*
AuFL	*Australian Folklore*
AuFolk	*Australian Folklore*
AuFS	*Australian Feminist Studies*
AuJL	*Australian Journal of Linguistics*
AUMLA	*Journal of the Australasian Universities Language and Literature Association*
AuS	*Australian Studies*
AuSA	*Australian Studies* (Australia)
AusCan	*Australian–Canadian Studies*
AusPl	Australian Playwrights
AuWBR	*Australian Women's Book Review*
AvC	*Avalon to Camelot*
AY	*Arthurian Yearbook*
BakhtinN	*Bakhtin Newsletter*
BALF	*Black American Literature Forum*
BARS Bulletin & Review	(British Association for Romantic Studies) *Bulletin & Review*
BASAM	*BASA Magazine*
BathH	*Bath History*
BB	*Bulletin of Bibliography*
BBCS	*The Bulletin of the Board of Celtic Studies*
BBCSh	BBC Shakespeare
BBN	*British Book News*
BBSIA	*Bulletin Bibliographique de la Société Internationale Arthurienne*

BC	*The Book Collector*
BCan	*Books in Canada*
BCMA	*Bulletin of Cleveland Museum of Art*
BCS	*B. C. Sudies*
BDEC	*Bulletin of the Department of English* (Calcutta)
BDP	Beiträge zur Deutschen Philologie
Belfagor	*Belfagor: Rassegna di Varia Umanità*
BEPIF	*Bulletin des Etudes Portugaises et Brésiliennes*
BFLS	*Bulletin de la Faculté des Lettres de Strasbourg*
BGDSL	*Beiträge zur Geschichte der Deutschen Sprache und Literatur*
BHI	*British Humanities Index*
BHL	*Bibliotheca Hagiographica Latina Antiquae et Mediae Aetatis*
BHR	*Bibliothèque d'Humanisme et Renaissance*
BHS	*Bulletin of Hispanic Studies*
BI	*Books at Iowa*
Bibliotheck	*The Bibliotheck: A Scottish Journal of Bibliography and Allied Topics*
Biography	*Biography: An Interdisciplinary Quarterly*
BIS	*Browning Institute Studies: An Annual of Victorian Literary and Cultural History*
BJA	*British Journal of Aesthetics*
BJCS	*British Journal of Canadian Studies*
BJDC	*The British Journal of Disorders of Communication*
BJECS	*British Journal for Eighteenth-Century Studies*
BJHP	*British Journal for the History of Philosophy*
BJHS	*The British Journal for the History of Science*
BJL	*Belgian Journal of Linguistics*
BJPS	*The British Journal for the Philosophy of Science*
BJRL	*Bulletin of the John Rylands University Library of Manchester*
BJS	*British Journal of Sociology*
Blake	*Blake: An Illustrated Quarterly*
BLE	*Bulletin de Littérature Ecclésiastique*
BLJ	*The British Library Journal*
BLR	*The Bodleian Library Record*
BN	*Beiträge zur Namenforschung*
BNB	*British National Bibliography*
Boundary	*Boundary 2: A Journal of Postmodern Literature and Culture*
BP	*Banasthali Patrika*
BPMA	*Bulletin* (Philadelphia Museum of Art)
BPN	*The Barbara Pym Newsletter*
BQ	*Baptist Quarterly*
BRH	*Bulletin of Research in the Humanities*
Brick	*Brick: A Journal of Reviews*
BRMMLA	*Bulletin of the Rocky Mountain Modern Language Association*
BSANZB	*The Bibliographical Society of Australia and New Zealand Bulletin*

BSE	Brno Studies in English
BSEAA	Bulletin de la Société d'Etudes Anglo-Américaines des XVIIe et XVIIIe Siècles
BSJ	The Baker Street Journal: An Irregular Quarterly of Sherlockiana
BSLP	Bulletin de la Société de Linguistique de Paris
BSNotes	Browning Society Notes
BSRS	Bulletin of the Society for Renaissance Studies
BSSA	Bulletin de la Société de Stylistique Anglaise
BST	Brontë Society Transactions
BSUF	Ball State University Forum
BTHGNews1	Book Trade History Group Newsletter
BTLV	Bijdragen tot de Taal-, Land- en Volkenkunde
BunyanS	Bunyan Studies
BuR	Bucknell Review
BurlM	The Burlington Magazine
BurnsC	Burns Chronicle
BWPLL	Belfast Working Papers in Language and Linguistics
BWVACET	The Bulletin of the West Virginia Association of College English Teachers
ByronJ	The Byron Journal
CABS	Contemporary Authors Bibliographical Series
CahiersE	Cahiers Élisabéthains
CAIEF	Cahiers de l'Association Internationale des Études Françaises
Caliban	Caliban (Toulouse, France)
Callaloo	Callaloo
CalR	Calcutta Review
CamObsc	Camera Obscura: A Journal of Feminism and Film Theory
CamR	The Cambridge Review
CanD	Canadian Drama/L'Art Dramatique Canadienne
C&L	Christianity and Literature
C&Lang	Communication and Languages
C&M	Classica et Medievalia
CanL	Canadian Literature
CAnn	The Carlyle Annual
CanPo	Canadian Poetry
CapR	Capilano Review
CARA	Centre Aixois de Recherches Anglaises
Carib	Carib
Caribana	Caribana
CarR	Caribbean Review
Carrell	The Carrell: Journal of the Friends of the University of Miami Library
CASE	Cambridge Studies in Anglo-Saxon England
CaudaP	Cauda Pavonis
CBAA	Current Bibliography on African Affairs
CBEL	Cambridge Bibliography of English Literature
CCRev	Comparative Civilizations Review

CCrit	Comparative Criticism: An Annual Journal
CCTEP	Conference of College Teachers of English Studies
CCV	Centro de Cultura Valenciana
CD	The Critics Debate
CDALB	Concise Dictionary of American Literary Biography
CDCP	Comparative Drama Conference Papers
CdIL	Cahiers de l'Institut de Linguistique de Louvain
CdL	Cahiers de Lexicologie
CE	College English
CEA	CEA Critic
CEAfr	Cahiers d'Études Africaines
CE&S	Commonwealth Essays and Studies
CentR	The Centennial Review
Cervantes	Cervantes
CFM	Canadian Fiction Magazine
CFS	Cahiers Ferdinand de Saussure: Revue de Linguistique Générale
Chapman	Chapman
Chasqui	Chasqui
ChauR	The Chaucer Review
ChH	Church History
ChildL	Children's Literature
ChiR	Chicago Review
ChLB	Charles Lamb Bulletin
CHLSSF	Commentationes Humanarum Litterarum Societatis Scientiarum Fennicae
CHR	Camden History Review
CHum	Computers and the Humanities
CI	Critical Idiom
CILT	Amsterdam Studies in the Theory and History of the Language Sciences IV: Current Issues in Linguistic Theory
CISh	Contemporary Interpretations of Shakespeare
Cithara	Cithara: Essays in the Judaeo-Christian Tradition
CJ	Classical Journal
CJE	Cambridge Journal of Education
CJH	Canadian Journal of History
CJIS	Canadian Journal of Irish Studies
CJL	The Canadian Journal of Linguistics
CJR	Christian Jewish Relations
CL	Comparative Literature (Eugene, Oreg.)
CLAJ	CLA Journal
CLAQ	Children's Literature Association Quarterly
ClarkN	The Clark Newsletter: Bulletin of the UCLA Center for Seventeenth- and Eighteenth-Century Studies
CLC	Columbia Library Columns
ClioI	Clio: A Journal of Literature, History, and the Philosophy of History
CLQ	Colby Library Quarterly
CLS	Comparative Literature Studies

Clues	*Clues: A Journal of Detection*
CMCS	*Cambridge Medieval Celtic Studies*
CML	*Classical and Modern Literature*
CN	*Chaucer Newsletter*
CNew	*The Carlyle Newsletter*
CNIE	*Commonwealth Novel in English*
CogLing	*Cognitive Linguistics*
ColF	*Columbia Forum*
Collections	*Collections*
CollG	*Colloquia Germanica*
CollL	*College Literature*
Comitatus	*Comitatus: A Journal of Medieval and Renaissance Studies*
Commentary	*Commentary*
Commonwealth	*Commonwealth*
Comparatist	*The Comparatist: Journal of the Southern Comparative Literature Association*
CompD	*Comparative Drama*
ConL	*Contemporary Literature*
Connotations	*Connotations*
ConnR	*Connecticut Review*
Conradian	*The Conradian*
Conradiana	*Conradiana: A Journal of Joseph Conrad Studies*
ContempR	*Contemporary Review*
Cosmos	*Cosmos*
CP	*Concerning Poetry*
CQ	*The Cambridge Quarterly*
CR	*The Critical Review*
CRCL	*Canadian Review of Comparative Literature*
CRev	*The Chesterton Review*
CRevAS	*Canadian Review of American Studies*
Crit	*Critique: Studies in Modern Fiction*
CritI	*Critical Inquiry*
Criticism	*Criticism: A Quarterly for Literature and the Arts*
Critique	*Critique* (Paris)
CritQ	*Critical Quarterly*
CritT	*Critical Texts: A Review of Theory and Criticism*
CRNLE	*The CRNLE Reviews Journal*
CRUX	*CRUX: A Journal on the Teaching of English*
CS	*Critical Survey*
CSLBull	*Bulletin of the New York C. S. Lewis Society*
CSR	*Christian Scholar's Review*
CTR	*Canadian Theatre Review*
CulC	*Cultural Critique*
CulS	*Cultural Studies*
CUNY	*CUNY English Forum*
Current Writing	*Current Writing: Text and Reception in Southern Africa*
CV2	*Contemporary Verse 2*
CVE	*Cahiers Victoriens et Edouardiens*
CW	*Current Writing: Text and Perception in Southern Africa*

CWAAS	*Transactions of the Cumberland and Westmorland Antiquarian and Archaeological Society*
CWS	*Canadian Woman Studies*
DA	*Dictionary of Americanisms*
DAE	*Dictionary of American English*
DAEM	*Deutsches Archiv für Eforschung des Mittelalters*
DAI	*Dissertation Abstracts International*
DAL	*Descriptive and Applied Linguistics*
D&S	*Discourse and Society*
Daphnis	*Daphnis: Zeitschrift für Mittlere Deutsche Literatur*
DC	The Dickens Companions
DerbyM	*Derbyshire Miscellany*
Descant	*Descant*
DHLR	*The D. H. Lawrence Review*
DHS	*Dix-Huitième Siècle*
Diac	*Diacritics*
Diachronica	*Diachronica*
Dialogue	*Dialogue: Canadian Philosophical Review*
Dickensian	*The Dickensian*
DicS	*Dickinson Studies*
Dictionaries	*Dictionaries: Journal of the Dictionary Society of North America*
Dionysos	*Dionysos*
Discourse	*Discourse*
DLB	Dictionary of Literary Biography
DLN	*Doris Lessing Newsletter*
DM	*The Dublin Magazine*
DMT	Durham Medieval Texts
DNB	*Dictionary of National Biography*
DOE	*Dictionary of Old English*
Dolphin	*The Dolphin: Publications of the English Department, University of Aarhus*
DOST	*Dictionary of the Older Scottish Tongue*
DownR	*The Downside Review*
DPr	*Discourse Processes*
DQ	*Denver Quarterly*
DQR	*Dutch Quarterly Review of Anglo-American Letters*
DQu	*Dickens Quarterly*
DR	*Dalhousie Review*
Drama	*Drama: The Quarterly Theatre Review*
DrS	*Dreiser Studies*
DSA	*Dickens Studies Annual*
DU	*Der Deutschunterricht: Beiträge zu Seiner Praxis und Wissenschaftlichen Grundlegung*
DUJ	*Durham University Journal*
DVLG	*Deutsche Vierteljahrsschrift für Literaturwissenschaft und Geistesgeschichte*
DWPELL	*Dutch Working Papers in English Language and Linguistics*
EA	*Études Anglaises*
EAL	*Early American Literature*

E&D	Enlightenment and Dissent
E&S	Essays and Studies
E&Soc	Economy and Society
EAS	Essays in Arts and Sciences
ESt	Englisch Amerikanische Studien
EC	Études Celtiques
ECan	Etudes Canadiennes/Canadian Studies
ECCB	Eighteenth Century: A Current Bibliography
ECent	The Eighteenth Century: Theory and Interpretation
ECF	Eighteenth-Century Fiction
ECI	Eighteenth-Century Ireland
ECLife	Eighteenth Century Life
ECon	L'Epoque Conradienne
ECr	L'Esprit Créateur
ECS	Eighteenth-Century Studies
ECW	Essays on Canadian Writing
EDAMN	The EDAM Newsletter
EDH	Essays by Divers Hands
EdL	Études de Lettres
EdN	Editors' Notes: Bulletin of the Conference of Editors of Learned Journals
EDSL	Encyclopedic Dictionary of the Sciences of Language
EEMF	Early English Manuscripts in Facsimile
EHR	The English Historical Review
EI	Études Irlandaises (Lille)
EIC	Essays in Criticism
EinA	English in Africa
EiP	Essays in Poetics
EIRC	Explorations in Renaissance Culture
Éire	Éire-Ireland
EiTET	Essays in Theatre/Etudes Théâtrales
EJ	English Journal
ELangT	ELT Journal: An International Journal for Teachers of English to Speakers of Other Languages
ELet	Esperienze Letterarie: Rivista Trimestrale di Critica e Cultura
ELH	Journal of English Literary History
ELN	English Language Notes
ELR	English Literary Renaissance
ELS	English Literary Studies
ELT	English Literature in Transition
ELWIU	Essays in Literature (Western Illinois Univ.)
EM	English Miscellany
Embl	Emblematica: An Interdisciplinary Journal of English Studies
EMS	English Manuscript Studies, 1100–1700
EMu	Early Music
Encyclia	Encyclia
English	English: The Journal of the English Association
EnT	English Today: The International Review of the English Language

EONR	*The Eugene O'Neill Review*
EPD	*English Pronouncing Dictionary*
ER	*English Review*
ERR	*European Romantic Review*
ES	*English Studies*
ESA	*English Studies in Africa*
ESC	*English Studies in Canada*
ESQ	*ESQ: A Journal of the American Renaissance*
ESRS	*Emporia State Research Studies*
EssaysMedSt	*Essays in Medieval Studies*
ESTC	*Eighteenth Century Short Title Catalogue*
EWIP	*Edinburgh University, Department of Linguistics, Work in Progress*
EWN	*Evelyn Waugh Newsletter*
EWPAL	*Edinburgh Working Papers in Applied Linguistics*
EWW	*English World-Wide*
Exemplaria	*Exemplaria*
Expl	*The Explicator*
Extrapolation	*Extrapolation: A Journal of Science Fiction and Fantasy*
FCEMN	*Mystics Quarterly* (formerly *Fourteenth-Century English Mystics Newsletter*)
FCS	*Fifteenth-Century Studies*
FDT	Fountainwell Drama Texts
FemR	*Feminist Review*
FH	*Die Neue Gesellschaft/Frankfurter Hefte*
Fiction International	*Fiction International*
FJS	*Fu Jen Studies: Literature and Linguistics* (Taipei)
FLH	*Folia Linguistica Historica*
Florilegium	*Florilegium: Carleton University Annual Papers on Classical Antiquity and the Middle Ages*
FMLS	*Forum for Modern Language Studies*
FNS	Frank Norris Studies
Folklore	*Folklore*
FoLi	*Folia Linguistica*
Forum	*Forum*
FranS	*Franciscan Studies*
FreeA	*Free Associations*
Frontiers	*Frontiers: A Journal of Women Studies*
FS	*French Studies*
FSt	*Feminist Studies*
Futures	*Futures*
GAG	Göppinger Arbeiten zur Germanistik
GaR	*Georgia Review*
GEFR	*George Eliot Fellowship Review*
GEGHL	*George Eliot–George Henry Lewes Newsletter*
GeM	*Genealogists' Magazine*
Genders	*Genders*
Genre	*Genre*
GER	*George Eliot Review*

Gestus	*Gestus: A Quarterly Journal of Brechtian Studies*
Gettysburg Review	*Gettysburg Review*
GHJ	*George Herbert Journal*
GissingJ	*The Gissing Journal*
GJ	*Gutenberg-Jahrbuch*
GL	*General Linguistics*
GL&L	*German Life and Letters*
GlasR	*The Glasgow Review*
Glossa	*Glossa: An International Journal of Linguistics*
GLS	*Grazer Linguistische Studien*
GR	*The Germanic Review*
Gramma	*Gramma: Journal of Theory and Criticism*
GrandS	*Grand Street*
Granta	*Granta*
Greyfriar	*Greyfriar: Siena Studies in Literature*
GRM	*Germanisch-Romanische Monatsschrift*
GSE	Gothenberg Studies in English
GSJ	*The Gaskell Society Journal*
GURT	*Georgetown University Round Table on Language and Linguistics*
H&T	*History and Theory*
Harvard Law Review	*Harvard Law Review*
HatcherR	*Hatcher Review*
HBS	Henry Bradshaw Society
HC	*The Hollins Critic*
HE	*History of Education*
Hecate	*Hecate: An Interdisciplinary Journal of Women's Liberation*
HEdQ	*History of Education Quarterly*
HEI	*History Of European Ideas*
HeineJ	*Heine Jahrbuch*
HEL	*Histoire Épistémologie Langage*
Helios	*Helios*
Hermathena	*Hermathena: A Trinity College Dublin Review*
HeyJ	*The Heythrop Journal*
HistJ	*The Historical Journal*
HistR	*Historical Research*
History	*History: The Journal of the Historical Association*
HJR	*The Henry James Review* (Baton Rouge, La.)
HL	*Historiographia Linguistica*
HBL	*Harvard Library Bulletin*
HLQ	*The Huntington Library Quarterly*
HNCIS	Harvester New Critical Introductions to Shakespeare
HNR	Harvester New Readings
HOPE	*History of Political Economy*
HPT	*History of Political Thought*
HQ	*Hopkins Quarterly*
HRB	*Hopkins Research Bulletin*
HSci	*History of Science*
HSE	*Hungarian Studies in English*

HSELL	Hiroshima Studies in English Language and Literature
HSJ	Housman Society Journal
HSL	University of Hartford Studies in Literature
HSN	Hawthorne Society Newsletter
HSSh	Hungarian Studies in Shakespeare
HSSN	The Henry Sweet Society Newsletter
HSt	Hamlet Studies
HT	History Today
HTR	Harvard Theological Review
HudR	Hudson Review
HumeS	Hume Studies
HumLov	Humanistica Lovaniensia: Journal of Neo-Latin Studies
HUSL	Hebrew University Studies in Literature and the Arts
HWJ	History Workshop
HWS	History Workshop Series
IAN	Izvestiia Akademii Nauk S.S.S.R. (Moscow)
I&C	Ideology and Consciousness
I&P	Ideas and Production
ICS	Illinois Classical Studies
IEEETrans	IEEE Transactions on Professional Communications
IF	Indogermanische Forschungen
IFR	The International Fiction Review
IGK	Irland: Gesellschaft und Kultur
IJAL	International Journal of Applied Linguistics
IJECS	Indian Journal for Eighteenth Century Studies
IJES	Indian Journal of English Studies
IJPR	International Journal for the Philosophy of Religion
IJSL	International Journal of the Sociology of Language
IJSS	Indian Journal of Shakespeare Studies
IJWS	International Journal of Women's Studies
ILR	The Indian Literary Review
ILS	Irish Literary Supplement
IMB	International Medieval Bibliography
Indexer	Indexer
IndH	Indian Horizons
IndL	Indian Literature
InG	In Geardagum: Essays on Old and Middle English Language and Literature
Inklings	Inklings: Jahrbuch für Literatur und Ästhetik
Inquiry	Inquiry: An Interdisciplinary Journal of Philosophy
Interlink	Interlink
Interpretation	Interpretation
IowaR	The Iowa Review
IRAL	IRAL: International Review of Applied Linguistics in Language Teaching
IS	Italian Studies
ISh	The Independent Shavian
ISJR	Iowa State Journal of Research
Island	Island Magazine
Islands	Islands

IUR	*Irish University Review: A Journal of Irish Studies*
JAAC	*Journal of Aesthetics and Art Criticism*
JAAR	*Journal of the American Academy of Religion*
JAF	*The Journal of American Folklore*
JAfM	*Journal of African Marxists*
JAIS	*Journal of Anglo-Italian Studies*
JAL	*Journal of Australian Literature*
JAmC	*Journal of American Culture*
JAMS	*Journal of the American Musicological Society*
JAmS	*Journal of American Studies*
JArabL	*Journal of Arabic Literature*
JAS	*Journal of Australian Studies*
JBeckS	*Journal of Beckett Studies*
JBS	*Journal of British Studies*
JCAKSU	*Journal of the College of Arts, King Saud University*
JCanL	*Journal of Canadian Literature*
JCC	*Journal of Canadian Culture*
JCF	*Journal of Canadian Fiction*
JChL	*Journal of Child Language*
JCL	*The Journal of Commonwealth Literature*
JCP	*Journal of Canadian Poetry*
JCPCS	*Journal of Commonwealth and Postcolonial Studies*
JCSJ	*The John Clare Society Journal*
JCSR	*Journal of Canadian Studies/Revue d'Etudes Canadiennes*
JCSt	*Journal of Caribbean Studies*
JDECU	*Journal of the Department of English (University of Calcutta)*
JDHLS	*D. H. Lawrence: The Journal of the D. H. Lawrence Society*
JDJ	*John Donne Journal*
JDN	*James Dickey Newsletter*
JDTC	*Journal of Dramatic Theory and Criticism*
JEDRBU	*Journal of the English Department, Rabindra Bharati University*
JEGP	*Journal of English and Germanic Philology*
JEH	*The Journal of Ecclesiastical History*
JELL	*Journal of English Language and Literature*
JEn	*Journal of English* (Sana'a Univ.)
JEngL	*Journal of English Linguistics*
JENS	*Journal of the Eighteen Nineties Society*
JEP	*Journal of Evolutionary Psychology*
JEPNS	*Journal of the English Place-Name Society*
JES	*Journal of European Studies*
JETS	*Journal of the Evangelical Theological Society*
JFR	*Journal of Folklore Research*
JGE	*JGE: The Journal of General Education*
JGH	*Journal of Garden History*
JGN	*The John Gower Newsletter*
JH	*Journal of Homosexuality*

JHI	*Journal of the History of Ideas*
JHLP	*Journal of Historical Linguistics and Philology*
JHP	*Journal of the History of Philosophy*
JHSex	*Journal of the History of Sexuality*
JIES	*The Journal of Indo-European Studies*
JIL	*Journal of Irish Literature*
JIPA	*Journal of the International Phonetic Association*
JIWE	*Journal of Indian Writing in English*
JJ	*Jamaica Journal*
JJA	*James Joyce Annual*
JJB	*James Joyce Broadsheet*
JJLS	*James Joyce Literary Supplement*
JJQ	*James Joyce Quarterly*
JL	*Journal of Linguistics*
JLH	*The Journal of Library History, Philosophy and Comparative Librarianship*
JLP	*Journal of Linguistics and Politics*
JLS	*Journal of Literary Semantics*
JLVSG	*Journal of the Loughborough Victorian Studies Group*
JMemL	*Journal of Memory and Language*
JMGS	*Journal of Modern Greek Studies*
JMH	*Journal of Medieval History*
JML	*Journal of Modern Literature*
JMMD	*Journal of Multilingual and Multicultural Development*
JMMLA	*Journal of the Midwest Modern Language Association*
JModH	*Journal of Modern History*
JMRS	*Journal of Medieval and Renaissance Studies*
JNLH	*Journal of Narrative and Life History*
JNPH	*Journal of Newspaper and Periodical History*
JNT	*Journal of Narrative Technique*
JNZL	*Journal of New Zealand Literature*
JoyceSA	*Joyce Studies Annual*
JP	*The Journal of Philosophy*
JPC	*Journal of Popular Culture*
JPCL	*Journal of Pidgin and Creole Languages*
JPhon	*Journal of Phonetics*
JPJ	*Journal of Psychology and Judaism*
JPrag	*Journal of Pragmatics*
JPRAS	*Journal of Pre-Raphaelite and Aesthetic Studies*
JPsyR	*Journal of Psycholinguistic Research*
JQ	*Journalism Quarterly*
JR	*Journal of Religion*
JRH	*The Journal of Religious History*
JRMMRA	*Journal of the Rocky Mountain Medieval and Renaissance Association*
JRSA	*Journal of the Royal Society of Arts*
JRUL	*Journal of the Rutgers University Libraries*
JSA	*Journal of the Society of Archivists*
JSaga	*Journal of the Faculty of Liberal Arts and Science, Saga University*

JSAS	*Journal of Southern African Studies*
JSSE	*Journal of the Short Story in English*
JTheoS	*The Journal of Theological Studies*
JWCI	*Journal of the Warburg and Courtauld Institutes*
JWIL	*Journal of West Indian Literature*
JWMS	*The Journal of the William Morris Society*
JWSL	*Journal of Women's Studies in Literature*
KanQ	*Kansas Quarterly*
KB	*Kavya Bharati*
KCLMS	King's College London Medieval Series
KJ	*The Kipling Journal*
KN	*Kwartalnik Neofilologiczny* (Warsaw)
KompH	*Komparatistische Hefte*
KPAB	*Kentucky Philological Association Bulletin*
KR	*Kenyon Review*
KSJ	*Keats–Shelley Journal*
KSR	*Keats–Shelley Review*
Kuka	*Kuka: Journal of Creative and Critical Writing* (Zaria, Nigeria)
Kunapipi	*Kunapipi*
KWS	*Key-Word Studies in Chaucer*
L&B	*Literature and Belief*
L&C	*Language and Communication*
Landfall	*Landfall: A New Zealand Quarterly*
L&H	*Literature and History*
L&L	*Language and Literature*
L&LC	*Literary and Linguistic Computing*
L&M	*Literature and Medicine*
L&P	*Literature and Psychology*
L&S	*Language and Speech*
L&T	*Literature and Theology: An Interdisciplinary Journal of Theory and Criticism*
L&U	*The Lion and the Unicorn: A Critical Journal of Children's Literature*
LangF	*Language Forum*
Language	*Language: Journal of the Linguistic Society of America*
Lang&S	*Language and Style*
LangQ	*USF Language Quarterly*
LangR	*Language Research*
LangS	*Language Sciences*
LanM	*Les Langues Modernes*
LB	*Leuvense Bijdragen*
LBR	*Luso-Brazilian Review*
LCrit	*The Literary Criterion* (Mysore, India)
LCUT	*The Library Chronicle of the University of Texas at Austin*
LDOCE	Longman Dictionary of Contemporary English
LeedsSE	*Leeds Studies in English*
Legacy	*Legacy: A Journal of Nineteenth-Century American Women Writers*

LeS	Lingua e Stile
Lexicographica	Lexicographica: International Annual for Lexicography
Lexicography	Lexicography
LFQ	Literature/Film Quarterly
LH	Library History
LHY	The Literary Half-Yearly
Library	The Library
LibrQ	The Library Quarterly
LIN	Linguistics in the Netherlands
LingA	Linguistic Analysis
Ling&P	Linguistics and Philosophy
Ling&Philol.	Linguistics and Philology
LingB	Linguistische Berichte
LingI	Linguistic Inquiry
LingInv	Linvisticæ Investigationes
LingP	Linguistica Pragensia
Lingua	Lingua: International Review of General Linguistics
Linguistics	Linguistics
Linguistique	La Linguistique
LiNQ	Literature in Northern Queensland
LIT	LIT: Literature, Interpretation, Theory
LitH	Literary Horizons
LitR	The Literary Review: An International Journal of Contemporary Writing
LittPrag	Litteraria Pragensia: Studies in Literature and Culture
LJGG	Literaturwissenschaftliches Jahrbuch im Auftrage der Görres-Gesellschaft
LJHum	Lamar Journal of the Humanities
LMag	London Magazine
LockeN	The Locke Newsletter
LongR	Long Room: Bulletin of the Friends of the Library, Trinity College, Dublin
Lore&L	Lore and Language
LP	Lingua Posnaniensis
LPLD	Liverpool Papers in Language and Discourse
LPLP	Language Problems and Language Planning
LR	Les Lettres Romanes
LRB	London Review of Books
LSE	Lund Studies in English
LSLD	Liverpool Studies in Language and Discourse
LSoc	Language in Society
LST	Longman Study Texts
LTM	Leeds Texts and Monographs
LTP	LTP: Journal of Literature Teaching Politics
LTR	London Theatre Record
LuK	Literatur und Kritik
LVC	Language Variation and Change
LWU	Literatur in Wissenschaft und Unterricht
MÆ	Medium Ævum
MAEL	Macmillan Anthologies of English Literature

Mana	*Mana*
M&H	*Medievalia et Humanistica*
M&L	*Music and Letters*
M&N	*Man and Nature/L'Homme et la Nature: Proceedings of the Canadian Society for Eighteenth-Century Studies*
Manuscripta	*Manuscripta*
MAR	*Mid-American Review*
MarkhamR	*Markham Review*
Matatu	*Matatu*
Matrix	*Matrix*
MBL	*Modern British Literature*
MC&S	*Media, Culture and Society*
MCI	Modern Critical Interpretations
MCJNews	*Milton Centre of Japan News*
McNR	*McNeese Review*
MCRel	*Mythes, Croyances et Religions dans le Monde Anglo-Saxon*
MCV	Modern Critical Views
MD	*Modern Drama*
Meanjin	*Meanjin*
MED	*Middle English Dictionary*
Mediaevalia	*Mediaevalia: A Journal of Mediaeval Studies*
MedPers	*Medieval Perspectives*
Melus	*MELUS: The Journal of the Society of Multi-Ethnic Literature of the United States*
Meridian	*Meridian*
MESN	*Mediaeval English Studies Newsletter*
MET	Middle English Texts
METh	*Medieval English Theatre*
MFN	*Medieval Feminist Newsletter*
MFS	*Modern Fiction Studies*
MHL	Macmillan History of Literature
MHLS	*Mid-Hudson Language Studies*
MHRev	*The Malahat Review*
MichA	*Michigan Academician*
MiltonQ	*Milton Quarterly*
MiltonS	*Milton Studies*
MinnR	*Minnesota Review*
MissQ	*Mississippi Quarterly*
MissR	*The Missouri Review*
MJLF	*Midwestern Journal of Language and Folklore*
MLAIB	*Modern Language Association International Bibliography*
MLJ	*The Modern Language Journal*
MLN	*[Modern Language Notes]*
MLNew	*Malcolm Lowry Review*
MLQ	*Modern Language Quarterly*
MLR	*The Modern Language Review*
MLS	*Modern Language Studies*
MMD	Macmillan Modern Dramatists

MMG	Macmillan Master Guides
MMisc	*Midwestern Miscellany*
MOCS	*Magazine of Cultural Studies*
ModA	*Modern Age: A Quarterly Review*
ModM	Modern Masters
ModSp	*Moderne Sprachen*
Monist	*The Monist*
MonSP	*Monash Swift Papers*
Month	*The Month: A Review Of Christian Thought and World Affairs*
MOR	*Mount Olive Review*
Moreana	*Moreana: Bulletin Thomas More* (Angers, France)
Mosaic	*Mosaic: A Journal for the Interdisciplinary Study of Literature*
MP	*Modern Philology*
MPHJ	*Middlesex Polytechnic History Journal*
MPR	*The Mervyn Peake Review*
MQ	*Midwest Quarterly*
MQR	*Michigan Quarterly Review*
MR	*Massachusetts Review*
MRDE	*Medieval and Renaissance Drama in England*
MRTS	Medieval and Renaissance Texts and Studies
MS	*Mediaeval Studies*
MSC	Malone Society Collections
MSE	*Massachusetts Studies in English*
MSex	*Melville Society Extracts*
MSh	Macmillan Shakespeare
MSNH	Mémoires de la Société Néophilologique de Helsinki
MSpr	*Moderna Språk*
MSR	*Malone Society Reprints*
MSSN	*Medieval Sermon Studies Newsletter*
MT	*The Musical Times*
MTJ	*Mark Twain Journal*
MusR	*Music Review*
MW	*The Muslim World* (Hartford, Conn.)
MysticsQ	*Mystics Quarterly*
Mythlore	*Mythlore: A Journal of J. R. R. Tolkien, C. S. Lewis, Charles Williams, and the Genres of Myth and Fantasy Studies*
NA	*Nuova Antologia*
Names	*Names: Journal of the American Name Society*
N&F	*Notes & Furphies*
N&Q	*Notes and Queries*
Narrative	*Narrative*
Navasilu	*Navasilu*
NB	*Namn och Bygd*
NCaS	New Cambridge Shakespeare
NCBEL	*New Cambridge Bibliography of English Literature*
NCC	*Nineteenth-Century Contexts*
NCL	*Nineteenth-Century Literature*

NConL	*Notes on Contemporary Literature*
NCP	*Nineteenth Century Prose*
NCS	New Clarendon Shakespeare
NCT	*Nineteenth Century Theatre*
NDQ	*North Dakota Quarterly*
NegroD	*Negro Digest*
NELS	*North Eastern Linguistic Society*
Neoh	*Neohelicon*
Neophil	*Neophilologus*
NEQ	*The New England Quarterly*
NERMS	*New England Review*
NewA	*New African*
NewBR	*New Beacon Review*
NewC	*The New Criterion*
NewComp	*New Comparison: A Journal of Comparative and General Literary Studies*
NewF	*New Formations*
NewR	*New Republic*
NewSt	*Newfoundland Studies*
NewV	*New Voices*
NF	*Neophilologica Fennica*
NfN	*News from Nowhere*
NGC	*New German Critique*
NGS	*New German Studies*
NH	*Northern History*
NHR	*The Nathaniel Hawthorne Review*
NJL	*Nordic Journal of Linguistics*
NL	*Nouvelles Littéraires*
NL&LT	*Natural Language and Linguistic Theory*
NLH	*New Literary History: A Journal of Theory and Interpretation*
NLitsR	*New Literatures Review*
NLR	*New Left Review*
NLWJ	*The National Library of Wales Journal*
NM	*Neuphilologische Mitteilungen*
NMAL	*NMAL: Notes on Modern American Literature*
NMer	New Mermaids
NMIL	*Notes on Modern Irish Literature*
NMS	*Nottingham Medieval Studies*
NMW	*Notes on Mississippi Writers*
NN	*Nordiska Namenstudier*
NNER	*Northern New England Review*
Nomina	*Nomina: A Journal of Name Studies Relating to Great Britain and Ireland*
NoP	*Northern Perspective*
NOR	*New Orleans Review*
NortonCE	A Norton Critical Edition
Novel	*Novel: A Forum on Fiction*
NOWELE	*North-Western European Language Evolution*
NPS	New Penguin Shakespeare

NR	*The Nassau Review*
NRF	*La Nouvelle Revue Française*
NRRS	*Notes and Records of the Royal Society of London*
NS	*Die Neueren Sprachen*
NSS	New Swan Shakespeare
NTQ	*New Theatre Quarterly*
NVSAWC	*Newsletter of the Victorian Studies Association of Western Canada*
NwJ	*Northward Journal*
NWR	*Northwest Review*
NWRev	*The New Welsh Review*
NYH	*New York History*
NYLF	New York Literary Forum
NYRB	*The New York Review of Books*
NYT	*New York Times*
NYTBR	*The New York Times Book Review*
NZListener	*New Zealand Listener*
OA	Oxford Authors
OB	*Ord och Bild*
Obsidian	*Obsidian II: Black Literature in Review*
OBSP	Oxford Bibliographical Society Publications
OED	*Oxford English Dictionary*
OENews	*Old English Newsletter*
OET	Oxford English Texts
OH	*Over Here: An American Studies Journal*
OHEL	Oxford History of English Literature
OhR	*The Ohio Review*
OL	*Orbis Litterarum*
OLR	*Oxford Literary Review*
OPBS	Occasional Papers of the Bibliographical Society
OpenGL	Open Guides to Literature
OpL	*Open Letter*
OPLiLL	*Occasional Papers in Linguistics and Language Learning*
OPSL	*Occasional Papers in Systemic Linguistics*
OralT	*Oral Tradition*
Orbis	*Orbis*
OS	Oxford Shakespeare
OSS	Oxford Shakespeare Studies
OT	*Oral Tradition*
Outrider	*The Outrider: A Publication of the Wyoming State Library*
Overland	*Overland*
PA	*Présence Africaine*
PAAS	*Proceedings of the American Antiquarian Society*
PacStud	*Pacific Studies*
Paideuma	*Paideuma: A Journal Devoted to Ezra Pound Scholarship*
P&C	*Pragmatics and Cognition*
P&L	*Philosophy and Literature*

P&P	*Past and Present*
P&R	*Philosophy and Rhetoric*
P&SC	*Philosophy and Social Criticism*
PAPA	*Publications of the Arkansas Philological Association*
PAPS	*Proceedings of the American Philosophical Society*
PAR	*Performing Arts Resources*
Parabola	*Parabola: The Magazine of Myth and Tradition*
Paragraph	*Paragraph: The Journal of the Modern Critical Theory Group*
Parergon	*Parergon: Bulletin of the Australian and New Zealand Association for Medieval and Renaissance Studies*
ParisR	*The Paris Review*
Parnassus	*Parnassus: Poetry in Review*
PastM	Past Masters
PaterN	*Pater Newsletter*
PAus	*Poetry Australia*
PBA	*Proceedings of the British Academy*
PBerLS	*Proceedings of the Berkeley Linguistics Society*
PBSA	*Papers of the Bibliographical Society of America*
PBSC	*Papers of the Biographical Society of Canada*
PCL	*Perspectives on Contemporary Literature*
PCLAC	*Proceedings of the California Linguistics Association Conference*
PCLS	Proceedings of the Comparative Literature Symposium (Lubbock, Tex.)
PCP	*Pacific Coast Philology*
PCS	Penguin Critical Studies
PEAN	*Proceedings of the English Association North*
PE&W	*Philosophy East and West: A Quarterly of Asian and Comparative Thought*
PELL	*Papers on English Language and Literature* (Japana)
Performance	*Performance*
Peritia	*Peritia: Journal of the Medieval Academy of Ireland*
Persuasions	*Persuasions: Journal of the Jane Austen Society of North America*
Philosophy	*Philosophy*
PHist	*Printing History*
Phonetica	*Phonetica: International Journal of Speech Science*
PHOS	Publishing History Occasional Series
PhRA	*Philosophical Research Archives*
PhT	*Philosophy Today*
PIL	*Papers in Linguistics*
PIMA	*Proceedings of the Illinois Medieval Association*
PinterR	*Pinter Review*
PJCL	*The Prairie Journal of Canadian Literature*
PLL	*Papers on Language and Literature*
PLPLS	*Proceedings of the Leeds Philosophical and Literary Society, Literary and Historical Section*
PM	Penguin Masterstudies
PMHB	*Pennsylvania Magazine of History and Biography*

PMLA	Publications of the Modern Language Association of America
PNotes	Pynchon Notes
PNR	PN Review
PoeS	Poe Studies
Poetica	Poetica: Zeitschrift für Sprach- und Literaturwissenschaft (Amsterdam)
PoeticaJ	Poetica: An International Journal of Linguistic-Literary Studies (Tokyo)
Poetics	Poetics: International Review for the Theory of Literature
Poétique	Poétique: Revue de Théorie et d'Analyse Littéraires
PoetryCR	Poetry Canada Review
PoetryR	Poetry Review
PoetryW	Poetry Wales
POMPA	Publications of the Mississippi Philological Association
PostS	Post Script: Essays in Film and the Humanities
PoT	Poetics Today
PP	Penguin Passnotes
PP	Philologica Pragensia
PPMRC	Proceedings of the International Patristic, Mediaeval and Renaissance Conference
PPR	Philosophy and Phenomenological Research
PQ	Philological Quarterly
PQM	Pacific Quarterly (Moana)
PR	Partisan Review
Pragmatics	Pragmatics: Quarterly Publication of the International Pragmatics Association
PrairieF	Prairie Fire
Praxis	Praxis: A Journal of Cultural Criticism
Prépub	(Pré)publications
PRev	The Powys Review
PRIA	Proceedings of the Royal Irish Academy
PRIAA	Publications of the Research Institute of the Åbo Akademi Foundation
PRMCLS	Papers from the Regional Meetings of the Chicago Linguistics Society
Prospects	Prospects: An Annual Journal of American Cultural Studies
Proteus	Proteus: A Journal of Ideas
Proverbium	Proverbium
PrS	The Prairie Schooner
PSt	Prose Studies
PsychR	Psychological Reports
PTBI	Publications of the Sir Thomas Browne Institute
PubH	Publishing History
PULC	Princeton Univeristy Library Chronicle
PURBA	Panjab University Research Bulletin (Arts)
PVR	Platte Valley Review
PY	Phonology Yearbook

QI	*Quaderni d'Italianistica*
QJS	*Quarterly Journal of Speech*
QLing	*Quantitative Linguistics*
QQ	*Queen's Quarterly*
Quadrant	*Quadrant* (Sydney)
Quarendo	*Quarendo*
Quarry	*Quarry*
RadP	*Radical Philosophy*
RAL	*Research in African Literatures*
RALS	*Resources for American Literary Study*
Ramus	*Ramus: Critical Studies in Greek and Roman Literature*
R&L	*Religion and Literature*
Raritan	*Raritan: A Quarterly Review*
RB	*Revue Bénédictine*
RBPH	*Revue Belge de Philologie et d'Histoire*
RCEI	*Revista Canaria de Estudios Ingleses*
RCF	*Review of Contemporary Fiction*
RDN	*Renaissance Drama Newsletter*
RE	*Revue d'Esthétique*
ReAL	*Re: Artes Liberales*
REALB	*REAL: The Yearbook of Research in English and American Literature* (Berlin)
RECTR	*Restoration and Eighteenth-Century Theatre Research*
RedL	*Red Letters: A Journal of Cultural Politics*
REED	Records of Early English Drama
REEDN	*Records of Early English Drama Newsletter*
Reinardus	*Reinardus*
REL	*Review of English Literature* (Kyoto)
Ren&R	*Renaissance and Reformation*
Renascence	*Renascence: Essays on Value in Literature*
RenD	*Renaissance Drama*
RenP	*Renaissance Papers*
RenQ	*Renaissance Quarterly*
Rep	*Representations*
RES	*The Review of English Studies*
Restoration	*Restoration: Studies in English Literary Culture, 1660–1700*
Rev	*Review* (Blacksburg, Va.)
RevAli	*Revista Alicantina de Estudios Ingleses*
Revels	Revels Plays
RevelsCL	Revels Plays Companion Library
RFEA	*Revue Française d'Etudes Américaines*
RFR	*Robert Frost Review*
RH	*Recusant History*
Rhetorica	*Rhetorica: A Journal of the History of Rhetoric*
Rhetorik	*Rhetorik: Ein Internationales Jahrbuch*
RHist	*Rural History*
RHL	*Revue d'Histoire Littéraire de la France*
RHT	*Revue d'Histoire du Théâtre*
Ricardian	*The Ricardian: Journal of the Richard III Society*

RL	Rereading Literature
RLC	Revue de Littérature Comparée
RLM	La Revue des Lettres Modernes: Histoire des Idées des Littératures
RLMC	Rivista di Letterature Moderne e Comparate
RLT	Russian Literature Triquarterly
RM	Rethinking Marxism
RMR	Rocky Mountain Review of Language and Literature
RMS	Renaissance and Modern Studies
RMSt	Reading Medieval Studies
RomN	Romance Notes
RomQ	Romance Quarterly
RomS	Romance Studies
ROO	Room of One's Own: A Feminist Journal of Literature and Criticism
RORD	Research Opportunities in Renaissance Drama
RPT	Russian Poetics in Translation
RQ	Riverside Quarterly
RR	Romanic Review
RRDS	Regents Renaissance Drama Series
RRestDS	Regents Restoration Drama Series
RS	Renaissance Studies
RSQ	Rhetoric Society Quarterly
RUO	Revue de l'Université d'Ottawa
RuskN	Ruskin Newsletter
RUUL	Reports from the Uppsala University Department of Linguistics
SAC	Studies in the Age of Chaucer
SAD	Studies in American Drama, 1945–Present
SAF	Studies in American Fiction
Saga-Book	Saga-Book (Viking Society for Northern Research)
Sagetrieb	Sagetrieb: A Journal Devoted to Poets in the Pound–H.D.–Williams Tradition
SAJL	Studies in American Jewish Literature
Sal	Salmagundi: A Quarterly of the Humanities and Social Sciences
S&S	Sight and Sound
SAntS	Studia Anthroponymica Scandinavica
SAP	Studia Anglica Posnaniensia
SAQ	South Atlantic Quarterly
SAR	Studies in the American Renaissance
SARB	South African Review of Books
SatR	Saturday Review
SB	Studies in Bibliography
SBHC	Studies in Browning and His Circle
SC	The Seventeenth Century
Scan	Scandinavica: An International Journal of Scandinavian Studies
ScanS	Scandinavian Studies
SCel	Studia Celtica

SCER	*Society for Critical Exchange Report*
SCJ	*The Sixteenth Century Journal*
SCL	*Studies in Canadian Literature*
ScLJ	*Scottish Literary Journal: A Review of Studies in Scottish Language and Literature*
ScLJ(S)	*Scottish Literary Journal Supplement*
SCN	*Seventeenth-Century News*
ScottN	*Scott Newsletter*
SCR	*The South Carolina Review*
Screen	*Screen* (London)
SCRev	*South Central Review*
Scriblerian	*The Scriblerian and the Kit Cats: A Newsjournal Devoted to Pope, Swift, and Their Circle*
Scripsi	*Scripsi*
Scriptorium	*Scriptorium: International Review of Manuscript Studies*
SD	*Social Dynamics*
SDR	*South Dakota Review*
SECC	*Studies in Eighteenth-Century Culture*
SECOLB	*The SECOL Review: Southeastern Conference on Linguistics*
SED	*Survey of English Dialects*
SEEJ	*Slavic and East European Journal*
SEL	Studies in English Literature
SEL	*Studies in English Literature 1500–1900* (Rice Univ.)
SELing	*Studies in English Linguistics* (Tokyo)
SELit	*Studies in English Literature* (Tokyo)
SELL	*Studies in English Language and Literature*
Sem	*Semiotica: Journal of the International Association for Semiotic Studies*
Semiosis	*Semiosis: Internationale Zeitschrift für Semiotik und Ästhetik*
SER	*Studien zur Englischen Romantik*
Seven	*Seven: An Anglo-American Literary Review*
SF&R	Scholars' Facsimiles and Reprints
SFic	*Science Fiction: A Review of Speculative Literature*
SFNL	*Shakespeare on Film Newsletter*
SFQ	*Southern Folklore Quarterly*
SFR	*Stanford French Review*
SFS	*Science-Fiction Studies*
SH	*Studia Hibernica* (Dublin)
ShakB	*Shakespeare Bulletin*
ShakS	*Shakespeare Studies* (New York)
Sh&Sch	*Shakespeare and Schools*
ShawR	*Shaw: The Annual of Bernard Shaw Studies*
Shenandoah	*Shenandoah*
Shiron	*Shiron*
ShJE	*Shakespeare Jahrbuch* (Weimar)
ShJW	*Deutsche Shakespeare-Gesellschaft West Jahrbuch* (Bochum)

ShLR	*Shoin Literary Review*
ShN	*The Shakespeare Newsletter*
SHR	*Southern Humanities Review*
ShS	*Shakespeare Survey*
ShSA	*Shakespeare in Southern Africa*
ShStud	*Shakespeare Studies* (Tokyo)
SHW	*Studies in Hogg and his World*
ShY	*Shakespeare Yearbook*
SIcon	*Studies in Iconography*
Signs	*Signs: Journal of Women in Culture and Society*
SiHoLS	Studies in the History of the Language Sciences
SiM	*Studies in Medievalism*
SIM	*Studies in Music*
SiP	Shakespeare in Performance
SIR	*Studies in Romanticism*
SJS	*San José Studies*
SL	*Studia Linguistica*
SLang	*Studies in Language*
SLCS	Studies in Language Companion Series
SLitI	*Studies in the Literary Imagination*
SLJ	*Southern Literary Journal*
SLRev	*Stanford Literature Review*
SLSc	*Studies in the Linguistic Sciences*
SMC	Studies in Medieval Culture
SMed	*Studi Medievali*
SMELL	*Studies in Medieval English Language and Literature*
SMLit	*Studies in Mystical Literature* (Taiwan)
SMRH	*Studies in Medieval and Renaissance History*
SMS	*Studier i Modern Språkvetenskap*
SMy	*Studia Mystica*
SN	*Studia Neophilologica*
SNew	*Sidney Newletter*
SNNTS	*Studies in the Novel* (North Texas State Univ.)
SOÅ	*Sydsvenska Ortnamnssällskapets Årsskrift*
SoAR	*South Atlantic Review*
Sociocrit	*Sociocriticism*
SocN	*Sociolinguistics*
SocT	*Social Text*
SohoB	Soho Bibliographies
SoQ	*The Southern Quarterly*
SoR	*The Southern Review* (Baton Rouge, La.)
SoRA	*Southern Review* (Adelaide)
SoSt	*Southern Studies: An Interdisciplinary Journal of the South*
Soundings	*Soundings: An Interdisciplinary Journal*
Southerly	*Southerly: A Review of Australian Literature*
SovL	*Soviet Literature*
SP	*Studies in Philology*
SPAN	*SPAN: Newsletter of the South Pacific Association for Commonwealth Literature and Language Studies*

SPAS	*Studies in Puritan American Spirituality*
SPC	*Studies in Popular Culture*
Spectrum	*Spectrum*
Speculum	*Speculum: A Journal of Medieval Studies*
SPELL	Swiss Papers in English Language and Literature
SphereHL	Sphere History of Literature
Sphinx	*The Sphinx: A Magazine of Literature and Society*
SpM	*Spicilegio Moderno*
SpNL	*Spenser Newsletter*
Sprachwiss	*Sprachwissenschaft*
SpringE	*Spring: The Journal of the E E Cummings Society*
SPub	*Studies in Publishing*
SPWVSRA	*Selected Papers from the West Virginia Shakespeare and Renaissance Association*
SQ	*Shakespeare Quarterly*
SR	*The Sewanee Review*
SRen	*Studies in the Renaissance*
SRSR	*Status Report on Speech Research* (Haskins Laboratories)
SSEL	Stockholm Studies in English
SSELER	Salzburg Studies in English Literature: Elizabethan and Renaissance
SSELJDS	Salzburg Studies in English Literature: Jacobean Drama Studies
SSELPDPT	Salzburg Studies in English Literature: Poetic Drama and Poetic Theory
SSELRR	Salzburg Studies in English Literature: Romantic Reassessment
SSEng	*Sydney Studies in English*
SSF	*Studies in Short Fiction*
SSL	*Studies in Scottish Literature*
SSt	*Spenser Studies*
SStud	*Swift Studies: The Annual of the Ehrenpreis Center*
Staffrider	*Staffrider*
STAH	*Strange Things Are Happening*
STC	*Short-Title Catalogue*
STGM	Studien und Texte zur Geistegeschichte des Mittelalters
StHum	*Studies in the Humanities*
StIn	*Studi Inglesi*
StLF	*Studi di Letteratura Francese*
StQ	*Steinbeck Quarterly*
StrR	*Structuralist Review*
StTCL	*Studies in Twentieth Century Literature*
Style	*Style* (De Kalb, Ill.)
SUAS	Stratford-upon-Avon Studies
SubStance	*SubStance: A Review of Theory and Literary Criticism*
SUS	*Susquehanna University Studies*
SussexAC	*Sussex Archaeological Collections*
SVEC	*Studies on Voltaire and the Eighteenth Century*
SWPLL	*Sheffield Working Papers in Language and Linguistics*

SWR	Southwest Review
SwR	The Swansea Review: A Journal of Criticism
TA	Theatre Annual
Tabu	Bulletin voor Taalwetenschap, Groningen
Talisman	Talisman
T&C	Text and Context
T&L	Translation and Literature
T&P	Text and Performance
TAPS	Transactions of the American Philosophical Society
TCBS	Transactions of the Cambridge Bibliographical Society
TCE	Texas College English
TCL	Twentieth Century Literature
TCS	Theory, Culture and Society: Explorations in Critical Social Science
TD	Themes in Drama
TDR	The Drama Review
TEAS	Twayne's English Authors Series
TEBS	Edinburgh Bibliographical Society Transactions
Telos	Telos: A Quarterly Journal of Post-Critical Thought
TenEJ	Tennessee English Journal
Te Reo	Te Reo: Journal of the Linguistic Society of New Zealand
TexasSLL	Texas Studies in Language and Literature
Text	Text: Transactions of the Society for Textual Scholarship
TH	Texas Humanist
THA	Thomas Hardy Annual
Thalia	Thalia: Studies in Literary Humor
ThC	Theatre Crafts
Theater	Theater
TheatreS	Theatre Studies
Theoria	Theoria: A Journal of Studies in the Arts, Humanities and Social Sciences (Natal)
THES	The Times Higher Education Supplement
Thesis	Thesis Eleven
THIC	Theatre History in Canada
THJ	The Thomas Hardy Journal
ThN	Thackeray Newsletter
ThoreauQ	The Thoreau Quarterly: A Journal of Literary and Philosophical Studies
Thought	Thought: A Review of Culture and Ideas
Thph	Theatrephile
ThreR	The Threepenny Review
ThS	Theatre Survey: The American Journal of Theatre History
THSLC	Transactions of the Historic Society of Lancashire and Cheshire
THStud	Theatre History Studies
THY	The Thomas Hardy Yearbook
TiLSM	Trends in Linguistics Studies and Monographs

TJ	*Theatre Journal*
TJS	*Transactions* (The Johnson Society)
TkR	*Tamkang Review*
TL	*Theoretical Linguistics*
TLR	*The Linguistic Review*
TLS	*TLS: The Times Literary Supplement*
TMLT	Toronto Medieval Latin Texts
TN	*Theatre Notebook*
TNWSECS	*Transactions of the North West Society for Eighteenth-Century Studies*
TP	*Terzo Programma*
TPLL	*Tilbury Papers in Language and Literature*
TPr	*Textual Practice*
TPS	*Transactions of the Philological Society*
Traditio	*Traditio: Studies in Ancient and Medieval History, Thought, and Religion*
Transition	*Transition*
TRB	*The Tennyson Research Bulletin*
TRHS	*Transactions of the Royal Historical Society*
TRI	*Theatre Research International*
TriQ	*TriQuarterly*
Trivium	*Trivium*
Tropismes	*Tropismes*
TSAR	*The Toronto South Asian Review*
TSB	*Thoreau Society Bulletin*
TSL	*Tennessee Studies in Literature*
TSLang	Typological Studies in Language
TSLL	*Texas Studies in Literature and Language*
TSWL	*Tulsa Studies in Women's Literature*
TTR	*Trinidad and Tobago Review*
TUSAS	Twayne's United States Authors Series
TWAS	Twayne's World Authors Series
TWBR	*Third World Book Review*
TWQ	*Third World Quarterly*
TWR	*The Thomas Wolfe Review*
TYDS	*Transactions of the Yorkshire Dialect Society*
UCrow	*The Upstart Crow*
UCTSE	*University of Cape Town Studies in English*
UCWPL	UCL Working Papers in Linguistics
UDR	*University of Dayton Review*
UE	*The Use of English*
UEAPL	*UEA Papers in Linguistics*
UES	*Unisa English Studies*
Ufahamu	*Ufahamu*
ULR	*University of Leeds Review*
UMSE	*University of Mississippi Studies in English*
Untold	*Untold*
UOQ	*University of Ottawa Quarterly*
URM	*Ultimate Reality and Meaning: Interdisciplinary Studies in the Philosophy of Understanding*

USSE	*University of Saga Studies in English*
UTQ	*University of Toronto Quarterly*
UWR	*The University of Windsor Review*
VCT	Les Voies de la Création Théâtrale
VEAW	Varieties of English around the World
Verbatim	*Verbatim: The Language Quarterly*
VIA	*VIA: The Journal of the Graduate School of Fine Arts, University of Pennsylvania*
Viator	*Viator: Medieval and Renaissance Studies*
Views	*Viennese English Working Papers*
VIJ	*Victorians Institute Journal*
VLC	*Victorian Literature and Culture*
VN	*Victorian Newsletter*
Voices	*Voices*
VP	*Victorian Poetry*
VPR	*Victorian Periodicals Review*
VQR	*The Virginia Quarterly Review*
VR	*Victorian Review*
VS	*Victorian Studies*
VSB	*Victorian Studies Bulletin*
VWM	*Virginia Woolf Miscellany*
WAJ	*Women's Art Journal*
WAL	*Western American Literature*
W&I	*Word and Image*
W&L	*Women and Literature*
W&Lang	*Women and Language*
Wasafiri	*Wasafiri*
WascanaR	*Wascana Review*
WBEP	Wiener Beiträge zur Englischen Philologie
WC	World's Classics
WC	*The Wordsworth Circle*
WCR	*West Coast Review*
WCSJ	*Wilkie Collins Society Journal*
WCWR	*The William Carlos Williams Review*
Wellsian	*The Wellsian: The Journal of the H. G. Wells Society*
WEn	*World Englishes*
Westerly	*Westerly: A Quarterly Review*
WestHR	*West Hills Review: A Walt Whitman Journal*
WF	*Western Folklore*
WHASN	*W H Auden Society Newsletter*
WHR	*Western Humanities Review*
WLT	*World Literature Today*
WLWE	*World Literature Written in English*
WMQ	*The William and Mary Quarterly*
WoHR	*Women's History Review*
WolfenbüttelerB	*Wolfenbüttele Beiträge: Aus den Schätzen der Herzog August Bibliothek*
Women	*Women: a cultural review*
WorcesterR	*Worcester Review*
Word	*WORD: Journal of the International Linguistic Association*

WQ	*The Wilson Quarterly*
WRB	*Women's Review of Books*
WS	*Women's Studies: An Interdisciplinary Journal*
WSIF	*Women's Studies International Forum*
WSJour	*The Wallace Stevens Journal*
WTJ	*The Westminster Theological Journal*
WTW	Writers and Their Work
WVUPP	*West Virginia University Philological Papers*
WWR	*Walt Whitman Quarterly Review*
XUS	*Xavier Review*
YCC	*Yearbook of Comparative Criticism*
YeA	*Yeats Annual*
YER	*Yeats Eliot Review*
YES	*The Yearbook of English Studies*
YEuS	*Yearbook of European Studies/Annuaire d'Etudes Européenes*
YFS	*Yale French Studies*
Yiddish	*Yiddish*
YJC	*The Yale Journal of Criticism: Interpretation in the Humanities*
YLS	*Yearbook of Langland Studies*
YM	*Yearbook of Morphology*
YNS	York Note Series
YPL	*York Papers in Linguistics*
YR	*The Yale Review*
YULG	*Yale University Library Gazette*
YWES	*The Year's Work in English Studies*
ZAA	*Zeitschrift für Anglistik und Amerikanistik*
ZCP	*Zeitschrift für Celtische Philologie*
ZDA	*Zeitschrift für Deutsches Altertum und Deutsche Literatur*
ZDL	*Zeitschrift für Dialektologie und Linguistik*
ZGKS	*Zeitschrift der Gesellschaft für Kanada-Studien*
ZGL	*Zeitschrift für Germanistische Linguistik*
ZPSK	*Zeitschrift für Phonetik, Sprachwissenschaft und Kommunikationsforschung*
ZSpr	*Zeitschrift für Sprachwissenschaft*
ZVS	*Zeitschrift für Vergleichende Sprachforschung*

Volume numbers are supplied in the text, as are individual issue numbers for journals that are not continuously paginated through the year.

2. Publishers

AAAH	Acta Academiae Åboensis Humaniora, Åbo, Finland
AAH	Australian Academy of Humanities
A&B	Allison & Busby, London
A&R	Angus & Robertson, North Ryde, N.S.W.
A&U	Allen & Unwin (now Unwin Hyman)
A&UA	Allen & Unwin, North Sydney, N.S.W.
A&W	Almqvist & Wiksell International, Stockholm
AarhusUP	Aarhus UP, Aarhus, Denmark
Abbeville	Abbeville Press, New York
ABC	ABC Enterprises
ABDO	Association Bourguignonne de Dialectologie et d'Onomastique, Dijon
AberdeenUP	Aberdeen UP, Aberdeen
Abhinav	Abhinav Pubns, New Delhi
Abingdon	Abingdon Press, Nashville, Tenn.
ABL	Armstrong Browning Library, Waco, Texas
Ablex	Ablex Pub., Norwood, N.J.
Åbo	Åbo Akademi, Åbo, Finland
Abrams	Harry N. Abrams, New York
Academic	Academic Press, London and Orlando, Fla.
Academy	The Academy Press, Dublin
AcademyC	Academy Chicago Pubs., Chicago
AcademyE	Academy Editions, London
Acadiensis	Acadiensis Press, Fredericton, New Brunswick, Canada
ACarS	Association for Caribbean Studies, Coral Gables, Fla.
ACC	Antique Collectors' Club, Woodbridge, Suffolk
ACCO	ACCO, Leuven, Belgium
ACP	Another Chicago Press, Chicago
ACS	Association for Canadian Studies, Ottawa
Adam Hart	Adam Hart Publishers Ltd, London
Addison-Wesley	Addison-Wesley, Wokingham, Berks.
Adosa	Adosa, Clermont-Ferrand, France
AEMS	American Early Medieval Studies
AF	Akademisk Forlag, Copenhagen
Affiliated	Affiliated East-West Press, New Delhi
AFP	Associated Faculty Press, New York
Africana	Africana Pub., New York
A-H	Arnold-Heinemann, New Delhi
Ahriman	Ahriman-Verlag, Freiburg im Breisgau, Germany
AIAS	Australian Institute of Aboriginal Studies, Canberra
Ajanta	Ajanta Pubns, Delhi
AK	Akadémiai Kiadó, Budapest
Al&Ba	Allyn & Bacon, Boston, Mass.
Albatross	Albatross
Albion	Albion, Appalachian State Univ., Boone, N.C.
Alderman	Alderman Press, London
AligarhMU	Aligarh Muslim Univ., Uttar Pradesh, India
Alioth	Alioth Press, Beaverton, Oreg.

Allen	W. H. Allen, London
Allied Publishers	Allied Indian Publishers, Lahore
Almond	Almond Press, Sheffield
AM	Aubier Montaigne, Paris
AMAES	Association des Médiévistes Angliciste de l'Enseignement Supérieur, Paris
Amate	The Amate Press, Oxford
AmberL	Amber Lane, Oxford
AMP	Aurora Metro Press, London
AMS	AMS Press, New York
Amsterdam	Amsterdam
AMU	Adam Mickiewicz Univ., Posnan
Anansi	Anansi Press, Toronto
Anma Libri	Anma Libri, Saratoga, Calif.
Antipodes	Antipodes Press, Plimmerton, New Zealand
Anvil	Anvil Press Poetry, London
APA	APA, Maarssen, Netherlands
APH	Associated Pub. House, New Delhi
APL	American Poetry and Literature Press, Philadelphia
APP	Australian Professional Pubns, Mosman, N.S.W.
Appletree	Appletree Press, Belfast
APS	American Philosophical Society, Philadelphia
Aquarian	The Aquarian Press, Wellingborough, Northants.
ArborH	Arbor House Pub., New York
Archon	Archon Books, Hamden Conn.
ArchP	Architectural Press Books, Guildford, Surrey
Ardis	Ardis Pubs., Ann Arbor, Mich.
Ariel	Ariel Press, London
Ark	Ark Paperbacks, London
Arkona	Arkona Forlaget, Aarhus, Denmark
Arlington	Arlington Books, London
Arnold	Edward Arnold, London
ArnoldEJ	E. J. Arnold & Son, Leeds
ARP	Australian Reference Pubns, N. Balwyn, Vic.
ARRC	No details
Arrow	Arrow Books, London
Artmoves	Artmoves, Parkdale, Victoria
ASB	Anglo-Saxon Books, Middlesex
ASECS	American Society for Eighteenth-Century Studies, c/o Ohio State Univ. Columbus
AshfieldP	Ashfield Press, London
Ashton	Ashton Scholastic
Aslib	Aslib, London
ASLS	Association for Scottish Literary Studies, Aberdeen
ASU	Arizona State Univ., Tempe
Atheneum	Atheneum Pubs., New York
Athlone	Athlone Press, London
Atlas	Atlas Press, London
Attic	Attic Press, Dublin
AucklandUP	Auckland UP, Auckland

AUG	Acta Universitatis Gothoburgensis, Sweden
AUP	Associated Univ. Presses, London and Toronto
AUPG	Academic & Univ. Pubs. Group, London
Aurum	Aurum Press, London
AUU	Acta Universitatis Umensis, Umeå, Sweden
AUUp	Acta Universitatis Upsaliensis, Uppsala
Avebury	Avebury Pub., Aldershot, Hampshire
Avero	Avero Pubns, Newcastle upon Tyne
A-V Verlag	A-V Verlag, Franz Fischer, Augsburg, Germany
AWP	Africa World Press, Trenton, N.J.
BA	British Academy, London
BAAS	British Association for American Studies, c/o Univ. of Keele
Bagel	August Bagel Verlag, Düsseldorf
Bahri	Bahri Pubns, New Delhi
Bamberger	Bamberger Books, Flint, Mich.
B&B	Boydell & Brewer, Woodbridge, Suffolk
B&J	Barrie & Jenkins, London
B&N	Barnes & Noble, Totowa, N.J.
B&O	Burns & Oates, Tunbridge Wells, Kent
B&S	Michael Benskin and M. L. Samuels, Middle English Dialect Project, Univ. of Edinburgh
BAR	British Archaeological Reports, Oxford
Barn Owl	Barn Owl Books, Taunton, Somerset
Barnes	A. S. Barnes, San Diego, Calif.
BathUP	Bath UP, Bath
Batsford	B. T. Batsford, London
BBC	BBC Pubns, London
BClarkL	Bruccoli Clark Layman
BCP	Bristol Classical Press, Bristol
Beacon	Beacon Press, Boston, Mass.
Beck	C. H. Beck'sche Verlagsbuchandlung, Munich
Becket	Becket Pubns, London
Belin	Editions Belin, Paris
Belknap	Belknap Press, Cambridge, Mass.
Belles Lettres	Société d'Edition les Belles Lettres, Paris
Bellew	Bellew Pub., London
Bellflower	Bellflower Press, Case Univ., Cleveland, Ohio
Benjamins	John Benjamins, Amsterdam
BenjaminsNA	John Benjamins North America, Philadelphia
BennC	Bennington College, Bennington, Vt.
Berg	Berg Pubns., Oxford
BFI	British Film Institute, London
BGUP	Bowling Green Univ. Popular Press, Bowling Green, Ohio
BibS	Bibliographical Society, London
Bilingual	Bilingual Press, Arizona State Univ., Tempe
Bingley	Clive Bingley, London
Binnacle	Binnacle Press, London
Biografia	Biografia Pubs., London

Birkbeck	Birkbeck College, University of London
Bishopsgate	Bishopsgate Press, Tonbridge, Kent
BL	British Library, London
Black	Adam & Charles Black, London
Black Cat	Black Cat Press, Blackrock, Eire
Blackie	Blackie & Son, Glasgow
Black Moss	Black Moss, Windsor, Ont.
Blackstaff	Blackstaff Press, Belfast
Blackwell	Basil Blackwell, Oxford
BlackwellR	Blackwell Reference, Oxford
Blackwood	Blackwood, Pillans & Wilson, Edinburgh
Bl&Br	Blond & Briggs, London
Blandford	Blandford Press, London
Blaue Eule	Verlag die Blaue Eule, Essen
Bloodaxe	Bloodaxe Books, Newcastle upon Tyne
Bloomsbury	Bloomsbury Pub., London
BM	Bobbs-Merrill, New York
BMP	British Museum Pubns, London
Bodleian	The Bodleian Library, Oxford
Bodley	The Bodley Head, London
Bogle	Bogle L'Ouverture Pubns, London
BoiseSUP	Boise State UP, Boise, Idaho
Book Guild	The Book Guild, Lewes, E.Sussex
Borealis	Borealis Press, Ottawa
Borgo	Borgo Press, San Bernardino, Calif.
BostonAL	Boston Athenaeum Library, Boston, Mass.
Bouma	Bouma's Boekhuis, Groningen, Netherlands
Bowker	R. R. Bowker, New Providence, N.J.
Boyars	Marion Boyars, London and Boston, Mass.
Boydell	The Boydell Press, Woodbridge, Suffolk
Boyes	Megan Boyes, Allestree, Derbyshire
Bran's Head	Bran's Head Books, Frome, Somerset
Braumüller	Wilhelm Braumüller, Vienna
Breakwater	Breakwater Books, St John's, Newfoundland
Brentham	Brentham Press, St Alban's, Herts.
Brepols	Brepols, Turnhout, Belgium
Brewer	D. S. Brewer, Woodbridge, Suffolk
Brewin	Brewin Books, Studley, War.
Bridge	Bridge Pub., S. Plainfield, N.J.
Brill	E. J. Brill, Leiden
Brilliance	Brilliance Books, London
Broadview	Broadview, London, Ont. and Lewiston, N.Y.
Bookside	Brookside Press, London
Browne	Sinclair Browne, London
Brownstone	Brownstone Books, Madison, Ind.
BrownUP	Brown UP, Providence, R.I.
Brynmill	Brynmill Press, Harleston, Norfolk
BSA	Bibliographical Society of America
BSB	Black Swan Books, Redding Ridge, Conn.
BSP	Black Sparrow Press, Santa Barbara, Calif.

BSU	Ball State Univ., Muncie, Ind.
BuckUP	Bucknell UP, Lewisburg, Pa.
Bulzoni	Bulzoni Editore, Rome
Burnett	Burnett Books, London
Buske	Helmut Buske, Hamburg
Butterfly	Butterfly
CA	Creative Arts Book Co., Berkeley, Calif.
CAAS	Connecticut Academy of Arts and Sciences, New Haven
Cadmus	Cadmus Editions, Tiburon, Calif.
Cairns	Francis Cairns, Univ. of Leeds
Calaloux	Calaloux Pubns, Ithaca, N.Y.
Calder	John Calder, London
CALLS	Centre for Australian Language and Literature Studies, English Department, UNewE, N.S.W.
Camden	Camden Press, London
C&G	Carroll & Graf, New York
C&W	Chatto & Windus, London
Canongate	Canongate Pub., Edinburgh
Canterbury	Canterbury Press, Norwich
Cape	Jonathan Cape, London
Capra	Capra Press, Santa Barbara, Calif.
Carcanet	The Carcanet New Press, Manchester, Lancs.
Cardinal	Cardinal, London
CaribB	Caribbean Books, Parkersburg, Iowa
CarletonUP	Carleton UP, Ottawa
Carucci	Carucci, Rome
Cass	Frank Cass, London
Cassell	Cassell, London
Cavaliere Azzurro	Cavaliere Azzurro, Bologna
Cave	Godfrey Cave Associates, London
CBA	Council for British Archaeology, London
CBS	Cambridge Bibliographical Society, Cambridge
CCP	Canadian Children's Press, Guelph, Ont.
CCS	Centre for Canadian Studies, Mount Allison Univ., Sackville, N.B.
CDSH	Centre de Documentation Sciences Humaines, Paris
Century	Century Pub., London
Ceolfrith	Ceolfrith Press, Sunderland, Tyne and Wear
CESR	Société des Amis du Centre d'Etudes Superieures de la Renaissance, Tours
CFA	Canadian Federation for the Humanities, Ottawa
CH	Croom Helm, London
C-H	Chadwyck-Healey, Cambridge
Chambers	W. & R. Chambers, Edinburgh
Champaign	Champaign Public Library and Information Center, Champaign, Ill.
Champion	Librairie Honoré Champion, Paris
Chand	S. Chand, Madras
ChelseaH	Chelsea House Pubs., New York, New Haven, and Philadelphia

Children's Lit. Association	Children's Literature Association
Christendom	Christendom Pubns, Front Royal, Va.
Chronicle	Chronicle Books, London
Chrysalis	Chrysalis Press
ChuoUL	Chuo Univ. Library, Tokyo
Churchman	Churchman Pub., Worthing, W. Sussex
Cistercian	Cistercian Pubns, Kalamazoo, Mich.
CL	City Lights Books, San Francisco
CLA	Canadian Library Association, Ottawa
Clarendon	Clarendon Press, Oxford
Claridge	Claridge, St Albans, Herts.
Clarion	Clarion State College, Clarion, Pa.
Clark	T. & T. Clark, Edinburgh
Clarke	James Clarke, Cambridge
Classical	Classical Pub., New Delhi
CLCS	Centre for Language and Communication Studies, Trinity College, Dublin
ClogherHS	Clogher Historical Society, Monaghan, Eire
Clunie	Clunie Press, Pitlochry, Tayside
CMAP	Caxton's Modern Arts Press, Dallas, Tx.
CMERS	Center for Medieval and Early Renaissance Studies, Binghamton, N.Y.
CML	William Andrews Clark Memorial Library, Los Angeles
CMST	Centre for Medieval Studies, Univ. of Toronto
Coach House	Coach House Press, Toronto
Colleagues	Colleagues Press, East Lansing, Mich.
Collector	The Collector Ltd, London
College-Hill	College-Hill Press, San Diego, Calif.
Collins	William Collins Sons, London
CollinsA	William Collins (Australia), Sydney
Collins & Brown	Collins & Brown, London
ColUP	Columbia UP, New York
Comedia	Comedia Pub. Group, London
Comet	Comet Books, London
Compton	The Compton Press, Tisbury, Wilts.
Constable	Constable, London
Contemporary	Contemporary Books, Chicago
Continuum	Continuum Pub., New York
Copp	Copp Clark Pitman, Mississuaga, Ontario, Canada
Corgi	Corgi Books, London
CorkUP	Cork UP, Cork, Eire
Cormorant	Cormorant Press, Victoria, B.C.
CornUP	Cornell UP, Ithaca, N.Y.
Cornwallis	The Cornwallis Press, Hastings, E. Sussex
Coronado	Coronado Press, Lawrence, Kansas
Cosmo	Cosmo Pubns, New Delhi
Coteau	Coteau Books, Regina, Saskatchewan, Canada
Cowley	Cowley Pubns, Cambridge, Mass.
Cowper	Cowper House, Pacific Grove, Calif.

CPP	Canadian Poetry Press, London, Ont.
Crabtree	Crabtree Press, Sussex
Cresset	Cresset Library, London
CRNLE	Centre for Research in the New Literatures in English, Adelaide
Crossing	The Crossing Press, Freedom Calif.
Crossroad	Crossroad Pub., New York
Crown	Crown Pubs., New York
Crowood	The Crowood Press, Marlborough, Wilts.
CSAL	Centre for Studies in Australian Literature, Univ. of Western Australia, Nedlands
CSLI	Center for the Study of Language and Information, Stanford Univ.
CSU	Cleveland State Univ., Cleveland, Ohio
CTHS	Editions du Comité des Travaux Historiques et Scientifiques, Paris
CUAP	Catholic Univ. of America Press, Washington, D.C.
Cuff	Harry Cuff Pubns, St John's, Newfoundland
CULouvain	Catholic Univ. of Louvain, Louvain, Belgium
CULublin	Catholic Univ. of Lublin, Poland
CUP	Cambridge UP, Cambridge, New York, and Melbourne
Currency	Currency Pres, Paddington, N.S.W.
Currey	James Currey, London
CV	Cherry Valley Editions, Rochester, N.Y.
CVK	Cornelson-Velhagen & Klasing, Berlin
CWU	Carl Winter Universitätsverlag, Heidelberg
Da Capo	Da Capo Press, New York
Dacorum	Dacorum College, Hemel Hempstead, Herts.
Daisy	Daisy Books, Peterborough, Northants.
Dalkey	Dalkey Archive Press, Elmwood Park, Ill.
D&C	David & Charles, Newton Abbot, Devon
D&H	Duncker and Humblot, Berlin
D&M	Douglas & McIntyre, Vancouver, B.C.
Dangaroo	Dangaroo Press, Mundelstrup, Denmark
Dawson	Dawson Publishing, Folkestone, Kent
DBP	Drama Book Pubs., New York
De Boeck	De Boeck-Wesmael, Brussels
Dee	Dee
De Graaf	De Graaf, Nierwkoup, Netherlands
Denoël	Denoël S.A.R.L., Paris
Dent	J. M. Dent, London
DentA	Dent, Ferntree Gully, Vic., Australia
Depanee	Depanee Printers and Pubs., Nugegoda, Sri Lanka
Deutsch	André Deutsch, London
Didier	Didier Erudition, Paris
Diesterweg	Verlag Moritz Diesterweg, Frankfurt-on-Main
Dim Gray Bar Press	Dim Gray Bar Press
Doaba	Doaba House, Delhi
Dobson	Dobson Books, Durham
Dolmen	Dolmen Press, Portlaoise, Eire

Donald	John Donald, Edinburgh
Donker	Adriaan Donker, Johannesburg
Dorset	Dorset Publishing Company
Doubleday	Doubleday, London and New York
Dove	Dove, Sydney
Dovecote	Dovecote
Dovehouse	Dovehouse Editions, Canada
Dover	Dover Pubns, New York
Drew	Richard Drew, Edinburgh
Droste	Droste Verlag, Düsseldorf
Droz	Librairie Droz S.A., Geneva
DublinUP	Dublin UP, Dublin
Duckworth	Gerald Duckworth, London
Duculot	J. Duculot, Gembloux, Belgium
DukeUP	Duke UP, Durham, N.C.
Dundurn	Dundurn Press, Toronto and London, Ont.
Duquesne	Duquesne UP, Pittsburgh
Dutton	E. P. Dutton, New York
DWT	Dr Williams's Trust, London
EA	The English Association, London
Eason	Eason & Son, Dublin
East Bay	East Bay Books, Berkeley, Calif.
Ebony	Ebony Books, Melbourne
Ecco	Ecco Press, New York
ECNRS	Editions du Centre National de la Recherche Scientifique, Paris
ECW	ECW Press, Downsview, Ont.
Eden	Eden Press, Montreal and St Albans, Vt.
EdinUP	Edinburgh UP, Edinburgh
Eerdmans	William Eerdmans, Grand Rapids, Mich.
EETS	Early English Text Society, c/o Exeter College, Oxford
Elephas	Elephas Books, Kewdale, Australia
Elm Tree	Elm Tree Books, London
ELS	English Literary Studies
Ember	Ember Press, Brixham, South Devon
EMSH	Editions de la Maison des Sciences de l'Homme, Paris
Enitharmon	Enitharmon Press, London
Enzyklopädie	Enzyklopädie, Leipzig
EONF	The Eugene O'Neill Foundation, Danville, Calif.
EPNS	English Place-Name Society, Beeston, Notts.
Epworth	The Epworth Press, Manchester
Eriksson	Paul Eriksson, Middlebury, Vt.
Erlbaum	Erlbaum Associates, NJ
Erskine	Erskine Press, Harleston, Norfolk
ESI	Edizioni Scientifiche Italiane, Naples
ESL	Edizioni di Storia e Letteratura, Rome
EUFS	Editions Universitaires Fribourg Suisse
EUL	Edinburgh Univ. Library, Edinburgh
Europa	Europa Pubns, London
Exile	Exile Editions, Toronto, Ont.

Eyre	Eyre Methuen, London
FAB	Free Association Books, London
Faber	Faber & Faber, London
FAC	Fédération d'Activités Culturelles, Paris
FACP	Fremantle Arts Centre Press, Fremantle, W. A.
FALS	Foundation for Australian Literary Studies, James Cook Univ. of North Queensland, Townsville
F&F	Fels & Firn Press, San Anselmo, Calif.
F&S	Feffer & Simons, Amsterdam
Farrand	Farrand Press, London
Fay	Barbara Fay, Stuttgart
F-B	Ford-Brown, Houston, Texas
FDUP	Fairleigh Dickinson UP, Madison, N.J.
FE	Fourth Estate, London
Feminist	Feminist Press, New York
FictionColl	Fiction Collective, Brooklyn College, Brooklyn, N.Y.
Field Day	Field Day, Derry
Fifth House	Fifth House Publications, Saskatoon, Saskatchewan, Canada
FILEF	FILEF Italo-Australian Pubns, Leichhardt, N.S.W.
Fine	Donald Fine, New York
Fink	Fink Verlag, Munich
Flamingo	Flamingo
Flammarion	Flammarion, Paris
FlindersU	Flinders Univ. of South Australia, Bedford Park
FlorSU	Florida State Univ., Tallahassee, Fla.
FOF	Facts on File, New York
Folger	The Folger Shakespeare Library, Washington, D.C.
Folio	Folio Press, London
Fontana	Fontana Press, London
Footprint	Footprint Press, Colchester, Essex
FordUP	Fordham UP, New York
Foris	Foris Pubns, Dordrecht
Forsten	Egbert Forsten Pub., Groningen, Netherlands
Fortress	Fortress Press, Philadelphia
Francke	Francke Verlag, Berne
Franklin	Burt Franklin, New York
FreeP	Free Press, New York
FreeUP	Free UP, Amsterdam
Freundlich	Freundlich Books, New York
Frommann-Holzboog	Frommann-Holzboog, Stuttgart
FSP	Five Seasons Press, Madley, Hereford
FW	Fragments West/Valentine Press, Long Beach, Calif.
FWA	Fiji Writers' Association, Suva
FWP	Falling Wall Press, Bristol
Gale	Gale Research, Detroit, Mich.
Galilée	Galilée, Paris
Gallimard	Gallimard, Paris
G&G	Grevatt & Grevatt, Newcastle upon Tyne
G&M	Gill & Macmillan, Dublin

Garland	Garland Pub., New York
Gasson	Roy Gasson Associates, Wimborne, Dorset
Gateway	Gateway Editions, Washington, D.C.
Girasole	Edizioni del Girasole, Ravenna
GL	Goose Lane Editions, Fredericton, N.B.
GlasgowDL	Glasgow District Libraries, Glasgow
Gleerup	Gleerupska, Lund
Gliddon	Gliddon Books Pubs., Norwich
Gloger	Gloger Family Books, Portland, Oregon
GMP	GMP Pub., London
GMSmith	Gibbs M. Smith, Layton, Utah
Golden Dog	The Golden Dog, Ottawa
Gollancz	Victor Gollancz, London
Gomer	Gomer Press, Llandysul, Dyfed
GothU	Gothenburg Univ. Gothenburg
Gower	Gower Pub., Aldershot, Hants.
Grafton	Grafton Books, London
Granta	Granta Publications, London
Granville	Granville Pub., London
Grasset	Grasset & Fasquelle, Paris
Grassroots	Grassroots, London
Graywolf	Graywolf Press, St Paul, Minn.
Greenhalgh	M. J. Greenhalgh, London
Greenhill	Greenhill Books, London
Greenwood	Greenwood Press, Westport, Conn.
Gregg	Gregg Publishing, Surrey
Greymitre	Greymitre Books, London
Groos	Julius Groos Verlag, Heidelberg
Grove	Grove Press, New York
GRP	Greenfield Review Press, New York
Grüner	B. R. Grüner, Amsterdam
Gruyter	Walter de Gruyter, Berlin
Guernica	Guernica Editions, Montreal, Canada
Gulmohar	Gulmohar Press, Islamabad, Pakistan
Haggerston	Haggerston
HakluytS	Hakluyt Society, c/o British Library, London
Hale	Robert Hale, London
Hall	G. K. Hall, Boston, Mass.
Hambledon	Hambledon Press, London
H&I	Hale & Iremonger, Sydney
H&M	Holmes & Meier, London and New York
H&S	Hodder & Stoughton, London
H&SNZ	Hodder & Stoughton, Auckland
H&W	Hill & Wang, New York
Hansib	Hansib Pub., London
Hans Zell	Hans Zell
Harbour	Harbour Pub., Madeira Park, B.C.
Harman	Harman Pub. House, New Delhi
Harper	Harper & Row, New York
Harrap	Harrap, Edinburgh

HarvardUP	Harvard UP, Cambridge, Mass.
HBJ	Harcourt Brace Jovanovich, New York and London
HC	HarperCollins, London
Headline	Headline Book Pub., London
Heath	D. C. Heath, Lexington, Mass.
Heinemann	William Heinemann, London
HeinemannA	William Heinemann, St Kilda, Vic.
HeinemannC	Heinemann Educational Books, Kingston, Jamaica
HeinemannNZ	Heinemann Pubs., Auckland (now Heinemann Reed)
HeinemannR	Heinemann Reed, Auckland
Helm	Christopher Helm, London
Herbert	Herbert Press, London
Hermitage	Hermitage Antiquarian Bookshop, Denver, Colorado
Hern	Nick Hern Books, London
Heyday	Heyday Books, Berkeley, Calif.
HH	Hamish Hamilton, London
Hilger	Adam Hilger, Bristol
HM	Harvey Miller, London
HMSO	HMSO, London
Hodge	A. Hodge, Penzance, Cornwall
Hogarth	Hogarth Press, London
Hong KongUP	Hong Kong UP, Hong Kong
Horwood	Ellis Horwood, Hemel Hempstead, Herts.
HoughtonM	Houghton Mifflin, Boston, Mass.
Howard	Howard UP, Washington, D.C.
HRW	Holt, Rinehart & Winston, New York
Hudson	Hudson
Hueber	Max Hueber, Ismaning, Germany
HUL	Hutchinson Univ. Library, London
HullUP	Hull UP, Univ. of Hull
Humanities	Humanities Press, Atlantic Highlands, N.J.
Huntington	Huntington Library, San Marino, Calif.
Hutchinson	Hutchinson Books, London
HW	Harvester Wheatsheaf, Hemel Hempstead, Herts.
HWWilson	H. W. Wilson, New York
Hyland House	Hyland House Publishing, Victoria, Australia
Ian Henry	Ian Henry Pubns, Hornchurch, Essex
IAP	Irish Academic Press, Dublin
IBK	Innsbrucker Beiträge zur Kulturwissenschaft, Univ. of Innsbruck
ICA	Institute of Contemporary Arts, London
IHA	International Hopkins Association, Waterloo, Ont.
IJamaica	Institute of Jamaica Pubns, Kingston
Imago	Imago Imprint, New York
Imperial War Museum	Imperial War Museum Publications, London
IndUP	Indiana UP, Bloomington, Ind.
Inkblot	Inkblot Pubns, Berkeley, Calif.
IntUP	International Universities Press, New York
Inventions	Inventions Press, London

IonaC	Iona College,. New Rochelle, N.Y.
IowaSUP	Iowa State UP, Ames, Iowa
IOWP	Isle of Wight County Press, Newport, Isle of Wight
IP	In Parenthesis, London
Ipswich	Ipswich Press, Ipswich, Mass.
ISI	ISI Press, Philadelphia
Italica	Italica Press, New York
IULC	Indiana Univ. Linguistics Club, Bloomington, Ind.
IUP	Indiana Univ. of Pennsylvania Press, Indiana, Pa.
Ivon	Ivon Pub. House, Bombay
Jacaranda	Jacaranda Wiley, Milton, Queensland
JadavpurU	Jadavpur Univ., Calcutta
James CookU	James Cook Univ. of North Queensland, Townsville
Jarrow	Parish of Jarrow, Tyne and Wear
Jesperson	Jesperson Press, St John's, Newfoundland
JHall	James Hall, Leamington Spa, Warwickshire
JHUP	Johns Hopkins UP, Baltimore, Md.
JIWE	JIWE Pubns, Univ. of Gulbarga, India
JLRC	Jack London Research Center, Glen Ellen, Calif.
Jonas	Jonas Verlag, Marburg, Germany
Joseph	Michael Joseph, London
Journeyman	The Journeyman Press, London
JT	James Thin, Edinburgh
Junction	Junction Books, London
Junius-Vaughan	The Junius-Vaughan Press, Fairview, N.J.
Jupiter	Jupiter Press, Lake Bluff, Ill.
JyväskyläU	Jyväskylä Univ., Jyväskylä, Finland
Kaibunsha	Kaibunsha, Tokyo
K&N	Königshausen & Neumann, Würzburg, Germany
K&W	Kaye & Ward, London
Kansai	Kansai Univ. of Foreign Studies, Osaka
Kardo	Kardo, Coatbridge, Scotland
Karia	Karia Press, London
Karnak	Karnak House, London
Karoma	Karoma Pubs., Ann Arbor, Mich.
KC	Kyle Cathie
KCL	King's College London
Kegan Paul	Kegan Paul International, London
Kenkyu	Kenkyu-Sha, Tokyo
Kennikat	Kennikat Press, Port Washington, N.Y.
Kensal	Kensal Press, Oxford
KenyaLB	Kenya Literature Bureau, Nairobi
Kerosina	Kerosina Pubns, Worcester Park, Surrey
Kerr	Charles H. Kerr, Chicago
Kestrel	Viking Kestrel, London
K/H	Kendall/Hunt Pub., Dubuque, Iowa
Kingsley	J. Kingsley Publishers, London
Kingston	Kingston Pubs., Kingston, Jamaica
Kinseido	Kinseido, Tokyo
Klostermann	Vittorio Klostermann, Frankfurt-on-Main

Knopf	Alfred A. Knopf, New York
Knowledge	Knowledge Industry Pubns, White Plains, N.Y.
Kraus	Kraus International Pubns, White Plains, N.Y.
KSUP	Kent State UP, Kent, Ohio
LA	Library Association, London
Lake View	Lake View Press, Chicago
LAm	Library of America, New York
Lancelot	Lancelot Press, Hantsport, N.S.
Landesman	Jay Landesman, London
L&W	Lawrence & Wishart, London
Lane	Allen Lane, London
Lang	Peter D. Lang, Frankfurt-on-Main and Berne
LATR	*Latin American Theatre Review*, Center of Latin American Studies
LC	Library of Congress, Washington, D.C.
LCP	Loras College Press, Dubuque, Iowa
LeedsUP	Leeds UP, Leeds
LehighUP	Lehigh University Press, Pennsylvania
LeicsCC	Leicestershire County Council, Libraries and Information Service, Leicester
LeicUP	Leicester UP, Leicester
LeidenUP	Leiden UP, Leiden
Leopard's Head	Leopard's Head Press, Oxford
LeuvenUP	Leuven UP, Leuven, Belgium
Lexik	Lexik House, Cold Spring, N.Y.
LF	LiberFörlag, Stockholm
LH	Lund Humphries Pubs., London
Liberty	Liberty Classics, Indianapolis, Ind.
Libris	Libris, London
Liguori	Liguori, Naples
Limelight	Limelight Editions, New York
Lime Tree	Lime Tree Press, Octopus Publishing Group, London
LittleH	Little Hills Press, Burwood, N.S.W.
Liveright	Liveright Pub., New York
LiverUP	Liverpool UP, Liverpool
Livre de Poche	Le Livre de Poche, Paris
Llanerch	Llanerch Enterprises, Lampeter, Dyfed
Locust Hill	Locust Hill Press, West Cornwall, Conn.
Loewenthal	Loewenthal Press, New York
Longman	Longman Group, Harlow, Essex
LongmanC	Longman Caribbean, Harlow, Essex
LongmanNZ	Longman, Auckland
Longspoon	Longspoon Press, Univ. of Alberta, Edmonton
Lovell	David Lovell Publishing, Brunswick, Australia
Lowell	Lowell Press, Kansas City, Mo.
Lowry	Lowry Pubs., Johannesburg
LSUP	Louisiana State UP, Baton Rouge, La.
LundU	Lund Univ., Lund, Sweden
LUP	Loyola UP, Chicago
Lutterworth	Lutterworth Press, Cambridge

Lymes	Lymes Press, Newcastle, Staffs.
MAA	Medieval Academy of America, Cambridge, Mass.
Macmillan	Macmillan Pubs., London
Madison	Madison Books, Lanham, Md.
Madurai	Madurai Univ., Madurai, India
Maecenas	Maecenas Press, Iowa City, Iowa
Magabala	Magabala Books, Broome, W.A.
Mainstream	Mainstream Pub., Edinburgh
Maisonneuve	Maisonneuve Press, Washington, D.C.
Malone	Malone Society, c/o King's College, London
Mambo	Mambo Press, Gweru, Zimbabwe
ManCASS	Manchester Centre for Anglo-Saxon Studies, Univ. of Manchester
M&E	Macdonald & Evans, Estover, Plymouth, Devon
M&S	McClelland & Stewart, Toronto
Maney	W. S. Maney & Sons, Leeds
Mansell	Mansell Pub., London
Manufacture	La Manufacture, Lyons
ManUP	Manchester UP, Manchester
Mardaga	Mardaga
MarquetteUP	Marquette UP, Milwaukee, Wisc.
Marvell	The Marvell Press, Calstock, Cornwall
MB	Mitchell Beazley, London
McFarland	McFarland, Jefferson, N.C.
McG-QUP	McGill-Queen's UP, Montreal
McGraw-Hill	McGraw-Hill, New York
McIndoe	John McIndoe, Dunedin, New Zealand
McPheeG	McPhee Gribble Pubs., Fitzroy, Vic.
McPherson	McPherson, Kingston, N.Y.
ME	M. Evans, New York
Meany	P. D. Meany Pubs., Port Credit, Ont.
Meckler	Meckler Pub., Westport, Conn.
MelbourneUP	Melbourne UP, Carlton South, Vic.
Mellen	Edwin Mellen Press, Lewiston, N.Y.
MellenR	Mellen Research UP
MercerUP	Mercer UP, Macon, Ga.
Mercury	Mercury Press, Stratford, Ontario
Merlin	The Merlin Press, London
Methuen	Methuen, London
MethuenA	Methuen Australia, North Ryde, N.S.W.
MethuenC	Methuen, Toronto
Metro	Metro Pub., Auckland
Metzler	Metzler, Stuttgart
MGruyter	Mouton de Gruyter, Berlin, New York, and Amsterdam
MH	Michael Haag, London
MHRA	Modern Humanities Research Association, London
MI	Microforms International, Pergamon Press, Oxford
Micah	Micah Pubns, Marblehead, Mass.
MichSUP	Michigan State UP, East Lansing, Mich.
MidNAG	Mid Northumberland Arts Group, Ashington, Northumbria

Milestone	Milestone Pubns, Horndean, Hampshire
Millenium	Millenium Books, E. J. Dwyer Pty Ltd, Newtown, Australia
Millstream	Millstream Books, Bath
Milner	Milner, London
Minuit	Editions de Minuit, Paris
MIP	Medieval Institute Pubns, Western Michigan Univ., Kalamazoo
MITP	Massachusetts Institute of Technology Press, Cambridge, Mass.
MLA	Modern Language Association of America, New York
MIM	Multilingual Matters, Clevedon, Avon
MLP	Manchester Literary and Philosophical Society, Manchester
Monarch	Monarch Publications, Sussex
Moonraker	Moonraker Press, Bradford-on-Avon, Wilts.
Moorland	Moorland Pub., Ashbourne, Derbys.
Moreana	Moreana, Angers, France
MorganSU	Morgan State Univ., Baltimore, Md.
Morrow	William Morrow, New York
Mosaic	Mosaic Press, Oakville, Ont.
Motilal	Motilal Books, Oxford
Motley	Motley Press, Romsey, Hampshire
Mouton	Mouton Pubs, New York and Paris
Mowbray	A. R. Mowbray, Oxford
MR	Martin Robertson, Oxford
MRS	Medieval and Renaissance Society, North Texas State Univ., Denton
MRTS	MRTS, Binghamton, N.Y.
MSUP	Memphis State UP, Memphis, Tenn.
MtAllisonU	Mount Allison Univ., Sackville, N.B.
Mulini	Mulini Press, A.C.T.
Muller	Frederick Muller, London
MULP	McMaster University Library Press
Murray	John Murray, London
Mursia	Ugo Mursia, Milan
NAL	New American Library, New York
Narr	Gunter Narr Verlag, Tübingen
Nathan	Fernand Nathan, Paris
NBB	New Beacon Books, London
NBCAus	National Book Council of Australia, Melbourne
NCP	New Century Press, Durham
ND	New Directions, New York
NDT	Nottingham Drama Texts, c/o Univ., of Nottingham
NEL	New English Library, London
NELM	National English Literary Museum, Grahamstown, S. Africa
Nelson	Nelson Pubs., Melbourne
New Endeavour	New Endeavour Press
NeWest	NeWest Press, Edmonton, Alberta

New Horn	New Horn Press, Ibadan, Nigeria
NewIssuesP	New Issues Press, Western Michigan University
NH	New Horizon Press, Far Hills, N.J.
N-H	Nelson-Hall, Chicago
NHPC	North-Holland Pub., Amsterdam and New York
NIE	La Nuova Italia Editrice, Florence
Niemeyer	Max Niemeyer, Tübingen, Germany
Nightwood	Nightwood Editions, Toronto
NIUP	Northern Illinois UP, De Kalb, Ill.
NLA	National Library of Australia
NLB	New Left Books, London
NLC	National Library of Canada, Ottawa
NLP	New London Press, Dallas, Texas
NLS	National Library of Scotland, Edinburgh
NLW	National Library of Wales, Aberystwyth, Dyfed
Northcote	Northcote House Pubs., Plymouth
NortheasternU	Northeastern Univ., Boston, Mass.
NorthwesternUP	Northwestern UP, Evanston, Ill.
Norton	W. W. Norton, New York and London
NorUP	Norwegian University Press, Oslo
NPF	National Poetry Foundation, Orono, Maine
NPG	National Portrait Gallery, London
NPP	North Point Press, Berkeley, Calif.
NSP	New Statesman Pub., New Delhi
NSU Press	Northern States Universities Press
NSWUP	New South Wales UP, Kensington, N.S.W.
NTC	National Textbook, Lincolnwood, Ill.
NUC	Nipissing Univ. College, North Bay, Ont.
NUP	National Univ. Pubns, Millwood, N.Y.
NUU	New Univ. of Ulster, Coleraine
NWAP	North Waterloo Academic Press, Waterloo, Ont.
NWP	New World Perspectives, Montreal
NYPL	New York Public Library, New York
NYUP	New York UP, New York
O&B	Oliver & Boyd, Harlow, Essex
Oasis	Oasis Books, London
OBAC	Organization of Black American Culture, Chicago
Oberon	Oberon
O'Brien	The O'Brien Press, Dublin
OBS	Oxford Bibliographical Society, Bodleian Library, Oxford
Octopus	Octopus Books, London
OdenseUP	Odense UP, Odense
OE	Officina Edizioni, Rome
OEColl	Old English Colloquium, Berkeley, Calif.
Offord	John Offord Pubns, Eastbourne, E. Sussex
OhioUP	Ohio UP, Athens, Ohio
Oldcastle	Oldcastle Books, Harpenden, Herts.
Olms	Georg Olms, Hildesheim, Germany
Olschki	Leo S. Olschki, Florence

O'Mara	Michael O'Mara Books, London
Omnigraphics	Omnigraphics, Detroit, Mich.
Open Books	Open Books Pub., Wells, Somerset
OpenUP	Open UP, Buckingham and Philadelphia
OPP	Oxford Polytechnic Press, Oxford
Orbis	Orbis Books, London
Oriel	Oriel Press, Stocksfield, Northumb.
OrientUP	Oriental UP, London
Orwell	Orwell Press, Southwold, Suffolk
Oryx	Oryx Press, Phoenix, Ariz.
OSUP	Ohio State UP, Columbus, Ohio
OTP	Oak Tree Press, London
OUCA	Oxford University Committee for Archaeology, Oxford
OUP	Oxford UP, Oxford
OUPAm	Oxford UP Inc., New York
OUPAus	Oxford UP, Melbourne
OUPC	Oxford UP, Toronto
OUPI	Oxford UP, New Delhi
OUPNZ	Oxford UP, Auckland
OUPSA	Oxford UP Southern Africa, Cape Town
Outlet	Outlet Book Co., New York
Owen	Peter Owen, London
Owl	Owl
Pacifica	Press Pacifica, Kailua, Hawaii
Paget	Paget Press, Santa Barbara, Calif.
PAJ	PAJ Pubns, New York
Paladin	Paladin Books, London
Pan	Pan Books, London
PanAmU	Pan American Univ., Edinburgh, Texas
P&C	Pickering & Chatto, London
Pandion	Pandion Press, Capitola, Calif.
Pandora	Pandora Press, London
Pantheon	Pantheon Books, New York
ParagonH	Paragon House Pubs., New York
Parousia	Parousia Pubns, London
Paternoster	Paternoster Press, Carlisle, Cumbria
Paulist	Paulist Press, Ramsey, N.J.
Paupers	Paupers' Press, Nottingham
Pavilion	Pavilion Books, London
PBFA	Provincial Booksellers's Fairs Association, Cambridge
Peachtree	Peachtree Pubs., Atlanta, Ga.
Pearson	David Pearson, Huntingdon, Cambs.
Peepal Tree	Peepal Tree Books, Leeds
Pelham	Pelham Books, London
Pembridge	Pembridge Press, London
Pemmican	Pemmican Publications, Winnipeg, Canada
Penguin	Penguin Books, Harmondsworth, Middx.
PenguinA	Penguin Books, Ringwood, Vic.
PenguinNZ	Penguin Books, Auckland
Penkevill	The Penkevill Pub. Co., Greenwood, Fla.

Pentland	Pentland Press Ltd, Ely, Cambs.
Penumbra	Penumbra Press, Moonbeam, Ont.
People's	People's Pubns, London
Pergamon	Pergamon Press, Oxford
Permanent	Permanent Press, Sag Harbor, N.Y.
Perpetua	Perpetua Press, Oxford
Pevensey	Pevensey Press, Newton Abbott, Devon
PH	Prentice-Hall, Englewood Cliffs, N.J.
Phaidon	Phaidon Press, London
PHI	Prentice-Hall International, Hemel Hempstead, Herts.
PhilL	Philosophical Library, New York
Phillimore	Phillimore, Chichester
Piatkus	Piatkus Books, London
Pickwick	Pickwick Pubns, Allison Park, Pa.
Pilgrim	Pilgrim Books, Norman, Okla.
PIMS	Pontifical Institute of Mediaeval Studies, Toronto
Pinter	Frances Pinter Pubs., London
Plains	Plains Books, Carlisle
Plenum	Plenum Pub., London and New York
Plexus	Plexus Pub., London
Ploughshares	Ploughshares Books, Watertown, Mass.
Pluto	Pluto Press, London
PML	Pierpont Morgan Library, New York
Polity	Polity Press, Cambridge
Polygon	Polygon, Edinburgh
Poolbeg	Poolbeg Press, Swords, Co. Dublin
Porcepic	Press Porcepic, Victoria, B.C.
Porcupine	Porcupine's Quill, Canada
PortN	Port Nicholson Press, Wellington, N.Z.
Potter	Clarkson N. Potter, New York
Power	Power Pubns, Univ. of Sydney
PPUBarcelona	Promociones y Publicaciones Universitarias, Barcelona
PrestigeB	Prestige Books, New Delhi
Primavera	Edizioni Primavera, Giunti Publishing Group, Florence, Italy
Primrose	Primrose Press, Alhambra, Calif.
PrincetonUL	Princeton Univ. Library, Princeton, N.J.
PrincetonUP	Princeton UP, Princeton, N.J.
Printwell	Printwell Pubs., Jaipur, India
Prism	Prism Press, Bridport, Dorset
PRO	Public Record Office, London
Profile	Profile Books, Ascot, Berks
ProgP	Progressive Pubs., Calcutta
PSUP	Pennsylvania State UP, University Park, Pa.
Pucker	Puckerbrush Press, Orono, Maine
PUF	Presses Universitaires de France, Paris
PurdueUP	Purdue UP, Lafayette, Ind.
Pushcart	Pushcart Press, Wainscott, N.Y.
Pustet	Friedrich Pustet, Regensburg
Putnam	Putnam Pub. Group, New York

PWP	Poetry Wales Press, Ogmore by Sea, Mid Glam.
QED	Q.E.D. Press of Ann Arbor, Mich.
Quarry	Quarry Press, Kingston, Ontario
Quartet	Quartet Books, London
RA	Royal Academy of Arts, London
Rainforest	Rainforest
Rampant Lions	Rampant Lions Press, Cambridge
R&B	Rosenkilde & Bagger, Copenhagen
R&L	Rowman & Littlefield, Totowa, N.J.
RandomH	Random House, London and New York
RandomHAus	Random House Australia, Vic.
Ravan	Ravan Press, Johannesburg
Ravette	Ravette, London
Reaktion	Reaktion Books, London
Rebel	The Rebel Press, London
Red Kite	Red Kite Press, Guelph, Ont.
Reference	Reference Press, Toronto
Regents	Regents Press of Kansas, Lawrence, Kansas
Reichenberger	Roswitha Reichenberger, Kessel, Germany
Reinhardt	Max Reinhardt, London
Remak	Remak, Alblasserdam, Netherlands
RenI	Renaissance Institute, Sophia Univ., Tokyo
Research	Research Pubns, Reading
RETS	Renaissance English Text Society, Chicago
RH	Ramsay Head Press, Edinburgh
RHS	Royal Historical Society, London
RIA	Royal Irish Academy, Dublin
RiceUP	Rice UP, Houston, Texas
Richarz	Hans Richarz, St Augustin, Germany
RICL	Research Institute for Comparative Literature, Univ. of Alberta
Rizzoli	Rizzoli International Pubns., New Yorks
RobartsCCS	Robarts Centre for Canadian Studies, York Univ., North York, Ont.
Robinson	Robinson Pub., London
Robson	Robson Books, London
Rodopi	Rodopi, Amsterdam
Roebuck	Stuart Roebuck, Suffolk
RoehamptonI	Roehampton Institute of Higher Education, London
Routledge	Routledge, London and New York
Royce	Robert Royce, London
RS	The Royal Society, London
RSC	Royal Shakespeare Co., London
RSL	Royal Society of Literature, London
RSVP	Research Society for Victorian Periodicals, Univ. of Leicester
RT	R.T. Pubns, London
Running	Running Press, Philadelphia
Russell	Michael Russell, Norwich
RutgersUP	Rutgers UP, New Brunswick, N.J.

Ryan	Ryan Pub., London
SA	Sahitya Akademi, New Delhi
SAI	Sociological Abstracts, San Diego, Calif.
Sage	Sage Pubns, London
Salamander	Salamander Books, London
Salem	Salem
S&A	Shukayr and Akasheh, Amman, Jordan
S&D	Stein & Day, Briarcliff Manor, N.Y.
S&J	Sidgwick & Jackson, London
S&M	Sun & Moon Press, Los Angeles
S&P	Simon & Pierre, Toronto
S&S	Simon & Schuster, New York and London
S&W	Secker & Warburg, London
Sangam	Sangam Books, London
Sangsters	Sangsters Book Stores, Kingston, Jamaica
SAP	Scottish Academic Press, Edinburgh
Saros	Saros International Publishers
SASSC	Sydney Association for Studies in Society and Culture, University of Sydney, N.S.W.
Saur	Bowker-Saur, Sevenoaks, Kent
Savacou	Savacou Pubns, Kingston, Jamaica
S-B	Schwann-Bagel, Düsseldorf
Scarecrow	Scarecrow Press, Metuchen, N.J.
Schäuble	Schäuble Verlag, Rheinfelden, Germany
Schneider	Lambert Schneider, Heidelberg
Schocken	Schocken Books, New York
Scholarly	Scholarly Press, St Clair Shores, Mich.
ScholarsG	Scholars Press, Georgia
Schöningh	Ferdinand Schöningh, Paderborn, Germany
Schwinn	Michael Schwinn, Neustadt, Germany
SCJP	Sixteenth Century Journal Publications
Scolar	Scolar Press, Aldershot, Hampshire
SCP	Second Chance Press, Sag Harbor, N.Y.
Scribe	Scribe Publishing, Colchester
Scribner	Charles Scribner's Sons, New York
Seafarer	Seafarer Books, London
Seaver	Seaver Books, New York
Segue	Segue, New York
Self-Publishing Association	Self-Publishing Association
Semiotext(e)	Semiotext(e), Columbia Univ., New York
Seren Books	Seren Books, Bridgend, Mid Glamorgan
Serpent's Tail	Serpent's Tail Pub., London
Sessions	William Sessions, York
Seuil	Editions du Seuil, Paris
7:84 Pubns	7:84 Pubns, Glasgow
Severn	Severn House, Wallington, Surrey
SF&R	Scholars' Facsimiles and Reprints, Delmar, N.Y.
SH	Somerset House, Teaneck, N.J.
Shalabh	Shalabh Book House, Meerut, India

ShaP	Sheffield Academic Press
Shearwater	Shearwater Press, Lenah Valley, Tasmania
Sheba	Sheba Feminist Pubs., London
Sheed&Ward	Sheed & Ward, London
Sheldon	Sheldon Press, London
SHESL	Société d'Histoire et d'Épistemologie des Sciences du Langage, Paris
Shinozaki	Shinozaki Shorin, Tokyo
Shinshindo	Shinshindo Pub., Tokyo
Shire	Shire Pubns, Princes Risborough, Bucks.
Shoe String	Shoe String Press, Hamden Conn.
SIAS	Scandinavian Institute of African Studies, Uppsala
SIL	Summer Institute of Linguistics, Academic Pubns, Dallas, Texas
SIUP	Southern Illinois University Press
Simon King	Simon King Press, Milnthorpe, Cumbria
Sinclair-Stevenson	Sinclair-Stevenson, London
SingaporeUP	Singapore UP, Singapore
SIUP	Southern Illinois UP, Carbondale, Ill.
SJSU	San Jose State Univ., San Jose, Calif.
Skilton	Charles Skilton, London
Skoob	Skoob Books Pub., London
Slatkine	Editions Slatkine, Paris
Slavica	Slavica Pubs., Columbus, Ohio
Sleepy Hollow	Sleepy Hollow Press, Tarrytown, N.Y.
SLG	SLG Press, Oxford
Smith Settle	Smith Settle Ltd, W. Yorkshire
SMUP	Southern Methodist UP, Dallas, Texas
Smythe	Colin Smythe, Gerrards Cross, Bucks.
SNH	Société Néophilologique de Helsinki
SNLS	Society for New Language Study, Denver, Colo.
SOA	Society of Authors, London
Soho	Soho Book Co., London
SohoP	Soho Press, New York
Solaris	Solaris Press, Rochester, Mich.
SonoNis	Sono Nis Press, Victoria, B.C.
Sorbonne	Pubns de la Sorbonne, Paris
SorbonneN	Pubns du Conseil Scientifique de la Sorbonne Nouvelle, Paris
Souvenir	Souvenir Press, London
SPA	SPA Books Ltd
SPACLALS	South Pacific Association for Commonwealth Literature and Language Studies, Wollongong, N.S.W.
SPCK	SPCK, London
Spectrum	Spectrum Books, Ibadan, Nigeria
Split Pea	Split Pea Press, Edinburgh
Spokesman	Spokesman Books, Nottingham
Spoon River	Spoon River Poetry Press, Granite Falls, Minn.
SRC	Steinbeck Research Center, San Jose State Univ., San Jose, Calif.

SRI	Steinbeck Research Institute, Ball State Univ., Muncie, Ind.
SriA	Sri Aurobindo, Pondicherry, India
Sri Satguru	Sri Satguru Pubns, Delhi
SSA	John Steinbeck Society of America, Muncie, Ind.
SSAB	Sprakförlaget Skriptor AB, Stockholm
StanfordUP	Stanford UP, Stanford, Calif.
Staple	Staple, Matlock, Derbyshire
Starmont	Starmont House, Mercer Island, Wash.
Starrhill	Starrhill Press, Washington, D.C.
Station Hill	Station Hill, Barrytown, N.Y.
Stauffenburg	Stauffenburg Verlag, Tübingen, Germany
StDL	St Deiniol's Library, Hawarden, Clwyd
Steel Rail	Steel Rail Pub., Ottawa
Steiner	Franz Steiner, Wiesbaden, Germany
Sterling	Sterling Pub., New York
SterlingND	Sterling Pubs., New Delhi
St James	St James Press, Andover, Hampshire
St Martin's	St Martin's Press, New York
Stockwell	Arthur H. Stockwell, Ilfracombe, Devon
Stoddart	Stoddart Pub., Don Mills, Ont.
StPB	St Paul's Bibliographies, Winchester, Hampshire
STR	Society for Theatre Research, London
Strauch	R. O. U. Strauch, Ludwigsburg
Studio	Studio Editions, London
Stump Cross	Stump Cross Books, Stump Cross, Essex
Sud	Sud, Marseilles
Suhrkamp	Suhrkamp Verlag, Frankfurt-on-Main
Summa	Summa Pubns, Birmingham, Ala.
SUNYP	State Univ. of New York Press, Albany, N.Y.
SUP	Sydney University Press
Surtees	R. S. Surtees Society, Frome, Somerset
SusquehannaUP	Susquehanna UP, Selinsgrove, Pa.
SussexUP	Sussex UP, Univ. of Sussex, Brighton
Sutton	Alan Sutton, Stroud, Gloucester
S-W	Shepheard-Walwyn Pubs., London
Swallow	Swallow Press, Athens, Ohio
SWG	Saskatchewan Writers Guild, Regina
Sybylla	Sybylla Feminist Press
SydneyUP	Sydney UP, Sydney
SyracuseUP	Syracuse UP, Syracuse, N.Y.
Tabb	Tabb House, Padstow, Cornwall
Taishukan	Taishukan Pub., Tokyo
Talonbooks	Talonbooks, Vancouver
TamilU	Tamil Univ., Thanjavur, India
T&H	Thames & Hudson, London
Tantivy	Tantivy Press, London
Tarcher	Jeremy P. Tarcher, Los Angeles
Tate	Tate Gallery Pubns, London
Tavistock	Tavistock Pubns, London

Taylor	Taylor Pub., Bellingham, Wash.
TaylorCo	Taylor Pub., Dallas, Texas
TCG	Theatre Communications Group, New York
TCP	Three Continents Press, Washington, D.C.
TCUP	Texas Christian UP, Fort Worth, Texas
TEC	Third Eye Centre, Glasgow
Tecumseh	Tecumseh Press, Ottawa
Telos	Telos Press, St Louis, Mo.
TempleUP	Temple UP, Philadelphia
TennS	Tennyson Society, Lincoln
TexA&MUP	Texas A & M UP, College Station, Texas
TextileB	Textile Bridge Press, Clarence Center, N.Y.
TexTULib	Friends of the Univ. Library, Texas Tech Univ., Lubbock
The Smith	The Smith, New York
Thimble	Thimble Press, Stroud, Glos.
Thoemmes	Thoemmes Press, Bristol
Thornes	Stanley Thornes, Cheltenham
Thorpe	D. W. Thorpe, Australia
Thorsons	Thorsons Pubs., London
Times	Times of Gloucester Press, Gloucester, Ont.
TMP	Thunder's Mouth Press, New York
Tombouctou	Tombouctou Books, Bolinas, Calif.
TorSVP	Sister Vision Press, Toronto
Totem	Totem Books, Don Mills, Ont.
Toucan	Toucan Press, St Peter Port, Guernsey
Touzot	Jean Touzot, Paris
TPF	Trianon Press Facsimiles, London
Tragara	Tragara Press, Edinburgh
Transaction	Transaction Pubs., New Brunswick, N.J.
Transcendental	Transcendental Books, Hartford, Conn.
Transworld	Transworld, London
TrinityUP	Trinity UP, San Antonio, Texas
TTUP	Texas Technical University Press, Lubbock
Tuduv	Tuduv, Munich
TulaneUP	Tulane UP, New Orleans, La.
TurkuU	Turku Univ., Turky, Finland
Turnstone	Turnstone Press, Winnipeg, Manitoba
Turtle Island	Turtle Island Foundation, Berkeley, Calif.
Twayne	Twayne Pubs., Boston, Mass.
UAB	Univ. of Aston, Birmingham
UAdelaide	Univ. of Adelaide, Adelaide
UAlaP	Univ. of Alabama Press, Tuscaloosa
UAlbertaP	Univ. of Alberta Press, Edmonton
UAntwerp	Univ. of Antwerp, Antwerp
UArizP	Univ. of Arizona Press, Tucson
UArkP	Univ. of Arkansas Press, Fayetteville
UAthens	Univ. of Athens, Athens, Greece
UBarcelona	Univ. of Barcelona, Barcelona
UBCP	Univ. of British Columbia Press, Vancouver

UBergen	Univ. of Bergen, Bergen
UBrno	J.E. Purkyne Univ. of Brno, Brno, Czechoslovakia
UBrussels	Univ. of Brussels, Brussels
UCalgaryP	Univ. of Calgary Press, Calgary
UCalP	Univ. of California Press, Berkeley
UCAP	Univ. of Central Arkansas Press, Conway
UChicP	Univ. of Chicago Press, Chicago
UCopenP	Univ. of Copenhagen Press, Copenhagen
UDelP	Univ. of Delaware Press, Newark
UDijon	Univ. of Dijon, Dijon
UDur	Univ. of Durham, Durham
UEA	University of East Anglia, Norwich
UErlangen-N	Univ. of Erlangen-Nuremberg, Germany
UEssex	Univ. of Essex, Colchester
UExe	Univ. of Exeter, Exeter
UFlorence	Univ. of Florence, Florence
UFlorP	Univ. of Florida Press, Florida
UGal	Univ. College, Galway
UGeoP	Univ. of Georgia Press, Athens
UGhent	Univ. of Ghent, Ghent
UGlasP	Univ. of Glasgow Press, Glasgow
UHawaiiP	Univ. of Hawaii Press, Honolulu
UIfeP	Univ. of Ife Press, Ile-Ife, Nigeria
UIllP	Univ. of Illinois Press, Champaign
UInnsbruck	Univ. of Innsbruck, Innsbruck
UIowaP	Univ. of Iowa Press, Iowa City
UKanP	Univ. of Kansas Press, Lawrence
UKatowice	University of Katowice Press, Poland
UKL	Univ. of Kentucky Libraries, Lexington
ULavalP	Les Presses de l'Université Laval, Quebec
ULiège	Univ. of Liège, Liège, Belgium
ULilleP	Presses Universitaires de Lille, Lille
ULondon	Univ. of London, London
Ulster	Univ. of Ulster, Coleraine
U/M	Underwood/Miller, Los Angeles
UMalta	Univ. of Malta, Msida
UManitobaP	Univ. of Manitoba Press, Winnipeg
UMassP	Univ. of Massachusetts Press, Amherst
Umeå	Umeå Universitetsbibliotek, Umeå
UMel	Melbourne University Press, Victoria, Australia
UMichP	Univ. of Michigan Press, Ann Arbor
UMinnP	Univ. of Minnesota Press, Minneapolis
UMirail-ToulouseP	University of Mirail-Toulouse Press, France
UMIRes	UMI Research Press, Ann Arbor, Mich.
UMissP	Univ. Of Missouri Press, Columbia
UMP	University of Mississippi Press, Lafayette Co, Mississippi
UMysore	Univ. of Mysore, Mysore, India
UNancyP	Presses Universitaires de Nancy, France
UNCP	Univ. of North Carolina Press, Chapel Hill

Undena	Undena Pubns, Malibu, Calif.
UNDP	Univ. of Notre Dame Press, Notre Dame, Ind.
UNebP	Univ. of Nebraska Press, Lincoln
UNevP	Univ. of Nevada Press, Reno
UNewE	Univ. of New England, Armidale, N.S.W.
Ungar	Frederick Ungar, New York
Unicopli	Edizioni Unicopli, Milan
Universa	Uitgeverij Universa, Wetteren, Belgium
UNMP	Univ. of New Mexico Press, Albuquerque
UNott	Univ. of Nottingham, Nottingham
UNSW	University of New South Wales
Unwin	Unwin Paperbacks, London
Unwin Hyman	Unwin Hyman, London
UOklaP	Univ. of Oklahoma Press, Norman
UOslo	Univ. of Oslo, Oslo
UOtagoP	Univ. of Otago Press, Dunedin, New Zealand
UOttawaP	Univ. of Ottawa Press, Ottawa
UPA	UP of America, Lanham, Md.
UParis	Univ. of Paris, Paris
UPColorado	UP of Colorado, Niwot
UPennP	Univ. of Pennsylvania Press, Philadelphia
UPFlor	Univ. Presses of Florida, Gainesville
UPittP	Univ. of Pittsburgh Press, Pittsburgh
UPKen	Univ. Press of Kentucky, Lexington
UPMissip	UP of Mississippi, Jackson
UPN	Université de Paris Nord, Paris
UPNE	UP Of New England, Hanover, N.H.
Uppsala	Uppsala Univ., Uppsala
UProvence	Univ. of Provence, Aix-en-Provence
UPValery	Univ. Paul Valery, Montpellier
UPVirginia	UP of Virginia, Charlottesville
UQP	Univ. of Queensland Press, St Lucia
URouen	Univ. of Rouen, Mont St Aignan
URP	University of Rochester Press
USalz	Institut für Anglistik und Amerikanistik, Univ. of Salzburg
USantiago	University of Santiago, Spain
USCP	Univ. of South Carolina Press, Columbia
USFlorP	University of South Florida Press, Florida
USheff	Univ. of Sheffield, Sheffield
Usher	La Casa Usher, Florence
USPacific	Univ. of the South Pacific, Institute of Pacific Studies, Suva, Fiji
USzeged	Univ. of Szeged, Hungary
UtahSUP	Utah State UP, Logan
UTampereP	University of Tampere Press, Finland
UTas	Univ. of Tasmania, Hobart
UTennP	Univ. of Tennessee Press, Knoxville
UTexP	Univ. of Texas Press, Austin
UTorP	Univ. of Toronto Press, Toronto
UTours	Université de Tours

UVerm	Univ. of Vermont, Burlington
UVict	Univ. of Victoria, Victoria, B.C.
UWalesP	Univ. of Wales Press, Cardiff
UWAP	Univ. of Western Australia Press, Nedlands
UWarwick	Univ. of Warwick, Coventry
UWashP	Univ. of Washington Press, Seattle
UWaterlooP	Univ. of Waterloo Press, Waterloo, Ont.
UWI	Univ. of the West Indies, St Augustine, Trinidad
UWiscM	Univ. of Wisconsin, Milwaukee
UWiscP	Univ. of Wisconsin Press, Madison
UYork	Univ. of York, York
Valentine	Valentine Pub. and Drama, Rhinebeck, N.Y.
V&A	Victoria and Albert Museum, London
VanderbiltUP	Vanderbilt UP, Nashville, Tenn.
V&R	Vandenhoeck & Ruprecht, Göttingen, Germany
Vantage	Vantage Press, New York
Variorum	Variorum, Ashgate Publishing Group, Hants
Véhicule	Véhicule Press, Montreal
Verso	Verso Editions, London
VictUP	Victoria UP, Victoria Univ. of Wellington, New Zealand
Vieweg	Vieweg Braunschweig, Wiesbaden
Vikas	Vikas Pub. House, New Delhi
Viking	Viking Press, New York
VikingNZ	Viking, Auckland
Virago	Virago Press, London
Vision	Vision Press, London
VLB	VLB Editeur, Montreal
VR	Variorum Reprints, London
Vrin	J. Vrin, Paris
Wakefield	Wakefield Press
W&N	Weidenfeld & Nicolson, London
Water Row	Water Row Press, Sudbury, Mass.
Watkins	Paul Watkins, Stamford, Lincs.
WB	Wissenschaftliche Buchgesellschaft, Darmstadt
W/B	Woomer/Brotherson, Revere, Pa.
Webb&Bower	Webb & Bower, Exeter
Wedgestone	Wedgestone Press, Winfield, Kansas
Wedgetail	Wedgetail Press, Earlwood, N.S.W.
WesleyanUP	Wesleyan UP, Middletown, Conn.
West	West Pub., St Paul, Minn.
WHA	William Heinemann Australia, Port Melbourne, Vic.
Wheatsheaf	Wheatsheaf Books, Brighton
Whiteknights	Whiteknights Press, Univ. of Reading, Reading
White Lion	White Lion Books, Cambridge
Whitston	Whitston Pub., Troy, N.Y.
Whittington	Whittington Press, Herefordshire
WHP	Warren House Press, Sale, Cheshire
Wiener	Wiener Pub., New York
Wildwood	Wildwood House, Aldershot, Hampshire

Wiley	John Wiley & Sons, Chichester, New York, and Brisbane
Wilson	Philip Wilson, London
Winter	Carl Winter Universitätsverlag, Heidelberg, Germany
Winthrop	Winthrop Pubs., Cambridge, Mass.
WIU	Western Illinois Univ., Macomb, Ill.
WL	Ward Lock, London
WLUP	Wilfrid Laurier UP, Waterloo, Ont.
WMP	World Microfilms Pubns, London
WMU	Western Michigan Univ., Kalamazoo, Mich.
Woeli	Woeli Publishing Services
Wo-No	Wolters-Noordhoff, Groningen, Netherlands
Wolfhound	Wolfhound Press, Dublin
Wombat	The Wombat Press, Wolfville, N.S.
Woodstock	Woodstock Books, Oxford
Woolf	Cecil Woolf, London
Words	Words, Framfield, E. Sussex
WP	The Women's Press, London
WPC	The Women's Press of Canada, Toronto
WSUP	Wayne State UP, Detroit, Mich.
WVUP	West Virginia UP, Morgantown
W-W	Williams-Wallace, Toronto
WWU	Western Washington Univ., Bellingham
Xanadu	Xanadu Pubns, London
YaleUL	Yale Univ. Library Pubns, New Haven, Conn.
YaleUP	Yale UP, New Haven, Conn. and London
Yamaguchi	Yamaguchi Shoten, Kyoto
YorkP	York Press, Fredericton, N.B.
Younsmere	Younsmere Press, Brighton
Zed	Zed Books, London
Zena	Zena Pubns, Penrhyndeudraeth, Gwynedd
Zephyr	Zephyr Press, Somerville, Mass.
Zomba	Zomba Books, London
Zwemmer	A. Zwemmer, London

English Language

KATARZYNA JASZCZOLT, NICOLA WOODS, OLGA FISCHER,
WIM VAN DER WURFF, CAROLE HOUGH, and JEAN JACQUES WEBER

This chapter has the following sections: 1. General; 2. Dialectology and Sociolinguistics (including Creolistics); 3. Morphology; 4. Syntax; 5. Onomastics; 6. Stylistics. Section 1 is by Katarzyna Jaszczolt; section 2 is by Nicola Woods; sections 3 and 4 are by Olga Fischer and Wim van der Wurff; section 5 is by Carole Hough; and section 6 is by Jean Jacques Weber.

1. General

The linguistics-semiotics-literary criticism interface enters the arena of general linguistics this year with an abundance of new ideas to offer. *Beyond Superstructuralism: The Syntagmatic Side of Language* by Richard Harland presents a new insight into how syntagmatic relations work, reconsidering Saussure, Barthes and Derrida, but also taking a stance towards theories that constitute landmarks in linguistics such as Chomsky's generative, autonomous syntax or Austin, Searle's and Grice's approach to discourse. The first is refuted since syntagmatic theory shows how meaning constrains syntax, whereas the latter is praised as linguistics should place *parole* over *langue* and emphasize what the speaker does by language. The book is written in a witty and confident style, and its informativeness is enhanced by the diaphanous presentation of how words really relate to one another horizontally. Sections on syntagmatic theory and literature and syntagmatic theory and textual interpretation have to be praised for reducing the hiatus between theoretical linguistics and literary studies. After all, the conclusion is important for both: meaning is subtractive, there is less in the syntagm than the meaning that comes into it. The book comes just at the time for those willing to rethink Saussure: *Saussure's Third Course of Lectures on General Linguistics (1910–1911)* appeared edited and translated by Eisuke Komatsu and Roy Harris, advancing a new perspective on this revolutionary teaching. It is based on the notes by Emile Constantin which were not utilized by the editors of the 1916 edition, Bally and Sechehaye, as they only came to light in 1958. The book, published with facing French and English text, is organized differently from the original edition of Saussure's lectures and provides praiseworthy insight into the course, offering multiple examples and diagrams.

However, one would wish to impose further editorial work on some Saussure lovers and hope that they come up with an *oeuvre* which unifies existing materials and renders 'Saussure pour de vrai' instead of 'Saussure through the eyes of his pupil'. To continue on the interface note, Richard Bradford contributes *A Linguistic History of English Poetry* in the Routledge Interface Series. He poses an intriguing question as to how poetry can be described as a linguistic structure. His approach is methodical: distinguishing the 'poetic line' as a surface pattern and the sentence with its deep structure underneath, he asks how this double patterning works, i.e., how these two levels of interpretation interact. The result is 'a sliding scale', a means of measuring the relationship between the deep, syntactic, cognitive dimension and the textual dimension, the latter comprising metre, sound pattern, line division, and some other aspects. To raise a point of weakness, the scope of the book is exceptionally broad. There are chapters concentrating on separate works, writers or epochs, the latter with an extensive historical background, and the former two with large examples of works followed by detailed exegesis and criticism, *and* linguistic analysis on top. The work is not sufficiently focused and frequently the aim of the enterprise seems to be lost.

We also witnessed the appearance of the second volume of Creel Froman's *Language and Power I–V*. The leitmotif that all that is known is known in language and that those who have power over language control knowledge and reality reappears in the second volume which is composed of three books: on the 'irreal' language of games and sports, on language as a form of oppression (racism, sexism, ageism, speciesism), and on various social, semantic and political matters respectively. The style and language of the book is not for the uninitiated, although Harland's rethinking of the linguistic sign reviewed above may help, as well as a grounding in deconstruction. The notes on proper names in Book V require special attention: as they introduce individuals, they 'make' them into real objects and create new differentiations, *and* simultaneously, inequality. The interweaving of perspectives makes this work a real challenge for those who are not indoctrinated. For those carefully avoiding reinventing the wheel in twentieth-century semiotics and the 'revolutionary' idea of the linguistic sign, a spark from the long-gone fiery debates on language is on offer. Lia Formigari's masterly conducted investigation into the philosophy of language in the Enlightenment deserves great applause. *Signs, Science and Politics: Philosophies of Language in Europe 1700–1830*, published in the series Studies in the History of the Language Sciences takes the reader through the multifarious influence of Locke's theory of signs on the views on language and politics held by the central figures of the Enlightenment in Europe, but also brings to light ideas neglected in historiography and with them less central figures of the period. The power of language to influence nature and society reappears as the central concern of the philosophers of the period. Accounting also for the birth of German idealism, the work provides a thorough, wide-ranging and reliable perspective of the various roles performed by language in society. In spite of its heavy italocentrism, Formigari's contribution to the historiography of linguistic ideas is indelible. The social dimension of the power of language was also taken up by Robert Hodge and Gunther Kress in *Language as Ideology* which acquired its second edition and although many of its claims are of a rather sensational nature, the arguments are appealing: rules of language are dependent on social power, syntax is interwoven with language use and the study of society.

The Routledge series Translation Studies is represented by two very different but equally attractive contributions. *Contemporary Translation Theories* by Edwin Gentzler vindicates the study in the title to the status of an independent discipline which, as we find out, it acquired in the 1980s. Gentzler discusses with insight the reality which underlies the 'translation boom' in the 1960s: modern poetry, Buddhism, the hippie ideology, the pop music of The Beatles all contributed to the emergence of new, alternative value systems and their increasing acquisition of institutional support. On a more methodological note, the author presents various theories of translation, stresses the need for applying a scientifically sound methodology to any translation enterprise and discusses the notion of equivalence upon which such an activity relies. Among the components of this equivalence we can find aesthetic, syntactic, literary and social factors. After illuminating observations on the thorough treatment translation receives from the advocates of *différance* like Derrida, the concluding follow-up is optimistic: translation acquired a methodological approach of a wide scope; it accounts for the influence a translated text has on semiotic behaviour of language and on discourse rather than merely for the rendering of the source text in the target text. A recommendable book, and for those in need of examples, Romy Heylen offers *Translation, Poetics, and the Stage: Six French 'Hamlets'*, also in Routledge Translation Studies. Heylen stresses the importance of accounting for the functioning of the translation in the receiving culture and illustrates the value of this stress by the case studies of French translations of *Hamlet*, from the eighteenth-century version to the more recent twentieth-century versions. The main thesis is the rejection of normative theories of translation based on absolute equivalence and replacing them with a historical-relative, socio-cultural model since translation is decision-making rather than rule-following. And although the enterprise is not exhausted in linguistics as a discipline, the book can be of interest to many representatives of that profession.

Two commendable dictionaries are on offer. Larry Trask's *A Dictionary of Grammatical Terms* requires special praise for the idea and for filling the existing gap in linguistics reference books. It covers about 1,500 terms in syntax and morphology, as well as some other theoretical concepts and mathematical and computational linguistics terminology. It contains examples, pronunciation guidelines, and symbols used in linguistics. And although one might wish for more thorough definitions, the generality of the explanations is not detrimental to the value of the work: there are ample references and, as the dictionary is more focused than its predecessors, the search for definitions is much more successful. The explanations of the entries combine to provide considerable information about certain theories and phenomena even for the uninitiated. There is also something to be recommended to five-year-olds: *My First Oxford Dictionary* compiled by Evelyn Goldsmith and colourfully and wittily illustrated by Julie Park is bound to be fun to read and a pleasure to learn from. The dictionary is published by Oxford University Press and contains 1,500 words, 550 of them illustrated, as well as a simple grammar (plurals, irregular verbs, irregular comparative and superlative grades of some adjectives). There is also rudimentary semantics: homonymy and synonymy can become great discoveries at that age! Definitions of the type 'Steam is very hot water that has turned into a cloud' do not presuppose much knowledge about the physical world. Tables of related words such as flowers, body parts, or means of transport train us to recognize semantic relation and the componentiality of meaning. The list of 'words we often use' convinces us that not everything can be drawn: there are forms like 'this', 'up', 'any' which often do their job unnoticed.

Discourse studies obtained a diversified treatment. François Recanati's *Direct Reference. From Language to Thought* provides a long awaited synthesis of the theories of reference, presenting arguments for and against a popular standpoint that a proper name and a demonstrative contribute only reference to the proposition expressed by the sentence in which they occur. The second part of the work is of particular interest to linguists as it concerns pragmatics. His well-supported claim that pragmatic information is a part of the proposition expressed contributes significantly to explaining the opacity of some types of constructions such as propositional attitude contexts. Although Recanati's own position seems eclectic and difficult to place in the tradition of theories of reference, perhaps it signifies a landmark in the debate as to the semantic content of propositions: the differences between various linguistic and philosophical camps are smaller than they are commonly believed to be. After all, as Recanati convinces us throughout, a pragmatic approach to communication has to account for the relations between utterances and thoughts. It also has to account for cultural and linguistic differences between societies and nations, as we learn from a series of stimulating and very informative essays in *Interlanguage Pragmatics* edited by Gabrielle Kasper and Shoshana Blum-Kulka. This is the second contribution from these authors to the topic, following *Cross-cultural Pragmatics* of 1989, co-edited also by Juliane House and containing papers written in a similar spirit. Elite Olshtain and Liora Weinbach discuss 'Interlanguage Features of the Speech Act of Complaining' across Hebrew, British English and American English, backing their description of native and non-native speakers of these languages with interesting empirical evidence: a lot of enticing evidence for speech act theorists and those unconvinced.

A *Festschrift* for Malcolm Coulthard prepared by John M. Sinclair, Michael Hoey and Gwyneth Fox as *Techniques of Description* sums up the achievements in describing texts to date. The contributions are significantly diversified, ranging from papers on discourse and conversation, to mention only one on discourse structure by John Sinclair, through the study of polarity and the English finite clause by M. A. K. Halliday and Z. L. James, to pedagogical implications of grammar and lexis by Dave Willis and a series of contributions on language in literary fiction. Although one could think of many other ways texts are described, the volume offers a valuable cross-section of approaches and, as such, acknowledges the important role of its addressee Malcolm Coulthard in building up the study of conversation. Another diversified volume on discourse is contributed by William A. Foley who edited proceedings from a conference on the interface between linguistic theory and the description of natural language which was held in Ocho Rios, Jamaica in 1987, and which gave the book its title: *The Role of Theory in Language Description*. Published in the Mouton series Trends in Linguistics, it covers a variety of issues: grammar, discourse, culture and conversational inference, grammaticalization, and other issues, all across exotic languages such as Chichewa, Burmese, Malay, Thai and others. The papers seem to be permeated with one central discussion as to whether separate languages require separate descriptions or else fit the standard grammatical frameworks which claim to be applicable to all languages such as GB and LFG. The multifarious relation between sentence structure and text is masterly undertaken by Michael Silverstein in 'The Expanse of Grammar in the "Waste" of Frames', a sociocultural study of how the structure of Chinook grammar shapes the cohesion of Chinook narratives. He discusses a narrative recorded by E. Sapir and sees text as a 'poetic structure' of indexical relationships, not transparent to grammar, and performance as not directly related to competence. How do we then set up a framework for the analysis of communication which would account for both its linguistic and socio-cultural aspects? This question is taken up by John Gumperz in 'Culture and Conversational Inference' and receives a thorough, although not ultimately conclusive, analysis. Generally, the collection is highly commendable for its abundance and variety of data and techniques used.

Cognitive enterprise comes to the fore this year with many commendable texts. Robert Schreuder and Bert Weltens collected 12 state-of-the-art articles on *The Bilingual Lexicon*, concerning research on bilingual lexicology. The recurring thought is the importance of mental lexicon for any model of language processing and the importance of the issue as to which information the speaker shares for both languages in the bilingual lexicon. Semantic priming and cross-language interference provides evidence for common representations across languages and the issue is carried further in the contributions concerning the creation of a model for speech production and the practical applications for teaching and learning vocabulary. As for model construction, the conclusion of David Green's 'Towards a model of L2 Comprehension and Production' is perhaps the most representative for the collection; an ideal theory would relate sentence meaning to the meaning of its constituents, parallel to relating the thought to the concepts. The paper deserves special praise for its perspective, presentation, and the accuracy of its judgements. The book is an informative, well-organized contribution to cognitive linguistics and lexicology and, what is most significant, brings lexicon to the fore of linguists' attention in the era of syntax-driven theories of language acquisition. The leading ideas of language being linked with other cognitive domains, and language structure being dependent on conceptualization reoccur in *Conceptualization and Mental Processing in Language*, papers from a cognitive linguistics conference held in Duisburg, Germany in 1989, supplemented by other invited contributions and edited by Richard Geiger and Brygida Rudzka-Ostyn in the Mouton series Cognitive Linguistics Research. Anna Wierzbicka argues there that since meanings can be either language-independent or language-specific, we need a framework for explaining both; Wolf Paprotté discusses constructing computational lexicon; John Taylor writes about a pedagogical grammar of English based on cognitive principles; and other contributions in this voluminous compilation deal with meaning (including an account of metaphor), structure and function of lexical and morphosyntactic categories, and discourse from the cognitive, cross-linguistic and cross-cultural perspective. Béatrice Lamiroy and Pierre Swiggers studied the imperative in Romance languages and mobilizing the hearer for discourse interaction by various means, and Ronald Geluykens claims that left-dislocation shows an interaction of syntactic, semantic and functional perspectives. This is a heterogeneous collection but certainly worth some attention.

Patterns in the Mind is a new book on mental grammar by Ray Jackendoff. Language, as well as other mental capacities such as experience, music, vision, and thought receive an original treatment: if language is similar to other biological capabilities of the brain, then there should be analogous principles governing other human activities and experience. The ability to understand visual images and music is said to be governed by patterns similar to those that govern linguistic behaviour and there is mental grammar for language, vision and music, as well as for social behaviour, and experience. The thesis of the biological basis of language is strengthened and scientific evidence is put to use in an attempt to answer the question: how does the brain change when a child learns a language? Provocative and inspiring, the book cannot be ignored by the followers and the opposers.

Pragmatics and Cognition is a promising new journal launched by Benjamins. Anna Wierzbicka inaugurates it with her 'Reading Human Faces. Emotion Components and Universal Semantics' (*P&C* 1–23) in which she argues for the 'Natural Semantic Metalanguage' as a framework for analysing components of emotions cross-linguistically. The 'component' approach represents meaning by lexical universals ('I feel something good now' as a meaning of a smiling face) and shows how this meaning is put together ('I want to do something + I think I can't do it now + I didn't think this would happen' for a frown). On a different note, T. Givón discusses text coherence as a natural cognitive process depicting the organization of episodic memory in 'Coherence in Text, Coherence in Mind' (*P&C* 171–227). The journal deserves a warm welcome as it reflects the increasing interest in the issue already mentioned by the present reviewer in her discussion of Recanati, namely the necessity to investigate the relation between utterances and corresponding thoughts.

On similar subjects, *Lingua* presents the second volume of articles devoted to Relevance Theory, edited by Deirdre Wilson and Neil Smith. The special issue (*Lingua* 90.1–220) deals with explicit and implicit communication, discourse particles in communication, constructions from various languages which encode procedural and conceptual information, and other issues researched in the relevance-theoretic framework. On this subject, Billy Clark's 'Relevance and "Pseudo-Imperatives"' (*Ling&P* 16.79–121), requires mentioning as a stimulating and readable contribution to the study of discourse. In the following issue of *Lingua*, Neil Smith, Ianthi-Maria Tsimpli, and Jamal Ouhalla allow us to trace the progress in their study of linguistic capabilities of a polyglot *savant*, 31-year-old Christopher, this time exposed to an Afro-Asiatic language Berber and Epun, an invented language violating universal grammatical principles. In 'Learning the Impossible: The Acquisition of Possible and Impossible Languages by a Polyglot Savant' (*Lingua* 91.279–347), the authors provide evidence against parameter resetting in learning a second language and conclude that acquisition of the second language is a joint function of transfer effects from the first language and the principles of Universal Grammar. The language acquisition topic is also taken up from an unusual perspective by Robin Clark and Ian Roberts in 'A Computational Model of Language Learnability and Language Change' (*LingI* 24.299–345). The question posed concerns the explanation of language change. The learner is said to converge to a target grammar in the process of learning a language. But if each generation converges to the adult grammar, how do languages change? The answer is the 'genetic algorithm': learning is a special case of natural selection. Acquisition is seen here in a 'pre-polyglot-*savant*-paradigm', i.e. as fixing parametric values. 'Cognitive Status and the Form of Referring Expressions in Discourse' by Jeanette Gundel, Nancy Hedberg and Ron Zacharski (*Language* 69.274–307) offers a cognitive explanation of the use of 'it', 'this', 'the' and other referring expressions by postulating a hierarchy based on their being perceived as *given*, to a greater or lesser degree. The authors call the degrees the cognitive statuses and claim their universality across languages, while their usage is governed by Grice's Maxim of Quantity: if a weaker form on the scale is used, it indicates that the stronger one did not apply. This is a readable, informative and well-supported study. Semantics is a vast and rapidly expanding area which does not easily yield to summaries. This year Peter Gärdenfors in his 'The Emergence of Meaning' (*Ling&P* 16.285–309) makes a successful attempt to answer a question of general interest, namely, how speakers can mean the same thing, or what is the relation between individual speakers and their communal language. The main thesis is that the social meaning emerges from individual meanings through the network of linguistic power in the society (in line with the books on language and power reviewed at the beginning of this contribution). In effect, the problem is that of a missing translator: if we have individual conceptual structures, why do we have intelligible languages rather than Babel? The emergence of meaning from conceptual schemes is convincingly claimed to result in the social meaning of language. The formalism of the approach does not confine the audience to those already initiated; it is gently composed into the structure of clearly spelled out arguments.

The abundance of textbooks is on a par with their quality this year. Ronald Wardhaugh's *Investigating Language: Social Problems in Language*, is not an ordinary introductory textbook. It addresses the question *why* we talk about language, facing the issues of the psycholinguistic side of speaking and understanding, variation among languages, use of language in everyday activities and language acquisition. It is readable, encouraging, and informative. Philip Carr's *Phonology* and Francis Katamba's *Morphology* are accessible, well-organized sources of information for undergraduates and other interested parties, simple in style and containing precise definitions. The Modern Linguistics Series launched by Macmillan and edited by Noel Burton-Roberts and Andrew Spencer, although by no means threatening the popularity of the CUP textbook series, provides a more introductory alternative for those unfamiliar with the ideas and concepts in theoretical linguistics. Similar praises can be proclaimed about another work in the above-mentioned series, Vivian Cook's *Linguistics and Second Language Acquisition*. The broad scope of the latter enterprise, accounting for the advancements in syntax, methodological soundness, thoroughness of the accounts of the principles and parameters syntax, Universal Grammar model, and, on the other hand, cognitive approaches, make the text widely utilizable as both a textbook and a reference book. The study of the sequences on second language acquisition and the treatment of the Input Hypothesis by Krashen, as well as that of learning and communication strategies complete the scope and merits of the work. In spite of the open-mindedness of the presentation, the author seems to be a committed proponent of Universal Grammar in second language acquisition, giving, however, credence to the opposition.

Linda Thomas's *Beginning Syntax* from Blackwell will be welcomed by both tutors and undergraduate students of linguistics. The introduction to word and phrasal categories and to tree diagrams could hardly be more accessible and exercises could hardly be less frustrating: clear guidance to every particular phenomenon in syntax is put to use in a series of simple exercises (with answers) and manages to avoid all the metaphysics of contemporary syntactic theories that grow more and more sophisticated. The practical analysis of sentences like the one offered by Linda Thomas is more and more valuable in times when syntactic analysis is also of use to specialists in disciplines other than theoretical linguistics. A more advanced and specialized reference book is offered for those wishing to find their way through some non-constituent-structure grammars. Mary McGee Wood's *Categorial Grammars* presents a cross-section through contemporary approaches and a history of the discipline. She also provides an account of the separate levels in linguistic analysis in these approaches. The work is published in the Routledge series Linguistic Theory Guides edited by Dick Hudson and is aimed at linguists wanting to keep up with recent theories for various purposes such as improving their teaching of mainstream syntax. As the treatment of semantics in syntax is attractive to computational linguists, the work is also likely to attract this group. Wood begins by introducing the tradition of categorial grammars and passes to the main unifying principles of these approaches such as that language is seen in terms of functions and arguments rather than constituent structure, homomorphism of syntax and semantics, favouring monotonicity as opposed to movement or deletion found in transformational grammars, lexicalism about combining words into phrases, i.e. words provide all the necessary information, language as a system of oppositions rather than positive terms, i.e. categories are defined by stating what they combine with and what is formed as a result. Although accessible to all, the book does not lose on its informativeness, which signifies the masterly handling of the endeavour. For those convinced by the mutual full translatability of syntax and semantics, there is a magnificent and long awaited coursebook from Kluwer on Discourse Representation Theory by Hans Kamp and Uwe Reyle, *From Discourse to Logic*. Logic is seen there as a science of inference, and discourse representation structures are offered for interpreting language and accounting for everyday logical deduction, rather than for providing truth conditions of sentences. Although perhaps it is not a text of general interest, it cannot be ignored in this section as an excellent introductory coursebook. The book is published in the Kluwer series Studies in Linguistics and Philosophy and although other contributions to the series are more specialized, two of them have to be mentioned here as linguistics and philosophy interface is not covered by any other sections of this chapter: Alessandro Zucchi's *The Language of Propositions and Events* discusses syntax and semantics of nominals, and *Semantics and the Lexicon* edited by James Pustejovsky presents representative research in lexical semantics, knowledge representation and lexicon design in computational linguistics and contains papers from a workshop held at Brandeis University in 1988. Ray Jackendoff talks there about the semantics of concepts and Lakoff follows suit with the study of metaphor in cognitive semantics. The increase of interdisciplinary studies that involve linguistic research can be seen from the abundance of excellent papers such as those in Pustejovsky's volume.

Realms of Meaning by Th. R. Hofmann in a Longman series Learning About the Language aims at accounting for many issues related by their pertaining to the study of meaning: what is meaning, how conversation works, the study of opposites, negatives, deixis, modals, time, prepositions, reference, suffice as headings to indicate problems with terminology and the overlapping of this enterprise. To raise a more detailed point, reference is presented from an angle far from clear and comprehensive, and the traditional distinctions between reference and denotation or reference and meaning are not preserved. Moreover, propositions and sentences are not juxtaposed and the remarks on quantification in natural language are so general that they are on the verge of being uninformative. Background knowledge and componential analysis also require further treatment. The work is unfortunately an example of oversimplification and erroneous focusing: avoiding technical vocabulary and the lack of commitment to specific theories seems not to pay off in semantics; simplicity is achieved at the great expense of informativeness and clarity.

The study of conversation is enriched by Jacob Mey's *Pragmatics* from Blackwell and Jan Renkema's *Discourse Studies* from Benjamins. In the first, the accessible style and the speed of leading the reader through the subject matter is reconciled with providing a generous portion of knowledge as to what pragmatics is, how micropragmatics studies reference, implicature and speech acts, and macropragmatics accounts for the role of society and context, as well as for the data-driven conversation analysis, with particular emphasis on certain aspects of the sub-field such as the description of various types of social contexts, culture dependence of discourse, and the theoretical and the applied nature of pragmatics. Comprehensive and informative, it will be welcomed by those finding Levinson's *Pragmatics* (1983, CUP) too dense at times. Passing to the other introductory textbook on discourse, Renkema offers a clear, well-organized, and useful coursebook and teaching material covering speech act theory, textuality and cohesion, discourse connections, written and spoken language, styles and types of discourse, the derivation of information and the process of producing utterances. Equipped with examples, questions, and an extensive bibliography, it is likely to be appreciated by linguists both on the learning and the teaching side of the enterprise. To sum up, this rather successful year witnessed the appearance of many stimulating works on general linguistic issues and the proportions of the chosen area or viewpoint seem to have been well balanced with the valuable addition of books on translation theories and linguistics-literary criticism interface.

2. Dialectology and Sociolinguistics (including Creolistics)

Milroy and Milroy's (eds) *Real English: The Grammar of English Dialects in the British Isles* (Longman's Real Language series) provides a much needed addition to the relatively scarce amount of research on syntactic variation in British English dialects. Organized into three parts – Dialect in Education, Regional Variation in English Grammar, and Resources (for the study of dialects in the British Isles) – the volume includes eight papers which have as their common theme the identification of grammatical diversity, and the promotion of syntactic variation as an important object of sociolinguistic study. Jenny Cheshire's paper on 'Non-standard English and Dialect Levelling' achieves both of these objectives: she highlights variability in the syntax used in urban centres despite patterns of contact and consequent levelling which take place in these contexts. Case studies included in the volume provide accounts of Scottish English (Jim Miller), Irish English (John Harris), the dialects of Tyneside and Northumbrian (Joan Beal), and Southern English (Viv Edwards). Viv Edwards also provides a summary of resources – from books to sound recordings – on British English varieties.

Another 1993 publication in Longman's Real Language series is Mark Sebba's *London Jamaican: Language Systems in Interaction*. Based on research undertaken in the early 1980s, Sebba provides a careful and thorough description of this variety by means of detailed analysis of conversational data. In the introduction, Sebba outlines the history of creole development in the Caribbean, and the origins of the use of a creole variety in London. Having pointed to Jamaica and Jamaican culture as the focus for black youth in the UK, he then discusses such issues as how this variety can best be detailed and described, and also examines the functions that London Jamaican (LJ) fulfils. In later chapters, Sebba employs a Conversation Analysis method to describe patterns of code-switching between LJ and London English, and finds that, while London English is employed for stretches of discourse classified as asides and insertions, LJ is typically used to express more salient parts of speakers' utterances. Sebba concludes his work by considering the future that LJ may have in the British education system. Also on Jamaican Creole – but on its use in the USA rather than in Britain – *WEn* (12.2) includes Yvonne Pratt-Johnson's analysis of the problems encountered by student speakers of Jamaican Creole in New York City public schools (257–64). Finally on this topic of the relationship between linguistic and cultural identity, we should recommend Paul Ghuman's text *Coping With Two Cultures* in which the author discusses historical and contemporary issues relating to the position of British-Asian and Indo-Canadian youths in the maintenance of their bicultural identities.

'Welsh and English in the City of Bangor' (*LSoc* 22.1–17) is the title of Cora Lindsay's analysis of the relationship between English and the use of one of Britain's older mother tongues. Having warned that the types of relationship between these two languages are as plentiful as the different areas and towns in Wales, Lindsay assesses whether the linguistic situation found in Bangor can be termed 'diglossic'; criteria examined include the prestige, acquisition, and standardization of Welsh and English, as well as the degree to which these two languages are functionally differentiated. Lindsay finds that the relationship between Welsh and English in Bangor is more complicated than a traditional definition of diglossia allows. For example, in terms of prestige, Lindsay reports that, although traditionally English has been perceived as the language of status and Welsh has been stigmatized, the situation is now rapidly changing with Welsh having the greater prestige in certain domains of use. Similarly, Lindsay finds that patterns of acquisition do not reveal the 'natural' acquisition of one language and the (educational) imposition of the other, as is the general expectation in a diglossic situation. Rather, she observes that while some children acquire Welsh in the home and English through formal education, others acquire English 'naturally' and develop bilingual competence in Welsh in the school context. Also on the topic of the relationship between Welsh and English, James *et al.*'s paper on 'Welsh Bilinguals' English Spelling' (*JMMD* 14.287–304) poses the question to what extent, and in what respects, the second language English spelling of young Welsh–English bilinguals is systematically idiosyncratic. From the basis of analysing the writing of 10- and 11-year-old school children, in which over 38 per cent of misspellings were seen to be attributable to Welsh L1 pronunciation and spelling rules, an 'unreservedly affirmative' answer is given. Turning from Wales to language use in Scotland, *EWW* 14.1 (part 2 remains unseen at time of writing) includes two articles on Scots this year. One is Derrick McClure's review and analysis of individual and regional variation in contemporary and recent Scots literary narrative prose (1–22). The other is Iseabail Macleod's 'Research in Progress' account of the Scottish National Dictionary Association's ongoing aim to 'spread Scots more widely' through the compilation of an English–Scots Dictionary and Thesaurus (115–28).

Examining the use of English in the wider European context, Kaplan discusses 'The Hegemony of English in Science and Technology' (*JMMD* 14.151–72). He finds that it is only work in English which has global appeal and interest in this domain, and that as a (rather unsurprising) consequence, Hungarian scholars are at a linguistic disadvantage. On the relationship between English and other languages in Europe, Ager, Muskens, and Wright edit a collection of papers on the topic of *Language Education for Intercultural Communication* which includes a number of case studies reporting on initiatives in multilingual and multicultural education in the European community. Finally, although not on English *per se*, we should nevertheless record the publication of Guus Extra and Ludo Verhoeven's *Immigrant Languages in Europe*. This collection, based on presentations given at a colloquium on immigrant languages which took place in the Netherlands in 1990, includes a wide variety of papers dealing with topics as diverse as 'South Asian Languages in Britain' by Safder Alladina (55–66); 'Code-Copying in Immigrant Turkish' by Lars Johanson (197–222); and 'Romani at the Crossroads' by Donald Kenrick (285–96). Finally, on a contemporary political theme, François Grin considers 'European Economic Integration and the Fate of Lesser-Used Languages' (*LPLP* 17.ii.101–16). Grin argues that certain languages are likely to benefit and others are likely to lose from the planned patterns of integration in the European Union. Specifically, she claims that varieties likely to prosper include those which are (i) in contact with a majority language of importance in intra-EC trade; (ii) can be used in an urban setting; and (iii) enjoy some degree of official recognition. Languages which Grin claims fall into this category include Catalan and Basque, and languages which do not, and are thus likely to be disadvantaged, include Irish, Breton and Occitan.

Turning our attention from the linguistic situation in Europe to the use of English in Asia, Man-Siu Yau's paper on the 'Functions of Two Codes in Hong Kong Chinese' (*WEn* 12.i.15–24) examines the use of English in a variety of written modes including textbooks, magazines and popular entertainment books. Results show that while English is used in all of these genres, it is most often to be found in texts dealing with science and technology, and business and commerce. Eddie Kuo and Bjorn Jernudd's paper 'Balancing Macro- and Microsociolinguistic Perspectives in Language Management: The Case of Singapore' (*LPLP* 17.1–17) examines the increasing use and status of English *vis-à-vis* the three other official languages of Singapore. The authors comment that, because English is the only non-Asian official language and is thus 'neutral', it is emerging as the language of Singaporean supra-ethnic identity. Reporting on the use of English in specific contexts, Kuo and Jernudd comment that English has been retained as the administrative language in independent Singapore, and that it has seen an increase in status and representation in such domains as higher education, international trade, modern industry and technology. Also on the sociolinguistic situation in Singapore, Anne Pakir discusses the bilingual state of this nation (*JMMD* 14.73–90), and argues that, for young Singaporeans, bilingualism is becoming synonymous with speaking English. Pakir shows how young speakers in Singapore have increased the range and functional use of their English particularly within the home domain, and how this shift and increase in the use of English has led to a simultaneous change in cultural values from Eastern to Western norms. Finally on Singapore, Anna Kwan-Terry examines the political, socio-cultural and economic changes which have occurred over the past decade, and consequent new initiatives for the teaching of English in this nation (*WEn* 12.75–84).

In contrast with the increasing use of English in Singapore, Ozog's analysis of 'Bilingualism and National Development in Malaysia' (*JMMD* 14.59–72), highlights the demise of English in this nation. Ozog reports on how the phasing out of bilingual education since the 1960s, and the abolition of English medium education, has led to a greatly reduced use of English among young Malaysians; particularly among those social classes who relied on the education system to provide them with instruction in the English language. However, Ozog finds that while, ostensibly, proficiency in English is no longer a requirement for higher education and career advancement, nevertheless, in practice, English is still a necessary prerequisite to educational, social and occupational mobility. Ozog thus points a tension between the theory and practice of the use of English in Malaysia, and he concludes that, while English is recognized as being important for national development, 'in Malaysia it is not wise to praise English without at the same time praising Malay'. In 'Standards and Pedagogical Norms for Teaching English in Malaysia' (*WEn* 12.223–38), Saran Kaur Gill identifies different varieties of Malaysian English (on a continuum of basilectal to acrolectal) and argues that future research should aim to identify which forms are suitable for 'international' communication (and thus taught to those learning English as a foreign/second language), and which are appropriate only in the domain of 'intranational' usage.

Other analyses of Asian varieties this year include descriptions of Pakistan, Japanese and, more unusually, Egyptian English. In his paper 'The Power of English in Pakistan' (included in *WEn*'s *Symposium on Power, Politics and English*, 12.147–56), Shemeem Abbas discusses how social, political and economic control are implemented through language hegemony in Pakistan and in the 'Third World' in general. Abbas examines the linguistic and sociolinguistic position in Pakistan (and specifically identifies the competition between Urdu and English in this context), and concludes that while competence in English may be required if Third World countries are to be included as members of the larger 'world community', the teaching of English in these nations should be carried out within a '*Third World*' theory of literacy orality and aesthetics'. Daisuke Nagashima charts the consequences of contact between European languages and Japanese in her text 'Bilingual Lexicography in Japan: The Dutch–Japanese to the English–Japanese Dictionary' (*WEn* 12.249–55). Finally, 'Illocutionary Acts Across Languages: Editorializing in Egyptian English' (*WEn* 12.35–46) is the title of Dudley Reynolds's article comparing 'acts of passing judgement' (as accomplished in editorial writing) in Egyptian English, American English, and Egyptian Arabic. Reynolds's analysis reveals that while Egyptian English editorials are unlike their American counterparts, this is *not* due to the influence of Egyptian Arabic. Rather, Reynolds concludes that differences in illocutionary acts (e.g. Representatives, Directives, Commissives and Expressives) are best explained by reference to Grice's maxims of conversational behaviour: while American English editorials place more emphasis on the maxim of Quality, Egyptian English editorials place more importance on the maxim of Quantity.

From the Pacific, Anders Kallgard reports on 'Present Day Pitcairnese' (*EWW* 14.71–114). The paper begins with an account of the origins and history of this variety, and proceeds to provide a description of contemporary Pitcairnese in terms of its spelling, phonology and vocabulary. Kallgard's approach is broadly sociolinguistic: historical development is charted with reference to such major political events as the opening of the Panama canal; and contemporary synchronic description provides information on patterns of socially motivated (particularly age-related) variation. In concluding his paper, Kallgard considers the future for Pitcairnese, and suggests that its maintenance may be best assured by changing islanders' negative perception of their language. Kevin Kawamoto writes on 'Hegemony and Language Politics in Hawaii' *(WEn* 12.193–207), and reports that the enforced patterns of English language assimilation which occurred with American colonization are being reversed by contemporary initiatives. Specifically, Kawamoto finds that sovereignty claims relating to the reclamation of land, traditional practices, and culture are leading to a resurgence of the Hawaiian language as a marker of native identity.

Unfortunately, we have little to report on Australian or New Zealand English this year. *AJL* did not include anything of direct interest to readers of *YWES* in its first issue, and the second issue remains unseen at the time of writing. Those who have access to *Te Reo* – the journal of the Linguistic Society of New Zealand – will find papers on 'The Australian Influence on Melanesian Pidgin English' by Philip Baker (36.3–68); 'Chairpersons and Goddesses: non-sexist usages in New Zealand English' by Janet Holmes (36.99–114); and '"Hey Yous!": The Maori-NZE Interface in Sociolinguistic Rules of Address' by Lorraine Johnston and Shelley Robertson (36.115–27).

In contrast to Southern Hemisphere Englishes, the growing interest and research into African English has provided a wealth of publications this year. A number of these have examined the linguistic consequences of the social revolution in South Africa. Sheila Onkaetse Mmusi's 'Ethnic Labels in South African English' *(WEn* 12.47–58) focuses on the question of the relationship between social, political and economic factors, and semantic shifts in the 'labelling of others' under the Apartheid system. Mmusi's engaging paper points to the tension between self-labelling and government-labelling of indigenous peoples, and to how different semantic connotations emerge in reaction to political activity (e.g. the melioration of 'black' during the 1970s due to the 'Black Consciousness' movement). In concluding her paper, Mmusi points to the importance of labelling procedures and practices for the newly emerging post-apartheid South Africa. Another paper which looks at the relationship between politics and language use is Elizabeth De Kadt's 'Language, Power, and Emancipation in South Africa' *(WEn Symposium on Power, Politics and English* 12.157–68). Kadt first seeks to develop a more general model of the 'power of language' and then uses this model to assess English language use in South Africa. In particular, she aims to assess the implications of using English as a common language, and argues that 'accepting English as a lingua franca means simultaneously – and generally unwittingly – accepting a particular interpretation of the world, and at that one which is located in the context of colonialism and apartheid'. Kadt concludes with a discussion of how language planning, particularly in the form of strategies for promoting individual bi- and multilingualism, can be used as a mechanism of emancipation in South Africa. Finally on language use in this nation, we should recommend Ralph Adendorff's 'Ethnographic Evidence of the Social Meaning of Fanakalo in South Africa' *(JPCL* 8.1–28). Fanakalo is a creole variety (born out of contact between speakers of English, Zulu and Afrikaans) which is restricted to certain – particularly non-affective – domains, and has unfavourable connotations associated with its use. Adendorff seeks to explain the value system and ideology which Fanakalo encodes by examining its employment in a number of *unmarked* and *marked* domains. Analysis reveals that while in unmarked/ typical settings the creole variety is used as a means of 'entrenching asymmetrical power relations and of limiting the rights of blacks', in marked contexts, use of the creole fulfils a more positive function of creating solidarity between speaker and listener.

Carol Myers-Scotton's *Social Motivations for Code-Switching: Evidence from Africa*, provides a detailed and delicate description of patterns of language use in Kenya and Zimbabwe. Although her main objective in drawing on the African data is to support a theory of Markedness to explain code-switching, as a background to this, Myers-Scotton considers the use of English as an official language, and identifies the difficulties which arise in promoting indigenous varieties to official status. For example, noting the problem faced in contexts such as Nigeria where the major groups — Yoruba, Ibo and Hausa — are each unwilling to see another group's language prevail, Myers-Scotton points out that it is because of this internal variation, division and competition that the languages of colonization — French and Portuguese as well as English — remain as official languages in Africa. However, while these languages have the virtue of being alien and thus relatively 'neutral' as far as indigenous ethnic groups are concerned, nevertheless, their elitist connection means that they represent a negative choice. In essence, the 'neutrality' of English is purely theoretical, in practice, access to English, and other colonial varieties, comes only through an extended formal education which is available to the privileged alone. Regarding her theory of Markedness to explain code-switching, Myers-Scotton's theory rests on the assumption that participants enter into conversations with similar expectations regarding unmarked code choices and/or unmarked communicative intentions. To explain this knowledge, and the patterns of switching which occur as a result, Myers-Scotton emphasizes social context and contextual norms, and draws from work in the Sociology of Language, Pragmatics, Social and Linguistic Anthropology. Myers-Scotton also has a paper in *LSoc* this year entitled 'Common and Uncommon Ground: Social and Structural Factors in Code-switching' (22.475–503).

The competition between indigenous languages for the status of official language in African countries is also mentioned in Oladejo's paper 'How not to Embark on a Bilingual Education Policy in a Developing Nation: The Case of Nigeria' *(JMMD* 14.91–102). Oladejo reports on how language planning strategies in this nation have been designed to ensure that the high position occupied by English is shared with indigenous languages. However, because of the failure of these policies, and particularly because of their 'over ambitious' and 'unrealistic' aims, Oladejo reports that English remains the '*de facto*, if not the *de jure*, official language of Nigeria'. Also in *JMMD*, Rugatiri Mekacha examines the use of English, Kiswahili and various ethnic community languages in Tanzania. Her main thesis is that the complex linguistic situation which holds in Tanzania cannot, as has been suggested, be described as triglossic. For example, Mekacha shows that English has no 'communicative status' for the vast majority of speakers in Tanzania; and that Kiswahili and ethnic community languages show little functional specialization or stability. Casmir Rubagumya's *Teaching and Researching Language in African Classrooms*, published by Multilingual Matters, also looks at the linguistic situation in Tanzania — as well as in Botswana, Burundi, Zaire and Zimbabwe — and provides an educational perspective on the issue of language use in Africa. Multilingual Matters, who have been responsible for publishing so much of the material on varieties of English outside of the UK and North America, also release Gerda Mansour's *Multilingualism and Nation Building* this year: a text which examines the linguistic, social and political factors surrounding multilingualism in West Africa. Finally, *JMMD* includes two further papers on English in Africa. Kembo Sure considers the 'Grammatical and Phonological Integration of English Loanwords into Dholuo' *(*14.329–44), and argues that patterns of borrowing reflect political and cultural interaction (and particularly patterns of cultural superiority) between the Luo and immigrant European population. Bobda writes on 'English pronunciation in Cameroon' (14.435–45) where it seems that 'British-based' accents and specifically, although somewhat surprisingly, 'RP' features are winning out against American and Nigerian features in the pronunciation of English in the Cameroon.

Glowka and Lance's *Language Variation in North American English: Research and Teaching* is a collection of 39 essays all addressing the question of how best to teach language variation; a number of the papers also aim to give guidance to students beginning research on this topic. The papers are organized into seven parts: General; Regional Variation; Ethnic and Social Variation; Sex, Gender and Language Variation; Variation in Historical Contexts; Standard Language and Questions of Usage; Language Variation and Composition. Apart from its use as a textbook, there are a number of papers in the section on Ethnic and Social Variation which may be of more general interest; for example, John Baugh's 'Research Trends for Black American English'; and Salikoko Mufwene's 'Investigating Gullah Difficulties in Ensuring "Authenticity"'. On the topic of texts for teaching, this is perhaps the best place to note the second edition of Freeborn, French and Langford's *Varieties of English: An Introduction to the Study of Language* – a beginner's guide to variation including discussion of the relationship between Standard English and non-standard varieties; the English of speech and writing; and stylistic variation in English. The use of illustrations, examples and suggestions for discussion topics makes the text suitable for students taking introductory courses in English Language and Sociolinguistics.

Guillermo Bartelt's 'Urban American Intertribal Discourse' (*EWW* 14.57–70) is an ethnographical account of the discourse structures characteristic of American Indian public dance celebrations – *powwows*. Analysis of speech in this setting reveals that the discourse strategies employed – e.g. indirectness, reticence and non-authoritarianism – reflect the social conventions common to many tribes, and thus mark the *powwow* as a social setting in which the development of an intertribal identity of Indianness is being developed in an urban context. 'A U.S. Colony at a Linguistic Crossroads: The Decision to Make Spanish the Official Language of Puerto Rico' (*LPLP* 17.120–39) is the title of Velez *et al.*'s report on the rationale leading to the 1991 act which made Spanish the sole official language of Puerto Rico, and the consequent political, social and economic repercussions. The authors examine the place of English in contemporary, officially 'monolingual', Puerto Rico, and consider the claim that the real purpose of making Spanish the sole official language was to 'challenge and, if possible, minimize the presence of English' in this nation.

Providing us with a link between American English and creole varieties, John Lipski writes on '*Y'all* in American English: From Black to White, from Phrase to Pronoun' (*EWW* 14.23–56). Through charting the geographical and chronological development of this form together with making an examination of its syntactic evolution, Lipski argues that *y'all* had its origins in the creole of plantation settlements and entered into white Southern American English from Black English in the mid-nineteenth century. Lipski suggest that the transmission followed two tracks: from Black English speaking nursemaids (and their children) to the children of wealthy plantation owners; and from the close contact between speakers of Black English and working-class White Southern English speakers (from colonial times to the present day). On English-based and English-influenced creoles *per se*, first mention should go to Lise Winer's report on 'Right Throughs, Rings and Taws: Marbles Terminology in Trinidad and Tobago' (*LSoc* 22.41–66). Winer's analysis suggests that although these gaming terms are British in origin, they also reveal East Indian, French-Creole and possibly African influences. As well as the development of the terms, Winer looks at the linguistic characteristics of those who use them. In particular, she reports on a gender-related pattern where men's speech in the game of marbles is shown to be 'competitive' and 'confrontational'. Another paper which examines Trinidadian Creole in order to draw wider and more general conclusions is Valerie Youssef's 'Children's Linguistic Choices: Audience Design and Societal Norms' (*LSoc* 22.257–74). In her latest paper on this creole variety, Youssef examines pre-school children's variable production of Trinidadian Creole and Standard English verb forms, and finds that children's use of the two varieties changes even when audience factors remain constant. She concludes that factors such as topic, setting, discourse mode and level of emotionality have a style determining function independent of audience design, and that the social and psychological constraints which modify audience design must be accounted for in explaining linguistic behaviour.

Sali Tagliamonte and Shana Poplack's 'The Zero-Marked Verb: Testing the Creole Hypothesis' (*JPCL* 8.171–206) examines 'early' black Englishes, and draws valuable conclusions for the explanation of creole language development generally. The authors analyse data from two sources: native English-speaking descendants of American ex-slaves who settled on the Peninsula of Samana in the Dominican Republic; and recordings of 11 former slaves born in the Southern States of America. Using a variable rule analysis to examine morphological marking of past temporal reference structures, Tagliamonte and Poplack provide evidence which counters the assumption that creole grammars feature a different tense/mood/aspect system from that of their lexifiers. 'Pionnier and Late Nineteenth Century Bislama' (*JPCL* 8.207–26) is the title of Tony Crowley's latest paper on this Melanesian pidgin. Crowley outlines the grammatical account of Bislama published by Pere Pionnier in 1913, and uses this to provide support for his argument that many lexical and grammatical forms in contemporary Tok Pisin can be traced to late nineteenth-century Melanesian pidgin.

IJSL includes two papers on the relationship between English and French-based creoles represented in the Caribbean. David Frank's article 'Political, Religious, and Economic Factors Affecting Language Choice in St. Lucia' (102.39–56), examines the history of the use of English as the 'official' language, and French-creole as the 'national' language in this nation. Frank shows that, although traditionally the national creole has been stigmatized and suppressed, the recent 'Creole Movement' has led to a change in the prestige and, simultaneously, an elaboration of the functions fulfilled by the local language. A similar picture is painted in Stephanie Stuart's 'Dominican Patwa – Mother Tongue or Cultural Relic?' (102.57–72). Stuart shows that, as in St Lucia, the local creole variety has traditionally been stigmatized, but that due to the work of the

'Standing Committee on Creole Studies', attitudes have changed and Patwa is now represented, albeit in a limited way, in such domains as education, government administration and radio. Stuart concludes that the future of the local creole language can only be assured if Patwa continues its extension into official domains, and, more specifically, if young speakers are taught to value the use of this variety in formal as well as informal contexts.

On the topic of English as an international language, and particularly with reference to the teaching of English internationally, we should record the publication of the following papers: Kimberley Brown's 'World Englishes in Tesol Programs: An Infusion Model of Curricular Innovation' (*WEn* 12.59–73). Marc Gerard Deneire's 'Democratizing English as an International Language' (*WEn* 12.169–78); Jeffra Flaitz's 'French Attitudes toward the Ideology of English as an International Language' (*WEn* 12.179–91); and, staying with the English–French connection, Douglas Kibbee's 'World French takes on World English: Competing Visions of National and International Languages' (*WEn* 12.209–21). On the question of testing English cross-culturally, *WEn* 12 includes four papers (originally given at the conference on World Englishes Today, Illinois, 1992): Bernard Spolsky's 'Testing Across Cultures: An Historical Perspective' (87–93); Peter Lowenberg's 'Issues of Validity in Tests of English as a World Language: Whose Standards?' (95–106); Cathy Wesolek *et al.*'s 'The Philippine Refugee Processing Centre: A Case Study' (107–12); and Fred Davidson's 'Testing English Across Cultures: Summary and Comments' (113–25).

Finally, to bring this review of the use of English around the world to a close, we should recommend the fourth edition of Albert Baugh and Thomas Cable's *A History of the English Language*. Although this volume fits more neatly into another section, it is worth mentioning here because of the authors' attention to the social and political factors which have influenced the spread and development of English. This is particularly true of the fourth edition which, among numerous other revisions, includes new sections dealing with the use of English in the Caribbean, Singapore, Hong Kong and Malaya.

Although there are no textbooks on Sociolinguistics or Dialectology *per se* published this year, there are a number of general volumes which deserve to be mentioned. First, we should highly recommend Ronald Wardhaugh's *Investigating Language: Central Problems in Linguistics,* in which the author aims not simply to introduce the reader to concepts, theories and paradigms of Linguistics, but rather asks *why* it is that linguists are preoccupied with particular concepts and concerns. The concise nature of the volume's chapter headings – Do Only Humans Talk?; Does the Mind Matter?; Why do Languages Vary So? – are indicative of the general nature of the text which, by avoiding jargon and providing clear and engaging discussion, makes the volume essential reading for all students seeking a general introduction to the study of language. Another textbook which deserves to be mentioned is David Silverman's *Interpreting Qualitative Data: Methods for Analysing Talk, Text and Interaction.* In this, his second work on qualitative procedures, Silverman provides hints on 'Beginning Research' as well as detailed discussion of the methods of qualitative analysis; for example, chapters on Observation and Interview Data. In later chapters he considers the implications of using qualitative techniques for linguistic analysis – e.g. chapters on 'Validity and Reliability' and 'The Practical Relevance of Qualitative Research'. The essential and important theme of the volume is that qualitative analysis cannot be defined merely in terms of 'what is not quantitative', but rather constitutes an independent theory and set of methods in its own right. Silverman's use of exercises and worked examples, together with his clear exposition of concepts, makes this a valuable text for students interested in the interface between sociology, social anthropology and linguistics, as well as for those seeking an introduction to the area of discourse analysis.

Staying with the topic of discourse and interaction, this year has seen the publication of numerous texts on conversational speech. A brief scan of the literature highlights John Shotter's *Conversational Realities: Constructing Life Through Language* – a text which provides an in-depth discussion of the ways in which speakers use conversational language in order to construct different kinds of social relationship; the text may be of most interest to those concerned with the more 'social' side of the sociolinguistic. Cecilia Ford's *Grammar in Interaction: Adverbial Clauses in American English Conversations* brings together linguistic and social considerations to provide an illuminating account of the use and functions of adverbial clauses in conversational American English. Finally, Peter Hartley provides an introductory text dealing with defining, describing and explaining *Interpersonal Communication*; the text is suitable for students seeking a clear and simple beginner's guide to this topic. From conversational to institutional speech, Vijay Bhatia's *Genre Analysis* provides another in the increasing number of texts dealing with language use in professional settings. Bhatia begins with an overview of different approaches which have been taken to this topic – grammatical, functional, interactional – and argues for the importance of a genre analysis (more usually associated with the study of literature) which emphasizes professional language as goal-orientated, highly structured and conventionalized.

On the relationship between language and culture, Brian Street edits an enlightening collection of papers on the theme of *Cross-Cultural Approaches to Literacy*. The collection includes papers by Don Kulick and Christopher Strand on literacy in Papua New Guinea; Peter Probst on literacy and religion in western Nigeria; and Miriam Camitta on the vernacular writing of high school students in Philadelphia. *Language and Culture*, edited by David Graddol, Linda Thompson and Mike Byram, includes papers presented at the 24th meeting of the British Association of Applied Linguistics. The volume opens with a paper by Gunther Kress on 'Cultural Considerations in Linguistic Description' in which Kress charts past developments and future paths for Applied Linguistic Study. Arguing that *Linguistic* Linguistics is 'a-social' and 'a-historical', Kress highlights the potential of *Applied* Linguistic study as a dynamic and dialogic approach to language use. Other papers in the volume include Brian Street's 'Culture is a Verb: Anthropological Aspects of Language and Cultural Process'; Norman Fairclough's 'Discourse and Social Change in the Enterprise Culture'; and Romy Clark's 'Developing Practices of Resistance: Critical Reading for Students of Politics'. Although not on English, Daniel Wagner's *Literacy, Culture and Development*, which examines the acquisition of literacy in Morocco, certainly deserves a mention. Finally, we should record Roberta Stein and Carol Eastman's paper 'The Negotiation and Outcome of Language and Culture Contact' (*LPLP* 17.238–53) in which the authors examine case studies of contact and their results. From the basis of their comparisons, Stein and Eastman conclude that integration into a new group 'is not so much a matter of speaking with complete structural accuracy as it is a matter of gaining access to the institutions of the dominant society and acquiring communicative competence'.

Linking the factor of age and language use, Nikolas Coupland and Jon Nussbaum edit a collection of papers entitled *Discourse and Lifespan Identity*. The papers take as their general theme the topic of how maturation, ageing and change are reflected and represented in social interaction, and in doing so meet, in part at least, Coupland's recent call for increased attention to the elderly as a speech community worthy of recognition and study (see report in *YWES* 73). The publication (for the first time in paperback) of *Language, Memory and Aging*, edited by Leah Light and Deborah Burke, also provides data on this theme but concentrates not so much on Sociolinguistic as Psycholinguistic issues: e.g. Salthouse's 'Effects of Aging on Verbal Abilities'; Kemper's 'Geriatric Psycholinguistics: Syntactic Limitations of Oral and Written Language; and Huff's 'The Disorder of Naming in Alzheimer's Disease'.

On the relationship of gender and language use, first mention should go to the publication of the second edition of Jennifer Coates's excellent textbook on the topic – *Women, Men and Language: A Sociolinguistic Account of Gender Differences in Language*. This revised edition includes up-to-date information and references on topics ranging from the relationship between gender and communicative competence, gender-related variation and linguistic change, and the social consequences of gender-related linguistic differences. Coates's clear and compelling style, together with the exhaustive review of research in the field, makes this text the standard introductory book for all those interested in the topic of women's language and male–female linguistic differences. Linking the topics of *Language, Minority Education and Gender*, David Corson considers such issues as Bilingual Education; Gender and Language Policy in Education; and the Dynamics of Teacher–Pupil Interaction. In the final chapter of his work, Corson considers how social injustice can be addressed through the development of explicit policies on language awareness. Janet Holmes reviews the literature pertaining to 'Immigrant Women and Language Maintenance in Australia and New Zealand' (*IJAL* 3.159–79) and finds that, while women tend to maintain ethnic minority languages for a longer period than men, nevertheless this is not at the expense of acquiring new languages: Holmes cites a number of studies which reveal that women often take a leading role in language shift. Finally, on a related topic, James and Lesley Milroy consider the interaction between gender, social network and social class in their paper 'Mechanisms of Change in Urban Dialects' (*IJAL* 3.57–78). In contrast to a long-held belief in sociolinguistic enquiry, the Milroys suggest that gender-based patterns of variation are not always explicable by reference to social class differences, but rather that, in stark contrast to this, gender is 'often prior to social class'. Among many specific points on language change, Milroy and Milroy find that women are leading in a supra-local shift towards the use of glottal stops in Britain. This conclusion, together with that drawn by Janet Holmes, adds to the mounting evidence that females are not as linguistically 'insecure' and 'conservative' as has traditionally been believed.

3. Morphology

We start by noting the publication (in 1992) of a paperback version of Laurie Bauer's *Introducing Linguistic Morphology* (hardback published in 1988, but not reviewed in *YWES* at the time). This work provides a convenient introduction to the main issues in the study of morphology. After presenting fundamental concepts like the morpheme, allomorphy, affixation, and compounding in Part I, Bauer elaborates on these in Part II, which addresses topics like the definition of 'word', productivity, the distinction (and difference) between inflection and derivation, and the morphology–syntax and morphology–phonology interfaces. In Part III, some current models and areas of research are presented (lexicalist morphology, word-and-paradigm morphology, morphological universals of the Bybeean and Carstairean kind, and natural morphology). There are study questions and exercises at the back of the book. Many of the examples dealt with are from English, and this fact, together with the book's clarity and emphasis on essential ideas of a range of approaches rather than on technical details, should make it a good choice as a textbook for an introductory general course on morphology. For a course that is more slanted towards the generative approach to morphology, we would recommend Francis Katamba's *Morphology*. The first few chapters cover much the same ground as Bauer's (since this book too is meant for complete novices), but after this the emphasis is very much on generative work. Lexical morphology and prosodic morphology in particular receive extensive discussion, but the student is also acquainted with notions such as grammatical function changing processes, the mirror principle, incorporation, and the right-hand head rule. Examples mainly come from English, African languages and Arabic. Each chapter concludes with a set of exercises, and there are also some in-text questions.

Apart from these two textbooks, there are some general theoretical items published this year that deserve our attention. In *Simplicity in Generative Morphology*, Harry Bochner puts forward a model that he calls 'lexical relatedness morphology'. He argues that related words (e.g. *declare*, *declaration*, and *declarative*) are all in the lexicon and are related by matching against morphological patterns (e.g. [/X/, V, Z] ↔ [/Xation/, N, ACT of Zing] ↔ [/Xive/, Adj, PRONE to Zing]). Inflection is also handled in this way. Bochner shows in some detail how his model would deal with various cases of lexical relation in English (including the *receive-reception* pattern) and other languages. He also compares his model with that of lexical morphology, which he criticizes for failing to take into account historical explanations (e.g. the ungrammaticality of **incheerful* can be attributed to the fact that *in-* has never become productive enough to attach to native bases, rather than to its level-ordering, and the restrictions applying to specific elements (e.g. **Darwinismian* is out because *-ian* productively attaches only to names, not because it is at level 2).

Bochner's model implies that words do not consist of morphemes; in this respect (and others), it is close to Anderson's important *Amorphous Morphology*, published last year. We reviewed that work very briefly in *YWES* 73.24–5, but fuller reviews have now appeared. We would note in particular the one by Andrew Carstairs-McCarthy, in *YM* 1992.209–33; he concludes that, for at least some purposes, words must have a certain degree of internal structure, since some word formation rules must be able to inspect it. To account for *mutable* vs *debatable*, for example, the rule in question must know that *-ate* can be truncated only if it is a suffix. The existence of cases like this will probably not surprise Rochelle Lieber, whose *Deconstructing Morphology* we also briefly reviewed last year (*YWES* 73.25), since in her model words have a full-blown phrase marker associated with them. Of the reviews of her book that have appeared this year, we mention only that by Richard Sproat (in *YM* 1992.235–58), who points out some problems for her analysis of anaphoric islands (why is *When Reagan entered, he$_i$ waved to all the Reagan$_i$ites* possible, in spite of the apparent violation of binding principle C?) and for her analysis of synthetic compounds, which cannot distinguish *American history teacher* from **apple on a stick taster*.

A general model of morphology which combines features of both Anderson's and Lieber's models is proposed by Morris Halle and Alec Marantz in 'Distributed Morphology and the Pieces of Inflection' (in Hale and Keyser). They postulate the existence in the grammar of a separate level of Morphological Structure (positioned in between S-structure and Phonetic Form). Terminal nodes (including affixes) are inserted in phrase markers at D-structure as bundles of semantic and morphosyntactic features, but receive phonological features only at the level of Morphological Structure. At that level, and also at S-structure and D-structure, there are several operations (addition of terminal nodes; movement; merger of adjacent nodes – such as Tense and Verb in English, which is discussed in detail; fusion of, for example, Case and Number, etc.) that can bring about mismatches between morphosyntax and phonology.

Turning now to publications whose focus is on English rather than the general theory of morphology, we find a number of studies on verbal morphology, two of which appear in Stein and Tieken-Boon van Ostade (eds), *Toward a Standard English 1600–1800*, a book which is concerned with processes of standardization. Jenny Cheshire looks at 'Standardization and the English Irregular Verbs' synchronically by comparing standard forms with the range of variants that are found in present-day dialects. Since dialect forms are less prone to standardization, 'it is possible to identify some of the effects of standardization and literacy on the verbal morphology of English' (p. 116). She notes, for instance, that the preservation of irregular verbal forms is stronger in the standard than in the dialects, suggesting that a social/psychological force may have been at work here. On the other hand, those verbs that are still irregular in dialects are usually not very salient in standard discourse so they would not be used by standard speakers to establish a social divide. Cheshire also finds evidence that [ʌ], which became a marker of pastness in the sixteenth to eighteenth centuries (cf. Hogg 1988), is still used as such in dialects. Finally, the use of the *-en*-less form for the strong past participle, a tendency stopped by normative grammarians, is still current in the dialects. The other article in this book, by Roger Lass, is diachronic but complementary to Cheshire: 'Proliferation and Option-cutting: The Strong Verb in the Fifteenth to Eighteenth Centuries'. After some important preliminary methodological points about the use of a corpus (in his case the Helsinki corpus), Lass looks at the paradigm restructuring that has taken place in the class of strong verbs as a result of two general reorganizations: (i) a typological trend towards an invariant-base morphology, isolating the strong verb, and (ii) the erosion of number and stabilization of tense as the main inflection on the verb, leading to the loss of one of the preterite vowels (but not without creating a lot of junk first that could be and often was exaptated). Lass next discusses the tendencies that are at play to resolve the resulting complex and variable strong verb system, such as the preterite-to-past-participle shift, the transfer to the weak verbal system etc., illustrating these by means of a number of case histories. He ends his contribution by considering what the effects of normative grammar have been on the ironing out of these variants.

A partial regularity in the strong verb system is noted by Hubert Gburek, in 'A Morphonological Rule for the Past Tense Formation of Irregular English

Verbs' (in Aertsen and Jeffers). He argues that, after forms like *chid*, *kept*, and *met* had developed a short vowel through the operation of various unrelated processes, the short vowel came to be interpreted as a marker of past tense, which led to its use also in *ate*, *fell*, *fled*, *held*, *said*, etc. This rule was partially productive in Shakespeare's time (hence rhymes like *proved-loved*), and has left traces in many present-day verbs.

Developments in present-tense morphology are studied by Merja Kytö, who uses the Helsinki Corpus to write about the 'Third-Person Present Singular Verb Inflection in Early British and American English' (*LVC* 5.113–39). She looks at the decline of the *-th* form (zero forms were already relics) in favour of the *-s* form and notes that quite a number of factors played a role here, such as the type of verb (e.g. *do* and *have* are among the last to change), the phonological shape of the stem-final element (vowels showing a longer preference for *-th*), text type, style and author's sex. The *-s* ending was already the colloquial norm before English became established in America, but, contrary to expectation, the rate of change was more rapid in the new world than it was at home. Also concerned with the ending of the third person is the following study by Michael Montgomery, Janet Fuller and Sharon DeMarse, ' "The Black Men has Wives and Sweet Harts [and third person plural *-s*] Jest like the White Men": Evidence for Verbal *-s* from Written Documents on 19th-century African American Speech' (*LVC* 5.335–57). This is a very worthwhile contribution which may throw light on the controversy between the 'creole-hypothesis' and the 'British dialect-hypothesis' among researchers of Black (or African American) Vernacular English (BVE). A comparison of letters by nineteenth-century semi-literate African Americans and the contemporary McCullough letters written by a family of Scots–Irish descent shows clear similarities in the use of verbal *-s*, both obeying the same constraints. Thus, it is clear that the nature of the subject (especially pronominal vs nominal) plays an important role in the presence or absence of *-s* in the third person plural (the singular usually had *-s*), and so does the proximity of the subject (here also first and second person tend to acquire *-s* when the subject is not adjacent). These constraints are like the ones found in early Northern, especially Scottish English (cf. the study by Meurman-Solin below), and therefore support the idea that at least some of the features of BVE are not based on an earlier creole.

There has been a lively exchange this year in *Views* on the nature of Old English weak verb class II (infinitive ending in *-ian*). Roger Lass poses the question: 'Old English *-ian*: Inflectional or Derivational?' (*Views* 2.26–34). He takes some 200 verbs of this class and argues that nearly all can be regarded as derivational (e.g. *fiscian*, *gearwian*, *sarian*, *cunnian*, etc.). His conclusion is that, although it is also in a sense conjugational (i.e. inflectional), class II looks much like a bit of derivational morphology. Lass's piece sparked off four reactions. Support for Lass's views is expressed by Alfred Bammesberger in his 'Old English *acsian*: Word-Formation and Etymology' (*Views* 2.68–70); he provides a possible base for *acsian* (which Lass had listed among the verbs having no clear nominal source) and points out that at least two of the other apparently source-less verbs in class II are hapaxes. No support for Lass's ideas is expressed by Nikolaus Ritt, who asks: 'What Exactly is it that Makes OE *-ian* Derivational? Reply to Lass' (*Views* 2.35–9). He argues that the relation between the presumed base (e.g. *ar*, *synn*, *andsæc*) and the related class II verb (*arian*, *syngian*, *andsacian*) has neither a constant formal marker (since both base and verb have many different inflectional forms; e.g. *ara* can be a form of the noun or the verb) nor a systematic semantics (*arian* is 'to endow with *ar*', *syngian* 'to commit *synn*', and in the case of *andsacian* the verb seems more basic than the noun). Hence an analysis in which both verb and noun/adjective derive from a syntactically neutral root seems more appropriate to him. Christiane Dalton-Puffer ('How Distinct are Inflection and Derivation? Reply to Lass and Ritt', in *Views* 2.40–4) does not entirely agree with Ritt. She points out that some derivational markers (e.g. present-day English -*al*, as in *musical*, *industrial*) can express many meanings. To accommodate Lass's points, she suggests that inflection and derivation should be viewed as endpoints on a scale. A further contribution to the debate comes from Dieter Kastovsky ('Inflection, Derivation and Zero – Or: What Makes OE and German Derived Denominal Verbs Verbs?', in *Views* 2.71–81). He suggests that the structure of verbs like *arian* (or the comparable form *ehren* in Modern German) is [ᵥ [ₙ *ar*]φ]*ian*, with zero-derivation of noun to verb (much like conversion in present-day English), and -*ian* and the other verbal endings being added as inflectional markers. He also sketches the possible development of this verbal class from a Proto-Germanic or even Proto-Indo-European system with a thematic vowel which was derivational but later reinterpreted as inflectional. Finally, in 'Old English Class II: More VIEWS' (*Views* 2.104–10), Roger Lass himself reacts to some of the points made in connection with his ideas. He agrees with Ritt that the meaning of class II is too unspecific to call it derivational, and with Dalton-Puffer on the idea that inflection and derivation define a scale. The position of class II on this scale may have been one of 'geriatric derivationality'. Although Lass does not say so, his reaction implies disagreement with Kastovsky's analysis.

There are three studies of back-formation this year. Alan Slotkin and Robert Bode write about 'A Back(-to-the-Future)-Formation' (*AS* 68.323–7), by which they mean the use of *contrapt* as a verb (attested as participle and gerund). They also survey the possible origins of *contraption* (derivation from *contrive*, in a manner similar to *deceive-deception*? blend of *contrivance*, *trap* and *invention*?). A more theoretical study is Paval Štekauer's 'On some Issues of Back-Formation in English' (*Linguistica Pragensia* 2/93.81–8). His main point is that back-formation is a productive, specific word-formative process, which is independent of (zero) suffixation and which is important also from a theoretical, synchronic point of view (in contrast to Marchand (1960, 1969), who saw it as a purely diachronic process). Štekauer advocates the 'onomasiological method'. He believes that back-formation both formally and semantically (as a process of recategorization) is in fact much closer to conversion than to derivation; he rejects, therefore, the term zero-suffix. To support his case further, he shows that there are also cases of back-formation, such as *pease > pea*, which are not related to an omitted derivational suffix. Thomas Becker's 'Back-Formation, Cross-Formation, and "Bracketing Paradoxes" in Paradigmatic Morphology' (in *YM* 1993.1–25) is a plea for the paradigmatic analysis of words, in particular those resulting from back-formation (which involves a rule that is less productive than its inverse) and cross-formation (e.g. *a breed-to breed*; no difference in productivity).

Makiyo Niwa's 'Nominalization Suffix and Argument Structure: A Note on *The Canterbury Tales*' (*Ling&Philol.* 13.25–42) is far less general. She notes that of the suffixes that create abstract nouns (which may also have acquired a concrete sense, such as *building*) from verbs, such as -*ment*, -*age* etc., -*ing* is the only one that has survived from OE. The purpose of this paper is to examine whether *The Canterbury Tales* show any differences between the 'loan'-nominalization structures and the original OE one. It is found that the loan nominalizations occur less with PPs and genitive arguments than the native structure in -*ing*, showing (and this doesn't really come as a surprise) that the new structures needed time to integrate into the overall structure of the language. There have been some studies of other noun suffixes as well. Laurie Bauer presents 'More -*ee* Words' (about 40 of them) in *AS* 68.222–4. They include *bowee, conjuree* and *pleasee*, for which the example given is: *In all my relationships I'm usually the pleaser, not the pleasee.* As this example shows, many of the -*ee* words occur in close vicinity either to the verbal base or the -*er* word. Bauer has come across three non-human -*ee* words, all created by – yes indeed – linguists (*governee, controllee* and *cliticee*). Janet Holmes has studied 'Sex-Marking Suffixes in Written New Zealand English' (in *AS* 68.357–70). In the Wellington Corpus, only -*ess* words (and the isolated forms *heroine* and *suffragette*) are found, at a lower frequency than in the LOB corpus (which is 25 years older, although, of course, it also represents another regional variety). The decline of sex-marking suffixes (which is slow: Holmes notes that -*ess* words were being declared moribund as early as the eighteenth century) is held up by Michael Shapiro ('Drift as an Organic Outcome of Type', in Aertsen and Jeffers) as one consequence of the analytic nature of English, which favours phrasal over suffixal formations.

The mechanisms of present-day English derivation have also received some attention this year. The scarcity of category-changing prefixes in present-day English is the topic of Michael Hammond's 'On the Absence of Category-Changing Prefixes in English' (in *Lingl* 24.562–7). He notes that the few prefixes of this type that exist (*en-, be-, de-*) are restricted to underived bases when they are category-changing (*enable, enchain, endear*) but can occur with complex bases when not category-changing (*encapsulate, enliven*). He attributes this to processing constraints similar to those responsible for the badness of centre-embedding. On the subject of adjectives, Robert Beard argues for 'Simultaneous Dual Derivation in Word Formation' (*Language* 69.716–41). In *a rusty knife*, for example, the adjective can be derived from the noun *rust* either by means of a grammatical function [POSSESS (rust)], or by a process of transposition which changes noun into adjective but leaves the semantic properties (such as: [substance; brown/red; corrode; etc]) intact, with the nature of the noun modified determining which will be selected (in the case of *knife*, all of them). For the phrase *rusty hair*, only [brown/red] will be selected; moreover, in this case the adjective can also be derived by means of a function [SIMILAR TO (rust)]. All adjectives of this type, Beard claims, have a dual derivation, one through transposition and subsequent selection of the appropriate semantic properties, and one through a grammatical function.

The adjective *unhappier* continues to inspire. Beom-mo Kang's '*Unhappier* is Really a "Bracketing Paradox"' (*Lingl* 24.788–94) is a reply to Sproat's 1992 piece on this word (see *YWES* 73.32). Sproat's claim that *unhappier* means 'the opposite of *happier*' i.e. 'less happy' is shown to be dubious, since *John is unhappier than Bill* implies that they are both unhappy, while *John is less happy than Bill* does not imply this. Kang suggests that relation-denoting expressions do not allow *un-* (note **unsenior, *unbetter, *undifferent* etc.), so that *un[happier]* is not allowed as a semantic structure.

Compounding, finally, is the topic of Paul Rastall's 'On the Attributive Noun in English' (in *IRAL* 31.309–13). He notes the increasing use of pluralized attributives (as in *antiques dealer* and *fares increase*) where traditionally the form used to be singular. In forms like *medal(s) winner*, this allows one to make meaning distinctions. Rastall points out that as a result N+N combinations come to look like syntactic constructs, as certain other facts indeed also suggest (i.e. order determining meaning, as in *palm oil* vs *oil palm*; constituency, as in *door-and-ignition key*; and ambiguity, as in *jet fuel container*).

4. Syntax

(a) Modern English

We start with a big book (1029 pp.). In their preface, Jacobs et al., the editors of *Syntax: An International Handbook of Contemporary Research* (Vol. 1) say that this work tries to document as completely as possible the various interpretations of the tasks and methods of syntactic research. And this is indeed what the book does, on a lavish scale. It contains articles on the syntactic components of all the major linguistic theories (with some emphasis on generative approaches), and also descriptions of the way various syntactic phenomena are realized cross-linguistically. For anyone wanting to be instructed on particular syntactic theories or issues that are prominent in contemporary research, this is the book to turn to. If one is more ambitious, and wants to get a comprehensive picture of the state of the art, we would first recommend the article by Peter Matthews, 'Central Concepts of Syntax', which gives an excellent survey of traditional and recent thinking about syntactic units, relations, functions, categories and realizations. After this, the reader could profitably turn to the two articles by Wolf Thümmel, 'Der europäische Strukturalismus' and 'Der amerikanische Strukturalismus', to see how such topics have been developed in structuralist terms. Once this has been digested, one is ready to tackle structuralism's most vigorous offshoot, the generative approach to syntax. Its early successes and squabbles can be traced in Gisbert Fanselow's 'Die frühe Entwicklung bis zu den "Aspekten"', and Frederick Newmeyer's 'Diverging Tendencies' (on the rise and fall of generative semantics). Of course, these papers do not enable one to cope with the most recent issues of, say, *Linguistic Inquiry*. To understand the nature of many of the problems still being addressed in such journals today, one should next read James McCloskey's 'Constraints on Syntactic Processes', which recounts the discovery of what used to be called island constraints, such as Complex Noun Phrase Constraint, Wh-island Constraint, Subjacency and Opacity. By this time, one's appetite will have been whetted for hearing the Master's own words, and one should therefore proceed to 'The Theory of Principles and Parameters', written by Noam Chomsky together with Howard Lasnik; this article provides a very accessible outline of the underlying assumptions and concrete properties, though not in any great formal detail, of the various levels and modules of the theory as it stands today. This piece could be followed by Arnim von Stechow's 'Die Aufgaben der Syntax', which has more discussion of fundamental issues in the principles and parameters model. To familiarize oneself further with specific topics that are prominent in generative research, one should certainly also read Wolfgang Sternefeld's 'Anaphoric Reference', which explains terms and concepts such as bound variable, name, quantifier, crossover, sloppy identity, e-type anaphora, and binding, and perhaps also, while at it, take in Jürgen Pafel's 'Scope and Word Order'.

Should one like to sample some alternatives to the principles and parameters model, one could try 'Phrase Structure Grammar' (by Robert Borsley), or 'Lexical-Functional Grammar' (by Tibor Kiss). Next, there is quite a bit of dependency syntax (Hans Jürgen Herringer writes about 'Basic Ideas and the Classical Model' and 'Formalized Models', while Richard Hudson discusses 'Recent Developments in Dependency Theory') and categorial grammar, which is described by Mark Steedman (in a piece entitled 'Categorial Grammar', which appears in exactly the same form – but with a shorter bibliography – in *Lingua* 90.221–58). We also note here another overview of categorial grammar that has appeared this year, Mary McGee Wood's *Categorial Grammars*; this expounds the basic principles and applications of this approach for newcomers – it includes an explanation of the Lambek calculus, something also handy to know in reading current syntactic research. But perhaps one should first finish *Syntax: An International Handbook of Contemporary Research*. More functionally inspired approaches than those discussed so far are represented in this work by Peter Sgall, who writes about 'The Czech Tradition' (i.e. functional sentence perspective), Machtelt Bolkestein ('General Ideas of Functionalism in Syntax'), and Simon Dik, who describes in some detail his own model of 'Functional Grammar'. Finally, there are various articles focusing on specific syntactic phenomena rather than on any theoretical model. These include Hans-Jürgen Sassen's 'Syntactic Categories and Subcategories' (on word classes), Edith Moravcsik's 'Government' (viewed in terms of dependence of case and/or syntactic function), Robert van Oirsouw's 'Coordination', Anna Siewierska's 'On the Interplay of Factors in the Determination of Word Order' (it describes grammatical, semantic and pragmatic factors, and various hierarchies that have been proposed), Bernard Comrie's 'Argument Structure', Östen Dahl's 'Negation' and Ekkehard König's 'Focus Particles'. Obviously, to sum up a work of this scope is difficult, so we leave it at this very brief review, hoping to have made the point that here the reader can find syntax galore. We noted only one omission: no item on cognitive grammar is included. On the whole, not so much work in this area has appeared this year; however, there is 'A Selected and Annotated Bibliography of Recent Publications with a Cognitive Perspective' by Rainer Schulze (in *CogLing* 4.75–88), containing items published from 1990 onwards.

The theoretical notion of 'head' receives a volume of its own this year: *Heads in Grammatical Theory*. In their introduction, the editors, Greville Corbett, Norman Fraser and Scott McGlashan, briefly review earlier thinking on heads, focusing on Zwicky's eight criteria for headhood (semantic argumenthood, determinant of concord, morphosyntactic locus, governorhood, distributional equivalence, etc.). Richard Hudson is a firm believer in heads, and uses them to argue for dependency grammar and against phrase marker grammar in his 'Do We Have Heads in Our Mind?'. His position is that the notion of head brings together various properties (having to do with order, government, subcategorization, hyponymy and agreement) and that the head–dependent relation should be directly represented in the grammar, as it is in dependency grammar. Phrase marker grammars do not do this, and sometimes even use traces to mediate the relation. But Hudson is no believer in traces. He argues, for example, that positing traces implies that the following sentence should be very hard to process (because *in which$_i$* has to be kept in store while *on which$_j$* – t_j is being processed): *John found* *the box in which$_i$ I put [the tray in which$_j$ Mary placed the dish t$_j$] t$_i$.* John Hawkins, who is also interested in processing but from a cross-linguistic perspective, does not think heads should be primitives, at least in the area of word order. His theory is that word order should enable hearers to recognize syntactic grouping and ICs as rapidly as possible (the rapidity being quantifiable). Mother node constructing categories (such as Det, N, V, Adj, which determine a phrasal mother node), rather than heads are important for this. Heavy NP shift, for example, makes more rapid recognition of the ICs of VP possible. In 'Heads in Head-Driven Phrase Structure Grammar', Robert Borsley considers the status of the head feature principle (which says that the features of mother and head are identical), suggesting that in both HPSG and government-binding theory this principle is a default principle which can be overridden (e.g. X-bar theory ensures that head and mother differ in bar-level, theta-theory that X' will not inherit the internal theta-role, etc.).

Ronnie Cann's contribution to the book, 'Patterns of Headedness', investigates English V+NP, Aux+VP, Det+N, Dem+N, Adj+N, COMP+S, and Wh+S with the use of a set-theoretic formulation of Zwicky's criteria, with somewhat mixed results. He puts forward a slightly revised X'-theory to account for the patterns. The question whether NPs are really DPs is the topic of John Payne's 'The Headedness of Noun Phrases: Slaying the Nominal Hydra'. His answer is that they are not. He shows, for example, that V determines the nature of a following COMP (a head) and also some aspects of the following verb (e.g. *I insist that he play for England* vs. *I know that he plays for England*). Since V can determine the nature of a following noun, but not of its determiner or quantifier, we should not posit a DP. In the same volume, Andrew Radford goes 'Head-Hunting: On the Trail of the Nominal Janus'. He posits not only a DP but also other heads above NP, since he analyses adjectives and quantifiers as heads that can take a NP complement. In *black sheep*, for example, *black* is the immediate head, while its complement is *sheep*, which may be called the ultimate head. The idiomaticity of many combinations of this type is comparable to that of V plus object (*break the ice*), showing that indeed there is a head-complement relationship. Johanna Nichols writes on 'Heads in Discourse: Structural versus Functional Centricity'. She uses her earlier proposals about head-marking vs dependent-marking languages, and wonders whether there is a correlation between type of marking and the type of element left after gapping, deletion and ellipsis. She finds that there is no clear correlation. English, for example, is largely dependent-marking, but both heads and dependents can be isolated: e.g. in *What did you look it up in?*, the head *in* remains, but in *(What did you give him?) A book*, only the dependent *a book* remains. The final item in this head volume is Arnold Zwicky's 'Heads, Bases and Functors'. He proposes that headedness is made up of three separate notions: semantic functor (the internally central element), base (central w.r.t. semantic interpretation and lexical subcategorization by external elements) and head (central w.r.t. agreement and government morphology). These three notions are associated by default.

Some further work on general theoretical issues within principles and parameters theory has appeared. Noam Chomsky sketches 'A Minimalist Program for Linguistic Theory' (in Hale and Keyser). The minimalism in the title refers to the attempt to do away with the levels of D-structure and S-structure, leaving only Logical Form (representing the meaning aspect of sentences) and Phonological Form (representing the sound aspect). Within Chomsky's new approach, phrase markers are constructed by means of a generalized transformation. In case of movement operations, the phrase marker can undergo spell-out, i.e. be linked to a particular Phonological Form, at any point, so before or after movement. Various economy considerations (e.g. 'Procrastinate': delay all operations until Logical Form if possible) bear much of the burden of constraining the grammar. A powerful argument in favour of Chomsky's general approach is that there is no longer a need for yoyo-movement of AGR to V and back again, since verbs can now be inserted in fully inflected form, with their inflectional features being checked against the relevant functional heads in the course of the derivation. This is also true for the Case-features of NPs, for which there are the functional projections AGR-S Phrase (for checking of subject NPs) and AGR-O Phrase (for object NPs). Proposals similar in spirit are made by Michael Brody, in 'Theta-Theory and Arguments' (*LingI* 24.1–23). He takes as his starting point several apparent problems for the theta-criterion: (i) at D-structure, Wh-elements can be arguments, but not at Logical Form; (ii) parasitic gap constructions seem to have two theta-positions in one chain; (iii) there is no apparent reason why PRO must always be an argument. He suggests that the theta-criterion should be abolished, and that D-structure should be regarded as all positions involved in thematic projection, rather than as a separate level. Some further principles (having to do with chain-uniformity and visibility) ensure that the apparent problems he starts out with are solved. Chomsky's checking approach to inflection is further developed by Shichiro Tanaka in 'Case-Checking as Noun Incorporation' (*LingA* 23.274–322). Tanaka suggests that, for A-chains, checking of Case can be reduced to incorporation of N into V at the level of Logical Form. For A'-chains, there is Spec–Head agreement checking.

The relation between economy and optional movement (such as extraposition or heavy NP shift) is the topic of Naoki Fukui's 'Parameters and Optionality' (*LingI* 24.399–420). Since economy principles like Procrastinate forbid movement if it can be avoided, the question is why there can be movement that is neither forbidden nor unavoidable (i.e. it is optional). Fukui's answer is that there is a parameter value preservation measure, which says that movement is free if it creates a structure consistent with the parameter setting of the language; in English, which has a head-initial VP, extraposition and heavy NP shift preserve the parameter setting, and are indeed optional. Other cases of movement are not possible in English (e.g. scrambling) unless they have some driving force (e.g. Spec–Head agreement, or checking), as with passive and Wh-movement. This implies that topicalization, although it looks optional, must have a trigger (perhaps some form of Spec–Head agreement – there can indeed only be one topicalization per clause). Eric Reuland and Wim Kosmeijer deal with related topics in 'Projecting Inflected Verbs' (in Fanselow). They note that the SOV Germanic languages have VP-internal subjects, liberal scrambling, and mixed nominalizations (like the following Dutch example: *dat vervelende stiekem stenen bij de buurman in de tuin gooien van die kinderen* 'that annoying sneakingly stones at the neighbour's in the garden throwing of those children'), while the SVO languages have none of these properties. They derive this difference from the (non-)uniformity of government direction in VP and IP: the SVO languages have NP I V O (V but not I is initial), and the SOV languages have NP O V I (both V and I are final). In the latter type of language, V and I can merge, and the authors show in detail how this one parameter can explain the three differences between the language types. The status of parameters as such is scrutinized by

Hubert Haider, 'Principled Variability: Parametrization without Parameter Fixing' (in Fanselow). He argues that parametrization is an epiphenomenon of UG, since UG cannot guide the cognitive mechanisms that should scan and process the input data. He prefers to regard UG as a filtering and reinforcing device on specific data structures. We also mention here Johan Kerstens's *The Syntax of Number, Person and Gender: A Theory of Phi-Features*. He proposes that DP and IP can be given a unified analysis as AGRP, with N and V raising from complement position to AGR, which is coindexed with and shares phi-features with its specifier (Det, Adj, or subject). Although Kerstens uses Dutch examples to illustrate the theory, the unification should also be possible for English (with interesting differences between Modern English and earlier stages).

We now turn to works which in one way or another deal with argument structure, mainly of verbs. Gary Miller's *Complex Verb Formation* offers a well-considered and important contribution to the question of what role morphology plays in syntax, which as we have just seen, is an important issue in the most recent work within the principles and parameters approach to syntax. The title 'complex verb formation' should be interpreted very widely: it is any kind of derivation (syntactic as well as morphological) that has 'alter[ed] the form, meaning, or argument structure of the base verb (or verb 'root')'. The author wants to test how far the syntactic principles and parameters approach can account for morphological forms, and which forms can only be explained by a lexical approach. The key notions here are 'opacity' and '(in)visibility to syntax'. Through a number of case studies, Miller wants to determine on what part of the cline morphological form belongs, the cline running from syntactic incorporation via increasing opacity to lexicalization. It is not surprising that the historical dimension plays an important role here since morphological forms usually start off life as syntactic incorporations and only slowly (if at all) become syntactically opaque when they develop exceptions (or become exceptional due to other external developments), so that full lexicalization may result. Miller looks in detail at the various components of the principles and parameters theory and discusses in each case which are (and in how far they are) of importance to morphology. Thus, he illustrates the importance of case theory, theta theory, the projection principle, binding theory, X-bar theory for an understanding of how morphology works, concluding at the same time, however, that 'lexical and syntactic solutions are complementary rather than contrary, supporting the conventional hypothesis about language change, that what originates in syntax or elsewhere in the system can become lexicalized'.

The argument structure of lexical items is also the topic of several smaller studies, all of them firmly rooted in the generative framework. We only briefly mention two reviews of Grimshaw's important 1990 *Argument Structure*, by Edith Moravcsik (in *SLang* 17.455–67) and by Masataka Ishikawa (in *Word* 44.101–5). Both have much to say about Grimshaw's use of 'prominence' to regulate argument structure assignment. The argument structure of causatives (using the term comprehensively) is investigated in four articles. Ray Jackendoff's 'The Combinatorial Structure of Thought: The Family of Causative Concepts' (in Reuland and Abraham) presents an analysis of verbs of causation (e.g. *pressure*), and also verbs of helping, letting, transfer of possession, and reaction, with the aid of conceptual roles. These are organized into two tiers: a thematic tier (with the functions Cause, Go, Be, Stay), and an action tier (which deals with Actor–Patient relations). *Harry pressured Sam to go away*, for example, has the following (simplified) thematic tier: CAUSE ([Harry] [GO] ([Sam], [away])); its action tier is: AFFECT ([Harry], [Sam]). It turns out that, within such an analysis, verbs of logical relation (*entail, imply, reinforce, support* etc.) resemble verbs that express the action of pushing things around in space. In 'Lexical Mapping' (in Reuland and Abraham), Jill Carrier and Janet Randall also use conceptual roles to analyse resultative transitives (*John watered the tulips flat*) and intransitives (*John ran the pavement thin*). Having examined the syntactic structure of resultatives in 1992 (see *YWES* 73.36), this year they address the question where these structures (which are not the same for transitives and intransitives) come from. They argue that in both cases the same general principles operate to create predicate-argument structure from underlying lexical-conceptual structure. For transitive resultatives, the latter structure would be something like 'that John caused water to come to be on the tulips caused the tulips to be flat', while the former has a ternary branching VP (with *the tulips* receiving two theta-roles, one from *water* and one from *flat*). A different syntactic analysis for this construction is proposed by Tova Rapoport, in 'Stage and Adjunct Predicates: Licensing and Structure in Secondary Predication Structures' (in Reuland and Abraham): verb and adjective are said to form a complex predicator (*water flat*), which assigns one thematic role to the object NP. Exactly the same structure, the author suggests, underlies VPs like *make someone angry* and *find someone incompetent*. A different case is represented by *eat meat raw*, in which *raw* is a sister to *eat meat*; the fact that only stage-level adjectives occur in this construction is discussed in some detail. Causative and other uses of the verb *have* form the topic of Elizabeth Ritter and Sara Thomas Rosen's 'Deriving Causation' (in *NL&LT* 11.519–55). They note that in a sentence like *John had his students walk out of class, John* can be interpreted either as causer or experiencer, and derive both readings from the assumption that *have* plus its argument *John* (which is thematically unspecified) are added to the event *the students walk out of class*. The effect is that the duration of this event is extended to include the new participant, pushing back either the beginning point (leading to a causative interpretation), or the end point (producing an experiential interpretation). In syntactic terms, *have* takes a VP complement (unlike *make*, which takes an IP; cf. *I didn't make/*have John write the article, but he did it anyway*). This analysis of *have* as a thematically 'empty' verb is also applied to some of its other uses (*John had a good time* – experience; *he had a dinner party* – creation; *he has a new car* – possession; *the car has a stereo in it* – location).

More general questions of argument structure and conceptual structure are addressed in Ray Jackendoff's 'On the Role of Conceptual Structure in Argument Selection: A Reply to Emonds' (in *NL&LT* 11.279–312). He defends the view that words, phrases and sentences are triples of phonological structure, syntactic structure and conceptual structure, pointing out that an approach employing argument linking (i.e. general principles for deriving argument structure from conceptual structure) makes it possible to dispense with much stipulation of subcategorization. For example, if we say that *be* is followed by a Property, nothing need be said about category, since all categories that can express a Property (AP, NP, PP) are found following *be*. It is only for cases like *get* (which is also followed by a Property, but it must not be expressed as a PP: **he got out of his mind*) that subcategorization is still necessary. In 'Topic ... Comment' (*NL&LT* 11.557–8), David Pesetsky, looking at slightly different facts, suggests that no categorial information need be stated in lexical entries. For *worry*, for example, the lexical entry could specify that the thematic object may not bear morphological case. This would mean there can be a CP object, or an athematic NP object (*he worried himself to death*), but no thematic object NP.

Jaklin Kornfilt and Nelson Correa do not specifically address questions of subcategorization, but they endorse Jackendoff's general approach in 'Conceptual Structure and its Relation to the Structure of Lexical Entries' (in Reuland and Abraham). They propose that predicate-argument structure derives from lexical-conceptual structure (which contains thematic information) via a projection rule. As they show in some detail, a thematic hierarchy will be needed to regulate the process of projection. However, not everybody believes in theta-roles. In Kenneth Hale and Samuel Jay Keyser's 'On Argument Structure and the Lexical Expression of Syntactic Relations' (in Hale and Keyser), it is suggested that theta-roles are nothing but reflections of structural relations; an agent, for example, is the role of a Specifier NP in a structure in which one event is a proper part of another event. The fact that there are so few theta-roles can then be explained by the limited number of categories (N, V, A, P) and positions in their projections. As the authors note, this idea is still quite programmatic. At a more concrete level (if this is the right word), they propose analyses for unergative verbs like *laugh*, which they derive through incorporation of the noun *laugh* into an empty verb whose complement it is, and for verbs like *shelve*, which is derived in Larsonian fashion, by incorporation of *shelf* into its (empty) governing preposition, which incorporates into its governing V, and from there into a higher V. Inchoatives and middles are also considered. A last item in this group is Jane Grimshaw and Sten Vikner's 'Obligatory Adjuncts and the Structure of Events' (in Reuland and Abraham). They propose that sentences not only have a thematic structure, but also an event structure. Its syntactic relevance is demonstrated by the ungrammaticality of a sentence like *this house was built*. The reason why adding a phrase like *yesterday* or *by me* will rescue the sentence is that accomplishment verbs such as *build* denote an event made up of two parts, a process and a state. Both subevents need to be identified. Since the agent-phrase *by me* can do so, but the passive morpheme cannot, it appears that the passive morpheme should not be analysed as the external argument.

No doubt the very idea of such an analysis would find little favour with the author of the next work we turn to, which is Talmy Givón's two-volumed *English Grammar: A Function-Based Introduction*, a welcome addition to the library of English grammars. With this work, Givón has written a complete grammar meant for use by native speakers (to teach them to communicate coherently in spoken as well as written form) and second language learners. It does not come as a surprise from this author that the grammar is unashamedly function-based: he sees grammar as a set of strategies that are employed to produce coherent communication, not a set of rules to produce grammatical sentences (which has been and still is the more restricted aim of generative grammarians). In his judgement, autonomous syntax is 'pernicious nonsense'. He believes instead that grammar is a biological organism whose 'structural design is adapted through protracted evolution to perform specific functions'; from which it follows that grammar is interconnected with other areas such as semantics, phonology etc. and cannot be studied in isolation. All this entails that grammatical rules are in principle transparent, functional. Opaque rules may arise in two ways: through historical accident (however, often such rules or vestiges of it may become transparent again through exaptation), or because there is a clash between the semantic proposition of a clause and its discourse function. Another point that he makes is that grammatical rules are not hard and fast. There is always some fuzziness, some frayed edges (where of course change may start), where certain regular rules do not apply because of subtle differences in context. This again shows that one cannot study grammar outside context. The two volumes deal with the structure of the simple clause and that of the complex clause respectively. Givón calls the simple clause the 'theme', which can be understood in terms of theme alone, i.e. it is a straightforward semantic proposition. Complex clauses, on the other hand (this also includes interrogatives, negatives) are called variations on the theme and must be understood in terms of the theme but also in terms of discourse. Discourse function therefore plays an important role in grammar. The various chapters that follow give a full view of the way in which segments (morphemes, words, NPs, VPs, clauses) are used and should therefore provide a highly useful tool in grammar teaching.

Another work in which generative grammarians are taken to task for leaving function and discourse out of the picture is Susumu Kuno and Ken-ichi Takami's *Grammar and Discourse Principles: Functional Syntax and GB Theory*. The authors examine various syntactic phenomena (e.g. *that*-trace, argument-adjunct asymmetries, subjacency, multiple Wh-questions, coreference and scope with psych-verbs etc.), and in each case argue that the syntactic principles put forward by GB-grammarians are *ad hoc* and inadequate; they propose various functional principles instead (or in addition: Kuno and Takami do not deny the existence of grammatical principles). One specific case will have to suffice to give a flavour of their approach: after reviewing GB-proposals for psych-verbs meant to explain their unexpected binding patterns (as in *pictures of himself₁ don't bother John₁*), they present some data that these proposals cannot explain (e.g. *A picture of himself₁ with a feature story in the Boston Globe gave John₁ a big moral boost*, featuring a non-psych-verb with the same binding pattern), and then propose that the data can be accounted for by a functional principle to the effect that if the referent of a reflexive is aware that the referent of a picture-noun depicts him, a reflexive is obligatory. They dub this the 'Awareness Condition'; since psych-verbs usually imply awareness, the reflexive is found with them. Altogether, the authors put forward some 15 principles of this type, many of them being construction-specific and the relation between them remaining somewhat unclear.

Several grammatical studies of specific topics have appeared in which discourse also plays a leading role. First there is Cecilia E. Ford, *Grammar in Interaction: Adverbial Clauses in American English Conversations*. The book is intended as a contribution to our knowledge of how grammar is used in discourse and how grammars may change through use. It concentrates on dialogue (the database consists of 13 taped natural conversations, so not interviews) rather than stories, which so far have been the more usual object of discourse studies. The methodology used is that of 'Conversation Analysis', as developed by scholars like Sacks, Schegloff and Jefferson, who have investigated turn-taking strategies and the sequential structure of discourse. The focus is on adverbial clauses because there has already been quite a bit of discourse research in this area (mainly based on written texts), which showed that these clauses provide important discourse clues. Her findings do indeed show (confirming this earlier work) that the functions of initial adverbial clauses are different from those of final ones. Initial clauses function as discourse-structuring devices, whereas final ones tend to work more locally: they narrow down main clause meaning or provide additional background information. The function expressed by clause position also explains the preference of specific types of adverbial clauses for either initial (e.g. conditional clauses) or final position (e.g. causal clauses). Roughly the same difference between initial and final adverbial clauses is described by Gary Prideaux and John Hogan in 'Markedness as a Discourse Management Device: The Role of Alternative Adverbial Clause Orders' (*Word* 44.397–411). They studied stories (recounting, in speech and writing, an episode in a film) and also found that adverbial clauses (i.e. clauses starting with *when, since, before, after, while,* and *as*) in initial position serve as directions to the hearer/reader that there is a discourse unit boundary. Final adverbial clauses do not have such a specific function, and could be called unmarked.

A book very similar to Ford's is Elizabeth G. Weber, *Varieties of Questions in English Conversation.* It also deals with the relation between linguistic form and interactive or social meaning; it is likewise based on a corpus of spoken language and uses the same methodology of Conversation Analysis. The book has two main goals. First, to describe what morphosyntactic forms (in combination with intonation, which cannot be separated from it) speakers use to do 'the social action of questioning'. In practice, this means that not so much the standard types of interrogatives will be considered but the non-typical forms, such as declaratives and non-clausal questions, which serve the function of asking a question. Weber is especially interested in the lexical and morphosyntactic forms that characterize these non-interrogative questions, and what their functions are, especially how they function differently from the typical interrogative questions. The second goal is to consider how the various morphosyntactic question markers are motivated by their function, with the ultimate aim of showing that syntactic forms emerge through discourse, in the spirit of the work done by 'grammaticalization-linguists' like Hopper, Thompson and Traugott. Context also plays a part in another study dealing with questions, Juhani Rudanko's 'On Some Aspects of Rhetorical Questions in English' (*SN* 65.29–36). It offers an elaboration of the description of both *yes-no* questions and *wh*-rhetorical questions as given previously by scholars such as Pope (1976) and Quirk *et al.* (1985) in that, for instance, positive rhetorical *yes-no* questions carrying constituent negation (in contrast to those carrying sentence negation) expect *only* negative answers. Furthermore, it shows that in the interpretation of *wh*-questions, context plays a more important role than hitherto assumed.

Rodney Huddleston contributes two items on questions. In 'Remarks on the Construction *You won't believe who Ed has married*' (in *Lingua* 91.175–84), he argues that this type of Wh-clause is not exclamative (as has been claimed), but interrogative. One piece of evidence is the fact that main clause exclamatives only allow *how* and *what.* An alleged piece of evidence for exclamative status, i.e. the impossibility of **you won't believe whether Ed has married,* is shown to be inconclusive, since some predicates select only certain types of questions (cf. *I doubt whether it is true* vs **I doubt who has done it*). Huddleston also writes 'On Exclamatory-Inversion Sentences in English' (in *Lingua* 90.259–69), which means sentences like *Boy, is syntax easy.* In the past, various arguments have been adduced for saying that these are not questions, but Huddleston demonstrates that none of them are convincing. He concludes that such sentences are syntactically and semantically like questions (although not inquiries for information), but are different pragmatically.

Ronald Geluykens deals with the pragmatic or discourse task of 'Topic Introduction in English Conversation' (*TPS* 91.181–214). He discusses the various ways in which new topics are marked in the conversations in the Survey of English Usage corpus, summarizing them by means of a scale of explicitness of marking, which goes from declarative clause via other clause types (in particular, questions) to unattached NPs (left dislocation, quasi-left dislocation) and explicit phrases ('Now I'll tell you something else'). The same kind of approach to the same kind of data is found in a paper by Peter Collins, 'Extern Constructions in English' (*AJL* 13.23–37), which is on three particular constructions used for topic management: left dislocation (*John, I know him*), right dislocation (*I know him, John*) and topicalization (*John I know*). In the informal spoken corpus analysed, their specific functions turn out usually to be: identification of a topic that is being reestablished (left dislocation), identification of a current topic (topicalization), and reinforcement of a salient topic (right dislocation). In 'Cleft Sentences in English: A Comprehensive View' (in *Word* 44.1–30), Edward Fichtner regards clefts (*it*-clefts, Wh-clefts, and pseudo-clefts) as devices to reshape an underlying sentence so that it conforms more closely to the sequence of ideas (which can be captured by the terms affirmation, specification, and definition respectively for the three types). The series of operations that are carried out in the process of reshaping are described in some detail; the first step in each case is assigning FOCUS to an item. The role of *it*-clefts in information structure is investigated somewhat more closely by Gunther Kaltenböck in 'A Brief Discussion of *it*-Clefts in Spoken English' (*Views* 2.4–25). He takes an earlier classification of *it*-clefts by Declerck (with three types, depending on where the new information is found) and finds that, in the spoken part of the Survey of English Usage corpus, it is most often the 'focused' element (nearly always a NP) that is new and highlighted. Further aspects of the data (such as relative length of focused element and following 'relative' clause, the nature of the 'relative' marker used, etc.) are also discussed.

Two studies deal with the syntax of a type of language far removed from speech: legal writing. Jeffrey Kaplan writes about 'Syntax in the Interpretation of Legal Language: The Vested versus Contingent Distinction in Property Law' (*AS* 68.58–82), finding that the position of the contingency expression in a phrase marker of the relevant sentence will determine its interpretation as either vested or contingent. On a somewhat less arcane legal topic, there is Judith Levi's 'Evaluating Jury Comprehension of Illinois Capital-Sentencing Instructions' (in *AS* 68.20–49). It turned out the instructions were difficult to comprehend and could create a bias towards choosing the death penalty rather than imprisonment, due to various syntactic, semantic, and pragmatic features of the text.

Discourse and pragmatics remain in the foreground also in two studies dealing with definiteness. The first, 'Definite Possessives and Discourse Novelty' (*PRMCLS* 28.26–41), by Chris Barker, starts off from the notion that definite descriptions can only be used if the entity referred to is familiar from previous discourse. Barker is interested in definite expressions that seem to defy this 'familiarity condition'. He concentrates on the type containing definite possessives, as in *That man's daughter*. In order to accommodate the interpretation of these possessives, he proposes to revise the familiarity notion in such a way that the above construction may count as familiar whenever only the possessor phrase (*that man's*) is familiar. In addition, a distinction has to be made between relational possessives and lexical possessives in order to factor out examples that are not grammatical, i.e. *A man came in.*His giraffe was with him*. In 'A Pragmatic Account of the Definiteness Effect in Existential Sentences'

(*JPrag* 19.39–55), Barbara Abbott deals with examples such as *There is everyone in the room*, which are commonly starred as being ill-formed syntactically and/or semantically. Abbott shows that definite NPs are not by definition ungrammatical, but that one can only account for this type of sentence and also, *Well, there is the left-over chicken from last night* and *There was the usual smell of pot all over the apartment*, by looking at pragmatic factors. For instance, anaphoric definitions such as *There is everyone in the room* 'require a predicational slot in the existing discourse, and the locational phrase *in the room* must be interpretable as part of the focus NP [*everyone*] for full acceptability'. She also concludes that definite NPs cannot be easily defined in syntactic terms since there is a continuum of definiteness running from most definite (anaphoric pronouns) to least (exclamatory superlatives, as in *There is the most beautiful house for sale in the next block!*). We also include here two rather different studies of (in)definiteness. Elisabeth Löbel writes 'On the Parametrization of Lexical Properties' (in Fanselow). She identifies two lexical parameters of nouns: determined (i.e. definite or indefinite) vs. not determined, and countable vs. non-countable. These parameters relate to the functional categories DP and QP. Keumsil Kim Yoon's 'Challenging Prototype Descriptions: Perceptions of Noun Countability and Indefinite vs. Zero Article Use' (*IRAL* 31.269–89) is an investigation of article use by Japanese learners and native speakers of English. It was found that many Japanese subjects who judged a word in isolation (e.g. *dependency*) to be [–count] used the zero article also if the word was presented in a context where the indefinite article was called for. Native speakers in such cases used the indefinite article, whatever their judgement of the word in isolation had been. Learners, apparently, often (mistakenly) go by some perceived inherent property of the word, rather than by context.

The status of subjects (mainly expletive) is addressed by Caroline Heycock in 'Topics and Subjects in Germanic' (*PRMCLS* 27.219–32). She argues, following Rothstein (1983, 1989) and *contra* Fukui (1986), that Chomsky's (1981) Extended Projection Principle is in fact part of a more general principle namely the principle that 'predicates must have subjects'. Thus any head that is [+V] is syntactically a predicate, which requires that a subject is supplied. It is claimed that this approach leads to a unified account of expletives in a number of Germanic languages such as English, German and Yiddish. Another analysis of expletive subjects is provided by Ellen Brandner in 'The Projection of Categories and the Nature of Agreement' (in Fanselow). She focuses on the difference in the type of expletive found in the Germanic languages (*there*, an adverb, in English; the pronoun *es* in German; an empty element in Swedish). Arguing against expletive *pro*-drop, she proposes that expletives have a role to perform w.r.t. licensing, an XP being licensed only if X is inherently strong and/or Spec XP is filled. Independent properties of X and the various types of expletives determine which type of expletive can occur where.

There is an interesting exchange this year on the nature of null subjects in English child language. Are they grammatically null or grammatically full but null due to performance factors? Nina Hyams and Kenneth Wexler place their bets 'On the Grammatical Basis of Null Subjects in Child Language' (*LingI* 24.421–59). They say that a production account (as advocated by Paul Bloom and others) cannot explain why there are many more null subjects than null objects in child language, since there is no evidence that processing problems are heavier at the beginning of sentences than elsewhere. Hyams and Wexler instead propose that null subjects result from topic drop; since children have no topicalization, the object cannot be moved into the appropriate position. In 'Grammatical Continuity in Language Development' (*LingI* 24.721–34), Paul Bloom strikes back, claiming that (i) Hyams and Wexler seem to waver between a *pro*-drop analysis and a topic-drop of null subjects; (ii) it is *ad hoc* to assume that children cannot topicalize; (iii) subjects are more often omitted than objects because they more often represent given information; (iv) it does seem that initial portions of a sentence are especially difficult to process, since articles are more often omitted from subject NPs than from object NPs; (v) the data show a very irregular decline of null subjects over time, which a parameter resetting cannot account for.

That the underlying position of the subject is relevant to reconstruction is shown in James Huang's 'Reconstruction and the structure of VP: Some Theoretical Consequences' (in *LingI* 24.103–38). He notes the asymmetry between *Which pictures of himself did John think that Bill saw t* (where *himself*, part of a fronted argument, may be bound by either *John* or *Bill*) and *Criticize himself, John thought Bill would not t* (where *himself* is part of a fronted predicate, and can only be bound by *Bill*). The explanation is that in the former case, the complete wh-phrase can be reconstructed either to the embedded Spec CP (leading to binding of *himself* by *John*) or to its base position (then *himself* will be bound by *Bill*). In the latter case, the fronted predicate is a VP (or perhaps even AGRO-P); if it assumed that subjects are base-generated in VP, a fronted VP will include the trace of the subject and the trace will bind *himself*. It is not difficult to agree with Huang that these facts provide strong (and interesting) further support for the VP-internal subject hypothesis. There is more on subjects, in relation to their predicates, in 'The Syntax of Predication' by John Bowers (in *LingI* 24.591–656). He proposes that all subjects are base-generated in the Spec of the functional category Predication Phrase, whose complement can be any of the major categories. The relation between Spec and complement is predication. PredP itself is always a complement in IP or VP. Bowers supports his proposals by showing how they would apply to structures with conjoining and gapping, with adverbs, ECM constructions with floated quantifiers (which can feature raising-to-object), pseudo-reflexives (*he ate himself sick*), anaphors in fronted VPs, various infinitival complements, and also double object constructions (which involve an empty higher causative V).

Indirect objects are also addressed in Joseph Emonds, 'Projecting Indirect Objects' (*TLR* 10.211–63). In this contribution Emonds wants to save the structure-preserving analysis of the rule (involving the indirect object) originally proposed by him (in 1972). This involves a sharpening and formalization of the Projection Principle into a universal and meaning-free device of syntax, and a new account of the triggering mechanism. This done, he claims that the locality of indirect object movement, as well as the lack of traces will follow automatically. In order to show this, Emonds looks at great length at both the surface structures of prepositionless datives in a number of languages, among them English (he analyses the P-less datives and the P-datives as basically the same) and at their deep structure (where P-less datives are derived from P-datives). A different, cognitive approach to double objects is taken in Adele Goldberg's 'The Inherent Semantics of Argument Structure: The Case of the English Ditransitive Construction' (in *CogLing* 3.37–74). The basic semantics of the construction (so not of the V as such) is said to be that of transfer, with the subject intending the transfer, and the object being a willing recipient. Apart from the central sense

CAUSE Object1 to RECEIVE Object2, the construction also allows INTEND TO CAUSE ... (with *bake, make*, etc.), ENABLE Object1 to RECEIVE Object2 (*permit, allow*, etc.), and various other senses. Goldberg argues that this approach will enable us to dispense with restrictions like: 'the construction allows verbs of communicated message (*tell* etc.), but not manner of speaking verbs (*shout* etc.), and no verbs with non-initial stress (*announce* etc.)', which have been proposed in the earlier literature on the construction.

We will now discuss a very large group of primarily theoretical studies which are all written within the generative framework, and all involve movement processes of one type or another. First, there is Marcel den Dikken and Alma Naess, 'Case Dependencies: The Case of Predicate Inversion' (*TLR* 10.303–36). It deals with the proper analysis of so-called locative inversion of the type, *Down the hill rolled the baby carriage*, showing that there are problems with both the 'movement' and the 'raising to subject' approach and advocating a blend of the two, in which the PP is raised first to subject position but next undergoes topicalization. This is shown to work for English, but empirical support is mainly found in Norwegian, where there is a much richer variety of these constructions. We could not make much of Yusaku Oteki's account 'On the Necessity of Quantifier Raising' (*Ling&Philol*. 13.95–103), because the English in which it is written is rather poor and the account itself is purely theory internal. What he seems to want to illustrate is the advantages of having a Quantifier Rule over and against the disadvantage of not having one. In 'Negation and Contraction' (*PRMCLS* 28.297–317), Susumu Kuno and Ken-ichi Takami show that extraction out of negative clauses (as in *Who don't you like*) is not dependent on the argument or adjunct nature of the extracted element, nor on whether it is referential or not. Rather, the extraction is conditioned primarily (apart from a pragmatic factor) by the scope relation of the negation: i.e. the extracted element may not be in the scope of negation before fronting.

Most of these studies deal with A′-gaps of one kind or another. There are three on the so-called Complementizer-Gap Constraint: Anna Roussou's 'I-to-C Movement and the *that-t* Filter' (*UCWPL* 5.103–27), Hubert Haider's 'ECP-Etuden: Anmerkungen zur Extraktion aus Eingebetteten Verb-Zweit-Sätzen' (*LingB* 145.185–203), and Peter Culicover's 'Evidence Against ECP Accounts of the *that-*t Effect' (*LingI* 24.557–61). The first one is interested in the asymmetry between sentences such as *Who do you believe (*that) left* and *The man *(that) left is my neighbour*. Both sentences involve a subject gap, but in the first one the complementizer *that* must be absent whereas in the second one it must be present. The author works out what the different properties of each of these constructions are, and how they interact with the presence/absence of *that*. It is concluded that the latter is linked to the phenomenon of I-to-C movement. Although Haider's paper is concerned with the fact that in German complement clauses not introduced by a complementizer, the verb must appear in first position rather than second (which is linked to a general theoretical discussion about the application of ECP), what is of interest is the parallel that he draws between these constructions (e.g. *Wie hat man dir gesagt sei das Problem/*das Problem sei zu lösen*) and the *that*-trace phenomenon in English, as in *What do you think (*that) bothers her*, stating that both constructions must be explained within the theory in the same way. Peter Culicover argues against an ECP account of *that*-trace, since it cannot explain why the insertion of certain adverbials can make such structures acceptable: *the man that they said that *(to all intents and purposes) t was the* *mayor of the city* and *Leslie was the person who I said that *(under no circumstances) t would run for any office.* Culicover concludes that the *that*-trace filter is still the only empirically adequate account of the facts.

Still on the subject of gaps created by A'-movement, there are two contributions dealing with null operators: 'On Null Operator Structures' by Helen Contreras (in *NL&LT* 11.45–64), and 'The Range of Null Operators: Evidence from Clefting', by Lorie Heggie (*NL&LT* 11.65–84). Contreras argues that null operators are freely assigned the features [±pronominal] and [±anaphor]. In structures such as *easy to please, pretty to look at, too important to ignore,* and purposive infinitivals, the CP is an adjunct, and the null operator will be an ungoverned [+pronominal]. In parasitic gap structures, the operator is governed and [–anaphor], [–pronominal], which makes it subject to principle C and the ECP. Heggie's paper is about null operators in *it*-clefts, which are divided into normal clefts and meta-linguistic clefts (e.g. *It's not always that I am lazy (just sometimes)*). Normal clefts have a null operator (which must obey the 'null operator generalization' proposed by Heggie) in COMP. The operator can restructure with C, and come to resemble a relative pronoun.

There are other papers on further aspects of A'-movement. Joseph Aoun and Yen-hui Audrey Li write about '*Wh*-Elements in Situ: Syntax or LF' (*LingI* 24.199–238). They propose the existence of a functional category XP (above VP), with X = [±Question], [±Wh]. If X = [+Question], [+Wh], it must agree with an appropriate element in Spec XP. In Chinese, there is an operator in that position, which raises to Spec CP and licenses the Wh-element in situ. In English, there is no operator, so the Wh-item must raise to Spec XP (for agreement to take place) and from there to Spec CP. In multiple Wh-questions, only one element need move. Koji Fujita thinks otherwise: his 'In Defense of LF Pied-Piping' (*Lingua* 90.291–334) is based on the idea that in a multiple Wh-question, one Wh-item moves in the syntax and the other one(s) at LF. He proposes that such LF-movement is also subject to Subjacency, which results in LF structures like [*the man who bought what*]$_k$, who$_i$ [$_{IP}$ t$_i$ saw t$_k$], with t$_k$ being due to pied-piping. To solve some problems for pied-piping w.r.t. superiority, weak crossover, and anaphor binding, a reformulation of crossing constraints and the bijection principle is necessary, and Affect α must be allowed to do some reindexing.

Paul Postal makes some 'Remarks on Weak Crossover Effects' (in *LingI* 24.539–56), in which he finds fault with the suggestion, due to Lasnik and Stowell, that weak crossover only occurs when a true quantifier is moved (so with e.g. questions, ?*who$_i$ did his$_i$ sister call t$_i$ a moron?*, but not with e.g. parasitic gaps and topicalization, *Frank$_i$, his$_i$ sister called t$_i$ a moron*). Postal presents facts that do not fit this idea (e.g. **Harry$_i$, a picture of him$_i$ fell on t$_i$,* and *Harry$_i$, I am sure his$_i$ dismissal/*your dismissal of him$_i$ will drive t$_i$ mad*) and also shows that in some cases strong crossover also fails unexpectedly. The conclusion is that weak crossover is an even more mysterious phenomenon than it might have seemed before. J.-Marc Authier's 'Nonquantificational *Wh* and Weakest Crossover' (*LingI* 24.161–8) is also inspired by Lasnik and Stowell's suggestion about weak crossover. Authier observes that echo-questions provide another example of non-quantificational A'-movement (witness the grammaticality of *the claim that he$_i$ was drunk bothered WHO$_i$?*). However, quizmaster questions are also immune to weak crossover (*For $1000, do you know which EC$_i$ its$_i$ antecedent must A-bind t$_i$ at S-structure?*), in spite of the fact that they seem to be quantificational (for one thing, they show scope interaction: *For $1000, what did everyone eat?* is ambiguous, just like a true question). Just like Postal, Authier concludes that weak crossover remains a mystery.

Eun-Ji Lee has looked at 'Superiority Effects and Adjunct Traces' (in *LingI* 24.177–83), and disagrees with Lasnik and Saito, who have argued that adjunct traces can be deleted. Lee points out that the traces are needed to explain superiority effects such as **Why did who buy the books?* vs. *(?)Why did you buy what?*. An attempt to reduce superiority to the ECP is shown not to work. Katalin Kiss has looked at 'Wh-Movement and Specificity' (*NL&LT* 11.85–120). This involves contrasts like *??What grade did who get t?* vs. *What grade did which student get t?*. The reason for such contrasts, Kiss suggests, is the fact that an operator may only have wide scope if it is specific (i.e. it quantifies over a set familiar to the discourse participants). *Which* (but not *who* and *what*) is always specific. The same mechanism is at work in *Everybody met a politician*, in which *a politician* must have narrow scope if it is non-specific. The well-known contrast *Who did you see a/*his portrait of*, which also has to do with specificity, is studied in Frank Drijkoningen's 'Movement Theory and the DP-Hypothesis' (*Linguistics* 31.813–53). He assumes that NP is contained within a DP, and postulates that Spec DP is an A-position if it is filled. It will then block Wh-movement out of NP, since there will have to be movement across NP (a barrier) and DP (a barrier by inheritance) in one step. In 'Some Defective Paradigms' (*LingI* 24.347–64), Paul Postal studies another asymmetry: *John, I assure you to be the best* but **I assure you John to be the best*. In the standard account, these facts are made to follow from the idea that Case assignment involves the COMP position. But Postal shows that there are further facts for which this will not work (e.g. *they alleged t to be pimps all of the Parisians the CIA had hired in Nice*). He provides an account in terms of Metagraph Grammar (*sic*), in which the relevant NP raises to object position, but cannot surface there.

Next, there are three papers on parasitic gaps. One of these is also by Postal: 'Parasitic Gaps and the Across-the-Board Phenomenon' (*LingI* 24.735–54). His main purpose is to argue against the idea that parasitic gap constructions (pgs) involve any across-the-board (ATB) processes (which would make them similar to coordinate structures). He does so by pointing out six empirical differences between parasitic gaps and ATB (e.g. pgs, but not ATB, are restricted to NPs; ATB, but not pgs, can involve the subject of a finite clause; pgs, but not ATB, can generally alternate with an overt pronoun; etc.). Robert Frank writes on 'Parasitic Gaps and Locality Conditions' (*PRMCLS* 27.167–81). Like many of the other papers in this group, this is a highly theoretical contribution, in which the author shows with the help of some data concerning parasitic gaps, which involve long distance movement (e.g. *Which car$_i$ did Bill understand how the mechanic had fixed t$_i$ without dismantling e$_i$*) that the standard Barriers analysis of parasitic gaps is not adequate and that the use of locality conditions in this analysis has to be changed. This is done by means of TAG (Tree Adjoining Grammar). Rita Manzini, in 'Parasitic Gaps and Locality Theory: A Conclusion' (*UCWPL* 5.55–73) takes another, and possibly conclusive, look at the phenomena of parasitic gaps. According to her they can now all be understood in terms of the theorem of Minimality. Any locality behaviour that does not fall under this follows an ordering constraint which is independently motivated. The final item in this large group of papers on Wh-movement is 'A Principled Characterization of Dislocated Phrases: Capturing Barriers With Static Discontinuity Grammars', by Veronica Dahl, Fred Popowich and Michael Rochemont (in *Ling&P* 16.331–52). It presents a computational model of a parser for A′-movement *à la Barriers*, in which all principles and constraints apply on one single structure. Gaps are also present in coordination structures. Hee-Rahk Chae deals with one of these in 'Right Node Raising and a Licensor Feature' (*PRMCLS* 27.46–59). Traditionally, Right Node Raising (as in *Alice composes, and John performs, Philadelphia-style punk rock music*) has been seen as a type of movement. Chae shows that there are empirical facts that do not agree with a displacement analysis, and that later, non-displacement analyses cannot account for all the characteristics either. His proposal entails that the displaced element (the 'factor') remains in the second conjunct and that the gap in the first conjunct is licensed by it. In 'Dependency Categorial Grammar and Coordination' (*Linguistics* 31.855–902), Martin Pickering and Guy Barry argue that the flexibility of constituency allowed in dependency categorial grammar (which has no problems with *he went into the room*, in which both *went into* and *into the room* appear to be constituents) makes that model eminently suitable for the analysis of various types of coordination. They provide the formalizations needed for this. One more formally-oriented study, Norbert Corver's 'A Note on Subcomparatives' (*LingI* 24.773–81), is devoted to arguing that subcomparatives (i.e. structures such as *Mary bought more cookies than Pete had sold [e candies]*) are coordinate-like. Various empirical similarities are discussed (e.g. Right Node Raising, ATB movement, and gapping) and an analysis is provided by which, for the sentence just given, *more* is raised at LF and then ATB-fashion A′-binds both [e] and its own trace.

Another study into the facts of coordination is not restricted to formalization. In 'Elliptische Koordination: Strukturen und Prozesse Lokaler Textkohärenz' (*LingB* 146.312–42), U. Günther, W. Kindt, U. Schade and L. Ichelschmidt plead for a homogenous theory of ellipsis that tries to do at least three things: to provide (i) a precise definition, (ii) a typology of ellipsis and how the types differ, (iii) an evaluation of existing competing explanations. The language discussed is German, but the discussion is relevant for all languages with ellipsis phenomena. There are two types of explanation for ellipsis: (a) the deletion approach: ellipsis is reduced sentence structure and always goes back to a perfect/full structure, (b) the composition approach, which believes that fragments of phrases are immediately combined/integrated to produce a unitary structure. The difficulty with (a) is that it often cannot account for variation in reference, with which (b) has no problem. Semantic factors may also influence the interpretability of gapped constructions (see pp. 327–8). Next they have performed experiments to elicit the kind of cognitive processes at work in ellipsis based on chronology measurements. These show that the composition theory works better. No evidence was found that thematic factors facilitate the interpretation of gapped clauses. Anne Lobeck looks at three cases of ellipsis in 'Strong Agreement and Identification: Evidence from Ellipsis in English' (*Linguistics* 31.777–811). They are VP-ellipsis (*Because I couldn't [e]*), N-ellipsis (*These are John's [e]*) and sluicing or IP-deletion (*We wanted to invite someone but didn't know who [e]*). She suggests that in each case [e] is non-NP *pro*, which is licensed by a functional head which is specified for strong agreement (i.e. [+plural], [+Poss], [+tense,+AGR], or [+WH]. The last item in this group is a study of the regional distribution of prop *do*: 'Propredicate *do* in the English of the Intermountain West', by Marianna di Paolo (in *AS* 68.339–56). The author reports that uses like *Did he love nature? He must have done*, often held to be British/Australian, also occur (perhaps even function as an ethnicity marker) in the Mormon Dominance Area in the Intermountain West of the US; she attributes this to the effects of migration from England from 1850 to today. As in other years, there is also a good crop of work on binding and (co)reference. Ray Jackendoff, Joan Maling and Annie Zaenen argue that '*Home* is Subject to Principle A' (in *LingI* 24.173–7), on the basis of sentences like *Elliot expected ET to phone home*, which must mean 'to ET's home'. Of course, there is no coreference between *home* and its 'binder', but there is referential dependence. The authors reject an analysis as [$_{PP}$ [$_P φ$] [$_{NP}$ PRO house]], and propose that *home* must be bound in its clause, possibly by an implicit antecedent which is coreferential with an argument in a higher clause. The problem of long-distance reflexives, which appear to violate principle A, is the topic of Priya Bondre's 'Parameter Setting and the Binding Theory: No Subset Problem' (in Fanselow). The difference between Icelandic *sig* (a long-distance reflexive) and *himself* is argued to be due to their different morphological make-up (φ+SELF vs. pronoun+SELF). Subjunctive AGR also plays a role, since it can extend the binding domain. If this is accepted, Wexler and Manzini's parametric approach to this problem, and with it the subset principle, can be abandoned. In 'Object Movement and Binding at LF' (*LingI* 24.381–8), Koji Fujita notes that recent ideas about object movement to AGRO-P at LF imply that the object might sometimes bind a reflexive subject. *Pictures of herself please Mary* is put forward as an actual case. The question then arises why this binding is usually impossible, and Fujita suggests various reasons for this, one of them being that only Cause-subjects originate inside VP (compare also the analysis in Kuno and Takami's book, mentioned above).

A classification of apparent violations of principle C is provided by Joseph Malone, in 'Referring Expressions in Bound Position: Infraction of Principle C of the Binding Theory' (*GL* 33.1–56). He distinguishes three classes: cases with disruption by a disjunct or other obstacle (*The mind, with the mind's uncanny attribute of irrelevant recapitulation, ...*), cases with an 'attributive' NP or a stereotyped epithet (*The speaker has a repertoire of semantic procedures ... that equip the speaker to use ...*), and metalinguistic usage (*This cannot mean that Sue loves Sue*). Some of these classes are also investigated in 'The Innateness of Binding and Coreference', by Yosef Grodzinsky and Tanya Reinhart (in *LingI* 24.69–101). The authors make a distinction between variable binding (principles A and B) and coreference. Coreference can take place across and within sentences; in the latter case, coreference is possible only if distinguishable from a bound-variable reading. Both binding and coreference are innate, but children will have processing problems with intersentential coreference, since that requires them to compare two possible representations. An even more thorough-going reformulation of the traditional binding theory is proposed in Tanya Reinhart and Eric Reuland's 'Reflexivity' (*LingI* 24.657–720). They assume two principles: a reflexive-marked predicate must be reflexive, and a reflexive predicate must be reflexive-marked. In *Max criticized himself*, e.g., the predicate is reflexive-marked (because *himself* is an argument of *criticized*) and indeed also reflexive (because *himself* is coindexed with a co-argument). In **Max$_i$ criticized him$_i$*, the predicate is reflexive (*him* is coindexed with a coargument), but not reflexive-marked. Cases like *There were five tourists apart from myself* are grammatical because *myself* is not an argument of the predicate, which is therefore neither reflexive nor reflexive-marked. The authors also assume a separate chain condition, which takes care of various other facts.

Ljiljana Progovac continues her attempt to unify negative polarity and binding (cf. *YWES* 73.37) in 'Negative Polarity: Entailment and Binding' (*Ling&P* 16.149–80). Negative polarity items like *any* must be bound by either negation or an operator in COMP. However, there cannot be such an operator in an upward entailing clause. Matters dealt with are the relation between inversion and negative polarity, language variation in polarity behaviour, theoretical Wh-questions and the behaviour of *only* under polarity. The relation between free-choice *any* and negative polarity *any* is the topic of Nirit Kadmon and Fred Landman's 'Any' (*Ling&P* 16.353–422). They suggest that *any N* is the indefinite version of *a N*, with some additional semantic and pragmatic characteristics (i.e. widening and strengthening). Free-choice *any* is an indefinite interpreted generically.

The following three items all investigate (co)reference, but not from the perspective of binding theory. Jeanette Gundel, Nancy Hedberg and Ron Zacharski look at 'Cognitive Status and the Form of Referring Expressions in Discourse' (in *Language* 69.274–307). Cognitive status basically means degree of givenness, for which the authors propose a hierarchy with the following positions: 'in focus of attention' > 'activated in short-term memory' > 'familiar' > 'uniquely identifiable' > 'referential' > 'type-identifiable'. This is reflected in the forms that can be used, which for English are: pronouns > *this N/this/that* > *that N* > *the N* > *this N* > *a N*. Some examples of natural discourse show that the hierarchy is obeyed. Two Gricean maxims are used to account for the use of a particular form where a form higher up the hierarchy would have been possible (e.g. *the N* instead of a pronoun). In *Discourse Structure and Anaphora: Written and Conversational English*, Barbara Fox investigates the use of full NPs vs. pronouns in English conversation and expository writing. It turns out that the strategies used depend on text type, but in any event the idea that greater distance promotes the use of a full NP (so prominent in work inspired by Givón) is much too simple. In conversation, for example, use of a full NP often signals that a sequence has closed, or that disagreement or an assessment is being expressed. On the other hand, even when there are two possible antecedents, a pronoun is sometimes used, often with some kind of repetition of phrasing (e.g. *Ward's not letting him talk about what he wanted to talk about. He's making him talk about something else*). In expository writing, the choice to a great extent depends on rhetorical structure, as Fox shows in some detail. Mary Carroll and Christiane von Stutterheim compare English and German descriptions of objects in 'The Representation of Spatial Configurations in English and German and the Grammatical Structure of Locative and Anaphoric Expressions' (*Linguistics* 31.1011–41). English speakers tend to use an object-based perspective for describing (using expressions like 'an L-shape', 'the west side', 'at 3 o'clock') while German speakers take a speaker-based perspective. The authors tie this in with the zero-anaphoric nature of English phrases like *on top*, which will link to the NP last mentioned rather than to the speaker as a deictic centre, whereas German *oben* is usually grounded in the speaker. Various other differences are noted, and related to differing patterns of information organization in the two languages.

Verbal complementation is usually a topic that receives some attention. Juhani Rudanko continues his investigation of verbs governing *to-ing* (cf. *YWES* 73.34) in '*Reducing someone to grovelling*: Aspects of an Object Control Pattern in Present-day English' (*ES* 74.485–95). The aims he sets himself and the questions he asks are the same as last year except that the construction is different. This time he is concerned with object control structures, last year he looked at subject control, as in *John resorted to borrowing money.* Howard Lasnik and Mamoru Saito write 'On the Subject of Infinitives' (*PRMCLS* 27.324–43). Their study deals with the asymmetry in acceptability between finite and non-finite clauses containing an infinitival subject such that *John proved the defendants to be guilty with one accusation each* is ok, whereas a *that*-clause in the same example is hardly acceptable. The question then is, what is at issue here: boundary strength (as argued e.g. in Chomsky 1981 (S-bar deletion)) or structural height (cf. Postal's 1974 subject to object raising)? Another look at the data suggests that there must be some operation that raises the infinitival subject to matrix clause position and that this must take place prior to S-structure. This would entail that Chomsky's proposal of LF movement of accusative NPs to the Spec position of AGR-O cannot adequately account for all cases.

Peter Erdmann has an interesting contribution on how 'Die *for ... to*-Konstruktion nach dem Verb *want*' (*ZAA* 41.124–32) is used in real life. On the basis of a large corpus of British and American English, Erdmann notes that the *for ... to* construction seldom appears immediately after *want*. Often an adverbial phrase occurs in between, or the *for* construction is found in combination with an earlier object, or it appears in focus (cleft) clauses of the type *All/What I want is for him ...*. For the non-contiguity of *want* and *for*, Erdmann refers to ideas expressed by Givón about the amount of integration of main and subclause. Since the semantic bond between *want* and *for* is not very strong, syntactic integration is also less intimate. The second reason is that *want* does not, as a rule, admit a *that*-clause, which is another sign that with *want*, main and subclause are less intimately connected than with verbs like *hate* or *like*. Satomi Niwa presents a rather theory internal account of 'The Complement of Causative and Perception Verbs and PF Identification' (*Ling&Philol.* 13.105–22). It is an attempt to explain the obligatory presence of *to* in infinitival complements after passive perception verbs and causatives (as in *I was made to eat it*) in terms of Roberts's (1993) theory of PF identification. Just as NP objects in passive constructions are raised to subject position because verbs in the passive lose the ability to PF-identify the NP (assign it case, in the old terms), in the same way the infinitive after a passive perception verb or causative must be PF-identified by means of the 'inflection' *to*. One wonders whether this adds anything to a true understanding of the construction (i.e. why *to* is obligatory). William Bennett asks: 'What is Infinitival *to*?' (in *SAP* 25/27.155–68). He argues, on the basis of the distribution of *for*, *that* and *to*-clauses, that *to* is actually in COMP. *For* is said not to be in COMP.

Geart van der Meer has some rather programmatic 'Remarks on the "Object-with-Infinitive"' (in *NOWELE* 21/22.89–109). He argues that in cases like *I saw John cross the street* and *I hate you to talk like that*, there are no good reasons for considering the NP to be part of the infinitival complement syntactically. Intuitions to that effect are based on the semantics of the construction. Perhaps, the author suggests, syntactic terminology should be pared down (e.g. the terms subject and clause could be restricted to finite groups), with semantics taking care of the rest of things. Another study that looks at perception verbs is Nikolas Gisborne, 'Nominalisations of Perception Verbs' (*UCWPL* 5.23–43). It explores in how far a particular semantic class (in this case the group of perception verbs and nouns) shows semantic similarities of behaviour and what the correspondences are between semantic and syntactic structure. It looks especially at correspondences in argument structure between nouns and verbs, in particular concerning the semantics of possession (including *of*-phrases), and at the occurrence of perception nominalizations after so-called light verbs (as in *have a look* etc.). Kunihiro Iwakura addresses the distribution of *that*-clauses and infinitival CPs in 'A Syntactic Restriction on Sister Categories' (*LingA* 23.253–73). He explains the ungrammaticality of sentences such as **I blame that we can't go on you* by proposing a 'sister category principle', which bars base-generated sisters of which one is [+V] and the other [–V]. The categories NP, AP, and PP are [–V], while CP and IP are [+V]. Finally, there is a comparative study of control in 'A Cognitive Approach to Obligatory Control Phenomena in English and German' by Klaus-Uwe Panther and Klaus-Michael Köpcke (in *FoLi* 27.57–105). They try to provide a meaning-based account of the fact that subject-control is much more usual than object control, but that control-shift is sometimes possible (as in *I promised him to be promoted*). They point out that control-verbs prototypically take a following action predicate. PRO will therefore be an agent, and will choose the matrix agent as controller. If, however, PRO is beneficiary, it will choose the matrix beneficiary, yielding control-shift. In an empirical study, the authors found that in English, control-shift is sometimes resisted (e.g. in *Mary requested Barbara to be helped with her work*).

There are several worthwhile contributions based on corpus work. The widest in scope is 'Clause Patterns in Modern British English: A Corpus-Based (Quantitative) Study' by Nelleke Oostdijk and Pieter de Haan (*DWPELL* 28.1–34). The authors have looked at the frequency of various sentence patterns (transitive, intransitive, intensive, complex, finite, non-finite, embedded clauses in NP, AdjP, AdvP, PP, adverbial types, marked word orders, etc.) in the Nijmegen corpus of (written) English. Their investigation yields a lot of firm data on frequency and distribution, which can take the place of earlier impressionistic statements on these matters. Richard Hudson just happened to stumble on some interesting distribution facts concerning 'Word-Classes in Performance' (*UCWPL* 5.45–54). He looked at the number of word-classes that appear in written texts and comes to the 'surprising' conclusion that the distribution of word-classes across texts shows a very clear statistical trend, around 47 per cent in any text represent nouns, 7 per cent adjectives and 18 per cent verbs, and that this figure also works more or less for languages other than English. He does not have an answer (yet) why this should be so. Flor Aarts, '*Who, Whom*, and in Two Corpora of Spoken English' (*EnT* 9:iii.19–21) is a reaction to an earlier article (in *EnT* 8:4) on the diglossic variants *who* and *whom*. Aarts argues that one cannot really discuss this without paying attention to the other options available, i.e. *that* and zero. He notes that *who* is the most frequent pronoun in subject position in a number of corpora he looked at, much more frequent than *that*, and that *that* and zero are very clearly favoured in object position (to the detriment of *whom*).

In another article in the same volume of *EnT* (10–17), 'A Question of Concord', David S. Taylor notes the present uncertainty and confusion about concord between subject and verb. Many instances that occur cannot be understood by the principles concerning concord given in the Quirk *et al.* (1985) grammar. Taylor thinks that subject/verb concord is undergoing further erosion and may disappear altogether. He concentrates on two types, those with singular subject and plural verb, and plural subject and singular verb, and discusses the validity of the Quirkean principles of notional concord, proximity and coordination in connection with them. The lack of concord between the form *they* and an indefinite antecedent such as *everyone, a person* or *the student* is the topic of Miriam

Meyers's 'Forms of *they* with Singular Noun Phrase Antecedents: Evidence from Current Educated English Usage' (in *Word* 44.181–92). She reports that this usage is found in both educated speech and writing, in spite of normative pronouncements about its incorrectness (which are reviewed, together with earlier descriptive statements).

Studies of tense, aspect and auxiliaries are, as usual, well represented. Bonnie McElhinny writes on 'Copula and Auxiliary Contraction in the Speech of White Americans' (in *AS* 68.371–99). Among 20 white speakers studied, the effect of following grammatical environment (adj/verb+*ing*/noun/locative/gonna) differed from individual to individual. This situation is contrasted with that of deletion in the black vernacular, for which following environment has a uniform effect. This, the author suggests, may be evidence that there is a fundamental difference between the black and white systems, and that there has been no diffusion from one variety to another. In *AS* 68.241–52, Cecily Hancock notes that 'If he would have and if he didn't' are nowadays quite common. The former, however, seems to be restricted to speech and speech-based writing; Hancock attributes its origin to reanalysis of *if he'd have* (from *if he had have*) and/or a desire for symmetry (it allows the use of the same verb forms in protasis and apodosis). Perhaps connected with the form *if he didn't* (as in *If I didn't have my seat belt on, I'd be dead*) is the occasional use, also noted by the author, of *may have* in counterfactual conditionals (as in *We may never have known about this if David had not told us*). Another usage which is not noted in most grammars is analysed by Osvaldo Jaeggli and Nina Hyams in 'On the Independence and Interdependence of Syntactic and Morphological Properties: English Aspectual *come* and *go*' (*NL&LT* 11.313–46). The facts are as follows: aspectual *come* and *go* (mainly found in American English) resist all overt inflection (one can say *Come talk to me*, or *I will go talk to them*; but not **He often comes/came talk to me*). Jaeggli and Hyams propose a generative analysis, in which *come* and *go* head their own VP, and select the lexical VP. They assign a secondary agentive theta-role to the subject, and for that reason it may not raise either in the syntax or at LF. The trace of any affix lowered to *come* or *go* will therefore be ungoverned at LF. This account necessitates some revision in the analysis of affix movement and also *do*-support, which the authors provide.

Galia Hatav has a shot at 'The Aspect System in English: An Attempt at a Unified Analysis' (in *Linguistics* 31.209–37). Using Reichenbach's notions of time of E(vent), S(peech), and R(eference), but interpreting them as intervals, Hatav analyses tense as involving the relation between R and S (which can be one of anteriority, simultaneity, or posteriority). Aspect has to do with E and R: simple aspect has E included in R, progressive aspect has R included in E, and perfect aspect has E preceding R. A puzzle that cannot be solved by this analysis (which works well enough for some other data, as Hatav shows) is the ungrammaticality of **John has left yesterday*; the author has to resort to stipulation here. A rather different approach to tense and aspect is found in Frank Vlach's 'Temporal Adverbials, Tenses and the Perfect' (*Ling&P* 16.231–83). In his analysis, the choice between e.g. past and present perfect depends at least partly on the nature of temporal adverbials (which may be 'understood'). Thus, an adverbial indicating 'extended now' will trigger use of the perfect, while an adverbial which does not indicate this will trigger the past tense. In view of the varying uses of one and the same form, such an approach may eventually turn out to be more adequate than one in which tense and aspect forms themselves project meaning. In 'The Use of the Present Perfect in English and Dutch: A Look behind the Scenes' (in *Lingua* 89.1–37), Lia Korrel draws on her 1991 book on this topic (see *YWES* 72.47). She notes three usage differences between English and Dutch past and perfect forms (the obligatory use of the perfect in English, but not Dutch, for extended-now contexts; the incompatibility in English, but not Dutch, of definite past time adverbials with the present perfect; the strong implication of current relevance of the perfect in English but not Dutch), and tries to derive these facts from a subtle difference in the interpretation of the present moment: in English, the present moment is regarded as about to be actualized, while in Dutch it is considered just to have been actualized. Interaction with the meaning of the perfect itself (which presents 'the aftermath phase of a situation') then yields the facts.

Two entire books deal with general questions of aspectuality. In *Aspect in the English Verbs*, Yishai Tobin argues for the pervasive influence of the features Process and Result on the English verb. They affect lexical items (e.g. *make* is marked for Result, while the near-synonym *do* is unmarked, i.e. can indicate Process and/or Result), grammar (e.g. *get* is marked for Result, and can therefore be used in resultative passives; dummy *do* can be regarded as a process-marker), and perhaps also morphology (e.g. English irregular verbs may have in common the fact that they are marked for the feature Result). The book bristles with data from all kinds of sources, and it is made clear enough that the notions of Process and Result are important for their interpretation; what seems to be lacking, however, is an attempt to relate these notions systematically to other features of English verbs and/or an attempt to formalize the analysis. Such formalization is the strong point of Henk Verkuyl's *A Theory of Aspectuality: The Interaction Between Temporal and Atemporal Structure*. The central question that is addressed here is: how do sentences express aspectual properties (in particular, terminative, bounded aspect vs. durative, unbounded aspect)? The answer proposed is that aspect is determined compositionally from properties of V and its arguments. For V, the relevant property is [±ADD TO] (i.e. dynamic and/or expressing movement), and for NP it is [±Specified Quantity]. In *John ate three sandwiches*, for example, *ate* is [+ADD TO], and *three sandwiches* is [+Specified Quantity], which makes the VP [+terminative]. Since the subject is also [+Specified Quantity], the clause as a whole is [+terminative]. To determine when a NP is [±Specified Quantity] and a V [±ADD TO], and what their interaction is, Verkuyl uses generalized quantification theory and set theory.

A very different investigation of tense and aspect is John Singler's 'An African-American Linguistic Enclave: Tense and Aspect in Liberian Settler English' (in Aertsen and Jeffers). Singler examines tense-aspect marking in the English of the Liberian Settlers (descendants of Black American immigrants in the nineteenth century). He argues that they preserved many features of (earlier) Black English, and were little influenced by Yoruba and Kru. To find pattern in confusion is Donald Winford's aim in 'Variability in the use of Perfect *have* in Trinidadian English: A Problem of Categorial and Semantic Mismatch' (*LVC* 5.141–87). The article is primarily interested in an important methodological point, i.e. how one decides upon the possible semantic equivalence of morphosyntactic variants within more than one grammatical system, or how the concept of the sociolinguistic variable may be applied to levels other than phonology. It focuses on the perfect variants in the Trinidadian English creole continuum, where *have* varies with such forms as zero, *done*, progressive -*in* etc., with *have* being used in all standard perfect senses, the others being restricted to subsenses such as resultative, continuative and experiential. Patterns of variation can be distinguished on the basis of class, the type of perfect used and predicate type. A second aim is to find out more about contact-induced variation and the changes that are the result of this.

The items by Singler and Winford provide a good transition to several studies dealing with the grammar of particular varieties of English. One of these is Wayne O'Neil's 'Nicaraguan English in History' (in Jones). Although published in a book on historical linguistics, this paper does not focus on the study of creole as a laboratory for language change, but simply wants to present the present-day grammatical facts of Nicaraguan English and how they came to be that way. As far as the (inflexional) morphology is concerned (we skip the section on phonology), O'Neil notes the almost total loss of standard English inflexions and the emergence of new ones such as the suffix -*dem* to indicate the plural of (only) definite nouns, and the use of proclitic *do/did* to indicate tense in verbs. In syntax, he looks at a number of constructions that are different from the standard, e.g. question-formation (lack of inversion in wh-questions), copular verbs (the variation in use between *is*, *de*, and zero verb), a larger use of null NPs (which in many ways resembles OE, such as an unexpressed pronominal object, more extensive use of arbitrary PRO), and the use of serial verbs. Gabriella Mazzon describes 'English in Malta' (*EWW* 14.171–208), focusing on status and attitudes, but also making some observations on grammatical peculiarities. These involve the (non-)use of the definite article, a tendency to omit subject and object *it*, usage of prepositions, verbal -*s*, frequent use of topicalization, and progressives with stative verbs. A very special type of English is that found in code-mixing; Helena Halmari writes about it in 'Structural Relations and Finnish-Finnish-English Code-Switching' (*Linguistics* 31.1043–68). The data show violations of many proposed constraints on code-mixing; there are, for example, frequent switches between stem and bound morpheme (as in *rhym-aa* 'rhyme-3pl'). A modified version of the government constraint (see Di Sciullo et al., 1986) seems the best explanation for the data.

James and Lesley Milroy have edited a volume entitled *Real English: The Grammar of English Dialects in the British Isles* (one wonders about the implications of the word *real* in the title). In the first article of the book, Jenny Cheshire and Jim Milroy write about 'Syntactic Variation in Non-Standard Dialects: Background Issues'; the topics discussed include the history and social background of standardization, the rule-governed nature of social and regional variation, and the problems arising from the use of non-standard grammar (esp. from an educational viewpoint). In the next article, 'Sociolinguistics in the Classroom: Exploring Linguistic Diversity', Jenny Cheshire and Viv Edwards describe the set-up of the Survey of British Dialect Grammar (conducted from 1986 to 1989), which asked pupils at 87 schools in Britain to report on grammatical features of the speech of their area. A questionnaire with 196 features was used for this. To prepare the pupils, outlines for lessons on language variation were sent to the teachers. These apparently yielded some very interesting work by the pupils themselves. One particular specimen of this must be the cutest item reviewed in *YWES* 74; it is a poem written by a 12-year-old Pakistani girl, in Lancashire dialect, on the subject of going to the disco and her grandmother (given by the authors on p. 47). The results of the questionnaire are described in 'Non-Standard English and Dialect Levelling', by Jenny Cheshire, Viv Edwards and Pamela Whittle. Features reported very frequently included the use of demonstrative *them*, expressions like *two pound*, *what* as a relative marker, the use of *was sat/stood* as intransitives, adverbs without *-ly*, and *ain't*. Other features showed regional distribution (e.g. double negation was mainly Southern, as was past tense *done*).

These articles are followed by four descriptive pieces on the grammar of specific regions: Jim Miller writes on 'The Grammar of Scottish English', John Harris on 'The Grammar of Irish English', Joan Beal on 'The Grammar of Tyneside and Northumbrian English', and Viv Edwards on 'The Grammar of Southern British English'. The book concludes with 'A Directory of English Dialect Resources: The English Counties' by Viv Edwards, which lists relevant books, sound materials, local centres and societies for each region.

We now come to a number of studies on adjectives. Chris Barker and Christopher Culy write on 'Nominal Control of Misplaced Modifiers' (*PRMCLS* 28.42–55). The paper deals with constructions such as *The tabloid published naked pictures of the candidate*, where *naked* modifies the candidate in spite of its position before *pictures*. Their (rather obvious) point is that the linking here depends solely on the lexical entailments and presuppositions of the adjective and the NP it controls, and does not show any syntactic constraints as in the control properties of for instance PRO as in *I want PRO to leave*. Isn't this a phenomenon we see a lot of in spoken discourse (in the anticipation of words or speech-sounds) or poetry ('prolepsis')? Connor Ferris, in *The Meaning of Syntax: A Study in the Adjectives of English* promotes a particular view of syntax by applying it to the adjectival constructions of English. The various concepts of his syntactic model (which is strongly semantically based; a prominent role is played by the relations of 'qualification', 'equation', and 'assignment') are brought to bear on constructions with attributive adjectives (both ascriptive and associative, prenominal and postnominal), predicative adjectives, predicate-qualifying adjectives (*He brought his gun loaded*), adverbial adjectives (*He rubbed it clean*), clausal adjectives (*He considers it hopeless*), extra-clausal adjectives (*Furious, he ordered their arrest*), etc. Many interesting observations are made on the meaning of specific patterns; indeed, Ferris contends that each pattern typically has its own semantics. Attributive adjectives, e.g., qualify N, while predicative adjectives assign a property to the subject.

John Taylor deals with one adjective in 'Old Problems: Adjectives in Cognitive Grammar (*CogLing* 3.1–35). He describes the different senses of *old friend* ('friend who is old', absolute reading; 'friend of long standing' and 'former friend', synthetic readings), and explains them by positing three senses for *old*. The choice depends on elements in the semantic structure of the noun. Predicative *old* only has the absolute reading because *old* can activate semantic elements only of N, not of NP. Jan Nuyts investigates the difference between *It is probable that they ran out of fuel* and *Probably they ran out of fuel* (in 'Epistemic Modal Adverbs and Adjectives and the Layered Representation of Conceptual and Linguistic Structure', *Linguistics* 31.933–69). He suggests that the modal adverb is only used if the following conditions are met: (i) the modal qualification is not salient in the discourse; (ii) no evidentiality is involved; (iii) the speaker is committed to the epistemic modality. The modal adjective is always possible.

The small words *so* and *such* each receive one contribution this year. Jacob Hoeksema and Donna Jo Napoli compare 'Paratactic and Subordinate *so* (*JL* 29.291–314), i.e. *I fainted, the sun was so hot* vs. *The sun was so hot I fainted*. They describe various differences between the two sentence types (e.g. the possibility of inserting *that*, inversion, binding into the second clause by a quantifier, and negative polarity licensing), and conclude that the second type has a subordinate clause. The first type, they argue, is not an example of clause coordination (since it only allows two clauses, and does not permit conjunction reduction), but of syntactic parataxis (i.e. it has two juxtaposed matrix clauses). Eric Schiller and Barbara Need are all for 'The Liberation of Minor Categories – *Such a nice idea*' (*PRMCLS* 28.484–98). The article considers the semantics as well as the syntax of elements such as *such*, showing that, syntactically, the use of *such* is difficult to capture within X-bar theory. They reject the suggestion of treating *such a* as a 'super-word' (*sucha*) because it cannot deal with structures like *too good/big/rich a ....* Instead, they propose a constituent structure within Autolexical theory. They also show that the odd structure of *such a* can only be understood from a diachronic point of view.

Four items deal with passives. Miki Saito looks at two types of passive (verbal and adjectival passives) in terms of differences in their argument structure, using Grimshaw (1990) (in 'The Argument Structure of Passive Participles', *Ling&Philol.* 13.123–40). She makes the not very stunning proposal (because it represents a mere terminological solution) that there are two different passive suffixes (one for verbal, one for adjectival past participle) that induce their different argument structures and the other properties involved. Grant Goodall writes 'On Case and the Passive Morpheme' (in *NL&LT* 11.31–44). He takes issue with the popular idea that the passive morpheme is an argument which requires a theta-role and Case. Although this may be adequate for English, data from other languages (Kannada, Finnish, Ukrainian, Norwegian, Nepali) show in different ways that the correlation between theta-role and Case does not hold. The same type of data are also discussed by Shalom Lappin and Ur Shlonsky in 'Impersonal Passives' (*Linguistics* 31.5–24). They suggest that the passive morpheme occupies Spec VP, and may be [±theta-role bearer] and [±Case absorber]. If it can bear a theta-role (which it can't in English), intransitive impersonal passives can be formed (as in German); if it is [−Case absorber] (which it isn't in English), in situ objects are possible (as in Norwegian). Ellen Woolford's 'Symmetric and Asymmetric Passives' (in *NL&LT* 11.679–728) is about the passive of double object sentences, which in English is asymmetric (*Pat was sent a letter* vs. **A letter was sent Pat*). She compares English with several other languages, and proposes that differences are due to the level at which the passive morpheme is attached.

The proper analysis of middle constructions continues to occupy the minds of generative scholars. Last year we reviewed Thomas Stroik's analysis (see *YWES* 73.49). This year it is criticized by Anne Zribi-Hertz ('On Stroik's Analysis of English Middle Constructions', in *LingI* 24.583–9). She cannot agree with Stroik's suggestion that middles have a PRO agent, adjoined to VP, which can bind anaphors, as in *Books about oneself never read poorly*. She adduces examples like *Books about oneself are often worrisome*, in which a non-middle has the same anaphor, and points out that anyway anaphors do not always obey binding principle A. She proposes that middles imply an implicit (semantic) arbitrary agent argument, which can license *oneself*. A completely new analysis for middles is given in Teun Hoekstra and Ian Roberts's 'Middle Constructions in Dutch and English' (in Reuland and Abraham). They posit a D-structure for middle sentences which is roughly: $[_{IP} \text{ e INFL } [_{VP} \text{ pro } [_{V'} \text{ bribe bureaucrats easily}]]]$, with *pro*, the non-overt counterpart to *one*, as VP-internal subject. This *pro* (quite indirectly) interferes with Case-assignment by *bribe* to the object *bureaucrats*, which then moves to the empty Spec IP. The affectedness condition to which middles are subject (*It didn't admit easily*) is interpreted by the authors as a difference in Case-marking by verbs that are (non-)affecting.

Genitives form the topic of D. J. Allerton's 'Problems of Modern English Grammar III. Classifying Genitives: Putting the Apostrophe in its Place' (*ES* 74.559–67). It is about the problem of whether one has to write *girl's school* or *girls' school*, and therefore looks at sequences with an irregular noun to see what is what, such as *woman's college* vs. *women's college*. This leads to a further argument about what the difference may be between (1) *a child's bike* and (2) *a children's bike*, and the relation to compounds such as *student union* (from earlier *students' union*). The parameters that are important in these cases are individual (cf. (1)) vs. generic (cf. (2)), whether the head noun is a mass noun or not (with a mass noun the plural is more likely cf. *children's blood* vs. **child's blood*), and whether the genitive is classifying or identificatory. Ronald Langacker analyses possessive constructions (*my watch, our host, the cat's fleas*) in 'Reference-Point Constructions' (*CogLing* 4.1–38). His view is that the possessor is invoked as a reference point for establishing mental contact with the possessed entity. This idea is also applied to *have*, dative shift, topics and presentationals, the conclusion being that reference-point organization is a very basic cognitive ability.

Finally, some didactic items. In 'Triggering Science-Forming Capacity Through Linguistic Inquiry' (in Hale and Keyser), Maya Honda and Wayne O'Neil report on their development of linguistics lessons for secondary schools, which had the aim of developing awareness of the nature of scientific inquiry (and were taught in science classes). Topics the pupils were encouraged to explore (through data analysis, hypothesis formulating and testing) included *wanna* contraction, plurals of nouns, past tenses, and binding of reflexives. Materials for university students needing an introduction to the syntactic analysis of English are found in Linda Thomas's *Beginning Syntax*. The book deals with word and phrase categories and functions, types of VP, verbs, the structure of NPs, subclauses and coordination. A large number of tree diagrams are provided, and many questions are given (with a key occupying 80 pages, again full of tree diagrams). We think this will be a good textbook for an elementary introductory course. We finish with a book that is useful for somewhat more advanced students of linguistics to have, i.e. R. L. Trask's *A Dictionary of Grammatical Terms in Linguistics*. It concentrates strictly on syntax and morphology, so unlike Crystal's *Dictionary* it contains no information on phonetic and phonological terms. It is up to date in including the most recent GB terms and some terms from other well-established theories such as General Phrase Structure Grammar, Lexical Functional Grammar etc. However, since many of those terms are highly theory-specific, it seems to us that the descriptions as provided will not in all cases help the reader to understand what is meant without her/him doing quite a lot of cross-referencing.

(b) Early English

Quite a few books and articles of theoretical interest to syntactic change, and indeed language change in general, have appeared this year, and it is interesting to note that most of these turn away from a strictly synchronic point of view concerning the locus of change, and in fact from many ideas voiced by diachronic grammarians working within the generative (or if you like Minimalist) school of thought. We would like to discuss first Paul J. Hopper and Elizabeth Closs Traugott's important contribution to our knowledge about *Grammaticalization* processes, and, in general, about how grammar evolves. Although this book, strictly speaking, does not deal with English grammar proper, many of the case histories it presents are drawn from the history of English. It is a perfect book to read in conjunction with Givón's *English Grammar* (discussed in the previous section) in that both call into question the discreteness of categories and rules, and the rigid Saussurian distinction between synchronic and diachronic dimensions; grammaticalization, of course, being a prime example of a process that may cut across all these distinctions. Hopper and Traugott's book studies grammaticalization from two different perspectives, which have been combined. From a historical point of view, it looks at the linguistic changes through which lexical items may become more grammatical (semantic bleaching plays an important role here). More synchronically (although this clearly has historical dimensions too), it discusses to what extent grammaticalization is the result of discourse pragmatic forces; here the changes occur by shift rather than linearly. All the well-known problems that exist in relation to grammaticalization are lucidly described and, as far as possible, explained, such as the question of unidirectionality, the common core of source words amenable to grammaticalization, the type of domains in which pragmatic shifting takes place, the (dis)continuity of the process, and especially the relations/differences with other well-known mechanisms of change, such as reanalysis, analogy and parametric change.

A lively, funny and interesting article (and a good antidote if one has had an overdose of autonomous syntax and/or purely theory internal considerations) that goes well with the arguments presented in Hopper and Traugott's book is John Haiman's 'Life, the Universe, and Human Language (A Brief Synopsis)' (*LangS* 15.293–22). Haiman shows that grammaticalization may be understood as a kind of ritualization, as the creation of stereotypes that slowly move away from concrete reality. He gives examples of ritualization in real life (the development of the mannequin archetype, the 'fool as hubby' etc.) and shows the similarities between this and what happens in language. The keyword is motivation. Although language structures often seem unmotivated, this is only because they have become ritualized; motivation for them can be found in the past. He thus sees a parallel between language functions (from expressive to ritual) and types of language structure (from motivated to largely arbitrary). This article is in a volume of *Language Sciences* that is completely devoted to the question whether knowledge of language is distinct from knowledge of the world. In the introduction to this volume, Philip Davis calls into question the notion of language as a structure separate from other human cognitive activities, and also the idea that language is discrete in terms of morphological and syntactic entities. P. Swiggers's contribution '"Synchrony" and "Diachrony" in Sapir's *Language*' (*NM* 94.313–22) also stresses the absence of a clear dichotomy, in this case between synchrony and diachrony. This was true, he argues, for Sapir's seminal work in spite of the fact that many linguists have read this dichotomy into it. Sapir was no Saussurian; rather, he wished to show that there is an intimate connection between the structure of language and its evolution in that the 'global pattern of language ... traces the path for its evolution'. In other words, the fundamental causes of language change are to be found in the language itself and not in such principles as 'least effort' or 'generational transmission'.

There are two articles that address themselves to the way parameter-setting has been used (in a GB kind of approach) to explain syntactic change. The first one is in a book, Charles Jones (ed.) *Historical Linguistics: Problems and Perspectives*, that in itself is of great methodological interest to diachronic linguists. Most of the papers in it, however, do not deal with English proper and will therefore only be briefly mentioned here. The papers tackle all the relevant sub-areas in historical linguistics such as (concentrating on what is relevant to syntax) the contribution of typology to language change (Bernard Comrie on 'Typology and Reconstruction'), the relation between language acquisition and change (David Lightfoot on 'Why UG Needs a Learning Theory: Triggering Verb Movement'), the role of external as well as internal factors in borrowing (Nancy Dorian on 'Internally and Externally Motivated Change in Language Contact Settings: Doubts about Dichotomy'), '[On] the Social Origins of Language Change' (James Milroy), in how far language change may be said to be remedial (Theo Venneman on 'Language Change as Language Improvement'), and the risks we run when we use language history to illustrate theoretical positions, especially when we interpret reconstructions of the past (such as Grimm's Law) as factual data (Roger Lass 'How Real(ist) are Reconstructions?'). The English syntax paper in the book relevant for this section (there is one more, by O'Neill, discussed above) is John Anderson's 'Parameters of Syntactic Change: A Notional View'. Anderson's aim is to show that language change involves or is restricted to minimal modifications to categories, and that categorial changes as suggested e.g. by Lightfoot (1979 etc.) are unlikely and perhaps impossible. In Anderson's theory of notional grammar there is a set of notional components or features (i.e. P for predicative and N for Nominal) out of which larger structures or more complex categories are built. He wants to show by means of case studies from the history of English (the 'reanalysis' of the modals, the development of infinitives, and of gerund and participles) that changes involve local, minimal modifications of the notional categories, and that only three types of change are likely to occur: (i) realignment of categories, (ii) conflation of categories, (iii) differentiation of categories. He ends with a plea for more work on the articulation of a restrictive theory of syntactic categories. The other contribution, by Dorothy Disterheft, also dealing with 'Parameter Resetting' (in van Marle) is not so much interested in whether it is features or categories that are reset, but rather in the methodology of parameter-setting as used by e.g. Lightfoot. Once again the modal story is used as an illustration. Lightfoot argued that a parameter is reset once the majority of constructions no longer show variation. For Disterheft, however, the appearance of variant forms itself in their early stages is an indication that a parameter has been reset because only the resetting can account for the gradual emergence of variant constructions. In short, for Disterheft parameter resetting is a purely abductive process, whereas for Lightfoot (according to Disterheft at least) it is achieved inductively. It seems to us that a middle road must be possible because, if the resetting is purely abductive as the author claims, then still the abduction will have to be triggered by some earlier changes; otherwise why would the process start at all? In that sense we agree with Lightfoot that there must be changes (variants) both before and after resetting.

A book that stands out here in that it is not functional but strictly 'Minimalist', observing a strict separation between synchrony and diachrony, and following the GB type of parameter setting, is Elly van Gelderen's *The Rise of Functional Categories* (some of the material is also found in her separate paper 'Tense and *to* in Layamon', in *FLH* 13.133–42). The title of the book refers both to the emergence of functional categories in Chomskyan linguistics (as pointed out in the previous section, in minimalist theory, verbs or nouns no longer move to pick up their inflections, but instead are 'checked' against features present in the functional head/category), showing their usefulness as a theoretical construct, as well as, more specifically, to the 'factual' rise of the functional category T(ense) in English. Van Gelderen argues that T was not present in OE (nor in most other Germanic languages, also discussed), because OE does not show constructions which need a tense node, such as split infinitives, exceptional case-marking constructions (i.e. *I believe him to be* ...), the use of *do*-support etc., which all according to the author appear at about the same time (end of ME period). The appearance of T is further also associated with the gradual loss of Verb second. Although the book contains some interesting ideas, especially for minimalist theory, we feel that it is rather superficial from a functional and from a more philological point of view. First of all, it does not become clear *why* the category T was introduced in English (we are simply told that it was), i.e. what internal and/or external changes led to this development. Similarly, but on a smaller scale, it is often not clear why a construction is structured the way it is. For instance, in OE bare infinitives are said to be both CPs and VPs, but there is no explanation offered for why there is this choice and what the difference is between them. More problematic, however, is the fact that we feel that the reader may not be able to trust quite a few of the examples adduced. Thus, of the four examples which are given (on pp. 60–1) as evidence for the occurrence of 'pro-infinitives', only one is clear, two do not give enough context so that the reader cannot possibly decide that they indeed show the intended phenomenon, and one is plain wrong. Facts like these limit the book's usefulness, and there is a danger that it will appeal only to adherents of the theoretical framework chosen. Works of that type are bound to disappoint the majority of students of early English syntax. Kirsti Peitsara, in a review in *Word* 44.121–30, shows in some detail that Moessner's 1989 *Early Middle English Syntax* is definitely such a work (confirming our own impression, see *YWES* 70.111–12).

It is interesting to compare van Gelderen's book with David Denison's *English Historical Syntax: Verbal Constructions*, because the very strong point of this book is the extreme care that the author has given to the presentation of examples. In this book it is quite clear that the data are far more important than the theory, on which the author is frankly eclectic. This also has its drawbacks, in that the reader is at times as it were overwhelmed by the data; one is not always given enough direction to get a feeling for what the change may be about, or indeed that there is any necessary direction to the change at all. In other words, it does not always become clear why a change would have moved in one way and not in another. It seems to us, however, that overall Denison's book will be very useful because the interested student is given enough reliable data to come up with their own theory of the change. The book concentrates on changes in the verbal constructions: the relation between the subject and the VP, changes in verbal complementation, and especially the rise and use of periphrastic verbs. Apart from that, there is a handy resumé of what happened diachronically in morphology and word order, areas which provide the groundwork for further changes. The book is a useful tool for both students and researchers in that it provides a very wide coverage of data and succinctly deals with all the relevant work that has appeared on each particular topic discussed.

From the sections in Denison's book which describe earlier work, it becomes clear that there have not really been many changes in English that can be straightforwardly attributed to grammatical borrowing. However, according to Fred Weerman the important change from OV to VO may have been one: in 'The Diachronic Consequences of First and Second Language Acquisition: The Change from OV to VO' (*Linguistics* 31.903–31) he argues that the Vikings who acquired English as a second language overgeneralized the use of VO order found in many OE main clauses (due to the rule of Verb-second). He points to the same kind of overgeneralization of VO by foreigners learning Dutch or German (which are like OE in having underlying OV, but Verb second in main clauses), and also considers the sociolinguistic factors that may have promoted the further spread of VO. If this is indeed a case of grammatical borrowing (although Denison, who discusses a pre-publication version of Weerman's paper in his book, is not convinced), it would still be one of only a few. We also note that Lilo Moessner denies foreign (i.e. Latin) influence on OE relatives in 'How English are Old English Relative Constructions?' (in *SAP* 25/27.95–107). She considers two types of OE relatives (those with successive cyclic movement, and those with a resumptive pronoun), and concludes that they cannot be due to borrowing from Latin, since they do not always translate a Latin relative (and, in fact, Latin has no resumptive pronouns). While on the subject of borrowing, we would also like to mention Lyle Campbell's wide-ranging article 'On Proposed Universals of Grammatical Borrowing' (in Aertsen and Jeffers), which makes clear that there are counter-examples to nearly all proposed universals in this area (such as: 'There must be structural compatibility between donor and recipient language'; 'There cannot be non-lexical borrowing unless there has been lexical borrowing'; 'Derivational affixes are borrowed before inflectional affixes', etc).

The rise of periphrastic verbs has always attracted a lot of attention in English historical linguistics. This year we are particularly fortunate in that it witnesses the long-awaited publication of Anthony Warner's book on *English Auxiliaries: Structure and History*. Its main aim is to show how the present-day system of auxiliaries grew out of its historical roots. The book therefore is of interest to both synchronic and diachronic linguists, while at the same time it shows that it pays to take the history of a particular construction into consideration when describing its present-day structure. What makes this book so valuable is the care with which the author has treated the available data (and he has indeed looked at a lot of data) and considered earlier accounts. His main question throughout the book is: how is the class of modals organized and how is it related to the class of verbs? He does not agree with the usual view that the modern auxiliary is categorically distinct. Instead, he proposes a new lexical account for their fixed order and for their restricted availability morphologically. He shows that this lexical account is a worthwhile proposition in terms of e.g. observational adequacy and learnability. The lexical treatment of auxiliaries is further nicely supported by the fact that like words they are 'anaphoric islands', and in the way that it accounts for some very interesting changes that are taking place in late Modern English (e.g. the loss of morphological agreement, the occurrence in inverted structures of full verbs, the development of the double -*ing* constraint, the rise of the progressive passive, and the use of *of* for *have*). A major part of the book is devoted to the development of the auxiliaries as a subcategory of the verb in OE and ME. Warner shows that this subcategory developed formal aspects which were always embryonically present. That is, the so-called pre-auxiliaries already had a distinctive status before the sixteenth century, not on semantic grounds (as argued in Brinton 1988 and Goossens 1987), but on the basis of their formal properties (so he disagrees with a cataclysmic account of the change *à la* Lightfoot 1979 etc.). These formal differences with full verbs concern, among other things, 'their occurrence before contexts of ellipsis, transparency to impersonal constructions', and especially with reference to modals, their 'preterite present morphology' and 'their subcategorization for the plain infinitive'.

There are several other papers showing interest in the history of the auxiliaries. The first one is by Bonnie McElhinny, 'The Interaction of Phonology, Syntax and Semantics in Language Change: The History of Modal Contraction in English' (*PRMCLS* 28.367–81). It looks at the development of modals from full verbs to auxiliaries in connection with the phonological reduction that modals (can) undergo, which according to the author had not been considered before Warner (1990) (but see, however, Plank 1984: 330, 339–40). She examines in more detail than before how modal contraction became possible and how it interacts with other changes modals undergo connected with grammaticalization. Her findings disagree with Warner, who had written that contraction only occurred *after* the reanalysis of the modals as a kind of additional property. Ans van Kemenade reanalyses Lightfoot's modals story in 'The History of English Modals: A Reanalysis' (in *FLH* 13.143–66). Instead of saying that the pre-modals were ordinary verbs in OE, she suggests that there were no less than three possible structures: modal as V with a theta-marked subject and NP or VP complement (deontic reading), modals as raising V with VP complement (epistemic reading), and modal as INFL (purely futural meaning of *sceal/will*). She also discusses the factors leading to all modals being reinterpreted as INFL-elements.

Double modals are also popular this year. Michiko Ogura writes on '*Shal (not) mowe*, or Double Auxiliary Constructions in Middle English' (RES 34.539–48). She considers the origin of the construction in the title, which is not found in OE and occurs for the first time in the *Orrmulum*, suggesting that there may have been some ON influence behind it. She also looks at the way the construction is used, rejecting Mustanoja's idea that it represents a periphrastic future. Finally, she lists the other combinations of auxiliaries occurring in ME. The starting point for Stephen Nagle's 'Double Modals in Early English' (in Aertsen and Jeffers) is the existence of combinations like *might could, may can, might can*, and *might should* in the speech of many American Southerners (a fact usually not noted in descriptions of the modals). He examines the double pre-modals occurring in OE (among the 15,000 pre-modal tokens he has looked at, there are some 40 examples of *sceal/scolde/mot/moste* followed by *agan* and *cunnan*), and notes that they differ from the present-day double modals in the identity of the modals that are combined, and also in the fact that the second modal in OE is very clearly an infinitive, which is not the case in present-day English (as data on question formation and negation show). In ME, *shall may* and *shall can* are predominant (perhaps because *can* remained a full V longer than other modals). The conclusion is that the modern instances do not derive from Old or ME, and must represent a Modern English development. Nagle continues this story (this time with Michael Montgomery as co-author) in 'Double Modals in Scotland and the Southern United States: Trans-Atlantic Inheritance or Independent Development?' (in *FLH* 14.91–107). The differences and similarities between Scottish and Southern American double modals are discussed, and the authors point out that the earliest attestations (around 1760 in Scotland, one century later in the

USA) may postdate their actual use by a long time since double modals are very much a characteristic of interactive uses of language which are poorly represented in historical writings. They suggest that the phenomenon originated in Scots (with the item *can*, still often a full V in Scots, playing an important role), from there entered Ulster English (for which there is both historical and contemporary evidence for the existence of double modals), and was then taken along to the American South. After this, there must have been further independent development. Altogether, this seems to us a plausible account. This is apparently also Barbara Fennell's opinion, since her 'Evidence for British Sources of Double Modal Constructions in Southern American English' (in *AS* 68.430–437) includes several references to Montgomery and Nagle's paper, and presents basically the same sketch of the historical development.

The auxiliary *be* is dealt with in two studies. Janusz Malak writes on 'The Function of the Present Participle in Predicative Position in Old English' (in *SAP* 25/27.123–41). After surveying some earlier descriptions and analyses of the pattern *beon* + present participle in OE, he argues that the participle functions as a predicative adjective. Evidence adduced consists of the fact that it can take modifiers such as *swiðe*, can be coordinated with an adjective, and can take a comparative ending. The construction is therefore very different from the Modern English progressive. The development of the OE and ME construction *this is to do* ('this can/should be done') is compared with that of its German counterpart by Ulrike Demske-Neumann in 'Sprachwandel im modalen Passiv' (in *FLH* 13.65–91). They are claimed to be similar until the Early Modern period, after which there was reanalysis of *zu* + infinitive + *sein* in German but not in English, which became SVO. The construction *this is easy to do* is also included in the discussion but, for English at least, the range of facts considered is quite narrow, and the analysis therefore not very convincing.

The auxiliary *do* has not been forgotten either this year. Mieko Ogura tackles some large, methodological questions involved in the rise of *do* in her 'The Development of Periphrastic *do* in English: A Case of Lexical Diffusion in Syntax' (*Diachronica* 10.51–86). She argues against Kroch's (1989) idea that the changes involving *do* have the same starting- and end-points across the different contexts (i.e. interrogative, negative etc.) and involve the same slope. She also disagrees with his conclusion that a grammatical reanalysis took place in the middle of the sixteenth century. She tries to show, rather (the paper is not exactly easy to read), that different contexts have different slopes, *do* first evolving in contexts where an adverb blocked affix hopping, thus forcing *do*-insertion. Later this was followed by other contexts where *do* was not restricted in that way. In other words, there was no grammatical reanalysis, but slow diffusion, in which high-frequency words were affected later, but changed more quickly than low-frequency ones. In Ian Roberts's *Verbs and Diachronic Syntax: A Comparative History of English and French*, we find, among many other things, a discussion of the development of *do* in a generative framework. Within this framework, Roberts allows not only for XP, X′ and X° but also for X⁻¹ (an element that will trigger a particular type of head-to-head movement), and he suggests that *do*, which earlier on may have had some aspectual meaning, in the sixteenth century came to function as a substitute for AGR⁻¹, which used to trigger verb-movement (this is another topic discussed in detail in the book) but was being lost due to the erosion of verbal agreement. Roberts also notes that *do* in negatives lags behind somewhat, and attributes this to the status of *not* as a specifier rather than a head until the seventeenth century. Other changes analysed by Roberts, using the same kind of theoretical concepts, include the loss of verb-second and the development of the modals. It is not possible, in the very limited space available here, to do justice to this work, which puts the various constructs of generative grammar to good use in providing an account of syntactic change that recognizes both its gradualness and its domino-like quality. A final item on *do* is Anneli Meurman-Solin's 'Periphrastic *do* in Sixteenth- and Seventeenth-Century Scots' (in Rissanen et al.). Her aim is to provide more information on the use of *do* in older Scots, and to compare her findings to earlier studies, as well as analyse the linguistic and extra-linguistic factors that condition its use. She finds that *do* is much more frequent in texts that reflect spoken discourse, where it lends emphasis to what takes place. Its stylistic use (as described in Stein 1990: Ch. 4) is confined to argumentative prose, where it correlates with other characteristics of emphatic language.

There is a contribution on *have* by Laurel Brinton, 'The Differentiation of Statives and Perfects in Early Modern English: The Development of the Conclusive Perfect' (in Stein and Tieken-Boon van Ostade). Language historians have usually interpreted the so-called conclusive perfect (*She had it all worked out*) as a development from the earliest OE perfects, which were initially resultative in meaning and usually had the object preceding the past participle. In this paper, however, Brinton argues that the conclusive perfect is an innovation in the Modern English period 'modeled on earlier *have* + object + past participle constructions expressing indirect causation, indirect passive, and experiental passive'. As evidence for this point of view Brinton cites the almost complete non-occurrence of the conclusive perfect in the Helsinki Corpus for the Early Modern period, and the fact that already in OE most perfects were no longer resultative. There remains the fact, however, that in OE and ME the perfect could still have conclusive meaning even if it was not tied to the pre-participial object order (which, of course, it is now). We feel that not enough is made of the loss of exbraciation in late ME, which would have forced out the use of the pre-participial object order as a 'regular' perfect, with the result that the conclusive meaning could remain the only one still appropriate for the 'old' order. It seems clear, however, from the evidence Brinton gives, that the use of the old pre-participial object order in a conclusive sense was strengthened by the occurrence of the above-mentioned constructions, and also by the rise of the *got*-passive (see also Givón and Yang to appear in *YWES* 75).

We have slowly drifted towards grammatical questions that have a relation with word order. A contribution directly involved with word order is Susan Pintzuk's 'Verb Seconding in Old English: Verb Movement to INFL' (*TLR* 10.5–35). This paper is based in part on Chapter 3 of the author's doctoral dissertation. Her main assertions are (i) that Verb seconding in OE main clauses involves verb movement to clause medial INFL rather than to COMP (the position usually assumed to be the landing site), and (ii) that this movement applies also in subordinate clauses. This assertion is based on a new proposal, the so-called 'double-base hypothesis', which holds that OE shows synchronic variation in the underlying position of INFL, i.e. that it can be both clause medial and clause final. In testing this hypothesis, it is crucial to know more about the order in which auxiliary and verb occur in OE. Daniel Donoghue's book that appeared in 1987 (discussed in *YWES* 69) was an attempt to discover more about the early position of the auxiliary via OE poetry. This book is critically considered by

James Keddy in his 'Testing the Test: How Valid is *The Test of the Auxiliary*' (*SP* 90.1–28). Keddie wants to test the accuracy of Donoghue's statistics by looking at just one aspect, i.e. the verbal auxiliary half-line as it applies to *Beowulf*. Keddie disagrees with many of Donoghue's general and specific conclusions on *Beowulf*, and with some of his methods, e.g. the way in which he deals with (ambiguous) *þa* clauses, and with the length poems should have to make them statistically useful. It is Donoghue's belief that in *Beowulf* the order of verb and auxiliary is not only influenced by metrical considerations (as Bliss believed) but also by grammatical function, and that grammatical function played an even more important role for the other poets. Keddie shows (while admitting that *Beowulf* is different from other poems) that when one looks beyond the verbal auxiliary half-lines themselves, it becomes clear that metrical considerations played a far greater role than Donoghue wants to admit. Donoghue does not note, for instance, that the verbal auxiliary half-lines are practically restricted to the off-verse, and as a rule follow an on-verse which lacks the standard double alliteration.

There are several Dutch contributions to the field of word order in early English this year. Apart from Weerman's piece on OV/VO (discussed above), there are articles by Koopman and van Kemenade. Koopman's 'The Order of Dative and Accusative Objects in Old English and Scrambling' (in *SAP* 25/27.109–21) is aimed at establishing the underlying order of DAT and ACC objects in OE; the conclusion (reached quite elegantly on the basis of the kinds of binding facts that have also been used to establish the order in Modern English) is that the underlying structure is DAT [ACC V]. Either of the objects can be scrambled out of its base position, which leads to a wide array of surface patterns (especially if the clause also features Verb (Projection) Raising, as Koopman shows in detail). Van Kemenade's 'Verbal Position in Old English: Evidential Problems' (in *SAP* 25/27.81–94) is more concerned with OE verbal position per se. After outlining the basics (underlying OV, Verb-second in main clauses, Verb Raising, rightward movement of complements), she considers in more detail the occasional failure of Verb-second, the ambiguity of many surface orders, and the evidence for clause-medial position of INFL (agreeing with Pintzuk that this evidence is quite strong). Van Kemenade also writes about 'Syntactic Changes in Late Middle English' (in Aertsen and Jeffers), noting the following three changes in this period: (i) gradual loss of Verb-second; (ii) loss of impersonals without a nominative subject; (iii) loss of weather-verbs without subject. Using a generative framework, she argues that these changes are in fact related, and were triggered by the reanalysis of pronominal subject clitics as ordinary NPs. The result was that Verb-second was lost, which meant that the feature in COMP that triggered Verb-second was also lost; since this feature was responsible for licensing expletive *pro*, expletive *pro* also became impossible, so that constructions without an overt subject disappeared. More details on the feature in COMP that triggered Verb-second and licensed expletive *pro* are given in a paper written by Ans van Kemenade and Aafke Hulk, 'Subjects, Nominative Case, Agreement, and Functional Heads' (*Lingua* 89.181–215). A distinction is drawn between COMP-oriented and INFL-oriented languages, and shown to be applicable to various Germanic and Romance languages.

Three more papers that are concerned with word order in OE are Ruta Nagucka, 'Changes in Noun Modifier Orders in Late Old English' (*FLH* 12.3–19), R J. Reddick, 'Heavy noun phrases in pre-900 Prose' and Kari Haugland, 'A note on cleft and existential sentences in Old English' (the last two in *ES* 74, pp.

369–80 and 407–13 respectively). Nagucka explores the order of NP constituents in several OE texts, finding that the usual order is: Dem/Poss Num Adj Gen N RelCl (with a few examples of N Adj and N Gen occurring). Nagucka suggests that the strict order facilitated the decline of inflectional endings. Reddick questions the validity of the idea that heavy NPs occur late in the clause because they are heavy syntactically. Investigating a number of OE texts he finds that relative weight does not seem to matter as far as position is concerned. What does matter is text type, because it is only in the *Orosius* that heavy NPs tend to occur late. The *Orosius* is different from other texts in that it conveys a lot of 'new' information. In OE prose, initial position is usually reserved for the theme, while new information is typically given in final position. The author concludes therefore that it is not syntactic weight that determines position but thematic ordering: weight seems to be involved only because new information is usually 'weightier' than given information. Haugland notes that the two types of sentences mentioned in her title, which are distinguished in PrDE by the use of *it* and *there* respectively, are not so easily distinguishable in OE because *þær*-sentences alternate with zero subject sentences, and so do *hit*- or *þæt*-sentences. This means that if one wants to investigate the history of cleft sentences in English (a project this writer has embarked upon), one will need to differentiate between OE clefts and existentials on semantic and pragmatic grounds. The article discusses how this can/should be done.

Tracy Crouch's 'Observations on the Old English se' (in *FLH* 14.109–23) looks at two special features of *se*: its use as a demonstrative and as a pronoun, and the co-occurrence in the paradigm of forms starting with *s*- as well as *þ*. She does not posit any connection between these facts apart from suggesting, on the basis of comparative evidence, that they go back to PIE. Another article that we will also discuss at this point because we cannot fit it in anywhere else is Laurel Brinton's 'Episode Boundary Markers in Old English Discourse' (in Aertsen and Jeffers). Brinton has found that phrases like *ða gelamp/gewearð/gesælde ðæt* ... are used to mark episode boundaries in OE narrative. Very often these phrases include an adverbial of time or reason, making them similar to preposed adverbial clauses in PrDE both in form and function, as the many examples discussed show. This is a good example of the kind of work that applies modern discourse approaches (as found in, e.g., Cecilia Ford's work, reviewed in the previous section) to historical texts; it is a pity that there is so little of it around to report on here.

The subject of impersonals seems to have petered out a bit this year. Kazuhisa Ishikawa claims in his 'On the Demise of Impersonal Constructions' (*Ling&Philol.* 13.69–94) that (i) the OE and ME impersonals should be treated like the Italian *piacere*-constructions, i.e. that the non-nominative experiencer occupies subject position and (ii) the obsolescence was caused more by the loss of verbal inflections than the loss of case. Thus, the loss of the impersonal is related to the character of INFL (INFL being the category that takes care of agreement features). In OE, INFL could still bear a nominative case feature (OE is seen as a null subject language). When this feature got lost the experiencer object which moved to subject position had to acquire nominative case because oblique case would have resulted in a case clash. It seems to us that this theory-internal solution (which should be compared with van Kemenade's account, discussed above) does not really show that loss of case was not involved. Case also plays a role, but in rather different ways, in two papers concerned with case

variants found after prepositions. Else Fausbøll's 'A Contribution to the Study of
Ælfric's Use of Accusative/Dative/(Genitive) after Prepositions' (*ES* 74.295–
323), is rather factual. She wishes to place on a firmer footing the conclusion of
earlier studies about which cases are used after the prepositions, *emb(e)*, *ofer*,
ongean, *oþ*, *þurh*, *wiþ* and *for* (and verbs prefixed with these) by looking at works
written by Ælfric not considered before. Some of the tendencies noted before are
confirmed but not all, such as the tendency for pronouns to occur in the accusative
rather than the dative, and for plural nouns to occur more often with the dative.
Peter Kitson's study dealing with similar phenomena ('Geographical Variation in
Old English Prepositions and the Location of Ælfric's and Other Literary Dialects', also in *ES* 74.1–50) is much more wide ranging, both in its scope and the
conclusions he draws from it. Kitson shows in this important contribution that it
is possible to get a much more precise picture of the OE dialect situation (both
of the provenance of literary texts and of the dialect on which the WS standard
was based) by looking at the evidence of boundary survey charters. The main part
of the article presents evidence about the dialectal position of Ælfric's language.
By looking at the phonetic variants of prepositions and the variants in case form
that they govern, Kitson concludes that is is highly likely that Ælfric's dialect was
not of the Winchester area (as often assumed) but of 'the northern fringe of
Wiltshire and/or extreme south-east Gloucestershire'.

More on prepositions can be found in Tom Lundskær-Nielsen's *Prepositions
in Old and Middle English: A study of Prepositional Syntax and the Semantics
of* at, in *and* on *in some Old and Middle English Texts*. The syntactic part of this
work, unfortunately, is less interesting than the semantic part, since no new data
or analyses are presented in it. The author describes the most important characteristics of prepositions in OE (the cases they take, their position with respect to
their complement) and discusses the relation between more frequent use of
prepositions and loss of case endings. This point figures prominently in the
chapter on the syntax of prepositions in ME, in which the author suggests (and
he is certainly not the first) that the shift from OV to VO may have been partly
caused by the high frequency of post-verbal PPs.

Finally, there is a paper 'On the Historical Transition of Genitive Case
Assigner' (the English used leaves something to be desired) by Mitsuhiro
Ohmura (*Ling&Philol.* 13.141–57), which is rather similar to Janda's proposal in
1980 (not referred to), in that it suggests that the *-es* ending is not a case ending
but a 'relational element' (Janda suggested it had been reanalysed as a possessive
pronoun). The analysis is a purely theory internal one, in which it is proposed that
the functional category D(eterminer) in PrDE, but not in OE, contains a nominal
AGR element which assigns 'Case to its specifier and regulate[s] the morphological agreement on the head of its complement NP'. The reason that D could
become a case assigner is due to a number of changes that had taken place in the
DP structure in the course of time.

We will now turn to a more recent period and studies concerned with the
forces of standardization. Wim van der Wurff writes on 'Gerunds and their
Objects in the Modern English Period' (in van Marle). He wishes to explain the
reduction in the number of ways in which the gerundial object could be expressed. This has usually been ascribed to the influence of prescriptive grammarians, but van der Wurff argues that this is only part of the story. It may explain
the disappearance of *The writing this book was a difficult job* but not of *Writing
of this book* .... The author presents an analysis of the late Mod. Eng. gerund in

terms of a hybrid construction, i.e. the gerund was both [+V] and [+N]. In PrDE polarization has taken place, that is, the gerund must now either be completely verbal or completely nominal; the reason for this being (i) the steady increase in the number of verbal nouns which are lexically derived such as *blockage, colonization* etc., which pressured the semantically and morphologically similar gerunds into becoming pure nouns too; and, on the other hand, (ii) the verbal character of the progressive form, which was becoming very frequent at around this time, which 'purified' the verbal gerund.

The next five studies are all concerned with the pronominal system in Early Modern English. Ingrid Tieken-Boon van Ostade's 'Standard and Non-Standard Pronominal Usage in English, with Special Reference to the Eighteenth Century' (in Stein and Tieken-Boon van Ostade) focuses on the extent to which the (normative) descriptions of the eighteenth century grammarians were in conflict with actual usage at the time, concentrating mainly on subject oblique pronouns as found in private letters and diaries. Inspired by a claim made by Walpole that it is mainly women who sin against the norm, the author analyses the writings of four women and four men, and finds that this claim is clearly false. What is striking, however, is the use of *-self* pronouns in positions where variation is likely to occur e.g. *Miss Allen and I/me/myself. -Self* seems to have been used as a modesty device – it was not part of an avoidance strategy. Education does not seem to have been a factor in the variable pronoun use, but regional differences may well have played a role. In the same volume, Terttu Nevalainen and Helena Raumolin-Brunberg write about '*Its* Strength and the Beauty of *it*: The Standardization of the Third Person Neuter Possessive in Early Modern English'. They consider the paradigm of the variant possessive forms during the period which sees the rise of *its* (the main variants are: *it, his, of it, it's, (the), thereof*), and trace the (non)-linguistic circumstances that promoted the innovation. The rise of *its* in itself is not surprising in that it fills a systemic gap due to the loss of the gender system, but the authors show that the change did not take place in a linear manner, but was promoted/obstructed by various factors. One of these is whether the possessive pronoun was used anaphorically, which clearly promoted prenominal position (so *his/its* rather than of *it/thereof*). Factors impeding the change were the typological drift from synthetic to analytic and the tendency to preserve the inflected possessive for animate nouns. Extra-linguistic factors did not play a decisive role. Edgar Schneider's 'The Grammaticalization of Possessive of *which* in Middle English and Early Modern English' (*FLH* 14.239–57) is about the development of the relative counterpart to *its*. Using data from the Helsinki corpus, he first traces the competition between *whose* (which slowly declined after 1570), *of which* (which slowly rose in importance, first mainly in prenominal position, like *whose*), and *whereof* (which rose and declined in the period 1500–1700). The function of *of which* as a definite possessive relative is used to explain the occasional addition of *the*, of *his/their*, and of the antecedent itself (*of which wall ...*). The origin of *of which* is connected with the tendency to mark the human/non-human distinction; Schneider notes, however, that the situation has not settled yet, since *of which* is often felt to be structurally and stylistically awkward, and *whose* semantically odd – further change may be expected here. First and second person possessives are the topic of Herbert Schendler's '*My/mine, thy/thine*: Aspects of their Distribution in Early Modern English' (in *Views* 2.111–20). He notes that the conventional idea that a following *h* promotes the use of *mine/thine* just as much as a vowel is incorrect, and gives full figures for the occurrence of the variants in a corpus of texts from 1500–1633. The conclusion is that there is a development from phonological conditioning (practically always *mine/thine* before a vowel) to stylistic conditioning (*my/thy* before vowel first being informal, later the normal form) to lexical conditioning (*mine/thine* only used before *own/ear/eye* etc.). Finally, Jonathan Hope shows in his 'Second Person Singular Pronouns in Records of Early Modern "Spoken" English' (*NM* 94.83–100) how Early Modern court records may be used as evidence in historical research, since they (or at least sections of them) represent a type of language that is closer to original speech than any of the records investigated so far. Hope uses these data to give a qualitative and quantitative analysis of the use of *thou*, in which he shows that the pronoun is invested with much more complex semantic content than has generally been assumed, and that *thou* had become the unmarked form in speech much earlier than in writing.

Perhaps we should also mention here Roman Kopytko's *Polite Discourse in Shakespeare's English*. In the first part of the book, its author finds a lot to criticize in earlier views on politeness, but eventually seems quite content to count occurrences of Brown and Levinson's strategies of positive and negative politeness in four comedies and four tragedies by Shakespeare. Unfortunately perhaps, address forms have been excluded from the analysis. Moreover, in the absence of any strict criteria for inclusion and exclusion, it seems to us that not much significance can be attached to the final figures arrived at (363 positive politenesses, 137 negative politenesses). For those with fewer qualms, Kopytko offers some general pronouncements about the development of politeness in Britain based on a comparison of his figures with conventional ideas about politeness in present-day Britain.

In 'Democratic *you* and Paradigm' (*SAP* 25/27.143–53), Hanna Mausch considers the generalization of *you* as the pronoun of address from the point of view of morphological and phonological patterning, relating it to the effect of the GVS on *thou* but not *you*, the difficult matching of *thou-thee* to *ye-you*, and the loss of verbal endings in the plural. The nature and origins of the new plural pronoun *y'all* are investigated by John Lipski ('*Y'all* in American English: From Black to White, from Phrase to Pronoun', in *EWW* 14.23–56). He finds earlier and more solid attestations of this form in Black English Vernacular than in White English, and suggests that it was passed on to White English in the period 1800–1850. During its development, *y'all* turned from phrasal quantifier into 'strong' pronoun (i.e. it resisted being bound by *you/y'all*) and from there to ordinary pronoun, partly as a result of phonetic reduction.

Corpus linguistics, or at least the use of corpora, is playing an increasingly important role in historical linguistics. We have already seen that many of the studies described above have made use of the Helsinki Corpus. Two of the makers of this corpus, Matti Rissanen and Merja Kytö, have now, together with Minna Palander-Collin, edited a new book welcome to anyone working with or planning to work with the Helsinki Corpus, which is still the only structured, diachronic corpus available. This study, entitled *Early English in the Computer Age: Explorations Through the Helsinki Corpus* introduces the reader in a non-technical way to the various parts of the corpus (OE, ME, early Mod. Eng., Older Scots and early Am. Eng.) showing how they were built up and indicating the special problems/characteristics of each period. The second part of the book presents a number of pilot studies illustrating how the corpus has been/may be used. Quite a few of these deal with lexis/semantics or style/genre and will not be discussed here. Of syntactic relevance are the contributions by Matti Kilpiö, Kirtsi Peitsara (on the *by*-agent, similar to the one discussed in *YWES* 73.30–1), Anneli Meurman-Solin (referred to above), and Kytö and Rissanen. Kilpiö's 'Syntactic and Semantic Properties of the Present Indicative Forms of the Verb *to be* in Old English' deals with the existence of two different paradigms for the verb *to be* in OE, i.e. the one derived from IE **es*, **er* and from IE **bheu*, wishing to find out whether the differences with respect to tense and aspect, and dialect, suggested by scholars over the years, can be confirmed by the corpus. In his conclusion the author notes that too sharp a line cannot be drawn between the two paradigms, but that the following differences are clear: (i) *is* is more typical in actional, *be* in stative passives; (ii) *be* is preferred with future reference; (iii) only *be* can be given an iterative interpretation, and is more common with a durative reading; (iv) *be* is more frequent in generic sentences. Kytö and Rissanen show in their contribution how the grammatically untagged Corpus can still be used with good effect for syntactic searches if one uses some ingenuity. This is illustrated by means of a search for three constructions, all of which occur in the title, ' "By and by Enters [this] my Artificiall Foole ... who, when Jack Beheld, Sodainely He Flew at Him": Searching for Syntactic Constructions in the Helsinki Corpus': i.e. (1) the combination of a demonstrative and a possessive pronoun, (2) the use of the so-called push-down relative element, (3) inversion after non-negative adverbs. They discuss the (dis)appearance of these constructions, and how they are spread according to text type, which may tell us more about their origin. Another, separate study which is bound up with the Helsinki Corpus is Anneli Meurman-Solin's dissertation, *Variation and Change in Early Scottish Prose: Studies Based on the Helsinki Corpus of Older Scots*. This study contains an overview of the rise of the Scottish Standard and the effects of anglicization on it, and a description of the various text types found in the corpus. The aim of its main section is to provide 'statistically significant information about extralinguistically and linguistically conditioned frequencies and distributions of distinctively Scottish features, and about diachronic changes in the use of these features'. For more information see also the author's publication on *do* mentioned above, and the one discussed in *YWES* 73.27.

Finally, we must discuss four general works on the history of the English language, three of which are re-editions. The one that is new is by Orrin Robinson, *Old English and its Closest Relatives: A Survey of the Earliest Germanic Languages*. This book was written to provide background material for an introductory class on the Germanic languages. A need was felt, in order to get the students interested, not just to give the linguistic details of the various languages but also historical and literary information to put the whole thing into some kind of perspective. In this the author has succeeded very well. He first discusses the Germanic language family, next the separate Germanic languages, and rounds it off by a discussion of the relations and similarities between the various members. To give some idea how each chapter is presented, we will look briefly at the OE section. First we are given a survey of the historical and political developments among the Anglo-Saxons. Next follows a discussion of the types and number of texts found, in both poetry and prose, illustrated with excerpts (with glossary), and finally, we are given an overview of the most important aspects of OE grammar: spelling and pronunciation, phonology and morphology, but also a quite lengthy, and welcome, piece on the more tricky topic of syntax. Attention is paid to word order, the development of periphrastic verbs and of clause subordination, all put in the wider perspective of the other, sister languages (syntax is only treated in this chapter).

The re-editions are Albert Baugh and Thomas Cable *A History of the English Language*, Thomas Pyles and John Algeo *The Origins and Development of the English Language* and Charles Barber *The English Language: A Historical Introduction*. The aim of the first book has remained the same as in earlier editions, namely, to provide students with 'a knowledge of the path which it [English] has pursued in becoming what it is' in such a way 'as to preserve a proper balance between what may be called internal history ... and external history ...'. To show what English has become, the sections on Vernacular Black English and English as a world language have been expanded; for the first time sections on Chicano English, Caribbean English, and English in Singapore, Malaysia and Hong Kong have been incorporated. Some other sections have been brought more up to date. This also involved the addition of two sections on OE and ME syntax. Attention is drawn to the difficulty of recognizing hypotaxis and parataxis in OE texts as noted among others by Mitchell (1985). For ME the work of Mitchell (1964) is also referred to with respect to the changes in word order taking place. Although these are both important syntactic matters, the description of the changes in syntax remains disappointingly small. As before, the emphasis in the Pyles and Algeo book, in contrast to Baugh, is on the internal history of the language. The presentation of the book has been changed so that the information is more easily accessible; this is particularly true for the way the various paradigms have been laid out. All the sections are updated. The section on OE syntax is rather different from Baugh & Cable in that it provides mainly a summing up of differences between OE and ME. One of the important topics in historical syntax nowadays is changes in word order and the repercussions this has for other parts of the syntax. This is barely touched here (most attention is paid to (changes in) morphology); rather, the authors emphasize that OE and ME have 'much the same word order' as Modern English (pp. 129, 162). This seems to us somewhat oversimplified. Finally, it is good to see Barber's book again, in a revised version and with a more academically respectable publisher. The main part of the book still presents in quite digestible form the basic linguistic facts (i.e. the levels of sounds, morphology (especially word formation), selected lexical matters, some syntax) and social background of the various periods in the history of the language. The updating of the book shows mainly in the general discussion of language change and its causes.

5. Onomastics

The fourth edition of Dunkling and Gosling's *Everyman Dictionary of First Names* was published this year, with around 4,500 entries on British and American personal-names. Most of the errors noted in Peter McClure's detailed review of the first edition (*Nomina* 8.96–100) have been corrected, and this is now a very useful book, attractively presented and reasonably priced. Information is given on the origins, meaning and history of each name and on its usage and popularity at different times, offering many hours of pleasurable reading to the browser or prospective parent.

Also by Leslie Dunkling, the sixth edition of *The Guinness Book of Names* presents a highly enjoyable discussion of names of all kinds, from hat names,

apple names, and lipstick names, to criminal nicknames and popular dog names.
The emphasis throughout is on psychological aspects of naming rather than
etymological interpretation, but Dunkling overstates his case in arguing that an
'amateur' approach to name studies has more to offer than the techniques applied
by 'heavyweight' scholars like Ekwall. Not surprisingly, the least successful
sections of the book are those where a philological approach is essential. The
treatment of English place-names is particularly unsatisfactory. Tuesley, for
instance, is no longer considered to contain the name of the God *Tiw*, nor is
Gateshead believed to refer to paganism; and Hawkesbury is as likely to refer to
a hawk as to a man called *Hafoc*. The criteria for inclusion in the index are
unclear. Taking as a sample the sixteen place-name words discussed on p. 19,
nine are indexed while the remaining seven remain untraceable (lorry names are
wrongly indexed to p. 21 instead of p. 219). Nevertheless, the book abounds in
enthusiasm and fascinating facts, and one can only admire the dedication which
leads Dunkling not only to undergo arrest by a police dog but even to pursue his
researches at the Parisian Crazy Horse Cabaret.

Adrian Room's *The Naming of Animals* investigates naming patterns for
various types of animals and provides a handy source of reference on the names
of famous animals, whether real or fictional. Much of the information is anecdotal, deriving from accounts provided by 'young children, who tell how they chose
a name for their kitten or hamster' or 'retired folk, who reflect on the names of
dogs and cats they have known and loved in the past', and the book will probably
be of more interest to animal-lovers than to onomasts. The same author's *Brewer's Dictionary of Names* (*YWES* 73.66), has been re-issued this year in a
paperback volume representing excellent value for money.

Nomina 15 (1991–2) includes a report on the Twenty-Third Annual Study
Conference of the Council for Name Studies in Great Britain and Ireland in April
1991 as well as several papers from the conference, some of which will be
mentioned below. Although not directly concerned with English name studies, W.
F. H. Nicolaisen's 'Pictish Place-Names as Scottish Surnames: Origins, Dissemination and Current Status' (7–20) contains some pertinent observations on the
interaction between different types of names, and in particular on the relationship
between place-names and surnames. A paper by the late Cecily Clark entitled
'Personal-Name Studies: Bringing them to a Wider Audience', first read at the
inaugural meeting of the Society for Name Studies in Britain and Ireland in
October 1991, appears in the same volume (21–34).

In the field of literary onomastics, Charlotte Templin demonstrates how
'Names and Naming Tell an Archetypal Story in Margaret Atwood's *The
Handmaid's Tale*' (*Names* 41.143–57), and Hassell Simpson discusses 'A Pair of
Desert Saints: Name Symbolism in Peter Shaffer's *Equus*' (*Names* 41.183–93).
Richard Crider, in 'Yahoo (Yahu): Notes on the Name of Swift's Yahoos', argues
in favour of the view that Swift intended the name as an ironic echo of *Yahu* from
the Hebrew Bible (*Names* 41.103–09). In 'Jane Austen and the Name "Richard"'
(*N&Q* 40.38), F. B. Pinion suggests that the derogatory reference to the name of
the heroine's father towards the beginning of *Northanger Abbey* may be an
allusion to George Sand's *Mauprat*. Robert F. Fleissner's 'Prufrock-Shmufrock?
An Appendage to J. Alfred's Nomenclature' (*Names* 41.15–22) is largely a
critique of an earlier article by Michel Grimaud concerning the significance of the
name of the anti-hero in T. S. Eliot's *The Love Song of J. Alfred Prufrock*.
Grimaud returns to the theme in the same journal (5–14), discussing alternative

approaches to literary onomastics in 'Whither Literary Onomastics? "Prufrock" Revisited'.

On the place-name front, two major texts have been re-issued in paperback this year: Margaret Gelling's *Place-Names in the Landscape*, first published in 1984 (*YWES* 65.59) and recently out of print, and A. D. Mills's *A Dictionary of English Place Names*, a newcomer in 1991 (*YWES* 72.58). Richard Coates's excellent book on the place-names of Hampshire (*YWES* 70.132) has also appeared in paperback, with the revised title *Hampshire Place-Names*. The text is unaltered.

John Field's *A History of English Field-Names* is a fascinating book for both the specialist and general reader alike. It is the second title in the series Approaches to Local History, and maintains the same high standards of scholarship and readability as McKinley's *A History of British Surnames* (*YWES* 71.163). The opening chapter provides a concise introduction to the techniques of field-name study – a theme returned to at the end of the book in the chapter on 'Work in progress and prospect' – but for the most part the approach is thematic, exploring the origins and meaning of field-names under such headings as 'Common fields and the process of enclosure', 'Field-names and the landscape', 'Woodlands and wild life', 'A living from the land', 'Tenure and endowment', 'Buildings, transport and manufacturing industry', and 'Religion, folk customs and assembly places'. The treatment of field-name vocabulary is impeccable throughout, and alternative interpretations – as, for instance, whether the word 'honey' refers to land where honey was produced, to land held by a food rent of honey, or to sticky soil – are lucidly discussed. Photographs exemplify landscape terms such as *hield* 'slope' and *hamm* 'land in a river-bend', and illustrate farming practices referred to in early field-names. More than 2,500 field-names are discussed during the course of the book and most, but not all, are taken from the county volumes of the English Place-Name Society. The provision of an index to field-names in addition to the general subject index ensures that Field's book will become not only a standard text but a valuable reference tool.

Field-names are also the subject of two *JEPNS* articles. In '*Harrow* Fields in Heswall-cum-Oldfield' (25.9–10), Prudence Vipond argues that several fields named *Harrow* in Heswall-cum-Oldfield on the Wirral, Merseyside, may derive from OE *hearg*, indicating the site of a pagan shrine. As Margaret Gelling points out in her contribution 'Paganism and Christianity in Wirral?' (25.11), this has considerable significance in extending the distribution of place-names referring to Anglo-Saxon paganism further west than has previously been recognized. D. P. Dymond's 'Place-Names as Evidence for Recreation' (25.12–18) is less wide-ranging than its title suggests, focusing on the field-name *Camping Close*. It adds little to Dymond's earlier and much fuller treatment of the same subject in 'A Lost Social Institution: The Camping Close' (*Rural History* [1990] 1.165–92).

Local history is well served by John D. Beasley's *Origin of Names in Peckham and Nunhead*, a collection of some 800 names from this area of south-east London. The majority are street names, but coverage includes the names of business premises, parks, pubs, schools, churches and other buildings in a single alphabetical list keyed to an extensive bibliography. Philological detail is hazy for names with a long history (e.g. Hatcham, Peckham Rye), but most entries are well researched, providing a useful catalogue of information on local people, industries, and events.

In 'Why Aren't We Speaking Welsh?' (*ASSAH* 6.51–6), Margaret Gelling discusses the role of place-name evidence in assessing the degree of contact between Welsh and English speakers during the early Anglo-Saxon period and in charting the gradual replacement of the Celtic language by Old English. She estimates that a general change from Welsh to English names had occurred by the mid-ninth century, and addresses the problem of the low incidence of Celtic survivals in areas such as Shropshire and Devon by pointing to the high proportion of directional and functional names in both counties. These, it is suggested, may have replaced earlier British names.

There are some short pieces on individual names. Jason St. John Nicolle has 'A Note on the Identification of "Alvestone" in Wiltshire Domesday' (*The Wiltshire Archaeological and Natural History Magazine* 86.151–2). He suggests that it may be identical with Kelston in Somerset, the manor having been entered in *Domesday Book* as an appurtenance of Bradford on Avon since both properties were held by the nuns of Shaftesbury Abbey. Susan Rands traces occurrences of the lost place-name *Bikenham* in Somerset ('West Pennard: Chronicle of a Lost Place Name' *Notes and Queries for Somerset and Dorset* 33.201–3). Margaret Gelling summarizes the evidence relating to 'The Place-Name Mucking', which she considers more likely to represent a singular -*ing* formation than a plural -*ingas* one (H. Hamerow, ed., *Excavations at Mucking. Vol. 2: The Anglo-Saxon Settlement*, 96). David Smith suggests that the duplication of entries in the Hertfordshire section of Domesday Book for 'Titeberst in Aldenham' may reflect conflicting land claims (*Hertfordshire's Past* 35.9–14). John Insley examines the etymology of 'The River-Name *Wenning*', and suggests an OE **Wenninga ea* 'the river of Wenna's people' as a possible though unusual formation (*Anglia* 111.75–81).

In 'Tingwall, Dingwall and Thingwall' (*NOWELE* 21/22.53–67), Gillian Fellows-Jensen examines eleven place-names in the British Isles which may be related to the Icelandic *Þingvellir*. Four are in England, although Dingbell Hill, Northumberland, is of very doubtful etymology, and the precise location of the lost *Thingwala* in the North Riding of Yorkshire cannot be established. The remaining two, Thingwall in Wirral and Thingwall in Lancashire, were, according to Fellows-Jensen, probably inspired by Tynwald on the Isle of Man, itself named by Norwegian settlers in the ninth century.

'Tide-End Town, which is Teddington (or is it?)' (*Verbatim* 19.iii.31–2) is a rather slight piece in which Adrian Room draws attention to some of the many false place-name etymologies that may still turn up in print.

Several articles on North American place-names appear in *Names*. Gerald Cohen traces 'The Origin of NYC's Nickname *The Big Apple*' to racing jargon of the 1920s (41.23–8). Rowland Berthoff's 'In a Tavern, in a *Caverne*: Explicating Missouri Names' (41.29–43), explores the significance of the name 'Tavern' as applied to creeks and caves in French-speaking areas of Missouri. Although previously taken to represent the sites of early taverns, Berthoff argues that the name derives from a pun on the French words *caverne* and *taverne*. *Names* also has an article on political aspects of place-naming by J. Timmons Roberts, focusing particularly on the Brazilian state of Pará ('Power and Placenames: A Case Study From the Contemporary Amazon Frontier' (41.159–81)).

Studies of place-name elements include some good work this year. In '*Lin* in the Landscape' (*Nomina* 15.61–8), Mary Higham argues convincingly that many field-names containing this element do not represent places where flax was grown, as stated in volumes of the *English Place-Name Survey*, but places where it was processed or retted (i.e. soaked in water). Ann Cole investigates 'The Distribution and Use of *mere* as a Generic in Place-Names' (*JEPNS* 25.38–50), drawing particular attention to the location of such names along routeways. She makes the interesting suggestion that they may have formed part of a deliberate naming system to indicate to travellers where water was available. Gillian Fellows-Jensen ('Place-Names in *-þorp*: In Retrospect and in Turmoil' (*Nomina* 15.35–51)) re-assesses the criteria for deriving English place-names in *-þorp* and *-þrop* from the Old Danish settlement-word *þorp* rather than from the Old English cognate of similar meaning. Her conclusion is that whereas in all probability the majority of these names were coined by Danish settlers, the evidence is less clear-cut than for place-names containing *bý* or *þveit*. Örjan Svensson examines 'The *Worthy*-Names of Devon', arguing that most were created during the Middle English period and represent the holdings of single individuals (*Nomina* 15.53–9). He also suggests that many of the personal names compounded with *worðig* in Devon place-names are those of freemen of the franklin class. In the *Beng Pamp Festschrift* (*Nordiska Orter Och Ord: Festskrift till Bengt Pamp på 65-årsdagen den 3 November 1993*), Gillian Fellows-Jensen suggests that OE '*Pamp(e)*' may mean 'mire' or 'mud' rather than 'hill' (72–4), and Gillis Kristensson demonstrates that some of the place-names attributed to OE *fyrs* 'furze' in Smith's *English Place-Name Elements* are more likely to derive from 'Old English **fers* (Angl), **fiers* (WSax) "heifer"' (142–4). In 'OE *hyll* in the East Midlands in late Middle English' (*NOWELE* 21/22.69–79), Kristensson uses place-name evidence to establish dialect boundaries in the early fourteenth century.

The first of Bengt Lindström's 'Notes on Two Words in Shakespeare' (*ES* 74.133–7) concerns the word *sloth* 'muddy pool', one occurrence of which is in an early name for St Stephen's Street in Norwich. Although usually taken to be a variant of OE *sloh* 'slough', Lindström suggests that the word may derive from ME *sloth* 'sluggishness' in a secondary sense 'sluggish water'. He partly withdraws from this position in an addendum noting the occurrence of *sloth* 'muddy pool' in an Old English charter, long before *sloth* 'sluggishness' entered the language, but since the charter in question is of doubtful authenticity, the suggestion should be allowed to stand.

'Some Notes on the History of the English Place-Name Society' are provided by Aileen M. Armstrong, Margaret Gelling and Kenneth Cameron (*JEPNS* 25.1–8), documenting the progress of EPNS from its inception in 1923 to the present day. No EPNS volume has been published this year.

Several articles focus on charter boundaries. Della Hooke's 'Charters and the Landscape' (*Nomina* 15.75–96) is a wide-ranging paper which discusses the value of Anglo-Saxon charter bounds as evidence for landscape history. In 'Interrogating Anglo-Saxons in St Dennis' (*Cornish Archaeology* 32.67–75), Peter Herring and Della Hooke examine the bounds of a charter drawn up in 1049 to grant part of Trerice in Cornwall to King Edward's minister Eadulf. Paul Everson and G. C. Knowles present a detailed analysis of 'The Anglo-Saxon Bounds of Æt Bearuwe' (*JEPNS* 25.19–37), demonstrating that the estate granted by King Edgar to Bishop Æthelwold in 971 probably included the modern parish of Barton upon Humber as well as that of Barrow itself. Mary Higham provides a summary of her findings on 'The Medieval Boundary of Burton Chase: Identification and Implications' (*Nomina* 15.69–73). Finally, place-name scholars should not miss Peter Kitson's 'Quantifying Qualifiers in Anglo-Saxon Charter

Boundaries' (*FLH* 14.29–82), a statistical analysis of qualifying elements in the corpus of Anglo-Saxon charter boundaries. Written in his usual inimitable style and supported by detailed statistical tables, this is a major piece of research with important implications for the interpretation of place-name elements such as *har*, **filde/filden*, and *wifel*.

6. Stylistics

In the mid-1980s, in another publication, I deplored the lack of studies exploring the ideological dimension of the critical concept of point of view. This gap has at last been filled by the publication of Paul Simpson's *Language, Ideology and Point of View* in Routledge's Interface series. The first three chapters introduce, respectively, deixis for the analysis of spatial and temporal point of view, modality for the analysis of point of view on the psychological plane, and Halliday's transitivity model for the analysis of point of view on the ideological plane. The next chapter firmly places this analytic framework within a pragmatic model of communication, and the final chapter applies it in an investigation of the ideology of gender. The wide range of practical analyses (of narrative fiction, newspaper reports and advertising texts) illustrate the underlying premise of the book that 'language use cannot be regarded as neutral, value-free or exempt from at least some "angle of telling". Rather, it is shaped by a mosaic of cultural assumptions, political beliefs and institutional practices – in other words, ideologies'. My only criticism – wish rather than criticism – is that Simpson could have put more emphasis on the ideological dimension of point of view in narrative fiction, by concentrating on whole works instead of confining his discussion to brief extracts.

Two more books were published in Routledge's highly successful Interface series: Richard Bradford's *A Linguistic History of English Poetry* and Peter Verdonk's *Twentieth-Century Poetry: From Text to Context*. According to Bradford, the *differentia specifica* of poetic discourse is the 'double pattern', or interaction between syntactic and metrical structures. He examines how poets exploit this double pattern and how tensions created by the double pattern influence the reader's interpretation of poems. He refers to the interaction between sentence and line as the 'sliding scale', with, for example, free verse at one extreme foregrounding the 'cognitive' (syntactic) elements of language and the sonnet at the other end highlighting 'conventional' (metrical) features. (The choice of words is rather unfortunate here since syntactic structures, too, are conventional.) Shifts in the sliding scale are then related to the intertextual, historical and social context.

Bradford charts the changing relationship between the two elements of the double pattern through literary history, from the sixteenth century to the present. A large variety of topics are covered, including deixis in metaphysical poetry, the heroic couplet as a means of cohesion in Augustan poetry, the exploitation of their readers' cultural expectations by Romantic poets, the Victorian poets' sense of balance between the functional and structural conditions of poetry and the free verse techniques of modernist poets. I cannot resist ending with a quote about the Victorian poets' awareness of a need for balance, in which the author shows himself to be admirably straight-faced: 'For the Victorians the relationship between the conventional and the cognitive elements of the double pattern was comparable to the relationship between men and women. The marriage was necessary.'

Verdonk's introductory textbook for undergraduates aims at the development of a receptive and sensitive language- and context-based literary criticism. The chapters move from close textual analysis to a greater awareness of contextual (social, cultural, historical, intertextual) factors. Mick Short's 'To Analyse a Poem Stylistically: "To Paint a Water Lily" by Ted Hughes' is a model analysis of foregrounded linguistic features. In 'Person to Person: Relationships in the Poetry of Tony Harrison', Henry Widdowson shows how Harrison uses terms of reference and of address in 'Long Distance II' to construct a theme of simultaneous involvement and estrangement. Michael Toolan's 'Approaching Hill's "Of Commerce and Society" Through Lexis' offers a fascinating 'lexically-driven voyage' through the poem. Walter Nash ('The Lyrical Game: C. Day Lewis's "Last Words"') analyses the linguistic playfulness of the poem, charting a movement from doubt and hesitation to certainty and reassurance. According to Ronald Carter's 'Between Languages: Grammar and Lexis in Thomas Hardy's "The Oxen"', Hardy's linguistic choices appear caught between established poetic diction and colloquial everyday language. Richard Cureton ('The Auditory Imagination and the Music of Poetry') applies his new theory of rhythm to Frost's 'Nothing Gold Can Stay', distinguishing between three rhythmic components: metre, grouping and prolongation.

The following chapters place greater emphasis on contextual factors. In 'Teach Yourself "Rhetoric": An Analysis of Philip Larkin's "Church Going"', Katie Wales analyses the Bakhtinian polyphony of voices in Larkin's monologue, especially the dialogic interaction between an overtly cynical, colloquial voice and a more reflective, sensitive one. Ruth Waterhouse's '(Non)-Communication in the Park' shows how paradigmatic and syntagmatic choices reveal the poet's attitudes. Peter Verdonk ('Poetry and Public Life: A Contextualized Reading of Seamus Heaney's "Punishment"') looks at deictic and other contextual factors to bring out the tension between the poet's artistic and political commitments. Roger Sell's 'The Difficult Style of *The Waste Land*: A Literary-Pragmatic Perspective on Modernist Poetry' argues that Eliot's increasingly extreme floutings of Gricean maxims of communication in 'A Game of Chess' build up as what he calls an 'affective crescendo'. He moves beyond stylistic analysis towards a more fully contextualized reading, which also considers aspects of the production and reception history of *The Waste Land*. With Balz Engler's 'The Poem and Occasion', the reversal of text and context is complete: he argues for the primacy of context over text. He shows to what extent the circumstances of reading (the 'occasion') and the paratextual features (visual presentation, title, ...) influence our interpretation of Dave Etter's 'Summer of 1932'. Finally, Mary Louise Pratt ('"Yo soy La Malinche": Chicana Writers and the Poetics of Ethnonationalism') brings in the ideological dimension, tracing the 'transculturation' of the Mexican figure of La Malinche in bilingual Chicana poems from traitor and victim to cultural and revolutionary ideal.

A direct competitor for the Verdonk volume, but more traditional and less exciting in its approach, is Lesley Jeffries's *The Language of Twentieth-Century Poetry*, published by Macmillan in the Language of Literature series. After a brief historical survey, she documents the spread of non-standard varieties in twentieth-century poetry written in English. The central chapters of the book examine the predilections of twentieth-century poets in the following areas: sound effects, word-formation and combination, word-choice and meaning, grammar, cohesion and what she calls 'orientation'. Under this last label she includes a discussion of the favourite addressees of twentieth-century poems and notes the popularity of storytelling, descriptive, testimonial, and hypothetical modes. The last chapter presents three sample analyses of poems by Amy Clampitt, Philip Larkin and Carol Rumens. The choice of poets is highly commendable both here and throughout the book, as Jeffries quite deliberately quotes extensively from women poets.

Monika Fludernik's *The Fictions of Language and the Languages of Fiction* is a comprehensive survey of previous research findings in the area of speech and thought representation and an impressive display of erudition. Interestingly, Fludernik concentrates on 'non-standard' free indirect discourse (FID), i.e. FID outside literary third person past tense narrative. She looks exhaustively at both the shifted (or narratorial) features of FID and its unshifted (expressive, subjective) features. She deconstructs the representational model of FID and substitutes for it an alternative, non-mimetic model, the model of schematic language representation, based on typification and evocation. The mechanism of typification and schematization (the way in which language is used to represent a typical or schematic image of a linguistic expression) is illustrated, and strategies of linguistic typification not only in FID but also in direct discourse and oral discourse are discussed.

In this model, expressive elements are seen to function as signals evoking voice and subjectivity. However, there is a problem of attribution here: these expressive elements can be attributed either to narratorial or to figural subjectivity. The problem is solved within a frame-theoretical model of reading: attribution of subjectivity is related to verisimilitude within the particular frame of understanding that has been activated in the reader's mind. Fludernik's title aptly epitomizes her main point by stressing the invented nature of all representation: the fictions of language are the illusory effects of mimetic representation that language is able to evoke by means of the languages of fiction (such as FID).

Peter Tan in *A Stylistics of Drama* advocates a 'more aggressive breed of stylistics', in which linguistic and pragmatic analysis is complemented by contextual and intertextual analysis. However, the author's conception of context and contextual analysis is limited: it boils down to an exploration of the multi-layered nature of dramatic discourse, and how writers play with discourse levels in an attempt to destabilize the audience or to generate humour. The chapter on intertextual analysis is more convincing: Tan sets up a typology of intertextuality, discussing similarities and differences between such intertextual techniques as parody, irony, and allusion. In the second half of the book, he applies his model to Stoppard's *Travesties* and in particular shows how the sections of Act I under Carr's control are informed by a Wittiness Principle which overrides the constraints of the Politeness and Cooperation Principles and gives a manic quality to the discourse.

In *The Mediation of Interpretive Criteria in Literary Criticism*, Sirpa Leppänen looks at how critics imply a particular view of literary text, author, reader and context, and how they suggest that one or more of these play a decisive role in interpretation. She describes the linguistic strategies by means of which the critics implicitly or covertly mediate to their readers that certain interpretive criteria are relevant in the understanding of literary texts. She compares two essays on *King Lear*, written from very different theoretical and critical orientations: one by G. Wilson Knight and the other by Jonathan Dollimore.

Interestingly, she finds that despite the theoretical differences between them, the two critics use highly similar linguistic strategies to mediate highly similar interpretive criteria. In this way, she uncovers a quite surprising and fascinating contradiction between Dollimore's theory and practice: in his actual analysis of *King Lear*, he implicitly relies on a highly conservative model of interpretation which is 'monistic, normative and text-based'!

Before turning to periodicals, I just have space here to mention Jürgen Esser's *English Linguistic Stylistics*, a general overview of stylistic theories and approaches, which however was not available in time in order to be fully reviewed. In an interesting theoretically oriented article, Glenn Most ('The Languages of Poetry', *NLH* 24.545–62) offers an interpretive approach to literariness, suggesting that it is the prominence, frequency and interaction of a broad range of phonetic, syntactic, lexical, semantic, and pragmatic features that determine a text as more or less poetic. Keith Green ('Relevance Theory and the Literary Text', *JLS* 22.207–17) lucidly discusses the relevance of relevance theory in literary studies. *RBPH* 71.3 is a special issue on *New Horizons in Stylistics* and includes, among others, Leo Hickey's 'Stylistics, Pragmatics and Pragmastylistics' (*RBPH* 71.573–86), which advocates the use of pragmalinguistic principles and methods in stylistics, and Jose-Luis Martinez-Duenas's 'Words, Women, and Orders: The Stylistics of Anglican Discourse' (*RBPH* 71.677–85), which presents a discourse-stylistic study of the debate concerning the ordination of women. It also contains a number of interesting contributions on genre, but there is not the space to review those here.

Sonia Cunico's 'Patterns of Foregrounded Deviations in "A Refusal to Mourn the Death, by Fire, of a Child in London" by Dylan Thomas' (*LeS* 28.149–58) is a fairly traditional and formalist analysis of phonological, metrical, syntactic and semantic deviations in the poem. Also traditional in its approach is John Schmit's '"I only said – the Syntax –": Elision, Recoverability, and Insertion in Emily Dickinson's Poetry' (*Style* 27.106–24). He looks at elisions, both recoverable and non-recoverable, which introduce an element of uncertainty into the poems but which nevertheless tend to follow a number of consistent patterns. And in 'The Skeptical Verbs of Shelley's *Alastor*' (*Lang&S* (1990) 23.119–23), Marcia P. Halio argues that the poet's attitude of uncertainty and scepticism is set forth by his choice of verbs.

Drama is the focus of a couple of discourse-based stylistic studies. Neil Bennison's 'Discourse Analysis and the Dramatic "Character": Tom Stoppard's *Professional Foul*' (*L&L* 2.79–99) presents a detailed study of Anderson's conversational strategies, showing how changes in his conversational behaviour refract his developing views. In 'Conversation Analysis and the Structure of Shakespeare's Dialogue' (*SN* 65.169–85), Anthony J. Gilbert illustrates by means of many examples how Shakespeare exploits conversational sequence and indexicality in order to achieve many distinctive dramatic effects.

Among the other discourse-stylistic studies, I found Jeffrey W. Karon's 'Cohesion as Logic: The Possible Worlds of Marvell's "To His Coy Mistress"' (*Style* 27.91–105) rather disappointing. He examines the logical relationships underlying Marvell's connectives, something that was already done in a better and clearer way more than 35 years ago by Francis Berry. Sheryl Stevenson ('"Poetry Deleted", Parody Added: Watergate, Spark's Style, and Bakhtin's Stylistics', *ArielE* 24.71–85) studies hybrid constructions and parodic quotations in Muriel Spark's *The Abbess of Crewe*. In 'The Relevance of Reformulations' (*L&L* 2.101–

20), Diane Blakemore carefully examines, in relevance-theoretic terms, how reformulations can convey a wide array of weak implicatures, and thus achieve poetic effects. Bernhard Lindemann ('Readers and Mindscapes', *JLS* 22.186–206) shows how cognitive structures which he calls 'mindscapes' help the reader to interpret Robert Coover's chaotic story 'The Babysitter'. Val Gough and Mary Talbot's '"Guilt Over Games Boys Play": Coherence as a Focus for Examining the Constitution of Heterosexual Subjectivity on a Problem Page' (*LSLD* 1.3–22) is an interesting critical-linguistic analysis of the 'discoursal common sense' that the reader needs to draw upon in order to construct coherence for a problem page letter and reply.

A number of papers deal with point of view and the problem of attribution: Arthur L. Palacas ('Attribution Semantics: Linguistic Worlds and Point of View', *DPr* 16.239–77) gives a semantic account of point of view: more particularly, of how as a default meanings expressed in a text are assigned to the 'linguistic world' (LW) that captures the speaker's point of view, and how temporal, stylistic and other shifts signal the creation of a subordinate LW (LWs are highly reminiscent of Paul Werth's 'text worlds', though Werth is not cited here). Lucy Pollard-Gott's 'Attribution Theory and the Novel' (*Poetics* 21.499–524) is a study of how readers' attributional responses to characters are influenced by the author's manipulation of point of view and available information in Forster's *A Passage to India* and Austen's *Pride and Prejudice*. David Herman ('Towards a Pragmatics of Represented Discourse: Narrative, Speech and Context in Woolf's *Between the Acts*', *Poetics* 21.377–409) sets up a new typology of forms of represented discourse stretching along a pragmatic continuum from context-backgrounding to context-foregrounding types, with the latter including cases where the represented discourse is undecidably attributable to more than one character. In 'Language, Subject, Self: Reading the Style of *To the Lighthouse*' (*Novel* 26.192–213), Rebecca Saunders looks at passages of 'unclaimed consciousness' (which resist attribution to any single character), as well as at Woolf's use of passive constructions and of the pronoun 'one'. And in *PoT* 14.691–714, Stefan Oltean offers a useful 'Survey of the Pragmatic and Referential Functions of Free Indirect Discourse'.

Other studies of narrative which are relevant to stylistics include Monika Fludernik's 'Second Person Fiction: Narrative *You* as Addressee and/or Protagonist' (*ArAA* 18.217–47), which sets up a typology of second person fiction and then applies the model to Joyce Carol Oates's short story 'You'. In a brief paper ('The Implied Author Once Again', *JLS* 22.68–75), Nilli Diengott argues in favour of a depersonified understanding of implied author. Paul Tucker ('Displaced Deixis and Intersubjectivity in Narrative', *JLS* 22.45–67) shows convincingly that displaced deixis (the non-deictic use of deictic expressions) is not exclusively an index of free indirect discourse, but rather that both free indirect discourse and displaced deixis are indices of what he calls planar-type (as opposed to linear-type) narratives. Also of interest is J. A. Alvarez Amoros's discussion of intertextual saturation in the second half of Joyce's *Ulysses* ('Intertextuality and the Suspension of Narrative Coherence in *Ulysses*', *LangF* 1.1–17). Finally, *Style* 27.3 is a special issue on the short story, with ten chapters ranging from Gerald Prince's attempt to provide a generic definition of the short story ('The Long and the Short of It', *Style* 27.327–31) to Harold F. Mosher Jr's analysis of the non-narrated and the disnarrated in *Dubliners* ('The Narrated and Its Negatives', *Style* 27.407–27).

In the area of metaphor studies, Donald Freeman's ' "According to my bond": *King Lear* and Re-Cognition' (*L&L* 2.1–18) is an interesting cognitive-linguistic analysis of the metaphors in the opening scene of Shakespeare's play. He shows how Lear conceptualizes family relationships and filial love in terms of a BAL-ANCE schema within an overall scenario of financial accounting. But this scenario is subverted by Cordelia's radically different understanding of family relations in terms of a LINKS schema. 'Metaphor, Simile and Cognition in Golding's *The Inheritors*' by Elizabeth Black (*L&L* 2.37–48) is yet another study of how Golding contrasts the Neanderthal people's conceptual system with the reader's, and more specifically how he uses metaphor to represent the Neanderthalers' experiential world. In an interesting functional-linguistic (Hallidayan) study of metaphors of speech and music, their incongruent lexicogrammatical patterns and their main source domains, Anne-Marie Simon-Vandenbergen ('Speech, Music and Dehumanisation in George Orwell's *Nineteen Eighty-Four*', *L&L* 2.157–82) examines how the above contribute to Orwell's themes of dehumanization of the individual and absolute control by the Party. In 'Poetic and Non-Poetic Simile: Structure, Semantics, Rhetoric' (*PoT* 14.1–23), David Fishelov sets up a number of principles which characterize non-poetic simile (NPS) and defines poetic simile as a complex cluster of deviations from the NPS model. Tamar Sovran ('Metaphor as Reconciliation: The Logical-Semantic Basis of Metaphorical Juxtaposition', *PoT* 14.25–48) argues that the initially perceived semantic incompatibility of a metaphorical juxtaposition is resolved on a higher plane of abstraction by a number of reconciling functions. J. Glicksohn and C. Goodblatt's 'Metaphor and Gestalt: Interaction Theory Revisited' (*PoT* 14.83–97) brings together Gestalt psychology and Interaction theory in an analysis of Dylan Thomas's Sonnet VII, from his 'Altarwise by Owl-Light' sequence, showing how the chain of metaphors forces the reader into a continuous act of perceptual restructuring. Ruth Waterhouse and John Stephens ('The Tyranny of the Syntagm in the Literary Uses of Language', *Lang&S* (1990) 23.45–72) study the interaction of the signifier/ signified relationship with the syntagm/ paradigm relationship with particular reference to metaphor. Final mention is due to Joanna Thornborrow's 'Metaphors of Security' (*D&S* 4.99–119), a study of metaphor in the tradition of critical discourse analysis, dealing with the non-literary register of defence discourse in the post-cold-war period. She shows how Europe is metaphorically conceptualized as a three-dimensional architectural structure in the process of construction, and discusses the ideological implications of this discursive practice.

Books Reviewed

Aertsen, Henk, and Robert J. Jeffers, eds. *Historical Linguistics 1989*. Current Issues in Linguistic Theory. Benjamins. pp. 538. hb Dfl 195. ISBN 90 272 3608 9.

Ager, D., G. Muskens, and S. Wright. *Language Education for Intercultural Communication*. MlM. pp. 213. hb £35, pb £11.95. ISBN 1 853 59190 4, 1 853 59204 8.

Barber, Charles. *The English Language: A Historical Introduction*. Cambridge Approaches to Linguistics. CUP. pp. 299. hb £30, pb £8.95. ISBN 0 521 42622 7, 0 521 41620 5.

Bauer, Laurie. *Introducing Linguistic Morphology.* EdinUP (1992; hb edn 1988). pp. 272. pb £11.95. ISBN 0 85224 582 3.

Baugh, Albert C., and Thomas Cable. *A History of the English Language,* 4th edn. Routledge. pp. 444. pb £12.99. ISBN 0 415 09379 1.

Beasley, John D. *Origin of Names in Peckham and Nunhead.* South Riding Press. pp. 100. pb £5.95. ISBN 1 874401 01 2.

Bhatia, V. *Genre Analysis: Theory, Practice, and Application.* Longman. pp. 246. £14.99. ISBN 0 582 08524 1.

Bochner, Harry. *Simplicity in Generative Morphology.* Publications in Language Sciences 37. Mouton. pp. 247. hb DM 128. ISBN 3 11 013594 9.

Bradford, Richard. *A Linguistic History of English Poetry.* Routledge. pp. 240. hb £35, pb £11.99. ISBN 0 415 07057 0, 0 415 07058 9.

——. *A Linguistic History of English Poetry.* Routledge. pp. 225. pb £10.99. ISBN 0 415 07058 9.

Carr, Philip. *Phonology.* Macmillan. pp. 324. hb £40, pb £12.99. ISBN 0 333 51907 8, 0 333 51908 6.

Coates, J. *Women, Men, and Language: A Sociolinguistic Account of Gender Differences in Language,* 2nd edn. Longman. pp. 228. £12.99. ISBN 0 582 07492 4.

Coates, Richard. *Hampshire Place-Names.* Ensign. pp. 193. pb £6.95. ISBN 1 85455 090 X.

Cook, Vivian. *Linguistics and Second Language Acquisition.* Macmillan. pp. 313. hb £40, pb £12.99. ISBN 0 333 55533 3, 0 333 55534 1.

Corbett, Greville G., Norman M. Fraser, and Scott McGlashan, eds. *Heads in Grammatical Theory.* CUP. pp. 340. hb £37.50. ISBN 0 521 42070 9.

Corson, D. *Language, Minority Education and Gender: Linking Social Justice and Power.* MlM. pp. 263. hb £35, pb £11.95. ISBN 1 853 59210 2, 1 853 59209 9.

Coupland, N., and J. Nussbaum. *Discourse and Lifespan Identity.* Sage. pp. 338. hb £37.50, pb £18.95. ISBN 0 8039 5105 1, 0 8039 5106 X.

Denison, David. *English Historical Syntax: Verbal Constructions.* Longman Linguistics Library. Longman. pp. 530. pb £24.99. ISBN 0 582 29139 9.

Dunkling, Leslie, and William Gosling. *Everyman Dictionary of First Names,* 4th edn. Dent. pp. 305. pb £4.99. ISBN 0 460 861859.

Dunkling, Leslie. *The Guinness Book of Names,* 6th edn. Guinness. pp. 255. pb £9.99. ISBN 0 85112 595 6.

Esser, Jürgen. *English Linguistic Stylistics.* Niemeyer. pp. 192. pb DM 29.80. ISBN 3 484 40124 9.

Extra, G., and L. Verhoeven. *Immigrant Languages in Europe.* MlM. pp. 326. ISBN 1 853 59179 3.

Fanselow, Gisbert, ed. *The Parametrization of Universal Grammar.* Linguistik Aktuell 8. Benjamins. pp. 232. hb Dfl 100. ISBN 90 272 2728 4.

Ferris, Connor. *The Meaning of Syntax: A Study in the Adjectives of English.* Longman Linguistics Library. Longman. pp. 235. pb £11.99. ISBN 0 582 21012 7.

Field, John. *A History of English Field-Names.* Longman. pp. 285. hb £29, pb £12.50. ISBN 0 582 08157 2, 0 582 08158 0.

Fludernik, Monika. *The Fictions of Language and the Languages of Fiction.* Routledge. pp. 536. hb £50. ISBN 0 415 09226 4.

Foley, William A., ed. *The Role of Theory in Language Description.* Gruyter. pp. 467. hb DM 198,–. ISBN 3 11 013516 7.

Ford, Cecilia E. *Grammar in Interaction: Adverbial Clauses in American English Conversations*. Studies in Interactional Sociolinguistics 9. CUP. pp. 165. hb £30. ISBN 0 521 41803 8.

Formigari, Lia. *Signs, Science and Politics: Philosophies of Language in Europe, 1700–1830*. Benjamins. pp. 261. hb Hfl. 125,–. ISBN 90 272 4557 6.

Fox, Barbara A. *Discourse Structure and Anaphora: Written and Conversational English*. Cambridge Studies in Linguistics 48. CUP (hb edn 1987). pp. 173. pb £11.95. ISBN 0 521 43990 6.

Freeborn, D., with P. French and D. Langford. *Varieties of English: An Introduction to the Study of Language*, 2nd edn. Macmillan. pp. 269. £10.99. ISBN 0 333 58917 3.

Froman, Creel. *Language and Power I–V*. Humanities. Books 1–2 pp. 312. hb £49.95. ISBN 0 391 03733 1. Books 3–5 pp. 280. hb £45. ISBN 0 391 03764 1.

Geiger, Richard, and Brygida Rudzka-Ostyn, eds. *Conceptualization and Mental Processing in Language*. Gruyter. pp. 825. hb DM 258,–. ISBN 3 11 012714 8.

Gelderen, Elly van. *The Rise of Functional Categories*. Linguistik Aktuell 9. Benjamins. pp. 224. hb Dfl 100. ISBN 90 272 2729 2.

Gelling, Margaret. *Place-Names in the Landscape*. Dent. pp. 326. pb £9.99. ISBN 0 460 86086 0.

Gentzler, Edwin. *Contemporary Translation Theories*. Routledge. pp. 240. hb £35, pb £10.99. ISBN 0 415 09171 3, 0 415 09172 1.

Ghuman, P. *Coping With Two Cultures*. MIM. pp. 190. hb £35, pb £11.95. ISBN 1 853 59202 1, 1 853 59201 3.

Givón, Talmy. *English Grammar. A Function-Based Introduction*. 2 vols. Benjamins. pp. 318, 363. pb Dfl 200. ISBN 90 272 2117 0.

Glowka, A. W. and D. M. Lance. *Language Variation in North American English: Research and Teaching*. MLA. pp. 417. ISBN 0 873 52389 X, 0 873 52390 3.

Goldsmith, Evelyn. *My First Oxford Dictionary*. OUP. pp. 128. hb £7.95, pb £3.95. ISBN 0 19 910236 8, 0 19 910275 9.

Graddol, D., J. Maybin, and B. Stierer. *Researching Language and Literacy in Social Context*. MIM. OpenUP. pp. 229. hb £33, pb £10.95. ISBN 1 853 59222 6, 1 853 59221 8.

Graddol, D., L. Thompson, and M. Byram. *Language and Culture*. British Studies in Applied Linguistics no. 7. MIM. OpenUP. pp. 152. £11. 95. ISBN 1 853 59207 2.

Hale, Kenneth, and Samuel Jay Keyser, eds. *The View From Building 20: Essays in Linguistics in Honor of Sylvain Bromberger*. Current Studies in Linguistics 24. MITP. pp. 273. hb $53.95, pb $25.50. ISBN 0 262 08223 3, 0 262 58124 8.

Hamerow, Helena, ed. *Excavations at Mucking*. Vol. II. *The Anglo-Saxon Settlement*. English Heritage, British Museum Press. 1993. ISBN 1 85074 274 X.

Harland, Richard. *Beyond Superstructuralism: The Syntagmatic Side of Language*. Routledge. pp. 272. hb £37.50, pb £12.99. ISBN 0 415 06358 2, 0 415 06359 0.

Hartley, P. *Interpersonal Communication*. Routledge. pp. 215. £8.99. ISBN 0 415 01385 2.

Heylen, Romy. *Translation, Poetics and the Stage: Six French 'Hamlets'*. Routledge. pp. 188. hb £35. ISBN 0 415 07689 7.

Hodge, Robert, and Gunther Kress. *Language as Ideology*. 2nd edn. Routledge. pp. 240. hb £35, pb £11.90. ISBN 0 415 04678 5, 0 415 04679 3.

Hofmann, Th. R. *Realms of Meaning*. Longman. pp. 352. pb £13.99. ISBN 0 582 02886 8.

Hopper, Paul J., and Elizabeth Closs Traugott. *Grammaticalization*. Cambridge Textbooks in Linguistics. CUP. pp. 348. hb £35, pb £12.95. ISBN 0 521 36655 0, 0 521 36684 4.

Jackendoff, Ray. *Patterns in the Mind*. Harvester Wheatsheaf. pp. 264. hb £45, pb £11.95. ISBN 0 7450 0962 X, 0 7450 0963 8.

Jacobs, Joachim, Arnim von Stechow, Wolfgang Sternefeld, and Theo Vennemann, eds. *Syntax: An International Handbook of Contemporary Research*. Vol. 1. Gruyter. pp. 1029. hb DM 740. ISBN 3 11 009586 6.

Jeffries, Lesley. *The Language of Twentieth-Century Poetry*. Macmillan. pp. 178. pb £10.99. ISBN 0 333 45937 7.

Jones, Charles, ed. *Historical Linguistics: Problems and Perspectives*. Longman Linguistics Library. Longman. pp. 405. pb £15.99. ISBN 0 582 06085 0.

Kamp, Hans, and Uwe Reyle. *From Discourse to Logic*. Kluwer. pp. 728. hb £112, pb £40. ISBN 0 7923 2403 X, 0 7923 1028 4.

Kasper, Gabrielle, and Shoshana Blum-Kulka. *Interlanguage Pragmatics*. OUP. pp. 253. hb £35. ISBN 0 19 506602 2.

Katamba, Francis. *Morphology*. Modern Linguistics Series. Macmillan. pp. 354 hb £40, pb £12.99. ISBN 0 333 54113 8, 0 333 54114 6.

Kerstens, Johan. *The Syntax of Number, Person and Gender. A Theory of Phi-Features*. Linguistic Models 18. Mouton. pp. 277. hb DM 148. ISBN 3 11 013603 1.

Komatsu, Eisuke, and Roy Harris, eds. *Saussure's Third Course of Lectures on General Linguistics (1910–1911)*. Pergamon. pp. 320. hb £49. ISBN 0 08 041922 4.

Kopytko, Roman. *Polite Discourse in Shakespeare's English*. Seria Filologia Angielska 24. AMU. pp. 122. pb. ISBN 83 232 0516 7.

Kuno, Susumu, and Ken-ichi Takami. *Grammar and Discourse Principles: Functional Syntax and GB Theory*. UChicP. pp. 221. hb $59.95, pb $21.95. ISBN 0 226 46202 1, 0 226 46204 8.

Leppänen, Sirpa. *The Mediation of Interpretive Criteria in Literary Criticism*. JyväskyläU. pp. 390. ISBN 951 34 0023 9.

Light, L., and D. Burke. *Language, Memory and Aging*. CUP. pp. 281. hb £40, pb £13.95. ISBN 0 521 32942 6, 0 521 44876 X.

Lundskær-Nielsen, Tom. *Prepositions in Old and Middle English: A Study of Prepositional Syntax and the Semantics of* at, in *and* on *in some Old and Middle English Texts*. NOWELE Supplement 9. OdenseUP. pp. 203. pb Dkr 200. ISBN 87 7492 922 4.

Mansour, G. *Multilingualism and Nation Building*. MIM. pp. 160. hb £35, pb £11.95. ISBN 1 853 59175 0, 1 853 59174 2.

Marle, Jaap van. *Historical Linguistics 1991: Papers from the 10th International Conference on Historical Linguistics*. Current issues in Linguistic Theory 107. Benjamins. pp. 395. hb Dfl 170. ISBN 90 272 3609 7.

McGee Wood, Mary. *Categorial Grammars*. Routledge. pp. 184. hb £35, pb £11.99. ISBN 0 415 04954 7, 0 415 04955 5.

Meurman-Solin, Anneli. *Variation and Change in Early Scottish Prose: Studies Based on the Helsinki Corpus of Older Scots*. Annales Academiae Scientiarum Fennicae Dissertationes Humanarum Litterarum 65. Suomalainen. pp. 336. pb. ISBN 951 41 0707 1.

Mey, Jacob. *Pragmatics*. Blackwell. pp. 368. hb £40, pb £12.99. ISBN 0 631 18689 1, 0 631 18691 3.

Miller, D. Gary. *Complex Verb Formation*. Current Issues in Linguistic Theory 95. Benjamins. pp. 381. hb Dfl 140. ISBN 90 272 3595 3.

Mills, A. D. *A Dictionary of English Place Names*. OUP. pp. 388. pb £6.99. ISBN 0 19 283131 3.

Milroy, James, and Lesley Milroy, eds. *Real English: The Grammar of English Dialects in the British Isles*. Real Language Series. Longman. pp. 344. pb £14.99. ISBN 0 582 08176 9.

Myers-Scotton, C. *Social Motivations for Code-Switching: Evidence from Africa*. OUP. pp. 177. £20. ISBN 0 198 23905 X.

Pustejovsky, James, ed. *Semantics and the Lexicon*. Kluwer. pp. 416. hb £92. ISBN 0 7923 1963 X.

Pyles, Thomas, and John Algeo. *The Origins and Development of the English Language*, 4th edn. HBJ. pp. 381. pb £9.50. ISBN 0 03 097054 7.

Recanati, François. *Direct Reference. From Language to Thought*. Blackwell. pp. 420. hb £40. ISBN 0 631 18154 7.

Renkema, Jan. *Discourse Studies*. Benjamins. pp. 224. hb Hfl. 90,–, pb Hfl. 45,–. ISBN 90 272 2136 7, 90 272 2137 5.

Reuland, Eric, and Werner Abraham, eds. *Knowledge and Language*, Vol. II: *Lexical and Conceptual Structure*. Kluwer. pp. 238. hb $124. ISBN 0 7923 1790 4.

Rissanen, Matti, Kytö Merja, and Minna Palander-Collin, eds. *Early English in the Computer Age. Explorations Through the Helsinki Corpus*. Topics in English Linguistics 11. Mouton. pp. 296. hb DM 168. ISBN 3 11 013739 9.

Roberts, Ian. *Verbs and Diachronic Syntax: A Comparative History of English and French*. (pb, hb 1992). Studies in Natural Language and Linguistic Theory 28. Kluwer. pp. 373. hb Dfl 210, pb Dfl 85. ISBN 0 7923 1705 X, 0 7923 2495 1.

Robinson, Orrin W. *Old English and its Closest Relatives. A Survey of the Earliest Germanic Languages*. Routledge (1993: hb edn. 1992). pp. 290. pb £12.99. ISBN 0 415 10406 8.

Room, Adrian. *Brewer's Dictionary of Names*. Helicon. pp. 610. pb £8.99. ISBN 0 09 177954 5.

———. *The Naming of Animals: An Appellative Reference to Domestic, Work and Show Animals Real and Fictional*. McFarland. pp. 231. $35. ISBN 0 89950 795 6.

Rubagumya, C. *Teaching and Researching Language in African Classrooms*. MIM. pp. 160. hb £35, pb £11.95. ISBN 1 853 59175 0, 1 853 59174 2.

Schreuder, Robert, and Bert Weltens, eds. *The Bilingual Lexicon*. Benjamins. pp. 307. pb Hfl. 60. ISBN 90 272 4110 4.

Sebba, M. *London Jamaican: Language Systems in Interaction*. Longman. pp. 191. hb £30, pb £11.99. ISBN 0 582 08096 7, 0 582 08095 9.

Shotter, J. *Conversational Realities: Constructing Life Through Language*. Sage. pp. 201. hb £35, pb £11.95. ISBN 0 803 98932 6, 0 803 98933 4.

Silverman, D. *Interpreting Qualitative Data: Methods for Analysing Talk, Text, and Interaction*. Sage. pp. 240. hb £35, pb £11.95. ISBN 0 803 98757 9, 0 803 98758 7.

Simpson, Paul. *Language, Ideology and Point of View*. Routledge. pp. 198. pb £9.99. ISBN 0 415 07107 0.

Sinclair, John M., Michael Hoey, and Gwyneth Fox, eds. *Techniques of*

Description. Routledge. pp. 228. hb £40. ISBN 0 415 08805 4.

Stein, Dieter, and Ingrid Tieken-Boon van Ostade, eds. *Toward a Standard English 1600–1800.* Topics in English Linguistics 12. Mouton. pp. 325. hb DM 178. ISBN 3 11 013697 X.

Street, B. *Cross-Cultural Approaches to Literacy.* CUP. pp. 321. hb £35, pb £13.95. ISBN 0 521 40167 4, 0 521 40964 0.

Tan, Peter K. W. *A Stylistics of Drama.* SingaporeUP. pp. 248. pb $28. ISBN 9971 69 182 5.

Thomas, Linda. *Beginning Syntax.* Blackwell. pp. 224. hb £37.50, pb £10.99. ISBN 0 631 18827 4, 0 631 18826 6.

Tobin, Yishai. *Aspect in the English Verb: Process and Result in Language.* Longman Linguistics Library. Longman. pp. 398. pb £22. ISBN 0 582 06831 2.

Trask, R. L. *A Dictionary of Grammatical Terms in Linguistics.* Routledge. pp. 335. pb £10.99. ISBN 0 415 08628 0.

Upton, C., D. Parry, and J. Widdowson. *Survey of English Dialects: The Dictionary and Grammar.* Routledge. pp. 506. £90. ISBN 0 415 02029 8.

Verdonk, Peter, ed. *Twentieth-Century Poetry: From Text to Context.* Routledge. pp. 194. £10.99. ISBN 0 415 05863 5.

Verkuyl, Henk J. *A Theory of Aspectuality: The Interaction Between Temporal and Atemporal Structure.* Cambridge Studies in Linguistics 64. CUP. pp. 393. hb £40. ISBN 0 521 44362 8.

Wagner, D. *Literacy, Culture and Development.* CUP. pp. 367. hb £40, pb £16.95. ISBN 0 521 39132 6, 0 521 39813 4.

Wardhaugh, Ronald. *Investigating Language: Social Problems in Language.* Blackwell. pp. 304. hb £40, pb £11.99. ISBN 0 631 18753 7, 0 631 18754 5.

Warner, Anthony R. *English Auxiliaries: Structure and History.* Cambridge Studies in Linguistics 66. CUP. pp. 291. hb £35. ISBN 0 521 30284 6.

Weber, Elizabeth G. *Varieties of Questions in English Conversation.* Studies in Discourse and Grammar 3. Benjamins. pp. 252. hb Dfl 100. ISBN 90 272 2613 X.

Wood, Mary McGee. *Categorial Grammars.* Linguistic Theory Guides. Routledge. pp. 180. hb £35, pb £11.99. ISBN 0 415 04954 7, 0 415 04955 5.

Zucchi, Alessandro. *The Language of Propositions and Events.* Kluwer. pp. 288. hb £69. ISBN 0 7923 2437 4.

II

Old English Literature

E. M. TREHARNE

This chapter is arranged into the following sections: 1. Bibliography; 2. Manuscript Studies, Palaeography and Facsimiles; 3. Social, Cultural and Intellectual Background; 4. Literature: General; 5. The Exeter Book; 6. The Poems of the Vercelli Book; 7. The Junius Manuscript; 8. The *Beowulf* Manuscript; 9. Other Poems; 10. Prose. The review of R. D. Fulk in section 4 is by C. B. McCully, University of Manchester.

1. Bibliography

Anglo-Saxon England 22, the *International Medieval Bibliography,* and the *Old English Newsletter* (26.4) have provided full bibliographies for 1992 this year. *OENews* 26.2 contains reviews of Old English studies for 1991. *OENews* 26 and 27 include conference, and exhibition information, and project reports (on the *Dictionary of Old English*, by Joan Holland, 27.1.25–9; 'Ambrose in the *Sources of Anglo-Saxon Literary Culture*', by Jessica Wegmann and Dabney Anderson Bankert, 27.1.30–4; 'Opening the "Electronic *Beowulf*"' by Kevin Kiernan, 27.1.35–40; and '*Fontes Anglo-Saxonici*: Eighth Progress Report', by Joyce Hill, 26.3.12–13). Brief articles include Jonathan Wilcox's 'King Alfred Speaks: William L'isle's Defense of Anglo-Saxon, 1623' (*OENews* 27.1.42–3), 'Images of Women in Anglo-Saxon Art IV: First Target of a Demonized Eros in the Paris Psalter' (*OENews* 27.1.44–6) by Carol Neuman de Vegvar, 'The Will of Wulf' by Simon Keynes (*OENews* 26.3.16–21), and Thomas H. Ohlgren's 'Martial Iconography in the *Harley Psalter*: Dubbing or Drubbing' (*OENews* 26.3.36–8).

Robert J. Hasenfratz's *'Beowulf' Scholarship: An Annotated Bibliography, 1979–1990* is of immense value to scholars. It continues the 1980 bibliography of *Beowulf* criticism by Douglas D. Short. Hasenfratz gives relatively full summaries of articles and books by chronological and alphabetical sequence and includes useful indexes to author, subject, word, and line references. It is a comprehensive volume detailing all works, including articles and reviews appearing in some of the less accessible periodicals.

Gopa Roy has produced a useful research tool in her 'Female Saints in Male Disguises – the Old English *Lives* of St Eugenia and St Euphrosyne: A Bibliographical Guide' (*MSSN* 31.47–53).

2. Manuscript Studies, Palaeography and Facsimiles

Boydell and Brewer have once again published impressive works on manuscript studies which concern Anglo-Saxon England. Patrick W. Conner's monograph, *Anglo-Saxon Exeter: A Tenth-Century Cultural History* is a wide-ranging book which contains a great deal to interest palaeographers, historians, and textual scholars, thus dissolving disciplinary boundaries; it exemplifies new approaches and certainly advances current scholarship on this most important of codices, and its milieu. Not only is Conner's work of considerable importance for the issues of the dating and provenance of the Exeter Book (and the many related manuscripts), and the fulcral role played by Exeter in tenth- and eleventh-century Anglo-Saxon England, but also his investigative methodology is exemplary, fascinating, and usually convincing. It represents a quite remarkable scholarly achievement and is well worth the price, as it is unlikely to be superseded. In Chapter I, Conner outlines the 67 manuscripts associated with Exeter provenance before the twelfth century. Of those, half are from the second half of the tenth century and half from the second half of the eleventh century. Conner discusses the latter period of scriptorium activity in the light of Bishop Leofric's removal of the Devon see from Crediton to Exeter in 1050, then asks why the former period should be so well represented, as opposed to the first half of the eleventh century, for example. Considering the historical context, Conner adduces that the Benedictine Reform period led to the copying of manuscripts at Exeter: it is these manuscripts which were incorporated into Leofric's collection and which, thus, account for the strong representation of later tenth-century books. Conner focuses on 'The Leofric Missal' which he concludes is of Exeter origin and not Glastonbury as previously thought. Chapter II traces the development of Exeter as a religious centre from the refoundation by Athelstan in 932 until the Leofric episcopate. Conner concentrates on documentary evidence relating to Exeter and the four surviving relic-lists. The evidence points to a 'continuous institution' at Exeter, even before the eleventh century, during which time Exeter appears to have been relatively wealthy. Chapter III, in an extensive discussion using historical, palaeographical, and contextual evidence, asks the fundamental question for this volume: how much can we know about a scriptorium prior to Leofric's episcopate? Conner examines six manuscripts which may have originated at Exeter in the second-half of the tenth century. He reconsiders the evidence offered by Leofric's donation list to suggest it may not be inclusive of all that was at Exeter; and indeed, some of the manuscripts included on it may have been at Exeter beforehand. Chapter IV examines manuscripts which contain the kind of script (clear and relatively unabbreviated) which might have influenced the Exeter Book scribe and those of related manuscripts. Conner discusses the skill of the Exeter Book scribe in producing a regularity of aspect; he provides a comparative analysis of individual letter forms with other tenth-century manuscripts, in particular, the various annals of The Parker Chronicle. His detailed examination suggests a date for the Exeter Book of $c.950 - c.970$. In Chapter V, Conner analyses, in great detail, the codicology of the Exeter Book, paying attention to the theory that it was originally comprised of three booklets. These booklets demonstrate the chronology of the manuscript, and the evolution of the scribe's skill. Chapter VI then moves into the cultural and poetic history and context of the manuscript; the three booklets represent 'three distinct periods of time'. The second booklet ('Azarias' to the first eight words of 'The Partridge'),

Conner argues, is the oldest of the three, and represents a collection based on Continental models; the second booklet to have been produced is now third in the manuscript ('The Partridge' to the end of the Riddles); the third booklet composed is now the first in the manuscript (containing the 'Christ' and 'Guthlac' poems) and is firmly rooted in the Reform period of the tenth century. As these booklets were produced over a period of time, the manuscript 'must reflect a major shift of a cultural paradigm'. Conner takes us through this paradigm to show that the changes imposed by the Benedictine 'Revolution' were 'swifter and more thorough than we often imagine'. A useful set of appendixes containing primary source material (including the Exeter Relic lists), and 'The Preservation of the "Exeter Book" since 1100' follow Chapter VI.

David Dumville has once again produced a scholarly volume (his third in two years) that, like Conner's, employs a variety of methods and encompasses a number of approaches: *English Caroline Script and Monastic History: Studies in Benedictinism A.D. 950–1030* provides a new assessment of the four styles of Anglo-Caroline minuscule that Dumville detects in use at one or another time during the period, and re-interprets the material in the light of various monastic scriptoria and their concerns. Style I, a 'monumental' script is associated with Æthelwold or Oswald; Style II which incorporates Insular minuscule features and is localizable to Canterbury, is associated with Dunstan; Style III is comprised of a number of versions of the script that can be attributed to Worcester in the early eleventh century; and Style IV, which originates from Style I (with an intermingling of Style II), was a Christ Church script of *c.*1020 associated, in particular, with 'Eadwig Basan': this script disseminated to other scriptoria and was thence used throughout the eleventh century 'wherever Latin script was written.' These variations of Anglo-Caroline are, of course, far more complex than has been suggested here, and Dumville examines these complexities and relationships with admirable clarity. In linking these styles to participants and houses associated with the reformation in Benedictine monasticism (Chapter II, for example, examines the influence of Dunstan on the nature and form of book-production at Christ Church), Dumville deduces a great deal about the nature of the movement and its manifold concerns. He also demonstrates attitudes towards language from the scripts employed in copying, for example, bilingual versions of the Benedictine Rule: Corpus Christi College, Oxford, 197 is such a text, and Dumville provides a very full account of its origins within an Æthelwoldian scriptorium by a scribe who seems to have come in from outside such an institution. All in all, this is a volume which is meticulously researched, contains a vast array of information, and makes a notable contribution to our knowledge of tenth- and eleventh-century methods of, and attitudes towards, manuscripts and their production.

James E. Cross and Jennifer Morrish Tunberg have produced an immaculate work of scholarship in their edition of *The Copenhagen Wulfstan Collection: Copenhagen Kongelige Bibliotek Gl.Kgl.Sam. 1595* for EEMF. As the Preface states: this edition 'makes available to scholars an important manuscript ... in one of the libraries not habitually visited by Anglo-Saxonists.' According to Morrish Tunberg, the manuscript, dated to 1002–23, appears to have been compiled on the instruction of Wulfstan, Bishop of Worcester and Archbishop of York, judging by the extensive annotations found throughout the codex which can be confidently attributed to him. The manuscript is shown to be comprised of seven sections, each of which is provided with physical and individual palaeographical analyses. These sections do not appear to have been produced for incorporation into a single volume. The probable origin of some of these sections, however, can be ascertained by showing that certain scribes in the Copenhagen manuscript (sections II and IV–VI) also contributed to other manuscripts associated with Worcester. It is probable, then, that the manuscript was collated at one of the centres with which Wulfstan was connected. Notably, the manuscript may still have its original binding which Morrish Tunberg describes meticulously for the first time. She suggests that GKS 1595 may have found its way to Denmark from Worcester or, indeed, Evesham as a result of the English influence in the Christianization of Scandinavia and, particularly, contacts with Odense. The contents of the manuscript, described by Cross, include Wulfstan's own compositions, texts by Ælfric, sermons by Abbo of Saint-Germain-des-Près (see also section 10, below), and a number of other items, some of which Cross suggests may now be attributed to Wulfstan's *oeuvre*. Cross provides a detailed summary of each textual item, including parallel occurrences in other manuscripts. This introduction is a thorough examination which throws light on the facsimiles in the edition, particularly those of the binding. There is no doubt that this manuscript is of great importance; the careful research of the two editors will provide even greater recognition for the testimony it bears to eleventh-century manuscript production in general, and the methods of Wulfstan's textual compilation in particular.

The editors of *A Palaeographer's View: Selected Writings of Julian Brown*, Janet Bately, Michelle Brown and Jane Roberts, have gathered together an invaluable set of well-chosen and well-edited papers which provide an excellent collection of this notable scholar's contributions to the fields of palaeography and Insular manuscript studies. The volume is divided into three parts which reflect the author's main concerns. Part I contains 'Palaeography since Traube', 'Names of Scripts – A Plea to all Medievalists', 'Palaeography: an Overview', 'Palaeography: Latin and Western European Vernacular', and 'Punctuation' which are all previously published, though some remarks which were excised in the initial publication have been re-incorporated here. In 'What is Palaeography?', an essay printed for the first time, Brown outlines the nature of the subject and its value to, and inter-relatedness with, other disciplines. This section of the volume ranges broadly through the fundamental principles of palaeography, covering scripts throughout the centuries, punctuation, and the production of manuscripts. Part I alone is essential reading for all students of the subject. In Part II, the editors have collected six essays dealing with the early Insular manuscript tradition: previously published are 'Northumbria and the Book of Kells', 'The Distribution and Significance of Membrane Prepared in the Insular Manner', 'An Historical Introduction to the Use of Classical Authors in the British Isles from the Fifth to the Eleventh Century', 'The Irish Element in the Insular System of Scripts to c. A.D. 850', and 'The Oldest Irish Manuscripts and their Late Antique Background'. Unpublished hitherto is 'Tradition, Imitation, and Invention in Insular Handwriting of the Seventh and Eighth Centuries' which is the Chambers Memorial Lecture from 1978–9. Here, Brown details elements of Insular manuscript production which are similar to Continental practices such as the quires of eight, and methods of pricking before folding. Abbreviations in Insular books are notably different from those in use on the Continent; and major features of script, both Irish and Anglo-Saxon, are outlined to demonstrate the evolution of, and major influences on, these systems. Part III contains two important papers, reprinted from earlier publications, 'The St Ninian's Isle Silver Hoard: The Inscriptions', and 'The Detection of Faked Literary Manuscripts'. Appended to the volume are a bibliography of Brown's writings, a glossary of terms, and a concordance of manuscripts mentioned. The latter, in itself, amply demonstrates Brown's wide range of learning and reference. This is a volume which no university library can afford to be without; the price reflects the high quality of the book's production which includes over 100 illustrations.

Michael Lapidge has much to say about 'The Edition, Emendation, and Reconstruction of Anglo-Saxon Texts' in Roberta Frank, ed., *The Politics of Editing Medieval Texts*. He tackles the controversy between conservative and liberal editors, which revolves around the perceived status of the manuscript text, and puts this into context by surveying the predecessors of present-day Old English editors, such as Kemble, and Trautmann. Lapidge is eager to see closer alliances between editors of Latin texts (who are applauded for critical emendation), and Anglo-Saxonists (who are derided for such liberal editorial judgements), and he provides several examples of the type of emendations that could be made to Old English texts were the principles of Latin editing to be adopted; this includes the 'reconstruction' of a portion of the twelfth-century copy of the *Soliloquies* in BL Cotton Vitellius A.xv as the Alfredian original might have been composed. Allen Frantzen (in 'The Living and the Dead: Responses to Papers on the Politics of Editing Medieval Texts', also in Frank, ed.) comments that Lapidge is 'long on confidence in the author and editor and short on confidence in the scribe and the manuscript' and notes that Lapidge is primarily concerned with textual criticism, and not specifically editing; Frantzen points out that there are differences between the Latin manuscript tradition and the vernacular, which must be taken into account by respective editors. He notes that in reconstructing later copies of Old English material into 'idealised concepts' of the earlier text, the editor is merely creating an alternative text which may well be as far from Alfred's original as the post-Conquest version (which does, at least, provide 'testimony to lived language experience').

In many respects *contra* Lapidge (above), Katherine O'Brien O'Keeffe writes on practices of editing as the 'body of procedures on which any criticism of Old English verse necessarily depends' in an excellent essay, 'Texts and Works: Some Historical Questions on the Editing of Old English Verse' (in Cox and Reynolds, eds). She points out that editions have a double function: to present scholarly knowledge which is limited by the degree of information available at the moment of that edition's creation; and to select the knowledge presented, according to the editor's judgement of what is important. She cites examples of editions, notably Cædmon's *Hymn* and *Solomon and Saturn I* from the Anglo-Saxon Poetic Records. In the latter instance, manuscript evidence is blurred in order to provide a 'complete' poem. Important textual variants are assigned to the apparatus and thus this 'modern redaction ... conflates two distinct moments in the history of the poem'; in effect, a 'new' poem is created. Editorial techniques usually involve presenting the text in a version which is as close as possible to 'authorial' but which often involve ignoring the 'scribal format'. O'Brien O'Keeffe observes that 'The details of scribal usage ... are the material condition for the presentation of Old English verse'. What most verse editors provide is an 'idealized' text which 'may hide as much as it reveals', whereas 'A realized text ... is that object which is written down ...', '... is made real and given history'. As such, an idealized text 'hides from the modern reader the condition of early literacy'. O'Brien O'Keeffe advocates that 'a poem's material condition and its situation in the world require recognition and representation in an edition.' She proposes that editors might consider 'an edited version faced by a scrupulously archaeological mapping of the manuscript in print' although she is painfully aware of the implied costs of such an edition. O'Brien O'Keeffe's proposal is a sound and responsible alternative to the subjectivity of the traditional edition, but regardless of the costing implications, it bears its own difficulties: a printed 'mapping' of the manuscript page, in itself, hides the palaeographical information that the manuscript yields. It may be that the only alternative lies in an edition similar to Klinck's (costly) *Old English Elegies* (*YWES* 73.97–8) in which facsimiles are provided, albeit not in the most effective *en face* arrangement.

David Ganz reports on 'An Anglo-Saxon fragment of Alcuin's letters in the Newberry Library, Chicago' (*ASE* 22.167–77). He provides physical and palaeographical details of the tenth-century fragment which is one of the earliest examples of Square minuscule. Comparisons can be made with Lambeth Palace 218, part III, localizable to Winchester, or East Anglia, or London. The copying of Alcuin's letters shows an interest in politics, commensurate perhaps with the patriotism or search for Carolingian models of kingship of Athelstan's reign. Lawrence Nees provides a detailed reassessment of 'Utlán the Scribe' in his article in *ASE* 22.127–46. This scribe, or more probably, illuminator, working in Ædeluulf's monastery in the first-half of the eighth century, owes his fame to Ædeluulf's *De abbatibus* from which most conclusions about his work have been drawn. Nees analyses the available information from *De abbatibus*, looking closely at phrases describing Utlán (*comptis notis ornare libellos*, for example), to conclude that, ultimately, many scholars have been over-enthusiastic in assigning particular manuscripts to this scribe. Nees demonstrates that, in fact, we have little that is concrete to allow an identification of Utlán with specific early eighth-century codices.

In 'Not St Dunstan's Book?' (*N&Q* 40.431–3), B. C. Barker-Benfield challenges the acceptance of 'Dunstan' as the reading of the twelfth-century inscription on the spine of Bodleian MS Hatton 42 (and for further scholarship on this manuscript see David Dumville's article 'Wulfric Cild' in *N&Q* 40.5–9). Barker-Benfield shows that the medial *t* is omitted in this inscription, thus reading 'LIBER Sᶜ DUNSANI'; significantly, the third letter of the name is shown to be an *F* and not an *N*; and, furthermore, the initial *D* may be a wynn, producing a reading of 'WUFSANI'. The candidate for this inscription is, then, St Wulfstan (*d*. 1095), with the subsequent elimination of any Canterbury connection for the manuscript which resulted from a reading of 'Dunstan'.

Richard Gameson discusses 'The Romanesque Artist of the Harley 603 Psalter' in *EMS* 4.24–61. The illustrations of the Utrecht Psalter are the source of three extant copies, and Gameson focuses on those in the Harley Psalter which were completed by a twelfth-century illustrator. The detailed discussion shows that the artist concerned was an individualist when his work is compared to other examples of twelfth-century manuscript decoration at Canterbury.

The interest in the sixteenth-century collection and use of Anglo-Saxon and medieval manuscripts will be aided by R. I. Page's publication of his 1990 Sandars Lectures, *Matthew Parker and his Books*. This handsome volume is made the more so by the inclusion of 63 plates illustrating many aspects of Parker's use of the manuscripts he gathered. Page, not surprisingly, concentrates on Corpus

Christi College, Cambridge manuscripts. He looks at Parker as a book collector, his methods, and the range of material he gathered. Page pays attention to the Register contained in CCCC 575 to discuss the information it provides about the history of the collection as it was in the sixteenth century, and as it is today. He then moves into a closer investigation of Parker's interest in, conservation of, and publication of historical documents. Parker's 'curious examples' of conservation include the provision of beginnings and ends of defective manuscripts, and his damage to manuscripts by the removal of 'intrusive or ugly' pages. A focus on Parker as annotator and reader of his collection, shows the interest in Old English in the sixteenth century. Page discusses the ways that Parker and his circle may have learned Old English, and their subsequent manipulation of Old English texts. *The Peterborough Chronicle*, for example, was examined and marked up by Parker for use in the writing of his *A defence of priestes mariage* published in 1566/7. The volume concludes with an outline of the 'vast field of research' required on Parker's work including detailed study (and an edition) of the Register, and close analysis of this with the manuscripts listed in it. Page's book ought to inspire further scholarly interest in this area.

3.   Social, Cultural and Intellectual Background

(See also section 9, below: Janet Cooper, ed., *The Battle of Maldon: Fiction and Fact.*)

Michael Lapidge has published a collection of 16 of his essays in *Anglo-Latin Literature 900–1066*. Included among these reprints are some seminal works such as 'Schools, Learning and Literature in Tenth-Century England', and 'The Hermeneutic Style in Tenth-Century Anglo-Latin Literature'. The collection aims 'to serve as a preliminary guide' to the history of pre-Conquest Anglo-Latin literature, and it includes additional notes which provide up-dated bibliographical and scholarly material.

Anglo-Saxon England 22 contains a wealth of cultural and intellectual, as well as literary, information among its 13 articles. Michael Parker Pearson, Robert van de Noort and Alex Woolf are interested in identifying to whom the burials at Sutton Hoo belong in 'Three Men and a Boat: Sutton Hoo and the East Saxon Kingdom' (*ASE* 22.27–50). They use archaeological, genealogical and historical evidence to build a case for the mounds belonging to Sæberht and his sons (of the East Saxon royal house) rather than to Rædwald. They determine the influence – Saxon or Anglian – on the artefacts discovered at the site to conclude that 'their "centre of gravity" converges on Essex rather than East Anglia'. In so doing, they meticulously reassess the problems in associating Sutton Hoo with the East Anglian dynasty and provide fresh impetus for further research into this long-debated subject. David A. Hinton with Robert White are also concerned with archaeological matters in 'A Smith's Hoard from Tattershall Thorpe, Lincoln-shire' (*ASE* 22.147–66). They publish details of the artifacts discovered in 1981 when this important site was excavated. Among the finds are an anvil, hammer-heads, scabbard-mounts, a scrap-box, some glass fragments, and bones. The finds indicate an early date (sixth or seventh century), and possible Flemish contacts for their 'high status' owner whose burial 'does not conform to the usual English practices of disposal behaviour'.

In 'An Unreported Early Use of Bede's *De natura rerum*' (*ASE* 22.85–91),

Vernon King focuses on an unnoticed use of Bede's work in the *Aratus latinus*. Various ultimate sources for this text have already been determined but King notes an important number of occasions where the author has drawn upon Bede. Presented cumulatively, King states '[these passages] present a strong case for the *De natura rerum* being the immediate source'; this presents additional evidence for the place of origin of the *Aratus latinus* – the northwestern Frankish kingdom, specifically perhaps, Corbie. In 'Aldhelm's *Enigmata* and Byzantine Riddles' (*ASE* 22.51–64), Celica Milovanovic-Barham examines how aware Aldhelm may have been of the Roman and Greek riddlic tradition when he composed his *Enigmata*. She shows him to be more aware of this tradition than previous scholars have suggested: features apparent in the *Enigmata* are also present, for example, in Byzantine riddles. She proposes that Aldhelm's knowledge of Greek may have been gleaned from his teacher, Theodore, archbishop of Canterbury. T. O'Loughlin and H. Conrad-O'Briain discuss Latin and Celtic influences in 'The "Baptism of Tears" in Early Anglo-Saxon Sources' (*ASE* 22.65–83). In the *Vita S. Gregorii*, Gregory weeps for the soul of Trajan, thereby 'baptising' him. O'Loughlin and Conrad O'Briain trace this controversial episode and incorporate biblical and patristic writings, and penitential literature. It seems that Origen's conception of penitential tears entered Irish literature from where the motif disseminated ultimately becoming confused with baptismal tears as in the Whitby *vita* of St Gregory. Staying in Northern England, Donald Bullough asks 'What has Ingeld to do with Lindisfarne?' (*ASE* 22.93–125). He demonstrates that the answer is 'nothing' by focusing on Alcuin's letter to Speratus. Bullough investigates the identity of the recipient of the letter, and thoroughly investigates its contents, printing the letter in full in translation as an appendix. Also in *ASE* 22 is a well-written and documented article by Ian McDougall: 'Serious Entertainments: An Examination of a Peculiar Type of Viking Atrocity' (201–25). McDougall looks at the historical accuracy of the Viking tortures in Abbo's *Vita S. Edmundi* and the martyrdom of Ælfheah in the *Anglo-Saxon Chronicle* concentrating on their 'human bullseye' practice of throwing javelins and bones at hostages prior to execution. For Abbo's hagiography, no such parallel incident occurs in contemporary *Chronicle* entries, but the very nature of the text as saint's life, links the torture of Edmund (having javelins thrown at him) with St Sebastian's. Likewise, Ælfheah's torture (by boning as opposed to stoning) and death, even in the *Chronicle*, is described as a martyrdom. McDougall expands his discussion of Viking atrocities to Irish and Scandinavian literary sources illustrating the well-attested propensity of the Vikings for pelting their hostages with a variety of missiles, usually over supper! It would seem that historical authenticity, as opposed to mere hagiographical elaboration, is supported for both the *Vita S. Edmundi* as well as the *Chronicle*'s account of Ælfheah's death.

There are a number of essays dealing with lexical and etymological issues. P. R. Kitson criticizes the editors of the Toronto *Dictionary of Old English* for their failure to take etymologies into account in 'No *blere, blerig* "bald" in Old English' (*Neophil* 77.637–52). He analyses the use of 'blere' and 'blerig' in Old English to suggest that the basic meaning may be '(having) a white patch' as opposed to 'bald' as given in the *DOE*.

Alfred Wollmann deals with 'Early Latin Loan-words in Old English' (*ASE* 22.1–26) furthering work by scholars such as Campbell in this area. He deals with the difficulty of assessing the periodization of loan-words, a difficulty that requires the grouping of such loans by linguistic appearance and assignment to an historical or geographical origin in order to yield dating evidence. Phonological integration into Old English, for example, illustrates the early adoption of the Latin lexeme; usually such loan-words are traced, with some difficulty, by their origin from both Continental and Insular sources. Wollmann concludes that it is more profitable to discuss pre-600 loans in terms of 'early' and 'late' rather than geographical origin. Helmut Gneuss is also concerned with loanwords in his Sir Israel Gollancz Memorial Lecture, '*Anglicae linguae interpretatio*: Language Contact, Lexical Borrowing, and Glossing in Anglo-Saxon England' (*PBA* 82.107–48). In this paper, Gneuss outlines the history of loan-word scholarship to examine 'how far the work from Skeat to Funke and that of their successors have stood the test of time'. He discusses contact and its periodization between Old English and other languages: Latin, Greek, Hebrew, Celtic, Scandinavian, Germanic dialects, French (where he states that a more critical attitude is required by scholars working on loan-words); different types of borrowing including lexical and structural, and the relation of loan-words to interlinear, continuous glossing where frequent loan-formations and semantic loans occur. This is a learned and informative essay which covers an enormous amount of scholarly ground in its 40 pages.

Andrew Breeze continues his work on Celtic influences on Old English: he suggests 'Celtic Etymologies for Old English *cursung* "curse", *gafeluc* "javelin", *stær* "history", *syrce* "coat of mail", and Middle English *clog(ge)* "block, wooden shoe", *cokkunge* "striving", *tirven* "to flay", *warroke* "hunchback"' (*N&Q* 40.287–97); and suggests an etymological link between '*Wered* "sweet drink" at Beowulf 496: Welsh *gwirod* "liquor, drink"' (*N&Q* 40.433–4). Roland Torkar examines 'The Aldhelm Gloss *Constantina*: *demera* (ClGl 1)' in Cotton Cleopatra A.iii (*N&Q* 40.428–31). He demonstrates that the gloss 'demera' (gen. pl.), meant to render *praetorum*, was mismatched by the scribe with a chapter rubric in the source which read *Constantina*.

4. Literature: General

Charles D. Wright's years of scholarship concerning Celtic influences on Anglo-Saxon literary production have culminated in *The Irish Tradition in Old English Literature*, a thorough, extensive, and ground-breaking work. Wright modestly states that the book provides a 'preliminary thematic and stylistic inventory of Irish influence', and while it certainly lives up to that claim, it is also much more. Wright, for example, discusses methods of religious literary composition in Anglo-Saxon England, and demonstrates conclusively the influence of Irish and Anglo-Saxon missionaries on the early transmission of the sermon on the Continent; he also traces certain motifs through to their employment in Middle English texts, thus illustrating the popularity and longevity of the Irish influence. The work focuses on a number of motifs that occur primarily in Old English religious prose such as the Vercelli and Blickling Homilies, and the Prose *Solomon and Saturn Pater Noster Dialogue*. The 'enumerative style' is common to Anglo-Saxon and Irish literatures: among these, the listing of the 'three deaths' and 'three lives' in Vercelli IX (printed as an appendix), Wright suggests, may have been transmitted from a Hiberno-Latin florilegium, a 'commonplace book to be plundered and modified according to the practical needs of the preacher'. Other motifs are those that developed in the Insular tradition from the *Visio S. Pauli* such as 'The Hanging Sinner', and the account of Grendel's mere in *Beowulf*. Wright also discusses the rhetorical force of the theme of 'The Devil's Account of the Next World' found in texts such as *Judith*, and the *Life of St Margaret*, which may have derived from the Irish hagiographic tradition. In his chapter on 'The literary milieu of Vercelli IX and the Irish tradition in Old English literature', Wright shows that the influence of Irish topoi affected later Anglo-Saxon England 'especially in the realm of apocryphal eschatology and cosmology'. In this later period, the two most famous homilists, Ælfric and Wulfstan, were relatively unaffected by Irish texts and traditions, making something of a conscious decision to avoid Hiberno-Latin works, it seems. In his analysis of Vercelli IX and the prose *Pater Noster Dialogue*, Wright's stylistic examinations are so meticulous that he is able to attribute them to a 'common workshop' which he suggests may have been Mercia during King Athelstan's reign thus showing how late Irish influence was felt in Anglo-Saxon England. Wright's work, then, undoubtedly provides new information and analyses as well as an innovative approach for further research to continue from this very important beginning. David F. Johnson, in 'The Five Horrors of Hell: An Insular Homiletic Motif' (*ES* 74.415–31) also demonstrates the influence of the Irish literary tradition on Old English homiletic texts.

Another work which explores the links between Celtic and Anglo-Saxon literature is Sarah Lynn Higley's *Between Languages: The Uncooperative Text in Early Welsh and Old English Nature Poetry*. Higley is concerned to elucidate the relationship and differences between these two literary traditions. She uses philological and theoretical approaches to examine poems which focus on 'the plight of lonely people' and the reflection of the macrocosmic on internal turmoil. Chapter I deals with the familiar motif of 'The Natural Analogy'. *The Wanderer*'s use of nature is analysed with *The Sick Man of Abercuawg*, for example, to show 'What is lacking in the Old English is an intricacy of poetic requirement and a play of sounds that is absolutely required in Welsh poems'. In looking at the 'formal expression' of the motif, Higley proposes 'three dimensions' to the study – the natural analogy operating 'as a juxtaposition or parataxis which sets up a triangulation'. It may be that modern interpretation forms the third element or it may be an empathetic approach: Higley does not make this clear (very occasionally, clarity in her expression is lacking). In Chapter II, the figurative register of *The Seafarer*, and, in particular, the use of 'forþon', is considered with reference to Welsh analogues, and other Old English elegies such as *The Wife's Lament*. Chapter III widens the discussion by employing metrical and stylistic analyses: the Old English texts are examined as 'The Continuous Style' (paratactic and sequential) where stanzaic arrangement is rare. This leads into a debate on 'Oral Formula' in which it is proposed that 'Old English poets were not confined to the formulas of their poetic trade'. Higley looks at *The Ruin*, moving into an examination of 'Style and Latin Influence' in such poems as *Judith* and Welsh analogues, which deduces that the homiletic and didactic poetic style was better suited to Old English than early Welsh. In the second section of the book, 'The Image and Connection', Higley discusses the use of gnomes in *Maxims I* and *II* and Welsh wisdom texts highlighting the deliberate ambiguities of gnomic verse when using the nature image. In the third section, 'The Private Connection', 'intentional difficulties' in early Welsh poems, and 'Clarity and Obscurity in Old English Poetry', especially *Wulf and Eadwacer* and Riddles, are the main focus.

Higley suggests that the *Wulf and Eadwacer* poet may have used 'the prerogative of the poet to keep things hidden or to present them with alternative interpretations', in a similar manner to Welsh court poetry in which '"difficulty" ... was looked upon as an attribute'. Ambivalence, it seems, was 'much more tolerated' by the Welsh poets. In concluding, Higley suggests that the Old English elegies may be 'companion pieces' and variations on a theme, perhaps 'an assignment set to aspiring poets'. An appendix contains translations of and commentary on some of the works discussed including *The Seafarer*, *Maxims II* and *Wulf and Eadwacer*. In contrast, a comparative analysis of Scandinavian and Anglo-Saxon wisdom literature is the subject of Carolyne Larrington's *A Store of Common Sense: Gnomic Theme and Style in Old Icelandic and Old English Wisdom Poetry* (Oxford).

Karen Cherewatuk addresses the 'Germanic Echoes in Latin Verse: The Voice of the Lamenting Woman in Radegund's Poetry' (*Allegorica* 14.3–21). She identifies the Germanic tradition of the lamenting women in Radegund's 'De excidio Thoringiae' and 'Ad Artachin' which can be paralleled in *Beowulf*, *The Seafarer*, *The Wanderer*, *The Wife's Lament* and *Wulf and Eadwacer*. The use of this motif strengthens the claim of authorship of these Latin texts by Radegund and demonstrates 'a powerful oral tradition that predates poetry written in a Germanic vernacular'.

Richard J. Schrader is interested in tracing the influence of the 'law of succession' for reading Anglo-Saxon literature in *Old English Poetry and the Genealogy of Events*. Schrader reassesses the importance of Augustine and, notably, Orosius to the Anglo-Saxons' perception of their place in secular and salvation history. The main poetic foci for Schrader's analysis of literary representations of history are *Genesis, Daniel, Judith, Elene, Widsith, Deor, Guthlac A* and *Beowulf* (as well as a chapter devoted to Laȝamon's *Brut*). The lengthiest attention is devoted, not surprisingly perhaps, to the 'complex sense of time' in *Beowulf*, where Schrader points to the main emphasis as one of 'succession' which he links to historical English concerns of stability and 'Anglo-Danish harmony'. The discussion of the *Brut* illustrates its mythological approach to history; one more akin to the Anglo-Saxon perception than to the secular orientation of the Anglo-Norman historiographers.

A worthwhile purchase this year is Fred C. Robinson's *The Tomb of Beowulf and Other Essays on Old English*. It is comprised of a collection of 20 previously printed essays, and three new works. Four essays deal with 'Literary Interpretation: *Beowulf*', seven with 'Literary Interpretation: Several Poems', four with 'Women in Old English Literature', four with 'Names in Old English Literature', and four with 'Old English in the Twentieth Century'. Robinson has updated footnotes, and added the occasional 'Afterword 1992'. Two new essays which give a different and fascinating perspective on Old English scholarship might appropriately be discussed here; the third is reviewed in section 9 below. In 'Ezra Pound and the Old English Translational Tradition', Robinson considers the success of Pound's translation of *The Seafarer* in the light of less successful attempts at Old English translation by Conybeare, Tennyson and George Stephens. William Morris published an alliterative and metrical translation of *Beowulf* in 1898 which, Robinson shows, may have influenced Pound's methods. A more important influence on Pound, however, was Stopford A. Brooke whose *The History of English Literature* included his own version of *The Seafarer*. Robinson provides a comparative analysis of the translations of Pound and

Brooke to demonstrate the 'similar echoes of phrasing' which may have helped Pound create one of the more evocative modern renditions of the poem. In 'The Afterlife of Old English: A Brief History of Composition in Old English after the Close of the Anglo-Saxon Period', Robinson examines a manuscript, composed and written by Alistair Campbell, and now deposited in the Dictionary of Old English archives in Toronto. The manuscript contains, among other texts, Campbell's Old English translations of parts of the *Aeneid* and *The Song of Roland*. This leads Robinson into a discussion of post-Conquest compositions in Old English: these range from twelfth- and thirteenth-century compositions, annotations and expansions in earlier or contemporary manuscripts, to the sixteenth-century interest in the language. 'Old English' poems by Humphrey Wanley and William Elstob were published in 1700 to lament the death of Queen Anne's son, and Robinson moves through the centuries incorporating material such as Grundtvig's own poems on *Beowulf* in Old English and Danish.

The last ten years have seen a striking renaissance of work on English metrics, and on the prosodic structure of Old English in particular. R. D. Fulk's *A History of Old English Meter* arrives, then, in an exciting environment and among significant scholastic activity. It is immediately apparent that Fulk's contribution is very important indeed, allowing conceptual depth to meet with philological rigour, and marrying historical phonology to metrics and dialectology, often in completely original ways. On ever-closer inspection, it becomes increasingly obvious that Fulk's mastery of detail is virtually complete. Complementarily, he retains his interest in the wider conclusions inherent in the smallest historical change: cases in point are the consideration of Kaluza's law in Chapter VI, and the succeeding chapter on tertiary stress. Let it be said forthwith that Fulk's achievement is a magnificent piece of scholarship, and knowledge of his work will be obligatory from now on for all those interested in Old English poetry as well as those interested in how poetry is transmitted, in how it is constrained, and in diachronic and diatopic variation in verse tradition(s). Given a book of such richness – eleven chapters, with Introduction, Conclusion, four Appendices, and four Indices – it is difficult to summarize. For their complexity and Fulk's intellectual elan in the treating of them, three areas are notable for the links that Fulk creates between them: (i) the nature of historical argumentation and its relationship with prosodic analyses; (ii) the nature of syllables, stress and their deployment in verse; and (iii) linguistic evidence, dating and chronology. These are issues constantly revisited by Fulk. Kaluza's law merits a chapter in Fulk in which he rightly points out that Kaluza's original formulation carried too many exceptions, but he also amplifies on Kaluza's further demonstration that the distinction between long and short endings is relevant to the first foot in Sievers's types A and E. Fulk's analysis runs to several pages, and also treats widely of Bliss's revisions of Kaluza's law. Simplifying the detail, Fulk's treatment of the suspension of resolution is, on historical grounds, rather more convincing than Cable's 1991 postulation of an 'Antepenultimate Rule', and Fulk's conclusions support the hypotheses that *Beowulf* must have been composed before the shortening of long endings, and that the poem is compositionally unified. In his chapter on Tertiary Stress, Fulk's examination runs to over 60 pages, but perhaps the most important sub-part of his analysis is that he (re)introduces the role of syllable length as a determining factor of stressedness. Fulk consistently works by argument leading to discussion of specifics (syllable-length, stress, rule of the coda) leading to chronology (empirical analysis of dating) leading back to argument ('coda-constraints' in verse may well be universal). It is brilliantly done. One question, though, remains to be asked: if Fulk is correct then what kind of poetry was Old English verse? Given the structures and constraints explicit here, Old English poetry seems to be a staggeringly complex artefact. Fulk suggests that the process by which the scop learned his art 'cannot have been essentially different from child language acquisition [where] ... grammar is ... learned by the child's own observation .... The only way a scop can have learned the quantities of final vowels by mere observation is if there was a phonological difference [between long and short vocalic endings].' The invocation of child language acquisition may be unwise. Genetic endowment, for example, seems to play a role in language acquisition; likewise, overgeneration of syntactic processes is common; there is also a maximal age-range in which language can be most readily acquired. Nothing specifically in metrics would support the idea of metrical competence being a result of any of these factors. One must therefore ask again: what kind of poetry is Old English verse? Its structures – apparently of rare complexity – are not altogether consistent with the notion of spontaneity or, perhaps, orality. Spontaneous oral genesis in Old English may not be consistent with the artefact explored by Fulk, or indeed, by Bliss, Russom and Cable. The poetry seems altogether more 'scriptist', even more 'artificial': the poem seems to lie on the page more readily than in the vocal tract. Is it conceivable that the past century of work on Old English metrics is coming to suggest that the extant poetry is an anachronistic artefact which bears the same relation to the Old English language as, six centuries or so later, 'classical' experiments in English quantitative metres were to bear to the language of Shakespeare? Both forms of poetry would then be characterized as arcana, distinguished not by their 'natural' relationship to the underlying language, but by their artificiality. And certainly, both kinds of verbal construct eventually shared the same fate. [C. B. McCully]

In a considerably less weighty volume than Fulk's, F. H. Whitman provides *A Comparative Study of Old English Metre*. It is an accessible work which includes an Appendix of verse scansions from *Beowulf*, *Cædmon's Hymn*, *The Dream of the Rood*, and *The Rhyming Poem* that indicate Whitman's proposed methodology. Whitman's objective is to advance the study of Old English metrics beyond the well-established paradigms of Sievers's and Heusler's, and, to that end, many synopses of current metrical theories (e.g. those of Bliss, Pope and Cable) are discussed. Whitman's comparative approach involves analyses of Italic and Germanic accentual (as opposed to quantitative) alliterative verse as the former may yield 'primitive metrical patterns that might underlie the [Germanic] traditions' under consideration. Whitman discusses the accentual nature of medieval Latin that some scholars believe to have been influenced by vernacular verse; here, he proposes that the accentual tradition may be traced back to the pre-classical Italic period, concomitant therefore with Celtic and Germanic stress patterned verse. In Chapter 1, 'The Earliest Accentual Verse', scansion of Umbrian and Old Latin verse and its features are described. In Chapter 2, 'German Accentual Verse' is analysed, including snippets of *Beowulf* and *The Dream of the Rood*, for which Sievers's model is shown to be inadequate, 'an artificial thing', because it offers 'a metrical system that ignores time'. Kaluza's observation of the difficulties in Sievers's Types B and C is the subject of Chapter 3 which focuses on initial syllables, and the various interpretations of these offered by Heusler and Pope, among others. Chapter 4 deals with 'Light Lines' which can be scanned as variants of the 'normal' half-line or which can be seen to demonstrate a need for the re-analysis of stress-bearing categories (since many begin with finite verbs). In Chapter 5, 'Clashing Stress', Whitman looks at this common phenomenon in Old English verse and deduces that most instances of 'clashing' stress might be attributable to 'syllabic loss, primarily the loss of stem vowels between stressed items'. Chapter 6, 'Towards a New Paradigm', summarizes the critical debate concerning the nature of the foot: whether one can impose a chronometric analysis onto Old English verse. The boundary, stressed and unstressed syllables, resolution, and other aspects of metrics are scrutinized in the light of comparative Italic and Greek verse. Whitman concludes by looking at 'Rhythmic Principle' especially the 'curious mixture of two-, three-, and four-measure half-lines in Old English verse' which is regarded as somewhat unbalanced. Drawing attention to scholarship which has examined similarly constructed Greek lyric poetry and concluded that there are four major rhythmic classes, Whitman suggests that an understanding of Old English verse might benefit from such investigations.

Benjamin H. Carroll looks at 'Metrical Resolution in Old English' in *JEGP* 92.167–78. His study focuses on the nature and importance of the constraints which operate on the length of the second syllable in resolved halfstresses. Carroll reappraises Bliss's examination of resolved halfstresses and shows that there is 'remarkably clear and consistent logic in the distribution of the long and short endings, a logic that cannot come from decay [as Bliss proposes]'. The theory is that these constraints are a result of 'the correlation of quantity, accent, and rhythm which were presumably native to the Old English language'. Also dealing with constraints is Edwin Duncan's 'Weak Stress and Poetic Constraints in Old English Verse' (*JEGP* 92.495–508). Duncan notes that Old English is traditionally regarded as having three levels of stress: primary, secondary, and weak and proposes that weak stress classification ought to be sub-divided into two varieties, a finding that 'not only calls for a re-evaluation of phonological descriptions of OE stress but also reveals some unrecognized and important poetic constraints'.

John W. Schwetman provides 'An Assessment of Kuhn's Laws of Stress in Old English Poetry' (*NM* 94.47–60). In this article, Schwetman is concerned to demonstrate that Kuhn's rules are adequate as descriptions of stress patterns only, and are not sufficient as 'linguistic rules'. He comments that 'While Kuhn's Laws may describe many of the lines that exist in poetry, they can hardly be accurate statements as laws governing the composition of poetry' as some scholars have tended to employ them. Viewed as such, they 'present an overly simplistic view of the poetic language of Old English'; Schwetman advocates a more humble approach to the study of Old English grammatical rules. Taking a somewhat similar view is B. R. Hutcheson's 'Stress of Quantitative Adjectives and Some Common Adverbs in Old English Poetry: An Alternative to Kuhn's Law' (*LeedsSE* 24.27–56). Hutcheson analyses temporal and directional adverbs, and adjectives such as *fea*, *fela* and *eall* from a corpus which includes *Beowulf*, *Brunanburh* and *The Dream of the Rood* to determine patterns of stress. He provides statistical and analytical evidence to suggest that Kuhn's law 'is useless for determining stress in Old English poetry'; and that it is alliteration which provides the major key to the stressing of particular classes of adjectives and adverbs.

Joseph D. Wine's book, *Figurative Language in Cynewulf*, develops the close examination of the Cynewulfian canon (and other Old English poems) hinted at in his article '*Juliana* and the Figures of Rhetoric' (*YWES* 73.99). His aims here include a definition of the style of this poet, and the proposal of methods for studying poetic figures which emphasizes linguistic criteria (such as verbal and aural repetition, and parallelism), which Wine considers not to have been sufficiently appraised by earlier Cynewulf scholars. A slim volume, it nevertheless provides detailed investigation of the percentage occurrences of particular figures (homoeoteleuton, paronomasia etc.) to conclude that Cynewulf carefully varied his rhetorical hoard in his 'intricately structured' works; that such rhetorical devices are more frequently used by Cynewulf than other Old English poets (with the possible exception of the composer of the *Phoenix*); and that the application of the stylistic figures, working 'on the surfaces of language', is suited to the individual thematic or character aspects of each poem. An appendix includes a list of figures discussed in the text. Rhetorical analysis can be a complex subject, but Wine manages to make his investigation approachable and clear, to produce a work which is suitable for use by students of Old English, and to illustrate a number of methodologies which can be equally well applied to other poetic texts.

M. S. Griffith examines 'Convention and originality in the Old English "beasts of battle" typescene' (*ASE* 22.179–99) to show that the scene is more conventional that has previously been thought and that many of the variations in its use occur, even so, within conventional parameters. He discusses *Genesis A*, *Judith* and *Elene* where the battle-scenes, including the motif of the beasts, indicate an adherence to poetic form rather than any sources. Griffith also analyses audience expectation (the wolf, for example, is usually associated with slaughter), and lexical limitation within the scene's composition. Other poems that Griffith deals with are *Maldon*, *Brunanburh* and *Exodus* as well as Celtic and classical texts. An appendix of poetic excerpts illustrates his points. He concludes by proposing that formulaic analysis in Old English studies has shifted to the 'manner of composition' rather than the mode; such analysis ought therefore to concern itself with 'the development of a rhetoric that can most economically describe the stylistic features of the texts themselves'.

The discernible shift from manner of composition to mode is reflected also in Roberta Frank's Toller Memorial Lecture which addresses orality, a topic close to the heart of many Anglo-Saxonists. In 'The Search for the Anglo-Saxon Oral Poet' (*BJRL* 75.11–36), Frank reminds us of the precarious nature of the evidence for assessing the nature of the scop. She ranges through centuries of Anglo-Saxon scholarship and, in so doing, encompasses attitudes of post-Conquest historians such as William of Malmesbury to their Anglo-Saxon forebears, to illustrate the legendary aspects of much that is 'known' about the Old English poet. Frank reminds us that debates which seek to find the elusive scop, are, ultimately, concerned with the 'unknown and unknowable'; with the exception of Bede's account of Cædmon, scholars are dealing with 'a disembodied voice' which has left only manuscript words as compositional testimony.

Tracing the transition from orality to literacy is the central concern of Nicholas Howe's 'The Cultural Construction of Reading in Anglo-Saxon England' (in Boyarin, ed.). He looks at reading as a 'public, spoken act', a 'shared, cultural practice' and reinforces his discussion with an analysis of the semantic development of Old English *rædan* and *ræd*. These forms often refer to the explanation of 'something obscure or solving a riddle', later evolving into the practice of reading aloud (translating *legere*), under the influence of the monastic community. By looking at *rædan* and its variants, Howe demonstrates 'that reading in

Anglo-Saxon England cannot be understood by any facile opposition of orality and literacy', and that scholars must beware of understanding 'reading' from the modern perception of literacy. Joseph A. Dane looks at the evidence for oral composition provided by ring patterns in 'The Notion of Ring Composition in Classical and Medieval Studies' (*NM* 94.61–7). With reference to *Beowulf* and the *Iliad*, for example, he attempts to show that the existence of ring composition is more a result of 'critical methods' than textual actuality, and thus cannot be employed in supporting theories about oral composition.

In an essay which requires some grammatical attention (for example, 'Why the difference? The watershed of the Crucifixion.'), Catherine Brown Tkacz analyses the occurrences of *wlite*, *gewemman* and *scufan* to illustrate various uses of 'Christian Formulas in Old English Literature: *næs hyre wlite gewemmed* and its Implications' (*Traditio* 48.31–61). The 'Three Young Men' of the Book of Daniel, employed to illustrate the redemptive power of God, can be traced as a hagiographic motif in Old English prose (such as Ælfric's homilies) and in poems such as *Azarias*, *Daniel*, *Juliana*, *Genesis A* and *Andreas*. She provides a detailed contextual reading of the instances of this formula; her discussion of its use in *Andreas* shows it to be a 'deliberate, ironic reversal of Daniel material'. Tkacz states that 'the existence of this compositional material in Old English literature at last proves the existence of Old English formulas that were Christian from the start, as opposed to Christian adaptations of already existing formulas'.

Alfred Bammesberger offers 'A Note on Old English *gedræg/gredreag*' (*NM* 94.243–8), alternate spellings which occur variously in *Beowulf*, *Andreas*, *Christ III*, *The Wife's Lament* and *Riddle 6*. Bammesberger notes from the contexts of the words, that if they both represent variants of the same lexeme, they cannot be connected to *dragan*. Etymologically and phonologically, they may be derived from Germanic *-drauga-*, the meaning of which may be interpreted as 'action of warfare', or those who carry out that action: namely, 'a noisy company'.

Paul Cavill draws attention to shared maxim formulas in '*Beowulf* and *Andreas*: Two Maxims' (*Neophil* 77.479–87). The half-line conclusion, 'gif/þonne his ellen deah', for example, occurs at *Beowulf* line 573, and *Andreas* line 460, and illustrates a 'process of crafting which has gone into the *Andreas* version in order to transform the maxim [from which the phrases derive] into a fully Christian *sententia*'. Cavill's exposition of this maxim and other shared maxims, leads him through a detailed discussion of Christian and Germanic parallel occurrences, to conclude that the poet of *Andreas* knew *Beowulf*, and 'was working within the tradition of which *Beowulf* is the principal extant monument'.

Kathleen Herbert provides fictionalized accounts of some Old English poems in the first part of *Spellcraft: Old English Heroic Legends*. *The Wife's Lament*, for example, is the inspiration behind 'The Third Game Wins the Match' in which the events leading to the exile of the poem's speaker are imaginatively created. In the second section of the book, information on source material (such as *The Husband's Message* and *Waldere*) is provided.

5. The Exeter Book

Patrick Conner, as well as producing *Anglo-Saxon Exeter* (for which, see section 2, above) has written on 'Source Studies, the Old English *Guthlac A*, and the

English Benedictine Reformation' (*RB* 103.380–413). This is an excellent study that immediately enters the current debate on source studies within Old English scholarship: Conner declares that, to date, source studies 'ignores the fact that an intensely textual culture would support composition by allusion to things read and remembered as easily as it would support composition from actual models present at the time of composition'. He suggests the word 'resource' be used instead of 'source' and advocates the seeking of 'sign systems [in texts] whose referents extend to systems in other texts' to determine conscious, or unconscious use of sources. It is from this stand that he approaches *Guthlac A* which other commentators have found 'anomalous' but which Conner does not. He examines the poem within the literary environment of intertextuality in the Benedictine Reform, employing *The Rule of St Benedict* and Smaragdus's *Expositio* to illuminate *Guthlac A*'s linked system of signs. Conner believes the poem to be examinable as a 'model of training of the soul within the monastic rule' which demonstrates such a definable knowledge and use of the *Rule* and *Expositio* that they may well be primary sources. As such, Conner proposes that the poem be placed firmly in the milieu of the Reform movement, as it 'could not have been composed much before *c.*960'.

Conner has, in this article, illustrated a contextualization of his subject-text in precisely the scholarly manner that T. A. Shippey calls for: Shippey has some stirring words to say in 'Old English Poetry: the Prospects for Literary History' (in *Segundo Congreso Internacional de la Sociedad Espanola de Lengua y Literatura Inglesa Medieval*, ed. Antonio Leon Sendra, Oviedo). He begins by lamenting the reluctance of critics to attempt to date the surviving corpus of Old English poetry [I take it that the constant attention paid to *Beowulf*'s date of composition is excluded here], or 'to establish a relative chronology for the poems surviving'. Shippey pays particular attention to the result of Amos's work, *Linguistic Means of Determining the Dates of Old English Literary Texts*, which is an 'impasse' 'accepted increasingly readily'. He notes that to attempt to contextualize poetry by means of, for example, 'the changing history of the Anglo-Saxon Church', would at least produce 'sense-richer meanings' than the limbo which critics often find themselves in. To illustrate this point, Shippey examines, among other works, *The Phoenix* and *Guthlac A*: for the latter (in sharp contrast to Conner's more convincing findings above), Shippey finds that the poem may have been produced in a period of ecclesiastical tension such as existed in ninth-century Anglo-Saxon England. He states that the historical context was not 'the Æthelwoldian one': 'it is evident that the poet of *Guthlac A* cannot have been an Æthelwoldian'. Linguistic, as well as historical, evidence is used in this wide-ranging discussion. Shippey ultimately points out that Anglo-Saxonists need not give up hope of establishing a plausible chronology for the corpus of existing verse.

Thomas N. Hall proposes 'A Gregorian Model for Eve's *biter drync* in *Guthlac B*' (*RES* 34.157–75). He addresses 'the metaphor of death as a bitter drink' at lines 863b–70a and 980b–91a in the poem. The origin of the metaphor in these two passages, expansions of the *Vita Sancti Guthlaci*, has caused some critical debate (which extends to analogous passages in *Beowulf* and *Andreas*). Hall outlines the debate and previous proposals for the possible sources of the 'drink of death', and suggests that the use of the metaphor in *Guthlac B* may derive from Gregory's homily for Easter Thursday which is shown to have had a considerable influence. Thus, *Guthlac B*, as well as being dependent on Felix's

Vita, also invokes 'themes and images familiar from medieval exegetical literature, so that the poem can be seen to take part in a broader literary tradition'. John C. Pope presents a convincing argument for 'What the Seraphim Do in Line 396a of the Old English *Advent*: A Scribal Cover Uncovered' (*Speculum* 68.1–5). This wittily entitled article tackles a word which, Pope believes, shows the erratic spelling by the manuscript scribe of 'wearð' which has been emended by editors since Thorpe as 'wearðian'. The emendation to 'to guard' makes sense in the poetic context: 'and with their wings [the seraphim] [guard] the face of the Lord Almighty', unlike the senseless original manuscript reading. Pope proposes, however, that the emendation is unnecessary, as the scribe might simply have transposed the *r*, meaning to write 'wreað' ('cover'). Illustrating his case with linguistic, metrical, and authoritative source evidence (from the Vulgate Isaiah 6.2), Pope cogently re-interprets the text to read that the Seraphim are covering the Lord's face with their wings, rather than guarding it.

Robert Hasenfratz writes on the '*Wanderer*, lines 45–57 and the Birds of Diomede' (*JEGP* 92.309–24). The interpretative problems of these lines of *The Wanderer* are well known (who are 'secga geseldan' and what are the 'floating ones'?). Hasenfratz proposes that an interesting parallel to the shift that occurs from the companions of the Wanderer's dream to the seabirds can be drawn from Book XI of the *Aeneid*. In the *Aeneid*, Diomede is made to wander the ocean as an exile; furthermore, his men were transformed into seabirds. The use of this story is traced by Hasenfratz through Pliny's *Historia Naturalis* to Augustine and Isidore, all authors known to the Anglo-Saxons; none of these are sources, however. The notable similarities between the birds in relevant passages of *The Wanderer* and the *Aeneid* do, however, suggest that the latter text may be a source, or was at least familiar to the Old English poet.

Marcella McCarthy proposes 'A Solution to Riddle 72 in the Exeter Book' (*RES* 44.204–10). Solutions previously offered include 'cuttlefish', 'swan', 'siren', and 'writing', none of which satisfy the poem's details. McCarthy revives a solution, first put forward in 1861, of 'sun' which seems to relate to many of the paradoxes inherent in the riddle and can be reinforced by images from other poems including *The Phoenix* and *The Order of the World*.

6. The Poems of the Vercelli Book

Thomas D. Hill draws attention to a 'quasi-dramatic Anglo-Saxon liturgical custom' in the *Regularis Concordia* and its implications for understanding the Passion in *The Dream of the Rood* in 'The Cross as Symbolic Body: An Anglo-Latin Liturgical Analogue to *The Dream of the Rood*' (*Neophil* 77.297–301). The *Regularis Concordia* states that on Good Friday a cross is to be placed in a receptacle representing Christ's tomb until Easter Sunday. This cross is identified in the ceremony as 'a symbol of the body of Christ'. Such a rite is analogous to the crucifixion scene in the poem where the cross becomes symbolic of the human suffering of the divine Christ.

7. The Junius Manuscript

B. R. Hutcheson, in '*Genesis A* 1786a: A Proposed Emendation' (*N&Q* 39.1–2), uses morphological and metrical evidence provided by a portion of the Old English poetic corpus to show that the half-line in question is unique for its type in lacking double alliteration. He proposes an emendation based on this evidence from 'domfæst wereda' to 'domfæst duguþa'.

John Vickrey discusses the four occurrences of the motif 'tacen (-)iewan' in 'Adam, Eve, and the Tacen in *Genesis B*' (PQ 72.1–14). The motif and its contexts centre around the apportionment of guilt in the temptation. The Old Saxon *Genesis* is examined in close detail for the philological evidence it yields.

Other articles on the Junius Manuscript this year include 'Some Codicological Considerations in the Interpretation of Junius Poems' (*ELN* 30.iv.1–10) by Laurel Amtower; and A. N. Doane's 'Interdialectics and Reading in *Genesis B*' (in Laurie Bauer and Christine Franzen, eds, *Of Pavolova, Poetry and Paradigms: Essays in Honour of Harry Orsman*, Wellington, NZ).

8. The *Beowulf* Manuscript

Sam Newton's *The Origins of 'Beowulf' and the Pre-Viking Kingdom of East Anglia* will certainly fuel the debate concerning the poem's date of composition. The central hypothesis of the volume is that *Beowulf* is dateable to eighth-century East Anglia, and, to this end, all evidence is clearly and logically directed. Newton provides a step-by-step explanation of his theory which incorporates current debate, as well as much new information and some refreshingly different perspectives. This volume involves linguistic, archaeological, genealogical and historical approaches. In the first chapter, 'The *Beowulf* Manuscript', Newton rejects proposals that the poem is a composite and that the manuscript copy represents an autograph version. In discussing the poem as a copy of an earlier version, Newton notes the use of *d* for eth or thorn and states this is 'an orthographic equivalence not current later than the eighth century' which thus gives (very) tentative evidence for an early date. (Such orthography, it should be noted, is not uncommon in very late Old English manuscripts.) Newton discusses the language of the poem, its dialectal forms, and the possible use of a 'poetic register', noting syntactic, metrical and lexical considerations, many of which may point to a date of composition 'between the late seventh and early ninth centuries, perhaps in an Anglian kingdom'. The second chapter concerns itself with 'The Question of the Poem's Origins', and here, Newton traces the historical and literary contexts which might support an early date. An examination of *Beowulf* with Northern heroic material, provides evidence that the transmission of the legend of the Scyldings is 'long before the Viking period'. In Chapter 3, '*Beowulf* and the Old English Royal Pedigrees', the focus is on the Danish names in the poem which correspond with Old English genealogical concerns: the 'pedigree of King Offa' is analysed with lines 1954–62 of the poem to show that 'the allusion to Offa in *Beowulf* appears thus not to be necessarily of exclusively Mercian significance'; the pedigree of King Æthelwulf of Wessex, where it corresponds with the poem, probably shows an 'ultimate derivation from a common Old English source, perhaps a genealogy in verse'. Chapter 4 gives a detailed account of 'The Royal Name *Hroðmund*' which occurs in the poem and in the pedigree of King Ælfwald of East Anglia where it 'may have been regarded as being associated with an East Anglian dynastic origin legend' (herein, the crux of Newton's theory). Newton undertakes a very close reading of the Scylding victory-feast in *Beowulf* to show the doubts raised by this episode for a permanent peace with the Danish royal family. In so doing, his main concern is to 'wonder if Hroðmund is to share the same fate as his brother Hreðric'. In this discussion, the Eanmund and Eadgils episode (*Beowulf* 2379–96) is utilized as a parallel to the sons of Hroðgar: Hroðmund may have also gone into exile after his brother's murder. Newton suggests that the Hroðmund of the poem and that of Ælfwald's pedigree may be 'the same proto-historical figure'. Chapter 5 deals with 'Wuffings and Wulfings' (the East Anglian dynastic eponym, *Wuffa*, may perhaps have been thought of as a descendant of the Wulfings in *Beowulf*, line 471) and continues the focus on pedigrees to show that Hroðmund's mother, Wealhtheow, may have been a Wulfing princess prior to her marriage; it is she who may 'represent a vital genealogical link between the sixth-century Northern world of *Beowulf* and its Old English audience'. Thus, the occurrence of Hroðmund in Ælfwald's patrilineal pedigree might indicate 'an explicit Wuffing claim to descent from the legendary Danish' Scyldings. East Anglia, during the reign of Ælfwald (c.713–49) might be the most likely place of origin to have promoted the poem's 'prominent Danish dynastic concerns'. Newton proposes two further pieces of evidence to support this: 'the royal rite of ship-funeral', and 'Grendel and East Anglia'. In the latter, Newton points out that the *Vita Sancti Guthlaci* commissioned by Ælfwald, features fen-dwelling demons similar to Grendel and his mother. Indeed, East Anglian folklore preserves the legend of the 'Shuck' (OE *scucca*) inhabiting the fens. All in all, this is a well-executed volume which involves a great deal of scholarship, thought, and intelligent argument. It is focused at all times on the central argument and it is always clear what Newton is building up to; he is aware of the tenuous nature of some of his evidence and is not averse to presenting counter-arguments. Much of what Newton says is convincing in context, although, of course, this is not the last word on the subject.

In contrast to Newton's findings are John D. Niles's: he asks 'What are the cultural questions to which *Beowulf* is an answer' in his essay 'Locating *Beowulf* in Literary History' (*Exemplaria* 5.79–109). He observes that the extensive amount of criticism on the poem may have obscured an understanding of *Beowulf* as 'a socially embedded act'. To remedy this to a degree, Niles places the poem in its socio-historical context as a textual representative of 'a broad collective response to changes' which had affected Anglo-Saxon England up to the time of the poem's composition. Niles sees *Beowulf* as rooted in oral culture and depicting such a culture 'in imaginary guise' and gives evidence for this from his own fieldwork into oral traditions. The discussion leads Niles to a tenth-century date for the poem, a date which reflects the 'textualization' of a legendary era consistent with the concerns of the tenth-century period of 'nation-building that followed the ninth-century Viking invasions'. It may be that the *Beowulf* poet was 'a master of the aristocratic oral tradition who happened to be enlisted in an effort to reify this poem in the form of a material text'. The result is a text that reinvents the 'ancestral past in the light of Christian doctrine and Viking presence'.

J. Michael Stitt provides an intelligent exposition of important and traditional saga motifs with convenient translations in *Beowulf and the Bear's Son: Epic, Saga, and Fairytale in Northern Germanic Tradition*. He examines saga analogues in considerable detail to determine the folktale origins of Beowulf and texts such as *Grettis Saga Asmundarsonar*, and the modern-day *Märchen*, and the motifs common to these dragon-slayer legends. His survey is broad, covering, for example, Iranian traditions which share narrative features with the medieval 'mythic-heroic' texts. Focal points of the study include 'The Two-Troll Tradition', and the 'Gravemound Battle Tradition' discussed in comparison with parallels. The comparative approach shows that the transmission of these motifs is non-linear: 'the aesthetic of transmission results in variation around a stable narrative core'. At the centre of these traditions is the warrior-hero, and, of course, the villain. Stitt observes that the Grendel episode in *Beowulf* owes more to the Scandinavian tradition than any other, although each poet, including the *Beowulf*-poet, created 'specific versions' of the theme. The tradition is, ultimately, 'a sequence of motifs related in structurally constant patterns'.

S. R. Jensen is also concerned with parallel texts, historical, and contextual evidence in *Beowulf and the Swedish Dragon* in which the dragon-slaying motif is explored in the tradition of human transformation into dragon (as in *Bærings Saga*, for example). Jensen seeks to discover: 'Could it be that this dragon represents a shape-shifted man, a villainous, human opponent who acquires and holds a vast quantity of treasure?' The dragon in *Beowulf* might then characterize the leader of a neighbouring, and malevolent, tribe. Jensen's proposal is placed in the context of Geatish vengeance against Onela for the slaying of Heardred, and linked with the use of Wiglaf's sword, originally Eanmund's. Onela himself thus becomes Jensen's 'shape-shifter' dragon (see especially *Beowulf* lines 2391–400).

In 'The Tomb of Beowulf' (in Robinson), Fred C. Robinson foregrounds the problematic nature of the poem's close at lines 3137–82 where two distinct ceremonies – cremation and burial – are provided for Beowulf. Robinson notes that the second ceremony is often seen as indicating poetic confusion about pagan burial customs; he proposes a specific significance for this second rite, however: 'that at least some in the poet's audience would have seen in the final ceremony of the poem suggestions of an apotheosis'. To demonstrate this, Robinson traces the cultural and literary context of herotheism from classical to Anglo-Saxon and Scandinavian evidence. He shows that 'allusions to deification of heroes, to worship of the dead ... are prominent in Old English and Anglo-Latin writings [such as Ælfric and Wulfstan] right up to the end of the Anglo-Saxon period'. The devotional nature of the warriors' chant at lines 3173–7 gives a 'prayer-like quality' which is suggestive of deification; furthermore, the monument that is built to house Beowulf's ashes and the treasure, can be viewed as a shrine. 'For those in the audience who thought of pagan deification, the closing rites would have been a powerful culmination of the pervasive tension throughout the poem between inspiring heroism and the sad shame of heathenism'.

T. A. Shippey approaches the speeches in *Beowulf* using modern discourse analysis in 'Principles of Conversation in Beowulfian Speech' (in John M. Sinclair, Michael Hoey and Gwyneth Fox, eds, *Techniques of Description: Spoken and Written Discourse: A Festschrift for Malcolm Coulthard*, Routledge). There are 44 speeches in Beowulf, and Shippey proposes that the application of discourse analysis (particularly the Co-operative Principle, the Politeness Principle and the Face Threatening Act) might be productive. Three things might be accomplished by this exercise: that 'speech in Old English obeys many of the laws, principles and maxims now inferred from modern English'; that 'it may bring out some distinctive qualities in the speech of Old English characters, thus indicating particularly literary or stylistic effect'; and that such an analysis might raise questions concerning whether or not 'speech is a reflection of cultural ethos'. He looks at lines 1168–88 to demonstrate that readers need to understand the 'implicature' of Wealhtheow's speech, not the implications; he analyses lines 2047–56 to show 'the speech as a whole ... constitutes an unmistakable example of the deliberate and carefully honed Face Threatening Act', a 'Conflictive Principle' (Shippey's own theory) in particular. This is a refreshing article and one which outlines the valid application of modern linguistic theories.

B. R. Hutcheson provides a close reading of '*Beowulf* 162: An Impossible Emendation' (*N&Q* 39.3–5). The manuscript line, 'hyrde ic þelan cwen', has been variously emended by the poem's editors into readings Hutcheson believes to be metrically and syntactically incorrect. Allying himself most closely with Malone's reading of 'hyrde ic þæt [Yrse wæs to On]elan cwen', Hutcheson adds that the name supplied ('Yrse') might more satisfactorily be one beginning with *h* for alliterative balance.

Richard J. Schrader discusses 'The Language on the Giant's Sword Hilt in *Beowulf*' in *NM* 94.141–7. His argument focuses around lines 1687–98, where he comments particularly on the word 'runstafas' which he interprets as '(mysterious/secret) letters'. His theory is that the inscription on the hilt is meant to be imagined as created by antediluvian giants (possibly writing in Hebrew), and that the poet has presented the words for his audience in a comprehensible language.

Jeffrey Jerome Cohen looks at the 'monstrous content' of *Beowulf*, *The Wanderer* and Ælfric's *Passio Apostolorum Petri et Pauli*, as well as some Germanic texts, in 'Old English Literature and the Work of Giants' (*Comitatus* 24.1–32). He shows the giants to be perceived as historical, in the sense that they are derived from biblical sources (though coupled with Classical, Germanic, and apocryphal material) and that the discourse (concerning giants in Old English texts) proceeded mainly in theological terms, unlike developments in their portrayal in the post-Conquest period. In 'Prey Tell: How Heroes Perceive Monsters in *Beowulf*' (*JEGP* 92.1–116), Ward Parks approaches the issue of the monsters in *Beowulf* from a modern behavioural perspective, looking at the ambivalence of Grendel and the way in which Beowulf faces him, for example, as a 'distinction between predatorial and agonistic aggression'. These two forms of aggression form the central focus for Ward's argument – while Grendel acts as predator attacking prey, Beowulf engages his foe in 'the high style, as between conspecific adversaries'; as such, the poem stands as testimony to 'the vindication of human courage in the face of a hostile world'.

Lenore Abraham analyses *Beowulf* in three parts (lines 1–1008, 1009–2199 and 2200 to the end) in 'The Decorum of *Beowulf*' (*PQ* 72.267–87). She sees these three parts as representative respectively of youth (beginnings, and impetuous faults of youth here associated with Grendel), middle age (present time, and faults associated with middle age as represented by Grendel's mother), and old age (endings, plenitude, and where the dragon represents the cursed nature of the past) linked by Beowulf's rise and fall. She discusses Christian virtues prominent in the poem which suggest an Anglo-Saxon or Anglo-Danish 'argument to newly converted Scandinavians ... and of their dire need for the Providence of a Christian God'.

In '*Murnan* or *Wrecan*: The Idea of Vengeance in *Beowulf*' (in Ruud, ed.), Thomas J. Gasque sees the concepts of 'mourning' and 'revenge' as central to the poem. He examines a selection of points in the poem which feature retribution to attempt to show that the poet 'rejects not only the system [of revenge] but the values of Beowulf himself'.

Mary Flavia Godfrey looks at the symbolism of the head in '*Beowulf* and *Judith*: Thematizing Decapitation in Old English Poetry' (*TSLL* 35.1–43). She focuses on *Beowulf*'s 'abiding interest in the potent symbolism of dismemberment' as seen, for example, in Beowulf's return from the mere to Heorot clutching the head of Grendel. Godfrey illustrates that the head was regarded as the locus of intellect and creation, and that parts of the body form a point of 'poetic elaboration' generating characters' own versions of events preceding the victory. Godfrey's aim is to 'offer an explanation for the power of heads as literary and cultural symbols' in *Beowulf* and *Judith*. *Judith*, she proposes, is included in Cotton Vitellius A.xv precisely because of scenes similar to those in *Beowulf* involving decapitation and dismemberment. (In this part of her discussion, she takes much for granted involving the date and provenance of the Nowell Codex.) In comparing the scenes of Grendel's head viewed by Heorot, and Holofernes's viewed by the Hebrews, Godfrey points out the shared features: 'heads, for Judith and Hroþgar, are objects for gaze and study'; these scenes 'are moments of narrative recitation by their heroic characters'.

Finally, E. L. Risden has produced a translation of *Beowulf* in *Beowulf: A Student's Edition*. The aim is to give an accurate translation which is uncluttered by on-the-page apparatus. The admirably readable translation is thus printed in the same manner as edited verse, with the two half-lines split by the caesura; alliteration is not retained. A useful glossary of names and (very) select bibliography accompany the text.

9. Other Poems

Janet Cooper has edited an extensive and important volume that asks, among other things, how authoritative *The Battle of Maldon* might be as an historical source, and how the poem might have distorted scholars' views of the real battle. In *The Battle of Maldon: Fiction and Fact*, 13 essays, from a variety of disciplinary approaches, deal with a range of issues concerning the poem, its reception history, its cultural and historical contexts, and other available forms of historical evidence for England in the late tenth century. It is a valuable companion to D. G. Scragg's edited volume published in 1991 (*YWES* 72.91–2). Among the essays are P. Sawyer's 'The Scandinavian Background', 'Early Medieval Warfare' by Karl Leyser, 'A Geological Reconstruction of the Site of the Battle of Maldon' by George and Susan Petty, and 'The Battle of Maldon and the Minting of Crux Pennies in Essex: *Post Hoc Propter Hoc*' by D. M. Metcalf and W. Lean. Warwick Rodwell uses place-name, archaeological, military and geographical information to discover the site of the Battle of *Assandun* in Essex in 1016. In his 'The Battle of *Assandun* and its Memorial Church: A Reappraisal', Rodwell meticulously sifts through the evidence for four possible sites, concluding that Ashdon in North Essex is the most probable location for the battle. James Campbell, in the opening essay, places *The Battle of Maldon* in its most immediate cultural context in 'England, *c.*991'. He discusses, for example, Ramsey Abbey and Ely and their links with wealthy secular patrons – links which extend to historical interests and attitudes common to the monastic and aristocratic milieu. Campbell examines literacy, and literary composition in England at that time, which ultimately results in his supposition that the poem may have been 'composed for recitation at such a *convivium* as ... concluded the great court day on which the foundation of Eynsham was confirmed'. Absence of certain textual features in the poem, such as any emphasis on the 'holy war' of the Christian English against the Vikings, leads Campbell to conclude that the poem may have been composed shortly after the battle itself, 'before the full seriousness of the new wave of Viking invasions was apparent', and that it may be 'a product ... of the relative peace and order of the 990s'. Cyril Hart provides a detailed historical and demographic context for the poem in his thorough essay on 'Essex in the Tenth Century', while Pauline Stafford analyses 'Kinship and Women in the World of *Maldon*: Byrhtnoth and his Family'. She looks at the heroes of the poem and their relationships and descendants, such as Æthelgyth, the last-known survivor of Byrhtnoth's family, and a wealthy woman at the time of the Domesday survey. Much of what we know of the hero in *Maldon* is due to the will of the female survivors which ultimately illustrates how much women were affected by the issue of lordship and the male world of battle and lordship with their due rewards.

A comment by D. G. Scragg in his essay reminds us of the importance of *The Battle of Maldon* as history as well as literature: 'If the only contemporary reference to survive had been the few lines in the *Anglo-Saxon Chronicle*, the battle of Maldon nowadays would be no more than the briefest footnote in the history books.' Scragg's '*The Battle of Maldon*: Fact or Fiction' examines the reliability of the account of the battle in the poem. He assesses critics' views of the historicity of the text beginning with its earliest edition by Thomas Hearne in 1726. The tradition of viewing the poem as an historical document is well-attested (Stenton, for example, treats it as such) until recent reappraisals which have considered the work as partially fictional – 'fictional because such facts as it reports are given in a way that forces the audience to see them in a particular light'. Scragg's point is that as readers we must beware of the poet's manipulation, and read all the more carefully to distinguish between reality and invention, art and truth. Scragg provides an overview on such critical debates, focusing on the issue of the poem's date: how soon after the battle was the poem composed? Using convincing orthographical evidence, Scragg postulates a late tenth-century date. To conclude, he compares the unity of art and selective actuality in Tennyson's *Charge of the Light Brigade* with *Maldon* in an effective examination of poetic tone which demonstrates how reality and poetic art are intermingled. For after all, as Scragg states: 'in his imagery, in his characterisation and in the interspersed comments of the authorial voice, ... the poet is saying: Honour the dead, they died well'. Paul E. Szarmach also compares *Maldon* with other battle poems in 'The (Sub) Genre of *The Battle of Maldon*' by placing *Maldon* in the context of earlier continental texts that also deal with Christian versus Viking and which are thus, also a cross between literature and history. The comparative texts are *Das Ludwigslied*, which celebrates Louis III of France's victory over the Danes in 881, and *Bella Parisiacae Urbis*, composed by Abbo of Saint-Germain-des-Près, which relates to events in 885–96. From his analyses, several 'generic' elements common to these texts can be elucidated; for example, the moral framework, 'the positive depiction of *aristeia*', and the commemoration of Christian heroes. These texts thus illuminate the issue of 'ofermod' in *Maldon*, and its relatively secular spirit, and thereby provide readers of *Maldon* with a valuable analogous setting to gain 'a better view of the literary choices the *Maldon* poet made'. Ute Schwab regards the poem as something of a panegyric in '*The Battle of Maldon*: A Memorial Poem'. She concentrates on the '"non-realistic" sphere' of the poem – the speeches of Byrhtnoth and his retainers by placing the poem within the larger framework of European heroic poetry. She begins, for example, by looking at the 'rites of death' within a broad range of texts to show how the *Maldon* poet adheres to conventions like the dying speeches of heroes; other traditions are abandoned by the *Maldon* poet, however, such as the *dissonis vocibus* which is replaced by 'one funerary service alone: vengeance'. This is a fascinating survey which throws new light onto the compositional techniques of the poem. Finally in this volume is Roberta Frank's entertaining and informative '*The Battle of Maldon*: Its reception, 1726–1906'. These chronological parameters are set by the first edition of the poem and the publication of Le Queux's novel *The Invasion of 1910*. Between these two dates the Old English poem 'seems to have lived as something of a recluse, rarely going out into society', an odd phenomenon considering the nineteenth-century's love of the heroic. The poem in this latter period was popular among scholars, but did not, it seems, capture the public's imagination. Frank believes this to be the case even today: 'Maldon is a losing battle in more ways than one; for all its fine words and fragmentary splendour, the Old English poem has not yet become a household word.' It is probably the case that even a fine volume such as Cooper's is unlikely to alter the situation!

Thomas D. Hill analyses *Solomon and Saturn I* from a comparative viewpoint in 'Tormenting the Devil with Boiling Drops: An Apotropaic Motif in the Old English *Solomon and Saturn I* and Old Norse-Icelandic Literature' (*JEGP* 92.157–66). Highlighting the difficulties in determining the literary form and function of the poem (Hill suggests it may be a gloss on a Pater Noster amulet), Hill focuses on the claim in a passage surviving in two versions of the poem that the devil can be tormented by drops of blood from the Pater Noster. He provides a translation of the passage which reinterprets 'stigað' at line 44 to mean 'fall on'. Literary analogues support Hill's reading: *Laxdæla saga*, for example, and *Heimskringla* share the motif of a saint's prayers burning a demonic foe. Earlier images from which this motif may have developed are found in Christian-Latin *oratio fervens*, as well as Germanic heroic myth and literature where it is attested that 'tears can disturb the rest of the beloved dead'.

Miriam Youngerman Miller uses modern technology in an attempt to recreate Old English verse, reporting on her findings in 'Isochrony in Old English Poetry: Two Performances of *Cædmon's Hymn*' (*OralT* 8.324–54). Using recordings of the poem taken from the Moore manuscript read by Thomas Cable and Robert Creed, Miller analyses the results of the sound spectrograph and Visi-pitch output. She bases her discussion firmly within the context of the debate on isochrony in Old English verse (and, indeed, English as whole), and finds that there appears to be some degree of 'freedom in regard to duration as long as [the] performance contained a core of roughly isochronous metrical units'.

M. J. Toswell considers the relationship between 'The Metrical Psalter and the *Menologium*' (*NM* 94.249–57), poems contained in Paris, Bibliothèque nationale MS lat. 8224, and BL Cotton Tiberius B.i respectively. These texts are closely linked as three lines that occur in the latter approximate to Psalm 117.22 of the *Paris Psalter*. Toswell examines the available evidence for the manuscripts to determine if date, place or origin can be ascertained by the demonstrable link between them. She deduces that the *Menologium* may be connected to Canterbury in the tenth-century Reform period, and that it descends from a different exemplar to the *Paris Psalter*. This indicates that versions of the metrical psalms were in circulation in southern England and were found to be useful to manuscript compilers of the later tenth and early eleventh centuries. Rolf H. Bremmer Jr identifies 'An Old English Rhyming Curse' (*N&Q* 40.434–5) which appears to have been current at Bath Abbey towards the end of the eleventh century. The curse, 'Crist hine ablende þis gewrit awende', occurs five times at the close of manumissions in CCCC 140. Bremmer points out that the preference for rhyme over alliteration may foreshadow poetic developments in Middle English.

10. Prose

Susan Irvine has edited *Old English Homilies from Bodley 343* for EETS. The publication of newly edited twelfth-century prose is to be warmly welcomed. Irvine uses the opportunity to present new codicological and linguistic data though rather more detailed palaeographical information would have been helpful. The codex appears to have derived from a single exemplar, itself a compilation from a number of individual booklets: this presents a complex network of sources, and lack of overall chronological or thematic design for Bodley 343. Evidence suggests that the manuscript was produced for devotional reading and pastoral instruction for the secular clergy. Irvine's study of the manuscript's make-up has important implications for our understanding of the way in which twelfth-century codices were compiled; for the reasons behind production in the vernacular; and for the material that was available to the scriptoria where English texts were copied.

Irvine edits seven homiletic texts conservatively: four are by Ælfric, and new data are provided to reinforce this ascription: she prints the texts as verse to emphasize the alliterative and metrical flow of the style. The remaining three homilies, printed as prose, are anonymous; they are derived from Old English exemplars but exhibit twelfth-century linguistic alteration. The apparatus and notes are, in themselves, useful tools for ascertaining scribal misreadings, later uses of the manuscript, and Latin sources. As is the EETS custom, each text is preceded by an introduction which also provides valuable source information.

Bodley 343, according to Irvine's linguistic and contextual analysis, was produced in the West Midlands at a centre near Worcester, though probably not in Worcester itself. Her research has been taken one step further by Peter Kitson in his article 'Old English Dialects and the Stages of Transition to Middle English' (*FLH* (1992) 11.27–87), which is more precise than Irvine in assigning the production of Bodley 343 to Hereford. If Kitson is correct, this will be of considerable importance to researchers working in the field of twelfth-century vernacular manuscript studies.

Joyce Hill writes on 'Reform and Resistance: Preaching Styles in Late Anglo-Saxon England' (in Hamesse, ed.), in which she surveys the homiletic tradition in late-tenth- and early-eleventh-century England. She concentrates on Ælfric's concerns to emulate monastic reform within the secular church and on his compositions which tended away from error by omitting unorthodox material. Such omissions, coupled with Ælfric's statements in the prologues to his Pastoral letters, show that he 'knew himself as a reformer'. This self-positioning of Ælfric in relation to the Reform movement and to those who came after him is Hill's main focus: Ælfric is both traditionalist (adhering ultimately to patristic sources) and 'modern' (in his use of intermediate sources written as a result of the Reform). His attempts to control his authorial and authoritative position were thwarted by his successors who 'plundered' his texts. Hill outlines the 'selective appropriation' of Ælfric's 'eventful' texts, an appropriation and re-use that would, presumably, have alarmed Ælfric, and she calls for greater scholarly attention to be paid to the evidence of reader-response that these later Old English uses of Ælfric can yield.

Mary Clayton writes a detailed account of 'Of Mice and Men: Ælfric's Second Homily for the Feast of a Confessor' (*LeedsSE* 24.1–26). This homily 'becomes chiefly one on the superiority of the religious state, and of teachers in particular' which, in its second part, concentrates on the vengeance of God. Clayton shows by an historical contextualization, that the period in which the homily was composed (*c.*1007) was a turbulent one which may be directly reflected in the nature of its composition. The use of divine retribution within the homily may indicate a warning on Ælfric's part to those in power in the last years of Æthelræd's reign, 'an urgent wish to make known his dismay and his opposition to recent developments'.

In 'Ælfric's Devils' (*N&Q* 40.286–7), Margaret Locherbie-Cameron examines Ælfric's creative processes in the portrait of the devil in *De Auguriis*. It is a portrait which does not fully derive from Ælfric's cited source, Caesarius of Arles. The devil is shown as flying throughout the world, a motif which is used elsewhere in Ælfric's corpus. Locherbie-Cameron identifies 'wicked flying spirits' in Bede's commentary and a Gregorian homily (texts known to Ælfric) and suggests that this demonstrates further Ælfric's memory and 'ability to meld material from divergent sources'.

Two articles deal with the use of language in the Ælfric corpus. Else Fausboll makes 'A Contribution to the Study of Ælfric's use of Accusative/Dative (/Genitive) after Prepositions' (*ES* 74.295–323) where she focuses on texts which have not, as yet, been studied extensively such as the *Heptateuch* and *De temporibus anni*, and finds that nearly all texts have more accusatives than datives. Peter Kitson provides extensive data in 'Geographical Variation in Old English Prepositions and the Location of Ælfric's and Other Literary Dialects' (*ES* 74.1–50). Kitson challenges the findings of Gneuss and others in their analyses of a Winchester vocabulary. He offers boundary surveys of land charters as sources of dialectal information to review the evidence for assigning provenance to manuscripts based on scribal forms in literary texts.

J. E. Cross and Alan Brown illustrate Wulfstan's use of 'the miscellaneous collection of homilies and sermons' composed by Abbo of Saint-Germain-des-Près ('Wulfstan and Abbo of Saint-Germain-des-Près', *Mediaevalia* 15 [1993 for 1989].71–91). A complex discussion of the manuscripts in which Wulfstan's hand is thought to appear provides information for determining the transmission of Abbo's texts as appropriated by Wulfstan. The nature of the adapted sources indicates a particular interest on the part of the compiler of the manuscripts (probably Wulfstan himself) in which these sermons appear: Corpus Christi College, Cambridge, 190, pp. 247–9, and pp. 249–52 provide such examples. Significant textual expansions and abbreviations in Abbo's sermons, and those of Wulfstan, are noted in a finely detailed argument concerning the transmission of the texts; for example, chapter numbers within Copenhagen Royal Library *Gl.Kgl.S* 1595 (for which, see section 2 above) suggest that the compiler may well have drawn upon an extensive collection of Abbo's sermons.

Staying with the Reform in tenth-century Anglo-Saxon England, Lucia Kornexl has edited *Die 'Regularis Concordia' und ihre altenglische Interlinearversion*. The introduction provides a great deal of information about the text: she examines the issue of authorship, its contents (by manuscript chapter), its historical source, and political context. A very useful linguistic analysis of the Old English gloss suggests that it may have been composed at Christ Church, Canterbury. Kornexl bases her edition on the versions of the *Regularis Concordia* in BL Cotton Faustina B.iii and Cotton Tiberius A.iii (which is continuously glossed in the vernacular) which date from the middle of the eleventh century using as her fair text the Tiberius version with collated readings from Faustina. Full apparatus and notes make this a most impressive and useful piece of scholarship; there seems little doubt that this will become the definitive edition for the text.

Beate Günzel has edited *Ælfwine's Prayerbook (London, British Library, Cotton Titus D.xxvi + xxvii)* for the Henry Bradshaw Society series. The manuscripts, originally one volume (with Titus D.xvii being the first part), come from New Minster, Winchester, and are dateable to the first half of the eleventh century. Günzel describes the manuscripts' palaeography, codicology and miniatures, and provides a detailed analysis of the contents, which include a calendar, computistical texts, prognostications, Ælfric's *De temporibus anni*, prayers, offices, a collectar and a litany. The Old English texts, with analogous examples, are examined contextually and linguistically; they are composed in a late West Saxon dialect. The editions themselves are immaculate and clearly laid out; they are followed by appendices which detail Anglo-Saxon manuscripts containing computistical material, and private prayers (the latter appendix also contains elaborate collation tables). This edition is a valuable research aid; as the manuscripts' contents are so varied, their availability in this scholarly work will be of considerable importance.

A note on an anonymous homily is given by Sarah Cutforth in 'Delivering the Damned in Old English Homilies: An Additional Note' (*N&Q* 40.435–7). This motif of delivering the damned is found in CCCC 41 and CCCC 303. Part of the motif in the former is omitted in CCCC 303's version. Cutforth suggests the omission may be the result of eyeskip, or may be the deliberate excision of theologically problematic material such as that condemned by Ælfric himself.

M. Mc. Gatch provides an evaluation of the evidence relating to ecclesiastical buildings in the *Vision of Leofric* in 'Miracles in architectural settings: Christ Church, Canterbury and St Clement's, Sandwich in the Old English *Vision of Leofric*' (*ASE* 22.227–52). The first vision at Christ Church provides information about the building before it was burnt in 1067: specifically, details about the main public entry to the church at the south tower can be gleaned. The second vision, also at Christ Church, details the interior of the building – the monks' seats and the physical arrangement of altars and crosses. The third vision at Sandwich gives the earliest evidence for the interior of St Clement's Church: in particular, for a cross standing in the northeastern corner with a *dextera Dei* upon its upper arm. Gatch shows by his methodical and detailed discussion that important information can be gained from a close and intelligent reading of Anglo-Saxon texts, including those which are often neglected by scholars.

Turning to saints' lives, Allen Frantzen writes on female saints in the edition of *Speculum* (68.2) devoted to 'Studying Medieval Women: Sex, Gender, Feminism'. His essay, 'Why Women Aren't Enough' (445–71), he declares is the contribution of the volume's 'token man'. He discusses the Old English lives of Agatha, Eugenia, and Euphrosyne as examples of the 'manly woman'. Agatha transcends, albeit briefly, the female body; Eugenia and Euphrosyne, as transvestite saints, demonstrate 'The secondariness of the female [which] is reinforced since the women can be saved only by becoming like men'. Within his discussion, Frantzen covers a vast amount of medieval and modern ground examining grammatical gender in Old English, what 'gender studies' have come to mean, and the role of the contemporary university. This is a politically and intellectually astute essay that tackles, with characteristic forthrightness, issues and areas of scholarship that ought to be of key interest to the discipline. Jonathan Wilcox is concerned with the endings of saints' lives in 'Famous Last Words: Ælfric's Saints Facing Death' (*EssaysMedSt* 10.1–13).

Timothy Graham edits 'The Old English Liturgical Directions in Corpus Christi College, Cambridge, MS 422 (*Anglia* 111.439–46). This composite volume – also known as The Red Book of Darley – dates from the mid-tenth to the twelfth centuries. Graham has been able, with various lighting tools, to read previously illegible portions of the text and provides a detailed edition of his findings from pages 367–421 which include rubrics and directions in Old English for baptism, and anointing the sick; and pages 555–70 and 491–506 which contain rubricated directions and headings for services in Holy Week and Easter Saturday.

Two pieces this year deal with *The Anglo-Saxon Chronicle*. Fredrik J. Heinemann discusses ' "Cynewulf and Cyneheard" and *Landnamabok*: Another Narrative Tradition' in *LeedsSE* 24.57–89. He shows that the Old Icelandic text can be regarded as something of a parallel text to the Old English chronicle entry. Heinemann argues that neither can withstand the 'close rhetorical analysis' devoted to them by scholars (particularly in the case of the famous Old English narrative) as both are summaries of stories rather than elaborate prose compositions. John G. Johansen looks at 'Language, Structure, and Theme in the "Cynewulf and Cyneheard" Episode' (*ELN* 31.3–8) to show that the annal reveals an artistry (of three sub-divisions, verbal parallels etc.) which emphasizes 'the glorification of Cynewulf and those loyal to him for their embodiment of heroic values'.

The Alfredian translation of Bede's *Ecclesiastical History* provides the source for Gerald Russello's 'Bede and Cædmon' (*ELN* 31.1–2) in which it is noted that *surgebat a media caena et ...* in Bede is translated as 'þonne aras he for scome from þæm symble ond ...' Russello suggests that the translator mistook *caena* for *caenum* ('befoul', 'filthy') and subsequently gave his mistranslation a moral connotation. Michael Treschow has found 'Echoes of the *Periphyseon* in the Third Book of Alfred's *Soliloquies*' (*N&Q* 40.281–6) which concern the soul's condition in the afterlife. He notes that Alfred abandoned Augustine's *De Vivendo Deo* in this portion of the *Soliloquies*, but that such unconventional elements of Alfred's works are similar to those found in John Scottus Eriugena's *Periphyseon*. Alfred's knowledge of this work may have been a result of contact with his circle of scholars, among them, Grimbald or John the Old Saxon, who knew of, or may have had copies of, Eriugenian works.

There are a number of articles on legal prose: Carole Hough uses comparative linguistic and contextual evidence to offer 'A Reappraisal of Æthelberht 84' (*NMS* 37.1–6) which reads 'Gif gængang geweorðeþ xxxv scill' 7 cyninge xv scillingas'. She reinterprets 'gængang' as akin to 'to block someone's way' or 'to obstruct' and does not accept earlier translations of 'pregnant' or 'return'. Christine Fell, in 'An Appendix to Carole Hough's Article "A Reappraisal of Æthelberht 84"' (NMS 37.7–8) offers a further interpretation of 'gǣngang' as 'fight' (the fight being between two men over a woman when put in the context of Æthelberht 82 and 83). The important implication of both these articles is that Anglo-Saxonists should, as Fell puts it, 'cease to take on trust the desperate suggestions of earlier lexicographers' when other interpretations offer better lexical, contextual, and legal sense.

Simon Keynes has travelled far in his search for material relating to Anglo-Saxon England, and in so doing has come across Brussels, Bibliothèque Royale, 7965–73 (3723), formerly MS 157 in the Bollandists' Library ('A lost cartulary of St Albans Abbey', ASE 22.253–79). This manuscript, transcribed from a variety of sources in the seventeenth century by the Bollandists, contains a number of items of interest to Anglo-Saxonists. Keynes concentrates on one of these items – a transcript of a St Albans cartulary containing copies of pre- and post-Conquest charters, and a collection of papal privileges, all of which derive from a manuscript now lost. Keynes catalogues these charters which date from Offa's reign to the twelfth century, and goes on to discuss the pre-Conquest texts which 'are not authentic in their received form'. An appendix gives an edition and translation of the will of Eadwine of Coddington (c.1050) with commentary.

In 'Never say nefa again' (NM 94.27–35), Kathryn A. Lowe looks at the use of the word nefa and its meanings in the Anglo-Saxon corpus of charters, where it is used only three times. Usually assumed to mean 'nephew', Lowe demonstrates through careful analysis of the charter material, and by means of reconstructed genealogies, that the meaning of nefa is likely to approximate more generally to '(younger or contemporary male) relative'. In another article, '"As Fre as Thowt"?: Some Medieval Copies and Translations of Old English Wills' (EMS 4.1–23), Lowe asks how accurately do post-Conquest copies of pre-Conquest legal texts represent the original. She finds that the closer in date to the original the copy is, the less reliable it may be as a witness to the exemplar; the later copyists tended to adhere as closely as possible to their exemplars, transcribing rather than altering, probably because they did not fully understand the language with which they were dealing.

Books Reviewed

Bately, Janet, Michelle Brown, and Jane Roberts, eds. A Palaeographer's View: Selected Writings of Julian Brown. HM. pp. 371. £48. ISBN 0 905203 20 8.

Boyarin, Jonathan. ed. The Ethnography of Reading. UCalP.

Conner, Patrick W. Anglo-Saxon Exeter: A Tenth-Century Cultural History. Studies in Anglo-Saxon History IV. B&B. pp. 279. £45. ISBN 0 85115 307 0.

Cooper, Janet. The Battle of Maldon: Fiction and Fact. Hambledon. pp. 265. ISBN 1 85285 065 5.

Cox, Jeffrey N., and Larry J. Reynolds, eds. New Historical Literary Study: Essays on Reproducing Texts, Representing History. PrincetonUP. pp. 337. pb. ISBN 0 691 01546 5.

Cross, James E., and Jennifer Morrish Tunberg, eds. The Copenhagen Wulfstan Collection: Copenhagen Kongelige Bibliotek GL. KGL. SAM. 1595. EEMF XXV. R&B. intro. pp. 62. pb, lb. ISBN 87 423 0515 2, 87 423 0517 9.

Crossley-Holland, Kevin, trans. *The Exeter Book Riddles*. rev. edn. Penguin. pp. 124. £5.99. ISBN 0 14 043367 8.

Dumville, David N. *English Caroline Script and Monastic History: Studies in Benedictinism, A.D. 950–1030*. Studies in Anglo-Saxon History VI. Boydell. pp. 196. £35. ISBN 0 85115 323 2.

Frank, Roberta, ed. *The Politics of Editing Medieval Texts. Papers Given at the Twenty-Seventh Annual Conference on Editorial Problems, University of Toronto, 1–2 November, 1991*. AMS. pp. 181. $29.50. ISBN 0 404 63677 2.

Fulk, R. D. *A History of Old English Meter*. Middle Ages Series. UPennP. £40. pp. 466. ISBN 0 8122 3157 0.

Günzel, Beate, ed. *Ælfwine's Prayerbook (London, British Library, Cotton Titus D.xxvi + xxvii)*. Henry Bradshaw Society CVIII. Boydell. pp. 227. £25. ISBN 1 870252 04 7.

Hamesse, Jacqueline. ed. *De L'Homélie au Sermon: Histoire de la Prédication Médiévale*. Univ. of Louvain. Brepols. pp. 380.

Hasenfratz, Robert J. *'Beowulf' Scholarship: An Annotated Bibliography, 1979–1990*. Garland Medieval Bibliographies 14. Garland. pp. 442. $66. ISBN 0 8153 0084 0.

Herbert, Kathleen. *Spellcraft: Old English Heroic Legends*. ASB. pp. 283. £6.95. ISBN 0 9516209 9 1.

Higley, Sarah Lynn. *Between Languages: The Uncooperative Text in Early Welsh and Old English Nature Poetry*. PSUP. pp. 314. £37. ISBN 0 271 00876 8.

Irvine, Susan, ed. *Old English Homilies from MS Bodley 343*. EETS o.s. 302. OUP. pp. 242. £20. ISBN 0 19 722304 4.

Jensen, S. R. *Beowulf and the Swedish Dragon*. ARRC. pp. 18. ISBN 0 646 16911 4.

Kornexl, Lucia. *Die Regularis Concordia und Ihre Altenglische Inter-linearversion*. Texte und Untersuchungen zur englischen Philologie 17. Fink. pp. 423. DM 158. ISBN 3 7705 2868 9.

Lapidge, Michael. *Anglo-Latin Literature, 900–1066*. Hambledon. pp. 506. ISBN 1 85285 012 4.

Newton, Sam. *The Origins of 'Beowulf' and the Pre-Viking Kingdom of East Anglia*. Brewer. pp. 177. hb £35, pb £12.95. ISBN 0 85991 361 9, 0 85991 472 0.

Page, R. I. *Matthew Parker and His Books*. MIP. pp. 133. $40. ISBN 1 879288 20 6.

Risden, E. L., trans. *Beowulf: A Student's Edition*. Whitston. pp. 99. $6.50. ISBN 0 87875 455 5.

Robinson, Fred C. *The Tomb of Beowulf and Other Essays on Old English*. Blackwell. pp. 335. £45. ISBN 0 631 17328 5.

Ruud, Jay, ed. *Proceedings of the First Dakotas Conference on Earlier British Literature*. NSU Press. pp. 117. ISBN 1 883120 004.

Schrader, Richard J. *Old English Poetry and the Genealogy of Events*. Medieval Texts and Studies 12. Colleagues (USA). B&B (Eur.). pp. 206. £19.50. ISBN 0 937191 52 3.

Stitt, J. Michael. *Beowulf and the Bear's Son: Epic, Saga, and Fairytale in Northern Germanic Tradition*. Garland (1992). pp. 247. ISBN 0 8240 7440 8.

Whitman, F. H. *A Comparative Study of Old English Metre*. UTorP. pp. 170. $66. ISBN 0 8020 0540 3.

Wine, Joseph D. *Figurative Language in Cynewulf.* Lang. pp. 153. £31. ISBN 0 8204 1936 2.

Wright, Charles D. *The Irish Tradition in Old English Literature.* Cambridge Studies in Anglo-Saxon England 6. CUP. pp. 321. £37.50. ISBN 0 521 41909 3.

III

Middle English

CATHERINE BATT, GILLIAN RUDD and ALAN FLETCHER

This chapter has the following sections: 1. General and Miscellaneous; 2. Alliterative Poetry; 3. The *Gawain*-Poet; 4. *Piers Plowman*; 5. Romances; 6. Gower, Lydgate, Hoccleve; 7. Middle Scots Poetry; 8. Lyrics and Miscellaneous Verse; 9. Malory and Caxton; 10. Other Prose; 11. Drama. Sections 1, 5, 6 and 9 are by Catherine Batt; sections 3, 10 and 11 are by Alan Fletcher; and sections 2, 4, 7 and 8 are by Gillian Rudd.

1. General and Miscellaneous

Feminist perspectives continue to offer lively insights into medieval literature and its contexts, and the most perceptive contributions redefine and refine the theoretical frames of discussion as they re-read the literature. Many of the pieces are highly elaborate, the subtlety of the argument (and sometimes the wordiness of expression) making it difficult to paraphrase without risking misrepresentation and (as with other books and articles reviewed) lack of space precludes detailed analysis of, and engagement with, their methodology and the topics they present. Among the challenging volumes to have appeared this year, *Feminist Approaches to the Body in Medieval Literature*, edited by Linda Lomperis and Sarah Stanbury, expressly seeks to break down boundaries and hierarchies between modern theory and medieval literature, and is a welcome addition to the growing mass of critical work in this field. The essays concentrate on a range of medieval literature, although all are linked by an interest in the relation between the physical and the textual. Margaret Brose, in 'Petrarch's Beloved Body: "Italia mia"', considers how Petrarch's figuring of Italy as a mutilated woman reinforces the notion of power, in politics as in poetry, as masculine. In 'Unruly Bodies and Ruling Practices: Chaucer's *Physician's Tale* as Socially Symbolic Act', Linda Lomperis argues that the notion of the body as a site of instability evident in this text exposes and facilitates the decline of the late medieval monarchy's political power. Peggy McCracken, 'The Body Politic and the Queen's Adulterous Body in French Romance', focusing especially on *Cligés*, studies the complex of contradictory metaphors describing the queen's body in romance, and how she figures as a threat to notions of unity and to narrative propriety alike. Theresa Coletti, 'Purity and Danger: The Paradox of Mary's Body and the En-gendering of the Infancy Narrative in the English Mystery Cycles', suggests that the playwriters employ the paradox of Mary's body as virginal and pregnant to challenge rather than to endorse traditional discourses of gender, both in their own right and as part of the exposition of the Christian mystery. Sarah Stanbury's thoughtful 'Feminist Masterplots: The Gaze on the Body of *Pearl*'s Dead Girl', uses film and psychoanalytic theory to consider the nature of the Dreamer's relation to the Pearl-Maiden, but as she shows, the poem itself, through its shifting presentation of the Maiden as 'daughter, lover, mother', conveys a far richer sense of loss than does a 'phallocentric' theoretical perspective. Gayle Margherita, in 'Originary Fantasies and Chaucer's *Book of the Duchess*', similarly employs psychoanalytic theory, to suggest that in this poem the author explores 'the tension between an ideologically necessary recuperative impulse and a fantasmatic identification with the position of lack'. In 'Medieval Medical Views of Women and Female Spirituality in the *Ancrene Wisse* and Julian of Norwich's *Showings*', Elizabeth Robertson considers to what extent male authors are influenced by medical lore in their construction of female spirituality, and argues that in her own practice Julian appropriates such preoccupations with the body positively. For Wendy Harding, 'Body into Text: *The Book of Margery Kempe*', Kempe's expression of her spirituality through her female body challenges hierarchies and binary oppositions, looking forward instead to a dialogic relation between body and text, male and female. E. Jane Burns's clever exposition of the body in 'This Prick Which Is Not One: How Women Talk Back in Old French Fabliaux', wittily charts the breakdown in fabliau of distinctions between mind and body through the phenomenon of talking vaginas, to claim the female body challenges the male hierarchy. Helen Solterer, 'At the Bottom of Mirage, a Woman's Body: *Le Roman de la Rose* of Jean Renart', claims that in moving between the literal and the metaphoric in its representation of the female body the text indicates a broader range of representation for the feminine in medieval narrative than some current critical perspectives allow for. A useful bibliography on 'The Body, Gender, and Sexuality in History and Theory' completes the volume. The thoughtful reader will find much to contest as well as much to agree with, regarding both methodologies and conclusions, but this remains a valuable book, both for mapping out the work in this area and for stimulating debate on the subject.

Ulrike Wiethaus has edited *Maps of Flesh and Light. The Religious Experience of Medieval Women Mystics*, interdisciplinary essays that through a range of critical approaches demonstrate the diversity of women's religious experiences and their creativity throughout the medieval period. Jo Ann McNamara, in 'The Rhetoric of Orthodoxy: Clerical Authority and Female Innovation in the Struggle with Heresy', considers the measure of independence allowed to female religious in spite of the Church's increasing tendency to silence women, and how constructions of women's spirituality made their position precarious when the Church took a stand against heresy. Laurie Finke, 'Mystical Bodies and the Dialogics of Vision', taking as her examples male-authored lives of women mystics and work by Gertrude the Great, Angela of Foligno, and Julian of Norwich, stresses the roles of suffering and creativity in women's mystical experience and language, and how women found a voice in their claim to be instruments of the Divine. Ellen Ross also emphasizes suffering in '"She Wept and Cried Right Loud for Sorrow and for Pain": Suffering, the Spiritual Journey, and Women's Experience in Late Medieval Mysticism', but from a more theological point of view, emphasizing that both Margery Kempe and Julian of Norwich develop an idea of suffering as part of an understanding of God's compassion. E. Ann Matter's 'Interior Maps of an External External: The Spiritual Rhetoric of Maria Domitilla Galluzzi d'Acqui', has a gloomier assessment of woman's spirituality in a sixteenth-century context, tracing how the *imitatio Christi* has, by this time, been transformed from a radical to an institutionalized means of spiritual expression. Margot Schmidt, 'An Example of Spiritual Friendship: The Correspondence Between Heinrich of Nördlingen and Margaretha Ebner', looks at the spiritual support of friendships between religious men and women, and, in the case of Margaretha, what a male–female correspondence can reveal about the deep respect in which a female religious could be held. Ulrike Wiethaus's own contribution, 'In Search of Medieval Women's Friendships: Hildegard of Bingen's Letters to Her Female Contemporaries', addresses what she sees as the freer parameters of female friendships, and explores how such relationships offer support within a female community.

The last two articles offer different perspectives on the place of art in women's religious experience. 'Reality as Imitation: The Role of Religious Imagery Among the Beguines of the Low Countries', by Joanna E. Ziegler, shows how the images in Beguinages encourage a preoccupation with spiritual motherhood as the central means of religious experience, although the question of the extent to which the Beguines are therefore 'manipulated' by external authority is open to question, while in 'Text and Context in Hildegard of Bingen's *Ordo Virtutum*', Patricia A. Kazarow emphasizes Hildegard's autonomy in her artistic creativity.

Ulrike Wiethaus has also co-edited, with Karen Cherewatuk, a series of essays *Dear Sister. Medieval Women and the Epistolary Genre*, and in their introduction they point out how, if women 'always wrote at the margins of a realm staked out by male authors', their letters can none the less by their very nature afford us tantalizing glimpses of their lives – both public and private – and reveal something of the sophisticated nature of their literary creativity. The first three essays concentrate on the work of women writing in Latin: Karen Cherewatuk, 'Radegund and Epistolary Tradition', shows how the sixth-century saint, in the letters ascribed to her, draws on models of literary personae from both classical and Germanic sources to poetic effect, while her letters also have an important political function. Gillian T. W. Ahlgren, 'Visions and Rhetorical Strategy in the Letters of Hildegard of Bingen', finds that Hildegard, acutely aware of her position as woman visionary, deploys particular strategies to describe her visions, a language carefully nuanced according to the status and sex of her addressee, and by such means she can affirm her authority as a visionary in the eyes of men. '"Wholly Guilty, Wholly Innocent": Self-Definition in Héloïse's Letters to Abélard', by Glenda McLeod, looks at the letters as expressive of Héloïse's sense of self as a conflict between love of God and love for Abelard, and considers the consequences of this for her definition. Karen Scott, in '"Io Caterina": Ecclesiastical Politics and Oral Culture in the Letters of Catherine of Siena', describes the nature of the saint's correspondence: the 382 letters that survive show great variety and an alertness to the particular needs of her addressees. Scott also considers how their construction suggests that Catherine saw them as a natural extension of her speech, rather than written documents. Ulrike Wiethaus's study, '"If I Had an Iron Body": Femininity and Religion in the Letters of Maria de Hout', outlines the historical context of this sixteenth-century Beguine's life, and examines the nature of the 14 extant letters she wrote, which reveal different constructions of her character depending on the audience, and suggest de Hout had to negotiate her social and spiritual positions very carefully.

In '"No Writing for Writing's Sake": The Language of Service and Household Rhetoric in the Letters of the Paston Women', Diane Watt ascertains what Margaret Paston's epistolary style owes to oral forms, and also concludes from the letters that her influence, as controller of a large household, must have been considerable. Earl Jeffrey Edwards, in '"Seulette a part": The "Little Woman on the Sidelines" Takes Up Her Pen: The Letters of Christine de Pizan', shows how Christine de Pizan succeeds in synthesizing the courtly, the medieval Latin, and, especially, the humanist epistolary traditions, and also how she constructs and develops a new female voice in which to address universal human issues. This collection offers some astute readings in a promising area of study where there is still much to be done in terms of discovering and reconstructing communities of readers and writers.

The above volume shows the extent to which medieval women work within a range of cultures, within learned languages as well as the vernacular. *Women and Literature in Britain 1150–1500*, edited by Carol M. Meale, is a welcome project that gauges women's access to literature and its production in Latin and in the vernaculars current in Britain during that period. Some of the essays offer documentary evidence of women's involvement in literature and literary production, others are more speculative in their relation of art to life. The first three essays concentrate on romance in Britain: Judith Weiss, 'The Power and the Weakness of Women in Anglo-Norman Romance', raises the question of the relation between historical patrons and the characterization of women in romance narrative as powerful. Flora Alexander, 'Women as Lovers in Early English Romance', interprets romances as a site for wish-fulfilment on the part of the women in the audience. Jennifer Fellows, 'Mothers in Middle English Romance', suggests that where clerical writings tend to idealize or denigrate women, this genre allows for a more generous, but also more nuanced, presentation of mothers' characters.

Other essays bring an awareness of the difficulties of retrieving and reconstructing the nature of the relation between writing and reader reception, orality and the uncertain nature of literacy, to bear on particular aspects of women's contributions to medieval culture. Jocelyn Wogan-Browne's meticulous '"Clerc u lai, muïne u dame": Women and Anglo-Norman Hagiography in the Twelfth and Thirteenth Centuries' examines women's production and consumption of saints' lives, and makes the valuable point that we cannot be sure what particular use a female audience might have made of male-authored texts. Bella Millet, 'Women in No Man's Land: English Recluses and the Development of Vernacular Literature in the Twelfth and Thirteenth Centuries', looks at the role of vernacular religious literature in the move from oral to written during this period, and the importance of lay anchoresses in its development (although not necessarily its production).

Felicity Riddy, in 'Women Talking about the Things of God': A Late Medieval Sub-culture', adduces evidence for a 'spiritual sub-culture' among women, a supportive community which makes possible the production of female-authored texts. Carol M. Meale, '"... alle the bokes that I haue of latyn, englisch, and frensch": Laywomen and Their Books in Late Medieval England', brings together a wealth of detail about female ownership of books, and suggests ways we can find out more about women's roles as owners and patrons and their specific

contribution to medieval culture. Julia Boffey employs her expertise with manuscripts to consider the difficulties of teasing apart women's literature and literary
impersonations of women, and the special interpretative problems posed by those
works composed by women but mediated through men, and identifies the need for
a different vocabulary, one 'free from lettered associations' to discuss the nature
of women's literature, and for different approaches to its recovery. Ceridwen
Lloyd-Morgan, 'Women and their Poetry in Medieval Wales', shows how important oral composition was to women poets who were largely excluded from a
written 'tradition'.

Part 2 of volume 68 of *Speculum* contains a number of often densely argued
articles on the general theme of 'Studying Medieval Women: Sex, Gender,
Feminism'. Judith M. Bennett, 'Medievalism and Feminism', considers the role
and status of women medievalist historians in the academy in the recent past and
the present, and celebrates the new opportunities feminism offers for medieval
studies. Madeline H. Caviness, 'Patron or Matron? A Capetian Bride and a Vade
Mecum for Her Marriage Bed' (333–62) examines the tiny prayerbook, now New
York Metropolitan Museum of Art, Cloisters, 54.1.2, probably made for Jeanne
d'Evreux at the time of her marriage to Charles IV of France in 1324, and
concludes from a study of its iconography, and especially its marginalia, that it
expresses above all masculine control and construction of Jeanne and her role as
queen. Carol J. Clover, in 'Regardless of Sex: Men, Women, and Power in Early
Northern Europe' (363–87), argues from a study of the sagas and laws of
Scandinavia that one can resolve the apparent paradox by which strong women
and a contempt for the female co-exist, by concluding that this society has no
specific notion of womanhood, which makes for some fluidity in both men and
women's social status. Kathleen Biddick's intricate argument in 'Genders, Bodies, Borders: Technologies of the Visible' (389–418), offers a critique of Caroline
Walker Bynum's understanding of women's bodies and their significance, arguing that the terms of her discussion bypass the problems of understanding gender
within medieval Christianity. Nancy F. Partner, 'No Sex, No Gender' (419–43),
criticizes recent theories that see gender as wholly socially constructed, suggesting instead that ideas of sex and gender, and body as distinct from society, are
insufficient to address difficult issues of 'psychosexual identity and collective
culture'.

Sarah Beckwith, in her book *Christ's Body: Identity, Culture and Society in
Late Medieval Writings*, brings together recent theory on social and metaphorical
interrelations of body and society to examine how Christ's body, inherently
ambivalent through its very nature as flesh and spirit or, as Beckwith has it,
symbol of 'transcendence and immanence', can function both to legitimize authority and to resist such authority. Beckwith illuminates the essential ambiguity
of Christ's body, and the importance of its material nature, through expositions
of attitudes to the Eucharist, of the extraordinary imagery of devotional texts such
as *The Prickynge of Love*, and of Margery Kempe, whose attitude to Christ's body
emerges as typical rather than extraordinary. This is an important book, though
sometimes the prose, in its attempt to articulate all the issues at once, obscures
rather than elucidates.

In 'The Uses of Manuscripts: Late Medieval English' (*HBL* 4.iv.30–6), Derek
Pearsall touches lightly on the problems confronting the would-be editor of
medieval manuscripts and endorses the current trend for manuscript study as a
means to achieving a greater understanding of medieval literature and its cultural

milieu. Alexandra Barratt makes sophisticated use of manuscript evidence in 'Feminist Editing: Cooking the Books' (*AUMLA* 79.45–57), to emphasize how important to our understanding of women's writing in the medieval and Renaissance periods is an awareness of its cultural context, the circumstances surrounding its production, and its contemporary reception. Sylvia Huot's *The Romance of the Rose and Its Medieval Readers: Interpretation, Reception, Manuscript Transmission*, is an exemplary work. Her fine detailing of the rich manuscript tradition that contextualizes and constitutes the different versions of the *Roman* both demonstrates the wide range of medieval literary responses to this influential poem and shows us something of the cultural background that made such diverse responses possible.

The basic premise of A. C. Spearing's *The Medieval Poet as Voyeur: Looking and Listening in Medieval Love-Narratives*, provides a useful general introduction to this area of medieval literature, suitable for the lecture courses for which it was apparently conceived: a brief survey of modern and medieval theories of looking prefaces readings of a wide range of well-known and less familiar texts, from the Tristan legend to Chrétien de Troyes, Marie de France and anonymous romances, to Chaucer, Dunbar and Skelton. Spearing uses psychoanalytic material to investigate the relation between the public and the private, and the paradox of making public, in the act of writing literature, the self-declaredly intensely private love experience. The whole is perhaps disappointing, however, in that we seem hardly to progress beyond the insistence on the voyeuristic, which seems to work better for some texts than others, and ultimately suggests a depressingly prescriptive perspective on both narratorial positioning with regard to, and reader response to, the fictional text. The discussion of *Lanval* as a 'male fantasy, that of the son who gets the mother all to himself', is a change from the general thesis, admittedly, but does not itself seem to sit very happily with Marie de France's text. John Burrow's *The William Matthews Lectures 1993: Thinking in Poetry: Three Medieval Examples*, takes a rather different tack, although the lecture-form allows for only cursory animadversions on the absorbing theme of the uses of fiction as a means of debating ethical issues – specifically, in episodes from *Pearl, Piers Plowman* and *St Erkenwald*, concerning soteriology.

Gwendolyn A. Morgan's *Medieval Balladry and the Courtly Tradition. Literature of Revolt and Assimulation* claims that the ballad is the literature of the lower orders in the fourteenth and fifteenth centuries, and accordingly ballads debunk courtly posturings with commonsense and realism. In view of such a thesis (which itself requires a rather narrow understanding of what constitutes the courtly and its literary influence, or at least some very careful supporting historical evidence, if it is to be convincing), the readings of the ballads are puzzlingly lacking in all but the most general contextualization. References to manuscripts are rare and frustratingly vague (see, for example, p. 32), and there is barely any acknowledgement, critical or otherwise, of the problems accompanying the ballads' textual instability and their complex oral origins. Colin Richmond, meanwhile, in 'An Outlaw and Some Peasants: The Possible Significance of Robin Hood' (*NMS* 37.90–101), suggests more convincingly, from an examination of the relevant pre-sixteenth-century ballads and a play fragment, that Robin Hood, associated as he often is with the yeomanry, a particularly fluid class of society during the period 1350–1500, is a 'hero for a society in transition'.

Interpretation: Medieval and Modern, edited by Piero Boitani and Anna Torti, is a varied collection of essays that, as the title intimates, make use of diverse critical approaches to medieval literature. In a characteristically precise essay, Rita Copeland, 'Rhetoric and the Politics of the Literal Sense in Medieval Literary Theory: Aquinas, Wyclif, and the Lollards', looks at ways of reconciling literal sense with rhetoric's ambiguity when one wants to assert the truth of Scripture, and emphasizes their interdependence, concluding that 'rhetoric is precisely what is political about the literal sense. If the literal sense is always the site of contest over control of the text, rhetoric is the means of that control'. Renate Haas, 'Pope Joan and Patient Griselda as "Top Girls": Late Medieval Literature Via Poetic Deconstruction', carefully charts how Caryl Churchill's play deconstructs the ideology that makes these two medieval figures remarkable, and she offers at the same time a critique of medieval masculine interpretations of Griselda. George H. Brown, 'The Meanings of *Interpres* in Aldhelm and Bede', defines the Latin terms as embracing several meanings, but denoting especially a 'go-between', and sees these two masters of Latin literary forms precisely as intermediaries between Latin learning and Anglo-Saxon cultures. Karl Reichl, 'The Literate Fallacy: Interpreting Medieval Popular Narrative Poetry', looks at the evidence we have for oral performance of medieval stories and asks, from the internal evidence of the description of the cloak in this romance, whether *Émaré* is an oral text, and should therefore be assessed differently from examples of 'literary discourse'.

Juliette Dor, '*Traduttore Cicerone*: The Translator as Cross-Cultural Go-Between', looks at questions raised by twentieth-century writers on translation, among them Benjamin and Genette, and counters the image of the translator as 'traitor' with a positive view of the translator as someone who allows access to the literature of different times and different cultures. H. Ansgar Kelly, 'Interpretation of Genres and by Genres in the Middle Ages', investigates the scarcity of the term 'tragedy' in the Middle Ages, and discusses medieval writing on genre in such a way as to foreground Chaucer as a 'generic innovator', while also stressing the variety of medieval interpretations, and sometimes misapprehensions, of genre. Francesi Bruni, 'Interpretation Within the *Decameron*', contends from a reading of six episodes of the *Decameron* that the themes he traces of understanding and misunderstanding are to be understood in the context of a text that has no allegorical, but only a literal, sense.

Vincent Gillespie, 'Postcards from the Edge: Interpreting the Ineffable in the Middle English Mystics', provides an excellent introduction to different authors' approaches to the problem human language poses in that it is inadequate to express what is beyond the human. James Simpson's assured '*Ut Pictura Poesis*: A Critique of Robert Jordan's *Chaucer and the Shape of Creation*', challenges Jordan's interpretation of medieval poetics in general as being concerned with the 'rhetorical surface' of literature rather than with the agency of the author, by detecting interest in the latter element in twelfth-century poetic theory and practice. John V. Fleming, in 'The *Fidus Interpres*, or From Horace to Pandarus' advances the opinion that mention of Lollius shows Chaucer's debt to Horace and that in *Troilus and Criseyde* he makes dramatic as well as thematic use of the concept of the *fidus interpres*.

Some pieces reflect on criticism and its methodology. Stephanie Trigg brings together, in *Medieval English Poetry*, a series of articles published over the last 20 years by established scholars, from David Aers and Stephen Knight to Sheila Delany and Jill Mann: an introduction discusses recent trends in medieval studies, especially what we understand by the term 'medieval', and how modern theory can inform a medieval poetic. Trigg contextualizes the authors and their work and prefaces each piece with a summary of the argument. This should be a useful handbook for students who want a brief overview of mainstream approaches to medieval poetry together with examples of their practical application and an indication of the possibilities for debate between critical perspectives on texts, and between criticism and text. R. Howard Bloch, 'The Once and Future Middle Ages' (*MLQ* 54.67–76), also traces concerns of medieval studies over the past two decades, albeit in a different format, and sees the present developments in interdisciplinary approaches in a positive light.

Joseph A. Dane, 'The Notion of Ring Composition in Classical and Medieval Studies. A Comment on Critical Method and Illusion' (*NM* 94.61–7) questions 'ring composition' as a critical idea and pronounces it arbitrary, arguing that the patterns it arrives at are the products of critical method, and not descriptive of compositional practice. Gina L. Greco and Peter Shoemaker, 'Intertextuality and Large Corpora: A Medievalist Approach' (*CHum* 27.349–55), draw examples primarily from Chrétien de Troyes to illustrate their argument for the suitability of computer methodology to medieval studies. They endorse Mark Olsen's proposal that one move away from the single text towards a large 'corpora' of texts that would enable the study of 'socially constructed discourses', and suggest computerized systems would provide the best means for comparison of manuscripts. On medieval rhetoric, Mary Carruthers, 'The Poet as Master Builder: Composition and Locational Memory in the Middle Ages' (*NLH* 24.881–904), looks at the correspondence between rhetorical invention and actual buildings, 'previsualized' in the same manner as one might plot a poem or a prayer.

Arthurian Literature XII, edited by James P. Carley and Felicity Riddy, is an excellent addition to the series. Martin B. Schichtman and Laurie A. Finke, in 'Profiting from the Past: History as Symbolic Capital in the *Historia Regum Britanniae*', provide a full and imaginative discussion of Geoffrey of Monmouth's attitude towards patronage as evidenced in this text, and examine how one can read Merlin and his magic in the context of Geoffrey's concept of historical writing, and concerns about 'the circulation of intellectual property ... within the economy of feudal patronage'. N. M. Davis, 'Gawain's Rationalist Pentangle', painstakingly reconstructs a concept of proportion for *Sir Gawain and the Green Knight*, from speculative mathematics, and from medieval understanding of the *Nichomachean Ethics*, to show that the poem and its hero operate within a normative philosophical tradition, while the poem also signals that human life is not naturally tractable to 'reasoned order'.

Felicity Riddy, in 'John Hardyng's Chronicle and the Wars of the Roses', fleshes out a political context for Hardyng's work, especially with regard to propaganda for Edward IV. Articles by Helen Phillips on *The Awntyrs off Arthure*, and by Bonnie Wheeler and by Richard Barber on Malory, are reviewed in sections 5 and 9 below. Shorter pieces in the collection raise a number of different issues. Jeremy duQuesnay Adams, 'Sidonius and Riothamus: A Glimpse of the Historical Arthur?', examines a letter of Sidonius which, he suggests, offers further evidence to connect Riothamus with Arthur. Anne Dooley, 'Arthur in Ireland: The Earliest Citation in Native Irish Literature', looks at the political contexts for the fourteenth-century Gofraidh Fionn Ó Dálaigh's mention of Arthur. John Carmi Parsons, 'The Second Exhumation of King Arthur's Remains at Glastonbury, 19 April 1278', sees Edward I's exhumation and reburial of

Arthur and Guinevere as motivated by an interest in asserting himself as rightful successor to the Arthurian imperium. Michelle P. Brown and James P. Carley, 'A Fifteenth-Century Revision of the Glastonbury Epitaph to King Arthur', compare versions of the epitaph on Arthur's monument, and suggest from the manuscript contexts a lively interest in this aspect of the Arthur legend in the mid-fifteenth century.

Alison André, 'Geoffrey of Monmouth's Portrayal of the Arrival of Christianity in Britain. Fact or Fiction?' (*RMSt* 19.3–13) concludes from a survey of Geoffrey's source-material that the author should, when he mentions religion, be credited with telling the truth, but the piece could be a little more precise, both in its definition of 'historical truth' and in its contextualization of material. Deborah Crawford, in 'St. Joseph in Britain: Reconsidering the Legends: I' (*Folklore* 104.86–98) interestingly reviews literature on the Grail, and prepares the ground for her further investigation of how the personality of Joseph came to be associated both with the Grail and with the bringing of Christianity to Britain.

Middle English Historiography, by Robert A. Albano, is rather less inclusive and more specialized than its title might suggest, as it primarily concerns itself with what one can learn of Anglo-Scottish affairs during this period, and, in particular, what this tells us of medieval historians' ideological stances, from an examination of the relevant parts of the Prose *Brut*, John of Trevisa's *Polychronicon*, John Barbour's *Bruce*, Andrew of Wyntoun's *Orygynal Cronykil of Scotland* and Laurence Minot's political poems. The introduction offers a sound overview of critical writings on historiography, and individual chapters focus on how the fourteenth-century historians have different approaches to narrativizing historical events: Albano's general argument, however, is that these writers share an interest in motifs of treachery and loyalty, and place events within a religious moralistic framework that sees God intervening in human history. This is a useful basic comparative study.

Nicholas Birns, 'The Trojan Myth: Postmodern Reverberations' (*Exemplaria* 5.45–78), offers a sophisticated appraisal of the associations of Troy for a late-medieval audience, and argues that the diversity of response to the 'self-consciously fictive' aspect of the historical myth also challenges visions of 'wholeness' a modern mind might project onto other medieval institutions. Martha Rampton, in 'The Peasants' Revolt of 1381 and the Written Word' (*Comitatus* 24.45–60), notes, as part of her argument that the common people sought not ultimately to overturn the system, but to better their condition within it, the significance to them of written documentation. The rebels destroyed records, but they also sought to draw up new agreements and charters within an already recognized legal framework.

Anne Rooney, *Hunting in Middle English Literature*, is an excellent student guide to this theme, describing lucidly a range of literature on the hunt, from manuals of the chase through discussion of related motifs – the devil as hunter, the hunt of love, religious allegories of the hunt – to expositions of the significance of the hunt in *The Book of the Duchess* and *Sir Gawain and the Green Knight*. In the former she identifies the hunt as image of worldly bliss that has a thematic function in this poem of mourning, while in the latter the poet subtly deploys different associations of the hunt to play on readerly expectations. This serves as a sound introduction to an important aspect of medieval literature.

Medieval Political Theory – A Reader: The Quest for the Body Politic, 1100–1400, edited by Cary J. Nederman and Kate Langdon Forhan, makes accessible in modern translation extracts from a number of key medieval political theory texts, including Bernard of Clairvaux, Marie de France, John of Salisbury, Thomas Aquinas, and William of Ockham. Designed as an introductory handbook for students of political theory, there is none the less much here to interest the literature student. An introduction helps to place and define medieval political thought in general, and to identify some of its major preoccupations in the context of feudal society: this will be especially useful to read in conjunction with other medieval literary texts treating of the nature of kingship.

Two books consider other aspects of Latin culture in the Middle Ages. Jan M. Ziolkowski, *Talking Animals: Medieval Latin Beast Poetry, 750–1150*, is an enthusiastic introduction to its subject: his discussion of the wide range of material that the term covers, from the work of the Carolingian poets to dramatic beast-dialogues and the *Ysemgrimus*, alerts us to the fact that these were by no means the productions of a closed society, but that they owe as much to oral as to literary models. He shows that far from offering prescriptive readings of human behaviour, how we are to relate animal to human is often an intrinsic part of the challenge of reading this literature. Translations of 32 beast poems accompany this volume.

Peter Allen, *The Art of Love: Amatory Fiction from Ovid to the 'Romance of the Rose'*, argues convincingly for continuity in the influence of Ovid's texts on love, linking Andreas Capellanus's *De Amore* and Jean de Meun's *Roman de la Rose* by means of their common interest in Ovid's work. Allen wisely contends that these are works about poetics rather than handbooks of love, and ingeniously traces the inherent contradictions of the medieval authors' works to the form of Ovid's *Ars Amatoria* and of the *Remedia Amoris*.

In her volume, Maria Picchio Simonelli offers a commentary on *Inferno III*, the text and translation of which prefaces the detailed exposition of its major themes, its form, and its relation to the rest of Dante's *Inferno*.

Several articles contribute to or synthesize knowledge of medieval culture and learning. Joanne Jasin, 'The Compiler's Awareness of Audience in Medieval Medical Prose: The Example of Wellcome MS 225' (*JEGP* 92.509–22), detects in the presentation of a fifteenth-century work of uroscopy the intention to give general lay access to technical knowledge. Alauddin Samarrai, 'Beyond Belief and Reverence: Medieval Mythological Ethnography in the Near East and Europe' (*JMRS* 23.19–42), considers the longevity of fanciful tales of geography in both areas, and shows what myths about unknown places such as the Germanic North and the Far East, European and Near Eastern texts have in common. Lawrence D. Roberts, 'Medieval Doctrines of Human Freedom' (*Mediaevalia* [1993 for 1989] 15.279–98), outlines views on the subject from the fourth to the thirteenth centuries, from Augustine to Duns Scotus. Wilbur R. Knorr, 'Two Medieval Monks and their Astronomy Books: MSS. Bodley 464 and Rawlinson C.117' (*BLR* 14.269–84), finds evidence that Michael of Northgate and John of London, both of St Augustine's, Canterbury, collaborated in their interests in astronomy, astrology and medicine, but suggests also that the abbey itself was not specifically a centre for the development of scientific interests. A. Leslie Harris, 'Instructional Poetry for Medieval Children' (*ES* 74.124–32), demonstrates that in its prescriptions for moral and social behaviour, instructional literature presents the child from an adult perspective.

Scholarly work continues in the area of manuscript-to-print studies. A. S. G. Edwards and Carol M. Meale, 'The Marketing of Early Printed Books' (*Library*

15.95–124), point out the new economic aspect to patronage in the relationship between printer and dedicatee in the marketing of books, focusing especially on de Worde's practice. Julia Boffey, '*The Treatise of a Galaunt* in Manuscript and Print' (*Library* 15.175–86), compares the broad and flexible manuscript context of this diatribe against sartorial excess (where it appears with religious and historical material) with its more fixed context in print.

Finally, bibliographers will be pleased to note the issue of *A Catalogue of the Fifteenth-Century Printed Books in the Harvard University Library Volume II. Books Printed in Rome and Venice*, by James E. Walsh.

2. Alliterative Poetry

Helen Barr's edition of *Pierce the Plowman's Crede, The Crowned King, Richard the Redeless* and *Mum and the Soothsegger* in *The Piers Plowman Tradition* for Everyman provides a clear, brief précis of the historical background and literary perspective of this group of texts, giving readers new to the material a sense of *terra firma* and those familiar with it a clear indication of the context Barr regards as most relevant, which is made central by a witty use of cover illustration. Each poem is awarded an individual section of the general introduction which allows for consideration of them as independent pieces as well as elements within a tradition. Here *Crede* is defended somewhat uncertainly as both 'a poem of some merit' albeit 'on its own terms' and also as containing in the Dominican as fine an example of grotesque as could be found in any medieval poem. The history of 'Richard the Redeless' is briefly sketched in and Barr provides a summary of the debate about whether or not *Mum and the Soothsegger* forms a second part to this text. Barr herself sides with Embree's view that they are two separate works by the same author. The texts themselves have been edited with the aim of producing 'texts that could conceivably have been read at the time' and are clear reading texts with the familiar marginal gloss of the Everyman style. Unfortunately, there is no general gloss at the end of the book, which raises the problems of restrictive interpretation suffered by the Schmidt edition of *Piers Plowman* for so long. It is a pity that Everyman have not automatically used the same form for this edition, which in many ways is a companion to their *Piers*. Andrew Breeze suggests an addition to the *PP* tradition in the form of Iolo Goch's poem of c.1380–1390s, which he discusses in *N&Q* (40.142–51). According to Breeze this Welsh lyric, which uses a ploughman, may possibly be one of the earliest imitations of *Piers*. In the light of Wheatley's article, which precedes Breeze in the same volume (discussed under section 4 below), this claim may be open to further argument.

The apparent tautology of the first line of *St Erkenwald* is explained by John Burrow ('*Saint Erkenwald* line 1: At London in Englond', *N&Q* 40.22–3) as reflecting Cheshire's semi-autonomous status of county palatine, not liable for tax, but without representation in Parliament.

3. The *Gawain*-Poet

One book from 1992 eluded notice: *Sir Gawain and the Green Knight: Sources and Analogues*, compiled by Elisabeth Brewer, is a second edition of her earlier work of 1973, *From Cuchulainn to Gawain*. Her selection of sources and analogues, translated into modern English, helps to illustrate how *Sir Gawain and the Green Knight* relates to its cultural matrix, both in points of comparison and contrast. It conveniently brings together a wide range of pertinent materials. (Casey Finch, Malcolm Andrew, Ronald Waldron and Clifford Peterson, eds *The Complete Works of the Pearl Poet* (Berkeley: University of California Press, 1993) was not received for review.)

Karen Cherewatuk finds 'Echoes of the Knighting Ceremony in *Sir Gawain and the Green Knight*' (*Neophil* 77.135–47) in the fourth fitt. She argues that a parody of the knighting ceremony underlies Gawain's encounter with the Green Knight at the Green Chapel, and that through this parody the poet summarizes his reflections on the theme of the discrepancy between ideal behaviour and fallen practice which threads through the poem, and causes the audience to reflect on the meaning of knighthood itself. In 'The Name and Fame of Gawain in *Sir Gawain and the Green Knight*' (*SN* 64 [1992].141–7), Robert J. Blanch examines Gawain's search for identity, illustrating how the poem strips Gawain of his legendary reputation and invests him with an identity which, although flawed, is at once more human. With Julian N. Wasserman, he also reviews 'The Current State of *Sir Gawain and the Green Knight* Criticism' (*ChauR* 27.401–12), traversing, in the main, studies of its poetic closure (or lack of it), its semiotics and its critiques informed by Marxist and feminist agendas. They propose that fruitful future studies might include one of the New Historicist sort, 'What does it mean to write *Sir Gawain and the Green Knight* in Lancashire or Cheshire at the end of the fourteenth century?', and issues raised by considering all four poems as an *oeuvre*, not as independent units. In 'Undressing Lady Bertilak: Guilt and Denial in *Sir Gawain and the Green Knight*' (*ChauR* 27.305–24), Harvey De Roo looks afresh at Gawain's anti-feminist diatribe after he has received the return blow from the Green Knight at the Green Chapel, and decides that it is central for any understanding of Gawain: it expresses sexual guilt and is the end result of a series of denials which Gawain has made throughout the course of the poem.

Further work this year has been done on the poet's three other works. '*Pearl*, Penitence and the Recovery of the Self' (*ChauR* 28.164–86), by Gregory Roper, traces the process of the narrator's redefinition in *Pearl*, shifting from self-preoccupation and self-interest, to a contemplation of this state of selfhood, and finally to its abandonment for a self remodelled on the spiritual exemplar to which the narrator has been introduced. This movement, Roper interestingly argues, is analogous to the medieval practice of penance. Kevin Marti describes the 'Traditional Characteristics of the Resurrected Body in *Pearl*' (*Viator* 23.313–35), showing how although the bodies of all the maidens referred to in *Pearl* decay 'in clottez' in the earth, for the sake of his narrative art the poet has been obliged to manufacture for them bodies and form of some sort. The only forms available to him are those with which souls are endowed in orthodox theological descriptions of the resurrected bodies of the saved, but since the General Resurrection, when these bodies are conferred, has not yet occurred, the poet has in effect produced a work that wavers between conformity and non-conformity to religious orthodoxy. In 'The Self Mourning: Reflections on *Pearl*' (*Speculum* 68.54–73), David Aers traces *Pearl*'s treatment of the bereaved self, seeking to explicate some of the complexity of its psychological and theological implications. He sensitively reviews the claims of the competing discourses of dreamer and maiden.

Lara Ruffolo, in 'Verbs in *Patience*: God's Patience in Action' (*SN* 65.141–55), seeks to shift critical emphasis to the text of *Patience* itself, especially to its verbal system, and to recommend deferral of discussions of the 'external' matter of the poem's cultural instantiation that she thinks have dominated critical attention hitherto. She finds in the verbal texture evidence of the construction of an ideal of the virtue of patience which is action-packed rather than passively enduring: God is seen as the exemplar of this strenuous variety of patience, and a cause for the readers to reflect on how far this sort of patience may be possible for themselves. In 'Alain de Lille and the Prologue to *Patience*': A Bibliographical Correction' (*MÆ* 62.292–3), Francis Cairns points out that he had himself already published in *SN* 59 (1987) the substantial findings presented in Professor John Scattergood's article in *MÆ* 61. The editors of *MÆ* express regret at their oversight in not having caught this.

Lastly, Donna Crawford provides an intriguing study of 'The Architectonics of *Cleanness*' (*SP* 90.29–39), in which she attempts to account for the numerical patterns and proportional relations underlying the placement of the 13 decorated capital letters that appear in the manuscript text of *Cleanness*.

4. *Piers Plowman*

Prophecy and ploughmen have come in for some scrutiny this year, while discussions about text continue. Edward Wheatley suggests in 'A Selfless Ploughman and the Christ/Piers Conjunction in Langland's *Piers Plowman*' (*N&Q* 40.135–42) that the figure of the virtuous ploughman may have been familiar to Latinate readers of the thirteenth to fifteenth centuries from Walter of England's *Liber Catonianus* whose fables were used for teaching and where the ploughman appears in 'De Duello Militis et Aratoris'. As mentioned under section 2 above, this may leave Breeze's desire to add to the corpus of *Piers* descendants open to further debate. Andrew Breeze has, however, added to our understanding of a detail of Langland's poem by pointing out that 'tikes' at B.XIX.37 is related to the Welsh 'taeog', meaning serf or bondman ('"Tikes" at *P.P.* B.XIX.37: Welsh "Taeog" "serf, bondman"', *N&Q* 40.443–5). Thus the Jews are being termed bondsmen rather than dogs, which, although clearly still a term of abuse, is a more intricate one as bondsmen inherited their position by blood, creating a kind of nation. Langland's verbal density is further demonstrated by Alan Spearman in 'Langland's "Corlew": Another Look at *Piers Plowman* B.XIV.43' (*MÆ* 62.242–58). Spearman capitalizes on the two very different birds each of which could be 'corlews' (the modern curlew and quail) to show the deliberate use of both alternatives at this point in the poem. After presenting readings of the line with each definition of 'corlew' in turn, it becomes apparent that a more literal reading of the line will incline us towards the plover-like curlew while the quail fits well with a moral reading. Spearman follows Simpson and Carruthers in asserting that 'no simple correspondence may exist between one word and one thing' in the poem and that since Patience is the speaker it may be desirable to read in a more figurative than literal manner here. Overall, however, he sees the 'Corlew' of this line as 'functioning as a symbol of the interpenetration of the physical and spiritual' which is found not only in exegesis of the word but also at large in *Piers Plowman*.

On more familiar ground, Langland is presented as a poet who questions, but finally protects and affirms, the prevailing ideology by moving beyond the realm of praxis into that of faith in Alan Fletcher's article 'The Social Trinity of *Piers Plowman*' (*RES* 44.343–61). Langland's use of the social Trinity of the three estates is regarded as so deeply rooted that its effect is greater than previously acknowledged. Selecting the exchange between Piers and the knight of B.VI and the conflation of Samaritan, Piers and Christ in B.XVIII, Fletcher provides a fairly detailed but also straightforward account of how these passages are founded upon estates thinking which acknowledges, yet in the end silences, the existence of alternative social concepts.

Also on a familiar topic is Anne Savage's consideration of translation as food for the soul (*'Piers Plowman:* The Translation of Scripture and Food for the Soul', *ES* 74.203–21). Knowledge/wisdom is one of the fundamental oppositions in the text and the use of knowledge of Latin as both beneficial and an impediment is briefly rehearsed via *The Book of Vices and Virtues* before Savage goes on to concentrate on two metaphors in particular; these are the again familiar pairing of consuming the Scriptures and consuming food. It is a clear working through of the intersection between food and Scripture which Langland uses so much in the poem, but one which seems to add very little to the discussions already available on this aspect of the poem. However, as Savage states that this is part of a larger project perhaps more may emerge at a later date.

Ernest Kaulbach's study of the poem is dense and demanding of both text and reader. While reading *Imaginative Prophecy in the B-Text of 'Piers Plowman'* one is obliged to take Kaulbach's overview of the poem on trust and work within its parameters. This study is firmly in the tradition of offering a pattern by which to explain the whole text. Having suggested that the poem be regarded as a kind of dream journal, Kaulbach more or less abandons his Jungian references and turns to Avicenna's notion of the perfected prophet instead. It transpires that the status of perfect prophet is denied the waking Will as his and others are encumbered by pride and need and so cannot be free. Throughout Kaulbach parallels Thoght and Ymaginatif as different parts of Anima (the human and animal respectively) in a way which is not always utterly convincing – statements such as 'Ymaginatif is simply the twin of Thoght' jar. The conclusion – that the adoption of an Avicennan view-point renders the structure of the poem clear verges on the laughable, but none the less, this book is laudable for its use of the idea of prophecy and the perfection of it, for the detail of its application of Avicennan ideas, for its careful and illuminating reading of the two inner dreams and for the assertion of the importance of the poem's Malvern provenance and influence.

John Burrow is, as ever, comprehensible, lucid and thought-provoking in discussing the uses of poetic fiction in *Piers Plowman*. Dreams; uncertainty as a result of a divided mind; the fiction of history and self-creation and autobiography form the main chapters of *Langland's Fictions*, flanked by an introduction and afterword which touch on the appeal *Piers Plowman* has for unbelievers and also advocate giving due credit to the literal level of the text. A footnote laments the C-Text's 'unfortunate tendency ... to treat the literal story with insufficient respect'.

The essays collected to honour David Fowler, *Suche Werkis to Werke*, provide varied and interesting reading. Detailed treatments of precise literary elements of the text may be found in Alford's appraisal of the figure of Repentance, Dolan's swift and to the point piece on shame, and Emmerson's analysis of Anima's first appearance. Higgs counterbalances Emmerson in arguing that Piers's doing well needs to be adjusted just as much as Conscience's right thinking, which is why the two figures are rarely found together and Need's role in the destruction of Unity is delineated. Across a wider canvas Martin explores the central role of ideas of syntax in the poem, pointing out how individual words come in for close scrutiny and grammatical relations are used as analogies for other systems, specifically social ones. Consistently the indirect relation in any system is the rebellious one. There is a brief treatment of the influence of gender on personification, which is worth reading in conjunction with Cooper's article on the same in *YLS* 1991 (31–48), and some intriguing ideas about direct and indirect speech. Meanwhile Dahl attacks the current prevalent reliance on certain editions which have established a form of textual *status quo* thereby obstructing better understanding of fundamental textual issues. We are reminded of the diversity of the copies we have and roundly told to take note of them. The slightly rebarbative tone enlivens this detached survey and may well be a way of making the discussion of *text* interesting to undergraduates as well. Lawton and Vaughan study textual matters in their contributions on alliterative metre and the endings of the A-Text respectively. As one progresses through Lawton's resumé and application of Duggan's metrical analyses the compelling nature of this type of study becomes manifest, as do the conflicting desires for rules to establish a metrical pattern and exceptions to prove the individuality of texts. Prophecy again crops up here as having a precise metrical form, evident in *Piers*, and the essay ends by recommending that generic and metrical scholarship be recognized as mutually informative. Vaughan's study of the A manuscripts bears out Lawton's claim as he shows how various scribes have sought to resolve problems of interpretation arising from a suspicion of incompleteness. Finally a plea is issued for these texts to be regarded seriously and in terms of literary relations between versions, regardless of assumptions concerning single authorship. This last serves as a riposte to Emmerson's views. Consideration of individual manuscripts is provided by Clifton and Pearsall. Pearsall's contribution is a slightly expanded version of his introduction to the facsimile C-Text (reviewed in *YWES* 73.128–9) which allows for a more general discussion of the effect of illustration, as Pearsall at first cautiously debunks the favoured dream that illustrations are usually witty commentaries on the accompanying text and then points out how some of the Bodleian Library MS Douce 104 do just that. Clifton uses the fact that a copy of the A-text is found in the Vernon manuscript to assert *Piers*'s place among contemplative writing, a claim which surely no longer needs assertion, but which here precedes a nice enough discussion focusing on the dangers of jangling, in which Will is seen to get the reward for curbing jangling that *The Benjamin Minor* promises, namely, discretion and contemplation in the persons of Patience and Conscience. The security of the claim that Conscience can be regarded as contemplation is left uninterrogated, but here that scarcely seems to matter. Naturally included in this volume is an appreciation of David Fowler and an annotated bibliography of his work which is a useful resource in itself as well as being a tribute to the man.

Further explicitly textual considerations of *Piers* will be found in this year's volume of *The Yearbook of Langland Studies*, where Peter Barney provides an index to each line's discussion in the Athlone editions; an enterprise which will certainly expedite consultation of these editions for particular points (*YLS* 7.97–114). In slightly different vein, Ralph Hanna answers Ian Doyle's call for fuller descriptions of *Piers Plowman* manuscripts in 'Studies in the Manuscripts of

Piers Plowman' (*YLS* 7.1–25) with a description of the C-Text fragment designated by Kane's sigil H. The description provides further testimony for a Worcestershire circulation of the C-Text. This leads into a consideration of MS Bodley 851 against a background of A and Z dissemination, which leaves Hanna more inclined to regard this version as a result of separate production forming part of a series of additions to John Wells's book than as part of the original core selection. His final conclusion is that the author of Z was a Langland enthusiast who 'responded to the poem and its metre'. The piece is neatly topped by a plate of the C-Text (H) folio 1r and tailed by a reduced description of MS Bodley 851. This year's volume also contains a treatment of prophecy and *Piers*, here by Richard Emmerson, who begins by declaring a sceptical position as to its role in the poem and ends by asserting that this particular line of enquiry has gone as far as it fruitfully can: he sees 'no critical value in searching for an all-encompassing movement in which to place Langland'. Instead, he advocates historicizing the connections between *Piers* and prophecy both synchronically and diachronically. The following contribution by Stephen Manning, 'Langland and the Tradition of Spiritual Growth' (*YLS* 7.77–95), illustrates what happens when terms are studied in their appropriate contexts. He focuses on Dowel, Dobet and Dobest, and argues that although they have analogues in the mystical tradition they 'cannot be reduced to any other schema'. While this is not exactly breaking new ground, Manning does bring together much of the range of mystic and spiritual writing which has a bearing on this triad and defends the apparent imprecision of Langland's vocabulary. Most usefully he also shows how the notion of *epectasis*, with its connotations of endless stretching forward, underpins the principle of progress so many readers find in the poem. In contrast to this, Nicole Clifton points out Langland's use of Romance conventions in B.XVIII, and M. Jane Toswell pinpoints the penitential motif of Gloton's 'cawdel'.

The consideration of translation found in George Kane's very negative review article on Schmidt's translation of *Piers* for the World's Classics series (see *YWES* 73.128–9) is characteristically definite (*YLS* 7.129–56). It could prove invaluable in prompting critical consideration of translations in those heaviest of consumers of them, the undergraduates, as well as demonstrating the inevitable pitfalls of any translation in the lexis section, in which Kane disagrees in detail with many of Schmidt's translation decisions.

5. Romances

Several books this year address romance motifs and themes, and the nature of the genre. *Noble and Joyous Histories: English Romances 1375–1650*, edited by Eileán Ní Chuilleanáin and J. D. Pheifer, is a chronologically broad-ranging collection of essays that includes work on major romances from Chaucer to the Renaissance. The editors' introduction traces romance from its classical origins to its European manifestations, to emphasize that the English romances are part of an international tradition. By the sixteenth century, they note, English romance writers have to negotiate rather more delicately their relationship to the genre, although women as readers of romance gain a new prominence in the Renaissance, and both Spenser and Sidney address the question of women's relation to political power. Articles here on Middle English romance, which address notions of continuity in rather different ways, range from *Gawain* to Malory. The two pieces on the latter are reviewed in section 9 below. Piotr Sadowski, 'Time

Structure in the Narrative Framework of *Sir Gawain and the Green Knight*', examines time-frames relating to the quest, to cyclicity, to human life, and the liturgy, to suggest allegorical layers that make the poem 'a rare example of a poetic synthesis of the crucial concepts regarding man, society, and religion'. Helen Cooney addresses romance and philosophy in 'Wonder and Boethian Justice in the *Knight's Tale*', and reads the text as a critique of Boethius's account of divine justice. Cathalin Buhrmann Folks, 'Gentle Men, *Lufly* and *Loothly* Ladies, *Aghlich Maysters*: Characterization in *The Wife of Bath's Tale* and *Sir Gawain and the Green Knight*', considers how in Chaucer's tale the 'flawed hero' is transformed into *gentilesse*, while in the latter poem the hero moves from 'perfection' to 'imperfection', while both narratives go against traditional generic expectations in their presentation of the protagonists' education. Lesley Johnson's 'King Arthur at the Crossroads', is a judicious article that examines the ethical issues the alliterative *Morte Arthure* raises, concentrating especially on its complex view of history, its questioning 'whether, and how far, the quest for an empire is compatible with that for salvation'. David Scott-MacNab, 'Burlesque Romance and the Bourgeoisie', makes the valuable observation, from a study of the *Tournament of Tottenham*, the *Hunting of the Hare*, and the *Felon Sew*, that these poems were probably not intended for a middle-class audience contemptuous of romance, but rather that chivalry is the vehicle of comedy, not the butt of the joke, and that the texts were possibly intended primarily for the nobility.

In *Counsel and Strategy in Middle English Romance*, Geraldine Barnes identifies counsel as a central concern, of romance as of the later medieval English feudal political scene: she carefully consolidates earlier criticism as she traces the importance of counsel and strategy in *Ywain and Gawain*, *Havelock*, *Athelston*, and in nine romances from the Auchinleck MS, and ends with a discussion of how, in *Sir Gawain and the Green Knight*, the hero neglects heavenly counsel for earthly stratagem. One might want to counter that Gawain's problem lies rather in the difficulty of interpreting the possible spiritual import of the signs around him, but this is none the less a sound book, drawing attention to an important aspect of Middle English romance.

Corinne J. Saunders also considers one motif, in *The Forest of Medieval Romance*, but this study is less successful, perhaps because she covers the great range of material – from classical through medieval to Shakespearean examples – in such a way as makes for general description rather than analysis. Ambitious though the study is in its attempt to trace across time the complex of literary resonances in diverse representations of the forest in romance texts, what emerges is a series of rather conservative readings of major works that rarely engage with recent critical arguments relevant to the topic.

Two articles in *Arthurian and Other Studies Presented to Shunichi Noguchi*, edited by Takashi Suzuki and Tsuyoshi Mukai, consider the Stanzaic *Le Morte Arthur*: Ján Šimko, 'Modernity of the Middle English Stanzaic Romance *Le Morte Arthur*', gives a positive, if also somewhat general, appraisal of the poem's 'human' values. Tadahiro Ikegami, meanwhile, in 'The Structure and Tone of the Stanzaic *Morte Arthur*', compares the poem with its French source, *La Mort le Roi Artu*, and argues that the English poem has a bipartite structure, but he similarly emphasizes the 'human' aspect of the drama, although its designation as 'an English Arthurian popular romance' perhaps needs sharper definition. Essays in this collection relating to Caxton and Malory are listed in section 9 below. Helen Phillips has written on '*The Awntyrs off Arthure*: Structure and Meaning. A Reassessment' for *Arthurian Literature XII*. She contests the 'bipartite' structure others have seen for this poem, and uses manuscript evidence to suggest instead a more engaging and complex pattern of repetitions and of episodes which frame other episodes, 'through which the secular becomes a context for the spiritual and the spiritual for the secular'.

Françoise Le Saux has produced a useful edition of *Amys and Amylion*, based on Douce MS 326. Apart from a helpful introduction, appendices offer summaries of variations on the story, in Latin, *chanson de geste* and Anglo-Norman versions. Unfortunately, this edition is rather more expensive than *Of Love and Chivalry: An Anthology of Middle English Romance*. Jennifer Fellows's accessible student edition, for Everyman, includes six romances: *Amis and Amiloun* (here edited largely from the Auchinleck MS), *King Horn*, *Floris and Blanchefleur*, *Sir Launfal* and the *Erl of Toulous*, together with the less well-known *Sir Tryamowre*. Fellows's edition of Middle English romances also has the advantage of complementing the collection of Anglo-Norman romances translated by Judith Weiss in *The Birth of Romance* (*YWES* 73.132). For those with no French, Patricia Terry and Nancy Vine Durling offer a translation (albeit sometimes uneven-sounding to a British ear) of Jean Renart's early thirteenth-century *The Romance of the Rose or Guillaume de Dole*, a romance significant for its innovative intercalation of lyric in the prose narrative.

There are some interesting observations on the interrelation of hagiography and romance. Jennifer Fellows, in 'St George as Romance Hero' (*RMSt* 19.27–54), detects an increasing interest, from Jacobus de Voragine's *Legenda Aurea* onwards, in the account of St George's battle against the dragon and, noting some similarity between the George legend and *Bevis of Hampton*, proposes a romantic tradition for the figure of St George. Anne B. Thompson, 'Jaussian Expectation and the Production of Medieval Narrative: The Case of "Saint Eustace" and *Sir Isumbras*' (*Exemplaria* 5.387–407) approaches the issue of the relation between hagiography and romance by asking how readerly expectation might have influenced the production of medieval narrative. She suggests that the version of the Eustace legend in the *South English Legendary* successfully and boldly achieves its effects by incorporating romance elements into its narrative, whereas *Sir Isumbras* is more confused, and depends on a knowing readership to supply its deficiencies. Linda Marie Zaerr and Mary Ellen Ryder, 'Psycholinguistic Theory and Modern Performance: Memory as a Key to Variants in Medieval Texts' (*Mosaic* 26.iii.21–35), excite curiosity with a review of critical arguments for and against oral transmission of Middle English romances, and a summary of a modern performer's experience of learning the *Tournament of Tottenham*, as a means of considering to what extent memorized transmission could account for corruptions in a fifteenth-century manuscript of the romance, Cambridge University Library Ff.5.48.

6. Gower, Lydgate, Hoccleve

Georgiana Donavin begins her monograph *Incest Narratives and the Structure of Gower's 'Confessio Amantis'*, with an examination of the double meaning of incest, in its literal sense and in its allegorical sense of mystical union with God. Both meanings are integral, she claims, to an understanding of the *Confessio*, where incest narratives appear in five of the eight books. Donavin synthesizes and develops earlier criticism by linking the incest stories to Amans's spiritual progress from delusion to self-knowledge, from concupiscence to higher love. This study emphasizes, especially in the discussion of the play of literal and metaphorical in the representation of incest, an important motif in the text.

Volume 16 of *Mediaevalia* (1993 for 1990) is a collection for John Hurt Fisher of 17 articles on John Gower, some examining a particular topic, some placing Gower in a general cultural or historical context. Some aim to recover something of Gower's political affiliations: George B. Stow, 'Richard II in John Gower's *Confessio Amantis*: Some Historical Perspectives' (3–31), reviews Gower's theories of kingship and considers the poet's revisions of his poem in the light of Ricardian policy, 1390–1, suggesting Gower is particularly alienated from Richard's centralization of rule and disregard of law and order. Judith Ferster, 'O Political Gower' (33–53), concentrates especially on what Gower's works reveal of his understanding of advice literature and the role of 'the people' in government, and finds that he is highly flexible in his use of the 'discourse of advice', pragmatic in his response to the king's actions.

Edward Donald Kennedy, meanwhile, in 'Gower, Chaucer, and French Prose Arthurian Romance' (57–90), concludes from his investigations that while Chaucer probably knew no Chrétien, he must have had a sound knowledge of the French Prose *Lancelot*, but that perhaps he found the central characters of Arthurian romance 'morally offensive', or that there was a general shift in court taste away from longer narratives. Gower by contrast is more specific in his allusions to French romance. William Calin's findings in 'John Gower's Continuity in the Tradition of French *Fin' Amor*' (91–111), follow naturally upon Kennedy's conclusions, for he produces a wholly plausible argument against the idea that Gower rejects French court culture, even suggesting that the *Confessio* is best seen in the context of Jean de Meun's writings. Helen Cooper, ' "Peised Evene in the Balance": A Thematic and Rhetorical Topos in the *Confessio Amantis*' (113–39), traces Gower's use of a rhetoric of measure and balance that corresponds to his desire for order. Anthony E. Farnham, 'Statement and Search in the *Confessio Amantis*' (141–58), takes as his point of departure Dorothy Sayers's distinction between the poetry of 'search' and of 'statement', and proposes that the *Confessio Amantis* itself shifts progressively from the latter to the former category. James Simpson's engaging 'Genius's "Enformacioun" in Book III of the *Confessio Amantis*' (159–95) looks at the ramifications of the term 'enformacioun', its designation of a body of knowledge, and its effect on both literary form and moral content: Simpson suggests that Genius is Amans's imaginative faculty and seeks to make the will conform to reason. R. A. Shoaf, ' "Tho Love made him an hard eschange" and "With fals brocage hath take usure": Narcissus and Echo in the *Confessio Amantis*' (197–209), sees in Gower's condemnation of Narcissus as presumptuous, and in Echo as emblem of erotic excess, evidence of Gower's prescriptive style where Chaucer is more 'indeterminate'.

A. C. Spearing, 'Canace and Machaire' (211–21) compares Gower's treatment of the legend in Book III of the *Confessio Amantis* with the Ovidian source and notes that Gower excludes from the description of letters 'the problematics of female authorship' which is integral to Ovid's account. A. S. G. Edwards similarly notes a lack of interest in the female in 'Gower's Women in the *Confessio*' (223–37), arguing against Derek Pearsall's view that Gower treats women sympathetically by pointing out that either their suffering is made little of, or they are blamed for what they do to men.

Chauncey Wood, 'Petrarchanism in the *Confessio Amantis*' (239–56) finds echoes in the *Confessio Amantis* of the attitudes towards literature Petrarch voices in his 'Letter to Posterity'. Alan T. Gaylord '"After the forme of my writynge": Gower's Bookish Prosody' (257–88), is a defence of Gower's versification and an attempt to define more rigorously the nature of Gower's rhetoric while being at the same time appreciative of the interplay of the philosophical and the poetic. N. F. Blake, 'Early Printed Versions of the *Confessio Amantis*' (289–306) looks at Caxton's edition of 1483, and at Berthelette's edition of 1532, which emphasizes above all the moral and exemplary value of Gower's work, and concludes that he was respected more as a teacher and communicator of wisdom than as a poet.

Thomas H. Bestul, 'Gower's *Mirour de l'Omme* and the Meditative Tradition' (307–28), considers this text as a work of private devotion, and shows how it draws on traditions of devotional literature, in Latin but also in Anglo-Norman, for its most telling language. Andrew Galloway, 'Gower in His Most Learned Role and the Peasants' Revolt of 1381' (329–47) looks at how Gower in the *Vox Clamantis* views his political role as an intellectual in the guidance of the State. Charles R. Blyth, 'Thomas Hoccleve's Other Master' (349–59) compares Gower's version of the story of Lycurgus with Hoccleve's account in the *Regement of Princes*, and finds that the latter is rather more practical in his attitude to the problems of abiding by over-strict laws, where Gower is more idealistic about law's perfectibility. Stephen J. Lynch, 'The Authority of Gower in Shakespeare's *Pericles*' (361–78) assesses Shakespeare's debt to the *Confessio* and sees the choric Gower at odds with the play's dynamic: Shakespeare uses the Gower figure not to frame the play but draw attention to authorial control even as he suggests the limitations of the author.

Russell A. Peck contributes an article on 'The Problematics of Irony in Gower's *Confessio Amantis*' to *Mediaevalia* 15.207–29, a special volume in honour of Bernard S. Levy. He argues against recent criticism that sees the poet undermining the ethical framework of his own poem, and proposes a more even-handed approach that appreciates the nature of Gower's irony.

Work on Hoccleve and Lydgate is scarce this year. Karen Winstead, '"I am al othir to yow than ye weene": Hoccleve, Women, and the *Series*' (*PQ* 72.143–55), thought-provokingly deduces from the narratives in the *Series* that the whole is an anti-feminist continuation of the *Letter of Cupid*, a joke at the expense of women readers, and specifically a criticism of Joan Beaufort, to whom the Durham MS of the text is dedicated. David Lorenzo Boyd, 'Reading Through the *Regiment of Princes*: Hoccleve's *Series* and Lydgate's "Dance of Death" in Yale Beinecke MS 493', (*FCS* 20.15–34) argues that the late fifteenth-century manuscript presents the poems as all relating to the control and regulation of the self. The juxtaposition of the three texts reinforces their socio-political thrust.

7. Middle Scots Poetry

Dunbar's authorship of 'Bewty and the Prisonier' is cast into doubt by Josephine Bloomfield in 'A Test of Attribution: William Dunbar's *Bewty and the Prisonier*' (*ELN* 30.11–19). Her case rests on words and phrases, anomalies in rhyme scheme, stanza form, genre and subject matter. The poem is revealed as a genuine allegory of real courtly love and as being positive about marriage, all of which, apparently, are antipathetic to Dunbar. It is a confident challenge to the attribution, with the full text provided as if to clinch the argument.

Henryson receives more extensive treatment this year with a book on the relation of his poetry to medieval rhetoric and several articles. Robert Kindrick's book *Henryson and the Medieval Arts of Rhetoric* is puffed by the general editors of the series as 'one of the first open "thesis" books on Henryson' and expands on his previously published work in this area. Although it does supply a fairly useful resumé of the *artes* and their history, the prime focus is on Henryson and his 'synthetic genius'. Thus several extensive treatments of individual poems and their relations to other texts in terms of rhetorical devices are to be found here, and are probably worth the discovery. Henryson's independence as a poet, even when following in others' footsteps, is asserted by Anne McKim in 'Tracing the Ring: Henryson, Fowler and Chaucer's *Troilus*' (*N&Q* 40.449–51). The end of the *Testament* is not a mis-remembering of Chaucer, but a deliberate invocation of Troilus's signet ring which sealed his love-letter to Criseyde. This leads McKim to discuss *The Late Epistle of Creseyde to Troyalus* attributed to Fowler.

The representation of history and the gradual separation of history and literature is the general subject of R. James Goldstein's *The Matter of Scotland*. The basis of the book is what he terms 'the war of historiography' and it provides an interdisciplinary approach to the recording and interpreting of historical events. John of Fordun's *Chronica Gentis Scotorum*, Barbour's *Bruce* and Hary's *Wallace* receive detailed treatment and, by the end of the book, one emerges with a fair idea of what one had to be to qualify as a Scot. It is interesting to see mild concern with historical accuracy being replaced with concern with ideological accuracy as literature becomes a political force. Grace G. Wilson adds to this area of debate in her quotation-packed article 'History and the Common Reader? Robert Lindsay of Pitscottie's *Cronicles*' (*FMLS* 29.97–110). It is an engaging account of Pitscottie's 'unevenness and unpredictability' which defends him as 'indispensable for details that occur nowhere else' (although she declines to consider whether that makes him more or less trustworthy where such details are concerned) and perceptively suggests that in the later sections of his chronicles Pitscottie 'came up most sharply against the difficulty of disseminating a history while in the process of living it'.

8.   Lyrics and Miscellaneous Verse

Henry Hargreaves publishes and describes the previously unpublished poem 'Stirps Anne Beate', found in AUL MS.123 and noted by Professor Robbins (*ELN* 31.9–18). Hargreaves offers an explanation for the relation of numerology and this poem about St Anne's family, pointing out the relevance of the diagram which precedes the text in the manuscript, whose record of the marriages and family tree may allow for the computation of degrees of kinship between numbers. The poem itself, written in NW dialect, has a 'curious' metre and scheme. Although it is 'by no means one of the masterpieces of ME literature', it does have a certain appeal and is kindly presented here. Meanwhile, in the previous volume (*ELN* 30.5–10), David Parker suggests that The Corpus Christi Carol is generically a riddle, as it is a trait of this genre that the texts conspicuously ignore their subject. This also accounts for its inclusion in Hill's MS, as Hill loved lists and enigmas. Parker points out the importance of ceremony in the mass in the early 1500s and suggests that the hall of the carol is the altar fully hung in its lenten purple. When Gray's explication of the white falcon as Anne Boleyn is added, the whole carol becomes a lament for the Roman Church in the days following the Act of Supremacy. It is a neat and satisfying argument. Another lenten lyric, 'Lenten Ys Come', draws the attention of Andrew Breeze (N&Q 40.14–15). It transpires that we have been severely underestimating the meaning of the assumed Welsh source of the word 'mil': it usually denotes a large monster, not a mere animal. With similar precision Breeze concludes that the ME 'tromchery' found in Harley 913, A Satire of the People of Kildare, does not after all mean 'rubbish', as Sisam suggested, but is linked to the Irish 'tromchoi', meaning 'liver' or 'heavy heart'. Liver thus joins the tripe and cow's feet sold by the 'hokesters' of the poem and so reflects attitudes to the Irish language, which might be respected beyond the Pale, but is the domain of offal sellers within it.

More fuel is added to the debate about the categorization of *Judas* as a ballad by Karin Boklund-Lagopoulou in *MÆ* (62.20–34). She considers the context provided by the manuscript, the narrative structure of the text and its 'point of view', by which we are led to identify with Judas, a fact she regards as 'clearly in opposition to the fundamental intent of the devotional poetry'. After some consideration of the poem as religious ballad, the category she finally offers is that of 'tragic, popular ballad' with the further suggestion that Chambers may have been right in suggesting that the composer was a cleric. Charles of Orleans's right to be regarded as the author of the English verse ascribed to him is vigorously defended by Mary-Jo Arn (*ES* 74.222–35).

In contrast to these elucidations of the details of individual lyrics, Maureen Boulton discusses lyrics and other songs found within longer texts (*The Song in the Story: Lyric Insertion in French Narrative Fiction, 1200–1400*). The precise area of her study is the lyric insert in French romance texts of the thirteenth and fourteenth centuries, yet her suggestions and conclusions about the use of lyric insertion as a general literary technique, whereby the lyrics remain independent songs, stressing the performative aspects of these texts and their ability to address two audiences simultaneously (one inside, one outside the text) raise interesting questions for the English free-standing lyrics as well as those which are found in longer narratives, such as *The Book of the Duchess*.

9. Malory and Caxton

P. J. C. Field seems indefatigable this year, and has produced a great deal of material, much of it documentary, relating both to Malory and to his text. His *The Life and Times of Sir Thomas Malory* considers all one can glean of Malory's family, his life, and his involvement in politics, in a persuasive argument for identifying Sir Thomas Malory of Newbold Revel as the author of the *Morte Darthur*. Field is, however, cautious about the possibilities of reading the *Morte* in the light of this man's extraordinary career, suggesting that although some changes to the sources reflect this 'strikingly unacademic' writer's troubled times, the subject-matter of the *Morte* takes precedence over any consideration of Malory himself. This leaves much room for others to determine the possible interrelation of art and life. In 'Malory and the French Prose Lancelot' (*BJRL*

75.79–102), Field carefully correlates the ten sections of Malory's 'The Noble Tale of Sir Launcelot du Lake' with its French source material, and concludes (not surprisingly) that the edition of the *Lancelot* by Micha is closer to the version of the French romance Malory knew than the manuscript Sommer edited that Vinaver chose for source-study. In 'Malory and *Perlesvaus*' (*MÆ* 62.259–69), meanwhile, he finds evidence that Malory must have worked directly from *Perlesvaus* material, rather than being familiar with only a little of this text by means of a postulated interpolation in a manuscript of the 'Agravain' section of the Prose *Lancelot*. Field's contribution to *Noble and Joyous Histories: English Romances 1375–1650*, 'Author, Scribe, and Reader in Malory: The Case of Harleuse and Peryne', discusses the factual inconsistencies regarding Malory's minor characters, and examines the ways others have accounted for them, before suggesting that they constitute part of the narrator's tendency to fallibility and factual error which is subordinate to the author's feel for the 'nobility' of his subject-matter. Field contributes to *Arthurian and Other Studies Presented to Shunichi Noguchi* a piece on 'Hunting, Hawking, and Textual Criticism in Malory's *Morte Darthur*', which suggests that Malory's additions to his sources show an enthusiasm for hunting and hawking but that the Winchester MS scribe does not necessarily share Malory's specialized knowledge, which makes for some error. Field also co-writes with Gillian Rogers a note on 'Malory's Trapdoor and the Name Estorause' (*N&Q* 40.23–5), which sensibly corrects to 'escurys', 'stables', Mellyagaunte's invitation to Lancelot to see his castle's 'esturys', and emends the name Estorause to Escorause.

Other contributions to Malory studies include the excellent 'Romance and Parataxis and Malory: The Case of Sir Gawain's Reputation', by Bonnie Wheeler in *Arthurian Literature XII*, which ranges widely across the *Morte* to relate the nature of Malory's prose style to the particular demands made of the reader by the author's presentation of character and to the difficulties with accounts of causation in Malory's text: Wheeler concludes that Gawain serves as 'exemplary index of Malory's paratactic causality'. In the same volume is Richard Barber's 'Malory's *Le Morte Darthur* and Court Culture Under Edward IV', which sees Malory's interests in the *Morte* – especially in the description of tournaments – as best understood in the context of contemporary entertainments at the English court: Barber proposes a specifically courtly status for the author. Derek Brewer offers another perspective on Malory's literary style in his paper 'Hauberk and Helm in Malory's *Le Morte Darthur*', in *Arthurian and Other Studies*, noting that while Malory will use military detail necessary to individual scenes, he takes for granted a general knowledge of armour, and is more interested in stirring the imagination than in conveying a precise sense of realism. Gregory J. Kember, in the same volume, writes of 'Chaucer and Malory: Signs of the Times', comparing Chaucer's interest in the transformative with Malory's use of written signs as registering 'an attempt to contain and understand the irrational and the numinous', to claim that both authors reflect a pre-Renaissance trend of 'increasingly rational thinking'. It is interesting to compare these observations on signs with Roy Rosenstein's ingenious work, 'D'Eden à Armageddon, ou la Pomme et le Serpent: Sir Thomas Malory, *Laudator Temporis Acti*' (*Sénéfiance* 33.457–74). For Rosenstein, Malory regrets the passing of the Arthurian idyll and thus informs his account of the demise of the Round Table with motifs – the poisoned apple, the serpent, fratricide – that recall the end of Eden, the time of 'legend', and the beginning of 'history', while the deployment of such motifs implicates all the major characters in the fall of the society.

In *Arthurian and Other Studies*, Edward Donald Kennedy has an astute reading of 'Malory's "Noble Tale of Sir Launcelot du Lake", the Vulgate *Lancelot*, and the Post-Vulgate *Roman du Graal*', which concludes that Malory selected source-material that would relate Lancelot's adventures in this section to earlier and later portions of the *Morte*. J. D. Pheifer's 'Malory's Lancelot', in the collection *Noble and Joyous Histories*, covers much the same ground, but suffers in comparison with Kennedy's work, for this is a summarizing rather than an analytical piece which traces in a somewhat pedestrian fashion Lancelot's appearances in French romance and in Malory, to conclude for the superiority of Malory's account of Arthurian legend.

Several papers discuss the 'Tristram' section, compare the heroes Tristram and Lancelot, and consider the social complexities of its world. Danielle Morgan MacBain, 'The Tristramization of Malory's Lancelot' (*ES* 74.57–65), argues that Lancelot's character is continually redefined by reference to Tristram, which makes the former darker, less idealized and more tragic in consequence. In a similar vein, but also more specifically, Françoise le Saux, '*Pryvayly and Secretely*: Personal Letters in Malory's "Book of Sir Tristram de Lyones"' (*EdL* 3.21–33), sees the exchange of letters among the characters as forming a nexus of relationships that underlines the parallels between Arthur's court and that of Mark: and while letters can serve as plot devices, they also come to illustrate 'the gradual bankruptcy of authority which leads to the fall of the Round Table'. Le Saux also makes some interesting observations on the nature of public and private as mediated through language. Kevin T. Grimm, 'Fellowship and Envy: Structuring the Narrative of Malory's *Tale of Sir Tristram*' (*FCS* 20.77–98), considers how we can see the interplay of these two forces in the text as a commentary on social and literary contexts. Elizabeth Sklar, in 'The Undoing of Romance in Malory's *Morte Darthur*' (*FCS* 20.309–27), takes Gareth's *Tale* as the 'paradigmatic romance' against which one reads the less fortunate experience of Alexander, at approximately the mid-point of the *Morte*, to show how, in Malory, the form of the romance system and its ideals break down in the face of 'human frailty'. Corinne Saunders, meanwhile, in 'Malory's *Book of Huntynge*: The Tristram Section of the *Morte Darthur*' (*MÆ* 62.270–84), bypasses social complexity and sets the hero apart as one defined principally by 'the mirth and delights of the hunting world', an innocent in 'the more sinister world of politics'.

Two contributions to a general and unscholarly collection of Arthurian material, *The Arthurian Myth of Quest and Magic: A Festschrift in Honor of Lavon B. Fulwiler*, edited by W. E. Tanner, are relevant to this section: Lavon B. Fulwiler, 'The Myth Fulfilled', briefly argues for Arthur as hero, and especially as a type of Christ, and Donna Lea Skeen Shelton, 'Malory's Use of Dream Vision: Medieval and Contemporary Strategies for Interpretation', barely has space to hint at the structural significance of dreams in the *Morte*. Rather more rigorous, and more rewarding, are those articles in *Arthurian and Other Studies* that consider the *Morte*'s textual history: in 'Some Scribal Differences in Malory', Tomomi Kato charts the similarities between, and idiosyncrasies of, Scribes A and B of the Winchester MS. Yuji Nakao, 'On the Relationship Between the Winchester Malory and Caxton's Malory', offers further linguistic support for the argument (and evidence) that Caxton made use of the Winchester MS. Toshiyuki Takamiya, 'Editor/Compositor at Work: The Case of Caxton's Malory', meanwhile, offers intriguing evidence of his own, based on a study of textual errors, that the copy Caxton used to prepare his edition had lines slightly longer than those of the Winchester MS. Tsuyoshi Mukai, 'De Worde's Displacement of Malory's Secularization', combines perceptive notes on Malory's attachment to earthly chivalry with a thoughtful consideration of Wynkyn de Worde's motives in changing the flavour of Malory's text, especially in his didactic interpolation in Book 21, which Mukai thinks may draw on *Troilus and Criseyde*. He notes that ultimately, however, such moralization cannot override the *Morte*'s secular interests and emotional power.

Kiyokazu Mizobata, 'Caxton's Revisions: the *Game of Chess*, the *Mirror of the World*, and *Reynard the Fox*', in the same collection, argues that the more meticulous production of the second edition of the first text in comparison with the errors in the second editions of the *Mirror* and *Reynard* supports the idea that the *Game of Chess* is a courtly work, and has to meet the higher requirements of the courtly audience as opposed to a bourgeois readership: but such assumptions about audience and reception are surely open to debate. Seth Lerer discusses Caxton in *Chaucer and His Readers*, an engaging and inventive assessment of the reception of Chaucer in the fifteenth century (although sometimes one suspects the material accommodates itself to his thesis, rather than the other way around). He argues persuasively, however, that Caxton's attitude to Chaucer demonstrates the printer's general displacement of authority from writer to reader, 'from the originator of a text to those who transmit and interpret it'. V. M. O'Mara, 'From Print to Manuscript: The *Golden Legend* and British Library Lansdowne MS 379' (*LeedsSE* (1992) 23.81–104) shows that the scribe of this manuscript has copied and adapted sections of a later edition of Caxton's *Golden Legend* (published first in ?1483) and identifies the compilation of material as a homily collection.

10. Other Prose

Michael G. Sargent's splendid edition of *Nicholas Love's Mirror of the Blessed Life of Jesus Christ* was missed for review in 1992. It is cheering to have this important early fifteenth-century work available again in so carefully presented a form. Sargent's introduction discusses the pseudo-Bonaventuran *Meditationes Vitae Christi* upon which the *Mirror* is based, the author of the *Mirror*, Nicholas Love, and what Love did with his source, including his anti-Lollard stance. Sargent also discusses contemplative literature and English bourgeois piety, and describes the textual tradition of the *Mirror*. The edition is accompanied by a standard apparatus.

The *Two Wycliffite Texts* edited by Anne Hudson are the sermon of William Taylor, preserved uniquely in Oxford, Bodleian Library, MS Douce 53, and the testimony of William Thorpe, whose sole surviving medieval copy, Oxford, Bodleian Library, MS Rawlinson C. 208, is used as a base text. Appendixes and standard apparatus are included.

Helen Leith Spencer's *English Preaching in the Late Middle Ages*, an eight-chapter study of preaching in late medieval England, and a study mainly of the preaching records preserved in Middle English, offers an abundance of material of interest to students of prose. It is impossible to do justice to so rich an offering in a review as short as this, but it might be mentioned that the substantial chapters of her book reflect on the phenomenon of preaching in medieval England in general, on medieval views of how preaching was to be conducted, on how preaching the gospel and pastoralia were to be managed, on sermon form and on what the manuscripts add to our knowledge of preaching. This book, graced additionally with a supple and dignified prose, is the best book-length study of Middle English preaching to have been written since the works of G. R. Owst. John Edward Damon usefully demonstrates that the source of the opening Latin formula of 'An Early Middle English Homily for the Common of an Apostle' (*N&Q* 40.10–11), which occurs in Lambeth Palace Library, MS 487 and Cambridge, Trinity College, MS B.14.52, is an antiphon for the Common of an Apostle.

Ancrene Wisse has done well this year. The *Concordance to Ancrene Wisse: MS Corpus Christi College Cambridge 402*, presented by Jennifer Potts, Lorna Stevenson and Jocelyn Wogan-Browne, is based on Tolkien's diplomatic version of the Cambridge manuscript, checked against the original. After their huge labour, students should be better able to inform their discussions of this text while we await the new edition currently in progress from Bella Millett. From an analysis of the religious habits which are variously 'Black, White and Grey in *Hali Meiðhad* and *Ancrene Wisse*' (*MÆ* 62.69–78), Alan J. Fletcher unfolds the various possible referrents that the author(s) of these texts may have had in mind. By a process of elimination, he is able to suggest that the 'greie cuuel' of *Ancrene Wisse* probably referred to the Franciscan habit, and that if so, the composition of *Ancrene Wisse* in its earliest form should now be dated to some time shortly after 1224. Also on the topic of clothing, Mary C. Erler convincingly illustrates how 'Margery Kempe's White Clothes' (*MÆ* 62.78–83) would have signalled not only vowed chastity in the lay state, but also in the specific choice of white an unusual distinction: a lay woman vowed to chastity, but wearing the garments of symbolic virginity. Another piece by Alan J. Fletcher demonstrates that what the 'The Dancing Virgins of *Hali Meiðhad*' (*N&Q* 40.437–9) were doing was dancing a ring dance, and more specifically, a *carole en ronde*. As the aristocrats of the court of heaven, the author of the text has presented his virgins as being just as capable of courtly pastime as their more secular counterparts in texts like the *Roman de la Rose*.

Päivi Pahta has produced a useful edition of 'The Middle English Legend of St Faith in MS Southwell Minster 7' (*NM* 94.149–65). It includes in its apparatus a discussion of St Faith's cult, a manuscript description and notes on the text. In 'The Compiler's Awareness of Audience in Medieval Medical Prose: The Example of Wellcome MS 225' (*JEGP* 92.509–22), Joanne Jasin illustrates thoroughly how the compiler of the Middle English treatise on uroscopy in Wellcome MS 225 shows himself sensitive to the reading requirements of a broader audience than a narrowly academic one acquainted with French and Latin. She describes the means he uses to make academic medical information available for wider use. On a similar medical theme, Elaine E. Whitaker shows how 'Reading the Paston Letters Medically' (*ELN* 31.19–27) provides evidence of the growing displacement of women from the medical sphere during the later Middle Ages, a displacement confirmed by other historical sources.

Oliver S. Pickering notes 'A London Chronicle in Yorkshire: An Addition to Handlist VI of the *Index of Middle English Prose*' (*N&Q* 40.305–7), in Bradford District Archives, MS 32D86/42. Folios 1–33 of this manuscript contain a London chronicle, written in a hand of the mid-fifteenth century. Pickering briefly locates its text in the field of other contemporary London chronicles. Andrew Breeze contributes two notes. In 'Welsh Babau "Baby" and *Ancrene Wisse*' (*N&Q* 40.12–13), he argues that 'babau' ('baby') in *Ancrene Wisse* is a Welsh loan word, and in 'Welsh *Geneu* "Mouth, Jaws" and the Middle English *Seinte Margarete*' (*N&Q* 40.13–14), he argues that the word *genow/geneow* was a fairly recent loan word into English at the time when *Seinte Margarete* was composed.

Finally, Marion Glasscoe has written a fluent and absorbing study of the *English Medieval Mystics: Games of Faith*. After an introductory chapter, Glasscoe devotes a chapter each to the landmark writers of mystical prose in Middle English: the flamboyant prose of Richard Rolle, Walter Hilton's comparatively methodical charting of the religious life, the astringent apophatic mysticism of the *Cloud*-Author and his *Book of Privy Counselling*, Julian of Norwich, who is treated to a vision-by-vision commentary, and Margery Kempe. Throughout the study meanders the metaphor of mysticism as a game, and this metaphor surfaces from time to time in the various chapters. Glasscoe stresses the essential points of unity that these otherwise very diverse writers seem to share.

11. Drama

This section is divided into the following sections: (a) Editions and General Studies; (b) Chester; (c) York; (d) Moralities and Non-Cycle Plays.

(a) Editions and General Studies

Missed for review in 1990, but well worth retrospective mention here, is Gordon Kipling's edition of *The Receyt of the Ladie Kateryne* for the Early English Texts Society. Kipling has been specializing in the study of London royal entries for some years, and what he has had to say has always proved worthwhile reading. This edition is no exception. The *Receyt*, edited from London, College of Arms, MS 1st M. 13, describes the arrival of Katherine of Aragon in England at the beginning of the sixteenth century, the extraordinary pageantry devised for her triumphal entry into London, her marriage to Prince Arthur with its disguisings and tournaments, and Arthur's funeral a few months later at Ludlow and Worcester. The edition is a model of care and attention; it comes also with a standard apparatus of introduction, notes and glossary. Another edition is to be reported under this heading, that by Clifford Davidson of *A Tretise of Miraclis Pleyinge*. The importance of the *Tretise* as a piece of theoretical writing about the function and perception of medieval drama has long been recognized, and now we have been presented with a full and convenient edition of it. Davidson has set the work in context, and written a lively introduction which incorporates an extremely useful study of the written dialect of the sole surviving copy of the *Tretise* (London, British Library, MS Additional 24202, ff 14–21) contributed by Paul A. Johnston Jr. This edition will be a welcome item on the shelves of students of early drama.

'Structure, Characterization, and the New Community in Four Plays of Jesus and the Doctors' (*CompD* 26 [1992–3].344–57), by Daniel T. Kline, is a straightforward rehabilitation of the extant Middle English plays, apart from that in the N. Town collection, on Jesus and the Doctors, and a salvaging of them from Rosemary Woolf's dismissal as 'dull and infelicitous'. He argues that, contrary to Woolf, each play is important in its own right, and that in each the presentation of Christ is nuanced and distinct. Meg Twycross has added 'More Black and White Souls' (*METh* 13 [1993 for 1991].52–63) to her earlier collection and study of depictions of the saved and the damned at the Judgement. Her new source is Oxford, Bodleian Library, MS Douce 134, a lavishly illustrated copy of the French prose *Livre de la Vigne de Nostre Seigneur*, made about 1450–70. Illustrations from the manuscript are reproduced. Bruce Moore's thorough sifting of the evidence for 'The Banns in Medieval English Drama' (*LeedsSE* 24.91–122) leads him to conclude that, unlike the banns read in advance of the northern play cycles, the delivery of those prefacing more southerly plays may have featured condensed play performances, or have been announced with mimed accompaniment.

(b) Chester

Since the articles gathered in *The Chester Mystery Cycle: A Casebook* and edited by Kevin J. Harty were reviewed in earlier issues of the *YWES*, it would be otiose to review each of them again. However, Harty's collection should be noted as it assembles between two covers some important work on Chester published between 1960 and 1987.

(c) York

Another valuable article on the playing places of the York cycle and their social implications has been written, this time by David J. F. Crouch in 'Paying to See the Play: The Stationholders on the Route of the York Corpus Christi Play in the Fifteenth Century' (*METh* 13 [1993 for 1991].64–111). His article, in dealing with the fifteenth-century evidence, serves as a useful prelude to the superb analysis by Eileen White (see *YWES* for 1987) on similar aspects of the cycle in the sixteenth century.

(d) Moralities and Non-Cycle Plays

Sarah Carpenter writes sensitively on 'Masks and Mirrors: Questions of Identity in Medieval Morality Drama' (*METh* 13 [1993 for 1991].7–17), tracing the theatrical manipulations of masks and mirrors to explore and body forth moments of self-discovery in a selection of fifteenth- and sixteenth-century English plays. Victor I. Scherb's analysis of 'Frame Structure in *The Conversion of St. Paul*' (*CompD* 26 [1992].124–39) seeks to repair the damage which he believes scholarly emphasis upon that play's staging has done to our understanding of its dramatic focus. He discovers in the play a sophisticated arrangement of framing techniques, comparable to those in the contemporary visual arts, which help to bring together narrative, devotion and didacticism. In 'Stage Properties and Iconography in the Early English Drama' (*Mediaevalia* 15 [1993 for 1989].241–54), Clifford Davidson makes further important contributions towards fleshing out our understanding of what early stage productions actually looked like by recourse to medieval iconography.

Books Reviewed

Albano, Robert A. *Middle English Historiography*. American University Studies. Series IV, English Language and Literature Vol. 168. Lang. pp. 254. hb £35. ISBN 0 8204 2136 7.

Allen, Peter L. *The Art of Love: Amatory Fiction from Ovid to the 'Romance of the Rose'*. UPennP. pp. 178. hb £22. ISBN 0 8122 3188 0.

Barnes, Geraldine. *Counsel and Strategy in Middle English Romance*. Brewer. pp. 163. hb £29.50. ISBN 0 85991 362 7.

Barr, Helen. *The 'Piers Plowman' Tradition*. Everyman. Dent. pp. 375. pb £5.99. ISBN 0 460 87238 9.

Beckwith, Sarah. *Christ's Body. Identity, Culture and Society in Late Medieval Writings*. Routledge. pp. 200. hb £37.50. ISBN 0 415 04420 2.

Boitani, Piero, and Anna Torti, eds. *Interpretation: Medieval and Modern*. Brewer. pp. 212. hb £29.50. ISBN 0 85991 382 1.

Boulton, Maureen. *The Song in the Story: Lyric Insertion in French Narrative Fiction, 1200 –1400*. UPennP. pp. 327. hb $39.95. ISBN 0 8122 3199 6.

Brewer, Elisabeth. *Sir Gawain and the Green Knight: Sources and Analogues*. B&B (1992). pp. 160. hb £29.50, pb £12.95. ISBN 0 85991 358 9, 0 85991 359 7.

Burrow, John. *Langland's Fictions*. OUP. pp. 130. ISBN 019 811293 9.

——. *The William Matthews Lectures 1993: Thinking in Poetry: Three Medieval Examples*. Birkbeck. pp. 32. pb £5. ISBN 0 907904 70 X.

Carley, James P., and Felicity Riddy, eds. *Arthurian Literature XII*. Brewer. pp. 200. hb £35. ISBN 0 85991 397 X.

Cherewatuk, Karen, and Ulrike Wiethaus, eds. *Dear Sister. Medieval Women and the Epistolary Genre*. UPennP. pp. 218. hb £31.50, pb £13.95. ISBN 0 8122 3170 8, 0 8122 1437 4.

Chuilleanáin, E. Ní, and J. D. Pheifer, eds. *Noble and Joyous Histories. English Romances 1375–1650*. IAP. pp. 294. hb £27.50. ISBN 0 7165 2379 5.

Davidson, Clifford. *A Tretise of Miraclis Pleyinge*. MIP. hb $36, pb $15. ISBN 1 879288 31 1, 1 879288 32 X.

Donavin, Georgiana. *Incest Narratives and the Structure of Gower's 'Confessio Amantis'*. English Literary Studies, University of Victoria Monograph Series, No. 56. UVict. pp. 104. Can$9.57. ISBN 0 920604 64 1.

Fellows, Jennifer. *Of Love and Chivalry: Anthology of Middle English Romance*. Dent. pp. 288. £4.99. ISBN 0 460 87237 0.

Field, P. J. C. *The Life and Times of Sir Thomas Malory*. Arthurian Studies XXIX. Brewer. pp. 220. £29.50. ISBN 0 85991 385 6.

Glasscoe, Marion. *English Medieval Mystics: Games of Faith*. Longman. pp. 256. hb £43, pb £15.99. ISBN 0 582 49516 4, 0 582 49517 2.

Goldstein, R. James. *The Matter of Scotland*. UNebP. pp. 386. ISBN 0 8032 2144 4.

Harty, Kevin J. *The Chester Mystery Cycle: A Casebook*. Garland. pp. 344. hb $51. ISBN 0 8153 0497 8.

Hudson, Anne, ed. *Two Wycliffite Texts: The Sermon of William Taylor, 1406 – The Testimony of William Thorpe, 1407*. EETS o.s. 301. OUP. pp. 182. £20. ISBN 0 19 722303 6.

Huot, Sylvia. *The 'Romance of the Rose' and its Medieval Readers: Interpretation, Reception, Manuscript Transmission*. CUP. pp. 404. hb £40. ISBN 0 521 41713 9.

Kaulbach, Ernest. *Imaginative Prophecy in the B-Text of 'Piers Plowman'*. Piers Plowman Studies VIII. Brewer. pp. 158. hb £29.50. ISBN 0 85991 357 0.

Kindrick, Robert. *Henryson and the Medieval Arts of Rhetoric*. Garland. pp. 345. ISBN 0 8153 1246 6.

Kipling, Gordon, ed. *The Receyt of Ladie Kateryne*. EETS o.s. 296. OUP (1990). pp. 296. £25. ISBN 0 19 722298 6.

Le Saux, Françoise, ed. *Amys and Amylion*. UExe. pp. 150. £9.95. ISBN 0 85989 411 8.

Lerer, Seth. *Chaucer and His Readers: Imagining the Author in Late Medieval England*. PrincetonUP. pp. 320. hb £30. ISBN 0 691 06811 9.

Lomperis, Linda, and Sarah Stanbury, eds. *Feminist Approaches to the Body in Medieval Literature*. UPennP. pp. 256. hb $36.95, pb $16.95. ISBN 0 8122 3117 1, 0 8122 1364 5.

Meale, Carol M. *Women and Literature in Britain, 1150–1500*. CUP. pp. 224. hb £30. ISBN 0 521 40018 X.

Morgan, Gwendolyn A. *Medieval Balladry and the Courtly Tradition. Literature of Revolt and Assimulation*. American University Studies. Series IV, English Language and Literature Vol. 160. Lang. pp. 148. £25. ISBN 0 8204 2042 5.

Nederman, Cary J., and Kate Langdon Forhan, eds. *Medieval Political Theory – A Reader: The Quest for the Body Politic, 1100–1400*. Routledge. pp. 258. hb £37.50, pb £12.99. ISBN 0 415 06488 0, 0 415 06489 9.

Potts, Jennifer, Lorna Stevenson, and Jocelyn Wogan-Browne. *Concordance to Ancrene Wisse: MS Corpus Christi College Cambridge 402*. Brewer. pp. 1280. hb £120. ISBN 0 85991 395 3.

Rooney, Anne. *Hunting in Middle English Literature*. Brewer. pp. 214. £32.50. ISBN 0 85991 379 1.

Sargent, Michael G. *Nicholas Love's Mirror of the Blessed Life of Jesus Christ*. Garland. pp. 496. hb $80. ISBN 0 8240 5896 8.

Saunders, Corinne J. *The Forest of Medieval Romance*. Brewer. pp. 236. hb £35. ISBN 0 85991 381 3.

Simonelli, Maria Picchio. *Inferno III*. (With a new translation of the Canto by Patrick Creagh and Robert Hollander.) UPennP. pp. 124. ISBN 0 8122 3229 1.

Spearing, A. C. *The Medieval Poet as Voyeur. Looking and Listening in Medieval Love-Narratives*. CUP. pp. 321. £40. ISBN 0 521 41094 0.

Spencer, H. Leith. *English Preaching in the Late Middle Ages*. Clarendon. pp. 542. hb £48. ISBN 0 19 811203 3.

Suzuki, Takashi, and Tsuyoshi Mukai. *Arthurian and Other Studies Presented to Shunichi Noguchi*. Brewer. pp. 273. £49.50. ISBN 0 85991 380 5.

Tanner, William E., ed. *The Arthurian Myth of Quest and Magic. A Festschrift in Honor of Lavon B. Fulwiler*. CMAP. pp. 200. $14. ISBN 0 9635769 0 9.

Terry, Patricia, and Nancy Vine Durling. *'The Romance of the Rose' or 'Guillaume de Dole', by Jean Renart*. UPennP. pp. 118. hb £23.50, pb £11.95. ISBN 0 8122 3111 2, 0 8122 1388 2.

Trigg, Stephanie, ed. *Medieval English Poetry*. Longman Critical Readers. Longman. pp. 300. hb £32, pb £11.99. ISBN 0 582 08260 9, 0 582 08261 7.

Vaughan, Miceál, ed. *Suche Werkis to Werke*. Colleagues. pp. 292. hb £29.50. ISBN 0 937191 36 1.

Walsh, James E. *A Catalogue of the Fifteenth-Century Printed Books in the Harvard University Library Volume II. Books Printed in Rome and Venice*.

Medieval and Renaissance Texts and Studies Vol. 97. MRTS. pp. 674 + 16 plates. $50. ISBN 0 86698 111 X.

Wiethaus, Ulrike, ed. *Maps of Flesh and Light. The Religious Experience of Medieval Women Mystics.* SyracuseUP. pp. 206. hb $34.95, pb $17.95. ISBN 0 8156 2560 X, 0 8156 2611 8.

Ziolkowski, Jan M. *Talking Animals. Medieval Latin Beast Poetry, 750–1150.* UPennP. pp. 354. £33.95. ISBN 0 8122 3161 9.

IV

Middle English: Chaucer

VALERIE ALLEN and MARGARET CONNOLLY

This chapter is divided into four sections: 1. General; 2. *Canterbury Tales*; 3. *Troilus and Criseyde*; 4. Other Works.

1. General

Mark Allen and Bege K. Bowers have produced 'An Annotated Chaucer Bibliography 1991' (*SAC* 15.309–83), and Bege K. Bowers has also compiled 'Chaucer Research, 1992: Report No. 53' (*ChauR* 28.187–203).

Michael Seymour's study of Chaucerian manuscripts continues with two useful articles considering 'The Manuscripts of Chaucer's *Legend of Good Women*' (*Scriptorium* 47.i.73–90) and 'The Manuscripts of Chaucer's *Parlement of Foules*' (*Scriptorium* 47.ii.192–204). Each essay gives a brief account of the poems' origins and contemporary readership, and comments on the textual history and composition of the manuscripts, which, for the most part, are compiled in booklets; the discussion of the *Parliament of Fowls* also includes a note on the authenticity of the roundel which follows stanza 97 in the text. The extant manuscripts for both texts are described according to the same set of principles, but to avoid duplication the seven manuscripts which contain both poems are described fully in the former article, and given only brief additional entries in the latter. Two brief notes in *Medium Ævum* are of interest to Chaucerians: A. S. G. Edwards finds some annotations prompted by Chaucer's work in a manuscript of Trevisa's *Polychronicon* ('A Chaucerian Reader of Trevisa', 62.288–9), and J. W. Binns offers some comments on the reception of Chaucer in the seventeenth century ('Wenceslas Clemens' Homage at the Tomb of Chaucer, 1636', 62.289–92). In another short piece A. S. G. Edwards considers 'The Chaucer Portraits in the Harley and Rosenbach Manuscripts' (*EMS* 4.268–71), accounting for their similarity by suggesting that the Rosenbach portrait was copied from the Harley portrait. Noted and to be reviewed next year is Ian Lancashire's edition, *Computer-Based Chaucer Studies*, a collection of essays all of whose analyses are based on computer-assisted research.

Several pieces concentrate on aspects of Chaucer's language. Peter Richardson contributes 'Chaucer's Final -E: Some Discourse Considerations' (*ChauR* 28.83–93) to a long-running linguistic debate, but aims to alter the traditional direction of scholarship in this area by employing principles of narrative pragmatics. For Richardson, the issue of Chaucer's final *-e* is not just a question of versification, but an aspect of Chaucer's narrative style, and, using examples from the *Miller's Tale* he attempts to show how final *-e* and tense interact, claiming that Chaucer systematically manipulates tense for his own narrative purposes. C. P. Biggam explores 'Aspects of Chaucer's Adjectives of Hue' (*ChauR* 28.41–53), investigating 37 lexemes and their subjects, and discovering that Chaucer had an exceptional colour vocabulary; she finds that his use of adjectives is both sophisticated and subtle, despite his preference for basic colour terms. In his presidential address to the New Chaucer Society's Eighth International Congress in Seattle, 1992, Alfred David considers '*Old*, *New*, and *Yong* in Chaucer' (*SAC* 15.5–21). Following an insight of Louise O. Fradenburg's that Chaucer's poetry is deeply concerned with the experience of loss, David detects Chaucerian patterns of disillusionment, grief and pain, by examining the word *old* in its oppositions with its antonyms *new* and *yong*. His essay covers the *Romaunt of the Rose*, some of the dream poems, *Troilus and Criseyde*, and the *Canterbury Tales*; paradoxically he finds the latter 'a more youthful work' than works which predate it chronologically. The festschrift for John Leyerle, *The Centre and its Compass: Studies in Medieval Literature in Honor of Professor John Leyerle*, edited by Robert Taylor et al., contains 17 contributions including five on Chaucer, each of which is noted in the appropriate section below.

There is some interest in biographical issues this year. In a brief article relating to Chaucer's involvement in a *raptus* suit, 'Geoffrey Chaucer, Cecilia Chaumpaigne, and Alice Perrers: A Closer Look' (*ChauR* 28.78–82), Marta Powell Harley argues against the identification of Cecilia Chaumpaigne as the stepdaughter of Alice Perrers, Edward III's mistress. More substantially, Christopher Cannon writes of the *raptus* in '*Raptus* in the Chaumpaigne Release and a Newly Discovered Document Concerning the Life of Geoffrey Chaucer' (*Speculum* 68.74–94). Cannon notes the lack of critical consensus on the meaning of the word *raptus* – whether it implies forced coitus or, less severely, abduction. To resolve the dilemma, Cannon turns to cases of *raptus* in unpublished court documents just prior to Chaumpaigne's document of release. Distinguishing between 'ravishment' (meaning elopement) and *raptus* (meaning forced coitus), Cannon shows that the word carried the same serious implications to Chaucer's contemporaries as it carries to a twentieth-century audience. In support of this view, Cannon brings to light a 'memorandum' in the *coram rege* rolls for 3 Richard II which purports to record the language of the Chaumpaigne release. Significantly, this document has omitted the key phrase *de raptu meo* in favour of more general and less grievous wrongs. Although cautious about speculating how the change came about, or who was responsible for it, Cannon argues that the phrase was eliminated because of its gravity and offensiveness – an argument that neatly resolves our semantic dilemma over the word *raptus*.

Seth Lerer's important book, *Chaucer and His Readers: Imagining the Author in Late-Medieval England*, considers Chaucer's reception in the fifteenth century, and his various transformations from mere maker to laureate poet, and subsequently to dead *auctor*. Part of Lerer's argument is that the way in which Chaucer is constructed by his fifteenth-century readers depends on elements already present in his poetry, and accordingly each of the book's first four chapters is built around Chaucerian figures. In the first chapter, Lerer argues that Chaucer's Clerk, a narrator caught between the demands of *auctor* and patron, served as a model for writing, for fifteenth-century poets in general, and for Lydgate in particular. Lydgate's achievement in designating Chaucer as both laureate and aureate poet is explored, as is the interchangeability of these terms, and this chapter includes a most persuasive account of the illustrations in Huntington Library, MS HM 268 and the *Troilus* frontispiece in Corpus Christi College, Cambridge, MS 61. Moving from writing to reading, Lerer argues in Chapter 2 that the figure of Chaucer's Squire shapes the literary values of the fifteenth century, firstly as the son of the Knight, by encouraging a genealogical perception of literary history, and secondly, as the lover *par excellence*, by guiding literary taste for love poetry. Lerer's evidence here is based on Clanvowe's *Book of Cupid* in its earliest manuscript context. He reads MS Bodley Tanner 346 in two different ways: from end to end, and from centre outwards; though interesting, these analyses would have proved easier to grasp had he first provided a clear list of the manuscript's contents, as he did, for example, when discussing the manuscripts in Chapter 3. In Chapter 3, following a different tack, and noting the qualities attributed to Chaucer by the late fifteenth-century didactic poem, the *Book of Curtayse*, namely, clarity and brevity, Lerer distinguishes another Chaucerian construction: Chaucer as children's writer, a natural development, he claims, following the propagation of the image of a 'father' Chaucer. His discussion centres on two manuscripts usually dismissed as 'bad' texts, but Lerer takes nothing on trust, and indeed the strength of this book lies in his detailed, careful and fresh approach to some well-worn manuscript evidence. Here, he considers the Helmington manuscript's childish marginalia and suggests that this was a volume both intended for and used by a childish readership throughout its history; further, that its abridgment of *The Tale of Melibee* and the *Pardoner's Tale* is a systematic scribal reduction of the complexities of Chaucer's texts which rewrites literature into moral compilation, a refashioning which also characterizes the version of the *Clerk's Tale* in Huntington Library, MS HM 140. In approaching this latter anthology, Lerer uses critical terminology borrowed from John Shirley's headnotes, and since Shirley is a figure who has haunted the discussion somewhat during the book's opening chapters, it is a relief to find his influence considered more centrally in Chapter 4. Based on a discussion of Chaucer's short poems, this section assesses Shirley's contribution to the making of the Chaucer canon. Borrowing a phrase from Paul Strohm, Lerer discerns in Shirley's anthologizing and annotation the creation of a 'social Chaucer', a public poet of occasion. His controlling image for this chapter, the figure of the wayward scribe, Adam Scriveyn, is appropriate enough, especially since this poem survives only in Shirley's hand; less apt is his other analogy drawing Shirley as 'a kind of romance hero'. The chapter on Shirley concludes with a brief mention of John Stowe and his printing of the Latin epitaph supposedly engraved on Chaucer's tomb. This epitaph is discussed at length in the following chapter, whose focus is Caxton, and here Lerer returns to the notion of laureateship to show how the perceptions of the new print culture towards the end of the fifteenth century, as well as the political milieu, provoke the displacement of the English poetic tradition by the classical, and allow the deposition of Chaucer as poet laureate by the university-educated John Skelton. Chaucer is constructed instead as a dead *auctor*, his name invoked by Hawes and Skelton only for its citability, and from this point on Lerer's argument is that Chaucer is dead and buried, a figure removed to the past; given this argument it should not surprise us that these final two chapters have less to say about Chaucer than do the earlier sections of the book. Parodying the fifteenth-century works with which it has been concerned, *Chaucer and His Readers* concludes with an envoy entitled 'All þis ys said under correctyon'. Lerer reminds us here, as he does too often elsewhere in the volume, of his agenda, but his thesis, most succinctly described by its subtitle, 'Imagining the Author in Late-Medieval England', is thought-provoking, imaginative and argued with authority.

By far the most unusual item received for review this year is *Chaucer's Checklist: The Poet's Life List of all the Birds in All His Works*, the first in a series of four illustrated books by Michael Jeneid, listing the birds mentioned by Chaucer, Dante and Shakespeare. The volume begins with a bland summary of Chaucer's life, followed by some comments on his references to birds (530 in total, including 50 different species), and an attempt to identify some unfamiliar Chaucerian bird names. The book's largest section is that entitled 'Field and Literary Notes'; more field than literary, and certainly more about birds than Chaucer, this section comprises an eclectic gathering of snippets, sometimes summarizing the plots of Chaucer's stories, but at other points assuming more knowledge on the part of the reader. The section on birds of prey is the most informative, and sheds light on the *Parliament of Fowls* (another volume devoted to the poem alone is promised); but the style is often irritatingly chatty, the notes hard to locate (and not always apparently relevant to the text), and the inclusion of three different indexes seems like overkill for such a slim volume. Linne R. Mooney's interesting essay, 'The Cock and the Clock' (*SAC* 15.91–109) is not about birds but about telling the time. By examining two almanacs written by Chaucer's contemporaries, and by paying minute attention to Chaucer's own references to time, Mooney lucidly expounds the various methods by which one might calculate the time in the fourteenth century; she explains the distinction between 'artificial' and 'common' time, and outlines the growing acceptability of 'clock time' during this period, despite the relative scarcity of clocks in Chaucer's England.

Janette Dillon's *Geoffrey Chaucer* appears in a series ('Writers in Their Time') whose stated aim is to place writers and works 'in the specific and detailed contexts of their time'; with such a big aim for quite a small book, it is hardly surprising if the result sometimes falls between two stools. The opening chapters deal straightforwardly enough with Chaucer's life and times, with the mechanics of a manuscript culture, and with the structure of medieval society; later chapters explore philosophy, attitudes to death, and the critical reception of Chaucer's work, and the volume also contains discussion of several key Chaucer texts, addressed by a variety of critical approaches. The strength of the book lies in just such variety, and in its ability to mix literature and history; so, for example, a discussion of women and the clergy moves naturally to a consideration of the Wife of Bath's *Prologue*, and includes a lucid explanation of Lollardy. But the more difficult material attempted in Chapter 5, '"Greet altercacioun": The Influence of Philosophy' is not so successfully synthesized, and one might question its inclusion given the book's direction at an audience of absolute beginners, and especially since, as Dillon admits, 'Chaucer ... shows no sign of direct familiarity with the works of either Ockham or Wyclif'. Nevertheless, this book will be useful supplementary reading for undergraduate courses on Chaucer.

On the gender issue, there are two books, only one of which deals exclusively with Chaucer. The one that does not, Linda Lomperis and Sarah Stanbury's edition of *Feminist Approaches to the Body in Medieval Literature* contains an essay on the *Physician's Tale* and an essay on the *Book of the Duchess* which are reviewed below. Margaret Hallissy's *Clean Maids, True Wives, Steadfast Widows: Chaucer's Women and Medieval Codes of Conduct* is a consideration of Chaucer's women in the context of medieval conduct guides and the common-place division of the woman's life into three 'estates': virginity, wifehood, and widowhood. Hallissy sees such an estate division (which already presupposes we are talking here about secular, not religious, women) as so pervasive that it informs Chaucer's representation of female experience both consciously and unconsciously. The first two chapters sketch out the legal, religious and cultural contexts in which woman's submission to and identification in terms of men can be understood; they also look at a selection of fourteenth-century codes of conduct – 'The Good Wife Taught Her Daughter', the *Goodman of Paris*, and the *Book of the Knight of the Tower*. In Chapter 3, Hallissy notes the hagiographical examples of saints who suffered for their chastity and allies the notion to the *Legend of Good Women* where she sees Chaucer questioning the necessary connection between chastity and suffering – a connection that gets interrogated even further in the *Franklin's Tale*. In this tale, chastity is no longer seen as the chief virtue of a woman but now ranks alongside a virtue characteristically male, 'trouthe'; and the marriage relationship between Dorigen and Arveragus is celebrated as 'egalitarian', even if humanly flawed. The centrality (or otherwise) of chastity is the dominant theme again in the chapter on virginity. The *Physician's Tale* is seen to articulate the truism 'better to die a meek maid than to live a bold wife'. Domestic harmony is explored through the example of Griselde in the *Clerk's Tale*. Hallissy hears Chaucer speaking less in the tale and more in the 'Envoy' where women are encouraged not to follow Griselde's example or the example of the conduct guides, but to speak their minds. In the act of gossip (the Wife of Bath being the obvious instance), Hallissy sees not only negative female disruption but also the positive assertion of female companionship. The *Man of Law's Tale* demonstrates the 'spatial instability' of woman in motion. Travelling alone, Custance is vulnerable and must be restored to the domestic interior of the protector's (be it father's or husband's) house. Architectural space (as well as clothing) serves as 'metaphor for the integrity of the female body'. Criseyde sums up the vulnerability of the estate of widowhood which is invoked as at least a partial explanation for her betrayal of Troilus. The book ends with an analysis of the *Wife of Bath's Prologue and Tale* as a discourse on the importance of woman's speech and the need for men to listen to women. This is a very thorough and informative book; however, the question of how we might read a book of conduct and a fictional poem differently is not really addressed (despite the brief final chapter on books) and it leaves one wondering how Hallissy salvages Chaucer from his anti-feminist pilgrim narrators in order to assert that '"Chaucer liked women", real women'.

A theoretical piece comes from Andrew Taylor, in 'Chaucer our Derridean Contemporary?' (*Exemplaria* 5.471–86), in which he addresses complaints that the so-called theoretically informed criticism reductively describes whatever medieval text they are talking about to a deadening 'self-subversion and irresolvable ambiguity' (quoting A. C. Spearing). Taylor recognizes the justice of the criticism but argues for medievalists as a special case, describing them as 'struggling to keep abreast of the New Philology', and as divided between the master of a 'radical method' (i.e. deconstruction) and the master of medieval purism; 'for us the challenge of theory is particularly overwhelming'. On the basis of his plea for medievalism as an extenuating condition, Taylor permits that to some extent we will 'misunderstand the force of Derrida's negative ontology'. His defence is based on an unshaken belief in disciplinary specialism: there is medieval specialism and deconstructive specialism and, by definition, we can only do justice to one. The possibility that inasmuch as deconstruction is seen to deny the boundaries of history, it also denies the boundaries of discipline (its own and medieval) is not addressed. The point that nobody can read everything is hardly debatable; it is debatable that having more time to read more Derrida would better the quality of the bulk of medieval criticism. 'Lik an asse to the harpe ...'

2.   *Canterbury Tales*

Firstly, some computer-assisted developments deserve notice. Norman Blake and Peter Robinson have edited the first volume of a series of occasional papers describing *The* Canterbury Tales *Project.* The project's origins lie partly in a dissatisfaction with the editorial work of J. M. Manly and E. Rickert, and partly in an awareness of the new possibilities offered by increasingly sophisticated methods of computer analysis; its stated aim is 'to make available, in computer-readable form, transcripts, images, collations, and analyses of all eighty-four extant manuscripts and four pre-1500 printed editions of the *Canterbury Tales*'. In the first essay, Norman Blake discusses the complexity of the textual tradition of the *Canterbury Tales* and outlines what the project can and cannot do; two subsequent essays explain the principles used in transcription (Peter Robinson and Elizabeth Solopova), and the techniques of cladistic analysis and database analysis used in the reconstruction of the history of the *Canterbury Tales* (Robert O'Hara and Peter Robinson). Two further contributions consider possible applications for the project: Daniel Mosser proposes a new type of electronic descriptive catalogue, which might include colour facsimiles and linguistic profiles as well as codicological descriptions; Stephen Partridge calls for a re-examination of the marginal and interlinear glosses in the manuscripts of the *Canterbury Tales*. The establishment of such an ambitious project deserves applause, but it remains to be seen whether the outcome will, as Norman Blake promises, 'alter our attitude to what we mean by a text'. A different sort of text is proposed in Paul G. Remley's article, 'An Electronic Reading-Text of Chaucer's *Canterbury Tales*' (*Æstel* 1.77–110). Remley describes the project named in the title, an enterprise designed to assist undergraduates reading Chaucer in the original Middle English, and emphasizes how the proposed text will differ from the diskette release of the *Riverside Chaucer*. Helpful aspects of this article are its survey of computer-assisted developments in humanities research over the last 25 years (including mention of some as yet unfulfilled promises), and its inclusion of extensive bibliographical notes summarizing publications in this area. Remley tries hard not to lose his reader in the realms of computer-speak, though he does not always succeed. Nor does Ian Lancashire in his scrutiny of Chaucer's habits of phrasal self-repetition, 'Chaucer's Repetends from The General Prologue of *The Canterbury Tales*' (in Taylor et al., 315–65). With the aid of computer analysis, Lancashire seeks to solve the problems of identifying and classifying repeated phrases. The result is a lengthy and abstruse article amply illustrated with ferocious diagrams, graphs, and tables. For all this effort some of the findings are disappointingly inconclusive, for example, the statement that 'the repetend ... seems to belong to writing generally'; but some of the possibilities are intriguing, such as the suggestion that the occurrence of repetends might be used as a 'fingerprint' of authorship, of help in dating Chaucer's work. Diagrams and tables also characterize Charles Moorman's study, *The Statistical Determination of Affiliation in the Landmark Manuscripts of the 'Canterbury Tales'*. By using common statistical procedures, Moorman aims to devise a method for discerning 'statistically meaningful relationships' among the manuscripts of any given work, in this case the *Canterbury Tales*. He applies his method not to all of the *Canterbury Tales* manuscripts, but to one particular group: those produced within a decade of Chaucer's death which establish independent lines of transmission, termed the 'landmark' manuscripts by Germaine Dempster. In effect this means that Moorman uses the Hengwrt manuscript as a base-text, partly because of its age, partly through sheer convenience. But he is anxious to distinguish his procedures from those of Manly and Rickert, and to explain that his primary interest is not in justifying their findings but in ascertaining the *degree* of manuscript relationship in the *Canterbury Tales*. One of his more interesting conclusions concerns the relationship of the Hengwrt and Ellesmere manuscripts, which he shows to be both 'statistically unrelated in tale after tale', and also, most of the time, 'statistically opposed'. Moorman also sets out some other conclusions, or 'conjectures', as he prefers to call them, but he also admits to being less interested in these than in the figures themselves. Indeed, he expresses the hope that critical attention to his study might focus on his texts and tables, and accordingly displays his data in four appendices: these cover more than a hundred pages, a fact which is slightly disguised because the pages of the appendices are not numbered, although page numbers do reappear for the brief bibliography and index.

Manuscript studies are further discussed in Charlotte Morse's 'The Manuscripts of the *Canterbury Tales*' (*N&Q* 40.19–22), a review article, in which Morse recommends that Charles Owen's book (of the same title) 'should become standard reading for all students of Chaucer'. Morse sets Owen's thesis above both Norman Blake's tendentious privileging of Hengwrt and Larry Benson's privileging of Ellesmere, in that Owen's own dependence on the Manly–Rickert edition is itself subjected to dispassionate, careful analysis that takes into account *all* the manuscript evidence, even fragments and later fifteenth-century collections.

In an introduction that doesn't stint on self-confidence, Wolfgang E. H. Rudat, in *Ernest Exuberance in Chaucer's Poetics*, promises a reading of 'bawdy puns and innuendoes' that banishes the ennui of jaded critics and offers a 'definitive' version of the Pardoner. Acknowledging his debt to Laura Kendrick's *Chaucerian Play* (*YWES* 69.183), he claims to take her ideas further in a 'palimpsestic' mode of reading that is both intertextual and intratextual. This is a reading that interests itself more in allusion than in source, because al-lusion means 'playing to'. The uncharitable amongst us might feel that this is a justification for linking Chaucer's text to anything, but such a reading is, although it does not announce itself thus, a deconstructive one that sees all texts as interconnected. The question of source, then, becomes virtually redundant. The claimed originality and definitiveness of the palimpsestic reading turn out, however, to be sanctioned by an authority that is as (old) New Critical as you can get: a 'close-reading of the text' that lets the text 'speak for itself'. This letting the text speak for itself involves, for example, Alison's buttocks and thighs extending out the window in the *Miller's Tale* being imagined as a gigantic pair of scissors about to cut off Absolom's coiffure in a Delilah-act of castration. The Flood is the ejaculate of a divine and cosmic act of onanism. The narrative of the stuffing of the little boy's corpse into a privy in the *Prioress's Tale* is a *confessio* by the Prioress, who is a 'severely disturbed person', about an illicit abortion of her own. The Pardoner is *both* homosexual and eunuch (this is the 'definitive' version). The domestic disaster of Walter and Griselde is a comment upon the tyranny of the matrimonial and reproductive imperatives. The target in all this, Rudat argues, is Pope Innocent III's declaration on the uncleanness of the sperm from which man is formed and the sexually repressive nature of papal policies. The extent of the satire against the 'sexo-economic politics' of the church is in direct proportion to the bawdiness of the tales. The readings are not without an ingenious merit but, in the light of the untempered claims of the introduction, they have too high an expectation to live up to.

A general book with specific chapters on Chaucer's individual fabliaux is John Hines's *The Fabliau in English*, in which Hines argues for its independence from the French fabliau tradition. Even as far back as the early fabliau of the *Shipman's Tale*, Chaucer is seen to be defying and modifying the genre by using 'a fabliau to place fabliau in a critical light'. This impulse is noted throughout Chaucer's texts: the *Reeve's Tale* is morally inconclusive; the *Merchant's Tale* is a tale about the problems of hermeneutic interpretation; the *Miller's Tale* reveals strong continuities with its chivalric forerunner, the *Knight's Tale*; the Wife usurps the traditionally male role of fabliau-storyteller by telling her own tale. Hines also finds parallels of such problematization of genre in other non-Chaucerian fabliaux and texts with fabliau elements. What this amounts to is a distinctively English ironic treatment of the fabliau form of sufficient consistency to constitute the English fabliau as an autonomous type.

In *The Wives of the Canterbury Tales and the Tradition of the Valiant Woman of Proverbs 31:10–31*, Frances Minetti Biscoglio claims that the Hebraic tradition of the *mulier fortis* runs counter to both fourteenth-century misogyny and twentieth-century feminism and that it exerts a profound influence on Chaucer's depiction of the feminine in the *Tales*. Whereas the Hebraic *mulier fortis* is both literal wife and allegorical type of wisdom, the Christian *mulier fortis* is more narrowly symbolic of *Ecclesia* as *sponsa Christi* or of some aspect of Christian virtue. Chaucer's 'rich diversity' of human experience in the *Tales* and his interest in character rather than allegory suggests a sympathy with the more ancient tradition. Biscoglio sees Chaucer's wicked wives as parodically subverting the wifely ideal of the woman of Proverbs – a subversion that implicitly affirms rather than undermines such an ideal. On the other hand, his ideal wives are saved from simple allegorization in the manner in which they dominate their tales, being active in their very passivity, and paradoxically participating in both sacred and secular genres.

In '"Amonges Othere Wordes Wyse": The Medieval Seneca and the *Canterbury Tales*' (*ChauR* 28.135–45), Grace G. Wilson considers Seneca's medieval reputation and the use of his name in individual tales. Noting that the total number of references to Seneca in the *Canterbury Tales* 'is greater than the number to any other philosopher except Solomon', she helpfully lists these references in the endnotes; she also tries to discern whether Chaucer sees Seneca as moral philosopher or hackneyed aphorist. Brenda Deen Schildgen finds

Jerome's arguments about hermeneutics useful when approaching the *Canterbury Tales*, and her essay 'Jerome's *Prefatory Epistles* to the Bible and *The Canterbury Tales*' (*SAC* 15.111–30) has much to say about subjectivity and the problems of interpretation. She shows how both writers demonstrate an awareness of the 'potential arbitrariness of literary response', but argues that whilst Jerome sought to control this response, Chaucer delighted in constructing a fictional audience of pilgrims who might represent the entire anarchical gamut of interpretative possibilities. H. Ansgar Kelly looks at some of Chaucer's allusions to religious practices in 'Sacraments, Sacramentals, and Lay Piety in Chaucer's England' (*ChauR* 28.5–22). Focusing particularly on scenes of liturgical life, he finds that many questions relating to this area remain unanswered, or even unasked, and that in their investigation many hitherto neglected sources remain to be explored. In his attempt to chart these 'unplumbed sources', he devotes as much space to his footnotes as to his text, thus compressing a wealth of useful information into a short article.

The fine line between science and magic is the subject of Joyce Tally Lionarons's 'Magic, Machines, and Deception: Technology in the *Canterbury Tales*' (*ChauR* 27.377–86). Lionarons looks at how the two are intimately connected in Chaucer – how technology often has supernatural effects and how magic is mechanically based. The 'hors of bras' in the *Squire's Tale* with all its pins and gadgets is a classic example of such interconnection. Citing a number of scattered instances, Lionarons suggests that Chaucer betrays a profound mistrust in the esoteric arts and their capacity to dupe the uneducated.

George R. Petty Jr, in 'Power, Deceit, and Misinterpretation: Uncooperative Speech in the *Canterbury Tales*' (*ChauR* 27.413–23), looks at rhetorical strategies in Chaucer whereby characters, placed in situations in which they are on the defensive, counterattack to gain the offensive by a careful misinterpretation or 'flouting' of the text. Such a case is Oswald the Reeve's misinterpretation of the Miller's attack upon his character as defamatory speech about women; or the Monk's careful ignoring of the Host's request for a bawdy story. The instances are numerous, but we might note the Wife of Bath as misinterpreter *par excellence* and how she subordinates truth to rhetorical effectiveness. In a culture where she is disempowered by dint of her sex, the form her resistance takes is discursive. Chaucer the poet also 'misinterprets' his own text in the *Miller's Prologue*; when he anticipates objections to its moral quality. Like the Wife, he subordinates the intrinsic (im)morality of his poetry to the value of the marketplace. If you don't like it, don't read it; there are other customers not so precious about what they consume.

Miriam Youngerman Miller provides a useful survey of 'Illustrations of the *Canterbury Tales* for Children: A Mirror of Chaucer's World?' (*ChauR* 27.293–304). Her informative essay briefly reviews the history of children's book illustration, and covers 18 illustrators, whose names are listed in an appendix. Concentrating on nineteenth- and twentieth-century illustrators she shows how, rather than imitate models or seek inspiration from Chaucer's own words, these artists preferred instead to rely on contemporary conventions; thus she answers the question of her subtitle: 'Instead of mirroring Chaucer's world, they have mirrored their own'.

Light of Learning: Selected Essays of Morton W. Bloomfield 1970–1986, edited by Elizabeth Walsh and Susie M. Barrett, is not a festschrift but a tribute to Morton W. Bloomfield (d. 1987) which gathers together and republishes 24 essays written by him during the last 17 years of his life. Roughly a third of the volume is dedicated to Chaucer: the first section, entitled 'Chaucer', contains eight items, and two further pieces on Chaucer are included in subsequent sections. One essay deals specifically with *Troilus and Criseyde* and is noted in the appropriate section below; another piece, 'Fourteenth-Century England: Realism and Rationalism in Wyclif and Chaucer' (*YWES* 54.110) ranges more widely and presents Chaucer as an ultra-rationalist; but otherwise these essays are mostly concerned with the *Canterbury Tales*, and their approach is one which is closely textual. 'The *Canterbury Tales* as Framed Narratives' (*YWES* 64.149) treats the frame not just as a unifying device, but as a separate part of the poem; 'The *Miller's Tale*: An Un-Boethian Interpretation' (*YWES* 51.116) contrasts the irrationality and injustice of the *Miller's Tale* with the rationality and justice of the neighbouring *Knight's Tale* and *Reeve's Tale*; the '*Friar's Tale* as a Liminal Tale' (*YWES* 64.152) explores the concept of liminality; '*The Franklin's Tale*: A Story of Unanswered Questions' (*YWES* 64.103) argues that despite questions raised and left unanswered, the *Franklin's Tale* achieves harmony and closure. In '*The Merchant's Tale*: A Tragicomedy of Neglect of Counsel' (*YWES* 59.112), Bloomfield considers questions of genre, parody, and irony. He exaggerates the amount of sympathy due to January, but his comments on the tale's multiple violations of boundaries are well-placed. Two pieces deal with *The Man of Law's Tale*: '*The Man of Law's Tale*: A Tragedy of Victimization and a Christian Comedy' (*YWES* 53.112) examines the nature of this pathetic tale, but also flirts with too many large topics, such as the nature of medieval and Renaissance tragedy, and the influence of the *contemptus mundi* tradition; 'Contemporary Literary Theory and Chaucer' includes a structural analysis of this tale, whilst also addressing wider issues, specifically the non-application of modern literary theory to Chaucer. First published in 1981, this essay thus shows its age, as does 'The Gloomy Chaucer' (*YWES* 53.110) which discusses changes in attitude towards Chaucer's humour 'today', today being 1972. The overwhelming impression of this volume is one of datedness – an unfair criticism, perhaps, since the nature of the undertaking admits no revision, but one which has to be voiced. In general this collection is difficult to review, since what is under scrutiny is not merely one person's scholarship, but that scholarship selected and presented by others. There is merit in this enterprise, since it brings to wider attention a number of items previously published in more obscure locations, but one or two of these pieces are now making their third appearance in print, which seems excessive. Annoyingly, there is no index; nor is there a bibliography of Bloomfield's work, though this is quite proper, since one features in his festschrift, *The Wisdom of Poetry* (G. H. Brown, 1982). Another reprint, but one which will be welcomed by undergraduate students and those planning their courses is Derek Pearsall's *The Canterbury Tales*, first published in 1985 (*YWES* 66.172) and reissued this year.

The reference in the *General Prologue* to the Pardoner coming from Rouncivale is discussed in David K. Maxfield's 'St Mary Rouncivale, Charing Cross: The Hospital of Chaucer's Pardoner' (*ChauR* 28.148–63). Maxfield asks why Chaucer chose this particular hospital as the sponsor for the doubtful character of the Pardoner. He points out that hospitals in that time were dedicated as much to the care of the soul as to that of the body, and that part of their support came from the sale of indulgences by their pardoners who themselves acted as corrupt middlemen, making a profit directly from the penitent buyer. From detailed charting of the fortunes of St Mary Rouncivale, Maxfield concludes firstly, that Chaucer's Pardoner's bulls were almost certainly based on forged papal bulls; secondly, that the hospital had a questionable reputation throughout Chaucer's time; and finally, that Chaucer chose this hospital in particular for his Pardoner because of its 'plenitude of ironical possibilities'. The Variorum edition of the *General Prologue*, Parts One A and B (hereafter referred to as A and B), appeared this year. A contains the critical commentary, the textual commentary, the text and textual notes, and the bibliographical index; while B, an enormous volume, contains the explanatory notes. Malcolm Andrew is responsible for the critical commentary (A 3–60), which itself is subdivided into a number of sections. Key structural aspects of the poem – the spring opening, portraits, sources, etc. – are briefly reviewed especially in terms of the most influential scholarship done on them. He then provides a survey of the reception history of the *General Prologue* of which the earlier periods are most concisely covered. The survey of the scholarship of the last two decades inevitably begins to get more diffuse and to an extent there is, perhaps inevitably, some overlap between this and the next section in which he turns to more particularized topics and interpretations. Daniel J. Ransom's textual commentary is particularly valuable for a bird's-eye view of the 49 extant manuscripts of the *General Prologue*, referencing all the spurious lines, and giving a description and table of correspondences between the base-group manuscripts. The printed editions are also covered, including all the early editions as well as the key modern editions: Skeat, Robinson (1933), Manly–Rickert, Robinson (1957) and Pratt (the Riverside edition is briefly noted but not covered in detail). The edition is explicitly minimalist in its presentation of the Hengwrt text, allowing the collations and textual notes, which are printed on the same page as the text, to speak for themselves as much as possible. As usual, the effect of this is positively Derridean, with the page trisected horizontally and a formidable amount of textual footnote which constitutes a narrative all of its own. Charles Moorman is responsible for the text and collations, while the textual commentary is the work of both Moorman and Ransom. An appendix offers possible sources of and analogues for the spring opening, and Andrew's bibliographical index covers material cited in A and B. The explanatory notes occupy all of B and are the work of Andrew. Each portrait begins with a chronology of interpretations, where, again, the succinctness of the broad sweep is particularly valuable. Although 1985 is the cut-off year for citation of scholarship, material from the *Middle English Dictionary* extends up to 1989. It is true that the mid-1980s necessarily jettisons much recent scholarship. And it is also true that the *General Prologue*, perhaps more than the other tales, has generated a higher percentage of historical (rather than interpretative) commentary. Nonetheless, the edition is decidedly cautious about touching on recent scholarship informed by theory. The passing acknowledgement to feminist scholarship and the work of H. Marshall Leicester in the critical commentary does not really convey the sense in which conventional character criticism (which constitutes a huge percentage of *General Prologue* criticism) has been fundamentally undermined in recent years. The edition is still, however, a *tour de force* and the scholarship impeccable.

Frieda Elaine Penninger, in *Chaucer's Troilus and Criseyde and the Knight's Tale: Fictions Used*, juxtaposes the tale alongside *Troilus and Criseyde* in a pattern of contrasts that nevertheless affirm an overarching unity. Where *Troilus and Criseyde* is seen as a tragedy, the *Knight's Tale* has affinities more with comedy; likewise, Criseyde and Emelye are opposed as positive to negative. Both poems, however, reveal their subordination to a capricious Fortune. Despite this depiction as comedy, the *Knight's Tale* is seen as an ironic poem where tyranny masquerades as virtue and where the ideology of chivalry fails to cover up the ugliness of death and conquest. Chivalry, a gendered institution, 'pursues goals hardly worth the while of serious players on the world's stage'. The final consolation of the *Knight's Tale* lies not in the narrative as such but rather in the 'failure of the narrative to provide a satisfactory answer to the human quest'. How this can be a consolation remains somewhat unclear. For further comments, see section 3 below.

Joseph A. Dane, in 'The *Syntaxis Recepta* of Chaucer's "Prologue to the Miller's Tale", Lines 3159–61' (*ELN* 31.iv.10–17), argues that these lines have been misread since the earliest editions of Chaucer. The translation he offers is: 'I would not take on myself more than what the oxen in my plow can handle, that is, I would not deem myself a cuckold'. In contrast, editorial history has generally read the lines as approximating to: 'I wouldn't admit to being a cuckold even if offered all the oxen in my plow as an exchange'. A small point, perhaps, but Dane fairly queries the logic of being offered what is already your own. The problem of interpreting the line disappears when we ignore the editorial tradition (a tradition Dane charts) of enclosing the key phrase 'for the oxen in my plogh' within punctuation marks. In '"Upon the Viritoot": A Chaucerian Portmanteau?' (*ELN* 31.ii.1–9), Jeffrey L. Singman offers a possible definition for the phrase 'upon the viritoot' (*Miller's Tale*, line 3770), positing a connection with children's games, and suggesting that 'viritoot' may be some kind of top. In 'The Flemish Analogue to Chaucer's *Miller's Tale*: Three Notes' (*N&Q* 40.445–9), David F. Johnson praises Stith Thompson's translation of the Middle Dutch *Heile van Beersele*, but offers retranslations from three separate places in the text. For line 34 in Thompson, Johnson explains the literal translation of the idiom 'her thumb did not fail her', meaning that Heile was in complete control of the situation. For lines 78–9 in Thompson, Johnson offers: 'The priest proceeded to declaim many a word from the Gospels.' And finally, for line 113 in Thompson, Johnson retranslates: 'You never saw such a good joke'. R. T. Lambdin, in 'Chaucer's *The Miller's Tale*' (*Expl* 52.27–9) queries the consensus of the meaning 'churl' for 'gnof'. Indeed, Lambdin offers a brief revisionist reading of John's entire character, arguing against the prevailing view of the carpenter as gullible and loutish. After all, the carpenter loves Alison 'moore than his lyf' (Lambdin conveniently ignores, however, the disparity between their ages). Unfortunately, Lambdin does not offer a preferred reading for 'gnof' and the final assertion – that the representation of the carpenter as a 'caring, concerned man adds depth to its [the tale's] hilarity' – leaves one wondering how.

A study of Chaucer's special interest in a generally ignored character of the *Reeve's Tale* is given by Tamarah Kohanski who is 'In Search of Malyne' (*ChauR* 27.228–38). Kohanski notes how the assumption that Malyne is sexually willing – like the stereotypical fabliau wench and like her prototype in *Le meunier et les II clers* – has little foundation in the text. The complexity Kohanski notes in her character is borne out in her looks, which are a mixture of the coarseness of her father and more refined features from her mother's side. Her silence at the moment of being 'swyved' should not be read as unconditional surrender, while her loving words to Aleyn the following morning are suggestive of pathos rather than comedy. Kohanski sees Malyne as 'the human victim of a masculine power struggle' within the tale and argues that the lengths to which Chaucer has gone to differentiate Malyne from the regular fabliau wench call into question the justice of the 'poetic justice' that is so central to the fabliau form. Richard Firth Green's investigation of the phrase 'fee simple' in 'Chaucer's Man of Law and Collusive Recovery' (*N&Q* 40.303–5) leads him, as he admits, 'into some very obscure avenues of legal history' and suggests that the Man of Law is ingenious, if unethical. Patricia J. Erble argues in 'The Question of Authority and the Man of Law's Tale' (in Taylor et al., 111–49) that this tale and its prologue offer a critique of the 'descending' theory of political authority espoused by the king and challenged by the 'Wonderful Parliament' of 1386. This leads her to call for a re-thinking and expansion of the so-called 'Marriage Group' as a cluster of tales more centrally concerned with the concept of authority in the age of Richard II, an idea that would be interesting to see developed.

Catherine S. Cox, in 'Holy Erotica and the Virgin Word: Promiscuous Glossing in the *Wife of Bath's Prologue*' (*Exemplaria* 5.207–37), recognizes that the Wife's discourse is no transparent statement of feminine perspective, constructed as it is by literary genre, by anti-feminist traditions and by Chaucer the male author. It is not a question, then, of whether or not the Wife is a feminist, but of how, through her, Chaucer tests the limits of discourse. The essay places 'glossing' at the centre of discourse in the *Wife of Bath's Prologue*, an activity that is both textual and sexual in its element of 'pleye' and its association with antifeminist texts such as Jankyn's book. Cox connects this glossing with the Wife's voracious appetite – both for language in the way that one text generates another (its gloss) and for sexual play. In such a mutual identification of 'sexual rhetoric', text is sexualized and sex is textualized. The 'virgin word' of Cox's title comes fairly late in the essay where she argues that the Wife attempts to appropriate meaning by harbouring it as a secret to herself, by lying and covering her words in 'autoerotic delight'. This harbouring of meaning is likened to the miserly harbouring of the virginal body. The Wife's 'privatization of eros leaves her hungry for more, and she remains – both sexually and textually – isolated and constrained within the parameters of the masculine discourse'. Cox sees the Wife, then, as a deeply problematic figure, and as a fictional statement by Chaucer on sexual difference and its discursive construction that ultimately remains unresolved. Lynne Dickson considers the Wife of Bath's challenge to anti-feminism in 'Deflection in the Mirror: Feminine Discourse in *The Wife of Bath's Prologue and Tale*' (*SAC* 15.61–90). She divides her discussion into five sections, beginning with Christine de Pizan's resistance to patriarchy before considering Chaucer's position as a male writer 'revising and resisting antifeminist discourse'. Her conclusion is that 'both Wife of Bath texts', by which she means the *Prologue* and the *Tale*, challenge anti-feminism by emphasizing the tyranny of a patriarchal mode of understanding, and by disrupting any purely masculine response, inviting readers instead to respond as complex sexual beings. She also claims that Chaucer's texts suggest an alternative to patriarchy – a feminine community of readers and speakers – but that this suggestion is a mere gesture, defined only in imaginary terms. Laura F. Hodges explores the significance of what the Wife of Bath wears in 'The Wife of Bath's Costumes: Reading the Subtexts' (*ChauR* 27.359–76). In an article bristling with notes, she analyses the Wife's Sunday wear and her travel outfit, finding both social and moral implications in the details. In 'Voices of Translation: Poet's Voice and Woman's Voice' (*PCP* 28.3–19), Katherine M. Morsberger interprets translation as a process which may cross time and gender as well as language, and in this context she discusses Dryden's translation of the *Wife of Bath's Tale* and Pope's translations of the *Wife of Bath's Prologue* and the *Merchant's Tale*. Manuel Aguirre's 'The Riddle of Sovereignty' (*MLR* 88.ii.273–82) takes the *Wife of Bath's Tale* as its point of departure, but is more centrally concerned with the tale's analogues, both English and Irish; he claims these are to be regarded as a continuous tradition, accounting for their differences as a subversion, rather than as a loss, of meaning. Joerg O. Fichte also considers the analogues to the *Wife of Bath's Tale* in his discussion of 'Images of Arthurian Literature Reflected in Chaucer's Poetry' (*Archiv* 230.52–61), but with three theses and a three-part intertextual model with which to analyse them, Fichte is too ambitious about what can be achieved in a short article.

In a brief piece, '*Friar's Tale*, D 1489: "At oure Prayere"' (*ChauR* 28.146–7), A. S. G. Edwards suggests that the phrase 'at oure prayere', attested by the majority of manuscript readings, should be emended in favour of the smaller, but significant, number of manuscripts which read 'at oure pray'. In context, 'prayere', meaning request, makes little sense; but 'pray', meaning prey, fits the sense of the predatory devils being permitted by God to torture the body only but also instructed to leave the soul unscathed.

Although he cannot prove his thesis, V. A. Kolve nevertheless suggests a convincing iconographic source for the ending of the *Summoner's Tale*. In 'Chaucer's Wheel of False Religion: Theology and Obscenity in *The Summoner's Tale*' (in Taylor et al., 265–96), Kolve takes the tale's ultimate image of the cartwheel and finds parallels to it in the manuscript illustrations which accompany Hugh of Fouilly's text *De rota verae et falsae religionis*: The essay is generously illustrated. D. Thomas Hanks, Jr, in '"Savour", Chaucer's "Summoner's Tale", and Matthew 5:13' (*ELN* 31.iii.25–9), notes that Chaucer's phrase 'ye been the salt of the erthe and the savour' has been usually assumed to refer to Christ's words from Matthew 5. But 'savour' appears in no version (Latin or English) available to Chaucer at that time. Rather, Hanks refers us to a more precise reference in Gower's *Vox clamantis*. And he further concludes that the now familiar phrase from the Geneva Bible 'but if the salt have lost its savour' was probably written with Chaucer's text in mind.

Mary R. Bowman explores female subjectivity and its representation in men's discourse in '"Half as She Were Mad": Dorigen in the Male World of the *Franklin's Tale*' (*ChauR* 27.239–51). The tale's final question, 'Which was the mooste fre?' asks us to evaluate the actions of the male characters whilst ignoring Dorigen's deeds as irrelevant, but Bowman disagrees with the traditional premise that the tale's male economy of moral value is equally valid for Dorigen, contending instead that Dorigen's moral values may be different from those of the men in the tale, or indeed, from those of the Franklin himself.

The unfortunate aesthetics of the *Physician's Tale* are considered by John C. Hirsh in 'Modern Times: The Discourse of the *Physician's Tale*' (*ChauR* 27.387–95). Noting the difficulty critics have had in appreciating it, Hirsh finds the reasons for such difficulty in the tale's apparent lack of motivation or causality, in the 'studied two-dimensionality' of the characters, in its digressions, and in its disproportion between emotional extremity and narrative brevity. To explain these so-called shortcomings, Hirsh turns to the narrator of the tale, the Physician. Describing him as a 'practising nominalist', interested in individual (and expensive) cases rather than systems, theories, or ideologies, Hirsh sees the Physician and the text as thoroughly 'modern' in the sense of sceptical and anti-teleological. Linda Lomperis's 'Unruly Bodies and Ruling Practices: Chaucer's *Physician's Tale* as Socially Symbolic Act' (in Lomperis and Stanbury, 21–37) sees criticism of this tale as patriarchal and anti-corporeal, that is, as having focused on the tale primarily as an exemplum of virginity. But for Lomperis, the *Physician's Tale* abounds with an abundant and transgressive sexuality that threatens at every point to break the controlling strategies the narrative imposes upon it. The apostrophe to governesses and to parents is such a case in point. A discourse that so attempts to ward *off* sex ends up obliquely as discourse *about* sex. The essay also contains some historical material on the conditions of women amongst fourteenth-century English aristocracy. Lomperis is drawing out the tensions that existed in England (and in the tale) between women's transgressive ability for self-determination and their class-determination by the exigencies of aristocratic lineage. In the *Physician's Tale*, Lomperis evaluates how these conflicting desires are not so much in opposition to each other as they are mutually productive of each other. Noting that only in this version is Virginia killed at home, the spheres of the private and political begin to converge. The female body functions as site of resistance not from *without* the patriarchal order but from *within* it, as the productive body upon which the perpetuation of patriarchy depends.

In 'The Pardoner's Pants (and Why They Matter)' (*SAC* 15.131–45), Richard Firth Green relates the Pardoner's invitation that the Host should kiss his 'olde breech' to 'The Friar's Pants', a particular version of a general folktale type, identified by Green as 'Adulteress Outwits Husband'. The weakness of his argument is that he cannot find any fourteenth-century English examples of this tale, but he manages to locate so many other examples that we are convinced of its popularity and wide dissemination, and amenable to the suggestion that Chaucer might have been familiar with it. Having thus established a popular allusion, Green then uses this as further support of his (and C. David Benson's) previously stated position that current interpretations of the Pardoner's sexual identity are built on shaky foundations; in his eyes the Pardoner is neither eunuch nor hermaphrodite nor homosexual but a 'randy troublemaker'. The Pardoner's sexuality is addressed more directly by Michael A. Calabrese in '"Make a Mark that Shows": Orphean Song, Orphean Sexuality, and the Exile of Chaucer's Pardoner' (*Viator* 24.269–86), where Calabrese argues that Chaucer is less interested in analysing the actual sexual condition of the Pardoner (be that of homosexual, eunuch or hermaphrodite) than he is in 'exploring actions that dramatize moral identity and spiritual essence'. Calabrese links his portrayal with Orpheus, the artist and homosexual of Ovid and of Jean de Meun, but argues that this does not make the Pardoner homosexual as such. Indeed, Calabrese takes pains to distinguish modern discourses of homosexuality from the ambivalence of Chaucer's text. The useful evidence he provides, however, does seem to argue for homosexuality: namely, Genius's speech about Orpheus in the *Roman de la Rose*. In this speech, the links between sex, language, and death are made clear – a connection found also in the Pardoner. Paul Sheneman, in 'The Tongue as a Sword: Psalms 56 and 63 and the Pardoner' (*ChauR* 27.396–400) points out a number of instances throughout Chaucer's work – and most notably in the reference to the Pardoner who can 'wel affile his tonge' – where the tongue is imaged as a sword. On this basis, Sheneman suggests that 'affile' means to 'sharpen' in this context rather than to 'polish' (as Lawrence Besserman has previously argued). This preferred reading places greater emphasis on the Pardoner's malicious intent.

Janet Thormann, in 'The Circulation of Desire in the "Shipman's Tale"' (*L&P* 39.1–15), looks at how three symbolic systems – speech, money, and sex – circulate in an economy of transference and exchange. Such words as 'taille' and 'busyness' register the semantic exchanges at work in the narrative. Indeed, it is the 'potential of speech for duplication, uncertainty, and ambiguity' that facilitates the circulation of the wife's body and the hundred francs. Thormann notes the importance of privacy in the poem as the space in which exchange is transacted. The tale also interests itself in a female desire that Thormann suggests is represented through metaphors of money and language.

'Chaucer's Monk: The Poetics of Abbreviation, Aggression, and Tragedy' (*ChauR* 27.260–76), by Jahan Ramazani, sets up the Monk's conservative poetics in opposition to Chaucer's larger and more flexible vision. Drawing parallels between the prosodic analysis of the tale and the impression we gain of the Monk from references to him dispersed across the *Canterbury Tales*, Ramanzani portrays the Monk as an anal-retentive type, an obsessive collector of tragic stories, fixatedly avaricious, and wearisomely repetitive. Moreover, the qualities are all suggestive of each other. Chaucer is seen to distance himself from identification with the Monk by incorporating the Monk's *de casibus* narratives parodically into other tales. It is not that Chaucer rejects the tragedy as such but rather the Monk's reduction of it into a formula. Referring also to his portrait in the *General Prologue*, Christine Herold identifies Chaucer's Monk with victims of Fortune in 'The Unfortunate Iconography of Chaucer's Wayward Monk' (*ELN* 31.iv.5–9). Herold reads the Monk as pilgrim and his tale simultaneously as parodic of tragedy and yet also as genuinely tragic. Noting two aspects of the Monk's appearance which are not the traditional material of estates satire (his bald head and gleaming eyes), Herold suggests a link between the bald, shiny head and the glass cap Chaucer's Fortune places on her victim (*Troilus and Criseyde* 2,867–8); and between the bulging, burning eyes and the victims of Fortune (Virgil's Dido and Seneca's Oedipus).

Dryden's *Fables Ancient and Modern* is the focus of discussion about the reception of Chaucer in Stephanie Trigg's 'Singing Clearly: Chaucer, Dryden, and a Rooster's Discourse' (*Exemplaria* 5.365–86). Most of the time, Trigg notes, critics pay attention to Dryden's Preface to the *Fables* rather than to the actual translations of the tales. Of all the tales' fluctuating fortunes in popularity over the centuries, the *Nun's Priest's Tale* has remained a constant favourite and is particularly notable for the consistent tendency to align Chaucer the author with the narrating voice of the tale. Dryden's own evaluation of Chaucer is ambivalently pitched between praise of the *fons et origo* of English poetry and the persistent opinion that he is in need of improvement as well as of translation. In Dryden's abstraction of the tale from out of the frame of the pilgrimage, the relationship between teller and tale becomes significantly de-emphasized. In the differences between the Dryden and Chaucer versions that Trigg notes, she speaks of Dryden's 'far less ambiguous tyranny of Chanticleer over Partlet' alongside his 'fine modulations of the religious and political features of the tale'. That is, the misogyny latent in Chaucer's tale is made explicit in Dryden's. On the basis of this, Trigg shows how the discourses of critical reception and translation over the centuries are not homogenous and how, when we appeal to a received tradition of Chaucer reception, we should pay attention to what is excluded as well as included. Kathleen Ann Kelly argues that 'An Inspiration for Chaucer's Description of Chaunticleer' (*ELN* 30.iii.1–6) may be found in the description of the phoenix in Mandeville's *Travels*.

The *Canon's Yeoman's Tale* is addressed by Michael Calabrese in 'Meretricious Mixtures: Gold, Dung, and the *Canon's Yeoman's Prologue and Tale*' (*ChauR* 27.277–92). Here an analogy is drawn between the arts of alchemy and the arts of love. To support this analogy, Calabrese turns to an anonymous fourteenth-century poem, the *Antiovidianus*, which has not hitherto been related to Chaucer's tale. Although there are no generic similarities between the works, both the poet's attack on Ovid and the Yeoman's text attempt to expose the deceptions of the false artist. Where Ovid is accused of making dung masquerade as gold ('aurified dung') by his deceptive rhetoric, alchemical treatises castigate false alchemists who use similar materials. The alchemists are sterile in that they uselessly 'spill their seed', producing nothing but the false image of creation. The sexual metaphor for alchemy certainly holds, although Calabrese's reading offers more of a general context of associated ideas in which we can think about Chaucer's tale, rather than any specific, textual relation. A more detailed and extended study is by Lee Patterson in 'Perpetual Motion: Alchemy and the Technology of the Self' (*SAC* 15.25–57), which offers both a reading of the *Canon's Yeoman's Tale* and of both alchemy and Chaucer in general. The essay opens with a review of criticism on the tale, in which Joseph Grennen's opposition of the tale's multiplicity to the unity of the *Second Nun's Tale* and Charles Muscatine's assessment of the tale as censorious of a dangerous modernity are reaffirmed by Patterson. Turning to the *Canon's Yeoman's Tale* itself, he notes its preoccupation with textuality and with 'a discourse of radical deferral'. The Yeoman's multiplying words that nevertheless fail to represent essential meaning is a condition Patterson identifies with the alchemical enterprise. For alchemy deals with realms beyond the sensory, with prime matter; it is an exquisitely metaphysical language yet deeply textual in its attempts both to communicate and veil its esoteric truths; which is not to make alchemy just another form of mysticism, for it is also a mechanical science, a technology – in short, a materialist utopianism. It is because of this technologism and materialism that alchemy was placed on the margins of orthodox medieval knowledge; and it is in this simultaneous marginality and modernity that Patterson identifies alchemy's affinity with Chaucer, who is 'socially indefinable: neither courtier nor merchant nor clerk, he participates in all three social formations without fully according with any'.

3. *Troilus and Criseyde*

Two books on *Troilus and Criseyde* appeared this year. Frieda Elaine Penninger's *Chaucer's Troilus and Criseyde and the Knight's Tale: Fictions Used* (see also section 2) counterpoints the two poems in an analysis that is centred on two famous distinctions from two famous texts: between *cupiditas/caritas* in Augustine's *De doctrina christiana*; and between transient *Fortuna* and constant *Philosophia* in Boethius's *De consolatione philosophia*. Penninger sees *Troilus and Criseyde* as a tragedy dominated by the fickleness of Fortune. Criseyde, of course, is the archetype of falseness here, but Chaucer is seen to have 'done his best by her'. The poem also narrows the divinity and breadth of *caritas* to self-gratification and to the games of *cupiditas* in which actions are undertaken 'to pass time and conceal truth'. If this seems a Robertsonian reading, it isn't really, in that the poem is defended as a diversion whose consolation is precisely that it offers nothing other than a diversion. 'The poems charm as narratives even while they are invalidated as ideal models for life.' As a whole, the book devotes more space than is interesting to narrative description (the Preface contains summaries of the two poems and of Augustine's and Boethius's texts) and to quotation. For example, a substantial percentage of Chapter 2 is devoted to listing and describing the imagery of play in *Troilus and Criseyde*. More selective and detailed exemplification would have lent greater depth to the argument.

Allen J. Frantzen's *Troilus and Criseyde: The Poem and the Frame* is a useful guide for students, containing a brief history of the reception of Chaucer's poem as well as a prefatory attempt to set Chaucer into social and historical context. The concept of the 'frame' informs Frantzen's analysis as a device that destabilizes the opposition between inside and outside, or between art and life, rather than setting the one apart from the other. In this sense, the 'frame' marks the point where the text ceases to be an autonomous entity and begins to be seen as inherently relational and discursively constructed. Therefore, the 'frame' becomes a metaphor for theoretically aware literary criticism. In his reading of the text of the poem, which constitutes the bulk of the book, Frantzen shows how the frame can be understood on many levels, not just in terms of the relation between the literary text and its social milieu. Within the poem itself, we can see the framing of private interior selves within the public and cultural construction of the self. There is the frame of history: the ancient embedded within the medieval embedded within the contemporary. And there is the frame of literary genre, the codes of courtly love, epic and romance which symbolically construct the 'characters' of the poem. His schema is as follows: Book I is framed by the narrator (in his drawing of disjunctions between past and present, source and story, pagan and Christian); Book II by Pandarus (the surrogate of the narrator, who reports and mediates the seduction by Troilus of Criseyde); Book III by the Boethian concept of universal love (an ideology that links the private world of the lovers to an ideal cosmology thereby valorizing and authorizing that private world); Book IV by war (which supersedes the imperatives of love); Book V by fate (in which individual agency is redescribed as necessity and where symbolic values overcome social values). The book is very readable and balances well between critical survey, theoretical discourse, and specific reading of the text. We note also Stephen Barney's *Studies in Troilus: Chaucer's Text, Meter, and Diction* to be reviewed next year.

In 'The Psychic Struggle of the Narrative Ego in the Conclusion of *Troylus and Criseyde*' (*PQ* 72.i.15–31), Gale C. Schriker's psychoanalytic approach to *Troilus and Criseyde* takes as its point of departure E. Talbot Donaldson's remark that the poem's narrator is suffering, by the end of his task, 'a kind of nervous breakdown in poetry'. Far from obeying D. W. Robertson Jr's dictum not to read Chaucer from a modern perspective, Schriker asserts that modern psychology provides the key to understanding the behaviour of Chaucer's narrators. In particular, Schriker uses Freud's model of psychic functions to illuminate what is termed the narrator's 'neurotic crisis' at the end of the poem. Four different and opposing components which the narrator must juggle are identified, and it is argued that these may be understood respectively through reference to the four components of Freud's psychical apparatus; the narrator's mediation between the pagan tale and its Christian epilogue may be seen as the operation of the ego in relation to the id and super-ego. The argument is detailed and persuasive, but the conclusion reached – that the narrator thus proves himself a human being – hardly seems to justify the effort. Freud is invoked again in Jeremy M. Downes's '"Streght to My Matere": Rereading Chaucer's *Troilus and Criseyde*' (*JNLH* 3.155–178). Here Downes notes the centrality of Criseyde in the poem and, more significantly, the special female audience of the poem alluded to by the narrator: 'wommen that bitraised be'. The shift of emphasis within epic from arms to love is linked, for Downes, with the gradual representation of epic as a written rather than oral event and with a concomitant evolution from a more transparent discourse (oral) to polysemous ambivalence (written). Using Freud's scopophilic instinct as explanatory frame, Downes investigates the relationship between sexuality and textuality in the poem. Linked to epistemophilia, scopophilia is fundamental both to the formation of childhood sexuality and to the issues addressed by *Troilus and Criseyde*. Indeed, Downes sees medieval courtly love as the precursor of Freud's scopophilic instinct. Criseyde, however, deconstructs this patriarchal control by remaining irreducible to an object of either the male gaze or of the exegetic act of 'reading like a man'.

Chaucer's use of Boethian philosophy in *Troilus and Criseyde* is addressed by several critics. Noel Harold Kaylor Jr finds 'Boethian Resonance in Chaucer's "Canticus Troili"' (*ChauR* 27.219–27) and offers this as an explanation for Chaucer's decision to incorporate this translation of a Petrarchan sonnet into *Troilus and Criseyde*. Ruth Morse investigates the nature of Chaucerian tragedy in 'Absolute Tragedy: Allusions and Avoidances' (*PoeticaJ* 37.1–17), finding that it consists of 'disappointment, disillusionment, and disaster, but not a lot of evil'. Discussing passages from the *Knight's Tale*, the *Franklin's Tale*, and the *Nun's Priest's Tale*, as well as *Troilus and Criseyde*, Morse discovers also a lack of resolution, the latter because 'Chaucer defers what he cannot solve to another story, the story told by Boethius'. In 'Chaucer's Boethius and Thomas Usk's *Testament of Love*: Politics and Love in the Chaucerian Tradition' (in Taylor et al. 29–70), David R. Carlson considers Usk's debt to Chaucer's *Boece* and *Troilus and Criseyde*. He demonstrates that Usk's figure of Love is equivalent to both Lady Philosophy and Dame Fortune, and shows that the concept of love articulated in the *Testament of Love* is fundamentally similar to that expressed in *Troilus and Criseyde*; he also claims that Usk's complex literary dependence on Chaucer may have been motivated by political considerations.

In 'The Ends of Fiction: Narrative Boundaries and Chaucer's Attitude Toward Courtly Love' (*ChauR* 28.54–66), Adam Brooke Davis identifies and discusses a number of narrative strategies in *Troilus and Criseyde* which function either as introductory or concluding devices. In 'Figuring Criseyde's "Entente"' (*ChauR* 27.342–58), Jennifer Campbell considers authority, narrative, and Chaucer's use of history, examining the narrator's changing relationship with his sources and the narrative disclaimers of Books II and III, in order to interpret Book IV, in which she finds both a reassertion of history and an expansion of Criseyde's point of view. She questions Chaucer's purpose in thus problematizing both his narrator and his heroine and concludes that *Troilus and Criseyde* is 'a feminist work that fails to liberate women'; but she blunts the effectiveness of her point by overqualifying her final remarks, saying that this is 'perhaps' one of the uses to which Chaucer has put history.

Several short articles and notes discuss particular sections of the poem. In 'Venus and the Virgin' (*ChauR* 27.252–9), Sumner Ferris compares the Proem to Book III, a hymn to the goddess Venus, with the Prologue to the *Prioress's Tale*, a hymn to the Blessed Virgin Mary. Showing a range of topical similarities between the two pieces, Ferris argues that Chaucer is praising both human love and divine love. Julia Dietrich writes a brief note on 'Chaucer's *Troilus and Criseyde*, book 3, line 1093' (*Expl* 51.139–41) to comment on the significance and possible irony of the line: 'This was no litel sorwe for to se'. Morton W. Bloomfield's reprinted essay 'Troilus' Paraclausithyron and its Setting' (in Walsh and Barrett, 71–81) (*YWES* 53.118), examines in detail Troilus' contemplation of Criseyde's empty house (*Troilus and Criseyde* v.519–602).

Dealing with later versions or later receptions of *Troilus and Criseyde*, we have 'Tracing the Ring: Henryson, Fowler, and Chaucer's *Troilus*' (*N&Q* 40.449–51), in which Anne M. McKim considers the token of the ruby ring in the Middle Scots version of the legend. And two essays from *Exemplaria*: Clare Kinney, in 'Lost in Translation: The Vicissitudes of the Heroine and the Immasculation of the Reader in a Seventeenth-Century Paraphrase of *Troilus and Criseyde*' (*Exemplaria* 5.343–63), opens with a distinction made by Carolyn Dinshaw (and by now something of a critical topos – see Downes above) between 'reading *like* a man' and 'reading *as* a man'. In the former, one reads in a totalizing way, suppressing the (feminine) disorderliness of the equivocal, while the latter merely refers to one's literal sex. Where Dinshaw had relegated the poem's narrator to the totalizers, Kinney seeks to vindicate him in that he explicitly refuses to draw the conventional anti-feminist conclusions about Criseyde's fickleness. Kinney then looks at how a Renaissance 'translation' of *Troilus and Criseyde*, Jonathan Sidnam's 'A Paraphrase vpon the three first Bookes of Chaucer's Troilus and Cresida', itself reads the poem 'like a man' by suppressing the narrator's moral ambivalence over Criseyde. Moreover, Kinney finds Sidnam not alone amongst his contemporaries in damning Criseyde and suggests that the reason may be found in part in the tradition of Renaissance Petrarchanism which privileges the representation of masculine desire and agency. On the other hand, Tim William Machan, in 'Kynaston's *Troilus*, Textual Criticism and the Renaissance Reading of Chaucer' (*Exemplaria* 5.161–83), reads the period more sympathetically (Kynaston's publication being 1635 and Sidnam's composition speculated at around 1630). In Kynaston, Machan sees a paradox at the heart of English humanism: the need to valorize the present by keeping it at a safe distance from the past; and the need for the continuity of an English tradition. The ambivalence is observed most in the attitude to Middle English language: Chaucer is both an exquisite poet and yet writes in a language that is obsolete. Kynaston's solution is to translate *Troilus and Criseyde* into Latin, a *lingua franca* that reaches beyond the confines of even modernized English vernacular, to celebrate Chaucer as the English Virgil. What Kynaston offers, then, are the two versions 'as simultaneously distinct and identical poems'. The paradoxical desire both to archaize and modernize Chaucer is also demonstrated by some meticulous and insightful analysis of the edition's typeface and topography of the page.

4.   Other Works

In a posthumously published article, 'Chaucer's Dream-Vision Poems and the Theory of Spatial Form' (*Parergon* 11.i.79–90), Marcella Ryan applies Joseph Frank's theory of spatial form to the dream visions, concentrating on Chaucer's use of myth in these poems.

The *Book of the Duchess* has had a bumper year. In 'Portrait of a Lady: Blaunche and the Descriptive Tradition' (*ES* 73.324–42), Valerie Allen claims that Blaunche goes virtually unmentioned in contemporary Chaucer criticism (or had done until this year), and blames this absence on Blaunche's unproblematical conventionality. Oddly, two articles published this year concentrate on Blaunche's description: the other is James Miller's contribution 'How to See Through Women: Medieval Blazons and the Male Gaze' (in Taylor et al. 367–88). Miller takes the 'interminable blazon' of Blaunche (*Book of the Duchess*, lines 939–60) and argues that there is more going on in this passage than meets the eye. After considering three other examples of medieval gynophany, he concludes that in this case the motivation is therapeutic: the Black Knight is encouraged to see through love-objects of this world to a higher world beyond; mental stripping and eroticism are thus transformed into 'pure lokyng'. Allen's discussion is more detailed, and deals with the whole portrait (lines 817–1033), not just one section. She explores the history of the medieval *descriptio feminae* and its components, drawing attention to its binary structure which incorporates both physical and moral description; she also reviews the portrait's critical reception, before returning to the binary division to examine how physical and moral are connected in Blaunche's description. Blaunche's portrait is also considered, more tangentially, by Phillipa Hardman in 'Ars Celare Artem: Interpreting the Black Knight's "Lay" in Chaucer's *Book of the Duchess*' (*PoeticaJ* 37.49–57). Hardman discusses the Man in Black's two songs, especially the first with its missing line (line 480), and she uses the narrator's remembrance of these songs to interpret his relationship with the Black Knight, seeing this as parallel to the relationship between poet and patron: the patron provides the poet with subject material, and the poet turns this into art. Because Chaucer collapses the separate stages of this process into one, the raw material of the experience itself becomes the poem's commemorative portrait: 'the portrait of the lady is not presented as the product of poetic art. It is the plain unvarnished truth, which is most appropriately delivered by the bereaved lover himself'. Carol A. N. Martin discusses 'Mercurial Translation in the *Book of the Duchess* (*ChauR* 28.95–116), an article adapted from a chapter of her dissertation. She argues that Chaucer uses the figure of Mercury as a unifying device, and claims that both Juno's unnamed messenger, and the whelp that the dreamer follows, are mercurial figures. She admits that Chaucer's overt references to Mercury are 'deliberately sparse', but explains the anonymous nature of Mercury's presence in the *Book of the Duchess* as characteristic elusiveness; other mercurial characteristics – speed, shape-shifting – are linked to ideas of revision, mutability, translation and wordplay, with Mercury held up as a veritable patron saint of translation. Glenn Burger, in 'Reading Otherwise: Recovering the Subject in the *Book of the Duchess*' (*Exemplaria* 5.325–41), thinks about the derivativeness of Chaucer's poem in the light of Michel Foucault's speculations on 'indifference' to authorial presence. Granted that we do not want to return to old assertions of authorial intentionality, Burger nevertheless argues for the possibility of an authorial subjectivity: 'Decentering the subject ... need not lead to its disappearance'. Thus, reading the problems of the *Book of the Duchess* (Chaucer's conventionality, the absence of Blaunche, the inconclusiveness of the narrator, the reticence of the Black Knight) as expressive of an anxiety about finding one's subject position is not the same thing as asking about the author and characters as autonomous selves. Burger sees the subjects in the poem achieving self-consciousness through otherness. The

Black Knight's acceptance of Blaunche's death may involve the recognition that that which was lost was never fully present in the way he had imagined; that his therapeutic construction of a fictional stability of the signifying subject was in order to regulate the ultimate acceptance of its instability (presumably much as Freud's little boy of one and a half does in the *Fort/Da* game). Although Burger develops his ideas in relation to the characters of the poem, he does not make it clear how his reading applies to the problem of authorial originality/conventionality. Gayle Margherita, in 'Originary Fantasies and Chaucer's *Book of the Duchess*' (in Lomperis and Stanbury, 116–41), links the loss of Blaunche with what she calls desire for the lost origin – a desire that haunts both the psychoanalytic enterprise in its search for primal pleasure and medieval (and Robertsonian) exegetics in its belief in a recoverable history. The question of loss is related to the body and Margherita sees in the elegy a 'site of a certain kind of recuperative impulse within a patriarchal literary tradition'. It is out of loss that poetic utterance arises. Her question is to what extent the *Book of the Duchess* masters loss through representation, most notably, of Blaunche. Where the Black Knight laments the loss of Blaunche at length, Alcyone has no words that can substitute for her lost husband. Elegy as 'patriarchal literary tradition' thus affirms its positive, substitutionary value against woman as negative or loss. The article is densely written but offers a persuasive case for 'the instability at the heart of a paternalist poetics'.

The unresolved problems of the *House of Fame* continue to interest critics. Describing the poem as 'a riddle without a key', John M. Steadman sets out to elucidate some of the work's enigmas in '*The House of Fame*: Tripartite Structure and Occasion' (*Connotations* 3.i.1–12). He explains the poem's seemingly incoherent structure of three unrelated episodes as a feature of its initial performance, suggesting that it was designed for recitation over three successive days. This proposal conveniently allows the fictional date of the poet's dream (10 December) to be linked with that of the feast of St Lucy (13 December), and thus Steadman can suggest an occasion for the poem's first performance. He supports this by noting various associations of Chaucer's eagle, but his argument is preceded by the proviso that his solution 'must necessarily remain hypothetical, and largely speculative', and this weakens his case. Steven F. Kruger is also concerned with how the poem is held together. In his essay 'Imagination and the Complex Movement of Chaucer's *House of Fame*' (*ChauR* 28.117–34), he claims that the poem achieves unity by 'a consistent, if complicated, pattern of movement'. This pattern involves three stages: firstly, a self-reflexive foregrounding of poetic issues; secondly, a movement both outward, to the world of external phenomena, and upward, to a transcendent realm of abstract and universal ideas; and thirdly, when the contradictory pressures of this second movement become too great, the poem returns to self-exploration and self-consciousness. Lara Ruffolo is more concerned with the poem's meaning than with its structure. In 'Literary Authority and the Lists of Chaucer's *House of Fame*: Destruction and Definition Through Proliferation' (*ChauR* 27.325–41), she draws attention to the poem's many lists, highlighting their general movement away from organization towards chaos. Her object is to show how Chaucer here denies the traditional idea that literary authority rests in historical and moral truths, redefining it as the very fact of being read or heard. The *House of Fame* also features, briefly, in Beryl Rowland's essay, 'The Artificial Memory, Chaucer, and Modern Scholars' (*PoeticaJ* 37.1–14). Referring to her own earlier work in this area, Rowland describes some of the poem's mnemonic devices, and argues that here Chaucer is demonstrating the workings of the Artificial Memory; her article is mostly a survey of modern critical attention to this phenomenon, and is not otherwise about Chaucer.

The biggest event in Boethian studies this year is A. J. Minnis's edition of *Chaucer's Boece and the Medieval Tradition of Boethius*. In this book, Minnis examines Chaucer's debt to Nicholas Trevet and challenges the ubiquitous assumption that Trevet was an inferior commentator to William of Conches. Chapter 1, by Minnis and Lodi Nauta, looks at how the received tradition has represented Trevet as having Aristotelianized Conches' Neoplatonism. Rather, Trevet is seen as sympathetic to Conches' Neoplatonism. Minnis and Nauta attempt to get away from the opposition between Neoplatonism and Aristotelianism in order to emphasize the unity between the commentators as Christian academics. Trevet's effort constitutes an attempt to modernize Conches and harmonize obvious points of difference between Neoplatonism and Aristotelianism. The key Platonic doctrines touched on in *Boece* are as follows: knowledge through recollection; the eternity of prime matter; the nature and status of the world soul; and the pre-existence of human souls. Minnis and Nauta show how Trevet does not attempt to deny Plato's doctrines, but rather to reconcile them with Aristotelian theories of causation and of faculty psychology. Chapter 2 contains extracts from Trevet's commentary in Latin (text by E. T. Silk) and in English (text by A. B. Scott). These excerpts deal with the key Platonic doctrines described above. Chapter 3, by Minnis, is on the relation between Trevet's commentary and Chaucer's *Boece*. This is not an easy relation to establish in that Chaucer used not only Trevet but also other texts including Jean de Meun's *Li Livres de Confort*. Minnis sees no systematic privileging of one over the other in Chaucer and attempts instead to establish the extent of the debt to Trevet, concluding that that debt is far greater than has been appreciated. And finally, in Chapter 4, Minnis and Tim William Machan look at the *Boece* as an example of late medieval translation, contending that it is a fine example of its genre. Minnis and Machan bring out the controversial nature of translation in an age only too well aware of the Babelish confusion and mendacity of language. Translation is thus a form of exegesis in itself and highly interpretative – a point that accords well with Phillip's arguments below. In terms of the genre of translation, Chaucer's style is flexible and literal, attempting to be close and faithful both to *verba* and *sententia*. This is a fine piece of scholarship and a landmark in *Boece* studies. On translation also, Paul Beekman Taylor subjects one short passage from *Boece* (Book 3, prosa 8, 35–49) to a detailed examination in 'Chaucer's Eye of the Lynx and the Limits of Vision' (*ChauR* 28.67–77). Taylor alights on a line which is not in Boethius's text, Chaucer's reference to the 'eyghen of a beeste that highte lynx', and argues for the centrality of this image to his poetry; Taylor takes it to be a figure that represents 'the limits of the artist's ability to see and express the perfection of form beneath the ugly matter of things'.

Andrew Galloway, in 'Chaucer's *Legend* of *Lucrece* and the Critique of Ideology in Fourteenth-Century England' (*ELH* 60.813–32), discerns within her an uneasy relationship between private and public consciousness. Lucrece has never been read as any easy exemplar of virtue as her zeal for honour and fame was stoutly criticized by Augustine, and subsequent commentators viewed her with similar ambivalence. Nonetheless, she is clearly a figure whose concern for *fama* fascinated late-medieval intellectuals. Galloway traces in detail a tradition of English commentary (Trevet, Waleys, Ridevall and Higden) on Lucrece's suicide. Although there are marked differences between the commentators, Galloway notes that they all, in some measure, attempt to historicize Lucrece's predicament, showing an awareness of some critical differences between Roman and Christian ideologies. Galloway suggests that the fourteenth century in England and Italy represented a threshold of consciousness, or anxiety, about differing cultural kinds of knowledge. Women in particular seem to be a focal point of articulation and mediation of ideological contradiction. Often, Chaucer uses the female perspective as the means through which he interrogates 'masculine or pagan or clerical social assumptions'. Lucrece is a key case in point. Chaucer bypasses the question of Lucrece's agency in, or complicity with, the rape by having her faint. He reverses Augustine's condemnation of her by turning the censure upon the Roman ethos which produced her. In Galloway's reading of Lucrece, Chaucer turns her into a self-conscious victim and covert critic of that Roman ethos.

Helen Phillips examines Chaucer's practice as a translator in two articles, 'Chaucer's French Translations' (*NMS* 37.65–82) and 'Chaucer and Deguileville: The *ABC* in Context' (*MÆ* 62.1–19). In the former, although qualifying her findings as 'necessarily tentative', she distinguishes four different techniques of translation, illustrating these with examples from *Melibee*, the *Romaunt of the Rose*, the *Complaint of Venus*, the *Complaint of Mars*, and the *ABC*, arguing that the distinction between translation and creativity is not as clear-cut as has previously been suggested. In the second article, she concentrates on one poem, the *ABC*, and one technique, which she calls 'redistribution', using this to examine the relationship between Deguileville's *ABC* and Chaucer's poem. Again criticizing previous studies for oversimplifying matters, she shows that to compare Chaucer's poem with the French prayer without considering the larger context of the *Pèlerinage de la Vie Humaine* is unsatisfactory. John Thompson argues for the importance of a different type of context for the *ABC* in 'Chaucer's *ABC* in and out of Context' (*PoeticaJ* 37.38–48), an essay so densely packed with information it is difficult to summarize. He examines the textual tradition of the poem's sixteen extant manuscripts, and considers how the survival of these witnesses may have shaped the poem's reputation prior to its appearance in print; he then marshalls evidence to show that Thomas Speght's decision to include the poem in his second edition of Chaucer's works in 1602 (and hence the poem's inclusion in the Chaucer canon), may have been influenced by John Stow.

Julia Boffey considers Chaucer's lyrics in two substantial articles, 'The Lyrics in Chaucer's Longer Poems' (*PoeticaJ* 37.15–37) and 'The Reputation and Circulation of Chaucer's Lyrics in the Fifteenth Century' (*ChauR* 28.23–40). In the former she first sets out the sheer quantity and variety of the lyrical and epistolary interpolations in Chaucer's narrative poems, before concentrating on one particular category, those 'clearly differentiated and potentially different poems' which occur in the *Book of the Duchess*, *Troilus and Criseyde*, *Prologue to the Legend of Good Women* and *Parliament of Fowls*. As well as enumerating the various functions of these lyrics in their narrative contexts, a discussion which contains a particularly lucid account of the letters of Troilus and Criseyde, Boffey considers matters of textual presentation, specifically how the lyrics in these poems are made to stand out from the narrative. As elsewhere in her work, she calls for greater attention to manuscript context, though in this instance the poor and 'uninformative' quality of the manuscripts hardly helps her. The same problem besets her in the second article, where she mentions some of the same examples, but here her focus is on the influence of Chaucer's lyrics on later writing. Her task is a difficult one; as she admits, 'borrowings and echoes ... can be traced in the output of almost every fifteenth-century writer of courtly verse', but her caveats about the difficulty of locating specific borrowings seem unnecessary given the convincing discussion which follows. She outlines three ways in which Chaucer's lyrics influence other fifteenth-century lyric writing, substantiating these points by including the texts of two anonymous lyrics, both from manuscript and otherwise not readily accessible to scholars; she also brings together a mass of evidence about the knowledge and use of Chaucer's lyrics by other fifteenth-century writers.

Noted here, but to be reviewed next year, is *The Authorship of the 'Equatorie of the planetis'* by Kari Anne Rand Schmidt (Brewer). Peter J. Hager and Ronald J. Nelson have an article in *IEEETrans* 36.87–94, entitled, 'Chaucer's *A Treatise on the Astrolabe*: A 600-year-old Model for Humanizing Technical Documents'. Dealt with from the perspective of rhetoric and technical writing, the essay looks particularly at how Chaucer tempers the 'logico-rational' self with the 'tonal glue' [*sic*] of the 'humanistic' self – this latter self being familiar and fatherly (the *Treatise* is of course addressed to his son and the title appearing in a number of manuscripts is *Bread and Milk for Children*). The thesis depends on a rather trite opposition between subjective and objective voice but one which might nevertheless have some foundation since the article presents a description of the astrolabe's technical construction that is more clear and detailed than much of the more interpretative scholarship. Hagar and Nelson note, generally with favour, the user-friendliness of Chaucer's repetitions and metadiscourse (i.e. authorial intrusion), but ultimately, they censure the work for not conforming to the requirements of modern technical writing, finding Chaucer's text too digressive in details, too verbose and too complicated in sentence construction. Poor old Chaucer.

As a parting thought, Joseph A. Dane's review article, 'The Importance of Importance' (*HLQ* 56.307–17), is noted. In it he considers two books and a cluster of articles on Chaucer published during 1992, after posing two provocative opening questions: 'Who cares about Chaucer? or worse, about Chaucerians?' At least the former can be answered in a positive fashion.

Books Reviewed

Andrew, Malcolm, Charles Moorman, and Daniel J. Ransom, eds. *A Variorum Edition of the Works of Geoffrey Chaucer: The General Prologue: Part One A&B*. UOklaP. pp. 298, 623. hb $115. ISBN 0 8061 2552 7.

Biscoglio, Frances Minetti. *The Wives of the Canterbury Tales and the Tradition of the Valiant Woman of Proverbs 31:10–31*. Mellen Research UP. pp. 272. hb $89.95. ISBN 0773 49803 6.

Blake, Norman, and Peter Robinson, eds. *The Canterbury Tales Project: Occasional Papers*, vol. I. Office for Humanities Communication Publications, 5. Office for Humanities Communication. pp. 97. pb £10. ISBN 1 8977961 06 2.

Dillon, Janette. *Geoffrey Chaucer*. Macmillan Writers in Their Time Series. Macmillan. pp. 212. hb £35, pb £10.99. ISBN 0 333 54202 9, 0 333 54203 7.

Frantzen, Allen J. *Troilus and Criseyde: The Poem and the Frame.* Twayne's Masterwork Studies, 113. Twayne. pp. 158. hb $22.95, pb $12.95. ISBN 0 8057 9427 1, 0 8057 8581 7.

Hallissy, Margaret. *Clean Maids, True Wives, Steadfast Widows: Chaucer's Women and Medieval Codes of Conduct.* Contributions in Women's Studies, 130. Greenwood. pp. 224. hb $49.95. ISBN 0 313 27467 3.

Hines, John. *The Fabliau in English.* Longman. hb $68.95, pb $25.95. ISBN 0 58203732 8, 0 582037336.

Jeneid, Michael. *Chaucer's Checklist: The Poet's Life List of all the Birds in All his Works.* Pandion. pp. 130. $11.95. ISBN 0 963 61690 0.

Lerer, Seth. *Chaucer and His Readers: Imagining the Author in Late-Medieval England.* Princeton UP. pp. 309. hb $39.50. ISBN 0 691 06811 9.

Lomperis, Linda, and Sarah Stanbury, eds. *Feminist Approaches to the Body in Medieval Literature.* UPennP. pp. 272. hb $36.95, pb $16.95. ISBN 0 8122 3117 1.

Minnis, A. J., ed. *Chaucer's Boece and the Medieval Tradition of Boethius.* B&B. pp. 265. $70. ISBN 0 85991 368 6.

Moorman, Charles. *The Statistical Determination of Affiliation in the Landmark Manuscripts of the 'Canterbury Tales'.* Mellen. pp 209. hb $69.95. ISBN 0 7734 9276 3.

Pearsall, Derek. *The Canterbury Tales.* Routledge. pp. 380. pb £12.99. ISBN 0 415 09444 5.

Penninger, Frieda Elaine. *Chaucer's Troilus and Criseyde and the Knight's Tale: Fictions Used.* UPA. pp. 126. hb $39.50. ISBN 0819 19218 X.

Rudat, Wolfgang E. H. *Ernest Exuberance in Chaucer's Poetics: Textual Games in the Canterbury Tales.* Mellen. pp. 340. hb $99.95. ISBN 0 7734 9381 6.

Taylor, Robert A., James F. Burke, Patricia J. Erble, Ian Lancashire, and Brian S. Merrilees, eds. *The Centre and its Compass: Studies in Medieval Literature in Honor of Professor John Leyerle.* Studies in Medieval Culture 33. MIP. pp. 474. hb $40, pb $20. ISBN 1 879288 29 X, 1 879288 30 3.

Walsh, Elizabeth, and Susie M. Barrett, eds. *Light of Learning: Selected Essays of Morton W. Bloomfield 1970–1986.* Lang. pp. 347. hb DM 91. ISBN 0 8204 1766 1.

V

The Sixteenth Century: Excluding Drama after 1550

SUSAN BRUCE

This chapter has three sections: 1. General; 2. Prose; 3. Poetry. Some items are by R. E. Pritchard.

1. General

It seems apposite to begin this chapter with the interdisciplinary *Culture and History 1350–1600: Essays on English Communities, Identities and Writing* (ed. David Aers), which questions conventional divisions between the Medieval and early Modern periods (as do several studies appearing this year). Aers's own essay, 'A Whisper in the Ear of Early Modernists; or, Reflections on Literary Critics Writing the "History of the Subject"' challenges claims that modern subjectivity dates from the sixteenth century, arguing that this view represses both earlier labour struggles, and the earlier emergence of a pre-capitalist market economy and its contingent communities, seeming, moreover, to be 'committed to reproducing aspects of the ideology which gave us the term "Renaissance"'. 'A Whisper' rather understates the tone of the article (more a blast of the trumpet), but it is a well-defended and challenging blast that's well worth reading. Judith M. Bennett's 'Medieval Women, Modern Women: Across the Great Divide' shares much in common with Aers's own essay, also attacking the view that the Medieval and Early Modern worlds are distinct: women's work, Bennett argues, 'provides ... evidence ... of continuity between 1300 and 1700'. The medieval family economy was never the egalitarian haven historians have assumed; similarly, possibilities for a wage differential between female and male labour were as apparent to, and as exploited by, Medieval employers as (Early) Modern ones. The other essays are on pre-sixteenth-century topics and sixteenth-century drama (and so, ironically, given Aers's diatribe, beyond the remit of this chapter).

Periodization is also the concern of *The Work of Dissimilitude: Essays from the Sixth Citadel Conference on Medieval and Renaissance Literature* (ed. David G. Allen and Robert A. White). This aims to address differences between Medieval and Renaissance world views, and (somewhat unusually in conference collections) its main concern is respected by most of its contributors, who in one way or another do try to engage these boundaries. Arthur F. Kinney's 'Figuring

Medieval and Renaissance Literature', for instance, invokes Jakobson's distinction between metonymy and metaphor to argue for the continued relevance of periodization, arguing that Renaissance writers distinguish themselves from their Medieval predecessors by opting for metaphor rather than metonymy; seventeenth-century writers return to metonymy, but do not relinquish metaphor. O. B. Hardison, Jr, discusses competition between romance, quantitative verse, and the new vernacular prosody in 'Crosscurrents in English Sixteenth-Century Prosody', arguing that recognition of the second and third types in the early sixteenth century subjected the first to critical scrutiny. Despite the anxieties the author expresses about the 'idea of a definite break in history', Laviece C. Ward, in 'Historiography on the Eve of the Reformation in an Early-Sixteenth-Century English Manuscript, *e Museo 160*' reads *e Museo 160* as exemplifying a moment when medieval theology and ideas of historiography were replaced by those of the Renaissance and Reformation, a claim Ward bases on the author's encouragement of 'active reader participation'. Finally, in his deconstructive essay, '"For There Is Figures in All Things": Juxtology in Shakespeare, Spenser and Milton', R. A. Shoaf argues that a characteristic mark of the Renaissance is 'its awareness that its difference from earlier periods is difference itself'. Other essays in this volume are discussed in the following paragraph, and below.

Three of the essays in *The Work of Dissimilitude* discuss social and/or historical topics. In 'The Desanctification of the Beggar in Rogue Pamphlets of the English Renaissance', Mark Koch adopts a methodology influenced both by Marx and (more explicitly) by Weber to argue that representations of the beggar in the emergent capitalist economy of sixteenth- and seventeenth-century Northern Europe reject the sanctity previously associated with almsgiving, replacing it instead with a rational, secular charity. David Read's interesting and well-argued 'Ralegh's *Discoverie of Guiana* and the Elizabethan Model of Empire' (one of the best essays in this volume) takes issue with the belief that there existed in 'the Elizabethan cultural matrix a stable sense of what empire meant'. No official policy on colonialism existed in the period, he argues: when Ralegh uses the word 'empire', he denotes not the emergent Empire of England, but the Empire of Guiana, the only 'meaningful "model of empire" for most Elizabethans'. Mary B. Campbell's 'The Illustrated Travel Book and the Birth of Ethnography: Part I of De Bry's *America*', which is also very good, reads Hariot's text and White's pictures as originating the genre of the travel book: it is 'in the relations between the verbal and visual texts of De Bry's book that we find the most hauntingly "modern" of its implications'. She discusses a tension between the pictures, 'motivated, in part, by the absence of an ethnographic language', and the text, linked to 'ethnography proper' by its refusal of narrative; both, she claims, constitute one of the earliest examples of erotic exoticism in European art. In 'Representations of Blacks and Blackness in the Renaissance' (*Criticism* 35.4.499–527), Peter Erikson argues that visual representations of blacks in the period exhibit 'a specific awareness of racial blackness' which both participates in and exposes ideologies surrounding colonial expansion; his article concludes with an examination of similar concerns in Shakespeare's comedies.

Empire is also the concern of *New World Encounters* (ed. Stephen Greenblatt), a cross-disciplinary collection which largely, and very usefully, reprints articles which appeared originally in *Representations*, such as Louis Montrose's 'The Work of Gender in the Discourse of Discovery', Jeffrey Knapp's 'Divine Tobacco', and Michel de Certeau's 'Travel Narratives of the French to

Brazil'. The volume also includes Sara Castro-Klaren's, 'Dancing and the Sacred in the Andes', and Margarita Zamora's 'Columbus's "Letter to the Sovereigns": Announcing the Discovery', which translates into English a different version of this letter. Greenblatt's introduction claims that the articles all concentrate on 'the vision of the vanquished'; many, however, concern primarily the victors. The other articles reprinted in the volume are Mary Fuller on *The Discoverie of Guiana*, and essays on Spanish and Spanish-American writing.

Addressing representations of another New World is David Fausett's *Writing the New World: Imaginary Voyages and Utopias of the Great Southern Land*. Fausett provides an overview of representations of Australasia from classical times (Plato, for example, and Lucian) through the seventeenth century, his intention being, he says, to assess how earlier modes of writing about societies function as a vehicle for speculative thought in later eras. Much of the discussion in the chapters relevant to this essay is descriptive rather than analytic; it is heavily influenced by other secondary sources, which too often serve as alternatives to engagement with the texts themselves (he reads *Utopia*, for instance, almost entirely through Louis Marin). Other chapters in the book discuss 'Baroque Allegories', and 'Utopia and Seventeenth-Century Rationalism'.

Nationalism and empire is also the subject of several of the essays in *Renaissance Culture in Context: Theory and Practice* (ed. Jean R. Brink and William F. Gentrup). The first group of essays in this conference collection deals with nationalism and with the interdisciplinary theory and practice of British literature. R. D. S. Jack discusses the formation of a canon of Scottish literature, arguing that decisions about what ought to form part of the canon should not be taken on political, but only on aesthetic grounds. Arthur F. Kinney offers an interesting source study of *Macbeth*, reading the play as a pointed study of imperial thinking, whilst Bart Westerweel uses Bakhtin's theory of the chronotope to discuss time in *As You Like It* and *Twelfth Night*. The second group of essays is devoted to Renaissance geography, religion and history, and the third discusses issues relevant to humanism; these are mentioned below.

Closer to home, John Michael Archer's *Sovereignty and Intelligence* examines 'Spying and Court Culture in the English Renaissance', departing from the broadly Foucauldian paradigms he initially discusses by arguing that sovereignty and surveillance are far more continuous modes of power than Foucault would suggest. Techniques of surveillance were already operative in pre-Enlightenment court politics: paranoia underlies subjectivity in the Renaissance, as in the post-Enlightenment state. Chapter 1 offers a Lacanian reading of Montaigne, reading Montaigne's search for self-knowledge as a form of self-spying. In Chapter 2, Archer examines the impact and effect of sexual anxiety within court culture in the *Arcadia*, in which the pastoral becomes the vehicle through which this anxiety is registered: in the *Arcadia*, Archer argues, Sidney constructs a paranoid relationship between sovereign surveillance and heterosexual romance. The remaining three chapters of the book examine Marlowe, Jonson and Bacon.

A different aspect of court politics underlies Susan Frye's impressive feminist study of *Elizabeth I: The Competition for Representation*, which considers how Elizabeth contested patriarchal gender definitions to create her own identity. Frye argues that Elizabeth's self-representation as virgin queen acknowledged her gender and allowed her to 'elude her subjects' representation of her as female, passive, possessible and always exposed to scrutiny', declaring herself instead 'active and self-possessed, virtuous in terms that God only could judge'. In defence of this thesis, Frye traces alterations in the iconography of the queen throughout her reign: her coronation entry, for example, Kenilworth (which Frye reads in terms of a competition between Dudley and Elizabeth, and later Gascoigne), and *The Faerie Queene* (where Frye examines Spenser's patriarchal redefinition of the chastity Elizabeth adopted: allegory, she argues, became 'an important locus of representational conflict' in which prevailing masculinist codes competed with an evolving court discourse of Elizabeth's self-possession). One wonders whether the players in this representational genre really were as conscious of the strategies in which they were engaged as Frye tends to suggest.

This approach to iconography would be challenged by some of the articles in *The Art of the Emblem: Essays in Honor of Karl Josef Höltgen* (ed. Michael Bath, John Manning and Alan R. Young), which covers English emblem art from the Early Modern period to the nineteenth century. John Horden, for example, in 'The Connotations of Symbols,' argues that 'even familiar symbols ... can contain "snares that lie ... obscure to the eye"', especially as those connotations vary according to 'modifications in the prevailing climate of opinion'; that opinion is shared by Clifford Davidson in his discussion of 'The Transformation of Symbols in English Emblem Books', which examines the figure of the pelican in *King Lear*. The best essay in the volume, Roy Strong's '"My Weeping Stagg I Crowne,": The Persian Lady Reconsidered' examines Marcus Gheeraerts the Younger's 'The Persian Lady', together with its accompanying (Spenserian?) sonnet. Strong's rich reading of the iconography of this 'most complex of all Elizabethan allegorical portraits' elaborates the signification of Persia in the Elizabethan imagination, pointing out how different previous interpretations of this painting and its iconography have been. Other essays in the volume include '*De Morte et Amore*: A Story-telling Emblem and its Dimensions' (Judith Dundas), 'Samuel Daniel and Abraham Fraunce on the Device and the Emblem' (Denis L. Drysdall), and Alciato in Whitney's *A Choice of Emblemes* (Mary Silcox).

Frye's tacit assumptions about the legibility of iconography and the consciousness of individuals' manipulation of its strategic possibilities, then, perhaps need a little qualification. That said, *The Competition for Representation* is an interesting and challenging discussion, well-argued and well-defended. Readers interested in this subject might also be interested in Stephen W. May's review article on 'Recent Studies in Elizabeth I' (*ELR* 23.345–54) and in Margaret Christian's 'Elizabeth's Preachers and the Government of Women: Defining and Correcting a Queen' (*SCJ* 24.561–76) which examines tensions between 'spiritual and temporal authority', arguing that 'preachers protected their own privileged authority by stressing [Elizabeth's] dependence on [God] and therefore on themselves'.

Four more books which wholly or partly concern royal figures can be mentioned at this point. Marc Shell's brilliant and fascinating study, *Children of the Earth: Literature, Politics and Nationhood*, which examines conceptions of kinship in cultural manifestations as diverse as the family pet and Siamese twins, and authors as diverse as Racine and Mark Twain, includes a chapter on Elizabeth I's self-representation which is more fully discussed below, as a version of the essay also appears in Shell's *Elizabeth's Glass* (*Children of the Earth* also, incidentally, includes an original and provocative reading of incest in *Hamlet*). Similarly, Wendy Wall's *The Imprint of Gender* (also discussed more fully below) includes a chapter on 'Author(iz)ing Royal Spectacle,' in which Wall, like

Frye, examines courtiers' interpretations of Elizabeth's sovereignty. Finally, *Henry VIII in History, Historiography and Literature* (ed. Uwe Baumann) is an interdisciplinary collection of essays, mainly (very) old historicist and/or (very) new critical, which treat of representations of the king in literature and art. The book also includes 26 black and white reproductions of illustrations (portraits, drawings and some film stills), a select bibliography and a brief chronology of Henry's reign. Essays pertinent to this chapter cover panegyric poetry on the King's Coronation (Beate Lusse), Skelton's *Magnyfycence* (Rainer Holtei), Henry VIII's love-letters and songs (Theo Stemmler), the chronicles of Hall and Holinshed (Jurgen Beer), Scottish chronicles (Ulrike Moret and Sonja Vathjunker), and William Thomas and Ulpian Fulwell (Uwe Baumann). None of them, unfortunately, is very strong. The best are substantially catalogues of references; the worst degenerate into poorly argued hagiographical character studies of the King. Almost all are lamentably ill-informed about developments in critical studies over the last 25 years, and some are appallingly proof-read: someone, surely, ought to have caught repeated misspellings such as 'Herny'.

From royalty to religion and popular belief: John W. O'Malley's *Religious Culture in the Sixteenth Century: Preaching, Rhetoric, Spirituality and Reform* reprints a number of essays (rather bizarrely with their original pagination, on the ground that this will make articles easy to refer to for readers who have used them before). Two articles concern Renaissance Rome, others cover the content, rhetorical form and influence of sixteenth-century treatises on preaching, Luther, the place of St Charles Borromeo in the history of preaching, the rhetoric of Erasmus, and the Jesuits.

Sharon L. Jansen brings to bear a more political interpretation of the text she examines in her '"And he shall be called Edward": Sixteenth-Century Political Protest and Folger MS Loseley b.546' (*ELR* 23.227–43), claiming that in the sixteenth-century manuscript, 'The Sayings of the Prophets', we can read political subversion perhaps directly related to cases such as the execution of Sir Rhys ap Griffith in 1531. Also attentive to subversion is Christopher Marsh's valuable account of *The Family of Love in English Society, 1550–1630*, a notorious sect denounced and persecuted as extremist, subversive and sexually outrageous; writers such as Jonson and Middleton mocked them, as they became figures for sexual license; others (possibly including Donne) were affected by their beliefs. Marsh's careful historical study discusses their beliefs and modest practices, and explores their place in English society (from the court of Elizabeth to East Anglian villages), and should be useful to those interested in the influence of religious radicalism on the literature and culture of the time. [REP] Several essays on religious topics, not directly English ones, also appear in *Culture and Identity in Early Modern Europe 1500–1800*, ed. Barbara B. Diefendorf and Carla Hesse.

In his well-argued '"Holy Cozenage" and the Renaissance Cult of the Ear' (*SCJ* 23.47–65), Bryan Crockett invokes the work of Victor Turner in his discussion of sermons by preachers such as Playfere, Browning, Adams, Andrewes and Donne, arguing that 'the peculiar cultural conditions developing out of the Protestant Reformation engendered in England a "cult of the ear", a sensibility marked by heightened aural receptivity to performances evoking a sense of wonder by their manipulation of paradoxical terms'. Crockett's interest in oral culture is shared by Elizabeth S. Cohen, in her lively and fascinating account of the social meaning of a (very funny) illustrated love letter from early seventeenth-century Rome (in Diefendorf and Hesse, eds, *Culture and Identity in Early Modern Europe*). The meaning of the ill-fated letter, Cohen argues, derived from the partially literate culture in which the two lovers found themselves: illiterate folk such as the hapless receiver of the letter in question, she argues, 'readily sacrificed privacy in order to participate in the imposing, if sometimes dangerous, domain of a written culture'. Oral culture, albeit of a different sort, is also the subject of Linda Woodbridge's 'Patchwork: Piecing the Early Modern Mind in England's First Century of Print Culture' (*ELR* 23.5–45). Like Crockett, Woodbridge uses anthropological studies in her discussion of (mainly Shakespearean) plays, which she sees as influenced by oral literature, especially the folk tale. This influence, she argues, challenges the more accepted view of 'sources', which reflects a capitalist, patriarchal conception of literary influence where only named authors, holders of literary property and fathers of their texts, are credited with influence on canonical drama.

Woodbridge's is only one of the large number of works which appeared this year on subjects related to gender and sexuality. One of the most important is Wendy Wall's extremely accomplished *The Imprint of Gender: Authorship and Publication in the English Renaissance*, which looks at how writers of nondramatic texts 'began to represent ... print's cultural, literary, and political potential', arguing that there developed, over the period, a rhetoric of publication which 'described the relationship between writers, texts and their readers by expressing problems of status as gendered issues'. Wall first offers a detailed examination of the relation of early printed sonnet sequences to manuscript culture, showing how writers such as Sidney, Spenser, Drayton and Daniel use their literary mistresses as figures for the reader, and arguing that the reformatting of the sonnet for the printed sequence changed the way the reader was asked to imagine gendered authority; books became figured by writers as 'unruly women who ... relied on the care and supervision of their publishing authors'. Chapter 2 examines writing about spectacle, offering very convincing readings of works such as Gascoigne's *The Princely Pleasures at Kenelworth Castle* and Sidney's *The Lady of May*, in terms similar to Frye's: gendered discourses of pastoral romance and courtly love, Wall argues, are used to question the terms of Elizabeth's rule. Chapters 3 and 4 elaborate different strategies adopted in response to print's ability to occlude social difference: reading became figured as an act of trespass, for example, and prefaces frequently engaged in an 'eroticized rhetoric of disclosure'. Greene, Drayton, Heywood, Jonson, Daniel, Lodge, Nashe, Spenser, Sidney, Shakespeare, and the complaint poem all come under discussion in these chapters. The final chapter examines the 'alternative modes of expression and self-authorization' developed by women writers, and includes discussions of Isabella Whitney, Amelia Lanyer, Mary Sidney and Mary Wroth. Wall's book is an important study, a rich and complex account impressive in its illustration and convincing in its argument.

Quite the reverse argument to Wall's is offered by Mary Erler in 'The Books and Lives of Three Tudor Women', which appears in *Privileging Gender in Early Modern England* (ed. Jean R. Brink). Erler examines the library of the Fettyplace sisters, half-siblings of Sir Thomas Elyot, arguing that the advent of printing meant that reading began to transcend class and, to a lesser extent, gender boundaries. *Privileging Gender* includes three other essays pertinent to this chapter. Margaret Hannay's '"Unlock my lipps": the *Miserere mei Deus* of Anne Vaughan Lok and Mary Sidney Herbert, Countess of Pembroke' compares two verse translations of Psalm 51 by these writers, arguing that both invoke a male persona as a means of justifying their own speech. Phyllis Rackin's rather more sophisticated 'Historical Difference/Sexual Difference' argues that whereas modern gender ideology invokes physical difference to construct its oppositions, Renaissance sexual distinctions 'were grounded ... in the ... more traditionally privileged discourses of theology and history'. Consequently, masculine desire for women in authors such as Shakespeare and Sidney is 'coded as effeminate', whereas 'extreme virility is often expressed in erotic desire for another man; and masculine behaviour in women associated with heteroerotic promiscuity'. Margaret Downs-Gamble, in 'The Taming-School' reads Shakespeare's *The Taming of the Shrew*, and *A Pleasant Conceited History, called The Taming of a Shrew* (1594) in the context of Agricolan and Erasmian educational programmes which conflated 'Woman and language' to impose 'upon female scholars a nonnegotiable position as subject, object, and medium of study'.

The essays in *Renaissance Discourses of Desire* (ed. Claude J. Summers and Ted-Larry Pebworth) are mainly concerned with seventeenth-century literature, although the editors' introduction discusses attitudes to love and sexuality in Elizabethan poetry: ambivalence, and the fear of sexuality are, they argue, the dominant impulse of most love poetry and theory of the period. Several essays in the volume discuss homoerotic desire: Raymond B. Waddington's 'The Poetics of Eroticism: Shakespeare's "Master Mistress"' examines Shakespeare's Sonnet 20 in the context of medical attitudes towards sex transformation and bisexuality, and sixteenth-century interpretations of bisexual myths, whilst Stella P. Revard analyses 'The Saphic Voice in Donne's "Sapho to Philaenis"'. Same-sex desire is also the concern of Janel Mueller's 'Troping Utopia: Donne's Brief for Lesbianism', which appears in *Sexuality and Gender in Early Modern Europe: Institutions, Texts, Images* (ed. James Grantham Turner). Guido Ruggiero's 'Marriage, Love, Sex and Renaissance Civic Morality', in the same volume, includes a brief discussion of the Renaissance 'subculture of sodomy'.

This excellent collection of essays also includes several others pertinent to this chapter. In 'The Semiotics of Masculinity in Renaissance England' David Kuchta examines male sartorial display in the Renaissance court. Constance Jordan considers 'Renaissance Women and the Question of Class': and concludes that although Renaissance women 'constituted an economic class in themselves', this class was 'also conditioned by its caste character', and that prostitution was the work most likely to escape male control. One of the best essays in the volume is Katherine Eisaman Maus's rich and provocative article 'A Womb of His Own: Male Renaissance Poets in the Female Body', suggesting that Renaissance writers (such as Sidney, Greville and Milton, amongst others) associated creative imagination with the female body, which 'provides a risky but compelling model for the structure of male poetic subjectivity' in the period. Other essays in the volume cover William Shakespeare and Elizabeth Cary, Lady Mary Wroth's *Urania*, and Madeleine de Scudéry's *Clélie*, *Paradise Lost*, and Renaissance Italian painting and (some French) poetry.

Three other articles worthy of mention are the following. Mark Breitenberg's well-argued 'Anxious Masculinity: Sexual Jealousy in Early Modern England' (*FSt* 19.377–98) examines Shakespeare, conduct books, and pamphlets about jealousy in support of a claim that sexual jealousy is 'constitutive and symptomatic of the normative operations of patriarchy'. Breitenberg is influenced by Stanley Cavell (whom he also attacks); his essay also invokes Lacan in a discussion of the construction of woman in the period. In a feminist source study, 'Nicholas Breton reads Jane Anger' (*RenSt* 7.291–300), A. Lynne Magnusson argues convincingly that links between Breton and Anger are far more extensive than have hitherto been recognized, and that the originating author is Anger. Finally, in 'Taking the Pencil out of God's Hand: Art, Nature, and the Face-Painting Debate in Early Modern England' (*PMLA* 108.224–39), Frances E. Dolan examines Sidney's *Apologie for Poetry*, Puttenham's *The Art of English Poesie* and Shakespeare's *The Winter's Tale* to show how each invokes the discourses of art and nature, discourses which, Dolan argues, 'render poetry and face painting suspect as analogous effeminate enterprises'. The tradition of discussions of rhetoric and painting 'constructs display or spectacle as feminine and the spectator as masculine, associating pleasure and desire with the feminine and rendering them suspect'.

The last publication to be discussed in this context, Dudley Wilson's *Signs and Portents: Monstrous Births from the Middle Ages to the Enlightenment*, is something of a disappointment. Despite his provocative subject matter, Wilson seems strangely unwilling to analyse the cases that he details, so the book ends up reading more like a compendium of instances than an analysis of them, a 'Key to all Mythologies' written not by Casaubon, but by Mr Brooke ('in dealing with the seventeenth and eighteenth centuries in particular', Wilson states, 'we shall be on our guard against going too closely into intellectual and religious controversies'). This is a shame, because the book really is amply illustrated, both in pictorial terms and in its range of reference, and suggests a considerable amount of research into its source material.

Several studies of form appeared this year. One of the most substantial is Mindele Anne Treip's *Allegorical Poetics and the Epic: The Renaissance Tradition to Paradise Lost*, proposing Renaissance continuity with, and development from, earlier theory and practice of allegory, as in the influence of Tasso on Spenser. In addition, the book includes discussions of Boccaccio, Sidney, Bacon and John Harington, amongst others, and chapters on neoclassical epic theory and Le Bossu on the epic, as well as its lengthy discussion of *Paradise Lost*.

In *Framing Authority: Sayings, Self, and Society in Sixteenth-Century England*, Mary Thomas Crane argues that the practice of keeping a commonplace book was 'reformulated ... in response to complex ... insecurities about language': in 'gathering' and 'framing' textual fragments English humanists accumulated intellectual capital, participated in the commodification of knowledge, and attempted 'to create ... a stable place in society between the landed nobility and the deterritorialized merchant class'. Crane defends this thesis through discussions of More, Heywood, Wyatt, Gascoigne, Sidney and Shakespeare, amongst others. Between 1520 and 1550, she argues, humanists utilized the practice to seek preferment, articulating 'non-threatening supplements to the monarch's power', but the practice also implied an 'ideology opposed to aristocratic and mercantile values', as More's *Utopia* shows in its endorsement of a meritocratic hierarchy ruled by scholars. After the accession of Elizabeth, gathering and framing were adapted to suit the needs of a changing social situation, and to articulate concepts of selfhood, whose distinct modernity is inaugurated by Sidney. The book is occasionally rather theoretically undecided: as Crane herself states, she has been influenced by revisionist and Marxist historians, Derridean deconstruction, Foucauldian 'discipline', Lacanian subject-formation, Bourdieu's theory of cultural capital and Althusser's 'anti-humanism'.

Also worth reading is S. K. Heninger, Jr's amply illustrated *The Subtext of Form in the English Renaissance: Proportion Poetical*, which contextualizes its discussion within arts such as painting and architecture. Heninger aims to 'engage with the challenges of poststructuralism and ... to demonstrate a theory and a praxis that preserve interpretation while eluding the limitations of positivism as well as the pitfalls of poststructuralist thought, to license meaning in Renaissance texts in order to explore their negotiations within a larger context'. The opening chapter concludes that in the Renaissance a radical materialist aesthetic competes with an orthodox, theocentric one, as a consequence of which the 'analysis of any artifact from the period produces at least two competitive readings, one grounded in ... logocentrism, the other in the reality of matter and its palpable phenomena (hylocentrism)'. The centrepiece of this chapter is a discussion of Surrey. Chapter 2 discusses the meaning of poetry for writers such as Harrington and Puttenham, invoking the architectural principle of *Ratio*; Chapter 3, using examples from Petrarch, Wyatt and Shakespeare, argues that in the sonnet 'subtext of form becomes a counterpoint to what the words themselves might say'. The fourth chapter examines the discourse of sexual otherness in companion poems, whilst the final chapter offers an interesting discussion of 'the rhetoric of perspective', arguing that literary narratives in the Renaissance increasingly used strategies first employed in painting, such as framing devices. This chapter is illustrated by discussions of *Utopia*, *Astrophil and Stella* and *Euphues*.

Far less challenging a publication is Iva Beretta's *'The World's a Garden': Garden Poetry of the English Renaissance*. Very similar to a doctoral thesis, this book examines the relation between the literary and the physical Renaissance garden from the beginning of the sixteenth century to 1660, discussing Classical and Christian paradises and gardens, Italian and English Renaissance gardens, Paradise and the English garden and the contemplative garden. Finally, Peter Mack has edited a collection of papers on *Renaissance Rhetoric*. In this, Lawrence Green and Lisa Jardine consider early Renaissance uses of Aristotle and Agricola, respectively, and Kees Meerhoff discusses Melanchthon's use of rhetoric in scriptural interpretation. Dilwyn Knox examines the relationship between rhetoric teaching and school organizations, Brian Vickers discusses English rhetoric textbooks, David Norbrook argues that exposure to rhetoric education would have affected judgement of the arguments for degree in *Troilus and Cressida* and Sir John Davies's *Orchestra*, George Hunter distinguishes between the principles underlying modern literary criticism and Renaissance rhetorical thinking, and Patricia Rubin suggests that rhetorical approaches might help in the appreciation of Raphael. Mack himself offers interesting and lucid analyses of rhetorical technique in Greene's *Mamillia* and *Pandosto*, and Lodge's *Rosalynde*. [REP]

Several editions of hitherto hard-to-come-by works have been made available this year. The University of Nebraska Press has done an excellent job of producing Marc Shell's wonderful edition of *Elizabeth's Glass*. 'The Glass of the Sinful Soul' is Elizabeth I's translation of Marguerite of Navarre's *Le Miroir de l'âme pécheresse*, published in several editions in 1548, 1568, 1582 and 1590. Shell's edition of the text includes a transcription and reproduction of Elizabeth's manuscript, and a transcription of the 'epistle dedicatory' and conclusion added by John Bale, who produced the 1548 edition, as well as shorter introductions to Bale's additions to Elizabeth's text, a glossary of names, and a brief chronology of Elizabeth's life. The central concern of Shell's introduction will be recognizable to readers familiar with his 1988 book *The End of Kinship*: 'Elizabeth', he argues, 'was concerned to transform physical incest (of the sort that she had reason to fear in her childhood) and libertine incest (of the sort that she represented in the 'Glass') into a kind of political incest based in the unity of the English people as a single family'. He reads the 'Glass' as a kinship riddle, in terms of a complex of problems revolving around the doctrine of universal siblinghood. This is an original and challenging essay, and the edition is a very fine and useful one.

Elizabeth's resistance to marriage is also, in part, the subject of Valerie Wayne's informative introduction to her edition of Edmund Tilney's entertaining dialogue, *The Flower of Friendship*. Wayne's introduction has three main aims: to defend the 'relevance of humanist thinking about marriage ... to sixteenth-century English culture; ... to demonstrate the presence of ... residual, dominant, and emergent ideologies of marriage within Tilney's text ...; [and] to show how and why the emergent view of marriage that *The Flower* releases is not contained by its dominant ideology'. She offers a different explanation from Shell's of Elizabeth's resistance to marriage: in her opinion marriage would have threatened to circumscribe Elizabeth's power.

Robert C. Evans and Barbara Wiedemann have published an edition of an autobiographical poem by Martha Moulsworth, 'The Memorandum of Martha Moulsworth/Widdowe' which, written in 1632, refers to events in Moulsworth's life between 1577 and 1632. The poem itself is only five pages long; the rest of the book, (entitled *'My Name Was Martha': A Renaissance Woman's Autobiographical Poem*), thus constitutes a rather long prologue to the tale Moulsworth more succinctly describes. The book, apparently aimed at undergraduates, includes chapters on the poem as a work of art, its historical contexts, the poem as autobiography, an overview of the feminist theoretical contexts in which one might want to read the poem, and textual notes (some rather self-evident) to the poem itself.

Extraordinarily good value for money is Elizabeth Story Donno's edition of *Three Renaissance Pastorals: Tasso, Guarini, Daniel*: Tasso's *Aminta*, Battista Guarini's *Pastor Fido* and Samuel Daniel's *Queenes Arcadia*. Both Italian texts are reprinted in their early seventeenth-century English translations; Daniel's play has hitherto only been available in a limited edition of the *Works*, edited by A. B. Grosart. A succinct general introduction offers a publishing history of the texts and discusses the accuracy of the translation; brief introductions to the individual texts are also included, and each play has brief notes. Also of interest is Barrett L. Beer's edition of John Hayward's *The Life and Raigne of King Edward the Sixth*, which includes, in addition to the text, an introduction covering Hayward's life and work, and a discussion of the text, which Beer sees as 'less a study of the life of Edward the Sixth than a narrative of conflict among leading court nobility'. Also included is a select bibliography, and an index. Finally, Victor Houliston in (*ELR* 23.382–427) publishes the Latin original, with an English translation, of an allegorical playlet, *Breuis Dialogismus*, of uncertain authorship, the first dramatic text from the English Jesuit School at St Omer, written around the turn of the century.

Three reference tools need mentioning here. Volume 132 of the *Dictionary of Literary Biography* (ed. David A. Richardson) covers 'Sixteenth-Century British Nondramatic Writers'. Individual entries generally include a bibliography of texts and contemporary editions, illustrations (woodcuts, portraits, and/or reproductions of contemporary editions, for example), an essay on the author, with his or her biographical details and descriptions of the major works, and a list (of very variable length and usefulness) of twentieth-century criticism. The introduction maintains that each volume 'includes the major writers ... and those standing in the ranks immediately behind them'; that three literary forms recur frequently in this volume (autobiography and biography, dialogue, and satire); and that 'four large descriptive categories are conspicuous in the entries in this volume: literary innovations and forms, authorial origins and careers'. If these are the principles of selection, why are there entries for Henry VIII and Lady Jane Grey, for example, but not for Elizabeth, for John Knox, but not for More or Puttenham, for Dunbar and Wyatt, but not for Spenser or Surrey? Individual essays often (of course) refer to writers such as these, but the reader must go elsewhere to find out about them.

A useful research tool is the second volume of R. J. Fehrenbach and E. S. Leedham-Green's *Private Libraries in Renaissance England*, which catalogues 62 Oxford inventories surviving from 1507 to 1554, enabling us to see who owned (and presumably read) what in the period. Each list is preceded by a paragraph or so – occasionally about a page – of biographical and bibliographical matters relating to owner and collection (rather grandly described as an 'essay' in the introduction). Also of interest here is William A. Ringler, Jr's *Index of English Verse in Manuscript 1501–1558*, prepared and completed by Michael Rudick and Susan J. Ringler, which aims to catalogue 'all identifiable English verse, from major long poems to scraps and extracts', transcribed between 1500 and 1558: it includes older books with verse added to them by owners and borrowers, manuscripts of single works, miscellanies, musical manuscripts, and prose works with verse added to them, and an exhaustive list of indexes. An introduction claims that the first 75 years of print affected the literary culture of manuscript at most in minor ways. Anne Ferry's review essay (*SEL* 33.209–43) examines 'Recent Studies in the English Renaissance'.

Of related interest to this chapter is Jonathan Dewald's *Aristocratic Experience and the Origins of Modern Culture*, which discusses the history of individuality in France, 1570–1715. Arguing against the view that the modern self developed in the emergent bourgeoisie, Dewald maintains that the nobility, preoccupied with issues of selfhood, increasingly doubted the value of the social conventions surrounding the self. Of considerable importance for those interested in *Interpretation and Meaning in the Renaissance* is Ian Maclean's book of that title. Although Maclean's focus, as his subtitle makes clear, is 'the Case of Law', his is an important intervention in the debate about meaning in the Renaissance: his admirable range of reference, both in Renaissance and in contemporary theory, and his lucid and intelligent exposition of his subject matter make this a book to be reckoned with by those interested in, amongst other things, the impact – or lack thereof – of the humanists on legal thinking, and on Renaissance thought about linguistic issues. There is little evidence, he concludes, to support the claim that Renaissance thinkers were approaching a conception of relational semantics.

One book on architecture, one on art history, and one on conversation might also be of interest. Simon Thurley has produced an extremely detailed architectural history of *The Royal Palaces of Tudor England*, which discusses the relation between architecture and court life 1460–1547. Superbly illustrated, this book examines the motivation behind the explosion of building under Henry VIII, the pattern to the distribution of the royal houses, and the reasons for the court's movement between them, and includes a wealth of information not only on the more glamorous aspects of courtly life, but also on matters such as kitchens, sanitation, recreation, chapels and so forth. In his *Refiguring the Real: Picture and Modernity in Word and Image, 1400–1700*, Christopher Braider examines the relationship between the painted and the verbal image, arguing that the traditional explanation of the former in terms of the latter is misguided, misrepresenting the impact of pictorial naturalism from the fifteenth century on. The book aims to 'reorient our sense of the essential reciprocity of the relation between image and text': texts demand interpretation in the light of images, and not just the other way around, and we must not, in interpretation, repress the visual experience to which the verbal imagery of, for example, the Cervantean or Cartesian text, appeals. This is an erudite and original book, full of insight on the individual paintings it discusses, as well as challenging in its main argument.

2. Prose

Reid Barbour's energetic *Deciphering Elizabethan Fiction* examines Early Modern prose narrative, arguing against accounts which read it as a forerunner of the novel: Elizabethan prose fiction, Barbour claims, challenges novelistic discourse rather than founds it. He proceeds through an analysis of three 'key words' of the prose of the period: 'deciphering', (whereby some prior truth which constitutes the meaning of the narrative is revealed by the narrator); 'discovering', in which, unlike deciphering, the reader is led by the narrator to elevate one narrative event over another; and 'stuff'. The former two are, Barbour argues, Greene's two main schemes, denoting his confidence in, and desire for, the possibility of a stable prose; Nashe's 'stuff', challenging rival literary traditions, parodies and replaces deciphering; Dekker 'works within the genres of discovery', but, less confident in the possibility of stability, uses Nashe's 'stuff' to vex Greene's conventions of discovery, privileging 'flux and hybridity over the purity of mode and genre'.

This is a lively and original account of Early Modern prose. Like Barbour, Lorna Hutson also challenges the view of critics who see the Renaissance prose narrative as a forerunner of the novel. Her semi-ironically titled 'Fortunate Travellers: Reading For the Plot in Sixteenth-Century England' (*Rep* 41.83–103) is an excellent and complex essay, which invokes Bakhtin's notion of the chronotope to argue that 'the word *plot* had stronger spatial connotations in the sixteenth century than it does now' and that Gascoigne, Lyly, Sidney, Boccaccio and Bandello exhibit a 'preference for plots which are brought about and resolved by the exhibition of skill ... reemplotting the circumstances of the problem itself so as to ensure the cooperation of otherwise doubtful or hostile (conceptual) forces'. Hutson's essay ends with a consideration of the gender-specific nature of the reading strategies she elaborates. Gender is also the defining category behind Juliet Fleming's 'The Ladies' Man and the Age of Elizabeth' (in Turner, ed. *Sexuality and Gender in Early Modern Europe*). Fleming examines 'ladies' texts' (texts such as *Euphues, A Petite Pallace of Pettie His Pleasure*, and *Rich His Farewell to Military Profession*, which are directed specifically to women); in these texts, she argues, class anxieties about print publication are displaced into the register of gender: 'in displaying their fictions as products of a prodigal phase Elizabeth's poets intended their writings first to explore and then to reject, female power and its most alarming consequences'. James Nielson's original and wide-ranging defence of manuscript study, 'Reading Between the Lines' (*SEL* 33.43–82) examines (amongst other things) differences between the handwritten and printed versions of drafts of the work of Gabriel Harvey (the former crammed with marginalia deleted from the printed texts), to argue that from Early Modern manuscripts we can extrapolate a theory of the 'textuality of personality'.

Several studies appeared this year which, in one way or another, chose to treat humanist subjects through an examination of their use of different forms of publishing. Just the opposite perspective from that of Mary Thomas Crane (discussed above) is taken by Lisa Jardine in *Erasmus, Man of Letters: The Construction of Charisma in Print*, which argues forcefully and persuasively, that Erasmus was the prime mover in the construction of his own reputation, manipulating the new media of painting (portraits by Holbein, Durer and Metsys, for example) and printed book, and exploiting them to represent himself as the pre-eminent Renaissance man of letters. 'The enduring image of Erasmus which seems to stand as some kind of reproach to our own ... intellectual efforts is Erasmus's own ... statement of the importance ... of his learning', Jardine argues: 'it ... was not the evaluation of the Europe he inhabited'.

Jardine's study is a well-researched and very well-written work of literary detection. Her conclusions are very similar to those of David R. Carlson, whose detailed but occasionally repetitive *English Humanist Books* examines 'Writers and Patrons, Manuscript and Print 1475–1525'. Carlson argues that 'humanists were more attuned to the complexity of systems of publication than anyone, and were quicker to exploit them', carefully adapting modes of publication to the ends they meant them to serve. Presentation copies, for example, crucial to the process of securing patronage (which, like Crane, Carlson understands as an investment in cultural capital), were carefully judged to fulfil certain criteria, such as fitness to current political concerns. Many humanists experimented with various methods of publication, from presentation copies to manuscript and printed collections of their writings. Like Jardine, Carlson also examines the Metsys diptych, though he arrives at a rather different reading of it; like Jardine, Carlson also concludes that Erasmus was the most sophisticated in his manipulation of the available media: 'twice the return for half the work underlies much of Erasmus's publishing'.

Other work that appeared on humanist topics this year includes Ari Wesseling's 'Dutch Proverbs and Ancient Sources in Erasmus's *Praise of Folly*' (*RenQ* 351–78), which examines the impact on Erasmus of his native language and lists classical sources and proverbs which appear in the *Praise of Folly*. David Baker's '"To Divulgate or Set Forth": Humanism and Heresy in Sir Thomas Elyot's *The Book Named the Governor*' (*SP* 90.46–57) discusses *The Governor* and More's *Utopia*, arguing that the publication of the former in the vernacular is an important determinant of their relationship, as Elyot 'attempts to control the interpretation of Utopian ideals ... by a vernacular public reading'. The third group of essays in *Renaissance Culture in Context* (ed. Brink and Gentrup) covers examples of the theory and practice of the humanist ideal of imitation, discussions of Neo-Latin poems and authors, and different aspects of the role of Italian humanism in the spread of Renaissance values. A. J. Carlson's '*Mundus Muliebris* The World of Women Reviled and Defended ca. 195 B.C. and 1551 A.D. and Other Things ...' (*SCJ* 24.541–60) examines William Thomas's hitherto lost translation from Livy's Fourth Decade of *Ab Urbe Condita Libri* which, Carlson argues, Thomas uses to comment on the events of 1551.

Volume 31 of *Moreana* is largely devoted to articles on More's *Utopia*, and to Clarence H. Miller's edition of seven of 'Thomas More's Letters to Frans van Cranevelt'. Miller provides photographic reproductions and English translations of the correspondence (31.117.3–66). William A. McClung's 'Designing Utopia' (31.118–19.9–28) discusses 12 visual representations of the island and its buildings, from the map accompanying the 1516 edition of the text to contemporary illustrations, in the context of an argument which claims that the text invites its readers to 'visualise not the thing itself ... but ... the kind of thing it is'. István Bejczy's '*L'Utopie* et le Moyen Age' (31.118–19.29–42) argues that Hythloday's description of the island suppresses Medieval culture, and that to succeed in this endeavour, Hythloday 'est obligé d'abroger l'histoire et ... sa propre existence historique'. Miguel Martínez López details similarities between 'The Life of the Essenes and the Life of the Utopians' (31.118–19.43–59) (such as their common abolition of property), whilst Hubert Demenier argues in his 'La Propriété en Utopie: réflexions d'un juriste' (31.118–19.85–101) that the Utopian 'parable' respects the priority of the individual over society by virtue of its familial emphasis. Cosimo Quarta's '*L'Utopia* come generatrice di "nuovi mondi"' (31.118–19.121–40) claims that critical relation of the birth of utopias to the discovery of geographical new worlds is misplaced, and that utopias are themselves generative of new worlds, whilst Nicole Morgan's 'Le petit singe cercopithèque mangeur du bibliothèque' (31.118–19.141–45) reads the monkey in More's text and the spatial voyage towards Utopia as metaphors for the foundation of knowledge.

Still in the same volume, Germain Marc'hadour discusses 'Edward Surtz's debt to G. C. Richards's Translation of *Utopia*' (31.118–19.155–65), and Roman A. Tokarczyk examines 'The Reception of Thomas More's *Utopia* in Poland' (31.118–19.169–201). John Freeman offers 'A Field Theory Approach to *Utopia*' in his 'More's "Island of Improvement"' (31.118–19.61–84), arguing that such an approach shows that the island is not cut off from history, but 'participates fully in the agrarian and social changes of early sixteenth-century England', being underwritten 'by feudal agrarian patterns [evoking] principles of landholding and social identity that were increasingly displaced in More's day'. George M. Logan offers a substantial review article of 'Ten Recent Studies and the Modern Critical Traditions' (31.118–19.203–58), as well as an article on '*Utopia* and Deliberative Rhetoric' (31.118–19.103–20) which analyses the text in terms of the tripartite scheme of rhetoric which, he argues, More adopted in writing it; in Book I, he concludes, Hythloday's strictures on European society reflect the position of the Stoic philosophers, whilst 'More' adopts a more traditional rhetorical stance.

More's relation to the Stoics is also the subject of A. D. Cousins's 'More and the Refiguring of Stoicism: The Prefatory Poems to *The Boke of Fortune*' (*Moreana* 30.115–16.19–32), which argues that through the refiguration of Boethian arguments, the poems prefigure More's creation of different personae. In the same volume, David Baker's 'First Among Equals: The Utopian *Princeps*' (30.115–16.33–45) discusses More's confusing adoption of the word 'princeps' in the *Utopia*, claiming that More uses the word intentionally, in order to critique European tyranny and also to point out the ubiquity of pride and ambition, from which the Utopians, as well as More himself, are not immune. This issue also includes Dale B. Billingsley's examination of More's sense of his changing readership, 'Readers and the Dangers of Reading in More's Work' (30.115–16.5–18), which argues that as a result of increased literacy in the period, More chooses in his later work to represent reading as 'a likely source of heresy', the remedy for which is face-to-face conversation.

3. Poetry

(a) General

Humanism is also the topic of Erik S. Ryding's *In Harmony Framed: Musical Humanism, Thomas Campion, and the Two Daniels*, which examines humanist treatments of musico-poetic relations in order to further an understanding of the Renaissance lyric. Ryding sees Campion's debate with Daniel over rhyme as one of the central issues of the Renaissance, 'a period whose art is constantly marked by the juxtaposition of medieval and classical elements'; it is 'the struggle between these two forces – the ancient versus the modern, the classical versus the nonclassical –' with which much of this book is concerned. The book is divided into three parts, on musical humanism and 'measured' verses in Germany, France, Italy and England; on Polemic and Song in Campion's *Observations* and Ayres, Daniel's *Defence*, and John Daniel's Songs; and on Fin'Amors and Eros in *Delia* and in Campion's Lyric Poetry.

Readers of this subject might also be interested in John Hollander's reprinted *The Untuning of the Sky* with a new, brief (largely bibliographical) preface by Hollander, referring to further critical studies and primary texts. The second edition of Gary Waller's *English Poetry of the Sixteenth Century* is rewritten in part to take account of the issues raised in the 1980s by the political criticisms, to a discussion of which the first part of Waller's introduction is largely devoted. The edition also includes a new chapter on issues of gender, in which Mary Sidney and Mary Wroth are lumped together with what Waller surely anachronistically terms 'gay voices' (quite why the women poets of the period have more in common with 'gay voices' than do the men eludes me; Waller also characterizes the latter as 'more disturbing' than the former, for reasons which are, again, not clear). Some readers might wish that Waller could be a little less dogmatic at times: '... the obscurities of our history of our culture's attempts to recognize and explore difference and multiplicity do not excuse us from trying to explore that spasmodic history'. Would a student who wanted to write, say, merely on metaphor, need to be 'excused' for doing so?

Wyatt was discussed by several critics this year. In 'Wyatt, the Heart's Forest and the Ancient Savings' (*ELR* 23.46–80), Michael Holahan examines Wyatt's version of Petrarch's *Rime 140*, arguing that the translation is a court poem, more public than private, whose audience is the King. His claim that the relationship of the two texts 'shifts from translation to imitation' distances him from Lisa M. Klein, who argues in 'The Petrarchanism of Sir Thomas Wyatt Reconsidered' (in *Dissimilitude*, ed. Allen and White) that Wyatt's love poetry expresses a fundamental affinity with Petrarch's which transcends the later poet's rejection of the earlier. Laura's contradictory attributes, she argues, are a function not of her character, but of 'the lover's inner division ... under the force of desire'; it is this Petrarchan sense of the lover's internal divisions and tensions which proves so useful to Wyatt. Perez Zagorin's lively 'Sir Thomas Wyatt and the court of Henry VIII: The Courtier's Ambivalence' (*JMRS* 23.113–41) also explores Wyatt's ambivalence, reading Wyatt in the context of Sir Francis Bryan's translation of Guevara's *Menosprecio*, and accepting at face value what Holahan more laboriously defends: Wyatt's translations, Zagorin argues, are more 'free adaptations or ... inspired imitations than literal versions of the original'. Like Holahan, Zagorin sees Wyatt's audience as courtiers; he also asks why Wyatt turned from secular to religious themes at the end of his career, concluding that in so doing 'he sought ... spiritual resources ... to arm himself against the temptations ... of the courtiers' life'. This is also the question addressed by Jan Lawson Hinely in '"Freedom Through Bondage": Wyatt's Appropriation of the Penitential Psalms of David' (also in Allen and White, eds): she claims that the psalms reflect the concerns of the secular poems, recast in spiritual terms as Wyatt uses the persona of David to resolve the emotional tensions established in the secular poems. Finally, Colin Burrow's 'Horace at Home and Abroad: Wyatt and Sixteenth-century Horatianism' in *Horace Made New: Horatian Influences on British Writing from the Renaissance to the Twentieth Century* (Charles Martindale and David Hopkins, eds) argues that unlike most sixteenth-century writers, who found Horace incomprehensible, Wyatt-the-diplomat utilized, in his satires, Horace's method of simultaneously hiding his identity and asserting his opinion.

(b) Sidney

One full-length study of Sidney appeared this year: Katherine J. Roberts's *Fair Ladies: Sir Philip Sidney's Female Characters*. Roberts argues that Sidney's oeuvre exhibits the author increasingly departing from existing models of gender to offer more complex representations of women. An opening chapter examines virtues and vices attributed to women in texts from the Middle Ages to Renaissance; this chapter, unfortunately, is more a synopsis of other critics' arguments than an engagement with the texts themselves, and makes claims that could do with more defence, the major one being that 'the female characters in the works of Sidney's literary predecessors are static, either good or evil'. Out with the old, in with the new: Sidney reverses all these stereotypes, Gynecia being a 'strongly individual character' but not evil, unlike representations of strong women before, Stella being 'neither the cruel mistress nor the plaster saint', responding to 'Astrophel's love with all the desire and fear an Elizabethan woman – not a star – might have felt as she contemplated adulterous love'. This is a book which would have benefited from some more revision, and some more reading, before being rushed into print.

In *The Reinvention of Love: Poetry, Poetics and Culture from Sidney to Marvell*, Anthony Low argues that Sidney is representative of older ways of thinking about love, but is also among the first to discover that such modes of loving were no longer satisfactory: the last great exemplar of Petrarchanism, Sidney also reveals the fissures of its forthcoming dissolution. Sidney's model for a lover's behaviour, Low argues, remained nostalgically feudal – courtly Petrarchan desire impelled the lover faithfully to serve his lady just as a feudal servant served his lord. Renée Pigeon's '"An Odious Marriage With a Stranger": Sidney's *Arcadias* and the French Match' (*ELN* 31.28–40) argues that both the versions, in the *Old* and *New Arcadias*, of the citizens' riot against Basilius allude to the proposed marriage between Elizabeth and the Duke of Anjou: in the *Old Arcadia*, the 'rebellion serves as a cautionary reminder of what a people stirred to unrest ... might do; ... the ambiguous tensions of the episode in the *New Arcadia* reflect an increasing awareness of, and ambivalence about, the risks of protest, ... [an] ambivalence ... epitomized in the figure of the maimed artist'. In

'Charactonymic Structures in Sidney's *Arcadias*' (*SEL* 33.1–19), Marvin Hunt offers a Saussurian linguistic analysis of Sidney's narratology, arguing that 'a character in Sidney's poetics acquires meaning by its placement within the plot', and that Sidney adopts a 'structuralist characterology by giving the appearance of substance to signifiers and at the same time denying that possibility' in *A Defence of Poetry*; in the *Arcadias*, such a characterology expresses plenitude.

(c) Spenser

Two editions aimed at college students appeared this year. Particularly welcome is Douglas Brooks-Davies's Everyman edition of *The Faerie Queene, Books I to III*, that should do much to restore, or even to introduce, Spenser's great work to college syllabuses. The introduction is clear, energetic, and up-to-date, exploring the poem's deeper ambiguities and 'double vision'. Included also are useful outlines of each book's subject, method, sources and structure, a chronology, concise but informative notes, a good glossary and selective reading list: excellent value for money. [REP] A third updated edition of the Norton Critical Anthology of *Edmund Spenser's Poetry* (ed. Hugh Maclean and Anne Lake Prescott) includes extracts from *The Shepheardes Calender* and *The Faerie Queene* (Books I and III in their entirety, and extracts from the others and the *Mutabilitie* cantos), 'Amoretti', 'Epithalamion' and 'Prothalamion', 'Muiopotmos', and 'Colin Clouts Come Home Again'. All selections include footnotes and have been updated to reflect recent critical interest in 'bodies masculine, feminine and politic' and recent critical commentary on the sonnet sequence amongst other topics. Editorial notes follow, and a good selection of criticism includes three pre-twentieth-century accounts and extracts by commentators from Virginia Woolf, through Northrop Frye and A. C. Hamilton, to Louis Montrose and David Lee Miller. This would be an excellent teaching edition of the texts. Willy Maley has compiled a remarkably detailed and illuminating *Spenser Chronology*, skilfully combining the relatively familiar England-based literary history with details of Spenser's work and life in Ireland, both as secretary of Lord Grey and as landowner and 'undertaker' at Kilcoman, set in the context of the turbulent Irish history of the time. [REP]

Spenser's secretarial career is also the subject of Richard Rambuss's informative and provocative *Spenser's Secret Career*, which addresses the relation between Spenser's careers as secretary and as poet. The former, Rambuss argues, provided a model that shaped both Spenser's poetry and his self-conception as a poet: secrecy, central to both careers, is deployed in the poems as a strategy for self-promotion. Many of Spenser's poetic choices are a function of his careerist ambitions, Rambuss claims, reading *The Shepheardes Calender* in terms of Spenser's desire to advance his career as secretary to the Bishop of Rochester, and discussing the relationship between secretary and master in terms of a system of male affective relations in which 'secretaryship entails becoming the simulacrum of the master himself'. The move from the 1590 *Faerie Queene* to the *Complaints* he sees as enacting a 'renegotiation of Spenser's relation to the court and his terms of literary management': whereas the 'impulse of [Spenser's] poetry up through the 1590 *Faerie Queen* was to keep secrets; the impulse in 1591 *Complaints* is to expose them'.

Patrick Cheney concentrates on a rather more traditional understanding of Spenser's career in his *Spenser's Famous Flight: A Renaissance Idea of a*

Literary Career, arguing that in images of flight, Spenser represents a 'Christian-ized Virgilian career that aims to demonstrate to English culture the utility of poetic fame to Christian glory'. Cheney examines three career models open to Spenser: the Ovidian, the Augustinian, and the Virgilian: Spenser, he argues, 'reinvents the Virgilian wheel: rather than a narrowly circumscribed Virgilian ideal of pastoral and epic, [Spenser] works from an Orphic ideal of pastoral, epic, love lyric and hymn'. In each stage Spenser identifies the Poet with a specific species of bird: the nightingale in the pastoral (*The Shepheardes Calender*); the dove in both epic (*The Faerie Queene*), and love lyric (the *Amoretti* and *Epithalamion*), the hawk in the hymn (*Fowre Hymnes*) and finally, in the turn back to courtly poetry in the *Prothalamion*, the swan. This four-career generic model forms for Spenser a myth of identity in which the 'male poet "sympathises" with feminine power for poetic authority' since the 'source of the male poet's art is the female's great creative nature'. This ideal is prophesied at the beginning of Spenser's career, and fulfilled at its end.

Thomas Francis Bulger's *The Historical Changes and Exchanges as Depicted by Spenser in 'The Faerie Queene'* reads the poem as a fiction about the historical process itself. The book has a threefold approach, aiming to contextualize the text's attitudes towards history within traditions of Renaissance history and historiography, to explore the relevance of these perspectives to the episodes in which they are voiced, and to 'define the most significant ramifications of Spenser's concepts of historical being and becoming'. The narrative of the poem endorses apparently incompatible views of history, which is represented as linear, cyclic, progressive, static, chaotic and exemplary. For Spenser, Bulger argues, 'historical fulfilment is obtained when the purposes of divine, human, and natural history coincide', and the 'ambiguous temporal framework of the poem, is ... intended to ... call attention to the unexpected ways in which the past and the present continually interact'.

Two articles address various Spenserian episodes from feminist perspectives. Mary Villeponteaux's '*Semper Eadem*: Belphoebe's Denial of Desire' (in Claude J. Summers and Ted-Larry Pebworth) reads Spenser's Belphoebe in the context of the merging of erotic and political discourses circulating around the figure of the queen, who, like Belphoebe, both demanded and forbade desire, thus existing outside the realm of male power: Spenser's 'portrait of Belphoebe suggests [that] "political Petrarchanism" poses a threat to masculine power'. Dorothy Stephens, in her '"Newes of devils": Feminine Sprights in Masculine Minds in *The Faerie Queene*' (*ELR* 23.363–81), argues that 'by conceiving the human imagination in gendered terms, Spenser ends up rearranging the architecture of the self', confus-ing the issue of 'good' versus 'bad' and privileging this confusion. Questions raised in Greville's and Sidney's lyrics about 'the relationship of artistic self-containment to feminine images of confusion become allegorized and generalized in *The Faerie Queene*', she argues, where 'feminine delusions sometimes become inextricable from poetic conception itself'. In '"Mother of laughter, and welspring of blisse": Spenser's Venus and the Poetics of Mirth' (*ELR* 23.113–33), Laurel L. Hendrix uses Bakhtinian theory to argue that Renaissance perspec-tives on laughter see it not only as a signifier of joy, but also, when inspired by folly, as an 'outward sign of inward scorn or disdain'. In a prelapsarian world Venus's laughter on the rape of Amoret might be conciliatory and recreative; in a postlapsarian world it is instructive and corrective, and it is this latter function (misunderstood by Scudamour) which underlies Venus's mirth.

Three source studies for episodes of *The Faerie Queene* were published this year. Arnold A. Sanders's 'Ruddymane and Canace, Lost and Found: Spenser's Reception of Gower's *Confessio Amantis 3* and Chaucer's *Squire's Tale*' (in Allen and White) argues that Gower's appropriation of Ovid's tale of Canace is a source for the *Squire's Tale* and for the image opening Guyon's quest. The move in the treatment of the tale from the *Confessio Amantis* to the *Squire's Tale* enacts a 'patriarchal revision of a powerful depiction of incest', completed by Spenser who eliminates 'the original tale's pagan indictment of ruthless control over sexuality and reproduction'. John Watkins, in '"Neither of idle shewes, nor of false charmes aghast": Transformations of Virgilian ekphrasis in Chaucer and Spenser' (*JMRS* 23.345–63), proposes that Spenser's appropriations of Virgil 'challenge the longstanding reception of Aeneas as a character who comes to a full understanding of the world that he inhabits. ... By suggesting that only those called to virtue can aspire to be virtuous', Watkins argues, 'Spenser brings the Virgilian allegorical tradition to an end'. A very different kind of source study is offered in Anthony Esolen's 'Spenser's "Alma Venus": Energy and Economics in the Bower of Bliss' (*ELR* 23.267–86), which proposes Biblical and Lucretian sources for the Bower episode, arguing that 'these sources suggest ... a net of nature worship, sexual license, and Epicureanism in *The Faerie Queene*, all of which might be linked ... to islands of social dysfunction within any realm whose success depends on the local service of its aristocracy'. He reads the Bower as an oral, ungenerative area: Book II of the poem is the book of the mouth and anus, consumption and expenditure, Book III of the genitals and heart, reproduction and love.

Norman K. Farmer, one suspects, probably wouldn't like Esolen's reading very much. In 'The World's New Body: Spenser's *Faerie Queene* Book II, St Paul's Epistles and reformation England' (in Brink and Gentrup), Farmer argues, against 'procrustean new-historicist theory', that St Paul's distinction between *sarks* (man's appetitive nature, flesh, sin, corruption) and *soma* (man's spiritual nature, the vehicle of resurrection) is what really lies behind the image of the body in the Bower of Bliss episode, and that Book II is Spenser's allegorical anatomy of the body politic which is the British nation, of Christ's Body which is the reformed church, and of the microcosmic individual body. Ake Bergvall's more theoretical discussion of 'The Theology of the Sign' (*SEL* 33.21–42) analyses the relation of the Legend of Holiness to Augustine's *The City of God* and *On Christian Doctrine*. Redcrosse, he argues, is not only named for a sign, but is one, a sign whose validity needs to be 'anchored in the transcendental logos': Spenser's allegory is 'simply an extension of the basic reading of signs'. Finally, Gordon Teskey's complex article, 'Mutability, Genealogy, and the Authority of Forms' (*Rep* 41.104–22), invokes Nietzsche to examine the *Mutabilitie* cantos' question as to 'whether the basis of judgements of value in human affairs ... is in a metaphysics promoted by the authority of visual forms' or in 'the experience of the body in the *agora* of collective, political life'. In the cantos, Teskey argues, Mutabilitie is a figure for political memory, and genealogy undermines the more coordinated allegorical world as Spenser undoes the 'illusion necessary to allegory by inverting the priority ... of metaphysics and politics'.

The Shepheardes Calender had one book devoted entirely to it in 1993: Robert Lane's *Shepheards Devises: Edmund Spenser's Shepheards Calender and the Institutions of Elizabethan Society*. Lane resists what he sees as the 'predominant tradition of literary criticism with its essentialist perspective, organized around transcendent categories of human nature and aesthetics that exclude social and political dimensions from their purview'. Attacking the claim that Renaissance poetry was a thoroughly aristocratic phenomenon, he argues that the *Calender* appeals to a wider audience, challenging courtly aesthetics, inaugurating an alternative poetry with very different social affiliations and political functions, '[incorporating] the voices of those we do not expect to find in poetry – the people' and '[revealing] its affinities with a pattern of resistance to authoritarian royal power'. Lane defends this claim through a consideration of the way in which 'Spencer's [sic] language intersects nonliterary usage' (such as the husbandry image in February, and the phrase 'motherly care' in May); and by a discussion of Spenser's invocation of the moral authority of religious pastoral yoked to the perspective of the lower classes. Nowhere does he address what would seem to be the main objection to his argument, which is the reconciliation of this view of Spenser's political sympathies with his more immediate and personal relationships with the power structures of Elizabethan society, and his representation (however vexed) of the epitome of that power in *The Faerie Queene*.

In ' "Ryse Up *Elisa*" – Woman Trapped in a Lay: Spenser's "Aprill" ' (*Ren&R* 27.63–73), Marianne Micros attempts to bring a mixture of French and American feminisms to bear on *The Shepheardes Calender*, arguing that embedded in the poem is a contest between masculine and feminine qualities: despite the fact that all the speakers in the poem are male, and that it is solely their voices through which women are represented, Elisa's voice, she claims, is allowed to undermine the male poet's authority. Roy Eriksen analyses metamorphoses in the 'mythological machinery' of the *Prothalamion* in his 'Spenser's Mannerist Manoevres: *Prothalamion (1596)*' (*SP* 90.143–75) to read the poem in terms of a bid for patronage: 'the wedding actually anticipated in the *Prothalamion* ... is Spenser's poetic courtship to regain Essex's favour' and the relationship between the Petrarchan lover and his lady a 'translation' of that between poet and patron. Finally, M. Thomas Hester's ' "If thou regard the same": Spenser's Emblematic Centerfold' (*ANQ* 6.4.183–9) offers a brief note on the poems placed between the *Amoretti* and *Epithalamion*, arguing that they are emblems for the *Amoretti* and the *Epithalamion*.

Books Reviewed

Aers, David, ed. *Culture and History 1350–1600: Essays on English Communities, Identities and Writing*. WSUP (1992). pp. 213. hb $29.95, pb $15.95. ISBN 0 8143 2415 0, 0 8143 2416 9.

Allen, David G., and Robert A. White, eds. *The Work of Dissimilitude: Essays from the Sixth Citadel Conference on Medieval and Renaissance Literature*. UDelP (1992). pp. 292. £32.95, $42.50. 0 87413 435 8.

Archer, John Michael. *Sovereignty and Intelligence: Spying and Court Culture in the English Renaissance*. StanfordUP. pp. 203. £24.95, $35. ISBN 0 8047 2079 7.

Barbour, Reid. *Deciphering Elizabethan Fiction*. UDelP. pp. 175. £26.50. ISBN 0 87413 450 1.

Bath, Michael, John Manning, and Alan R. Young, eds. *The Art of the Emblem: Essays in Honor of Karl Josef Höltgen*. AMS. pp. 272. £61.95. ISBN 0 4046 3710 8.

Baumann, Uwe, ed. *Henry VIII in History, Historiography and Literature*. Lang. pp. 327. £36.90. ISBN 3 631 44143 6.

Beer, Barrett L. ed. *The Life and Raigne of King Edward the Sixth*, by John Hayward. KSUP. pp. 195. £31.50, $35. ISBN 0 87338 475 X.

Beretta, Iva. *'The World's a Garden': Garden Poetry of the English Renaissance*. Uppsala. pp. 208. ISBN 91 554 3155 0.

Braider, Christopher. *Refiguring the Real: Picture and Modernity in Word and Image, 1400–1700*. PrincetonUP. pp. 314. £33, $42.50. ISBN 0 691 06957 3.

Brink, Jean R., ed. *Privileging Gender in Early Modern England*. Sixteenth Century Essays and Studies 23. pp. 250. $35. ISBN 0 940474 24 7.

Brink, Jean R., and William F. Gentrup, eds. *Renaissance Culture in Context: Theory and Practice*. Scolar. pp. 232. £45, $69.95. ISBN 0 85967 950 0.

Brooks-Davies, Douglas, ed. *The Faerie Queene, Books I to III*. Dent. pp. 575. £6.99, $9.95. ISBN 0 460 87391 1.

Bulger, Thomas Francis. *The Historical Changes and Exchanges as Depicted by Spenser in 'The Faerie Queene'*. Mellen. pp. 208. £39.95, $89.95. ISBN 0 7734 9342 5.

Carlson, David R. *English Humanist Books: Writers and Patrons, Manuscript and Print 1475–1525*. UTorP. pp. 275. £32.50, $50. ISBN 0 8020 2911 6.

Cheney, Patrick. *Spenser's Famous Flight: A Renaissance Idea of a Literary Career*. UTorP. pp. 360. £39, $60. ISBN 0 8020 2934 5.

Crane, Mary Thomas. *Framing Authority: Sayings, Self, and Society in Sixteenth-Century England*. PrincetonUP. pp. 281. £30, $37.50. ISBN 0 691 06947 6.

Dewald, Jonathan. *Aristocratic Experience and the Origins of Modern Culture: France, 1570–1715*. UCalP. pp. 231. £28, $35. ISBN 0 520 07837 3.

Diefendorf, Barbara B., and Carla Hesse, eds. *Culture and Identity in Early Modern Europe 1500–1800*. UMichP. pp. 280. $49.50. ISBN 0 472 10470 5.

Evans, Robert C., and Barbara Wiedemann, eds. *'My Name Was Martha': A Renaissance Woman's Autobiographical Poem*. Locust Hill. pp. 117. $22.50. ISBN 0 933951 53 1.

Fausett, David. *Writing the New World: Imaginary Voyages and Utopias of the Great Southern Land*. SyracuseUP. pp. 237. hb $42.50, pb $17.95. ISBN 0 8156 2585 5, 0 8156 2586 3.

Fehrenbach, R. J., and E. S. Leedham-Green, eds. *Private Libraries in Renaissance England: A Collection and Catalogue of Tudor and Early Stuart Book-Lists*, vol. II, PLRE 5–66. MRTS. pp. 283. $25. 0 86698 099 7.

Frye, Susan. *Elizabeth I: The Competition for Representation*. OUP. pp. 228. £25, $35. ISBN 0 19 508023 8.

Gaisser, Julia Haig. *Catullus and His Renaissance Readers*. OUP. pp. 446. £45, $75. ISBN 0 19 814882 8.

Greenblatt, Stephen, ed. *New World Encounters*. UCalP. pp. 344. £12, $15. ISBN 0 520 08021 1.

Heninger, Jr, S. K. *The Subtext of Form in the English Renaissance: Proportion Poetical*. PSUP (1994). pp. 214. $35. ISBN 0 271 01070 3.

Hollander, John. *The Untuning of the Sky: Ideas of Music in English Poetry 1500–1700*. 2nd edition. Archon. pp. 467. $47.50. ISBN 0 208 02351 8.

Jardine, Lisa. *Erasmus, Man of Letters: The Construction of Charisma in Print*. PrincetonUP. pp. 284. $14.95. ISBN 0 691 00157 X.

Lane, Robert. *Shepheards Devises: Edmund Spenser's Shepheards Calender and the Institutions of Elizabethan Society*. UGeoP. pp. 240. $40. ISBN 0 8203 1514 1.

Low, Anthony. *The Reinvention of Love: Poetry, Poetics and Culture from Sidney to Marvell.* CUP. pp. 258. £35, $44.95. ISBN 0 521 45030 6.

Mack, Peter, ed. *Renaissance Rhetoric.* Macmillan. pp. 188. £42.50. ISBN 0 333 52354 7.

Maclean, Hugh, and Anne Lake Prescott, eds. *Edmund Spenser's Poetry.* Norton Critical Edition. Norton. 3rd edition. pp. 842. £9.95, $13.95. ISBN 0 393 96299 7.

Maclean, Ian. *Interpretation and Meaning in the Renaissance: The Case of Law.* CUP. pp. 236. £30, $54.95. ISBN 0 521 41546 2.

Maley, Willy. *A Spenser Chronology.* Macmillan, B&N. pp. 120. £47.50. ISBN 0 333 53744 0.

Marsh, Christopher W. *The Family of Love in English Society, 1550–1630.* CUP. pp. 305. £35, $59.95. ISBN 0 521 44128 5.

Martindale, Charles, and David Hopkins, eds. *Horace Made New: Horatian Influences on British Writing from the Renaissance to the Twentieth Century.* CUP. pp. 330. £40, $64.95. ISBN 0 521 38019 7.

O'Malley, John W. *Religious Culture in the Sixteenth Century: Preaching, Rhetoric, Spirituality and Reform.* Variorum. £42.50, $79.95. ISBN 0 86078 369 3.

Rambuss, Richard. *Spenser's Secret Career.* Cambridge Studies in Renaissance Literature and Culture 3. CUP. pp. 164. £32.50, $44.95. ISBN 0 521 41663 9.

Richardson, David A., ed. *Sixteenth-Century British Nondramatic Writers, First Series.* Dictionary of Literary Biography 132. Gale. pp. 466. n.p. ISBN 0 8103 5391 1.

Ringler, William A. Jr. *Index of English Verse in Manuscript 1501–1558*, prepared and completed by Michael Rudick and Susan J. Ringler. Mansell (1992). pp. 315. £110, $190. ISBN 0 7201 2099 3.

Roberts, Katherine J. *Fair Ladies: Sir Philip Sidney's Female Characters.* Renaissance and Baroque Studies and Texts 9. Lang. pp. 130. ISBN 0 8204 2145 6.

Ryding, Erik S. *In Harmony Framed: Musical Humanism, Thomas Campion, and the Two Daniels.* SCJP. pp. 223. $45. ISBN 0 940474 22 0.

Shell, Marc. *Children of the Earth: Literature, Politics and Nationhood.* OUP. pp. 353. £27.50, $35. ISBN 0 19 506864 5.

Shell, Marc. *Elizabeth's Glass.* UNebP. pp. 365. £30.95, $40. ISBN 0 8032 4216 6.

Story Donno, Elizabeth, ed. *Three Renaissance Pastorals: Tasso, Guarini, Daniel.* MRTS. pp. 260. $20. ISBN 0 86698 118 7.

Summers, Claude J., and Ted-Larry Pebworth, eds. *Renaissance Discourses of Desire.* UMissP. pp. 284. £39.95, $44.95. ISBN 0 8262 0885 1.

Thurley, Simon. *The Royal Palaces of Tudor England: Architecture and Court Life 1460–1547.* YaleUP. pp. 283. £29.95, $50. ISBN 0 300 05420 3.

Treip, Mindele Anne. *Allegorical Poetics and the Epic: The Renaissance Tradition to Paradise Lost.* UKL. pp. 368. $43. ISBN 0 8131 1831 X.

Turner, James Grantham, ed. *Sexuality and Gender in Early Modern Europe: Institutions, Texts, Images.* CUP. pp. 345. £12.95, $17.95. ISBN 0 521 44605 8.

Wall, Wendy. *The Imprint of Gender: Authorship and Publication in the English Renaissance.* CornUP. pp. 373. $45.95. ISBN 0 8014 2765 7.

Waller, Gary. *English Poetry of the Sixteenth Century*. 2nd edition. Longman Literature in English. Longman. pp. 317. £14.99. ISBN 0 582 09096 2.

Wayne, Valerie. *The Flower of Friendship: A Renaissance Dialogue Contesting Marriage*. CornUP. pp. 198. £10.95. ISBN 0 8014 9705 1.

Wilson, Dudley. *Signs and Portents: Monstrous Births from the Middle Ages to the Enlightenment*. Routledge. pp. 215. £50. ISBN 0 415 03236 9.

VI

Shakespeare

BENJAMIN GRIFFIN, DERMOT CAVANAGH, PAULINE KIERNAN and DEBORAH CARTMELL

This chapter is divided into the following sections: 1. Editions and Textual Matters; 2. Shakespeare in the Theatre; 3. Criticism. Section 1 is by Benjamin Griffin; section 2 is by Dermot Cavanagh; section 3(d) is by Deborah Cartmell; and section 3(a), (b), (c) and (e) is by Pauline Kiernan.

1. Editions and Textual Matters

I begin, not with the customary rundown of Oxford and Cambridge editions, but with what must be regarded as the year's most-needed contribution. Despite recent developments in the textual criticism of *King Lear*, there has not been a modernized, parallel-text edition since the nineteenth century. René Weis's new Longman Annotated Texts *King Lear* is not only compact and beautifully designed, it is a masterly production and will be essential for any student of the play. It is especially useful for introducing 'literary' students to the texts without encumbering them with bibliographical arcana, but even the most advanced student or scholar will constantly find it useful. Weis presents modernized texts of Q and F on facing pages, with a minimum of emendation. He thus preserves, as far as is possible, the relation between the existing *texts*, rather than reconstruct hypothetical performance versions, as the 1986 Oxford edition did. Weis's introduction is a model of clarity and judgement. On the genesis of textual variation, he is commendably sceptical; but if an 'authorial' *Lear* were to be sought, his bias, refreshingly, inclines towards Q. The commentary calls attention to the major variants for each scene. This edition contains no record of emendations to the copy-texts, so it cannot be used to reconstruct the exact readings of Q and F in their raw states; this is a justifiable decision, since Michael Warren's parallel-text photofacsimile edition (*YWES* 70.254) serves this need better than an edited text can. Checks show that Weis's texts are highly accurate, and his few emendations are sound. The space that might have gone to a collation has gone instead to excellent glosses and longer notes on the textual variations, the play's language and its historical context. The texts are not broken up into line-for-line parallel; each runs smoothly down its page, so that a single version can be read through comfortably. For a full collation, account of the sources, etc., Muir's NA

edition or some other must be consulted; but in our present state of knowledge –
which may last a long time – Weis's text is the one to have.

The OS single-play volumes, in their paperback format, now appear in the
World's Classics series at a lower price (and with handsome new covers in place
of the funereal old ones). Susan Snyder's *All's Well That Ends Well* has an
elegant and clarifying critical introduction. For Snyder, this is still emphatically
a problem play, but the presence of problems is itself not as problematic as it
seems once to have been. The play is now *about* problems – of class, sex, merit,
endings, marriages, story-books and historical realities. Snyder handles it all with
great intellectual energy. Her approach emphasizes the play's shocks and
discontinuities, the way it works by 'getting inside awkward moments rather than
simply gliding over them', so that a mood of 'uneasy questioning' is generated.
The text is treated conservatively, even to the point of retaining F's 'make rope's
in such a scarre' at IV.ii.38, which is a fine idea, since, as Snyder says, 'none of
the proposed emendations is convincing'. Of the many emendations invented by
the Oxford *Complete Works,* Snyder has admitted only the most probable, particularly those clarifying the stage action. Here, as in Wells-Taylor, the heroine
is invariably 'Helen' in place of F's vacillation between that form and 'Helena';
for this regularization there seems to be no reason apart from a love of tidiness.
There are some reproductions of emblems illustrating the play's proverbial
language, appendices detailing editorial matters, and reprints of the major
sources (including Erasmus's *Colloquia*).

Alan Brissenden's *As You Like It* is also excellent. The commentary is much
fuller than is usual in this series, and it is always appealingly characterful – try
the note at V.iv.45, on the financial risks courtiers inflicted upon tailors, or I.i.5,
on how Orlando says 'school' for university, 'like modern American university
students'. The annotation, in fact, is generally superb; it is particularly distinguished by the huge range of Renaissance works cited as parallels or elucidations.
The flipside of polymathic brilliance is hobby-horsical perverseness, and in this
category I would put Brissenden's frequent detections of improbable or impossible bawdry (his interpretation of Jaques's 'I met a fool i'th' forest' speech has to
be seen to be believed). He is more cautious, and rightly so, about his suggestion
that publication of the play was 'stayed' in 1600 because 'Jaques' puns on 'jakes'
which refers to *The Metamorphoses of Ajax* which recalls Harington's association
with Essex. The introduction concentrates on the play's concern with
'doubleness', which includes such things as puns, cross-dressing and 'paired'
characters such as Touchstone and Jaques, Orlando and Oliver, and Dukes Senior
and Frederick; under these double-headings Brissenden is especially helpful on
fools, melancholy, and satire. Especially outstanding is the section on the play in
performance. We expect a full account of this perennial stage favourite, and
Brissenden weighs in with 30 pages, of which eight are devoted to productions in
the USA, Europe, Canada and Australia, plus a section on outdoor performances!
Other editors should follow Brissenden and raise their eyes above the horizons of
London and Stratford. There are 21 captivating illustrations. This edition shows
the results of much original research, and is recommended unreservedly, although
there are more misprints than we expect from this kind of series; perhaps these
can be corrected in future reprints.

Jay L. Halio's *The Merchant of Venice*, compared with Snyder's *All's Well*,
doesn't really get inside its play's contradictions and problems. Halio's introductory essay tends to shut down options instead of exploring them. He has little to

say to the multitude of readers who have found Shylock something more than inconvenient; he points to Shylock's maltreatment in the past as the thing which has made him so 'intransigent', and in this way he tries to save the character as a 'comic villain'. Little sense is imparted of the long critical tradition which finds Shylock *more* sympathetic than his adversaries. Halio addresses the play's complexity, but he cannot shake the desire to push it into shape, and the result is vagueness. There is a full stage history, which concentrates on the play's capacity to stir up controversy. All round, this lags some way behind the NCaS and the ancient NA edition.

Sheldon P. Zitner's *Much Ado About Nothing* is solid and careful. Zitner begins his introduction with a discussion of how our overfamiliarity with the 'three great romantic comedies' can lead to boredom, and he suggests *Much Ado* as a corrective to this mood; but his own appreciation of the play is decidedly cool. Sometimes he is uncomfortably oblique, as when he suggests reasons for the organization of the cast into 'contrasting dyads and triads': it facilitates 'rapidity in orientating audience attention and easing the writer's task of generating dialogue'. At such moments it is hard to remember it is Benedick and Beatrice we are talking about. For Zitner the play's distinction lies in its language, a 'Utopia of discourse', and in his annotations he tries to stay out of its way. Zitner has written elsewhere on the advisability of keeping footnotes short and few (*YWES* 65.192); here he puts his preaching into practice. To this reader the notes seem positively sparse; they are almost entirely brief glosses. However, the text is sound, based on Q, which is conventionally interpreted as deriving from Shakespeare's foul-papers; there are several new emendations, all of which are convincing, and it is here the edition's greatest contribution lies.

Among the virtues of the Oxford Shakespeare is that of eliciting interesting reviews, and two long review-essays may be noted here. Brian Vickers has strong reservations about practically every aspect of two 1990 OS editions (*RS* 7.229–41). Laurie E. Maguire makes some sharp points about the 'parent' Wells-Taylor edition in her review essay (*MRDE* 6.204–16).

Only one NCaS edition came forth this year, Michael Hattaway's *The Third Part of King Henry VI*. Hattaway's introduction is consistently rewarding. He sees the play as a corrosive essay in politics in which chivalry is shown up as the cloak of cruelty and ferocity. He emphasizes the play's craftsmanship, its 'extraordinarily deft shaping of shapeless material'. There is a good stage history and a section on 'Date and occasion', in which Hattaway ably sifts the familiar, ambiguous clues to the genesis of the whole trilogy (he favours Shakespearean authorship for all three plays, and composition in order of the historical events, but does not argue these points in any detail). The text is accurate and soundly constituted on the whole, but gives some minor grounds for regret. By comparison with the Oxford edition, which is peppered with variants from the 1595 Octavo, Hattaway adheres closely to F; but he is prepared to admit chunks from O where he thinks they may be 'lacking' in F. Hattaway, in fact, has recourse to O in more than one place where even the Oxford editors restrain themselves. Spelling is sensitively modernized, and metrical irregularity tolerated. Punctuation, however, is something of a problem: sometimes F's pointing is retained where it is fussy, sometimes it is emended where it was clear. The number of traditional emendations accepted into the text, while pleasingly low, could have been still lower. Nevertheless, this is a satisfying capstone to Hattaway's editions of Parts 1 and 2, and, taken together, the NCaS *Henry VI* represents an enormous advance on all other editions.

Harvester's Shakespearean Originals series, edited by Graham Holderness and Bryan Loughrey, offers unemended texts of the 'bad quartos'. As such, it will not please conventional textual scholars; but neither will it satisfy every school of quarto-enthusiasts (those, for example, who would see the quartos as early versions by Shakespeare – the whole notion of 'authorship' is firmly problematized here). A general introduction discusses the history of Shakespeare's text, but the lumbering jargon in which this is written will obscure the issues for anyone not already in the know. With regard to plays which differ between Quarto and Folio, a conceptual distinction is drawn between the perception of them as 'variants of a single work' on the one hand, and 'discrete textualizations independently framed within a complex and diversified project of cultural production' on the other; but if there is a difference, we do not learn what it is. Interestingly, the series is gaining in confidence as it goes forward. The two volumes published in 1992 (*Hamlet* and *A Shrew*) were circumspect, the latter, for instance, being cautiously offered 'in its own right as a brilliantly inventive popular Elizabethan play'. But the jacket of *Henry the Fifth* (published 1993) claims to present 'the original text of *Henry V*' – a claim not endorsed by the general introduction, which proffers the early versions only as 'facets of Shakespearean drama'. The effect of retaining all the printer's errors intact and unemended is irritating enough in the text, but it becomes positively bizarre in the commentary, which is forced into glosses such as: '*guardyour*: guard your.' Surely this is *why* we correct errors in reading editions: who wants to read notes like that? Whatever the nature of the copy-texts, the volumes themselves are not very accurate reprints, so that the (admitted) errors in the quartos are embellished with new errors. The editors include in each volume 'a sample of the original text in photographic facsimile', intended to make their own editorial practice 'as open as possible'; in *Henry V*, this 'sample' actually reproduces some pages from an 1875 edition. Another apparent oversight: at several points in the *Hamlet* volume, the commentary refers to the text as presented in traditional editions, so it makes no sense with reference to the Q1 text actually printed herein – for example, it refers to 'Polonius' instead of 'Corambis'. These editions have the unintended effect of reminding us that error and corruption do, after all, exist; a reflection with serious consequences for the school of textualists who promote the sanctity of the historical object at the expense of the text as instrument of communication.

These editions were at the (nominal) centre of a debate carried on in the *TLS*, starting with Brian Vickers's hostile review of the *Hamlet* volume (24 December 1993), and carrying on in the Letters columns for 21 January 1994, 4 February, and 11 February. The correspondence is wide-ranging; it includes the views of some actors (who find the memorial-reconstruction theory implausible) as well as scholars of various persuasions. In general, there is more discussion of the bad quartos themselves than of the Harvester editions.

Gary Taylor and John Jowett's *Shakespeare Reshaped: 1606–1623* collects three essays on post-authorial alterations to Shakespeare's text; this is a long-awaited volume in the OSS series, which has as its function the exposition and documentation of the OS's textual decisions. The first essay, Taylor's 'The Structure of Performance', is convincing in support of the traditional view that at some time around 1607 the adult companies began to perform plays with musical 'intervals' between the acts, which had not been their custom before that time. But plays before 1591 sometimes have act divisions, and this situation still awaits exploration. Taylor has some insightful comments on how Jacobean stagings of

Shakespeare's plays might have been affected by the presence of musical *entr'actes*. In "Swounds Revisited' Taylor takes us through the issue of expurgation in the Folio texts – which entails a tour of the conjectured nature of the printer's copy, especially for *King John* and *2 Henry IV*. Taylor's thesis is that the expurgation of profanity is generally attributable to the theatre, not the printing-house; scribes making private transcripts would not have been expurgating, but following their copy. (This runs counter to T. H. Howard-Hill's investigation of Ralph Crane's transcripts of Middleton, *ShS* 44.113–29.) He concludes with sweeping recommendations for the restoration of oaths in suitable places ('missed opportunities for swearing'). Here, as elsewhere, Taylor proceeds on the assumption that theatre practice and Shakespeare's personal practice (in spelling, swearing and stagecraft) were perfectly uniform at any given period (once more against Howard-Hill, who says 'the single editorial virtue Crane lacked was consistency'). His project of bringing Shakespeare into conformity with a conjectural statistical norm – itself derived from the much-mediated textual evidence – must be suspect. Many of the arguments in this book are based on Shakespeare's linguistic and orthographical 'preferences' (between 'O' and 'Oh', for example); and yet on the evidence of Hand D we know Shakespeare was capable of spelling 'Moore' three ways in the space of one line. The longest essay, 'With New Additions' (by Taylor and Jowett) argues that two passages in *Measure for Measure* 'should be stigmatized as unShakespearian interpolations' written by Middleton. There can be no doubt that *Measure* is an oddly dishevelled text, especially in the places under discussion; once again the question is, can the-text-as-Shakespeare-wrote-it be excavated from F with any reliability at all? Taylor and Jowett are sure that any reconstruction is preferable to the adaptation, but I admit to being unconvinced. A 'Post-script' details something readers may be wondering about: can this be the *Oxford* editors talking about 'ur-texts' and 'theatrical interpolations'? Taylor's answer is that the cut-off point is the first-night performance; everything judged to have gone in before that point has implicit authorial approval, and everything after, if not itself authorial, is an interpolation. On this point, it must be confessed that the book seems incomplete without an account of the Middleton additions to *Macbeth*, which were such a visible aspect of the Oxford edition; for this we must presumably wait for Taylor's edition of Middleton.

Alternative versions, naturally, are the focus of most of the periodical articles on Shakespeare's text this year. The two versions of *The Merry Wives of Windsor* are the quarry for Arthur F. Kinney's 'Textual Signs in *The Merry Wives of Windsor*' (*YES* 23.206–34). Kinney observes that F's sense of specific locality and its frank mercantilism are both muted in the text of Q, and argues that it was the dearth, poverty and political uncertainty of the 1590s that compelled both these obfuscations: 'The play has no distinctly persistent setting in the Quarto text (despite four references in passing to Windsor) since all places suffered, and no authentic suffering would do in a play which pretended to be a farce'; while in the F version, 'Shakespeare relies on his audience's knowledge of the authentic Windsor, their authentic world – a real place characterized by starvation, theft, and death'. If that doesn't sound much like *The Merry Wives of Windsor*, then I don't know what you can do about it. It seems a bit much to say that Q is distinguished by its 'unlocated geography'; presumably, a really urgent need to dis-locate the play would have done something about the title page and the remaining references to Windsor, and I cannot believe any audience, or any authority, would have thought that the Q version was set in Utopia. At the opposite end of the spectrum, an attitude towards textual divergence similar to René Weis's *Lear* edition (reviewed above) is evident in the chapter on 'Plays and texts' in R. A. Foakes's *Hamlet versus Lear: Cultural Politics and Shakespeare's Art* (a book, not an article, reviewed here for thematic coherence). This is a clear-headed analysis of contemporary editorial quarrels over the editing, or un-editing, of these plays. Foakes accepts that authorial revision has been established in both plays, but thinks the significance of the revisions needs further investigation. In particular, he doubts the dogma that what we possess is multiple autonomous versions of each play, preferring to see 'evidence of a process of change' in the text of a single play, and suggesting that the 'destabilizing' aspect of the revisions has been exaggerated.

Eric Sams unconvincingly maintains that there never was a version of *1 Henry IV* in which Falstaff was called Oldcastle ('Oldcastle and the Oxford Shakespeare', *N&Q* 40.180–5); contemporary references to a scandalous Oldcastle play must therefore refer to *The Famous Victories*, which is itself by Shakespeare. 'Cavalier' is a gentle word for Sams's way with evidence, as habitual readers of this review will already know. Sams is ill-served by the running order of *N&Q* in this issue, for in the very next item, 'A Catholic Oldcastle', R. W. F. Martin produces a 1634 devotional work which quotes the bouncing knight's sentiments on 'honour' and assigns them to '*Syr Iohn Oldcastle*' (*N&Q* 40.185–6). This partisan endorsement should have its uses in debate on the reception of 'Falstaff' as well as the textual argument surrounding the name. Y. S. Bains, in 'The Incidence of Corrupt Passages in the First Quarto of Shakespeare's *Hamlet*' (*N&Q* 40.186–92), argues that Q1 is a 'legitimate text' which preceded Q2 in order of composition, and purports to demonstrate that everything which has been thought a corruption could also be an authorial variant. Bains does not undertake to show that the variants are *more likely* to be authorial – nor does any such sense emerge from the discussion.

Hamlet Q1 appears in the opposite light in E. A. J. Honigmann's 'The First Quarto of *Hamlet* and the Date of *Othello*' (*RES* 44.211–19). Honigmann reconsiders the proposition that the reporter (here unabashedly called the 'pirate') behind *Hamlet* Q1 borrowed from *Othello* in making his reconstruction; *Othello* would thus have to have existed before 1603. In support of a date of 1601–2, Honigmann examines the original parallels amassed by Alfred Hart, and presents some new parallels of his own detection. Not all the observations are of equal weight, but the case for an Elizabethan and not a Jacobean *Othello* emerges looking stronger than ever. Also on chronology and making use of inter-play 'echoes', David Farley-Hills's 'The Position of *Antony and Cleopatra* in the Canon' (*N&Q* 40.193–7) proposes an unconventional order of composition for Shakespeare's later tragedies (*Timon, Lear, Antony, Macbeth, Coriolanus*), building on his observation that Shakespeare sometimes 'echoes plays he has just finished in the new play he is writing'. It is an interesting direction to pursue, although it assumes the writing of the plays was a sequence of discrete acts of composition, whereas if Shakespeare's completion of one play overlapped with his reading-up for the next, then the *next* play's source (e.g. Plutarch) could 'contaminate' an almost-finished play (e.g. *Macbeth*) rather than the other way around.

On the frontier between textual and cultural studies, Peter Stallybrass in 'Editing as Cultural Formation: The Sexing of Shakespeare's Sonnets' (*MLQ*

54.91–103), expands on Margreta de Grazia's contention (reviewed *YWES* 72.156) that it was Malone who 'constructed' our 'modern' Shakespeare. Stallybrass examines the ways in which eighteenth- and nineteenth-century editors responded to the Sonnets' homosexuality, and, by extension, the sexuality of Shakespeare. Stallybrass unearths a lot of interesting testimony from perturbed poets and critics, but it is not literally true that 'until Edmond Malone's 1780 edition, the history of the publication of the *Sonnets* was that of the reproduction of John Benson's edition of 1640': the 1609 Quarto text was reprinted by Lintott in 1711 and by Steevens in 1766 (Rollins, edn 1944, II, 36–9). De Grazia's *Shakespeare Verbatim* itself gets a searing review from T. H. Howard-Hill, who is troubled by the way de Grazia makes Malone stand at the head of the modern tradition while absolving him of eighteenth-century antecedents ('Shakespeare Edited, Restored, Domesticated, Verbatim and Modernized', *Rev* 15.115–25). Howard-Hill questions de Grazia's claim to avoid such misleading concepts as chronology and genealogy, mainly by observing that she doesn't in fact avoid them. He classes her with other members of a school 'that seems not to need texts or editions, or even works, but merely the writings of other critics'. Howard-Hill might almost have been referring to an article written by de Grazia and Stallybrass together, 'The Materiality of the Shakespearean Text' (*SQ* 44.255–83). This, the footnotes indicate, was originally intended as the introduction to a collection of essays by Randall McLeod, and it is definitely introductory in character. The essay 'is an attempt to interrogate what we take to be the four categories basic to the dominant post-Enlightenment treatment of Shakespeare'; these are the 'work', the 'word', the 'character', and the 'autonomous author'. Each of these categories, the authors contend, masquerades as whole and stable but is radically indeterminate; 'there *is* no monadic "original" and hence no authenticity either'. Their suggestion is that we 'take our minds off the solitary genius immanent in the text' and concentrate on 'the complex social practices that shaped [...] the Shakespearean text'. While abolishing the category of the 'autonomous author', I would enter a plea that studies of this kind would occasionally treat some other playwright. It is hard to see why each battle has to be fought over Shakespeare alone, especially since these claims are being made for culture at large, not for an individual *oeuvre*; presumably, there is no monadic original to Jonson's texts either, or Chapman's, or Ulpian Fulwell's. On the subject of 'post-Enlightenment' editions, Antonia Forster's article on an eighteenth-century edition that never came to fruition reminds us of an important fact: not everyone at this time was driven by a fetishistic craving for 'authentic Shakespeare'. The object of her study, 'like many editors', wanted 'first a money-maker and second a place to show off' ('Eighteenth-Century Shakespeare: Samuel Badcock, A Would-Be Editor', *SQ* 44.44–53). This amusing article gives us a view of that world, at least as journalistic as it was scholarly, in which the early editing tradition was mostly carried on.

Studies of authorship in the canonical and apocryphal plays are many this year, all of them using linguistic evidence. MacD. P. Jackson contributes two more articles in a continuing series on evidence for George Wilkins's part-authorship of *Pericles*. Jackson admits that his investigation of 'Rhyming in *Pericles*' (*SB* 46.239–49) suggests divided authorship generally, rather than Wilkins specifically. Much the same is true of the other article, 'The Authorship of *Pericles*: The Evidence of Split Infinitives' (*N&Q* 40.197–200). Robert A. J. Matthews and Thomas V. N. Merriam use new computerized techniques of linguistic analysis in 'Neural Computation in Stylometry, I: An Application to the Works of Shakespeare and Fletcher' (*L&LC* 8.203–9). This article contains an introduction to neural computation, which is certainly too technical for me to evaluate; but it apparently teaches computers to recognize patterns by repeated exposure to data. The result is meant to help them discriminate between individuals' styles even in 'noisy' samples, like the texts of collaborative plays. The tests are of the function-word type employed by Gary Taylor in the Oxford *Textual Companion* (1987). *Henry VIII* turns out 'strongly Shakespearian', with some hesitation over the fifth act; while *The Two Noble Kinsmen* suggests collaboration. It is harder to know what to make of the findings on *The London Prodigal* and Theobald's *The Double Falsehood*. On this evidence, both exhibit 'Fletcherian' characteristics; but since the only two authors sampled for the test were Shakespeare and Fletcher, this is not so much an argument for Fletcher's authorship of these plays as an argument that they are *more* like Fletcher than Shakespeare. T. V. N. Merriam has published an article which proposes, using the function-word test, to locate 'Marlowe's Hand in *Edward III*' (*L&LC* 8.59–72). The section of the play which is said to show a Marlovian quality is not the 'Countess scenes' but III.i and III.ii. I suppose that takes us pretty far from 'textual studies of Shakespeare', but Shakespeareans will want to keep up with the debate over *Edward III* generally; the play is increasingly accepted as partly or wholly Shakespeare's, and is now to be edited for the NCaS by Giorgio Melchiori.

I have not been able to see *HSt* 15, which contains an article on *Hamlet* Q1 by the late M. C. Bradbrook. Kristian Smidt's final instalment of investigations into the Shakespearean Muddle, *Unconformities in Shakespeare's Later Comedies* (Macmillan), will be reviewed in *YWES* 75.

2. Shakespeare in the Theatre

This year saw the publication of some innovative studies in an often conservative area of criticism. In *Foreign Shakespeare*, Dennis Kennedy has edited an exciting collection of essays which extend the frame of reference in which future studies of performance must be located. Kennedy's aim is to explore 'Shakespeare's vast importance in the theatre in languages other than our own', and so uncover the diversity of cultural understandings of the plays. Later in the volume, John Russell Brown attacks the complacency that assumes a shared language bequeaths the Anglo-American tradition a uniquely privileged access to textual meaning. He reminds us that any production is always an interpretation of remote cultural meanings, and that contemporary translations of Shakespeare can clarify obscurities, return immediacy to the archaic and recover undiscerned strains of implication – especially political and polemical emphases. The latter point is exemplified in Lawrence Gunter's account of Shakespeare production in East Germany which charts the use of plays as a critical commentary on unacknowledged social conflicts and contradictions. The volume offers a consistently stimulating introduction to the variety of (mainly) European performance traditions, with analyses of the process of translation itself, studies of individual directors (Peter Zadek, Girgio Strehler, Yuri Lyubimov, Daniel Mesguich), the fortunes of plays in specific national traditions of production (*The Merchant of Venice* in Israel, *Hamlet* and *Antony and Cleopatra* in the Soviet Union), and contains some fascinating attempts at intercultural comparison. This study suggests new methods of approach to neglected areas and builds a comprehensive picture of key cultural shifts in theatre practice from the postwar to the postmodern.

One effect of Kennedy's collection is to make other work appear circumscribed in its assumptions and parochial in its concerns. One now encounters, with a certain weariness, study after study using the cultural politics of the RSC as the sole context for production-based criticism. Despite adopting 'radical' approaches to performance traditions, much of the year's work is still absorbed by what Kennedy terms 'the myth of cultural ownership'. Michael Scott's 'Shakespearean Choice and Current Practice' (*CS* 5.313–22) is a critique of the timidity of current Shakespearean practice and its Anglo-American bias towards the psychology of key protagonists, yet this conclusion is arrived at only through the example of the RSC, and his suggestion that leading figures need to be 'decentred' is hazily-argued. Penny Gay – an Australian academic – has published a study of Shakespeare's 'unruly women' in *As She Likes It*, an attempt to challenge 'essentialist' understandings of romantic comedy by analysing the changing definitions of femininity expressed in the performance-history of transgressive female figures. However, this involves only consideration of the postwar RSC, a factor indicative of a wider lack of independent thinking. Gay makes some sensible points about the theatrical and social significance of women characters who refuse prevailing gender codes in five comedies, but her case is heavily dependent on quotation from contemporary reviews and has too much inert summary of productions.

Robert Shaughnessy, in *Representing Shakespeare: England, History, and the RSC*, has some sharp words for performance-criticism which relies on a nostalgic re-creation of atmosphere and visual effect and on the RSC's fostering of academic approaches which preserve its institutional prestige. Shaughnessy analyses the Company's use of the English history plays as cultural dialogues with their historical moment and as legitimations (and occasionally contestations) of a dominant understanding of Shakespeare's sense of history: heroic-individualist, male-dominated, cyclical. There are provocative reflections on the ideological effects of different theatre-spaces and on the RSC's recurrent investment in historical cycles – including the grand ventures of the Hall-Barton *The War of the Roses* (1963–4) and Adrian Noble's *The Plantagenets* (1988) – as explorations of both the RSC's and the nation's prevailing aspirations and anxieties. Shaughnessy stresses a common patriarchal emphasis on generational struggles between fathers and sons, on the battlefield as the locus of historical change, and on a performance tradition which has often simplified, displaced and resolved contemporary social conflicts. However, his study does replicate some of the critical tendencies it disparages, not only in its fixation with the RSC, but in a disregard for the portrayal of women and subordinate groups and in some crudely developed relationships between social context and performance. The final section is the strongest, with a tendency towards broad speculation reined in, and there are stimulating accounts here of John Barton's bizarre *King John* (1974) and Deborah Warner's treatment of the same play as a satire on the infantilism of masculine modes of Shakespearean history play production.

Still, any sympathy one has for the exhaustively analysed Company is soon qualified when reading the banalities pronounced by its current director, Adrian Noble, in an interview with Paul Nelsen: 'Noble Thoughts on Mighty Experiences: An Interview with Adrian Noble' (*ShakB* 11.5–10). Critical vigilance seems a necessary quality in the face of Noble's ill-defined vision of a 'classical repertoire' and the confession that his vague intuitions about the plays are drawn from exhibitions, poetry, movies and Frances Yates. Noble would do well to read John Russell Brown's sensibly pointed remarks on the possibilities of interchange between theatrical production and scholarship in 'Research in the Service of the Theatre: The Example of Shakespeare Studies' (*TRI* 18.25–35). This contains some practical recommendations on how academic information can enrich knowledge of the text, outline perimeters for casting and suggest social and historical locations.

In *Cross-Cultural Performances: Differences in Women's Re-Visions of Shakespeare*, Marianne Novy has edited a collection of essays many of which – like *Foreign Shakespeare* – also explore the under-regarded plurality of performance-traditions, but from the historical perspective of women's responses to Shakespeare. A number of contributors analyse particular strategies of appropriation performed by women actively involved in production as acts of accommodation to, or confrontation with, dominant modes of cultural reception. Julie Hankey's 'Helen Faucit and Shakespeare: Womanly Theatre' is an incisive study of the cultural influences that led to this leading Victorian actress enacting idealized notions of womanhood. The possibilities of women utilizing the patriarchal Bard are explored in three subsequent essays. In 'Shakespeare at the Fun Palace: Joan Littlewood', Dympna Callaghan has a lively revaluation of the Theatre Workshop movement and Littlewood's commitment to a politically challenging – but pleasurable – demonstration of how traditional institutions and practices could be transformed. Littlewood's innovatory approach to theatre practice and her revolt against the late-Edwardian decorums of verse-speaking and set-design, still prevalent in the 1950s, led to electrifying versions of *Richard II, Henry IV* and *Macbeth*. Joyce Green MacDonald's 'Women and Theatrical Authority: Deborah Warner's *Titus Andronicus*' establishes how a tradition of male directors – principally Peter Brook and Trevor Nunn – defused the text's explosive sexual and political conflicts. Warner foregrounded an alternative view of the relationship between the bonds of family, gender and imperial dominion, and enquired into masculine political absolutism with the patriarchal family as the instrument whereby political order is maintained or shattered. Lizbeth Goodman explores 'Women's Alternative Shakespeares and Women's Alternatives to Shakespeare in Contemporary British Theatre' through the examples of Fiona Shaw's exploration of gender boundaries (and Tilda Swinton's rejection of them) and the establishment of feminist theatre projects and companies performing 'reinventions' of Shakespeare texts. Finally, and on a different note, Ania Loomba's '*Hamlet* in Mizoram', engages in a critique of Pankaj Butalia's film *When Hamlet Came to Mizoram* (1989). This is a finely argued response to key facets of postcolonial and poststructuralist theories of resistance and to the intricate local circumstances of this staging of Shakespeare. It reflects on how challenges to literary authority can also be conflictual exercises, especially in terms of how gender issues alert us to how even subversive productions can both displace as well as display resistance.

Further fresh lines of research are suggested by Meredith Anne Skura's already comprehensive *Shakespeare the Actor and the Purposes of Playing*. This is an erudite and often suggestive analysis of Shakespeare's plays in the context of their performance conditions, especially that of the subculture of the Elizabethan actor. The book begins with some over-pitched comparisons between the condition – somewhat melodramatically evoked – of modern actors (significantly all male) and their Elizabethan counterparts. However, it settles down with an excellent chapter on the sociological and cultural significance of the Elizabethan player, where the continuities observed in the exercise of mimetic power and performative charisma seem more convincing. The regressive psychological concerns inherent in acting and in its confrontation with a volatile audience are then seen as recurring concerns in a number of plays, for example *Richard III* (seen as 'a psychological myth of origin for actors') and the ambitions and dependencies charted in the players of the 'great house plays' (*Love's Labour's Lost*, *The Taming of the Shrew* and *A Midsummer Night's Dream*). Skura's study has a tendency to indulge liberally in speculation – especially on Shakespeare's inner psychological development – and is less attuned to political implications, but it is extremely well-informed on contemporary theories of acting and theatrical context, and it draws on a wide range of texts to suggest some intriguing interpretative possibilities.

3.   Criticism

(a)   General

This year Brian Vickers published his 500-page denunciation of current literary criticism, *Appropriating Shakespeare: Contemporary Critical Quarrels*, predictably to reflect responses from both sides. It might be helpful, then, to attempt at least some kind of objective assessment of the validity of his counter-argument to what he sees as the progressive, multiplying-of-errors effects of post-structuralism's distortions, misrepresentations and partial readings of the authorities on which they base their theories. First, no one aware of the circumstances of the publication of Saussure's posthumous *Cours de Linguistique Générale* can refute Vickers's statement that its editors and commentators emphasized the concept of language as a self-contained system and underplayed his complementary approach to language as a social phenomenon: even elementary students of linguistic theory in the late 1960s (including this reader) knew that in 1916, the editors added to the text its programmatic concluding sentence to the effect that linguistics should study language for its own sake as an end in itself.

An awareness of this fragmenting of Saussure's unified concept of the sign is important because, as Vickers goes on to demonstrate, on this initial distortion was built the notion of language existing outside human agency which has been adopted by different critical schools during the last 20 or so years. It is when the book leaps from this to its second contention (the post-structuralists are wrong) that Vickers's subjective judgement confuses the argument. If he wants to accuse critics of distorting Saussure, Freud and Marx in order to legitimize the 'disabling of language', the flight of the subject, the banishing of an originating author, and all the other 'imperialistic' strategies the book attacks, and if he wants to demolish pieces of criticism for sloppy scholarship and faulty logic, Vickers is entitled to condemn the enterprise. But this does not afford him the right to claim a privileged licence for the interpretation of Shakespeare texts, and it is this which undermines his polemic.

Vickers's demolition work on the 'specious arguments' of post-structuralist criticism which he terms a 'can't-fail enterprise' is executed, in the main, with erudition, if not much subtlety, bulldozing specific readings of Shakespeare plays one after the other in order to re-erect an aesthetic of literature which forbids any other way of approaching texts. His exposure of basic errors in the expositions of Saussure's ideas in the critical theory of the last three decades, and of the dubious provenance of theses on which many current works of criticism are based is, for me, the important part of the book, and it has to be said that his detailed demonstrations of wilful misrepresentations, elementary mistakes, and faulty logic in oft-recycled works (e.g. Stephen Greenblatt's ubiquitous 'Invisible Bullets') provide solid support for his counter-argument.

But to support his plea for pluralism he might have included rather more examples than the few offered of post-essentialist work that does fulfil his requirements for literary criticism to be based on sound argument supported by reference to the text. More unhelpfully, Vickers is unwilling to concede that important insights into the plays have been produced by, and within, the different strands of criticism he repeatedly rejects. He seems to think that for any reading to be valid, one has to embrace the whole critical 'school' behind it (a charge that is, of course, equally relevant to his 'enemies'). The book is at its strongest when it cites the reception given to Derrida, Foucault, Lacan and Althusser from their respective disciplines to show that it is only literary criticism which has taken up their assertions (Vickers refuses to call them theories); and at its weakest when it resorts, with unintended irony, to generalized protestations against the 'unpleasant intolerances' of 'avant-garde or post-whatever critics', and when it too often calls in support from like-minded critics. But the underlying thesis of this book − that a body of literary criticism, now institutionalized, is based on the recycling of misrepresentations which other disciplines have rejected − warrants a considered response.

In *Hamlet versus Lear: Cultural Politics and Shakespeare's Art*, R. A. Foakes is also concerned with reclaiming the aesthetic, but he does make an attempt to accommodate recent critical developments in Shakespeare textual studies and some post-structuralist theory. His main focus is on the history of the reception of the two contenders for Shakespeare's 'greatest' tragedy; to discover why and how critical response to *Hamlet* and *King Lear* has changed over the years; why the first has been seen as representative of modern anxieties since 1800, and why criticism of the latter has been marked by an evasion of politics before the 1960s. Foakes's commendable attempt to put all this into critical practice in the second half of the book to recover the artistry and organic unity of the two tragedies may not have very interesting results, but the book as a whole represents a willingness to reassess the question of an aesthetic criticism in the light of new critical theory, and shows a reasonableness not found, for example, in the seemingly endless squabble between Richard Levin and Linda Charnes which rears its yawn-inducing head again this year (*TPr* 7.i.50–5 and 56–9); nor in Jonathan Hart's rambling 'New Historical Shakespeare: Reading as Political Ventriloquy' (*English* 42.193–219) which does nothing to contribute to the debate.

Maynard Mack takes the opportunity, in his preface to *Everybody's Shakespeare: Reflections Chiefly on the Tragedies*, to distance himself from what he describes as the 'tribal wars and Byzantine pedantries that now balkanize professional students of literature' into 'cells of the elect' to insist that his book is for all who enjoy Shakespeare and read him for pleasure. The book is a collection of his reprinted essays, notably the influential 1962 'Engagement and

Detachment in Shakespeare's Plays', the even more influential 1953 *Hamlet* essay, and his 1964 metaphysical reading of *King Lear* in which he argued against previous 'sentimentalized' interpretations of the tragedy.

Mack concludes his preface by stating that his concern has been with how 'great works of art manage to affect us as profoundly as they do'; and turning to a new work, we find another defence of the aesthetic being expressed by one of the younger generation of critics, Jonathan Bate, whose 'avowed aim' is to show that literature 'can still work the traditional magic of poetry ... by awakening our wonder'. It is good to be able to say that the full-length study of Ovid and Shakespeare we have been waiting for is much more than a traditional source study. Bate's *Shakespeare and Ovid* goes some way towards fulfilling criticism's long-felt need to explore the complex and wayward processes involved in Shakespeare's creative responses to his classical predecessor. Bate is excellent on demonstrating the ways in which Shakespeare (and Marlowe) sidestepped Golding's judgemental moralizing of Ovidian metamorphosis to respond directly to the classical poet's treatments of destructive passion, sexual degradation and unbearable mental pain. On the story of Myrrha, which he describes as 'an ironic, darkening pre-text' for Ovid's tale of Venus and Adonis, and which he rightly sees as exercising a significant pressure on Shakespeare's poem, Bate writes: 'This kind of presentation of the mind under the stress of conflicting emotions is Ovid's prime gift to the Elizabethan narrative poets'. The book's overarching thesis is that it is the psycho-pathological concerns of Ovid which exert the greatest influence on Shakespeare, in both the early and late work and, in more complex transformations of origins, in the mature tragedies; to which I would want to add the artistic concerns of Ovid's works as an equally pervasive presence in Shakespeare, which are more discernible in the original than in Golding. This partly explains my one disappointment with the book: that more of Ovid's Latin might have accompanied the passages of Golding's translation. Bate has given us an outstanding study. He has succeeded in re-animating Renaissance mythography with a learned and lively engagement with the interaction of classical and Shakespearean texts, and I particularly valued the ways in which he demonstrates Shakespeare's workings of Ovid in the context of the Renaissance tradition of multiple interpretation of precursory texts: how 'the moral and historical, what we might now call the universalizing and the political, are not mutually exclusive'. Perhaps this approach might usefully be adopted by the modern academy's squabblers discussed earlier.

Classical influence on Shakespeare is the subject of some of the best essays this year. In *Drama and the Classical Heritage: Comparative and Critical Essays* (ed. Clifford Davidson, Rand Johnson and John H. Stroupe), Douglas Bruster offers a stimulating analysis of Shakespeare's aristocratic versions of the Plautine *poeta*, arguing that his conception of the controlling playwright figure was based not only on the Vice/Machiavel but also on this powerful prototype from New Comedy; and his reading of Theseus's imagination speech is particularly suggestive. Elizabeth Truax's essay 'Macbeth and Hercules: The Hero Bewitched' (see *YWES* 70.281) is reprinted in this volume, and the other essays in the collection will be discussed in their place.

If the left-wing historian Victor Kiernan (no relation) had been able to bring out his *William Shakespeare: Poet and Citizen* when it was first drafted in the fifties, one would have been able to say that it broke some new ground in its aim to show that Shakespeare's 'men and women are rooted in the conditions of his time'. Unfortunately its solid, readable account of the shifts from feudalism to individualism accompanies rather pedestrian readings (curiously, only the plays up to *Hamlet*).

In contrast, Richard Wilson's *Will Power: Essays on Shakespearean Authority* is a robust and stimulating, if at times circumscribing, attempt to 'restore history to historicism' by arguing that the 'most power-laden meaning is local in its social logic': Southwark sweatshop workers rioting, agrarian conflict and unrest, Stratford famine, public execution, the introduction of imprisonment ('earlier than Foucault imagined'), the medical case-notes of Shakespeare's son-in-law, John Hall — all are examined and sharply used to demonstrate the book's thesis that it was 'the actual social process that moved the drama and determined that dramaturgical decisions were neither random nor without historical significance'. The final chapter on *King Lear* and the far-reaching implications of changing attitudes towards wills in the period is thought-provoking. One quarrel, though: the often unnecessary reliance on its theoretical underpinning. The book is at its best when using precise contemporary documentation to illuminate its arguments, and usually at its weakest when Foucault is dutifully coerced into service. Wills are the subject of two books this year which I have not been able to see: Joyce Rogers's *The Second Best Bed: Shakespeare's Will in a New Light* (Greenwood), and *Playhouse Wills, 1558–1642: An Edition of Wills by Shakespeare and his Contemporaries in the London Theatre* by E. A. J. Honigmann and Susan Brock (ManUP). Two other biographical items this year are: Mary Edmond's account of the career of 'Peter Street, 1553–1609: Builder of Playhouses' (*ShS* 45.101–14) which provides much interesting detail on the building of the Globe, and Honan Park's note in 'Shakespeare's Bible and the Harts' (*N&Q* 40.231–2) that 'it seems possible' that a Bible once belonging to Shakespeare was kept by the linear descendants of his sister, Joan, late in the eighteenth century.

There is so much of interest in Brian Gibbons's *Shakespeare and Multiplicity*, each chapter warrants more attention than is here allowed. As an exercise in historicizing a play to open up new, important perspectives in a clear, subtle and engaging style, his chapter on *Cymbeline* and Britain is exemplary, and this standard of criticism is sustained throughout the book: there is a stimulating discussion of *Antony and Cleopatra* in relation to Marlowe, an enlightening examination of the issue of persecution that 'unites *Titus* and *Shrew*', and an excellent piece on the influence of *Arcadia* on *As You Like It*. All this, *and* a consistently lively engagement with the plays as theatre, make this a stimulating and important study.

Patricia Carlin's full-length general study *Shakespeare's Mortal Men: Overcoming Death in History, Comedy and Tragedy* argues, that in the context of the transition from a feudal to an early modern society, the shaping force of Shakespeare's work is the wish to confront and master death. The book makes a rather earnest and not always very successful attempt to support this view with much reliance on other critics (too much Lawrence Stone), particularly in the lengthy footnotes. Two books particularly helpful to undergraduates are Maurice Charney's accessible commentaries on the plays and poems in *All of Shakespeare*, and Susan Bassnett's *Shakespeare: The Elizabethan Plays*, a valuable introduction, being particularly useful on the historical and cultural contexts.

Shakespeare in psychoanalysis is the subject of *After Oedipus* by Julia Reinhard Lupton and Kenneth Reinhard, a subtle and learned study focusing on the interrelation of *Hamlet* and *King Lear*, to show how the dominant Oedipal readings of *Hamlet* are countered by both Freud and Lacan by the figure of the mother as the bearer of loss and language, and how the theme of nothingness in *Lear* presents psychosis as a model for the canon and its discontents. This is a richly argued book offering substantial discussions of classical allusions in the two plays: I particularly liked their fresh insights into the Senecanism of *Hamlet*. B. J. Sokol (ed.) *The Undiscover'd Country: New Essays on Psychoanalysis and Shakespeare* is a collection of essays by academics and practising psychotherapists (and one by Jonathan Miller) with the aim of finding 'many kinds of reference beyond the text' in 'the dark, "undiscover'd" side of human relations'. Most of the essays take a circuitous route *via* (mostly Kleinian) psychoanalytic readings of the texts to arrive at conclusions already well-rehearsed by Shakespeare criticism. Philip K. Bock argues for a more psychologically realistic reading of *The Phoenix and the Turtle* than conventional allegorical interpretation; M. D. Faber sees in Hamlet a 'reactivation' of the infant's feeling for the bad maternal object; B. J. Sokol discusses Prospero's stay on the island as 'a kind of self-exile from self'; and Lyn Stephens finds 'surprising savagery and ruthlessness' in *The Merchant of Venice*, in a reading that sees Antonio as a mother figure. The volume contains a bibliography of psychoanalytical and psychological Shakespeare studies in English from 1979–89 to add to the two previous ten-year bibliographies.

General articles were very much a mixed bag this year. *YES* 23 was devoted to 'Early Shakespeare' and contained some interesting work, notably Ann Blake's 'Children and Suffering in Shakespeare's plays' (293–304) which draws attention to a neglected topic: 'with the exception of William Page, all Shakespeare's named children are fated to suffer'; their sufferings and deaths 'constitute an image of human evil at its most ruthless'. Her sense of theatrical impact helps to make her discussion of the fates of Macduff's children in Act IV of *Macbeth* and the blinding of Arthur with hot irons in *King John* particularly enlightening, and she makes the suggestive point that comparisons with tragedies of Shakespeare's contemporaries are remarkably free from child figures. This is a topic that would seem to hold much promise. In the same volume, Richard Dutton ('Shakespeare and Marlowe: Censorship and Construction', 1–29) takes issue with Jonathan Dollimore's construction of Elizabethan and Jacobean playwrights as uniformly alienated and marginalized figures, constantly subjected to repressive censorship, to argue that Shakespeare and Marlowe received identical treatment from their licensers and censors. Dutton very plausibly claims that equally potent, if less melodramatic, constructions (than those of Marlowe the demon and the scholar-poet) of Shakespeare can be found in early commentary on him.

Andrew Gurr's 'Three Reluctant Patrons and Early Shakespeare' (*SQ* 44.159–74) is a fascinating, detailed examination of why Chamberlain and Pembroke 'seem to have spent a lot of their time not becoming patrons of major London playing companies', giving an account of how and why the new acting companies were established and what was involved in the management of playing during the time of Shakespeare's early works. Also in the same volume, James P. Lusardi's 'The Pictured Playhouse: Reading the Utretcht Engraving of Shakespeare's London' (*SQ* 44.202–27) is copiously illustrated with valuable details of the engraving; and William L. Pressly ('The Ashbourne Portrait of Shakespeare: Through the Looking Glass', *SQ* 44.54–72) surveys the painting's history and the passions it has aroused. Theodore Leinwand (*SQ* 44.284–303) argues for an expansion of the category of the 'middling sort' in Shakespeare, and puts the case for including in it the citizens in *Coriolanus*.

Gillian West, in 'The Second-Meaning Pun in Shakespeare's Emotional Verse' (*SP* 90.247–76), argues that 'where it uncloses the depths of the speaker's trauma, punning has incalculable dramatic power'; and among the examples usefully discussed are: 'Access' in *Measure for Measure* II.iv.18–22; and 'Blanket' in *Macbeth* I.v.50–4. Another article on language is J. Gilbert's 'Conversation Analysis and the Structure of Shakespeare's Dialogue' (*SN* 65.169–85) which examines examples in *Lear*, *Comedy of Errors* and *Hamlet* of the way an utterance 'gains its full meaning from its position in the sequence of exchanges'.

Two articles in this year's *E&S*, whose theme is 'Literature and Censorship', are on Shakespeare: Jonathan Bate's 'Faking It: Shakespeare and the 1790s' (74.63–80) discusses forgery and authenticity to argue that Edmond Malone's exposure of William Henry Ireland's forged Shakespeare manuscripts was part of the political battlefield of the time, both men being in the business of presenting Shakespeare selectively, i.e. of censoring Shakespeare's text. In the same volume, Richard Wilson, in 'The Kindly Ones: The Death of the Author in Shakespearean Athens' (1–24), suggests that in *A Midsummer Night's Dream* Shakespeare 'encodes the conditions of his own freedom of expression' in linking this with the play's half-hidden portrayal of social control. Mention must be made in this section of *Foreign Shakespeare: Contemporary Performance* (ed. Dennis Kennedy), an important, valuable, and long-needed attention to foreign productions of Shakespeare, which will I hope have the effect of achieving Kennedy's aim 'to open a discourse for a subject much ignored by Anglo-centred Shakespeare commentators'. A similar aim of counterbalancing the British insularity of Shakespeare criticism is expressed by Jerzy Limon and Jay L. Halio who have edited *Shakespeare and His Contemporaries: Eastern and Central European Studies* to bring to a wider audience the work of scholars from Eastern and Central Europe. A collection of essays by non-Anglo-American critics mainly published over the past 20 years, it includes three essays on *Hamlet*: Emma P. Szabó on Pasternak's poem; Piotr Sadowski's 'The "Dog's Day" in *Hamlet*: A Forgotten Aspect of the Revenge Theme'; and Marta Gibinska on the play scene as the 'central point in the play' in '"The Play's the Thing": An essay on Subjectivity and Discourse in *The Tempest*' by Martin Procházka; and a playfully provocative essay by István Géher, 'Morality and Madness: A Hungarian Reading of *Measure for Measure*', which asks 'What if the good Duke ... is in fact deranged?' and answers: 'Then the play suddenly makes sense in the theatre of the absurd'; and invites us all to feel free to express our indignation at his outrageous suggestion, but not before adding a conclusion (that for me, almost justifies his argument), which gives thanks for the world of tragedy: 'For that other world beyond reason in which it is impossible to live but worthwhile to die is better and more humane than this deranged world in which it is not worthwhile to live and impossible to die'.

The British Academy Shakespeare Lectures 1980–89 are published this year. Those relevant to this section include R. A. Foakes on stage illusion; E. A. J. Honigmann on *Measure for Measure*; A. D. Nuttall on *Hamlet*; Leo Salingar on Jacobean audiences; Stanley Wells on Shakespeare teaching methods; and Inga-Stina Ewbank on 'Shakespeare's Liars'.

(b) Comedies and Late Plays

There was nothing startlingly original, or particularly stimulating in the batch of full-length general studies on the comedies published this year. Kristian Smidt's *Unconformities in Shakespeare's Later Comedies*, which is the fourth and final volume in his series examining broken continuities in the plays (*YWES* 64.206–7; 67.231–2; 71.277), covers *Much Ado, As You Like It* and *Twelfth Night*, the 'dark' comedies and the final plays with much the same mix of hypothesis and overdetermination to detect failures or unavoidable difficulties in the execution of the plays' intended structure and characterization. More inspiring is G. Beiner, in *Shakespeare's Agonistic Comedy: Poetics, Analysis, Criticism*, who distinguishes 'agonistic comedy', an essentially punitive strategy, from 'comedy of love' and 'comedy of folly', to argue that there is a discernible pattern of conflict in the comedies between antagonistic forces, one of which is 'irredeemably negative, and finally defeated': the libidinal Falstaff versus the merry and chaste wives, the vindictive Jew and the Christians who hate him; Malvolio versus the festive revellers and so on. His analysis of what he terms the exposure, punishment and exclusion pattern (particularly in *The Merry Wives of Windsor* and *The Merchant of Venice*) opens up fresh perspectives on those negative figures in the comedies who receive such unpleasant and publicly displayed punishment and who cannot participate in the comic resolutions of them.

In *Shakespeare's Early Comedies: Myth, Metamorphosis and Mannerism*, Gunnar Sorelius proposes that these plays explore the way the individual self is constructed through love in a world of Ovidian metamorphic instability and change. The book draws some interesting parallels with classical texts and contemporary Mannerist art, but gives rather too many prescriptive readings of the plays. On *Dream* we are told, for example, that the wood is 'a place of sin', that the love of the young lovers is 'ignoble' and that 'it would be wrong to think of it as a play that celebrates (the imagination)'. Bottom does not escape stern moral judgement either: he 'remains throughout the same selfish and unobservant character'. Camille Slights argues in *Shakespeare's Comic Commonwealths* that the notion of subversion and containment is too crude to describe the early comedies, and repeatedly stresses that the hierarchies are not subverted or changed. Instead, these plays 'satirize the absurdities and celebrate the virtues of the civilized community'. *As You Like It* and *Twelfth Night* are rather predictably discussed as tracing 'the renewal of societies that have broken down', while *Shrew* endorses women's subordination within patriarchal marriage, making Kate's speech not ironic. More suggestive are the chapters on *Much Ado*, bringing out the political dimension of the play, and *Love's Labour's Lost*, which is purposively examined in relation to the impact of humanist education on a hierarchical society.

Naseeb Shaheen's *Biblical References in Shakespeare's Comedies* now joins its companion volumes (*Tragedies YWES* 68.243; and *History Plays YWES* 70.275).

There were a fair number of articles of note on individual plays this year. Douglas Lanier ('"Stigmatical in Making": The Material Character of *Comedy of Errors*', *ELR* 23.81–112) supports his proposition that 'by staging disruptions of identity-effects' *Comedy of Errors* is preoccupied with 'interrogating the curious material logic of Renaissance self-presentation' with a detailed examination of the play and its performance conditions, particularly those in its staging for the Gray's Inn revels. He argues that because Shakespeare demonstrates that character is an ongoing influence we make from outward marks, Shakespearean 'interiority persists, even in diminished form, in an age of post-essential criticism'. J. L. Simmons, in 'Coming Out in Shakespeare's *Two Gentlemen of Verona*' (*ELH* 60.857–77), proposes that the play represents Shakespeare's début and that the text of the play is traversed and thwarted by anxieties of 'coming out', with rather overbearing assertions to unoriginal effect. Michael D. Friedman (' "For man is a giddy thing, and this is my conclusion": Fashion and *Much Ado About Nothing*', *T&P* 13.267–82) argues that the play consistently employs fashion imagery to probe subtle class and sexual distinctions. Donald McGrady ('The Topos of "Inversion of Values" in Hero's Depiction of Beatrice', *SQ* 44.472–76) provides a note examining Hero's stratagem of inciting Beatrice to love Benedick as partly due to its use of the classical topos in which the lover characterizes the beloved's various physical or spiritual defects as laudable attributes; and that Beatrice's criticizing her lovers is a rhetorical commonplace.

Get past Lena Cowen Orlin's laboured theoretical jargon ('The Performance of Things in *The Taming of the Shrew*' *YES* 23.167–88), and one arrives at a reading that has been a given in traditional criticism: 'things purchase the consent that perpetuates the gendered social contract'; they enable the prevailing power relationship between men and women by grounding it in contractual terms 'by interposing the economic logic of exchange'. In contrast, a readable and stimulating discussion of the play is Michael Shapiro's 'Framing the Taming: Metahistorical Awareness of Female Impersonation in *The Taming of the Shrew*' (*YES* 23.143–66), a suggestive essay arguing that the Folio text provides a metatheatrical frame, a perspective for reading Kate's submission as the final incarnation of an elaborately but transparently constructed ideal of upper-class femininity: i.e. a doubly theatrical replication of a socially generated role. Instead of using Sly to subvert Petruchio as an icon of patriarchal authority as the Quarto does, Shapiro argues that the Folio playfully contrasts opposing stereotypes of the gentlewoman and the scold and juxtaposes the ideal fantasy with the dreaded nightmare, exploiting the audience's realization that these familiar cultural constructs or roles were theatrical illusions created by male performers.

In his full-length study *Shakespeare's Almanac: 'A Midsummer Night's Dream', Marriage and the Elizabethan Calendar*, David Wiles supports his argument that the play was commissioned for the wedding of the granddaughter of the Lord Chamberlain by means of extensive reference to its astrological allusions. On the whole, this scrupulous attention to precise planetary references, which is located within the broader context of a variety of contemporary discourses and social relations, is productive, and leads Wiles to some suggestive insights into the treatment of marriage in the play. His discussion of 'Pyramus and Thisbe' as a burlesque wedding masque is richly argued. In an essay on the same play, Howard Skiles ('Hands, Feet and Bottoms: Decentring the Cosmic Dance', *SQ* 44.325–42) finds élite and popular traditions of dancing unusually coextensive in the play and, rejecting traditional views of dance as a bland celebration of harmony, argues for the significance of the role of dancing practices in the play's complex negotiations of power.

Mark Thornton Burnett ('Giving and Receiving: and the Politics of Exchange', *ELR* 23.287–313) argues that *Love's Labour's Lost* negotiates the political crisis of the last decades of Elizabeth's reign in terms of the repercussions of the breakdown of gift exchange. It states, rather than demonstrates, that with the Princess and her entourage Shakespeare goes so far as 'to mount a radical critique of Elizabeth', dramatizing the challenges posed by women to patriarchy and the ramifications of their refusal to receive gifts. A thinly-argued piece.

There was less attention given to *As You Like It* this year. Cynthia Marshall's 'Wrestling as Play and Game in *As You Like It*' (*SEL* 33.265–87) is a rather strained attempt to argue that the wrestling match functions as mimetic violence, game, spectacle and metaphor, to demonstrate how 'social codes are continually being made, broken and remade'. Stuart A. Daley examines the 'pervasiveness and centrality' of 'The Idea of Hunting in *As You Like It*' (*ShakS* 21.72–95) with reference to classical and contemporary allusions and symbols; while Steven Doloff (*Expl* 51.143–5) provides a note on an overlooked Jovian oak reference to suggest Orlando's re-enactment of Hercules's third famous labour at 2.i.31–5.

Two articles on *Twelfth Night* concentrate on Malvolio. Chris R. Hassell ('Malvolio's Dark Concupiscence', *CahiersE* 43.1–11) sees a Malvolio who is 'rich in self-love, darkly ignorant, heathenish and concupiscent in righteousness' in the context of Luther's paradigm of the deluded self-righteousness of those who believe in salvation by merit rather than grace; while Maurice Hunt (*SP* 90.277–97) discusses Malvolio's notion of Providence as self-serving, to argue that Shakespeare satirizes his character's belief in unmediated, unearned blessing of the elect, and endorses a deity who works through secondary agents to reward those who have earned blessing by selflessly serving others. He reads the 'M.O.A.I' scene in the context of the private ciphers and hieroglyphics used by John Machin and Lord Harington for their spiritual pilgrimage (and Hooker's belief that puritanism sprang from a psychological disorder), and suggests that it may be a satire on the Puritan practice of literal interpretation of Biblical passages to create meanings to justify their narrow view.

The letter in the 'C.U.T' scene has in one sense 'become a cunt clamouring its desire', according to Dympna Callaghan ('"And all is semblative a woman's part": Body Politics in *Twelfth Night*', *TPr* 7.428–52) in a rigidly prescriptive reading which focuses on 'the absent-presence' of the 'monstrous female genitalia', to argue that the transvestite actor is as likely to be portraying women with contempt as with respect: the male body 'repeatedly and ritually enacts the displacement, exclusion and discipline of its female counterpart'. Karin Coddon ('"Slander in an Allow'd Fool": *Twelfth Night*'s Crisis of the Aristocracy', *SEL* 33.309–25), in a sloppily argued piece, claims that the play mockingly discloses the mutability and contingency of social rank, and 'demystifies' one of the Elizabethan authorities' 'central political fictions'; and goes on to make a forced effort to link the excesses of the nobility to the precarious limits of theatrical licence. Horst Breuer (*ES* 74.441–4), in a note on class, suggests that the play points to Fabian having the rank of esquire or independent landed gentleman, not necessarily a retained servant of Olivia.

There was little of real interest in the studies of *The Merchant of Venice* this year. Christopher Hardman ('"Trouble Being Gone, Comfort Should Remain": Tranquility and Discomfort in *The Merchant of Venice*', *YES* 23.189–205) sets out to examine the source of unease in the relationship between Antonio and Bassanio in a rambling fashion that does not get him (or the reader) very far. Nancy E. Hodge ('Making Places at Belmont: "You are Welcome Notwithstanding"', *ShakS* 21.155–74) discusses Belmont as an 'alternate site', an aristocratic retreat from a mercantile centre, using historical information on sixteenth-century Venice; while Herbert Berry ('Shylock, Robert Miles and Events at the Theatre', *SQ* 44.183–97) offers an intriguing argument for seeing the practices of Shakespeare's Venetian court depending on those at Westminster, and, in particular, the lawsuits involving James Burbage's share in the ownership of The Theatre; and Joan Ozark Holmer suggests Miles Mosse's *The Arraignment and Conviction of Vsurie* (1595) as a new source for the play (*ShakS* 21.11–44).

There are two suggestive and sharply argued essays on *The Merry Wives of Windsor*. Arthur F. Kinney's 'Textual Signs in *Merry Wives*' (*YES* 23.206–34) argues that the play is a burlesque of Jonson and humours comedies generally, and proceeds to examine the differences between the 1602 Quarto and the Folio text to demonstrate the effect of different economic climates on the setting and force of the play. In the Folio, Kinney points out, monetary thinking governs all transactions in Windsor but is never a theme in the Quarto. In the second piece, Robert S. Miola ('*The Merry Wives*: Classical and Italian Intertexts', *CompD* 27.364–76) discusses the ways in which Shakespeare arranges elements of its 'New Comedic substrata' in Italian style with its emphasis on jealousy, *senex amans*, *miles gloriosus*, and signature motif: a male disguised as a bride. He examines the 'striking' transformation of the classical matrona in Mrs Page and Mrs Ford, and the mixed ancestry of Falstaff as primarily a *miles gloriosus* figure, but also as *senex amans* or *Eunuchus*.

David Haley's full-length study of *All's Well That Ends Well, Shakespeare's Courtly Mirror*, is a rather eccentric book which argues that character is defined by Shakespeare in terms of a publicly determined persona reflected in the 'courtly mirror'. Both character and the play's design are analysed by means of concepts of 'heroic prudence' and 'reflexivity': 'the courtier's deliberation is guided by a reflexive, self-regulating prudence that is usually identified with honor or love', to turn Bertram's role into a heroic quest for self-determination, and Helena's into a much diminished one. After going back to it several times, I'm still not sure where this book led me. There is more of interest in Robert S. Miola's article 'New Comedy in *All's Well that Ends Well*' (*RenQ* 46.23–43), where he argues that 'Shakespeare's most Terentian play' is a sophisticated recension of New Comedic themes, conventions and characters, which draws on his earlier adaptations of Plautus and Terence. Miola finds unusual parallels between Malvolio and Parolles, and Bertram and Katherine, and sees Parolles and Bertram as a 'splitting' of the figure of the *miles gloriosus*. 'Shakespeare reveals in (Bertram) as he had in Claudio, the theatrical and moral limitations of the Plautine adulescens'.

Another substantial essay is Julie Robin Solomon's 'Mortality as Matter of Mind: Toward a Politics of Problems in *All's Well That Ends Well*' (*ELR* 23.134–69) which purposefully contextualizes Shakespeare's use of contemporary controversies over the limits of medical knowledge to conceptualize political changes as a process which proceeds by transgressing evolving distinctions between nature and culture. She argues that the play 'anatomizes the ways in which socio-political order is constituted as "real", "possible" and "natural"' and suggests how it explores altered perceptions of social worth. To support her view that the medical metaphor bears the largest burden in articulating the alteration of socio-political reality in its capacity to unsettle our sense of boundaries of matter and mind, Solomon discusses the way in which the metaphor develops at length the contrast between Galenic medicine's belief in the limits of knowledge and Paracelsian ambition as a figure for 'the play's series of oppositions between knowledge and mortality, private wish and public reality, and culture and nature'. This essay provides much helpful contemporary documentation and opens up the play to fresh lines of enquiry; and sent this reader back to the play (and to Richard Wilson's chapter on John Hall) with a new perspective.

Measure for Measure received much interest again this year, but of variable quality. Mario Di Gangi ('Pleasure and Danger: Measuring Female Sexuality in *Measure for Measure*', ELH 60.589–609) offers a way to read the play 'oppositionally'. She asserts that because it measures 'the perceived cost of woman's autonomy' in marital and reproductive affairs, it foregrounds female sexual desire 'only to deny the desirability of seeking pleasure for pleasure's sake'. I tried it: it works, if you don't look at the text or see a performance. The modish title of Laura Knoppers's 'Engendering Shame: *Measure for Measure* and the Spectacles of Power' (*ELR* 23.450–71) signals a routine reading of the play in relation to 'Church and State rituals which produced shame and generated it as specifically female'. In great contrast, a discerning, substantial, and judicious essay is Victoria Hayne's 'Performing Social Practice: The Example of *Measure for Measure*' (*SQ* 44.1–29) which provides fascinating contemporary documentation on betrothal and social practices for forming marriage, which genuinely illuminates the play, particularly the context of contemporary public debate about how to regulate moral behaviour, and of the 1650 law decreeing adultery punishable by death (which was rarely enforced because juries simply refused to find the defendant guilty). Christopher Baker (*Expl* 51.146–7) suggests another meaning for 'razed' at 1.ii.11 as 'erased', 'scrape out', and 'stole' at 146–7 later in the same scene as a masterpiece of thievery; James P. Bednarz re-examines the question of Shakespeare's 'purge' of Jonson through this play (*ShakS* 21.175–213); and T. A. Stroud (*ES* 74.84–95) argues for an incompleted but intentional balancing or doubling of Angelo and Lucio. I liked his observation of the opposition of the bed trick ('a comic element out of place in the serious plot') and the head trick ('a serious element out of place in a comic plot').

Troilus and Cressida is the subject of one of the best periodical articles this year. Gary Spears's lucid and well-argued discussion ('Shakespeare's "Manly" Parts: Masculinity and Effeminacy in *Troilus and Cressida*', *SQ* 44.409–22) explores the way the play repeatedly challenges culturally determined notions of masculinity by drawing attention to 'the effeminacy and emasculation of nearly every central figure'. Effeminacy is shown as an excess of masculinity: the very signs that mark a man as a virile warrior are 'the signs that, recontextualized, stigmatize him as effeminate, soft, weak, womanish'. Grace Tiffany ('Not Saying No: Female Self-Erasure in *Troilus and Cressida*', *TSLL* 35.44–56) argues against sympathetic valuations of Cressida that divest her of responsibility for choice, to insist that Cressida chooses her own self-erasure: she 'does not offer resistance, at every turn she chooses not to speak, not to acquiesce in male discursive practices'. *The Winter's Tale* received most attention among the Late Plays in periodical articles this year. Verna A. Foster in 'The "Death" of Hermione: Tragicomix Dramaturgy in *WT*' (*CahiersE* 43.43–56) argues against the critical conflation of wonder and surprise to describe the effect of the Statue scene to insist that tragic possibility is continuously deflected in the earlier part of the play to prepare for Hermione's resurrection. Her support for this is questionable: for example, 'the very physicality of Leontes's language (at 1.ii) undercuts the tragic potential of his jealousy'; the violence of Paulina's accusation (at III.175–202) 'anaesthetizes our capacity to feel the pain of Hermione's death'. Not in the theatre they don't.

Gillian West ('Fuelling the Flames: Inadvertent Double Entendre in *The Winter's Tale* at I Scene ii', *ES* 74.520–23) gives examples of the 'salacious ambiguities' of the language used in the exchanges between Hermione and Polixenes in the jealousy scene; Donna B. Hamilton argues that the relationships of Bohemia and Sicilia in *Winter's Tale* 'record and refigure' the divisiveness that threatened the social order at the time of James I's project of Union between 1604 and 1610 (*ShakS* 21.228–52); and Robert Henke sees the mixed genre of the play as exemplifying the 'unwritten poetics' of tragicomic dramaturgy as in Guarini. In an unusual essay, 'Machines for the Suppression of Time' (in Davidson, Johnson and Stroupe), Robert C. Ketterer examines the statue-come-to-life motif in Puccini's *Suor Angelica*, *The Winter's Tale* and Euripides's *Alcestis*, and offers the suggestion that the 'statue' of Hermione returns what has been lost but the return is incomplete; the reunion acknowledges that the suffering that has been done 'cannot be undone'.

There were several notes, and very few articles on *The Tempest*. Martin W. Walsh's note relates Caliban's song to the disenfranchised agricultural labourers' autumn hiring customs when the change of master was one of the few occasions when they could indulge in 'the illusion of freedom' (*CahiersE* 43.57–60); Victor Bourgy, in the same volume (35–42) argues in a rather unstructured, confusing piece that 'concentric ripples of meaning radiate' from Caliban, the play's 'invisible reference point'; and in a somewhat meandering piece, David Porter ('His Master's Voice: The Politics of Narragenitive Desire in *The Tempest*', *Comitatus* 24.33–44) argues that what he calls Prospero's 'reception anxiety' and 'obsession with asserting a form of narrative mastery' in the face of Sycorax who 'represents the most dangerous challenge to Prospero's sovereignty' explains why he pleads guilty in the epilogue: he has failed to consummate his creative will within the play. Mark Taylor ('Prospero's Books and Stephano's Bottle: Colonial Experience in *The Tempest*', *ClioI* 22.ii.101–13) links the interpretative mistakes shown in the scene where Stephano demands that Caliban 'kiss the book which is his bottle' with the analagous confusion described by Hariot of the Amerindians at the properties of the Bible.

Initial excitement at the prospect of a full-length study of *The Two Noble Kinsmen* rapidly evaporated on opening Richard Allan Underwood's *'The Two Noble Kinsmen' And Its Beginnings*, which tiresomely traces what he terms 'the masturbation motif' in the play back to the narrative poems to argue (with much help from A. L. Rowse's biography along the way) that Palamon is a figure for Southampton while Arcite represents 'the Essex/soldier/horseman aspect of Southampton' (evidence: Southampton's letters from prison are eloquent; Palamon is eloquent). The book proliferates in phrases such as 'my guess is …', 'I can't help thinking …', in order to arrive at the claim which the book has been hinting at all along: the Jailer's daughter is a figure for Shakespeare, which explains the role's 'mordant sweetness'. Shakespeare and Fletcher's *Two Noble Kinsmen* 'is a reproach' to Southampton. This is silly stuff.

(c) Poems

The best note on the Sonnets this year is M. L. Stapleton's '"My False Eyes": The
Dark Lady and Self Knowledge' (*SP* 90.213–30) which examines 'Will's panic
at the incompatibility of love, talent, and self-knowledge' expressed in nearly
every sonnet of the sub-sequence (127–54), in the light of the contrasting smug-
ness found in Ovid's *Ars Amatoria*, where the poet is able to continue 'dribbling
his elegaic couplets of falsehood'. 'My false eyes' (148.5) is read by Stapleton as
Will's 'appraisal of himself as too blind to judge his mistress with any reliability'. He also suggestively points out that the Sonnets in which Will insults the
Dark Lady most brutally are also some of the most masochistic: 'he rarely forgets
to lie or to admit his falsehoods'. Peter Stallybrass provides an engaging piece in
'Editing as Cultural Formation: The Sexing of Shakespeare's Sonnets' (*MLQ*
54.91–103) on the responses of those Shakespeare editors (including Steevens's
horror at the thought of gentle Shakespeare as contaminator and corrupter of
youth) which testify to 'the great obstacle that the Sonnets formed in the smooth
production of the national bard'. Nancy Martinez and Joseph Martinez ('Shakespeare's Sonnet 99: A Blighted Flower Garden in a Winter's Tale', *Expl* 51.76–
80) make rather heavy weather of arguing that Sonnet 99 uses the metaphor of
Henry Peacham's *Garden of Eloquence* to express the idea that 'writing during
the loved one's absence is akin to cultivating a flower garden in winter'. John Roe
('"Willobie His Avisa" and *The Passionate Pilgrim*: Precedence, Parody and
Development', *YES* 23.111–25) argues that *Willoughbie* Canto XLVII was written in direct reponse to 'When as thine eye'; and two pieces (James H. Sims and
Peter Milward, *Connotations* 3.64–71) examine 'Single Nature's Double Name'
in *The Phoenix and the Turtle*. Carolyn D. Williams's ambitious aim to examine
Lavinia and Lucrece in the light of Renaissance ideas about rape in poetry, drama,
in religious and legal writings and legal practices and modern theories about rape
('Silence, like a *Lucrece* Knife': Shakespeare and the Meanings of Rape', *YES*
23.93–110) produces a rather unoriginal and unfocused piece. Jonathan Bate's
important article on *Venus and Adonis* (*YES* 23.80–92) is reprinted in an expanded version in his *Shakespeare and Ovid* (see 3(a) above).

(d) Histories

This year's work on the histories can be best summarized as viewing Shakespeare
as a spokesman for the dominant culture – with the exception of the studies of the
plays in performance and Graham Bradshaw's *Misrepresentations: Shakespeare
and the Materialists* which challenges the very notion of a dominant culture. Half
of Bradshaw's book is devoted to *Henry V* setting his own reading of the play's
multiple perspectives over what he regards as the 'Either/Or' positions of old and
new historicists and cultural materials. His witty and detailed attack on the new
historicists and cultural materialists as 'inverted Tillyards' undoubtedly makes a
major contribution to the now fashionable 'After Theory' school, but the analysis
of the play's many dimensions is far from a new way of reading *Henry V*; in fact
this is the approach offered by most 'Shakespeare in performance' studies.

The strength of the most comprehensive of these approaches, in Barbara
Hodgdon's *Henry IV Part Two*, in the Shakespeare in Performance series, is in
the reading of productions as responses to particular historical and cultural
moments. She provides detailed analysis of five productions from 1951 to 1985.
Her scope, however, is limited by the choice of productions (all directed by

British directors); and, with the exception of a chapter on the BBC production, directed by David Giles, the analysis is confined to theatrical performances of the play. Her most insightful comments are aimed, as asides, at Orson Welles's *Chimes at Midnight*, which she uses throughout as a yardstick to measure other productions. A chapter devoted to *Chimes at Midnight* and Gus Van Sant's *My Own Private Idaho* (not mentioned by Hodgdon) would have improved a book in which the author struggles with the difficult task of separating this play from the other histories in the second tetralogy.

The inclusion of the BBC production in Barbara Hodgdon's selection reflects the critical attention that these plays continue to attract. This year, a notable proportion of research on Shakespeare is on film and television adaptations. In 'The BBC's Henriad' (*LFQ* 21.25–32), Ace G. Pilkington defends the concentration on Hal/Henry's straightforward linear development and the necessary darkening and diminishing of Falstaff in the Henry plays directed by David Giles. Another contribution to the discussion of the history plays on screen is made by E. A. Rawchut in 'The Siege Oration in Branagh's *Henry V* (*ShakB* 11.39–41) in which Henry's Harfleur oration, omitted from the Olivier film, is regarded as the cinematic *coup de main* of Branagh's movie. *King John* receives a rare mention in 'Shakespeare on screen' discussion in Luke McKernan's account of the discovery of Beerbohm Tree's film of *King John*; lasting just over one minute, it is the first Shakespeare film made ('Beerbohm Tree's *King John* Rediscovered: The First Shakespeare Film, Sept. 1899', *ShakB* 11.35–6).

The unambiguous, in fact mythic, representation of Henry V is seen in relation to the Chorus by Brownell Salomon ('The Myth Structure and Rituality of *Henry V*', *YES* 254–67). Salomon argues that the Chorus authenticates the play as ritual, thereby forestalling criticism of the story. The opposing interpretations of Henry V are read in the context of Shakespeare's foregrounding of conflicting discourses by Paola Pugliatti in what is now a conventional reading of the play ('The Strange Tongues of *Henry V*', *YES* 235–54). Susan E. Krantz, similarly, focuses on reception and looks at how audience response is complicated in *Henry VIII*, describing the play as a product of a destablilized culture and shaped accordingly like a funhouse mirror in which each section distorts our perception of the other ('Audience Response to *Henry VIII* and Cultural Destabilization', *UDR* 22.133–46).

In an outstanding essay, 'Masculine Negotiations in the History Plays: Hal, Hotspur and the Foolish Mortimer' (*SQ* 44.440–63), J. L. Simmons compares the chronicles with Shakespeare's histories and convincingly argues how women are seen to function in evoking masculine insufficiencies: lineage is thwarted in masculine historical discourses by female inheritance, loose women and imprudent marriages. In the second tetralogy, Hal seems uniquely untainted by female influence until the final act of *Henry V* where, ironically and disastrously, he emerges as a combination of his doomed 'feminized' enemies from *1 Henry IV*: Hotspur (in his plainspokenness with Catherine and in his soldiership) and Mortimer (in his claim to the throne through the female line and in his marriage to a woman who speaks in an unknown language). The feminine disruption to masculine historical discourse is developed by Phyllis Rackin in 'Engendering the Tragic Audience: the Case of *Richard III*' (*SLitI* 26.47–65). The conception of the effects of tragedy as feminizing is regarded in relation to the reconstruction of history as tragedy in *Richard III* and the male protagonist's appropriation of the subversive threat posed by women to masculine history-making. Unlike the previous histories, in this play, the representation of women (in their passivity), gender roles, and the family becomes more 'modern'. According to Rackin, this is exemplified in the final image of the patriarchal family (Richmond and Elizabeth) which legitimates both masculine authority and monarchical power. A similar view of women in the first tetralogy is found in Susan Bassnett's *Shakespeare: The Elizabethan Plays* in which the women are read, in keeping with the popular perception, as threats to a natural order; the increasing stylization of women in the later histories is noted, but not analysed by Bassnett who is not always successful in her declared purpose of reading the plays as rooted in Elizabethan society. Instead, she tends to project her own views onto the plays' popularity; for example, she asserts that '*Henry IV Part 2* and *Henry V* are not likeable plays; they disturb too much'.

The demonic disturbances in the first tetralogy are considered in relation to *Dr Faustus* by John D. Cox in 'Devils and Power in Marlowe and Shakespeare', *YES* 46–64. According to Cox, the difference between the devils in Marlowe and in *1* and *2 Henry VI* is that the former serve as a reflection of external demonic power, the latter, of the human lust for power. In Shakespeare's histories (unlike Marlowe's tragedy), it is the human figures rather than the devils who have the demonic gift of lying, a necessary prerequisite for the office of king. In considering Michael Bogdanov's and Adrian Noble's editorial decisions in their productions of the first tetralogy, Alan Dessen looks at the much maligned scene with the devils in *1 Henry VI* and, like Cox, sees the highly visible devils in terms of an ongoing pattern of images, thematically central to the play. Rather unconvincingly, Morton J. Frisch argues that we are invited to compare Caesar and Richard III in the final play of the first tetralogy which he reads as an essay in the delusions of power ('Shakespeare's *Richard III* and the Soul of the Tyrant', *Interpretation* 44.275–84).

In 'Shakespeare's Poor: *2 Henry VI*', in *The Politics of Shakespeare*, Derek Cohen examines the only play in the canon in which the poor pose a real threat to the political structure of patriarchal monarchy. Cohen argues that Shakespeare treats the poor in the play with anxiety, ultimately demonizing them through their fear of literacy which marks them off from the wealthy. Cohen argues that the play, in the end, confirms the relationship between wealth and literacy, power and literacy, and, finally, morality and literacy. Cohen stresses Shakespeare's defence of the dominant culture again in *Shakespeare's Culture of Violence*, in which a consideration of the second tetralogy forms half of the book. Essentially concentrating on the language of violence, Cohen demonstrates how the cohesive and therefore necessary violence of patriarchal power is contrasted to the ruptural (and therefore, dangerous) potential for violence in Eastcheap. A different view of Shakespeare's politics is offered by Eric Sterling ('Breaking Ideological Barriers: Shakespeare's *Richard II*', *PAPA* 19.33–43); by comparing the play with the chronicles, Sterling accounts for Shakespeare's darkening of King Richard, the ruler who has the strongest monarchical claim of any in the Shakespearean canon, as a subversive declaration of the right of political necessity over lawful succession.

The Oldcastle/Falstaff controversy is resurrected by R. W. F. Martin who approves of the 'restoration' of the name 'Oldcastle' for 'Falstaff' in the recent Oxford *Complete Works* and finds a possible paraphrase of Falstaff's – or Oldcastle's – catechism on honour, surprisingly, in support of Jane Owen's 1624 defence of English Catholics ('A Catholic Oldcastle', *N&Q* 40.185–6). Finally,

Eric Sams argues against Gary Taylor's decision to replace Falstaff with Oldcastle in the Oxford edition while collecting evidence in support of Shakespeare's authorship of *The Famous Victories* ('Oldcastle and the Oxford Shakespeare', *N&Q* 40.180–5).

(e) Tragedies

The first line of Zulfikar Ghose's *Shakespeare's Mortal Knowledge: A Reading of the Tragedies* tells you pretty much all you need to know about this book: 'The women die first'. The second paragraph tells us: 'From the bodies of women flows life, and it is life that is stopped with their death'. Direct quotation here seems to render commentary superfluous, but, for the record, Ghose writes on Bradley's Big Four in a continuous glossing exercise, that seems intended for nursery children, to little discernible purpose: '"If thou hast any sound or use of voice,/Speak to me." Speak to me. Use words. Construct a language so that I can know what I do not know and what I desperately desire to know'. I don't think I can bring myself to say any more.

There were many fewer articles on the tragedies than on the comedies this year. There was little of note in the studies of *Hamlet*. Marvin D. Hinten (*Expl* 51.145–46) examines an overlooked pun in *Hamlet* at I.ii.113–14: 'A dew' is a pun on 'adieu'; and, more substantially, R. V. Holdsworth provides evidence from Middleton's 1604 pamphlet *Father Hubbard's Tales* that 'nunnery' was a stock term in Elizabethan and Jacobean bawdy (*N&Q* 40.192–3). In a rather overdetermined reading, James O. Taylor examines, with reference to Vincetio Saviolo's fencing manual *Practices*, how the specific nature of rapier fencing is related to the language in Hamlet's thrust and parry of exchanges: 'the syntax, rhythm and rhetoric' correspond to the feinting and anticipation moves of the rapier duellist ('The Influence of Rapier-Fencing on Hamlet', *FMLS* 29.203–15). Luke Wilson ('Hamlet versus Petit and the Hysteresis of Action', *ELH* 60.17–25) examines the historical context of the legal ramifications of the suicide of Sir James Hale, Justice of the Court of Common Pleas in which the jury ruled his possessions be forfeited to the Crown. 'Legal language enters the play under the aspect of parody, but carries with it so high a charge of verbal energy that it seems both to generate and release itself from the attack against it'.

In *HSt* 15, Neil L. York ('Hamlet as American Revolutionary' (40–53) considers why American revolutionaries found the play and its protagonist so appealing; James R. Andreas (8–23) argues that the energy of the play is generated from the Bakhtian 'dialogical clash' of the vulgar (Hamlet) and the polite (Claudius); and Larry S. Champion (24–35) examines proverbs in the play. The volume also contains William E. Sheidley's introduction to, and translation of, Louis Henry's 1816 ballet version in which Hamlet becomes King at the end (54–80); and there is a weak and unconvincing piece by A. Banerjee on Osborne's Jimmy Porter as a modern Hamlet (81–92).

David Thatcher ('Horatio's "Let me speak": Narrative Summary and Summary Narrative in Hamlet', *ES* 74.246–5) makes the already well-rehearsed point that Horatio's claim to deliver a true account of events at V.ii.374–88 is questionable, in order to state that it is the kind of play which 'adamantly resists closure'. Another rather predictable reading is offered by P. K. Ayers ('Reading, Writing and *Hamlet*', *SQ* 423–39) who focuses on the 'inherent slipperiness of language' in the play.

King Lear New Casebook edited by Kiernan Ryan reprints essays selected from the last decade which, we are told with no apparent sense of irony, 'dissent from the traditional critical assumptions which have obstructed the reappraisal of this drama for our time'. It is a pity that more examples of interesting recent work on the play were not included; quite a few of those chosen are inferior or indifferent pieces. In a thoughtful essay, Geoffrey Aggeler reads the notion of 'Good Pity' in *King Lear* (*Neophil* 77.321–31) in the context of Stoic condemnation of pity (Seneca viewed *misericordia* as a mental defect), which, Aggeler says, the play as a whole rejects; but its representation of good pity as a prerequisite to moral growth is complex: Edgar must undergo a symbolic death of self to become an 'effective moral agent'. David Bergeron ('"Deadly Letters"' in *King Lear*', *PQ* 72.ii.157–76) offers a fairly superficial account of what he describes as the 'reliance on letters' in the Gloucester story which serves to open up a level of discourse in contrast to Lear's. More stimulating is Christopher Nielson's note (*Expl* 52.16–17) on Edmund's 'villainously indeterminate line' at 5.i.225: 'take my sword,/ Give it the captain', which can mean 'to hand over' or 'make an attack', and invites us to speculate that he remains unconverted at the end.

A mixed bag of articles on *Othello* this year, mainly on the questions of race and/or sexuality: James R. Aubrey examines Elizabethan attitudes to 'Race and the Spectacle of the Monstrous in *Othello*' (*ClioI* 22.221–38). Derek Cohen ('Othello's Suicide', *UTQ* 62.323–33) argues somewhat dogmatically that Othello's suicide raises more questions about the cultural dilemmas of the play than it answers. Cohen insists that an intense drama of self-hatred is played out 'signalling the final and total success of white culture', which comes with Othello's realization that he himself is 'a traitor both to Desdemona and the white world and to the black world': the 'circumciz'd dog' is both the malignant Turk and Othello.

The-text-as-pornographic-site fashion seems to be making its tedious way into Shakespeare studies now. According to Arthur Little ('An Essence That's Not Seen: The Primal Scene of Racism in *Othello*', *SQ* 44.304–24) from the opening words of *Othello* to its closing moments the play 'simulates some imagined or actual pornographic scene', and 'the play's pornography is deeply embedded in the ideological portrayal of Othello's blackness'. It gets worse: The 'uncovering of the homosexual scene' (Iago and Cassio in bed described by Iago at 3.3) is the play's 'most pornographic and immediate sexual event'. Such statements proliferate; evidence to support them does not. Meanwhile, Patricia Parker ('Dilation, Spying, and the "Secret Place" of Woman', *Rep* 44.60–95) returns to her continued concern with the word 'dilation' for an attempt to set *Othello* and *Hamlet* beside the contexts of 'the delator or informant as a secret accuser and the quasi-pornographic discourse of anatomy and early modern gynaecology that seeks to bring a hidden or secret place to light'. Unfortunately, an intense and scrupulous analysis of 'dilation' is not developed to any clear purpose. Sipahigil Teoman provides a note on specific parallels between the storm in *Othello* at 2.i.185–9 and descriptions of storms in Ovid's *Tristia* and *The Tempest* (*SQ* 44.468–71).

The best essay on *Macbeth* this year is Lorna Flint's excellent analysis, 'The Significance of Rime in Shakespeare's Plays' (*CahiersE* 43.13–20) which is particularly stimulating in its engagement with the theatrical impact of the play's rhyme. It opens, she reminds us, in rhyming dialogue to 'riveting effect', and she goes on to examine the ways in which rhyme points forward to half-foreseen consequences, and backwards to situations already established, and discusses the cumulative significance of rhyme in the play to purposeful effect. She points out that 10 per cent of all lines in Shakespeare are end-rhymed; in *Macbeth* there are 290 rhyming lines, 108 of them by human characters. Only five out of 31 scenes are totally without rhyme. Flint explores the subliminal functions of rhyme; e.g. controlling pace, distancing; the relationship between rhyme/non-rhyme and the play's themes of dissonance/harmony. Her analysis of 2.ii.20–41 is particularly astute: 'the word assaults are the aural equivalents of twenty trenchèd gashes on the head of Banquo's ghost'. I hope we'll be treated to some more examples of aural effects in other Shakespeare plays in such fine expositions from this critic.

Stanley Cavell's 'Macbeth Appall'd' (*Raritan* 12.ii.1–15 and 12.iii.1–15) is a highly personal, rambling meditation on and around several large topics (the relationship of Macbeth and his wife, of speech and silence and so on) which seemed to go nowhere. For J. O'Rourke (*ShakS* 21.213–27), *Macbeth* examines the problem of a Christian metaphysic. He sees the 'sound and fury' speech as 'subverting both halves of the Christian paradox', and becoming far more than an eloquent expression of Macbeth's despair: the concluding action of the play remains within 'the ironic command' of the representatives of the Wyrd. Taking Freud's unsolved question 'Why does Lady Macbeth collapse on reaching success?' as her starting point, Anny Crunelle-Vanrigh ('*Macbeth*: Oedipus Transposed', *CahiersE* 43. 21–33) argues that *Macbeth* is not concerned with the Oedipal scene but the pre-oedipal where the son kills the father to ensure permanent symbiosis with his mother. Lady Macbeth, she says, performs the symbolic castration that will give her what she lacks, and resex her after her ritual 'unsexing'.

Romeo and Juliet is the subject of the tenth volume in the Shakespearean Criticism series (John Andrews, ed., *Romeo and Juliet: Critical Essays*). This provides a thoughtfully selected mix of traditional and newer approaches, which has the merit of offering undergraduates the intellectual challenge of historicizing criticism of the play for themselves, something which nearly all current introductory anthologies so patronizingly fail to do – they either exclude recent developments, or ignore traditional ones. This collection, by contrast, includes Derek Traversi's metaphysical reading (1956); Harry Levin's 1960 essay on the play's aesthetics; Stanley Wells's on the theatrical impact of the Nurse's speech (1980); Coppélia Kahn's 'Coming of Age in Verona' (1978); and Marianne Novy's 'Violence, Love and Gender' (1984), to select only five out of the 25 essays, that are helpfully arranged in three sections covering, respectively, language and structure, the play in performance, and the play as a product of Elizabethan culture. Catherine Belsey ('The Name of the Rose in *Romeo and Juliet*', *YES* 23.126–42) makes the repetitious and laboured point that '*Romeo and Juliet* is a play about desire' in an article whose echoing-Eco title will amuse some more than others.

The Classical tragedies received scant attention this year. Charles Wells's book, *The Wide Arch: Roman Values in Shakespeare*, is an unadventurous but solid study; and the periodical articles were patchy in quality. In 'The Politics of Wealth: *Timon of Athens*' (*Neophil* 77.149–60), Derek Cohen adopts modish terminology to offer the hardly startling view that 'the whole of the social discourse' in this play 'is tied to the cash-nexus'. More suggestive is the comparison he goes on to make between the transformative impulses in Lear's discovery of poverty and the response of the rich to the poor in *Timon*.

Julius Caesar receives a fair amount of attention this year. In a stimulating essay, 'Lucan and the Self-Incised Voids of *Julius Caesar*', Clifford Ronan (in Davidson et al.) argues that Shakespeare imitates *Pharsalia* in making crucial use of the motif of self-mutilation and parricide to describe civil war; while in the same volume, J. A. Bryant discusses the play from a Euripidean perspective, offering suggestive parallels between Brutus and the Euripidean protagonist, to argue that in its fragmentation of the traditional hero's role, *Julius Caesar* is a play that picks up the examination of the world where Euripides left off: with dreams of metaphysical order discredited and the systems of value deprived of their sanctions. In the most dismal essay I've read all year ('Social Role and the Making of Identity in *Julius Caesar*', *SEL* 33.289–307), Sharon O'Dair defends Brutus in this embarrassingly naive and simplistic way: 'because I believe one's social roles, one's position in society are part and parcel of one's personal identity, I find it difficult to criticise Brutus'.

It was a relief to turn to Barbara L. Parker's intelligent essay, '"A Thing Unfirm": Plato's Republic and Shakespeare's *Julius Caesar*' (*SQ* 44.30–43) which provides fresh insights into the play by arguing that it is anchored solidly on precepts in Plato's *Republic*: the concept of contamination 'sullying the mind's metal' becomes 'a governing metaphor by which to explain the downfall of Caesar and Brutus'. In 'The Senecan Context of *Coriolanus*' (*MP* 90.465–78), John M. Wallace argues for a debt to *De Beneficiis* (complementing his piece on *Timon* in *MP* 86).

Antony and Cleopatra received little attention this year. Cynthia Marshall takes the Hank Williams ballad 'Man of Steel Done Got the Blues' as her starting point for a densely argued analysis of 'Antony as Melancholic Subversion of Presence in *Antony and Cleopatra*' (*SQ* 44.385–408), not very productively; while Paul Yachnin's 'Shakespeare's Politics of Loyalty: Sovereignty and Subjectivity in *Antony and Cleopatra*' (*SEL* 33.343–6) sees the play as a critique of absolutism, and asks: 'What can the play tell us about the theatricality of power and the power of theatricality?'. Unfortunately, the piece promises rather more than it delivers.

Books Reviewed

Andrews, John, ed. *Romeo and Juliet: Critical Essays*. Garland. pp. 440. $45. ISBN 0 8120 4795 8.

Bassnett, Susan. *Shakespeare: The Elizabethan Plays*. Macmillan. pp. 184. hb £35, pb £10.99. ISBN 0 333 43782 9, 0 333 43850 7.

Bate, Jonathan. *Shakespeare and Ovid*. Clarendon. pp. 292. £35. ISBN 0 19 812954 8.

Beiner, G. *Shakespeare's Agonistic Comedy: Poetics, Analysis, Criticism*. FDUP. pp. 302. $44.50. ISBN 0 8386 3467 2.

Bradshaw, Graham. *Misrepresentations: Shakespeare and the Materialists*. CornUP. pp. 322. £13.50. ISBN 0 801 48129 5.

Brissenden, Alan, ed. *As You Like It*. OS. OUP. pp. 245. hb £35, pb £3.99. ISBN 0 19 812948 3, 0 19 281955 0.

British Academy. *The British Academy Shakespeare Lectures 1980–9*, ed. E. A. J. Honigmann. OUP. pp. 280. hb £35, pb £9.95. ISBN 0 19 726139 6, 0 19 726133 7.

Carlin, Patricia. *Shakespeare's Mortal Men: Overcoming Death in History, Comedy and Tragedy*. Lang. pp. 250. $44.95. ISBN 0 8204 1563 4.

Charney, Maurice. *All of Shakespeare*. ColUP. pp. 424. hb £20, pb £10.95. ISBN 0 231 06863 8, 0 231 06862 X.

Cohen, Derek. *Shakespeare's Culture of Violence*. Macmillan. pp. 178. £37. ISBN 0 333 57088 X.

——. *The Politics of Shakespeare*. Macmillan. pp. 192. £35. ISBN 0 333 59886 5.

Davidson, Clifford, Rand Johnson, and John H. Stroupe, eds. *Drama and the Classical Heritage: Comparative and Critical Essays*. AMS. pp. 299. £37.50. ISBN 0 404 64301 9.

Foakes, R. A. *Hamlet versus Lear: Cultural Politics and Shakespeare's Art*. CUP. pp. 264. £35. ISBN 0 521 34292 9.

Gay, Penny. *As She Likes It: Shakespeare's Unruly Women*. Routledge. pp. 208. £11.99. ISBN 0 415 09696 0.

Ghose, Zulfikar. *Shakespeare's Mortal Knowledge: A Reading of the Tragedies*. Macmillan. pp. 171. hb £37.50, pb £13.99. ISBN 0 333 57909 1, 0 333 57910 0.

Gibbons, Brian. *Shakespeare and Multiplicity*. CUP. pp. 248. £32.50. ISBN 0 521 4406 3.

Haley, David. *Shakespeare's Courtly Mirror: Reflexivity and Prudence in 'All's Well That Ends Well'*. UDelP. pp. 320. £38. ISBN 0 87413 443 9.

Halio, Jay L., ed. *The Merchant of Venice*. OS. OUP. pp. 241. hb £30, pb £3.99. ISBN 0 19 812925 4, 0 19 281454 0.

Hattaway, Michael, ed. *The Third Part of King Henry VI*. NCaS. CUP. pp. 231. hb £29.95, pb £5.25. ISBN 0 521 37331 X, 0 521 37705 6.

Hodgdon, Barbara. *Henry IV Part Two*. ManUP. pp. 157. £29. ISBN 0 7190 2751 9.

Holderness, Graham, and Bryan Loughrey, eds. *A Pleasant Conceited Historie, Called The Taming of a Shrew* (1992). HW. pp. 106. hb £25, pb £4.95. ISBN 0 7450 1103 9, 0 7450 1104 7.

——, eds. *The Tragicall Historie of Hamlet Prince of Denmarke* (1992). HW. pp. 136. hb £25, pb £4.95. ISBN 0 7450 1099 7, 0 7450 1100 4.

——, eds. *The Cronicle History of Henry the Fift* [...]. HW. pp. 122. hb £25, pb £4.95. ISBN 0 7450 1101 2, 0 7450 1102 0.

Honigmann, E. A., and Susan Brock. *Playhouse Wills, 1558–1642: An Edition of Wills by Shakespeare and His Contemporaries in the London Theatre*. ManUP. £45. ISBN 0 7190 3016 1.

Kennedy, Dennis. *Foreign Shakespeare: Contemporary Performance*. CUP. pp. 311. £35. ISBN 0 521 42025 3.

Kiernan, Victor. *Shakespeare, Poet and Citizen*. Routledge. pp. 300. £19.95. ISBN 0 86091 392 9.

Limon, Jerzy and Jay Halio, eds. *Shakespeare and His Contemporaries: Eastern and Central European Studies*. UDelP. pp. 269. £32.95. ISBN 0 87413 475 7.

Lupton, Julia Reinhard, and Kenneth Reinhard. *After Oedipus: Shakespeare in Psycho-Analysis*. CornUP. pp. 288. hb $37.50, pb $14.95. ISBN 0 8014 2407 0, 0 8014 9687 X.

Mack, Maynard. *Everybody's Shakespeare: Reflections Chiefly on the Tragedies*. UNebP. pp. 279. £25. ISBN 0 8032 3161 X.

Novy, Marianne, ed. *Cross-Cultural Performances: Differences in Women's Re-Visions of Shakespeare*. UIllP. pp. 274. hb $49.95, pb $18.95. ISBN 0 252 02017 0, 0 252 06323 6.

Rogers, Joyce. *The Second Best Bed: Shakespeare's Will in a New Light*. Greenwood. £40.50. ISBN 0 313 28831 3.

Ryan, Kiernan, ed. *King Lear New Casebook*. Macmillan. pp. 208. hb £35, pb £9.99. ISBN 0 333 55529 5, 0 333 55530 9.

Shaheen, Naseeb. *Biblical References in Shakespeare's Comedies*. UDelP. pp. 260. £30. ISBN 0 87413 457 9.

Shaughnessy, Robert. *Representing Shakespeare: England, History, and the RSC*. HW. pp. 222. £12.95. ISBN 0 7450 1560 3.

Skura, Meredith Anne. *Shakespeare the Actor and the Purposes of Playing*. UChicP. pp. 325. ISBN 0 226 76180 0.

Slights, Camille Wells. *Shakespeare's Comic Commonwealths*. UTorP. pp. 290. £28. ISBN 0 8020 2924 8.

Smidt, Kristian. *Unconformities in Shakespeare's Later Comedies*. Macmillan. pp. 239. £37.50. ISBN 0 333 58450 3.

Snyder, Susan, ed. *All's Well That Ends Well*. OS. OUP. pp. 245. hb £30, pb £3.99. ISBN 0 19 812931 9, 0 19 281459 1.

Sokol, B. J., ed. *The Undiscover'd Country: New Essays on Psychoanalysis and Shakespeare*. ColUP. pp. 272. pb $21. ISBN 1 85343 197 4.

Sorelius, Gunnar. *Shakespeare's Early Comedies: Myth, Metamorphosis, Mannerism*. MRTS. pp. 218. pb £21. ISBN 91 554 3133 X.

Taylor, Gary, and John Jowett. *Shakespeare Reshaped: 1606–1623*. OSS. Clarendon. pp. 333. £40. ISBN 0 19 812256 X.

Underwood, Richard Allan. *'The Two Noble Kinsmen' And Its Beginnings*. Mellen. pp. 208. ISBN 3 7052 0928 0.

Vickers, Brian. *Appropriating Shakespeare: Contemporary Critical Quarrels*. YaleUP. pp. 528. hb £35, pb £11.95. ISBN 0 300 06105 6.

Weis, René, ed. *King Lear: A Parallel Text Edition*. LAT. Longman. pp. 314. pb £12.99. ISBN 0 582 04052 3.

Wells, Charles. *The Wide Arch: Roman Values in Shakespeare*. BCP. pp. 200. £25. ISBN 1 85399 088 4.

Wiles, David. *Shakespeare's Almanac: 'A Midsummer Night's Dream', Marriage and the Elizabethan Calendar*. Brewer. pp. 256. £35. ISBN 0 85991 398 8.

Wilson, Richard. *Will Power: Essays on Shakespearean Authority*. Wheatsheaf. pp. 289. pb £12.95. ISBN 0 7450 0971 9.

Zitner, Sheldon P., ed. *Much Ado About Nothing*. OS. OUP. pp. 214. hb £27.50, pb £3.99. ISBN 0 19 812992 0, 0 19 282620 4.

VII

Renaissance Drama: Excluding Shakespeare

EMMA SMITH and STUART HAMPTON-REEVES

This chapter has the following sections: 1. General Criticism; 2. Theatre History; 3. Marlowe. Section 1 is by Emma Smith; sections 2 and 3 are by Stuart Hampton-Reeves.

1. General Criticism

A number of essays this year address themselves to civic pageantry and court masques, and most are concerned with the political interpretation of these dramatic forms. Raymond D. Tumblesdown reads the London triumphs as a narrative of, and contribution to, the city's increasing importance during the sixteenth and seventeenth centuries. In 'The Triumph of London: Lord Mayor's Day Pageants and the Rise of the City' (in *The Witness of Times: Manifestations of Ideology in Seventeenth Century England*, ed. Keller and Schiffhorst), he states that by 1701 symbolic Triumphs were redundant because London had triumphed, although he does not substantiate this neat assertion, and concentrates largely on Middleton. Tumblesdown sees in Middleton's civic pageants the potential for the city comedian's satire, and views Middleton's contribution to the civic genre as symbolic of the 'ideological posture' of the city. In his assessment of the mayoral pageants as a symbol of the city as an alternative locus of power, Tumblesdown coincides with David M. Bergeron, who, in his 'Pageants, Politics and Patrons' (*MRDE* 6.139–52) writes of their reinforcement of the image of the mayor as royal substitute. Bergeron traces the pageants' increasing emphasis on the office of the mayor, as well as their overlap with political discourse in other spheres, such as James's first address to the English Parliament. The civic entertainments offer 'a running political commentary' on events during the pre-civil war period. In his essay on the genre, James Knowles emphasizes its didactic rather than commentary purpose. He argues in 'The Spectacle of the Realm: Civic Consciousness, Rhetoric and Ritual in Early Modern London' (Mulryne and Shewring) for an analysis of civic pageantry which extends beyond mayoral inaugurations to other rituals of the ceremonial year. This gives a picture of civic ceremony as the representation of models of behaviour for both governor and governed in its image of potential social conflict integrated by and into ritual. Sergei Lobanov-Rostovsky's reading, '"The Triumphes of Golde": Economic Authority in the Jacobean Lord Mayor's Show' (*ELH* 60.879–98) also stresses the didactic, pointing out the use of Error's temptation of the mayor in Middleton's 1613 pageant, and arguing for the pageants as implicit critiques of the commercial ideology they purport to celebrate. This radical potential is a feature also of city comedy according to Catherine Gimelli Martin's 'Angels, Alchemists and Exchange: Commercial Ideology in Court and City Comedy, 1596–1610' (Keller and Schiffhorst).

Lobanov-Rostovsky describes the Lord Mayor's show as an 'artistic medium shaped by an explicitly political context', and two articles in Mulryne and Shewring's collection treat the court masque as a similar genre. Graham Parry's 'The Politics of the Jacobean Masque' discusses the masques' inscription of the power play between Prince Henry and the king. Parry argues that a masque like that of 1610 written for Henry, 'Barriers', utilizes the genre of Arthurian romance to present the young prince as the chivalric embodiment of ancient virtue and militant Protestantism. This strikes an oppositional note in contrast to the adulatory tones of the masques from the early years of James's reign, therefore, for a brief period, the masques seem to speak of an alternative centre of power at court. Martin Butler's reading of Caroline masques as 'part of the machinery of government' rather than its substitute in 'Reform or Reverence? The Politics of the Caroline Masque' (in Mulryne and Shewring) also sees the genre as a vehicle for criticism as well as compliment. He sees a limited space for criticism and debate in the masque literature before 1634, and traces a more defensive, vindicatory tone in masques after that date.

Butler warns the reader to be aware both of the ways in which masques make meaning and the circumstances in which meaning is made, and it is this context of performance which concerns Matthew H. Wikander in his *Princes to Act: Royal Audience and Royal Performance*. Wikander distinguishes between Elizabeth's performative style of royal audience and the more isolated and reticent presence of James. He draws some interesting comparisons between *A Midsummer Night's Dream*, a play explicitly concerned with playing before royalty, Leicester's Kenilworth entertainment and that of Thomas Churchyard in Norfolk. In the Jacobean plays of Beaumont and Fletcher, Wikander sees a growing scepticism about the genre of masque, and an ironic, even satirical self-consciousness about its conventions. A concern for the circumstances of court performance also informs William H. Sherman's essay on *Old Fortunatus*, in which he analyses the contradictory implications of the trope of gold in the play and in Elizabethan England ('"Gold is the Strength, the Sinnewes of the World": Thomas Dekker's *Old Fortunatus* and England's Golden Age', *MRDE* 6.85–102). Sherman sees these ambivalences compounded, rather than resolved, in the presentation to Elizabeth of Fortune's golden purse at the end of the play. Against these political readings of the genre, Judith Dundas's bid for the appreciation of the aesthetics of the masque as 'an art that is above all ornamental' is a lone voice ('"Those Beautiful Characters of Sense": Classical Deities and the Court Masque', Davidson et al.). Dundas employs the aesthetics of Renaissance paintings to recover a sense of the beauty located in classical mythology, but finds in Rubens's ceiling at Whitehall a greater aesthetic against which masques 'cannot compete'. The politics of the masque are dismissed as 'propagandistic motives' which are subordinate to the real seriousness of the genre, its aesthetics and 'the conscience of the artist'.

Character types have received some attention this year, much of it unsatisfactory. William R. Dynes's treatment of 'The Trickster-Figure in Jacobean City Comedy' (*SEL* 33.365–84) is a near-exception to this, seeing Subtle and his like as focusing attention on the paradoxical contemporary views which, while endorsing individual ambition within a framework of nascent capitalism, also expresses profound anxiety about social mobility and ostentation. Thus, these figures offer an opportunity to examine these social tensions. Dynes offers two types of trickster: the altruistic and the egocentric, both living on the outskirts of community and thus enjoying the possibility of self-creation rather than the constraints of conformity. The reading of Moll Frith as a trickster is less convincing, but the social context for this persistent character type is well drawn. Discussing another frequenter of the drama of the period, the friar, Paul Voss also tries to establish the context for this literary presentation, usefully pointing out that since Catholicism had been a capital crime since 1581, few people by the turn of the century could have remembered seeing an actual friar ('The Antifraternal Tradition in English Renaissance Drama', *Cithara* 33.3–16). Voss's historical context is homogenized, however, and his survey of the type seems determined to see in Shakespeare, as in no other writer, the possibility for the 'voices of the Catholic faithful to be heard'. Other dramatists present friars as lecherous or immoral; in Shakespeare the friar works for the common good of the community and turns *Much Ado About Nothing* from potential tragedy into festive comedy. Voss does not comment on the disguised-as-friar tradition, which is a pity, as *Measure for Measure* might have been an interesting play to discuss in this context.

James Keller takes the character of the malcontent as the focus of his study, *Princes, Soldiers and Rogues: The Politic Malcontent of Renaissance Drama*. He begins by reintroducing the distinction between the malcontent and the figure of the melancholiac with which the character has become virtually synonymous. The alienated malcontent character offers the playwright the chance to intercede in the cultural process and the audience the opportunity for vicarious resistance to social change. Keller accepts the need to historicize his useful typology of the different incarnations of the malcontent as the prince, soldier and rogue of his title, but this he attempts only superficially. The chapter which cites the example of Earl of Essex as a paradigm for the malcontent prince is particularly inadequate, relying heavily on Strachey's *Elizabeth and Essex* for evidence in apparent preference to more recent or historically sophisticated works. There is a touch of *1066 And All That* in, for example, his distinction between Elizabethan and Jacobean rule: 'Whereas Elizabeth had been able to maintain order during her reign, the social order began to break down under James I who was infamous for his depravity and shameful excesses'. Betty Travitsky's work on 'Child Murder in English Renaissance Life and Drama' (*MRDE* 6.63–84) offers a different angle on the question of the relationship between drama and society. Rather than beginning with a common stage character, she chooses the figure of neo-naticide (child murder), which while it is a preoccupation of non-dramatic literature in the period, is rarely dramatized. Indeed, it is this very absence which, for Travitsky, forces a reappraisal of domestic drama as one in which 'Renaissance life intersects with art'. Her conclusion, reached through a reading of seven plays from *Gorboduc* to Beaumont and Fletcher's *Tragedy of Thierry and Theodoret*, is that the portrayal of mothers in the drama is overwhelmingly negative. It is a static interpretation of female characters in the drama which belies her argument that such comparisons can clarify thinking about the 'changing roles of women'.

Images of women are the subject of a number of articles, two of them on Middleton and Dekker's *The Roaring Girl*. Raphael Seligmann's note traces 'A Probable Early Borrowing from Middleton and Dekker's *The Roaring Girl*' (*N&Q* 40.229–31) in Richard Braithwait's conduct guide of 1631, *The English Gentlewoman*, speculating that either Braithwait saw the play in performance or owned a copy of the 1611 quarto, or that both texts refer to the same, as yet unknown source. Anthony B. Dawson's essay on the play examines the unusually self-reflexive relationship between stage and auditorium, actor and spectator which is established by its epistle, prologue and epilogue ('Mistris Hic & Haec: Representations of Moll Frith', *SEL* 33.385–404). There is nothing new in his view of Moll as an ambivalent and transgressive figure, but his juxtaposition of the play with Nathan Field's *Amends for Ladies* is more informative about the oblique relationship between theatrical conventions such as cross-dressing, and social conflicts and behaviours. Cross-dressing is the subject of Jean E. Howard's article 'Crossdressing, the Theater and Gender Struggle in Early Modern England', reprinted in *Crossing the Stage* (ed. Lesley Ferris). Reviewed in *YWES* 69, this essay was memorably described as sounding like 'Subtle out-Facing Mammon': maybe this tone has become so prevalent in the intervening years as to make Howard's article seem less remarkable in this respect. She argues forcefully that pamphlet literature, sumptuary laws, court records and plays signal a 'sex-gender system under pressure', and that cross-dressing is a practice of cultural struggle and resistance. Maureen Quilligan has a less optimistic view of the possibilities of subverting this system, in 'Staging Gender: William Shakespeare and Elizabeth Cary' (*Sexuality and Gender in Early Modern Europe: Institutions, Texts, Images*, ed. James Grantham Turner). Reading Kate's final speech in *The Taming of the Shrew*, she sees the sexual control of woman as ensuring her 'verbal blankness', and contrasts this with the speech of the self-sacrificing wife in Elizabeth Cary's *Tragedie of Mariam*, who must also pay the price for breaking wifely silence within a play which is itself similarly transgressive.

The spectacle of the chattering woman is linked in Gail Kern Paster's *The Body Embarrassed* to other kinds of bodily incontinence. Paster's study is a finely scatological and humoral contribution to the post-Foucauldian history of the body. She argues that the female body is imaged as a leaky vessel in medical treatises, proverbs, and plays such as *Bartholomew Fair* and *A Chaste Maid in Cheapside*, and that these representations seek to regulate and regularize the subject's experience of her/his body. Paster does not refer to the duel by flatulence between Trimtram and Captain Albo in Middleton and Rowley's *A Fair Quarrel*, for which Swapan Chakravorty offers 'Medwall's *Fulgens and Lucres* as a Possible Source for Middleton and Rowley's *A Fair Quarrel*' (*N&Q* 40.214–15). Chakravorty also has a note on 'Middleton's Michaelmas Term, Inductio 13–19' (*Expl* 51.209–11) which unpicks a series of quibbles which juxtapose urban dissipation with the plainness of rural life. Other notes on Middleton include Rick Bowers on 'Middleton's *A Trick to Catch the Old One*' (*Expl* 51.211–14) which reads the play's coarse comic realism as close to the Morality tradition, R. V. Holdsworth's 'Notes on *Women Beware Women*' (*N&Q* 40.215–22) which gives detailed, linguistic notes on the play, and Douglas Bruster's '*The Changeling* and Thomas Watson's *Hecatompathia*' (*N&Q* 40.222–4) which registers the similarity of diction in the play's madhouse subplot and Watson's 1582 sonnet collection.

In Duncan Salkeld's book on *Madness and Drama in the Age of Shakespeare*, the madhouse in *The Changeling* marks the shift towards confinement as a response to madness. Salkeld reads madness as a powerful trope for 'the failures of sovereignty and reason to guarantee the meaning of the Renaissance world', and an opportunity for women to speak and resist masculine authority. In an issue of *TD* devoted to *Madness in Drama* and edited by James Redmond, Arthur L. Little's reading of *The Changeling* is also concerned with the relation between gender and madness. His epigraph from Luce Irigaray indicates the methodology of his 'Transshaped Women: Virginity and Hysteria in The Changeling' (*TD* 15.19–42), which interrogates the 'politics of corporeality' at work in the play. The madhouse represents the enclosure of the feminine by patriarchy, and at the virginity test the audience becomes the speculum probing Beatrice's private self. Little sees madness as the stripping away of subjectivity, and, writing in the same volume, Karin S. Coddon makes a similar point at greater length. In '*The Duchess of Malfi*: Tyranny and Spectacle in Jacobean Drama' (1–18), she contrasts the early Jacobean tragic subjects with the emblematic madman whose madness is exterior and theatrical, arguing that in Webster's play, madness is a metonym of the public and spectacular world that constantly intrudes upon the private and subjective.

For Salkeld and for Coddon, stage madness questions authority, as does incest in Richard A. McCabe's book, *Incest, Drama and Nature's Law 1550–1700*. McCabe explains how the prevalent analogy between family and state, father and king lends a political significance to representations of incest. He points out that the use of classical models in the drama should not be assumed to be reactionary, but rather that these offer an opportunity for potentially radical dissent, tracing how normative ideals of natural law are superseded during the period by Calvinism, scepticism, rationalism and empirical science. McCabe discusses incest as an index of social and political confusion, and it is in these terms that Douglas F. Rutledge views 'The Politics of Disguise: Drama and Political Theory in the Early Seventeenth Century' (Keller and Schiffhorst). The social chaos evoked at the passing of one monarch and settled by the accession of the next is important to an understanding of early seventeenth-century culture, and Bruster illustrates this thesis with a discussion of plays dating from around the accession date which include the spectacle of monarchs disguising or lowering themselves. He does not, however, explain how these instances of the 'ritual of status inversion and elevation' are different from those which occur at other moments such as Greene's *George a Greene* (*c.*1590). The politics of theatrical representation is Margot Heinemann's focus in her 'Drama and Opinion in the 1620s: Middleton and Massinger' (Mulryne and Shewring) which reads the works of these playwrights as articulating a new popular public opinion and a disrespect for hierarchy.

The Protestant plays of the Tudor period are the subject of Paul Whitfield White's *Theatre and Reformation: Protestantism, Patronage and Playing in Tudor England*. White challenges the received wisdom of antitheatrical Protestantism with an analysis of the ways in which Protestant authorities in Reformation England patronized the drama as a means of disseminating their political and religious ideals. This revisionist history reinstates the church as a significant site of dramatic performance, rather than as the antithesis of the theatre, and establishes playing, along with printing and preaching, as a key practice in shaping Protestant culture. The conflict between religion and magic in the Protestant dramaturgy of Bale is discussed in Kurt Tetzeli von Rosador's 'The Sacralizing Sign: Religion and Magic in Bale, Greene, and the Early Shakespeare' (*YES* 23.30–45), who sees the binary opposition of true religion and Catholic magic as undone by its theatrical representation. Two articles, 'Woman's Wit and Woman's Will in *When You See Me, You Know Me*' by Kim H. Noling (*SEL* 33.327–42) and Julia Gasper's 'The Reformation Plays on the Public Stage' (Mulryne and Shewring) deal with Jacobean dramatizations of early Tudor history. Noling sees Rowley's play as a source for Shakespeare's *Henry VIII*, although she views its female characterization as more challenging than those of the later play. Shakespeare's play implicitly endorses the use of queens as the means to male heirs, whereas Rowley combines feminine will and wit in his portrayal of Katherine Parr. Gasper's essay is concerned with the Tudor dramas of the period following Essex's rebellion as expressive of contemporary 'doubt, conflict and dilemma', over the continuing uncertainties of the Reformation and its impact on government.

Numerous short notes offer explanations of detailed points on the drama. In *N&Q* 40, Philip J. Finkelpearl proposes the Reverend Thomas Pestell for 'The Authorship of the Anonymous "Coleorton Masque" of 1618' (224–6), Duncan Salkeld traces a conscious allusion to the death of Absalon in the killing of Horatio in Kyd's *The Spanish Tragedy* ('Kyd's Absalon', 177), and Jameela Lares suggests that Webster's *Duchess of Malfi* may recollect Catherine of Valois, the widow of Henry V who married in secret a poor but noble Welshman whom she promoted to Clerk of her Wardrobe ('*The Duchess of Malfi* and *Catherine of Valois*', 208–11). Also on 'Webster's *The Duchess of Malfi* 2.1.1–21', David Carnegie and David Gunby gloss Castruchio's ambition to become an 'eminent courtier' as a reference to the legal profession, rather than one who frequents court (*Expl* 51.208–9).

Other miscellaneous pieces this year include Mark E. Bingham's 'The Multiple Plot in Fletcherian Tragi-comedies' (*SEL* 33.405–23) which argues that Fletcher uses the multiple plot to approach simultaneously the emotional intensity of tragedy and comedy's sense of containment. Carolyn Prager offers an interesting analysis of an Elizabethan playwright's reworking of a classical text in 'Heywood's Adaptation of Plautus' *Rudens*: The Problem of Slavery in *The Captives*' (Davidson et al.). She argues that Heywood's play is an intervention into early modern discourse on liberty and slavery, and thus presents a thoroughly contemporary modification of his source. Ton Hoenselaars's survey of 'Europe Staged in Renaissance Drama' (*YEuS* 6.85–112) is little more than a list of dramatic references to Europe. Assertions such as 'in all his comedies, Shakespeare transported his audience abroad' go unchallenged and unelaborated. Hoenselaars is not interested in how 'abroad' and 'home' are constructed in the drama, nor in investigating the easy parallel he draws between the representation of the world in Ortelius's *Theatrum Orbis Terrarum* and on the stage of the Globe theatre. Despite some fascinating illustrations, including the 1598 depiction of 'Elizabeth I as Europe', Hoenselaars's discussion of gendered representations is disappointingly unsophisticated. Also concerned with Anglo-European relations is Kenneth Richards, whose 'Elizabethan Perceptions of the *Commedia dell'Arte*' (in *Cultural Exchange Between European Nations During the Renaissance*, ed. Sorelius and Srigley) concludes that while Italian drama found limited favour at court, English dramatists were either hostile to, or apparently ignorant of, its methods and conventions.

In conclusion, there has been a rather nervous approach to questions of methodology in some of the general books on the drama this year. J. R. Mulryne's tentative introduction to the volume of essays edited with Margaret Shewring, *Theatre and Government Under the Early Stuarts*, seems to exemplify this uncertainty and lack of commitment. Mulryne's cautious response to the 'new scholarship' and the vagueness of his claim that these ostensibly 'non-theoretical' essays 'assume in their methods and their interests many of the conclusions of recent theory' mark the uncertainties of the study of Renaissance drama at this juncture. Despite the book's interdisciplinary title, only one of the ten essays, Simon Adams's 'Early Stuart Politics: Revisionism and After' is from an historian. While Adams's contribution is an interesting historiographical survey, it is strangely out of place in the volume, pointing to the lack of discussion between disciplines whilst nodding towards a symbiotic future 'collaboration of historical and literary scholarship'. Kathleen McLuskie's 'Politics and Dramatic Form in Early Modern Tragedy' is hesitant and inconclusive in its questioning of the 'availability' of seventeenth-century plays as a locus for political criticism, and as a whole the volume seems to lack direction.

Elsewhere, other approaches also end in uncertainty. T. V. N. Merriam's 'Marlowe's Hand in *Edward III*' (*L&LC* 8.59–72) applies computerized stylometric analysis to the play. Three sides of text and eleven of tables and graphs later, Merriam concludes that Marlovian authorship of the first two scenes of Act III 'is not beyond the bounds of literary credibility'. M. W. A. Smith's use of Principle Component Analysis on the problem of authorship of '*Edmund Ironside*' (*N&Q* 40.202–5) concludes negatively – it is not a Shakespeare play, but does not offer an alternative attribution. Sara Jayne Steen's book on Middleton seems to state a clear methodology in its subtitle, *Ambrosia in an Earthen Vessel: Three Centuries of Audience and Reader Response to the Works of Thomas Middleton*, but her introduction begs certain questions about the way that her information is edited for her readers. Reading the selection, it is striking how little Middleton's reputation has changed: his work is predictably compared with Shakespeare, favourably by his supporters and unfavourably by his detractors. The title quotation, taken from an 1886 review of Middleton's work which fears that the ambrosia of his poetic genius may be tainted by the earthen vessel of his coarse expression, is strangely apt for the volume. Steen's contribution to the centuries of reader and audience response is to choose which responses are most 'useful', but this editorial function is mystified by the claim to objectivity in this 'reference volume'.

If only everything in this year's work in Renaissance drama studies were as knowable as the fine empiricism of David Carnegie, whose note 'Webster's *The White Devil* 4.2.170–1' (*Expl* 52.18–19) decisively clears up the matter of Webster's command of ferret-lore, expressing in a footnote its author's thanks to 'friends who grew up in the working-class north of England'.

2.   Theatre History

The story of Peter Street, Carpenter and Freeman of London, is really the story of the late Elizabethan theatre; he grew up in Coleman Street, where two other theatre families, the Braynes and the Burbages, lived close by, and he may have been involved with the building of The Theatre in 1576. In 'Peter Street, 1553–

1609: Builder of Playhouses' (*ShS* 45.101–14), Mary Edmond takes us sensitively through the many documents that relate to Street, beginning with his father's fortuitous stumble into the records of John Foxe and ending with Street's death just a few weeks before the reopening of the Blackfriars playhouse. One of Street's buildings, the Fortune playhouse (which he built for Henslowe in 1600), was explicitly based on the Globe; this has attracted the attention of John Orrell, the principal historical adviser on the rebuilding of the Globe. In his article 'Building the Fortune' (*SQ* 44.127–44), Orrell studies the Fortune accounts (including an entertainments account for Henslowe's lunches with Street) in order to reconstruct the narrative of its construction, from which we learn that Peter Street completed the whole building in less time than his modern imitators have taken to raise one section. There is a lesson here, although I'm not sure what it is.

John Orrell's article is the first of six consecutive essays in *SQ* 44 (125–227) devoted to Elizabethan theatre. In her introduction, editor Barbara Mowat points to a new vigour in our field, which has its origins in the archaeological discoveries of 1989 and the establishment of the Globe centre. This is certainly true, although Mowat overlooks the additional (and perhaps more important) momentum being developed by researchers of provincial playing. Their work is represented in this volume by Sally-Beth MacLean; her contribution 'The Politics of Patronage: Dramatic Records of Dudley's Household Books' (*SQ* 44.175–82) analyses the accounts of the Earl of Leicester and observes that Leicester's Men took Dudley's name all across the country in return for his patronage, at a time when he was looking for popularity and further influence through local appointments. Back in London, S. P. Cerasano's 'Philip Henslowe, Simon Forman and the Theatrical Community of the 1590s' (*SQ* 44.145–58) looks into the murky world of the occult and its relationship to theatre practitioners, especially Philip Henslowe, who paid two visits to the famous astrologer Simon Forman. On looking at Forman's casebooks, Cerasano ventures some thoughts about *Doctor Faustus*, and proposes 1555/6 as the year of Henslowe's birth, based on Henslowe's own report to the astrologer. This last point is worth noting, although a glance at the court cases detailed by William Ingram in *The Business of Playing* (see review below) shows that Henslowe's contemporaries were not always reliable – or even consistent – witnesses of their own age. In 'Three Reluctant Patrons and Early Shakespeare' (*SQ* 44.159–74) Andrew Gurr asks why Carey and Herbert (until the early 1590s) 'spent a lot of their time not becoming patrons of major London playing companies'. The litigious squabbles over the Theatre are rehearsed again by Herbert Berry, who makes an intriguing leap to *The Merchant of Venice* in his article 'Shylock, Robert Miles, and Events at the Theatre' (*SQ* 44.183–201); and James P. Lusardi offers us an exercise in 'graphical archaeology' in his engaging paper, 'The Pictured Playhouse: Reading the Utrecht Engraving of Shakespeare's London' (*SQ* 44.202–27). These articles are all fine in themselves but they do not complement each other in any special or revealing way.

I turn now to two studies of the business practices of the first London theatres, beginning with James H. Forse's *Art Imitates Business: Commercial and Political Influences in Elizabethan Theatre*. Forse is not a literary man but a historian; he combines the academic rigour of his profession with the naiveté of an amateur enthusiast. I will be kind and overlook the more fanciful chapters of this book, where Will Kempe is an industrial spy and Shakespeare is his own leading lady. Forse's central thesis is that the Elizabethan theatre was an institution where capitalism and art walked hand in hand, where Burbage and his fellow sharers (especially Shakespeare) made every effort to exploit a public hungry for entertainment and diversion. This is not an original point, of course, and there is some truth in it, but Forse's argument is undermined by an unhistorical use of the word 'business', which transports modern concepts of business and economics back into the Early Modern period. In William Ingram's superior study *The Business of Playing: The Beginnings of the Adult Professional Theater in Elizabethan London*, the familiar world of the 1570s is turned on its head; Ingram argues that it was a flourishing time for playing companies and playgoers, rich and varied in its range of material and styles of playing, until successive attempts to restrict city playing and the fatal political manoeuvring of the aldermen drove them into the regulated world of the playhouse. The key document in this book is the Act of the Court of Common Council of 6th December 1574, in which the sponsors of performances (that is, the innkeepers) were required to obtain a civic licence. The conditions of the licence included a rigorous assessment and a variable fee. No wonder, then, that innkeepers became reluctant to sponsor plays, forcing the playing companies to buy their own venues.

The business of the player is contrasted, perhaps ironically, with the business of the historian. Ingram devotes nearly a quarter of his book to a discussion of how historical research should proceed and in one sense the rest of his book is a case study for his theoretical gambit. This gives the book a highly original structure which attends to the gaps and the inconsistencies of history, putting them on display rather than trying to explain them away. Andrew Gurr, in his essay 'The Chimera of Amalgamation' (*TRI* 18.85–93), has a similar agenda, which he calls (rather innocently) 'the kaleidoscope principle' (where one sees different patterns by rearranging the same pieces). The essay focuses on the fashion for large-cast plays which began in the late 1580s and ended abruptly in 1594. Gurr argues that we cannot simply summon from the ether an amalgamated company capable of meeting their requirements to account for this historical peculiarity. In a cogent analysis, Gurr demolishes this 'chimera' (originally a hypothesis proposed by E. K. Chambers) but he does not seek to replace it with a chimera of his own.

Brayne, Burbage and Street are certainly no strangers to the academy this year, as they appear yet again, this time in their own words, in E. A. J. Honigmann and Susan Brock's *Playhouse Wills 1558–1642: An Edition of Wills by Shakespeare and his Contemporaries in the London Theatre*. Together with 70 or so wills that will be familiar to seasoned scholars, the editors have uncovered another 30 wills that will be new to the theatre historian. The range is extensive, including the wills of actors, playwrights, theatre builders, managers and widows of theatre practitioners. I have no doubt that this volume will prove to be an invaluable tool for the Elizabethan theatre researcher. However, it is not recommended bedtime reading; the wills are written to a strict legal formula and demand to be read carefully and knowledgeably. The editors' introduction goes some way towards unlocking the technical mysteries of the legal document, but their decision to eschew editorial commentary of the individual wills may alienate some students. It may be that Susan Brock and E. A. J. Honigmann are hoping for a second bite of the cherry with a companion volume. Let's hope so.

In 'Direct Evidence, Audience Response and *Twelfth Night*: The Case of John Manningham of the Middle Temple' (*ShakS* 21.109–54), Henk K. Gras turns our attention to John Manningham's diary and its rare account of a performance of *Twelfth Night*. Manningham's famous comments on *Twelfth Night* are (and always will be) more tantalizing than they are informative; to his great credit, Gras squeezes every last drop of significance out of them. By comparing Manningham's review with the rest of his diary, Gras maps the 'mind-set' of a 'typical' *Twelfth Night* spectator, with some valuable insights for students of Manningham and Shakespeare. Phillip Ronald Stormer takes a wider view of audiences in 'Development and Influence of Tragicomedy During the Early Stuart Period' (*RORD* 32.101–20). In this essay, the change in audiences' dramatic tastes from the 1590s to 1642 is traced through a collection of statistics designed to chart the rise of tragicomedy in the seventeenth century and the concurrent demise of the genres it supplanted. Stormer's figures suggest that the demands of the private theatres and the court increasingly dominated new writing in the early Stuart theatre. I wonder how Gras would describe the mind-set of an audience which develops a taste for tragi-comedy just before the revolutionary years of the Civil War?

Mark Eccles's essential, annual series draws to a conclusion with 'Elizabethan Actors IV: S to End' (*N&Q* 39.165–76). Among the lives documented by Eccles are James Sands, Jerome Savage, John Shanke, John Sincler, Martin Slater, Richard Tarlton and the interestingly named Eyllaerdt Swanston. Strangely, one actor, William Shakespeare, is left off the list. All of Mark Eccles's actors are men but, as Sandra Richards reminds us in *The Rise of the English Actress*, there were also women players in the sixteenth century. In Richards's narrative, these players are an historical oddity, disconnected from the tradition of the English Actress. In his article 'Women and Mimesis in Medieval and Renaissance Somerset' (*CompD* 27.176–96), James Stokes refutes this premise and makes the claim that there is a clear, historical continuity between the medieval and early modern actresses and the restoration theatre. Stokes is adamant that we should not overlook the large number of records of women's involvement in the theatres, especially (but not only) in provincial, local affairs, as itinerant players, dancers, travelling musicians, balladeers and patrons.

In *Theatre and Reformation: Protestantism, Patronage and Playing in Tudor England,* it is Paul Whitfield White's thesis that the early Protestant authorities were actively involved in the theatre rather than opposed to it, as patrons, players and audiences. White is right to maintain that there is a traditional reluctance to admit to this curiously symbiotic situation between the two institutions of religious reform and playing, especially considering the extent to which later Puritanism tried to sabotage the theatre tradition. But he is wrong to overstate the case as an unshakeable orthodoxy – by which I mean that White's book is engaging and valuable but not as startlingly original as its dust-jacket triumphantly proclaims. White presents a clever analysis of the political and religious pressures on the reformation theatre, which has the Catholic interludes being appropriated by the new Protestant régime and put to work on a paradoxically anti-theatrical project. John Bale's *King Johan* emerges as a treatise against the empty truths of spectacle, which White reads as a critique of the Catholic reliance on ceremony and ritual. By encouraging a distrust of things seen, Bale helped to establish an idea of theatre as illusion rather than truth. Later chapters deal intelligently with education and youth plays and there is a welcome (although too brief) discussion of the church as a playing place. The post-reformation theatre is also considered by Jeffrey Knapp in his article 'Preachers and Players in Shakespeare's England' (*Rep* 44.29–59). Knapp wonders if the players were really antithetical to religion and the church, or were actually better at preaching good values. The preachers, in this account, are deeply anxious because they are losing their audience to a rival form of spiritual entertainment. 'Elizabethans', he writes, 'were capable of regarding the theatre as a spiritually valuable institution.' Stop sniggering at the back.

Finally, Graham C. Adams claims to have found an English playhouse in Kassel, Germany. *The Ottoneum Theatre: An English Survivor from Seventeenth Century Germany* is a worthy collection of documents relating to this odd playhouse, which was built at the beginning of the seventeenth century. It was used until around 1613 by a touring troupe of English players and is still standing today. In his introduction, Adams makes the claim that the Ottoneum Theatre was not only built for English players, but built by them, although later on Adams wavers, not sure whether this really is an English playhouse or an international hybrid. Could this be one of those chimeras that Andrew Gurr warned us about?

3. Marlowe

1993 may not be a vintage year for Marlovian scholars, but there is some excitement in the form of a new series of the plays from ManUP which was launched this year with a parallel text edition of *Doctor Faustus*, edited by Eric Rasmussen and David Bevington. Eric Rasmussen has also written a companion volume in which he reflects upon his editorial adventures. *A Textual Companion to Doctor Faustus* wades ambitiously into the bibliographical problems that the two texts of the play present and demonstrates (convincingly in my view) that the A-text was set in type from the manuscript whilst the B-text represents a post-performance revision of the text. Rasmussen picks over the bones of Greg's assertion that the A-text is a 'memorial' reconstruction and comes to the conclusion that the A-text is in fact an authoritative rendering of Marlowe's play. The methods that Rasmussen uses are clear and effective, his arguments are thorough and hard to refute for the most part; but even so, it is interesting that when the B-text was generally favoured, arguments for its authenticity were found, and now that the A-text has a wider currency, Rasmussen emerges to slay the ghost of memorial reconstruction and give bibliographical credence to our critical tastes.

Emily C. Bartels's first book *Spectacles of Strangeness: Imperialism, Aliena-tion, and Marlowe*, together with her articles 'Marlowe, Shakespeare and the Revision of Stereotypes' (*RORD* 32.13–26) and 'The Double Vision of the East: Imperialist Self-Construction in *Tamburlaine Part One*' (*RenD* 23.3–24), presents a competent modern re-reading of Marlowe's works. In Bartels's version of the Marlovian world, Marlowe exploits and challenges his society's fascina-tion with the strange, the alien and the exotic by examining the stereotypes of alien figures and the way they have been constructed to underwrite an emerging imperialist ideology. Bartels proceeds to look at all of Marlowe's dramatic work (except for *The Massacre at Paris*, which is conspicuously ignored) dividing the plays into works which deal with external aliens or the outer 'others' (represented by the Turks, the Jews and the Africans), and internal 'others' (the magician and the sodomite). All of these are placed on the wrong side of a self/other axis, where an Elizabethan audience self-fashions a cultural identity and an imperial destiny through the theatrical demonization of the 'other'. A similar argument is more skilfully developed by Margo Hendricks; in her article 'Managing the Barbarian:

The Tragedy of Dido, Queen of Carthage' (*RenD* 23.165–88), Marlowe is impli-cated in the ideology of imperialism that he attempts to subvert. The principal source of anxiety about England's place in the world in the late sixteenth century was the threat from Spain, a threat that was simultaneously territorial and ideological, in the sense that Spain, the imperial power of the age, thwarted the 'imperial aims' of English ideology. With no glorious imperial present to defend themselves with, the English were compelled to look back into their past. *Dido*, Hendricks reminds us, is about England's past: the legend of Aeneas, through the founding myth of Brutus, recuperates an imperial destiny for the English nation and affirms the superiority of its lineage over that of Spain. Marlowe is shown deconstructing this new-found 'Englishness' at the very moment that it is being established, by examining the media and the mechanisms of its invention and upsetting the logic of its ideology, which depends on a fixed notion of gender and race. Thus Aeneas is read as a man who is clothed in femininity when he is blinded by exotic desire and has to recover his lost masculinity through imperial conquest; Dido's 'independence, power and desirability, as well as her African femaleness' make her a threat to Aeneas.

The subversive, enigmatic Christopher Marlowe of Bartels and Hendricks appears in three further studies this year. Dena Goldberg's ' "Whose God's on First?": Special Providence in the Plays of Christopher Marlowe' (*ELH* 60.569–88) sets out to uncover the devices that Marlowe used to circumvent censorship and undermine the ideology of special providence, a theme which Goldberg believes is central to the Marlovian project. This essay relies on a modern totalizing concept of censorship which radically misunderstands the function and the politics of the Master of the Revels. In 'Cultures of Surveillance: Marlowe in the 1950s' (*RORD* 32.27–44), Curtis Breight turns a sceptical eye on the tradition that Marlowe was a spy, a tradition which takes the gaps in Marlowe's biography and eroticizes them (and his works) with an espionage fantasy. Breight deftly dismantles the idea of a patriotic Marlowe heroically working to uphold his nation's interests, and replaces it with the counter-myth of a double agent shaking the structures of Elizabethan society. The doubts raised in this paper about Marlowe's true status as a spy are fair enough, although Breight might find many of his questions already answered by Charles Nicholl's *The Reckoning* (*YWES* 73.222). Karl H. Kregor's 'Doubled Roles in English Renaissance Drama: Prob-lems, Possibilities and Marlowe's *Edward II*' (*THStud* 13.149–62) argues that Gaveston and Lightborn should be played by the same actor, so that Edward's lover becomes Edward's executioner. This is a fine and intelligent reading that plays ironically with the issues of sodomy, Edward's death and the repressed anger that links the homosexual lover and the hired killer. The only thing I am not sure about is the number of statistics employed by Kregor to 'prove' his reading of *Edward II*, that this doubling pattern is an implicit and integral part of the play, and a trace of its original staging. I believe that in this case the critic doth protest too much.

N&Q (39) published four short pieces on Marlowe this year. In ' "This Blessed Sight": Marlowe's *Doctor Faustus* and the Conventions of the *Icones Illustrium*' (39.154–7), John Manning resorts to a study of Guillaume Rouille's *Prontuario de le Medaglie de piu illustri, e fulgenti huomini e donne* (a sixteenth-century *Icones Illustrium*) in order to rid us of 'an inappropriate petty and narrow morality' which reads Faustus's conjuring of simulacra of the famous as sympto-matic of his irredeemable depravity. In 'Christopher Marlowe's *The Jew of Malta* and Two Newsletter Accounts of the Siege of Malta (1565)' (39.157–60), Michael G. Brennan draws our attention to a recent reconstruction from various fragments of a 1566 newsletter which may have been one of the sources for *The Jew of Malta*. Neglected source material is also the concern of Maureen Godman in her note 'Stow's *Summarie*: Source for Marlowe's *Edward II*' (39.160–3). Although the *Summarie* would not have given Marlowe any information that was not also in the recognized sources, Godman argues that it 'provided Marlowe with a concise, suggestive map' for his play. 'Early Responses to *Tamburlaine*' (*N&Q* 39.176–7) is a brief note by Richard Levin, who agrees with David Womersley that a number of references to Tamburlaine in the 1590s probably used Marlowe's two plays as the most available source.

In his study 'Marlowe's Cambridge Years and the Writing of *Doctor Faustus*' (*SEL* 33.249–64), G. M. Pinciss shows how the doctrinal debates raging in Cambridge during Marlowe's undergraduate years informed the structure of *Doctor Faustus* and the ambiguity of its ending. The nature of free will, Pinciss tells us, was a key battleground between the Anglicans and the more passionate Calvinists, who gained a solid grip on the university in the later parts of the sixteenth century. The question of Faustus's possible salvation can be translated into an unresolved conflict between a Calvinist universe (where Faustus's damnation is predestined) and an anti-Calvinist universe (where Faustus's damnation is a consequence of his own actions). Marlowe's failure to provide an answer is particularly problematic: perhaps, Pinciss suggests tentatively, Marlowe wanted to avoid being embroiled in religious debate. I am slightly worried by this argument; if Marlowe wanted to avoid religious controversy, why did he write this play? Finally, A. D. Wraight's overlong book *Christopher Marlowe and Edward Alleyn* is an undistinguished addition to the lists of amateur literary scholarship and has little to offer to the serious student.

Books Reviewed

Adams, Graham C. *The Ottoneum Theater: An English Survivor from Seventeenth Century Germany*. AMS. pp. 93. $39.50. ISBN 0 404 62332 8.

Bartels, Emily C. *Spectacles of Strangeness: Imperialism, Alienation, and Marlowe*. PSUP. pp. 221. £28.50. ISBN 0 8122 3193 7.

Bevington, David, and Eric Rasmussen, eds. *Doctor Faustus, by Christopher Marlowe*. Revels. ManUP. pp. 298. pb £8.95. ISBN 0 7190 1554 5.

Davidson, Clifford, Rand Johnson, and John H. Stroupe. *Drama and the Classical Heritage: Comparative and Critical Essays*. AMS Ancient and Classical Studies 1. AMS. pp. 299. $47.50. ISBN 0 404 64301 9.

Ferris, Lesley, ed. *Crossing the Stage: Controversies on Crossdressing*. Routledge. pp. 198. pb £10.99. ISBN 0 415 06269 1.

Forse, James H. *Art Imitates Business: Commercial and Political Influences in Elizabethan Theatre*. BGUP. pp. 298. hb $39.95, pb $15.95. ISBN 0 87972 594 X, 0 87972 595 8.

Honigmann, E. A. J., and Susan Brock. *Playhouse Wills 1558–1642: An Edition of Wills by Shakespeare and His Contemporaries in the London Theatre*. RevelsCL. ManUP. pp. 273. £40. ISBN 0 7190 3016 1.

Ingram, William. *The Business of Playing: The Beginnings of the Adult Professional Theater in Elizabethan London*. CornUP (1992). pp. 255. $38.50. ISBN 0 8014 2671 5.

Keller, James R. *Princes, Soldiers and Rogues: The Politic Malcontent of Renaissance Drama.* American University Studies Series IV, English Language and Literature vol. 153. Lang. pp. 185. £25. ISBN 0 8024 1972 9.

Keller, Katherine Z., and Gerald J. Schiffhorst. *The Witness of Times: Manifestations of Ideology in Seventeenth Century England.* Studies Language and Literature Series 15. Duquesne. pp. 308. $44.95. ISBN 0 8027 0252 8.

McCabe, Richard A. *Incest, Drama and Nature's Law 1550–1700.* CUP. pp. 362. £35. ISBN 0 521 43173 5.

Mulryne, J. R., and Margaret Shewring, eds. *Theatre and Government Under the Early Stuarts.* CUP. pp. 271. £35. ISBN 0 521 40159 3.

Paster, Gail Kern. *The Body Embarrassed: Drama and the Disciplines of Shame in Early Modern England.* CornUP. pp. 285. £12.50. ISBN 0 8014 8060 4.

Rasmussen, Eric. *A Textual Companion to Doctor Faustus.* RevelsCL. ManUP. pp. 114. £35. ISBN 0 7190 1562 6.

Richards, Sandra. *The Rise of the English Actress.* Macmillan. pp. 305. £40. ISBN 0 333 45601 7.

Salkeld, Duncan. *Madness and Drama in the Age of Shakespeare.* ManUP. pp. 168. £35. ISBN 0 7190 3787 5.

Sorelius, Gunnar, and Michael Srigley. *Cultural Exchange Between European Nations During the Renaissance.* Studia Anglistica Upsaliensia 86. AUP. pp. 244. SEK200. ISBN 91 554 3316 2.

Steen, Sara Jayne. *Ambrosia in an Earthen Vessel: Three Centuries of Audience and Reader Response to the Works of Thomas Middleton.* Studies in the Renaissance 31. AMS. pp. 240. $45. ISBN 0 404 62331 X.

Turner, James Grantham, ed. *Sexuality and Gender in Early Modern Europe: Institutions, Texts, Images.* CUP. pp. 345. £12.95. ISBN 0 521 44605 8.

White, Paul Whitfield. *Theatre and Reformation: Protestantism, Patronage and Playing in Tudor England.* CUP. pp. 268. £40. ISBN 0 521 41817 8.

Wikander, Matthew H. *Princes to Act: Royal Audience and Royal Performance 1578–1792.* JHUP. pp. 348. £40.50. ISBN 0 8018 4428 2.

Wraight, A. D., *Christopher Marlowe and Edward Alleyn.* Adam Hart. pp. 503. £20. ISBN 1 897763 00 X.

VIII

The Earlier Seventeenth Century: Excluding Drama

MELANIE HANSEN

This chapter has three sections: 1. General; 2. Poetry; 3. Prose.

1. General

There have been four major studies of women writers in the Renaissance published this year, comprising two collections of essays and two book-length studies of a range of women writers. The collection of essays *A History of Women in the West: Renaissance and Enlightenment Paradoxes*, ed. Natalie Zemon Davis and Arlette Farge, is the third volume in a series to illuminate women's voices and lives in Early Modern Europe. The aim of the collection is to counter the standard myth of women's 'invariable oppression', to testify instead to 'a shifting zone in which women found and used a multitude of strategies outside the roles of inevitable victims or exceptional heroines to make themselves active agents in history'. Focusing on the historical problems of gender difference and the 'shifting forms of male–female tension', the essays explore the lives of women from a diversity of social and economic backgrounds and concentrate on issues such as women, work and the family, the female (and the 'beautiful') body, daughters, virgins and mothers, women in politics, literature, theatre, philosophy, science and medicine; the volume also includes much needed critical and historical enquiry into women journalists, witches, prostitutes, criminals and protesters.

In *Sexuality and Gender in Early Modern Europe: Institutions, Texts, Images* edited by James Grantham Turner, the essays are interdisciplinary in focus and centre on the historicity of sex and gender, the conflict of violence and idealization, and the connection between the punitive and the normative. Collectively, the essays seek to 'transform the bodily realm (reproductive or seductive) into figures of larger significance for the practice of art, for the maintenance of masculine identity at court, or for the institutional treatment of women' and all explore the 'reciprocal constitution of institutions and representations, whether image or text'. The essays are diverse in content and include the discussion of Shakespeare, Donne, Cary, Milton and seventeenth-century women's fiction. Margaret J. M. Ezell's *Writing Women's Literary History* presents an immensely erudite and important re-evaluation of our critical approach to the recent 'discovery' of women writers of the Early Modern period. In this challenging and thought-provoking study, Ezell questions the theoretical model of women's literary history and the construction of women's literary studies as a field, and seeks instead to 'historicize' self-consciously and to 'gender' history. Her provocative and polemical study considers the present status of women's literary history, explores the formation of a canon of women's writing in twentieth-century anthologies, examines the tradition behind the twentieth century's historiography and analyses the eighteenth- and nineteenth-century anthologies, which have had a considerable influence upon twentieth-century assumptions regarding women's writing of this period, and concludes with a 'call for re-visioning of critical assumptions in a case study of a particular group of early women writers lost to us at the present time in current models of women's literary history, the Quaker women writing between 1650 and 1672'. In this final chapter of what will undoubtedly become a central text for Renaissance women's studies, Ezell argues that 'existing assumptions about modes of literary production and about historiography can be recovered by a re-visioning of the literary past'. Barbara Kiefer Lewalski's *Writing Women in Jacobean England* examines the work of nine women writers of the Renaissance period, Queen Anne, Princess Elizabeth, Arabella Stuart, the Countess of Bedford, Anne Clifford, Rachel Speght, Elizabeth Cary, Aemilia Lanyer and Mary Wroth in their cultural and literary context and illuminates the way in which they conceptualized the self, gender role, womankind, and their own writing. Throughout this study, Lewalski identifies the way in which these writers individually constructed themselves as writers according to class status and access to patronage and, collectively, the way in which they challenged the patriarchal construct of women as 'chaste, silent and obedient'. Finally, in 'Writing and Reaction: Seventeenth-century Sectarian Englishwomen's Struggle for Authorship' (Institute for Advanced Research in the Humanities, University of Birmingham, Occasional Paper No. 71), Hilary Hinds examines the conjunction and relationship between two related phenomena: the increased number of women's published texts, and the hostility of reaction that they received from men. Through her analysis of the various forms of sectarian writing, 'public' and 'political' texts, 'personal' and 'spiritual', Hinds offers 'explanations for this hostility of response by exploring the challenges offered by the so-called "private texts" and by assessing any common ground between these generically disparate writings' and concludes with a discussion of the limitations of the public/private distinction in relation to these writings.

The collection of essays, *The Art of the Emblem: Essays in Honour of Karl Josef Höltgen* edited by Michael Bath, John Manning and Alan R. Young arises out of the acknowledgement that Höltgen has 'done much to legitimize and de-marginalize the study of an art form, prominent in the Renaissance and Baroque periods, but largely neglected by modern literary students until relatively recently'. These essays are primarily concerned with English manifestations of the art of the emblem and they include examination of the work of Geoffrey Whitney, Henry Peacham, Marcus Gheeraerts, Francis Quarles, John Hall, Christopher Harvey, Andrea Alciator and George Wither. In 'The Early Stuart Epicure' (*ELR* 32.170–200) Reid Barbour traces the way in which Epicureanism challenged the concepts of sovereignty, divinity and freedom in early Stuart culture. Identifying the complexity of positions available within Stuart culture, Barbour considers the political currency of atomism and pleasure for the early Stuart court, and their religious import for Archbishop Laud's church and its enemies, and his discussion of Robert Burton's *Anatomy* illustrates how this text included conflicting values and ramifications of Epicureanism in the Stuart search for true liberty. The many forms of analogy that existed between the governments of the Household and the State in Early Modern culture is the subject of Constance Jordan's 'The Household and the State: Transformations in the Representation of an Analogy from Aristotle to James I' (*MLQ* 54.307–26). Jordan argues convincingly that whilst the analogy held a great deal of attraction for James I in justifying his paternal role, its implementation invariably elided consideration of his marital role, and reveals the pressures to which the idea of popular representation was subject in the Early Modern period, particularly as determined and problematized by reference to actual marriage practices and notions of womankind. Curtis Perry seeks to counter the oversimplification of critical response to laudatory accounts of Elizabeth as indicative of an unambiguous dissatisfaction with Jacobean failures of government in 'The Citizen Politics of Nostalgia: Queen Elizabeth in Early Jacobean London' (*JMRS* 23.89–111). Examining the various accounts of Elizabeth produced by and for the citizen classes of London during the first decade of James's reign, Perry demonstrates that accounts of Elizabeth were far from univocally critical of James, that localized economic, political and aesthetic interests inform the various Jacobean appropriations of Elizabeth and finally, that the social implications of Jacobean images of Elizabeth changed and developed over time. Raymond A. Anselment's ' "The Tears of Nature": Seventeenth-century Parental Bereavement' (*MP* 91.26–53) continues the refutation of Laurence's thesis on parental responses to infant mortality. In his analysis of diaries, autobiographies and elegiac poems, Anselment confirms the very real distress experienced by both mothers and fathers at the loss of their children.

Christopher Hill's lucid and informative *The English Bible and the Seventeenth-Century Revolution* constitutes a welcome exploration of the impact and function of the Bible in the lives of men and women during 'England's revolutionary seventeenth-century'. In considering the religious and political ends to which the Bible was put, its effect on economics, literature and social life, Hill examines the part that the Bible played in the emergence of an English nationalism, in the assertion of the supremacy of the vernacular, in its appropriation by Catholics and Protestants, radicals and conservatives, and in its centrality to intellectual and moral life, arts, sciences and literature; this erudite study will undoubtedly become a key text for any student of seventeenth-century politics, religion and literature. Confirming the significance of the Bible for English Renaissance literary studies is John R. Knott's *Discourses of Martyrdom in English Literature 1563–1694,* a fascinating and insightful analysis of the way in which Protestant writers endeavoured to create a drama of suffering that was profoundly influenced by stories in the Bible, accounts of the primitive church and Foxe's *Acts and Monuments*, all of which were used to present an ideal of Protestant heroism. By means of his discussion of seventeenth-century writers such as Milton, Bunyan, George Fox, and of Quaker texts, Knott moves beyond questions of influence, however, to illustrate how 'these writers engaged with the tradition of suffering in name of God that Foxe did much to shape and popularize'. Whilst *Acts and Monuments* constitutes a major concern in this book (and a welcome one, too), Knott further examines Foxe's account of John Rogers, the London minister who was the first to die in the Marian persecution and one who constructed his own drama of martyrdom, and assesses the critical influence of John Bale upon Foxe's conception of Protestant martyrdom. Knott also identifies in Foxe's text the contrast of Protestant plainness and Catholic ceremonialism, as well as this Protestant writer's presentation of the joyfulness and peace of mind of the martyrs in their suffering, and the graphically represented horrors of their actual executions. Cynthia Garrett explores the critically neglected manuals of private prayer that were produced between 1600 and 1660 in 'The Rhetoric of Supplication: Prayer Theory in Seventeenth-Century England' (*RQ* 46.328–57). Employing the methods of historicism, phenomenology of religion and a particular examination of the rhetorical features of private prayer manuals, Garrett illuminates the way in which they reveal a complex theory of prayer, one that acknowledges the problematics of communication with the divine, and suggests that the ambivalence that characterizes these manuals has 'wide implications for the study of post-Reformation English views of God, language and the self'. Megan Matchinske's 'Holy Hatred: Formations of the Gendered Subject in English Apocalyptic Writing, 1625–1651' (*ELH* 60.349–77) constitutes a fascinating study of apocalyptic writings. Through her close examination of this material, Matchinske explores the connection between a rhetoric of holy hatred (a marked aggression towards a perceived enemy), that sought to provoke a moral catechism on correct behaviours and the repercussions of failing to abide by its tenets, and the simultaneous construction of national and individual consciousness. For Matchinske, her approach responds to the previous neglect of adequate acknowledgement of the 'shift', as it is articulated in apocalyptic writings, in state and subject formation prior to the Civil War and, specifically, in relation to notions of gender. In '"Not I, But Christ": Allegory and the Puritan Self' (*ELH* 60.899–937), Thomas H. Luxon considers a range of texts that centre on the constructions of individuals as pseudo-Christ or prophetic figures, noting their particular popularity during the interregnum years, a popularity that generated alternatively enthusiastic or anxious responses.

In *Miracles and the Pulp Press during the English Revolution: The Battle of the Frogs and Fairford's Flies*, Jerome Friedman examines 'the newsbooks and pulp press from 1640–1660 to assess how ordinary English people conceived of the English Revolution'. Drawing upon an immense range of sources, Friedman concentrates on the several hundred newsbook accounts of ghosts, miraculous events, witches and witchcraft, ancient prophecy, popular heroes, master criminals, sects and religious cults, monsters, and peculiar natural occurrences, as well as pamphlets that argue the various merits of tobacco, marijuana, liquor and liberated sexuality. Friedman argues that the pulp press and common newsbooks 'tell us much about how Englishmen actually conceived of the revolution, not only if they were for or against it, but also about the ideas and concepts that determined how catastrophic events might be evaluated' and reveals how these texts further illustrate 'gender hatred, fear of the unknown, mindless reverence for authority, blame of the weak, and victimization of the innocent'. In 'Soapboilers Speak Shakespeare Rudely: Masquerade and Leveller Pamphleteering' (*CS* 5.235–43) Nigel Smith examines Leveller pamphleteering strategy to suggest that the texts of leading Leveller propagandists skilfully exploited martyrological and heroic codes by means of their subtle adoption of different kinds of speaking voice, and describes how their pamphleteering provided their audience with a political education. Brian Patton discusses the impact that the Civil War had upon women's lives and political expression in 'The Women are Revolting? Women's Activism and Popular Satire in the English Revolution' (*JMRS* 23.69–87).

Through his discussion of the women's petitions and their satirical responses, Patton shows how women despite constraints on their public expression, achieved political action through their access to the press. Timothy Raylor's 'Providence and Technology in the English Civil War: Edmond Felton and his Engine' (*RS* 7.398–413) centres on Edmond Felton's design and promotion of an engine of war for use by the Parliamentary army. Whilst the initial focus is on Felton's family and its immediate history, Raylor also examines in detail the invention of the engine as constituting not only an important episode in the history of the Civil War but also an historical event that 'affords an insight into contemporary puritan attitudes towards technology and warfare', and illustrates 'the difficulties involved in preserving an appropriate balance in war between human action and faith in the operation of providence'. In 'Francis Quarles and the Crisis of Royalism' (*CS* 5.252–62), Robert Wilcher illustrates the way in which Quarles's *The Profest Royalist: His Quarrel with the Times* both indicates a profession of allegiance and is 'representative of the kind of internal debate that must eventually have persuaded many supporters of moderate reform to embrace the cause of royalism'.

2. Poetry

The Varieties of Metaphysical Poetry by T. S. Eliot (The Clark Lectures at Trinity College, Cambridge, 1926 and The Turnbull Lectures at Johns Hopkins University, 1933), edited and introduced by Ronald Schuchard, provides access to lectures written under intense pressure during a period of great personal difficulty. Schuchard's critical introduction and annotation of these lectures shows how they provide a crucial insight into Eliot's 'disintegration of the intellect' in three metaphysical moments of European literature – Dante and Cavalcanti in the thirteenth century, Donne and Crashaw in the seventeenth, Laforgue and Corbière in the nineteenth. For Schuchard, publication of these lectures 'will have as much impact on our revaluation of his critical mind as did the facsimile edition of *The Waste Land* (1917) on our comprehension of his poetic mind'. Joseph H. Summers's *Collected Essays on Renaissance Literature* assembles both published and unpublished lectures and essays, spanning his long and immensely productive career. Omitting any essay which has been published in a volume that Summers has previously written or edited, the collection includes essays on George Herbert, Marvell, Shakespeare and Milton, 'Notes on Recent Studies in English Literature' of 1965 and 'Stanley Fish's Reading of Seventeenth-Century Literature'. Eruditely written and offering incisive readings of seventeenth-century literature, these essays represent a clear sense of the development of one of the English Renaissance's most eminent scholars.

Ambivalence towards sexuality, the oscillation between frustration and satisfaction of sexual desire that pervades seventeenth-century love literature, is the focus of a new collection of essays, *Renaissance Discourses of Desire*, edited by Claude J. Summers and Ted-Larry Pebworth. Employing a diversity of critical methods sensitive to the cultural specificity of sexual attitudes, these essays 'confront important questions about the relationship between sexuality and textuality in the period, about the intertwining of political and sexual discourse, about attitudes towards gender and the differences between men and women as desiring subjects, about the representation of homoerotics and the discourses of homosexuality (and homophobia), about the impact of economic and social ideologies on love poetry and sexual expression, and about the erotics of criticism'. The text studies in this fascinating and informative collection include exploration of the work of Donne, Carew, Suckling, Herrick, Katherine Philips and Aphra Behn. With love rather than sexuality in mind, Anthony Low's *The Reinvention of Love: Poetry, Politics and Culture from Sidney to Milton* is concerned with 'ways of loving, under changing cultural, political, and economic circumstances, as expressed in poetry from Sir Philip Sidney to John Milton'. Arguing that 'Love remains my central concern, not the varieties of "sexual politics"' (although the latter is alluded to throughout his study) and deliberately limiting his study to male poets, Low centres his discussion on how cultural, economic and political change transformed the ways in which Sidney, Donne, Herbert, Crashaw, Carew and Milton thought and wrote about love. Through close reading of the poetry, Low explores how these poets attempted to replace Petrarchanism by reference to their more immediate cultural circumstances and how they engaged with the interrelationship between secular and divine love. In *Forms of Reflection: Genre and Culture in Meditational Writing*, David Hill Radcliffe discusses the 'continuities and discontinuities between forms of reflection used by contemporary critics'. Rather than offering a 'cultural history of literature', Radcliffe posits instead a 'literary history of culture' that identifies the way in which one particular genre functioned as an agent of change in the Early Modern period, and, by means of that identification challenges the ways in which criticism is practised today. Throughout the study, Radcliffe considers the way in which the 'changes taking place in forms of reflection as values of courtly deference yield to values of civil refinement, and those to later values of genius and universal humanity, courtesy modulating into cultivation, cultivation into culture'. The first chapter on Donne provides an insightful analysis into the poet's reflections on method that reveals 'the need to reformulate relations between text and context, literature and history, and individual authors and institutional structures' and in the second chapter on Denham Walton and Cowley, Radcliffe describes the different procedures adopted by these three georgic writers to undermine courtly deference and propose instead decentred communities in which differences of rank are subordinated to differences of manners. The remaining chapters deal with the work of Defoe, the eighteenth-century Hertford Circle, and Shaftesbury and Coleridge. Iva Beretta's *'The World's a Garden': Garden Poetry of the English Renaissance* offers an interdisciplinary exploration of the interaction in English Renaissance poetry, between the garden of literary tradition and the physical Renaissance garden, that exemplifies the treatment of the relationship between Art and Nature, the mythological, scientific, philosophical and architectural preoccupations of the poets, and the recreation of the earthly paradise. Poets studied include Spenser, Chapman, Cowley, Marvell, Carew and Milton.

The Poems of Aemilia Lanyer: 'Salve Deus Rex Judaeorum' (Women Writers in English 1350–1850 Series) edited by Susanne Woods is a very welcome edition of this poet, although the price of £22.50 will unfortunately place it completely out of the reach of most students. This is a shame, because Lanyer is now the subject of increasing scholarly attention and is beginning to be taught (in selected form) on many undergraduate courses. Woods includes a lucid and informative introduction, the Huntington Library copy retains the original spelling but adds some useful modernization, and clearly annotates throughout. This is an undoubtedly much-needed edition of this poet and will be a useful reference text for both scholars and students. Ann Baynes Coiro's 'Writing in Service: Sexual Politics and Class Position in the Poetry of Aemilia Lanyer and Ben Jonson' (*Criticism* 35.357–76) responds to the refiguring of the Renaissance canon brought about by the 'discovery' and publication of women writers of this period. In placing Lanyer next to Jonson in the canon and thereby contesting the criteria of that canon, Coiro raises questions about Renaissance authorship and print culture as they apply to class *and* gender (with the added dimension of race, as Lanyer was from a Jewish family) and in doing so, offers new and thought-provoking readings of the work of both poets.

Using as a starting point Jonson's personalization of his name and his insistence on its correct spelling in all publications, Bruce Thomas Boehrer's 'The Poet of Labor: Authorship and Property in the Work of Ben Jonson' (*PQ* 72.289–312) investigates Jonson's literary practice in the prose work 'Timber, or Discoveries'. Boehrer analyses Jonson's emphasis on literary labour, his philosophy of authorship throughout his career and his contemporaries' reactions to the idea of Jonsonian authorship. For Boehrer, considerable irony lies in the fact that despite Jonson's theoretical stance, 'his work – even his own name – becomes appropriable by others, and thus it resists Jonson's own insistence upon the determinacy of authorial labour, essence, and property'. Continuing the focus on Jonsonian authorship, Martin Butler's 'Jonson's Folio and the Politics of Patronage' (*Criticism* 35.377–90) reviews recent historicist work on the publication significance of the 1616 Jonson Folio. Although Butler acknowledges the critical unravelling of the writerly self-consciousness of Jonson's volume and all that it implies for its impact on seventeenth-century print culture, he argues that 'though the Folio makes Jonson's genius seem monumental and self-contained, it cannot in fact decisively extricate itself from the politics of patronage relationships in 1616' and that it remains nevertheless 'implicitly embedded in that patronage economy which its publication appears to transcend'. In 'To Write Sorrow in Jonson's "On My First Sonne"' (*JDJ* 9.149–56), Lauren Silberman notes that while many critical studies have cited Genesis 35:16–20 as the source for the opening line of Epigram 45, 'On My First Sonne', few have expanded upon its significance for a reading of this poem, and argues that Jonson 'has used poetic language to perform his valediction and enact his loss, rather than just memorialize his son'.

Empson's seminal work on Donne, including previously unpublished material, is brought together in *William Empson: Essays on Renaissance Literature* (Vol. 1): *Donne and the New Philosophy* edited and introduced by John Haffenden. In the introduction to this collection of essays, Haffenden places Empson's radical readings of Donne, that posit the profound influence of new scientific discoveries upon the poet, in their critical context. Eruditely exploring the critical controversy centring on Donne's response to the 'New Philosophy', Haffenden brings to life Empson's often passionate approach in which he 'aimed to free the poet from the dual straitjacket of stemmata and sanctimoniousness, scoffing at Gardner's editorial methods and critical findings'. Also included are essays on Copernicanism, Thomas Digges and 'Godwin's voyage to the moon'. *John Donne: 'Pseudo-Martyr'* edited and introduced (with Commentary) by Anthony Raspa, seeks to be a definitive edition of this most neglected of Donne's prose works written in 1610 when Donne was still a lawyer. Raspa identifies key issues for the study of this text and sets it in its historical context, noting how it functions both as an autobiographical document which reveals how Donne resolved his own lapse from Catholicism as well as illuminating the way in which the text constituted an attempt to convince English Roman Catholics that they could remain loyal to the spiritual authority of Rome and still take the oath of allegiance to the British Crown and thereby avoid persecution. Raspa also includes a discussion of source texts, biblical and manuscript sources and the two copies of *Pseudo-Martyr*, that serve jointly as copy texts for this edition.

Richard Halpern's 'The Lyric in the Field of Information: Autopoiesis and History in Donne's *Songs and Sonnets* (*YJC* 6.185–216) constitutes a radical and sophisticated approach to Donne's lyrics and the question of lyric autonomy. Eschewing Marxist, New Historicist and Poststructuralist theoretical frameworks as problematic in explicating lyric autonomy, Halpern applies the theory of autopoiesis or self-referring systems, a biological model of increasing benefits to the human sciences and specifically to the study of cultural phenomena, to analyse the Renaissance love lyric and its focus on sexuality. The article concludes with considering the role that autopoietic theory can play in examining the boundaries of Marxist criticism itself. In 'Taking Liberties: Eliot's Donne' (*CS* 5.278–87), Peter Carpenter extends discussion of the influence of Donne on the work of Eliot to identify close connections between them: 'For both, the play between text and speech was analogous to the relationship between body and soul'. Through this identification, Carpenter explores the way in which both writers were preoccupied with 'creative, bodily and spiritual health and malaise, and the links between them'. Graham Roebuck's 'Elegies for Donne: Great Tew and the Poets' (*JDJ* 9.125–36) both questions the comparative lack of elegies in the 1633 edition of *Poems, by J.D. with Elegies on the Author's Death* and considers the way in which the sequence of elegies by Henry King, Edward Hyde, Thomas Browne and others reveals more about the contest to appropriate Donne's intellectual legacy.

On individual poems, Dayton Haskin's 'A History of Donne's "Canonization" from Izaak Walton to Cleanth Brooks' (*JEGP* 92.17–36) posits that the original marginality of this poem derives in part from Walton's biography, that invokes a seventeenth-century reader response to the poem as delineating Donne's attempt to justify his marriage. In 'Radical Donne: "Satire III"' (*ELH* 60.283–322), Richard Strier asserts the restoration of a nineteenth- and early twentieth-century understanding of the 'young John Donne' and his early poetry in which 'a sense of boldness, radicalism, and freethinking' abounds. Taking as its initial starting point Empson's interpretation of 'Satire III' as a poem that embraces a radical argument for freedom of conscience, Strier argues that the poem, whilst not always consistent in that radicalism, illustrates nevertheless a strain of radicalism that is profoundly and deliberately expressed. Also on Donne's satires, Joshua Scodel's 'The Medium is the Message: Donne's "Satire 3," "To Sir Henry Wotton" ("Sir, more than kisses"), and the Ideologies of the Mean' (*MP* 90.479–511) argues succinctly that Donne's utilization of the ethics of mean between excess and deficiency illuminates the relationship between Early Modern subjectivity and cultural institutions and interprets 'Satire 3' and 'To Sir Henry Wotton' as poems that invoke the mean in order to expand the sphere of individual freedom and the self's freedom to manoeuvre.

In 'Donne and the Real Presence of the Absent Lover' (*JDJ* 9.113–24), Anne Barbeau Gardiner sets a reading of Donne's 'A Valediction: Forbidding Mourning' within contemporary debates concerning Christ's Real Presence at the Lord's Supper, and suggests that underlying the lyric song of farewell, Donne reiterates

British and European conceptions of Real Presence wherein Christ's love for the Church would not allow him to be absent. Donne's 'A Valediction: Forbidding Mourning' receives an alternative treatment in Eileen Reeves's 'John Donne and the Oblique Course' (*RS* 7.168–83) in which, instead of reading the poem in terms of the Real Presence, she argues that all interpretations must take into account the presence of the New Science. Contextualizing the poem with reference to the *Sermons* and other notable cartographic passages, Reeves considers the alliance of poetry and technology together with the loxodromic problem of Early Modern cartography to suggest specific parallels in Donne's work between cartographic and poetic representation. In 'Lyric Autobiography: John Donne's *Holy Sonnets*' (*HTR* 86.293–308), Frederick J. Ruf grounds a discussion of Donne's Holy Sonnets with reference to the lyric voice, juxtaposing his analysis with anthropological studies of autobiographical 'unruliness'. Ruf locates a self-absorption in the poems that has an intricate impact on the social character of Donne's lyrics. Also, M. Thomas Hester's '"Let them sleepe": Donne's Personal Allusion in "Holy Sonnet IV"' (*PLL* 29.346–50) indicates that in addition to this poem's allusion to the prophetic vision of the Apocalypse in Revelations, the first lines evoke details of St John's vision, an evocation that clarifies the note of frustration on which this poem concludes. Donne's critically neglected exercise in biblical translation is the focus of John Klause's 'The Two Occasions of Donne's *Lamentations of Jeremy*' (*MP* 90.337–59). Countering early criticism that the poetry represents the poet in a mood of deep self-abnegation, Klause is centrally concerned with investigating the complexity that surrounds the dating of this poem (there having been suggested two separate versions of the poem produced in the late 1580s or early 1590s and following his ordination). Finally, in 'Notes on an Important Volume of Donne's Poetry and Prose' (*JDJ* 9.137–40), John T. Shawcross rectifies the incomplete and erroneous description of the privately owned volume which binds together exempla of John Donne's 1633 *Poems* with a poetic manuscript, and the 1633 *Juvenilia* (first edition) with a prose manuscript contained in Peter Beal's updating of 'More Donne Manuscripts' (*JDJ*, 1987). Apart from describing the contents anew, Shawcross reports that the volume is now being included in the textual information of the *Variorum Edition of the Poetry of John Donne*.

In *Authority, Church and Society in George Herbert: Return to the Middle Way*, Christopher Hodgkins reaffirms the importance of setting Herbert's work within its religious and political context. Seeking to rediscover and define Herbert's 'middle way' of Anglicanism (exemplified through his advocacy of parish ministry, simplicity in liturgy, poetry and church architecture) Hodgkins argues that Herbert 'even more than the Elizabethan Settlement, which formed his ecclesiastical ideal, was Calvinist in the essentials of his theology'. By means of a 'reconstructive rather than a deconstructive or reductionist project', Hodgkins explores Herbert's ambivalence towards applying state coercion in spiritual matters, the parson's power, motives and pastoral vision in *The Country Parson*, and the individual's sometimes conflicting obligations to church and nation, and concludes with a speculation on how Herbert might have reacted to the national upheaval that occurred not long after his death. *A Life of Glory: A Selection of Poems by George Herbert for Reflection*, edited and introduced by Marianne Dorman, includes an introduction to the life of Herbert and a selection of poetry in modernized spelling, arranged in order that they can be used for the preparation for public worship, assistance with private meditation and for receiving the Holy Sacrament. *George Herbert: A Portrait* by Nick Page discusses the poet's life in relation both to his family and to the major historical events of the period. In particular, Page concentrates on the influences on Herbert of his mother and elder brother, illustrating the way in which both had a profound effect on Herbert's life, opinions and actions.

The industry of Herbert Critical Studies itself is the remit of Stanley Stewart's 'Investigating Herbert Criticism' (*RQ* 45.141–58). Stewart locates the origins of Herbert criticism with Nicolas Ferrar's focus on the poet's character and motivations, a focus that has generated a range of critical questions underlying which are issues of knowledge and belief. Such questions, Stewart argues, remain encoded with Herbert criticism, and furthermore suggests a 'renewed interest in what Coleridge calls the "constitutional predisposition" of the critic', a predisposition that necessarily determines contemporary questioning and interpretation of Herbert's poetry. In 'Title in George Herbert's "Little Book"' (*ELR* 23.314–44), Anne Ferry considers in detail the titling of poems and asserts that in distinction to the more usual seventeenth-century casual and inconsistent practice, Herbert's concern with titling was pivotal to his technique. Contrasting the organizing of poems in *Poems, by J.D.* together with close examination of titling principles encoded with *The Temple,* Ferry illustrates that the titling can illuminate our understanding of what Herbert 'thought a poem should be or do, about his notions of collecting his poems into a "little Booke", and about how it should be read'. Moreover, Ferry also examines the principle determining Herbert's division of secular and sacred and the way in which 'Herbert used titling as a way of defining the nature of his poems and the collection in which he arranged them'. Anthony Low scrutinizes Herbert's difficulty in accommodating the traditional biblical tropes of love and marriage, bride and bridegroom in 'George Herbert: "The Best Love"' (*RQ* 45.159–78). Whilst for Donne, such biblical tropes facilitated the multifaceted exploration and expression of human sexuality, Low argues that in Herbert's poetry the tropes that posit the positions of masculine and feminine are replaced by the trope of another love relationship altogether, that of father and son. Through this replacement of tropes, Low attests that Herbert is able to avoid 'the point where courtship gives place to consummation and marriage', and employ alternatively 'the marital trope for longing love, the parental trope for satisfied love'. In 'Herbert and the Real Presence' (*RQ* 45.179–98), R. V. Young contests traditional readings of *The Temple* that posit that the poetry either embraces an unequivocal 'Protestant Poetics' or an obvious Anglican theology, and advocates instead that the Eucharist elements in Herbert's Eucharistic poems are far from 'merely metaphorical', so that 'it must be inferred that Herbert believed in the Real Presence as firmly as Thomas Cranmer disbelieved'. Also taking issue with more recent criticism, Esther Gilman Richey's '"Wrapt in Nights Mantle": George Herbert's Parabolic Art' (*JDJ* 9.157–72) disputes the analysis of Herbert's narrative poems as primarily autobiographical sketches or fictions designed to catechize the reader, and stresses the poet's parabolic technique, that can be productively explored in relation to Herbert's commentary on parable in *The Country Parson.* On individual poems, Jeffrey Powers-Beck examines Herbert's employment of the dual image in '"Whence com'st Thou ... So Fresh and Fine?": The King's Stamp and the Origins of Value in Herbert's "Avarice"' (*ELN* 30.14–23). Powers-Beck offers a reading of 'Avarice' that stresses Herbert's conceptualization of monetary power 'in the paradoxical image of an ennobling and disgracing, incarnating and desecrating, stamp'. And in '"Me Thoughts I Heard One Calling, *Child!*": Herbert's "The Collar"' (*RQ* 45.197–214), John R. Roberts illuminates the way in which in this lyric poem 'Herbert has articulated in very precise theological terms an attitude toward religious service that far transcends mere pietistic platitudes or conventional religious posturing'.

In a thought-provoking reading of Herrick's love poetry, Browen Price's 'The Fractured Body – Censorship and Desire in Herrick's Poetry' (*L&H* 2.23–4) counters more traditional criticism that either alleges an explicit nostalgia in his poetry or, more recently, an identification of a seemingly dehistoricized and depoliticized element in his pastoral poetry, to illustrate instead that the love poetry evinces a profoundly disturbed sexual politics, that is 'bound up within an emerging bourgeois economy and discourse of subjectivity, where the female body is frequently the site of conflicting claims'. Continuing the focus on Herrick's erotic play, Lillian Schanfield's '"Tickled with Desire": A View of Eroticism in Herrick's Poetry' (*L&P* 39.63–83) traces a psychology to the narrator(s) of his poetry. Through critical examination of his poetry, Schanfield argues that the narrators invariably exhibit a man with sexual problems related to immaturity, passivity and possibly impotence. In 'Robert Herrick on Predestination' (*ELN* 30.24–30), David W. Landrum considers the much neglected *Noble Numbers* N–215–N–221, poems that engage with predestination. Landrum demonstrates that whilst these poems testify to Herrick's anti-Calvinist stance and his affirmation of establishment Anglicanism, they also manifest a tension that Herrick felt with 'his position as a parish priest who had direct contact with the general population, and as one whose own roots were not in the ruling social class he found himself representing'.

3. Prose

In his compendious study, *Francis Bacon: History, Politics and Science 1561–1626*, W. H. G. Wormald has 'sought to muster "a kind of thoughtful prudence" against idols "either adventitious or innate"; also to interrelate the statement in Bacon's teaching, rejecting sharp separations between the departments of knowledge in which he makes contributions; also to combine sobriety and caution with audacity, despising "vain apprehensions"'. Through his exploration of Bacon's preoccupation with knowledge of the world of nature and with knowledge of policy, Wormald identifies the way in which the relationship or interplay between the two constituted a dilemma for Bacon, a dilemma that he resolved through 'arguing that he would perform in policy in ways which would help progress in knowledge of nature'. In this densely argued study, Wormald illuminates the way in which Bacon, through his teaching, through his practice and in his achievement, connected knowledge and policy through civil and natural history.

John Clavell 1601–43: Highwayman, Author, Lawyer, Doctor (With a Reprint of his Poem 'A Recantation of An Ill Led Life', 1634) by J. H. Pafford, is a fascinating study of a man from Dorset who took to a life of crime but repented in prison, where he wrote his 'Recantation', a classic although frequently plagiarized account of 'the tricks of the highwayman's trade'. Following his release from prison, Clavell went on to compose a five-act play, *The Sodder'd Cittizen,* and spent much of his remaining life in Ireland where he practised both as a lawyer and as a physician. Appended to Pafford's engaging biography and welcome reprint of the 'Recantation' are extracts from Clavell's *Notebook*, a text that includes poetry, correspondence, details of his relationship with Massinger, and copious lists of cures. *Sir Thomas Urquhart of Cromarty (1611–1660) Adventurer, Polymath and Translator of Rabelais* by R. J. Craik seeks to provide an extensive biography and commentary on Urquhart's multiplicity of interests. With chapters on his life and minor works *Ekskubalauron, Neaudethaumata*, and the translation of *Gargantua and Pantagruel*, Craik argues that despite the eccentricity of his writing, 'all of Urquhart's works, however disparate they may seem, are related both in Urquhart's view and in act, and that in his Rabelais translation his diverse talents and interests find their ideal application'.

Claire Preston's '"Unriddling the World": Sir Thomas Browne and the Doctrine of Signatures' (*CS* 5.263–70) explores Browne's belief in signatures, the signs of God embedded in all things. Preston illuminates the way in which the 'doctrine of signatures formed Browne's thought and guided his scientific activities', showing how Browne's major works are strongly determined, stylistically and thematically, by the necessity of discovering the divine text inscribed in the Creation.

Books Reviewed

Bath, Michael, John Manning, and Alan R. Young, eds. *The Art of the Emblem: Essays in Honour of Karl Josef Höltgen*. AMS. pp. 272. £61.95 ($62.50). ISBN 0 404 63710 8.

Berretta, Iva. *'The World's a Garden': Garden Poetry of the English Renaissance*. Uppsala. pp. 208. ISBN 0 915 43155 0.

Craik, R. J. *Sir Thomas Urquhart of Cromarty (1611–1666) Adventurer, Polymath and Translator of Rabelais*. Mellen. pp. 229. £39.95. ISBN 0 773 49269 0.

Davis, Natalie Zemon, and Arlette Farge, eds. *A History of Women in the West* (Vol. 3): *Renaissance and Enlightenment Paradoxes*. Belknap. pp. 595. £19.95. ISBN 0 674 40372 X.

Dorman, Marianne, ed. *A Life of Glory: A Selection of Poems by George Herbert for Reflection*. Pentland, St Mut (1992). pp. 74. pb £7.50. ISBN 1 872 79578 1.

Ezell, Margaret J. M. *Writing Women's Literary History*. JHUP. pp. 205. $39.50. ISBN 0 801 84432 0.

Friedman, Jerome. *Miracles and the Pulp Press during the English Revolution: The Battle of the Frogs and Fairford's Flies*. St Martin's. hb $45, pb $16.95. ISBN 0 312 09125 7, 0 312 10170 8.

Haffenden, John, ed. *William Empson: Essays on Renaissance Literature* (Vol. 1): *Donne and the New Philosophy*. CUP. pp. 296. £35.00. ISBN 0 521 44043 2.

Hill, Christopher. *The English Bible and the Seventeenth-Century Revolution*. Penguin. pp. 466. £30. ISBN 0 713 99078 3.

Hodgkins, Christopher. *Authority, Church and Society in George Herbert: Return to the Middle Way*. UMissP. pp. 231. £35.95. ISBN 0 826 20881 9.

Knott, John R. *Discourses of Martyrdom in English Literature 1563–1694*. CUP. pp. 278. £37.50. ISBN 0 521 43365 7.

Lewalski, Barbara Kiefer. *Writing Women in Jacobean England*. HarvardUP. pp. 431. £35.95. ISBN 0 674 96242 7.

Low, Anthony. *The Reinvention of Love: Poetry, Politics and Culture from Sidney to Milton*. CUP. pp. 258. £30. ISBN 0 521 45030 6.

Pafford, J. H. P., ed. *John Clavell 1601–43: Highwayman, Author, Lawyer, Doctor* (With a Reprint of his Poem 'A Recantation of An Ill Led Life', 1634). Leopard's Head. pp. 309. £12.50. ISBN 0 904 92028 3.

Page, Nick. *George Herbert: A Portrait*. Monarch. pp. 194. pb £7.99. ISBN 1 854 24180 X.

Radcliffe, David Hill. *Forms of Reflection: Genre and Culture in Meditational Writing*. JHUP. pp. 232. £32. ISBN 0 8018 4500 9.

Raspa, Anthony, ed. *John Donne: 'Pseudo-Martyr'*. McG-QUP. pp. 427. £52.25. ISBN 0 773 50994 1.

Schuchard, Ronald, ed. *The Varieties of Metaphysical Poetry by T. S. Eliot*. Faber. pp. 343. £25. ISBN 0 571 14230 3.

Summers, Claude J., and Ted-Larry Pebworth, eds. *Renaissance Discourses of Desire*. UMissP. pp. 284. £39 ($44.95). ISBN 0 826 20885 1.

Summers, Joseph H. *Collected Essays on Renaissance Literature*. Special Studies and Monographs. GHJ. pp. 269. pb $15.

Turner, James Grantham, ed. *Sexuality and Gender in Early Modern Europe: Institutions, Texts, Images*. CUP. pp. 345. pb $17.95. ISBN 0 521 44605 8.

Woods, Susanne, ed. *The Poems of Aemilia Lanyer: 'Salve Deus Rex Judaeorum'*. Women Writers in English Series 1350–1850. OUP. pp. 139. £22.50. ISBN 0 19 508037 8.

Wormald, B. H. G. *Francis Bacon: History, Politics, and Science, 1561–1626*. CUP. pp. 409. $45.00. ISBN 0 521 30773 2.

IX

Milton

THOMAS N. CORNS

The Norton Critical Edition of *Paradise Lost* appears this year in a second edition edited by Scott Elledge, and offers some advantages for teachers seeking a pedagogically useful version of the poem. It prints some very helpful secondary material (from Isobel Rivers and David Masson) on the context of the poem, and some astutely selected critical readings, both from 'Great Writers on Milton, 1688–1929' and from important modern criticism from Fish and Frye to Hill and Turner. There are useful sections containing the biblical sources for the poem and Milton's own writing, usually on themes adjacent to the poem. But annotation is too light and mainly concerned with glossing hard words, and I don't understand quite why it is felt necessary to so insistently give Greek and Latin etymologies, a process which can only reanimate those ghost Latinisms so effectively exorcised in Alastair Fowler's edition (1968). The editor has opted for modern spelling and capitalization, but retains original punctuation.

Marie-Madeleine Martinet has produced a French translation of Milton's prose, *John Milton: Ecrits Politiques*, with notes, introduction, '*Postface*', and the text of *Areopagitica* in English. The book contains a translation of the whole of *Areopagitica*, and substantial extracts from *Of Reformation*, *The Tenure*, *Eikonoklastes*, *Defensio Prima* and *The History of Britain*. The selection is plainly skewed towards Milton's republican writing, appropriately, since Martinet is, in part, concerned with issues relating to the French perception of Milton, especially in the republican period and in the nineteenth-century radical tradition. Milton has not been frequently translated into French (though *Areopagitica* was translated in 1788 and *Defensio Prima* in 1789). While her book will primarily serve a Francophone readership interested in the broadest tradition of European radicalism, it has its interests for any concerned with the afterlife of Miltonic thought and writing.

John T. Shawcross's new biography, *Milton: The Self and the World*, manifests a wealth of scholarship, close reading, and interpretative vigour, shrewdly, provocatively and sometimes rather strangely applied. Shawcross is, of course, a formidable scholar, and rarely can attention to textual and publishing history and to the details of manuscripts (here, the Commonplace Book and the Trinity Manuscript) have been so well rewarded with interpretative insights of a biographical nature.

There are other interpretations of considerable cogency. For example, Shawcross's reconstruction of Milton's tour through continental Europe discloses its unstructured, unplanned character: 'Milton did not know exactly where he would go and did not know exactly how long he would stay at any specific place in his plan'. Milton emerges from this account not as the programmic traveller assiduously educating himself (as he is usually represented), but as a young man losing himself in Europe. For me, this accords well with John Leonard's recent suggestion that his European jaunt was an attempt by his family to get him out of the country before he got himself into trouble with the Laudian clamp-down on puritan dissidents. Shawcross, however, always prefers psychological over political explanations for actions, and he seeks to relate the tour to the death of Milton's mother.

Indeed, old classics, mostly the Jung and Freud so loved by critics of a certain generation, stalk these pages: Shawcross drags the ghost of Milton to the psychiatrist's chair, but it is a chair endorsed 'Geneva, circa 1932'. Inherent in much of what Shawcross attempts (and it is inherent, too, in the psychological models which influence him) is an unacceptable essentialism which rejects the historical and social construction of much human conduct, especially human sexuality. For 'this different biography', as he terms it, returns persistently to explain the development of Milton's creative impulses in terms of hypotheses concerning his sexual impulses and frustrations, as though the desires and inclinations of a rather enigmatic young man some 350 years ago can be teased out by what we know (or think we know) about the desires of our own contemporaries, augmented by some mythic criticism and the help of Jung and Freud. Thus, in the 'Epitaphium Damonis' Shawcross finds, in Milton's purposeful use of 'female imagery of space, water, and enclosure, as well as phallic male imagery', evidence of 'the female personality bereft of male being'; 'Milton's insistence on Diodati's celibacy makes sense, really, only if Milton knew of or suspected nonheterosexual [sic] interests on Diodati's part'. Milton's status as 'the Lady of Christ's' leads Shawcross to ponder 'our world's penchant for assigning certain attributes to the male or to the female'... 'That there may have been homosexual experiences with Diodati does not demand a label of "homosexual" for Milton but rather a latent homosexualism that on occasion might possibly have emerged and a homoerotic personality that would seem to fit the total evidence of Milton's life'.

Shawcross may well be right; though as easily he could be wrong. What is extraordinary is the narrow and questionable base of his evidence. This is a view of human sexuality as indifferent to Foucault as to Lawrence Stone. What a commitment to celibacy may have meant to someone living in a society in which sexually available women were probably carriers of incurable venereal diseases, in which healthy women were encouraged to be chaste until marriage, in which acts of male homosexual penetration could be punished with the death penalty, cannot be surmised or projected from what we may feel we know about the sexual mores of late-twentieth-century undergraduates or from our knowledge of ourselves or from the dubious hypotheses of the founding fathers of European psychoanalysis. But we may be sure that the very category (or in his phrase 'label') 'homosexual' can scarcely have carried the same significance as it may now.

Shawcross approaches later phases of Milton's biography (and particularly the reconstruction of his desire and frustrations) in similarly speculative vein. My other major concern with this book, however, relates to acts of omission. Simply, the historical contextualization of some of Milton's most significant choices is often insubstantial. From this study emerges no real sense of the origins of Milton's commitment to Revolutionary Independency, rather than the other positions open to him. Shawcross simplifies the complexities of the mid-century conflict. For example, he is plainly wrong to assert that by 1637 'no longer was there a moderate group between the Puritans and the Laudians'. Again, I am puzzled by his decision to advance *The Tenure of Kings and Magistrates* as in some way a paradigmatic text, when arguably it is Milton's most eccentric, published after the victory of Revolutionary Independency but before his emergence as its spokesman. Again, Shawcross's view of the dissenter experience in the Restoration does not appropriately distinguish the very different phases of the 14 or 15 years between the return of Charles II and Milton's death.

Shawcross's biography, then, gives us too much of the self and too little of the world. Yet it is, by some way, the most significant book on Milton published this year; I have a sense that other Miltonists will quarrel with it for years to come.

Shawcross is not the only critic to develop this year a Jungian view of Milton. In the same series as *Milton: The Self and the World* comes James P. Driscoll's *The Unfolding God of Jung and Milton*. This is a treatise incapable of refutation, an unsinkable vessel, rigged to ride out any storm: 'Conventional critics ... find Jungian criticism often frustrating and at times downright maddening. "You're wrong," they'll cry, "Milton could never have intended that archetype to mean what you say it means." To which I must respond, "It wouldn't be an archetype if it obeyed Milton's conscious intentions"'. This is a study the validity of which can only be judged by the power of the interpretations it suggests.

The key to Driscoll's reading is the identification of the 'dualist archetype, those hostile brothers, the Son and Satan' (like Shawcross, he needs to address the problem of the missing feminine, but that comes later). Within *Paradise Lost* he finds a schema, not of Trinity, but of 'quaternity', a four-cornered structure which unites the Holy Spirit and the Father, the Son and Satan, but opposes the first to the second, and the third to the fourth. But Driscoll is no passive follower of Jung; rather he seeks to advance and refine him: 'So far as I know, neither Jung nor any of the Jungians have explicitly correlated individuation in Godhead and self with the four psychic functions; notwithstanding, the correlation seems justified'. And off he goes. ... The Paraclete relates to Intuition, the Son to Thinking, Satan to Feeling and Yahweh to Sensation. Why? I can find no explanation in Driscoll or the poem. But this is but the start of a reading of Milton's major poems as coherent and convincing as a consultation with the Tarot; no doubt those who want to believe will believe.

Nicholas von Maltzahn, in 'Naming the Author: Some Seventeenth-Century Milton Allusions' (*MiltonQ* 27.1–18), offers intelligent musing on the nature of allusions and references in the Early Modern period, before adding about 90 references to Shawcross's *Milton: A Bibliography, 1624–1700* (MRTS, 1984). Valerie Ronnick, in 'Five Sources Notes on the Introduction to Milton's *Pro Populo Anglicano Defensio Prima*' (*MiltonQ* 27.35–6), adds to the allusions noted in Martin Dzelzainis's edition, *Milton: Political Writings* (CUP, 1991).

R. A. Shoaf's bright and suggestive book, *Milton Poet of Duality: A Study of Semiosis in the Poetry and the Prose*, first published in 1985, has been reissued. To the new edition he adds a fascinating prefatory essay which shows in miniature the possibilities of analysing complex texts in electronic form.

The year's most sustained engagement with Milton's theology comes in Stephen R. Honeygosky's devout and earnest *Milton's House of God: The*

Invisible and Visible Church. Honeygosky defines and engages a fascinating and crucial question about how Milton conceptualizes the congregation of the godly and how that congregation relates to other Christians. As he observes, 'Separating and congregating are twin halves of the ecclesial condition'. He has a good understanding of the tradition and legacy of Luther and Calvin, and, like others who have written recently, he has returned with profit to consideration of G. F. Nuttall's work on radical protestantism. His study is focused on the prose, but, like others who search that oeuvre for stability and the coherent development of a body of philosophy, he faces the problem of its polemical imperatives. For me, he seems never sufficiently to factor in the circumambient political context of Milton's vernacular prose. Inevitably, he is thrown substantially onto *De Doctrina Christiana*; *Milton's House of God* is another book that will need more than a little revision if that treatise proves to be non-Miltonic.

Milton could read three ancient Oriental languages, Hebrew, Aramaic and Syriac. 'Milton's Syriac' (*MiltonQ* 27.74–7) by Gordon Campbell and Sebastian Brock considers the ways in which Milton learned and used the language.

In 'Milton and Tradition' *(MiltonS* 29.121–41), E. R. Gregory considers all the examples of how Milton uses the word 'tradition', noting the shaping forces of context and the exigencies of debate, but nevertheless concluding that he held that 'tradition at its best was the record of men and women responding freely and lovingly to a living message'.

In 'Milton's Diatribal Voice: The Integration and Transformation of a Generic Paradigm in *Animadversions*' (*MiltonS* 30.3–26), Maureen Thum relates Milton's refutation of Joseph Hall to the genre of the diatribe, attempting to identify his transformation of a received form. In 'From Polemic to Prophecy: Milton's Uses of Jeremiah in *The Reason of Church Government* and *The Readie and Easie Way*' (*MiltonS* 30.27–44), Reuben Sanchez concludes, and few will register much surprise, 'Whereas sincere, albeit naive, optimism characterizes *The Reason of Church Government*, rhetorical optimism characterizes *The Readie and Easie Way*, an optimism that masks Milton's realistic understanding of the unfolding history in which he participates'. Rather subtler is James Egan's 'Creator-Critic: Aesthetic Subtexts in Milton's Antiprelatical and Regicide Polemics' (*MiltonS* 30.45–66), though once more the issues are familiar. He soundly argues that 'The most significant way in which Milton's sensibilities as a polemicist exceed those of his opponents is his cultivation of historical occasions as opportunities for sustained aesthetic deliberation'.

Andrew Barnaby's '"Another Rome in the West?": Milton and the Imperial Republic, 1654–1670' (*MiltonS* 30.67–84) considers 'Milton's use of republican Rome, understood as the exemplar of the imperial republic, to figure the redemptive promise of history as it is to be carried out through the agency of the English commonwealth'. He offers an intelligent mapping of the transformation of Milton's representation. Sharon Achinstein offers as acute a reading of *Eikon Basilike* as she does of Milton's response in 'Milton Catches the Conscience of the King: *Eikonoklastes* and the Engagement Controversy' (*MiltonS* 29.143–63).

'"New Light on Milton and Hartlib", with an appendix on the supporters of Felton's engine' (*MiltonQ* 27.19–31), by Timothy Raylor, is based on a document discovered among the Hartlib papers which apparently demonstrates that Milton supported the development of a piece of military hardware (unless the Milton in the document was one Major John Milton, who was known to be living in London at the time). The article argues that Milton's interest in this project, which had the patronage of Samuel Hartlib, is evidence that there was no rift between the men in the mid-1640s, as is sometimes hypothesized.

A collection of new essays edited by Brendan Bradshaw, Andrew Hadfield and Willy Maley, *Representing Ireland: Literature and the Origins of Conflict, 1534–1660*, contains a provocative essay by Maley on Milton's *Observations Upon the Articles of Peace with the Irish Rebels*. As well as engaging the issue of how Milton read Spenser's *View*, he challenges Miltonists with an evasive silence on Milton's justification of Cromwellian policy towards Ireland, in contrast with recurrent indictments of Spenser's apologia for imperialism.

In '"Plainly Partial": The Liberal *Areopagitica*' (*ELH* 60.57–78) William Kolbrenner ponders perspectives developed on *Areopagitica* in liberal and radical critical traditions, while in 'Printing the Mind: The Economics of Authorship in *Areopagitica*' (*ELH* 60.323–47) Sandra Sherman fascinatingly teases open potential contradictions in its informing polemical strategy. R. D. Bedford in 'Milton's Journeys North: *A Brief History of Moscovia* and *Paradise Lost*' (*RS* 7.70–85) relates that curious prose work to some allusions in the epic. In 'Milton's Vituperative Technique: Claude Saumaise and Martial's *Olus* in the *Defensio Prima*' (*N&Q* 40.314–15) Valerie Ronnick notes the richness of wordplay and allusion in Milton's armoury of abuse.

William B. Hunter returns to his recent concern with the provenance of *Christian Doctrine*. In 'The Provenance of the *Christian Doctrine*: Addenda from the Bishop of Salisbury' (*SEL* 33.191–207) he adduces the views of Thomas Burgess (1756–1837), Bishop of Salisbury, an early sceptic about the Miltonic authenticity of the treatise. The article is an important supplement to the views he has expressed in recent years.

An astute article by J. Martin Evans, 'A Poem of Absences' (*MiltonQ* 27.31–35), engages the argument that the Nativity Ode records an experience of Milton's life. Rather, Evans contends that the ode is 'the most rigorously depersonalized of all Milton's nondramatic works ... a poem that faces not inward but outward, a poem that casts the reader rather than the poet in the role of the convert'.

Virgil Nemoianu and Robert Royal offer in *Play, Literature, Religion: Essays in Cultural Intertextuality* a curious and interestingly conceived collection of new essays by several hands, including 'Milton "Ridens": Reinventing the Temporality of Tradition and Faith' by Sanford Budick. This is an attempt to tease out from the concluding line of 'Lycidas' large conclusions about the representation of futurity by Milton and others: 'Milton's use of "tomorrow" and "new" ... is promissory and performative. It is also without subject, without verb, and therefore without tense. Accordingly, the form of the statement, taken together with its ostensible content, stakes a vast yet almost unintelligible claim on a portion of futurity'. Perhaps it would be churlish to argue that the elliptical phrase clearly allows readers to recognize primarily through its deictics a deleted or implied subject (the speaker of the lament for Lycidas) and a tense (the future; the day after that speech act) and a place (woods and pastures different from the ones in which that speech act has been occurring); not only Milton should be 'ridens'.

In '"Once more, O ye Laurels": *Lycidas* and the Psychology of Pastoral' (*MiltonQ* 27.48–57), William Collins Watterson identifies 'a pastoral of sublimation, one in which the psychodynamics of envy are at once expressed and repressed in Milton's reworking of the Theocritan *agon*'. The inevitable two-handed engine reappears in Jason Isaac Mauro's 'Engine Trouble in Milton's "Lycidas"' (*ELN* 30.25–30).

In Milton's '*Elegia Septima*: The Poetics of Roman Elegy and a Verse Translation' (*MiltonQ* 27.131–8), Brian Striar argues for his new translation, appended to the article, as delivering 'to students otherwise untrained in Latin a truer and more helpful sense of the various tones and influences these poems present'. In an article which shares some of the concerns of Striar, 'Artistry and Originality in Milton's Latin Poems' (*MiltonQ* 27.138–49), John K. Hale once more brings his rich appreciation of Greek and Latin literary culture to the service of Milton studies, pondering resonances, juxtaposing Miltonic and classical themes, and finding a subtle relationship between Milton's notions of *amicitia* and national identity and those of Rome.

An exchange of significance reaches another phase in 'The Politically Correct *Comus*: A Reply to John Leonard' (*MiltonQ* 27.149–55), William Kerrigan's response both to Leah Marcus's historicist account of *Comus*, first published in 1983, and John Leonard's attack in *MiltonQ* 25 on Kerrigan's Freudian reading in *The Sacred Complex: On the Psychogenesis of 'Paradise Lost'* (HarvardUP, 1983). This debate has a grimly adversarial air. Kerrigan scores some stern points against the Marcus argument (that the immediately pertinent context for the masque is a rape case in which Bridgewater was involved as President of the Council of Wales), though he concedes something to Leonard, who proves a harder target to hit. This controversy is far from over.

A brief note by James Ogden, 'The Title of Milton's Masque' (*MiltonQ* 27.155–6), clarifies the process by which it came to be called *Comus* in the eighteenth century.

In 'The Intertextuality of *Comus* and Corinthians' (*MiltonQ* 27.59–70), Susan M. Felch offers the most biblical reading of the masque in recent years, though one may be more convinced of Milton's pervasive debt to Pauline values than by the specific parallels she identifies; after all, many texts open and close 'with the eternal perspective on the world'. More intertextuality in Maggie Kilgour's '*Comus*'s Wood of Allusion' (*UTQ* 61.316–33): Kilgour concludes that 'allusions themselves serve as one model for a way of knowing others without consuming them, of incorporating them without completely identifying them with oneself'.

In 'A Musical Source for *L'Allegro*?' (*MiltonQ* 27.72–4), in appropriately speculative vein, Raymond B. Waddington ponders the possible influence of Oratio Vecchi's entertainment, *Mascherata della Malinconia*, on Milton's poem. There is a new account of the poem, incorporating some elements of reader-response in Hermine J. van Nuis's 'Surprised by Mirth: The Seductive Strategy of *L'Allegro*' (*MiltonQ* 27.118–26), though it is premised on an improbably naive 'rapid reading' before an enforced 're-reading' and 'reassessment'. A rather different connection with music provides the starting point of Marc Berley's 'Milton's Earthy Grossness: Music and the Condition of the Poet in *L'Allegro* and *Il Penseroso*' (*MiltonS* 30.149–61), which on relatively slender evidence attempts a sweeping reading of these early works as seminal to his epic vision. Mary Elizabeth Basile's 'The Music of *A Maske*' (*MiltonQ* 27.85–98) profitably revisits some questions relating to Milton's relationship with Henry Lawes and the character of Lawes's setting.

Sonnet 23 is interpreted as exhibiting 'a complexity [which] arises at least partly from its concern with differing ways of experiencing loss' in B. J. Sokol's 'Euripides's *Alcestis* and the "Saint" of Milton's Reparative Twenty-third Sonnet' (*SEL* 33.131–47). A complex and fascinating argument from Louis Schwartz, '"Spot of child-bed taint": Seventeenth-Century Obstetrics in Milton's Sonnet 23 and *Paradise Lost* 8.462–78' (*MiltonQ* 27.98–109), explores the previously recognized echoes of Milton's lament for his 'late espoused Saint' in Adam's recollection of his birthing of Eve in terms of male guilt in the context of the horror of contemporary obstetric practice, noting that the latter passage in part parallels the male surgeons' role in dismembering and removing through the vagina embryos dead *in utero*. The gynaecological focus remains for Mary Adams's 'Fallen Wombs: The Origins of Death in Miltonic Sexuality' (*MiltonS* 29.165–79), which ponders the various references to wombs, especially in *Paradise Lost*, *en route* to her conclusion that 'to Milton, perhaps, the shame of lust, in the light of the possibility of perfect sexual love, might have seemed the fittest and most moving emblem of the fallen condition'.

This year sees the publication in CUP's 'Landmarks of World Literature' series of a valuable introductory study of *Paradise Lost* by David Loewenstein. Much less tendentious than the radical post-structuralism of Catherine Belsey's *John Milton: Language, Gender, Power* (Blackwell, 1988) or the quite narrowly focused feminism of Stevie Davies's *Milton* (Harvester, 1991), Loewenstein's book can appropriately find its way into the recommended reading of university teachers of all theoretical orientations. He works patiently, closely and surefootedly through the major areas of interpretative interest (though perhaps skirting the currently unfashionable topic of Milton's style), showing a sensitive awareness of textual nuances and a fine command of the critical issues as defined in recent studies. This, however, is a rather constrictive series (as the curious metaphor of its title suggests, a little fusty in its conception), and the constraints do tell. Loewenstein is an accomplished historicist critic, who has brought much originality to interpreting especially the concluding historical rhapsody of *Paradise Lost* and to defining the radicalism of Milton's last poems; I should have liked to see him cut loose a little to develop more personal readings here. Landmarks are static things, and the best parts of this book are where its author does pull and nudge Milton's text in fresh and distinctive ways. The book constitutes an appropriate entry-level study for smart undergraduates, for neophyte postgraduates, and for teachers looking rapidly to update their knowledge of Milton studies. The chronology of Milton's life and times is judicious and the suggestions for further reading are full and sensible.

Much narrower in focus and in its intended audience, David Reid's *The Humanism of Milton's 'Paradise Lost'* nevertheless manifests a similar level of careful preparation and sustained high competence. Reid richly contextualizes Milton's poetic agenda and psychological assumptions inscribed in his epic in a precisely defined tradition of neoclassical humanism. Shrewdly and persuasively he argues for an intellectual topography manifesting no major fissures between neoclassical humanism and evangelical Protestantism; what separates Erasmus from Luther, in these terms, is 'more of a difference than a true conflict'. Again, Reid is alert to the importance of identifying the neoclassical literary tradition before its subsequent eighteenth-century deformations and Anglocentric appropriations. Reid's Milton is truly a European writer, negotiating a complex position in dialogue with a continental Renaissance.

William M. Porter's *Reading the Classics and 'Paradise Lost'* fascinatingly complements Reid's work and deserves equal attention. Porter is an academic classicist and, as he self-effacingly observes, an amateur Miltonist. What he does is to ponder the rich fabric of Miltonic allusion to classical texts from the perspective of someone at least as interested in Latin and Greek literature as in

Milton. What he finds is a profound dialogue between Milton and classical writers, an open discourse inviting readers' participation in judging quite what critique or stricture or *hommage* is produced in Milton's poem: 'Milton has not wholly determined the meaning of this engagement [with the classics]. Instead he has made it contingent upon the reader's own understanding of the classics. In other words, he has put upon us readers a burden that is almost too much for us to bear'. Porter, who is not always at his most generous in engagement with other Miltonists, manages the burden pretty well himself, and his book not only contains many valuable local readings but also suggests a whole strategy for negotiating the classical intertext of *Paradise Lost*.

A rather different analogue is considered by Harry Redman in 'J. B. Sanson de Pongerville, Anne d'Urfe's *Hymne des anges* and *Paradise Lost*' (*EA* 46.328–33).

Diane Kelsey McColley's splendid *A Gust for Paradise: Milton's Eden and the Visual Arts* richly contextualizes Milton's depiction in the visual art of the late medieval and Renaissance periods. She shows a sensitivity to pictorial interpretation as fine as her critical perspective. This is, moreover, a book informed with a deep and infectious enthusiasm, as much for Milton's visual analogues as for the poem itself. It is illustrated with 60 splendid plates, of paintings, of murals, of manuscript illustrations, of woodcuts and engravings, even of a rather fine painted cabinet depicting, in its panels, scenes from the Genesis account.

In 'Rule, Self, Subject: The Problem of Power in *Paradise Lost*' (*MiltonS* 30.85–108), David Weisberg offers a bold and confident reading, deeply influenced by Foucault. He concludes, 'the power God wields operates through specific methods, such as domination, influence, permission, and prohibition, and through specific knowledges of the material world and the working of the mind. In the poem it is these methods and knowledges that create subjects (and readers) who are aware of the contradictory position of one who simultaneously chooses for oneself and is ruled from outside. This type of contradiction is precisely indicative of the modernity of *Paradise Lost*'. Catherine Gimelli Martin's 'Self-Raised Sinners and the Spirit of Capitalism: *Paradise Lost* and the Critique of Protestant Meliorism' (*MiltonS* 30.109–34) with fine insight juxtaposes discussion of the fallen angels, attempts to improve their lot and the role of the godly in the fallen world: 'Milton consistently argues that the faithful individual must uproot the idea of God as a petty Protestant accountant, replacing it with the conception of a Being who blesses not only repentant Eves, humbled Adams, and struggling Samsons, but also all those who can no longer gloriously strive, and so must merely "stand and wait"'.

Kristin Puritt McColgan in '"God is also in sleep": Dreams Satanic and Divine in *Paradise Lost*' (*MiltonS* 30.135–48) examines the verbal, thematic echoes and parallels in Eve's dreams, seeing in the dream which matches Adam's experience of the prophetic visions of Books XI and XII 'a poetically just, divinely authored revision of the satanic script of loss through self-exaltation'.

In 'Satan's Death Trip' (*MiltonQ* 27.41–8), despite its unpromising title, William Shullenberger produces a characteristically subtle reading of the psychology of Satan's relationship with the Father. Hye-Joon Yoon sometimes puzzles the reader in '"The Fiend Who Came Thir Bane": Satan's Gift to *Paradise Lost*' (*MiltonS* 29.3–19), though the essay has some suggestive power, especially in its reading of the concluding scene of the poem, of its 'serene beauty ... punctuated by a human figure, a laborer at that, whose toil and sweat transform the created nature, the gift of God, to a humanized drama of secular history'. That same scene is the final resting point of Arnold Stein's meditative and wide-ranging 'Imagining Death: the Ways of Milton' (*MiltonS* 29.105–20). 'Losing a Position and Taking One: Theories of Place and *Paradise Lost*' (*MiltonS* 29.21–33) by Jon Whitman, sets Milton's poem against the background of several contrasting attitudes to the concept of place in antiquity.

In ' "Reformed Eloquence": Inability, Questioning, and Correction in *Paradise Lost*' (*UTQ* 62.232–55), Ronald W. Cooley returns to the mature critical debate about Milton's attitude to rhetoric. Another question of some antiquity is revisited by Jane Melbourne in 'The Narrator as Chorus in *Paradise Lost*' (*SEL* 33. 149–65), namely, the relationship of the poem to classical Greek drama. She contends that 'we are to read the narrator of *Paradise Lost* ... as a new creation, a narrator as chorus – an attempt through the person of the narrator, as representative of the reader, to involve the reader in the central epic of human history', perhaps a difficult position to maintain, given the deeply personal and thoroughly Miltonic timbre of that voice. Eve's mirror episode, so fascinating to psychological and feminist critics, finds an intertextual response in Richard J. Durocher's 'Guiding the Glance: Spenser, Milton, and "Venus Looking Glas" ' (*JEGP* 92.325–41). An issue previously well established in the work of Lewalski, Rajan, Low, Labriola and others, that *Paradise Lost* manifests an encyclopedic approach to genre, takes a new turn in Paul J. Klemp's 'Milton's Pastourelle Vision in *Paradise Lost*' (*EA* 46.257–71). His focus is on Milton's appropriation, in depiction of Satan's regard of Eve, of pastourelle, 'a short lyric poem that offers a first-person account of a knight's recent brief journey to a rural area' where 'he hears a shepherdess singing'. Satan's encounter, not with Eve but with her angelic security guards, is the subject of Catherine Gimelli Martin's 'Ithuriel's Spear: Purity, Danger, and Allegory' (*SEL* 33.167–90), a sustained reading which concludes that the passage accomplishes 'a positive, naturalistic reorientation of the antiquated symbol system of allegory'. The same passage receives closing reading of another sort in John Leonard's 'Ported Spears and Waving Corn: *Paradise Lost* IV, 977–980' (*N&Q* 40.315–18), which relates the arms drill of the angels to their moral posture facing Satan. Leonard has another slight but nuanced reading in 'Inured in Fire: A Buried Pun at *Paradise Lost* 2.216' (*ELN* 31.41–3). John Leland's '*Ars Belli*, or Why Cannon Roar' (*ELN* 30.16–29) relates the account in Book VI to other Renaissance depictions of artillery.

Keith N. Hull's 'Rhyme and Disorder in *Samson Agonistes*' (*MiltonS* 30.163–81) returns to the issue of the play's prosody, though readers may wonder whether his narrowly based technical analysis supports his thematic conclusions that 'rhyme is a troublesome indicator of accident as well as God's intention'. David Gay's ' "Honied Words": Wisdom and Recognition in *Samson Agonistes*' (*MiltonS* 29.35–58) takes a new route through the old argument about its structure, but more valuable still is Derek N. C. Wood's essay, 'Aristotle, the Italian Commentators, and Some Aspects of Milton's Christian Tragedy' (*MiltonS* 29.83–104). This has rather less to say about the Italian commentators on Aristotle than about Aristotle himself (perhaps there is useful work still to be done here). However, Wood feeds well on Margaret Arnold's fascinating suggestion that Milton compressed the action of a classical Greek trilogy into *Samson Agonistes*, though he concludes instead that Milton simulates precisely the effect of one play within a trilogy: 'It is true ..., as it might be in the first or second play in a Greek trilogy, that the dramatic action in Milton's play appears to be complete, but the predicate lies in the future with the unfolding of Christian history'.

Paradise Regained received scant attention this year, though Samuel Smith writes well on its apocalyptic dimension in '"Christs Victorie Over the Dragon": The Apocalypse in *Paradise Regained*' (*MiltonS* 29.59–82).

An interesting case of Miltonic influence provides the subject of Taylor Corse's 'Dryden and Milton in "The Cock and the Fox"' (*MiltonQ* 27.109–18). Corse argues that the Miltonic allusions in Dryden's rendering of *The Nun's Priest's Tale* constitute a central part of its meaning: 'Dryden treats the fall of Chanticleer as a version of the Fall of man; and he handles his subject with as much skill and as much recognition of Milton's genius as went into the making of any previous work'.

An early response to *Paradise Lost* is the subject of Nicholas von Maltzahn's fascinating article, 'Laureate, Republican, Calvinist: An Early Response to Milton and *Paradise Lost* (1667)' (*MiltonS* 29.181–98). Von Maltzahn ponders the hitherto unrecorded references to Milton in the correspondence to Evelyn of John Beale (1608–83), a 'rural virtuoso' and country member of the Royal Society. Beale, while deeply critical of Milton's politics (and sensitive to their presence in his epic), has a lively appreciation of his literary achievements, and manifests an early concern with many abiding issues of Milton's studies, including prosody, the depiction of Satan, and the origin of Miltonic inspiration.

Nancy Armstrong and Leonard Tennenhouse have produced a splendid meditation on the representation of Milton in American culture in their substantial study *The Imaginary Puritan: Literature, Intellectual Labor, and the Origins of Personal Life*. Roland Barthes's *Mythologies* inspires this work. Explaining why an early, major chapter is termed semi-facetiously 'The Mind of Milton', they remark, 'If this phrase has a familiar ring to it, that is perhaps because we have tried to think of Milton much as Barthes thought of Einstein in "The Brain of Einstein", Garbo in "The Face of Garbo", or humankind in "The Great Family of Man". That is to say, we have assumed the object of our analysis to exist, in Barthes's words, as "a kind of nebula, more or less hazy, of a certain knowledge"'. This is an American book, addressing an American audience on what it represents as an American problem: 'by providing an English prototype for American poetry and fiction ... Milton has almost single-handedly perpetuated the twin beliefs that English literature is *our* [i.e. American] national literature and that Britishness is a distinctive feature of our national culture'. The argument is fascinating, closely wrought and yet wide-ranging, embracing not only Milton, but Locke, Defoe and Richardson, and their relationship with American high culture's sense of its own identity and its notions of what constitute the personal life.

The Imaginary Puritan is complemented by another study of Milton in America, K. P. Van Anglen's *The New England Milton: Literary Reception and Cultural Authority in the Early Republic*. This is an altogether less theorized account of Milton's impact on antebellum America, addressing the significance of Milton for writers such as Emerson, Thoreau, Cooper, Hawthorne, Melville and Whitman.

Revived interest in twentieth-century illustrators of Milton, recently manifest in the critical rediscovery of Mary Groom, recurs in Bruce Lawson's 'Unifying Milton's Epics: Carlotta Petrina's Illustrations for *Paradise Regained*' (*MiltonS*

30.183–218). The secondary title-pages reproduced here show an artist with a powerful sense of design and a fine command of detail. Lawson's analysis demonstrates her to be, as Milton's best illustrators always are, a subtle reader of and commentator on his poetry.

MCJ News 14 contains abstracts of papers presented to symposia on Milton in Japan in 1992 and a bibliography of publications in Milton studies in Japan in 1991.

Books Reviewed

Armstrong, Nancy, and Leonard Tennenhouse. *The Imaginary Puritan: Literature, Intellectual Labor, and the Origins of Personal Life.* UCalP. pp. 275. £28. ISBN 0 520 07756 3.

Bradshaw, Brendan, Andrew Hadfield, and Willy Maley, eds. *Representing Ireland: Literature and the Origins of Conflict, 1534–1660.* CUP. pp. 235. £37.50. ISBN 0 521 41634 5.

Driscoll, James P. *The Unfolding God of Jung and Milton.* UPKen. pp. 248. $33. ISBN 0 8131 1809 3.

Elledge, Scott. ed. *Paradise Lost.* Norton Critical Edition. Norton. pp. 685. £7.95. ISBN 0 393 962293 8.

Honeygosky, Stephen R. *Milton's House of God: The Invisible and Visible Church.* UMissP. pp. 255. £35.95. ISBN 0 8262 0876 2.

Martinet, Marie-Madeleine, ed. *John Milton: Ecrits Politiques.* Belin. pp. 335. ISBN 2 7011 1037 8.

Loewenstein, David. *Paradise Lost.* Landmarks in World Literature. CUP. pp. 160. £6.95. ISBN 0 521 39899 1.

McColley, Diane Kelsey. *A Gust for Paradise: Milton's Eden and the Visual Arts.* UIllP. pp. 305. $49.95. ISBN 0 252 01828 1.

Nemoianu, Virgil, and Robert Royal, eds. *Play, Literature, Religion: Essays in Cultural Intertextuality.* SUNYP. pp. 221. $16.95. ISBN 0 7914 0936 8.

Porter, William M. *Reading the Classics and 'Paradise Lost'.* UNebP. pp. 222. £28.50. ISBN 0 8032 3706 5.

Reid, David. *The Humanism of Milton's 'Paradise Lost'.* EdinUP. pp. 186. £30. ISBN 0 7486 0401 4.

Shawcross, John T. *Milton: The Self and the World.* UPKen. pp. 358. $35. ISBN 0 8131 1808 5.

Shoaf, R. A. *Milton Poet of Duality: A Study of Semiosis in the Poetry and the Prose.* UFlorP. pp. 225. £17.95. ISBN 0 8130 1192 2.

Van Angen, K. P. *The New England Milton: Literary Reception and Cultural Authority in the Early Republic.* PSUP. pp. 225. $40. ISBN 0 271 00848 2.

X

The Later Seventeenth Century

STUART GILLESPIE, ROGER POOLEY and JAMES OGDEN

This chapter has three sections: 1. General; 2. Dryden; 3. Other Authors. Sections 1(b) and 3(b) are by Roger Pooley; section 2(b) is by James Ogden; and the rest is by Stuart Gillespie.

1. General

Restoration's biannual round-ups of 'Some Current Publications' were compiled this year by Darin E. Fields and Jocelyn Coates (17.57–71, 135–50). As usual, the 'some' is not strictly necessary given the extensive coverage. Susan Staves was *SEL*'s reviewer of 'Recent Studies in the Restoration and Eighteenth Century' (33.659–97). Easily the most durable-looking work of reference to appear this year was the second part of the second volume of Mansell's *Index of English Literary Manuscripts*. Peter Beal's *Lee-Wycherley* completed this stage of the project, which will be rounded off by an index to Volumes I and II. In reviewing Part 1 of the current volume in 1987, *YWES* (68.6) thought it 'hard to find high enough praise for Peter Beal's volume or for the series as a whole', and it is even harder now that the task is finished. If further evidence were needed of Beal's sedulous devotion to scholarly duty, one might add that the most extensive entry here by some way – almost three times as long as Milton's at 94 pages – is that pertaining to William Strode.

Howard D. Weinbrot's *Britannia's Issue: The Rise of British Literature from Dryden to Ossian* is also a hefty volume. Its subject is the creation of a British literary consciousness through a complex set of negotiations with 'classical' norms. We have discussion of Cowley as the founder of the English ode; of Dryden's combative nationalism in the *Essay of Dramatic Poesy* and his development of the pindaric in the Killigrew Ode (recent 'ironic' readings of which Weinbrot rejects); of Oldham's contribution to the growing repute of the imitation. But most of these parts are not satisfactorily separable from the rest of a book which in all respects comes to rest in the eighteenth century, relying heavily on later material in its polemical objectives (we are to see 'Augustanism and neoclassicism, Augustan humanism, and the anxiety of influence as well-meaning muddles', for instance). Thus, Chapter XII can only wave Weinbrot off on his journey; for an account of his travels, see Chapter XIII. Meanwhile, one short

paper also requires mention here. David R. Evans was responsible for 'Charles
II's "Grand Tour": Restoration Panegyric and the Rhetoric of Travel Literature'
(*PQ* 72.53–71). Evans shows how Restoration verse and prose panegyrics –
Waller, Flecknoe, Dryden, Howell – endorse the restored monarchy by representing Charles II's exile during the interregnum as 'an occult benefit to the king's,
and therefore the nation's, well-being'. Charles was compared to Ulysses, or
represented as a ship 'fraught' with 'ruling wisdom' garnered on his 'travels'.
This may indeed be an example of discontinuity in the imagery of kingship on
either side of the interregnum, but even when viewed in this light most of the
texts discussed fail to look all that exciting.

(a) Poetry

Paul Hammond pursues two related subjects in 'Anonymity in Restoration Poetry' (*SC* 8.123–42) and 'Censorship in the Manuscript Transmission of Restoration Poetry' (*E&S* 45.39–62). The *SC* article is the first of a batch of papers to
be reviewed in this chapter from the special issue of that journal on 'Forms of
Authority in Restoration England', edited by Hammond himself. The issue maintains a notably high standard throughout. This item is a fine essay on the possible
ways of using, and of interpreting, anonymity, drawing on a wide range of
illustrations from manuscript and printed evidence, especially among the work of
Dryden, Oldham and Rochester. It is deft and often suggestive, for example in
observing that we might see the manuscript circulation of poems as an invitation
to readers to adapt them, and in drawing attention to the fact that the names of
the writers of prologues and epilogues for the Restoration stage were usually not
known to the audience. Hammond's *E&S* article proposes a model for our
understanding of censorship in the period which involves not a central authority
but a 'network of power' in which writers, scribes and readers 'struggle
for ... control'. This tends to make 'censorship' into a fairly indistinct concept.
For practical purposes, however, Hammond focuses on how and why professional
manuscript copyists altered or excised what they did not approve in two areas –
political poetry, and the work of Rochester. The how proves easier to ascertain
than the why, since many of the alterations he adduces are capable of more than
one explanation. Either the copyist is performing an act of censorship, or he is
dozing off after a heavy lunch: we draw conclusions at our peril.

A further paper of Hammond's, '"The Miseries of Visits": An Addition to the
Literature on Robert Julian, Secretary to the Muses' (*SC* 8.161–3), is an edition
of a short satire Hammond dates to 1680, found, among other sources, in a
manuscript now in the Brotherton Collection. The poem concerns one of the men
whose business it was to arrange scribal copying of poetry for private purchasers
around this date, and leads us directly into the ambit of Harold Love's *magnum
opus*, *Scribal Publication in Seventeenth-Century England*, not least because
Love happens to print another text of the same satire. But that is the smallest of
his book's attractions. The value of Love's work on scribal publication has been
recognized by *YWES* reviewers on numerous occasions in recent years (*YWES*
68.7, 322, 820, 823, for example), and sections of the present book draw on his
previous articles. But then we knew in part, and we prophesied in part; now we
see the whole, in more ways than one. As Love says, the growth since about 1960
in our knowledge of Restoration verse manuscripts has mostly come from investigation of individual texts; until now, little has been done on the culture of

transmission in general or on the larger manuscript anthologies. Furthermore, Love argues, scholars in this field have failed to draw together knowledge on the seventeenth century as a whole, whereas it is essential to see scribal transmission as part of the sociocultural picture over a substantial period. But these wide perspectives are opened up through discussions of local documentary detail which are important assemblages of information in their own right, on, for example, what Love calls 'Restoration scriptorial satire'. Love's work is a most impressive study of a crucially important phenomenon, and will be a resource for a generation of scholars to come.

William C. Horne's *Making a Heaven of Hell: The Problem of the Companionate Ideal in English Marriage Poetry, 1650–1800* also treats our period as part of a larger picture, taking in Dryden, Behn, Philips, Prior, Rochester, Sedley, Butler and smaller fry too numerous to mention. The ways in which the chapters are organized – thematic, generic, chronological – ensure that we never stay with one poem (or poet) for more than a paragraph or two, and very minor work is mixed up with the major. In some ways we find ourselves more in the field of social history than literature. On the other hand, Horne attempts a complete overview of 'marriage poems' in this long eighteenth century, providing a comprehensive checklist of them in an appendix, so that there is some justification for the claim on the cover that the book is a 'research tool'. It is, in fact, thus that the book will be most used, so I hope it does not sound too slighting to say that its actual theses, about the hesitant but gradual rise of the 'companionate ideal' over the period, are not inordinately interesting from a literary point of view. There is a cornucopia of information here, and if we want to contextualize the anti-marriage passage in 'To my Honour'd Kinsman', or to know what epithalamia were composed after the seventeenth century, this is the place to go.

Finally under this heading, and bearing little connection with anything else, there is 'A New Parliament of Birds: Aesop, Fiction, and Jacobite Rhetoric' (*ECS* 27.235–54) by Tomoko Hanazaki. This shows how fable writing develops from the 1690s onwards so as to deal with day-to-day political issues at a popular level. The discussion spills over quickly into the eighteenth century, but one connection with our period is that these pamphlets and collections 'were clearly intended ... often for an audience familiar with Dryden's *The Hind and the Panther*'.

(b) Prose

This has been a good year for studies of prose as a vehicle for ideas. *Political Discourse in Early Modern Britain*, edited by Nicholas Phillipson and Quentin Skinner, is a tribute to J. G. A. Pocock and covers much of his distinctive territory, particularly in the political ideas of the mid- to late seventeenth century. As well as important discussions of Hobbes (Skinner on his rhetoric, Richard Tuck on 'civil religion'), Harrington (Jonathan Scott), and Hume (Phillipson, Istvan Hont and John Robertson), there is a piece on Samuel Parker by Gordon Schochet which ought to be read by everyone who simply thinks of him as the occasion for Marvell's *Rehearsal Transpos'd*. Arminianism, Whigs and anti-clericalism all come in for fresh discussion (William Lamont and Mark Goldie seem particularly noteworthy). Pocock's own response at the end of the volume is also considerable; he ought to be more used by literary critics presently in thrall to less substantial writers on the thought of the period.

In *Fallen Languages: Crises of Representation in Newtonian England, 1660–1740*, Robert Markley continues his work on the history of representation begun in *Two-Edg'd Weapons* (see *YWES* 69.317). Despite the title, the focus is on Boyle as much as Newton, and, in particular, on those works of 'physico-theology' (Walter Charleton's term, gratefully appropriated) which relate science and theology. Theology, he argues, was these writers' principal theory. His main aim is to question the persistently progressivist accounts we have of both language and science in the period. By driving the story well into the eighteenth century, he is able to show how Boyle was rewritten out of a theological and gentlemanly context into a narrative of scientific and technological progress. Along with Kroll's *Material Word* and a host of articles from various disciplines, Markley's book argues for a significant change in the way modern science's myths of its own origins are allowed to affect our sense of the late seventeenth century. On the same area and with a similar theoretical predisposition as Markley's second chapter, Frank D. Walters's 'Taxonomy and the Undoing of Language: Dialogic Form in the Universal Languages of the Seventeenth Century' (*Style* 27.1–16) applies a Bakhtinian model to the project of universal language, and Wilkins's *Real Character* in particular. While he makes some interesting points about the relation of semantics and syntax to ontology and taxonomy, the overall conclusion reverts to the old anti-Ciceronian explanations for scientific language.

Richard Kroll, Richard Ashcraft and Perez Zagorin have edited *Philosophy, Science and Religion in England, 1640–1700*, which focuses on Latitudinarianism and its wider significance for cultural and intellectual issues in our period. Kroll's introduction stresses the link between debates about language and social behaviour, especially with enthusiasm's 'resistance to representation, the refusal to perform all individual acts under the social gaze'. The contributors generally stick to a model of history of ideas within a framework of political struggle (the substance of Ashcraft's contribution). There are two main sections. The first, on the Cambridge Platonists, includes Allison Condert on 'Henry More, the Kabbalah, and the Quakers', about convergent emphases on the religion of the heart, a perceptive note by Sarah Hutton on the different attitudes to Plato in Mire and Stillingfleet's *Origenes Sacra*, and Alan Gabney offering a rather more speculative link with the new science in 'Cudworth, More, and the Mechanical Analogy'. Zagorin's essay on 'Cudworth and Hobbes on Is and Ought' deals with the law/liberty distinction. The second section, on the Restoration settlement, has Margaret Osler demonstrating the influence of Gassendi on Boyle, an important revisionary piece on Sprat's *History of the Royal Society* by Michael Hunter, and two pieces on Locke: G. A. J. Rogers on the argument for tolerance from ignorance, and John Marshall on Locke's knowledge of the Latitudinarians.

Steven Zwicker's *Lines of Authority: Politics and English Literary Culture, 1649–1689* ranges wider than prose – the poetry of Marvell, Milton and Dryden feature as well – to establish a thesis that relates polemic and poetics in a period defined by the execution of one king and the deposition of another. After a purposeful introduction on the relation between invention and authority in Renaissance poetics, there follow chapters on *Eikon Basilike* and *Eikonoklastes*, *The Compleat Angler* and *The First Anniversary*, *Annus Mirabilis*, *Last Instructions* and *Paradise Lost*, *Absalom and Achitophel* and Locke's *Two Treatises* (a brilliant comparison), and Dryden's *Don Sebastian* as a masterpiece of reaction to William's revolution. Zwicker shows what can be done with good poems when one knows one's history and political theory – not so much new historicism as political historicism – and in doing so, constructs a persuasive model of the contested nature of aesthetics in and around the Restoration.

A number of important articles from *JHI*, mostly from the 1970s and 1980s, are reprinted in John W. Yolton (ed.) *Philosophy, Religion and Science in the 17th and 18th Centuries*. The main focus is on Locke and Newton and the inter-relation of the three fields in the title. Samuel G. Wong, on 'The Composition of Light in Newton's *Opticks*' (*PSt* 16.119–47), perceptively delineates the literary richness of Newton's text, its 'idealized narrative' of experimentation, its use of analogy, and its selective use of past authorities. Roger Pooley's *English Prose of the Seventeenth Century, 1590–1700* discusses a range of writers from this period under generic and thematic headings – narrative, religious prose, essays and scientific and political discourse.

The importance of Foxe's *Acts and Monuments* for English Protestantism's sense of itself has long been recognized, but John R. Knott's *Discourses of Martyrdom in English Literature, 1563–1694* manages to be both fresh and systematic in its approach to Foxe's influence. In particular, he details a discourse of faith as resistance in Foxe and a range of others, quietly showing the limita-tions of William Haller's work on the one hand and the application of Foucault on the other. He is particularly interesting on Lilburne, and there are substantial and revealing chapters on Milton (a nice discussion of 'aggressive martyrdom'), Bunyan and George Fox.

In a contribution to the history of sexuality, Emma Donoghue's 'Imagined More than Women: Lesbians as Hermaphrodites' (*Women's History Review* 2.199–216) traces the imputed link between lesbian desire and hermaphrodite anatomy in a range of treatises and a couple of literary texts, a poem of Aphra Behn's, and *The Memoirs of Count Grammont*. These things happen in France and Egypt rather than England, naturally. The footnotes suggest some fascinating possibilities for further work.

2.   Dryden

Two books, by Steven N. Zwicker and Phillip Harth, share some common ground; however, their approach differs. Zwicker's *Lines of Authority: Politics and English Literary Culture, 1649–1689* is more on Dryden than any other writer, although it also has material on Milton, Marvell, Locke, Izaak Walton and others. *Annus Mirabilis*, *Absalom and Achitophel* and *Don Sebastian* are paired in turn with texts from opposing sides of the contemporary political divide in an attempt to 'complicate the way we read literature'. One might have thought it was already sufficiently complicated, but we are now required, for instance, to find in Milton's 'Hail wedded love' passage 'topical urgency' and 'polemical point'. Happily, Zwicker is on firmer ground in seeking such things in the Dryden works, but his own evident bias towards the Whigs gets in the way of a balanced treatment of them. The premise of Harth's *Pen for a Party: Dryden's Tory Propaganda in its Contexts* is that the immediate contexts of the Dryden works he discusses must be sought in the contemporary propaganda campaigns rather than the actual historical events those works treat. Harth's knowledge of the primary literature is formidable, and he uses it to bring a new coherence to our understanding of the Tory campaigns of the early 1680s (he distinguishes them, and detects successive phases within them), solving some smaller-scale puzzles along the way. As for Dryden's work, we have detailed readings, usually persuasive, of the period from *Absalom and Achitophel* to *Albion and Albanius*, the latter now revealed as part of a propaganda offensive.

A collection of ten published essays by the late Thomas H. Fujimura was edited by Robert W. McHenry Jr and aptly entitled *The Temper of John Dryden*. All the essays have been reviewed in *YWES* and are reviewed again by McHenry in his introduction. More than most critics of his generation, Fujimura admired Dryden and pursued a biographical approach. His early essays on the heroic plays (*YWES* 41.172) and *Religio Laici* (42.177) mainly concerned Dryden's ideas, but later ones on 'The Personal Element' (YWES 55.303–4) and 'The Temper of John Dryden' (56.226) emphasized more the human appeal of the poet's personality. Finally, Fujimura applied biography to Dryden's Virgil (*YWES* 64.279) and the late works generally (65.324–5). His last essay, 'Dryden's Changing Political Views' (*YWES* 67.305), expressed his sense of a conflict between Dryden's natural aggressiveness and his Christian convictions. Although I thought he sometimes strained himself to represent Dryden as a romantic figure, I miss the regular eruptions of Fujimura on distant Hawaii. [J.O.]

Our miscellany of shorter items begins with *Literary Transmission and Authority: Dryden and Other Writers*, a mixed, and uncapacious, bag of four essays plus an introduction, edited by Earl Miner and Jennifer Brady. The editors write respectively on Dryden's Ovid and Dryden's relations with Jonson and Congreve; Greg Clingham contributes an essay on Johnson's Dryden, and David Kramer one on Dryden's Corneille. All the contributions are remarkably different in method, manner, and even ultimately in the nature of their subject matter. In other words, the individual items should perhaps have been published as articles instead, and the volume, although not a bad idea in principle, lacks coherence. All the same, the stronger essays, by Clingham and Brady, are worth having in any form. Nor should one assume that Brady's 'Collaborating with the Forebear: Dryden's Reception of Ben Jonson' (*MLQ* 54.345–69) might be a mere recycling of the Jonson material in her contribution: it is, in fact, a different and fuller treatment of the subject with some stimulating reflections on Dryden's work as a collaborator in general. Robert W. McHenry Jr takes a phrase from *Annus Mirabilis* for his title, 'Dryden and the "Metropolis of Great Britain"' (*SVEC* (1992) 303.145–8), But this short discussion avers that 'his poetry as a whole shows surprisingly little interest' in many aspects of contemporary London. McHenry appears to think that only fully fledged descriptive treatment of the city can count as evincing 'interest', as though Dryden were obliged to be some sort of Pevsner *de ses jours* to qualify as a true urban poet. Hence he ignores the many references to London life in, for example, Dryden's versions of Latin satires; he also ignores such works as *The Spanish Fryar* and *Albion and Albanius* altogether. Jerome Donnelly's 'John Dryden and the failure of political categories' (*SVEC* (1992) 305.1392–4) is a tantalizingly short conference presentation setting out a programme for 'de-mythologis[ing]' Dryden's 'conservatism'. Intelligent support is adduced for the view that 'Tory supporter though he was, Dryden's politics ultimately transcend either party'. We must await the article(s) Donnelly has to write if he is to give his opinions a more thorough airing.

(a) Poetry

Most of the above items draw heavily, although not exclusively, on Dryden's poetry, which is compensation for the leanness of the year's work specifically in this category. It consists of only one student edition, one essay and a clutch of short notes on possible sources for poems and parts of poems. The edition need not detain us long. Donald Thomas's *John Dryden: Selected Poems* is a perfunctory attempt to compete in the cheap paperback market; it has no new ideas and an unseemly error quotient in factual information provided. It is unlikely that students will be inspired by the critical pointers thrown out in the introduction. 'In [Dryden's] use of metaphor alone', Thomas writes, 'there is a universality of appeal in much of his writing. So there is in the truth of his maxims ... His insults have a craft that weathers the passage of the years.' The same cannot be said of Thomas's critical assumptions, heavily redolent as they are of the early to mid-twentieth century. Stuart Gillespie's 'Horace's *Ode* 3.29: Dryden's "Masterpiece in English"', in Martindale and Hopkins, speaks up for an undervalued part of the corpus in that period, the translations. This one, Gillespie argues, is 'a poem which compels our fullest attention', both as a reading of Horace's poem and as in itself 'one of [Dryden's] most attractive renderings from the classics in his wide and varied work on them'.

David Hopkins sees 'Nahum Tate's "On Their Majesties Pictures" as a Source for Dryden's "To Sir Godfrey Kneller"' (*N&Q* 40.322–3). Hopkins argues that the Tate poem is to be preferred to Richard Lovelace's 'Peinture' as the main source for Dryden's praise of Kneller, on several counts. Perhaps none is finally decisive, but if we require a source for the passage in question, this one is certainly made to seem more plausible than its rival. Taylor Corse offers 'A Note on Dryden and Larks' (*Restoration* 17.53–6), sketching a literary background in Milton, Spenser and other poets for Dryden's image of 'mounting Larkes' at the close of the Killigrew Ode. The lark has 'no mythological ancestry', and so, Corse thinks, had to be emblematized independently by English poets; but he does not examine any poetry from the European tradition. The same commentator's 'Roman Skies in *Threnodia Augustalis*' (*N&Q* 40.321) explains what does not need explaining by reference to something that does not explain it. Why, he asks, should the 'thunder-clap' in line 16 be 'so startling'? But thunder-claps are usually thought to be startling, so there was no need for Corse's laboured attempt to relate this one to Horace's *Ode* I.34. Margaret Duggan's 'Medievalism and *The Hind and the Panther*' (*SVEC* (1992) 305.1394–7) briefly reviews some sources and analogues for the poem's use of animal fable. This is a kind of 'medievalism', she contends, that 'many of Dryden's contemporaries understood and approved', and which if recovered would help make the poem 'available' once more. Really?

Three notes on *Absalom and Achitophel* complete the rather small-scale picture for this section. Taylor Corse finds 'An Echo of Virgil in *Absalom and Achitophel*' and 'An Allusion to Horace in *Absalom and Achitophel*' (*N&Q* 40.318–19, 319–20). Monmouth's effect on his supporters, Corse says, recalls Alecto's possession of Amata in *Aeneid* VII; Dryden's description of Shaftesbury as a 'pilot' can be related to Horace's Ode II.10. The evidence on both counts is inconclusive, but even if they are taken the points make little difference to one's reading of the poem. Heidi Kelchner's brief discussion 'Dryden's *Absalom and Achitophel*' (*Expl* 51.216–19) notes Renaissance sources for the notion that bastards were superior to legitimate progeny because they were 'got with a greater gust', as Dryden puts it, ironically, in describing Absalom near the beginning of the poem. Perhaps this is useful, but if one had wished to know about it, a short spell with a bibliography on *King Lear* would surely have done the trick.

(b) Plays

Dryden 'appears never to have much pleased himself with his own dramas', according to Johnson, and this year he did not much please his critics either, especially those occupied on his more serious plays. Two essays related the heroic plays to colonialism. J. E. Svilpis's 'Orientalism, Kinship, and Will in Restoration Drama' (*SVEC* (1992) 303.435–9) briefly considers *The Conquest of Granada*, *Aureng-Zebe*, Elkanah Settle's *The Empress of Morocco* and Nicholas Rowe's *Tamerlane*, to conclude that 'in creating an imaginary non-European world of unnaturally misused power, this drama set the stage on to which the white man would shortly carry his burden in the later, much darker play of colonialism'. In short, this drama was not genuinely enlightened. Nandini Bhattacharya's 'Ethnopolitical Dynamics and the Language of Gendering in Dryden's *Aureng-Zebe*' (*CulC* 25.153–76) interprets this play as 'a proto-text of colonial expansionism'. Its Indian hero is noble but effeminate, so that non-Western culture can be shown as essentially vulnerable, 'therefore seeming fair target for penetration and possession'. Of these two essays I found Svilpis's the more stimulating as it is shorter, less verbose and more wide-ranging. Marcie Frank's 'Staging Criticism, Staging Milton: John Dryden's *The State of Innocence*' (*ECent* 34.45–64) argues that opposition to revolutionary politics informs both Dryden's adaptation of *Paradise Lost* as a rhymed drama and his comments on Milton as a literary authority. Dryden's creation of a critical discourse in which Milton could be thought great but harmless seems to Ms Frank especially deplorable, but as Milton was a man too I would have thought that from her perspective there was something to be said for it. N. I. Matar's interesting essay on 'The Renegade in English Seventeenth-Century Imagination' (*SEL* 33.489–505) maintains that Dryden's presentation of the renegade improves on those of Richard Daborn and Philip Massinger: Dorax in *Don Sebastian* has virtue and stature, both as renegade from Christianity and as convert back to it. But Dryden was alarmed by signs of a sympathetic attitude to Islam among Protestants.

Critics of the comedies were less partisan, more relaxed. Stephen P. Flores's 'Negotiating Cultural Prerogatives in Dryden's *Secret Love* and *Sir Martin Mar-all*' (*PLL* 29.170–96) reminds us that Samuel Pepys thought the former 'one of the best plays I ever saw', and that John Loftis thought the latter perhaps Dryden's most popular play in his lifetime. Flores explains these successes by the audience's interest in seeing both restorations of order and critiques of received ideas on gender, rank and merit. Less plausibly, he suggests that in *Sir Martin Mar-all* old Moody, who loses his daughter to an impoverished cavalier, might have been a supporter of Cromwell. 'Thomas Durfey's *A Fond Husband*, Sex Comedies and the Comic Sublime' (*SP* 90.371–90), by Christopher J. Wheatley, suggests that Dryden in *The Kind Keeper* ridicules Durfey's association of eloquence and adultery: in this play 'departures into the sublime are the province of cuckolds', and Limberham hears a voice saying 'Sleep no more; Tricksy has murdered sleep'.

There is an essay on the heroic plays in Thomas Fujimura's *The Temper of John Dryden*, and a chapter on *Don Sebastian* in Steven Zwicker's *Lines of Authority*. There are some comments on wit in the early comedies in Michael Gelber's 'Dryden's Theory of Comedy'. These items are reviewed elsewhere in this section.

(c)   Prose

Of five items belonging under this heading, three are general and two on individual prose works. All five discuss Dryden's criticism. Laura L. Runge's title is as wordy as her summary. In '"The Softness of Expression, and the Smoothness of Measure": A Model of Gendered Decorum from Dryden's Criticism' (*ELWIU* 20.197–212), she 'investigates Dryden's use of gender as a model of difference upon which he established literary judgment with the intent to prove the extent to which critical discourse intersects with the culturally specific ideology of gender'. But one should not be altogether put off by this ugly sample: the discussion is wide-ranging and fair-minded on its own terms, which are interestingly different from those of James Winn in '*When Beauty Fires the Blood*' (*YWES* 73.265), where Runge locates some of her starting-points. Paul Hammond's 'Figures of Horace in Dryden's Literary Criticism', in the Martindale and Hopkins volume, is a careful treatment of Dryden's use of Horace principally in his writing on drama to 1678, with special emphasis on the Dryden–Shadwell debate. Michael Werth Gelber offers to analyse 'Dryden's Theory of Comedy' (*ECS* 26.261–83). He starts by referring to the early comic plays ('low comedy') and concludes with examples from *An Evening's Love* and *Marriage A-la-Mode* (more 'urbane'). In between, Gelber explains the difference by expounding Dryden's comments on 'wit', but gets bogged down in disentangling the various implications of this chameleon term – he thinks we need to be shown, for example, that Dryden is not trying to write metaphysical poetry in his plays.

Gelber resurfaces to provide for 'Dryden's "Defence of the Epilogue": A Reinterpretation' (*PLL* 29.323–35). Or perhaps it is best described as a defence of Dryden's 'Defence': the essay, Gelber notes, 'has never been well received', and he seeks to reinstate it as clarifying 'a key moment in Dryden's thinking' about the history of English drama and literary language. If this is not wholly convincing – more emphasis seems needed on the essay's occasional status, for example as an episode in Dryden's abandoned projects for an English academy – Gelber does at least show how some of Dryden's ideas in these areas are developing in the early 1670s. Finally here, J. P. Vander Motten discovers yet another source for the form of Dryden's best-known critical work in '"Sometimes Admiration Quickens Our Endeavours": Dryden, Galileo, and the *Essay of Dramatic Poesy*' (*SP* 90.391–425). This essay proposes – at some length – a dialogue by Galileo, translated by Thomas Salusbury in the 1660s as *The Systeme of the World: In Four Dialogues*. While arguing that Galileo is at least as plausible as some of the other sources suggested over the years, Vander Motten is appropriately hesitant about the conclusiveness of his case. There is nothing inherently impossible in the thesis; neither is it irresistible.

3.   Other Authors

(a)   Poetry

There are those who imagine our period as a placid backwater in which nothing has changed for a generation or two. Almost everything in the ensuing section shows otherwise. For example, Cowley is being worked on once again. The six-volume UDelP *Collected Works of Abraham Cowley* is fully under steam, and

Part 1 of Volume II, containing *The Mistress*, comes up for notice this year. So comprehensive are the efforts of Thomas O. Calhoun and his colleagues here that less than a fifth of the 650-page volume is sufficient for the text itself. Over half is occupied by printings of and notes to the musical settings of the poems, evidently a labour of love on the part of J. Robert King. Is there an element of overdoing things? Clearly so; but hard-pressed librarians may console themselves with the reflections that a British publisher would charge twice as much for a volume of this size, and that they will not need to buy another complete Cowley for a very long time indeed. On a smaller scale, David Hopkins has an admirable essay on 'Cowley's Horatian Mice' in Martindale and Hopkins. Charles Tomlinson once called 'The Country Mouse' Cowley's 'finest single poem', and, partly through extensive comparison with earlier and later versions of the Horatian original, partly through a lucid demonstration of Cowley's relation to 'Epicureanism', Hopkins's essay persuasively bears out Tomlinson's judgement. It also goes further: the poem is a key episode in English Horatianism, for Cowley is, as T. S. Eliot said of Ezra Pound's translations, both 'giving the original through himself and finding himself through the original'. Stella P. Revard's 'Abraham Cowley's *Pindarique Odes* and the Politics of the Inter-regnum [*sic*]' (*Criticism* 35.391–418) is a thoroughgoing attempt to identify a hidden political agenda in Cowley's 1656 volume. It does not really work. Some of the contemporary references are not in doubt; but Revard tries to involve every ode, translations and originals, and wants the whole book to constitute 'a coded message to the people of England, one which those in the know may very easily decipher and read'. Since she is unable to provide evidence about how far people did so in this period (or any other), and since even she finds it very hard to 'decipher' many of the 'messages' she wishes to find, it is safe to go on assuming that the 'politics of the Inter-regnum' are an occasional presence in, not a *raison d'être* for, the *Pindarique Odes*.

Rochester has had a full year, as has lately become usual: editorial, biographical, critical, and other studies proliferated. Jeremy Lamb's *So Idle a Rogue: The Life and Times of Lord Rochester* (Allison and Busby) was not available for review, so we begin instead with Marianne Thormählen's *Rochester: The Poems in Context*. This is only the third modern monograph on Rochester; it is considerably bulkier than Dustin Griffin and David Farley-Hills's volumes of the 1970s (*YWES* 54.266–7, 59.228). They focused on literary connections and influences. Thormählen says she is more concerned with Restoration events and personalities, but is in fact informative on the literary connections as well: to take two different examples, the index entries for Montaigne and Butler will both repay attention. Like many other critics, Thormählen has trouble finding a proper academic frame of reference for some of Rochester's work, and it is almost touching to see her noting details of the contemporary trade in imported dildos in her chapter on the lampoons. She seems happiest with the weightier satires, to which, like her predecessors, she devotes a preponderance of her space. Here she is knowledgeable and thorough, and proves that it was indeed time to gather up the scattered strands of Rochester scholarship since the earlier books appeared. The other book-length contribution this year was Paddy Lyons's student edition of *Rochester: Complete Poems and Plays*. If anything it is too complete, for Lyons adds rather freely to the canon, not only by assigning *Sodom* to Rochester on the basis of J. W. Johnson's recent review of the evidence (found unconvincing in *YWES* 68.329; but Lyons is not alone in following him). And although it may be a defensible principle to use the first printed text of individual works in most cases, Lyons does not find space to explain it. This volume looks handy as making Rochester available *in toto* at an affordable price, but Frank Ellis's Penguin edition of *The Complete Works*, to be reviewed next year, is only a little dearer and much more generous with documentation, especially biographical. Still, if every penny counts, Lyons is able to offer reasonably extensive notes, although they do not extend to information on even major textual variants. Naturally, the texts are modernized; the letters are not included.

Gillian Manning wrote on 'Rochester's *Satire Against Reason and Mankind* and Contemporary Religious Debate' (*SCent* 8.99–121). This article is equally useful as a contribution to our knowledge of the context of Rochester's poem and, more generally, as an investigation of attitudes towards irreligion from the 1650s to the 1670s. In the latter area it is the essayists and controversialists, rather than the imaginative writers, to whom Manning directs her attention. With Rochester's poem, she confirms what has been suspected before – that it was to some degree occasioned by a contemporary debate – but shows that the debate in question is much more extensive than we thought. Two papers on manuscripts complete Rochester's subsection here. Harold Love's 'A Restoration Lampoon in Transmission and Revision: Rochester's(?) "Signior Dildo"' (*SB* 46.250–62) begins by quoting Keith Walker's judgement that with this poem 'there is general agreement on the title, but upon little else'. Love has risen bravely to the challenge, and the result is a complete collation of the ten known early texts, together with conclusions on filiation and an interesting review of the evidence on authorship in which the case for Rochester is found 'not particularly strong' – despite the fact that all Rochester's editors have admitted the poem. All this makes for a peculiar article: the collation, which takes up most of the space, might more naturally have been presented in an edition. Later editors will be thankful for Love's industry, but the article, however admirable as a piece of research, is of highly specialized interest as a piece of publication. Paul Hammond's 'An Unrecorded Elegy on Ossory, Rochester, and Bedloe' (*Restoration* 17.85–7) makes good the lack of recording in question by describing and printing an unattributed couplet poem of some 70 lines dating from 1680, from a possibly unique copy now in the Brotherton Collection. The unknown writer's main interest, extending over half the poem, is in Rochester as poet and wit.

Most of this year's contributions on the women poets Katherine Philips and Aphra Behn divide into gender studies and scholarship. Straddling this line uneasily is the final volume in the Stump Cross *Collected Works of Katherine Philips*. Two earlier volumes (*YWES* 71.351, 73.268) covered the poems and letters; the third, edited by Germaine Greer and Ruth Little, consists of *The Translations* – of Corneille, St Amant and others – together with a useful section collecting together 'Poems addressed to Katherine Philips' up to 1667. The text is elegantly printed, uniformly with the previous volumes, but there is considerable uncertainty about what else to include. Textual variants are recorded minutely, as are low-level glosses of proper nouns such as 'Philomel'; but there is a lack of contextual information about the works. The most peculiar features arise from the effort to do all this editing on proper feminist principles, so that allusions are explained wherever possible through reference to texts by seventeenth-century women writers, and Cowley is castigated quite pointlessly for the 'male supremacist' attitudes in his commendatory verses to Philips's *Poems*. It is also most unfortunate that Greer and Little were unable to use (although they do list in their bibliography, inaccurately) Elizabeth H. Hageman and Andrea Sununu's 'New Manuscript Texts of Katherine Philips, the "Matchless Orinda"' (*EMS* 4.174–219). These two American professors are engaged on another edition of Philips, and more collaboration should obviously have gone on; this important article takes forward work done for the Stump Cross edition in documenting new manuscript items, including three autograph poems and evidence on the currency of Philips's writing in the late seventeenth century. Two single finds of these types are recorded in other publications this year. Joan Applegate's title explains her purpose: 'Katherine Philips's "Orinda upon Little Hector"': An Unrecorded Musical Setting by Henry Lawes' (*EMS* 4.272–80) is a thorough little paper documenting a setting of Philips's touching lament on the death of her infant son, preserved only in manuscript. And, as a supplement to the last two *EMS* articles, Peter Beal records 'Orinda to Silvander: A New Letter by Katherine Philips' in the same volume (4.281–6). Although short and unexciting, this is only the third autograph letter we have; it was written to her close friend Sir Edward Dering ('Silvander') and may date from around 1650.

The remaining Philips items are distinctly in the gender studies category. James Biester's 'Gender and Style in Seventeenth-Century Commendatory Verse' (*SEL* 33.507–22) is in fact a reading of a single text, the 'Philo-Philippa' eulogy 'To the Excellent Orinda'. Biester is concerned with how writers are characterized in gendered terms, and hence it would be helpful if we knew whether 'Philo-Philippa' was male or female. However, Biester does enough to show us this work's clear lead over most of its competitors in what is an increasingly popular area for study, Restoration poems on women writers; it is rare to find a single text being made so much of in this connection. In '"Manly Sweetness": Katherine Philips among the Neoclassicals' (*HLQ* 56.259–79), Paula Loscocco locates and tries to account for several phases in Philips's critical reception up to the eighteenth century. But it will not do to explain all the developments in terms of 'attitudes towards gender in the neoclassical literary environment'. Even if that were plausible, we would still have to worry about the accuracy of Loscocco's information. She thinks, for example, that in the Killigrew Ode, which refers to Anne Killigrew as a 'Virgin-Daughter', a Sappho, a 'Vestal', and a 'sweet saint', Dryden 'scrupulously avoids characterizing her virtues and achievements as sweet or feminine in any way'.

Work on Aphra Behn can also be divided into the factual/editorial and the gender studies types. Two paperback editions appeared: Malcolm Hicks's *Aphra Behn: Selected Poems* and Janet Todd's *Aphra Behn: Oroonoko, The Rover and Other Works*. The latter includes only nine poems as a pendant to longer prose works, so Hicks is plainly to be preferred by anyone seeking a large sample of Behn's verse. His business-like edition suffers from a shortage of space for notes – four pages only, making this virtually a 'plain text'. Yet it is, in fact, the only selected version available for the moment. Todd, whose complete *Poetry* of Behn was issued last year (YWES 73.268), might as well have called the present Penguin 'Selected Works': in addition to the handful of poems, there are two plays and three prose items (apart from those in the title, they are: *The Fair Jilt, Love-Letters to a Gentleman* and *The Widow Ranter*). Curiously, these two editors' suggestions for further reading have hardly anything in common.

Three other publications were also by Janet Todd, but not much is new in them. 'Aphra Behn: A Female Poet' (*SVEC* (1992) 304.834–7) is an abbreviated version of an essay in her *Gender, Art and Death*, which itself is a collection of mostly previously published work, including two papers on Behn. The introduction to the essay-collection *is* (apparently) new, and in looking back over the last few decades here Todd acutely diagnoses the reasons for Behn's recent rise to prominence, recapitulates some of the debates, and quarrels with the New Historicists, whose language of 'gesturing' and 'evacuation' she understandably finds off-putting. In collaboration with Francis McKee, Todd presented 'The "Shee Spy": Unpublished Letters on Aphra Behn, Secret Agent' (*TLS* 4719.4–5). This relates to Behn's activities as a spy in Antwerp, when, as we know from letters printed in W. J. Cameron's *New Light on Aphra Behn*, her senior colleague in the field was one Thomas Corney. The present article reprints parts of these letters; what is new is some excerpts from Corney's correspondence, preserved in the Public Record Office, together with some speculation about the vexing gaps they leave in our knowledge.

Rereading Aphra Behn: History, Theory, and Criticism, edited by Heidi Hutner, is a substantial collection of essays intended to show how Behn's 'literary vision challenges traditional critical assumptions about Restoration literature and culture'. Too often, it is the contributors' vision that seems to do the challenging, and Behn is a peg on which they hang their predilections. There is much transgressing, revisioning, destabilizing, and legitimizing, and it is apparent that the contributors' ultimate ambition is not merely to challenge received wisdom but to erect a wholly new order in place of the old. Although this millennium is still some way off, however, the current norms are less antediluvian than they are represented here. One of the two essays included on the poetry, Judith Kegan Gardiner's account of 'Utopian Longings in Behn's Lyric Poetry' (in which, incidentally, we are informed that misogyny 'increased during the late seventeenth century'), singles out pastoral verse as an area in which women writers were able to sidestep some of their difficulties. This is the starting-point for Elizabeth V. Young's 'Aphra Behn, Gender, and Pastoral' (*SEL* 33.523–43). Pastoral, Young thinks, is a particularly 'subversive form', so Behn uses it to 'transform ... participants in an exploitative relationship to participants in a mutually rewarding relationship', and, indeed, in general, to 'bring about change' by 'reversing gender roles'. These readings are questionable on many counts, both in matters of local interpretation and in overall ideological bias. Returning us to Behn biographical documents, James Fitzmaurice's 'Aphra Behn and the *Abraham's Sacrifice* Case' (*HLQ* 56.319–27) is a note on a manuscript letter in the Huntingdon Library, including a transcript. The letter, dealing with a ship seized by the English during the Second Dutch War, may (or may not) suggest that Behn was concerned with merchant shipping in Holland, and was indeed at some time a married woman. As Fitzmaurice says, the correspondence 'unfortunately does not help us with solid information about any of the key persons in Behn's life in the 1660s'.

Richard Terry's '*Hudibras* amongst the Augustans' (*SP* 90.426–41) is a small-scale example of a kind of study we see much of nowadays, the account of the fortunes of a text or a writer's reputation over a historical period. Terry shows how Butler's early readers worried over the resistance *Hudibras* posed to generic classification (worries still being voiced today, as in the next item reviewed here). By the later eighteenth century, however, some critics were singling it out as paradigmatic of comic literature. A limitation is that Terry never makes quite clear how the critics' judgements relate to Butler's popularity at large – Pepys, for example, commented simply: 'I cannot, I confess, see where enough of the wit lies', and this kind of puzzlement was doubtless common. Terry mentions but does not dwell on writers of Hudibrastics from Swift to Byron. David J. Rothman's 'Hudibras and Menippean Satire' (ECent 34.23–44) is by no means so specialized as the title might suggest, and is in some ways complementary to Terry's article in reviewing the more recent critical literature. Rothman writes well about the difficulties of classifying the poem as 'carnivalesque', and even, despite his title, as Menippean. Hence it becomes a work of the kind we postmodern readers find abordable: 'the poem invites critical confusion and paralysis, upbraiding our attempts to make systematic sense'. The same author's 'Hudibras in the Doggerel Tradition' (Restoration 17.15–29) is an attempt to relate Butler's versification to 'menippeanism', but it has little to add about the 'doggerel tradition' as such, and in its brevity slides over several of the problems noted in the longer ECent discussion. David Parkes's 'Documents Relating to Samuel Butler' (N&Q 40.324–5), our last Butler contribution, is on gleanings from manuscripts. Parkes describes two items found in the Bellot papers now in the John Rylands collection. One is a protection from arrest written for Butler by Richard Vaughan, Second Earl of Carbery, in 1667. The other is a transcript of verses known in another, more fragmentary form in a BL manuscript, and its significance, Parkes says, is that the arrangement given in the Bellot manuscript may make possible reconstruction of this unpublished segment of Butler's work, a 'Satyr upon the Imperfection of Human Learning'.

Two short items appeared on Oldham. The late H. A. Mason's 'A Note on Martial' (CQ 22.430–7) is, in one of its aspects, a recommendation of Oldham's 'An Allusion to Martial' as a way into the Latin original. Perhaps because of its format, that of a brief discussion paper, Beth Barnes's 'From Satyr to Satire: John Oldham's Satyrs upon the Jesuits' (SVEC 1992 305.1390–2) is superficial in its discussion of the Satyrs as 'transitional' works, 'both old-fashioned and anticipatory' in style – this is to say no more than what we have long known. James Fitzmaurice's paper on 'Some Problems in Editing Margaret Cavendish', in the Hill volume, embodies no new research, and raises few general issues, but does review what is known succinctly. Editors in search of a project may wish to note that Fitzmaurice's expression 'in editing' is proleptic, and he is not engaged in any such work himself. 'It is clear', he writes in conclusion, that Cavendish 'looms ever larger in the landscape of seventeenth-century English literature'. But this is the only item on her this year, and I doubt whether she has really arrived in the foreground as yet. 'The Deist: A Satyr on the Parsons', an unpublished poem found, with various names, in several Restoration manuscripts, is edited by Gillian Manning under this title in SCent (8.149–60). It is a rollicking and obscene 116-line attack on many of the things that occupied the period's satirists: clerics, kings, conventional sexual morality. The poem has been attributed both to Charles Blount and to Charles Sackville; Manning favours the former ascription. Finally, our record of Taylor Corse's year's work (see above) is not yet quite complete. His article 'The Ekphrastic Tradition: Literary and Pictorial Narrative in the Epigrams of John Elsum, an Eighteenth-Century Connoisseur' (W&I 9.383–400) may commend itself to the attention of those interested in the 'sister arts' in the period, and it pursues comparisons with Dryden's work in translating Du Fresnoy. Elsum's 167 Epigrams upon the Paintings of the Most Eminent Masters (1700), describing pictorial works from antiquity to the seventeenth century (he had of course never seen the earlier ones; he may never have seen the later), provide some evidence on contemporary taste and aesthetic assumptions. But Corse's comments on Elsum's 'couplet art' are wildly inappropriate for the often abominable doggerel in which they are composed.

(b) Prose
The quantity and quality of work on Aphra Behn's fiction continues to increase. *Rereading Aphra Behn* (ed. Heidi Hutner) is a substantial collection, covering the range of her writing, and unified by a desire to link feminist with historical perspectives, and to align Behn's increasing reputation with other revisionist readings of Restoration culture. There are five essays on the fiction: Ellen Pollak, in 'Beyond Incest: Gender and the Politics of Transgression in Aphra Behn's *Love-Letters Between a Nobleman and His Sister*' pursues a complex analogy between incest and sedition, and has useful formulations of the ironies of libertinism's association with royalty in the period. Ros Ballaster pursues a parallel theme, the popularity and political significance of the female love victim in Behn's fiction. Charlotte Sussman's 'The Other Problem with Women: Reproduction and Slave Culture in Aphra Behn's *Oroonoko*' extends the now commonplace analogy between being a woman and being a slave to the significance of Imoinda's pregnancy. Jacqueline Pearson, in 'The History of *The History of the Nun*' traces the complex afterlife of the novella in Southerne, Garrick, and Jane Barker's adaptations. In a less historicist piece, Ruth Salvaggio's 'Aphra Behn's Love: Fiction, Letters and Desire' flirts with the old biographical approach to Behn, although she ends up with some interesting remarks about the characteristic love plots in the fiction and an Irigarayan call to arms. All in all, a necessary collection. Stephanie Athey and Daniel Cooper Alarcón question *Oroonoko*'s status as a paradigmatic feminist and anti-colonialist text in '*Oroonoko*'s Gendered Economies of Honor/Horror: Reframing Colonial Discourse Studies in the Americas' (*AL* 65.415–43). The honour/horror doublet is actually from a textual crux in Southerne's play, but most of the discussion is about the novel. They criticize the tendency (also exemplified in studies of *The Tempest*) to reduce colonialism to a psychodrama by making one literary relationship stand for it all. This is tied in with an original reading of Behn's treatment of Imoinda, the white female voice commenting on the black female body. Margaret Ferguson has a chapter entitled 'Transmuting Othello: Aphra Behn's *Oroonoko*' in *Cross-Cultural Performances: Differences in Women's Re-visions of Shakespeare* (ed. Marianne Novy). The theme is, turning Shakespeare to *her* advantage. In Restoration critical opinion, Shakespeare is the great unlearned playwright, whose example permits a certain kind of erotic writing in his would-be successors. In this light, Ferguson examines interestingly the differences between Imoinda and Desdemona, and the similarities between Othello and Oroonoko. Robert A. Erickson discusses 'Mrs A. Behn and the Myth of Oroonoko-Imoinda' (*ECF* 5.201–16), less a thesis than a number of pertinent points, particularly about the double narration and the relation between the hero and the dedicatee.

For all its virtues, Hill's biography of Bunyan and his church did not say much that was new about Bunyan's writings. By contrast, Kathleen M. Swaim, in *Pilgrim's Progress, Puritan Progress*, confidently analyses Bunyan's works, while relating them to late Puritan culture. She regards Bunyan more as a greatly talented explicator than an innovator, and one could, *mutatis mutandis*, say the same of her. Her sense of context, both theological and political, is rich and illuminating. Like many recent critics, she has a strong sense of the importance of Part II of *The Pilgrim's Progress* and *The Holy War*. However, the value of the book is not just in the detailed synthesis of what has happened in Bunyan scholarship over the last 20 years, but more in charting the change in Bunyan's focus from internal psychodrama to church community, and, in the last works, a defensive holding action in the face of believers' complacency and secularization. 'Progress' of an ambivalent sort. Another sort of 'progress' in Bunyan's writing emerges as Sid Sondergard reinterprets the effects of Bunyan's imprisonment in '"This Giant has Wounded Me as Well as Thee": Reading Bunyan's Violence and/as Authority', a chapter in Keller and Schiffhorst's *The Witness of Times: Manifestations of Ideology in Seventeenth Century England*, a wide-ranging collection mostly concerned with the earlier part of the century. He usefully charts a shift between the early works, with their emphasis on experience as learning, with the more confident authority over violence in the later works like *The Holy War*. Thomas H. Luxon, in '"Not I, but Christ": Allegory and the Puritan Self' (*ELH* 60.899–938), investigates the 'pseudo-Christs' of the Interregnum such as Franklin and Gadbury, with their literal interpretation of union with Christ, to illuminate Bunyan's 'nervous and contradictory relation to allegory' as a less radical practice of representation.

Rachel Trubowitz discusses 'The Reenchantment of Utopia and the Female Monarchical Self: Margaret Cavendish's *Blazing World*' (*TSWL* 11:2 (1992) 229–45). It makes major claims for the book as a revision of the utopian into the magical and the fantastic, and an expression of the monarchical female imagination very different from the modest self-image of Cavendish's autobiography, and is particularly interesting on the competing assumptions in Cavendish's work.

In an interesting and various special Restoration edition of *SC* (8), edited by Paul Hammond, Nigel Smith disinters Richard Franck's *Northern Memoirs* (1694) as a republican alternative to Walton's *Compleat Angler*.

The new *British Journal for the History of Philosophy* contains three articles of interest. John Milton's 'Locke's Essay on Toleration: Text and Context' (45–63) discusses the 1667 essay rather than the translation of the *Epistola*, and in '"Philanthropy, or the Christian Philosophers"' (64–6) presents an edition of a brief manuscript essay by Locke. Sarah Hutton, in 'Damaris Cudworth, Lady Masham: Between Platonism and Enlightenment' (29–54) gives an account of a member of Locke's circle and his first biographer; and makes a shrewd assessment of her deriving arguments for women's education from Locke. The title of G. G. Meynell's illustrated article, 'John Locke's Method of Common-Placing, as seen in his Drafts and his Medical Notebooks, Bodleian MSS Locke d.9, f.21 and f.23' (*SC* 8.245–67) tells it all.

Gerard Reedy SJ. regards Archbishop Tillotson as one of the great and misunderstood writers of the century, a formative figure for post-Restoration culture. 'Interpreting Tillotson' (*HTR* 86.81–103) argues for the importance of the late 1693–5 sermons, with their 'wit of reader entrapment' and their stress on the interdependence of reason and revelation.

Isabel Rivers, in '"Galen's Muscles": Wilkins, Hume, and the Educational Use of the Argument from Design' (*HistJ* 36.577–97) considers the influence of John Wilkins's *The Principles and Duties of Natural Religion* (1675), and Hume's parodic inversion of his method.

Books Reviewed

Beal, Peter. *Lee-Wycherley. Part 2. 1625–1700.* Vol. II. *Index of English Literary Manuscripts.* Mansell. pp. 656. hb £250. ISBN 0 7201 1977 9.

Calhoun, Thomas O., et al., eds. *The Mistress. Part 1. Poems (1656).* Vol. II. *The Collected Works of Abraham Cowley.* UDelP. pp. 649. hb £60. ISBN 0 87413 408 0.

Fujimura, Thomas H. *The Temper of John Dryden,* ed. Robert McHenry Jr. Colleagues. pp. 245. hb $38. ISBN 0 937191 25 6.

Greer, G., and R. Little, eds. *The Translations.* Vol. III. *The Collected Works of Katherine Philips, The Matchless Orinda.* Stump Cross. pp. 266. pb £14.95. ISBN 1 827029 20 5.

Harth, Phillip. *Pen for a Party: Dryden's Tory Propaganda in its Contexts.* PrincetonUP. pp. 352. hb £27.50. ISBN 0 691 06972 7.

Hicks, Malcolm, ed. *Aphra Behn: Selected Poems.* Carcanet. pp. 128. pb £6.95. ISBN 1 85754 017 4.

Hill, W. Speed, ed. *New Ways of Looking at Old Texts.* MRTS. pp. 319. ISBN 0 86698 153 5.

Horne, William C. *Making a Heaven of Hell: The Problem of the Companionate Ideal in English Marriage Poetry, 1650–1800.* UGeoP. pp. 384. hb £42.95. ISBN 0 8203 1474 9.

Hutner, Heidi, ed. *Rereading Aphra Behn: History, Theory, and Criticism.* UPVirginia. pp. 336. hb £39.95, pb £16.50. ISBN 0 8139 1442 6, 0 8139 1443 3.

Keller, Katherine Z., and Gerald J. Schiffhorst, eds. *The Witness of Times: Manifestations of Ideology in Seventeenth Century England.* Duquesne. pp. 320. £41.95. ISBN 0 8207 0252 8.

Knott, John R. *Discourses of Martyrdom in English Literature, 1563–1694.* CUP. pp. 278. £37.50. ISBN 0 521 43365 7.

Kroll, Richard, Richard Ashcraft, and Perez Zagorin, eds. *Philosophy, Science and Religion in England, 1640–1700.* CUP, 1992. pp. 287. £40. ISBN 0 521 41095 9.

Love, Harold. *Scribal Publication in Seventeenth-Century England.* Clarendon. pp. 379. hb £40. ISBN 0 19 811219 X.

Lyons, Paddy, ed. *Rochester: Complete Poems and Plays.* Dent. pp. 300. pb £5.99. ISBN 0 460 87223 0.

Markley, Robert. *Fallen Languages: Crises of Representation in Newtonian England, 1660–1740.* CornUP. pp. 268. $35. ISBN 0 8014 2588 3.

Martindale, Charles, and David Hopkins, eds. *Horace Made New: Horatian Influences on British Writing from the Renaissance to the Twentieth Century.* CUP. pp. 330. hb £37.50. ISBN 0 521 38019 7.

Miner, Earl, and Jennifer Brady, eds. *Literary Transmission and Authority: Dryden and Other Writers.* CUP. pp. 163. hb £30. ISBN 0 521 44111 0.

Novy, Marianne, ed. *Cross-Cultural Performances: Differences in Women's Re-visions of Shakespeare.* UIllP. pp. 274. $18.95. ISBN 0 252 06323 6.

Phillipson, Nicholas, and Quentin Skinner, eds. *Political Discourse in Early Modern Britain.* CUP. pp. 444. £40. ISBN 0 521 39242 X.

Pooley, Roger. *English Prose of the Seventeenth Century, 1590–1700.* Longman. pp. 325. hb £40, pb £15.99. ISBN 0 582 01658 4, 0 582 01659 2.

Swaim, Kathleen M. *Pilgrim's Progress, Puritan Progress.* UIllP. pp. 368. $44.95. ISBN 0 252 01894 X.

Thomas, Donald, ed. *John Dryden: Selected Poems*. Dent. pp. 306. pb £4.99. ISBN 0 460 87230 3.

Thormählen, Marianne. *Rochester: The Poems in Context*. CUP. pp. 383. hb £30. ISBN 0 521 44042 4.

Todd, Janet, ed. *Aphra Behn: Oroonoko, The Rover and Other Works*. Penguin. pp. 384. pb. £6.99. ISBN 0 14 043338 4.

——. *Gender, Art and Death*. Polity. pp. 183. hb £39.50, pb £11.95. ISBN 0 7456 1054 4, 0 7456 1055 2.

Weinbrot, Howard D. *Britannia's Issue: The Rise of British Literature from Dryden to Ossian*. CUP. pp. 625. hb £35. ISBN 0 521 32519 6.

Yolton, John W., ed. *Philosophy, Religion and Science in the 17th and 18th Centuries*. URP (1991). pp. 539. £35. ISBN 1 878822 01 2.

Zwicker, Steven N. *Lines of Authority: Politics and English Literary Culture, 1649–1689*. CornUP. pp. 254. £27.95. ISBN 0 8014 2070 9.

XI

The Eighteenth Century

ALAN BOWER and NIGEL WOOD

This chapter has four sections: 1. Poetry; 2. Drama; 3. Prose; 4. The Novel. Sections 1 and 4 are by Alan Bower and sections 2 and 3 are by Nigel Wood.

1. Poetry

Donald Davie's *The Eighteenth-Century Hymn in England* bears revisionist witness to the power of close reading when the tools of explication are in the hands of a redoubtable intelligence. Davie has grown more determinedly non-conformist (in every sense) in the decades since the landmark of 1952 and *Purity of Diction in English Verse*: here he insists that the eighteenth century's remarkable outpouring of congregational lyricism has been all but obliterated by the newer literary history 'patented by Marxists and other atheists, indeed by agnostic "liberals"', and he wears his ideological unfashionability with combative pride. Yet the strength of his book lies, paradoxically, in the way its author's own 'articulate energy' undercuts his insistence on the necessary relationship between belief and judgement. Even the most committed deconstructionist would be hard pressed to deny the critical lucidity of, for example, Davie's old-style demolition of Wesley's 'sloppiness':

> The lack of fastidiousness is not in the carnal matters that Wesley readily refers to – on the contrary, as we seem to find in his treatment of babies, that is one of his strengths which is hard to parallel; the lack of fastidiousness that we may reprehend lies in his *art*, in the lack of control over his artistic medium, his language, which traps him into seeming to say things that he did not intend.

Davie works his way through the century of hymns he defines as characterized by poetic argument, from John Byram and Joseph Addison (of all people) to Cowper and John Newton – that epitome of muscular Christianity and 'The author of "Amazing Grace"' – but with all the twists, turns, cross-references and appeals to wider historical perspectives which enliven his own argument. So there is much to enjoy here, not least the erudition and eclectic eye for detail which Davie disposes so well to support his claim for affinity between Smart's 'elegance' and the rococo style of Francis Hayman. Blake's uncoupling of lyricism from doctrinal cerebration, Davie claims, brought that tradition to a dead stop.

In '"Aesthetics" and the Rise of the Lyric in the Eighteenth Century' (*SEL* 33.587–608) Douglas Lane Patey charts an alternative, if analogous, process by which the expectation of argument moving elsewhere sapped the energy and reputation of secular lyric; but Patey finds the faultlines inherent in 'Augustan' literary theory. He is particularly alert to the ironies of English misuse of French criticism in the battle of the books, and he throws out several intriguing possibilities, not least on the 'feminizing' of lyric (which, he suggests, was another source for Wordsworth's animus against Gray) and the resonance for both eighteenth and twentieth centuries in Abbé Trublet's projection: 'The first writers [...] were poets [...] they could hardly be anything else. The last writers will be philosophers.'

If contemporary 'aesthetic' critics were ambivalent about lyric, they were no less uneasy about the formal instabilities of *Hudibras*. Nevertheless, as Richard Terry demonstrates, 'hudibrastics' remained stubbornly resilient through the century, and not only in the verse of Swift and Prior ('*Hudibras* Amongst the Augustans', *SP* 90.426–41). The latter gets more attention than his more celebrated friend this year. Adrienne Condon, in '"The Syphilitic Lady" Revisited: A Second Opinion' (*Scriblerian* 25.221) challenges the reading of *The Lady's Dressing Room* by Herman J. Real and Heinz Vienken and finds support from the *OED* for her argument that Sylvia 'is more like a self absorbed young woman still wrestling with the blotches [...] rather than a victim of venereal disease'. Not so, retorts the first of those male critics ('More "Gum" to Chew On', 221–2), as he disposes a wider range of evidence to confirm the more harsh diagnosis. But this is little more than annotation. Nicholas H. Nelson mounts a more sustained and stout defence of his subject in 'Narrative Transformations: Prior's Art of the Tale' (*SP* 90.442–61), and bases his case on the four poems picked out for particular attention by Betrand Bronson in his 1968 essay which pitted Prior against Johnson in imaginary conversation. Prior enthusiasts have reason thus to stick together. For all the good sense in their insistence that Horatian satire is unjustly dismissed as mere light versifying, their sporadic complaints seem to make little impression; and Nelson does not enhance his argument when he strains towards claims that echo unconvincingly even in his own phrasing: 'Prior, I believe, stands near the beginning of the spread of the democratizing spirit that increasingly empathized with common humanity.' At least Nelson has immediate company in the familiar and better-founded appeal to qualities such as the deft characterization and hudibrastic cleverness of 'Matthew Prior's "An Epitaph"' (James L. Thorson, *Expl.* 51.ii.84–9). 'Prior's theme [writes Thorson], that retiring to the country is not an ideal but, to a thoughtful person, a sentence of mental and moral death, is beautifully exemplified here', and, by a curious coincidence, another instance of the humourist's concern with otium is placed securely within the canon this year. In 'An Autobiographical Ballad by Matthew Prior' (*BLJ* 18.163–70) H. Bunker Wright and Deborah Kempf Wright confirm as authentic and reproduce in its uncorrupted form 'A Ballad' of 1715/16 written when Prior was imprisoned while the vengeful Whig Parliament attempted to prove pro-French skulduggery in his conduct as negotiator at Utrecht: a 'product of imprisonment and no double boredom, it chronicles a period of his life that perhaps he came to feel was not worth celebrating', hence, perhaps, its exclusion from the *Poems* of 1718 and its relegation to an obscure corner of the Harley papers.

Pride of place on Pope this year must be given to a pair of complementary volumes from Pat Rogers, a collection of *Essays on Pope*, and *Alexander Pope: A Critical Edition of the Major Works* in the 'Oxford Authors' series. The blurb on the dust-jacket of the *Essays* claims that the first 13 reprinted pieces have been 'considerably revised'. Rogers himself is more cautious – 'For the most part I have confined revision to small acts of refurbishment, by way of an attempt to regularise forms of reference and to correct any mistakes' – and wisely so, since classic essays such as 'Pope and the Syntax of Satire' (Chapter 1) or 'A Drama of Mixed Feelings: The *Epistle to Arbuthnot*' (Chapter 7) read quite as persuasively today as they did when they first appeared in the journals. There are 'adjustments', of course, particularly in passages of the essays which deal with Pope's relations with women and with sexual politics, drawing on the work of such critics as Carol Fabricant, Ellen Pollak and Valerie Rumbold, although there is no place for the cultural materialists of the 'new eighteenth century'. Readers of *YWES* will be grateful to have all these repolished pieces between a single set of covers, and another generation of those new to Pope will have access to a distinguished body of work rather easier to access than by database and xerox. Both may also savour the only 'new piece' here, 'Pope and the Antiquarians' (Chapter 14), based on a paper delivered at the Yale tercentenary conference and a characteristic fusion of scholarship with critical acumen in its demonstration of the creative tension between scorn for and reliance on 'modern' scientific instincts in Scriblerian satire:

> Pope ransacked the world for mineralogical specimens, and he used William Borlase, a prime specimen himself of the antiquarian tribe, to find the choicest samples. It is a short step from this realization to move to a sense that *The Dunciad*, as set out on the page, represents a direct translation of the collector's habits into graphic terms, defined by print and white space. The poem, with its apparatus, textualizes tasteless antiquarian praxis. Indeed, the entire *Dunciad* has become a sort of cabinet of curiosities.

Revisionist scholarship and interpretative sharpness unite again in Rogers's critical edition of Pope for the 'Oxford Authors' series. This edition offers a modernized text based on Herbert Davis's 1966 volume but with a wealth of interspersed prose, from the whole of *Peri Bathous* to the resonant letter to Swift on the death of Gay (20 April 1733) printed illuminatingly between the *Essay on Man* and *The Fourth Satire of Dr John Donne Versified*. Not surprisingly, the original version of the *Rape* and *Dunciad* are excluded to make space for Pope as 'author', not just poet; but Rogers does squeeze in Book XVIII of *The Iliad*, so a few of those already wrestling with the complex of disagreements on Pope and the ladies (or the men) will have readily available part of the Homeric translation against which to best the explorations of gender in Carolyn D. Williams, *Pope, Homer and Manliness*. Williams amply justifies her subtitle, 'Some Aspects of Eighteenth-Century Classical Learning'; indeed, she is overly modest. This is the sort of book which gives scholarship a good name. Learning – almost a pun in the context of Pope's intent – is easily but tactfully and even entertainingly disposed as she establishes the broad contextual base in Part One ('Manliness in Early Modern Britain') for what is the heart of her concern, 'Gender in Pope's Homer', before moving out to consider how her readings might impact on the *Rape* and *Dunciad*. Williams picks her way carefully through the minefields of ancient, contemporary and modern semantics and is entirely persuasive on Pope's complex response to Homer no less than on his translation as a project to define manliness for his age and thus figure for himself a masculine role. So here again Rogers's extract from *The Iliad* is timely. Book XVIII contains the arming of Achilles through the agency of Thetis and the parallel was not lost on Pope; Madame Dacier, as Williams puts it, 'played Thetis to his Achilles: an obtrusively feminine presence, without whose aid he could achieve neither glory among his peers nor personal survival'. Moreover, if 'Achilles' acquisition of new armour concludes a sequence of feminine cover-ups', there are other, irresistible parallels between the epic hero's shield and the mock-heroic heroine's petticoat, which Williams suggests in her concluding section without speculating beyond the evidence. James McLaverty works with the relationship between the same two poems in a very different context in 'The Contract for Pope's Translation of Homer's *Iliad*: An Introduction and Transcription' (*Library* 15. 206–25) as he meticulously sifts the evidence for and against the thesis that the success of the *Rape* was the stimulus to the quarto edition of *The Iliad*. In doing so he also tells a more complex story about personal and economic relationships in the intricate world of London's literary producers. Two other male commentators return us to more familiar territory on the *Rape*. The late Francis Doherty's, '*The Rape of The Lock*: Stretching the Limits of Allusion' (*Anglia* 111.355–72) earnestly reaffirms and extends the approach to a poet 'whose method is to make jokes by concealing part or a good deal of his references' which stretches back to Winisatt and is here tuned to more evidence from Johnson, Tom Brown and commentators on the *beau monde*. Andrew Varney's 'Clarissa's Moral in *The Rape of The Lock*' (*EIC* 43.17–32) is more pugnacious in defence of the poem as a poem of praise to transient beauty: here Clarissa is a 'hypocritical moraliser' whose speech, 'Read carefully, [...] exposes not only the shallowness of the values of Clarissa's world but also the inadequacy of easy critiques grounded in a sententiousness alien to all the implications and strategies of the poem'.

Richard Terry's second essay on poetry this year, 'Pope's Miltonic Parody' (*ES* 74.138–42) revisits 'The Critical Specimen', an attack on John Dennis, with internal and external evidence to confirm the attribution first made by Norman Ault some six decades ago. Julian Ferraro performs a similar function for '"Sandy's Ghost": A New Manuscript' (*BJECS* 16.171–6) when he reports on a corrected holograph discovered in the Pierpoint Morgan Library; but a third bibliographical essay, by Michael Brennan, 'Alexander Pope's "Epistle to Robert Earl of Oxford, and Earl Mortimer": A New Autograph Manuscript' (*Library* 15.187–205) is altogether more substantial. Brennan picks up from McLaverty's work on the *Iliad* contract (see above) in this intriguingly multi-faceted analysis of an autograph discovered at Badminton House and almost certainly the copy used by Lintot for the poem which prefaced the 1722 edition of Parnell's *Poems on Several Occasions*. By this date, Pope had the clout to specify in detail the means of production: Brennan also anatomizes the confidence with which Pope significantly amended the text approved by Harley and preserved in the Longleat manuscript. It was all very different a decade earlier, and David Wheeler's '"So Easy to be Lost: Poet and Self in Pope's *The Temple of Fame*' (*PLL* 29.3–27) is a busy, close reading of Pope at the crossroads, objectifying in verse his choice between 'the ever-conflicting ideals of becoming a rich and famous poet and remaining a virtuous gentleman detached from professional, political and commercial strife'. Wheeler is persuasive on the consonance between historicized personalization in the later poems and this prefiguring verse; he is less convincing about the reality of an ambitious poet's dilemma. Self-consciousness transformed into cultural legitimacy is also the subject of Lucinda Cole's 'Distinguishing Friendships: Pope's *Epistle to a Lady* In/And Literary History' (*ECent* 34.169–92), an expansive reading which positively celebrates its debt to Nancy Armstrong and relates Pope to Hannah More and Mary Wollstonecraft. James McLaverty's second 1993 essay touches on similar concerns in a busy piece on Pope's book-making, with additional musings on the legitimacy of facsimile, in 'Facsimiles and the Bibliographer: Pope's *Dunciad*' (*Rev* 15.1–15): 'Pope's concern with the book as a form of self-expression and as a means of establishing authority in his dialogue with his critics makes it clear why facsimiles are important for literary criticism' he concludes, against the purists who would reject out of bibliographical hand publications such as David L. Vander Meulen's edition of the 1729 *Dunciad* in facsimile. Less contentious, and also less informative is B. W. Young's '"See *Mystery* to Mathematics fly!": Pope's *Dunciad* and the Critique of Religious Rationalism' (*ECS* 26.435–48) which reaffirms Book IV, lines 459–95 as the fulcrum of Pope's conservative attack on rationalist theology. Other publications on Pope this year are aimed at the student market. The one I have seen is Ian Gordon's second edition of *A Preface to Pope* and is an entirely serviceable reworking of his 1976 primer, with additional 'short introductory essays to a selection of Pope's major poems'. Two others, edited by Wallace Jackson and R. Paul Yoder, *Critical Essays on Alexander Pope* (G. K. Hall) and *Approaches to Teaching Pope's Poetry* (MLA), have not come my way but seem unlikely to prove the source of many surprises.

Thomas Gray: Contemporary Essays, edited by W. B. Hutchings and William Ruddick is a notable publication, and not only because it quotes this reviewer in its first sentence. Such assemblages are too often characterized by nuggets of value in a seam of indifferent quality. This, however is a remarkably well-balanced volume, for the editors have gathered together a group of literary historical scholars who deserve that title. Hutchings himself establishes the focus for what follows, and provides a more thorough guide than is possible here to the cross-connections and differences in emphasis between the various contributions, in a careful introductory chapter which dates 'Past Criticism and the Present Volume', and Vincent Newey – the other author of a recent book-length study of Gray – supports him splendidly in 'The Selving of Thomas Gray' which braces the 'biblio-selving' in the poetics of this ultimate 'man of letters', particularly in the two versions of the *Elegy*. Paul Williamson immediately turns the perspective glass through 180 degrees to focus on the same texts as defined rather by sensitivity to both sterilities and possibilities in the poetics of genre ('Gray's *Elegy* and the Logic of Expression'); and Richard Terry concludes the volume's first section by investigating the paradox of a poet made synonymous by the Romantic PR machine with the extremities of diction that he castigated in the work of others in his own time ('Gray and Poetic Diction'). A trio of equally substantial essays take that contemporaneity as their subject and investigate Gray in context: David Fairer on 'Thomas Wharton, Thomas Gray, and the Recovery of the Past', Paul Whiteley on 'Gray, Akenside and the Ode', and Anne

McDermott on '"The Wonderful Wonder of Wonders": Gray's Odes and Johnson's Criticism'. Three more explore the surprising variety and extent of oppositional language in later writers: Angus Easson's '"A Man of Genius" Gray and Wordsworth', Bernard Beatty's 'Unheard Voices, Indistinct Visions: Gray and Byron', and Malcolm Hicks's 'Gray Among the Victorians' (248–69). Even more unexpected, perhaps, are the two essays by T. W. Craik on 'Gray's Humorous and Satirical Verse' and by William Ruddick on 'Thomas Gray's Travel Writing'. Ruddick makes good his claim that 'Gray was to become almost the first of the truly influential travel writers in the second half of the eighteenth century', and Craik's sympathetically shrewd survey is as instructively brief as the corpus of surviving work. Mason's po-faced vandalism in destroying so much similar verse looms larger as Craik's analysis develops, so it is appropriate that the only other piece on Gray this year should be a note which tracks the origin of a Gray joke – 'As to posterity, I may ask, (with some body whom I have forgot) what has it ever done to oblige me' – to a 1714 *Spectator* (Barry Baldwin, 'Thomas Gray on Posterity', *N&Q* 40.328–9).

Other mid- and late-century canonical poets are the subject of single contributions. Indeed, one is represented by no more than a similarly brief note, by the indefatigable James Sambrook, correcting a persistent misprint in 'Cowper's "No More Shall Hapless Celia's Ears"' (*N&Q* 40.473), while Deborah Haller's 'Seeing but Not Believing: The Problem of Vision in Collin's Odes' (*TSLL* 35.103–23) reaffirms the value of literary historical discriminations, of the sort which informed all the essays in the Gray volume too, on the odes as a rejection of early-Enlightenment pictorialism in favour of insight. Shaun Irlam, by contrast, is hunting bigger game, and over open sights in 'Gerrymandered Geographies: Exoticism in Thomson and Chateaubriand' (*MLN* 108.891–2): here poems are of significance as 'Fabrications of geopolitical space [...] at a time when literature probably commanded a greater market share of cultural authority', particularly in the construction of nationhood when intimately related to colonial and imperial ambitions. In '"Origins of the Specious": James Macpherson's Ossian and the Forging of the British Empire' (*ECent* 34.132–50) Leith Davis ploughs a related ideological furrow and ingeniously disposes post-colonial theorists (notably Frantz Fanon and Homi Bhaba) to interrogate pre-colonial formation. *Thomas Chatterton: Early Sources and Responses* seemed to promise a storehouse of related material for cultural historians, but Routledge was reluctant to part with a review copy of the six-volume set. At £295, one would see the point, although this was mildly disappointing only until Claude Rawson's *TLS* review (6 May 1994) which relegated direct comment to a withering final paragraph on 'this overpriced and unintelligent compilation [...] no better than a set of Xeroxes'.

With the exception of significant publications on later-century women poets, only a couple of more modest but also more intelligent pieces remain. Thomas Lockwood tidies up the record on 'Early Poems By – And Not By – Fielding' (*PQ* 72.177–84) when he supplies the epitaph to the fugitive Coronation ode of 1727, then promptly torpedoes the ascription to Fielding of 'An Original Song' which external and internal evidence suggest to be the work of Tony Aston. As Lockwood notes, 'Little as he can afford to lose poetically, Fielding won't suffer anything by this loss; nor for that matter will Aston suffer much by the gain'. Paul William Child is equally hard-headed about the manuscript of 'Platonick Love' (*Scriblerian* 26.1–3), probably by the fashionable physician George Cheyne who so flattered the sensibilities of Richardson, Boswell and Gray by associating nervous sensibility with literary talent: 'If he does not have the talent [...] to be a poet – as this his only known poem suggests – he has at least the temperament'. Patricia Dehmers writes on the clash of two utterly opposed sorts of steely female personalities in '"For Mines a Stubborn and a Savage Will": "Lactilla" (Ann Yearsley) and "Stella" (Hannah More) Reconsidered' (*HLQ* 56.135–50) when she revisits the brief friendship and the long, bitter estrangement, 'sifting through the skewed and distorting rhetoric of the champions on both sides'. Moira Ferguson's 'The Unpublished Poems of Ann Yearsley' (*TSWL* 12.13–46) extends the record on one of those sides by reproducing a dozen poems found hand-written on blank pages in the first edition of what was probably Yearsley's own copy of *Poems on Several Occasions* unearthed in Bristol Public Library. Ferguson is obviously more inclined to her subject's version of the dispute with More, but the new poems help in that respect. Yearsley's fierce complaints and even more passionate philosophical convictions articulate an emotional integrity which could not allow either publication or moderation of sentiment to make publication possible: 'Contrary to her public reputation, she nurtures moderation, doing nothing to exacerbate her notorious reputation – flagged by More – as a trouble-maker'.

2. Drama

Theatre historians have reason to be especially grateful this year to two monuments to patient scholarship. The first, William J. Burling's *A Checklist of New Plays and Entertainments on the London Stage 1700–1737*, charts the enviable level of commitment to new writing before the Licensing Act. The list proceeds in chronological order, and for each entry gives details of date of premiere, venue, title, author or attribution, genre, publisher and/or printer, date of publication plus other notes of interest or explanation. Appendices then follow that provide information on new plays performed at minor London venues and also on unperformed plays. Burling's labours are thus a necessary supplement to *The London Stage*. Handel's operas are noted, as are foreign works (Racine and Corneille to the fore), although one is certainly left expecting more daring from his additional notes, which are usually just expository. In Appendix B, for example, Burling might have put his comprehensive reading a little more to work in hazarding some guesses as to why (pre–1737) certain obviously political works never made it to the public sphere. However, the net gains overwhelm such drawbacks, and one has now every reason to question the straightforward view that Lincoln's Inn Fields showcased just harlequinades and that the early century shunned French decorum (the New Haymarket most obviously Francophile in its tastes).

The second is *The Dublin Stage, 1720–1745: A Calendar of Plays, Entertainments, and Afterpieces*, compiled and analysed by John C. Greene and Gladys L. H. Clark. Advancing season by season, it traces the breadth of choice available at Smock Alley, and, from 1734, at Aungier Street, as well as the myriad of minor venues in the city. Each season is prefaced by a lucid introduction. There is also a very useful bibliography. The overall impression is of confidence and liberal tastes.

The year saw some welcome re-discoveries. In *The Dramatic Works of George Lillo*, edited by James L. Steffensen Jr, 'including *Silvia* edited by Richard

Noble', *The London Merchant* (1731) is no longer an isolated achievement, an occasional bourgeois tragedy that ends up in some developmental *cul-de-sac*. Fielding's verdict in *The Champion* for 26 February 1740, that Lillo was the 'best Tragick Poet of his Age', is almost feasible, given the ambition of his heroic *The Christian Hero* (1735), the ironies of his second domestic tragedy *Fatal Curiosity* (1736), and the posthumous *Elmerick* (1740). Long feted on the Continent for his originality, Lillo has often been the object in Britain of a sympathy that is ultimately patronizing and faint-hearted. Perhaps it has needed Steffensen's work (in the main) to alter this view. Besides his more well-known works, here is also his bawdy ballad opera, *Silvia; or, The Country Burial* (1730), a patriotic masque to celebrate the marriage of the Princess Royal to William, Prince of Orange, *Britannia and Batavia* (written, 1734, published, 1740 – but never performed [and no wonder]), his adaptations of *Pericles* (*Marina* [1738]), and the incomplete *Arden of Faversham*. Here is no easy sentimentalist, and Steffensen contributes a level-headed and judicious introduction plus succinct commentaries on theatre history and textual problems that offer a number of alternatives to the accepted one-play verdict – and, what is more, *The London Merchant* is granted for the first time a text that incorporates Lillo's own revisions, only found in what apparently seemed simple reprints. A full critical and textual apparatus is here provided; perhaps, all that remains is for the academic community actually to read and teach his work as an energetic and bold theatrical enterprise. Stephen L. Trainor's 'Suicide and Seneca in Two Eighteenth-Century Tragedies' (in *Drama and the Classical Heritage: Comparative and Critical Studies*, edited by Clifford Davidson, Rand Johnson and John H. Stroupe) pits the stoicism of Addison's *Cato* against Lillo's in *Fatal Curiosity*. It does much to help us to define the term better, whereas Tejumola Olaniyan's 'The Ethics and Poetics of a "Civilizing Mission": Some Notes on Lillo's *The London Merchant*' (*ELN* 29.33–47) is alive to the aesthetics of some of the play's moralizing touches, especially in the last act, yet could have done with Steffensen's work when generalizing on Lillo's theatrical experience.

Volume Two of the Wesleyan *Works* of Henry Fielding (*Miscellanies*) provides us with *Eurydice* (1736/7) and *The Wedding Day* (1742/3) (Introduction and Commentary by Bertrand Goldgar; text by Hugh Amory). The Commentary on *Eurydice* is particularly successful in unearthing its contemporary comments. An appendix gives us the Larpent MS of *The Wedding Day*. Tobias Smollett's stirring Jacobite blank verse tragedies, *The Regicide* and *The Reprisal* (both 1739), fill out our knowledge of his early life in his *Poems, Plays and 'The Briton'*, edited by Byron Gassman and O. M. Brack, Jr. Unfortunately, they emerge as little more than staging-posts on the way to less partisan and more finished work. David W. Lindsay's *The Beggar's Opera and Other Eighteenth-Century Plays* reproduces the 1928 Everyman texts of *Cato*, *The Conscious Lovers*, *The Tragedy of Tragedies*, *The London Merchant*, *She Stoops to Conquer* and *The School for Scandal* as well as the *Opera*. Lindsay provides biographical notes on the dramatists, chronologies of relevant historical and theatrical events, a conservative though trustworthy Suggestions for Further Reading and a straightforward introduction for a non-specialist or undergraduate audience. Certainly, easy access to *The Conscious Lovers* and *The London Merchant* is a real boon, but the lack of even rudimentary annotation or explanatory notes seems a little perfunctory and suggests a chance missed by Dent.

Perhaps we should peruse the plays with Calhoun Winton's *John Gay and the*

London Theatre in hand, for, although its organizing focus is an account of the 'critical biography' kind, it still manages to summon up a sense of a wider context and the complexity of Gay's theatrical associations. This it accomplishes with enviable lucidity and a clear-sighted purpose: to serve as an introduction to Gay's wider theatrical aims. Much of the material here, however, has already been worked on by others (an observation that Winton readily acknowledges). The severely chronological tread through Gay's life and works sometimes imposes an unduly teleological narrative, with gestures on more than one occasion to experiments that proved false steps or detours from a central aesthetic purpose. This seems a rather limiting figure of Gay, whose ability to regard his work as a series of fresh starts, full of alternative attempts to engage with the public, should not be minimized. Indeed, Winton's most helpful chapters are where he is most synchronic in his scope, '*The Beggar's Opera* in Theatre History' (Chapter 7) and '*Polly* and the Censors' (Chapter 9). There are also original attempts at commending Gay as a lyricist.

Paula R. Backscheider's *Spectacular Politics: Theatrical Power and Mass Culture in Early Modern England* takes seriously Habermas's perception that there could be a specifically literary public sphere. This superstructural world of civic discourse displayed in city and royal pageantry is most examined with relation to the seasons and occasions for ritual between 1659 and 1662 and then, concentrating on plays and prose fiction by women in 1695–6. There is then a jump towards the Regency Crisis of 1788–9 and the cultural anxiety manifested in Gothic drama. These case studies therefore do not purport to offer a synoptic survey. If anything, the real victor is Habermas himself, for Backscheider demonstrates how interesting his notion of the Public Sphere might be when applied to a number of different cultural contexts, especially when mapping alternative forms of audience response. In omitting most of eighteenth-century developments or shifts of taste (after all, Habermas's main pool of examples) one is left wanting a little more, so that the comparisons between Restoration and Regency sensibilities might have more bite. On the other hand, Backscheider does read a variety of playtexts with insight and offers some radical discoveries about the force of public opinion as an aesthetic power. On similar themes, but with less detail, I have just caught up with Joseph Roach's 1991 essay, 'The Artificial Eye: Augustan Theatre and the Empire of the Visible', in *The Performance of Power: Theatrical Discourse and Politics*, edited by Sue-Ellen Case and Janelle Einelt, which focuses on the figurative potential of the all-seeing eye and the construction of an Augustan insouciance in certain key plays.

Two other general accounts also prefer to skirt the eighteenth century. In Richard Braverman's *Plots and Counterplots: Sexual Politics and the Body Politic in English Literature, 1660–1730*, there is a full and theoretically sophisticated account of significant changes in the age's *episteme*, from the cyclical consolations of restoration and romance to the more linear plotting of the eighteenth century. Imperial themes derived from georgic allusions and adaptations supplant more nationalistic myths. For the purpose of this section it is as well that we note the treatment of *The Way of the World*, which conveys the belief that the 1688 Revolution was a 'negotiated settlement'. The same *topos* of on-stage contracts could just as easily be witnessed in Dryden's *Marriage à la Mode* (1671). *Genre and Generic Change in English Comedy, 1660–1710* by Brian Corman is one of that rare breed of monograph that actually might affect how we read turn-of-the-century literature. By focusing on six 'Representative Comedies' from 1670–1675 and then six from 1705–1710 Corman registers the implicit influence of the punitive Jonson and the sympathetic Fletcher. The latter case study takes in Farquhar's *The Recruiting Officer* and *The Beaux' Stratagem*, Vanbrugh's *The Confederacy*, Cibber's *The Double Gallant*, Susanna Centlivre's *The Busie Body* and Charles Shadwell's *The Fair Quaker of Deal*, and, whilst there is little discussion of just why these plays are of core interest, Corman's opening remarks on the 'mixed' genre do help to illuminate the variety of early century comic effect.

Sandra Richards's *The Rise of the English Actress* progresses from the seventeenth century to the present in rapid time, yet largely avoids too much summarizing. The desire to 'discover in what ways and to what degree women's experience differed from men' and to tell this story from the point of view of the actress is an attractive proposition, and one that has meant a great deal of collation and creative inference for the early periods. There are two chapters on the eighteenth century ('Early' and 'Late'), and it becomes clear that the novelty value of the Restoration actress provided an opportunity for later generations to hallmark individual styles, such as Kitty Clive's giggling (and knowing) chambermaid and the breeches parts especially written for Peg Woffington. The later years saw a generation of actresses emerge from provincial sources, such as Snow Baddeley and Dorothy Jordan, who, perhaps surprisingly, all became models of avant-garde fashion. There then follows a chapter on Sarah Siddons, a prime example of the actress's growing social and commercial influence.

There would seem to be a most promising extended study of the Augustan theatre in the offing from Peter Thomson. His 'Fielding, Walpole, George II and the Liberty of the Theatre' (*L&H* n.s.2.42–67) goes over ground that one may have regarded as well-trodden, yet Thomson takes pains to elicit some new details in a familiar overall picture. Marking Fielding's gradual recognition of Walpole's venality, Thomson dips into several apt and scatological examples of how the Prime Minister and his office were rendered in prints and their accompanying satirical tags. Dating from the gracefully ironic dedication to Walpole of *The Modern Husband* (1732), and through to his *Don Quixote in England* (1734), Thomson provides an admirably comprehensive account of how politically volatile the British electorate then were, and how Fielding capitalized on it. The route towards the Licensing Act was one that Walpole prepared with care, and he emerges from Thomson's account as one who had an uncanny rapport with political Britain. Fielding eventually became merely grist to the mill of Rabinocratic hyperbole.

The acceptable face of eighteenth-century theatre is provided by J. R. Oldfield in '"The Ties of Soft Humanity": Slavery and Race in British Drama, 1760–1800' (*HLQ* 56.1–14). Far from pandering to knee-jerk reflexes, several dramatists questioned the morality of slavery, and so helped pave the way to its eventual abolition. Oldfield praises Hawkesworth's adaptation of Southerne's *Oroonoko* (1759) for the inclusion of a more sympathetic first scene, and then proceeds to single out Isaac Bickerstaffe for particular praise for his characterization of noble slaves in Roxalana (*The Sultan* (1775) and Priscilla (*Love in the City* (1767)). William Kendall's perusal of theatre plans for the century puts obstacles in the path of easy generalization about the 'retreat' of the apron stage ('Did the Apron Stage Retreat?', *TN* 47.76–9). Comparing Wren's plans for Drury Lane from 1696 onwards with Adam's of 1775, the formula for the earlier design (one third of the stage depth for the scene and two thirds for the players) was reversed – not a retreat so much as an advance on the audience by greater scenic spectacle and actors more often than not thrust forward for greater prominence.

Ben Ross Schneider, Jr does much to rehabilitate George Granville's Shylock in his 'Granville's *Jew of Venice* (1701): A Close Reading of Shakespeare's *Merchant*' (*Restoration* 17.111–34). Granville may have read his Shakespeare attentively, but he still emerges as a conformist in racial matters. More generous is the estimate of George Colman, the Younger, in Linda V. Troost's 'Social Reform in Comic Opera: Colman's *Inkle and Yarico*' (*SVEC* 305 [1992].1427–9), where sentiment (and its occasional deflation) actually motivates more philanthropic impulses. A similar concern with commitment is evident in Anne McWhir's 'Revising Rowe's *The Fair Penitent*: Goldsmith, Holcroft, Wollstonecraft' (*SVEC* 304 [1992].827–30), where Rowe's original concern with female probity of 1703 is used for quite unforeseen purposes right up to the Romantic period. Goldsmith figures prominently in this survey, and it is perhaps fitting to examine such intertextuality given Rowe's own appropriation of Massinger in the first place. Goldsmith is exactly the kind of figure that would make a volume of *Goldsmith: Interviews and Recollections* (ed. E. H. Mikhail) a popular success. By his own admission, he seems to have brought over from Ireland nothing but his 'brogue and his blunders', and that inability to assimilate himself to a metropolitan culture is exactly what biographers find a central question about his literary successes. Mikhail serves his subject well. Here he has collected together testimonies from expected sources (Boswell, Johnson and Reynolds) as well as less available views. Richard Cumberland's character-study of Goldsmith from his own *Memoirs* (1806), William Hawes's unsparing account of his last illness from 1774 and John Tait's poetic posturing on Goldsmith's behalf from *The Druid's Monument* (1774) are not in common currency, and supply necessary additions to more canonical verdicts. Mikhail claims in his introduction that this collection is actually a form of biography. This is truer than similar claims made about other volumes in the series.

Robert Fahrner is kind about Garrick's political credentials in his 'A Reassessment of Garrick's *The Male-Coquette: or, Seventeen-Hundred Fifty-Seven* as Veiled Discourse' (*ECLife* 17.1–13). Here Garrick's creation of the Daffodil-figure is not regarded simply as a legacy of Restoration fops, but rather a specific glance at the effeminacy that was popularly understood to be hampering the national will in Britain's American war effort against the French. Using John Brown's *An Estimate of the Manners and Principles of the Times* (1757 – in its seventh edition by 1758), and Garrick's probable knowledge of it, Fahrner recovers a short-lived period of cultural anxiety. Garrick's celebrity is noted by Simon Varey (*N&Q* 40.335–6), and specifically the use of the term star to describe it. At a time when Johnson merely regarded the word as either possessing an astronomical reference or to an asterisk, Varey comes across two comments on Garrick in its more modern sense. I am afraid that I have not been able to trace David Wheeler's 'After the Restoration: David Garrick's *The Country Girl*' (*CLAJ* 36.430–9). Finally, Amy Elizabeth Smith adds to our knowledge of Sheridan's business acumen in her 'Casting and the Manager's Role in Sheridan's *A Trip to Scarborough*', (*TN* 47.170–1). Far from some disinterested homage to Vanbrugh's *The Relapse*, the play is actually a vehicle for astute and popular casting, reviving memories of John Lee's two-act farce, *The Man of Quality* (1773), an earlier adaptation, which had also featured James William Dodd, Frances Abington and William 'Gentleman' Smith. Memories of their recent roles coloured how they were to be received in Sheridan's new play.

3. Prose

1993 has been a quiet season for Swift studies; I have looked in vain for some general estimate of his work. Instead, there have been two collections of essays, one stocked mainly with reprinted material, the other conference papers.

Frank Palmeri's *Critical Essays on Jonathan Swift* stays near to the present critical moment for its representative examples. Palmeri's own introduction is succinct and impressively even-handed – a difficult task deftly accomplished. The fresh work (at least to me) comes from Frank Stringfellow ('Irony and Ideals in *Gulliver's Travels*') and Everett Zimmerman ('*A Tale of a Tub* and *Clarissa*: A Battling of Books'). Stringfellow shuttles lucidly between Swift's ideological parameters and the pervasive and relentlessly undercutting ironies of his narrative. Stringfellow realizes that if we want to convert this formal range to some unified comment, then we have to intervene rather clumsily, as one of the defining aspects of ideology is its basis in contradiction and disguise, most truthfully uttered in irony. It is with some surprise that Zimmerman is not here represented by an extract from his excellent *Swift's Narrative Satires* (1983), a precursor of much recent research on textual interpretation in the period. His essay here is formed by a basic comparison between the apparent intimacies of the Teller and Richardson's 'sincere' rhetoric in *Clarissa*.

There are also several inclusions one might have anticipated. Laura Brown's 1990 *ECS* piece on 'Reading Race and Gender' is a survey of numerous theoretical positions. Margaret Anne Doody's 'Swift Among the Women' appears from 1988. Carole Fabricant is heard again on his antipastoralism from 1982. Ellen Pollak's dissection of both Pope and Swift's fetishes ('The Difference in Swift') hails from 1988, and Palmeri himself weighs in with his illuminating comparison of Swift and Gibbon as satiric footnoters from 1990. Given the recent redoubled interest in Swift's cultural context, to afford him just one reading from a more obviously historiographical perspective is a mild surprise. F. P. Lock's assessment from 1984 of Swift's continued debt to Glorious Revolutionary debates is some recompense, but it could be argued that this has now become safely absorbed into modern accounts of Swift's politics. As one might expect, *Gulliver* attracts the fullest attention. Terry Castle's 1980 consideration of the Houyhnhnms' scriptophobia sits alongside much less deconstructive readings. Eric Rothstein from 1986 runs the rule over the impossibility of historical truth-telling from Book Three and Michael Seidel's identification of Swift's 'Strange Dispositions' is a welcome inclusion from his 1979 *Satiric Inheritance*. Arthur H. Scouten's 1981 essay on Swift's 'Progress from Prose to Poetry' isolates the altered circumstances that obliged Swift to return to poetry, and Anne Cline Kelly's 1988 analysis of his Utopian linguistic philosophy, 'How Possibly to Improve Discourse', wrings multiple meanings out of his *Proposal* for a bare academic denotation. There is no room for Rawson, Nokes or Downie – nor even Carol Houlihan Flynn, but in concentrating on less accessible work Palmeri is at the very least justifying the appearance of such collections.

Reading Swift: Papers From the Second Münster Symposium on Jonathan Swift (ed. Richard H. Rodino and Hermann J. Real, with the assistance of Helgard Stover-Leidig) derives from the Symposium of 1989, and now stands as a memorial also to Richard Rodino, whose death in 1990 robbed Swift studies of a particularly fair-minded and yet still incisive critic. This collection includes a wide variety of styles and approaches, and incidentally demonstrates what a broad church Swift scholarship can form – but first, a small, but necessary cavil: for those who may have been led to expect papers gathered with the common purpose of assessing a reader's response to his work (or 'entrapment', as Swift commentary has it), this is not the place to start. 'Reading' is here a most ecumenical term, that embraces monolithic historicism on the one hand and stops just short of killing the author on the other.

Part One, 'Theoretical Approaches', almost teases us with a 'Swift' lodged between an intentionalist being and a typographic creation. For Anne Cline Kelly, Swift is in quotes for all analytic purposes ('The Birth of "Swift"'), for, as a 'verbal construct' and as claimed by 'public discourse', the reference is a 'sign'. By segregating the public's appropriation of the name from the relics of actual existence, Kelly actually refuses the clean distinction between, say, a biographer's discoveries and the apocrypha that propelled 'Swift' to public notice – then as now. By dwelling on the pre-'Swift' Swift, that is, up to 1710, Kelly seems to dip into intention as well as depart from it. Thus, Swift *does* intend to project a self – the dependable shaper of Temple's *Miscellanea* and the occasional provider of Odes and Prefaces. Hence it was that the 'Swift' of the *Tale of the Tub* was a variable commodity. Wotton's *Observations* (1705) even identified Thomas Swift in the writing. The sea-change occurs in 1710 with Curll's *Complete Key* to the *Tale*. Swift enters an intertextual dialogue not only with his readers but also with his very self. Clive T. Probyn takes up this paper 'Swift' rather as Kelly leaves off. In 'Swift and Typographic Man: Foul Papers, Modern Criticism, and Irish Dissenters' the recent deconstructive relish for Print Culture is invoked to pick a way through eighteenth-century anxieties about the reader and the mass market. In so doing, he confronts the reticence of most Swift scholars to enlist modern theory when trying to comprehend ironic texts especially. The conclusion might be that Swift got there first. Who would now be confident that, say, a deconstructive reading of *Tristram Shandy* or *A Tale of the Tub* was not simply to play the game that Sterne/Swift had originally feared, and so, supplied? Probyn focuses on the 'orality' (to borrow Ong's term) of Swift's prose, its 'interrogative' effects undermining its apparent 'declarative' force, and he concludes with a detailed illustration of how Swift actually approached the answering of antagonists in a deconstructive spirit *avant la lettre*. His marginalia to the anonymous *Vindication of the Protestant Dissenters* (1733), itself a point-by-point rebuttal of his earlier and heavily ironic *Presbyterian Pleas of Merit*, demonstrates this. For Hermann J. Real (in ' "A Dish Plentifully Stor'd": Jonathan Swift and the Evaluation of Satire') pursues a laudable strategy: to clarify the reasons why we might *value* satire and its satirists. By rational demonstration – or, as Real here holds, by its *plausibility*? A parody might instil contempt for the original text, and we can detail its operations exhaustively, yet this is not getting us nearer to facing the problem as to whether the net effect of the tactic is well-founded in principle or productive of intelligent re-reading. The essay is well-stocked and its distrust of 'evaluative monism' is defensible – if your emphasis is going to be on delivering the exact constitution of some original text (which may not 'fit'). Swift appears here most artful when he allows his victims to betray themselves and he investigates the apparent but well-calculated 'plain-dealing' in the Bickerstaff Papers and his *Argument Against Abolishing Christianity*.

Part Two deals with 'Political and Biographical Concerns'. Jeremy Black draws on his wide expertise in early-century Foreign Policy in his 'Swift and

Foreign Policy Revised'. *The Conduct of the Allies* gets a new gloss as a serious, close reading of recent Whig pronouncements in order ultimately to promote a Tory reading of trade wars. The essay also carries a concise survey of recent historiographical opinion on the early years of Hanoverian Britain. Joseph McMinn's 'The Importance of Friendship in Swift's Writings' not only identifies personal relationships as a persistent theme in his letters, but also elevates it to the status of a presiding 'ethical value' – a lens through which to test other professions of warmth or intimacy, especially in the public sphere. McMinn is most persuasive when dealing with the Stella poems. Ian Campbell Ross attempts to unearth new information about Swift's early exile in Ireland and his continuing links with erstwhile Scriblerians in London in his 'The Scriblerians and Swift in Ireland' (pp. 81–9). In what has become a standard account he discovers a split loyalty – to the metropolitan culture he had just left behind and the bedrock of Irishness activated whenever he perceived the imperial harshness of this same London urbanity. This leads easily to Wolfgang Zach's 'Jonathan Swift and Colonialism' (pp. 91–9), which, while concentrating less on strictly biographical witness, applies these same perceptions in the main to *Gulliver's Travels* and *A Modest Proposal*.

Part Three deals with the poetry. Part Four, entitled 'The Prose Satirist', includes several forays into both political and historical concerns in order to comprehend Swift's formal variety in his prose pamphlets. Frank H. Ellis ('*An Argument Against Abolishing Christianity* as an Argument Abolishing the Test Act') promotes an entirely possible and original scheme to regard the *Argument* as a mock speech-in-Parliament. The scenario is set in the Commons where the Speaker assumes the task of speaking on behalf of a bill to repeal the test clause in Ireland. As a 'nominal Christian', he therefore is near to being an occasional conformist *ex officio*. The very act of speaking as he does, therefore, is paradoxical. Robert Phiddian returns to the play with names and identity in the Bickerstaff Papers in his 'A Name to Conjure With: Games of Verification and Identity in the Bickerstaff Controversy'. It also pursues this paper construction in several later 'editions', mostly tellingly in Steele's hands. Heinz-Joachim Müllenbrock concentrates on Swift's use, and development of, the essay medium, especially in *The Examiner*. Despite Swift's apparent distrust of Bacon, Müllenbrock makes a good fist of demonstrating the actual debt to his mix of forceful detail and structured argument ('Swift as a Political Essayist: The Strained Medium'). Swift, however, is no New Atlantean, as there are just as many gestures that ape the fashions of the eighteenth-century periodical essay. The same fruitful emphasis on generic matters can be found in Johann N. Schmidt's 'Talk That Leads Nowhere: Swift's *Complete Collection of Genteel and Ingenious Conversation*'. If generic consistency is expected, then this loose collation of assorted dicta will disappoint. Its communication of laboured compilation is actually a part of its method. The growing sense of the shallow and meretricious compiler holds the work together.

In Part Four, on *Gulliver* there are three essays that examine the generic indications in the work. Richard H. Rodino's ' "Splendide Mendax": Authors, Characters, and Readers in *Gulliver's Travels*' is reprinted from *PMLA* ([1991]106.1054–70). Rodino's awareness of how totalizing truths actually unravel is three parts Swift (as is fitting) and surely one part Rodino, and it leads into Brean S. Hammond's piece on 'Applying Swift', which is similarly sceptical about the battle-lines drawn up (Lock versus Downie among others) to debate the extent to which the work is allegorical. Remaining with pre-Augustan preoccupations with allegory as a fitting rhetorical mode, Hammond entertains the provocative assumption that Swift's deployment of 'allegory' was a deliberate attempt to present it as an outmoded and limited way of interpreting – much as the allegory of the Brothers and Coats dissolves in the *Tale*. Truth is a process of complex readerly judgement, not formulaic identification of simple basic premises.

Michael DePorte's 'Swift's Horses of Instruction' seems to pick up a topic upon which critics have worked so heavily that there would seem little room for novelty. De Porte notes Swift's love of riding and the common textbook association of heroes and irrationality, but DePorte goes further here to push the point that horses could also signify the freedoms of imagination. As Gulliver recognizes, the Houyhnhnms are poets. Perhaps instead of the cold calculators, they also stand for 'hard mouth'd' imagination, ready to throw the rider off at last. There is one paper on the prose in the sixth section, 'Canon': David Woolley's '*A Dialogue Upon Dunkirk* (1712), and Swift's "Penny Papers"', which comes equipped with a facsimile fold-out of the text. Woolley assigns the work to Swift and identifies it as one of the '7 Penny Papers' he confessed to have dashed off in July–August 1712. Six others have been found. His method is to pick out a shared vocabulary with several other contemporary works known to be by Swift. Collections such as this are notoriously uneven and usually resist a consistency of address and style. Perhaps that is their peculiar virtue, but Rodino and Real have done a thorough job here, and, although not all the contributions present new ideas, the aim, to provide examples of the range of recent critical work, is accomplished with conspicuous success.

Two Swift essays can be found in *Literature and Medicine During the Eighteenth Century*, edited by Marie M. Roberts and Roy Porter, the latest in the Wellcome Institute's series on the history of medical practice. Christopher Fox's 'Of Logic and Lycanthropy: Gulliver and the Faculties of the Mind' ponders the old conundrum of Gulliver's madness. The solitary Gulliver, enjoying his 'own Speculation' in the garden at Redriff, resists easy categorization. Recent work on contemporary ideas of logical reasoning usually just highlight one kind of intellectual effort, the Aristotelian. Here, Fox opposes a different strain, William Molyneux's, from 1692, in his *Dioptrica Nova*, where logic is more a matter of focusing on 'the nature and operation of the faculties than upon arguments and valid inference forms'. Gulliver's confusion between remembering and imaging is one unfortunate side-effect of melancholy and illogical fixation. The same preoccupation with proofs of sanity is explored in Michael DePorte's '"Mere Productions of the Brain": Interpreting Dreams in Swift'. Proceeding from the understanding that as many as 24 editions of Artemidorus's *The Interpretation of Dreams* appeared between 1606 and 1740, DePorte promotes the idea that the dual function of dreams, those 'growing out of everyday hopes and anxieties' and those 'containing clues to future events', haunted Swift. Decoding his dreams in the *Journal to Stella*, he is simultaneously fascinated and repelled by this nocturnal loss of reason, a drama he replicates in several poems. The third of DePorte's studies of Swift this year can be found in *SStud*: 'The Road to S. Patrick's: Swift and the Problem of Belief' (8.5–17). As the Richard Rodino Memorial Lecture, its aims are less specific than in the more usual *SStud* offerings. In discovering a perfectly straightforward Churchman, DePorte does not avoid the awkward questions posed by *A Tale of a Tub*: when does divine inspiration become ranting enthusiasm? If not proven by the miraculous, then religious faith needs to be content with a God 'remote and unknowable' – there's the rub: how to account for the ensuing isolation from all moral certainties.

Vaughan Hart explores 'Jonathan Swift and the Architecture of Nature' (*SStud* 8.100–5) by bringing out the comfort of architectonic forms in *Gulliver*. Starting from the premise that Houyhnhnm building exemplifies 'a simple, ancient harmony with nature', Hart notes the Vitruvian ideal of completely natural nest-building that sets the animal world apart from the human. Swift would have known of this distinction, and may have used it to lament the unnatural pursuit of reason that Swift (erroneously) sees in the Houyhnhnm world. Such a perception actually divorces the 'Modern' Gulliver from the 'garden of nature' – and Lord Munodi's natural temperance. This *anomie* Patrick Reilly traces in 'The Displaced Person: Swift and Ireland' (*SStud* 8.68–82), where the hybrid of Anglo-Irish stand for more fundamental instances of identity loss. Reilly is always an entertaining writer, but this is at best a fresh look at old material. *SStud* is at its best when it allows exegesis to follow textual discoveries. Here there are two studies that add to our knowledge of Swift's earlier self. N. F. Lowe and W. J. McCormack examine 'Swift as "Publisher" of Sir William Temple's *Letters* and *Miscellanea*' (*SStud* 8.46–57), by way of a close analysis of the marginalia of a recently discovered copy of Temple's *Letters to the King* in St Finbarr's Cathedral Library. Wishing to use Temple's celebrity in order to advance his own career, there is evidence that Swift's inscriptions on the fly-leaves of several copies of the *Letters* were to direct attention to his own labours. The authors conclude, though, that it is just as likely that the preface to the *Letters* show a growing disaffection with Temple – not, as Ehrenpreis suggested, that it was a rush job. Hermann J. Real is intrigued by the veneration Swift felt for a man he had never met: his paternal grandfather, Revd Thomas Swift. In 'The Dean's Grandfather, Thomas Swift (1595–1658): Forgotten Evidence' (*SStud* 8.84–93), Real reconstructs a plausible Royalist role model, who suffered extreme persecution for Charles I's sake. Edgar Mertner provides a note on 'Christian Martin Wieland's Criticism of Swift' (*SStud* 8.58–66), an outraged defence of human potential against Gulliver's closing diatribe.

Of the studies more exclusively on individual works, *Gulliver*, as usual, has excited the most comment. I have already mentioned Christopher Fox's work on Gulliver's Lycanthropy (in Roberts and Porter) and Stringfellow's essay (in Palmeri). Potentially the most suggestive of the rest is the recent discovery of Irvin Ehrenpreis's 'Show and Tell in *Gulliver's Travels*' (*SStud* 8.18–33), found in his papers at Munster and dating from the early eighties. The central focus of the paper can be found in the inevitable divorce between commentary and narrative, and, in a rather leisurely fashion, Ehrenpreis attempts to return us to the form of the book and take us away from yet more ruminating on the Yahoos. Drawing sustenance from a protracted comparison with *The Pilgrim's Progress*, this investigation identifies Gulliver as the well-travelled authority, heir to the comedy and despair usually associated with the work's close, and agonizingly self-conscious about a predicament we should eventually take to be ours. Thomas R. Cleary takes a lot of trouble to locate Swift's own particular terms of relativity and delves into Baroque theories of illusion in his 'Big and Little People: Size, Distance and Value in *Gulliver's Travels* and Baroque *trompe-l'oeil*' (*SVEC* 305.1493–5). Richard Crider reminds us that 'Yahu' is actually a variant of Yahweh, and perhaps incorporates, unconsciously or consciously, the Hebrew form of his own Christian name, 'Yehonatan', the gift of 'Yahu'. Is this ironic or not? Crider at least gives us the material for further interpretation ('Yahoo (Yahu): Notes on the Names of Swift's Yahoos' (*Names* 41.103–9)). Ronald Knowles reads the Yahoos as a possible figure for all of humanity in his 'Swift's Yahoos, Aphrodite and Hyginus Fabula CCXX' (*ELN* 31.44–6). The fable has Cura fashioning human form from 'clayey mud', which *might* (a big if, to my mind) suggest the Yahoos' source in 'corrupted mud and slime'.

Howard Erskine-Hill's *Jonathan Swift: 'Gulliver's Travels'* in the Landmarks of English Literature series is an admirably condensed account both of a varied critical history and of a large body of ultimately suggestive and so inconclusive scholarship into contemporary philosophical and theological debates. The form of the book is orthodox: introduction, then individual chapters on each book with a final chapter that draws together individual threads with some comments on Critical Reception. Erskine-Hill is at his best when isolating the ironic use of the 'reader-figure' and also when cutting through the plethora of interpretation to revive the importance of the actual experience of reading. One can appreciate this and yet, due doubtless to my having to assimilate all shades of Swift criticism these last few years, I cannot help regarding the emphasis as much less original than he does. What we do get are trenchant reminders of the actual circumstances of Swift's composition – necessary first steps often ignored in the rush for complication and ingenuity.

This dismantling of the consolation that works spring fully formed from the writer's head at some single moment is a necessary and valuable legacy of the newer, textual criticism. Some of this creative scepticism is evident in Judith C. Mueller's 'Writing Under Constraint: Swift's "Apology" for *A Tale of a Tub*' (*ELH* 60.101–15), a fresh look at the role of the 1710 additions. Proceeding from the questionable assumption that there is still a considerable body of commentary that accepts the 1710 'Apology' as (more or less) reliable and straight Swiftian comment, Mueller comes upon it as a parody of the sub-genre of self-conscious prefatory *diminutio*, so beloved of contemporary freethinkers, whilst also turning the charges of immorality levelled at the 1704 volume back onto the too ingenious reader. Such hurt innocence at the tyrannical power of reader over text effectively announces the most persistent keynote of the *Tale* 'proper'. This is Anne Barbeau Gardiner's guiding principle in her valuable piece of historical scene-setting in 'Licking the Dust in Luggnagg: Swift's Reflections on the Legacy of King William's Conquest of Ireland' (*SStud* 8.35–44). Here this tyranny is the ortho- doxy of Anglophone power, and, due to a precise reading of the Luggnagg episode in *Gulliver* and competing Irish views of the events of 1690, she comes to the conclusion that the Irish understood their oppression as a sort of release from a worse state of affairs. Indeed, this myth of achieved 'wholeness' is a form of idolatry and a betrayal of Irish liberty.

Lisa Herb Smith's ' "The Livery of Religion": Reconciling Swift's *Argument and Project*' (*ELN* 31.ii.27–33) attempts to square the apparently ironic *Argu- ment Against Abolishing Christianity* with his more direct *Project For the Advancement of Religion*. The process by which Swift is apparently advocating nominal observance in the *Argument* is consistent with his realization in both works that society (with a last shrug of the shoulders) cannot furnish the condi- tions for exact Christian morals. Peter Nocon's 'The Dramatic Fortunes of Isaac Bickerstaff' (*SStud* 8.109–12) continues the after-life of the notorious pen-name in the 1947 play by Paul Hennings – interesting in its realization of the charlatan Bickerstaff and (a surprise) to the cynical Gulliver, but not more than that.

Finally, W. A. Speck seeks to provide a sea-change in the assessment of Swift's journalism with his '*The Examiner*: Re-Examined' (in *Telling People What To Think: Early Eighteenth-Century Periodicals From the Review to the Rambler*, ed. J. A. Downie and Thomas N. Corns). What we get is an exercise in academic point-scoring with the targets Claude Rawson and F. P. Lock who seem to have ignored Speck's work unjustly. Submerged under this are some timely reminders that Swift was a pivotal figure in the formation of Tory ideology up to 1714 – but to get a full flavour of Speck's argument I suspect that you would have had to have attended the right conferences.

4. The Novel

'Perceptions of women as entirely limited by their sex are perhaps more frequent in novels by women than by men, but by no means [...] so ubiquitous as critics sometimes have implied' writes Mona Scheuermann in the introduction to *Her Bread to Earn: Women, and Society from Defoe to Austen*; but that even-tenored qualification opens out into wide historical vistas and an impressively sustained challenge to short historicist agendas. She is impatient with *Clarissa*'s distorting mirror, foregrounds the self-empowering energies of Defoe's heroines rather than their dependency, and castigates Fielding for his inconsistent stereotypes, before moving on to the radical novelists of the 1790s (both male and female) where her briskly confident readings are at their most impressive. There is a good deal of story-telling here, for Scheuermann is tactfully aware that many of her readers will not have such an eclectic store of knowledge, but her summaries are frequently enlivened by analytical enthusiasm, as on her favourite: 'The women in Robert Bage's *Hermsprong* are both admirable and amicable [...] and its heroines are two of the smartest women in these novels. *Hermsprong*'s tone is wry, its images sunny yet always just abutting shadow [...] a world where reason and good do triumph, but they win out by very narrow margins over the ubiquitous insanities of eighteenth-century England's laws, social customs, and patterns of male–female relationships.' Scheuermann's Wollstonecraft, on the other hand, is an atypically angst-ridden source for the hegemony of woman-as-victim criticism whether in its openly tragic or comically subversive forms. K. G. Hall's *The Exalted Heroine and the Triumph of Order: Class, Women and Religion in the English Novel, 1740–1800* starts from a similar premise in its design to encourage a wider reading of the period's fiction; it also gives *Hermsprong* as much room as *Pamela* (and consigns *Clarissa* to a parenthetical mention in a chapter on *The Vicar of Wakefield*). But here the resemblances end. Hall's book is a journeyman survey by a Marxist sociologist aimed at a readership which might not even be familiar with canonical texts and which does little more than accept the Richardsonian model as the singular bourgeois template for subsequent variation or modulation. Both books focus unreservedly on money as the root of all power, but Scheuermann gives better literary critical value for it.

Still, the middle class is always being reinvented. John P. Zomchick's *Family and the Law in Eighteenth-Century Fiction: The Public Conscience in the Private Sphere* is energized by Lawrence Stone – and by Lennard J. Davis, Michael McKeon, Bakhtin, Althusser, Gramsci, Foucault, Habermas, plus Hume, Ferguson, Blackstone, and virtually everyone else – to revisit the proposition that the rise of economic individualism in a secularizing society replaced the communal values of Christian humanism with the contentious specificities of law. Once through the 'survey of the literature' in an overlong introduction (which perhaps betrays the book's origin in a thesis) Zomchick's intellectually agile reading of the 'juridical subject' in his six chosen novels – *Roxana, Clarissa, Roderick Random, Amelia, The Vicar of Wakefield* and *Caleb Williams* – is enriched by his facility with a variety of interpretative frameworks. The result is an intricate progression of case histories to advocate that 'the law and the eighteenth-century novel displace the subject from a contentious civil society to the newly emergent nuclear family, which is in turn represented as the natural home of the rational, pleasure-seeking individual', although the prescribed intensity of Zomchick's cross-examination raises questions about the applicability of his matrix beyond its six components. Coincidentally, that objection is implied by another choice of texts and a different focus. In last year's *SECC* Elizabeth Kraft trailed her concern with 'Public Nurturance and Private Civility: The Transposition of Values in Eighteenth-Century Fiction' (22.181–93) which urged responsible readers to reconsider the comic novelists precisely because 'although the eighteenth-century novel responds to the seductive pull of private identity, it also harbours a resilient commitment to the social self'. This year she gives us the full treatment. *Character and Consciousness in Eighteenth-Century Comic Fiction* is a passionate book, explicitly committed to reading as an ethical quest, on five novels (*Tom Jones, The Female Quixote, Tristram Shandy, Peregrine Pickle, Cecilia*), as a challenge to the atomization of modern life no less than postmodern criticism such as that which foregrounds strategies to seize individual empowerment. A third of the book expounds her general thesis, and here Kraft is at her animated best; for example, in her treatment of comic and tragic possibilities which moves assuredly from McKeon on indeterminacy through Mack on the logics of opposed modes to an appropriately mischievous analogue between Clarissa in her closet and Molly Seagrim in her attic. Yet Kraft's mission to persuade us that seriousness does not require solemnity, or that novels figure complex fascination with the social games that people play, is curiously at odds with her own tendency to earnest inflexibility on the individual texts. *Cecilia*'s 'masquerade set piece suggests that character must conform to certain established conventions to avoid being ridiculous, but that in so doing it becomes trapped in a rigid form that is ultimately self-annihilating', declares Kraft. The titles of two other monographs seem to suggest that those who would disagree are just as active and more numerous, but I have not seen either Catherine Craft-Fairchild's *Masquerade and Gender: Disguise and Female Identity in Eighteenth-Century Fiction by Women* (PSUP), or Susan Fraiman's *Unbecoming Women: British Women Writers and the Novel of Development* (ColUP).

Ann Jessie Van Sant makes an original contribution to the later twentieth-century's renewed interest in *Eighteenth-Century Sensibility and the Novel*. Subtitled *The Senses in Social Context*, this well-written and impressively researched book argues that 'the story of sensibility is the story of the relation between sight and touch that arises from the philosophical and psychological sensationalism of the eighteenth century'. It fully justifies its claim for an irresistible parallel between the novel's rhetoric of sensibility and the other 'novel' languages of physiological and psychological enquiry. Particularly striking is Van Sant's own careful investigation of the public spectacle offered by the Magdalen House Philanthropic Society – and Dr Dodd's sermons designed to loosen the heart and purse strings of those who came to view penitent prostitutes

– which modulates provocatively into 'Gazing on Suffering' in *Clarissa*. Her range of reference is very tightly drawn; there is, for example, little Hume or Wollstonecraft, and even less of the critics from Jean Hagstrum to Tom Keymer. Yet she certainly reaches the end she seeks in demonstrating the consonance between literary and scientific discourses. On the way she launches lines of enquiry which might have defied exhaustive pursuit even if that had been her intent: 'I argue that the body of sensibility, which leads to both sentimental and satiric reports on the world, is inherently parodic ... [and] that despite definition by reference to a feminized standard of delicacy, this body is not a woman's body and could not become the sustained location of women's experience.' What follows is a brief but important analysis of sensibility as a 'miniaturizing and physicalizing force' in *A Sentimental Journey* and a range of challenges to other critics. One of those might well be Carolyn Woodward. Van Sant cites the softly pornographic 'Narrative of a Florentine Lady of Quality' to support her proposition that 'an experimental woman of feeling would be an adventuress, remarkable for her promiscuity. She could not, as Yorick does, feel her way across France.' In ' "My Heart so Wrapt": Lesbian Disruption in Eighteenth-Century British Fiction' (*Signs* 18.838–65) Woodward writes with expansive engagement on two women doing exactly that, in *The Travels and Adventures of Mademoiselle de Richlieu* (1744); but of course this is a transgressive narrative which has to move outside the patriarchal novel form to enclose its lesbian love story in a travelogue. Woodward also speculates, very tentatively, that the translation may have been by Lady Mary. Isobel Grundy is obviously well qualified to pursue that notion, or any other matter related to ' "Trash, Trumpery, and Idle Time": Lady Mary Wortley Montagu and Fiction' (*ECF* 5.293–310). Grundy's engrossing essay surveys Lady Mary's experience of fiction, first as a juvenile dabbler then a lifelong, voracious consumer, both attracted and resistant to Richardson, and conscious of her position as a wealthy expatriate (thus doubly reading 'from the fringes') with an instinctive recourse to neo-classical precepts: 'Ambivalent over didacticism but adamant over verisimilitude, Lady Mary subordinated all other requirements to a second essential; that her reading should engage and delight her.' By chance, the two themes of household pleasures and transgression are united in Cynthia Wall's 'Gendering Rooms: Domestic Architecture and Literary Acts' (also *ECF* 5.349–72), an essay no less sinuous in its use of historicist theory than Van Sant's work, but here applied to 'the fictional habitation of culturally and sexually determined interior space within otherwise widely dispersed canonical works' (*Roxana*, *Clarissa* and *Pride and Prejudice*). Barbara Claire Freeman's horizons were much wider last year, in 'The Rise of the Sublime: Sacrifice and Misogyny in Eighteenth-Century Aesthetics' (*YJC* 5.81–99) but she was no less concerned with female space, the growth of female authorship and blossoming interest in the sublime: 'in each case the feminine protagonist's victimization is crucial for narrative closure as well as the triumph of masculine authority [...] suggesting that feminine authorship must be understood not only as a crucial sign of women's rise to power, but also as helping to instantiate the very ideology its readers were beginning to resist'. How appropriate then that the last general 1993 essay on the novel I saw was Richard C. Taylor's 'James Harrison, *The Novelist's Magazine*, and the Early Canonizing of the English Novel' (*SEL* 33.629–43), a crisp account of one remarkable niche marketing enterprise which, along with circulating business, did much to entrench 'the novel' as a body of 'classic writing' in the later eighteenth century – at that time one that included Eliza

Haywood, Sarah Fielding and Charlotte Lennox – when the novel was under particular attack but before the more prescriptive canon-making of the early nineteenth century.

Defoe enthusiasts will take pleasure in two particularly weighty essays, by Gary Hentzi and Carl R. Lovitt. Hentzi projects Defoe's complex of responses to '"An Itch of Gaming": the South Sea Bubble and the Novels of Daniel Defoe' (*ECLife* 17.32–45), via its perceived threat to the integrity of English society, into the fictions: 'the achievement of *Moll Flanders* and *Colonel Jack* lies in the success with which they represent the compelling psychological power of that threat, as well as the conflicts it creates with reason and religion alike'. Lovitt, by contrast, traces a thoroughgoing if discursive logic in *Moll Flanders* which employs every device to reunite Moll with Jemy in a way which satisfies all four conditions for closure, 'Marriage, Wealth, Love and Gentility' ('Defoe's "Almost Invisible Hand": Narrative Logic as a Structuring Principle in *Moll Flanders*', *ECF* 6.1–28); but perhaps Lovitt's most intriguing accomplishment is to construct an elegant case for the proposition 'that Moll's agendas do not govern her narrative' without recourse to either armed camp on irony. Pat Rogers also steers his readers away from interpretative circularity as he urges them back to the imaginative immediacy of early eighteenth-century life in his introduction to the Everyman edition of *Moll Flanders*; but Jeffrey Hopes returns to familiar ambivalences – here the discourses of Providence on the one hand and unstable contemporaneity on the other – in a routine essay on 'Les Contradictions de Defoe: Providence, Stratégies et Discours Didactiques dans *A Journal of the Plague Year*' (*EA* 46.129–39); and Takau Shimada seems ultimately more concerned with oriental self-respect than with the materials on high Chinese culture he finds culled from various 'Sources for *The Exploits of Robinson Crusoe*' (*N&Q* 40.348–51). By contrast, *Roxana* has had an unusually good year. Zomchick and Scheuermann privilege that novel for extended analysis in the monographs noted already, and so does John Z. Zhang in 'Defoe's "Man-Woman" Roxana: Gender, Reversal and Androgyny' (*EA* 46.272–88). However, this clogged Marxist reading of the novel 'in terms of female power', which can be a force that disrupts the male monopoly and threatens patriarchy when perceived as the Kristevan maternal 'chora', is for the theoretical expert only, and Scheuermann will be preferred by anyone who wishes to explore Roxana as 'Man-Woman' without a prior struggle through barely penetrable prose. Another option is the brevity of witty thrust and counter-thrust on a religious allusion in Roxana's despair; a lunge by Melvyn New, 'On a Passage from John Richetti's "The Public Sphere and the Eighteenth-Century Novel"' (*ECLife* 17.85–6), countered by 'A Reply to Melvyn New' (86–8) which accepts the accuracy of the gloss but parries with the accusation that New remains 'unresponsive to the narrative dynamics of Defoe's book which is precisely about an emerging secular consciousness profoundly troubled by a lingering and imperfectly internalised religious ideology'. Yet it would be unjust to mention New's characteristically (and enjoyably) waspish aside on the contemporary meaning of 'Marxist critic' without also commending Zhang's intelligently ingenious speculations on the 'fictive' projections of Susan's fate, an issue which receives strangely scant attention in Zomchick's otherwise exhaustive treatment of the 'juridical subject' in that novel.

Murray L. Brown believes we are still 'Learning to Read Richardson: *Pamela*, "Speaking Pictures", and the Visual Hermeneutic' (*SNNTS* 25.129–51) and he works with a will to prove that Richardson's first fiction outlined the template for

his other novels by creating a text 'awash in idiomatic emblemata' from the
Puritan tradition. He is, however, alone in his conviction that this 'inconotext' is
well designed to guide the visually astute reader through the imperfect responses
of the novel's own interpreters to its Christian signification: other essayists have
their eyes too firmly fixed on secularized puritanism. Robert Folkenflik, for
example, finds an ingeniously new angle of approach to the old issues for
'*Pamela*: Domestic Servitude, Marriage, and the Novel' (*ECF* 5.253–68) by
applying Erving Goffman's research into institutionalization to Pamela the model
servant, as figured in the 'ruling-class hysteria' of conduct literature, at precisely
those points where modern readers find her most unacceptably self-abnegating;
and John A. Dussinger's well-shaped essay, 'Masters and Servants: Political
Discourse in Richardson's *A Collection of Moral Sentiments*' (*ECF* 5.239–52)
reads all the fictions refracted through the bourgeois writer's own compilation to
reveal the stark outline of a man enjoying his 'radical, even revolutionary cake'
while tucking into his 'paranoiac fear of [the lower class] predilection to cheat
and subvert the master's authority'. That contradiction is the source of Albert J.
Rivers's dilemma in another lively contribution to the class debate, 'The Place of
Sally Godfrey in Richardson's *Pamela*' (*ECF* 6.29–46), which begins with the
near-literal aristocratic hysteria of Lady Danvers (about the novel's alternative
domestic-as-object-of-desire) to deny auspicious readings of Pamela's success
and to ask that we 'question [...] our ethical responsibility' as interpreters in a
world sensitized to the sexual politics of class. Terri Nickel, '*Pamela* as Fetish:
Masculine Anxiety in Henry Fielding's *Shamela* and James Parry's *The True
Anti-Pamela*' (*SECC* 22.37–49) was, last year, no less troubled by modern
criticism 'that undercuts a carefully constructed homogeneity postulated on the
authority of the phallus as a signifier', but only, she feared, within the textual
world of castration-haunted dispute that excluded the female. Laura Fasick's
feminist essay, 'The Edible Woman: Eating and Breast-Feeding in the Novels of
Samuel Richardson' (*SoAR* 58.17–31), is altogether more confidently sustained
as she combines fictional desire with feeding and suckling to accuse Richardson
of an all-embracing compulsion that seeks the internalization of patriarchy:
'straightforward sexual exploitation of the female body proves a relatively feeble
instrument of control compared to the ability to impose an interpretation of the
body's significance'. Lovelace is Richardson's surrogate and both exhibit the
'male urge for mastery' in Elizabeth W. Harries's 'Fragments and Mastery: *Dora
and Clarissa*' (*ECF* 5.217–38), which contrives to distinguish Freud and a
Freudian novelist's dream of 'a seamless and seemly narrative' from the untidy
fictional reality in which 'sexual difference and narrative economies alternately
sort themselves out and merge'. Richard Hannaford's 'Playing her Dead Hand:
Clarissa's Posthumous Letters' (*TSLL* 35.79–102) brooks no such equivocation.
Here a combination of Bakhtin and psychoanalytical attention to the novel's
gamesters proves Clarissa the most intensely self-contained (if disordered) high
roller: 'the caustic condemnation in the posthumous letters suggest a shrewd and
manipulative Clarissa fully capable of playing her "dead hand"'. By a neat
coincidence the last journal piece to be noted takes Murray L. Brown's concern
with 'Speaking Pictures' into one of the late twentieth-century's multimedia
options. '"Is it Easier to Believe?" Narrative Innocence from *Clarissa* to "Twin
Peaks"' (*ArQ* 49.137–58) by Helen Deutsch is a sinuous discourse on David
Lynch's television blockbuster with regular flashbacks to Richardson: 'What
Lynch accomplishes [...] is to unite the sado/masochistic, ironic/sentimental,

masculine/feminine adversaries of Lovelace and Clarissa in the figure of the viewer, who must simultaneously acknowledge and disavow complicity in the "neere sadism" that makes innocence visible by testing and raping it.' And that, in turn, takes us back to Van Sant's rhetoric of experimentation. No doubt there will be more metahistorical layering to note in 1994's publications. That will also be the time to report on Tassie Gwilliam's *Samuel Richardson's Fictions of Gender* (StanfordUP) which arrived too late for inclusion here.

The Correspondence of Henry and Sarah Fielding, edited by Martin C. Battestin and Clive T. Probyn, contains no letters between brother and sister but a wealth of introductory comment and annotation on correspondences in which, despite Henry's dislike of non-profitable writing, he outscores his sister in the ratio of 2:1. But even that is an achievement of some proportions, and for the editors no less than the insecure sister of a famous brother. Twenty years ago only 31 holographs were known out of the 110 reproduced here in the unmodernized, unstandardized form which, as their editors point out, allows us to gauge relationships with recipients by attending to the degree of care taken over formal presentation. James Harris, Member of Parliament and polymathic scholar, the subject of Probyn's *Life and Works* in 1991 (*YWES* 72.248), is also the addressee of the most revealing new letters from both Fieldings. Henry writes to an intimate and valued scholarly equal, Sarah more decorously and tentatively in a contrast which is more instructive than many a modern essay on the dilemmas that faced women who wrote in a man's world, particularly when, like her, they pursued their frustrated thirst for classical learning into print. In the journals only Henry exercised the critics this year, although the shortest piece, Isobel Grundy's 'Innoculation in Salisbury' (*Scriblerian* 26.63–5), adds a few details to Battestin's *Life* of the male novelist and is similarly concerned with 'family networking', here orchestrated by Lady Mary against the threat of smallpox. Battestin's critical analysis of the Gypsy King episode is the starting point for Ricardo L.Ortiz in 'Fielding's "Orientalist" Moment: Historical Fiction and Historical Knowledge in *Tom Jones*' (*SEL* 33.609–28), mediated through Said and Todorov. Given to sentences which run into the teens of lines, this appears to be the distillation of a thesis which has been made indigestible through compression. Class anxieties were more exclusively to the fore in 'Joseph Andrews as Exemplary Gentleman' by Treadwell Ruml II (*SECC* 22.195–207), a 1992 essay on Fielding's 'model for upwardly aspiring tradesmen [... and] critique of downwardly behaving oligarchs'.

Evelina is the subject of both pieces on Burney in the journals. Raymond F. Hilliard's contribution, 'Laughter Echoing from Mouth to Mouth: Symbolic Cannibalism and Gender in *Evelina*' (*ECLife* 17.46–61), is a theoretically sophisticated application of Elias Canetti (on crowd behaviour) supplemented by Eli Sagan and Peggy Reeves Sanday, who explain ritual cannibalism 'as a fundamental form of institutionalized social aggression', to extend the significance of the novel's codified violence. Irene Tucker also steps away from the text for 'Writing Home: *Evelina*, the Epistolary Novel and the Paradox of Property' (*ELH* 60.419–39), but here to the near-contemporary Hardwicke judgement on Pope's action against Curll over the property of his correspondence, as her basis for a supple and thoughtful exploration of epistolarity and authorship. Another pair of essays help confirm the secure place Charlotte Lennox commands in the new canon. David Marshall's 'Writing Masters and "Masculine Exercises" in *The Female Quixote*' (*ECF* 5.105–35) weaves together an intricate network of evidence, from details of typography to the resonances of intertextuality, suggestive of 'Arabella's attraction to and identification with women involved with cross-dressing, sexual and gender transgression, and the masculine province in which male writers are masters'. Susan K. Howard attempts less while 'Identifying the Criminal in Charlotte Lennox's *The Life of Harriet Stuart*' (*ECF* 5.137–52), and on a novel with more historical than intrinsic merit, but she does draw some interesting conclusions about 'Captivity novels [as the] physical manifestation of the colonial woman's psychological situation'. Among the other work on later-century fiction is an equally solid but more wide-ranging analysis of the paradoxical gratifications offered by popular texts with inanimate narrators: 'Britannia's Rule and the It-Narrator' (*ECF* 6.65–82), by Aileen Douglas, pays particular attention to Charles Johnstone's *Chrystal: Or the Adventures of a Guinea*, 1760, in a persuasive account of the way such episodic fictions combined homiletic satire with confidence that 'the damage commerce does to human nature can be repaired once commerce is understood in terms of empire'. Historical constructs are also Steven Bruhm's subject in 'Roderick Random's Closet' (*ESC* 19.401–15), if here for a lively polemic on Captain Whiffle and Strutwell as, respectively, 'one of the first "authentic" representations of the modern gay man [... and the homosexual] who announces the birth of the closet and the dynamics of epistemology and regulation that dominate the closet' thereafter. Both characters are again listed, with a passing reference to their homosexuality, and little else, in Denise Bulckaen's *A Dictionary of Characters in Tobias Smollett's Novels*. Here too are 31 anonymous servants and 11 passing waiters dutifully listed among the 2,500 separate entries purportedly intended as 'a useful guide to the human maze introduced in the novels', but to no discernible purpose.

Sterne's mighty maze is certainly not without its plan in Pat Rogers's learnedly subtle reading of 'Ziggerzagger Shandy: Sterne and the Aesthetics of the Crooked Line' (*English* 42.97–107). Digressive yet progressively abrupt, angular movements, derived from frames of reference that united gardening with military engineering, were models useful to Corporal Trim and his creator alike: 'he needed a fictional model in which it was possible to change tack rapidly, to hold competing moods of comedy and sentiment on a par, and to combine discrete materials without privileging any individual motif as the grand central theme'. Roy C. Caldwell demonstrates a more self-regarding virtuosity with zig-zaggery in his valorization of mechanics in '*Tristram Shandy*, Bachelor Machine' (*ECent* 34.103–14), but one wonders why if the subject is 'a crackpot device which finally produces nothing other than the spectacle of its own functioning'. Elsewhere in the journals Madeleine Descargues reworks the old tension (or equilibrium) more tactfully if less inventively, for '*A Sentimental Journey*, ou le Cas D'Indélicatesse' (*EA* 46.407–19), and Mario Curreli reports carefully on 'Sterne in Italy: A Survey of Translations, 1792–1992' (*Scriblerian* 26.66–9). Similar sorts of endeavour have provided the backbone for the previous four annual volumes of *The Shandean*. In volume five they dominate all else. As usual, Kenneth Monkman is the mainstay: 'Towards a Bibliography of Sterne's Sermons' (32–109) describes all those copies he has collected for the library in Shandy Hall and does so with all the unique verve he brings to bibliographical annotation. This centrepiece work is supported by other scholarly if also more sober accounts: David Alexander, on 'Sterne, the 18th-Century Print Market, and the Prints in Shandy Hall' (110–24), and Agnes Zwaneveld on 'Laurence Sterne in Holland: The Eighteenth Century' (125–49) – with its fascinating account of translation as an expression of dissenting politics – to which Peter Voogd adds 'Laurence Sterne in Dutch (18th Century): A Bibliography' (150–9). Literally surrounding all this bibliographical endeavour are two essays which will be of interest to a wider range of *YWES*'s readers. Tom Keymer's 'Marvell, Thomas Hollis, and Sterne's Maria: Parody in *A Sentimental Journey*' (9–31) begins with an allusion to Marvell's 'Nymph Complaining for the Death of her Faun', builds a strong circumstantial case for a Sterne whose working knowledge of Marvell was transmitted by the great Whig propagandist, offers some intriguing extrapolations about satire and sentiment in Yorick's travels, and concludes with yet more evocative echoes of Marvell's 'Appleton House' in *Tristram Shandy*. Finally, Melvyn New's 'Sterne as Preacher: A Visit to St. Michael's Church, Coxwold' (160–7) returns *The Shandean*'s readers to the volume's keynote concern in a sympathetic reconstruction of the context for 'The House of Feasting and the House of Mourning Described' (a Lenten sermon probably written in 1745–55) with a stern warning that to take Sterne seriously as an Anglican clergyman does not require us to conclude that the novelist was either schizoid or hypocritical.

Books Reviewed

Backscheider, Paula R. *Spectacular Politics, Theatrical Power and Mass Culture in Early Modern England*. JHUP. pp. 296. $39.95. ISBN 0 801 84568 8.

Battestin, Martin C., and Clive T. Probyn. *The Correspondence of Henry and Sarah Fielding*. Clarendon. pp. 280. £37.50. ISBN 0 198 11273 4.

Braverman, Richard. *Plots and Counterplots: Sexual Politics and the Body Politic in English Literature, 1660–1730*. Studies in Eighteenth Century English Literature and Thought 18. CUP. pp. 337. £42.50. ISBN 0 521 35620 2.

Bulckaen, Denise. *A Dictionary of Characters in Tobias Smollett's Novels*. Presses Universitaires de Nancy. pp. 153. pb FF 120. ISBN 2 864 80790 4.

Burling, William J. *A Checklist of New Plays and Entertainments on the London Stage, 1700–1737*. AUP. pp. 240. £30.50. ISBN 0 838 63451 6.

Case, Sue-Ellen, and Janelle Einelt, eds. *The Performance of Power. Theatrical Discourse and Politics*. UIowaP (1991). pp. 306. hb $42.95, pb $16.95. ISBN 0 877 45317 9, 0 877 45318 7.

Corman, Brian. *Genre and Generic Change in English Comedy, 1660–1710*. UTorP. pp. 168. £39. ISBN 0 802 02885 3.

Davidson, Clifford., Rand Johnson, and John H. Stroupe, eds. *Drama and the Classical Heritage*. Ancient and Classical Studies 1. AMS. $47.50. ISBN 0 404 64301 9.

Davie, Donald. *The Eighteenth-Century Hymn in England*. CUP. pp. 169. £27.95. ISBN 0 521 38168 1.

Downie, J. A., and Thomas N. Corns, eds. *Telling People What to Think: Early Eighteenth-Century Periodicals from the Review to the Rambler*. Cass. £22.50. ISBN 0 714 64508 7.

Erskine-Hill, Howard. *Jonathan Swift: 'Gulliver's Travels'*. Landmarks of World Literature. CUP. pp. 123. hb £20, pb £6.95. ISBN 0 521 32934 5, 0 521 33842 5.

Goldgar, Bertrand (commentary and introduction). *Miscellanies by Henry Fielding Esq.* Ed. Henry Miller. Vol. 2 of the Wesleyan Edition of the Works of Henry Fielding. WesleyanUP. pp. 346. $98.70. ISBN 0 783 72622 8.

Gordon, I. R. F. *A Preface to Pope.* 2nd edn. Longman. pp. 275. pb £12.99. ISBN 0 582 089271 1.

Greene, John C., and Gladys H. Clark, eds. *The Dublin Stage, 1720–1745: A Calendar of Plays, Entertainments and Afterpieces.* LehighUP. pp. 480. £46.50. ISBN 0 934 22322 X.

Hall, K. G. *The Exalted Heroine and the Triumph of Order: Class, Women and Religion in the English Novel, 1740–1800.* Macmillan. pp. 172. £35. ISBN 0 333 54939 2.

Hutchings, W. B., and William Ruddick, eds. *Thomas Gray: Contemporary Essays.* LiverUP. pp. 279. £29.50. ISBN 0 853 23268 7.

Kraft, Elizabeth. *Character and Consciousness in Eighteenth-Century Comic Fiction.* UGeoP. pp. 216. £27.95. ISBN 0 820 31365 3.

Lindsay, David W. (introduction and commentary). *The Beggar's Opera and Other Eighteenth-Century Plays.* Dent. pp. 493. pb £6.99. ISBN 0 460 87314 8.

Palmeri, Frank. *Critical Essays on Jonathan Swift.* Critical Essays on British Literature. Twayne (Macmillan). pp. 200. $45. ISBN 0 7838 0003 7.

Real, Hermann J., Richard H. Rodino, with the assistance of Helgard Stover-Leidig. *Reading Swift: Papers From the Second Münster Symposium on Jonathan Swift.* Wilhelm Fink GmbH & Co. Verlags Kg. pp. 390. DM 98. ISBN 3 770 52300 8.

Richards, Sandra. *The Rise of the English Actress.* St Martin's. pp. 352. £45. ISBN 0 333 45601 7.

Roberts, Marie M., and Roy Porter. *Literature and Medicine During the Eighteenth Century.* Wellcome Institute Series in the History of Medicine. Routledge. pp. 304. £50. ISBN 0 415 07082 1.

Rogers, Pat, ed. *Alexander Pope. A Critical Edition of the Major Works.* Oxford Authors. OUP. pp. 737. hb £30, pb £11.95. ISBN 0 19 254182 X, 0 19 281346 3.

——. *Daniel Defoe: The Fortunes and Misfortunes of the Famous Moll Flanders.* Dent. pp. 316. pb £3.50. ISBN 0 460 87287 7.

——. *Essays on Pope.* CUP. pp. 263. £30. ISBN 0 521 41869 0.

Scheuermann, Mona. *Her Bread to Earn: Women, and Society from Defoe to Austen.* UPKen. pp. 296. $29. ISBN 0 813 11817 2.

Smollett, Tobias. *Poems, Plays and 'The Briton'.* UGeoP. pp. 592. $50. ISBN 0 820 31428 5.

Steffensen Jr, James L., ed. *The Dramatic Works of George Lillo.* Oxford English Texts. OUP. pp. 784. $145. ISBN 0 19 812714 6.

Van Sant, Ann Jessie. *Eighteenth-Century Sensibility and the Novel.* CUP. pp. 143. £27.95. ISBN 0 521 40226 3.

Williams, Carolyn D. *Pope, Homer and Manliness: Some Aspects of Eighteenth-Century Classical Learning.* Routledge. pp. 220. £37.50. ISBN 0 415 05600 4.

Winton, Calhoun. *John Gay and London Theatre.* UPKen. pp. 232. $22. ISBN 0 813 11832 8.

Zomchick, John P. *Family and the Law in Eighteenth-Century Fiction: The Public Conscience in the Private Sphere.* CUP. pp. 210. £32.50. ISBN 0 521 41511 X.

XII

The Nineteenth Century: Romantic Period

PETER J. KITSON, DAVID WORRALL, JOHN WHALE and SIV JANSSON

This chapter has three sections: 1. Poetry and Drama; 2. Non-Fictional Prose; 3. Fictional Prose. Section 1 is by Peter J. Kitson and David Worrall (Blake material); section 2 is by John Whale; section 3 is by Siv Jansson.

1. Poetry and Drama

This section has two categories: (a) Bibliographical and General Studies; (b) Works on Individual Poets. A number of books and articles were not available to me for review this year and, where this is the case, they have been mentioned without evaluative comment. The primary journals and newsletters relevant to British Romantic poetry and drama are: *BARS: Bulletin & Review* 3/4; *Blake* 26/27; *ByronJ* 21; *ChLB* 81–3; *ERR* 4; *KSJ* 42; *JCSJ* 12; *NCL* 48; the autumn issue of *SEL* 33; *SHW* 4; *SIR* 32; *WC* 24. The *BARS Bulletin & Review* is the newsletter of the British Association for Romantic Studies. Issues 2 and 3 appeared in February and October of this year. The Bulletin was edited this year by Stephen Copley, Kathryn Sutherland and John Whale. As well as containing many excellent reviews of recent work in the field, the Bulletin includes a brief article and notice of forthcoming events and conferences of interest to Romanticists. An important new journal of Romantic culture and criticism appeared in 1995; its contents will be reviewed in *YWES* 76. The journal is called *Romanticism*; edited by J. Drummond Bone, Nicholas Roe and Timothy Webb it will be published twice yearly (July and December) by EdinUP. *ANQ* 6.ii–iii is a special issue on 'Romantic Studies' edited by Karl Kroeber.

(a) Bibliographical and General Studies

This year, as last, has witnessed another substantial volume of studies relating to the Romantic period and Romantic poetry, so any individual attempting to review the year's work feels deluged by the quantity of the material. The main bibliographical work published this year is J. R. de J. Jackson's *Romantic Poetry by Women: A Bibliography 1770–1835*. Jackson's bibliography is just one of a number of works emphasizing notions of gender and highlighting the work of the women poets of the period: a strong feature of this year's work generally. Jackson's bibliography is impressively thorough, the product of substantial scholarship. It attempts to provide a record of 'all the volumes of verse published by women during the years 1770 to 1835'. Jackson helpfully provides biographical headnotes (where information is available) for his entries as many of the poets in his bibliography will be utterly unknown to even the most thorough researchers into the area. The bibliography also contains statistics concerning the annual rate of publication of women poets in the period derived from its author's researches which interestingly charts the great increase in their output which appears to almost double from c.40 titles published per year in 1806 to c.80 titles per year in 1807, remaining between 60 and 80 titles published per year up to 1835. This makes perfectly clear the point that the Romantic period witnessed an enormous growth in the productivity of female poets. An awareness of this fact has been re-shaping our notions of the period in criticism of the last decade. Jackson's bibliography is an important publication which will become an indispensable tool for those working on Romantic poetry. On a related note, I have been sent volume 133 of the *Dictionary of Literary Biography* edited by James Hardin and Siegfried Mews for review. This volume will be of interest both to readers of this chapter and of the Victorian chapter (Ch. XIII) in that it deals with *Nineteenth-Century German Writers to 1840*. The volume consists of biographical essays on such writers as Georg Büchner and Ludwig Feuerbach. The particular volumes which will be of most use to readers of this section remain, however, *German Writers in the Age of Goethe*, edited by James Hardin and Christopher Schweitzer *(DLB* 90); *British Romantic Poets, 1789–1832*, *(DLB* 93) and *British Romantic Prose Writers, 1789–1832*, both edited by John R. Greenfield *(DLB* 110). John Wells's 'Papers of Eighteenth- and Nineteenth-Century Literary Authors in Durham Libraries: A Brief Survey' describes manuscripts held in the libraries *(DUJ* 85[54].111–13).

The annual review essay in *SEL* on 'Recent Studies in the Nineteenth Century' is provided by Tilottama Rajan (33.875–937). Many of the works reviewed in this section are also reviewed in *SEL* 34 (1994) by Jonathan Loesberg. The autumn number of *WC* is the annual review issue of this important subject area journal, containing often substantial review essays by distinguished scholars of the Romantic period. I frequently draw upon the expertise of its reviewers in penning this section. Karen A. Weisman's 'Romantic Constructions' *(UTQ* 62.296–304) is also a review article. Last year Claire Lamont provided an overview of 'The Romantic Period (1780–1830)' in *An Outline of English Literature* edited by Pat Rogers (OUP [1992]) missed in *YWES* 73.

Only one collection of Romantic poetry has come my way this year: Jerome J. McGann's controversial *The New Oxford Book of Romantic Period Verse* which is designed 'partly as invitation and partly as argument'. While most of us who work on the literature of the period have been waiting for an anthology to teach from which includes both women poets and non-canonical male writers this collection is not the one. McGann's collection is certainly very interesting as he has chosen to arrange the poetry by year of first publication rather than by author: 'to include only those works that had been printed and distributed at the time'. This gives the reader an impression of what the period would look like year by year in terms of publication, rather than a more conventional view of the organic development of a series of poets' *oeuvre* through time. This means that Wordsworth's *The Prelude* (almost metonymic for Romanticism in traditional literary criticism) is not represented as it was not formally published until 1850, despite being known to a few influential literary friends, nor is Shelley's 'Epipsychidion'. McGann prints the first edition of Coleridge's 'The Rime of the Ancyent Marinere' with no critical apparatus to include its substantial revisions. McGann's introduction retreads the ground covered in his thoughtful article of last year 'Rethinking Romanticism', (*YWES* 73.358), specifically repeating the point that 'the romantic period and its correspondent breeze, the romantic movement are not the same thing' and it also again makes McGann's crucial point that Byronic romanticism, so influential in the period itself, has been replaced by Wordsworth and Coleridge's Romanticism which became so influential on later twentieth-century critics, such as M. H. Abrams and René Wellek. Nor is the romanticism of Wordsworth and Coleridge regarded as originary. McGann's selection and introduction emphasizes the importance of competing schools of influence, such as the Della Cruscan movement, the translations of Sir William Jones (whose profile in the period is undergoing substantial enhancement), and the early poems of Robert Burns. So too McGann's selection features generous selections from the work of the women poets of the period, Felicia Dorothea Hemans, Mary Tighe, Lady Morgan, Anna Laetitia Barbauld, Laetitia Elizabeth Landon and many others. Sadly, McGann includes only one poem by John Clare, 'My Mary'. This is an intriguing collection which should remind us of the counter-currents as well as the leading currents (to use a Romantic trope) which flowed throughout the period.

Moving on to general books of criticism of the literature of the period I will begin by noticing a work published in 1989 but missed that year and not reviewed in subsequent volumes. Rolf P. Lessenich's *Aspects of English PreRomanticism* is a serious and scholarly study of the notion of 'preromanticism' and its progress in the late eighteenth century and one which should have a wider audience among Romanticists. The neglect of this study probably stems from several causes. Its continental publication (Böhlau-Verlag, Köln) could account for its tardy appearance in subject-area bibliographies, and its undertheorized content and less than modish avocation of the comparative criticism of René Wellek could mark it out in the eyes of many Romanticists as perhaps one of the less pressing publications to be consulted among the substantial numbers of books that appear on the subject each year. This is a shame for the book contains much original research and thought and it certainly should be consulted by scholars working in the area. Lessenich accepts the notion and existence of preromanticism, relating its origin to the 'final outcome of all the liberalizing and individualizing and nationalizing regressive tendencies of the age'. He also accepts that in some ways Romanticism organically developed from this phase as a European phenomenon, seeing in various works 'the seeds of romanticism'. Lessenich's study is wide-ranging and covers subjects such as the development of feeling and sympathy, the lyric, originality and primitivism, and political libertarianism and prophecy. The book also contains extended discussion of sentimental drama and fiction and is generally replete with information and allusion. Lessenich writes in an attractive and accessible style, enhancing the value of his work.

Two general introductions to Romanticism as a literary concept have appeared this year. Stuart Curran edited *The Cambridge Companion to British Romanticism*, an excellent guide to issues relating to Romanticism. David Simpson provides an accessible and interesting account of critical theory and its involvement with Romantic literature, charting the various methodological from comparativist criticism to deconstruction and new historicism; Marshall Brown tackles the notion of preromanticism, Enlightenment and Romanticism; P. M. S. Dawson gives a fine and detailed account of the historical context of the Romantics; Peter Thorslev covers the German background; William Keach writes a fascinating piece on the linguistic theories of the Romantics; Marilyn Butler provides a cogent and knowledgeable overview of the importance of the periodical press in the period; Timothy Webb summarizes the debates among the Romantics concerning Greek aesthetic ideals; Gary Kelly deals with the Romantic novel; Morris Eaves helpfully discusses the visual arts in the period; and Stuart Curran writes on the women writers and readers in the period as well as contributing an overview of the literature of the period and how it has been perceived. This collection includes a useful bibliography and helpful guide to further reading. What the collection does not provide for the reader (and which is provided in some of the other *Cambridge Companions*) is any extensive treatment of the canonical poets and their work which makes this volume more suitable to a graduate student. This issue of intended readership is also raised by Cynthia Chase's collection of essays on *Romanticism* for the Longman Critical Reader series. This reader is presumably aimed at the general undergraduate student of Romanticism, yet the difficulty of Chase's introduction and of practically all of the essays contained in the volume renders it a rather specialized and advanced publication more suited to graduate level. Chase's introduction offers a sophisticated overview of the criticism of Romanticism from M. H. Abrams onward, including sections on deconstructive, psychoanalytical, new historicist, and feminist readings of Romanticism. The essays and extracts from books she selects are all strong readings with strong theoretical awareness, including writing by Geoffrey Hartman, Paul de Man, Neil Hertz, Caryl Caruth, Mary Jacobus, Karen Swann, Margaret Homans, Marjorie Levinson, Jerome Christensen and Carol Jacobs. This certainly will be a useful volume for the advanced student and scholar of Romanticism but its unwillingness to make concessions to the general reader new to the literature of the period render it a rather specialized affair.

Collections of essays relating to the Romantic period have been relatively abundant this year. The most important is Karl Kroeber and Gene W. Ruoff's substantial volume, *Romantic Poetry: Recent Revisionary Criticism*. This volume attempts to perform for criticism, mainly American and of the last two decades, the same function as M. H. Abrams's seminal collection *English Romantic Poets* (OUP, 1960). The editors do not claim that this selection is the best criticism of recent years, but rather that it is indicative of the ways in which contemporary Romantic criticism is evolving. Although the collection thus claims to be revisionary in this sense, it still remains a canonical collection including essays only discussing the big six Romantic poets. The collection has very generous selections of new historicist criticism (from the work of Jonathan Arac, Marilyn Butler, Jerome J. McGann, Alan Liu, Marjorie Levinson, David Simpson etc.) and fairly representative feminist writing (Alice Ostriker, Mary Jacobus, Karen Swann, Susan J. Wolfson etc.), but is rather more mean-spirited to deconstructive criticism (Frances Ferguson and Tilottama Rajan). Each poet has between three and six essays allotted to him, Keats doing best with six and William Blake receiving a miserly three. The volume contains some excellent criticism destined to become classic (including Geoffrey Hartman's 1975 essay on 'To Autumn', already assured of that status). Certainly this looks like a major collection which contains material to interest readers of differing levels of critical sophistication. The selection of material on Keats will probably be of most use.

Reflections of Revolution: Images of Romanticism, edited by Alison Yarrington and Kelvin Everest is an interesting collection of essays with an historicist bias derived from papers given at the conference on the French Revolution and British Culture at the University of Leicester in 1989. David Punter's 'Parts of the Body/Parts of Speech: Some Instances of Dismemberment and Healing' discusses the responses of the Romantic poets to the events in France in terms of the theories of Melanie Klein concerning infant development in a world of part-objects. Fred Botting's 'Reflections of Excess: *Frankenstein,* the French Revolution and Monstrosity' examines the appearance and effect of monsters in British political positions after the French Revolution and particularly in Mary Shelley's novel. Nigel Leask's 'Pantisocracy and the Politics of the "Preface" to *Lyrical Ballads'* presents an interesting overview of Coleridge and Southey's Pantisocratic scheme, clearly showing how Coleridge responded to contemporary events in France, but also to long traditions of republican thought stretching back through the work of Moses Lowman and James Harrington to the Hebrew Commonwealth itself. Leask, perhaps, makes too light of Southey's role in Pantisocracy and the by no means insignificant Godwinian elements which he brought to the scheme. The late William Ruddick's 'Liberty Trees and Loyal Oaks: Emblematic Presences in Some English Poems of the French Revolutionary Period' considers the politicizing of certain types of trees in radical iconography of the revolutionary period, commenting interestingly along the way on Coleridge's odd poem 'The Raven'. Chris Jones's essay 'Radical Sensibility' neatly summarizes the argument of his book-length study of the same title, also published this year and reviewed elsewhere in this chapter. George Crabbe's poetry is featured in Gavin Edwards's 'Crabbe's Regicide Households' which reveals the political nuances of his verse as represented in Crabbe's domestic subject matter. Angus Easson contributes a fascinating discussion of cannibalism in its relation to revolution (in both a literal and metaphoric sense). The relationship between poetry and the visual arts is the subject of the final three essays in the collection with David Bindman's '"My Own Mind is My Own Church": Blake, Paine and the French Revolution' retreading the familiar ground of Blake's problematic admiration for Tom Paine; William Vaughan traces British artistic disapproval of the work of Jacques-Louis David ('"David's Brickdust" and the Rise of the British School'); Claude Mitchell's 'Spectacular Fears and Popular Arts: A View from the Nineteenth Century' interrelates visual images, the language of nineteenth-century historians and that of art critics in an attempt to show how this interdependence informed and structured nineteenth-century discourse on the French Revolution; and, finally, Richard Wrigley's 'Breaking the Code: Interpreting French Revolutionary Iconoclasm' reappraises traditional artistic hostility to the Revolution's iconoclastic drives while also stressing its successive stage of renewal. Overall this is one of the better (if more tardy) collections of work occasioned by the bicentennial of the revolution.

Less historicist in its critical orientation is the *Festschrift, English Romanticism Preludes and Postludes: Essays in Honor of Edwin Graves Wilson* edited by Donald Schoonmaker and John A. Alford which contains a number of noteworthy essays. David Hadley's '"Public Lectures and Private Societies": Expounding Literature and the Arts in Romantic London', provides informative discussion of the lectures of Coleridge and Hazlitt in the metropolis, while D. Allen Carroll intriguingly discusses Keats's concealed use of economic imagery and language in 'Keats's "Chapman's Homer" and the Vagaries of Identification'. Donald

Schoonmaker's 'The Bittersweet of Keats's Liberal Imagination' provides a good overview of Keats's liberalism (in the broadest sense of the term) and relates this to Lionel Trilling's formulation of 'the Liberal Imagination': 'The poetry and the liberalism that he [Keats] shaped leaned on his core idea of the need for empathetic identification with nature and man in order to gain involved detachment'. Schoonmaker is, however, rather too dismissive of the actual context of Keats's liberalism in early nineteenth-century Britain, particularly when compared to Nick Roe's article, 'Keats's Lisping Sedition' reviewed last year (*YWES* 73.389). Finally for Romanticists this collection contains James Bunn's detailed analysis of Shelley's sentential style, 'The "True Utility" of Shelley's Method in *A Defence of Poetry*'. This is an interesting but hardly a major collection of essays.

Three studies have appeared which deal with the problematic notions of literary 'influence' and 'intertextuality' in one way or another. Two of these relate to the impact of Romantic writing on the later nineteenth century. The first of these *Influence and Resistance in Nineteenth-Century English Poetry* edited by G. Kim Blank and Margot K. Louis is another collection of essays and it deals with the subject of the persistence of Romanticism into the Victorian period. Although we are familiar with notions of the 'long eighteenth century' and the problematic separation of eighteenth-century from Romantic literature, less attention has been devoted to the equally unsatisfactory demarcation between Romantic and Victorian literature. The essays in Blank and Louis's collection redress this imbalance to some extent, as the editors put it: 'certainly this volume demonstrates how well the Romantics wrought, and with what ferocious diligence the Victorians engaged with, denied, affirmed, reworked the romantic vision'. Significantly, Shelley is featured as a major enabling figure for the Victorians, most surprisingly perhaps in the case of Christina Rossetti's *Goblin Market* as discussed in Barbara Charlesworth Gelpi's very strong piece '"Verses with a Good Deal about Sucking": Percy Bysshe Shelley and Christina Rossetti'. Wordsworth fares not so well, especially in Keith Hanley's 'In Wordsworth's Shadow: Ruskin and Neo-Romantic Ecologies' which seeks to discriminate Ruskin's from Wordsworth's world-view. Other essays in the collection tackle the subjects of Romantic and Victorian iconography of nature and perspectives of nature (John R. Reed and Ann Marie Ross), Shelley and Arnold (W. David Shaw), Arnold and the Romantics (Roland A. Duerksen), Wordsworth and Tennyson (Joanna E. Rapf), Swinburne's assimilation of a variety of Romantic sources (Herbert F. Tucker), Hardy's relation to the Romantics (Kerry McSweeney and U. C. Knoepflmacher), Christina Rossetti (Antony H. Harrison), and Robert Browning's relationship with Shelley and the Romantics (Theresa M. Kelley and Mary E. Finn). *Influence and Resistance in Nineteenth-Century English Poetry*, while lacking the sustained focus of a monograph study of the subject, is a substantial collection of essays which will be of great interest to scholars of Victorian poetry, and nineteenth-century poetry in general.

If the work of any one critic has coloured the year's output more than most it must be that of John Beer. In addition to his new edition of Coleridge's *Aids to Reflection*, the re-issue of his edition of Coleridge's poetry for Everyman, the publication of his Inaugural Lecture 'Against Finality' and the appearance of a *Festschrift*, *Coleridge's Visionary Languages: Essays in Honour of John Beer*, edited by Tim Fulford and Morton D. Paley (all to be reviewed later), Beer has also published a monograph entitled *Romantic Influences Contemporary-*

Victorian-Modern. This book defends, while complicating, traditional notions of literary influence, arguing that influence is best seen in this period as *influenza*, 'a kind of malaise, resulting from a loss of spiritual security'. For Beer, this state of insecurity became critical for the first time in the 1790s only to re-emerge again and again at later periods when thinkers would find that there was no longer an authoritative language that they could draw upon. To depict the ways in which writers thus influence one another, Beer adopts metaphors of flowing currents which eddy through the period and around the thinkers and writers in the period. Readers of this section will be most interested in Beer's early chapter on 'Prophetic Affluence in the 1790s' which elegantly surveys the development of the ideas of Wordsworth, Coleridge and Blake as they reacted to the political events of their time. *Romantic Influences* is a very different book from *Influence and Resistance* in that it is much more concerned with the impact of Coleridge's thought and personality on Victorian and early twentieth-century (Woolf, Hardy, Eliot, Lawrence) writing. Shelley is not featured so prominently as in Blank and Louis's volume. Similarly Beer is not as concerned with articulating his argument in the more critically current (or modish) terms of 'intertextuality'. For Beer, Coleridge is a key 'influence' in that he appeared to be asking the seminal questions of his own and of the later age. Beer writes a fine chapter on 'Coleridge's Elusive Presence Among the Victorians' which testifies to the importance of Coleridge for the Victorians: 'readers who found themselves in that country of doubt knew that Coleridge had been there before them'. Beer is apologetic for Coleridge whom he defends against Carlyle's famous criticism. Interestingly, Beer notes that Carlyle's celebrated depiction of Coleridge ('Coleridge sat on Highgate Hill') describes a view from the window which Carlyle could never have seen and that his powerfully memorable description involves second-hand knowledge. In all, this is a lucid, scholarly and intelligent volume full of detailed comment on the literary and philosophical matters affecting the nineteenth century, although it probably does not add much to Beer's previous work on Wordsworth, Blake and Coleridge. It is perhaps appropriate here to mention the publication of Beer's Inaugural Lecture 'Against Finality' delivered on 4 February 1993 which discusses the kind of investigation its author has devoted himself to, 'springing from an interest in the effects to be traced in literature and language when the metaphysical authority in the culture gives way to the deferred authority of empirical enquiry'. Beer spins an interesting narrative out of the theme of the weighing of words, arguing against the finality of interpretation in this elegant and knowledgeable disquisition.

Lucy Newlyn's superb *Paradise Lost and the Romantic Reader* approaches Romanticism and influence from the other direction by seeking out and discussing Miltonic allusions in the poetry of the Romantics. It is written on a similar theme to Robin Jarvis's recent *Wordsworth, Milton and the Theory of Poetic Relations* (*YWES* 72.288–9), although its scope is wider and its approach is much less sympathetic than that of Jarvis to the ideas of influence developed by Harold Bloom. Newlyn argues persuasively that an appreciation of Milton's influence on the Romantics is vital to an understanding of what Romanticism actually is. Her argument is more sophisticated than Beer's in terms of its understanding of influence as allusion which allows a duality to Milton's presence. Taking her critical bearings, at least as far as they relate to acts of recognition and interpretation, from Wittgenstein and Iser, Newlyn is more concerned with indeterminacies and ambiguities than the more corporeal influencings which John

Beer describes above. When the practices of allusion by different Romantic writers are analysed, she believes it to be possible to arrive at a 'Romantic reading' of *Paradise Lost*. The scope of this study is wide. Newlyn provides a fine overview of the history of Milton's reputation in the eighteenth and nineteenth centuries, tracing the appropriations of the 'Milton cult'. In separating out explicit invocations to the cult of Milton from intertextual references, Newlyn makes her most telling and original point, namely that there is a contradiction between the Milton who is constructed through such conscious and explicit acts of appropriation and the Milton who emerges from carefully receptive and imitative habits of allusion: 'The first is a model of authority [...] the second is a collocation of ambiguities and indeterminacies'. In showing us a Romantic Milton defined as indeterminate and open-ended, Newlyn has certainly enhanced our understanding of Milton's effect on the Romantics, as she moves away from the reception of the poet to the reception of the text itself. This leaves us with a Milton who is less of an authority figure, and a number of poets who are much less revisionary of their predecessor poet than previous scholarship has maintained. This sense of indeterminacy qualifies any more explicit moral message the poetry may possess. Rather than adopting a stance antipathetic to Harold Bloom's *The Anxiety of Influence* (OUP, 1973), as John Beer and many others have done (Thomas McFarland, Dustin Griffin, Jonathan Bate etc.), Newlyn sidesteps the issue by affirming 'that what is being termed as "anxiety" is a widespread phenomenon, and that this can be explained by considering the contested status of the imagination at a time when God was still very much alive'. Newlyn is very convincing about the damage done to literary studies by the overriding critical desire to prove Bloom's theories wrong.

Rather than analyse Milton's influence author by author, Newlyn adopts a thematic approach utilizing the headings: Politics, Religion, Sex, Subjectivity and Imagination (taking in Language and the Sublime) along the way. Newlyn's conclusions are perhaps more revisionary of previous scholarship than *her* Romantics are of Milton's poem. She argues that the traditional alignment of Milton and Satan is not so easily maintained on closer inspection: 'Satanic allusion is not the register of ideological certitude, but of moral and political *angst*: the Romantics turned to Milton when they are themselves preoccupied, as he had been, by the problematic relation of earthly politics to religious or moral truth'. Equally iconoclastic is Newlyn's treatment of Eve's fall and its reception in romantic texts. Newlyn believes it is possible to read *Paradise Lost* in feminized terms, suggesting parallels between Milton and Eve and enlisting the reader's sympathy for their shared plight. Newlyn has stimulating treatments of the theodicy of the Fall and its reception and of the sense of subjectivity which results and which, for the Romantics, is the price of experience. The ways in which Romantic ideas of Imagination encourage an alignment with the satanic perspective is also covered in Newlyn's most Bloomian chapter, before she concludes with an extended discussion of Blake's poem *Milton* which obviously represents the most sustained (and perhaps monolithic) wrestling with Milton's influence. *Paradise Lost and the Romantic Reader* is an important book, of interest to Romanticists, Miltonists and those interested in theories of intertextuality and of reading.

Historicist studies of the literature of the period are rather thinner on the ground this year than last; nevertheless three notable monographs have appeared which continue the process of critical rescue from the recent forceful imposition of formalist and deconstructive methods. David Simpson's major and challenging work *Romanticism, Nationalism, and the Revolt Against Theory* relates the traditional British distrust of system and method when applied to culture and politics to a long tradition of thinking which can be seen right back to the demystifying methodology of Peter Ramus in the sixteenth century and the Puritan revolutionaries of the 1640s: 'The "theory wars" occurring in today's humanities departments are to some degree a mediated response to the tensions generated by the French Revolution and by the English Revolution of the 1640s'. Simpson is interested in the way that hostility to theory has been associated with national characteristics whereby advocates of systematic method are depicted as inhuman rationalists. This hostility to theory persists in history and has resurfaced in recent attacks of literary theory in the United States: 'Theorists like Jacobins are seen as betraying a cause, that of a common culture and a common vocabulary'. One of the weaknesses of Simpson's argument is seen at the outset in that this work has no real theory of causation. Simpson's introduction circles the question but it is clear that he is deeply embarrassed by the similarity of this particular work to traditional scholarship in the history of ideas, which is how his book reads (at least in its early chapters). Simpson's point that political debates of the English Revolution prefigured those of the French Revolution which still seem to persist in the 1990s is a crucial one, and this persistence clearly does have some relation to national characteristics. Yet the issue seems more problematic than this. His argument for 'a narrative [...] holding together the established culture's responses to method as it appeared in the pedagogic and systematic reforms of the Ramists, in the appeals to a common "reason" made by the seventeenth-century radicals, and in the etymologically sanctioned organizational (and inspirational) abilities of the Methodists' goes some way to explaining the British response to the Declaration of the Rights of Man, yet it is sketchy and not entirely convincing, although deeply suggestive. Simpson seems hardly aware of the religious nature of 1640s radicalism, much removed from the Enlightenment rationalism of 1790s radicals like Thomas Paine and materialists like John Thelwall. Similarly, he does not explore (as one thinks he might) the very English nature of this thought. Most of the Puritan radicals of time (including Milton) accepted John Foxe's notion that it was the historic mission of the English nation to stand against Antichrist (Rome), and many thought in the 1650s that Oliver Cromwell's army would achieve the international overthrow of the forces of Antichrist prior to the establishment of the millennium. Simpson identifies revolutionary Puritanism with rational system and method, but surely if any group of thinkers were to be so identified in the mid-seventeenth century it would be the Oxford Latitudinarians (William Chillingworth and Falkland for instance) who were predominantly royalists, or the Cambridge Platonists whose sympathies were only moderately republican, if at all. Although Simpson is on surer ground when he turns to the late eighteenth century, his discussion of Methodist enthusiasm as a problematic example of 'method' is rather forced. Simpson cites the transgressive defence of polygamy by the Methodist Martin Madan as instancing the continuance of this antinomian debate from the Puritan Revolution, not mentioning that Madan had a celebrated controversy with the radical Unitarian minister Joseph Priestley about just who exactly were the heirs of this revolution. Madan accused Priestley of sympathy with the regicides and hostility to George III, Priestley replied by claiming, somewhat disingenuously, that if the Unitarians had predecessors they must be accounted the Presbyterian opponents of the execution of Charles I, purged from Parliament by Cromwell's forces in 1648.

Madan may have been a radical antinomian but he was radical in little else and it is a great mistake to assume that antinomian preachers in the 1790s are politically radical (this was also a tendency of Jon Mee's *Dangerous Enthusiasm* reviewed last year, YWES 73.342–4). Simpson's discussion of the debate over the French Revolution is much less controversial.

Simpson goes on to consider British representations of French and German excess as well as dealing with the gender aspects of a masculinist rational tradition and a feminized literature of sensibility, before turning to the Romantics themselves. He refreshingly turns away from recent new historicist writing to argue that there is a radical Wordsworth who attempts to locate his work somewhere between Burke and Paine: 'Wordsworth's democratic ideology was never a simple, uncompounded thing and never expressed itself as simply identical with any of the available models provided by Paine, Godwin, Mackintosh, Spence, or others'. Simpson points out that Wordsworth does use method of a kind in *The Prelude* and if this natural method is not exactly Ramist, it is not Burkean either. Wordsworth refuses any complete denunciation of reason and of the rational instinct. So, too, Simpson negotiates Blake's radicalism and its compatibility with the poet's famous hostility to the rational method as well as Shelley's plea for the creative imaginative faculty as prior to reason and progress, and also Keats's hostility to Enlightenment method despite his 'fastidious agnosticism' for anything else. Ultimately, for Simpson, despite their concentrated attempts, the Romantics failed to achieve a radical or reformist language because in steering clear of the discredited systematic and didactic mode they only ran aground instead on 'a form of inwardness whose variations are beyond prescription'. Simpson returns to the present in his final chapter, reflecting on current attacks on theory and lamenting that in the postmodern view of theory 'rational method has become the signature of an improper power, or aspiration to power, a masculine dream of reason that can only be for everyone else a nightmare'. The return to rational method, advocated in the 1940s by the Frankfurt School and nostalgically hankered after by Simpson, remains an impossibility for the 1990s. Nevertheless, in writing his history of these ideas of nationality and rationality, Simpson has contributed thoughtfully and effectively to a debate which is by no means near to conclusion. This is an important study.

Nigel Leask's *British Romantic Writers and the East: Anxieties of Empire* (dated 1992 but actually published this year according to CUP) is another important and very current study dealing with the orientalism of Byron, Shelley, De Quincey and other Romantic writers (including Southey, Samuel Rogers, Walter Savage Landor, Sir William Jones etc.). Leask's introduction is a model of clarity which sets out the debates concerning Romantic appropriations of the East. Rather than simply illustrating with period detail Edward Said's theory of Orientalism as a Western style for dominating the East, Leask is more interested in the instabilities and anxieties evidenced by Romantic projections of the oriental Other. Leask is surely right to disagree with Said who maintained that Orientalism was a 'closed system'. Leask argues that the '(plural) anxieties' of empire he examines in the work of Byron, Shelley and De Quincey 'cannot be laid on a procrustean bed' and that the representations of the oriental Other evince internal and external pressures undermining them which are more various than allowed in Said's insider/outsider view of the subject. Leask is very good indeed on the 'anxieties and contradictions which deconstruct the unitary imperative of Britain's "civilizing mission"'. His book contains a good survey of the oriental tale in the eighteenth century before moving on to Byron, Shelley and De Quincey. Leask maintains that although his subjects are suspicious of the more obvious aspects of imperialism, none of their orientalist works (with the possible exception of Byron) question the legitimacy of imperialism in its broader, historical guise as the expansion of the norms of European civilization over the whole globe. With Byron, Leask argues that the poet's gaze is fixed on the collapsing Ottoman Empire yet also turned back reflectively on his own culture as the world's dominant colonial power. Leask is most interested in Byron's awareness of his own complicity in British colonial power as a poet of Orientalism. He does not do full justice to the awareness that the dominant colonial power, albeit in decline, of the Eastern Mediterranean was, in fact, an Islamic power, Turkey, and there is a sense that Leask is anticipating British imperialism as it was *to be* developed later in the nineteenth century. Leask takes up the current debate about Shelley's Hellenism, arguing that the poet's admirers have tended to overlook the accommodation he makes with the question of imperialism. Leask's study of Romantic attitudes to India (Sir William Jones, Southey, Thomas Moore etc.) is very valuable and his suggestive treatment of *Prometheus Unbound* and its possible relation to Rammohun Roy's translation of part of the *Kena Upanishad* adds a further dimension to the depiction of Demogorgon, too often glossed as merely an imaging of historical necessity. Leask concludes with a discussion of De Quincey's *Confessions of an English Opium Eater* part of which was previously published in Peter J. Kitson and Thomas N. Corns (eds), *Coleridge and the Amoury of the Human Mind* (*YWES* 72.295). Leask's thesis here is that De Quincey represented the pains and pleasures of opium upon his nervous system as a metaphor for the effects of capitalism, in its imperialistic phase, upon the body politic. Much of this material is fascinating, although not as deftly dovetailed into the book's overall thesis as the material on Byron and Shelley. Leask is particularly good on the oriental dream sequences of the *Confessions*. This is another important book and one of the year's major publications.

Like Nigel Leask's book, Peter T. Murphy's lively and subtle *Poetry as an Occupation and an Art in Britain 1760–1830* is one in the series Cambridge Studies in Romanticism. It is a book about borders, both literal and figurative. It focuses on five poets of the period; James MacPherson, Robert Burns, James Hogg, Walter Scott and William Wordsworth. Murphy's book concerns the central interests of Romanticism: 'the Romantic interest in the primitive and simple; Romantic experiments with form; Romantic problematics of loss; the emergence of a new literary culture during the Romantic period'. The book is certainly historicist in its preoccupation with the forces that 'work to produce poetry'. MacPherson, Hogg and Burns all began their poetic careers with serious social and economic disadvantages and they chose to write a simple and plain kind of poetry as a means of, among other things, material advantage. Thus, for Murphy, poetry is 'a possible choice, an occupation, a kind of work' and he criticizes those decontextualized readings of the period which do not include some notion of material success or accomplishment. The book thus attempts to 'rescue "close reading" from formalism by producing a compellingly human picture of the force of form'. This process is complicated by the fact that four out of the five poets Murphy writes about are Scottish and the literary marketplace was dominated by the literary English of greater Britain. Rather than being a disadvantage, the four Scottish writers discussed show how marketable 'northernness' could be, spectacularly so in the case of Sir Walter Scott.

Murphy's book, however, is not about the Scottish aspects of Romanticism. In a larger sense it concerns the 'ballad revival' and Wordsworth is included as the most famous Romantic practitioner of the northern ballad. This study is in many ways a return to traditional literary history with its insistence on ethical and aesthetic judgements. MacPherson's fraudulent use of the primitive ballad in the celebrated 'Ossian' controversy is seen as dishonest, while Scott and Wordsworth possess 'integrity'. This is an interesting work which will be of great use to scholars of the poets discussed and those more generally interested in the rise of the primitive ballad in the late eighteenth and early nineteenth centuries. Peter T. Murphy's interesting paper on 'the most thoroughly dead' of Romantic poets Samuel Rogers, 'Climbing Parnassus, and Falling Off: Rogers and *The Pleasures of Memory*' is printed in *WC* (24.151–5).

While still with matters historicist, I should mention that Iain McCalman's *Radical Underworld: Prophets, Revolutionaries and Pornographers in London 1795–1840*, first published in 1988 (*YWES* 69.421), was issued in paperback by Clarendon this year. McCalman's straightforwardly historical study had a substantial effect upon British Romantic studies, particularly Blake studies, and its availability in paperback will be of great assistance to those working in the area. Of related interest is Kevin Gilmartin's 'The Press on Trial: Form and Imagination in Early Nineteenth-Century Radical Culture' which discusses the attempts of the popular radical press to report events and opinions of the time and the cross-overs of this discourse with Romantic values (*WC* 24.144–7).

Although discussions of gender are more often confined to the sections of this chapter concerning Prose and Non-Fictional Prose in the period, one major work on this issue has appeared which has far-reaching implications for interpretations of the poetry of both male and female writers. Anne K. Mellor's *Romanticism and Gender* is a challenging, lively and attractively written overview of the subject which provides an excellent overview of the feminist debate, as well as presenting the author's own arguments about the period. Mellor argues that the notion of Romanticism itself is heavily underwritten by gender biases and that 'a paradigm shift in our conceptual understanding occurs when we give equal weight to the thought and writing of the women of the period'. Commenting on the enormous body of female literary production, Mellor argues that the women writers of the period forswore the concerns of their canonical male peers with the capacities of the creative imagination, with the limitations of language, with the possibilities of transcendence, with the development of the autonomous self, and with the poet as the prophet of artistic, political or moral revolution. Rather, for Mellor, the female Romantic writers were more concerned with what Stuart Curran has described as the 'quotidian', the workings of the rational mind and the domestic conditions of life in the period. Most challenging and controversial of all is Mellor's use of a structural opposition to investigate gender bias. She hypothesizes that there existed in the period a 'feminine' and a 'masculine' Romanticism. This structural opposition leads to a gender distinction between literary form, such that the novel becomes a 'feminized' discourse and the epic and higher forms of drama appear as masculine Romantic forms. Mellor argues that by the end of the nineteenth century male authors and reviewers had created a distinction between the serious novel of historical and philosophical enquiry (that written by Sir Walter Scott and William Godwin for instance) and the lowbrow novel of feminine romance. So, too, the higher forms of poetic achievement, such as the epic and tragic drama, were the preserve of male poets, and women poets tended to stick to the more modest forms of poetic achievement such as Spenserian romances, odes, occasional verse, shorter verse narratives, nursery rhymes, songs and sonnets (the sonnet was itself later re-masculinized by Wordsworth). This is not to say that women writers did not contest this literary gender bias and in her chapter on Felicia Hemans, Mellor shows how the most popular poet of the time (after Byron) pitted a masculine public code of heroic chivalry against a feminine private code of domesticity, revealing the inadequacy of each.

Mellor's structural opposition of 'masculine' and 'feminine' Romanticism is not finally a binary distinction but what she describes as 'the endpoints on a continuum'. Thus individual writers of either sex may attempt to write in a mode opposite to their biological sex. Mellor instances the cases of Emily Brontë and John Keats, both writers whose work transgresses gender barriers. Both discussions are strong and detailed and Mellor does justice to the problems her contention causes. Her discussion is never simplistic but always aware of the difficulties raised in her treatment. After tracking Wollstonecraft's notion of an ideal and fully rational woman which demanded a 'revolution in female manners', she goes on to discuss what happens when a woman Romantic writer chooses to inhabit rather than reject the Burkeian–Rousseauian hegemonic construction of the beautiful and domestic ideal woman. Mellor, in a searching and sensitive chapter, explores the contradictions in the work of Laetitia Elizabeth Landon (L.E.L.) and Felicia Hemans who uphold the ideals of womanhood and domestic fidelity only to expose the fictive nature of both. Although very important in explicating the contradictions between the public and private spheres inhabited by men and women, Mellor provides no real aesthetic justification for the success of these poets and her interest in them appears at times almost forensic. *Romanticism and Gender* is bound to become a very influential work on gender in the period, both for its reading of the canonical male poets as well as its treatment of female writers.

'Romanticism and the Feminine' was also the subject of a special number of *SIR* (32.ii) containing two general essays relevant to this section. Elizabeth Fay's 'Romantic Men, Victorian Women: The Nightingale Talks Back' (211–24) concerns the Romantic topos of the nightingale poem and how the female voice in such poems is mythicized and 'dis-comprehended'. Sonia HofKosh's 'A Woman's Profession: Sexual Difference and the Romance of Authorship' poses an interesting consideration of the various class-inflected characterizations of femininity in the theory and practice of authorship in the early nineteenth century, particularly by Coleridge, Wordsworth and Hazlitt, arguing that 'when we read that writing then, writing which announces or defends the author's proprietary privilege, we should read it with an ear to the various cadences of the marketplace, including the voices of the women who have been silenced or separated out in the romance of authorship'. Still with matters feminine, Dorothy Wordsworth and Sara Coleridge are two women Romantic writers featured in K. T. Meiners's 'Reading Pain and the Feminine Body in Romantic Writing' (*CentR* 37.487–512) and Greg Kucich provides a fascinating account of the problems faced by female historians in the period in his 'Romanticism and Feminist Historiography' (*WC* 24.133–40). Joel Hafner discusses the canonical implications of women writers and Romanticism in '(De) Forming the Romantic Canon: The Case of Women Writers' (*CollL* 20.44–57).

The contrast between Mellor's *Romanticism and Gender* and Kathleen M.

Wheeler's intelligent and searching *Romanticism, Pragmatism and Deconstruction* is very marked. Wheeler's book is concerned with the aesthetics of 'high' Romantic writing, concentrating on the work of the German Romantics, Coleridge, Blake and Shelley, Hegel and Nietzsche, the pragmatists (William James, John Dewey and Richard Rorty), and the deconstructionists (especially Derrida). Wheeler's thesis, despite its sophistication and complexities, is quite straightforward. She argues that the philosophical questionings of her various subjects were anticipated in the work of classical philosophy (the Socrates of Plato's work) and that English and German Romantic ideas about critical theory and aesthetics reveal connections with modern theory, deconstruction, and Derrida. This itself is not an original point and the contrasts between a metaphysics of presence and a metaphysics of absence is quite a hackneyed one in Romantic studies. Wheeler's work, however, is more unusual in its attempt to elucidate these connections and contrasts in the implicit context of pragmatist philosophy and aesthetics, arguing that recent pragmatist aesthetic theories (such as those of Richard Rorty), based on John Dewey's work, relate very closely to Romantic aesthetic and critical principles. She also argues that Romanticism, pragmatism and deconstruction share a common insistence on the need for a method and theory of enquiry if literary criticism is to be more than merely transcribed received opinion. Wheeler begins her work with strong readings of the ways in which the German and English Romantics along with Hegel and Nietzsche privileged rhetoric over dogma through their concern with the constitutive role of metaphor and their notions of irony, symbol and allegory. Wheeler thus stresses the ironic aspects of Romantic writing over and above any claims for transcendence. She criticizes those who have seen Shelley's ideas and writings as indicating a belief in an ideal and transcendent reality, largely on the basis of his 'Defence of Poetry' and his fragmentary essay 'On Life'. This is probably truer to Shelley's work but it does evade some of the more idealistic statements of Shelley's later poetry (especially *Adonais*). So are we also presented with a very sceptical Coleridge who 'denied explicitly that he was engaged in any enquiry into ultimate grounds outside knowing'. More iconoclastic is Wheeler's surprising claim that Samuel Johnson is a precursor of Coleridge in establishing the notion that interpretation is not so much of objects, but of other people's prior interpretations, 'the "object" being understood as a kind of manifold of interpretations'. Texts are thus already interpreted entities. Most interesting is Wheeler's discussion of the deconstructive techniques to be found in Coleridge's poetry, with its shifts in narrative voice, its fondness for prefaces, notes and arguments, raising questions about the truth of interpretation. Although some might be themselves sceptical of Wheeler's fulsome defence of Coleridge's various irregularities as entirely motivated by the desire to encourage an active readership, this is a fascinating discussion of the connections and contrasts between the philosophical strategies adopted by the Romantics and their twentieth-century inheritors.

William H. Galperin's *The Return of the Visible in British Romanticism* is an ingenious revisionist reading of Romanticism. Galperin's study emphasizes the visible elements in Romanticism as opposed to the more commonly featured visionary strain. For the visionary nature of Romantic subjectivity to succeed, the visible has to be suppressed and the invisible world of inner vision revealed. Galperin finds that this suppression of the visible is met with resistance, whereby the visible will always return as the embodiment of that which is repressed. The visible, thus, is a remarkably fluid concept, including everything that has been repressed by the visionary imagination, including the 'material sublime' of panorama, diorama and theatrical spectacle generally. Galperin challenges the notion that a single philosophy characterized the art and culture of high Romanticism. Conversely, he argues that the culture of the period was a site of competing ideas. Galperin's book includes discussions of Wordsworth, Coleridge, Byron, Lamb and Hazlitt as well as the visual art of John Constable and Caspar David Friedrich. This study, which resembles new historicist criticism, in its insistence on present absence, as well as deconstruction in its challenging of the representative order, departs from both in claiming that Romanticism unwittingly *does* present a material visible reality. This is a challenging and provocative re-reading of Romanticism. The study of panoramas is clearly a growth area in Romantic criticism. In addition to Galperin's work, two Wordsworth articles engage with the theme. Ross King's 'Wordsworth, Panorama, and the Prospect of London' (*SIR* 32.57–73) argues that Book Seven of *The Prelude* 'consists in part of an exploration of the relationship between nature or reality and its figurative presentation, examining the collapse of the specular structure of representation in which the graphic image corresponds to, but distinguishes itself from, its referent in the world of nature'. King provides fascinating information about the panorama and the way it was perceived by Wordsworth and others who ranked it among the very lowest of artistic genres in its catching of the outward shape while neglecting the inward spirit or ideal form. King sees Wordsworth's unease with panoramic representation as deriving from his fear that the dead letter of such representation might disturb the hierarchy of things which separates it from the spiritual. The significance of King's important contribution is that he underscores the reasons why London remains so intractable a phenomenon for Wordsworth. This is a significant article. Phillip Shaw offers some more fascinating and detailed speculation about the kinds of panoramic displays Wordsworth might have seen in London which inform the poet's descriptions of '"Mimic Sights": A Note on Panorama and Other Indoor Displays in Book 7 of *The Prelude*' (*N&Q* 40.462–4).

Romantic repression of a different kind is also the subject of Steven Goldsmith's *Unbuilding Jerusalem: Apocalypse and Romantic Representation*, which is concerned with the Romantic aestheticization of the apocalypse, with the political purposes served by the claims of apocalyptic aesthetics to have transcended history. Goldsmith is right to emphasize how the authority of an apocalyptic text is predicated on its being perceived as separable or even antithetical to historical contingency. Thus the exaggerated formalism of the apocalyptic texts of Blake and Shelley is an ideological marker or a sign of their motivated participation in historical circumstance. Goldsmith's aim is to 'unbuild' Jerusalem to deconstruct texts which privilege the aesthetic while suppressing the historical conflicts that gave them being. Thus the Book of Revelation sponsors a cult of its own textuality: 'formal apocalypse evolved as a means of suppressing social conflict and, more specifically, of containing millenarianism'. So apocalypse in some circumstances can serve to legitimate and stabilize a given social order. The early part of Goldsmith's book deals with the Book of Revelation and three scholars of it from the seventeenth century to the present (Joseph Mede, Richard Hurd and Leonard Thompson). The second part of Goldsmith's book focuses on Romantic evocations of apocalypse in Blake, Paine, Percy Shelley and Mary Shelley. This is an important and searching study of a timely subject. In a sense it too functions as an evasion of history in its rather schematic and transhistorical structuring. The final book of a general nature which has come to my attention this year is Jonathan Wordsworth's *Visionary Gleam: Forty Books From the Romantic Period* which is a second collection of essays (*YWES* 72.270) based on the introductions written for the Woodstock Books series Revolution and Romanticism. These have been revised and a short preface to the volume has been added. Wordsworth's two collections of revised prefaces are very useful and informative. One cannot underestimate the importance of the Revolution and Romanticism series for students of the period. Once again, Bravo Woodstock!

Somewhat more traditional in its scope is Mark Trevor Smith's intellectual history of a theme or idea, *'All Nature Is But Art': The Coincidence of Opposites in English Romantic Literature*. This is a study of the pursuit of the reconciliation of opposites and its relationship to Romanticism in a number of writers, from Nicolas Cusanus, the fifteenth-century monk credited with developing the concept of the *coincidentia oppositorum*, through to Pope, Coleridge, Blake, Mary Shelley and Percy Shelley. Smith shows how Pope's own treatment of the idea is closer to that of his Romantic successors than one would at first suspect. The main focus of the book, however, remains on Blake who is accorded three chapters. Smith's book contains, as one might expect, much talk of concentric circles and centripetal forces, and although it is full of interesting material its rather unfashionable focus on the treatment of an idea is unlikely to make it prominent in Romantic studies.

A number of articles have appeared on general themes of interest to readers of this section. Marjorie Levinson discusses 'Romantic Poetry, the State of the Art' in *MLQ* (54.183–214). Alan Richardson presents a truly fascinating discussion of the literary representation of slave religion in 'Romantic Voodoo, Obeah and British Culture, 1797–1807' (*SIR* 32.3–28) and of the anxieties created among its audience. *ANQ* 6.ii–iii contains three articles of interest to Romanticists; Karen Swann continues her interest in the Gothic and sensational aspects of English Romanticism in 'Public Transport: English Romantic Experiments in Sensation' (136–42); Steven. E. Jones attempts to contextualize Romantic satire in 'Reconstructing Romantic Satire' (131–6), while Karl Kroeber presents an overview of 'The Next Wave of Romantic Criticism' (59–64). The Romantic Verse Letter is considered by James Mulvihill in 'An Inspiration of a Peculiar Sort: The Romantic Verse Letter' (*ESC* 19.439–55). David Perkins also contributes a fascinating account of 'Romantic Reading as Revery' in *ERR* (4.183–99). Perkins finds from an analysis of the views of such writers as Leigh Hunt, Francis Jeffrey, Joseph Priestley, Erasmus Darwin and Coleridge, among others, that the Romantics assumed that 'a creative, associative activity of mind is necessary and normal in the reading of all literature, whatever its stylistic features'. This state of reading was akin to reverie. This is an intriguing article. Jonathan Bate's 'Romantic Ecology Revisited' surveys his own response to new historicist criticism of Wordsworth and Romanticism, citing as perverse the new historicist wish to undertake a materialist critique of what is itself a materialist critique of capitalism in its high industrial phase, preferring instead a 'green' literary criticism (*WC* 24.159–62). This is also the subject of a short article by Bate, 'Toward Green Romanticism' in *ANQ* (6.ii–iii.64–9). Malcolm Kelsall writes on the role of place in Romanticism in 'The Sense of Place and the Romantic Cosmopolite' (*LittPrag* 3.28–41). The *Wordsworth Circle* for this year prints the papers from conferences of interest to Romanticists: The Wordsworth Summer

Conference of 1992 (*WC* 24.i.); The 1992 Wordsworth-Coleridge Association Meeting on the topic of 'Beyond Romanticism' (*WC* 24.iii.). Among the papers is Pamela Black's interesting discussion of some of the implications for Romanticists of postmodern literary theory, 'The Presence of the Unknowable: A Romantic Perspective on Postmodernism' (*WC* 24.29–34).

(b)   Works on Individual Poets
This year's work in Blake studies will probably prove to be a definitive moment, a year of extraordinary development such as is encountered only once in a generation. As well as an important sale of original Blakes, the year also saw two extremely significant works of historical contextualization, two splendid facsimile editions and, perhaps above all, Joseph Viscomi's *Blake and the Idea of the Book*, a work which provides far reaching new evidence about the techniques of producing the illuminated books.

The primary finding list for Blake studies continues to be the bibliographies and sales reports which appear in *Blake* (*Blake*). Scholars should start with D. W. Dörrbecker's 'Blake and His Circle: An Annotated Checklist of Recent Publications' and combine this with Robert N. Essick's 'Blake in the Marketplace, 1992' (*Blake* 26), which continues to be a prime source of reviews, reports and announcements on all matters relevant to Blake studies.

Joseph Viscomi's ground-breaking *Blake and the Idea of the Book* will replace much of G. E. Bentley Jr and David V. Erdman's scholarship on the status and dating of Blake's illuminated books, about which we must now also jettison many long-held beliefs.The first critical casualty is the idea that Blake worked on a 'commission' basis, only printing and colouring books when he found a buyer. Instead, Viscomi proves definitively that Blake produced 'editions', manufacturing each title (not each copy) in one or two sessions lasting a couple of days. This finding, even on its own, is of enormous significance. Such is Viscomi's practical familiarity with historically authentic print-making, that Blake's techniques can now be understood as a hybrid type of 'permanent manuscript', the artist probably writing his poetry onto scraps of paper before mirror-writing the text and design directly onto copper with an artisan's apprentice-served familiarity. That is, there were no intervening stages necessary to produce what we now have in the illuminated books. By examining such highly technical matters as paper type, plate size, indentation, inking and colour finishing, Viscomi renders a truly materialist account of Blake's texts. The days are now gone when critics could calmly, but naïvely, interpret these texts using methodologies unmediated by the implications of the production process.

Viscomi's is also a 'new' Blake, one who spent the majority of his life *not* writing and making illuminated books. Because the composition and production of the illuminated books are synonymous, we must now account Blake an extremely sporadic *author* of this type of work, the artist only writing them during very short periods within the years 1789–90; 1793–5; 1811; 1818–27. If this year's *YWES* Blake entry might also function as a guide to this highly technical branch of art history (whose leading practitioners, intriguingly, work in English departments), readers might first wish to turn to Viscomi's excellent 'see-at-a-glance' appendix table of printing dates. Everywhere in *Blake and the Idea of the Book* is Blake the artisan, using the backs of plates to engrave new works, reversing colouring/text inkings economically, discarding texts and pictures which failed to reach his professional standard, sometimes even bodging over slight imperfections.

Viscomi's findings, telescoped here, are based upon a comprehensive first-hand examination of the international collections. His scholarship will be very difficult to reproduce or re-examine adequately. The staggering logic and extrapolation of inferences from Blake's originals have made *Blake and the Idea of the Book* a densely technical read which is virtually 'state-of-the-art' art-history.

It is not an exaggeration to say that the centre of Blake studies is now occupied by bibliographical inquiries. Among the first fruits of this new wave are two further volumes in the series of splendid facsimiles published by the William Blake Trust in conjunction with the Tate Gallery. *William Blake: The Early Illuminated Books* edited by Morris Eaves, Robert N. Essick and Joseph Viscomi, incorporates many of the discoveries announced in *Blake and the Idea of the Book*. Effectively, one of the two facsimiles of *There is No Natural Religion* reproduced in this volume amounts to a 'new' work for Blake scholars because it represents a new sequence of plates when compared to the 'old' – but standard – Erdman sequence. 'Principles' I–VI of the 'old' *series (a)* are followed directly by 'Principles' I and II plus the plate which reads 'Therefore / God becomes as / we are, that we / may be as he / is' which comes from the 'old' *series (b)*. In other words, the Blake Trust edition clarifies how we are to read some of Blake's earliest and most emphatic philosophical statements. However, a *second* 'new' *There is No Natural Religion* is also identified by the editors who run (but this time not as facsimiles) the 'old' *series (a)* and *(b)* 'Principles' together so as to more clearly identify them as parallel sets of queries and answers. This is perhaps what Blake originally intended. Also (although students will find the rationale most clearly given in *Blake and the Idea of the Book*), both *All Religions are One* and all the significant impressions of *There is No Natural Religion* are dateable by watermark to a printing session in *c.*1794–5. Hitherto, internal evidence had suggested a date of *c.*1788 for both works. The copies of *There is No Natural Religion* employed are the Pierpont Morgan's copies G, I and L, while *All Religions are One* reunites copy A collated from the Fitzwilliam Museum and the Huntington Library. Volume 3 also reproduces *The Book of Thel* copy J (Harvard), a version printed and hand tinted in the same session, and within the same edition, as copies A–E, G–M and R in the early 1790s (but retouched by Blake *c.*1816). Only *Thel* copies F (*c.*1795), N and O (*c.*1818) were printed later than this first edition. The Blake Trust have also reproduced the colour-printed *Marriage of Heaven and Hell* copy F (Pierpont Morgan), a second (*c.*1794) printing of an edition which began with copies A, B, C and H before Blake turned some of the *Marriage* plates over and engraved *The Book of Urizen* on the other side of the copper. Finally, in this feast of delights, there is an excellent reproduction of *Visions of the Daughters of Albion* copy G (Houghton) a water-coloured copy which, uniquely, was paginated by Blake to run its frontispiece *after* its title page. Such is the pace at which our knowledge of Blake's originals is changing that many scholars may still not be aware that another copy of *Visions* (copy R) was discovered by D. W. Dörrbecker in the Bayerische Staatsbibliothek, Munich, in the late 1980s. As is usual in this Blake Trust series, significant variants are reproduced as supplementary illustrations. Volume 3 also contains a definitive description of Blake's distinctive methods of water colouring and colour printing. This will be a useful starting point for many scholars.

Many Blake scholars will find this necessity for bibliographic exactitude both daunting and intimidating, but the details need to be mastered because of the implications of their contextual significance. For example, the re-dating of *All Religions are One* and *There is No Natural Religion* to the mid-1790s now realigns both works as interventions into the materialist/deist debates forwarded by d'Holbach, Volney and, most closely to home, Paine's *Age of Reason*. Because of investigations of this type, the work of other scholars which had once been tentative, can now be considered as more firmly secured. For example, Peter A. Schock's investigation of '*The Marriage of Heaven and Hell*: Blake's Myth of Satan and its Cultural Matrix' notes the similarity (as well as the contrasts) in the positions of Blake and the French *philosophes* (*ELH* 60.441–70). Schock provides a rewarding investigation of the polarization of the Satan myth in contemporary ideological positions. As Daniel Isaac Eaton satirized it, 'the devil was the *first Jacobin*'. Being of 'the Devil's party' as Schock explains, 'acquires ideological resonance' because of the potential re-formation of traditional Christian myth which is implicit in these pro-revolutionary devils. Schock's essay provides a thorough cultural analysis of high art (James Barry, Philip de Loutherbourg) as well as figuring the significance of obscure political print caricaturists like William Dent (whose work Schock reproduces). In particular, Schock's essay usefully redresses the Blake Trust volume's down-playing of the *Marriage*'s contemporary political context.

Robert Essick and Joseph Viscomi, two of the team from the Blake Trust volume 3, also edited the Trust's volume 5, *Milton a Poem and the Final Illuminated Works: The Ghost of Abel, On Homers Poetry [and] On Virgil, Laocoön*. The copies reproduced are *Milton* copy C (New York Public Library), *The Ghost of Abel* and *On Homer/Virgil* copies A (Library of Congress and National Gallery of Art, Washington, D.C.) and *Laocoön* copy B (Robert Essick). These are rich examples of Blake's illuminated printing, the three smaller works being only rarely available before in facsimile while *Milton* benefits from a particularly sensible, reader-friendly introduction. As before, variants are shown in supplementary illustrations.

The dizzying political refractions of Blake's contemporary political culture were given a further complication by the resurfacing in a London salesroom of a unique but authentic printing of 'A Song of Liberty' (copy L), a work which Blake usually appended to the *Marriage*. Details and good photographs are given in the sale catalogue (no ISBN number), *Christies: Books and Prints by William Blake from the Collection formed by the late Frank Rinder, Esq.,* Tuesday, 30 November 1993. Ample discussion of this catalogue is included in this section of *YWES* because, although no author's name is given, it is very likely Joseph Viscomi acted as consultant to the sale. This probability notwithstanding, scholars must treat the Christies catalogue as an interim report pending definitive descriptions of this copy of 'A Song'. The sale copy of 'A Song of Liberty' turns out to be of enormous importance because it was printed by Blake onto a folded half-sheet of laid (as distinct to woven) paper, watermarked consistent with a date *c.*1790. Its significance lies in the fact that its production on folded laid paper is possibly suggestive of an embryonic pamphlet project similar to contemporary radical broadsides. The same Rinder sale also included *Jerusalem* copy C (watermarked 1818–20); *Milton* pl. 38; a posthumous *Jerusalem* pl. 25; a set of four uncut, relief etchings from copper preparatory for *The Pastorals of Virgil* (as distinct from the eventually used heavily trimmed wood engravings). Also offered in the sale were two impressions of *The Man Sweeping the Interpreter's Parlour* which are so widely different in colour, inking and printing that widely separated dates of *c*.1794 for one and *c*.1822 for the other are conjectured. Elsewhere, another work to resurface this year was a colour-printed headpiece from *The Book of Urizen* pl. 3, last sold at Sotheby's in 1970 but innocently lost from the sight of scholars in a private collection. Uniquely, the running flame-bound figure (which Blake usually genders as male) is distinguished by a quite distinct female breast. The impression is authoritatively described by Martin Butlin in 'Another Rediscovered Small Color Print by William Blake' (*Blake* 27.68).

There is still a lot to find out about Blake and his times. John D. Baird found a hitherto missed very early review of Blake's painting 'War Unchained by an Angel, Fire, Pestilence and Famine Following', which the *Morning Chronicle* described as exceeding 'most of the strange flights in our memory' ('Blake's Painting at the Royal Academy, 1784: A Reference', *N&Q* 40.458). Library burrowers can also now relocate, and find better transcribed, a misplaced short letter by Blake in the Beinecke Library, Yale University, written *c*.1800 (printed as Letter 20 in the Erdman and Bloom *Complete Poetry and Prose*, see G. E. Bentley, Jr, 'A Blake Letter Found', *YULG* (October) 60–4). Bentley has also written fascinatingly about John Marsh whose contemporary journal (now in the Huntington Library) gives a unique personal contextualizing of popular politics in Felpham, Sussex, at the exact time of Blake's traumatic trial for sedition. Marsh's journal suggests that Blake's prosecutors may have been trying to intimidate the unruly local Chichester militia and that Blake's own defiance of the military might have been greeted sympathetically in the locality (G. E. Bentley Jr, '*Rex v. Blake*: Sussex Attitudes Toward the Military and Blake's Trial for Sedition in 1804', *HLQ* 56.83–9).

Illustrative of the far-reaching implications of the bibliographical inquiries initiated by Essick and Viscomi, and the rapidity of their onset, is the displacement of Gerda S. Norvig's *Dark Figures in the Desired Country: Blake's Illustrations to The Pilgrim's Progress*, the first book-length study of this neglected series of drawings. Sensitive and intelligent though Norvig's readings are, and even though *Dark Figures in the Desired Country* is sumptuously produced with excellent colour photographs, she is fairly cavalier with the materiality of these watercolours (which is declared to be 'subordinate to my project of interpreting the phenomena before us'). The critical methodology employed ('a sort of cultural immaterialism') might be described as fine readings of compositional aspects of the *Progress* pictures intelligently informed by Jungian psychology. At its best, this may lead to some perceptive interpretations (often rendered as diagrams) such as the relationship of *Pilgrim's Progress* to the nineteenth emblem of *For the Sexes / The Gates of Paradise*. Norvig also writes illuminatingly about *The Man Sweeping the Interpreter's Parlour* (inevitably dated to *c*.1824). However, her attention to colour symbolism, and indeed the book's whole project of interpretive reading, is highly compromised by the neglect of the materiality of the pictures. It is disarming, to say the least, to find *Christian With the Shield of Faith* relegated to a tiny half-tone reproduction with truncated commentary even though (according to Butlin) it is probably the only picture in the *Progress* series to have been inscribed in Blake's hand and one of the few not retouched after Blake's death. Despite Norvig's excellent commentary and the wealth of plates detailing earlier illustrators of *Pilgrim's Progress*, conclusions and interpretations drawn from a series of watercolours which were rather crudely but extensively 'enhanced' after Blake's death, is unnerving at best and questionable at worst.

Similar compositional analysis/interpretation is offered in Marjean D. Purington's 'An Act of Theological Revisioning: William Blake's Pictorial Prophecy' (*CLQ* 29.33–42). According to Purington, relief etchings like *Lucifer and the Pope in Hell* 'challenge our preconceived mental constructs' and encourage 'us to reevaluate our own visions'. Purington's constant appeal to an imaginary, immaterialized community of 'us' and 'ours' is profoundly disorientating.

Blake's scores of illustrations to John Milton's poems are treated to a more eclectic set of positions in J. M. Q. Davies's *Blake's Milton Designs: The Dynamics of Meaning*. Davies provides learned readings of Blake's Milton designs illustrated with about 140 black-and-white photographs, about a quarter of which reproduce likely pictorial sources and analogies. Scholars are best advised to use *Blake's Milton Designs* for its close contextualization within Western art history and Milton's writings rather than for the book's presentation of an overall thesis. Davies is at his strongest in locating convincing visual sources, much after the fashion of Anthony Blunt or Jean Hagstrum. For example, traditions of a phallic Christ, apparent in early Renaissance woodcuts by Ludwig Krug, make suggestive visual links with some of Blake's more eroticized pictures such as the first state of *Milton* copy A pl. 38. Irritatingly, Davies does not consistently give details of media, date or provenance during much of this fascinating source-hunting.

Perhaps the most thoroughgoing contextual analysis of Blake's pictures, framed within an emphatically materialist knowledge of Blake's methods, is Morris Eaves's *The Counter-Arts Conspiracy: Art and Industry in the Age of Blake* (1992). It is rather more than merely an attempt to redress accounts of Blake's beleaguered and much-misunderstood place in his contemporary art-market. Eaves resituates Blake within the context of eighteenth-century fine-art discourse so that, by a process of refracting him from the context of other artists active at the time, Blake can be figured as a man more sensibly the product of his times. The phrase 'Counter Arts' comes from the manuscript *Public Address* of *c.*1809/10, where Blake uses it to describe the machinations (a key term in Eaves's lexicon) conspiring to depress English painting, engraving and particularly Blake's specialized corner of the visual arts. 'Commerce' is the counter-art on which Blake believed art to be skewered. Commercial engraving, with its division of labour into the 'Hands of Ignorant Journeymen', left Blake the visionary craftsman economically redundant and artistically isolated. Within Blake's fulminating *Public Address* lies a deeper experience of the frequently perceived paradox that English commercial and imperial success was contradicted by its neglect of its fine arts. To put it bluntly, how could Protestant England be a world leader if it borrowed its highest artistic ideas from Popish Italy? In the earlier part of *The Counter-Arts Conspiracy*, Eaves traces the pervasive disabling presence of this frustration in contemporary English fine art discourse.

If nationalism is implicated in the *Public Address*, Blake and other artists were eager to jump on the lucrative bandwagon which the commissioning of visual expressions of a suitably mythologized national pride might have offered. Eaves gives an extensive account of the failure of John Boydell's 'Shakespeare Gallery' which provides ample evidence of how Blake's craft as an engraver fundamentally impaired the commercial success of enterprises like Boydell's which might otherwise have given Blake creative independence. Eaves's account is very persuasive. Far from being the messiah of English engravers, Boydell became the booby: not only was his timing unfortunate (the French war was imminent), but engravers failed to meet production deadlines for his fine folios. This is not a new story, but Eaves recontextualizes the 'Shakespeare Gallery' in his account of an artistic tradition already pre-sensitized to failure by its perceived lack of patronage. Add to this cocktail an array of contradictory ideologies institutionalized within bodies like the Royal Academy, and Blake's self-righteous anger becomes readily understandable.

At the heart of *The Counter-Arts Conspiracy* is a deep argument about Blake's techniques of engraving which forms an extended dialectical sequel to the author's prize-winning 1977 *PMLA* essay on 'Blake and the Artistic Machine: An Essay in Decorum and Technology'. Ultimately, *The Counter-Arts Conspiracy* runs into some problems related to its specialization. Eaves is almost entirely concerned with Blake as an engraver, although Blake the painter and maker of illuminated books is implied throughout. Secondly, Eaves is dedicated to the centrality of the manuscript *Public Address*, tending to read it almost as Blake's complete unified theory of artistic production and English politics. Nevertheless, by making Blake's art intelligible within its own history of material production, Morris Eaves's *The Counter-Arts Conspiracy* is an original and very significant contribution to our knowledge of a major artist who lived during a turning point between a traditional craft and a mechanized reprographic industry.

Another suggestive, if more diffuse, contextualization of Blake's times is given in Marsha Keith Schuchard's 'The Secret Masonic History of Blake's Swedenborg Society' (*Blake* 26.40–51). Schuchard's thorough researching of very varied primary sources locates Emanuel Swedenborg as a royalist pro-French spy who visited London to merge himself in its shadowy religious subcultures between 1744–72. The cultural networks of individuals like the Swedish Mason and industrial spy Charles Bernhard Wadström in the mid-1770s (who had an interest in Swedenborgian publishing ventures) now make better sense in the light of the important work being done on the spiritual diversity of Blake's London by Jon Mee and Iain McCalman, as well as the book by E. P. Thompson noticed below.

The complexity of the historical context is also elegantly discussed in George Anthony Rosso, Jr's *Blake's Prophetic Workshop: A Study of The Four Zoas*. It includes a chapter giving a much-needed twentieth-century reception history of *The Four Zoas* in which Rosso briefly outlines the bias of cultural origins discernible in the critical writings of scholars as diverse as Damon, Frye, Bentley and Erdman. With a marked preference for historicist approaches, Rosso exemplifies his own position as perhaps being between Jackie DiSalvo's contextualist *War of Titans: Blake's Critique of Milton and the Politics of Religion* (UPittP, 1983) and Donald Ault's post-structuralist *Narrative Unbound: Revisioning William Blake 'The Four Zoas'* (Station Hill, 1987). While Rosso recommends *kerygma* ('a dynamic interplay between [rhetorical] force and form ... between readers and their social situations'), *Blake's Prophetic Workshop*'s theoretical structure is made solid without being overt. Given the complexities of the *Four Zoas* manuscript, it is good to find that Rosso adopts a night-by-night approach to the poem (and the pictures) which is sufficient to make the book a useful source of close reading, but *Blake's Prophetic Workshop* is also suggestive of important contexts in Paine's *Age of Reason*, Pope's *Essay on Man*, Lowth's *Lectures on the Sacred Poetry of the Hebrews* as well as Edward Young's *Night Thoughts*. It is Rosso's ability to remain faithful to the idea of *The Four Zoas* manuscript as

Blake's vacated 'workshop' (G. E. Bentley Jr's suggestive term), while at the same time invoking these important formative contexts, which makes the book so genuinely humanist in its sympathies.

Molly Anne Rothenburg's *Rethinking Blake's Textuality* shares many of Rosso's virtues of careful historicism and fine close reading. Rothenburg finds that Blake's visionary poems were validated by a historical context which had long undermined the authority of the Bible. In other words, Blake used his rhetorical powers to authenticate his visions. In *Jerusalem* (Rothenburg's core text), subjectivity centralizes 'reality' when it becomes the focal point of multiple inter-texts. In the exemplary *Jerusalem* pl. 98, 'the dim Chaos brightend beneath. above, around: Eyed as the Peacock / According to the Nerves of Human Sensation'. Here paradox and playfulness of sense (to invoke a Lacanian 'eye-I') displaces subjectivity for its authentication but without any resulting escape from 'Chaos' (which might equate with false ideology). Ultimately, Rothenburg argues that all this displacement will bring about only a modest political or social realignment in the visionary's relationship with the world. *Jerusalem* won't save us, we are cautioned, but it might help realign our spiritual selves. *Rethinking Blake's Textuality* is a subtle book but not a wilful one; everywhere is a careful sketching out of eighteenth-century Higher Criticism (excellent on Alexander Geddes); fine parallels with Thomas Gray, Kant and St Augustine; a sustained reading of the *Jerusalem* pl. 97 design and, throughout, a willingness to seek a historical placement for an essentially post-modernist reading of Blake.

Like Rothenburg, A. G. Den Otter's 'True, Right, and Good: Blake's Arguments for Vision in *Jerusalem*' (*PQ* 72.73–96) also takes as its starting point the rhetorical power of *Jerusalem*. Den Otter examines the poem's division into four chapters and argues that each is structured to reach an oratorical climax which is an attempt to reunify the fragmented religions into 'One Religion', 'The Religion of Jesus [...] the Everlasting Gospel'. The essay's consequent emphasis on the addressee as well as the addresser is interesting but the argument would be more convincing if it could be figured how the opening chapter of *Jerusalem*, 'To the Public', might have addressed Blake's increasingly rationalist or, at least, secularized, times. As it is, deists, Christians and Jews remain *Jerusalem*'s curiously unconstituted audiences, however much one might be persuaded by Den Otter's examination of the poem's oratory.

Two more critics offer advice for readers about to enter *Jerusalem*. Paul Youngquist's 'Reading the Apocalypse: The Narrativity of Blake's *Jerusalem*' (*SIR* 32.601–25) concludes that the poem 'is best read as a garden of forking paths, an open array of possible narrative trajectories that the activity of reading substantiates'. Disarmingly, Youngquist claims to 'in no way ... posit a reader prior to' *Jerusalem*. With a broadly similar focus on the act of reading, Hazard Adams's modestly toned survey of the same poem incorporates structural analyses broken down into several diagrams, concentric and otherwise. Adams is conscious of treading on the thin ice of reader theory: 'What I have said so far may seem to suggest that there isn't any story in *Jerusalem* and that the whole notion of story is actually negated'. In finding as much disorder as order in the poem, Adams likens *Jerusalem* to 'a great egg that is constantly turning itself inside out without breaking its shell' ('*Jerusalem*'s Didactic and Mimetic-Narrative Experiment', *SIR* 32.627–54). Both writers are scant in their attention to narrative complications engendered by *Jerusalem*'s pictures; indeed, you might not know there were any designs integrated onto Blake's plates. It is difficult to know where one goes from here. Both essays appear to present *Jerusalem* as if it were a poem beamed down by alien Eternals.

More substantial is the steady and continuing work being done recovering Blake's nineteenth-century audiences. Two essays by G. E. Bentley, Jr. and Keri Davies advance our knowledge further: '"Blake ... Had No Quaritch": The Sale of William Muir's Blake Facsimiles' (*Blake* 27.4–13); 'William Muir and the Blake Press at Edmonton with Muir's letters to Kerrison Preston' (*Blake* 27.14– 25). These well-documented, comprehensively researched essays provide important reception histories of Blake. Bentley's tables, for example, show that long-term sales of Muir's hand-coloured lithographic facsimiles of the prophetic books vended by Quaritch between 1885 and 1935 could be counted in scores in comparison to Blake's originals which sold in tens. A modest market indeed. Davies's essay provides an extraordinary biography of the granite quarry manager, inventor and publisher William Muir whose Edmonton, London, Blake Press was later shipped to a bothy on the isle of Iona. Another curious aspect of Blake's early reception history is detailed in Paula R. Feldman's 'Felicia Hemans and the Mythologizing of Blake's Death' (*Blake* 27.69–72) which reveals Hemans in her poetic drama 'The Painter's Last Work' modifying Allan Cunningham's then unpublished account of the artist's final day. Exceptionally, Hemans portrays William as noble, rather than eccentric, and Catherine as intellectual, rather than ignorant. Less sensitive than Hemans was an anonymous reviewer in an 1833 issue of the *Edinburgh Evening Post* who drew on Cunningham's recently published *Lives of the Most Eminent British Painters* when searching for examples which denote the physiological origins of 'visual phantasms' (David Groves, 'Blake and the *Edinburgh Evening Post*', *Blake* 26.51).

Blake's modern reception is also the subject of Angela Esterhammer's perceptive study of the introductory poems to the *Songs* ('The Constitution of Blake's Innocence and Experience', *ESC* 19.151–60). With elegant clarity, Esterhammer points out Northrop Frye's influential neglect of the performative status of the *Songs* introductions. Briefly, when we notice the poems' performative dimensions, the *Innocence* introduction communicates on a basis of equality with its reader while the 'Bard' of the *Experience* 'Introduction' makes an announcement of authority. Correctively to Frye, Esterhammer suggests we remember that language 'shapes identity' 'by its force or effect rather than its meaning, its use rather than its reference, its revelation of social authority and power relations rather than its revelation of mythic consciousness'. By reminding us of the social function of rhetoric, Esterhammer shows that the two poems address or represent distinct social ideologies.

Last but not least among the major works of both 1993 and our generation must be counted E. P. Thompson's long awaited *Witness Against the Beast: William Blake and the Moral Law*. Thompson, who died while the book was in press, gives us a new Blake, a man who was a product of his class and milieu rather than a tangential offshoot of its weirder tendencies. Like Viscomi's *Blake and the Idea of the Book*, *Witness Against the Beast* will necessitate a major readjustment in our knowledge about Blake's life and times. Modern scholars might initially cavil at Thompson's antique knowledge of recent tendencies in Blake studies, but his single most important finding is the Blake family's background in Muggletonianism. Thompson's diligence in the parish records of St James's, Westminster, strongly suggests that Blake's mother, Catherine

Harmitage or Hermitage, came from a Muggletonian family which probably included (what might have been) an uncle of William's, George Hermitage, a prominent poet and hymn writer in the small London Muggletonian community (which may have numbered less than 40 persons). *Witness Against the Beast* probably represents the professional historian's understatement of the *actualité*. While Thompson's book convincingly supplies a hitherto lost transmission model for Blake's antinomianism, from mid-seventeenth-century 'ranters' to late eighteenth-century skilled-trades religious sect, the present writer's examination of the Muggletonian archive in the Department of Manuscripts, British Library, reveals that Thompson only skims the surface of the likely connections between Blake's writing and Muggletonian rhetoric. Muggletonian writings illuminate a contemporary community who were spiritually self-sufficient and who, the archives show, shared William's extraordinary ability to sustain the act of writing for a tiny audience of readers, a sect who were profoundly pacifist in their politics, and, clearest of all, a group who strongly demonized Reason and continuously rewrote the Genesis account of creation.

At a stroke, *Witness Against the Beast* makes Blake understandable, a man who was the product of a definable strata of the London religious subculture. This *Year's Work* on Blake will prove to be profoundly influential and formative.

Wordsworth, along with Blake, continues to be the most written about Romantic poet and, as in recent years, a substantial number of monographs and articles have appeared on his work. Texts are few. Alan G. Hill has edited *The Letters of William and Dorothy Wordsworth* Volume VIII which is a supplementary volume to the standard edition of *The Letters of William and Dorothy Wordsworth* (Clarendon, 1967–88). This volume prints over 150 letters, most of them previously unpublished, from the 1790s to the poet's later years at Rydal Mount. Hill sees the most striking part of the fresh material to be the tender letters Wordsworth wrote to his wife Mary during periods of separation in 1810 and 1812. The new letters also show that there was more regular contact between the Wordsworths and the Vallon family and they shed fresh light on Wordsworth's relations with Annette. *The Fenwick Notes of William Wordsworth* edited by Jared Curtis about which I was somewhat confused last year (*YWES* 73.370–1) was in fact published *this* year by Bristol Classical Press which is an imprint of Gerald Duckworth & Co. This is a very welcome volume which prints the full notes which Wordsworth dictated to his friend Isabella Fenwick in 1843. The text is transcribed from the manuscript of the Notes in the Wordsworth Library at Grasmere. Most readers of Wordsworth are familiar with the more famous notes but only in the confines of notes to individual poems. Curtis presents them whole and in a form as close to the original as print will allow. He contributes a good introduction, precisely contextualizing the origin of the notes and he also includes substantial editorial notes and helpful glossary. This is a very accurate and welcome edition of the Notes which Wordsworth scholars will find particularly useful. A related volume published this year is Duncan Wu's *Wordsworth's Reading 1770–1799* which is a very careful and precise account of all the authors and books known with certainty to have been read by Wordsworth from his childhood until the age of 29 when he moved to Dove Cottage, as well as more speculative conjecture about the poet's likely reading. Wu prints a list of nearly 300 books that Wordsworth may have read and nearly 30 books which he possibly read. Wu also includes tantalizingly brief summaries of what little is known of the libraries of Francis Wrangham and Thomas Poole, as well as a very helpful descriptive summary of Coleridge's Bristol Library Borrowings 1797–8 which Wordsworth may have consulted (it would have been even more helpful for Coleridgeans if Wu had described the full list of Coleridge's borrowings, but that's another book!). Of course, there remain other libraries for Wordsworth to have obtained books and any list such as this must perforce remain provisional, yet, nevertheless, consultation of this scholarly and exhaustive volume will be essential for anyone working on Wordsworth's early period. The only editions of Wordsworth's poetry I have located this year are the Woodstock facsimiles of *The Prelude* (1850) and the paperback reprint of the facsimile of the 1798 *Lyrical Ballads* (published in hard covers in 1990) both for the marvellous series Revolution and Romanticism. *The Prelude* has an interesting introduction by Jonathan Wordsworth speculating on the question of its late publication: 'The great avant garde poem [...] had become instead the fossil wondered at by Victorian eyes for its otherness.'

Five substantial monograph studies of Wordsworth have come to my attention this year. Richard Bourke's *Romantic Discourse and Political Modernity* is an intriguing and provoking study of the relationship between political and literary discourse which takes the work and reception of Wordsworth as a case for analysis. Bourke seeks to interrogate and explicate the impossibility of Matthew Arnold's separation of the aesthetic domain from the political, 'not simply in so far as it presupposes the incorrigible disarticulation of the aesthetic domain, but rather because its promise to restore is *necessarily* put out of action by the literary pretence to irrevocable independence'. Bourke's argument is a difficult one but it grows out of previous scholarship on eighteenth-century notions of civic virtue (most notably Nigel Leask's *The Politics of Imagination in Coleridge's Critical Thought* [Macmillan, 1988]) and how such notions are transformed by the Romantic poet into the realm of aesthetics and the imagination. For Bourke, Wordsworth's investment in 'liberty' connotes the image of a virtuous commonwealth relying for its durability upon the frugal virtues of northern statesmen or independent freeholders protected from the vagaries of commercial indulgence. Bourke argues that Wordsworth after 1797 increasingly came to identify authority less with an exteriorized ideal, but instead with the inner resourcefulness of the individual, focusing more narrowly in later years on the elected or chosen individual: 'the intuition of a renovated consciousness acts as the model in terms of which an historically vanquished political liberty can be recommended'. Thus for Bourke this attempt to ground a political ideal, ultimately has no more validity than a myth in the poet's work, as 'Wordsworth's argument, even on its own terms, disenfranchises the very position which his work seems to occupy' and the 'public' as such disappears altogether, 'political association being dissolved into a natural, sympathetic association'. Bourke's study takes up Wordsworth's idea of culture, used to provide a theory of politics in the wake of the failure of the French Revolution and tracks it through Hazlitt, De Quincey, Mill, Arnold to T. S. Eliot (subject to particular scorn) and the intelligentsia of the twentieth century. This a major study, studded with a range of allusion and erudition that is, at times, quite breath-taking. Yet there are surprising omissions. *The Excursion* (1814) which was so important to Wordsworth's contemporaries in establishing his particular philosophy and the tone of his reputation is not discussed. Generally speaking, Bourke's 'Wordsworth' or Wordsworthianism assumes almost Hegelian dimensions, and, although his claim for Wordsworth's modernity is well-made, one is left with the feeling that too much is assumed about the coherence and programmatic nature of Wordsworth's *oeuvre*.

Psychoanalysis and the unconscious are the subjects of two studies of Wordsworth this year. Richard D. McGhee's *Guilty Pleasures: William Wordsworth's Poetry of Psychoanalysis* postulates a common identity of purpose between Wordsworth's poetry and Freud's psycho-analogy. McGhee argues that Wordsworth employed language as therapy, exploring expressive, rhetorical, and aesthetic levels of linguistic performance in his art. This is not a major study but will interest those concerned with the more traditional Freudian approach to psychoanalysis. Douglas B. Wilson's *The Romantic Dream: Wordsworth and the Poetics of the Unconscious* focuses on dreaming in Wordsworth's work. Wilson situates his work 'between ancient and Freudian dream interpretation' in order to 'gain a perspective on the oneiric moment of Romanticism'. Wilson develops an interesting account of dreaming in Wordsworth covering such subjects as Wordsworth's use of the 'uncanny', vision and the sublime, absence and death, ventriloquism and dreaming, reveries and nightmares, and imagination restored through dreaming. Chapter 6 of Wilson's book is an extended discussion of the Arab Dream from *The Prelude*. Wilson's approach, although heavily determined by key Freudian essays, is generally open and eclectic. This is a significant and very useful study for those interested in dream theory and Wordsworth's poetry.

Rather more involved and weighty than the previous two studies is David P. Haney's *William Wordsworth and the Hermeneutics of Incarnation,* a substantial philosophically informed exploration of Wordsworth's notion that language should be an 'incarnation' of thought. This notion of language as alternately 'incarnation' or 'counter-spirit' is one that has received much discussion, yet Haney goes beyond the merely linguistic aspects of the debate to argue that Wordsworth's incarnational metaphor is not simply a secularization of a Christian concept in the service of a theory of representation, but that it represents the process of a 'critical, nonrepresentational, historically engaged, concrete hermeneutic of both thought and language'. Haney discusses Wordsworth's notion of incarnation. He draws upon Christian conceptions of incarnation as well as the work of theoreticians such as Hans-Georg Gadamer, Charles Taylor, Emmanuel Levinas, and Stanley Cavell to explicate this idea. Haney argues that Wordsworth's incarnational rhetoric engages historical contingency and mortality by emphasizing the translation of spirit into mortal, historical humanity. Haney's aim is to 'preserve the theological bases of Wordsworth's thought *and* to rescue this side of his thought from charges of naïve logocentrism'. He explores the notion of language as incarnation from its Christian sources to the premises of Wordsworth's poetics and then considers the problem of the relationship between materiality and its effacement in Wordsworth's treatment of words as 'living things' and in his representations of death, discussing the Lucy poems and *The Prelude* in this context. Haney also discusses incarnation and autobiography in *The Prelude* before turning to *The Excursion* where he argues that Wordsworth attempts to work out an actual theory of incarnation as opposed to a rhetoric of incarnation. Haney's is a very interesting and erudite work on a topic of major interest to Wordsworthians and Romanticists.

Three studies of Wordsworth are aimed more towards the undergraduate reader. Antony Easthope's well-written *Wordsworth Now and Then: Romanticism and Contemporary Culture* seeks to evaluate the meaning of Wordsworth's poetry in the context of the 1990s, a context informed by all kinds of intertextualities in which being and meaning do not coincide so completely as Wordsworth wished. For Easthope, Romanticism remains a compensatory movement for the great economic and social changes of late eighteenth-century Britain: 'this compensatory movement itself constitutes Romantic ideology. And it is because that polarizing structure is still very much alive today that Wordsworth is our contemporary.' Easthope writes an engagingly sceptical account of Wordsworth's ideas and poetry peppered with references to contemporary modes of thinking. Nigel Wood's *The Prelude* is a contribution to the Theory in Practice series of applied theoretical readings of literary texts. It has a useful introduction by Wood to the debate over Wordsworth's *The Prelude* and Romanticism in general. This is followed by a number of theoretical applications to the text: John Cook applies De Manian deconstruction, Philip Shaw adopts a cultural materialist approach, Clifford Siskin uses Foucauldian and New Historicist approaches and Susan Wolfson applies hermeneutic theories. This is a helpful collection which shows theory in action on a substantial text. Slightly different in approach is John Williams's excellent collection of essays and extracts for his Macmillan New Casebook on *Wordsworth*. As well as a fine introduction dealing with criticism of contemporary trends in Wordsworth and Romantic criticism, the collection contains some outstanding criticism from a variety of different standpoints (although the collection's bias is very definitely towards the historicist, both old and new). This collection will no doubt prove extremely useful for undergraduates, although to be truly representative of current critical thinking about Wordsworth more work of a poststructuralist variety could have been included. Williams's collection will be supplemented by Peter J. Kitson's forthcoming collection of essays on *Coleridge, Keats and Shelley* in the same series. Of more general interest to readers of Wordsworth is Penelope Hughes-Hallett's attractively illustrated volume *Home at Grasmere: The Wordsworths and the Lakes* which tells the story of William and Dorothy's return to the lakes through the writings of the Wordsworths and their circle.

Two major articles on Wordsworth and economics by Mark Jones grace the year's output. The less satisfying of the two, 'Spiritual Capitalism: Wordsworth and Usury' (*JEGP* 92.37–56) presents a discussion of the inevitable infection of Wordsworth's poetry and spirituality with 'the logic and terminology of economics'. Jones provides some fascinating details of Wordsworth's usurious investments and applies the figural logic of usury to the providential economies of loss and gain in the poetry: ' "Tintern Abbey" advertises rather than veils the logic of usury, and in the form of leisure it registers a dividend both material and spiritual'. Although intriguing in many ways, Jones's piece cannot be anything other than reductive of the poetry itself. Much more open-ended is his article on a related theme in *PMLA*, 'Double Economics – Ambivalence in Wordsworth's Pastoral' (108.1098–113). This is an extended riposte to Marjorie Levinson's reading of 'Michael', convincingly arguing that the poem 'does not dramatize a selfish or heartless decision but shows Michael caught, like the other shepherd, between two systems and forced to suspend one valuation to realize the other. One valuation is spiritual and familial the other material and public, but at no point does the poem privilege either.' This is a sensitive and shrewd reading which really opens the poem up and demonstrates its real complexity of thought and feeling. Both of Jones's pieces are work-in-progress on a book on the Romantics writers and economics and I look forward to its publication. A comparison of the aesthetic theories of Wordsworth and Sir Joshua Reynolds is the subject of John L. Mahoney's 'Reynolds and Wordsworth: The Emergence of a Post-Enlightenment Aesthetic' (*SVEC* 305 (1992) 1502–5). Duncan Wu writes on

'Wordsworth's Metamorphoses' in *ChLB* (83.90–105) interestingly speculating on the use of metamorphoses in Wordsworth's juvenile poems and connecting this imaginative process with the poet's sense of loss at the death of his parents and his desire to accommodate the guilt arising from his failure of grief. Wu has two general pieces on Wordsworth in *N&Q*. The first 'Wordsworth and the *Morning Chronicle*' postulates a likely explanation for Wordsworth's meeting with James Gray and James Perry, editors of the *Morning Chronicle* through the person of Joshua Lucock Wilkinson, although Wu does not provide much detail of the association of Wilkinson with Perry or Gray beyond the mention of a pamphlet of Wilkinson's about a tour to revolutionary France which has an inscription, 'to Mr Perry with the Authors Com[pliments]' (40.39–40). Wu's second note 'Wordsworth's Reading of Marvell' (40.41–2) provides some fascinating speculation concerning Wordsworth's likely reading of the elder poet's works.

Moving on to articles on Wordsworth's poetry, Budick Sanford's 'Chiasmus and the Making of Literary Tradition: The Case of Wordsworth and "The Days of Dryden Pope"' (*ELH* 60.961–87) focuses on *chiasmus* as a means of describing the ways that literary traditions are made. For Sandford 'chiasmus creates a species of absences between its binary terms [...] not simply the antitheses or negations of the binary terms themselves'. Sandford's aim is to describe both the chiastic structures in Dryden and Pope that the Romantic writers miss as well as 'the historical, larger chiasmus in which their own antithetical claims participate *with* neoclassicism'. This is an interesting and involved discussion which problematizes the figure, or notion, of *chiasmus* so greatly that it almost becomes unrecognizable. Also in *ELH* (60.651–83) is Zachary Leader's 'Wordsworth, Revision, and Personal Identity' which casts a wry eye over the incessant debate about the various versions of Wordsworth's *ouevre*. Leader surveys this debate, including the various revisions to, and versions of, Stephen Maxfield Parrish's essays on the project of *The Cornell Wordsworth* before criticizing the current editorial consensus for its 'indifference to authorial experience and intention'. Leader argues that 'Revision [...] was only rarely seen by Wordsworth as "neverending". Though obsessive, its purpose was for the most part straightforward: the end of Wordsworth's efforts, he knew, would come with death, and he wished to be judged by the accomplishments – the final authorized versions – of his lifetime.' Leader's essay is a useful corrective to the critical consensus and his point that the virtues of many of Wordsworth's alterations have been undervalued is well taken, although his high notions of editorial 'honour' are rather farfetched: 'ignoring or denying authorial agency and intention means ignoring or denying one's responsibility to persons. As the example of Wordsworth's revisions so intelligently and honorably suggests, this responsibility ought to apply as much to dead persons – or the person one once was – as to the living.' Leader's faith in 'the dead hand' is touching.

Nicola Trott provides a valuable discussion of 'Wordsworth's Tranquillizers' arguing that rather than being a model of Victorian health and sanity, 'Wordsworth's emphasis on a sanity of heart and intellect constitutes its own kind of suppressed anxiety'. Trott surveys a number of instances of this double consciousness of terror and tranquillity in Wordsworth's poetry and relates his anxieties back to the historical point of the French Revolution (*WC* 24.38–47). Gordon Tweedie's 'Wordsworth and the Art of Imitation' (*WC* 24.12–18) analyses Wordsworth's interest in the notion of 'admiration' and tracks this through his 'Essay, Supplementary to the Preface' and the fragment 'We Live By Admiration' written for *The Prelude* in 1804.

Several articles have appeared concerning readings of individual poems. In 'Playing with Marbles' (*WC* 24.3–11), Eric Gidal discusses 'The Egyptian Maid; or, The Romance of Yarrow Revisited' in familiar terms, derived from Edward Said, and the poem's fusion of orientalist and medievalist discourse. Raimondo Modiano applies theories of sacrifice and gift exchange to 'Home at Grasmere' and discovers in this most joyous and edenic of Wordsworth's poems 'the terror of violence within both the human and the natural world' in 'Blood Sacrifice, Gift Economy and the Edenic World: Wordsworth's "Home at Grasmere"' (*SIR* 32.481–521).

Brian Barbour's '"Between Two Worlds": The Structure of "Tintern Abbey"' (*NCL* 48.147–68) rather abruptly and pompously dismisses recent historicist and new historicist writing on the poem, arguing, somewhat stridently that '"Tintern Abbey" is irrefragibly a religious poem in which Wordsworth sought to define and defend a realm of the autonomous spiritual – autonomous *contra* Christianity, spiritual *contra* the Enlightenment'. Barbour's reading divests the poem of almost all its contexts and reads it simplistically as a 'Romantic' text: 'Paragraph one is grounded in nature; paragraph two responds with active mind. Seldom in the history of ideas has an example crystallized with such clarity.' Barbour's somewhat leaden unfolding of the poem's 'drama of ideas' adds little that is new to criticism of the poem, even at the level of the close reading it exalts. More interesting is Fred V. Randel's 'The Betrayals of "Tintern Abbey"' (*SIR* 32.379–97*)* which elegantly discusses the poem in terms raised by recent critics, 'the topos and implied accusation of betrayal'. To charge the poem in this way is for Randel to ignore 'the poem's metaphoricity, negative rhetoric, intertextuality, and maverick historicity'. Randel makes the important point that 'When Wordsworth says that "nature never did betray," therefore, he makes a political and critical statement about what did betray, though it does not place him in either of the chief organized camps of his time and though it may be an unwelcome statement to readers identifying with one of those camps from the vantage point of a later time'. This wide-ranging discussion from the political (the Revolution's betrayal in invading Switzerland) to the personal (the betrayal of Annette Vallon) constitutes a major contribution to writing on 'Tintern Abbey' where 'the most seductive of betrayers is the trope of betrayal itself'. Less engaged with historicist critical discourse is Colin Pedley's 'Wordsworth's "Cheerful Faith": Echoes in "Tintern Abbey" and the Discourse of Visionary Recognition' (*RES* 44.37–46) which discusses the *credo* of the poem in terms of its various intertexts from eighteenth-century nature poetry, Romans 8, to Gilpin's picturesque writings. Pedley canters through these various intertexts to arrive at the conclusion that Wordsworth's 'visionary recognition' is nevertheless profoundly original.

Two short pieces on the 'Lucy Poems' have appeared this year. Philip L. Elliott's 'The Violet and the Star' discusses the treatment of the Venus and Adonis legend in the poem (*ELN* 30.41–3) and Mark Jones deals with the critical response to the poems in 'On Knowing the "Lucy Poems": Criticism as Containment' (*ANQ* 6.ii–iii.96–105). Similarly, not much of substance has appeared on *Lyrical Ballads*. The most interesting piece, Nigel Leask's 'Pantisocracy and the Politics of the "Preface to *Lyrical Ballads*"', is reviewed above. Also of interest is Thomas Pfau's treatment of language in the 'Preface' in '"Elementary Feelings" and "Distorted Language": The Pragmatics of Culture in Wordsworth's "Preface to the *Lyrical Ballads*"' (*NLH* 24.125–46). Duncan Wu discusses '*Lyrical Ballads* (1798): The Beddoes Copy' in *Library* (15.332–5) relating the volume to Beddoes 'Domiciliary Verses'. David Chandler has a brief piece on 'Wordsworth's "A Night-Piece" and Mrs Barbauld' in *N&Q* which finds a faint echo in the poem of Barbauld's 'A Summer Evening's Meditation' (40.40–1). Angela Esterhammer's 'Wordsworth's "Ode to Duty": Miltonic Influence and Verbal Performance' applies speech act theory to Wordsworth's Ode noticing its heavily Miltonic tone (*WC* 24.34–7). Surprisingly little has also been published on *The Prelude* this year. Two pieces on the panoramic representation and Book Seven (by Ross King and Phillip Shaw) have been discussed above. David Colling's 'A Vocation of Error: Authorship as Deviance in the 1799 *Prelude*' (*PLL* 29.215–35) deals with the notion of authorship in the poem, and W. J. B. Owen traces the history of the misinterpretation of Wordsworth's line 'The Props of My Affection' (*WC* 24.177–9). Grevel Lindop looks again at the episode of the stolen boat from Book One in 'Finding the Stolen Boat' (*TLS* 4694.14). Mary Wedd contributes a detailed and very interesting discussion of 'Industrialization and the Moral Law in Books VIII and IX of *The Excursion*' (*ChLB* 81.5–25), arguing that the poem is a 'brave and humane work' very relevant to modern times.

Nicola J. Watson contributes a solitary piece on *The White Doe of Rylestone*, 'Footnoting the Romantic: Forms of History and *The White Doe of Rylestone* (*WC* 24.141–3) which uses the poem to pose questions about Romantic historiography and the boundaries of Romanticism itself. On a related theme is Stephen Gill's excellent 'England's Samuel: Wordsworth in the "Hungry-Forties"' (*SEL* 33.841–58) which charts the creation of an image of Wordsworth as national saviour in the 1840s and broaches the question of the impact on the poet himself of this later fame. Gill presents much literary and historical detail of the indirect ways by which Wordsworth came to be regarded as the 'laureate of the Oxford Movement' and as a 'Christian poet, whose lofty vision encompassed both spiritual mysteries and the lives of the poor'. Gill instructively reminds us that Wordsworth 'was not only a precursor of Dickens, but a contemporary, a contemporary too of Carlyle, Disraeli, Kingsley, and Elizabeth Gaskell'. Gill is most revealing, however, in showing how some of Wordsworth's orthodox revisions to his earlier poetry were occasioned by the pressures exerted by the prevailing construction of himself as a Christian poet.

Finally, a few pieces concerning Wordsworth and other writers have appeared this year. David Chandler's '"Twisted in Persecution's Loving Ways": Peter Bayley Reviewed by Southey, Wordsworth and Coleridge' (*WC* 24.256–61) discusses the three poets' collaborative review of Bayley's *Poems* (1803); J. Hall's 'The Non-Correspondent Breeze, Melville and the Rewriting of Wordsworth in "Pierre"' (*ESQ* 39.1–19) considers Melville's appropriation of Wordsworth; and D. Dervin writes on 'A Psychoanalytic Approach to Language-Acquisition and Literary Origins' discussing Wordsworth, Beckett and Joyce (*Psychoanalytical Review* 80.265–91). I have come across only two pieces concerned with Dorothy Wordsworth: K. T. Meiners's 'Reading Pain and the Feminine Body in Romantic Writing' which looks at the examples of Dorothy Wordsworth and Sara Coleridge (*CentR* 37.487–512) and C. N. Jackson-Houlston's 'In Search of February's Solitary Strawberry Flower' which criticizes the botanical evidence for the alleged misdating of three entries in Dorothy's

Alfoxden Journal which has exercised contributors to *N&Q* in recent years (40.461–2).

This is very much the year of John Beer in Coleridge scholarship. The most important publication in the area is Beer's excellent edition of *Aids to Reflection* (volume nine of *The Collected Works of Samuel Taylor Coleridge*). This edition boasts full and detailed annotation combined with a substantial introduction which outlines the thought and ideas of *Aids* as well as the history of its genesis and composition and the text's influence and reception. Appendices to the volume include the surviving materials and a printing in full of James Marsh's influential preface to the first American edition. The year's other edition of Coleridge's prose writings, volume two of *Coleridge's Writings 'On Humanity'* edited by Anya Taylor (Macmillan) was not made available for review. John Beer has also reworked his edition of Coleridge's *Poems* for Everyman. This is an excellent and comprehensive edition of Coleridge's poetry which contains a helpful introduction. Most welcome is Beer's reprinting of the 1798 and 1828 versions of 'The Rime of the Ancient Mariner' as a parallel text making it possible to see the two most significant versions of the poem without recourse to cumbersome appendices. Beer also prints as parallel texts the 'Letter to Sara Hutchinson' and 'Dejection: An Ode'. Reasonably priced and carefully edited, this is the best teaching edition of Coleridge's poems. Beer may print just two versions of 'The Ancient Mariner' in his edition but, in line with much contemporary theorizings about multiple texts, Martin Wallen has helpfully produced an edition which features the 'three primary editions' of the poem (the 1798, 1800 and 1817 versions), *Coleridge's Ancient Mariner: An Experimental Edition of Texts and Revisions 1798–1828*. Wallen provides a useful commentary which sums up critical thinking about the poem and its revisions, although his conclusions themselves ('the gloss [...] obscures the poem under its moralistic framework') are hardly original. Unlike Beer's edition, we are actually left with no actual reading text for the poem, it being difficult to follow any of the three versions consecutively. Nevertheless, this edition does save the enquirer interested in the revisions a great deal of trouble and the very existence of this text emphasizes the problems posed by multiple versions.

As well as authoring his other publications reviewed above, John Beer is the subject of a very fine *Festschrift, Coleridge's Visionary Languages: Essays in Honour of John Beer* edited by Tim Fulford and Morton D. Paley. This is a collection of excellent essays about various aspects of Coleridge's work, linked by the notion of language back to Beer's pioneering work *Coleridge the Visionary* (1959) a work whose impact on Coleridge scholarship was profound and far-reaching. The work contains the following essays: 'The Whore of Babylon and the Woman in White: Coleridge's Radical Unitarian Language' by Peter J. Kitson; 'Coleridge and the Apocalyptic Grotesque' by Morton D. Paley; 'Coleridge and the Rhetoric of Secrecy: Figures of the Self in "Frost at Midnight"' by Jan Plug; '"Kubla Khan" and Orientalism' by John Drew; 'Coleridge's "Love": All He Can Manage, More Than He Could' by J. C. C. Mays; 'Coleridge and the Royal Family' by Tim Fulford; 'Coleridge, Wollstonecraft and the Rights of Women' by Anya Taylor; 'Coleridge on Human Communication' by Denise Degrois; Coleridge's Ekphrasis: Visionary Word Painting' by E. S. Shaffer; 'The Ache in the Missing Limb: Coleridge and the Amputation of Meaning' by Stephen Prickett; 'The Literature of Power: Coleridge and De Quincey' by Jonathan Bate; '"I See It Feelingly": Coleridge's Debt to Hartley' by David S. Miall; 'Aspects of the Distinction Between Reason and Understanding' by Thomas McFarland; and 'Coleridge, Language and History' by Mary Anne Perkins. The contributions are all of a very high standard and those by Fulford, Paley, Mays and Perkins I found to be especially interesting. This is an important collection the contents of which I expect to be frequently cited in future Coleridge scholarship. I highly recommend it.

The final full-length study of Coleridge's work is Charles de Paolo's excellent *Coleridge: Historian of Ideas* (1992) which was missed in last year's review and which certainly deserves a wide audience in its succinct and accessible discussion of the complex interrelationship between Coleridge's theological and historical thought. De Paolo is surely right to see Coleridge's intellectual career as involved with the central Christian problem 'What to do when the millennium failed to appear'. And his study documents in a scholarly and knowledgeable manner Coleridge's theological solutions to this problem of history, discussing typology, providence, creation theory, universality, periodicity and eschatology. This is an important study which I hope will be taken up in future writing on Coleridge's response to history. The final book of interest to Coleridge's readership for this year is the attractively written and illustrated *Coleridge and Wordsworth in the West Country* (1992) by Tom Mayberry which I neglected to review in last year's piece. Although written for the general reader this evocative narrative of Coleridge's association with the South West of England will provide much useful context about the milieu within which the two poets lived and wrote. Among the many fascinating illustrations is a photograph of the oak tree in the grounds of Alfoxden traditionally rumoured to be the 'huge oak tree' of 'Christabel'. Also interesting are the photographic illustrations of Tom Poole's house in Nether Stowey which for so long was off-bounds to Coleridge enthusiasts. I have not seen Christian La Cassagnère's collection of essays on Coleridge, *Coleridge: Études poétiques* (Didier, Paris) but note that it contains Kathleen M. Wheeler's 'Aesthetic Experience and Moral Good in S. T. Coleridge's Conversation Poems', François Piquet's 'Deux visions du millennium: Blake et Coleridge' and J. R. Watson's 'Coleridge's "Religious Musings" and Religious Musings' among other contributions mainly in French. I hope to locate a copy of this and review it in next year's work as it appears to be a volume of some importance.

WC 24.ii. contains a very welcome 'Selection of Papers from the Coleridge Summer Conference 1992' edited by David S. Miall. Although presented as near to the form of the papers as delivered, these papers contain much important scholarship and criticism on Coleridge's work and I would expect that the papers in this number would be often cited in future. The selection contains the following: 'Coleridge, Wordsworth and the Textual Abject' by Tilottama Rajan (61–8); 'Coleridge and Consubstantiality' by Pamela A. Black (69–73); '"Not, Properly Speaking, Irregular": The Metre of "Christabel"' by A. Elizabeth McKim (74–8); 'Speech Acts and Living Words: On Performative Language in Coleridge's 1798 Poems' by Angela Esterhammer (79–83); 'Paradise Rewritten? Coleridge's "The Blossoming of the Solitary Date Tree"' by Tim Fulford (84–90); 'Exorcising the Malay: Dreams and the Unconscious in Coleridge and De Quincey' by Daniel Sanjiv Roberts (91–6); '"Our Prophetic Harrington": Coleridge, Pantisocracy, and Puritan Utopias' by Peter J. Kitson (97–101); '"That Silent Sea": Coleridge, Lee Boo, and the Exploration of the South Pacific' by James C. McKusick (102–6); 'Coleridge, Polarity and the Contemporary Fate of Difference' by Peter Larkin (107–12); 'Coleridge and the Decadence of English Poetry' by Graham Davidson

(112–16); and 'Coleridge and the Object of Art' by E. S. Shaffer (117–28). The volume also contains John Beer's movingly affectionate tribute to 'Kathleen Coburn 1905–1991' (59–60). This is an excellent collection of papers on Coleridge matters and I was especially impressed by the contributions of Rajan, Esterhammer, Fulford, McKusick and Larkin.

Turning to general articles on Coleridge's work, Paul Bauschatz's 'Coleridge, Wordsworth, and Bowles' (*Style* 27.17–40) is a very insightful stylistic analysis of a number of the sonnets of William Lisle Bowles and their influence on Wordsworth and Coleridge. Bauschatz is good on Bowles and the eighteenth century pointing out that 'Bowles seems to be among the first English poets, if not the first, to conjoin the earlier rhetorical practice of Milton to the evolving English of his time', although he is less convincing on Coleridge in his rather straightforward analysis of 'To the Rev W. L. Bowles'. Bauschatz does not really explain why Bowles was so important for Coleridge, a question which was carefully discussed by James McKusick in his very important work *Coleridge's Philosophy of Language* (YaleUP, 1987). This article is also the year's single piece on Bowles that I could find. Nicholas Reid contributes a scholarly and intelligent discussion of the role of Platonism in Coleridge and Akenside in 'Coleridge, Akenside and the Platonic Tradition: Reading in *The Pleasures of the Imagination*' (*AUMLA* 80.37–56). Two pieces on Eastern influences on Coleridge's ideas have appeared. Aparajita Mazumder's 'Coleridge, Vishnu, and the Infinite' (*CLS* 30.32–52) discusses Coleridge's treatment of Vishnu and Hinduism, and Vincent Newey and A. R. Kidawi's 'The Outline Coleridge's and Southey's "Mohammed"' (*N&Q* 40.38–9) reports the rediscovery of the manuscript of an outline by Coleridge and Southey for their proposed poem on 'Mohammed'. H. J. Jackson's 'Coleridge's Women, or Girls, Girls, Girls, Are Made To Love' (*SIR* 32.576–600) concentrates on the explicit statements that Coleridge made about women and sexual difference from the letters, marginalia, notebooks and other scattered sources, commenting on, in particular, his concept of androgyny. Jackson is suspicious of claims made by Coleridge's admirers of his liberal views of women and she presents a strong case for Coleridge's intellectual dismissal of the feminine. More importantly, Jackson points out how Virginia Woolf was somewhat misled by Coleridge's account of 'androgyny' and that for Coleridge the androgynous state was always understood as a primarily masculine androgyneity. Still on a general note, Stanley Jones identifies three quotations in Hazlitt's work in 'Hazlitt, Coleridge, and Edward Young: Unidentified Quotations' (*N&Q* 40.470–1); Duncan Wu's 'Coleridge's "Great Circulating Library": A Footnote' (*N&Q* 40.470) prints information about Boosey's circulating library to which Coleridge was given a ticket by a stranger while at Christ's Hospital; and L. Stefanie Smith prints a corrected version of a Coleridge letter in 'Coleridge as Godfather: A Corrected Text of his 14 August 1828 Letter to Richard Cattermole' (*N&Q* 40.468–9).

Moving on to criticism on individual works, Paul Scott Wilson supplies one of the few articles on Coleridge's prose. His 'Coherence in *Biographia Literaria:* God, Self, and Coleridge's "Seminal Principle"' (*PQ* 72.451–69) looks again at Coleridge's formulation of the 'Primary Imagination' in an intelligent and aware manner, stressing the deconstructive aspects of the power. The year's other article on the *Biographia*, Richard E. Matlak's '*Licentia Biographica*: Or, Biographical Sketches of Coleridge's Literary Life and Plagiarisms' retreads the familiar ground of Coleridge's plagiarisms arguing that 'plagiarism is a metonymy for a distinguishing feature biographical pattern of Coleridge's life', a 'complex culmination of behavioural, psychological, and formal patterning' (*ERR* 4.57–70). David Aram Kaiser, in an important article on Coleridge's *On the Constitution of the Church and State* ('"The Perfection of Reason": Coleridge and the Ancient Constitution', *SIR* 32.29–55), argues that Coleridge is a thinker who tried to combine the common law traditionalism of the ancient constitution with the symbolic hermeneutics of Romanticism. Ultimately, for Coleridge, the constitution is based on a symbolic model of language which is inexhaustible in terms of meaning. This is a welcome reconsideration of Coleridge's ideas about 'Ideas' about the state. Kaiser's other contribution to Coleridge studies this year, 'The Incarnated Symbol: Coleridge, Hegel, Strauss, and the Higher Criticism, (*ERR* 4.133–50), examines Coleridge's famous definition of the symbol in *The Statesman's Manual* in the light of its context in German Higher Criticism. Kaiser stresses that Coleridge's formulation has its origins in his notion of the Incarnation and his article examines the particularities of Coleridge's concept of 'translucence'. This is a good contextualization and discussion of this aspect of Coleridge's thought. On a related subject, Nicholas Halmi's 'An Anthropological Approach to the Romantic Symbol' (*ERR* 4.13–33) negotiates the issue of the Romantic conception of the symbol, posing the question of whether the irrationality of the symbol did not serve some purpose for which reason was inadequate. This is a thoughtful and provocative article. H. J. Jackson's 'Writing in Books and Other Marginal Activities' (*UTQ* 62.217–31) comments on Coleridge's practice of compulsive marginal commentary and relates this, at times rather flippantly, to the issue of marginality in the larger sense. Finally for the prose, Michael Gamer comments on Coleridge's reviews of Radcliffe and Lewis and reprints a previously unidentified letter of apology to those of his readers angered by his praise of Radcliffe's *The Mysteries of Udolpho* in '"The Most Interesting Novel in the English Language": An Unidentified Addendum to Coleridge's Review of *Udolpho*' (*WC* 24.53–4). Julie A. Carlson writes on Coleridge's *Remorse* in 'Remorse for a Jacobin Youth' (*WC* 24.130–3). Carlson argues that the play stages the equivocations of his Jacobin history and the indispensability of theatre in proving the consistency of his mind. *Remorse* thus privileges individual morality over collective action, remorse over revenge, at the same time playing to the gallery and reanimating the radicalism of Coleridge's youth.

Three articles on *Christabel* have come to my attention this year but I was unable to see two of them. They are: Denis Bonnecase's 'Lire *Christabel*: narration, parole, texte' in *Coleridge: Études poétiques* (edited by Christian La Cassagnère) and Lore Metzger's 'Modifications of Genre: A Feminist Critique of *Christabel* and "Die Braut von Korinth"' (*SECC* (1992) 22.3–19). The third, Avery F. Gaskins's 'Dramatic Form, "Double Voice" and "Carnivalization" in "Christabel"' (*ERR* 4.1–12), discusses the narrative voices of the poem in terms derived from the theories of Mikhail Bakhtin. I can see that there is a dialogue among the narrators of this poem, as Gaskins points out, but I do not see in what sense this is Bakhtinian. Gaskins's suggestion that the narrators of the poem are of a somewhat radical turn of mind is interesting but unsubstantiated by any real argument. Like so many other invocations of Bakhtinian theories, Gaskins's article seems to be rather opportunistic and fails to engage with the substance of Bakhtin's ideas. *Christabel* is no doubt conducive to a systematic Bakhtinian analysis of its narrative effects, but Gaskin has not provided this here. Duncan Wu comments on a variant version of Coleridge's 'Nina-Thoma' in the *Morning*

Chronicle in *'Nina-Thoma*: An Addition to Coleridge Bibliography' (*N&Q* 40.468).

Not very much has come to my attention on 'The Ancient Mariner'. The most substantial piece of criticism is Anne Williams's 'An I for an Eye: "Spectral Persecution" in *The Ancient Mariner*' (*PMLA* 108.1114–27). This is a view of the poem as textual abjection which places it rather fixedly in a Kristevan perspective. Williams argues that the poem expresses 'the semiotic prehistory of a speaking subject [...] it traces the means by which meaning is constructed out of separation, need, fear, guilt, and a need to repair the primal break'. Williams shows several interesting insights into the poem, but overall the Kristevan shoe fits the Mariner all too easily for the reading to carry much weight. The other substantial article on the poem was published in the 1992 edition of *ACM* which I have not been able to consult when writing this piece. It is Vincent Newey's 'Indeterminacy of Meaning in Coleridge's *The Ancient Mariner*' (5.167–80). I will review it next year. *KR* contains William Empson's answer to Robert Penn Warren's seminal, sacramental reading of the poem re-edited by John Haffenden, '*The Ancient Mariner*: An Answer to Warren' (15.155–77).

Byron studies continue to flourish this year as last. The Oxford English Texts edition of *The Complete Works* of Lord Byron edited by Jerome J. McGann becomes complete this year with the publication of volume VII. This volume contains the poems from the last two years of Byron's life when he decided to leave Italy to aid the Greek struggle for independence. Included are the major poems *The Age of Bronze* and, the subject of much recent critical concern, *The Island*. Four new poems are added to the Byron corpus in an appendix to the volume. The comprehensive index to the whole edition is included in this final volume, along with detailed commentary to the poems it specifically contains. This is a fine, scholarly and authoritative volume in an obviously important series. Woodstock have published a facsimile of Byron's volume of poems *The Prisoner of Chillon (1816)*. In his introduction to the text Jonathan Wordsworth discusses the reasons why Byron turned briefly to Wordsworth in writing these poems, arguing that it was 'an unaccustomed vulnerability, a sense of his own "sad-unallied existence", that caused Byron in Switzerland to respond to Wordsworth's poetry'. Dover have also published an edition of *Selected Poems* in their series of Thrift Editions. The only other edition of Byron's works which I have tracked down is the facsimile by Garland: *Don Juan Cantos X, XI, XII, and XVII* edited by Andrew Nicholson. Despite my importunings Garland have not seen fit to provide me with a review copy of this work (or even reply to my letters of enquiry) so I am unable to comment further. Garland also were not prepared to supply a copy of their volume of essays on Byron, *Rereading Byron: Essays Selected from Hofstra University's Byron Bicentennial Conference* edited by Alice Levine and Robert N. Keane. This is a great shame as it appears from the *MLAIB* that this volume contains many interesting essays whose authors might have liked to have their work mentioned in *YWES*. It would seem appropriate to mention here Armand E. Singer's substantial annotated bibliography *The Don Juan Theme* which has been more than 40 years in the making. This bibliography contains over 3,000 entries and is divided into three sections: Origins (1–92); Versions (267–3081); and Chronological List of Versions. Singer's view of what is a version of the Don Juan legend is somewhat impressionistic (Byron's *Beppo* appears as 'A sort of *Don Juan* in miniature and Shelley's 'Epipsychidion' as 'A defense of free love'). Interestingly, it notes that Byron's *Don Juan* was adapted for the Russian stage in three parts in either 1963 or 1966. Singer also includes a checklist of continuations and imitations of Byron's treatment of the theme.

This year sees the publication of a major work on Byron, Jerome Christensen's strapping 400-page *Lord Byron's Strength: Romantic Writing and Commercial Society*. Christensen is a subtle and ingenious critic and he delights in overturning received opinion. His book deliberately avoids the issue of Byron's sincerity which he believes to be something of a red herring, to concentrate instead on that other aspect of Byron's poetry and persona, his 'strength'. Now 'strength' for Christensen can be described as 'a creatural capacity to take consequential action'. Byron's strength was enabled by the literary system of Byronism that was 'collaboratively organized in the second decade of the nineteenth century by coding the residual affective charge that still clung to the paraphernalia of aristocracy in order to reproduce it in commodities that could be vended to a reading public avid for glamour'. Thus Byron's strength is underpinned by the literary market for 'Byronism' as a commodity. Christensen, however, conducts a Romantic argument with political economy by attempting to rehabilitate poetic strength from functionalist accounts. Thus for Christensen, 'Lord Byron's career is the allegory of that imperative's [the family motto *Crede Byron*] residual strength in an age when the grounds of authority have been disclosed as being no more than nominal'. Christensen's book is thus a study of the production of 'Lord Byron' and 'Byronism' by the machinery of an emerging commercial society. Organized chronologically the study discusses Byron's transitions in style in order to demonstrate that Byron is the 'transitional figure between an aristocratic culture of honour and a middle-class culture of commerce'. Christensen works his way through Byron's career with this argument, digressing and elaborating with a range of theories and methods taken from widely different schools of thought. Christensen's style itself is very self-reflexive and it is not always easy to follow his point, which many will find discouraging and, perhaps, alienating. To do any kind of justice to this poststructuralist *tour de force* of wit and ingenuity would take up more time and space than the confines of my annual review for *YWES* allows and so I must regrettably leave this book with this partial and unsatisfactory notice. Nevertheless, this is clearly a major work of Romantic criticism which will no doubt remain influential and controversial for some time to come.

Byron's scepticism is the subject of Terence Allan Hoagwood's *Byron's Dialectic: Skepticism and the Critique of Culture*. Hoagwood attempts to provide an historical and analytical study of Byron's conceptual framework, identifying (from Adorno) a sceptical context of negative dialectic within which to situate Byron's work. The book's study of Byron's works consists of two parts. The first part deals with *Manfred, Childe Harold, Don Juan* and *Detached Thoughts*, arguing that these works are instances of a dialectical paradigm as well as simultaneously being subjects for dialectical analysis. The final chapter is an extended critique of *Cain* which is used to illustrate Hoagwood's contention that poetic drama embodies a criticism of ideology. This is a useful book which treats important aspects of Byron's work and its interpretation seriously. The year also sees the second publication in the OU series Theory in Practice edited by Nigel Wood. This volume concerns Byron's *Don Juan* and contains applied readings of the text by Laura Claridge (from a Lacanian perspective); Caroline Franklin (from a feminist perspective), Philip W. Martin (from a Bakhtinian perspective) and David Punter (from a pyschoanalytical perspective). The collection contains another useful and helpful introduction from Wood himself and it will function as an invaluable teaching aid. Several articles appeared this year on *Don Juan*. Catherine Addison's 'Foolscap Subjects: A Story of Reading Byron's *Don Juan*' (*ESC* 19.290–304) is a reader response treatment of the poem and her 'To Die of Love: Byron's *Don Juan* and the Antidote to Irony' (*UES* 31.20–8) deals with Romantic irony. Peter Cochran demonstrates Byron's indebtedness to Beckford's *Vathek* and Voltaire's *Candide* for the feast in Canto III of *Don Juan* and speculates upon the implications that these borrowings have for our view of the characters of Juan and Haidee in 'A Note on Some Sources for the Feasts in *Don Juan* Canto III' (*N&Q* 40.43–5). Cochran also has a short piece in *ByronJ*, 'Byron and Margutte' which discusses the sources of stanza 45, Canto III in Luigi Pulchi's *Morgante Maggiore* (21.80–6). R. W. Daniel notes 'Two Allusions to Ancient Novels in Byron's *Don Juan*' (*N&Q* 40.42–3) to Petronius's *Satyricon* and Apuleius's *Metamorphoses*. Charles H. Donelan's 'Morality and the Monosyllable: Freedom and Collective Memory in Byron's "*That There*" Sort of Writing' treats the issue of Byron's style and its relationship to memory (*ANQ* 6.ii–iii.114–21). Paul Elledge provides an interesting discussion of 'separation anxiety' using two scenes from Canto 5 in 'Byron and the Dissociative Imperative: The Example of *Don Juan* 5' (*SP* 90.322–46). Supplementing his other work on Romantic satire, Steven E. Jones writes informatively and attractively on the revival of Juvenalian satire under William Gifford's influence and applies this to *Don Juan* in 'Intertextual Influences in Byron's Juvenalian Satire' (*SEL* 33.771–83) and K. Gallafent's 'Byron's Hell' (*CQ* 22.263–83) applies a linguistic approach to Byron's treatment of God, Hell, laughter and despair in the poem. Finally for 'Donny Johnny' I should also note the appearance of Anthony B. England's discussion of self-consciousness in 'Byron's *Don Juan* and the Wakening of Conscious Intent' (*SVEC* 305 (1992).1413–15).

Two collections of conference papers involving Byron appeared this year. The first, *Rereading Byron: Essays Selected from Hofstra University's Byron Bicentennial Conference* edited by Alice Levine and Robert N. Keane and published by Garland, was not made available for review. The second, *Paradise of Exiles: Shelley and Byron in Pisa* edited by Mario Curreli and Anthony L. Johnson, is a collection of papers read at the International Conference of the same title in Pisa of 1985. This collection was originally published in 1988 and has been reissued in a new illustrated edition. The editors provide a good account of the poets' residence in Pisa and the collection contains the following articles on Byron: 'Lord Byron and Teresa Guiccioli in Pisa' by Erwin A. Stürzl; 'Byron, Shelley and Contemporary Poetry' by J. Drummond Bone; 'Byron: *The Vision of Judgment*' by Franco Buffoni; and 'Letteratura e Vita nelle lettere pisane di Byron' by Angelo Righetti.

Several general articles on Byron have appeared this year. John Clubbe's 'Byron and Napoleon, 1814–1816' (*LittPrag* 3.42–57) discusses Byron's views of Bonaparte. J. P. Donovan's 'Don Juan in Constantinople' (*ByronJ* 21.14–29) describes Byron's residence in Constantinople and provides reasons for his reluctance to put pen to paper while there. Two studies by Andrew Elfenbein concentrate on the reception of Byron's work during the Victorian period: 'Byronism and the Work of Homosexual Performance' (*MLQ* 54.535–66) and 'Carlyle, Byron, and Lockhart: A Note' (*CAnn* 12(1991).91–4). C. W. J. Eliot's 'Howe, Greece, and Byron's "Helmet"' (*JMGS* 10(1992).197–204) discusses Byron's sword and helmet in the collection of Samuel Gridley Howe. Annette Peach comments on a portrait of Byron held in the Bodleian Library in '"San fedele alla mia Biondetta": A Portrait of Lord Byron Formerly Belonging to Lady Caroline Lamb' (*BLR* 14.285–95). Byron's relationship to Jane Austen is the subject of an interesting article, 'Byron and Austen: Romance and Reality' by Doucet Devin Fisher in *ByronJ* (21.71–9) which speculates on Byron's possible knowledge of Austen's work and his likely attitudes to the woman author, despite the fact that there is no indication that his Lordship had perused even one of Austen's popular tomes. From the other end of the connection Peter Knox-Shaw's excellent '*Persuasion*, Byron, and the Turkish Tale' (*RES* 44.47–69) argues that Austen's engagement with Byron's texts is much more serious than has been thought, especially in her novel *Persuasion*. J. Drummond Bone insightfully approaches Byron's facility with the *ottava rima* stanza in '"Secular Criticism" and Byron's Ottava Rima Poems' (*LittPrag* 3.58–69). Jonathan Gross's 'Byron and *The Liberal*: Periodical as Political Posture' (*PQ* 72.471–85) discusses Byron's and Leigh Hunt's journal *The Liberal* and what the word 'liberal' meant for Byron: 'Byron defined a liberal as one interested in national sovereignty, not social reform'. This is an interesting discussion of Byron's changing conception of 'liberalism'. The Romantic lyric poem as handled by Byron is the subject of Jerome J. McGann's 'Byron and the Lyric of Sensibility' (*ERR* 4.71–83) which comments on the problems Byron's version of the lyric poses for critics of Romanticism. McGann points out that the Romantic lyric as practised by Wordsworth, Coleridge and Byron is a response to the earlier modes of lyric writing: 'Byron learned much of his art from several late eighteenth-century sentimental sources, including the Della Cruscans and Charlotte Smith'.

Moving on to criticism of other individual works of Byron, James Sonderholm discusses Byron's treatment of memory in *Manfred*, comparing his presentation of forgetting with that of Nietzsche in 'Byron, Nietzsche, and the Mystery of Forgetting' (*ClioI* 23.51–62). *Beppo* is the subject of James Fisher's '"Here the Story Ends": Byron's *Beppo*, a Broken Dante' (*ByronJ* 21.61–70) which notes that both *Beppo* and Dante's *Divine Comedy* end after 99 sections (cantos and stanzas) and intelligently considers the question as to whether or not Byron was imitating Dante. P. M. Curtis also writes on Beppo in 'Byron, Beppo, Digression and Contingency' (*DR* 73.18–33). A. R. Kidwai and Vincent Newey's '"A Vulgar Error": Byron on Women and Paradise' (*ByronJ* 21.87–8) comments on Byron's refutation in *The Bride of Abydos* of the common Western misconception that in Islamic belief women have no souls and cannot enter paradise. Also on the oriental tales is Cheryl Fallon Guiliano's 'Gulnare/Kaled's "Untold" Feminization of Byron's Oriental Tales' (*SEL* 33.785–807). Guiliano comments on Byron's gender-based hostility to women and his trick of ridiculing women writers by masculinizing them, but she notes an 'interesting twist' on this mockery of the phallic women in *The Corsair* and *Lara*. Guiliano argues that if '*Lara* is indeed a sequel to *The Corsair* and Kaled a transformed Gulnare, Byron may have continued the story [...] to undo what he did too well in *The Corsair*: to disempower the phallic woman who threatens to emasculate him (sexually and professionally)'. This is a good discussion of the relationship between gender and orientalist ideas in Byron.

The main event in Shelley scholarship this year is the publication of the first volume of *The Prose Works of Percy Bysshe Shelley* edited by E. B. Murray. This edition is to contain all of Shelley's prose writings except the early Gothic novels and the notes to *Queen Mab* and *Hellas* and includes a number of items appearing for the first time. This first volume contains all the original prose works written before the Shelleys left England in the spring of 1818. Where available, holograph manuscripts or transcripts have been used as basic texts with substantive variations and significant deletions recorded along with selected variants. With a few exceptions the texts of all of the original prose based on printed sources derive from first editions. The edition has a useful introduction and substantial editorial comment and is in every way a first-class scholarly edition of Shelley's prose works. The facsimile of *Shelley's "Devils" Notebook* edited by P. M. S. Dawson and Timothy Webb (Garland) was not made available for review. The only other edition of Shelley's work I have come across this year is the Dover Thrift Edition *Percy Bysshe Shelley, Selected Poems* which irritatingly does not include 'Mont Blanc'. Two articles of a bibliographical nature have appeared in a special issue of *DUJ* on Shelley material (reviewed below). P. M. S. Dawson reviews recent Shelley facsimiles in 'Textual Archaeology: New Editions of Shelley Manuscripts' (85[54].ii.239–7) and Paul Hamilton reviews recent Shelley criticism in '"Old Anatomies": Some Recent Shelley Criticism' (85[54].ii.303–9). *KSJ* also contains Shigetoshi Ishikawa's 'Shelley Studies in Japan: With a Bibliography Compiled by Hiroshi Harata' (42.142–207).

Surprisingly, I have come across no single monograph study of Shelley's work, although several collections of essays have appeared. Michael O'Neill has edited an excellent volume in the Longman Critical Readers series on *Shelley*. O'Neill provides a fine and helpful introduction which takes the reader through the history of Shelley criticism from T. S. Eliot and Leavis to recent approaches. The volume contains much of the best of recent representative Shelley criticism. O'Neill provides a good headnote to each essay explaining the theoretical orientation of the critic and he also provides an enormously useful annotated bibliography. This collection will probably be of most use to the advanced student of Shelley's poetry. O'Neill has also edited a fine Special Issue of *DUJ* (85[54].ii) on Shelley. This contains some excellent criticism of the poet's work by Shelley specialists including: Pamela Clemit, J. R. Watson, David Fuller, Timothy Clark, Kelvin Everest, Graham Allen, Vincent Newey and O'Neill himself. I especially enjoyed Timothy Clark's discussion of the prose fragment 'The Coliseum', 'Shelley's "Coliseum" and the Sublime' (225–36) and David Fuller's discussion of 'Shelley and Jesus' (*DUJ* 85[54].ii.211–23). The edition also contains useful review articles by Nicholas Roe, P. M. S. Dawson and Paul Hamilton. This is a very important collection which gives the reader a good idea of the state of Shelley studies. It is an essential collection for those working on Shelley. I will mention some of the essays from it in my review below.

James Hogg has edited *Shelley 1792–1992* in the Salzburg Studies in English Literature series published by Mellen which contains the proceedings of the Shelley Bicentenary Conference at Salzburg. The collection contains many articles of interest to Shelley scholars. A related publication is Fred Beake's essay *The Imaginations of Mr Shelley* which is also published by the University of Salzburg. Beake, a contemporary poet, comments on Shelley's poetry and attempts to look at the poet's actual processes of composition in the poems of the interior monologue. Mario Curreli and Anthony L. Johnson's *Paradise of Exiles: Shelley and Byron in Pisa* has already been mentioned above, but in addition to the Byron material it contains papers on Shelley by Stuart Curran, John Freeman, Alan Weinberg, Anna Maria Crinó, Lisa Maria Crisafulli Jones and Paolo Ottolenghi. I should also mention here the fine collection of poems by Robert Cooperman, *In the Household of Percy Bysshe Shelley* which contains poems about incidents in Shelley's life written as monologues by Shelley, Byron, Peacock etc. Also on a biographical note is F. S. Schwarzbach's '"Harriet 1812": Harriet Shelley's Commonplace Book' (*HLQ* 56.40–66) which comments on Shelley's relationship with Harriet Westbrook.

Pamela Clemit reviews Shelley's intellectual relationship with Godwin in 'Shelley's Godwin, 1812–1817' (*DUJ* 85[54].ii.189–201). This is one of the best brief discussions of the relationship between the two men, and one which takes Godwin's criticisms of Shelley's Irish project seriously. This is a fine and very helpful piece of writing by a serious scholar. The one work of reference on Shelley studies this year J. L. Bradley's *A Shelley Chronology* (Macmillan) was not made available for review.

The annual *KSJ* 42 contains much interesting material. Michael Scrivener writes, with great knowledge, on 'Shelley and Radical Artisan Poetry' (22–36). Scrivener is especially concerned with the plebeian poets Robert C. Fair and Allen Davenport who were influenced by Shelley's writings. Scrivener enhances our knowledge of the impact of Shelley among working-class radicalism, further negating the Arnoldian notion of Shelley as an 'aetherial angel' vainly beating his wings in the void. Two articles focus on Shelley's relationship to contemporary poetics: Michael Palmer's 'Some Notes on Shelley, Poetics and the Present' comments on the contemporary significance of Shelley's work 'in the light of the collapse of various melioristic futures' (37–47) and Michael Davidson's 'Refiguring Shelley: Postmodern Recuperations of Romanticism' considers the relationship of 'Shelley' (in its multiple meanings) to postmodern poetry (48–57). Davidson writes intelligently on Paul de Man's reading of *The Triumph of Life* as a commentary on its own figurality. The veteran Shelley scholar Donald H. Reiman discusses the 'Textual Authorities for Shelley' and describes the origin of the projects *Shelley and His Circle, The Bodleian Shelley Manuscripts* and *The Manuscripts of the Younger Romantics* published by Garland (58–65). Jerrold E. Hogle's 'Shelley's Texts and the Premises of Criticism' comments on the difficulty of grounding on actual texts and surveys the history of Shelley criticism lamenting that 'none of us can finally claim to be much freer of culturally-determined frames of understanding by which we define the provenance and ranges of reference in Shelley's texts' (66–79). Steven E. Jones 'Shelley's "Love, The Universe": A Fragment in Contest' surveys the textual history of Shelley's little-known fragment (80–96). Three contributors focus on *Epipsychidion*. Tatsuo Tokoo's 'The Composition of *Epipsychidion*: Some Manuscript Evidence' (97–103) pursues the genesis of the poem in the light of the evidence of Shelley's notebooks in the Bodleian Library, arguing that the poem is not a rhapsody but a highly polished work of artifice. Nancy Moore Goslee's 'Dispersing Emily: Drafting as Plot in *Epipsychidion* (104–19) provides a detailed account of Shelley's problems in translating Teresa Viviani from a person to a rhetorical figure. Agnes Péter's 'A Hermeneutical Reading of *Epipsychidion*' (120–7) analyses the shifts in modern interpretative paradigms using Shelley, Milton and Yeats as points of comparison. Finally for *KSJ* 42, Christine Berthin's '*Prometheus Unbound*, or Discourse and Its Other' (128–41) discusses the figural nature of the drama and how this very nature both shows how language deflects and complicates the poetic project and at the same time deflects language in order to launch the poetic project. I am not sure of the actual year of publication of *KSR* 7 (1992) and I have not seen the volume. I note, however, that it contains three considerations of

Shelley's poems: C. A. Adams's analysis of 'Tomorrow' (98–107); Nora Crook's discussion of 'The "Boat on the Sortie"' (85–9); and Kelvin Everest's consideration of 'Athanse' (62–7). In addition, the review contains Timothy Webb's consideration of Leigh Hunt's unpublished tribute to Shelley in 'The Religion of the Heart' (1–61).

Graham Allen writes on Harold Bloom's concept of 'transumption' and applies this to a reading of Shelley in one of the rare instances of a critic seriously engaging with Bloomian categories of influence in 'Transumption and/in History: Bloom, Shelley and the Figure of the Poet' (*DUJ* 85[54].ii.247–56). Gary Farnell's 'Rereading Shelley' (*ELH* 60.625–30) discusses the autobiographical quest to be 'named' in Shelley's poetry applying psychoanalytical attention to the poet's repeated and symptomatic use of shell imagery. Herbert Lindenberger interestingly compares the careers of Shelley and Rossini in 'Shelley and Rossini in Italy – 1819' (*WC* 24.19–29). Michael Neth discusses the relationship between Shelley, theory and literary criticism in 'Rehistoricizing the History of Ideas' (*ANQ* 6.ii–iii.89–96). Michael O'Neill's 'The Mind Which Feeds This Verse: Self- and Other-Awareness in Shelley's Poetry' (*DUJ* 85[54].ii.273–92) deals with the self-reflexive quality of Shelley's verse emphasizing that 'Shelley is alert to the creative, yet at times potentially deconstructive, nature of the medium' of poetry. Alan Tomlinson presents a somewhat unexpected reconsideration of Shelley's influence on the poetry of Wilfred Owen in 'Strange Meeting in a Strange Land: Wilfred Owen and Shelley' (*SIR* 32.75–95). Tomlinson's substantial article argues that Owen's Romanticism is a source of strength, and that he professes the Romantic creed as forcefully as Shelley.

Moving on to articles on individual works of Shelley, L. M. Findlay discusses the relationship of Shelley's drama *Hellas* to notions of nationalism in '"We Are All Greeks": Shelley's *Hellas* and Romantic Nationalism' (*HEI* 16.i–iii.281–6). A. A. Ansari discusses the 'Theme of Love in Shelley's *Prometheus Unbound*' (*ACM* 5(1992).199–212) and Kelvin Everest provides an interesting contextualization of *Prometheus Unbound* II.iii, which challenges the reader to confront the real difficulties of Shelley's very learned and allusive style (*DUJ* 84[54].237–45). A major article has appeared this year on *Adonais*. This is William A. Ulmer's deconstructive '*Adonais* and the Death of Poetry' (*SIR* 32.425–51). Ulmer brilliantly explores the poem's turn deathwards in the light of its own rhetorical structures and Shelley's displacement of immortality to literary tradition, itself displaced to the rhetorical structure of metalepsis. Ultimately for Ulmer the poem 'testifies to a deathliness inherent in poetic representation'. This is one of the strongest deconstructive readings of any Romantic poem that I have come across. *Alastor* is the subject of two contributions this year. Monika H. Lee discusses the way the text reflects contemporary language theories in '"Some Lone Ghost, Nature's Messenger": Rousseau and Organic Language in Shelley's *Alastor*' (*ESC* 19.417–38) and Vincent Newey writes on 'Shelley and the Poets: *Alastor* and "Julian and Maddalo", *Adonais*' (*DUJ* 85[54].ii.257–71). Newey intelligently discusses Shelley's relationship with Wordsworth and Byron which was a central part of his quest for poetic identity. J. R. Watson's 'Shelley's "Hymn to Intellectual Beauty" and the Romantic Hymn' (*DUJ* 85[54].ii.203–10) elegantly considers the form of the Romantic hymn and its long history before speculating on how Shelley modifies this form for his own ends. Christine Berthin comments on Shelley's 'The Pine Forest of the Cascine near Pisa' and its relationship to the Medusa of Leonardo da Vinci in '"The fragment of an uncreated creature"; Reprise et syncope dans la poésie de Shelley' (*Tropismes* 6.159–74). Monika H. Lee's second article of the year on Shelley, '"Nature's Silent Eloquence": Disembodied Organic Language in Shelley's *Queen Mab*' (*NCL* 48.169–93) makes intelligent reading on the subject of the clash between Enlightenment and Organic views of language in Shelley's work, using *Queen Mab* as an interesting example. For Lee, Shelley 'uses a Romantic language that, with its multiple tensions between idealism and irony, protects itself from its own dogmatism in a way that the empirical language of the Enlightenment cannot'.

1993 has been a very meagre year indeed for Keats studies and it is clear that publishers are keeping their powder dry for the Keats Bicentennial of 1995. I have come across only one new edition of Keats, *A Variorum Edition of Keats's 'Ode on a Grecian Urn'*. This is published by Lang who have not supplied a review copy (unusually for them). Two monographs have appeared. Unfortunately, I was not able to see Kara Alwes's intriguingly titled *Imagination Transformed: The Evolution of Female Characters in Keats's Poetry* (SIUP). The other monograph is Diane Brotemarkle's *Imagination and Myth in John Keats's Poetry* which is published by Mellen and is a version of a doctoral thesis. This study compares Keats's use of myth to that of Johann Winckelmann who recognized a historical style in art. Brotemarkle presents a good survey of Winckelmann's thought although I did not find the discussion of the poetry especially illuminating.

Turning to the handful of articles on Keats, we find John Bayley exploring 'that uniquely sensitive area in which Keats's great poetry can seem so close to being like bad poetry' in 'Keats and the Genius of Parody' (*EIC* 43.112–22). Bayley writes insightfully on this 'unmisgiving' aspect of Keats's verse across the range of his achievement. Michael G. Becker's 'Keats's Fantasia: "The Ode on Melancholy" Sonata Form and Mozart's "Fantasia in C Minor" for Piano, K.475' (*Comparatist* 17.18–37) compares Keats's poem to the work of Mozart. Keats appears to be a poet whose work is especially receptive to this kind of comparativist study (see *YWES* 73.388–9). Stanley Pumly writes on grief and its representation in birdsong in Keats's 'Ode to a Nightingale' (*APR* [1992] 21.11–16). One of the more substantial pieces of the year on Keats is 'The Erotics of Interpretation in Keats's "Ode on a Grecian Urn": Pursuing the Feminine' (*SIR* 32.225–43). Friedman writes on the circulation of desire within the poem and between the reader and the text as a kind of double analogy: 'the text suggests that the erotic scenes *on* the urn figure the charged relationships both *between* the speaker and the urn, and *between* the reader and the text'. Friedman argues that the speaker's eagerness to read and possess the meaning of the urn 'en-genders a story about gender, where interpretation is figured as male subject's sexual pursuit of a female object of desire'. This is an important and sophisticated contribution to criticism on the poem. Timothy Clark's 'By Heart, A Reading of Derrida's "Che Cose La Poesia' Through Keats and Celan' (*OLR* 15.43–78) applies Keatsian expertise to poststructuralist theory and A. Shepard's 'From Aristotle to Keats – Stephen's Search for the Good Life in *Portrait of the Artist as a Young Man*' (*ES* 74.105–12).

Continuing with the non-canonical poets of the period (although I accept that this term is somewhat problematic), I turn to Robert Burns. The poetry and prose of Burns is the subject of two substantial editions this year. Thoemmes Press and Routledge have very helpfully published the 1878–9 impression of *The Collected Works of Robert Burns* edited by William Scott Douglas in six volumes and published by William Paterson of Edinburgh. This edition is a facsimile and has no other apparatus than that supplied by Douglas. This is a useful edition to have and Thoemmes/Routledge are to be congratulated for reprinting it so handsomely. Routledge have also published the first comprehensive and unexpurgated excellent modern edition of *The Songs of Robert Burns* including all the discoverable songs of the poet edited by the distinguished Burns scholar Donald A. Low. Many of Burns's obscene or radical songs were not published in his lifetime. This is an excellent edition which prints the music for each song above the song itself and Low has accomplished a very tricky task in matching the song to the music as specified by Burns. Low provides full and detailed annotation to the songs as well as a good contextualizing introduction, which includes a rather unconvincing defence of Burns's bawdy songs. The only article on Burns poetry for the year that I have been able to track down is L. Zancu's 'Burns, Eminescu, and Whitman: Romantic Nationalism or Xenophobia' (*HEI* 16.351–7). The much underrated poet Thomas Lovell Beddoes features fitfully in the year's work. His finely gruesome tragedy, written at the age of 19, *The Bride's Tragedy 1822*, has been reprinted by Woodstock. This is excellent news for libraries not possessing an earlier copy, especially with the renewed interest in Romantic drama. Jonathan Wordsworth provides a shrewd and informative introduction, rightly claiming that Beddoes was a good poet, 'nearly a great one'. Beddoes's greatest work, the superb drama *Death's Jest Book*, is the subject of one article in German which I have not seen, Daniela Tandecki's 'Die Totentänze des Thomas Lovell Beddoes *Death's Jest-Book* und die Verneiung des Lebens' in Franz Link's (ed.) irresistibly titled *Tanz und Tod in Kunst und Literatur* (Duncker & Humblo: Berlin). *Library* has a useful article on 'The Publication of *The Farmer's Boy* by Robert Bloomfield' (15.75–94) and the year's one publication on William Lisle Bowles by Paul Bauschatz has been reviewed above.

Encouragingly the critical interest in John Clare continues to grow. No major monograph has appeared on his work but three new editions have been published. Carolyn Kizer's selection, *The Essential John Clare,* makes the claim that Clare is 'the most neglected great poet in our language'. Few today are embarrassed to write of Clare's greatness as a poet. Kizer's is a fair, if modest selection, and those interested in the poet would be better advised to go straight to the Oxford Authors *John Clare* (1984) edited by Eric Robinson and David Powell. Clare's popular long poem *The Shepherd's Calendar* edited by Eric Robinson, Geoffrey Summerfield and David Powell in 1964 has received a very welcome second 'new' edition. The original edition was very important in bringing a wider audience to Clare's work. The editors restored the poem to its form before Clare's publisher John Taylor mammocked it. Included are Clare's own punctuation, spellings and grammar, returning the poem to its early and vigorous state in line with the editorial principles of Greg/Bowers. This is a very welcome reprint. *JCSJ* 12 is a bicentenary number which abandons its usual format in favour of a more celebratory approach to its subject. Included are brief and evocative 'Bicentenary Thoughts' from a number of poets, writers and critics influenced by Clare, including Ronald Blythe, Gavin Ewart, Seamus Heaney, Andrew Motion, E. P. Thompson, John Barrell, Alan Brownjohn and John Wain. R. S. Thomas contributes a rather haunting and poignant poetic offering 'Lunar' (62–3) . Perhaps too often we easily forget the direct effect a poet's work can have in inspiring the creativity of others and we need not always refer, in Pavlovian fashion, to Bloomian theories every time influence is mentioned. Among the more substantial pieces in this issue are: Greg Crossnan's 'Celebrating John Clare' (18–25) which looks back on the various celebrations of the poet since his death; Bob Heyes's interesting speculation that the surpassingly large molehills in Clare's poetry are in fact anthills in 'Little Hills of Cushioned Thyme' (32–6); Edward Strickland's fine, sensitive discussion of the asylum lyric 'A Reading of "Song Last Day"' (40–50); and Richard J. Hand's 'John Clare on Stage: Edward Bond's *The Fool* and the Issue of Faction' (57–61) which comments on Bond's depiction of Clare and the effect of the dramatist's inventions. John Goodridge is to be warmly congratulated on his efforts for *JCSJ* which becomes more interesting with each issue. I should also mention here the publication of John MacKenna's fictional account of Clare's life, *Clare: A Novel*, told through the voices of Clare's womenfolk and Clare himself.

The only publication to appear on George Crabbe this year is Gavin Edwards's excellent essay 'Crabbe's Regicide Household' in *Reflections of Revolution: Images of Romanticism* edited by Everest and Yarrington and reviewed above. Not properly a poetry item, but historically minded readers of this section may be interested in Jon Mee's discussion of Daniel Isaac Eaton's *King Chanticlere* in '"Examples of Safe Printing": Censorship and Popular Radical Literature in the 1790s' (*E&S* 46.81–95). The fine and much neglected Irish Romantic poet James Clarence Mangan, so important for Yeats, is the subject of only one contribution, Dolores Buttry's 'The Negative Side of Fantasy: James Clarence Mangan's "The Thirty Flasks"' (*JIL* 22.38–46) as is that other Irish Romantic, Thomas Moore, whose *Irish Melodies* are looked at from the perspectives of colonialism in Leith Davis's 'Irish Bards and English Consumers: Thomas Moore's *Irish Melodies*' (*ArielE* 24.7–25). *SVEC* (1992) has a short piece on the poetry of Hannah More, 'The English Evangelicals and the Enlightenment: The Case of Hannah More' (303.458–62). The most celebrated female Romantic writer Felicia Dorothea Hemans, so interestingly discussed by Anne K. Mellor in *Romanticism and Gender*, is also the subject of Glennis Stephenson's 'Poet Construction: Mrs Hemans, L.E.L. and the Image of the Nineteenth-Century Woman Poet' in *ReImagining Women: Representations of Women in Culture* edited by Shirley Neuman and Glennis Stephenson (UTorP) which I have not seen.

SHW edited by Gillian H. Hughes for this year contains several notable articles on matters relating to the poet James Hogg and his circle. Jill Rubinstein's 'Varieties of Explanation in *The Shepherd's Calendar*' (4.1–11) discusses the ways in which Hogg's supernatural tales unsettle the reader by their sophisticated use of narrative. Ian Duncan's 'Shadows of the Potentate: Scott in Hogg's Fiction' (4.12–25) describes the ways in which each author fashioned his own vocational identity and the subjective relationships between the two authors, referring in particular to Hogg's cameo of Sir Walter in *The Three Perils of Woman* where Scott represents the 'harmoniously integrated cultural identity'. Also concerned with Scott and Hogg is Silvia Mergenthal's 'James Hogg and his "Best Benefactor": Two Versions of Hogg's Anecdotes of Scott' (4.26–36) which deals with the ambiguities of the writers' relations: Scott's admiration of Hogg's poetry but his dislike of the prose and his wariness of Hogg's behaviour in company. J. H. Alexander in 'Hogg in the *Noctes Ambrosiane*' (4.37–47) writes interestingly about Hogg's the persona in the *Noctes*. Alexander argues that this persona was a good deal closer to Hogg than has previously been recognized. I found this a fascinating article, full of detailed and informative comment. Giovanni Pelizza writes of 'The Fortunes of James Hogg in Italy' (4.48–56) discussing the translation and reception of Hogg's *Confessions* in Italy, and

Antony J. Hasler's 'Reading the Land: James Hogg and the Highlands' (4.57–82) describes Hogg's sly inspection of the Highland Mythopoesis. Douglas S. Mack's 'The Stirling/South Carolina Edition of James Hogg: Thoughts on Editorial Policy' (4.83–90) discusses the problems posed by Hogg's work for editors working on the new edition. *SHW* also prints an alternative version, hitherto unknown, of Hogg's poem 'A Sunday Pastoral by the Ettrick Shepherd' (4.94–108) edited by Peter Garside. *SHW* is a fine journal replete with information and discussion of the work of Hogg and the context of his works. Gillian H. Hughes has performed sterling service in putting it together.

An important publication for Romantic studies is Satya S. Pachori's *Sir William Jones: A Reader*. The importance of the work of Jones for an understanding of Romanticism has only recently become apparent as Nigel Leask's book (reviewed above) makes very clear. Future publications on Jones are imminent, but for the present we should be grateful for Pachori's selection from the work of this prominent philologist, poet, translator, orientalist, juror, and father of comparative studies. Jones's works have not been republished since 1807 and this is the first time they have been edited and annotated. This *Reader* is organized into three sections: Literature; Language and Linguistics; and Religion, Mythology, and Metaphysics. Included are Jones's translation of the entire *Gita-Govinda* of Jayadeva and the complete text of Kalidasa's drama *Shakuntala* which so captivated Goethe. This will be a very useful volume for university libraries to have. With that mention of Goethe I should also note here that Woodstock have reprinted in facsimile Goethe's *Faust 1833*.

Wonderful Woodstock have printed two more very useful facsimiles to own or for libraries to buy. The very influential orientalist poem by Walter Savage Landor, *The Gebir 1798* has been printed with a good introduction by Jonathan Wordsworth which tackles Landor's idiosyncratic, but ultimately rewarding style (and how Landor touches the 'eyeballs' of our hearts). But Woodstock's finest reprint of the year must be the handsome quarto of Southey and Coleridge's *Joan of Arc 1796*. Wordsworth's introduction to this epic poem concentrates on the intellectual contribution of Coleridge's ideas about an active universe. As Wordsworth puts it: 'Leaving aside Blake's *Songs of Experience* and *Book of Urizen* no work of the mid 1790s suggests so strongly the transmuting of political energies released by the Revolution into the new creative and spiritual impulse that is Romanticism'. Not available for review last year was Cornelis de Deugd's 'Friendship and Romanticism: Robert Southey and Willem Bilderdijk' in *Europa Provincia Mundi* edited by Joep Leerssen and Karl Ulrich Syndram (1992). This describes the friendship between the two men begun in 1825. Bilderdijk was a prolific writer of verse, author of the celebrated 'The Art of Poetry' and de Deugd finds many similarities between the two men. This biographical account of the two men's meeting and their mutual interests will be of much interest to Southey scholars.

Another important publication of the year is Stuart Curran's *The Poems of Charlotte Smith* in the series Women Writers in English 1350–1850. Smith is certainly an excellent poet who was extremely influential on the writers of her age, especially with regard to the sonnet revival. For Curran she is 'the first poet in England whom in retrospect we would call Romantic'. Curran argues that 'absorbed in style and thought into the mainstream of Romantic poetry, Smith's fate was to encourage the creativity of other poets and become herself by the second half of the nineteenth century largely forgotten by literary history'. Curran provides a fine introduction to Smith's life and work and clear unobtrusive annotations to the poetry. This is a good edition which will go a long way in raising Smith's profile as an important and influential poet of the period. I also note that a facsimile of Smith's late volume of poems *Beachy Head and Other Poems* was apparently published this year by Scholars's Facsimiles and Reprints but I have not seen a copy of this.

Little has appeared which is specifically on Romantic drama, although one major monograph has been published justifying my claim of last year that interest in the drama of the period has been much more prevalent in recent years, as work by Alan Richardson, Jeffrey N. Cox, Frederick Burwick and Julie Carlson has shown (*YWES* 73.393–4). Daniel P. Watkins's *A Materialist Critique of English Romantic Drama* is a Marxist account of several plays of the period, including Wordsworth's *The Borderers*, Coleridge's *Osorio*, Joanna Baillie's *De Montfort*, Charles Lamb's *John Woodvil*, Henry Hart Milman's *Fazio*, Thomas Lovell Beddoes's *The Bride's Tragedy*, Scott's *Halidon Hill*, and Byron's dramas. Watkins uses a materialist methodology to explain some of the historical dimensions of English Romantic drama. He is concerned primarily 'with the way meanings are put forward in dramatic texts produced under the pressures of the structural transformation of British society that culminated in the late eighteenth and early nineteenth centuries'. By writing on the drama Watkins strives to displace attention from the privileged Romantic lyric in order to challenge conventional literary critical approaches to Romanticism. Watkins takes up Raymond Williams's central point that English drama was unable to cope with the rise of nineteenth-century class structures and thus its work became artistically marginalized or vulgarized. Watkins argues that 'Romantic dramas portray (as dramas had done since the Renaissance) the actions of an aristocratic class, while, at another, deeper level, they betray (to a much greater extent than Renaissance drama) an antagonistic consciousness that is necessarily and powerfully bourgeois'. This point is illustrated in Watkins's account of *The Borderers* where the drama's 'decided resistance to bourgeois intellectualism – its condemnation of the villain, Rivers – leads it ideologically and inevitably into the trap of bourgeois subjectivity and sentimentality'. Watkins attempts to solve the enigma of the disparity between the fullness of the Romantics' poetry and their failure to write great drama by recourse to the alienation of the private from the public at the level of the political unconscious: 'this shift of imaginative emphasis from public to personal life paralyzes dramatic representation, which depends upon dynamic social exchange for its content'. So too does Coleridge's *Osorio* advance 'a bourgeois position not only against aristocratic authority but also against lower-class needs, desires, and claims'. Watkins's thesis makes sense, but he does not define his notion of the bourgeoisie to any great extent. To what degree were Wordsworth, Coleridge and the rest unconscious spokesmen of an ideology that had been arriving on the English stage for some considerable time is a question that Watkins does not address in any detail, and while the essays on the individual plays are suggestive, there is no real sense of late eighteenth-century theatrical context. In particular, what about the success of Sheridan's plays? Nevertheless, this is another important book of interest to students of Romanticism, Romantic drama, Marxist theory and, in particular, the plays of Byron. The final monograph I would like to mention in this year's piece is William C. Reeve's *Kleist on Stage, 1804–1987* which discusses the fluctuating fortunes of the German Romantic dramatist Heinrich von Kleist. Reeve's book is divided into seven chapters, each one discussing one of Kleist's seven completed plays. Especially interesting is Reeve's treatment of *Penthesilea* notoriously 'das meist gefürchtete Drama deutscher Sprache'.

2.   Non-Fictional Prose

Some of the best work this year is on women's writing and the connections between gender and politics. Helen Maria Williams features strongly alongside Mary Wollstonecraft. Mary A. Favret's *Romantic Correspondence: Women, Politics and the Fiction of Letters* attempts to 'revise the familiar fiction of the letter in literature' and to 'demonstrate how the sentimental fiction of letters disguises, in part, a revolutionary politics'. In her opening chapter, she reviews the significance of the letter in contemporary literary theory and details its historical importance by analysing the 'symbolic use of correspondence in England's reaction to the French revolution'. She sees the work of women writers in the Romantic period as a re-imagining of epistolary possibilities which questions the creation of a feminine space 'detached from the world of business, politics and philosophy'. Via a detour on spy correspondence in the 1790s involving Stone, Priestley, Cobbett and others, Favret addresses Helen Maria Williams's creation of 'a new and unsettling history in letters'. She carefully charts the differences between the various volumes of Williams's *Letters* showing how she 'abandons the strategies of spectacle and containment' to allow for change and movement in Volume 2, and how, more generally, the letter in Williams's texts moves through a loss of representational innocence to a recognition of its being the very substance of history. Through the kaleidoscopic and discontinuous nature of her *Letters*, Favret argues, Williams escapes the confinement of 'feminine' discourse. In her chapter on Wollstonecraft, Favret argues passionately for an understanding of *Letters Written During a Short Residence in Sweden, Norway, and Denmark* which moves beyond an appreciation of a proto-Romantic sensibility. Once again, she emphasizes the 'commerce' of Wollstonecraft's deployment of the multifaceted letter form and offers an insightful assessment of Wollstonecraft's strategic wooing of the public as the text trades between imagination and political economy. She then goes on to consider Austen and *Frankenstein* in the light of her thesis before concluding with a short chapter on De Quincey's *The English Mail-Coach* in which she cleverly focuses her concern for the transformations between the 'dangerously politicized letter and "helpless" femininity'.

In *Women, Writing, and Revolution 1790–1827*, Gary Kelly extends his thesis on Wollstonecraft in *Revolutionary Feminism* about the connection between gender, bourgeois revolution and print culture to include Helen Maria Williams, Mary Hays, and Elizabeth Hamilton. He divides his book neatly between the revolutionary decade and what he calls the 'revolutionary aftermath'; and each of the three women writers is given a separate chapter either side of this divide. Through a deft weaving together of biographical narrative, historical context and contemporary reception, Kelly presents an impressively detailed and lucidly argued account of the different ways in which all three writers attempted to feminize key modes of male-dominated literary culture. In particular, he is good at revealing how, in the 1790s, women writers deployed sensibility to suit their aims and how they rewrote the ideology of the domestic woman. He shows how Williams, in *Letters from France*, writes of revolution from the perspective of 'feminized domesticity', how Hays deploys sensibility in order to particularize philosophy, and how Hamilton, often for anti-Jacobin and anti-feminist purposes, in *Letters of a Hindoo Rajah* and *Memoirs of Modern Philosophers*, 'blend[s] discourses conventionally differentiated by gender'. In the second half of his book, Kelly argues convincingly for the inventiveness with which these writers resisted a process of 'remasculinization'. There is a good awareness of the changing relationship between genre and gender in Kelly's well-informed account of women's writing in this period − particularly travel writing and biography − even if, at times, the actual processes of feminization and remasculinization are too easily taken for granted.

Chris Jones's *Radical Sensibility: Literature and Ideas in the 1790s* usefully addresses the varieties of eighteenth-century sensibility which pre-date its manifestation in the revolutionary decade. Jones seeks to extend analysis of the subject beyond recent accounts which, he claims, have polarized it as either radical or conservative, and which have stressed its origin in physical matter. Following Raymond Williams, Jones wishes to elevate it into a 'structure of feeling'. He begins with a survey of earlier eighteenth-century theorists, including Locke, Shaftesbury, Hutcheson, Hume, Smith, Ferguson, Millar, Kames and Blair, in which he details how 'radical, conservative and self-indulgent forms of sensibility' were able to coexist in the earlier period. In his chosen revolutionary decade, however, Jones claims that the Hume/Smith line of sensibility was 'triumphant' and that Burke's *Reflections* was the major factor in separating its conservative and radical aspects. There are welcome chapters on Godwin and Wollstonecraft, Helen Maria Williams's *Letters from France*, and Charlotte Smith's novels, before the final chapter on Wordsworth. Throughout these detailed and conscientious commentaries, Jones shows how sensibility had great difficulty in attaching itself to the term 'radical', and Godwin emerges as the figure whose writings, for Jones, most articulately register the pressures and contradictions embodied in what he refers to as this 'Janus-faced' concept.

There are two high quality and substantial articles on the most prominent women prose writers in *Studies in Romanticism*. In 'Nasty Tricks and Tropes: Sexuality and Language in Mary Wollstonecraft's *Rights of Woman*' (*SIR* 32.177–209), Tom Furniss cleverly situates Wollstonecraft's engagement with femininity through Burke's aesthetics and the revolution controversy with Paine. Throughout, he is careful to define a politically and historically responsible act of deconstructive analysis which is alert to the complexity of Wollstonecraft's negotiation of femininity through manners and education. According to Furniss, 'Wollstonecraft's reading of Burke can therefore become an exemplary reading of the complexities of reading'. In her 'Spectatrice as Spectacle: Helen Maria Williams at Home in Revolution' (*SIR* 32.273–95), Mary A. Favret addresses the 'inside/out structure of Williams's correspondence' in which her home is 'a social space and mythologized space'. According to Favret, Williams 'domesticates public spectacle' in the act of representing revolution and claims the heart 'as the "natural terrain of politics"'. Janet Todd's *Gender, Art, and Death* contains two valuable chapters on Wollstonecraft. In 'Wollstonecraft and the Rights of Death' (102–19) she provides a fascinating cultural history of suicide in relation to gender and revolutionary rationalism in order to focus on the complex of meanings which mediate the writer's own suicide attempts. Given Wollstonecraft's complex intersection with the ideology of femininity, Todd is careful to stress that the suicide attempt at Putney Bridge is not 'a literary and heroic revolutionary event', but she wishes to retain the possibility that it 'may *also* be seen as both rational and revolutionary'. In the next chapter, entitled 'Thoughts on the Death of Fanny Wollstonecraft' (120–35), Todd meditates in a more straightforwardly biographical way on the complex of domestic, familial, literary and romantic contexts within the Godwin household which surround the death by suicide of Wollstonecraft's older daughter.

A much less prominent figure is dealt with in 'Anne Lister of Shibden Hall, Halifax (1791–1840): Her Diaries and the Historians' (*HWJ* 35.45–77), where Jill Liddington offers a scholarly and intriguing 'historiographical overview' of the 4 million word labyrinth of Lister's diaries. She carefully charts the successive images of Lister produced during the nineteenth and twentieth centuries from attitudes to the author's lesbian sexual identity and from varying degrees of access to the archive. She provides samples from the diaries and ends with some tentative questions as to the historical significance of Lister's writings.

Julie Carlson's 'Impositions of Form: Romantic Antitheatricalism and the Case Against Women' (*ELH* 60.149–79), following Schiller, addresses the relationship between the 'play-drive' and the state in Romantic writing's representation of, and response to, woman on the stage. She moves from Burke's aesthetic categories and his treatment of Marie-Antoinette in the *Reflections* to a detailed analysis of Hazlitt's engagement with women and theatricality. She exposes some of the strategies by which Romantic male writers domesticate women's power, and she offers a trenchant critique of the way in which Hazlitt 'reveals the male bonding at the heart of heterosexuality and the aesthetic nation' in his *Liber Amoris*. Her powerfully argued and stimulating essay concludes with an analysis of various responses to Mrs Siddons in the role of Lady Macbeth which, she argues, 'reflect[s] the logic and the limit of analyzing the period's antitheatricalism as a defense against women'.

There is also good work on male prose writers of the period. The link between Burke's *A Philosophical Enquiry into the Origin of our Ideas of the Sublime and Beautiful* and his *Reflections on the Revolution in France* has become a familiar topic of study, particularly for literary specialists. Tom Furniss's *Edmund Burke's Aesthetic Ideology* also focuses on the relationship between these two texts, but it offers a more wide-ranging and more sustained analysis than previous commentators have done. Furniss is rightly concerned to avoid the dangers of oversimplifying, psycho-biographical readings of Burke, and rather than attempting to resolve the apparent contradictions between Burke's texts, he is, instead, concerned to see the contradictions within them as evidence of a more general ideological formation. According to Furniss's argument, 'Burke's theory is constituted as a solution for problems intrinsic to the hegemonic struggle of the middle class in mid-eighteenth-century Britain'. His ideological critique of the grounding of the aesthetic of the sublime provides the base for a subtle analysis of the *Reflections* which resists the temptation to speculate on the timing of a switch in Burke's opinions. In Furniss's account, the *Reflections* comes alive as a text which sees the dangerous potential in the earlier treatise on the sublime not so much because of its prescience or its prophetic qualities as its ability to dramatize and engender its own critique. More consideration of Burke's aesthetic ideology in relation to India and Ireland would have been welcome, and more attention could have been given to Burke's significance as a political thinker for the nineteenth century, but, within the scope it sets for itself, Furniss's book offers an intense and thorough analysis of the *Enquiry* and the *Reflections*. Along the way there are valuable analyses of Burke's ideas on nature, gender and custom, and Furniss also offers some tentative, but fascinating, speculations on the relationship between Burke's vision of political economy and Romantic aesthetics.

In '"To forge a new language": Burke and Paine' (*PSt* 16.iii.179–92), Richard V. McLamore briefly examines Paine's critique of Burke's patriarchal ideology in his *Reflections on the Revolution in France*, and makes the claim that critics have underestimated the power of Paine's deconstruction of 'monarchist symbology' and his 'melding of kinship, language, and politics'.

There are two 'pioneering' essays on Cobbett. In 'The Medium of Landscape in Cobbett's *Rural Rides*' (*SEL* 33.825–40) James Mulvihill views Cobbett through the eyes of Romantic literary culture and identifies an incremental perspective and a 'civil grammar' operating in *Rural Rides*. Whereas his Romantic contemporaries Wordsworth and Coleridge 'may have found a medium of divine immanence' in landscape, Mulvihill argues that 'for Cobbett it was a medium of national immanence'. Lionel Basney's '"How the Matter Stood": Cobbett's Moral and Political Ecology' (*SR* 101.354–74) also makes out a belated pioneering case for the study of Cobbett's prose writings. Starting from the rather too straightforward position that 'Cobbett's only job is to see and record the significant fact', he moves on to a consideration of Cobbett's moral particularity, his persuasiveness and his bizarre theory of depopulation. Basney wishes, rightly, to defend Cobbett from the tag of simple nostalgia and looks to a period when he 'may be reclaimed from parody as a naïve nature lover and an assailant of policies he didn't understand' and when he can be 'seen more as a passionate diarist of a profoundly ecological vision'.

Notes and Queries contains three items on Romantic prose writers. In 'John Payne Collier's Contributions to the *Edinburgh Magazine* (1817–1826)' (*N&Q* 40.37), Oskar Wellens identifies ten essays by Collier on pre-Shakespearian dramatists, while Stanley Jones in 'Hazlitt, Coleridge, and Edward Young: Unidentified Quotations' (*N&Q* 40.470–1) provides references for four unidentified or wrongly identified quotations in the P. P. Howe edition of *The Complete Works of William Hazlitt*. In a more extended piece, Mark Philp gives us the benefit of his research on the manuscript of *Political Justice* which reveals an extensive false start and an indebtedness to French views on government in the draft material.

Highlights from this year's issues of the *Charles Lamb Bulletin* include Nicola Trott's '"The Old Margate Hoy" and Other Depths of Elian Credulity' (*ChLB* 83.47–59), which sees Lamb as an ironic fantasist who engages in oblique confession, and which offers an interesting insight into his theatrical imagination; Elena Yatzek's 'Godwin's *Life of Chaucer*: Making Virtue of Necessity' (*ChLB* 84.126–35) which addresses Godwin's 'twin doctrines of necessity and perfectibility' in the years after *Political Justice*; Bonnie Woodberry's 'Lamb's Early Satire of the Economists' (*ChLB* 81.26–30) which suggests that Lamb was less ignorant about economics than Hazlitt would have us believe; and, more briefly, Barry Symonds's '*The Stranger's Grave*: Laying a De Quinceyan Ghost' (*ChLB* 83.105–7) which establishes that the novel was, in fact, the work of George Robert Gleig. A new selection of Lamb's letters and essays is available in J. E. Morpurgo's edition *Charles Lamb and Elia: Selected Writings* which, as the title suggests, takes a rather straightforwardly biographical approach to its subject. The introduction is rather bland and the edition lacks any helpful notes.

The Wordsworth Circle this year has a good assortment of contributions on prose writers. Two of these concentrate on the significance of De Quincey's encounter with the Malay at the door of Dove Cottage which he relates in his *Confessions of an English Opium-Eater*. Charles Rzepka's 'De Quincey and the Malay: Dove Cottage Idolatry' (*WC* 24.180–5) explores the encounter in terms of social reputation and literary fame. He sees the Malay in De Quincey's text as a 'dangerous reader' who is, ingeniously, a *doppelgänger* of the younger De Quincey and 'in part, the demonic incarnation of Wordsworth'. By comparison, Daniel Sanjiv Roberts's 'Exorcising the Malay: Dreams and the Unconscious in Coleridge and De Quincey' (*WC* 24.91–6) lacks daring, but it does offer some useful observations on the fraught interaction between the two writers. In 'Thomas De Quincey, Clinician' (*WC* 24.170–7), John C. Lang argues from the evidence of De Quincey's writings that: 'Romantic medicine is not merely one of an amalgam of dialogisms; it is part of the structure and point of view, a model for mimesis, and a way of thinking about characters and events'. According to Lang, De Quincey 'sees and hears with a clinician's eyes and ears'. The more familiar territory of the relationship between narrative, consciousness and order in De Quincey's autobiographical writings is the subject of Curtis Perry's 'Piranesi's Prison: Thomas De Quincey and the Failure of Autobiography' (*SEL* 33.809–24). In his brief, but lucid contribution to this subject, he argues that in the *Confessions* De Quincey embarks on 'a remarkably fragile autobiographical project' in which 'the text both doubts and tests its own narrative control'. He then moves on to a consideration of 'The Household Wreck' in order to establish De Quincey's breaking down of the divide between autobiography and fiction.

There are three brief, but welcome contributions to the study of print culture in the period. Kevin Gilmartin has an interesting essay entitled 'The Press on Trial: Form and Imagination in Early Nineteenth-century Radical Culture' (*WC* 24.144–7) which focuses on Wooler and Cobbett in their attempts to 'forge an oppositional public sphere that united speech and print'. Gilmartin argues for a greater appreciation of the radical press in order to produce alternative literary histories of the period. Mark Schoenfield's 'Regulating Standards: The *Edinburgh Review* and the Circulations of Judgement' (*WC* 24.148–51) focuses on the *Edinburgh*'s attack on Wordsworth from the point of view of 'system', paper-money and the aesthetic judgements of the liberal market-place; and in 'Parody and the Anti-Jacobin' (*WC* 24.162–6) Graeme Stones argues that the magazine renewed 'the energy of parody as social critique' and made it a more respectable form of creativity. Following Iain McCalman's important work on the radical underworld of the 1790s, Jon Mee in 'Examples of Safe Printing: Censorship and Popular Radical Literature in the 1790s' (*E&S* 81–95) offers what he sees as a corrective to John Barrell's concentration on philosophical radicalism in his work on the Treason Trials where he foregrounds the 'dream of a language transparent in relation to Truth'. Mee stresses the distinction between philosophical and popular radicalism in order to show how the law of seditious libel determined the very different textual strategies of radicals such as Eaton and Spence, which include their reworkings of Spenser and Aesop.

Scholars working on political prose will be grateful for Gregory Claeys's handsome edition of Robert Owen's *Selected Works*. It contains an extensive and helpful introduction which provides a good guide to the life, the development of Owen's political thought, and to his publications.

3. Fictional Prose

A moderate year in terms of publications on the romantic novel, with probably the greatest emphasis being on Mary Shelley's *Frankenstein*, although some of Shelley's other novels have been given an airing and some critical commentary as well. A few books on Jane Austen, a lot of interest in the Gothic and a timely reprint of William Godwin's memoir of Mary Wollstonecraft are among other highlights.

Marie Mulvey Roberts and Roy Porter have provided us with an interesting angle on the eighteenth-century novel in *Literature and Medicine During the Eighteenth Century*. This is a varied collection of essays, some concentrating on specific writers, some on more general or historical aspects. The editors draw a parallel between literature and medicine by saying that 'medicine protects life and literature interprets it, that both are in some sense both diagnostic and therapeutic'. This is an interesting thought and though the connection between preservation and interpretation may seem tenuous, the significance of the growth in scientific thought during the Enlightenment and as a background to the rise of the novel is highly relevant, if not essential, and on this basis the book works fairly well. Pat Rogers's essay on 'The Novel And The Rise of Weight-Watching' is precise, detailed and contains the occasional surprise, as it describes what appears to be the beginnings of the dieting industry, informing the reader that a preoccupation with weight and diet was initially a male concern. Reasons immediately suggest themselves for this, particularly when one considers that late eighteenth- and early nineteenth-century male fashion required the masculine physique to be in good condition: it is one of the rare periods in costume history when male fashion was as restrictive, if not more so, than that for females. One can flick through the pages of novels set in this period and find constant reference to men needing 'a good leg' or 'good shoulders' or to men wearing very high starched shirt collars. Pat Rogers doesn't explore this, which is a pity, although the specific medical and historical detail he does provide is meticulous, including the first-known date of individuals actually weighing themselves. Rogers's chapter takes us into the nineteenth century, moving from brief discussions of *Sir Launcelot Greaves*, *Tom Jones* and *Pride and Prejudice* to *Martin Chuzzlewit*, and is ultimately vaguely unsatisfactory in that the amount of literary examples provided does not match the detail of the historical material. However, it offers new information on a subject which has been more extensively researched in recent years, and leads very nicely into Gloria Sybil Gross's essay on illness and Jane Austen. The subject of illness, particularly of hunger, and literature has merited much critical attention in recent years: Maud Ellman's *The Hunger Artists* and Helena Michie's *The Flesh Made Word* are just two examples which come to mind. Gross's chapter looks at the occurrence of nerves, jitters, palpitations and headaches as devices which are frequently the object of Jane Austen's satire, and she identifies, correctly, that these are usually female methods of manipulation or exertion of will (there are notable exceptions, of course, such as Mr Woodhouse in *Emma*). Gross's premise is not, however, that these 'flights into illness' were related to female powerlessness – a more usual reading of the cultural context of female illness – but that 'Jane Austen imagined the ignominy of "flights into illness" [...] There is a touching arrogance about Austen's wish that mind triumph over matter, that, like the blazoned heroes of old, we take our chances with the ineluctable forces of nature.' It is a nicely specific reading which, like Pat Rogers's preceding chapter, provides a different angle on some familiar ground. John Wiltshire, in a later essay, provides a reading on Fanny Burney and her health, which focuses squarely on her life rather than relating it to her fiction, and there are also essays on *Tristram Shandy*, *Gulliver's Travels*, Swift and Hogarth. I was rather surprised by the omission of *Clarissa* from any extended discussion, although Lynn Salkin Sbiroli's final essay on the biological and ideological role of women in pre-revolutionary and revolutionary France is an intriguing diversion in a book which concentrates on English literature. *Literature and Medicine* offers many new insights, but it failed to convince me completely of the editors' premise, stated earlier, concerning the connection between medicine and literature. This may well be because the organization of the book, and in some cases the structure of the essays, suggests a separation between medical and literary discourse, rather than a connection between or unification of them. However, this is still a very worthwhile book.

The Significance of Sibling Relationships in Literature is another collection of essays, edited by JoAnna Stephens Mink and Janet Doubler Ward. This hugely varied collection covers the eighteenth to the twentieth centuries, and includes essays on early sibling relationships in novels from Charlotte Lennox to Susan Ferrier, and sister/brother relationships in Fanny Burney, Emily Brontë and George Eliot. More wide-ranging – and therefore less focused – than Tess Cosslett's book on female friendship, or Lillian Faderman's *Surpassing the Love of Men*, this volume contains a lot of individually interesting observations rather than a clear and coherent overview of sibling relationships. The editors' introduction traces the biblical/historical context of sibling ties, but the ordering of the subsequent essays seemed rather odd, at least to this reader. The essays are collected to discuss only children, opposite-sex siblings and then same-sex siblings; unfortunately, this necessitates much historical and cultural jumping around, going from essays on George Eliot, *fin de siècle* and Eudora Welty, back to Charlotte Lennox and Susan Ferrier and forward again to Christina Rossetti and Toni Morrison. Certainly, the book would have benefited from sectioning the essays so that the principles of organization were more evident. This is not to denigrate the quality of the essays themselves, or indeed the editors' intentions: the introduction clearly demonstrates their commitment to their subject, although I think their discussion of the Biblical or historical aspects could have been extended. The book suffers, fundamentally, because of either a lack of structure or an explication of the structure it exhibits.

Chris Jones's *Radical Sensibility: Literature and Ideas in the 1790s* traces the manifestation of sensibility in the 1790s and its influence on the work of Godwin, Wollstonecraft, Helen Maria Williams, Charlotte Smith and Wordsworth. Closely researched and logically structured, Jones offers an historical and cultural context before placing the authors he chooses within it. Although he is concerned with the radical influence of sensibility, he doesn't ignore the 'other side', including a chapter on 'Sensibility in Reaction' which looks at the ways in which the backlash against sensibility was manifested. This is a specialized study, tightly focused and not straying from its premise, supplying a wealth of detail and information, whose complexity is suggestive in itself of the conflict and complexity of the period.

Birgitta Berglund's study of Radcliffe, Austen and Wollstonecraft in *Woman's Whole Existence: The House as an Image in the Novels of Ann Radcliffe, Mary Wollstonecraft and Jane Austen* considers the changes in women's roles during the eighteenth century, through the image of the house in some of the novels. As Berglund points out in her introduction, prior to the eighteenth century, because of the demands of home working, the house had been a very public domain, a place of industry with many servants and apprentices. By the eighteenth century this had changed considerably: the shift in working patterns, the growth of the middle class and the developing division between male and female roles meant that the house became a female domain: men went out to work, women remained at home. Berglund sees this as the beginnings of the cult of domesticity, of concern with home comfort, and the rise of the 'angel in the house'; but Berglund's premise is not just that the house was a place of confinement for women, a representation of their limited and marginalized role, but rather that the fictions of the period also contain a fear of expulsion from the house and a longing for the security which it provides, a viewpoint which has received far less critical consideration, perhaps because it could undermine the wish, which is sometimes manifested in feminist criticism, to appropriate all eighteenth- and nineteenth-century women novelists as feminists. Berglund's study explores this ambivalence, and points out, quite correctly, that although male writing of the period also concerns itself with imprisonment and liberty, male writers are far less equivocal in stating whether confinement is bad and liberty good, because, as Berglund states, they never have to consider the problems which 'liberty' can bring, problems which are, perhaps, essentially female. Berglund develops her discussion from Radcliffe, through Wollstonecraft (fiction and non-fiction) to Austen, in whose fiction the image of the house would seem to have a supreme significance, being intimately connected with money and property, and through these with courtship and marriage, all issues with which Austen is intimately concerned. Berglund sees Austen as a balance between Radcliffe and Wollstonecraft, between the paranoia (her word) of one, and the radicalism of the other: she exhibits some of the former, but is also able to ridicule it: she shows a clear awareness of the position of women, but instead of protesting or rebelling openly, she tries to deal with the conditions imposed on them, to find ways to survive and extend boundaries as far as possible. Of course, Austen is slippery, and difficult to pinpoint in terms of her stance on women's roles: and the implicit nature of her solution allows her, as Berglund says, 'to map out a pattern of survival for her young women without having to reveal what she really thinks of the society which they inhabit and which necessitates this strategy'. Berglund's study operates more as a comparative reading than as an exposition of a critical theory: her method is to work through a discussion of various works and suggest contrasts or similarities. I felt slightly frustrated by the brief conclusion, which seemed to side-step the issue by simply re-posing the question, and reiterating the differences already explored. However, individual discussions are close and detailed, and present a number of interesting observations.

Michelle A. Masse's *In The Name Of Love: Women, Masochism and the Gothic* (1992) actually moves a long way from the Gothic period, to considerations of how the Gothic motif operates in works such as *Jane Eyre*, *The Yellow Wallpaper*, *Rebecca* and *The Story of O*. The book is really about femininity and masochism, rather than Gothic fiction; Walpole's *The Castle of Otranto* and Radcliffe's *Mysteries of Udolpho* and *The Italian* are mentioned or discussed as examples, but Masse's intention lies more in examining the Gothic female archetype and its manifestation outside the realms of conventional Gothic. There is a lot on Freud; and Masse coins a new term, 'marital Gothic', which looks at the abuse or terrorization of women in marriage (one of the few times in which conventionally Gothic fictions are discussed). It is a very interesting approach: I only wonder if using the term 'the Gothic' in the title of the book is not slightly misleading, suggesting far more limitation than is actually there.

State of the Fantastic: Studies in the Theory and Practice of Fantastic Literature & Film, edited by Nicholas Ruddick (1992) falls slightly outside the area of this chapter, but includes essays on *Frankenstein* and M. G. Lewis. Based on conference papers, it meditates on fantasy and horror film through a variety of theoretical approaches and a range of subject-matter. Robert F. Geary's essay on Lewis is brief but interesting; there hasn't been much about Lewis this year.

Susan Wolstenholme has provided us with a delightful book on female Gothic, *Gothic (Re)Visions: Writing Women As Readers*. Dividing her book into two sections, 'What's Female About Gothic?' and 'Gothic Undone', Wolstenholme offers a reading of what she sees as female Gothic, and the relationships she perceives between notions of the Gothic and certain texts, including novels by Radcliffe, Shelley and Charlotte Brontë, and subsequently Harriet Beecher Stowe, George Eliot and Edith Wharton. It is a complex reading, as Wolstenholme takes us through a series of analyses which are based upon the idea of a multifaceted textual position for both the woman writer and reader. I particularly enjoyed the chapter on *Daniel Deronda*, which looks at the deployment of female Gothic through the lens of the mother, particularly the absent mother: and also the essay on *Villette*, which not only identifies Charlotte Brontë's propensity for the Gothic (fairly familiar ground) but also, as Wolstenholme puts it, describes her as 'rewriting Gothic to imitate, parody, and foreground the issue of what "Gothic vision" might be'. I have to say that the thread of Wolstenholme's argument is occasionally implicit rather than explicit: but nevertheless, this is a worthwhile read.

Anne K. Mellor's *Romanticism and Gender* is an exploration of constructions of gender in the work of both male and female writers of the period. Mellor looks at some female poets as well as novelists, and suggests that, rather than concerning themselves with either the sentimental or the sublime, these women were more interested in extolling the rational mind and thought process. Mellor argues very persuasively in her introduction that interpretations of romanticism have been gender-biased; and she structures her argument by looking first at gender in masculine romanticism, then in feminine romanticism, then at 'ideological cross-dressing', as she terms it, in John Keats and Emily Brontë. Mellor acknowledges the limitations of her model – 'the use of a model grounded on polarity is both theoretically dubious and critically confining' – and points out that binary models are already implicit and explicit in male romanticism. She suggests, therefore, the need to 'learn to think beyond a dialectic based on polarities'. Mellor's final premise is that 'masculine' and 'feminine' are ultimately 'endpoints on a continuum' – so, rather intriguingly, she structures her book on a certain model and then argues against it. This is probably one of the most important books to emerge on the subject, and certainly one of the most accessible: Mellor is always clear and concise, and the sense of overall vision remains explicit. An excellent book for scholars and students alike.

A substantial amount of work has appeared on Jane Austen this year. *Jane Austen at Play* by Kuldip Kaur Kuwahara describes her as a 'self-conscious novelist' who 'delights in playing with reality and illusion'. Kuwahara makes an argument in the introduction that all her novels are a kind of *Bildungsroman* for the hero and heroine, in which they make a journey and achieve a happy ending: 'In achieving balance and harmony within themselves and in their relationship, they learn to play'. I am not convinced that Jane Austen's endings are as unequivocally happy as all this: the hero and heroine may achieve a kind of understanding, but the problems which serve to keep them apart throughout the novel are not magically waved away by Austen at the end. I am, therefore, a little doubtful about Kuwahara's premise: also, the notion presented that Austen can 'play' because she is a 'serious novelist' or, at least, has serious concerns, seems to risk underestimating the sharpness, even occasional cruelty, of her satire. This is a close analysis, which makes many interesting points; but Kuwahara's own language is occasionally over-flowery (I have some difficulty in seeing Anne Elliott and Captain Wentworth as defining 'freedom and beauty' at the end of *Persuasion*) and the study has a tendency to interpret Austen one-sidedly.

Mansfield Park, edited by Nigel Wood, is a collection of critical essays, four to be exact, which look at both the novel specifically and issues to do with Jane Austen in general. I particularly liked Claudia L. Johnson's chapter on 'Gender, Theory and Jane Austen Culture', in which she makes reference to the 'theory resistant character of Jane Austen culture', and goes on to state that 'to the extent that I and others like me feel obliged to preface our discussion of theory, or feminism, or politics and Jane Austen with little apologies, we testify to the power of Janeism'. The intention of the chapter is to assert the possibility of gender-based readings of Austen, and to take issue with the concept that she cannot be read from such a perspective without substantial difficulty. As Johnson states, questions such as 'was Jane Austen a feminist?' are as irrelevant as questions as to whether, for example, she was a Tory. Johnson's argument rests, finally, on concluding that Austen displays no lack of awareness of the implications of her society specifically for women: and whether or not she is making political points, that awareness remains. This collection of essays is very useful for students looking at *Mansfield Park* (for whom, I presume, it was intended) since it covers a range of concerns in Jane Austen criticism, and is also a worthy addition for Austen scholars.

A Jane Austen Compendium: The Six Major Novels by Violet Powell, is an odd production: it summarizes and gives a précis of each of the novels, and relates them to aspects or events in Jane Austen's life. It is a curious, though interesting, project from a biographical point of view: but it leaves one simply with the desire to re-read the novels, which (seeing as Violet Powell is connected with the Jane Austen Society) may have been the intention. A book for fans, rather than scholars.

The Sayings of Jane Austen, edited by Maggie McKernan, is a collection of Austen's words of wisdom on such matters as love, marriage, folly and vice, ladies and gentlemen, etc. It reminds one of how very pithy and appropriate Austen always was, although it's a surprisingly slim volume for a writer whose novels contain so many observations. Quite useful for pulling out the odd quote, although, again, one is left with the longing to re-read the real thing.

Two editions of 'simplified' Jane Austen texts have been published this year. *Persuasion*, adapted by Robert Sellwood, has been published as part of Macmillan's Stories To Remember series and consists of a short Introduction followed by an abridged version of the novel. Designed for younger readers and non-native speakers, it also includes a glossary of terms. Similarly, Longman have brought out a simplified *Pride and Prejudice* which has been abridged by

Evelyn Attwood. It has an introduction as well as exercises for students written and devised by Gwyneth Roberts. This also includes a glossary of terms.

Pam Perkins's 'A Subdued Gaiety: The Comedy Of *Mansfield Park*' (*NCL* 48.1–25) suggests that Fanny and Mary are 'representative of two opposing comic traditions, those of sentimental comedy and laughing comedy'. Perkins intends to contrast the 'strengths and weaknesses of these two traditions, ultimately suggesting that neither is entirely satisfactory'. The article contrasts the verbal styles of the two girls in some detail and states that 'each woman has something to learn from the other'. *Mansfield Park* is perhaps, with the exception of *Persuasion*, the least 'comic' of Austen's novels, so it is interesting to come across a reading which attempts to locate it within a comic tradition: Fanny Price is, as Perkins says, not often perceived as funny. *SIR* contains Adela Pinch's 'Lost in a Book: Jane Austen's *Persuasion*' (32.97–117).

A number of works on Austen have not been available for review. These are: Jane Austen, *The Bedside Jane Austen* (Chancellor Press); Jane Austen, *Catharine and Other Writings*, edited by M. A. Doody and D. Murray (OUP); *The Complete Novels of Jane Austen* (HC); *The History of England by Jane Austen: A Facsimile of her Manuscript Written Aged 16, and Illustrated by her Sister Cassandra*, intro. Deirdre La Faye (Folio); Jane Austen, *Mansfield Park*, ed. P. Norris and intro. Peter Conrad (Wordsworth Classics); John Lauber, *Jane Austen* (Twayne); Alan Burton Melnick, *Everybody Requiring Something They Had Not: Fantasies of Sexual Identity and the Meaning of Jane Austen's Novels* (University de Lausanne); Maaja A. Stewart, *Domestic Realities & Imperial Fictions: Jane Austen's Novels in Eighteenth-Century Contexts* (UGeoP).

Two new editions of Maria Edgeworth's work have appeared this year, both published by Everyman. *Belinda*, Edgeworth's delightful comic novel, has been republished with an introduction by Eilean Ni Chuilleanain, and is an extraordinarily comprehensive version, including also a chronology, notes and critical extracts. Everyman have also republished *Letters For Literary Ladies*, edited by Claire Connolly, which also includes a chronology, introduction, notes and selected critical extracts. John G. Peters prints 'An Unpublished Letter from Maria Edgeworth to Eliza Fletcher' in *ELN* (30.44–52).

Work on Mary Shelley's fiction has been plentiful this year and several new editions of *Frankenstein* have appeared to compete with Johanna M. Smith's edition of the 1831 text in the Macmillan series Case Studies in Contemporary Criticism reviewed last year (*YWES* 73.404). Wordsworth Classics have offered their own cheap edition of the novel, using the 1818 text. I could not find any information about who edited this, although there is a short introduction. Nevertheless, Wordsworth Classics deserve praise for making this and other texts more cheaply available to students. Plume Books have published *The Essential Frankenstein: The Definitive Annotated Edition of Mary Shelley's Classic Novel* (as stated on the dust jacket) edited by Leonard Wolf with illustrations by Christopher Bing. This also uses the 1818 version, although it contains the 1831 introduction as well as an introduction by the editor, contemporary reviews, chronology, and selections from *Fantasmagoria*. This is a slightly lurid edition with fun illustrations. Another version of *Frankenstein* is aimed at a popular audience and to be found in a collection called Horror Classics, combining Shelley's novel with *Dracula* and *Dr. Jekyll and Mr. Hyde*. Billed on the dust jacket, in appropriate penny-dreadful style, as 'Terrifying Novels/Sensational Films', it uses the 1831 text and includes Mary Shelley's introduction. Finally for editions of *Frankenstein*, OUP in Hong Kong have included the novel in their Oxford Progressive English Readers series. This version is even more luridly and entertainingly illustrated than Woolf's. It is abridged and designed for non-native English learners. There is no information about editing or illustration, but it contains a section on Questions and Answers, intended to help with improving English.

Shelley's later novel *The Last Man* has also merited a new edition this year. UNebP have brought an edition, edited by Hugh J. Luke, Jr, and with an introduction by Anne K. Mellor. Mellor's introduction relates the issues of the novel to contemporary debates with great clarity: 'the novel articulates a profound critique of the dominant gender, cultural and political ideologies of the Romantic era, a critique so total that the novel becomes the first literary example of what we now call deconstruction'. This is an excellent edition, and Mellor has sectioned her introduction into accessible headings: biography, gender, romanticism, politics, deconstruction and AIDS. A brief chronology is also included.

Turning now to critical writing about Shelley's fiction. Jane Blumberg has written a study of other aspects of Mary Shelley's work. *Mary Shelley's Early Novels* is, at last, a work on Shelley which steers away from *Frankenstein* and reminds us that Mary Shelley did write other books. Blumberg does include an essay on *Frankenstein* – a study of Shelley's early novels could not really exclude it – but her reading is more focused on its place in the development of Shelley's thought than on any detailed reading of the text. This is the direction of the whole work: Blumberg's intent is to reconstruct Mary Shelley as an independent being with ideas and philosophies of her own, rather than perpetuating the image of her as chiefly an appendage of Shelley and Byron who just happened to write a rather extraordinary novel, by accident rather than design. Blumberg looks at early influences, and after dealing with *Frankenstein* she devotes space to discussions of *Valperga*, *The Last Man*, and, finally, to Shelley's role as literary executor of her husband's estate. Blumberg is not trying to establish that either *Valperga* or *The Last Man* are great novels, although *The Last Man* is becoming increasingly relevant to contemporary society. Rather, she is trying to trace the formulation and radicalism of Shelley's ideas, particularly as they began to move away from those of her husband and his circle. *The Last Man* also deserves the recent critical attention it is receiving because of its interest in 'plague' with all the contemporary resonances this carries. Blumberg's study is an admirable re-vision of Mary Shelley's work, life and attitudes, being both immensely readable as well as challenging.

Frankenstein: Mary Shelley's Wedding Guest, by Mary Lowe-Evans, is a short and original critical reading of the novel. Lowe-Evans bases her reading chiefly on the 1831 edition, for the reason that it 'is most widely available and discussed and the one that incorporates Mary Shelley's final revisions', although many Shelley editors now prefer the 1818 text which reflects more obviously Shelley's political and scientific interests at the time of composition. Lowe-Evans offers a new historicist reading, focusing particularly on the treatment in the novel of marriage, stating that 'The various marriage relationships in the novel represent an attempt to work out or write out not only Mary Shelley's but also her culture's discontents with the inequities implicit in the marriage-bond'. This is an unfamiliar if not original interpretation, although one that is not entirely convincing. I have not seen Audrey Fisch, Anne K. Mellor and Esther H. Schor, eds, *The Other Mary Shelley: Beyond Frankenstein* (OUP).

Vanessa D. Dickerson's 'The Ghost of a Self: Female Identity in Mary Shelley's Frankenstein' (*JPC* 27.79–91) argues that *Frankenstein* is a 'complex ghost story [...] the spectres of which are the female characters, whose spiritual and often passive role in the novel is such that the women are suspended in a shadow realm of powerlessness and potential power that ultimately skews their identity'. Dickerson explores the theme of the invisibility of *Frankenstein*'s women, finally concluding that, with the exception of Safie, they have only 'the ghost of a self'. An original and interesting article. Chris Baldick has contributed a short article about *Frankenstein* to *ER* (3.n.p.) which focuses chiefly on the gap between the *Frankenstein* media myth and the novel. Baldick also offers some brief suggestions on interpretations of Frankenstein. This is a much more general piece, for obvious reasons, than his other work on *Frankenstein* and the Gothic novel, but still very readable and attractively written.

Andrea Breemer Frantz has produced a short study called *Redemption and Madness: Three Nineteenth-Century Feminist Views On Motherhood and Childbearing*. The blurb on the back cover states that the 'discoveries and conclusions' of Ms Breemer Frantz are 'startling': I'm afraid I couldn't agree. Containing studies of *Frankenstein*, Gaskell's *Ruth* and Brontë's *Wuthering Heights*, each section is so brief and sketchy that I was hard pressed to find many conclusions or discoveries at all.

A fair amount of criticism on Scott has appeared this year. Three editions of his novels have been published as part of EdinUP's 'Edinburgh Edition of the Waverley Novels': *The Black Dwarf*, edited by Peter D. Garside; *Kenilworth*, edited by J. H. Alexander Scott; and *The Tale of Old Mortality*, edited by D. Mack. None were seen by me. Also unseen was Jane Stevenson's and Peter Davidson's edition of *Old Mortality* for World's Classics (OUP). One major collection of essays on Scott has appeared. *Scott In Carnival: Selected Papers from the Fourth International Scott Conference*, edited by J. H. Alexander and David Hewitt, is a huge collection of critical essays based on selected papers from the Fourth International Scott Conference in Edinburgh in 1991. The range of scholarship displayed is very impressive, including essays on Scott and historicism, Victorianism, in fact practically every aspect one could think of in connection with Scott. This is an essential collection for scholars of Scott. Paul A. Davis's 'Scott's Histories and Fiction in *Waverley* and the *Fictional Essays* (*R.E.A.L.: Yearbook of Research in English and American Literature* 9) aims to 'trace the use of oppositions such as truth/fiction and history/romance from late eighteenth century theory of historiography to Scott's use of the oppositions in his expository writing and, finally, in his historical romance'. *N&Q* contains Murray H. Pittock's 'Scott and the Templars: A Note on *Waverley*' (40.461). Regrettably, I have not seen Donald Sultana's *From Abbotsford To Paris and Back: Sir Walter Scott's Journey of 1815*; Richard Humphries's study of *Waverley* for CUP's series Landmarks in World Literature; Henri Suhamy's *Sir Walter Scott* (Editions de Fallois, Paris); Michael C. Gamer's 'Marketing a Masculine Romance: Scott, Antiquarianism, and the Gothic' (*SIR* 32.523–50); Michael Ragussis's 'Writing Nationalist History: England, the Conversion of the Jews and *Ivanhoe*' (*ELH* 60.185–215) or Katie Trumpener's 'National Character, Nationalist Plots: National Tale & Historical Novel in the Age of Waverley 1806–1830' (*ELH* 60.685–731).

Not too much has appeared this year on William Godwin. Woodstock Books have published a facsimile reprint of the 1798 edition of his *Memoirs of*

Wollstonecraft, with an introduction by Jonathan Wordsworth. The introduction is brief, but this is not a problem, since the autobiographical nature of the text, a celebration of Godwin's marriage to Wollstonecraft, is full of interest. Godwin gives a remarkably truthful account; he does not avoid the negative aspects or problems of their married life, and gives a fair evaluation of Wollstonecraft's work and ideas. But this memoir remains, primarily, a significantly tender tribute to their relationship. *The Political and Philosophical Writings of William Godwin* (7 volumes [P&C]) was not made available for review, and I have not seen A. Sullivan Garnett Jr's 'A Story to be Hastily Gobbled Up: *Caleb Williams* and Print Culture' (*SIR* 32.323–37) or Gary Handwerk's 'Of Caleb's Guilt and Godwin's Truth: Ideology and Ethics in *Caleb Williams*' (*ELH* 60. 939–60).

I have come across a very impressive edition of Charles Maturin's *Melmoth the Wanderer*, published by The Folio Society. Devendra P. Varma's short introduction places the novel in a historical and cultural context, and the edition is illustrated by Felix Zakar. The illustrations are extraordinary, both colourful and nightmarish, and the edition is beautifully bound and decorated with skulls and devils. It sounds lurid, but it isn't; definitely an item for collectors. Also on *Melmoth* is Amy Elizabeth Smith's 'Experimentation and "Horrid Curiosity" in Maturin's *Melmoth the Wanderer*' (*ES* 74.524–35).

I must briefly refer to a book that came to me which probably falls slightly outside the remit of this chapter: *The Apparition in the Glass: Charles Brockden Brown's American Gothic* by Bill Christophersen. This, as the title suggests, is concerned with American Gothic, specifically Brockden Brown's attempts, within his fiction, to reflect the new Republic of America in the 1790s, not only its celebration of a new-found freedom, but also its doubts and dilemmas that are an inevitable result of liberation. It is worth reading for its reflections on post-independence America. Although knowing little about the work of Brown, I found the chapters relating to American history of particular interest.

Finally, I have not seen the following books: Pamela Clemitt's *The Godwinian Novel* (OUP); Bradford K. Mudge, *British Romantic Novelists 1789–1832* (Gale, 1992), or Ann Radcliffe's *A Sicilian Romance*, ed. Alison Millbank (WC, OUP).

Books Reviewed

Alexander, J. H., and David Hewitt, eds. *Scott In Carnival: Selected Papers from the Fourth International Scott Conference*. AberdeenUP. ISBN 0 9488 7720 0.

Austen, Jane. *Persuasion*. Adapted by Richard Sellwood. Stories To Remember. Macmillan. pb £2.50. ISBN 0 333 58914 9.

——. *Pride & Prejudice Simplified*. Simplified by Evelyn Attwood and introduction by Gwyneth Roberts. Longman. ISBN 0 582 52913 1.

——. *Pride and Prejudice*. Edited by P. Norris and introduction by Peter Conrad. Dent. pp. 317.

Austen-Leigh, William, and Richard Arthur. *Jane Austen: Her Life and Letters. A Family Record*. Revised by Deirdre La Faye. Reprint Services Corporation. pp. 326. $99. ISBN 0 7812 7427 3.

Beake, Fred. *The Imaginations of Mr Shelley*. Usalz. pp. 68. pb £5. ISBN 3 705 20930 2.

Beddoes, Thomas Lovell. *The Bride's Tragedy 1822*. Revolution and Romanticism. Woodstock. pp.180. £25. ISBN 1 854 77130 2.

Beer, John. *Against Finality*. CUP. pp. 46. pb £5.95. ISBN 0 521 45954 0.

——. *Romantic Influences: Contemporary-Victorian-Modern*. Macmillan. pp. 303. £35. ISBN 0 333 43915 5.

Berglund, Birgitta. *Woman's Whole Existence: The House as an Image in the Novels of Ann Radcliffe, Mary Wollstonecraft and Jane Austen*. Lund Studies In English 84. LundU. pp. 244. Sek196, £19.95. ISBN 0 862 38332 3.

Blank, G. Kim, and Margot K. Louis, eds. *Influence and Resistance in Nineteenth-Century English Poetry*. Macmillan. pp. 306. £35. ISBN 0 333 56381 6.

Blumberg, Jane. *Mary Shelley's Early Novels*. UIowaP. pp. 257. $27.95. ISBN 0 87745 397 7.

Bourke, Richard. *Romantic Discourse and Political Modernity*. HW. pp. 353. £42.50. ISBN 0 745 01318 X.

Brotemarkle, Diane. *Imagination and Myth in John Keats's Poetry*. Mellen. pp. 164. $79.95. ISBN 0 773 42214 5.

Burns, Robert. *Collected Works of Robert Burns*. 6 vols. Routledge/Thoemmes Press. pp. 349. 351. 362. 391. 463. 435. £350. ISBN 0 415 09918 8.

——. *The Songs of Robert Burns*. Ed. Donald A. Low. Routledge. pp. 962. £120. ISBN 0 415 03414 0.

Byron, George Gordon, Lord. *The Complete Poetical Works*. Vol. VII. Ed. Jerome J. McGann. Clarendon. pp. 445. £50. ISBN 0 198 12328 0.

——. *Selected Poems*. Dover Thrift Editions. Dover. pp. 103. pb £0.95. ISBN 0 486 27784 4.

——. *The Prisoner of Chillon 1816*. Romanticism and Revolution. Woodstock. pp. 60. £18. ISBN 1 854 77133 7.

Chase, Cynthia. *Romanticism*. Longman Critical Readers. Longman. pp. 285. hb £29, pb £11.99. ISBN 0 582 05000 6, 0 582 04799 4.

Christensen, Jerome. *Lord Byron's Strength: Romantic Writing and Commercial Society*. JHUP. pp. 426. $29. ISBN 0 801 84355 3.

Christies: Books and Prints by William Blake From the Collection Formed by the Late Frank Rinder, Esq., Tuesday, 30 November 1993.

Christophersen, Bill. *The Apparition in the Glass: Charles Brockden Brown's American Gothic*. UGeoP. pp. 208. hb $35.00. ISBN 0 8203 1530 3.

Clare, John. *Cottage Tales*. Ed. Eric Robinson, David Powell and P. M. S. Dawson. Carcanet. pp. 159. pb £9.95. ISBN 1 857 54032 8.

——. *The Essential John Clare*. Selected by Carolyn Kizer. Ecco. pp. 115. pb $8. ISBN 0 880 01157 2.

——. *The Shepherd's Calendar*. New Edition. Ed. Eric Robinson, Geoffrey Robinson and David Powell. OUP. pp. 146. pb £6.99. ISBN 0 19 283154 2.

Coleridge, S. T. *Aids to Reflection. The Collected Works of Samuel Taylor Coleridge*. Vol. 9. Ed. John Beer. PrincetonUP. pp. 676. £85. ISBN 8 691 09876 X.

——. *Poems*. Ed. John Beer. Dent. pp. 535. pb £4.99. ISBN 0 460 87316 4.

Cooperman, Robert. *In the Household of Percy Bysshe Shelley*. UPFlor. pp. 104. hb £15.50, pb £9.95. ISBN 0 813 01180 9, 0 813 01181 7.

Curran, Stuart, ed. *The Cambridge Companion to British Romanticism*. CUP. pp. 311. hb £35, pb £11.95. ISBN 0 521 33355 5, 0 521 42193 4.

——. *The Poems of Charlotte Smith*. Women Writers in English 1350–1850. OUP. pp. 335. £32.50. ISBN 0 19 507873 X.

Curreli, Mario and Anthony L. Johnson, eds. *Paradise of Exiles: Shelley and Byron in Pisa*. Papers from the International Conference held in Pisa, 24–26

May 1985. Salzburg Studies in English Literature, Romantic Reassessment Series. 2nd edn. Usalz. pp. 191. pb £14. ISBN 8 877 41381 6.

Curtis, Jared, ed. *The Fenwick Notes of William Wordsworth*. BCP. pp. 229. £30. ISBN 1 853 99103 1.

Davies, J. M. Q., *Blake's Milton Designs: The Dynamics of Meaning*. Locust Hill Literary Studies No. 7, Locust Hill Press. pp. 346. 143 b/w plates. $40. ISBN 0 933951 40 X.

De Paolo, Charles. *Coleridge: Historian of Ideas*. ELS Monograph Series 54. English Literary Studies. 1992. pp. 110. pb $10.50. ISBN 0 920 60460 9.

Easthope, Antony. *Wordsworth Now and Then: Romanticism and Contemporary Culture*. OpenUP. pp. 153. hb £32.50, pb £9.99. ISBN 0 335 09461 9, 0 335 09460 0.

Eaves, Morris. *The Counter-Arts Conspiracy: Art and Industry in the Age of Blake*. CornUP. 1992. pp. 287. 91 b/w illustrations. £29.95. ISBN 0 8014 2489 5.

Eaves, Morris, Robert N. Essick, and Joseph Viscomi. *William Blake: The Early Illuminated Books*. Blake's Illuminated Books vol 3. The William Blake Trust /Tate and PrincetonUP. pp. 286. £48.00. ISBN 1 85437 119 3.

Edgeworth, Maria. *Belinda*. Edited by Eilean Ni Chuilleanain. Dent. pp. 474. pb. £6.99. ISBN 0 460 87228 1.

———. *Letters for Literary Ladies*. Edited by Claire Connolly. Dent. pp.95. pb £4.99. ISBN 0 460 87250 8.

Essick, Robert N., and Joseph Viscomi. *Milton a Poem and the Final Illuminated Works: The Ghost of Abel, On Homers Poetry [and] On Virgil, Laocoön*. Blake's Illuminated Books vol. 5. William Blake Trust/Tate and PrincetonUP. pp. 286. £48.00. ISBN 1 85437 121 5.

Favret, Mary A. *Romantic Correspondence: Women, Politics and the Fiction of Letters*. CUP. pp. 268. £35. ISBN 0 521 41096 7.

Frantz, Andrea Breemer. *Redemption and Madness: Three Nineteenth Century Feminist Views on Motherhood and Childbearing*. Ide House. pp. 100. $6. ISBN 0 866 63204 2.

Fulford, Timothy, and Morton D. Paley, eds. *Coleridge's Visionary Languages: Essays in Honour of John Beer*. Brewer. pp. 210. £25. ISBN 0 859 91388 0.

Furniss, Tom. *Edmund Burke's Aesthetic Ideology: Language, Gender and Political Economy in Revolution*. CUP. pp. 306. £35. ISBN 0 521 41815 1.

Galperin, William H. *The Return of the Visible in British Romanticism*. JHUP. pp. 327. £33. ISBN 0 801 84505 X.

Godwin, William. *Memoirs Of Wollstonecraft*. Edited by Jonathan Wordsworth. Revolution and Romanticism. Woodstock. pp. 198. pb £8.95. ISBN 1 85477 125 6.

Goethe, Johann Wolfgang von. *Faust 1833*. Revolution and Romanticism. Woodstock. pp. 280. £42. ISBN 1 854 77131 0.

Goldsmith, Steven. *Unbuilding Jerusalem: Apocalypse and Romantic Representation*. CornUP. pp. 324. hb £38.95, pb £15.50. ISBN 0 801 42717 7, 0 801 49999 2.

Haney, David P. *William Wordsworth and the Hermeneutics of Incarnation*. PSUP. pp. 269. £35. ISBN 0 271 00911 X.

Hardin, James, and Siegfried Mews. *Nineteenth-Century German Writers to 1840*. Dictionary of Literary Biography. Vol. 133. Gale. pp. 411. $128. ISBN 0 810 35392 X.

Hill, Alan G. *The Letters of William and Dorothy Wordsworth.* Vol. VIII. *A Supplement of New Letters.* Clarendon. pp. 308. £40. ISBN 0 19 818523 5.

Hoagwood, Terence Allan. *Byron's Dialectic: Skepticism and the Critique of Culture.* AUP. pp. 185. £26. ISBN 0 838 75245 4.

Hogg, James, ed. *Shelley 1792–1992.* Salzburg Studies in Literature, Romantic Reassessment 112. Usalz. pp. 366. ISBN 3 705 20628 1.

Hughes-Hallett, Penelope. *Home at Grasmere: The Wordsworths and the Lakes.* Collins & Brown. pp. 160. hb £14.99, pb £8.99. ISBN 1 855 85111 3, 1 855 85180 6.

Jackson, J. R. de J. *Romantic Poetry by Women: A Bibliography, 1770–1835.* Clarendon. pp. 484. £50. ISBN 0 19 811239 4.

Jones, Chris. *Radical Sensibility: Literature and Ideas in the 1790s.* Routledge. pp. 232. ISBN 0 415 07685 4.

Kelly, Gary. *Women, Writing, and Revolution 1790–1827.* Clarendon. pp. 328. £35. ISBN 0 19 812272 1.

Kroeber, Karl, and Gene W. Ruoff, eds. *Romantic Poetry: Recent Revisionary Criticism.* RutgersUP. pp. 508. hb $48, pb $17. ISBN 0 813 52009 6, 0 813 52010 X.

Kuwahara, Kuldip Kaur. *Jane Austen at Play: Self-Consciousness, Beginnings, Endings.* American University Studies, Series IV, English Language & Literature, vol. 159. Lang. pp. 187. $47.95. ISBN 0 8204 2040 9.

Lamb, Charles. *Charles Lamb and Elia: Selected Writings.* Edited by J. E. Morpurgo. Carcanet/Fyfield Books. pp. 290. pb £9.95. ISBN 1 857554 003 4.

Landor, Walter Savage. *The Gebir 1798.* Romanticism and Revolution. Woodstock. pp. 74. £21. ISBN 1 854 77128 0.

Leask, Nigel. *British Romantic Writers and the East: Anxieties of Empire.* Cambridge Studies in Romanticism. CUP. pp. 266. £35. ISBN 0 521 41168 8.

Leersen, Joep, and Karl Ulrich Syndram, eds. *Europa Provincia Mundi: Essays in Comparative Literature and European Studies Offered to Hugo Dyserinck on the Occasion of his Sixty-Fifth Birthday.* Rodopi (1992). pp. 518. Hfl 225. ISBN 9 051 83381 4.

Lessenich, Rolf P. *Aspects of English PreRomanticism.* 1989. Böhlau Verlag Köln Wien. pp. 490. DM 118. ISBN 3 412 00388 3.

Lowe-Evans, Mary. *Frankenstein: Mary Shelley's Wedding Guest.* Twayne. pp. 95. pb £6.95. ISBN 0 8057 8597 3.

MacKenna, John. *Clare: A Novel.* Blackstaff. pp. 181. £6.95. ISBN 0 856 490467 5.

Masse, Michelle A. *In The Name Of Love: Women, Masochism and the Gothic.* CornUP. (1992). pp. 301. pb. £13.50. ISBN 0 8014 9918 6.

Maturin, Charles. *Melmoth the Wanderer.* Introduction by Devendra P. Varma and illustrated by Felix Zakar. Folio. No details.

Mayberry, Tom. *Coleridge and Wordsworth in the West Country.* Sutton (1992). pp. 213. pb £12.99. ISBN 0 750 90628 6.

McCalman, Iain. *Radical Underworld: Prophets, Revolutionaries, and Pornographers in London, 1795–1840.* Clarendon Paperbacks. pp. 338. pb £12.95. ISBN 0 19 812286 1.

McGann, Jerome J. *The New Oxford Book of Romantic Period Verse.* OUP. pp. 832. £25. ISBN 0 19 214158 9.

McGhee, Richard D. *Guilty Pleasures: William Wordsworth's Poetry of Psychoanalysis.* Whitson. pp. 350. $35. ISBN 0 878 75431 8.

McKernan, Maggie, ed. *The Sayings of Jane Austen.* Duckworth. pp. 64. pb £4.95. ISBN 0 7156 2461 X.

Mellor, Anne K. *Romanticism and Gender.* Routledge. pp. 275. hb £35, pb £11.99. ISBN 0 415 90111 1, 0 415 90664 4.

Mink, JoAnna Stephens, and Janet Doubler Ward, eds. *The Significance of Sibling Relationships in Literature.* BGUP. pp. 174. pb $14.95, ISBN 0 87972 613 X.

Murphy, Peter. *Poetry as an Occupation and an Art in Britain, 1760–1830.* Cambridge Studies in Romanticism. CUP. pp. 270. £35. ISBN 0 521 44085 8.

Murray, E. B., ed. *The Prose Works of Percy Bysshe Shelley.* Vol. I. Clarendon. pp. 592. £65. ISBN 0 19 812748 0.

Newlyn, Lucy. *Paradise Lost and the Romantic Reader.* Clarendon. pp. 295. £35. ISBN 0 19 811277 7.

Norvig, Gerda S. *Dark Figures in the Desired Country: Blake's Illustrations to The Pilgrim's Progress.* UCalP. pp. 327. 28 colour plates. 58 b/w illustrations. £45. ISBN 0 520 04471 1.

O'Neill, Michael. *Shelley.* Longman Critical Readers. Longman. pp. 276. hb £29.99, pb £11.99. ISBN 0 582 08668 X, 0 582 08667 1.

Owen, Robert. *Selected Works of Robert Owen.* 4 vols. Edited by Gregory Claeys. Pickering Masters Series. P&C. £265. ISBN 1 85196 088 0.

Pachori, Satya S. *Sir William Jones: A Reader.* OUP India. pp. 230. £17.50. ISBN 0 19 562928 0.

Powell, Violet. *A Jane Austen Compendium: The Six Major Novels.* Heinemann. pp. 224. £15. ISBN 0 434 59964 6.

Reeve, William C. *Kleist on Stage, 1804–1987.* McG-QUP. pp. 238. £37.95. ISBN 0 773 50941 0.

Roberts, Marie Mulvey, and Roy Porter, eds. *Literature and Medicine During the Eighteenth Century.* The Wellcome Series in the History of Medicine. Routledge. pp. 293. £50. ISBN 0 415 07082 1.

Rosso, George Anthony, Jr. *Blake's Prophetic Workshop: A Study of The Four Zoas.* AUP. pp. 208. 9 half-tone illustrations. £26.95. ISBN 0 8387 5240 7.

Rothenburg, Molly Anne. *Rethinking Blake's Textuality .* UMissP. pp. 164. 2 half-tone illustrations. £34.95. ISBN 0 8262 0901 7.

Ruddick, Nicholas, ed. *State of the Fantastic: Studies in the Theory and Practice of Fantastic Literature and Film.* Greenwood. 1992. pp. 210. £42.50. ISBN 0 313 27853 9.

Schoonmaker, Donald, and John A. Alford. *English Romanticism Preludes and Postludes: Essays in Honor of Edwin Graves Wilson.* Brewer. pp. 166. £29.50. ISBN 0 937 19144 2.

Shelley, Mary. *Frankenstein, Dracula and Dr. Jekyll and Mr. Hyde.* Horror Classics. Chancellor Press. pp. 527. No details.

——. *Frankenstein.* Oxford Progressive English Readers Series. OUP (Hong Kong). pp. 121. pb £2.70. ISBN 0 19 581234 4.

——. *The Essential Frankenstein. The Definitive Annotated Edition of Mary Shelley's Classic Novel.* Edited by Leonard Wolf and illustrated by Christopher Bing. Plume Books. pp. 357. pb £8.99. ISBN 0 452 26968 7.

——. *The Last Man.* Edited by Hugh J. Luke Jr, introduction by Anne K. Mellor. UNebP. pp. 342. pb £8.95. ISBN 0 8032 9217 1.

——. *Frankenstein.* Wordsworth Classics. pp. 242. pb £1. ISBN 1 85477 117 5.

Shelley, Percy Bysshe. *Selected Poems.* Dover Thrift Editions. Dover. pp. 123. pb £0.95. ISBN 0 486 27558 2.

Simpson, David. *Romanticism, Nationalism and the Revolt Against Theory.* UChicP. pp. 254. hb $42, pb $16.95. ISBN 0 226 75945 8, 0 226 75946 6.

Singer, Armand E. *The Don Juan Theme: An Annotated Bibliography of Versions, Analogues, Uses, and Adaptations.* WVUP. pp. 415. ISBN 0 937 05832 7.

Smith, Mark Trevor. *'All Nature Is But Art': The Coincidence of Opposites in English Romantic Literature.* Locust Hill. pp. 282. $32. ISBN 0 933 95144 2.

Southey, Robert, and S. T. Coleridge. *Joan of Arc 1796.* Revolution and Romanticism. Woodstock. pp. 409. £75. ISBN 1 854 77134 5.

Thompson, E. P. *Witness Against the Beast: William Blake and the Moral Law.* CUP. pp. 234. 20 b/w plates. hb £17.95, pb £9.95. ISBN 0 521 22515 9, 0 521 46977 5.

Todd, Janet. *Gender, Art, and Death.* Polity Press. pp. 184. £39.50. ISBN 0 7456 1055 2.

Viscomi, Joseph. *Blake and the Idea of the Book.* PrincetonUP. pp. 453. 312 b/w illustrations, 13 colour plates. £40. ISBN 0 691 0692 X.

Wallen, Martin. *Coleridge's Ancient Mariner: An Experimental Edition of Texts and Revisions 1798–1828.* Station Hill. pp. 156. pb $16.95. ISBN 0 882 68148 6.

Watkins, Daniel P. *A Materialist Critique of English Romantic Drama.* UPFlor. pp. 246. hb £35.95, pb £15.50. ISBN 0 813 01240 6, 0 813 01241 4.

Wheeler, Kathleen M. *Romanticism, Pragmatism and Deconstruction.* Blackwell. pp. 302. hb £40, pb £14.99. ISBN 0 631 18964 5, 0 631 17012 X.

Williams, John. *Wordsworth.* New Casebooks. Macmillan. pp. 216. hb £32.50, pb £9.50. ISBN 0 333 54903 1, 0 333 54904 X.

Wilson, Douglas B. *The Romantic Dream: Wordsworth and the Poetics of the Unconscious.* UNebP. pp. 200. $35. ISBN 0 803 24761 3.

Wolstenholme, Susan. *Gothic (Re)Visions: Writing Women as Readers.* SUNY Series in Feminist Criticism & Theory. SUNYP. $57.50. ISBN 0 7914 1219 9.

Wood, Nigel, ed. *Don Juan.* Theory in Practice. OpenUP. pp. 186. pb £9.99. ISBN 0 335 09626 3.

——, ed. *Mansfield Park.* Theory in Practice. OpenUP. £9.95. ISBN 0 335 09628 X.

——, ed. *The Prelude.* Theory in Practice. OpenUP. pp. 205. pb £9.99. ISBN 0 335 09626 3.

Wordsworth, Jonathan. *Visionary Gleam. Forty Books From the Romantic Period.* Woodstock. pp. 243. £30. ISBN 1 854 77126 4.

Wordsworth, William. *The Prelude 1850.* Revolution and Romanticism. Woodstock. pp. 374. £42. ISBN 1 854 77135 3.

Wordsworth, William, and S. T. Coleridge. *Lyrical Ballads 1798.* Revolution and Romanticism. Woodstock. pp. 210. pb £8.95. ISBN 1 854 77124 8.

Wu, Duncan. *Wordsworth's Reading 1770–1799.* CUP. pp. 220. £40. ISBN 0 521 41600 0.

Yarrington, Alison, and Kelvin Everest. *Reflections of Revolution: Images of Romanticism.* Routledge. pp. 200. £35. ISBN 0 415 07741 9.

XIII

The Nineteenth Century: Victorian Period

INGA BRYDEN, LAUREL BRAKE, WILLIAM BAKER,
KENNETH WOMACK, EMMA FRANCIS and VICTOR EMELJANOW

This chapter has five sections: 1. Cultural Studies and Prose; 2. The Novel; 3. Poetry; 4. Periodicals and Publishing History; 5. Victorian Drama and Theatre. Section 1 (a) is by Inga Bryden (Pater material by Laurel Brake); section 2 is by William Baker and Kenneth Womack; section 3 is by Emma Francis; section 4 is by Laurel Brake; and section 5 is by Victor Emeljanow.

1. Cultural Studies and Prose

(a) General

As part of the Review Forum on Cultural Studies (*VS* 36.455–72) three Victorianists address the relevance for contemporary critics of Victorian culture of issues raised in *Cultural Studies*, edited by Lawrence Grossberg, Cary Nelson and Paula A. Treichler (Routledge, 1990). Stefan Collini expresses a concern that the work of the 'founding fathers' of cultural studies (Raymond Williams, E. P. Thompson and Richard Hoggart) has, in a sense, helped to perpetuate a stereotyped image of British nineteenth-century intellectual history, representing it as either 'the unfeeling rigidities of atomistic liberalism and political economy' or as 'the more generous but also more nostalgic responses of an essentially Romantic cultural criticism'. Furthermore, Collini voices reservations about a trend within the practice of contemporary cultural studies, that of the past being '"interrogated" but not listened to'. These sympathetic comments are certainly salutary for critics of Victorian culture. Happily, much of this year's critical work on Victorian culture and Victorian prose goes some way to challenging the binary oriented picture of Victorian intellectual history Collini refers to.

Robin Gilmour's book on the intellectual and cultural context of Victorian literature in the Longman Literature in English series, for example, is one account where the past is indeed 'listened to'. *The Victorian Period: The Intellectual and Cultural Context of English Literature 1830–1890* contains a useful chronology which presents key works of drama, verse and fiction in the context of 'other' works and of cultural and historical events. In addition there are general evaluative bibliographies for each chapter, sections on individual authors which include biographical notes, highlights of major works, suggestions for further reading and illustrations. Gilmour organizes his material into chapters on science (which has an insightful section on literature and science), religion, industrialization and the arts, 'The Life of Ideas and the Culture of Politics' (which includes discussion of the politics of empire and gender politics), and 'The Sense of Time and the Uses of History'. Gilmour sees the Victorian period as being shaped by two forces in particular: the discovery of 'deep time' which affected every aspect of intellectual life and, the social context of this, the emergence of new groups of people inspired by the prospect of reform and committed to the development of a modern, religiously plural society. His fascinating emphasis on the Victorians' fascination with time (revealed for example in the autobiographical pressure in writing or in the ideological uses of particular pasts) makes us look again at Victorian historiography and the impulses behind the preoccupation with 'tracing the genealogy of the present in the past'. In structuring his material in the light of these themes Gilmour does more than give his reader an introduction to Victorian intellectual and cultural life: he also reinterprets the past, having listened to what it has to say.

Among this year's publications the predominant preoccupations were the notions of representation and subjectivity: whether the focus was on generic categories, on the construction of sexual identities, or on the historical and intellectual record, questions of selfhood and agency were foregrounded.

In *A Community of One: Masculine Autobiography and Autonomy in Nineteenth-Century Britain*, Martin A. Danahay aims to present an analysis of the aesthetics of nineteenth-century masculine autobiography which will complement the recent and extensive interdisciplinary work by feminists studying female self-representation. The 'community of one', exemplified iconographically in the painting *Charles Reade in His Study* (attributed to W. C. Mercier and adorning the book's cover), articulates for Danahay the paradox of nineteenth-century masculine self-authorship. Masculine authors 'represent themselves in other words as autonomous individuals', but this inscription of autonomy is contingent on the effacement of labour (feminine domestic labour in the painting of Reade writing [working]) or 'the excluded principle of the social'. The 'principle of the social', Danahay argues, is textually valued and yet denied, figured in the writings of J. S. Mill, Ruskin, Edmund Gosse, and a whole host of romantic and Victorian autobiographers as a 'feminine other'. Contrastingly, in nineteenth-century women's and working-class autobiographies the social conditions that shaped the texts' production are foregrounded. The various theories mentioned in the introduction are not always fully followed through, but Danahay's main focus on Bakhtin's definitions of monologism and dialogism, Raymond Williams's definition of community, and Tönnies's *Gemeinschaft und Gesellschaft* allows him to successfully argue that 'community' represents a 'site of nostalgia' in the context of nineteenth-century individualism, and it is used in masculine autobiographies as an antidote to 'the deadly spectacle of the absolutely free self'. The book concludes nicely with an assessment of Woolf's critique of the 'masculine' narrative of Victorian autobiography – given this, further exploration of the gendering of cultural attitudes towards writing as 'labour' would have been useful.

For the purposes of Danahay's argument Mill's *Autobiography* documents an intellectual 'crisis of faith' represented as an isolated masculine consciousness: '"The doctrine of what is called Philosophical Necessity weighed on my existence like an incubus"'. This passage is also quoted by Amanda Anderson in *Tainted Souls and Painted Faces: The Rhetoric of Fallenness in Victorian Culture*. Anderson, in a different reading, notes the gendered nature of the 'incubus': the image is pivotal to her argument since it casts Mill's 'apprehension of being a fully determined subject' in feminine and sexual terms. For Mill, lacking autonomy as a rational subject is alike to being ravaged sexually. *Tainted Souls and Painted Faces* is an original and significant reassessment of the fallen woman figure in Victorian culture. Specifically it demonstrates that rather than being constituted as irredeemably 'other', the figure was one type of a mid-century rhetoric of fallenness, of 'attenuated autonomy', a rhetoric which constructed the fallen woman as a fragmented subject in opposition to the normative masculine subject. Carefully and persuasively argued, Anderson's book recontextualizes works by Dickens, Gaskell, Rossetti and Barrett Browning in the Victorian debate about selfhood and agency. Contemporary theoretical approaches to subjectivity and representation are evaluated in the Afterword. Here Anderson makes use of Habermas's theory of communicative action to highlight that the more extreme structuralist form of poststructuralist cultural criticism can ultimately 'reify' subjectivity. The foundation of Anderson's argument is precisely that the fallen woman 'is a figure who displaces multiple anxieties about the predictability of character itself'.

The year's spring issue of *Victorian Studies* was a special theme issue devoted to 'sexualities'. Camilla Townsend's article '"I am the woman for spirit": A Working Woman's Gender Transgression in Victorian London' (*VS* 36.293–314) should be mentioned as a piece of fascinating research directed towards examining the intersections of gender and historicity in cultural constructions of the past. Townsend, 'in an effort to underscore the tensions between two styles in which we write history', writes about Sarah Geals, a working woman who lived as a man in mid-Victorian London, in two different ways. The first account pieces together contemporary evidence in order to ascertain agency; the second uses the same evidence in conjunction with contemporary journalistic texts to talk about cultural 'performance'. The result is a revealing statement about the ways in which an individual human history intersects with the critical study of shifting cultural attitudes towards gender and class.

In 'Reimagining Masculinity in Victorian Criticism: Swinburne and Pater' (*VS* 36.315–32) Thaïs E. Morgan analyses the distinctive claims of Swinburne and Pater in their work as aesthetic critics in the 1860s, given that both reimagined masculinity as marginal to middle-class notions of manliness: their essays represent an 'aesthetic minoritizing discourse'. Morgan discusses the rhetorical tactics of each writer and the discursive effects on different readership groups. Drawing on Eve Sedgwick's theories (particularly the definition of 'the closet') Morgan concludes that whereas Swinburne's 'avant gardist agenda' during the 1860s involved the covering of a range of transgressive perversities, Pater focused on figuring male beauty as an aesthetic ideal (hermaphroditism, androgyny), thereby 'legitimizing' it.

Pater and the politics of desire was also the subject of other of the year's works. Lesley Higgins, for example, in her article 'Jowett and Pater: Trafficking in Platonic Wares' (*VS* 37.43–72) sees Pater's readings of Platonic texts as a reclaiming of the Platonic canon as a site of a 'valorized homoerotic culture'. Her study compares the translations (interpretive acts of rewriting) of Plato's writings for a late nineteenth-century audience undertaken by Pater and by Benjamin

Jowett. Whereas Pater's strategies allowed him to critique the dominant discourses of a 'heterosexist milieu', Jowett's rewriting served to encode texts in terms of those heterosexist tenets. Higgins also argues that this intellectual struggle over the Platonic canon was part of a wider cultural imperialist praxis: the Victorian intellectual appropriation of former cultures, whether of the Middle Ages or of the Classical past, was always a 'self-reflexive' act.

A further discussion of late nineteenth-century masculinities in this special issue of *VS* is Ed Cohen's 'The Double Lives of Man: Narration and Identification in the Late Nineteenth-Century Representation of Ec-centric Masculinities' (*VS* 36.353–76). Cohen's article centres on a major concern of this year's work: the relationship between autobiographical narration and identification. It is particularly concerned with the dynamics of the construction of personal and political identities 'in as much as they are explicitly reproduced by the process of narrativization colloquially known as "coming out"'. In a precise and historically contextualized reading of John Addington Symonds's *Memoirs* and 'Case 99' in the first English edition of Krafft-Ebing's *Psychopathia Sexualis* Cohen argues that the texts represent male subjectivity as 'split'. The representational strategy of 'doubleness', or the conscious 'conceptual bifurcation', develops other narrative possibilities for the affirmation of 'ec-centric' sexualities, directed at new audiences. Symonds's *Memoirs* constitutes the first 'coming out story' since it inscribes a '"dehiscence"' of the (male) subject.

The intersection of gender and genre is the project of *The Politics of the Essay: Feminist Perspectives*, edited by Ruth-Ellen Boetcher Joeres and Elizabeth Mittman. Katherine V. Snyder, in 'From Novel to Essay: Gender and Revision in Florence Nightingale's "Cassandra"', examines the 'transitional regendering' of the narrative persona as Nightingale revised the manuscript of 'Cassandra'. The shift from feminine to masculine subjectivity (the intervention of a masculine 'interpreter') marked a generic change of the text from autobiographical novel to non-fictional essay. However, Snyder locates this shift in the literary and social history in which the genres were produced, rather than in any essential gendering of the genres. The genre of the essay ultimately 'resolves the seeming paradox of Nightingale's equation of "self-command" with "concealment"'.

Christina Rossetti's prose receives critical attention (six volumes of devotional prose have been relatively critically neglected) in '"I Magnify Mine Office": Christina Rossetti's Authoritative Voice in her Devotional Prose' (*VN* 84.17–22). Joel Westerholm organizes his discussion around the question 'how could a woman write and publish what are printed sermons and biblical commentaries at a time when her church forbade women's preaching?' Contextualizing women's relation to preaching (and teaching) Westerholm goes on to analyse Rossetti's disclaimers to her devotional prose. Whereas readers read these declarations of limited authority at face value, Rossetti herself actively reinterpreted biblical passages and reassessed women's role within the church. Anderson writes about painted faces and tainted souls. The painted faces of women and the women artists who paint them are the subjects of one of the year's important contributions to Victorian cultural studies. Deborah Cherry's thorough *Painting Women: Victorian Women Artists* is a study of Victorian women artists as producers, consumers, and spectators. Cherry uses Elizabeth Cowie's theory of 'woman as sign', which allows distinctions to be made between a historical woman and written and visual representations of her, to explore the feminist significations for the sign 'woman' in the historical context of different communities of women. Challenging the masculine narrative of professionalization *Painting Women* makes an important contribution to contemporary theories about the representation of women and revises our knowledge of the relationship between gendered viewing practices and the structural model sub-culture/dominant culture. In Part Two of *Painting Women* Cherry focuses on women's representations of femininity in the categories of landscape, domesticity, and work. Whilst acknowledging the socially informed difference of women's art she insists on the participation, not the marginalization, of women in nineteenth-century cultural practices.

Visual representations of Queen Victoria are contextualized in terms of cultural debate about domesticity and the concept of female 'rule' in Margaret Homans's article '"To the Queen's Private Apartments": Royal Family Portraiture and the Construction of Victoria's Sovereign Obedience' (*VS* 37.1–41). In a clearly argued thesis, Homans shows that literary and visual representations which figured Victoria as both monarch and 'middle-class' wife were a 'public relations' exercise for the problem of female rule. Moreover, the representations were constituted as part of the emerging ideology of symbolic monarchy. Homans amply documents how the success of the monarchy was rooted in its transformation into a 'spectacle of royal domestic privacy'. 'Victoria is at once an exemplary construct of Victorian ideology and its fantasized author', a reciprocal shaping between the Queen and her subjects which achieves a remarkable degree of congruence between commercially produced and commissioned works.

Kate Flint's important work *The Woman Reader 1837–1914* investigates the participation of women in Victorian and Edwardian cultural debate about reading. Intertextual in approach, it is an impressively detailed and engaging assessment of how women readers were represented in, for example, New Woman fiction and sensation fiction, and of how a range of medical, psychoanalytic, and 'advice' texts constructed 'reading' and the 'woman reader'. Evaluating contemporary social research in a theoretically informed manner allows Flint to rehistoricize the concepts 'woman' and 'reading', an approach lacking in much current feminist analysis of reading practices. The study of reading in any period, Flint argues, 'involves examining a fulcrum: the meeting place of discourses of subjectivity and socialization'.

Women writing rather than women reading are the central concern of Dorothy Mermin's *Godiva's Ride: Women of Letters in England, 1830–1880*. Mermin's book belongs to the 'Women of Letters' series edited by Sandra M. Gilbert and Susan Gubar, a series designed to introduce the general (as well as the academic) reader to the notion of a female literary community or tradition, only recently 'excavated' by feminist critics. Mermin takes Lady Godiva as an enabling representative of the contradictions experienced by early and mid-Victorian women writers. Literature is located at the border between private and public; Godiva's story unites modesty and display, political involvement and family life. And for women writers, comments Mermin, imagining, writing and publishing are often figured as solitary travel, like Godiva's ride. Mermin discusses a range of fiction by canonical writers and religious and scientific prose, her main purpose being to show that their unifying factor is a pervasive consciousness of gender. This Mermin achieves, although, puzzlingly, the term 'women of letters' is ambiguously defined in the introduction.

Godiva's ride, representing the imagined travel of the woman writer, figured in another of the year's works: *Women and the Journey: The Female Travel*

Experience edited by Bonnie Frederick and Susan H. McLeod. This collection of essays focuses on 'physical movement, not just mental journeys' and on the gendering of the travel narrative. It includes an essay comparing the travel accounts of Isabella Bird and Hester McClung, besides an essay of interest to Victorian cultural critics, Birgitta Maria Ingemanson's 'Under Cover: The Paradox of Victorian Women's Travel Costume'. Theorizing in terms of closure and restraint, Ingemanson argues that far from being 'eccentric' and adopting a threatening persona, many Victorian women travellers presented a 'mask of normalcy' which allowed mobility and a degree of power. Paradoxically, the literal constraint of their costume guaranteed women travellers freedom and protection from the alienation and homelessness which formed part of the travel experience. Ingemanson explores the extent to which travel was figured as performance: 'the travelers were the actors emerging in full view; there was an audience and a kind of script'. Furthermore, travellers generally took enough luggage to be comfortable, creating a '*mise-en-scène* or stage setting with the props that best backed their roles'.

The confluence of gender, national identities, and representation, areas of interest characterizing much of this year's work, is thoroughly investigated in *Woman and Nation in Irish Literature and Society 1880–1935*. C. L. Innes explores the tradition of representation within the struggle for Irish nationality and identity which figures 'males as national subjects, woman as the site of contestation'. The author aims to rewrite this tradition paying particular attention to women's role in the creation of an Irish 'conscience', given that Ireland itself was mythologized as female. The book is in two parts: Part One deals with the historical, literary and cultural context in which women were constructed as representations of Irishness. Nineteenth-century portrayals of Ireland depicted the nation as maiden or as mother – and Innes argues that these were made more resonant by the threat to members of the Anglo-Irish Ascendancy class of dispossession. The threat of dispossession, based on the question of legitimacy (a recurring theme in nineteenth-century Anglo-Irish literature), necessitated a demonstration of a commitment to 'inheriting' the identity of the motherland. Part Two of the book examines how individual women, or groups of women, reacted to male constructions of Irish consciousness. The ethos of artistic collaboration underpinned the literary and cultural activity of women involved in national politics, in contrast to the self-construction of male artists as political heroes.

Flint makes the point in *The Woman Reader 1837–1914* that sensation and 'New Woman' fiction internally critiques the notion that women read uncritically, challenging the assumption that the woman reading is identifying with the central female character. Developing from this, it is the adulteresses and murderesses featured in the sensation novels who have a cathartic effect on middle-class readers. This point is made in Chapter 4 of Nicola Humble's and Kimberley Reynolds's *Victorian Heroines: Representations of Femininity in Nineteenth-Century Literature and Art*, an ambitious book which is perhaps more concerned with nineteenth-century attitudes towards sexuality than with attitudes towards femininity, and which deals more with literature than with art. There is a wealth of fascinating material, including discussion of autobiography and children's literature, and some particularly pertinent readings of the fictional representation of Victorian girls and of individual texts such as Tennyson's 'The Princess' where the use of 'inversion' effects 'a fusion between the sexual and desexualised images of women'. *Victorian Heroines* certainly covers a 'variety of perspectives' in dealing with the representation of nineteenth-century women, although the methodology behind the overall organization of material in this co-authored book is rather confusingly presented.

The year's interest in women and decadence, the daring of the New Woman and of her prose, is evident with Elaine Showalter's collection of eighteen short stories *Daughters of Decadence: Women Writers of the Fin de Siècle*. The collection includes biographical notes and in a useful contextual introduction Showalter highlights the recurring theme of a reimagining of the roles of artist and muse. The relationship between woman's body and her role as artist is directly addressed in 'The Yellow Wallpaper', but also included is the less well-known and terrifying story 'A White Night' by Charlotte Mew – a feminist counterpart of Conrad's *Heart of Darkness*, suggests Showalter – which also deals with issues of female entrapment.

Fin de siècle aesthetics were the focus of a cluster of writings, continuing last year's preoccupation with 1890s culture (although to a lesser degree). In 'Esthetes and Effeminati' (*Raritan* 12.iii.52–68) Linda Dowling continues her work on decadence and language, here focused on the moment of applause at Wilde's trial in April 1895 which she takes to signal the victory of a new ideal of Greek civilization over the tradition of classical republican thought that had dominated civic discourse in England throughout the seventeenth and eighteenth centuries (as revealed in the language of Wilde versus the Crown prosecutor). Dowling discusses an aspect of late nineteenth-century sexuality overlooked by recent gender criticism: that the effeminatus in classical republican theory is a symbol of civic enfeeblement and self-absorption rather than sexual debility. In this context civic alarm is a reponse to the threat of impotence to a 'metaphysics of community'.

Jay Losey's article 'The Aesthetics of Exile: Wilde Transforming Dante in *Intentions* and *De Profundis*' (*ELT* 36.429–50) also examines the linguistic construction of the artist pitted against institutional authority through a close reading of Wilde's references to Dante's *Commedia* in *Intentions* and *De Profundis* (a more convincing reading). Losey argues that the 'Aesthetics of Exile' become increasingly important in Wilde's work. Wilde appropriates Dante politically and aesthetically, to reinforce his position as political and artistic exile, and yet to make 'moral pronouncements on Victorian society'.

In *Spectrum of Decadence: The Literature of the 1890s* Murray Pittock ambitiously aims to recover the 'authentic' literary context of the *fin de siècle* and to investigate the development and values of Symbolism as an ideology 'across themes and artistic genres' (he defines Decadence as 'the performative aspects of symbolist ideology'). Pittock assesses Pater's intellectual achievement in the context of a native British symbolism rather than a pan-European context, and sees Pater and his artistic contemporaries as precursors of Modernism. Other chapters discuss the cult of beauty as a cultural phenomenon, the characteristics of decadent prose, literary periodicals, and the poetry of the Rhymers' Club. The most original and convincingly argued section is 'The rage for the past and the Celtic Twilight' where Pittock discusses the ways in which the emergence of a Neo-Jacobite movement with Celtic nationalist overtones was an attempt to create a political and literary agenda for the writers of the 1890s.

The construction of the category 'English Men of Letters' is deconstructed in David Amigoni's knowledgeable and closely argued study of Victorian biography, *Victorian Biography: Intellectuals and the Ordering of Discourse*. Amigoni usefully explores Victorian biography's role in relation to the emergence of the master-narratives 'literature' and 'history' in Victorian academic culture. Historicization of the rise of these disciplines is undertaken in the light of Bakhtinian and Foucauldian theories of discourse – a critique of the view of nineteenth-century biography as a 'cult of exemplarity'. Yet Amigoni goes further than this, employing theory to question current attitudes within the academy towards its own provenance. He argues that 'the emergence of the authoritative discipline of history in the nineteenth century was crucial in determining the subordinate space occupied by literature' and central to this is a focus on textual attitudes to rhetoric, on disciplines as acts of resistance to the dynamics of rhetoric. In this light Carlyle's rhetoric in texts such as *Sartor Resartus* and *Oliver Cromwell's Letters and Speeches* becomes a kind of literary and 'philosophical terrorism' – and J. R. Seeley's theory of the language of history, an attempt to discipline this terrorism.

The links between politics and discourse in Carlyle's work are the subject of John B. Lamb's article 'Utopian Dreams/Heterotopian Nightmares: Disease and Discourse in Carlyle's *Latter-Day Pamphlets*' (*VN* 83.11–14). With reference to Foucault's *The Order of Things*, Lamb argues that in *Latter-Day Pamphlets* Carlyle reads the present as a heterotopian nightmare of a body politic infected by 'babble'. Heterotopias, as Foucault indicates, '"dessicate speech"' and Lamb points out that the story of the Tower of Babel resonates throughout *Latter-Day Pamphlets*. Moreover, for Carlyle 'babble' has become a substitute for work (that is, social action): a symptom of *laissez-faire*. Lamb's thesis highlights the irony that it is only through discourse and the utopian imagination that Carlyle can create the ideal world of hero worship – he too is 'infected with words'. 'Heterotopias make clear the precarious nature of all cultural orderings, since they are ultimately dependent upon language'.

Victorian Biography, in the wake of Hayden White's questioning of nineteenth-century 'masculine' historiography, has obvious relevance for realignments of the literary canon in terms of gender. This year saw the publication as a paperback of Bruce Robbins's excellent *The Servant's Hand: English Fiction From Below* (originally published in 1986), a revaluation of the literary canon focused on class. Robbins successfully meets the theoretical challenge he sets himself – to accept the continuity and sameness in literary representations of the servant while 'refusing the independence of literature from social determination that appears to result from it'. His dissociation of literary realism from political effect allows him to reassess 'the political impact and import of commonplaces, that is, of what is most traditional about literary tradition'. *The Servant's Hand* is a highly readable and distinctive Marxist reading of the politics of representation. Servants are 'signs of the arbitrariness of signs' – as illustrated in Hazlitt's essay 'Footmen' – articulating the processes of acculturation and resistance. The hand is indeed a sign of productive value.

The servant's hand might signify housework, and passages which describe housekeeping, taken from a variety of texts, are discussed in Monica Feinberg's article 'Good Housekeeping: Job-Searching Victorian Fiction' (*VN* 83.7–10). The passages work to convey housekeeping as an ideological conception beyond the representational limits of the material detail so painstakingly recorded. This technique, Feinberg suggests, might be termed 'narrative montage' – montage in the cinematic sense of a rapid series of images having associations. Furthermore, the passages which construct housekeeping as a unified spiritual 'ideal' simultaneously give the sense of housekeeping as a business. Indeed, housekeeping is both 'busyness and business'. Here, referring to the 1851 census, Feinberg makes the interesting connection that the 'home' is acknowledged as a national ideal at the time when housewifery is being recognized as a demographically significant occupation.

The year saw the publication as an Oxford paperback of four self-contained studies originally written for the Past Masters series. *Victorian Thinkers* is a useful and timely assessment of the nineteenth-century cultural critics Carlyle, Ruskin, Arnold and Morris: the four studies are by A. L. Le Quesne, George P. Landow, Stefan Collini and Peter Stansky respectively.

The narrative of empire featured in the year's work in a context of postcolonial criticism and cultural rethinking. Empire Day itself, Queen Victoria's birthday, is remembered in various guises in the collection of mainly contemporary auto-biographical essays by women *Unbecoming Daughters of the Empire*, edited by Shirley Chew and Anna Rutherford. Marion Halligan recalls the tradition of Empire Day as 'a matter of being, not becoming', Cherry Clayton sees the authority of empire as being intertwined with patriarchal family control. 'Empire' is articulated as partly a fiction – and it is this 'fictive affiliation' in late nineteenth-century narratives which interests Thomas Richards in *The Imperial Archive: Knowledge and the Fantasy of Empire*. More precisely, Richards is concerned with the 'control of knowledge'. In a series of original, concise, and interesting readings of, for example, *Dracula*, *Kim*, *The Riddle of the Sands*, and *Tono-Bungay*, he demonstrates that the imperial archive was a 'fantasy of knowl-edge', 'a myth of a unified archive' developed from romanticism's project. Late nineteenth-century writing figures the rhetoric of the new disciplines of imperial science and morphology. In Chapter 1 Richards discusses representations that situated an archive-state in Tibet, drawing on Foucault (although this debt could be acknowledged more) in illustrating a shifting relationship between knowledge and state power. This is a fascinating and convincing account of how the imperial archive established itself at the centre of Victorian representation: in popular culture it was 'the key to the mythologies of Victorian life'.

(b) Individual Authors

Victorian travel from a masculine perspective forms part of this year's publica-tion of a collection of essays on Richard Burton, originally given as papers at a conference in 1990 to mark the centennial of Burton's death. *In Search of Sir Richard Burton: Papers from a Huntington Library Symposium* edited by Alan H. Jutzi aims to redress the balance where critical attitudes towards Burton are concerned, concentrating less on the infamous 'man of action' and more on the scholar and cultural critic. An essay on 'Burton and His Library' (Alan H. Jutzi), for example, attempts to classify the material in Burton's library and provides an interesting analysis of a 'remarkable observer's' reading practices. In the essay 'Burton as Autobiographer' John Hayman argues that Burton's textual 'detach-ment from the self' staged rather awkwardly in his autobiographical writings was replicated in the literal disguise he adopted on his travels.

Two notable essays on Darwin have appeared this year. *Textuality and Sexu-ality: Reading Theories and Practices* edited by Judith Still and Michael Worton, is a collection of theoretical essays which investigate the ways in which texts and the 'bodies' that read and write them are sexualized. Included in this collection is Gillian Beer's fascinating essay 'Four Bodies on the *Beagle*: Touch, Sight, and Writing in a Darwin Letter', an examination of Darwin's *positioning* within, how he is constituted by, the activities of representation. Darwin as anatomist and writer must dissect and describe: 'the hand as scalpel and as pen'. Beer offers a reading of a passage from a letter dated 23 July 1834, when the *Beagle* docked at Valparaiso in Chile after a difficult passage. She focuses on the naked 'bodies' of a Fuegian, Titian's Venus, and 'some small animal' mentioned in the passage (the fourth body of the title is Darwin's own) in order to throw into relief how Darwin's extreme 'proneness' before sense-experience reveals in his writing 'a form of nostalgia so intense that it may be called mourning'. The masculine autobiographers in Danahay's aforementioned *A Community of One* attained autonomy through positioning, for example, Nature as a feminine Other. Contrastingly, in Beer's analysis, Darwin did not inscribe Nature's femininity as difference. Indeed, Beer demonstrates that in Darwin's imagination there was no fixed sexual difference, rather an 'It' or 'one parent': 'It is *hors-sexe*, and almost *hors-texte*'.

A further essay on Darwin and knowledge could be said to epitomize the year's fascination with subjectivity, objectivity, and Victorian narrative: in particular, the threads of gender implications and epistemological crisis are knitted together. This essay, George Levine's 'By Knowledge Possessed: Darwin, Nature, and Victorian Narrative' (*NLH* 24.363–91), aims to discuss the implications of the metaphor that equates knowledge with the absence of qualities usually associated with life, focusing on the self-effacement of the observer (oppressor). In much nineteenth-century narrative, knowing means dying or killing. Levine suggests that the ideal of objectivity claimed by science is paralleled in fiction by the story of self-abnegation for the sake of 'truth' (which ends in literal and figurative deaths). He traces the traditions which contributed to the development of the scientific ideal of objectivity as a cultural value: Christian self-denial and the secular valuing of rationality. The thesis that 'the paradoxical assertion of death [is] a condition of knowing' in nineteenth-century prose is amply demonstrated. Nineteenth-century conceptions of selfhood, Levine argues, articulate an awareness that to be human is to be both the observer and the observed. This is demonstrated with examples of Darwin's attempts to repress the personal suggesting that the personal was central to his imaginative and scientific practice.

Mill's early essays on poetry, particularly 'What is Poetry?' are the subject of Timothy Gould's essay 'Utterance and Theatricality: A Problem for Modern Aesthetics in Mill's Account of Poetry' (in *Pursuits of Reason: Essays in Honor of Stanley Cavell*, edited by Ted Cohen, Paul Guyer and Hilary Putnam). Gould explores the limits and implications of Mill's claim to distinguish poetry from eloquence: the 'theatricality' of the essay's title is the manifestation in utterance of the speaker's awareness of an audience. The notion of the writer's consciousness of a listener is related to the 'anti-self-consciousness' theory Mill discusses in *Autobiography*. The work of Mill as political economist is discussed by Regenia Gagnier in 'On the Insatiability of Human Wants: Economic and Aesthetic Man' (*VS* 36.125–53). Gagnier pinpoints a tension in the concept of 'economic man' in the work of political economists from Smith to Mill. Under Neo-Classical economics (represented by Stanley Jevons and Carl Menger) economic man loses his critical and welfare function and comes to represent the end of history itself. Economic man is reinvented as the universal man of insatiable consumer desires, the precursor of 'revealed preference theory' in the 1990s. The second part of Gagnier's thesis relates these developments to a shift from normative to formal aesthetics (represented by Pater) where a universality is accorded the '*fin de siècle*' European consumer. Both the narratives of fiction and political economy are motivated by their exchange value and social base, promoting subjectivism, passive consumption, individualism and formalism. In a useful postscript Gagnier discusses the work of feminist economists.

This year saw the publication of *The Complete Novels and Selected Writings of Amy Levy, 1861–1889* (works previously not in print), edited by Melvyn New. The collection contains the novels *The Romance of a Shop* (1888) and *Reuben Sachs: A Sketch* (1888), which gives us a valuable picture of Anglo-Jewish life in the 1880s as a geo-physical reality and which generated hostility among the contemporary Jewish community in London. Also included by New is a good range of shorter fiction and essays on aspects of Jewish culture, and a selection of Levy's poetry, characterized by themes of love, death, mental anguish, and intellectual isolation. New presents Levy as an unmarried, urban intellectual: for him 'it seems possible that Levy's Jewishness has gotten in the way of a valid assessment of her achievements, most particularly as a feminist voice'.

One of the year's important contributions to our ways of interpreting nineteenth-century literature was Jeffrey Skoblow's invigorating and radical re-reading of Morris's *The Earthly Paradise, Paradise Dislocated: Morris, Politics, Art*. In common with Robbins (and Amigoni) Skoblow questions the cultural assumptions of critical discourse, alerting us to examine the notions of marginality and the 'traditional' canon. Indeed, Skoblow argues that *The Earthly Paradise* stands in a 'dislocated' relation to its critical context and to the assumptions of cultural production: in this sense the case of Morris is an example of the relationship between 'the modern imagination and the modern world'. This new context for Morris's utopian work is constructed in the light of nineteenth- and twentieth-century dialectical thought, primarily romanticism and the theories of the Frankfurt School. *Paradise Dislocated* literally bodies forth the stylistic techniques (ellipsis and circularity) of *The Earthly Paradise* – a methodology explained in the substantial introductory chapter. It is a refreshing and challenging reappraisal of how we might read the tensions in Victorian culture.

[There is little enough on Pater this year, and most of it is relational, linking Pater's texts with those of others. Anne Marie Candido, in 'Biography and the Objective Fallacy: Pater's Experiment in "A Prince of Court Painters"' in *Biography* (16.47–60), is the only critic this year to publish a piece exclusively on Pater's writing. This modest, patient piece which succeeds in making its point links Pater's alleged notions of aesthetic biography with Charles Whibley's advocacy of 'invention rather than knowledge' in 1897, and contrasts Pater's 'imaginative portraits' in both *Studies* and Watteau with Leon Edel's call for 'objective' biography and the avoidance of transference: the deployment of Marie-Marguerite's transference is an aesthetic device by which the portrait of Watteau, hers and the essay's, is crafted.

Murray G. H. Pittock devotes the first chapter of his *Spectrum of Decadence: The Literature of the 1890s* to 'Walter Pater and the French Connection' (15–44), but his treatment of Pater is far more general than the chapter title implies. His main argument is to show that Pater is precisely not a mere conveyor of French symbolism to Britain, but representative of a native British symbolism; unexpectedly he does not deal with Pater's 1890s writing but principally with the early essays and their later influence on younger 1890s' writers such as Johnson,

Dowson, Symons, Wilde, and Yeats. This reads like the work of a book in a hurry: Pater functions as an important origin of British Symbolist thought, and of Pittock's book. While the latter usefully draws attention to neglected aspects of Pater's work (e.g. its transformation of the Laudian aesthetic), it is far more categoric than evidence warrants on Pater's atheism ('Pater did not believe in God', 21) and, apart from a parenthetical phrase, avoids the question of gendered discourse altogether. The system of references is so concentrated that it is difficult to decipher some footnoted sources. This is not the place to send a neophyte to learn about Pater, but Pittock has some interesting, contestable observations on Pater's place within a spectrum of decadence.

One of the best publications this year, with a capacity to resonate through future Pater studies, is Thaïs E. Morgan's 'Reimagining Masculinity in Victorian Criticism: Swinburne and Pater' in *VS* (36.315–32). She takes up Swinburne's wry observation that Pater's early writing bore a resemblance to his own, and compares sets of texts, a review of Baudelaire with 'Diaphaneite', 'Notes and Poems and Reviews' with 'Winckelmann', and 'Notes on Designs of the Old Masters at Florence' with various aspects of *Studies*, with a view to showing that although both authors shared an 'aesthetic minoritizing discourse' and the project of extending extant boundaries of masculinity, they differed in the contents of that expansion: in a confrontational address Swinburne gave priority to transgression and perversion *per se*, with women fully included in the permutations of the androgyne and the hermaphrodite, while Pater consistently gave exclusive priority to its male beauty, and in language of persuasion and tact. These are both distinguishable from 'specifically homoerotic *desire*'.

Two pieces pertain to material in *Studies*. Joseph A. Kestner's principal interest in 'Constructing the Renaissance: Leighton and Pater' in *JPRAS* (ns. 2.1–15) is Frederic Leighton. Paying especial attention to the indebtedness of Pater to Leighton in his versions of Michelangelo and Giorgione, Kestner compares a lecture of Leighton's in 1887 on the Renaissance, and his pictures from 1848–72 with Pater's Renaissance essays between 1867 and 1872, the 1873 book, and Pater's review of J. A. Symonds's Renaissance volume in 1875. However, while Leighton's Renaissance is violent and militaristic as well as suffused with sweetness, Pater's is graceful, and oblivious to the violence of politics and religion.

In 'The Mona Lisa and the Symbol of Ideas. Pater's Leda as Mother to Yeats's Helen' (*CLQ* 29.20–32) Mark Jeffreys avers that Yeats's reading of Pater's *Studies* passage on the Mona Lisa was a 'primary model [...] for Yeats's treatment of Maud Gonne as a poetic subject' and more generally for his 'archetypal' metaphors, particularly of the feminine and the beautiful. Jeffreys is convinced that Yeats's reasons for adapting this Paterian passage for the first entry in *The Oxford Book of Modern Verse* remain unexplained, and lie beyond idiosyncrasy. Detecting evidence of Pater's influence in Yeats's early essay 'The Symbolism of Poetry', Jeffreys goes on to build his argument on readings of the Pater–Yeats connection in twentieth-century critics (Engelberg and F. C. McGrath), and to demonstrate by close reading that the echoes of Pater in Yeats are 'largely to be found in the Maud Gonne poems'. For both its hypotheses and its detail, this article repays reading.

In 'Pater and Carlyle in Eliot's "Little Gidding"' in *N&Q* (40.500–2) James F. Loucks suggests that the closing lines of the first movement of Eliot's poem may echo Pater's 'Animula Vagula' chapter from *Marius the Epicurean* or

Pater's 'best-known' English source for Goethe's America apothegm, Carlyle's *Sartor Resartus*. Lastly on Pater, Billie Andrew Inman has an important review article which is largely about Pater and the notion of authority (*NCP* 20.56–60). [LB]

How one reads a particular cultural figure and how that writer reads himself is the subject of Sheila Emerson's original and engrossing study (with illustrations) of Ruskin, *Ruskin: The Genesis of Invention*. The book is in two parts: the first dealing in detail with how Ruskin learned to write and to represent that learning, the second concentrating on Ruskin's later career and his reinvention of his genesis. Emerson demonstrates that Ruskin's application of his aesthetic principles (developed from childhood writing experiments) to his prose 'contradicts his pronouncements as a man but not his achievements as a child'. Her thesis draws on recent developments in linguistic, psychoanalytic, and feminist criticism; she is as interested in the gendering of the artistic parenting of a text as she is in an interrelated methodology. For Ruskin both the visual and the verbal are material languages. *Ruskin: The Genesis of Invention* has relevance for the history of discrimination between creative and critical writing.

Finally, mention should be made of the year's significant scholarly contributions to our knowledge of individual Victorian lives. A further three volumes (19–21) of *The Collected Letters of Thomas and Jane Welsh Carlyle*, edited by Clyde de L. Ryals and Kenneth J. Fielding (DukeUP), were published, as was volume five of Benjamin Disraeli *Letters: 1848–1851* (UTorP). Biographies included: *Lord Curzon: The Last of the British Moghuls* by Nayana Goradia (OUP); *Journey to Livingstone: Exploration of an Imperial Myth* by Timothy Holmes (Canongate); *Faith and Family: The Life and Circle of Ambrose Phillipps de Lisle* by Margaret Pawley (Canterbury); *George Green: Mathematician and Physicist 1793–1841, The Background to His Life and Work* by D. M. Cannell (Athlone). These texts will be reviewed in *YWES* 75. Other texts to be reviewed in *YWES* 75 are *Jeremy Bentham: Critical Assessments*, four volumes edited by Bhikhu Parekh (Routledge); *The Soul of Wit: Joke Theory from Grimm to Freud* by Carl Hill (UNebP); and *Clandestine Erotic Fiction in English 1800–1930: A Bibliographical Study* by Peter Mendes (Scolar).

2. The Novel

(a) General

The nature of the recent critical, historical, and biographical analyses regarding the Victorian novel remain similar to the commentary examined in recent surveys in the *YWES*. In addition to forays into feminism, deconstruction, New Historicism and textual and bibliographical study, recent criticism of the nineteenth-century novel features philological, linguistic, and postmodernist examinations, among a host of other critical pursuits. Additionally, the Victorian fictive canon continues to remain relatively stable, perennially including such predominant novelists as Dickens, Charlotte and Emily Brontë, George Eliot, and Hardy. It is refreshing to see the great diversity of work on the Victorian novel, particularly on such major figures as Thackeray, Trollope, Mrs Gaskell, Stevenson, Gissing and Disraeli, in addition to welcome attention to the writings of Stoker, Wilde, Conan Doyle, Carroll, Robert Surtees and Thomas Hughes, amongst others.

Several figures, however, have received scant attention in recent years, including Margaret Oliphant, Charlotte Mary Yonge, Grace Aguilar and William Harrison Ainsworth, to mention but a few, while writers such as Bulwer Lytton and Charles Reade remain shamefully neglected.

In *The 1890s: An Encyclopedia of British Literature, Art, and Culture* – the first reference work devoted to the cultural and literary fervour of the late-Victorian era – George A. Cevasco has assembled a wealth of information on a host of Victorian novelists, including individual entries on Thomas Hardy, George Gissing, William Mallock, Charlotte Mary Yonge, Leonard Merrick, Arthur Morrison, Edmund Yates, Rider Haggard and Mary Elizabeth Braddon, to mention just a few of the multitude of literary figures featured in the volume. In *Reverse Tradition: Postmodern Fictions and the Nineteenth Century Novel*, Robert Kiely offers readings of a diversity of works, including Charlotte Brontë's *Villette*, Thomas Hardy's *The Woodlanders*, and George Eliot's *Romola*. Kiely specifically considers such issues as the suppression of history and the genre of women writers who reconfigure the past – writers, Kiely argues, that are motivated by their historical relationships with their nineteenth-century feminine precursors. For this reason, Kiely affords particular attention to his poststructuralist argument that new women writers reconfigure the past through parody and historical suppression. Drawing upon this theoretical construct, Kiely considers such issues as the nature of ghost stories in Brontë's *Villette* and Toni Morrison's appropriation of Brontë's aesthetic in *Beloved*, while also examining what Kiely describes as the 'aesthetics of solitude' and the 'politics of exclusion', elements particularly exemplified through Louise Erdrich's reification of Hardy's *The Woodlanders* in *Tracks*.

Novel Images: Literature in Performance, edited by Peter Reynolds, features essays devoted to assessing the efficacy of television and film adaptations of well-known literary texts. John Collick's 'Dismembering Devils: The Demonology of *Arashi ga oka* (1988) and *Wuthering Heights* (1939), considers the mythical qualities of an early film production of Brontë's classic novel, while Grahame Smith's 'Dickens and Adaptation: Imagery in Words and Pictures' assesses the nature of Dickens adaptations on television and film. In 'Adapting Dickens to the Modern Eye: *Nicholas Nickleby* and *Little Dorrit*', Christopher Innes offers specific analyses of film adaptations of works by Dickens and reveals the manner in which animated images of literature reflect the ideological or cultural agendas of the eras in which they were produced. In Volume 46 of *Studies in Bibliography*, one article of relevance to the Victorian novel – apart from essays on 'The Life and Work of Fredson Bowers' and a Bowers bibliography – is Arthur Sherbo's 'From *The Bookman* of London', which sheds light upon the bibliographies of Thomas Hardy and Walter Pater, amongst others, and publishes extracts from a Wilkie Collins's letter of 15 March 1885 that reveals its author's response to Hall Caine's novel, *The Shadow of a Crime*. Sherbo also draws attention to other Collins's letters published in *The Bookman*, an interview with Hardy regarding the ending of *Tess*, and new revelations about the work of George Meredith.

In *Seeing Together: Friendship Between the Sexes in English Writing from Mill to Woolf*, Victor Luftig examines friendships between the sexes in the works of a host of English writers, including George Eliot, Hardy and John Stuart Mill, among others. Luftig affords particular attention to the difficult place of friendship in texts from the Victorian era, and reveals the troubling network of sexual, social, and political dynamics that underscore their narratives. Luftig argues that friendship for mid-Victorians originally functioned as a name for ostensibly sexless relationships between men and women, although the term later served as a vague phrase for otherwise explicitly sexual relationships. In addition to demonstrating that Victorian England lacked an adequate terminology for describing its own shifting social dynamics, Luftig examines such volumes as Eliot's *Daniel Deronda* and Hardy's *Jude the Obscure* in an effort to determine each author's idiomatic descriptions of fellowship in their texts. Through such analyses, Luftig offers a valuable insight into the divergent notions of friendship that mark the Victorian age and beyond.

John Maynard's exploration of *Victorian Discourses on Sexuality and Religion* reveals the central roles of erotic and spiritual language in the work of literary and ecclesiastical figures such as Arthur Hugh Clough, Charles Kingsley, Coventry Patmore and Hardy. Drawing upon the constructs of myth, anthropology, comparative religion, and the history of sexuality, Maynard explores the manner in which Victorian writers forged a central vocabulary in their debate regarding the relationship between sexual issues and religion. In his study of Hardy's *Jude the Obscure*, for example, Maynard discusses Hardy's usage of language and the ways in which meaning in his novel functions as a mechanism for deconstructing the fictive representations of sexuality in the work of his predecessors. Maynard likewise challenges prevailing arguments that establish the origins of Victorian sexual discourse within a single, ecclesiastical origin, and provocatively argues instead that writers such as Hardy derived their own parlance for engaging in the enduring social debate over the principal sexual issues that indelibly marked the Victorian era.

In *Outside the Pale: Cultural Exclusion, Gender Difference, and the Victorian Woman Writer*, Elsie B. Michie — using texts from nineteenth-century writers such as Mary Shelley, Charlotte and Emily Brontë, Elizabeth Gaskell and George Eliot — explores each author's divergent definition of femininity and contextualizes it within the varying historical moments in which each writer lived and worked. Michie also examines each author's concerns in her fiction with issues of gender and modes of production, class differences, the possession of property, colonial relations, and educational access. In addition to close readings of such novels as Shelley's *Frankenstein*, Gaskell's *Cranford*, and Eliot's *Middlemarch*, Michie explores the prevailing argument that the cultural exclusion of femininity can be adequately read in terms of history. Michie extends this argument through her useful readings of the works of her exemplars, and thus reveals the ways in which the pressure of economic, political, and social developments impinged upon and reconfigured the narrative pursuits of nineteenth-century women writers.

Bryan Cheyette also considers the manner in which history functions as a catalyst for narrative change in *Constructions of 'the Jew' in English Literature and Society: Racial Representations, 1875–1945*. In his study, Cheyette draws upon a wide range of literary texts and social and political perspectives from the 1870s to the 1940s in an effort to demonstrate the ways in which the emerging cultural identity of modern England constructed the racial conception of Jewishness. Cheyette employs cultural theory, discourse analysis, and new historicist insights in close readings of revelatory texts by Trollope, George Eliot and Kipling, among other Victorian writers. Cheyette argues that the image of 'the Jew' performs a central function in English literature and society as the embodiment of confusion and indeterminacy. Cheyette explores the cultural and literary role of semitism in the Victorian novel, and suggests that Eliot's *Daniel Deronda* exemplifies the manner in which a 'realist novelist' traverses beyond the dogma of liberal realism in order to depict the 'ultimately unknowable semitic "other"' (p. 42). In this way, Cheyette not only discounts the image of 'the Jew' as a static myth or stereotype, but also proffers an insightful discussion of the place of race in the larger body of English literature.

Using works by Dickens, Carlyle, Mill, George Eliot, Tennyson and Robert Browning, David Morse studies the cultural history of the Victorian age and its remarkable literary accomplishments in *High Victorian Culture*. Morse concentrates his examination upon Victorian issues of dislocation and uncertainty, as well as upon the strategic silences and democratic rhetoric that mark the era. Morse's analysis of the remarkably contradictory nature of Victorian social and cultural politics drives many of his literary conclusions regarding the Victorian age, and his careful readings of the works of his literary exemplars afford him the opportunity to trace Victorian national anxieties from the accession to the throne by Queen Victoria in 1837 to her proclamation as Empress of India in 1877. Morse demonstrates that during this era a growing national self-confidence was concomitantly thwarted by an undemocratic society driven by an ostensibly democratic cultural rhetoric. The convincing manner in which Morse traces these disparities in the fiction of such figures as Eliot and Dickens underscores the value of his study to an understanding of the divergent social fabric that marked the Victorian era.

In *Mechanism and the Novel: Science in the Narrative Process*, Martha A. Turner draws upon the tradition of mechanistic science as derived from Sir Isaac Newton, and traces the evolution of the concept of mechanism among science writers and novelists during the previous two centuries. Through close readings of nineteenth-century novels such as Jane Austen's *Pride and Prejudice* and Dickens's *Bleak House*, Turner identifies the principal elements of the mechanistic tradition and the mechanical philosophy that it forged within the narratives of later writers such as George Meredith, D. H. Lawrence and Doris Lessing. In addition to establishing a vital link between British fiction and the tradition of mechanistic science, Turner reveals the social quandaries fostered by the mechanistic world in *Bleak House*. While Turner's volume offers readers the opportunity to observe the valuable role of science in the Victorian aesthetic, James H. Reid in *Narration and Description in the French Realist Novel: The Temporality of Lying and Forgetting* performs a similar function through his study of French realism and the literary properties of memory and truthfulness. Moreover, this study of such major French realist novelists as Balzac, Flaubert and Zola affords students of Victorian literature the useful opportunity to explore the continental novelists who influenced the British realist novelists of the nineteenth century, including George Eliot and Dickens, among a host of others.

In addition to tracing the cultural history of walking in nineteenth-century English literature, Anne D. Wallace offers close readings of works by Dickens and Hardy in *Walking, Literature, and English Culture: The Origins and Uses of Peripatetic in the Nineteenth Century*. Wallace also surveys the current critical debate regarding Victorian relationships between industrialization and aesthetics, concluding that the assessment of images of walking in British literature affords critics the opportunity to understand the historical underpinnings of nineteenth-century literary plots and characterization strategies. Wallace offers close readings of a number of major works by the literary figures included in her study, although she also features refreshing analyses of several minor items, including Dickens's 'Night Walks'. In addition to considering issues of historical importance such as the land enclosure controversy or the assertion of footpath rights, Wallace demonstrates the value of a proper understanding of the peripatetic and its significant textual relationship with the larger English culture. Hers is an important work. Also of interest is Daniel Pool's *What Jane Austen Ate and Charles Dickens Knew: From Fox Hunting to Whist – The Facts of Daily Life in Nineteenth-Century England*, a volume that examines the social nuances of daily life in nineteenth-century England, as well as their value to an understanding of the literature of that era. In addition to studies of works by Thackeray, Dickens, Eliot, Trollope, and Charlotte Brontë, Pool's text offers readers valuable information about life in the nineteenth century, from details about the value of the Victorian-era British pound to the nature of British manners and society during the nineteenth century.

In *The Captured World: The Child and Childhood in Nineteenth-Century Women's Writing in England*, Penny Brown analyses the 'developments and implications of the theme of childhood' throughout the nineteenth century in a variety of genres, affording particular attention to Victorian fictive depictions of children in 'moral and didactic tales', as well as in 'domestic, family settings' (p. 1). Brown takes issue with Peter Coveney's classic text, *The Image of Childhood: A Study of the Theme in English Literature* (1957), and takes exception to his over-arching, exclusive focus upon male authors, save for George Eliot. Hence, Brown devotes special attention to the works of such writers as Mary Wollstonecraft, Maria Edgeworth, Mary Shelley, Charlotte Brontë, Austen, and Eliot. While Brown offers new explorations of the works of minor figures such as Maria Charlesforth, Catherine Sinclair, and other forgotten Victorian novelists, it cannot be said, however, that her discussions of Brontë's *Jane Eyre* or Eliot's *The Mill on the Floss* add anything particularly significant to the literature of Victorian criticism, despite her intention to 'throw more light on the importance of the child in nineteenth-century literature' (p. 11).

In *Subjects of Slavery, Agents of Change: Women and Power in Gothic Novels and Slave Narratives, 1790–1865*, Kari J. Winter compares the elements of female Gothic novels with slave narratives, and demonstrates that each genre exposes the sexual politics that motivate their creation and the terrifying aspects of life for women during that era. Drawing upon the works of female Gothic writers such as Emily and Charlotte Brontë, Ann Radcliffe and Mary Shelley, Winter assesses the routine brutality and injustice of the patriarchal family and of conventional religion. Additionally, Winter examines the narratives of American former slaves such as Harriet Jacobs and Nancy Prince and the corruptive practices of slavery. In this way, Winter demonstrates the manner in which the female authors of Gothic novels and slave narratives can usurp their roles as victims and mediators of the dominant order and instead become agents of historical change. Likewise, in *Gothic (Re)Visions: Writing Women as Readers*, Susan Wolstenholme assesses Gothic fiction and its critical perception as the special literary province of women, among them, Ann Radcliffe, Mary Shelley, Charlotte Brontë and George Eliot. In addition to exploring such issues as female sexuality, marriage and childbirth, Wolstenholme attempts to explain the 'female' qualities of the Gothic, while arguing that women write with an interest in negotiating their way through their double status as women and as writers, and to subvert the power relationships that hinder women writers. Wolstenholme also suggests that current theories of 'gendered' observation complicate the notion that Gothic fiction relies on individual scenes and visual metaphors to create its effect, while ultimately debunking the idea of a unified narrative in favour of a diffuse, multi-angled narrative quality.

In *The Early and Mid-Victorian Novel*, David Skilton assembles an impressive anthology of mid-nineteenth-century responses to the Victorian novel. Arranged thematically, Skilton's anthology reveals the diverse nature of the mid-Victorian critical debate. Skilton includes chapters on 'The Age of the Novel', 'Fiction with a Purpose', 'Social, Moral, and Religious Judgments', 'Realism and Idealism: The Imitation of Life' 'Plot and Character: Realism and Sensationalism', 'The Imagination and the Creative Process', and 'The Office of Novelist'. In addition to listing a host of contemporaneous critical approaches to works by such figures as George Eliot, Wilkie Collins, Anthony Trollope, Elizabeth Gaskell and Dickens, Skilton's collection offers useful insights into current assumptions about theme, genre, and the literary system in early- and mid-Victorian fiction. Eminently accessible for the scholar and student alike, Skilton's volume explores such worthy topics as literary form, the social responsibility of literature, the influence of criticism, realism, plot, and characterization strategies.

The logical successor to his 1986 volume, *Modes of Production of Victorian Novels*, N. N. Feltes's *Literary Capital and the Late-Victorian Novel* explores novel production during the 1880s and 1890s and traces the shift of the Victorian novel during these decades from a petty-commodity literary mode of production to a capitalist literary machine. Using a Marxist-structuralist interpretational methodology, Feltes argues that during this era novel publication emerged as a form of 'literary capital', and thus increased the gap between author and publisher as literary agents began appearing as mediators. In addition to his analyses of the diaries, publishers' records, and novels by such writers as Robert Louis Stevenson and Arnold Bennett, Feltes examines the various phenomena that literary capital propagated, from book collecting and 'best book' lists to international copyright laws and the privileging of male writers over their female counterparts. Feltes's expansive study contextualizes the capitalization of publishing within the late-Victorian era, while also cogently defining the concepts of form, format and genre and their evolution during this remarkable period of economic, cultural and literary flux.

Dennis W. Allen's *Sexuality in Victorian Fiction* rejects stereotypical notions of Victorian sexual repression and argues instead for the importance of sexuality as a central issue in Victorian culture and literature. Drawing upon historical, feminist, and psychoanalytic critical approaches, Allen reveals the manner in which the Victorian novel's erotic underpinnings reflect the larger difficulty of articulating mainstream Victorian views of sexuality within the ideological construct of nineteenth-century English culture. Using texts such as Austen's *Pride and Prejudice*, Elizabeth Gaskell's *Cranford*, Dickens's *Bleak House*, and Oscar Wilde's *The Picture of Dorian Gray*, Allen demonstrates that these authors attempted to produce and construct sexuality rather than repress it. Allen identifies the chaotic, anarchic and irrational qualities of these texts, and – using the theories of Michel Foucault regarding the history of sexuality – he reveals the Victorian tendency to categorize sexuality as a threat to the larger, ordered dichotomies of Victorian culture. In this way, Allen demonstrates that an awareness of the sexual strategies of Victorian fiction remains essential to an under-standing of nineteenth-century perceptions of the body, gender and the nature of the self.

In *The Inward Revolution: Troubled Young Men in Victorian Fiction, 1850–1880*, Alex J. Tuss explores the Victorian novel's depictions of the young middle-class male as he encounters the commercial *ethos* of the competitive marketplace. Tuss traces the development of this troubled young man through mid-Victorian fiction and periodicals. Using characters from the novels of Charles Kingsley, Dickens, Mary Elizabeth Braddon, George Eliot and Oscar Wilde, Tuss offers an illustration of the social fabric that marked the history and social commentary of the Victorian era. In addition to drawing upon feminist insights, Tuss examines the Woman Question of the late-Victorian era, and its propagation of the 'New Woman', the unstable gender identity that subverted the traditional narrative forms of the latter years of the nineteenth century. Tuss's attention to such issues, as well as his larger examinations of the geography of literary character, under-score the value of his volume in this otherwise previously unexplored region of Victorian studies. Additionally, Jim Reilly's *Shadowtime: History and Represen-tation in Hardy, Conrad, and George Eliot* addresses Adorno's assertion that the crisis of twentieth-century art is its inability to represent historical events, while arguing that this dilemma finds its roots in the nineteenth-century fiction of writers such as Eliot and Hardy. Drawing upon the theoretical insights of Benjamin, Foucault, Hegel, Nietzsche and Lukacs, Reilly reveals the complex relationship between realism, modernism, and the notion of history, while also considering issues of origination, antiquity, historical reconstruction, gender, possession, and the concept of the Real.

In *Allegories of Empire: The Figure of Woman in the Colonial Text*, Jenny Sharpe explores the appropriation of English womanhood for the perpetuation of the British Empire, and in this manner, introduces notions of race and colonialism to feminist theories of rape and sexual difference. Drawing upon the historical memory of the 1857 Indian Mutiny and its influence upon themes of rape in British and Anglo-Indian fiction, Sharpe argues that the idea of Indian men raping white women did not mark the colonial landscape until after the savage attack of mutinous Indian soldiers upon defenceless English women during the incident. In addition to demonstrating the manner in which contemporary theories of female agency impact the imperial past, Sharpe reveals the inappropriateness of such models both in the discussion of colonized women, as well as in their analysis of European women. Sharpe argues that feminist theory – if it truly intends to traverse the race-gender-class impasse – must operate from a premise that assesses notions of difference and dislocation rather than identity and correspond-ence.

Limited to 750 copies, designed by Polly Christensen, and also nicely typeset, Chester W. Topp's *Victorian Yellowbacks and Paperbacks, 1849–1905; Volume One: George Routledge* provides information on George Routledge, proprietor of one of the first publishing houses to issue 'yellowbacks', volumes sold largely at railway bookstalls and newsstands that made available to the general public more expensive three-decker novels. Chronologically arranged on an annual basis, and within years alphabetically arranged, this edition by Topp – an avid collector – provides a wealth of information ranging from price and format to wrappings and cover illustrations, as well as including dates from contemporary trade circulars and journals. Hopefully, subsequent volumes on other publishers will be more organized and draw upon archival material available on microfilm such as the Routledge publishing records, although, notably, the Routledge archives are more difficult to use and locate items in than Topp's edition.

(b) Individual Novelists

Susan S. Kissel recovers and reappraises the works of nineteenth-century writers and reformers in her volume, *In Common Cause: The 'Conservative' Frances Trollope and the 'Radical' Frances Wright*. Kissel considers the many contributions of both women to the most important political movements of their times, including the anti-slavery, women's rights, and industrial reforms. Kissel also argues that the myth of opposition often used in the study of these women's lives devalues the literary significance of their writings. In this way, Kissel reveals the manner in which stereotypes ultimately obscured the individual achievements of these writers during the nineteenth century, as well as within the scholarship of the present day. Similarly, Linda Abess Ellis's volume, *Frances Trollope's America: Four Novels*, addresses the author's quaternion of American novels — *The Refugee in America, The Life and Adventures of Jonathan Jefferson Whitlaw: Or, Scenes on the Mississippi, The Widow Wedded: Or, Adventures of the Barnabys in America*, and *The Old World and the New*. In her study, Ellis explores Trollope's infusion of American characters and institutions in her travel literature written between 1827, when she first departed for America, and 1848, when she finally settled upon Italy for her home. Patricia M. Ar's 'Charles Dickens and Frances Trollope: Victorian Kindred Spirits in the American Wilderness' (*ATQ* 7.293–306) discusses the treatment of American domestic manners and society in the various works of Dickens and Frances Trollope.

In *Robert Surtees and Early Victorian Society*, Norman Gash explores the landscape of Victorian social history and its representation in Surtees's novels. In addition to setting Surtees's writings within the appropriate historical context, Gash studies the novelist's unorthodox and sceptical views in terms of the geography of his texts, from the conservative world of the countryside and its small provincial towns to the seedier side of London. Gash's work should serve as a catalyst for reinvigorating the scholarship devoted to Surtees's often neglected fictional canon. Allan C. Christensen's 'Bulwer, Bloch, Bussotti, and the Filial Muse: Recalled and Foreseen Sources of Inspiration' (*Mosaic* 26.37–52) discusses the influence of Bulwer Lytton's novel, *Zanoni*, upon later works by Ernst Bloch and Sylvano Bussotti. Benjamin Disraeli's *Letters, Volume 5: 1848–1851*, edited by M. G. Wiebe, J. B. Conacher, John Matthews and Mary S. Millar, offers scholars a valuable tool for studying the writer's literary and personal associations with a number of significant Victorian figures, while Stanley Weintraub's magisterial *Disraeli: A Biography* considers the life and work of the great novelist and statesman in consummate fashion, illuminating his novels with biographical and interpretive underpinnings.

A rather thin year for Gaskell studies. In *Elizabeth Gaskell: A Habit of Stories*, Jenny Uglow offers a full literary biography devoted to the often-marginalized novelist Elizabeth Gaskell, and features close readings of her works from *Ruth* and *North and South* to *Sylvia's Lovers* and *Wives and Daughters*. Uglow also traces Gaskell's youth from her early years in rural Knutsford, to her married years in turbulent Manchester, and finally to her later years as a writer amongst her network of friends in London, Europe and America. Further, Andrea Lewis's 'A New Letter by Elizabeth Gaskell' (*ELN* 30.53–8), originally penned by the novelist in 1851, was written to Maria James and contains references to such Victorian figures as Walter Scott and Thackeray. In 'Mrs. Gaskell's Reference to Italian Punishment in *Mary Barton*' (*N&Q* 40.481–2), Stephen Derry reveals a source for Gaskell's 1848 novel. Also, in 'Cranford and the Victorian Collection' (*VS* 36.179–206), Tim Dolin examines Gaskell's *Cranford*, the Great Exhibition of 1851, and their relationships to Victorian culture. Alexander and Hewitt's *Scott in Carnival* – a volume that features selected papers from the Fourth International Scott Conference in Edinburgh in 1991 – includes Constance D. Harsh's 'Effaced by History: Elizabeth Gaskell's Reformulation of Scott', an essay that examines the influence of Scott upon the larger Victorian fictional aesthetic, and moreover, upon the historical ideology that marks Gaskell's writings.

In *Thackeray and Slavery*, Deborah A. Thomas traces themes of slavery, bondage, and racism in the novels of Thackeray. Through close readings of such works as *Barry Lyndon*, *Vanity Fair*, and *The Virginians*, Thomas examines the thematic value of the motif of slavery in Thackeray's canon, focusing particularly on the author's enduring interest in the history of slavery, as well as the operation of the caste system in his own historical era. In addition to considering the novelist's enduring interest in slavery as an historical construct, Thomas explores the relationship between the novelist's contemporary concerns with the abolition of slavery, his Indian background, and his mother's evangelistic predilections. Thomas fully and convincingly demonstrates the manner in which Thackeray exploits the potential of slavery as a subject. As her analyses reveal, Barry Lyndon's enslavement of his wife, the patterns of domination and subjection in *Vanity Fair*, and the marriage market in *The Newcomes* exemplify Thackeray's imaginative use of the auspices of slavery as an historical institution. Likewise, Thomas argues that Thackeray's approach to slavery remains remarkably ambiguous because of his abiding interest in presenting the fullness of human experience to his readers. In 'Colonial Discourse and William Makepeace Thackeray's *Irish Sketch Book*' (*PLL* 29.259–83), Kenneth L. Brewer, Jr explores the role of historiography in the writings of Thackeray, particularly in regard to the historical nature of Victorian England and the composition of the *Irish Sketch Book*.

Richard Pearson's 'W. M. Thackeray: An Uncollected Paris Letter from *The Constitutional* (1836–1837)' (*N&Q* 40.474–7) features a letter from Thackeray's series of foreign correspondence, and indicates his probable growing dissatisfaction with correspondence as a means for political commentary. In 'The Ex-Collector of Boggley-Wollah: Colonialism in the Empire of *Vanity Fair*' (*Narrative* 1.124–37), Sandy Morey Norton examines Thackeray's use of satire and his treatment of colonial issues in *Vanity Fair*. Sheldon Goldfarb's 'Thackeray and the Celebrated Wilkes of Paris' (*ELN* 31.40–3) discusses Thackeray's fictionalized treatment of John and Charles Wilkes in *Catherine*, while William J. Virker's 'Thackeray's Medical Fathers' (*VIJ* 21.71–86) addresses Thackeray's relationship to medicine and its treatment in his novels. In 'Manhood in *Vanity Fair*' (*CVE* 37.87–102), Max Vega-Ritter explores the treatment of masculinity and its relationship to desire in Thackeray's novel, while in 'Thackeray's Editors and the Dual Text of *Vanity Fair*' (*W&I* 9.39–50), Christopher Coates discusses the function of illustrations in Thackeray's text. Donald Bruce's 'Thackeray the Sentimental Sceptic' (*ContempR* 262.313–21) assesses Thackeray's depictions of urban life in London, particularly in *Vanity Fair*.

As with many of the principal figures in the Victorian canon – including the

Brontës, George Eliot, and Hardy, among others – the recent critical material devoted to the study of Dickens continues to be overwhelming. In *Charles Dickens and the Image of Woman*, David Holbrook employs psychoanalytic critical insights in his exploration of the various roles of women in Dickens's fictional canon, from angels, guides, whores and witches to mothers, libidinal sexual partners and emblems of death. Holbrook affords special attention to Dickens's recurring association of woman with images of murder and death, including the strange image of the hanging woman in *Great Expectations* to the appalling and visceral murder of Nancy in *Oliver Twist*. These images, Holbrook argues, define horrific moments of phenomenological meaning for Dickens and his narrative obsession with the dangers inherent to the culmination of sensual lust and the primal threat of sexual intercourse. Holbrook includes close readings of a number of Dickens's novels in his study, including *Bleak House*, *Little Dorrit*, *Great Expectations*, and *Our Mutual Friend*, while at the same time considering Dickens's use of themes of religion, sin and shame in his work. Holbrook concludes this fascinating study with a useful and provocative assessment of Dickens's own relationships with women and their likely role in the creation of his fictional aesthetic.

Natalie McKnight's *Idiots, Madmen, and Other Prisoners in Dickens* examines Dickens's fascination with prisoners of private worlds and arcane languages, and argues that nineteenth-century prison and asylum reforms and Dickens's own experiences with imprisonment influenced the novelist's attitudes toward these characters. McKnight also suggests that Dickens created such figures in an effort to rebel against the social limitations of Victorian norms, as well as to advocate a greater sense of openness to aberrance in his fictions. Despite his apparent intentions for reform, however, McKnight notes that Dickens's approach to his characters remained inconsistent. She argues that his own imprisonment within the strictures of his bourgeois values forced him to marginalize these figures despite his desires to celebrate them. Drawing upon the insights of feminism and Michel Foucault, McKnight also explores Dickens's marginal treatment of female aberrant characters and their voiceless portrayal in his writings. McKnight includes close readings of *Nicholas Nickleby*, *Barnaby Rudge*, *Dombey and Son*, and *Little Dorrit* in this valuable contribution to Dickens criticism.

The editors of *DSA* (22) include a variety of essays in their latest volume that employ a diversity of critical approaches in their analyses of Dickens, including historical, biographical, feminist and narratological critical methodologies. Anny Sadrin's 'Fragmentation in *The Pickwick Papers*' (21–34) explores the pejorative nature of the critical assumptions regarding the fragmentary nature of the narrative of Dickens's novel, while Kenneth M. Sroka's 'Dickens's Metafiction: Readers and Writers in *Oliver Twist*, *David Copperfield*, and *Our Mutual Friend*' (35–66) discusses Dickens's approach to the textual and mechanistic functions of his fiction. In 'Carnivalesque "Unlawful Games" in *The Old Curiosity Shop*' (67–120), Mark M. Hennelly, Jr examines the carnival references and qualities of Dickens's novel, while Gerhard Joseph's 'Construing the Inimitable's Silence: Pecksniff's Grammar School and International Copyright' (121–36) addresses Dickens's enduring angst regarding the nature of Victorian copyright laws and their effect on the international publication of his works, particularly *Martin Chuzzlewit*. Scott Moncrieff's '*The Cricket* in the Study' (137–54) examines the problematic critical reputation of Dickens's often neglected novel, *The Cricket on the Hearth*, while Margaret Flanders Darby's 'Dora and Doady' (155–70) explores the paradoxical qualities of the narrative structure of *David Copperfield*. In 'What's Troubling about Esther? Narrating, Policing, and Resisting Arrest in *Bleak House*' (171–94), Jasmine Yong Hall discusses Esther's vigilance and its function in Dickens's novel. Efraim Sicher's 'Acts of Enclosure: The Moral Landscapes of Dickens' *Hard Times*'s (195–216) addresses the historical and cultural qualities of Dickens's 'moral fable' in *Hard Times*, while Edwin M. Eigner's 'Dogmatism and Puppyism: The Novelist, the Reviewer, and the Serious Subject; The Case of *Little Dorrit*' (217–38) discusses the polemical qualities of Dickens's novel and its critical appropriation as a means for fomenting public debate. In 'Inimitable Double Vision: Dickens, *Little Dorrit*, Photography, Film' (239–82), Joss Lutz March critiques film versions of Dickens's writings, particularly the 1987 film production of *Little Dorrit*. The article is well illustrated with drawings and still photographs from the films of Dickens's works. In 'Trevelyan, Treasury, and Circumlocution' (283–302), Trey Philpotts examines Dickens's treatment of the Circumlocution Office in *Little Dorrit*.

In *Charles Dickens: The Uses of Time*, James E. Marlow explores the novelist's attitudes toward the past, present and future in his writings, thus clarifying the antinomies that mark his writings. Drawing upon Dickens's correspondence, journalistic essays and novels, Marlow traces the author's personal and literary development from his painful childhood to his dysfunctional marriage. Similarly, a variety of essays in the December 1993 issue of *Dickens Quarterly* explore the novelist's approach to narrative strategy and design. In 'Thackeray's First Fashioned Response to Dickens: *The Yellowish Papers* Cast a Cynical Eye on the "Admiral Boz's *Pickwick Papers*"', Mark Cronin assesses Dickens's celebration of life, language and community in *The Pickwick Papers*, while also examining Thackeray's response to Dickens's novel and its dark analysis of the perverse and corruptive elements that threaten to undermine the spirit of Dickens's optimistic narrative. William G. Wall's 'Mrs. Affery Flintwich's Dreams: Reading and Remembering in *Little Dorrit*' addresses the function of memory and dreams in Dickens's fictional aesthetic, particularly emphasizing the challenges of the serial novel in representing such narrative constructs. The issue concludes with Ella Westland's 'The Making of Dickens: Conflicts in Criticism, 1940–1970', which assesses the critical reception of Dickens during the twentieth century by such critics as F. R. Leavis and Edmund Wilson, as well as the place of Dickens in the larger university literary curriculum.

In *Eloquent Reticence: Withholding Information in Fictional Narrative*, Leona Toker offers a paradigm for understanding the narrative strategies of a number of classic novels, including Dickens's *Bleak House*. Through close readings of these texts, Toker demonstrates the manner in which the withholding of information affects the attitudes of readers, stimulates their personal reassessment, and leads them to a self-critical reorientation. Drawing upon descriptive poetics, reader-response criticism, and information theory, Toker analyses the characters of these novels and affords particular attention to their moments of silence and reticence within narratives. Similarly, in *Dickens's Rhetoric*, Sheila M. Foor discusses the function of language in the operation of Dickens's elaborate plot and characterization structures. Adam Roberts's 'Dickens Megalosaurus' (*N&Q* 40.478–9) examines the chronological puzzle that opens *Bleak House*, while Rodney Stenning Edgecombe's 'A Variant Reading of *Bleak House*' (*N&Q* 40.479) explores a likely proofreading oversight by Dickens during the production of his novel. In 'Locution and Authority in *Martin Chuzzlewit*' (*ES*

74.143–53), Edgecombe examines the novelist's use of Shakespearean and Ho-
meric proverbs, as well as their value to an understanding of Dickens's narrative.
In 'Bringing to Earth the "Good Angel of the Race"' (*VN* 84.25–8), Michael
Schiefelbein discusses the treatment of spirituality and the characterization of
Nell in *The Old Curiosity Shop*, while Monika Rydygier Smith's 'The W/Hole
Remains: Consumerist Politics in *Bleak House, Great Expectations*, and *Our
Mutual Friend*' (*VR* 19.1–21) examines the function of the consumer in the urban
societies of Dickens's novels. David Paroissien's '*Oliver Twist* and the Contours
of Early Victorian England' (*VN* 83.14–17) explores the treatment of Victorian
culture and its function within the narrative fabric of *Oliver Twist*.

In 'Bodies of Capital: *Great Expectations* and the Climacteric Economy' (*VS*
37.73–97), Susan Walsh argues that Miss Havisham functions as an important
index to the local economies operating beneath the ahistorical fairy tale motifs
that define the structure of *Great Expectations*. In addition to exploring the
influence upon Dickens by Victorian legislation such as the Limited Liability Act
of 1855, Walsh discusses the place of Miss Havisham in Dickens's novel as the
means by which the novelist demarcates the commercial parameters within which
Victorian men operated. Sue Zemka's 'From the Punchmen to Pugin's Gothics:
The Broad Road to a Sentimental Death in *The Old Curiosity Shop*' (*NCL*
48.291–309) addresses the manner in which Dickens's novel has dismayed
readers because of its 'disunity' and 'lack of design', and argues instead that
issues of class position and mobility afford the novel with properties of coherence
and narrative design. Steven Michael's 'Criminal Slang in *Oliver Twist*: Dickens's Survival Code' (*Style* 27.41–62) contains an analysis of criminal slang with
special reference to the Artful Dodger's focal scene. Michael concludes that 'the
Dodger uses language – whether translating flash language or dropping it altogether – to sustain his identity, to separate himself from a society whose Principle
of Good is a gossamer morality having little to do with humanity' (59). David M.
Wilkes in 'Dickens's *David Copperfield*' (*Expl* 51.157–9) discusses the other
characters' pejorative labels for David in the novel, while also exploring David's
relationship with Murdstone.

The 1993 incarnation of *Dickensian* (89), edited by Malcolm Andrews, features a number of essays devoted to the study of Dickens's enormous fictional
canon. Richard Lettis's '"How I Work": Dickens in the Writer's Chair' (5–24)
attempts to define the creative force that motivated Dickens during the act of
writing, while Valerie L. Gager's '"Our Pew at Church": Another Interpretation
by Way of Shakespeare' (25–31) explores the role of sculpture in *David
Copperfield* and its resemblance to William Shakespeare's memorial at his
graveside in Holy Trinity Church at Stratford-upon-Avon. Nancy E.
Schaumburger's 'The "Time Machine" of *Great Expectations*: Pip, Magwitch,
and Developmental Time' (32–5) assesses the roles of time and memory in the
characterization of Pip and Magwitch, particularly in regard to Dickens's structural strategies for the narrative of *Great Expectations*. In 'The "Glaring Fault"
in the Structure of *Bleak House*' (36–8), Gillian West interprets Lady Dedlock's
personal history as yet another instance of the tragic destruction caused by the
over-arching role of the Chancery in Dickens's novel, and moreover, she argues
that there is no 'fissure' in the structure of *Bleak House*, as J. Hillis Miller claims
in his introduction to the Penguin edition of the novel. Similarly, in 'Lady
Dedlock's Sin' (39–43), Maria Nicholls ascertains the nature of Lady Dedlock
and the causes of her unhappy life and pathetic death, while in 'The Influence of

King Lear on *Bleak House*' (45–9) Shifra Hochberg analyses the influence of Shakespeare's play upon the moral topography and character considerations in Dickens's novel.

Additional essays in *Dickensian* include Steven O'Connor's 'Dead? Or Alive?: *Edwin Drood* and the Work of Mourning' (85–102), which assesses Timothy Forder's film version of *The Mystery of Edwin Drood* and its failure to capture the spirit of Dickens's work. In 'He Played with Crummles: The Life and Career of William Pleater Davidge, Anglo-American Actor, Author, and Dickens Enthusiast (1814–1888)' (103–17), Robert Simpson MacLean explores the career of Davidge, as well as the actor's role in Dickens's life and work. Charles Forsyte's 'Charles Kent and Dickens's Last Birthday" (118–28) considers the textual background of Kent's pamphlet, *Charles Dickens's Last Birthday Celebration* (1899), while R. D. Butterworth's 'Dickens the Journalist: The Preston Strike and "On Strike"'(129–38) discusses the influence of the January 1854 Preston Strike upon the creation of Dickens's *Hard Times*. The *Dickensian's* special issue on *A Christmas Carol* includes 'The Reception and Status of the *Carol*' (170–6), in which Philip Collins explores the critical and popular reception of Dickens's novel, while in 'The Triumph of Humour: The *Carol* Revisited' (184–92), Michael Slater assesses the role of wit and humour in *A Christmas Carol*. Edwin M. Eigner's 'On Becoming Pantaloon' (177–83) examines the role of nineteenth-century pantomime in the narrative fabric of the *Carol*, while J. Hillis Miller defines 'The Genres of *A Christmas Carol*' (193–206) and their place in Dickens's Victorian England. In addition to the inclusion of David Dickens's biographical account, 'Dickens Was Dead: To Begin With' (207–13), the special issue includes Charles W. Callahan, Jr's 'Tiny Tim: The Child with a Crippling Fatal Illness' (214–17), an essay that explores Dickens's vague treatment of Tiny Tim's debilitating fatal disease. Finally, James J. and Patience P. Barnes's 'Solitude and Ghosts in Dickens's Christmas Books' (218–25) discusses the role of ghosts and spirits in the narratives of a number of Dickens's annual Christmas volumes.

A number of new corrected editions of Dickens's novels accent the wave of recent criticism of his writings. Margaret Cardwell's edition of *Great Expectations* marks the latest instalment in the great Pilgrim edition of Dickens's works. Inaugurated in 1966, Clarendon's deluxe series of editions of the novelist's classic texts features an array of useful front and back matter, including Cardwell's extensive textual introduction, a lavish selection of illustrative plates, and a valuable descriptive listing of editions of *Great Expectations* published between 1861 and 1868. The volume concludes with seven appendices, including notes on the novel's original ending, Dickens's compository notes, a listing for the instalments of *All the Year Round*, notes on the first five impressions of *Great Expectations*, and notes, illustrations, and headlines for later editions of the novel during the 1860s. Fred Kaplan's Norton critical edition of *Oliver Twist: Authoritative Text, Backgrounds and Sources, Early Reviews, Criticism* also offers a text particularly valuable for students. Although he departs from the Clarendon edition of the novel in several respects, he nevertheless employs the ten serialized instalments of the original 1846 edition of *Oliver Twist*. Kaplan includes a map of the city of London as it appears in the novel, a lengthy selection of Dickens's correspondence regarding the composition of the novel, and a special section devoted to the Poor Law Amendment Act of 1834 and its centrality to any understanding of the historical implications of *Oliver Twist*. The eminently accessible Everyman text of *A Tale of Two Cities*, edited by Norman Page, contains his succinct introduction to the novel. Ruth F. Glancy's *'A Tale of Two Cities': An Annotated Bibliography* offers scholars complete listings of the novel's dramatizations, film scripts and contemporary reviews, in addition to her inclusion of references to manuscripts, newspaper articles, journal articles and musical productions of *A Tale of Two Cities*. The publication of the seventh volume of the Pilgrim edition of *The Letters of Charles Dickens* covering the years 1853 to 1855, and edited by Graham Storey, Kathleen Tillotson, and Angus Easson, concludes a significant year in the promulgation of both new and authoritative editions of Dickens's writings. This continuing monumental work of scholarship contains as its first appendix an 'Addenda to Volumes I–VI (1820–1852)' featuring a wealth of new letters that 'came to light too late to include in the appropriate volume. Some are wholly new, others provide a fuller text, replacing a former catalogue extract, summary, or mention' (777). There are five other useful appendices to this significant volume in the Pilgrim edition of Dickens's correspondence. This and Margaret Cardwell's edition of *Great Expectations* are the highlights of yet another fervid year in Dickens scholarship and criticism.

Students of the novels of Trollope should note the publication of four new primary Trollope editions, including David Skilton's new edition of *He Knew He Was Right*, published in the Everyman series. In addition to featuring extensive corrections unavailable in earlier editions of the text, Skilton's volume includes a chronology and critical essay of particular value to students. Skilton also edits the first World's Classics edition of *The Golden Lion of Granpère*, an often neglected entry in Trollope's profuse literary canon. The World's Classics series likewise offers a new edition of Trollope's *John Caldigate*, edited by N. John Hall, the doyen of Trollope scholarship and biography, and appended with an extensive introduction and a selection of useful explanatory notes. Another fine scholar and critic, Graham Handley, offers an edition of *Trollope the Traveller: Selections from Trollope's Travel Writings* that features extracts from the novelist's travels to *The West Indies and the Spanish Main*, *North America*, *Australia and New Zealand*, and *South Africa*. Handley's edition provides readers with Trollope's important professional insights into the political, social and economic conditions that he encountered during his considerable travels, and these tracts are likewise valuable for their contribution to the critical understanding of the author's life and work during the nineteenth century.

In 'Reading Trollope: Whose Englishness Is It Anyway?' (*DSA* 22.303–29), Julian Wolfreys examines in a lively manner the question of Englishness and its problematized treatment in the Palliser novels of Trollope, particularly regarding crises of identity in the political and cultural discourses of the English bourgeoisie of the 1870s. Scott Moncrieff's '"It's the Life": Trollope's Fictional Autobiography' (*CVE* 37.95–105) discusses the role of Trollope's biographical life in his fictional autobiography, while two recent pieces trace the frequently tenuous state of Trollope's current literary reputation: N. John Hall's 'A Corner of Westminster Abbey That Will Always Be Anthony Trollope' (*NYTBR* 35) and Louise Weinberg's 'Is It Alright to Read Trollope?' (*ASch* 447–51). The critical reception of the works of Anthony Trollope are treated in Denise Kohn's '"The Journey to Panama": One of Trollope's Best "Tarts" – or, Why You Should Read "The Journey to Panama" to Develop Your Taste for Trollope' (*SSF* 30.15–22). In her essay, Kohn examines the nature of Trollope's short fiction and its place within his fictional canon. In 'Truth and Fiction in Trollope's *Autobiography'* (*NCL* 48.74–88), R. H. Super, the distinguished Arnold scholar, explores the composition of Trollope's *Autobiography* and his treatment of a number of his Victorian contemporaries, including Dickens. Also of interest are the World's Classics edition of the frequently marginalized Anglo-Irish author Sheridan Le Fanu's *In a Glass Darkly*, edited with a valuable biographical introduction by Robert Tracy, and Daniel Barrett's '*It Is Never Too Late to Mend* (1865) and Prison Conditions in Nineteenth-Century England' (*TRI* 18.4–15), an essay that considers the dramatization of Charles Reade's *It Is Never Too Late to Mend* and its commentary on the condition of Victorian prisons and the treatment of their inmates.

Elizabeth Imlay considers the writings of Charlotte Brontë in her volume, *Charlotte Brontë and the Mysteries of Love: Myth and Allegory in Jane Eyre.* In addition to analysing the novel in regard to Brontë's cultural and educational background, Imlay explores the novelist's reading material and the text of *Jane Eyre* in an effort to demonstrate how the novel conceals a brilliant reworking of the classic fairy-tale, *Cupid and Psyche*. Imlay argues that Brontë knew of the tale's relationship to the Platonic mystery tradition, and for this reason she employed it in her endeavour to describe a nineteenth-century figure in search of passionate love. Imlay also examines the Brontë family's intimate connection with Freemasonry, their knowledge of classical paganism and magic, and the implications of these issues within the narrative of *Jane Eyre*. In her reading of the novel, Imlay reveals the manner in which Brontë's wandering heroine travels through air, fire and water to ultimately emerge as a human soul that unites with love in a spiritual and physical union. Drawing upon feminist, and psychoanalytic critical approaches, Imlay's study offers a valuable contribution to the understanding of *Jane Eyre*'s classical origins. Also, in David Cowart's *Literary Symbiosis: The Reconfigured Text in Twentieth-Century Writing*, the literary borrowings and retellings of twentieth-century texts are explored, focusing in particular upon Jean Rhys's rewriting of *Jane Eyre* in *Wide Sargasso Sea.* Drawing upon the theoretical arguments of Lacan and Derrida, Cowart affords special attention to the examination of the concrete and explicit qualities of intertextuality, and argues that such texts assume a postmodern tendency towards self-consciousness and self-reflexivity, thus engaging in an 'epistemic dialogue' with the past. Cowart concludes that the intertextual qualities of such narratological relationships affect indelibly the manner in which readers experience the host text, in this instance, Brontë's *Jane Eyre*. *Approaches to Teaching Brontë's Jane Eyre*, edited by Diane Long Hoeveler and Beth Lau, reprints a variety of essays exploring Brontë's novel from a wealth of critical perspectives.

In *Charlotte Brontë and Her 'Dearest Nell': The Story of a Friendship*, Barbara Whitehead offers a similar, close textual reading of Charlotte Brontë's writings, in this instance, based on her voluminous and revealing correspondence with her 'dearest Nell', Ellen Nussey. Drawing upon letters from Brontë to Nussey, Whitehead tells the fascinating tale of the novelist's life, from her meeting with Nussey in 1831, through the composition and publication of her novels, to her marriage and death in the 1850s. Additionally, Whitehead's study offers close analysis of the themes, characters, and settings of *Jane Eyre* and *Shirley*, whose character of Caroline Helstone was based on Nussey. Whitehead also devotes attention to the study of Nussey's efforts on behalf of Brontë after the novelist's death, particularly her role in procuring Mrs Gaskell to write a posthumous biography of Brontë. Whitehead supplements this significant volume with a useful selection of manuscript listings and illustrations. Additionally, in '"That Kingdom of Gloom": Charlotte Brontë, the Annuals, and the Gothic' (*NCL* 47.409–36), Christine Alexander argues that Brontë employs conventional Gothic motifs in an effort to forge a 'New Gothic' that functioned upon a heightened sense of emotion, as well as the notion of a surreal and psychic disorder.

Patsy Stoneman's edition of *Wuthering Heights: Contemporary Critical Essays* features essays reprinted from a host of significant critics employing psychoanalytic, deconstructive, Marxist, historical and feminist approaches to Emily Brontë's classic novel. Selections include Stoneman's introduction; Q. D. Leavis's 'A Fresh Approach to *Wuthering Heights*'; Frank Kermode's '*Wuthering Heights* as Classic'; John T. Matthews's 'Framing in *Wuthering Heights*'; N. M. Jacobs's 'Gender and Layered Narrative in *Wuthering Heights*'; Lyn Pykett's 'Gender and Genre in *Wuthering Heights*'; Michael Macovski's 'Voicing a Silent History: *Wuthering Heights* as Dialogic Text'; Terry Eagleton's 'Myths of Power in *Wuthering Heights*'; Sandra M. Gilbert's 'Looking Oppositely: Emily Brontë's Bible of Hell'; Stevie Davies's 'The Language of Familial Desire'; and Patricia Parker's 'The (Self-) Identity of the Literary Text: Property, Proper Place, and Proper Name in *Wuthering Heights*'; Stoneman concludes her edition with a useful, although regrettably unannotated, listing of critical scholarship for further reading. Monica L. Feinberg's 'Homesick: The Domestic Interiors of *Villette*' (*Novel* 26.182–91) reveals Charlotte Brontë's use of a 'rhetoric of renunciation' in her treatment of the character of Lucy Snowe, particularly in regard to the trappings of Snowe's spinsterhood, while in 'Down Garden Paths: Charlotte Brontë's Haunts of Self and Other' (*VN* 83.35–43), Barbara Gates examines the function of the self and the 'other' in Brontë's fictive world. Gayla McGlamery's 'The Unlicked Wolf-Club: Anti-Catholicism in Charlotte Brontë's *Villette*' (*CVE* 37.55–71) explicates Brontë's complex attitude towards Catholicism and its role in the narrative of her novel. Also of interest is Everyman's latest republication of *Villette*, edited by Sandra Kemp, and featuring a comprehensive textual introduction and a valuable selection of biographical notes.

Russell Poole examines 'Cultural Reformation and Cultural Reproduction in Anne Brontë's *The Tenant of Wildfell Hall*' in *SEL* (33.859–74). Poole discusses the elements of theology and realism and their role in Brontë's narrative and characterization strategies. Poole argues that Brontë's depiction of her heroine Helen Huntingdon's struggle for purity, order and control simultaneously reforms and perpetuates the practices of the larger society in which Brontë lived and wrote. Drawing upon feminist, deconstructive, and Russian formalist critical approaches, Poole describes Brontë's novel as a text replete with conflicts and contradictions regarding theology and sexuality in a Victorian culture that both represses and liberates female desire, while simultaneously condemning and encouraging the male libido. As Poole concludes: 'Brontë's theology spares her female protagonist from the unequivocal extinction of her Desire, regardless of how corrupt that Desire may be' (871).

Scholars interested in Anne Brontë's second novel should also note the recent publication of the World's Classics edition of *The Tenant of Wildfell Hall*, edited by Herbert Rosengarten with an introduction by Margaret Smith, and based upon Rosengarten's splendid Clarendon edition of the novel (1991). Rosengarten's edition features a useful selection of textual notes, an Anne Brontë biographical chronology, and a variety of appendices of value to the scholar and student alike.

Additionally, students of the Brontës might note Robert G. Collins's recent edition, *The Hand of the Arch-Sinner: Two Angrian Chronicles of Branwell Brontë*. In addition to a detailed and extensive introduction, Collins includes the texts of two novellas by Patrick Branwell Brontë, including *The Life of Field Marshal ... Alexander Percy* and *Real Life in Verdopolis: A Tale*. Collins supplements this valuable edition with notes on his textual methodology, the unabridged manuscripts of Branwell Brontë's texts, a Branwell Brontë biographical chronology, and a useful selection of textual and explanatory notes vital to the reconstruction and recovery of these often forgotten chronicles by the brother of three of the Victorian age's most gifted novelists.

The consummate achievement of the year's work in George Eliot scholarship is Andrew Brown's superb critical edition of *Romola*. This is the sixth volume in the Clarendon edition of the novels of George Eliot, and contains a wealth of scholarly information. For his text, Brown chooses the *Cornhill* serial version, whilst providing at the foot of each page of text variants in other editions and in the manuscript. In addition to an 82-page introduction, there are 184 pages of extensive and detailed explanatory notes. Brown writes well and his edition is an *exemplum* of editing, laced with information on Eliot, her creative practices, and the collaborative relationship among author, printer and publisher in Victorian England.

Brian Spittles's *George Eliot: Godless Woman* supplies literary and social contexts for the principal issues that Eliot impinges upon in her fiction. He supplements his study with extensive analyses of Eliot's novels, letters, essays and poetry, as well as with the voices of a host of the novelist's nineteenth-century contemporaries, including Victorian feminist journals and tracts, newspapers, magazines and scientific theories. In *George Eliot and the Conventions of Popular Women's Fiction: A Serious Literary Response to 'Silly Novels by Lady Novelists'*, Susan Rowland Tush uses Eliot's *Westminster Review* 1856 essay on female novelists as a guide for examining the novelist's response to the literary conventions that prevailed in the fictions of Victorian women writers. In addition to exploring the six popular novels referred to by Eliot in her essay, Tush examines the role of these narratives in Eliot's *Adam Bede*, *The Mill on the Floss*, and *Middlemarch*.

Using texts by George Eliot and others, Leland Monk argues in *Standard Deviations: Chance and the Modern British Novel* that chance is the unrepresentable 'other' of narrative. Monk also traces the fictional treatment of chance to important historical constructs in the philosophical and scientific understanding of the nature of chance. In his analysis of the thematic properties of chance, Monk reveals the textual and theoretical problems inherent to understanding the role of chance in the reading experience of a novel. Monk argues that in *Middlemarch* Eliot proffers a new and distinctive vision of chance and its role in Victorian fiction, particularly through her break with the prevailing providential aesthetic and her adoption of a realistic aesthetic informed by scientific principles. Using such textual exemplars, Monk defines an aesthetic framework for understanding the novelist's paradoxical attempt to depict chance in a narrative form that ostensibly furnishes the reading experience with structures of order and design.

In '*The Mill on the Floss*, the Critics, and the *Bildungsroman*' (*PMLA* 108.136–50), Susan Fraiman addresses the two sibling tales that define the narrative of Eliot's novel, particularly the dialogic structure of the novel and its role in the emergence of feminist criticism and canon formation. In his mono-graph, *George Eliot and George Sand*, Daniel Vitaglione explores the compara-ble social, religious and aesthetic conceptions of the two women novelists. Vitaglione's volume also employs recently discovered correspondence in the examination of the friendship of Lewes and Sand, while also assessing the influence of the French writer on the development of Eliot's thought and aesthet-ics. Terence Dawson's '"Light Enough to Trusten By": Structure and Experience in *Silas Marner*' (*MLR* 88.26–45) argues that the narrative of *Silas Marner* includes numerous thematic concerns that suggest that the events that it describes are shaped by a psychological dilemma from Eliot's biographical life. Moreover, Dawson contends that the text's structure invites readers to read the novel as an expression of a woman's psychological concerns.

In 'Struggling for Medical Reform in *Middlemarch*' (*NCL* 48.341–61), Lilian R. Furst argues, perhaps hardly surprisingly, that Eliot's novel offers a number of revelations about Victorian medical organization and practices, while also ad-dressing the medical dimension of the novel and its value to understanding Eliot's thematic intentions. Margaret Homans's 'Dinah's Blush, Maggie's Arm: Class, Gender, and Sexuality in George Eliot's Early Novels' (*VS* 36.155–78) considers notions of propriety and the predominance of the Victorian middle-class he-gemony in novels such as *Adam Bede* and *The Mill on the Floss*. Similarly, in 'The Miser's Two Bodies: *Silas Marner* and the Sexual Possibilities of the Commodity' (*VS* 36.273–92), Jeff Nunokawa explores issues of gender and the body in his examination of the place and displacement of the family in Eliot's novel. In 'A Novel Sympathy: The Imagination of Community in George Eliot' (*Novel* 27.5–23), Forest Pyle discusses the 'figure of the imagination in *Adam Bede* and *The Mill on the Floss*'. Additionally, in 'George Eliot's Scrupulous Research: The Facts Behind Eliot's Use of the *Keepsake* in *Middlemarch*' (*VPR* 26.19–23), Meg M. Moring studies Eliot's passion for meticulous research, as evidenced by her notebooks, journals, correspondence and fiction. In addition to exploring the role of the Victorian periodical *Keepsake* in *Middlemarch*, Moring assesses the place of the text in Eliot's writings.

The September 1993 issue of *GEGHL* includes essays that explore Eliot and Lewes's work from a variety of critical perspectives. In 'George Eliot, George Henry Lewes, and Spinoza's *Tractatus Theologico-Politicus*' (1–16), Thomas Deegan examines the roles of Eliot and Lewes in the creation of Spinoza's *Tractatus*, while also addressing their failed attempts during the 1840s and mid-1850s to publish English translations of Spinoza's works. Eeyan Hartley's 'A Country House Connection: George Eliot and the Howards of Castle Howard' (17–21) reveals the nature of the friendship between Rosalind Howard and Eliot, as evinced by previously neglected materials housed in the Howard Archives. In 'The Two Georges' (22–31) Martha S. Vogeler explores the remarkable commonalities between the lives and literary heritages of Eliot and George Gissing. Edward H. Cohen's 'George Eliot and W. E. Henley: A Case of Influ-ence' (32–36) traces Henley's unabashed admiration for Eliot and her profound influence upon his poetic sequence, *In Hospital*. D. J. Trela's 'Two Margaret Oliphants Review George Eliot' (37–60) addresses the contradictory nature of Oliphant's many reviews and analyses of Eliot's novels, ranging from high praise to abject criticism. In 'Robert Louis Stevenson and the "High ... Rather Dry Lady"'(61–8), Laura Mooneyham assesses Stevenson's brash critical retort to Eliot's *Daniel Deronda*, a 'literary abomination', Stevenson wrote, by 'a woman of genius' (61). Finally, Robert Bates Graber's 'Herbert Spencer and George Eliot: Some Corrections and Implications' (69–83) comments on the relationship between Spencer and Eliot and its influence upon their respective writings, while also assessing Gordon S. Haight's account of their friendship.

A special issue of *GEGHL*, edited by William Baker and John Rignall, includes essays from a conference at the University of Warwick in July 1992 devoted to 'George Eliot and the Heart of England'. Barbara Hardy's 'Rome in *Middlemarch*: A Need for Foreignness' (1–16) explores the role of international scenes and images in Eliot's novels and stories, while Beryl Gray's 'The Power of Provincial Culture: *Felix Holt*' (17–35) discusses Eliot's acute awareness of her own tendency to be beguiled by an imagined past and the role of this phenomenon in *Felix Holt*. In 'Shakespeare at the Heart of George Eliot's England' (36–64), A. G. van den Broek explores Eliot's infusion of Shakespearian character, plot, and theatrical constructs in her novels. T. J. Winnifrith's '"Subtle Shadowy Suggestions": Fact and Fiction in *Scenes of Clerical Life*' (65–75) addresses the relationship between Eliot's biographical life and the narrative of *Scenes of Clerical Life*. The seminal Eliot biography bears scrutiny in Hugh Witemeyer's 'The Province of Scandal: Gordon S. Haight's Conception of the Biographer's Task' (76–92), an essay in which Witemeyer charges Eliot's biographer with 'revisionist interpretation'. Rosemary Ashton's 'Mixed and Erring Humanity: George Eliot, G. H. Lewes, and Goethe' (93–117) explores Goethe's role in forging the narrative voices of Lewes and Eliot, while Kevin Ashby's 'The Centre and the Margins in *The Lifted Veil* and Blackwood's *Edinburgh Magazine*' (132–46) discusses the relationship of the magazine to Eliot's early fiction. William Baker's 'Memory: Eliot and Lewes' "The Past Is a Foreign Country, They Do Things Differently There"' (118–31) addresses the function of memory and imagination in the writings of Eliot and Lewes. In 'History and the "Speech of the Landscape" in Eliot's Depiction of Midland Life' (147–62), John Rignall assesses the landscape of the Midlands and its role in the national life of England and its place in Eliot's fiction, particularly in *The Impressions of Theophrastus Such*. Finally, the late John Goode's 'Remembering Anywhere: Notes Towards the Definition of a Midlands Writer' (163–74) explores the function of the Midlands in the development of Eliot's fictional aesthetic.

Alan W. Bellringer's *George Eliot*, one of the latest instalments in Macmillan's 'Modern Novelists' series, features a study of Eliot's major works, including special attention to the important connections between her biographical and literary life. The sections on *Silas Marner*, *Romola* and *Middlemarch*, and the final chapter, 'George Eliot Criticism', are particularly valuable. The volume concludes with a selected unannotated bibliography of works by and about Eliot. In 'Safely to Their Own Borders: Proto-Zionism, Feminism, and Nationalism in *Daniel Deronda*' (*ELH* 60.733–58), Susan Meyer addresses the function of race in George Eliot's fiction, particularly in regard to the British gentile proto-Zionist activity of the mid-nineteenth century and its relation to Eliot's Zionist agenda in her novel. Anne Smith's edition of *Silas Marner*, published in the Everyman series, is based on the 1867 collected edition of Eliot's works. Smith supplements her edition with an Eliot biographical chronology, an extensive introduction, a textual apparatus, and useful secondary scholarship, including an appendix on 'George Eliot and Her Critics'. William Baker's '"Her Longest-Venerated and Best-Loved Romancist": George Eliot and Sir Walter Scott' – an essay that traces the influence of Scott upon Eliot's reading and her fiction – was published in J. H. Alexander and David Hewitt's *Scott in Carnival*.

In 'George Eliot to William Blackwood III: Two Unpublished Letters' (*GEFR* 23.31–3), David Finkelstein reprints letters that he discovered in the National Library of Scotland's Blackwood Archives, while in 'Martha Barclay to Isaac Evans' (*GEFR* 23.34–5), Kathleen Adams reproduces a letter from Eliot's school friend, Martha Barclay, regarding the fate and correspondence of Blackwood's late brother, George Frederick Blackwood. William Baker's 'George Eliot – "Original Manuscripts Bound In"' (*N&Q* 40.484–7) describes 53 leaves of notes by Eliot in the archives of the Harry Ransom Humanities Research Center at the University of Texas at Austin. These notes 'testify to her thorough research and absorption into a historical period prior to her writing and transforming her writings into fiction'. The Twenty-First George Eliot Memorial Lecture, entitled 'The Names of George Eliot' (*GEFR* 23.25–30) and delivered by Ruth Harris, considers the *mélange* of names that Eliot adopted during her lifetime. Henry Alley's 'George Eliot and the Ambiguity of Murder' (*SNNTS* 25.59–75) addresses the 'agents and victims of murderous behaviour' that mark Eliot's fiction, including such figures as Hetty Sorrel, Baldassare Calvo, Bulstrode and Gwendolen Harleth. Joseph Wiesenfarth explores with perceptive close readings 'Mythic Perspective in George Eliot's Fiction' (*GEFR* 23.41–6), concentrating on Eliot's use of myth in *Silas Marner* and *The Spanish Gypsy*. In 'Metaphor, Truth, and the Mobile Imagination in *The Mill on the Floss*' (*GEFR* 23.36–40), John Rignall discusses the linguistic texture of Eliot's novel, particularly regarding her use of metaphor as a vehicle for creating elements of unity and harmony within her narrative. Alain Barrat's '*Middlemarch*: A Darkening Vision of Provincial Life' (*CVE* 37.105–14) explores Eliot's treatment of provincial life and its agrarian ideals, while Deborah Guth's 'Strategies of Surprise in *Middlemarch*' (*CVE* 37.115–28) discusses Eliot's use of surprise as a narrative technique in her writings. Derek Miller's 'A Note on Hermione in *Daniel Deronda*' (*GEFR* 23.46) assesses the Shakespearian usage of *tableau vivant* in Eliot's novel, while John K. Hale's 'George Eliot's Mr. Casaubon as "A Bat of Erudition"' (*N&Q* 40.487) explores Petrarchan images in *Middlemarch*. Also, students of Eliot's life and work should note the recent re-publication of Volume 1 of her translation of the Reverend David Friedrich Strauss's massive text, *Das Leben Jesu, kritisch bearbeitet* [*Life of Jesus, Critically Examined*], edited by Yoesh Gloger.

Although it was a lean year for Wilkie Collins scholarship, the recently published and revised edition of Catherine Peters's *The King of Inventors: A Life of Wilkie Collins*, originally published in 1991, contains a new appendix on the author's first, unpublished novel, *Ioláni*, a manuscript of 160 quarto pages, set in Tahiti before the coming of the Europeans, that has recently resurfaced. Other recent Wilkie publications of interest include Peters's World's Classics edition of Wilkie Collins's *Hide and Seek*, compiled from the original 1854 text of Collins's third novel. Dedicated to Dickens, this often neglected text in Collins's *oeuvre* features a useful textual introduction by Peters, who is also Collins's principal biographer. Alan Sutton published three new 'Pocket Classics' editions of Collins's novels, including *Miss or Mrs?*, *The New Magdalen*, and *Legacy of Cain*. Susan Balée's 'Wilkie Collins and Surplus Women: The Case of Marian Halcombe' (*VLC* 21.197–216) explores the critical and social response to Collins's novel, *The Woman in White*. In 'Reopening the Mysteries: Colonialist Logic and Cultural Difference in *The Moonstone* and *The Horse Latitudes*' (*LIT* 4.215–28), Robert Crooks examines Collins's approach to issues of cultural identity and difference in his fiction. Ashish Roy's 'The Fabulous Imperialist

Semiotic of Wilkie Collins's *The Moonstone*' (*NLH* 24.657–81) discusses Collins's approach to imperialism and colonialism in his novels, while Stephen Bernstein's 'Reading Blackwater Park: Gothicism, Narrative, and Ideology in *The Woman in White*' (*SNNTS* 25.291–305) addresses the role of setting, social class and gender in Collins's novel. In '*Twin Peaks*: Rewriting the Sensation Novel' (*LFQ* 21.248–54), Melynda Huskey compares the sensational novelistic qualities of *The Woman in White* to the television series, *Twin Peaks*. In 'Agents of Empire in *The Woman in White*' (*VN* 83.1–7), Lillian Nayder explores Collins's treatment of imperialism in his novel.

Patricia O'Hara's 'Primitive Marriage, Civilized Marriage: Anthropology, Mythology, and *The Egoist*' (*VLC* 21.1–24) explores the connections between nineteenth-century social and biological theories and their relation to literary images of the self during that era, particularly as evinced by Meredith's text. In 'The Tailor Transformed: Kingsley's *Alton Locke* and the Notion of Change' (*SNNTS* 25.196–213), Alan Rauch explores the roles of science and religion in Charles Kingsley's novel, *Alton Locke: Tailor and Poet*, while Colin Manlove's 'Charles Kingsley, H. G. Wells, and the Machine in the Victorian Age' (*NCL* 48.212–39) discusses the treatment of machines in Kingsley's *The Water Babies*, as well as in works by Wells. Also of interest is Everyman's latest republication of Mary Kingsley's *Travels in West Africa*, edited by Elspeth Huxley, and featuring a comprehensive textual introduction and a valuable selection of biographical notes useful to the student and the advanced scholar alike. In 'Victorian Travel Writers in Iceland, 1850–1880' (*VLC* 21.99–116), Frederick Kirchhoff examines the proliferation of travel books on Iceland during the latter half of the Victorian era, including studies written by such figures as John Murray, Samuel Laing, Lord Dufferin. Additionally, Ernie Trory's *Truth Against the World: The Life and Times of Thomas Hughes, Author of Tom Brown's School Days* deals with the dramatic social aspects of Hughes's world and the author's interest in exposing social injustices as a barrister and a Liberal MP. Trory also devotes attention to Hughes's socialist activities as publisher of the *Workman's Advocate* during the 1860s, as well as his censure by Karl Marx in an 1865 letter to Engels describing Hughes as the leader of a 'sundry bourgeois'. Attempting to recover the place of Hughes in nineteenth-century letters, Trory concludes: 'Thomas Hughes fought against the world for the truth as he saw it. He does not deserve to be remembered only for his authorship of *Tom Brown's School Days*' (8). Harold Orel's 'Adapting the Conventions of Historical Romance: Rider Haggard's *Eric Brighteyes*' (*ELT* 36.40–59) explores the romantic narrative constructs of Haggard's novels, and his strong feelings about the significance of the romantic genre. In a comprehensive survey, Alan Richardson's 'Reluctant Lords and Lame Princes: Engendering the Male Child in Nineteenth-Century Fiction' (*ChildL* 21.3–19) utilizes feminist revisions of Freudian developmental theory and applies it in readings of the representation of juvenile male protagonists, including Thomas Hughes's Tom Brown, Mrs Craik's (Dinah Maria Mulock) Little Lame Prince, and Frances Hodgson Burnett's Little Lord Fauntleroy.

A number of recent texts also provide Victorian scholars with new and reprinted texts for the works of several neglected nineteenth-century writers. In the *Letters of George Augustus Sala to Edmund Yates*, for example, Judy McKenzie proffers an edition of 170 annotated letters housed in the Edmund Yates Archives in the University of Queensland Library. Although the presence of a small typeface detracts from the overall quality of McKenzie's edition, her compilation nevertheless offers readers the opportunity to examine this otherwise neglected yet fascinating selection of correspondence. The publication of *The Edmund Yates Papers in the University of Queensland Library: A Catalogue*, compiled by Peter Edwards and Andrew Dowling, offers scholars a useful tool for accessing the materials in McKenzie's edition, and includes descriptive entries for each of the Archive's 686 items. Also of interest is the recent World's Classics edition of Samuel Butler's *The Way of All Flesh*, edited and introduced by Michael Mason. In 'Disclosure and Cover Up': The Discourse of Madness in *Lady Audley's Secret*' (*UTQ* 62.334–55), Jill L. Matus explores the treatment of madness and the function of narrative disclosure in Mary Elizabeth Braddon's novel, while in 'Pre-Raphaelitism in *Lady Audley's Secret*' (*PAPA* 19.1–10), Pamela Didlake Brewer examines the place and treatment of the Pre-Raphaelites in Braddon's fiction. Finally, three essays offer analyses of the life and work of Lewis Carroll, including Sophie Marret's 'Metalanguage in Lewis Carroll' (*SubStance* 71–2.217–27), which discusses the function of metalanguage in the major works of Carroll. Robin Tolmach Lakoff's 'Lewis Carroll: Subversive Pragmatist' (*Pragmatics* 3.367–85) addresses stylistics, pragmatics, and the function of names in *Alice's Adventures in Wonderland* and *Through the Looking Glass*, while dialectics-at-work should see Jean Jacques Lecercle's somewhat esoteric 'Lewis Carroll and the Talmud' (*SubStance* 71–2.204–16), which applies the theories of Abraham Ettelsen to *Through the Looking Glass*. The Lewis Carroll Society of America also recently sponsored the publication of *The Pamphlets of Lewis Carroll*. Volume 1, edited by Edward Wakeling, includes Charles Lutwidge Dodgson's Oxford pamphlets, leaflets and circulars.

Recent scholarship regarding Hardy includes Dennis Taylor's *Hardy's Literary Language and Victorian Philology*, a volume that offers a detailed examination of Hardy's use of language and the critical response to his linguistic 'awkwardness'. Taylor also explores Hardy's association with the *Oxford English Dictionary* and treats the history of Victorian philology. In his study, Taylor argues that Hardy's language must be understood as a distinctive response to the philological concerns of his day, and suggests that Hardy deliberately infused his writing with a sense of the Victorian vernacular that influenced his aesthetic. Taylor also examines Hardy's interest in the prevailing Victorian historical study of language, a sense of history that, in Hardy's case, distinguishes his narratives from the ahistorical, synchronic aesthetic that marks the work of his modernist successors. Taylor concludes his study with a useful analysis of the influence upon Hardy's language by the founding and development during this period of the *Oxford English Dictionary*. Additionally, Jonathan Wike's 'The World as Text in Hardy's Fiction' (*NCL* 47.455–71) addresses Hardy's fictional canon and its landscape of 'legible faces'. *The Sense of Sex: Feminist Perspectives on Hardy*, edited by Margaret R. Higonnet, features essays that draw upon feminist critical insights in their analyses of the major novels of Hardy and their depictions of gender issues and female characters.

In *Hardy: The Margin of the Unexpressed*, Roger Ebbatson employs a number of poststructuralist theoretical perspectives in his analysis of minor texts by Hardy such as *Desperate Remedies*, *The Trumpet-Major*, *Our Exploits at West Poley* and *An Indiscretion in the Life of an Heiress*. In addition to attempting to challenge the dominance of Hardy's canonical texts among the novelist's literary *oeuvre*, Ebbatson explores Hardy's pervasive use of tone, language and conception in works that Ebbatson argues are marked by a circularity of desire and a language of self-enclosure. Ebbatson supplements his study by placing Hardy's texts firmly within the contradictory context of nineteenth-century literary production, and in this way, reveals the larger role of Victorian culture in the creation of Hardy's prose. In 'Appropriating the Word: *Jude the Obscure* as Subversive Apocrypha' (*VR* 19.48–66), Richard Nemesvari addresses Hardy's subversion of the Bible in his novel, and argues that Hardy attempts to re-write it as well. Nemesvari also suggests that Hardy's revision self-consciously involves the non-canonical books of the Apocrypha as a means for asserting the contingent natures of scriptural and textual authority in Hardy's writings, particularly in *Jude the Obscure*.

Originally published in 1976, Merryn Williams's updated *A Preface to Hardy* provides readers with an insightful introduction to the novelist's life, fiction and verse, while also highlighting the connections between the author's life, work and the creative environment that influenced his writings. In addition to an expansive section devoted to analysing the intellectual and cultural climate in which Hardy lived, Williams explores the nature of the major phases of his career, concentrating particularly upon the composition of *The Mayor of Casterbridge*. Williams also devoted sizeable attention to Hardy's career as a poet and short story writer, regions of Hardy study often neglected in favour of his novels. Williams offers special consideration to Hardy's remarkable verse epic, *The Dynasts*, and also provides readers with a valuable guide for researching the voluminous canon of available secondary scholarship devoted to Hardy. A leading Hardy scholar, Simon Gatrell in his *Thomas Hardy and the Proper Study of Mankind* furnishes students of Hardy with a valuable guide to the humanistic elements that mark the novelist's fiction. Gatrell treats a number of Hardy's major works, including *Under the Greenwood Tree*, *The Return of the Native*, *The Trumpet-Major*, *A Laodicean*, *Two on a Tower*, *The Mayor of Casterbridge*, *Tess of the d'Urbervilles* and *Jude the Obscure*. Gatrell also provides readers with intriguing analyses of the role of dance in Hardy's fiction, the place of the environment in his aesthetic, and the significance of traditional community in his novels.

In a collection of previously printed materials, Graham Clarke's four-volume *Thomas Hardy: Critical Assessments* likewise provides students of Hardy's writings with an expansive survey of more than a century of scholarship devoted to his work. In his collection, Clarke attempts to capture the remarkable ambiguity and complexity of Hardy criticism, while also attempting to reflect the range and depth of his aesthetic achievement. Volume I offers a range of reviews from the nineteenth and early twentieth centuries and establishes a distinctive guide to the nature of the critical response to Hardy's writing as it was originally published. In Volume II, Clarke assembles a selection of analyses of Hardy as poet, including a series of significant contemporary studies of his verse. Clarke features a collection of general contemporary essays in Volume III, as well as selected responses to Hardy's work by such figures as John Cowper Powys, Ezra Pound, T. S. Eliot, E. M. Forster, W. H. Auden, Thom Gunn and Philip Larkin, among others. The volume also includes studies of 'Wessex'. In Volume IV, Clarke includes a series of commentaries on Hardy's major novels, as well as a series of essays regarding general aspects of his aesthetic.

Joanna Gibson's 'Thomas Hardy: A Borrowing from Schopenhauer' (*N&Q* 40.492–3) illustrates the novelist's philosophical influences, while Elizabeth Bartsch-Parker's 'Further Hardy Debts to Hawthorne' (*N&Q* 40.493) explores Hardy's appropriation of Hawthorne's characterization strategies. In 'Hardy's

Noble Melancholies' (*Novel* 27.24–39), Brandon B. Bennett addresses the 'melancholy satisfaction' that accompanies notions of pain and death in Hardy's novels, particularly *The Woodlanders*. In 'Hardy: Versions of Pastoral' (*VLC* 21.245–72), Robert Langbaum explores Hardy's infusion of poetic, pastoral images into such novels as *Far from the Madding Crowd* and *The Return of the Native*. In 'Thomas Hardy, *Desperate Remedies*: Three Additional Notes by an Editor' (*N&Q* 40.60–1), C. J. P. Beatty discusses the problematic editorial nature of the extant edition of *Desperate Remedies*. Frank Jordan's 'The Scott Furrow in *The Mayor of Casterbridge*', another entry in Alexander and Hewitt's *Scott in Carnival*, explores the influence of the Waverley novels upon Hardy's creative aesthetic.

In *Hardy's Wessex Locations*, F. P. Pitfield rediscovers the countryside geography that defines the major novels of Hardy's fictional *oeuvre*. Pitfield provides his readers with chronological entries for each of the author's novels and stories in an effort to demonstrate the evolution of Hardy's use of place names. An abundance of previously overlooked Hardy locations enables Pitfield to offer a number of new revelations regarding the geography of Hardy's writings and to elucidate the value of 'Wessex' to an understanding of his novels. Similarly, a new Macmillan casebook on *Tess of the d'Urbervilles*, edited by Peter Widdowson, reprints eclectic responses published during the last decade to Hardy's novels, ranging from feminist and new historicist analyses to poststructuralist critical approaches. The editor's introduction, '*Tess of the d'Urbervilles*: Faithfully Presented by Peter Widdowson', is particularly clear and helpful to students of Hardy's classic volume. Scholars should also note the recent publication of two new editions of Hardy's novels. The World's Classics edition of Hardy's *Two on a Tower*, edited by Suleiman M. Ahmad, features a useful selection of explanatory notes, as well as a map of Hardy's Wessex. Pamela Norris's Everyman edition of *The Mayor of Casterbridge* provides readers with the original text of Hardy's novel and a comprehensive guide to the available scholarship regarding the novelist's life and work. Finally, Pamela Dalziel and Michael Millgate's splendid textual edition of Hardy's '*Studies, Specimens, &c*'. Notebook offers scholars an important source for Hardy's private observations about the people, places and things that impinged upon the novelist's life and work from the 1860s until the early years of the twentieth century. This is the highlight of the year's crop of Hardy studies.

Alison Case's 'Tasting the Original Apple: Gender and the Struggle for Narrative Authority in *Dracula*' (*Narrative* 1.223–43) discusses the roles of gender and power in Stoker's novel, while Troy Boone's '"He Is English and Therefore Adventurous": Politics, Decadence, and *Dracula*' (*SNNTS* 25.76–91) addresses Stoker's treatment of politics in *Dracula*. In 'Bram Stoker and C. S. Lewis: *Dracula* as a Source for *That Hideous Strength*' (*Mythlore* 19.16–22), Mervyn Nicholson examines the intertextual and influential relationships between Stoker's novel and Lewis's *That Hideous Strength*. Robin S. Appleby's '*Dracula* and Dora: The Diagnosis and Treatment of Alternative Narratives' (*L&P* 39.16–37) explores the comparable narratives of Stoker's novel and Sigmund Freud's *Bruchstuck einer Hysterie Analyse*. Also of interest is Carol A. Senf's edition exploring *The Critical Response to Bram Stoker*, which features contemporary critical examinations of the novelist's work, as well as analyses of Stoker's critical reception during the twentieth century.

Melvyn New's recent edition of *The Complete Novels and Selected Writings of Amy Levy, 1861–1889* offers a valuable biographical introduction to Levy's often neglected fictional canon, and also includes the text of her novel, *Reuben Sachs: A Sketch.* In *The Emblems of Margaret Gatty: A Study of Allegory in Nineteenth-Century Children's Literature*, Wendy R. Katz draws upon Gatty's correspondence in an effort to assess the author's life and work, particularly as they related to her 1872 novel for children, *A Book of Emblems.* Katz affords special attention to an analysis of the role of emblems in children's literature and the manner in which emblems functioned antithetically to Victorian sensibilities. In addition to tracing the various sources for Gatty's work, Katz examines the larger allegorical tradition that marks children's literature of the Victorian era, while also assessing the genesis of Gatty's interest in emblems and their value to her fictions. Lavishly illustrated with Gatty's sketches, Katz's volume concludes with a valuable appendix of Gatty's often neglected works.

The important but neglected Richard Jefferies (1848–87) is the subject of George Miller and Hugoe Matthews's extensive *Richard Jefferies: A Bibliographical Study.* In what is obviously a labour of love from two Jefferies devotees and avid Jefferies scholars, Miller, a book designer, and Matthews, a surgeon, have compiled, to employ the words of W. J. Keith's foreword, a 'detailed and scholarly bibliography'. The clear introduction outlines procedures, and is followed by five clearly enumerated and descriptive sections: 'Contributions by Jefferies to Periodicals: Works in which the Writings First Appeared in Newspaper and Magazine Form'; 'Books and Pamphlets by Jefferies: Works in which the Writings First Appeared in Book and Pamphlet Form'; 'Anthologies: Selected Passages, Collected Works: Separate Editions of Pieces Previously Collected in Book Form'; 'Manuscript material'; and 'Chronological List of Works about Jefferies in Books, Pamphlets, and Periodicals'. There is an extensive index to this goldmine of information regarding Victorian publishing, the novel and Jefferies, whose genius Q. D. Leavis wrote so well on in *Scrutiny* in March 1938. White Lion's reprint of Richard Jefferies's 1879 novel, *The Amateur Poacher*, includes a foreword by Ian Niall, as well as detailed wood engravings by Barbara Greg.

In *Robert Louis Stevenson: Poet and Teller of Tales*, Bryan Bevan explores the life of Stevenson and his career as novelist, essayist, travel writer, poet, writer of ballads and fables, correspondent and short-story writer. In addition to extensive analysis of the role of Stevenson's ill health in his writings, Bevan examines the influence of the author's Scottish descent and the Scottish highlands upon his work and his unwavering work ethic despite his physical ailments. Bevan devotes special attention to the study of Stevenson's major works, including *Treasure Island*, *Kidnapped* and *Dr. Jekyll and Mr. Hyde*, as well as to the author's less well-known works such as 'Thrawn Janet', *Beach of Falesá*, and his unfinished last novel, *Weir of Hermiston.* Bevan's volume finds its strength in his elucidation of Stevenson's final, difficult years in the South Seas before his death in Samoa at the height of his creative powers. Students of Stevenson's work should also note Dover's republication of an unabridged edition of *Treasure Island.* Using the text of Charles Scribner's Sons' 1905 edition of the novel, the Dover edition essentially reprints the original 1883 text of Stevenson's classic novel. In 'Stevenson's *Strange Case of Dr. Jekyll and Mr. Hyde*: A Textual Variant' (*N&Q* 40.490–2), Richard Dury addresses the early texts of Stevenson's novel and demonstrates the manner in which errors and misreadings entered the text of the first American edition of the novel, while in 'Overdetermined Allegory in *Jekyll and Hyde'* (*VN* 84.35–8), Cyndy Hendershot traces the properties of allegory in Stevenson's writings. Additionally, in 'Culture, Nature, and Gender in Mary Ward's *Robert Elsmere* and *Helbeck of Bannisdale'* (*VN* 83.25–31), Laura Fasick explores the treatment of cultural issues regarding nature and sexuality in the novels of Mary Ward. Also of interest is Barry Menikoff's edition of Stevenson's *Tales from the Prince of Storytellers*, a volume that includes a valuable textual apparatus and a number of useful textual and biographical notes.

The Collected Letters of George Gissing, Vol. 4: 1889–1891, edited by Paul F. Mattheisen, Arthur C. Young and Pierre Coustillas, offers scholars a vital research tool for understanding Gissing's pivotal years abroad, the publication of such volumes as *The Nether World* and *The Emancipated*, his problematic marriage to Edith Underwood, and his difficult relationships with his family and his publishers. This period also saw the publication of one of his best known works, the 1891 novel, *New Grub Street*. Using a diversity of sources, including newspapers, the author's memoirs, biographies and sales catalogues, the editors provide a valuable context for understanding this significant moment in the aesthetic shift between the Victorian age and the advent of modernism. The letters featured in this fourth instalment of Gissing's correspondence reflect the author's abiding interest in themes of poverty, socialism, class differences, social reform and the problems of women and industrialization. Fully annotated, this important edition of Gissing's work should serve for years to come as a central resource to Gissing scholars and students of late-Victorian culture. Also of interest is *George Gissing's 'American Notebook': Notes – G.R.G. – 1877*, edited by Bouwe Postmus, which assembles materials from the novelist's 1877 notebook chronicling his travels in America. Published in the World's Classics series and carefully edited by the late John Goode, the text of Gissing's classic novel *New Grub Street* includes a detailed introduction and a useful appendix on 'New Grub Street and London'. The April 1993 issue of *GissingJ* (29) features Martha S. Vogeler's 'People Gissing Knew: Dr. Jane Walker' (1–10), an essay that analyses the life of Gissing's physician and her role in his life. John Simpson's 'Gissing in the *OED*' (11–18) enumerates the 83 *OED* entries that cite works by Gissing for their literary or linguistic exemplars. Robert L. Selig's 'The Critical Response to Gissing in the *Chicago Times Herald*' (19–28) explores four favourable reviews of Gissing by *Times Herald* reporter Mary Abbott. Finally, Everyman recently published a new edition of Gissing's *The Day of Silence and Other Stories*, edited by that great Gissing advocate, Pierre Coustillas.

In 'Disraeli and Wilde's Dorian Gray' (*UES* 31.29–33), Stanley Weintraub explores the sources for the central character in Wilde's *The Picture of Dorian Gray*, while locating them in the works of Benjamin Disraeli. Two articles in *PAPA* 19 concern *Dorian Gray*: Amanda Witt's 'Blushings and Palings: The Body as Text in Wilde's *The Picture of Dorian Gray*' (85–96) explores the role of the human body in Wilde's narrative, while Elaine Smith's 'Oscar Wilde's *The Picture of Dorian Gray*: A Decadent Portrait of Life in Art, or Art in Life' (23–31) assesses Wilde's treatment of life and its relationship to art in his novel. Guy Willoughby explores the artistic and religious qualities of Wilde's fictional aesthetic in *Art and Christhood: The Aesthetics of Oscar Wilde*. Also of interest is Thomas Mikolyzk's *Oscar Wilde: An Annotated Bibliography*, which features listings for Wilde's primary works, as well as for more than a century of criticism devoted to the study of his prose and poetry. Students of Wilde's work should also note Dover's republication of an unabridged edition of *The Picture of Dorian*

Gray. In 'Subjectivity and Story in George Moore's *Esther Waters*' (*ELT* 36.141–57), Annette Federico discusses Moore's 1894 novel and its examination of gender, fiction and late-Victorian culture, while also considering Moore's commitment to challenge these issues through the formulation of the character of his heroine. In William H. D. Crewdson's 'C. J. Cutcliffe Hyne' (*ABMR* 20.20–5), the life and work of the neglected Victorian adventure novelist are enumerated, including Hyne's fourteen novels written under the pseudonyms of Chesney and Weatherby. A listing of the first editions of Hyne's novels concludes the article. Crewdson considers the similar fate of 'Robert Leighton' (*ABMR* 20.18–25), an active participant in the Victorian literary milieu of the 1890s, and the author of *In the Shadow of Guilt*. Drawing upon a New Historical critical approach, Bill Bolin's 'Olive Schreiner and the Status Quo' (*UES* 31.4–8) examines the Victorian era and its incarnation in South African literature, particularly within the fiction of Olive Schreiner and her narratives of social order such as *The Story of an African Farm*. Similarly, in 'Writing the Self on the Imperial Frontier: Olive Schreiner and the Stories of Africa' (*BuR* 37.134–55), Gerald Monsman discusses Schreiner's treatment of the self in her writings about the South African frontier of the nineteenth century.

Finally, the works of Sir Arthur Conan Doyle receive attention in two recent essays worthy of mention: Bernard Duyfhuizen's 'The Case of Sherlock Holmes and *Jane Eyre*' (*BSJ* 43.135–45) examines the influence of Charlotte Brontë upon Conan Doyle's short story 'The Copper-Beeches', while Kenneth Wilson's 'Fiction and Empire: The Case of Sir Arthur Conan Doyle' (*VR* 19.22–42) discusses Conan Doyle's treatment of British imperialism in his works. In *Narratives of Empire: The Fictions of Rudyard Kipling*, Zohreh T. Sullivan offers new readings of Kipling's fictional representations of India, particularly in such works as *Kim* and Kipling's later biography. Sullivan especially considers Kipling's troubled vision of the British empire, particularly through the author's depictions of the anxieties and contradictions that mark the empire's experience in India. Sullivan also examines Kipling's narratological link between history and fiction. In Christopher Collard's 'Gilbert Murray on Rudyard Kipling: An Unpublished Letter' (*N&Q* 40.63–4), a 1902 letter by Murray reveals the nature of his relationship with Kipling, while also discussing the work of the novelist. M. Flint's 'Kipling's Mowgli and Human Focalization' (*SN* 65.73–9) assesses the role of Mowgli in the narrative focalization of Kipling's short fiction, while Stephen D. Arata's 'A Universal Foreignness: Kipling in the *Fin-de-Siècle*' (*ELT* 36.7–38) explores the place of Kipling's writings in the literary promulgation at the turn of the century. In 'The "Ricksha That Happened": Norris' Parody of Rudyard Kipling' (*FNS* 15.1–4), Joseph McElrath, Jr, the bibliographer of Frank Norris, addresses Norris's fictional parody of Kipling in his writings.

3. Poetry

1993 saw the appearance of many important volumes, bringing a variety of theoretical and critical perspectives to Victorian poetry. Isobel Armstrong's general study *Victorian Poetry: Poetry, Poetics and Politics* spans the period, and deals with both 'major' and 'minor' poets. Publications on major canonical figures included two substantial volumes on Browning, Daniel Karlin's *Browning's Hatreds* and E. A. W. St. George's *Browning and Conversation*, Peter

Levi's biography *Tennyson* and two major collections of essays, Herbert F. Tucker's edition *Critical Essays on Alfred Lord Tennyson*, and a new anthology on Swinburne *The Whole Music of Passion: New Essays on Swinburne*, edited by Rikky Rooksby and Nicholas Shrimpton. A useful new perspective on the diversity of late-century poetry was opened up by the publication of the series of facsimile reprints from Woodstock, *Decadents, Symbolists, Anti-Decadents: Poetry of the 1890s*. It has been a particularly good year for annotated bibliographies; Aletha Andrews's *An Annotated Bibliography and Study of the Contemporary Criticism of Tennyson's Idylls of the King, 1859–1886*, Sandra Donaldson's *Elizabeth Barrett Browning: An Annotated Bibliography of the Commentary and Criticism 1826–1990* and Clinton Machann's *The Essential Matthew Arnold: An Annotated Bibliography of the Major Modern Studies*, open up scholarship in their respective fields.

Surely the most significant publication of the year was Isobel Armstrong's major study *Victorian Poetry: Poetry, Poetics and Politics*. Armstrong begins with the proposition that Victorian poetry is inextricably bound up with the discourses which structured Victorian culture – politics, philosophy, theology, theories of language, science. The meticulousness with which she works through writing and events related to these debates and traces the pattern they leave on poetic language means that this study is much more than just a history of the poetry of the period. It is a substantial contribution to the cultural and intellectual history, revealing Victorian culture in all its energy, contradiction and violence. Armstrong's introduction wrestles with the problematic status of Victorian poetry within modern literary cultures and its institutions, as unfashionable and consequently under-theorized. An incisive analysis of twentieth-century critical history points out that our perception of the poetry is still determined to a large extent by the snide dismissal of the Victorians as crude, sentimental and reactionary by the modernists. Utilizing Bakhtin's concept of dialogism, and Volosinov's account of the 'struggle for the sign', Armstrong argues that the Victorian poem is a site of struggle, a complex articulation of conflicting ideologies and the languages which speak them. The body of the analysis follows a broadly chronological structure. Part One focuses on the debates around the Tennyson and Browning groups during the 1830s and early 1840s. As Armstrong points out in her introduction, 'the Victorian poets were the first group of writers to feel that what they were doing was simply unnecessary and redundant'. This anxiety about the functional status of poetry gave rise to a split within literary theory which, borrowing a term from J. S. Mill, Armstrong calls 'two systems of concentric circles'. These articulated in the early parts of the period as the difference between the various kinds of 'conservatism' which structured Tennyson's work and the 'Benthamite formation' Browning struggled with. Part Two deals with the effects of the 'repeated shocks' which shook Victorian culture during the 1840s and 1850s, the Irish famine, Chartism, the European revolutions of 1848 and the Crimean war. Armstrong focuses on three major responses, by Clough, the radical, Arnold, the troubled liberal and Morris, who dramatically reformulated the politics of myth for a revolutionary analysis. Chapters on the mid-century work of Tennyson and Browning follow. The section rounds off with a substantial account of women poets, where Armstrong explores whether work by women across the century can be thought of as 'an expressive tradition'. Part Three addresses poetry written from the 1860s. During this period, Armstrong argues, language became 'a renewed site of ideological conflict', due to a more general crisis within culture caused by the excessive expansion, and the many crises of financial speculation at this time. Both language and money are systems of substitution and both became the subject of intense scrutiny and panic. Armstrong sets up a dazzling dialectic between Swinburne and Hopkins, both working within this problematic, both thrown back on the 'brute materiality' of language, compelled to 'create closed systems, poetic languages which arise from the empty material sign, the sign without a referent'. Later chapters in this section study the fraught accounts of sexuality in Meredith, Patmore and Rossetti and the atheism and anarchy of James Thomson's urban vision.

These are the broad strokes on Armstrong's canvas. In between them is a cornucopia of detail which gives a full account of 'major' and 'minor' figures of the period. It is Armstrong's great talent to draw out the links, ideological and aesthetic, between positions and poets who might seem utterly divergent. She produces some startling conjunctions, between Carlyle and Marx (both theorizing the alienation of labour), Arnold and Clare (both obsessed by gypsies), Caroll and Hyndman (both theorists of substitution: Caroll in relation to language, Hyndman in relation to money). The commitment to fully dialectical analysis allows Armstrong to reveal the doubleness of Victorian poetry, indeed the 'double poem', the poem which is under constant threat from another poem which struggles inside itself, articulating an oppositional politics and eroding the control the poem has over its own language, is one of Armstrong's major conceptual tools. This study should be read in its entirety by all critics and students of Victorian poetry. Its outstanding scholarship, massive intellectual energy and tenacious struggle with Victorian poems and the contradictions of the culture which produced them will transform the nature of work in this field. It is, arguably, one of the most important studies of Victorian poetry to appear this century.

1993 saw the appearance of the first instalment of an exciting and useful series of facsimile reprints from Woodstock Books, *Decadents, Symbolists, Anti-Decadents: Poetry of the 1890s*. Under the general editorship of R. K. R. Thornton and Ian Small, the series, now completed, collects 38 books of poetry, in 27 volumes, representing the work of 22 poets. Volumes to appear in 1993 include *In a Music-hall, 1891* and *Ballads and Songs, 1894* by John Davidson, collected in a single volume; Davidson's 1893 and 1896 volumes of *Fleet Street Eclogues* also bound together; Ernest Dowson's *Verses, 1896,* and *Decorations, 1899* in one volume; *Poems, 1898* by William Ernest Henley; two collections by 'Michael Field' *Sight and Song, 1892* and *Underneath the Bough, 1893* bound together; Lionel Johnson's *Poems, 1895;* Rudyard Kipling's *Barrack-room Ballads, 1892; The Book of the Rhymer's Club, 1892* bound together with *The Second Book of the Rhymers' Club, 1894;* Arthur Symons's *Silhouettes, 1896* and *London Nights, 1897* in one volume; and *Poems, 1894* by Francis Thompson. Future volumes will represent the work of a further variety of poets including Olive Custance, Alfred Douglas, John Gray, Thomas Hardy, A. E. Housman, Selwyn Image, Richard le Galliene, Henry Newbolt, Vincent O'Sullivan, Victor Plarr, Theodore Wratislaw, Oscar Wilde and William Butler Yeats. The editorial apparatus is sparse, each volume is prefaced by a short biographical note, a select bibliography of the poet's other work and a brief list of useful secondary sources for further study.

The series addresses a moment of crisis and transition in British poetry. The deaths of the major Victorian poets at this time – Arnold, Browning, Hopkins and

Tennyson – gave rise to diversification of critical taste and the fragmentation of cultural authority, 'a sense of new beginnings' which involved the poetry of the period in the rearticulation of national and imperial identities, engagement with French movements and new accounts of culture, politics and the aesthetic. It is to be applauded for representing the work of poets, like Housman, Kipling, Wilde and Yeats who have retained a position in the mainstream of literary culture of the late twentieth century alongside that of much less well-known writers such as Davidson, Image and Wratislaw. The series is priced for purchase by the library rather than the individual scholar, and should be examined in its entirety as, taken together, the volumes facilitate a reconsideration of diverse aesthetic and political movements which created the culture of the *fin de siècle*. It will be of interest not only to scholars of Victorian poetry, but to theorists concerned with any aspect of late-century culture. My only regret about this excellent project is that the work of only three women, 'Field' (Katherine Bradley and Edith Cooper) and Custance, is included. Not only are scholars in the rapidly expanding field of the study of Victorian women's poetry in great need of a similar resource, representing the work of 'major' and 'minor' figures of the 1890s to facilitate research and teaching, but lack of representation of the work of women distorts what is otherwise a comprehensive account of the diversity of the poetry of the period. On occasion, the editors do stretch their chronology outside of the 1890s and so it is surprising that a volume like Amy Levy's *A London Plane-Tree, and Other Verse, 1889*, which was among the first collections of the late-century to experiment with an urban aesthetic derived from Baudelaire, does not find a place in the list. Equally, works by Mathilde Blind, Alice and May Clarissa Gillington, Rosamund Marriott-Watson, Alice Meynell, Edith Nesbit, A. Mary F. Robinson and Katharine Tynan, for example, would have been an invaluable addition. Perhaps even Christina Rossetti's final collection of religious poetry *Verses* (1893), which is still largely inaccessible, would have lent a useful perspective to the series. However, during the 1990s Woodstock Press has demonstrated its commitment to the reprinting of a wide variety of work, including that of women poets. Its reprint of Felicia Hemans's *Records of Woman, 1828* under the aegis of Jonathan Wordsworth's Woodstock series *Revolution and Romanticism* in 1991 and the volumes by Sara Coleridge and Caroline Norton, which appeared in the same series in 1994, indicate that women's work is becoming increasingly important to such projects. Despite this caveat, *Decadents, Symbolists, Anti-Decadents* is a significant event in the scholarship of late Victorian poetry which will inject new energy into the field.

Volume 2 of Donald Thomas's edition *The Everyman Book of Victorian Verse: The Pre-Raphaelites to the Nineties*, was published this year. It provides a more satisfactory representation of the diversity of the period than that attempted in Thomas's earlier volume *The Post-Romantics* which was lamentably limited in scope, focusing on the 'big five' of the high-Victorian canon, Tennyson, Browning, Arnold, Clough and Swinburne. The 1993 edition includes poems by the working-class poet John Clare and several women including Elizabeth Barrett Browning, 'Michael Field', Jean Ingelow and Christina Rossetti, as well as 'minor' figures like Andrew Lang, Eugene Lee-Hamilton, Frederick Locker and Charles Stuart Calverley alongside texts by more mainstream names including Hardy, Hopkins, Kipling, Meredith and Dante Gabriel Rossetti. Thomas's introduction, however, fails to deal with the complex issues and conflicts written across the poetry of the later decades of the nineteenth century. It offers a brief history of the movements which frame the volume. Remarks on the Pre-

Raphaelites consist mostly of anecdote about the group's domestic arrangements and unorthodox social behaviour. The account of the 1890s is more adequately contextualized, although concentrating heavily on events surrounding Wilde's trial. Texts from the intervening period are organized under a series of rather quaint thematic headings which drastically depoliticize analysis of both the poetry and the period. For instance, Thomas makes no mention of feminism in his remarks on poems dealing with the theme of 'Men and Women' and no mention of class conflict in relation to poems he organizes under the heading of 'England, My England'. To include poems like Emily Brontë's unitarian 'No Coward Soul is Mine' and James Thomson's atheist 'City of Dreadful Night' under the Christian teleology of the heading 'The Way of the Cross' is extraordinary. The usefulness of the edition is restricted further by Thomas's failure to indicate the sources for his copy texts. In the year which saw the publication of Isobel Armstrong's politically, theoretically and analytically sophisticated study, the inadequacies of the conservative approach shaping this edition are revealed particularly clearly.

Publications devoted to Arnold's poetry were sparse in 1993, but the appearance of two volumes should be noted. *The Essential Matthew Arnold: An Annotated Bibliography of the Major Modern Studies*, compiled by Clinton Machann, is a selective survey of editions and criticisms of all aspects of Arnold's work which appeared from 1900 to 1991. Machann rejects simple chronology, and the almost 800 citations are grouped under generic and thematic headings. Major editions, important biographies, general studies, works on Arnold's sources and influences and assessments of his reception and the influence of his work on subsequent writers are listed at the start of the bibliography. The remaining space is devoted to lists of studies of the poetry, prose and, finally, to 'special topics', including 'Arnold and America', 'Arnold and the Classics', 'Arnold and Gender' and 'Arnold and Science'. Within each section, citations are listed alphabetically by author. Citations appear only once, within the most relevant section, and are supported by a system of cross-referencing between sections. The bibliography reveals that despite the increasing decline of his reputation as a poet during the twentieth century, a large amount of critical attention has still been paid consistently over the period to a number of poems: 'Dover Beach', 'Empedocles on Etna', 'Tristram and Iseult', 'The Scholar-Gipsy' and 'Thyrsis'. This volume will be of most interest to critics concerned with tracing the legacy of Arnold's theory of culture during this century. It allows the critic to trace the passionate reactions to Arnold's work, of both approval and hostility which have structured cultural theory this century, via Eliot and Leavis, through to Williams and his successors. Perhaps Machann's introduction could have drawn out more strongly the importance of Arnold as precursor of important strands of current literary theory and cultural studies, and the paradox that a writer who was adamant about the separation of literature and politics set the terms for the development of twentieth-century theories of the politics of culture. Many critics will appreciate the opportunity to consider the critical history of the poetry within this context.

As part of their project to refresh their series of the Victorian poets, Everyman have reissued Miriam Allot's 1978 edition of Arnold's *Selected Poems and Prose* with slightly revised introductory material and updated references to critical material.

Four major studies of Browning appeared this year. Clyde de L. Ryals's splendid *The Life of Robert Browning: A Critical Biography* explores Browning's work from *Pauline* to *Asolando* and treats chronologically and at some length the entire corpus of Browning's work. Ryals, somewhat against the grain, presents Browning as a writer both objective and subjective in that, Ryals argues, Browning's personality was both a 'biographical presence and biographical absence' in his poetry. For Ryals, Browning's description of his poems as performances is suggestive. The poet thus plays a part in the poetry as producer, presenter, actor and, sometimes, all three. This is a very useful book. Daniel Karlin's *Browning's Hatreds* is a perceptive and original study of Browning's obsession with the topic of hatred. Karlin analyses Browning's 'hatred' of such figures as Wordsworth, and more generally, tyranny and the abuse of power, and deceit or quackery in personal relationships or intellectual systems. Tracing this theme in its subtle windings through Browning's poetry, involving detailed discussion of individual poems, Karlin demonstrates how the poet's work displays an unequalled grasp of hatred as a personal emotion, as an intellectual principle, and as a source of artistic creativity.

E. A. W. St. George's *Browning and Conversation* is an attempt to provide new insight into Browning's longer and later poems. In an analysis which recalls Armstrong's account of the way in which criticism of Victorian poetry still has to bear the burdens laid upon it by modernism, St. George observes that 'we have forgotten how to read long poems, so ingrained is the model of the perfect lyric surrounded by white space on the page'. He argues that the difficulties posed by much of Browning's work can be elucidated by considering them as conversational systems: 'To value the conversational in Browning's poems is to embark on a view of poetry which values the unscripted and inordinate rather than the perfectly turned and perfectly suggestive line'. The opening chapter of the study is an interesting cultural history of Victorian conversation. The Victorians, St. George argues, hyper-invested in conversation as a form of social contract. Surveying a variety of texts from the 1840s to the 1880s, this chapter points to phenomena including the growth in the science of elocution, the role of public oratory within political culture and the perceived importance of reading aloud within the family circle. Chapter 2 presents contemporaneous testimony from a wide variety of sources about Browning's ability as a conversationalist. Later chapters of the study work through the thesis that '[c]omment on Browning's conduct as a talker provides the point of purchase for investigating the unique vigour and power which contemporary criticism noticed in his poems' by analysing particular texts, including 'Red Cotton Night-Cap Country', 'The Inn Album', 'Pacchiarotto', 'Jocoseria' and others. To the extent that St. George's thesis opens up the possibility of articulating a dynamic relationship between Browning's texts and various kinds of cultural discourse it is valuable. However, the tortured complexity of Browning's language registers more than just the 'discontinuities, interruptions, non-sequiturs and irrelevancies of conversation'. More than any other Victorian poet, Browning's work bears the strain of the huge functional demands which Victorian culture made upon language. St. George makes Browning's relationship with his culture – and with language – too comfortable. The final book on Browning is Richard S. Kennedy's study *Robert Browning's Asolando: The Indian Summer of a Poet*, which discusses Browning's final, and much overlooked, volume of poetry. Kennedy makes the not always convincing claim for the greatness of the volume, seeing it as one of the crowning achievements of Browning's life. He puts the collection into the biographical context of the poet's last years. Kennedy provides an overview of the poet's last years before turning to a critical commentary on each of the poems in the collection.

By contrast with this approach, some of the best essays on Browning to appear this year argue that the linguistic difficulty of Browning's poetry is the vehicle for his exploration of different forms of epistemological complexity. Herbert Tucker's brilliant piece 'Representation and Repristination: Virginity in *The Ring and the Book*' (in *Virginal Sexuality and Textuality in Victorian Literature*, edited by Lloyd Davis), deals with Browning's complex account of truth. By way of a case study of Caponsacchi and Pompilia's construction of their own putative virginity, Tucker explores the way in which Browning models truth according to the paradoxes of virginity, as something which may be lost, but never found. Thus, for Browning, history is the story of changes in historiography, truth 'does not exist outside the cultural representations that constitute our modernity'. Also focusing on a section of *The Ring and the Book*, Alexander Petit's essay 'Place, Time and Parody in *The Ring and the Book*' (*VP* 31.95–106) argues that Caponsacchi and Guildo are studies in geographical disjunction and temporal discontinuity who represent 'exhausted cultural and literary traditions'. In 'The Voices in Karshish: A Bakhtinian Reading of Robert Browning's "Epistle"' (*VP* 31.213–26), Cheryl Walsh utilizes the concept of dialogism to elucidate the contradictory accounts with which Karshish struggles in attempting to comprehend Lazarus's revival from death. Walsh argues that the event activates a crisis in the physician's world view: 'Karshish finds himself in what Mikhail Bakhtin has called 'the rupture-prone world of dialogue' where one voice is inadequate to express truth and the existence of more than one voice can threaten to produce chaos'.

A substantial new edition, *Thomas Hardy: Selected Poems* edited by Tim Armstrong appeared this year and will be reviewed in full, alongside other impending new editions of Hardy's poetry, in next year's *YWES*. One major monograph to appear on Hardy and matters Victorian is Dennis Taylor's *Hardy's Literary Language and Victorian Philology*. This is the first detailed exploration of Hardy's notorious linguistic 'awkwardness'. Taylor's pioneering study shows that Hardy's language must be understood as a distinctive response to the philological and literary issues of the time. Deeply influenced by the Victorian historical study of language, Hardy deliberately incorporated into his own writing a sense of language's recent and hidden history, its multiple stages and classes, and its arbitrary motivations. Indeed, Taylor argues that Hardy provides us with an example of how a writer 'purifies the dialect of a tribe' by inclusiveness, by heterogeneity, and by a sense of history which, in Hardy's case, distinguishes him from a more ahistorical, synchronic modernist aesthetic and which constitutes an ongoing challenge to literary language. Taylor provides a fascinating account of Hardy's relationship with the *OED*. This is a very important study of Hardy's use of language.

This year's crop of essays on Hardy's poetry include Pamela Dalziel's 'Hardy's Sexual Evasions: The Evidence of the "Studies, Specimens & c." Notebook' (*VP* 31.143–56) which examines the notebook of the 1860s for the evidence it provides of Hardy's development of a poetic vocabulary. Dalziel points to 'the extent to which that vocabulary was ... specifically erotic'. The difficulties registered in the notebook of this process of formulating a language for sexuality are mapped by Dalziel onto Hardy's fraught and problematic accounts of sexuality and of women in his published work. Neil Covey's 'The Decline of Poetry and

Hardy's Empty Hall' (VP 31.61–78) aims to shed new light on Hardy's conscious decision to move from prose to poetry in order to avoid hurtful public scrutiny in the 1890s. Covey provides a substantial account of the sociological history of poetry which demonstrates that Hardy's conception of it as a safe, élite space, insulated from popularist scrutiny was not just his personal 'mythology'. From well before the 1890s 'the rest of England was also partaking in the construction of the particular mythology, so as to make it a cultural fact that poetry was an ignored genre amenable only to outsiders'. In 'The Poetics of Interruption in Hardy's Poetry and Short Story' (VP 31.41–60), Norman D. Prentiss explores the 'structural awkwardness' – the abrupt juxtapositions, gaps in chronology, shifts in tone, philosophy or narrator's voice – throughout Hardy's work. Prentiss counters the claim that Hardy was simply 'a bad editor of his own work' with the assertion that these dissonances are central to Hardy's project in both his prose and, to an even greater extent, his poetry, to insist that 'philosophical consistency is impossible'.

Several new books have appeared on Hopkins's poetry this year. C. K. Williams has edited for Ecco Press The Essential Hopkins which prints a standard selection of the poems with an elementary introduction. The most substantial and important publication in Hopkins studies for the past two years must be Norman White's Hopkins: A Literary Biography (1992). White's biography is well-researched and fully documented, setting the development of his subject's work against the background and currents of Victorian intellectual life. Gerard Manley Hopkins and Critical Discourse edited by Eugene Hollahan is a collection of 20 essays by major scholars in the area (mainly American), including work by Jerome Bump, Paul G. Arakelian, James Finn Cotter, Richard F. Giles, Norman H. Mackenzie, Jude V. Nixon, David A. Downes, Howard W. Fulweiler, René Gallet, Lesley Higgins, Terence Allan Hoagwood, Marcella M. Holloway, Peter Millward S.J., Cary H. Plotkin, Kinereth Meyer and Rachel Salmon, William B. Thesing, Joseph J. Feney S.J., Catherine Phillips, Carla Valley, Tom Zaniello, and Pamela Palmer. This volume will be useful to those working on Hopkins in giving a good idea of the current state of Hopkins scholarship. James Olney's The Language(s) of Poetry: Walt Whitman, Emily Dickinson, Gerard Manley Hopkins explores the work of three seemingly disparate precursors of modernism. Olney writes against the grain of much contemporary scholarship in his contention that there exists a 'nearly ahistorical language' of poetry formed from certain poetic traits, such as 'heightened rhythmization'.

The 1992 Gerard Manley Hopkins Annual edited by Michael Sundermeier was not available for review last year. It contains several interesting articles on Hopkins's work, including Hugh Kenner's 'The Poetic of Detail', Norman White's 'Hopkins and the County Kildare', Guiseppe Serpillo's 'Moulding the Brute, Restraining Matter: Hopkins, His Translators, and Temporary Truth', Michael Sundermeier's 'Of Wet and Wildness: Hopkins and the Environment', Domenico Pezzini's 'Images of Friendship in Hopkins' Poetry', Joseph J. Feeney's 'The Collapse of Hopkins' Jesuit Worldview: A Conflict between Moralism and Incarnationalism', and Russell Murphy's 'Enough I Say/I Say Enough: Hopkins, Arnold, and Teilhard's Mind-Mastered Globe'. The 1993 Gerard Manley Hopkins Annual, which was also edited by Michael Sundermeier (with Desmond Egan), contains Guiseppe Serpillo's 'Poem Writing and the Quest for Silence', Angel Crespo's 'The Baroque Aeon in the Poetry of Gerard Manley Hopkins', John C. Hawley S.J.'s 'Hopkins and the Christian Imagination', Norman White's 'Hopkins: A Life', and James Finn Cotter's 'Hopkins' Notes on the Bible'. *The Hopkins Quarterly* (1992) contains two articles: James Hanvey S.J.'s '"The Leaden Echo and the Golden Echo" – Hopkins' Vision of a Christian Aesthetic', and Christopher Strathman's 'The Idea of Nature in Hopkins's "The Blessed Virgin" Compared to the Air we Breathe'.

A new collection of essays on Swinburne edited by Rikky Rooksby and Nicholas Shrimpton, *The Whole Music of Passion*, appeared this year, which will be reviewed in the next edition of *YWES*.

After the large number of excellent publications on Tennyson which appeared on the occasion of his centenary last year, one might have expected a paucity of material in 1993, but, nevertheless, several important volumes have appeared. *Critical Essays on Alfred Lord Tennyson*, a retrospective of some of the most important essays of the 1980s, edited by Herbert F. Tucker is outstanding. Tucker is one of the most intelligent critics of Victorian poetry but also one of the most lucid, and his concise introduction to the volume is a brilliant analysis of the way in which Tennyson scholarship 'holds larger implications for the state of scholarship within literary discourse and beyond that for the place of literature within modern culture'. Tucker summarizes trends in criticism of Tennyson from the 1830s to the 1980s. In his lifetime Tennyson was a public icon whose career was consulted and constructed as an index of the general state of culture. The Victorians used Tennyson to 'think themselves'; as their confidence in their institutions and practices grew from the 1830s to the 1860s Tennyson's reputation soared, but faltered in the face of increasing cultural anxiety after 1870. During the twentieth century Tennyson ceased to be viewed as a representative public figure and became the subject of scholarly scrutiny. The variety of approaches in the early twentieth century is an index of the forces which structured the professionalization of English studies; critics often looked to his work as a 'vehicle of indoctrination ... to reground academic humanism on English rather than classical literature'. For conservatives he 'served to focus a nostalgic and doctrinaire reprise of Victorian apologetics for hearth and empire', for Modernists he 'could be stigmatised as patently passé'. Tucker identifies two major trends in modern studies which correspond to the two most important movements in modern literary criticism. During the middle decades of this century, under the influence of the 'New Criticism', many critics ignored Tennyson's position as a public figure and the history of the interaction of his texts with Victorian culture, in favour of examination of the formalist complexity of his lyrics. Latterly, the attempt has begun to retrieve Tennyson's interaction with his cultural context, and many studies working from a variety of politicized perspectives, including Marxism and feminism, have been produced. The essays selected are chosen for the way in which they combine the best of each of these elements, close attention to textual detail and sophisticated cultural theory. They are too well known to require examination here. 'The Poet as Man of Letters' by Cecil Y. Lang and Edgar F. Shannon Jr, 'Tennyson's Breath' by Eric Griffiths and Timothy Pelatson's 'Tennyson's Philosophy: Some Lyric Examples' open the collection with discussions of broad topics across a range of texts. Eight essays follow which work through a variety of perspectives in relation to specific poems: 'The Skipping Muse: Repetition and Difference in Two Early Poems of Tennyson' by Matthew Rowlinson; 'A Blessing and a Curse: The Poetics of Privacy in Tennyson's "The Lady of Shalott"' by Joseph Chadwick; 'Personification in "Tithonus"' by Daniel A. Harris; 'Tennyson's *Princess*: One Bride for Seven

Brothers' by Eve Kosofsky Sedgwick; 'The Collapse of Subject and Object: *In Memoriam*' by Isobel Armstrong; ' "Descend, and Touch, and Enter": Tennyson's Strange Manner of Address' by Christopher Craft; '*Maud* and the Doom of Culture' by Herbert F. Tucker; and 'The Female King: Tennyson's Arthurian Apocalypse' by Elliot L. Gilbert. The volume ends with two essays which deal with later works in order to make a retrospective argument about the scope of Tennyson's preoccupations, 'The Contours of Manliness and the Nature of Woman' by Marion Shaw and Alan Sinfield's ' "The Mortal Limits of the Self": Language and Subjectivity'. The collection is outstanding, not just as a representation of the best in Tennyson scholarship of the 1980s but also of the best, historically and textually sensitive use of modern literary theory in reading Victorian poetry.

Aletha Andrews's *An Annotated Bibliography and Study of the Contemporary Criticism of Tennyson's Idylls of the King: 1859–1886* offers new insight into a poem whose complex historical articulation is now rarely tackled in its entirety. Organized chronologically, the volume is a record both of the poem's publication history, and of the changing critical responses to the poem's development. Andrews claims that as a serial, evolving progressively over a long period 'from the settled mid-Victorian period to the verge of the final cynicism of the last decade of the century, [the *Idylls*] put several theories of art to the test'. The changing tone of the criticism is an index of some of the most important shifts in Victorian culture. A meticulous analytic introduction to the bibliography draws out some of the most important developments, from the controversy surrounding Tennyson's concentration on female figures in the 1850 sections, through the critical enthusiasm for the moralistic emphasis of the 1870 additions and revisions, which led to the *Idylls* being hailed as a 'national poem' which celebrated the virtues of Englishness, to the decline of its reputation in the last quarter of the nineteenth century. Andrews also provides a summary of trends in twentieth-century criticisms of the poem.

Two biographies of Tennyson have appeared recently. Peter Levi's *Tennyson* is a work of substantial scholarship which places the poet in a relationship with some of the most important political, religious and literary debates of his period. The emphasis of the biography, particularly in the sections dealing with the latter part of the poet's life, is on Tennyson's family circle and intimate friends, but important links are made with significant events and movements in Victorian culture. In particular, Levi is meticulous in his account of Tennyson's reading, indicating not only the rigorous programmes of study he set himself in theology, philosophy, ancient and modern languages and natural and physical sciences, but also the influence on his poetry of the huge amount of 'popular' fiction and poetry he consumed – during some periods in his life he read a novel each night at bedtime – much of it written by women, who are now forgotten. As do all the finest biographies it has a sense of its nature as narrative. It reads rather like a Victorian novel, its subject characterized with depth, in Levi's beautifully crafted prose. It avoids the worst sin of literary biography, of reading the writer's texts as direct autobiographical representation of the events of his life. As Levi comments, this approach is particularly inappropriate for a reading of Tennyson as 'the usual inspiration of his idyllic narratives was not life but magazine fiction'. Perhaps the one shortcoming of Levi's approach is his aggressive repudiation of adverse contemporaneous criticism Tennyson's poetry received. He dismisses Wilson and Croker, for example, who had written important reviews of the early poetry as 'prancing poseurs of criticism'. He loses the opportunity to examine the cultural anxieties at stake in the conflicting responses to Tennyson's poetry. This biography will be of more interest to the general reader than the critic, but offers a fresh and intriguing perspective on the poet.

Michael Thorn's lively and authoritative biographical study *Tennyson* (1992) is aimed at the general reader and those particularly interested in biography as a genre. Thorn casts light on some of the more shadowy aspects of Tennyson's deeply complex character: the rumours of drug addiction, epilepsy, sexual frigidity and mental imbalance. This is a substantial and attractively written work. Leonée Ormond's *Alfred Tennyson: A Literary Life* in the Macmillan Literary Lives series is more concise than either Thorn's or Levi's work. It is a more systematic account of the social and political circumstances within which Tennyson was writing and which will perhaps be of more use to students and critics. Ormond deals in detail with the critical reception of each of Tennyson's collections, making many useful links with shifts in aesthetic and cultural theories during the period.

John Schad's essay 'The Divine Comedy of Language: Tennyson's *In Memoriam*' (*VP* 31.171–86) addresses the question of the usefulness of contemporary theory for reading Victorian poetry in a refreshing and intelligent way. Schad aims to 'reverse the usual practice of theoretically informed work not so much by employing post-structuralist literary theory to reread *In Memoriam* as by employing *In Memoriam* to reread various currents within poststructuralism'. He opens with the proposition that the poem is as much an act of mourning for language as one for Hallam. The poem's consciousness of the limit(ation)s of language forces it into a theoretical exploration of the nature of the language. Perhaps Schad throws his net too widely; dealing with Bakhtin, Baudrillard, Cixous, Derrida, Kristeva and Lacan, as well as with nineteenth-century theories of language, including Carlyle and Fox, in a piece of this length involves reduction of the complexity of and differences between the positions he engages with. However, in conception, this essay is a valuable rejoinder to the traditionalist objection to theory on the grounds that it distorts and simplifies texts to (post)modern agendas. Schad demonstrates the way in which the complexity of the Victorian can deconstruct the deconstructionists. David W. Shaw also focuses on *In Memoriam* in 'Impact and Tremor in Tennyson's Elegies: The Power of Genre' (*VP* 31.127–42). Looking to structuralism rather than post-structuralism to inform his argument, Shaw utilizes Tvetzan Todorov's essay 'The Origins of Genres' in his argument that the power of Tennyson's greatest poem of mourning lies in its transgression of the codes of elegy to creative 'tremors' within the genre. Three short articles attempt to tease out the political problems Tennyson's poetry poses to modern readers. Roger Platizky's 'Tennyson's "Angel in the House": Candy-Coated or Opiate-Laced?' (*VP* 31.427–33) defends the poet's sexual politics, arguing that he interrogates rather than just reproduces misogynist Victorian accounts of femininity. Platizky points out that Tennyson supported many feminist campaigns of the period, including lobbying for the Married Women's Property Act and female enfranchisement: 'Tennyson may sometimes politicize his angels in the house when we least expect it'. Linda Hughes re-examines Tennyson's relationship with imperialism in 'Victors and Victims: Tennyson's "Enid" as Postcolonial Text'. Hughes utilizes Ashis Nandy's dialectical account of colonialism as not just a binary system of victim and oppressor, but one which degrades and destroys the colonizer too, in her account of the poem. Working in the opposite direction is John McBratney's 'Rebuilding Akbar's "Fane": Tennyson's Reclamation of the East', which argues that 'Akbar's Dream' needs to be understood as a manifestation of Tennyson's orientalism, 'Tennyson's lifelong need to lift the East into an aesthetic, moral and spiritual realm dominated by what he himself called "the supreme Caucasian mind"'.

It is pleasing to note that critical interest in the work of women poets continues to grow. Two substantial publications will be of great interest to critics of Elizabeth Barrett Browning. Sandra Donaldson's *Elizabeth Barrett Browning: An Annotated Bibliography of the Commentary and Criticism 1826–1990* is a comprehensive account of the poet's critical history. Containing several thousand citations, the bibliography works from the early reviews of poetry, through the biographical and contextual accounts of the later nineteenth and earlier twentieth centuries, to the feminist readings of the 1980s. In her brief introductory remarks summarizing the relations of the bibliography to previous Browning scholarship, Donaldson raises the important point that, until comparatively recently, work on Barrett Browning was embedded in commentaries which also dealt with Robert Browning, whose titles often cited only his name, making identification difficult. Collecting citations together in this way constructs a fascinating retrospective on the agendas which have governed the critical history. As Donaldson comments, Barrett Browning is a 'wonderfully complicated subject', subject to hugely contradictory readings from the start of her career. As a radical, committed to a sexual politics of equality rather than difference, Barrett Browning differs from many women poets of the first half of the nineteenth century, and early reviews, particularly those of 'Aurora Leigh', were often more hostile and outraged than those received by Dora Greenwell, Jean Ingelow or Christina Rossetti. Later, however, her work became subject to many of the same critical constraints and prejudices that were imposed upon her contemporaries. The bibliography reveals that during the first half of the twentieth century she was frequently the subject of Masters theses, but rarely that of doctorates, indicating that 'there was indeed scholarly interest in her work but that such work was not encouraged at advanced levels until the last two decades or so'. Like many other Victorian women poets, she was often dealt with in biographical rather than analytic terms and her poetry 'was not highly regarded by literary critics when academic journals were controlled by the philologists or the New Critics'. It is useful that Donaldson includes references to the fictional romances about the Brownings, highlighting the role she has had in collective cultural fantasies. This bibliography will prove invaluable for critics working on Barrett Browning from all perspectives. Donaldson ends her introduction by pointing to the vast amount of work which remains to be done, especially in respect of the production of authoritative editions.

Elizabeth Barrett Browning: Selected Poetry and Prose edited by Meredith B. Raymond and Mary Rose Sullivan goes some way towards answering this need. Raymond and Rose are longstanding scholars of Barrett Browning who have previously produced definitive editions of the correspondence with Mary Russell Mitford. The scholarship of this volume is not quite as ambitious: the editors have not gone back to the manuscripts of the poems, but take their texts from Charlotte Porter and Helen A. Clarke's edition of the complete poems of 1900. It is similar in scope to Margaret Forster's edition *Elizabeth Barrett Browning: Selected Poems* (1988), reprinted last year by Everyman, which takes as its text Henry Frowde's *Oxford Complete Edition of the Poetical Works of Elizabeth Barrett*

Browning, of 1908. Nevertheless, Raymond and Rose's volume is to be celebrated as it makes accessible a range of poems from all periods of the poet's career, from the juvenile imitations of the eighteenth-century epic, through the nature poems of the 1820s, the verse dramas of the 1830s, sonnets of the 1840s and strong political poetry she was writing by the end of her life. A useful introduction summarizes the development of Barrett Browning's career and points out important elements of her theory of poetry, including her developing feminist analysis, which was always presented within a highly moralized, often explicitly religious context and her strong conception of her legitimacy as a poet. A small number of Barrett Browning's letters and specimens of her literary criticism at the back of the volume shed useful light on her poetic theory. The editors analyse the dramatic shifts in Barrett Browning's reputation from the great respect in which she was held in her own period to the neglect of the earlier twentieth century. It is to be hoped that the interest which this useful edition will provoke will stimulate more interest in the production of a modern authoritative edition of the work of this major poet.

An interesting essay by Dolores DeLuise with Michael Timko, 'Becoming the Poet: The Feminine Poet-Speaker in the Work of Elizabeth Barrett Browning' (in *Virginal Sexuality and Textuality in Victorian Literature*, edited by Lloyd Davis) argues that in the course of her career Barrett Browning gives different accounts of poetic identity. She begins with an unproblematic endorsement of the figure of the male poet as genius and an acceptance of female poetic inferiority, but in the later *Aurora Leigh*, Aurora 'usurps the role of poet-genius'. The trope of virginity is deployed in a subversive way in this poem, it is the province of the male-poet genius and 'Barrett Browning is comfortable with the idea of the poet as an experienced woman'.

Juliet R. V. Barker's *The Brontës: Selected Poems* appeared in re-edited form this year. As an affordable paperback in the Everyman library, which contains a substantial representation of work by each of the four Brontës, it will be of great use to students. The edition is a summary of existing scholarship, rather than a new appraisal. For the most part, Barker does not re-examine the manuscripts but takes her texts of the sisters' poems from the most established twentieth-century editions: Clement Shorter's 1923 editions, *The Complete Poems of Charlotte Brontë*, *The Complete Poems of Anne Brontë* and *The Complete Poems of Emily Jane Brontë* edited by C. W. Hatfield (1941) which, particularly in respect of punctuation are not always authoritative readings of the manuscripts. Emily Brontë's manuscript poems, for instance, are very sparsely punctuated and Hatfield often takes it upon himself to supply the deficit. It is pleasing to note, however, that like Gezari's fine edition *Emily Jane Brontë: The Complete Poems* (1992), Barker prioritizes the published texts of 1846 over their manuscript versions, acknowledging the importance of the editorial decisions made by the Brontë sisters over the form in which their poems became public. The texts of Branwell Brontë's poems are taken from more diverse sources, but here Barker also draws on the work of nineteenth- and early twentieth-century scholarship including John Drinkwater's *The Odes of Quintus Horatius Flaccus Book 1 Translated by Patrick Branwell Brontë* and F. A. Leyland's *The Brontë Family* (1886). The inclusion of a substantial number of poems by Branwell Brontë, who has been largely inaccessible during this century, is useful. Barker calls for a serious reconsideration of his talent, arguing that he is 'not only the most underestimated member of the Brontë family, but also one of the most underrated of English poets'. The volume also contains a small selection of relevant prose, including reviews of the 1846 edition *Poems by Currer, Ellis and Acton Bell*, Robert Southey's notorious letter to Charlotte Brontë, in which he advised her that 'literature cannot be the business of a woman's life', and Charlotte Brontë's *Biographical Notice of Ellis and Acton Bell* (1850). The volume opens with a biographical introduction and a chronology of significant events in the Brontës' lives and important political and literary events of their times. Perhaps the extensive textual commentary which concentrates primarily on the biographical context of each poem and thematic links with other parts of the Brontës' work, including Angria and Gondal texts, will be of more interest to the general reader than the scholar. The most pressing priority in Brontë studies is for close attention to the texts and textuality of the poems and their extrication from biographical mythology. But this revised edition is sure to aid this project. It responds to a real need for an accessible collection of Brontë poetry.

Melvyn New prints a selection of Amy Levy's poetry in his edition *The Complete Novels and Selected Writings of Amy Levy: 1861–1889*. This substantial volume is a much needed resource for Levy scholars, concentrating mainly on Levy's prose, including examples of her short stories and journalism as well as novels. It is disappointing that Levy's poetry is less fully represented, although examples from each of her published collections and, in particular, a substantial number of texts from her final, fascinating volume, *A London Plane-Tree, and Other Verse*, are included. New's introduction usefully outlines contexts relevant to a reading of Levy's work, including her feminism and the scandal created by her antagonistic depiction of the life of her own middle-class Anglo-Jewish community in her prose.

There was no major volume devoted to Christina Rossetti in 1993: critics (or publishers) are doubtless holding back for the centenary next year, but there were a number of interesting essays. Two critics are concerned with Rossetti's negotiation with the images of femininity deployed in the art and poetry of the Pre-Raphaelite brotherhood and by other male poets of the period. Barbara Garlick's essays 'The Frozen Fountain: Christina Rossetti, the Virgin Model, and Youthful Pre-Raphaelitism' (in *Virginal Sexuality and Textuality in Victorian Literature* edited by Lloyd Davis) explores Rossetti's resistance to, and revision of, the objectified images of women in Pre-Raphaelite art. Garlick argues that Rossetti uses virginity as an emblem of her rejection of patriarchal culture and her lyrics dramatize the 'active protection of the virginal self'. Similarly, in 'Feminine and Poetic Privacy in Christina Rossetti's "Autumn" and "A Royal Princess"' (*VP* 31.187–202), Kathy Alexis Psomiades outlines a comparative reading of Rossetti's poems with paintings by Dante Gabriel Rossetti and poems by Tennyson which depict women in private, enclosed spaces. Psomiades argues that '[w]omen can be used to represent artistic subjectivity because of an analogy Victorian culture sets up between the privacy of artists and the privacy of middle-class women'. This metaphor is more problematic for the female poet, however, who is subject to a double privacy which threatens to 'stifle poetry altogether'. Brilliantly tracing the way in which Rossetti revised resonances of, in particular, Tennyson's poems about enclosed women, Psomiades argues that Rossetti negotiates these perils to produce an account of herself as the 'best poet' because of her unflinching confrontation of the 'horrors of privacy'. Virginia Sickbert's essay 'Christina Rossetti and Victorian Children's Poetry: A Maternal Challenge to the Patriarchal Family' (*VP* 31.385–411) compares *Sing Song*, Rossetti's rarely read collection for children, with other children's poetry of the period. She argues that Rossetti 'transforms common themes and dramas to the point of critiquing ideology she is supposed to be upholding', refusing to make her poems authoritarian didacticism or sentimental moralizing, instead creating through them a vision of 'respectful, egalitarian' relationship between mother and child. Finally, in 'Incarnation and Interpretation: Christina Rossetti, the Oxford Movement, and "Goblin Market"' (*VP* 31.79–93), Mary Arsenau opens up a fresh perspective on 'Goblin Market', arguing that it should be read in the context of Rossetti's devotional writings. Arsenau charts the way in which Rossetti was influenced by Tractarian poetics, in particular Keble, to produce an account of the material world as a sign and passage to the spiritual. 'Goblin Market' is read within this context; Laura falls because she loses sight of this relation, and comes to regard the material, the goblin fruits, as sufficient for her. Lizzie saves her by restoring to her the capacity for typological understanding.

Finally, a book from 1991 which has escaped *YWES* so far is Linda K. Hughes and Michael Lund's *The Victorian Serial* which is a study of instalment literature in the period. The authors demonstrate how the serial format (a continuing story over an extended time with enforced interruptions) affected the way Victorian audiences interpreted sixteen major works of poetry and fiction. Hughes and Lund conclude that this publishing format became an essential factor in creating meaning and that the effects of this format have been overlooked by twentieth-century scholarship. Contributing to the Victorians' interest in the serial were their notion of life as rich and full; their capitalistic view of growth and progress; their sense of time; and their uniformitarian ethos. Among the serial poems discussed are works by Coventry Patmore, Robert Browning and Tennyson.

4. Publishing History

As the transition from quarterly to annual of *JNPH* resulted in no issues in 1993, the bulk of this year's yield pertains to the periodical press and publishing history, and may be found respectively in *VPR* and *PubH*; while the latter manifests a new and pronounced interest in the nineteenth century with the advent of an additional editor, *VPR*'s masthead records the farewell of a long-standing editor in 2 and her successor in 3. If *Macmillan's* is the journal which gets most attention, aspects of *Punch* and *Truth* also claim space, and there is a clutch of work on gender and the press.

Dennis Griffiths has edited *The Encyclopedia of the British Press 1422–1922*, the core of which is occupied by an idiosyncratic, alphabetical sequence of 3,000 items called 'Biographies/histories of newspapers'. Sandwiching the sequence are, to begin, a number of longer signed articles on press history mainly by scholars: Louise Craven, Jeremy Black, Lucy Brown, J. Baylen and Aled Jones. Latterly a series of signed, generally longer entries, may be found, again alphabetical, on institutions associated with the contemporary press – such as the Advertising Association, the Associated Press, and (NB) the Periodical Publishers Association – and on topics, such as the newspaper collector, newspaper design, and the uncomfortable add-on 'Women in British Journalism'. The volume closes with an uneven 'Thematic Bibliography'.

The core sequence of the *Encyclopedia* is overwhelmingly composed of biographical studies of journalists, with occasional short histories of titles and a very few terms ('hiring newspapers'). This exposes its limitations: although the term 'press' in the title of the volume appears to include periodicals, the listing is confined to newspaper titles. However, I did find two periodical titles in this unsystematic sequence (*The Oldie* and *Private Eye*), *and* periodical titles are mentioned, voluminously *within* biographies (justifying entirely the inclusion of Leslie Stephen), in *some* of the initial essays on the history of the press (by Lucy Brown but not J. Baylen), and irregularly in the 'British Press Chronology' (the *Fortnightly* but not the *Saturday Review* or the *Nineteenth Century*). This *Encyclopedia* promises to be as indispensable and awkward to use as the great index to Victorian periodicals compiled by W. F. Poole, whose biography and *Index* do not appear in the *Encyclopedia*, with Poole's lacking an author index and Griffiths's a periodical index.

Aled Jones's book on *Press, Politics and Society: A History of Journalism in Wales* approaches this cluster of problematics through the history of popular journalism in Wales, for both English and Welsh language communities. Here too, the focus is primarily, but systematically and not exclusively, on the newspaper press because 'the sophistication of the ... contents and the complexity of the motivation of their editors and contributors deserve fuller treatment than can be afforded here' (5). The five chapters – on Journalism, Production and Distribution, Ownership and Patronage, Conflict and Culture, and Traditions and Transformations (on the twentieth-century press) – are clearly argued, crisply organized, and well written. Throughout this lively book, Jones's terms of analysis relate its material directly to the ways in which journalism functions elsewhere in Britain at the time, while providing considerable insight into the detail of nineteenth-century journalism and politics in Wales.

Allan C. Dooley's *Author and Printer in Victorian England* is both a reference book which scholars will continue to consult in the course of work, and a textbook for postgraduates in Victorian literature, publishing history, and bibliography which reliably details the processes of author-publisher-printer relations from composition to reprinting. Over eight chapters, it argues and demonstrates that Victorian printing technology shapes texts, and proceeds through largely historical and empirical discussions of composition, proofing, printing and reprinting. It offers case studies of Arnold, R. Browning, Tennyson and Eliot and their reprints, and concludes with bibliographically oriented chapters on documents, technology and evidence; authorial control; and textual change and textual criticism. It is manifestly sensitive and vulnerable on two points: there is a standard disclaimer in the last paragraph of the introduction about theory (it is 'avoided as much as possible'!) and the penultimate paragraph explains defensively (and fatuously) that 'bookwork' is concentrated on because 'it is a fact that Victorian authors aimed at book publication'. Although Dooley is not venturesome, there is a wealth of patient and welcome details of printing technology and processes that generations of students and scholars will learn to their benefit.

One of the most interesting articles this year, on the history of publishing, is David Finkelstein's '"The Secret": British Publishers and Mudie's Struggle for Economic Survival 1861–4' (*PubH* 34.21–50). Finkelstein utilizes evidence in the Blackwood, Bentley and John Murray archives to show that 'over expansion and private extravagance' between 1861 and 1864 led to near ruin, not only of Mudie's but of these and other publishers. Identifying events between 1861 and 1864 which adversely affected Mudie's business, Finkelstein reveals that Mudie's bankruptcy was avoided initially by agreements from 1861 between

Smith and Elder, John Murray and Hurst and Blackett who, alone aware of Mudie's financial difficulties, deferred their payments from Mudie in favour of his other creditors; from 1862 Blackwood was drawn into the rescue attempt which, eventually, involved a significantly enlarged group of firms, with Bentley failing to cooperate. Appended to this useful and detailed account of business history are Sales and Subscription lists for 1858–65 for Blackwood, Smith and Elder, and John Murray; also for Bentley 1857–9 and 1864.

The title of Alexis Weedon's 'A Quantitative Survey: George Bell & Sons' also in *PubH* (33.5–35) refers to book production costs between 1860 and 1905; it is conceived as a contribution to a larger project of quantitative analysis of book production in the nineteenth century necessary for understanding the economics behind the cheapening of printed materials. Weedon adumbrates the *process* of the project – the design of the data base; the problems of bibliographical terms (the nineteenth century's and ours); the problems of the archives – before she reaches the specific case of Bell and its acquisition of the Bohn libraries: its printers, print-runs, binding and new editions and reprints, each of which is subjected to statistical analysis. She concludes with questions about the macro-discourse and some pertinent if wry observations about the micro-economics: while the new technology of the printers William Clowes *did* allow cheaper and faster longer print runs, Bell rarely used them, preferring his own stereotype printing process! There are appendices on Archival Sources and Printing Contracts.

In light of their record of publication of science, theology, poetry and literature, and their failure to capitalize on the lucrative genres of textbooks and annuals, and on the juvenile market, the publication books 1871–89 of Henry King and his successors Kegan Paul and Trench, suggest conflicting elements of capital and hegemonic literary taste in contracts with authors. This is one conclusion drawn by Leslie Howsam in 'Forgotten Victorians' (*PubH* 35.51–70). After summarizing briefly the history of the three firms, Howsam ascertains the variety of types of contracts issued – commission (all risks run by the author), the firm's purchase of copyright, and types of royalty and share profit arrangements – the genres favoured, and the gender factor. As the predominance of commission and the preponderance of non-fiction distinguish King, Kegan Paul and Trench from the typical trade practices, Howsam finally turns to the implications of commission or 'vanity' publishing for the Victorian literary middle class as typified by a Victorian author, Claude Conder. Howsam's research in the publication books moves substantially beyond quantitative conclusions to meaningful social and publishing history.

In a well-written, pithy piece in *PubH* 33 (59–76), Bernard Warrington limns the publisher William Pickering's contribution to the transformation of the appearance of retail books between 1820 and 1853, when responsibility for binding passed from the retail bookseller to the publisher, and from boards to cloth. 'William Pickering and the Development of Publishers' Binding in the Early Nineteenth Century' sorts through Pickering's reprints of older English literature to establish a detailed chronology of Pickering's experiments with cloth, lettering, gilt and decoration, and his innovations. Moving on to comment on Pickering's other types of binding as alternatives to cloth, of which leather remained an important example, Warrington looks at sale catalogues of 1854–6 to assess further Pickering's binding policies; he alleges that while Pickering was an innovator in the case of cloth, he was not responsible for the development of full-edition binding. *PubH* 34 (71–102) contains abstracts of papers from the 1993 SHARP conference, a number of which address nineteenth-century press and publishing history. Likewise *VPR* 26.1 (43–6) has Kathryne S. McDorman's 'Conference Report' for RSVP's Manchester conference in 1992.

Joel Haefner turns to an earlier period in *VPR*'s 'Pressures of the Marketplace: John Hunt's Editorial Philosophy and Strategies, 1805–1831' (26.92–100), John being Leigh Hunt's brother and partner in *The Examiner*, and Byron's publisher. Drawing effectively on Hunt's correspondence, Haefner clarifies his politics and the development of his journalism policy from a position in 1808 when an admixture of politics and literature ensured the success of *The Examiner*, to the 1820s when the failure of *The Liberal* convinced him that politics and literature must part company for either to sell respectively to the working and upper classes, and that advertising was repaid in sales. Haefner's shapely piece offers a clear view of a rapidly changing readership and its interpretation by a canny if radical publisher.

To move from named publishers to publishing history, in *VPR* (26.125–32) Robert Colby writes on the Chace Act of 1891 and the mutual efforts of the American and British authors, authors' groups and professional journals of authorship to achieve a binding copyright act in 'Authors United!: An Anglo-American Alliance'. Besant, the Society of Authors and the *Author* figure prominently here, along with *Literature* (the predecessor to the *TLS*), and their American counterparts Brander Matthews, the *Bookman* and the American Society of Authors which later became the Authors' League. Readers should be wary of the many printing errors which litter this article (resulting in the 'Chance Act') and the whole of *VPR* 26.3 and 26.4; corrections appear in *VPR* 27.178.

In *PubH* (33.37–58), Rosemary Scott examines 'Pious Verse in the Mid-Victorian Market Place: Facts and Figures' and demonstrates that Sunday verse was a commercial proposition for publishers such as Longman and their writers such as James Montgomery (1771–1854) and Catherine Winkworth (*Lyra Germanica*). As well as singling out prominent authors in this field, her subject comprises the pricing of works, print runs, the number of women authors, and the periodicals which represented the lower end of the market. The Appendices consist of fourteen tables.

Almost half of the papers in *Serials and Their Readers 1620–1914* edited by Robin Myers and Michael Harris pertain to the nineteenth century, and two of the three relate to more general aspects of publishing history. Aled Jones tackles 'Constructing the Readership in 19th-century Wales' (145–62), and what makes this article doubly interesting is its treatment of readership as a theoretical and methodological problem as well as relating to the particulars of Wales in the last century. A section on readership as imagined community looks at the limitations of dependence on periodicals' modes of address to readers to construct readerships, as well as readers' address to the periodical in the correspondence columns, and Jones goes on to consider distributors – such as chapels, pubs and trade unions – as cultural formations and the core readership which mediated between editors and shifting 'real' readers. The factor of distinct language domains is linked to distinct cultural and moral values, and competing notions of readership, and that of the commercial market such as railway bookstalls to a shift from the collective reading atmosphere of the pub, club or chapel to a pattern of individual purchase from a retail source.

Laurel Brake's ' "The Trepidation of the Spheres": the Serial and the Book in the 19th Century', also in Myers and Harris (82–101), argues that the apparent separateness of the two spheres during the period is mitigated by a profound interrelatedness. To make this case she shows links between the origins of periodicals and the publishers of books, the imitation of books by the early nineteenth-century reviews, the press functions of reviewing, originating, and advertising books, and the role of the serial in finally reducing the price of books towards the end of the century. In the course of the argument, a series of periodical essays on 'Contemporary Literature' in *Blackwood's Magazine* is drawn on, as is the role of the circulating libraries in the distribution and sale of serials.

It is good to report that Murray G. H. Pittock's *Spectrum of Decadence: The Literature of the 1890s* has a chapter 'Literary periodicals' (163–73) which outlines the articulations of decadence in the 1890s little magazines and the 'literary mainstream'. Though brief and synoptic, Pittock has done some periodical reading, musters some apt examples, and has some interesting things to say.

The Spring issue of *VPR* includes three articles on gender and journalism. In 'Redundancy and Emigration: The "Woman Question" in Mid-Victorian Britain' (26.3–7) Nan H. Dreher argues that the debate about middle-class female emigration in the press (1859–80) 'challenged and changed' notions of the 'redundant' woman, gender and class by establishing work and 'singlehood' as acceptable for middle-class women; it also influenced the early feminist movement and later feminist campaigns. This is an article about issues rather than the press which, except for *The Times* and *The English Woman's Journal* is largely invisible and transparent, and named only in footnotes: the 'debate' is presented as conducted through named individuals who are constituted as unmediated autonomous subjects/agents, and from the footnotes it appears that most of the 'journalism' cited was accessed in anthologies. Any 'debate' in the press remains to be located, analysed, proven.

It is revealing to compare Dreher's methods with those in Ken Lewandoski's piece on a related subject, 'A New Transportation for the Penitentiary Era: Some *Household Words* on Free Emigration' (*VPR* 26.8–18), which is rooted in a named and visible periodical to which the contemporary 'debate' is consistently related, as in '*Every* reformatory scheme outlined in *Household Words* during its ten-year run embraced emigration as an element of its teleology' (14). Lewandoski is interested in the popular weekly as a site of the contesting ideologies generated by the shift between the policy of transportation of criminals and the rise of the indigenous penitentiary, and he looks at fiction, documentary features, and reviews to that end. He finds that the periodical encourages emigration while regarding the new penitentiaries with suspicion, and that Australia, and free emigration, continue to flourish in the cultural imagination of *Household Words* as a site of reformation. This piece is impressive, both in its method and cultural profile.

In 'The Langham Place Circle and Feminist Periodicals of the 1860s' (*VPR* 26.24–7) Sheila Herstein argues that the periodicals stemming from the group – the *English Woman's Journal*, the short-lived *Alexandra Magazine*, the *Victoria Magazine*, and the *Englishwoman's Review* – were produced by editors and contributors who viewed themselves as reformers rather than professional journalists, and that the journals serve as 'reflectors' of the breakup of the Circle and as 'indicators' of the diverse commitments of their founders. This is a useful, succinct summary of the interrelations among these magazines, and their respective distinctive characters.

Margaret Shaw (*DSA* 21.195–212) examines mid-century overdetermined constructions of women by male critics such as G. H. Lewes, R. H. Hutton, Henry James and anonymous others, which show distinct 'masculine and feminine imaginations', whereby male reviewers separated themselves from the literacy of women writers and readers and their allegedly separate tradition. The contribution of reviews to the stratification of the new literacy of the period by class and gender and its use for political purposes are the terrain of 'Constructing the Literate "Woman": Nineteenth-Century Reviews and Emerging Literacies'; the privileging of a new 'man of letters' is the alleged result. While this version of publishing history offers close readings of some eight reviews, the attempt to address the issue of the feminization of Victorian literature is innocent of all reference to discussions of just this link between gender and literature by Gaye Tuchman, and the allegations of George Moore, Hardy and others in the 1880s and 1890s; moreover, it is astounding that no referee took issue with the allegation here that 'early periodicals did not recruit people in the professions', when it is well known that writers for early nineteenth-century reviews such as the *Edinburgh* and *Quarterly* included lawyers, MPs and government ministers.

In *VPR*'s 'Class and Gender Bias in Victorian Newspapers' (26.29–35) Judith Knelman quotes a range of interesting examples to show that a notable degree of sympathy in the press for women victims of crime or injustice in the 1840s gives way in the 1890s to hostility and intolerance for women, perhaps reflecting the perceived threat of the 'new woman' of the period.

Other groupings of articles treat aspects of history and literature – Ideas, single authors or titles – rather than periodicals or their history. 'Cultural Dissonance and the Ideology of Transition in Late Victorian England' (*VPR* 26.108–14) are explored by Mary Anderson in a survey of periodical material 1880–5. Although the method here involved reading runs of a number of journals over the five-year period, the resulting article deals with successive quotations, 'evidence' called up which floats in isolation without any meaningful link with the article, periodical and author which produced it, although the latter two names are given. Do not Dissonance and Ideology both stand to be enhanced, and pointed, through greater specificity in these matters?

Mary Lu MacDonald has a spirited piece in *VPR* (26.221–7) on 'English and French-Language Periodicals and the Development of a Literary Culture in Early Victorian Canada'. For most readers of *VPR* and *YWES* her intelligent mapping of the pre-1850 newspaper press briefly and the periodical press in detail will be enlightening, and her regular comparisons between the Canadian press, and its 'parent' journalism in Britain, France, and the USA are helpful in assessing the quality and nature of what Canada was producing. There is much of interest in this article, not least the distinction between the notions of national in the English and French periodicals.

In the same number of *VPR* (26.203–12) Jonathan Smith highlights scientific issues and their bearing on distinctions between poetry and science in 'DeQuincey's Revisions to "The System of the Heavens,"' an 1846 review for *Tait's Edinburgh Magazine* of a work by the astronomer J. P. Nichol. The mechanism of Smith's research is the differences between the article as it appeared in *Tait's* and its form in Masson's edition of DeQuincey which reproduces the author's responses to Nichol's objections to the original review in the light of new developments concerning the nebular hypothesis: the revisions show that, despite DeQuincey's apparent rejection of Nichol's views, he adjusted the piece to update it scientifically.

Crys Armbrust finds an unexpected connection between Tennyson's early work and the Chartists in 'Tennyson's Political Readers: W. J. Linton's *The National* and the Chartist Literary Canon' (*VPR* 26.199–202). Linton's reprinting of 'Mariana' and 'A Fragment' in *The National* in March and May of 1839 indicates a likely identification by Linton of Tennyson as a radical author, possibly due to the poet's connections with radicals such as Effingham Wilson, publisher of *Poems by Two Brothers*, and Leigh Hunt. Noting that 'A Fragment' first appeared in a sumptuous annual gift book, *The Gem*, Armbrust offers new readings of the two texts in a radical context which 'illustrate the transforming nature of the publishing process'.

Just such a gift book figures in 'George Eliot's Scrupulous Research: The Facts Behind Eliot's Use of the *Keepsake* in *Middlemarch*' by Meg M. Moring in *VPR* (26.19–23). She shows that the perusal of the *Keepsake* by Rosamund, Ned, and Lydgate in Chapter 27 is factually based on its 1829 edition, and that the engraving discussed in *Middlemarch* appears in the *Keepsake*, illustrating an anonymous story by Walter Scott, a favoured author of the young George Eliot, and anticipates the failures of the Vincy-Lydgate marriage.

Annuals figure in yet another article. Christine Alexander's '"That Kingdom of Gloom": Charlotte Brontë, the Annuals, and the Gothic' (*NCL* 47. 409–36) begins by providing an account of the history and nature of English annuals which were introduced into the UK by a Swiss engraver. Alexander goes on to use a combination of early writings by Brontë, biography, and copies made by Charlotte of eight Annual engravings, to establish that Brontë read and absorbed the visual and verbal contents of annuals such as *Friendship's Offering* (1829), *The Literary Souvenir* (1830), and the *Forget Me Not* (1831), and in particular the illustrations of John Martin, twenty-seven of which appeared in the annuals between 1826 and 1839, the years of Brontë's 'Glass Town Saga' and other juvenilia. Alexander concludes that the Gothic liberates Charlotte Brontë to imitate the Annuals, to indulge her love of the exotic and the mysterious, and to create anti-Gothic parodies and spectral spaces of the human psyche. This illustrated article accrues interest and weight as it proceeds, and uses its space to create prose worth reading and insights worth having.

All three of the nineteenth-century pieces in Myers and Harris have a noteworthy element of theory, and Bill Bell's 'Fiction in the Marketplace: Towards a Study of the Victorian Serial' (124–44) begins by situating itself within British Marxism. Beginning with discussion of a general question, the disappearance of the author in and through the commodity serial text, Bell goes on to explore the nature of fiction itself, here as narrative realism, as a determinate form. The bulk of this resonant article settles into Dickens, *Bentley's Magazine* and the text and serial issue of *Oliver Twist*; probing to what degree Dickens's early audience *was* inclusive of all classes, Bell establishes the ambiguity of Dickens and his readers, and identifies passages in the novel which address their readers as bourgeois, middle class.

Susan Balee has a short piece 'Correcting the Historical Context: the Real Publication Dates of *East Lynne*' (*VPR* 26.143–5), in which she shows that the generally repeated error that the novel had only begun to appear in the *New Monthly Magazine* by January 1861 is disproved both by the *actual* date it began publication (January 1860) and the topical material it incorporates (in the plot around Richard Hare on the subject of the harsh winter of 1860/61 and the breakdown in poor relief), both of which are visible to readers who consult the novel in its periodical context, a procedure which the author heartily recommends. The context of Victorian fiction is similarly Mark Turner's preoccupation in 'Gendered Issues: Intertextuality and *The Small House at Allington* in *Cornhill Magazine*' (*VPR* 26.228–34). Arguing that *Cornhill*'s policy of banning politics and religion gender it as female, Turner examines a single issue (November 1862) containing a serialized part of Trollope's novel, linking its treatment of the domestic ideal with a piece on 'Professional Thieves' in *Cornhill*, and of marriage with W. R. Greg's contemporary piece on 'redundant' women in the *National Review* (a male space), and responses to Greg in the press at large. Both Turner and Balee repay reading.

A number of scholars take individual periodical titles as their subjects, some unfamiliar and others as renowned as *Punch* and *Macmillan's*. If in 'Loudon's *Architectural Magazine* and the Houses of Parliament Competition' (*VPR* 26.145–53) Howard Leathlean is as interested in the editor in his own right as he is in this Longman monthly (1834–9), Leathlean capitalizes on this biographical streak by claiming that the general neglect of Loudon has made interest in his periodical a related casualty. This informative article has three topics: J. C. Loudon, landscape designer and editor; the first magazine to be devoted to architecture; and the style, alternative styles, and critique of the new Houses of Parliament, a topic explored in order to enhance our understanding of the journal.

In 'Unexpected Affinities: Slavic Literature in *The Illustrated Polytechnic Review*' (*VPR* 26.213–20) Roman Koropeckyj uses an anonymous review from 1843 of a Polish language edition of a course of lectures given at the College de France by Adam Mickiewicz, the greatest Polish poet of the period and the first Professor of Slavic literature at the College, to draw attention to the weekly *Illustrated Polytechnic Review* (1843–7). The identity of the anonymous reviewer, which is part of a complicated and absorbing narrative of detection, is aided by the discovery that his quotation from Mickiewicz and his early reference to Pushkin are translated from a German paraphrase of Mickiewicz's lecture on Pushkin, which appeared in the inaugural issue of *Jahrbucher* in 1843. In this unexpectedly interesting article, Koropeckyj considers the cultural and political reasons for this review.

Two articles in *VPR* concern *Punch*. Joe K. Law discusses its opera criticism in '*Punch* Goes to the Opera: The First Decade' (26.62–7), and Patricia Marks a species of its humorous poetry in '"Love, Larks, and Lotion": A Descriptive Bibliography of E. J. Milliken's "'Arry" Poems in *Punch*' (26.67–78). Law looks at the treatment of opera in all its manifestations which includes not only serious prose reviews, in which he notes the intrinsic value of opera is assumed, but also versified reviews, cartoons, satires, and parodies, all of which involve at least a basic knowledge of opera, but often considerable musical sophistication and instruction. Patricia Marks prefaces her Descriptive Bibliography with an informative essay explaining Milliken's involvement with *Punch*, 'Arry, '*Punch*'s anti-hero', and his Cockney verse letters which appeared irregularly from 1877 for twenty years. Preceding an economical conspectus of 'Arry's characteristics, Marks speculates that 'Arry survived two distinctive editorial regimes because he exposed the weaknesses of the upper as well as those of his own class. As for Milliken's contribution to *Punch*, Marks identifies him as an important member of the magazine's Table, the weekly dinner where editorial decisions were made, and as a writer of obituaries and introductions to volumes. The Bibliography includes illustrations as well as letterpress.

Ann Parry pursues her interest in the definition of the role of intellectuals in 'Theories of Formation: *Macmillan's Magazine*: Vol. 1, November 1859

Monthly. 1/0' which appears in *VPR* (26.100–4). Chary of the 'biographical' methods of writing the history of periodicals, Parry argues in this thoroughly theorized piece that 'in significant ways, a magazine is manifestly a process without an individual subject', that magazine texts are by nature composite, and that literary and political discourses in the first number function to conceal contradictions and create an illusion of a unified point of view. This is a fine and all too rare example of theory in relation to press history.

As though on cue, George J. Worth's 'Alexander Macmillan and His Magazine [I]' follows Parry's in *VPR* (26.105–7), arguing 'biographically' as it does that the disaffection of J. M. Ludlow in the mid-1860s, the death of F. D. Maurice in 1872, and the strong influence of Alexander Macmillan throughout the 1860s and 1870s, the last being the topic of this article, were important factors governing the character of *Macmillan's*. Worth deals briskly, and factually, with three elements of Alexander Macmillan's influence – his recruitment of Tennyson and Christina Rossetti to the *Magazine* and to the firm's list, his dealings with women contributors such as Margaret Oliphant and Caroline Norton, and his handling of controversy such as that occasioned by Arnold's adverse view of Colenso's higher criticism, and Carlyle's defence of slavery. In Part II (*VPR* 26.133–4) Worth details Alexander Macmillan's interference/participation in editing and his consequent difficulties in 1867 with the *Magazine*'s editor David Masson, who had moved in 1865 from London to Edinburgh to take up a Chair, and who resigned as editor in December 1867.

Worth looks at the 1860s from another perspective in *'Macmillan's Magazine* and the American Civil War: A Reconsideration' in *VPR* (26.193–8). Though also 'biographical', this interestingly includes textual analysis and shows, through texts in *Macmillan's* on the Civil War and correspondence of Alexander Macmillan, Maurice and Ludlow that the support of the *Magazine* for the North was fissured, in part as a result of *Macmillan's* policy of free expression and in part of Alexander Macmillan's belief in Carlyle's genius, and hence the validity of his claim in 'Ilias (Americana) in Nuce' that slavery involves the hiring of 'servants for life', rather than 'by the month or the day'. While Ludlow's outraged response to Carlyle's squib duly appeared in the following number, Worth's point is that this conflict between the dedication of the *Magazine* to the promotion of the principles of Christian Socialism and its commitment to diversity of opinions and freedom of expression was discernible from the first number. Parry would agree.

Two scholars in *VPR* discuss *Truth* (1877 ff.), Labouchere's and Horace Voules's Society weekly. In 'Henry Labouchere, *Truth*, and the New Journalism of Late Victorian Britain' (26.36–43) Gary Weber provides a factual profile – its origins, circulation, appearance and contents, but *not* its price, audience or frequency. While the article is illuminating on 'Entre Nous', the inclusive gossip feature which occupied 13 pages or 45 per cent of the non-advertising space in 1887, the dual emphasis on the investigative and entertainment elements of *Truth*, and the claim for both a popular and 'wealthier' readership generate a confusion (or complexity) which is not addressed, and complicates the question of *Truth*'s relations with the New Journalism.

Whereas the bulk of Weber's piece pertains to *Truth* as text and cultural product, Claire Hirshfield's 'Labouchere, *Truth*, and the Uses of Antisemitism' (*VPR* 26.134–42) closely links the policies of the journal with its hands-on editor. Reading against the notion of the 'composite' journal, the attribution of the entirety of *Truth*'s 'single political voice' to its 'sole owner' is strained, but

Hirshfield's article reveals a curve of Judaeophobia from a politically inspired campaign by (Gladstone and) the editor against Disraeli's policies on the Eastern Question to *Truth*'s rabid antisemitism in relation to Dreyfus and the Boer War, which stains its predominantly Liberal and progressive origins.

Arthur Sherbo's 'From *The Bookman* of London' (*SB* 43. 349–57), retrieves contributions (including letters) by Hardy, Chesterton, Wilkie Collins and Quiller Couch, which were overlooked by the compilers of *CBEL* and *NCBEL*. Short in comparison with his habitual work, Sherbo's piece gains in clarity and point from the welcome shaping of his material.

In '*Everyman*: An Experiment in Culture for the Masses' in *VPR* (26.79–87) Jonathan Rose brings to light not J. M. Dent's series of reprints but his inexpensive literary weekly ostensibly for a popular audience which appeared between 1912 and 1920. Edited and soon owned by Charles Sarolea, a modern languages scholar at the University of Edinburgh, *Everyman* placed more 'emphasis on the classics than on contemporary literature', a perverse decision for a weekly. Using Sarolea's papers, Rose provides a full introduction to the journal, and charts its rise and fall, citing sales and advertising revenue. Rose concludes that initially its political radicalism, its high moral stance, its dullness, its lack of funds to pay authors, its excessive publication of G. K. Chesterton and other Catholic writers, and Dent's abrasive relation with his editor presaged its failure with a popular audience, but notes ruefully that even when Sarolea bought Dent out in 1914, the periodical continued to castigate modernist texts in the name of older values.

VPR has introduced articles which are specifically oriented to aids to research. In 'Retrieving a Synchronic Perspective of Victorian Culture: The *Athenaeum* as a Research Tool' Monica C. Fryckstedt considers ways in which the *Athenaeum*'s numerous adverts for books and periodicals may be used in research. Her examples include analysis of different kinds of adverts for Mudie's, the identification of best-selling fiction now unfamiliar, recovery of lost reviews through press cuttings in publishers' adverts, and the contents of periodicals, some now lost, to supplement those included in *The Wellesley Index*. 'But What?', Eileen Curran's interactive and learned contribution to the Research element of *VPR* (26.183–92) consists of annotated Addenda and Corrections to *Wellesley*, and annotated queries (what? where?) concerning the suspected involvement of particular authors with particular journals. Based on three sources – applications to the Royal Literary Fund, biographies in *The Critic* (1852–3), and obituaries and biographical dictionary entries which derived from information from friends, the periodicals covered by Curran are restricted to those in *Wellesley*. David Finkelstein (*VPR* 26.191–2) confirms three author attributions for *Blackwood's*, involving George Chesney, Alexander Michie and William Tweedie. Readers and libraries who possess *Wellesley* take note and amend. These two pieces are part of *VPR*'s commitment to collect and publish corrections and addenda to *Wellesley*. Kathryn Ledbetter offers corrections to an older work in 'Boyle's *An Index to the Annuals*. Some Proofing Suggestions' (*VPR* 26.153–5), in which she introduces unwary readers to the many and various errors of an important research aid.

Lastly, in 'A Note on Ephemerides' (*VPR* 26.28) Josef L. Altholz usefully extends our knowledge of the hard copy of the British Library catalogue by noting categories for periodicals other than Periodical Publications, 'Ephemerides' being the largest with 394 columns. It comprises a miscellaneous variety of annuals such as almanacs, calendars, diaries, annual pocket-books, guides and some directories, and Altholz supplies a selection of representative titles.

5.   Victorian Drama and Theatre

George Rowell, together with Michael Booth, was largely responsible for bringing Victorian drama and theatre to the attention of scholars, and his book *The Old
Vic Theatre: A History* serves both as an account of a significant London theatre
with a long history and an admonition to contemporary theatregoers that there is
a need once again to come to its assistance. For our purposes, the book covers the
period from the founding of the theatre as the Coburg in 1818 to the beginning
of the First World War and the Shakespeare seasons of Philip Ben Greet. Unlike
the rival Surrey theatre whose heyday lay firmly in the Victorian period, the
Coburg, subsequently named the Royal Victoria in 1834, only acquired a respected status in the twentieth century despite the fact that Hazlitt, Dickens,
Mayhew and Kingsley all reported their visits, and Edmund Kean, Macready and
later, William Poel, had an association with it.

The theatre was built in the hope that its proximity to the new Waterloo
Bridge would attract a city audience across the river. The patronage of Princess
Charlotte and Prince Leopold of Saxe Coburg Gotha promised auspiciously. But
this proved short-lived and royalty, when it patronized the theatre, as the Duchess
of Kent and her daughter, Victoria did in November 1834, was only there
occasionally. Despite the efforts of managers like Thomas Dibdin, Davidge and
Osbaldiston to lend the theatre a particular distinctiveness, it was never able to
compete with the combined attractions of the Surrey and Astley's. Ironically,
audiences seem to have bypassed the Victoria. With the erection of Waterloo
station in 1847, visitors and suburbanites used the train services to facilitate their
visits to the West End and the attractions of the Strand. There was little to
encourage them to visit the Victoria. Effectively built on a crossroad, the theatre's
audiences reflected impermanence which constant changes in repertoire and
appeal to novelty throughout its career, reflected. Of all the 'minor theatres', the
Victoria was least able to find a secure audience base or a house style.

The only period of relative stability appears to have occurred during the
management of Osbaldiston and his partner Eliza Vincent between 1841 and
1856. During this period, a repertoire of domestic dramas reflecting local tastes
kept the theatre solvent. After this, attempts were made to open the theatre as a
music hall in 1871 but with little success. The final Victorian phase of the
theatre's history took place when it was sold to the Coffee Music Halls Company
in 1881 and Emma Cons began its operation as a temperance meeting hall whose
platform of reform was enlivened by ballad concerts, musical tableaux from
opera, and, from 1904, film nights. The programme of variety would remain the
theatre's staple form of entertainment until 1912 and a resident drama company,
the first since 1880, would be established in 1914.

Rowell's book is a straightforward, chronological account of the theatre's
history from its opening in 1818 as the Coburg, to the change of name in 1834 and
the assumption of management by Egerton and Abbott; from Osbaldiston's first
appearance as an actor until the change to a temperance music hall; and from
1880 to the resumption of dramatic performances and the outbreak of the war.
The book's value lies in revealing a tantalizing glimpse of a struggling nineteenth-century theatre whose influence in the twentieth century was to be so
profound. Rowell structures it as a series of ongoing searches for a stable identity.
He suggests that much needs to be done, particularly in the investigation of the
theatre's two periods of stability: the managements of Osbaldiston and Emma
Cons.

A comparison between the Victoria and other 'minor' theatres is illuminating. Recently, Jim Davis and others have written extensively about the Britannia Theatre in Hoxton. Davis, in fact, concludes the analysis of his discovery of the Frederick Wilton diaries which he had edited in 1992 by drawing attention to the continuing interest Wilton took in the Britannia after his retirement in 1875 and his subsequent emigration to Australia ('Reminiscences in Retirement: Theatrical References in the Post-Britannia Diaries of F. C. Wilton', *TN* 47.106–13). Allan Stuart Jackson's book *The Standard Theatre of Victorian England* is therefore particularly welcome in that it adds to our knowledge of London's East End theatres. The Standard, built in Shoreditch in 1835, remained a place of public entertainment, albeit as a music hall and cinema, until 1939. Like the Britannia, its heyday was associated with a particular enduring dynasty, that of the Douglasses from 1850 until 1888. Even when the Douglass family relinquished control of the theatre to Andrew Melville in December 1888, it would be retained by the Melville family until 1907. A comparison between the history of this theatre and that of the Victoria is particularly striking. While the Victoria appears to have gained little from the construction of Waterloo station, the Standard was fortuitously built just before the completion of the terminus of the Eastern Counties Railway, in a growing suburb characterized by light manufacturing industry and the clothing trade and increasingly acting as a conduit for the distribution of goods to the north and east from the London docks (24–5). The theatre was thus able to rely on a growing neighbourhood and, subsequently, on tourism for its support, certainly until the end of the 1870s.

John Douglass, who bought the Standard Theatre in 1848 was an experienced manager and a noted nautical performer whose popularity in sailor roles rivalled that of T. P. Cooke. From the outset the repertoire of the theatre contained a judicious mixture of nautical melodramas, novelty acts, plays of a moral or corrective tone (Jackson argues that probably the earliest adaptation of *Uncle Tom's Cabin* took place at the Standard in September 1852), and visiting guest performers in Shakespeare and even Byron's *Manfred*, which would include Samuel Phelps in 1857 and the Keans in 1860. Douglass decided to rebuild the theatre in 1850, making it, with its capacity of 4,000–5,000 seats, the largest theatre in Britain. Douglass also began his regular seasons of pantomimes which would eventually rival those of Drury Lane in their sumptuousness and spectacle – electricity was used for lighting effects as early as the 1850s. Throughout his management he relied on the loyalty of family groupings of actors like the Honners and the Nevilles which maintained a stable company particularly through the period 1848–60. As well he could depend on guest stars returning like James Anderson, Sims Reeves and Barry Sullivan. That the theatre's policy was a successful one can be measured by the increase in its size to over 5,000 seats in 1853.

From 1860 neighbourhood audiences started to decline so that changes in policy needed to be implemented to attract tourists and those increasingly using public transport. The result was a turning away from the classical repertoire to a reliance on sensational melodrama and pantomime and the tours of West End companies. This would remain the staple policy until the end of the Douglass era with visits, for example, of Buckstone and the Haymarket company in 1868, Irving and the Lyceum company in 1872 and the Bancrofts with Robertson's *Caste* and *Ours* in 1874.

The theatre was remodelled in 1864 to include orchestra stalls and a dress circle with individually numbered seats while backstage, hydraulic lifts were installed together with a huge tank for water effects. The theatre was now being referred to as 'the Eastern Drury Lane'. The theatre, however, burned down in 1866 and reopened under the management of the younger Douglass family in 1867. By the mid-1880s the size of the theatre was becoming a handicap as the composition of Shoreditch irrevocably changed and domestic realism called for new styles of acting. Massive tank dramas with realistic seaweed, water and real swans were simply not enough. Jackson quotes from an article which appeared in the *Illustrated Sporting and Dramatic News* in March 1888: 'it takes an inordinately long time between acts to get the stage ready for [the sensation effects], and when they come, the sole reward for one's waiting is a subdued picture in the theatre of what one can see a good deal better outside'. Jackson's book extensively utilizing the resources of the Rose Lipman, Guildhall and Westminster City Libraries and the memoirs of Albert Douglass, is lavishly accompanied by 200 illustrations. It is a valuable contribution to theatre history and will hopefully stimulate other scholars to investigate the remaining theatres of the East End.

As well as London theatres, the history of the provincial circuits has also received some notice. The Society for Theatre Research continues to produce invaluable records which document the history of British theatre and its publication of Anthony Denning's *Theatre in the Cotswolds: the Boles Watson Family and the Cirencester Theatre* forms part of this ongoing service to theatre historians. Denning was a private scholar with an interest in the theatre of the West Country particularly centred on Cirencester. He died before the manuscript was completed and the work has been extended and seen through the press by Paul Ranger who has provided an account of Georgian theatre in the provinces, extended the manuscript's history beyond 1819, and has fully documented the extensive Boles Watson circuit in the West Country and Wales. Though most of the book is concerned with provincial theatre in the eighteenth century, it has implications for the later period particularly as an example of the collapse of the provincial circuits, the result of demographic changes and the decline of traditional agricultural centres.

The book begins with Boles Watson, his formation of the Cheltenham Company of Comedians and the building of theatres in Cirencester between 1794 and 1799. The heyday of the circuit lasted beyond the death of Boles Watson in 1813 and into the management of his son, John Boles Watson II. At its peak the circuit contained 44 theatres serviced by travelling companies with Cheltenham and Cirencester as its centre. It was important enough to be visited by Master Betty, Sarah Siddons and Edmund Kean. But after the death of Boles Watson II the company began to decline, and, by the 1830s, theatre buildings were being sold off. The Theatre Royal, Cheltenham was burnt down in 1839 and the theatre at Cirencester had become a barrel store by 1842. It is an account which while sadly documenting the collapse of the travelling circuits, forms a most welcome complement to the histories by Kathleen Barker and others of the theatres in Bristol and Bath.

A comparison between the portraits of Shaw and William Archer is illuminating. Shaw with his Jaeger suit worn with the uncaring confidence of a flamboyant actor and his red (subsequently white) hair and beard deliberately unkempt; Archer meticulously turned out in a business suit with a high collar, with his hair meticulously groomed and a moustache to hide his bad teeth. Their eyes, however, give them away. Shaw's challenge the onlooker to become complicit in naughtiness; Archer's keep the onlooker at bay with their implacable earnestness. If there are hidden depths, these need to be quarried by someone who believes that they exist at all. And this is what Peter Whitebrook in his *William Archer: a biography* has tried to do. He makes a valiant attempt to turn Archer into an interesting person, a difficult task given Archer's expert emotional dissimulation.

His book is the first modern attempt to give Archer his critical due and Whitebrook's enthusiasm for his subject rarely flags. Archer's place in the history of nineteenth-century criticism has never been questioned. After all, he was almost single-handedly responsible for making Ibsen's plays accessible to the Victorian public and his translations remained the standard until after the Second World War. He was also responsible for getting Shaw his first journalistic positions and assisted the career of Granville Barker, both of whom remained his lifelong friends. The problem is that Archer lived through other people. Perhaps this explains why so much of this biography is concerned with the stories of others who were influenced by Archer.

Archer made his reputation as an uncompromising apostle of the New Drama. After commencing his London career in 1878 as the dramatic critic for the *London Figaro*, he succeeded Dutton Cook on the *World* in 1884 and stayed as its critic for 21 years. Yet, like Shaw, Archer enjoyed the very dramatic mode of melodrama which he ostensibly despised. Shaw used its form to parody its content. Archer had little grasp of irony and none of Shaw's self-assertive arrogance. Archer, in fact, attempted to write plays on a number of occasions. They were largely unsuccessful and the identity of the author was concealed behind a series of aliases. When Archer did write a successful play, *The Green Goddess* in 1920, its form and content mirrored the despised autumn melodramas that could be seen at Drury Lane at the end of the nineteenth century. Indeed, as Whitebrook is at pains to describe, Archer was a man of contradictions. He worked hard to help actors in their performances of Ibsen but his name didn't appear as either translator or dramaturge. He actively supported the Barker-Vedrenne season at the Court theatre and the formation of a Memorial Theatre at Stratford but his name remains conspicuously hidden yet again. It is therefore hardly surprising that Archer concealed his private life completely. Whitebrook uses his redoubtable skills as an investigative journalist to quarry original letters and diaries for hints about this private area. He reveals much about the relationship between Archer and Elizabeth Robins and about Archer's emotional detachment from his family which even affected his reception of the death of his only child Tom in the last years of the First World War.

Ultimately, however, Whitebrook is defeated by his subject and the reader loses interest in a man dedicated to dissimulation. Archer's public pronouncements continue to be stimulating, especially his views on a National theatre. His efforts to advance the causes of English playwriting and the work of Shaw in particular vindicate his claim to be a Victorian pioneer. He still remains, however, the dour Scot which his photographs suggest and which his contemporaries believed him to be, despite his emotional peccadillos which Whitebrook has documented and the sense of humour which Shaw insisted that he really possessed.

The year has also seen the publication of studies about particular plays and their performances. George Taylor's *Players and Performances in the Victorian Theatre* was published in 1989 but appeared in paperback for the first time in 1993. Its evident strengths remain: his analysis of Romantic performance and its relationship to the portrayal of domestic behaviour especially the performances of the Wigans, Macready and Faucit and the examination of key productions like Macready's *Richelieu* in 1839 to Poel's and Forbes Robertson's *Hamlet* in 1881 and 1897 respectively. The book is an admirable account of traditions and change in performance style through the Victorian period and should be required reading for all students of the later holistic views of actor-as-character. Routledge's proofing, execrable in the hardback edition, remains so. On the other hand, it is difficult to determine why anyone should have bothered to produce an edition of Charles Mathews's *Othello, the Moor of Fleet Street* accompanied by the detailed exegetical apparatus which Manfred Draudt provides. Part of the problem lies in the fact that the edition is almost entirely literary and fails to suggest why anyone might have thought it worth staging. At best, the play may have served as a vehicle for the Adelphi's principal low comedian John Reeve to parody Edmund Kean's performance as Othello. However, it appears to have had a very short stage life at the Adelphi where it was first performed in 1833. Much of the editorial apparatus is concerned with proving that Mathews might have contributed to the play (since no actual attribution can be documented) by comparing its style to the celebrated *At Homes*. The editor concludes that the work is probably the result of the collaboration between Mathews and R. B. Peake. The style of the burlesque mirrors the common reductive technique whereby literary or mythological characters are equated with contemporary figures, in this case an actual black street-crossing sweeper with whom audience members would have been familiar. Burlesques have a limited life unless they are animated by an enduring relationship to manners or intellectual discourse. This version appears to have been simply a vehicle for an actor's ability to imitate and caricature. The edition suggests little of the essential dimension of performance, and, without it, the play emerges as singularly unfunny.

Among the *desiderata* of Victorian dramatic scholarship are accounts of the major dramatists of the period prior to the emergence of Gilbert and Pinero. Douglas Jerrold has received some attention, as has T.W. Robertson. Nothing, however, has been written about Dibdin Pitt, Hazlewood or Moncrieff, a few of the most prolific dramatists of the period. Larry Clifton has tried to redress this with his account of the life and work of Edward Fitzball in *The Terrible Fitzball: the Melodramatist of the Macabre*. In many ways, Fitzball's career was typical of the dramatist of the period. He wrote at least 150 plays, a valuable autobiography, novels and poetry. He was highly regarded as being able to provide an accurate barometer of popular taste and his services as play reader were used by both Covent Garden and Drury Lane during the period 1835 to 1851. He was astonishingly eclectic and could adapt novels by popular writers as well as provide comic operas and burlesques. His principal skills were in harnessing the developing theatrical technology to astonish and delight his audiences. His 1833 play *Jonathan Bradford*, for example, exhibited probably the first appearance of a multiple set on stage and the use of red and blue fire ensured the continuing success of his 1827 *The Flying Dutchman*. Clifton usefully refers to Fitzball's cinematic techniques and, indeed, suggests that he would have felt quite at home with the engineers of today's filmic imagination. Clifton's exuberant support however is undercut by determinedly making Fitzball into a purveyor of the macabre. This is essentially reductive and takes no account of the variety in his writing, exacerbated by the insubstantial analysis of the highly selective number of plays which fit Clifton's thesis. There is little awareness of the conditions of performance and the assumption that Fitzball's plays were performed to, and appreciated by, an unsophisticated working-class audience cannot be substantiated. Equally quixotic is Clifton's determination to give Fitzball a literary pedigree by making his plays fit Aristotelian models rather than those of popular theatre, while his comparisons between Fitzball and the writers of late nineteenth-century Grand Guignol is both anachronistic and artistically misleading.

Scholars looked forward with keen anticipation to the appearance of W. D. King's *Henry Irving's Waterloo*. His article in *VS* in 1992 which described the descent and ascent of the Lyceum's huge roller curtain as a metaphor for death and rebirth, and, as Irving's career and tenure of the theatre was drawing to a close, as a triumphant defeat of death itself by the magician-actor (*YWES* 73.481), prepared us for a book which would throw a new light on Irving as actor, Irving as public figure and Irving as cultural icon. It is therefore a pleasure to record that King's is indeed an extraordinary book, challenging and provocative, which owes less to the 'new historicism' than to theatrical essayists like Lamb, Hazlitt and Lewes. Its wit and imaginative flair enliven a combination of theatre history, detective story and imaginative biography.

As the book's lengthy title suggests, it is about battles and battlefields. The two principal antagonists are Irving and Shaw. The battles however are between Irving's reputation as an actor and the determination of his antagonist, Shaw, to undermine it; between Irving's mesmeric grip on his audiences and fellow-actors, and Shaw's determination to expose the grip as fraudulent, self-serving and manipulative. In a way, the battle is fought between two Renaissance champions locked in mortal combat for supremacy. The result will be the defeat of the old order and the beginning of the new. The battle will also involve others: Ellen Terry, whose favours will be courted and allegiance will be appealed to by both sides, and her son Gordon Craig, who, deprived of his father, E. W. Godwin, would take his position as his godfather's champion in the lists against Shaw after Irving's death in 1906. The battle itself would begin with a skirmish on what might appear to be a trivial pretext, Irving's performance as Corporal Brewster in Conan Doyle's *A Story of Waterloo*. The play is a 40-minute one-act curtain raiser which opened in Bristol in September 1894 and which Shaw reviewed for the *Saturday Review* after it had been performed in London in May 1895.

King provides the reader with the text of Doyle's play, augmented by textual variants derived from various acting versions. But the very ordinariness and sentimentality of an elderly and senile survivor remembering a personal act of bravery during the battle of Waterloo gives no clue to the way it was performed and the astonishing reception which it was accorded. The missing element is, of course, Irving's performance which provided 'the apotheosis of the spirit of nineteenth-century English theatre, in the form of a heroic actor, amidst a thunderous crowd, thrilling the emotions, illuminating the ideal' (10). That Irving was able to harness a trivial vehicle to demonstrate his skills as a performer, and thereby to have that vehicle assessed as though it were a major dramatic *tour de force*, struck Shaw as insufferable. As a critic, Shaw refused to be overwhelmed by the seductive power of such histrionic 'inspiration'. As a proto-Brechtian critic, he saw Irving's performance as merely a series of masks, masquerading as the real. As a would-be successful playwright, he resented the overwhelming success of an actor who saw playwrights merely as instruments to be used and discarded. Shaw therefore used all his verbal brilliance to caricature Irving's performance and to ensure that this would really be the end of an era dominated by unscrupulous actor-managers. Irving was an obstacle to Shaw's aspirations and he used all the dirty tricks he could think of to displace Irving from his throne. Thus the play, in King's finely imagined reconstruction, becomes the battleground between the inspired actor and the inspired critic.

In his second and third chapters, King investigates the nature of Irving's audiences, that malleable crowd which Shaw wished to transform from theatregoers to playgoers. King shows the attention which Irving paid to shaping the Lyceum audience and the lengths he went to shaping its responses by fostering its sense of eliteness. Moreover, Irving manipulated the press deliberately (Shaw was able to resist the blandishments of first night chicken and champagne suppers) although he found himself constantly irritated by the detachment from the audience of the new critics – Archer, Walkley and Shaw – who challenged the very theatrical devices which a play like Doyle's seemed to perpetuate. In most theatregoers, however, Irving was able to provoke a form of collective hallucination. King refers to the seminal work on crowds by Gustave Le Bon to show that Irving shared the characteristic charisma of a great leader like Napoleon in order to mobilize an unthinking attachment to tradition on the part of his followers, thus making the Lyceum a site for the spectacle of absolute rule. He returns to this theme in Chapter Eight when he discusses the nature of personality. Irving's performances inscribed themselves on his audience and carefully shaped their self-image. It formed part of his technique of control.

The fourth and fifth chapters place the play and its performance within the traditions of nineteenth-century theatre: on the one hand, the tradition of Victorian pictorial realism exemplified in Irving's performance of roles like Louis XI, a combination of realistic detail within an idealistic, and hence fictive construction; on the other, the perspective of great events from the point of view of ordinary people. Melodrama constantly interprets socio-economic movements from an individuated perspective. Therefore there is little to differentiate Brewster from the sentimentalized 'kindly old man' whom Michael Booth has described in his *English Melodrama*. King points out that Waterloo was the first battle to have been accompanied by accounts from ordinary soldiers who emerged from anonymity to tell of their own experiences. Shaw, however, found this quasi-naturalistic approach to military history spurious. Doyle's play, like distant memories of Waterloo, demonstrated for him a romantic preoccupation with the past which was dangerous. The success of the play, however, infuriatingly showed him that the past in fact never dies and that great actors constantly regenerated themselves in performance.

King goes on to explain that Doyle's play came at a significant moment for Irving, just as Waterloo had been a climactic moment for Napoleon. It was the year of Irving's knighthood. The moment of the play's production and the moment of Waterloo marked the moments of supreme idolization of the two men. Nevertheless, these moments contained the seeds of destruction. In Irving's case, he would increasingly turn his back on new material, would lose his beloved theatre and would end his days as an itinerant actor.

Shaw was determined to change the terms of the battle. Six days after he saw Doyle's play he began *The Man of Destiny*. It was to be the gage thrown down before his ageing antagonist. His strategy was to confront Irving with the new by engaging the support of Ellen Terry who, he knew, was fretting at Irving's reluctance to provide her with an adequate role. The play was a curtain raiser not dissimilar to Doyle's. But while Doyle's play gives no indication as to Irving's

complex and finely detailed pieces of 'business', Shaw's is full of his characteristic stage directions to the actor. Shaw was not going to allow Irving any leeway.
The play thus becomes a tussle for domination of the stage itself between the
indisputable Napoleon of the stage and the greasy-haired Napoleon of Shaw's
play manipulated by the dictates of the playwright. Though Irving ultimately
turned the play down, his failure to pick up the gage sealed his own fate. As King
points out, the *Story of Waterloo* and *The Man of Destiny* formed moments of
maximum interpenetration by the antagonists of the other's lines.

The last two chapters of the book form, as it were, a slow recessional. The
correspondence between Shaw and Terry came to an end and Irving's death made
him ostentatiously immortal. Gordon Craig was not going to allow Shaw to
tamper with this deserved immortality and took up the gage on behalf of his
surrogate father. Ironically, Shaw found himself unable to exorcise Irving's ghost.
King sees the death of the old corporal in Doyle's play as a role which became
more and more a parallel for Irving's demise in his last years. The loyal soldier,
who had shared in one of the decisive moments of modern military history, dies
as he repeats the line he had shouted almost a century before: 'The Guards need
powder and, by God, they shall have it!'. In so doing, in King's summation, the
character, the actor and the play call up for the last time the edifice of English
values which modernism would steadily undermine (238). This is a complex book
which brings to life in a very personal and inimitable way the combatants in the
struggle for hearts and minds which characterizes the temper of English *fin de
siècle* theatrical culture.

Tracy Davis continues her exhortation to bring some understanding of business and economic history to bear on the analysis of theatre history in 'Reading
for Economic History' (*TJ* 45.487–503). As she states, this article is a 'position
paper' combining 'straightforward rhetorical analysis ... with the questions and
concerns of the subject field of historical economics' (490). She argues that the
biographies of noted theatre practitioners take little account of their abilities as
business people and these practitioners include Eliza Vestris, Emma Cons and
Vesta Tilley as well as Boucicault and Ben Webster. This forms part of a larger
argument that 'the motivating effects of economic theory' (496) are just as
significant as aesthetic influences. She takes issue with Dorothy Eshleman's
account of the Theatre Royal, Norwich and Ann Saddlemyer's edition of letters
between the Abbey Theatre's first three directors on the grounds that neither
discuss the workings of a theatre as a business and how these were affected by
larger economic circumstances. What Davis posits is the necessity to examine the
entertainment business which is interdisciplinary in terms of four broad categories: theatre history and aesthetics, business history and finance, social and
economic history, and women's history (499). She concludes by referring briefly
to two plays which have at their heart the interplay between human aspirations
and actions and the dramatization of economic principles: G. H. Lewes's *The
Game of Speculation* (1851) and Tom Taylor's *Still Waters Run Deep* (1855).
These form important examples of the mid-century's concern with economic
questions. The directions Davis suggests are useful although the article itself is
an uneasy mixture of rhetoric and recycled material written elsewhere. What her
examples, however, help to displace is the no longer tenable view that melodrama
merely provided escapist vehicles unrelated to contemporary anxieties and concerns. This is further explored in Daniel Barrett's 'It *is Never Too Late to Mend*
(1865) and Prison Conditions in Nineteenth-Century England' (*TRI* 18.4–15). He

begins by analysing the origins of this play by Charles Reade and its successful opening in Leeds in February 1865. Though the play has close connections with both the novel and stage version of *Gold* it uses elements which were absent from the earlier version, notably the harrowing prison scene in Act II whose realism provoked an angry intervention from its London audience when it was transferred to the Princess Theatre in October of the same year. Barrett goes to considerable lengths to show that Frederick Lloyds, the theatre's designer, conscientiously tried to replicate the realities of prison life that Mayhew and Binney had depicted in their *Criminal Prisons of London and Scenes of Prison Life* of 1862. Critics found the staging of the treadmill and its attendant horrors 'dismal and revolting' (10). 'If the proper role of art was to inspire, enlighten, and entertain, then such scenes had no place in the theatre' (12). It was an argument which would persist in Clement Scott's denunciations of Ibsen thirty years later. The fact that Vining the theatre's manager, refused to succumb to the first night audience's demands to end the play, and therefore its run, 'signalled the end of democracy in the Victorian theatre ... The age of the autocratic actor-manager had begun' (13). Barrett concludes by suggesting that Reade had succeeded in bringing to the popular stage a controversial subject and thereby had extended the stage's dramatic vocabulary.

The discussion of sexuality and gender roles finds expression in two articles, one by Anne Russell ('Gender, Passion, and Performance in Nineteenth-Century Women Romeos', *EiTET* 11.153–67) and the other by Laurence Senelick. In 'The Homosexual as Villain and Victim in *Fin-de-siècle* Drama" (*JHSex* 4.201–29), Senelick examines representations of homosexuality on stage in England, France and Germany. He finds it curious that neither the naturalist nor symbolist schools of modernism dealt with the new scientifically defined types of hysterical women and male homosexual. On the other hand, popular melodrama, sensitive to elements which impinged on public consciousness, was aware of both and the latter it elaborately clothed in the trappings of blackmail and blackmailers – the first play to identify a homoerotic relationship appears to have been *The Black-mailers* which was given a matinee performance at the Prince of Wales Theatre in June 1894. Senelick suggests that it was interpreted by most critics within the constraints of conventional morality although the audience of *cognoscenti* may well have interpreted it somewhat differently. In his analysis of the play he makes much of a textual as well as physical semiotic code which would have been instantly recognizable to an audience familiar, for instance, with Hitchins's novel *The Green Carnation*.

In Germany, the appearance of homosexuality on stage can be dated from Ludwig Dilsner's *Jasminblüthe* in 1899 (213), which again contains blackmail as a dramatic trigger. It set the pattern for other German playwrights who were unable, however, to define the homosexual accurately despite the considerable developments in psychology. The depiction of the homosexual in other than the clothing of melodrama would need to wait until after the abolition of censorship under the Weimar republic.

Homosexuality could easily be disguised as languid aestheticism and certainly in England prior to 1894, the languid aesthete had been pilloried with little or no overtly sexual implication. In France, however, Senelick maintains that aestheticism was seen in a more sinister light. Armory's society comedy *Le Monsieur aux Chrysanthèmes* placed a homosexual at the centre of the action and the play shows the perversion of cultural values by homosexuality (223). The play finds its place in a tradition of French comedy of manners which stretches back to Molière's *Tartuffe* but in this case the author replaces Tartuffe's religious deception by sexual deception and the play becomes a vehicle for a denunciation of society's endorsement of such decadence.

Just as Wilde's trial set back the possibility of any attempt to place the homosexual overtly on stage, so European scandals 'aborted the development of the homosexual character on the Continental stage' (227). Nevertheless, Armory's play, according to Senelick, 'helped to crystallise a particular image of the homosexual dandy as feline, neurasthenic, underhanded and manipulative in his dealings with others' (228) which, together with his 'louche gracility', became signs easily read by theatre and cinema audiences (229). As one expects from Senelick, the article is meticulously researched and authoritatively written.

Russell's analysis of females who undertook the role of Romeo also complements the interest in cross-dressing found in the examination of female Hamlets in, for example, Jill Edmonds's 'Princess Hamlet' in *The New Woman and Her Sisters* (*YWES* 73.472–3). Comic cross-dressing was an accepted nineteenth-century theatrical convention, and, indeed, survived well into the present century. Tragic cross-dressing presents a more complex phenomenon, and none more problematic than representations of Romeo. Russell points out that contemporary reviewers loaded 'cross-dressed Romeos with multiple and often contradictory readings' suggesting that the representation rehabilitated 'the passionate but effeminate youth from a victim of love to a model of idealized, virtually de-eroticized, heterosexual passion' (156). Romeo had, after all, been often criticized as a character whose thoughtlessness and ineffectuality disqualified him as a model of Victorian heroism. Russell quotes a comment from the *Athenaeum* of February 1855 which, as well, suggests a reason why actors may have avoided Romeo: 'There is a tenderness and delicacy of sentiment in the Shakespearian idea which has always made it difficult of representation to the actor' (158). The comment suggests that the role was essentially a 'feminine' one in terms of contemporary expectations of gender.

The first representation of Romeo by a female appears to have been that of Ellen Tree playing opposite Fanny Kemble at Covent Garden in June 1832. Inevitably a considerable element of the discussion revolves around Charlotte Cushman who commenced her performances of Romeo in the USA as early as 1837. Critics went to considerable pains to differentiate the performer and the role in both cases and laboured to prove that these performances clarified rather than blurred gender and sexual difference. Russell's article provides further evidence of the anxieties and tensions which pervade Victorian attitudes towards the construction of gender roles.

The depiction of a particular type finds further expression in Shearer West's article about racial typology ('The construction of Racial Type: Caricature, Ethnography and Jewish physiognomy in *Fin-de-siècle* Melodrama", *NCT* 21.5–40). West uses his art background to bring together evidence based on popular art, caricature and stage representation to examine the complex figure of the Jew in late nineteenth-century theatre. He relates this to contemporary theories of race and their manifestations in the analysis of physiognomy which were 'reinforced by the representations of Jews in art' (12). When Jewish characters proliferated in popular novels, especially those by Trollope and Thackeray, these were illustrated in a way which reinforced the visual referents. West concludes with an extensive reference to plays with prominent Jewish figures to show the congruence and sometimes clash between contemporary attitudes toward Jews and the enduring character type of melodrama. Inevitably these include the stage versions of *Oliver Twist* and *Trilby* with an extensive analysis of the performance and persona of Beerbohm Tree as Fagin and Svengali. These are amplified by reference to Tom Taylor's *Payable on Demand* and *Helping Hands*, both plays of the 1850s, as well as Hazlewood's *The Stolen Jewess* of 1872. West shows that the figure of the Jew was susceptible to change as British society was confronted both by 'the large presence of Jewish immigrants and the increasing respectability and assimilationist tendencies of the Jewish middle class' (23) at the end of the century. He concludes his article with reference to Zangwill's *Children of the Ghetto*, an 'authentic' Jewish voice of 1899 and shows that, ironically, Israel Zangwill's interpretations of Jewish characters maintain the stereotypical characteristics of the Jewish characters of nineteenth-century melodrama. West's article complements George Taylor's analysis of *Trilby* in the book referred to above and his article 'Svengali: Mesmerist and Aesthete" in *British Theatre in the 1890s* (*YWES* 73.475).

Four interesting theatre history footnotes conclude the survey. John Boyes-Watson has alerted us to E. W. Godwin's significant series of articles which he wrote for *The Architect* from 1874 to 1875 covering design ideas for the complete canon of Shakespeare's 37 plays. He has listed these, suggesting that they should be compiled and made more accessible ('E. W. Godwin's Articles on Architecture and Costume of Shakespeare's Plays', *TN* 47.164–7) while M. Lindsay Lambert offers 'New Light on Limelight' – an argument that suggests there is a case for the use of limelight at Vauxhall Gardens, somewhat earlier than the usual dating for its first use in December 1837 (*TN* 47.156–63). Laurence Senelick's other contribution to Victorian drama and theatre has been to explore the 1840 and 1850 volumes of Charles Rice's diaries omitted by Arthur Colby Sprague and Bertram Shuttleworth from their edition *The London Theatre in the Eighteen-thirties* which the Society for Theatre Research published in 1950. These volumes, in the Harvard Theatre Collection recount the precarious life of a part-time singer in the 'free and easies' of the period and round off our knowledge of the subsequent career of Rice ('Moonlighting in the Music Hall: the Double Life of Charles Rice', *ThS* 34.29–42). Paul Schlicke offers an interesting gloss on the popularity of Dickens on stage in 'Dickens in the circus' (*TN* 47 3–19). Dickens's immense popularity on the nineteenth-century stage is well known in the dramatizations by Stirling, Comyns Carr, Oxenford, Halliday and others. What is less well known are the circus appearances of characters from *Pickwick Papers* and *Oliver Twist*. Schlicke shows how the original characters illustrated by 'Phiz' found themselves realized, in Meisel's usage, on horseback by performers like Alfred Cooke at Astley's. These portrayals were immensely popular in Dickens's lifetime and indeed may well have delighted Dickens himself given his own propensity for the circus.

Books Reviewed

Alexander, J. H., and David Hewitt, eds. *Scott in Carnival*. ASLS. pp. viii + 600. £20. ISBN 0 948 877 20 0.
Allen, Dennis W. *Sexuality in Victorian Fiction*. UOklaP. pp. 150. pb $3.95. ISBN 0 8061 2547 0.

Allott, Miriam, ed. *Selected Poems and Prose, Matthew Arnold*. Dent. pp. 293. pb £4.99. ISBN 0 460 87392 X.

Amigoni, David. *Victorian Biography: Intellectuals and the Ordering of Discourse*. HW. pp. 206. hb £40.00. ISBN 0 745 00771 6.

Anderson, Amanda. *Tainted Souls and Painted Faces: The Rhetoric of Fallenness in Victorian Culture*. Reading Women Writing. CornUP. pp. 260. hb $35, pb $16.44. ISBN 0 801 42781 9, 0 8014 8148 1.

Andrews, Aletha. *An Annotated Bibliography and Study of the Contemporary Criticism of Tennyson's Idylls of the King, 1859–1886*. Lang. pp. 243. $43.95. ISBN 0 820 42084 0.

Armstrong, Isobel. *Victorian Poetry: Poetry, Poetics and Politics*. Routledge. pp. 545. £35. ISBN 0 415 03016 1.

Armstrong, Tim, ed. *Thomas Hardy: Selected Poems*. Longman. pp. 385. pb £15.99. ISBN 0 582 04061 2.

Barker, Juliet R. V., ed. *The Brontës, Selected Poems*. Dent. pp. 162. pb £3.50. ISBN 0 460 87282 6.

Bellringer, Alan W. *George Eliot*. Macmillan. pp. x + 166. £30. ISBN 0 333 51904 3.

Bevan, Bryan. *Robert Louis Stevenson: Poet and Teller of Tales*. St Martin's. pp. x + 197. £14.95. ISBN 0 948695 28 5.

Boetcher Joeres, Ruth-Ellen, and Elizabeth Mittman, eds. *The Politics of the Essay: Feminist Perspectives*. IndUP. pp. 236. hb £30.00, pb £11.99. ISBN 0 253 33109 9, 0 253 20788 6.

The Book of the Rhymers' Club, 1892, bound with *The Second Book of the Rhymers' Club, 1894*. Decadents, Symbolists, Anti-Decadents: Poetry of the 1890s. Woodstock. pp. 280. £28.50. ISBN 1 854 77136 1.

Brontë, Anne. *The Tenant of Wildfell Hall*, ed. Herbert Rosengarten with an introduction by Margaret Smith. WC. OUP. pp. xxxiii + 486. pb £4.50. ISBN 0 19 202989 0.

Brontë, Charlotte. *Villette*, ed. Sandra Kemp. Dent. pp. xxxiv + 542. pb $5.95. ISBN 0 460 87247 8.

Brontë, Patrick Branwell. *The Hand of the Arch-Sinner: Two Angrian Chronicles of Branwell Brontë*, ed. Robert G. Collins. Clarendon. pp. lvi + 243. £30. ISBN 0 19 812258 6.

Brown, Penny. *The Captured World: The Child and Childhood in Nineteenth-Century Women's Writing in England*. HW. pp. ix + 222. $39.95. ISBN 0 7108 1334 1.

Butler, Samuel. *The Way of All Flesh*, ed. with Intro. Michael Mason. WC. OUP. pp. xlvi + 472. £4.99. ISBN 0 19 282980 7.

Cannell, D. M. *George Green: Mathematician and Physicist 1793–1841, The Background to His Life and Work*. Athlone. pp. 291. ISBN 0 485 11433 X.

Cevasco, George A., ed. *The 1890s: An Encyclopedia of British Literature, Art, and Culture*. Garland. pp. xxi + 698. $95. ISBN 0 8240 2585 7.

Cherry, Deborah. *Painting Women: Victorian Women Artists*. Routledge. pp. 290. pb £12.99. ISBN 0 415 06053 2.

Chew, Shirley, and Anna Rutherford, eds. *Unbecoming Daughters of the Empire*. Dangaroo. pp. 207. hb £19.95, pb £12.95. ISBN 1 871 04962 8, 1 871 04997 0.

Cheyette, Bryan. *Constructions of 'the Jew' in English Literature and Society: Racial Representations, 1875–1945*. CUP. pp. xvi + 301. $54.95. ISBN 0 521 44355 5.

Clarke, Graham, ed. *Thomas Hardy: Critical Assessments*. 4 vols. Helm. pp. 384 (I), 432 (II), 464 (III), and 576 (IV). £295. ISBN 1 873 40308 9.

Clifton, Larry Stephen *The Terrible Fitzball: The Melodramatist of the Macabre*. BGUP. pp. 191. hb $39.95, pb $15.95. ISBN 0 87972 608 3, 0 87972 609 1.

Cohen, Ted, Paul Guyer, and Hilary Putnam, eds. *Pursuits of Reason: Essays in Honor of Stanley Cavell*. TTUP. pp. 413. $45. ISBN 0 896 72266 X.

Collins, Wilkie. *Hide and Seek*, ed. Intro. Catherine Peters. WC. OUP. pp. xxxii + 440. pb £5.99. ISBN 0 19 283092 9.

——. *Legacy of Cain*. Sutton. pp. ix + 326. pb £5.99. ISBN 0 7509 0454 2.

——. *Miss or Mrs?* Sutton. pp. xv + 126. pb £3.99. ISBN 0 7509 0455 0.

——. *The New Magdalen*. Sutton. pp. xiii + 290. pb £4.99. ISBN 0 7509 0453 4.

Cowart, David. *Literary Symbiosis: The Reconfigured Text in Twentieth-Century Writing*. UGeoP. pp. xii + 232. $30. ISBN 0 8203 1544 3.

Danahay, Martin A. *A Community of One: Masculine Autobiography and Autonomy in Nineteenth-Century Britain*. SUNYP. pp. 242. pb $21.95. ISBN 0 7914 1512 0.

Davidson, John. *In a Music-hall, 1891*, bound with *Ballads and Songs, 1894*. Decadents, Symbolists, Anti-Decadents: Poetry of the 1890s. Woodstock. pp. 294. £28. ISBN 1 854 77138 8.

——. *Fleet Street Eclogues, 1893*, bound with *A Second Series of Fleet Street Eclogues, 1896*. Decadents, Symbolists, Anti-Decadents: Poetry of the 1890s. Woodstock. pp. 258. £28. ISBN 1 854 77139 6.

Davis, Lloyd, ed. *Virginal Sexuality and Textuality in Victorian Literature*. SUNYP. pp. 257. hb $64.50, pb $21.95. ISBN 0 791 41283 0, 0 791 41284 9.

Denning, Anthony. *Theatre in the Cotswolds: The Boles Watson Family and the Cirencester Theatre*, ed. Paul Ranger. STR. pp. xvii + 254. ISBN 0 85430 054 6.

Dickens, Charles. *Great Expectations*, ed. Margaret Cardwell. OUP. pp. lxvii + 516. $90. ISBN 0 19 818591 X.

——. *The Letters of Charles Dickens*, eds. Graham Storey, Kathleen Tillotson, and Angus Easson. Vol. VII. Clarendon. pp. xxiv + 975. £85. ISBN 0 1981 2618 2.

——. *Oliver Twist: Authoritative Text, Backgrounds and Sources, Early Reviews, Criticism*, ed. Fred Kaplan. Norton. pp. xii + 611. pb $11.95. ISBN 0 3939 6292 X.

——. *A Tale of Two Cities*, ed. Norman Page. Dent. pp. xxiv + 413. pb £3.99. ISBN 0 6794 2073 8.

Disraeli, Benjamin. *Letters, Volume 5: 1848–1851*, eds. M. G. Wiebe, J. B. Conacher, John Matthews, and Mary S. Millar. UTorP. pp. lxiv + 591. $95. ISBN 0 8020 2927 2.

Dodgson, Charles Lutwidge. *The Pamphlets of Lewis Carroll, Volume 1: The Oxford Pamphlets, Leaflets, and Circulars of Charles Lutwidge Dodgson*, ed. Edward Wakeling. UPVirginia. pp. xxi + 382. $65. ISBN 0 8139 1250 4.

Donaldson, Sandra. *Elizabeth Barrett Browning: An Annotated Bibliography of the Commentary and Criticism, 1826–1990*. Hall. pp. 642. $55. ISBN 0 816 18910 2.

Dooley, Allan C. *Author and Printer in Victorian England*. UPValery. pp. xix + 192. ISBN 0 8139 1401 9.

Dowson, Ernest. *Verses, 1896*, and *Decorations, 1899*. Decadents, Symbolists, Anti-Decadents: Poetry of the 1890s. Woodstock. pp. 142. £25. ISBN 1 854 77142 6.

Draudt, Manfred, ed. *Othello, the Moor of Fleet Street (1833)*, Francke. pp. xv + 99. DM 34.80. ISBN 3 7720 2132 8.

Ebbatson, Roger. *Hardy: The Margin of the Unexpressed*. ShaP. pp. 160. £25. ISBN 1 8507 5373 3.

Edwards, Peter, and Andrew Dowling, compilers. *Edmund Yates Papers in the University of Queensland Library: A Catalogue*. Victorian Fiction Research Guides. pp. 104. Aus$10. ISBN 0 86776 492 9.

Eliot, George. *Romola*, ed. Andrew Brown. Clarendon. pp. lxxxii + 688. $125. ISBN 0 19 812594 1.

——. *Silas Marner*, ed. Anne Smith. Dent. pp. xxx + 206. pb £3.99. ISBN 0 460 87263 X.

Ellis, Linda Abess. *Frances Trollope's America: Four Novels*. Lang. pp. xiv +158. $36.95. ISBN 0 8204 1854 4.

Emerson, Sheila. *Ruskin: The Genesis of Invention*. CUP. pp. 288. hb £35.00. ISBN 0 521 41807 0.

Feltes, N. N. *Literary Capital and the Late-Victorian Novel*. UWiscP. pp. 171. $49.50. ISBN 0 299 13664 7.

Field, Michael. *Sight and Song, 1892*, bound with *Underneath the Bough, 1893*. Decadents, Symbolists, Anti-Decadents: Poetry of the 1890s. Woodstock. pp. 290. £28.50. ISBN 1 854 77143 4.

Flint, Kate. *The Woman Reader 1837–1914*. OUP. pp. 378. hb £25.00. ISBN 0 19 811719 1.

Foor, Sheila M. *Dickens's Rhetoric*. Lang. pp. x + 150. $37.95. ISBN 0 8204 2011 5.

Frederick, Bonnie, and Susan H. McLeod, eds. *Women and the Journey: The Female Travel Experience*. WSUP. pp. 271. pb $19.95. ISBN 0 874 22100 5.

Galef, David. *The Supporting Cast: A Study of Flat and Minor Characters*. PSUP. pp. viii + 228. $35. ISBN 0 2710 0885 7.

Gash, Norman. *Robert Surtees and Early Victorian Society*. Clarendon. pp. 407. hb £40. ISBN 0 19 820429 9.

Gatrell, Simon. *Thomas Hardy and the Proper Study of Mankind*. Macmillan. pp. ix + 195. £35. ISBN 0 333 56285 2.

Gilmour, Robin. *The Victorian Period: The Intellectual and Cultural Context of English Literature 1830–1890*. Longman. pp. 314. pb £13.99. ISBN 0 582 49347 1.

Gissing, George. *The Collected Letters of George Gissing, Vol. 4: 1889–1891*, eds Paul F. Mattheisen, Arthur C. Young, and Pierre Coustillas. OhioUP. pp. xxxii + 362. $60. ISBN 0 8214 1054 7.

——. *The Day of Silence and Other Stories*, ed. Pierre Coustillas. Dent. pp. 375. pb $6.95. ISBN 0 460 87242 7.

——. *George Gissing's 'American Notebook': Notes – G.R.G. – 1877*, ed. Bouwe Postmus. pp. ii + 95. $39.95. ISBN 0 7734 9227 5.

——. *New Grub Street*, ed. with Intro. John Goode. WC. OUP. pp. xxvii + 540. pb £5.99. ISBN 0 19 282963 7.

Glancy, Ruth F. *'A Tale of Two Cities': An Annotated Bibliography*. Garland. pp. xxviii + 236. $40. ISBN 0 8240 7091 7.

Goradia, Nayana. *Lord Curzon: The Last of the British Moghuls*. OUP. pp. 321. hb £17.50. ISBN 0 19 562824 1.

Griffiths, D., ed. *The Encyclopedia of the British Press, 1422–1922*. St Martin's (1992). pp. x + 694. ISBN 0 312 08633 4.

Hardy, Thomas. *The Mayor of Casterbridge*, ed. Pamela Norris. Dent. pp. 62. pb £4.95. ISBN 0 460 87279 6.

——. *Thomas Hardy's 'Studies, Specimens, &c.' Notebook*, eds Pamela Dalziel and Michael Millgate. OUP. pp. xxvii + 164. £25. ISBN 0 19 811757 4.

——. *Two on a Tower*, ed. with Intro. Suleiman M. Ahmad. WC. OUP. pp. xxxv + 315. pb £4.99. ISBN 0 19 282919 X.

Hemans, Felicia. *Records of Woman, 1828*. Revolution and Romanticism, 1789–1843. Woodstock (1991). pp. 344. £32.50. ISBN 1 854 77071 3.

Henley, William Ernest. *Poems, 1898*. Decadents, Symbolists, Anti-Decadents: Poetry of the 1890s. Woodstock. pp. 278. £32.50. ISBN 1 854 77146 9.

Higonnet, Margaret R., ed. *The Sense of Sex: Feminist Perspectives on Hardy*. UIllP. pp. xviii + 286. pb $15.95. ISBN 0 252 01940 7.

Hill, Carl. *The Soul of Wit: Joke Theory from Grimm to Freud*. UNebP. pp. 244. ISBN 0 803 22369 2.

Hoeveler, Diane Long, and Beth Lau, eds. *Approaches to Teaching Brontë's Jane Eyre*. MLA. pp. ix + 180. pb $19.75. ISBN 0 87352 706 2.

Holbrook, David. *Charles Dickens and the Image of Woman*. NYUP. pp. 194. £22.95. ISBN 0 8147 3483 9.

Hollahan, Eugene, ed. *Gerard Manley Hopkins and Critical Discourse*. AMS. pp. 372. $45. ISBN 0 404 63211 4.

Holmes, Timothy. *Journey to Livingstone: Exploration of an Imperial Myth*. Canongate. pp. 383. hb £17.99. ISBN 0 820 31598 2.

Hughes, Linda K., and Michael Lund. *The Victorian Serial*. UPVirginia (1991). pp. 354. $42.50. ISBN 0 813 91314 4.

Humble, Nicola, and Kimberley Reynolds. *Victorian Heroines: Representations of Femininity in Nineteenth-Century Literature and Art*. HW. pp. 205. hb £42.50, pb £12.95. ISBN 0 710 81301 5, 0 710 81302 3.

Imlay, Elizabeth. *Charlotte Brontë and the Mysteries of Love: Myth and Allegory in Jane Eyre*. Imlay (St Martin's Press). pp. xiv + 216. £10. ISBN 0 952 0842 0 1.

Innes, C. L. *Women and Nation in Irish Literature and Society, 1880–1935*. UGeoP. pp. 220. pb $18.00. ISBN 0 873 28140 3.

Jackson, Allan Stuart. *The Standard Theatre of Victorian England*. AUP. pp. 360. £35.00. ISBN 0 8386 3392 7.

Jefferies, Richard. *The Amateur Poacher*, Intro. Ian Niall. White Lion. pp. 185. £15.95. ISBN 1 874762 03 1.

Johnson, Lionel. *Poems, 1895*. Decadents, Symbolists, Anti-Decadents: Poetry of the 1890s. Woodstock. pp. 136. £25. ISBN 1 854 77149 3.

Jones, Aled. *Press, Politics and Society. A History of Journalism in Wales*. pp. xii + 317. UWalesP. ISBN 0 7083 1167 9.

Jutzi, Alan H. *In Search of Sir Richard Burton: Papers from a Huntington Library Symposium*. Huntington. pp. 141. £11.50. ISBN 0 873 28140 3.

Karlin, Daniel. *Browning's Hatreds*. Clarendon. pp. 272. £30. ISBN 0 19 811229 7.

Katz, Wendy R. *The Emblems of Margaret Gatty: A Study of Allegory in Nineteenth-Century Children's Literature*. AMS. pp. xii + 195. $57.50. ISBN 0 4046 3708 6.

Kennedy, Richard S. *Robert Browning's Asolando: The Indian Summer of a Poet*. UMissP. pp. 152. $27.50. ISBN 0 826 20917 3.

Kiely, Robert. *Reverse Tradition: Postmodern Fictions and the Nineteenth-Century Novel*. HarvardUP. pp. x + 302. $36.95. ISBN 0 6747 6703 9.

King, W. D. *Henry Irving's Waterloo: Theatrical Engagements with Arthur Conan Doyle, George Bernard Shaw, Ellen Terry, Edward Gordon Craig,*

Late-Victorian Culture, Assorted Ghosts, Old Men, War, and History. UCalP. pp. xxv + 303. $40. ISBN 0 520 08072 6.

Kingsley, Mary. *Travels in West Africa*, ed. Elspeth Huxley. Dent. pp. 175. pb £5.99. ISBN 0 460 87394 6.

Kipling, Rudyard. *Barrack-room Ballads, 1892.* Decadents, Symbolists, Anti-Decadents: Poetry of the 1890s. Woodstock. pp. 250. £28.50. ISBN 1 854 77150 7.

Kissel, Susan. *In Common Cause: The 'Conservative' Frances Trollope and the 'Radical' Francis Wright.* BGUP. pp. iv + 175. $38.95. ISBN 0 8797 2614 4.

Le Fanu, Sheridan Joseph. *In a Glass Darkly*, ed. with Intro. Robert Tracy. WC. OUP. pp. xxxiii + 347. pb £5.95. ISBN 0 19 282805 3.

LeQuesne, A. L., George P. Landow, Stefan Collini, and Peter Stansky. *Victorian Thinkers.* OUP. pp. 435. pb £8.99. ISBN 0 19 283104 6.

Levi, Peter. *Tennyson.* Macmillan. pp. 370. £20. ISBN 0 333 52205 2.

Luftig, Victor. *Seeing Together: Friendship Between the Sexes in English Writing from Mill to Woolf.* StanfordUP. pp. viii + 308. $35. ISBN 0 8047 2168 8.

Machann, Clinton. *The Essential Matthew Arnold: An Annotated Bibliography of the Major Modern Studies.* Hall. pp. 177. $50. ISBN 0 816 9087 9.

Marlow, James E. *Charles Dickens: The Uses of Time.* SusquehannaUP. pp. 272. $42.50. ISBN 0 945636 48 2.

Maynard, John. *Victorian Discourses on Sexuality and Religion.* CUP. pp. xii + 394. £40. ISBN 0 521 33254 0.

McKenzie, Judy. *Letters of George Augustus Sala to Edmund Yates.* Victorian Fiction Research Guides. pp. 272. Aus$10. ISBN 0 86776 491 0.

McKnight, Natalie. *Idiots, Madmen, and Other Prisoners in Dickens.* St Martin's. pp. x + 148. £22.95. ISBN 0 312 08596 6.

Mendes, Peter. *Clandestine Erotic Fiction in English 1800–1930: A Bibliographical Study.* Scolar. pp. 497. hb £75.00. ISBN 0 859 67919 5.

Mermin, Dorothy. *Godiva's Ride: Women of Letters in England, 1830–1880.* IndUP. pp. 200. pb £11.99. ISBN 0 253 20824 6.

Michie, Elsie B. *Outside the Pale: Cultural Exclusion, Gender Difference, and the Victorian Woman Writer.* CornUP. pp. 190. $34.95. ISBN 0 8014 2831 9.

Mikolyzk, Thomas A. *Oscar Wilde: An Annotated Bibliography.* Greenwood. pp. xiv + 489. $69.50. ISBN 0 313 27597 1.

Miller, George, and Hugoe Matthews, eds. *Richard Jefferies: A Bibliographical Study.* Scolar. pp. 832. $129.95. ISBN 0 85967 918 7.

Monk, Leland. *Standard Deviations: Chance and the Modern British Novel.* StanfordUP. pp. 199. $32.50. ISBN 0 8047 2174 2.

Morse, David. *High Victorian Culture.* Macmillan. pp. viii + 553. £45. ISBN 0 333 46811 2.

Myers, Robin and Michael Harris, eds. *Serials and their Readers 1620–1914.* pp. 170. StPB. OTP. £34. ISBN 1 873040 20 2 (UK), 1 938768 48 4 (USA).

New, Melvyn, ed. *The Complete Novels and Selected Writings of Amy Levy: 1861–1889.* UPFlor. pp. 566. hb $49.95, pb $24.95. ISBN 0 813 01199 X, 0 813 01200 7.

Olney, James. *The Language(s) of Poetry: Walt Whitman, Emily Dickinson, Gerard Manley Hopkins.* Georgia Southern University Jack N. and Addie D. Averitt Lecture Series, No 2. UGeoP. pp. 158. $27.50. ISBN 0 8203 1485 4.

Ormond, Leonée. *Alfred Tennyson: A Literary Life.* Macmillan Literary Lives. Macmillan. pp. 221. hb £37.50, pb £10.99. ISBN 0 333 43832 9, 0 333 43833 7.

Parekh, Bhikhu, ed. *Jeremy Bentham: Critical Assessments*. 4 vols. Routledge. pp. (I) 573, (II) 605, (III) 1093, (IV) 369. ISBN 0 415 04654 8.

Pawley, Margaret. *Faith and Family: The Life and Circle of Ambrose Phillipps de Lisle*. Canterbury. pp. 472. £25.00. ISBN 1 853 11073 6.

Peters, Catherine. *The King of Inventors: A Life of Wilkie Collins*. PrincetonUP. pp. 523. $29.95. ISBN 0 6910 3392 7.

Pitfield, F. P. *Hardy's Wessex Locations*. Dorset. pp. 96. £9.95. ISBN 0 948699 40 X.

Pittock, Murray G. H. *Spectrum of Decadence: The Literature of the 1890s*. Routledge. pp. vii + 221. £37.50. ISBN 0 415 07757 5.

Pool, Daniel. *What Jane Austen Ate and Charles Dickens Knew: From Fox Hunting to Whist – The Facts of Daily Life in Nineteenth-Century England*. S&S. pp. 416. $25. ISBN 0 671 79337 3.

Raymond, Meredith B., and Mary Rose Sullivan, eds. *Elizabeth Barrett Browning, Selected Poetry and Prose*. Labyrinth. pp. 236. pb $15.95. ISBN 0 939 46452 7.

Reid, James H. *Narration and Description in the French Realist Novel: The Temporality of Lying and Forgetting*. CUP. pp. xv + 219. £35. ISBN 0 521 42092 X.

Reilly, Jim. *Shadowtime: History and Representation in Hardy, Conrad, and George Eliot*. Routledge. pp. 208. $45. ISBN 0 415 08597 7.

Reynolds, Peter, ed. *Novel Images: Literature in Performance*. Routledge. pp. ix + 208. £35. ISBN 0 415 09102 0.

Richards, Thomas. *The Imperial Archive: Knowledge and the Fantasy of Empire*. Verso. pp. 179. hb £34.95, pb £11.95. ISBN 0 860 91400 3, 0 860 91605 7.

Robbins, Bruce. *The Servant's Hand: English Fiction from Below*. 2nd edn. DukeUP. pp. 273. pb £13.95. ISBN 0 822 31397 9.

Rooksby, Rikky and Nicholas Shrimpton, eds. *The Whole Music of Passion: New Essays on Swinburne*. Scolar. pp. 186. £35. ISBN 0 859 67925 X.

Rowell, George. *The Old Vic Theatre: A History*. CUP. pp. xii + 207. ISBN 0 521 34625 8.

Ryals, Clyde de L. *The Life of Robert Browning: A Critical Biography*. Blackwell Critical Biographies. Blackwell. pp. 291. £19.99. ISBN 1 557 86149 8.

Ryals, Clyde de L., and Kenneth J. Fielding, eds. *The Collected Letters of Thomas and Jane Welsh Carlyle*. Vols. 19–21. DukeUP. ISBN 0 822 30240 3.

Senf, Carol A., ed. *The Critical Response to Bram Stoker*. Greenwood. pp. xx + 195. $55. ISBN 0 313 28527 6.

Sharpe, Jenny. *Allegories of Empire: The Figure of Woman in the Colonial Text*. UMinnP. pp. x + 190. £28. ISBN 0 8166 2059 8.

Showalter, Elaine, ed. *Daughters of Decadence: Women Writers of the Fin de Siècle*. Virago. pp. 346. pb £6.99. ISBN 1 853 81590 X.

Skilton, David, ed. *The Early and Mid-Victorian Novel*. Routledge. pp. ix + 182. £35. ISBN 0 415 03256 3.

Skoblow, Jeffrey. *Paradise Dislocated: Morris, Politics, Art*. UPVirginia. pp. 221. ISBN 0 813 91439 6.

Spittles, Brian. *George Eliot: Godless Woman*. Macmillan. pp. xii + 209. pb £10.99. ISBN 0 333 57218 1.

St. George, E. A. W. *Browning and Conversation*. Macmillan. pp. 235. £45. ISBN 0 333 55907 X.

Stevenson, Robert Louis. *Tales from the Prince of Storytellers*, ed. Barry Menikoff. NorthwesternUP. pp. xi + 396. pb $16.95. ISBN 0 8101 1084 9.

——. *Treasure Island*. Dover. pp. 160. pb $1. ISBN 0 486 27559 0.

Still, Judith, and Michael Worton, eds. *Textuality and Sexuality: Reading Theories and Practices*. ManUP. pp. 242. hb £35.00, pb £12.99. ISBN 0 7190 3604 6, 0 7190 3605 4.

Stoneman, Patsy, ed. *Wuthering Heights: Contemporary Critical Essays*. Macmillan. pp. ix + 222. £11.95. ISBN 0 333 54594 X.

Strauss, David Friedrich. *Das Leben Jesu, kritisch bearbeitet*, translated by George Eliot, ed. Yoesh Gloger. Gloger. pp. 224. $20. ISBN 1 878632 53 1.

Sullivan, Zohreh T. *Narratives of Empire: The Fictions of Rudyard Kipling*. CUP. pp. xiii + 199. £27.95. ISBN 0 521 43425 4.

Symons, Arthur. *Silhouettes, 1896*, bound with *London Nights, 1897*. Decadents, Symbolists, Anti-Decadents: Poetry of the 1890s. Woodstock. pp. 240. £32.50. ISBN 1 854 77155 8.

Taylor, Dennis. *Hardy's Literary Language and Victorian Philology*. Clarendon. pp. xiii + 429. £40. ISBN 0 19 812261 6.

Taylor, George. *Players and Performances in the Victorian Theatre*. ManUP. pp. viii + 238. pb £14.95. ISBN 0 7190 4023.

Thomas, Deborah A. *Thackeray and Slavery*. OhioUP. pp. xvii + 245. $45. ISBN 0 8214 1038 5.

Thomas, Donald, ed. *The Everyman Book of Victorian Verse, The Pre-Raphaelites to the Nineties*. Dent. pp. 287. pb £5.99. ISBN 0 460 87310 5.

Thompson, Francis. *Poems, 1894*. Decadents, Symbolists, Anti-Decadents: Poetry of the 1890s. Woodstock. pp. 118. £22.50. ISBN 1 854 77157 4.

Thorn, Michael. *Tennyson*. Abacus. pp. 566. pb £9.99. ISBN 0 349 10471 9.

Toker, Leona. *Eloquent Reticence: Withholding Information in Fictional Narrative*. UPKen. pp. x + 225. $33. ISBN 0 8131 1811 5.

Topp, Chester W. *Victorian Yellowbacks and Paperbacks, 1849–1905; Volume One: George Routledge*. Hermitage. pp. xiii + 557. $135. ISBN 0 963 39200 X.

Trollope, Anthony. *The Golden Lion of Granpère*, ed. with Intro. David Skilton. WC. OUP. pp. xxv + 270. pb £4.99. ISBN 0 19 282843 6.

——. *He Knew He Was Right*, ed. David Skilton. Dent. pp. xxv + 766. pb £6.99. ISBN 0 460 87249 4.

——. *John Caldigate*, ed. N. John Hall. WC. OUP. pp. xxxiii + 621. pb £4.99. ISBN 0 19 282817 7.

——. *Trollope the Traveller: Selections from Trollope's Travel Writings*, ed. Graham Handley. P&C. pp. xxxiv + 249. £14.95. ISBN 1 85196 075 9.

Trory, Ernie. *Truth Against the World: The Life and Times of Thomas Hughes, Author of Tom Brown's School Days*. Crabtree. pp. 280. £8.50. ISBN 0 951 50982 9.

Tucker, Herbert F., ed. *Critical Essays on Alfred Lord Tennyson*. Hall. pp. 264. £21.95. ISBN 0 816 18864 5.

Turner, Martha A. *Mechanism and the Novel: Science in the Narrative Process*. CUP. pp. xi + 199. £30. ISBN 0 521 44339 3.

Tush, Susan Rowland. *George Eliot and the Conventions of Popular Women's Fiction: A Serious Literary Response to 'Silly Novels by Lady Novelists.'* Lang. pp. 178. $39.95. ISBN 0 8204 1894 3.

Tuss, Alex J. *The Inward Revolution: Troubled Young Men in Victorian Fiction, 1850–1880*. Lang. pp. 198. $38.95. ISBN 0 8204 1968 0.

Uglow, Jenny. *Elizabeth Gaskell: A Habit of Stories*. Faber. pp. xiii + 690. £20. ISBN 0 5711 5182 5.

Vander Meulen, David L., ed. *Studies in Bibliography, Volume 46.* UPVirginia. pp. 388. $35. ISBN 0 8139 1452 3.

Vitaglione, Daniel. *George Eliot and George Sand.* Lang. pp. 256. $48.95. ISBN 0 8204 2016 6.

Wallace, Anne D. *Walking, Literature, and English Culture: The Origins and Uses of Peripatetic in the Nineteenth Century.* OUP. pp. 256. £30. ISBN 0 19 811986 0.

Weintraub, Stanley. *Disraeli: A Biography.* Dutton. pp. xiv + 717. $30. ISBN 0 5259 3668 8.

White, Norman. *Hopkins: A Literary Biography.* Clarendon (1992). pp. 531. £35. ISBN 0 19 812099 0.

Whitebrook, Peter. *William Archer: A Biography*, Methuen. pp. xii + 435. £25.00. ISBN 0 413 65520 2.

Whitehead, Barbara. *Charlotte Brontë and Her 'Dearest Nell': The Story of a Friendship.* Smith Settle. pp. 298. £11.50. ISBN 1 85825 010 2.

Widdowson, Peter, ed. *Tess of the d'Urbervilles: Contemporary Critical Essays.* Macmillan. pp. xii + 211. pb £8.99. ISBN 0 333 54585 0.

Wiebe, M. G., J. B. Conacher, John Matthews, and Mary S. Millar, eds. *Benjamin Disraeli Letters: 1848–1851.* Vol. 5. UTorP. pp. 655. hb $95.00. ISBN 0 802 02927 2.

Wilde, Oscar. *The Picture of Dorian Gray.* Dover. pp. viii + 165. pb $1. ISBN 0 486 27807 7.

Williams, C. K. *The Essential Hopkins.* Ecco. pp. 83. $8. ISBN 0 88001 319 2.

Williams, Merryn. *A Preface to Hardy.* Longman. pp. xii + 200. pb £10.99. ISBN 0 582 09563 8.

Willoughby, Guy. *Art and Christhood: The Aesthetics of Oscar Wilde.* AUP. pp. 170. $32.50. ISBN 0 8147 9259 6.

Winter, Kari J. *Subjects of Slavery, Agents of Change: Women and Power in Gothic Novels and Slave Narratives, 1790–1865.* UGeoP. pp. xii + 172. $30. ISBN 0 8203 1420 X.

Wolstenholme, Susan. *Gothic (Re)Visions: Writing Women as Readers.* SUNYP. pp. xvi + 201. $44.50. ISBN 0 7914 1219 9.

XIV

The Twentieth Century

JULIAN COWLEY, MACDONALD DALY, SUSAN WATKINS, RICHARD
STORER, MARK RAWLINSON, STUART SILLARS, IAN SANSOM and
TREVOR GRIFFITHS

This chapter has the following sections: 1. Fiction; 2. Poetry; 3. Drama. Section
1 (a) is by Julian Cowley; section 1 (b) is by Macdonald Daly, Susan Watkins and
Richard Storer; section 1 (c) is by Mark Rawlinson; section 2 (a) is by Stuart
Sillars; section 2 (b) is by Ian Sansom; and section 3 is by Trevor Griffiths.

1. Fiction

(a) General Studies
Bernard Bergonzi's *Wartime and Aftermath: English Literature and its Background 1939–1960* is an unpretentious survey, well-suited to the reader seeking
a general introduction rather than specialist information on the specified period.
Bergonzi does, however, draw attention to some relatively overlooked authors
(Richard Hillary, Patrick Hamilton) and their work, amid the more familiar fare
of Orwell, Waugh, Dylan Thomas and Larkin. The Second World War and its
repercussions provide broad criteria for inclusion and exclusion, but limitations
of space mean that historical materials are sketchy, and their formulation is at
times clearly inadequate.

A more substantial historical sense emerges from D. J. Taylor's comparable
survey, *After the War: The Novel and English Society since 1945.* Taylor writes
as a literary journalist, trained as an historian, and his perception of the 'crucible
of social influence' from which literature emerges may prove problematic for
some readers. But the thematic focus on Englishness, class division, and historical decline grants the study a clear sense of direction. Too often, chapters
resemble catalogues, skipping from novel to novel in a way that can frustrate or
annoy, but when Taylor allows himself space to pursue further analysis (notably
in the case of A. S. Byatt) the discussion can be stimulating.

S. P. Rosenbaum has compiled an excellent anthology to form *A Bloomsbury
Group Reader.* The collection is arranged in ten categories: Forewords; Stories;
Biographies; Essays; Reviews; Polemics; Talks; Travel Writings; Memoirs; and

Afterwords. This classification generates some interesting comparisons and intriguing clusters of material. The familiar (Forster's 'What I Believe', Woolf's 'Mr Bennett and Mrs Brown') appear alongside the neglected (a review of Freud by Leonard Woolf, and John Maynard Keynes's essay 'Newton the Man'). The selection is diverse yet coherent, making this a splendid introduction to the writings of the Bloomsbury set.

The first volume of *Literature and Culture in Modern Britain*, edited by Clive Bloom, covers the period 1900 to 1929. Locating the production of literature (in its twin conceptions as self-conscious art and as middle-class entertainment) within the broad realization of historical change in newspapers, radio, cinema, painting and sculpture, popular music, and in various technologies, it makes possible a range of connections which will benefit undergraduate literary and cultural study. Jim Reilly's contribution, 'The Novel as Art Form', a deft and lively exercise in literary sociology, is startling in its succinctness.

The representation, or construction, of national identity in literature is the central concern of David Gervais's *Literary Englands*. The choice of authors scrutinized may hold few surprises: Edward Thomas, Forster and Lawrence, George Sturt (a refreshing inclusion), F. R. Leavis and T. S. Eliot, Waugh, Orwell, Larkin and Betjeman, and Geoffrey Hill. But as Gervais says in an 'Afterword', the book succeeds if 'what it says about the writers it discusses sparks off thoughts about the writers it appears to ignore', and the sureness of Gervais's critical touch does make it succeed. He takes the notion of 'Englishness' as a starting point rather than a culminating disclosure; it steers the reading of his chosen authors in ways that are suggestive and generally convincing, but Gervais is nevertheless content to leave conceptual England various and unfixed.

Robert Welch's approach to Irishness, in *Changing States*, is one of lyrical meditation on issues of tradition and transformation. This book will not suit those looking for sustained and rigorous analytical criticism, but it does provide a framework for reading the work of George Moore, Yeats, Synge, Joyce, Joyce Cary, Francis Stuart, Beckett, Brian Friel and Seamus Heaney, together with writers in the Irish language, Mairtín ó Cadhain and Seán ó Ríordáin. Not all readers will share Welch's sense of Heaney's putative 'renewing light', to cite one among numerous instances of such appreciative assertion.

Bryan Cheyette makes large claims in his *Constructions of 'the Jew' in English Literature and Society*; recognition of '"the Jew" within the writer', he asserts, 'places a semitic discourse at the heart of literary production in general'. Rather more easily digested is Cheyette's complication of oversimple perceptions of how Jewish racial characteristics were stereotyped in Victorian and early twentieth-century literature. His combinations of John Buchan and Kipling, Shaw and Wells, Belloc and Chesterton, Joyce and T.S. Eliot, indicate a set of broad categories into which such representations have fallen, while substantiating the argument that 'the Jew' has not in fact conformed to 'a fixed, mythic stereotype'. He sets out 'to understand the question of racial representations in terms of a dominant liberalism and not as an aberrant or exotic phenomenon', and that he achieves through intelligent and well-focused analysis.

Brian W. Shaffer's *The Blinding Torch* opens with an introductory chapter that gathers together a range of materials to illustrate the debate surrounding the state of 'civilization' in early twentieth-century Britain. This useful compendium might fruitfully have been expanded to book-length. As it is, Shaffer passes into a series of case studies, assuming a diversity of approaches, and only loosely related around the 'civilization' theme. They are, nevertheless, of considerable merit, with the chapters on Conrad (including comparison to Herbert Spencer) particularly clear-sighted. Woolf is read in combination with Clive Bell; Lawrence and Lowry with Spengler; and Joyce with Freud and the Frankfurt School.

Rosa Maria Bracco has performed a valuable service for those engaged with the literary history of the 1920s and 1930s. Her *Merchants of Hope* looks at responses to the First World War, over those two decades, in the work of British middlebrow writers. The term 'middlebrow' was coined during the 1920s, she points out, to identify writers making no attempt 'to deviate from comfortably familiar presentations'. R. C. Sherriff's *Journey's End* is the principal case study, but Bracco maps out the terrain with a range of examples from the interwar years, illustrating how the turbulence of the time was met with manufacture in fiction of an English identity, 'an anchor of meaning', homogeneous and middle class. She makes no exaggerated claims for the writing, but has produced an informative and highly readable survey.

Dorothy Goldman's 'Introduction' to the essays of *Women and World War 1* identifies the intention of drawing neglected writers from the margins; yet the writers in English who emerge from this varied collection as most worthy of serious attention are Virginia Woolf and Hilda Doolittle. There are French, Russian, German and American writers surveyed here, and a chapter is devoted to the Australian, Mabel Brookes, understandably (it seems) 'long forgotten now'. The surveys are useful, beyond the conventionalities of the editor's introductory comments.

Angela Ingram and Daphne Patai have compiled a collection of essays, *Rediscovering Forgotten Radicals*, which explores a submerged history of writing by women during the period 1889 to 1939. These dates signal London's East End dock strike and the commencement of the Second World War. The work that is traced here has a common engagement with socialism, pacifism and a range of other political concerns including suffrage, antivivisection and reproductive rights. The volume has an evident coherence and is a substantial addition to accounts of women's writing. Virginia Woolf is located as a political writer rather than an exemplar of autonomous aesthetics, and, as might be expected, the overall emphasis is on displacing canonical evaluations through focus on social issues to the detriment of concern for literary form.

M. Keith Booker's starting point in *Literature and Domination* is the contention that literary form and technique constitute a kind of domination, which he associates with coherence and unity. He explores how the difficulty of certain modern fiction permits a collaborative generation of meaning between text and reader, and argues that this counters tendencies for readers either to become submissive or to seek positions of mastery. If Booker's reader can accept these premises, and their extrapolation into more general consideration of issues of power in society, there are suggestive readings here, that effectively reclaim Woolf's *The Waves*, Beckett's *Watt* and *The Lost Ones*, and novels by Italo Calvino, Thomas Pynchon and Vladimir Nabokov, from the charge of aesthetic detachment from social concerns.

Aesthetic autonomy comes under close scrutiny in Marcia Ian's impressive book, *Remembering the Phallic Mother: Psychoanalysis, Modernism, and the Fetish*. Ian writes with admirable lucidity, while performing sophisticated analysis of current assumptions concerning the materiality of language. Her case is that postmodern thought derived from Lacan (as distinct from Freud), makes the foundational assumption that culture is a linguistic phenomenon, and so is able to affirm that we, as social beings, are made of culture, and therefore of language. As a result, she claims we have become 'politically, practically ineffectual', and literary critics are to the fore in treating language alone as 'real', while ignoring the actual consequences of this belief. Psychoanalysis is analysed as 'the exemplary modernist discourse', while the fetishization of language, and its ramifications for 'character' are pursued in the novels of James, Forster and Lawrence. Eliot, in particular, is considered in relation to the poem perceived as fetish. Some will find the argument here highly contentious, and partial, but it does provide a necessary challenge to facile assimilation of contemporary critical orthodoxies.

Concern for human disembodiment amid linguistic simulacra is at the heart of Maud Ellman's provocative work *The Hunger Artists*. Ellman draws materials from history and literature; Sylvia Pankhurst and Irish hunger strikers are considered alongside Richardson's *Clarissa*, and Kafka's hunger artist. A vampiric relationship is traced between proliferation of language and the wasting of human flesh, with writing and starvation considered as the 'arts of disincarnation'. This is a book guaranteed to stimulate and infuriate in equal measure, and as such it succeeds in its own terms. Following the adventures of metaphors, in the manner of Gaston Bachelard, this is a catalytic work that proceeds in the belief that, while venturing into this terrain, 'the language of imagination has more to offer than the language of statistics'.

The relationship of mechanistic science to the narrative process is the focus for Martha A. Turner's readings in *Mechanism and the Novel: Science in the Narrative Process*. Turner's thesis is that despite ostensibly having lapsed from its position of authority, towards the end of the eighteenth century, the Newtonian model of reality has an enduring legacy. After chapters on Austen, Scott, Dickens and Meredith, she presents analyses of Conrad's *The Secret Agent*, Lawrence's *Women in Love*, and Doris Lessing's *Canopus in Argos: Archives*. The readings are convincing enough, but this is scarcely the bridge between two cultures it promises to be, and, after an early chapter on 'The concept of mechanism', analysis veers towards less scientifically specific consideration of order and chaos, stability and instability, flux and fixity.

Joseph McAleer's *Popular Reading and Publishing in Britain 1914–1950* is a splendidly scholarly account of production and consumption of popular fiction during a period between the consolidation of a commercially managed, mass reading public, and challenges to the practice of reading posed by rival entertainments such as television. It is a carefully researched and admirably well-illustrated study of reading trends among both adults and children, further substantiated through examination of publishing strategies adopted by Mills & Boon, D. C. Thomson, and the Religious Tract Society. This is a considerable contribution to the growing academic engagement with the history of reading and publishing practices.

Rafael Sabatini and Georgette Heyer are among the writers considered by Helen Hughes, in her study of *The Historical Romance*. Hughes aims to show how the past has been packaged in popular fiction. She outlines the structure of the genre, analyses the constitution of its readership, and looks at its ideological horizons, especially in terms of class, national identity, and gender. The first half of the book is overladen with citations of secondary authorities (possibly the legacy of the book's origin in doctoral research), and too often the analysis appears tentative.

Contemporary science fiction is the domain explored in Scott Bukataman's *Terminal Identity*. His focus falls on the construction of the postmodern subject within the genre, and he presents a convincing taxonomy for analysis of 'terminal identity fictions' in print and on film. Most of the cyberpunk practitioners included are American, but stress is put on the innovative and influential presence of J. G. Ballard at the fountainhead of writing for an electronic environment. Bukataman's study is readable and informative, but takes a great deal for granted in its large assumptions concerning both theoretical positions and technological imperatives, which some readers will surely resist.

By way of contrast, Nicholas Zurbrugg's *The Parameters of Postmodernism* takes a challenging and critical stance towards fashionable theorists of the postmodern. Against proclamations of the demise of creative possibilities (which he calls the B-effect, from Beckett, Jean Baudrillard, and Peter Bürger, among others), he assembles an array of instances of creative practice among contemporary writers, composers, visual artists and performers. These practitioners are identified with the C-effect (after the exemplary practice of John Cage), and Zurbrugg performs the welcome service of drawing attention to aesthetic innovation that belies the apocalyptic jeremiads. Ian Hamilton Finlay and Leonora Carrington feature among this predominantly American and European group, while J. G. Ballard appears here also, as a liminal figure emerging from the B to join the C group.

Allan Chavkin has edited a collection of essays as *English Romanticism and Modern Fiction*, including chapters on Joyce's 'The Dead', Woolf's *Orlando*, and the novels of Alan Sillitoe. John Moses's contribution on *Orlando* as caricature of the Romantic poet is the most substantial of the essays on British fiction, but overall the collection suffers from too vague a definition of Romanticism, resulting too often in facile suggestion of parallels without a stable framework for analytical reference.

Mark Lilly's *Gay Men's Literature in the Twentieth Century* is an aggressively polemical work, aimed at first-year undergraduates and general readers. It contains a number of stark assertions that will disconcert some readers. Forster, we are told, is 'admired by homosexual reactionaries' and 'despised by gay radicals'. There may be some truth in this, but it exemplifies the kind of sweeping statement favoured by Lilly. In addition to Forster, the book treats First World War poets, Isherwood and Orton, as well as Wilde and Byron, Constantine Cavafy, Jean Genet, Yukio Mishima, and a selection of American gay writers. The analysis often elides the literary with the extra-literary, and this appears to be a deliberate strategy for a work designed to serve primarily gay studies rather than literary criticism.

Janice Rossen's study, *The University in Modern Fiction*, aims to map trends in fiction dealing with academic life. Her broad concerns are the University's power, the exclusion of, or terms of inclusion for certain groups (notably women and lower-class men), and the nature of academic success amid tensions generated by professional rivalry. Starting with Hardy's *Jude the Obscure*, Rossen ranges through Waugh and Forster, Dorothy L. Sayers, Barbara Pym, C. P. Snow, and Kingsley Amis, to David Lodge, Malcolm Bradbury, and A. S. Byatt. Although the book declares itself not a survey, it reads very much in that vein, hedging around critical treatment of power relationships and offering descriptive rather than significantly analytic readings. In short, this old-fashioned approach amounts to a lack of incisiveness, and the book may best serve as a general introduction, or a resource for bolder interpretation.

Moving away from representations of academic life, one of this century's more notable educators is celebrated in *Raymond Williams: Politics, Education, Letters*, edited by W. John Morgan and Peter Preston. The essays commissioned for this collection testify to the range of activity in which Williams invested his energies. The perspectives presented on the man and his work are accordingly of broad interest. Of particular relevance here are contributions from Jeff Wallace, on Williams's engagement with the writings of D. H. Lawrence, and James A. Davies on the significance of Wales in Williams's own fiction.

The American university and its influence on the development of Pound and Eliot as poets is Gail McDonald's concern in *Learning to be Modern*. There are a few diverting details here, but many of the materials deployed are familiar. Ostensibly a study of the formation of modernist aesthetics in relation to the academy, it is in those terms disappointing. Overall, McDonald confirms that these scholarly writers were inclined to assume pedagogical postures, while their attitudes toward institutional education ranged from ambivalence to overt hostility.

Vincent Sherry, in *Ezra Pound, Wyndham Lewis, and Radical Modernism*, has produced a penetrating study which aims to dispel the critical myth 'that modernism proclaims a poetics of colloquial music'. Sherry focuses upon the case made by these two artists for the intellectual potency of the eye, against the deficiencies of the ear. Not only do their artistic practices reflect commitment to visual primacy, but this commitment informs also their political alignment with the far right. The ear lends itself to democratic politics; the eye enables 'dictatorial command'. In the wrong hands, such assumptions can all too easily lead to spurious argument, but a scrupulous intelligence is evident in the construction of Sherry's case. The careful documentation and meticulous organization of materials in this book make it an important addition to the analysis of modernist aesthetics and the political orientation of their adherents.

That analysis is taken up by Toby Avard Foshay in his *Wyndham Lewis and the Avant-Garde*. Subtitled, 'The Politics of the Intellect', this study pursues Peter Bürger's distinction between modernism, concerned essentially with aesthetic autonomy, and the avant-garde, which addresses the role of art in social, political and economic life. Foshay notes how Lewis's 'visualist objectivism' grounded his opposition to the doctrines of socialism, but also distinguished him as an avant-garde rather than a modernist figure. Primarily a study of Lewis's work, Foshay's book unavoidably addresses issues involved in the taxonomy of modern culture.

(b) Individual Authors: 1900–45

Journal publications on Conrad continue, as we shall see, in unabated plenitude, but surprisingly the year threw up only one monograph devoted entirely to him, Andrea White's *Joseph Conrad and the Adventure Tradition: Constructing and Deconstructing the Imperial Subject*. This is a study exclusively concerned with Conrad's early work. As if this focus were not unfashionable enough, White is also concerned not to tread the familiar path of Conrad's relationship to the nineteenth-century masters of French realism. Instead, she concentrates on 'minor' English works in the 'adventure tradition' signified by Kingsley, Ballantyne, Marryat, Kipling, Henty and, above all, Haggard. Chapters on travel writing and adventure fiction are preliminary to a chapter exploring how such discourses mapped out a sense of 'them' and 'us' which was 'useful and appealing' in relation to the colonial project. There is then a chapter on Haggard, which argues that in his work begins a shift from 'a discourse that created and confirmed stereotypes supportive of British imperial ventures abroad, to one subversive of those endeavours, such as Conrad's was to become'. This may sound rather politically polite, but in a 'Coda' White makes clear her belief that 'Conrad certainly did not challenge all the myths' of imperialism. This rounds off a well-balanced, original, and circumspectly conducted study. The Conrad texts which come in for serious scrutiny, in the chapters which constitute the second half of the book, are *Almayer's Folly*, *An Outcast of the Islands*, 'An Outpost of Progress' and *Heart of Darkness*.

Indeed, *Heart of Darkness* continues to preoccupy Conrad commentators, some with a greater sense of originality than others. Susan J. Navarette, in 'The Anatomy of Failure in Joseph Conrad's *Heart of Darkness*' (*TSLL* 35.279–315) tries to persuade us to reposition Conrad's novella in two contexts which are fairly distant from the imperialism it is usually seen as scrutinizing: decadence and the late gothic. Her argument is long and excessively detailed (there are ten pages of footnotes in a 37-page article) but compelling. It doesn't reduce the pleasure of reading George Kurman's and Roger W. Rouland's 'Conrad's *Heart of Darkness* as Pretext for Barth's "Night-Sea Journey": The Colonist's Passage Upstream' (*IFR* 20.i.3–13), in which John Barth's celebrated story of a medita-tive spermatozoon's ovum-ward odyssey is related in 'narration, plot, and theme' to Conrad's tale (and if 'seaman'/'semen' puns are predictably noted, those on 'tale' and 'tail' come as more of a surprise). Edward Said's section in *Culture and Imperialism*, 'Two Visions in *Heart of Darkness*', eschews such playfulness: 'As a creature of his time, Conrad could not grant the natives their freedom, despite his severe critique of the imperialism that enslaved them'. Gail Fincham is more sanguine in 'The Representation of Cultural Difference in the Fiction of Joseph Conrad' (*SD* 19.i.52–65), believing that *Heart of Darkness* prepares its readers to approach 'other' cultures by gradually subverting Marlow's values and ways of seeing. However, her discussion of the novella is, like Said's, fairly attenuated: in large part the article is also concerned with William Burton, on whose legacy this issue of *Social Dynamics* centres, although his name doesn't make it into her title.

Another fairly benign South African perspective on the novella is offered by Myrtle J. Hooper in 'The Heart of Light: Silence in Conrad's *Heart of Darkness*' (*Conradiana* 25.i.69–76). 'At the University of Natal in Durban not too long ago students demanded', she tells us, that *Heart of Darkness* 'be dropped from their syllabus. At the University of Zululand student demands tend to be less academi-cally sophisticated, and so would not take quite such a form'. Nevertheless, she experienced 'intense and immediate' difficulties when attempting to teach the novel at the latter institution. She traces these problems partly to Chinua Achebe's well-known accusation that Conrad's text is racist, and her paper takes issue with this polemic. Samir Elibarby has looked at the main periodicals of the late nineteenth century – *Nineteenth Century*, *Fortnightly Review*, *Cornhill Magazine* and *Macmillan's Monthly Magazine* – and found in them a 'discourse of primitivism and degeneracy' which he relates to Conrad in '*Heart of Darkness* and Late-Victorian Fascination with the Primitive and the Double' (*TCL* 39.i.113–28). This article incorporates more quotation than any I have read in four years of reviewing for *YWES*. Brian W. Shaffer's '"Rebarbarizing Civilization": Conrad's African Fiction and Spencerian Sociology' (*PMLA* 108.45–58), as well as holding that 'An Outpost of Progress' is a parody of Spencer's ideas, also sees Spencer's 'Militant-Industrial' distinction and his notion of a 'Rebarbarized Civilization' as being of relevance to *Heart of Darkness*. A misreading of a passage in the latter provides the inspiration behind the title of Shaffer's book, *The Blinding Torch*, reviewed in section 1 (a) of this chapter.

Tony E. Jackson makes a fairly brisk genuflection to theory (two pages on Heidegger, Lacan, Foucault, Derrida and Nietzsche on Cartesian subjectivity) which even he admits is 'very abstract', before settling into the very concrete pew of Conrad's *Lord Jim* ('Turning into Modernism: *Lord Jim* and the Alteration of the Narrative Subject', *L&P* 39.iv.65–85). Marlow is again having trouble fixing his identity here: 'The Marlow who presently speaks the narrative has been changed by the narrative in such a way that the Marlow who in the past experienced the events "is" no longer the same'. Before the end of his article Jackson manages to effect a spiral return to Nietzsche and Heidegger to try to explain the alteration of this subject of the spiral return plot. It is a relief to turn to David Trotter's *The English Novel in History 1895–1920*, where, in the midst of an extremely brief chapter on Conrad and Kipling, we are told that 'There are an awful lot of fat greasy men in Conrad'.

ELT 36.3 has three articles on Conrad. The most remarkable is the text of a lecture by Leonard Woolf here given the title 'Conrad's Vision: the Illumination of Romance' (286–302) and printed for the first time from the Monk's House Papers in the University of Sussex Library. J. H. Stape, introducing the text in 'The Critic as Autobiographer: Conrad Under Leonard Woolf's Eyes' (277–85), points out that the untitled MS is not dated, but ascribes it, for reasons that are explained, to the period 1912–13. This is something of a scoop for *ELT*, and poses the moral question of whether a reviewer in this case has an obligation not to nullify the journal's efforts by summarizing and evaluating what Woolf had to say. Woolf himself, after all, is tempted not to say anything about Conrad: 'There are the books, you can buy them for 7^d or 4/6 at any bookshop, you can borrow them from any library. Nothing that I or anyone else can say will alter what is in them, and the best way for any one to find out what is in them is to read them'. But he doesn't follow his own advice: should I? Or should I ignore the piece on other grounds (namely that *YWES* was not in existence in 1912–13)? Or should I simply imitate the 'Eastern sage' quoted by Woolf, who told the thousands who had come to him, hearing 'that he had got to the foundations of everything, all life, all knowledge, all experience', after they had waited for three days, '"What is, is"'?

The third *ELT* article tries to show that what is *isn't*. Ray Stevens' 'The Muddle of Minutiae, or What Text Should We Read: the Case of an Omitted Paragraph in a Forgotten Conrad Book Review' (305–21) is not an entry in the Most Trivial Academic Article of the Century Competition, whose yellow jersey is still sported by myself and Alexander George for our '"It's" Misspelled: History of an Error in *The Waste Land*' (*BSANZB* 11.iv.169–70), although we seem hard-pressed by a recent article by Sengupta, Laha and Nanda reviewed in section 2 (a) of this chapter. On the contrary, Stevens insists, 'Rather than forget the importance of such gaps in our knowledge that may lead to a sounder literary criticism, as some urge, it is imperative that critics understand, to the extent possible, what happens in the composition of the text'. This is fine, but one wishes Stevens had a meatier example. The text in question is Conrad's book review, 'John Galsworthy', which he dashed off in 1906 and which was so insignificant that 'by 1921, Conrad had forgotten that he had written it, and failed to include it in *Notes on Life and Letters*'. Stevens is vexed by the missing paragraph, cut by Richard Curle, because he has to produce a text of the review for the forthcoming CUP Critical edition of Conrad's *Last Essays*. He expends 8,000 words worrying about it. No wonder there is such monumental delay in the emergence of the Cambridge Conrad!

Daniel Bivona investigates Conrad's continuation of late nineteenth century anti-bureaucratic sentiment in 'Conrad's Bureaucrats: Agency, Bureaucracy and the Problem of Intention' (*Novel* 26.ii.151–69). His discussion ranges from *Heart of Darkness* to *Nostromo* to *The Secret Agent*, and argues that Conrad lampoons Lord Cromer's apology for the extension of British bureaucratic rule. Robert Eric Livingston is concerned, in 'Seeing Through Reading: Class, Race and Literary Authority in Joseph Conrad's *The Nigger of the "Narcissus"*' (*Novel* 26.ii.133–59), with the perceived breakthrough effected by Conrad's third novel, the notion that his writing asserted his professional status as an author, and relates this to its audience: 'Reworking the languages of class and race for a new middle class audience, it seeks to recapture civility under the sign of control. Such a recovery is the premise for Conrad's emergence as a literary professional, his acceptance into the rank of authors'.

Two articles in *Conradiana* discuss Conrad and Ibsen. Cedric Watts sees 'curious similarities' in '*The Wild Duck* and *The Secret Agent*' (25.i.47–52) – most obviously, of course, in the relationship of Winnie and Verloc. Watts points out that the play first appeared in an English translation in 1904, and quotes from Conrad's correspondence to bolster his admittedly speculative case. But 'Conrad seemed at times not to take Ibsen seriously', Paul Kirschner begins by reminding us in 'Conrad, Ibsen and the Description of Humanity' (25.iii.178–206), which nevertheless offers a much more developed argument to the effect that the two writers exhibited shared concerns across the entirety of their writing careers. Elsewhere in *Conradiana*, Keith Carabine has a detailed study in manuscript and character evolution, 'From *Razumov* to *Under Western Eyes*: The Case of Peter Ivanovitch' (25.i.3–29); Reynold Humphries's 'Skirting the Strait and Narrow: Narrative and Representation in Conrad's *An Outcast of the Islands*' (25.i.31–46) appropriates and applies to Conrad's text a remark made by Terry Eagleton of another ('marooned between *langue* and *discours*, doctrine and experience, dominance and dissemination'); Catharine Rising relates Conrad's work to that of the late American psychoanalyst, Heinz Kohut, in 'Conrad and Kohut: Development Demystified' (25.iii.207–21); Gene M. Moore's 'Conrad, Dr Gachet, and the "School of Charenton"' offers some heavily illustrated musings as to the paintings Conrad might have seen and definitely hated (his word was 'cauchemaresque' [*sic*]) when he visited the Paris apartment of Dr Paul-Ferdinand Gachet in June 1891; and J. H. Stape charts Conrad's 'direct and unacknowledged borrowing' from other writers (Anatole France and Louis Garneray) in '"Gaining Conviction": Conradian Borrowing and the *Patna* Episode in *Lord Jim*' (25.iii.222–34).

'Old Mindsets and New World-Music in Conrad's *The Secret Agent*' is the title of a 15-page chapter in Martha Turner's *Mechanism and the Novel: Science and the Narrative Process*, but there is more old than new in the discussion, which is routine. Jim Reilly has a 39-page chapter, 'Stasis, Signs and Speculation: *Nostromo* and History' in his *Shadowtime: History and Representation in*

Hardy, Conrad and George Eliot which, among other things, briefly compares *Heart of Darkness* to Kipling's 'Thrown Away', examines Conrad's hatred of his Communistic characters, and posits a congruity between Conrad's writing practice in *Nostromo* and 'Lukács's analysis of capitalist fiction's descriptive deadlock and delivery of the reified image of a reified world'. Reilly has a tendency to over-allude and to quote in barrages, but his discussion, like the book as a whole, is complex and rewarding. 'Playing Old Maid: *Chance* and the Proper Name' is a substantial chapter of Leland Monk's *Standard Deviations: Chance and the Modern Novel*, an engagingly written study which dips into the history of thinking about chance (which 'is in general a history of its marginalization') as a prelude to its examination of the role chance plays in various modernist narratives. There are even some confessed anachronisms, one of which is signalled in a footnote in which Monk apologises for invoking the findings of quantum theory ('not established until the 1930s') to discuss *The Secret Agent* and *Chance*. Monk's examination of the latter focuses on how Conrad 'problematizes the narrative machinery that inevitably concludes that "it was *meant* to happen", thereby generating a fateful reading of the text' (he has already instructed us that chance is *not* fate). The subsequent discussion takes in Freud, Lacan, Poe and Derrida, and is essential reading for anyone working on *Chance* (a novel which gets pretty short shrift in Cedric Watts's *A Preface to Conrad*, which has been issued in a new edition).

The scattered nature of the large quantity of Conrad items means that, despite a concerted trawl, some have escaped my net this year. In at least one case this may not be an occasion for regret. P. Ebersole has a piece on *Lord Jim* in *PsychR* (72.i.31–4), the abstract of which offers an improbably garbled title, and states that in the piece 'Conrad's fictional character Jim's meaning in life is employed as an illustration of the application of DeVogler-Ebersole and Ebersole's scoring system for depth of meaning in life and their method for categorization of different types of meaning in life. Finally, the following issues are briefly covered: future research, an alternative conceptualization of Jim, and the failure of current measures of meaning in life depth to take into consideration the person's behaviour'. It sounds awful: one hopes the author was not responsible for the abstract. Also unseen are Bernard J. Paris's 'Marlow's Transformation' (*AJES* 15.i–ii.65–72), which, presumably succinctly, takes in *Youth, Lord Jim* and *Heart of Darkness*, R. W. Winks's 'Spy Fiction, Spy Reality, From Conrad to Le Carré' (*Soundings* 76.ii–iii.221–36), and A. Careywebb's '*Heart of Darkness, Tarzan* and the Third World: Canons and Encounters in World Literature' (*CollL* 20.i.121–41). The large number of articles in *ECon* 19 – 'Epiphany in Conrad's Novels', 'Conrad's Tale of Two Cities', 'Witold Gombrowicz', '*Princess Ivona* and Joseph Conrad's "Amy Foster"', 'Razumov and Raskolnikov: The Path of Torments', 'Betrayal, Self-Exile and Language Registers: the Case of *Karain: A Memory*', 'Where Does the Joke Come In?: Ethics and Aesthetics in Conrad's "The Informer"', 'Colonial Self-Fashioning in Conrad: Writing and Remembrance in *Lord Jim*' – have not proved obtainable. Likewise, the volume *Contexts for Conrad*, edited by Keith Carabine, Owen Knowles and Wieslaw Krajka (Boulder, East European Monographs, pp. 285, ISBN 0 88033 267 0), a sequel to the same three editors' *Conrad's Literary Career* (see *YWES* 73.499).

Michael Squires has undertaken the difficult task of producing the Cambridge edition of *Lady Chatterley's Lover*, a novel 'the contents, structure, texture, and coherence' of whose chapters, Dennis Jackson argues in 'Chapter Making in *Lady*

Chatterley's Lover' (*TSLL* 35.363–83), are superior to those in *John Thomas and Lady Jane*. Two articles this year wish to make *Lady C.* into an intertextual site. Adam Roberts, in 'D. H. Lawrence and Wells's "Future Men"' points out the similarities between the characterization of Clifford Chatterley and the 'human tadpoles' posited by Wells in an obscure article of 1897 (*N&Q* 40.67–8). Julie Fenwick's 'Women, Sex, and Culture in *The Moonlight*: Joyce Cary's Response to D. H. Lawrence' (*ArielE* 24.ii.27–42) argues somewhat diffusely that Cary's novel is a reaction to *Lady C.*, although it can offer no proof that Cary had read it at the time of writing *The Moonlight*. Fenwick gets round this with an ingenious ploy: 'internal evidence strongly suggests that Cary is exploiting the reading public's familiarity with the central situation of *Lady Chatterley's Lover* in order to refute ideas that Lawrence formulated more explicitly in *Fantasia of the Unconscious*, a copy of which Cary owned and is known to have read carefully in the 1920s'. Squires's edition of *Lady C.* and volume VII of *The Letters of D. H. Lawrence*, edited by Keith Sagar and James T. Boulton, which was also published by Cambridge this year, come with the extensive annotation and painstaking textual apparatus customary of this series.

Less noteworthy (for reasons that ironically require more detailed explanation) are the popular editions of Lawrence which have also appeared. *The Rainbow* and *Women in Love* were both issued in Everyman Classics, edited by Jan Hewitt and Linda Ruth Williams respectively. These editions clearly live up to their stated claim to be 'the most comprehensive paperback edition available, with introduction, notes, text summary, selected criticism and chronology of Lawrence's life and times'. The plethora of extra-textual material is undoubtedly useful for both A-level students and undergraduates. Williams even includes Lawrence's 'Foreword' and 'Prologue', thus making them more widely accessible than ever before. What lets both editions down is their lack of attention to textual problems. The editors have really done little more than adopt the texts established by two previous Penguin editors, John Worthen and Charles Ross respectively. More startlingly, neither Hewitt nor Williams so much as acknowledges the existence of, or the monumental efforts by the editors of, the Cambridge editions of these texts, and their annotation, given the density and richness of both novels, is remarkably thin. Williams says that her edition is based on the Seltzer text, but she includes the chapter titles, which were not in Seltzer's edition. They were added in the Secker edition, which she doesn't even mention. She also quotes Lawrence telling Seltzer of the proofs, 'There are only very slight incorrections'. But she doesn't point out that this was manifestly untrue. Hewitt's edition of *The Rainbow* suffers from a number of elementary proofreading errors which are nothing to do with Lawrence.

Jan Todd's *D. H. Lawrence: Selected Poems* appears in a series aimed specifically at the A-level market, and thus comes in a very sturdy paperback format. It has 104 pages of poems and 80 pages of notes and discussion. There are some real oddities in the chronology: '1908 Becomes teacher in a Croydon Secondary School. Introduction of old age pensions'. The first sentence is factually incorrect, and it is not at all clear why, of all the historical occurrences of 1908, the second sentence should isolate the one it does. The notes are not as innocent, however, as one might anticipate. Of 'Snake' Todd writes: 'The *fissure* (7) from which the snake emerges, the *burning bowels* (20) from which it originates, and the man's revulsion at its penetration of the *horrid black hole* (52), together with the phallic suggestiveness of the snake itself, have, under-

standably, excited speculation over the precise physical and psychological implications of the poem'. This comes close to saying that the poem is partly about
what I, for one, have seen A-level students interpret it as an exploration of: anal
intercourse. This reading has at long last been fully explored by James Morgan
in '"Thrice Adream": Father, Son and Masculinity in Lawrence's "Snake"' (*L&P*
39.i–ii.97–111). Unfortunately, having almost raised the issue, Todd banally
deflects it: 'Such a reading though justifiable, can lead to too narrow an interpretation of a poem which seeks a more generalized acceptance of the darker aspects
of human nature'. This lack of necessary boldness perhaps arises from the
perceived conventionality of the target audience. But if a *Selected Poems* of
Lawrence is required, Mara Kalnins's 1992 Everyman edition (*YWES* 73.517)
remains to be bettered.

In *D. H. Lawrence: Aesthetics and Ideology*, Anne Fernihough has done
considerably more than systematize a disparate body of texts. She has also
interrogated the denial by generations of critics of any fraternity between Lawrence's aesthetics and those of his presumed ideological *bêtes noires*. In particular, she debates the placement of Lawrence in or against fascism, Freudian
psychoanalysis, and Bloomsbury, and explores a comparison with Martin
Heidegger. In each instance she establishes a convincing case for, and begins the
work of, re-evaluating commonplace opinion. Her first chapter pulls no punches
about Lawrence's affinities with German *völkisch* ideologies of the 1910s and
1920s 'from which, among other cultural and political phenomena, both
Heideggerian philosophy and Nazism emerged'. One of the implications for
Lawrence biographers, which Fernihough does not spell out, is the need to
explore the neglected *ideological* as well as merely 'personal' influence on him
of Frieda von Richthofen, who introduced him to this school of thought. She also
bears responsibility for exposing Lawrence to the work of Freud, a 'clash' on
which Fernihough sheds more theoretical illumination than any previous commentator. The high point of the volume, however, is a staggering exposition, in
three chapters, of Lawrence's deep-seated, unconscious, and universally denied
alliance with the Bloomsbury aesthetics of Clive Bell and Roger Fry. It is this
which will mark the book as a definitive step forward in Lawrence studies, and
make it required reading for all concerned with his work.

Another seemingly unlikely conjuncture is that of Lawrence and film. Linda
Ruth Williams makes this coupling in *Sex in the Head: Visions of Femininity and
Film in D. H. Lawrence*, in which she offers the thesis that 'Lawrence's corpus
as a whole [...] offers itself as a case history in visual disavowal'. Thus it is more
properly Lawrence's condemnation of visuality (of which his sporadic denunciations of film were part and parcel) in favour of the 'darkness' of the other senses
(particularly touch) which this book tackles, but it cleverly uses feminist film
theory to do so. Williams argues closely that Lawrence is every bit as fascinated
by visuality as he is concerned to revile it, and that his dealings with it reveal a
divided, deviant, perverse subject, lacking the integration accorded to him by
certain ideologies of the artist. Lawrence's texts are shown not just to be
attacking women, but in doing so to be attacking *themselves*, a fact which of
necessity prompts Williams to a reassessment of the feminist debate on Lawrence
over the past 20 years. All of this is original enough for the book to merit serious
attention. But Williams has a keen sense of humour too: she punctuates her text
with playful sub-titles ('Phallus in wonderland'; 'The public and the pubic'; 'The
closet queen and the invisible man'), and generally displays a pervasive wit,

which makes the book a real pleasure to read. Texts discussed in some detail include 'The Blind Man', *Fantasia of the Unconscious*, *The Plumed Serpent*, *The Rainbow*, *Women in Love* and the various *Chatterley* versions.

Paul Poplawski's *Promptings of Desire: Creativity and the Religious Impulse in the Works of D. H. Lawrence* is less novel in approach than the two books just discussed, but it is far more engaged and engaging in tone. In other words, he is much closer to Lawrence, and wants us to be, than either Fernihough or Williams, whose books are both exercises, for us and them, in distantiation. He defines 'creativity' in terms which, he freely admits, are derived from Lawrence: '*creativity* refers to the human capacity to explore, continually throughout life, one's various changing limitations, in a committed attempt to discover ways of transcending them and of embracing qualitatively new forms of behaviour and experience'. It is also, for Lawrence, essentially a *religious* capacity, as the title of one of Poplawski's four conceptualizing chapters, 'Creative Evolution: The Early Formation of Lawrence's Religious Thought', indicates. There follows a chapter on 'Nature, Art and Belief in the Early Novels' (focusing mainly on *Sons and Lovers*) and two chapters on *The Rainbow*, which is clearly, of all the novels, the one in which Lawrence is most ostentatiously religious. A further chapter explores the underside of this aspect of his work, offering 'a dialectical critique of the counter-creative trends' it entails. The final chapter, 'Consolidation: 1915–30', is a bit of a breathless sprint across a large tract of chronological and textual space, but Poplawski deserves credit for being able to demonstrate critical passion in these bleak days of postmodernist *laissez faire* shoulder shrugging.

One wishes one could say the same about Brian and Margaret Buckley's *Challenge and Renewal: Lawrence and the Thematic Novel*. 'When this book was first written, 15 or 20 years ago', Brian Buckley states in the preface, 'it contained references to current academic trends and opinions. Almost without exception these have now been dropped – in the interval they'd lost credit and appeal, replaced by others which were no more essential to our argument'. He clearly thinks the book's neglect of academic approaches to literature is something in its favour. But it isn't. The text rambles in and around notions which are ill-defined from the very beginning – 'the factors that contribute to the breakdown of an individual's competence to cope with a full life, and the factors that promote recovery' – and having done so with respect to Lawrence for four chapters, wanders off in search of similar will-o'-the-wisps emanating from the works of Hawthorne, Melville, Dickens, Dostoevsky, Conrad, Joyce, Huxley, Orwell, Ford, Waugh, Woolf and Beckett. These dozen authors are encompassed by only 74 pages of large-type text. Nothing new, and indeed nothing old that is of any import, is said about any of them.

Putatively a memoir of Lawrence, less than half of the late Enid Hopkin Hilton's *More Than One Life: A Nottinghamshire Childhood with D. H. Lawrence* is about what its title says it is about. In fact, the lion's share of the book describes her time as an adult social worker in California. Those expecting to see reprinted here Hilton's well-known memoir of Alice Dax will be disappointed. Instead, Hilton regales us with anecdotes, including one in which she apparently smuggled prohibited Lawrence material into England in her knickers. The trustworthiness of some of these tales is, however, in doubt. Hilton herself is continually pointing out the possible faults in her memory, and she gets a lot of very basic things (such as claiming that Lawrence attended Nottingham University when no such institution existed) wrong. At least, however, the material is original and not speculative, unlike Elaine Feinstein's *Lawrence's Women: The Intimate Life of D. H. Lawrence*, which adds yet another novelist's name (one thinks of Philip Callow and Anthony Burgess) to the toll of negligible Lawrence biographers. If abundance of sympathy compensated for poverty of original research, Feinstein's enterprise would be praiseworthy. Indeed, she probably extends too much sisterly understanding to women (such as Frieda Lawrence) who don't need or deserve it. But, if we were to ask why this book of recycled secondary sources and unscholarly imagination is necessary or desirable, we would not be able to give an answer. It will probably, nevertheless, sell better than the biographies which matter.

The most ground-breaking article of the year was undoubtedly Jeff Wallace's 'Language, Nature and the Politics of Materialism: Raymond Williams and D. H. Lawrence', in *Raymond Williams: Politics, Education, Letters*, edited by W. John Morgan and Peter Preston. This article attempts to pave the way for 'more affirmative evaluations of Lawrence from the Left' by ingeniously linking Raymond Williams's ongoing and evaluatively vacillating engagement with Lawrence with Williams's own ambivalences about the 'ordinary' language of community, to which he was ideologically committed, and the 'abstract' language of intellectual discourse, in which that commitment was perforce pronounced. Lawrence's apparent rejection of politics, with which Williams repeatedly struggled, is traced to precisely the same division. There can have been fewer more persuasive expositions of the way in which a critic works through his or her own intellectual concerns in the course of literary analysis. The only pertinent point Wallace neglects to make in his brilliant discussion is that Williams and Lawrence both attempted to negotiate the crisis of language they identified by manipulating a wide range of generic codes, from fiction to conceptual prose, refusing to reside exclusively within the bounds of any single discursive form.

Martha Turner has a run-of-the-mill 18-page chapter on *Women in Love* in *Mechanism and the Novel: Science in the Narrative Process*, a novel which, alongside 'New Eve and Old Adam', is also the focus of Sung Ryol Kim's 'The Vampire Lust in D. H. Lawrence' (*Novel* 25.436–48). Nadia Fusini's 'Womangraphy', first published as 'Donna-grafia' in *Memoria* in 1982, is translated by Sharon Wood in Sandra Kemp and Paola Bono's edited volume, *The Lonely Mirror: Italian Perspectives on Feminist Theory*. It opens with some Lawrence-illuminated etymological meditations on pornography, Fusini wishing to show that 'like Lawrence I too think that in the Novel, in the Book, pornography cannot exist'. One might stop to ponder the consequences of ignoring the fact that 'novel' and 'book' are not co-extensive terms, but it would be inappropriate for me to do so here, as Fusini is essentially using Lawrence as a launching pad for a theoretical discussion which it is not my brief to assess. 'D. H. Lawrence: Cliques and Consciousness', Jim Reilly's contribution to *The British Critical Tradition: a Re-evaluation*, edited by Gary Day, looks at Lawrence's 'fraught and contradictory conception of individuality, with particular reference to his relation to and commentary on nineteenth-century and Edwardian fiction'. Reilly sees individuality as a 'troublesome Ur-issue' behind Lawrence's many disparate concerns. 'The dialectic of confinement and liberation in the rhetoric of the narrative' is what concerns Gerald Doherty in 'The Dialectics of Space in D. H. Lawrence's *Sons and Lovers*' (*MFS* 39.327–43). He thus continues to probe the metaphorics of Lawrence's writing with the consummateness of his previous work in this field (see *YWES* 73.495–6). Doherty is particularly good at explicating several of the aporetic exchanges in the novel, such as Paul's enigmatic remarks to Clara about the 'wild men of the woods' in Chapter IX. However, as the Cambridge edition of the novel (see *YWES* 73.491–2) makes clear, some of these textual 'black holes' were the result of Garnett's editing. Doherty's article was written too early to make use of this: by default he uses Keith Sagar's unreliable 1981 Penguin edition. His attention may be tropical, then, but it isn't topical.

M. M. Lally has a chapter, '*The Virgin and the Gypsy*: Rewriting the Pain', in *Aging and Gender in Literature: Studies in Creativity*, edited by Anne M. Wyatt-Brown and Janice Rossen. The discussion is couched in terms about Lawrence's life laid down by obsolete or incompetent biographies, and is riddled with rhetorical irritations. For example, of Lawrence's relationship with the estranged wife of his ex-Professor, we are told 'his new life rested on a fault of guilt and pain; he knew that her distant children – silent and powerless though they might seem to be – could at any time displace him. He lived for years angry, fearful, and powerless'. This is, of course, preparatory to expounding the familiar thesis that the composition of *The Virgin and the Gypsy* ('does not this novella betray, after all, some slight shudder of guilt and regret in Lawrence?') offered Lawrence a belated opportunity to unburden himself of his inner venom and insecurity. John Zubizarreta wants to show that the supposedly antithetical 'Eliot and Lawrence have more in common than most readers are willing to admit' in 'T. S. Eliot and D. H. Lawrence: The Relationship and Influence' (*ELN* 31.i.61–72). His exposition is clear but routine. Zubizarreta surveys Eliot's attitude to Lawrence, but most of the connections he claims are superficial and negligible. The strongest example he offers is the potential parallel between Ursula's intellectual quest in *The Rainbow* and that of the [*sic*] speaker in *The Waste Land*, much being made of the shared invocation of Spenser's 'Sweet Thames, run softly till I end my song'. Apart from gesturing at these possible links, the article achieves very little. Harbour Winn's 'Parallel Inward Journeys: *A Passage to India* and *St Mawr*' (*ELN* 31.ii.62–6) is hardly a more satisfying enumeration of the 'substantive associations [which] exist between the two works'. The main link involves Mrs Moore and Lou Witt who are said to undergo 'recognizably similar experiences or stages in a mythical journey toward self-knowledge'.

DHLR continues to be seriously behind schedule – no volumes have appeared dated later than 1992, although the most recent were published in 1994. Still, volumes 23 (1991) and 24 (1992) are now complete. *DHLR* 23.ii–iii is a double issue which publishes some of the contributions to the 1990 Lawrence conference held at Montpellier. As an indication of just how massive the Lawrence industry has become, this issue alone has 38 book reviews. These are probably the most informative regular feature of *DHLR*. The articles are a mixed bag of, at best, interesting but not intellectually challenging work (such as Ginette Katz-Roy's 'D. H. Lawrence and "That Beastly France"', 23.ii–iii.143–56) or archival reports (such as Christa Jahnson's 'D. H. Lawrence and His German Translators', 23.ii–iii.157–66) and, at worst, expatiations on trumped-up pseudo-subjects (Karl Henzy's 'Lawrence and Van Gogh in Their Letters', 24.ii.145–60) or displays of literary critical pedestrianism (Keith Sagar's 'Open Self and Open Poem: The Stages of D. H. Lawrence's Poetic Quest', 24.i.43–6). The most amazing thing in these two volumes is neither an article nor a review, but Jill Farringdon's note, '"The Back Road" and the Linguistic Voice of D. H. Lawrence' (24.i.57–64), a scientific report, complete with eight line graphs, of the 'cusum' technique, which she applied, at John Worthen's request, to 'a story first published in the 2 June 1913 issue of *Everyman* magazine, and recently attributed to D. H. Lawrence'. The procedure is 'based on adapting a statistical method of averaging samples by cumulative sums (hence its name, the "cusum" technique). This method can plot a person's language-use so as to produce a graph showing deviation from the average of sentence length, and of an identifying feature within the sentence. It has demonstrated that each person's language habits remain consistent, whatever the form (or genre) of utterance.' Lawrence, it is argued, can be shown to have a 'cusum "fingerprint"' which is not in evidence in 'The Back Road'. The author informs us that she has homogeneous graphs representing the writing styles of Sylvia Plath, Edward Thomas, Henry Fielding and Gerard Manley Hopkins. She is currently writing a book on the subject.

It is surprising to discover that the market for biographical excursions into Orwell territory has not been exhausted by Crick, Shelden and a host of others. Steven Marcus's 'George Orwell: Biography as Literature' (*PR* 60.i.42–50) isn't much more than a belles-lettrish 'preliminary sketch of Orwell's awareness of a cultural tradition of representation, and of his own situatedness in it, as well as of the kind of analysis that might do justice to the dense convergence of material from a variety of contexts that is to be found in his writing', which takes as its starting point the limitations of Michael Shelden's (1992) biography. Stephen Ingle's *George Orwell: A Political Life* (in MUP's very affordable Lives of the Left series) is refreshingly brief and breezy. If it is also self-consciously working class ('it is proper that I declare my position'), it seems nevertheless not to be self-consciously political ('Orwell's ideas deserve to be discussed with critical detachment') until the final chapter, 'Orwellian Socialism Today', which gets down, in a discourse that sounds remarkably like a Fabian Society lecture, to the brass tacks of discussing whether or not Orwell offers an answer to the problems bedevilling the present-day British Labour Party. Ingle thinks that he does and, moreover, considers him to have a lot in common with Vaclav Havel. This should at least do what more academic books ought to do: provoke discussion and debate. Of course, such practical stuff won't satisfy literary critics or theoreticians, who will be disappointed that the politics is not interlaced with discussions of narrative structure, or that the statutory exposition as to how we can read Orwell in the light of Derrida seems to be absent.

Anthony Crabbe, in 'George Orwell: The Practical Critic', in Gary Day's edited volume, *The British Critical Tradition: a Re-evaluation*, confronts four issues: 'First, given Orwell's own literary career, what he saw the nature of literature to be; second, how far Orwell explicitly took note of established critical theory and tradition; third, how far we might detect implicit systems or orthodoxies in his own critical approach; and fourth, at the end of the day, what insights Orwell affords into both his chosen subjects and the practice of criticism in general'. He does so very readably. On the other hand, R. K. Meiners' 'Dialectics at a Standstill: Orwell, Benjamin, and the Difficulties of Poetry' (*Boundary* 20.ii.116–39) so stylistically compromises itself with subordinate clauses, parenthetical irrelevance, pretentious footnoting and general sonorousness that its specific focus is lost. Take the following (part of a footnote): 'In other contexts, it would be important to consider what "Blair" knew that "Orwell" did not know, and whether either of these was not quite other than what *Nineteen Eighty-Four* allows "Winston Smith" to know. This would inevitably lead to, among other things, some consideration of what version of mimetic figuration is achieved, at what cost, and to whom; or, who is victimized by which species of fiction, and what are the consequences for an imagined future or for a retrospective critical recovery?' The indefiniteness of 'in other contexts' and 'among other things' is dispensable; more seriously, the points made are gratuitous, never mind prolix. Is it that I am reading with undue solemnity an attempt by Meiners to humour me?

The annual trickle of work on Wyndham Lewis continues. There is a 13-page chapter devoted to him in David Trotter's *The English Novel in History 1895–1920*, where he is characterized 'as a writer importuned by the negative; an innovator, certainly, but one limited in his departures by the scope of his subject-matter'. Trotter briefly traces Lewis's development between the prose sketches of 1908 and *Tarr* (1918). Toby Avard Foshay examines 'the most enigmatic in a collection of intentionally polemical and explosive position pieces', *Enemy of the Stars*, in 'Wyndham Lewis's Vorticist Metaphysic' (*ArielE* 24.ii.45–63), and identifies it as 'a work of formidable thematic substance' which questions, Nietzsche-like, 'the very grounds and possibility of both truth and goodness in a post-classical world'. Andrew Hewitt points out in 'Wyndham Lewis: Fascism, Modernism, and the Politics of Homosexuality' (*ELH* 60.527–44) that 'Lewis's analysis of modernity – his critique of contemporary politics, and his original enthusiasm for Nazism – is structured taxonomically in terms of an analysis of homosexuality'. The texts under scrutiny are Lewis's *On the Art of Being Ruled* (1926), *Hitler* (1931) and *The Hitler Cult* (1931). Hewitt argues that the traditional political polarization of fascism and democracy may be deconstructed by the 'caricature of homosexuality' which Lewis offers – a fact, he adds, which is 'no more comforting to gay theory than it would be to Lewis'. He goes on to show that, 'while using homosexuality as a moral smoke-screen for his political distancing from fascism [...] Lewis in fact rejects Hitler not because he *is* homosexual – but because he is *not*'. G. Woodcock's '*The Enemy*, Symbol of Our Century (Wyndham Lewis in Canada)' (*QQ* 100.525–33) and M. Miller's 'Wyndham Lewis "Figures"' (*BCMA* 80.iv.174–9) have not been seen.

The starting point of Vincent Sherry's *Ezra Pound, Wyndham Lewis and Radical Modernism* is the often thought (but never so well expressed) point that most modernists are 'avant-garde and retro-grade: the disparity between the aesthetics and the sociology of the modernists continues to define a riddle central to their problematic achievement'. Pound consumes most of Sherry's attention – he has half of the book – but the first chapter succinctly describes the cultural turbulence in Europe between 1889 and 1925 (its sections are entitled 'Musical Empathy', 'Political Aesthetics', 'European Vortex' and 'This Hulme Business') and there is a 50-page chapter on Lewis's work between the two wars. Sherry's aim is to establish that Lewis had a 'seasoned awareness' of continental literature that is often underestimated. He traces this in Lewis's visual as well as literary productions. Andrea Freud Loewenstein's *Loathsome Jews and Engulfing Women: Metaphors of Projection in the Works of Wyndham Lewis, Charles Williams and Graham Greene* is the second volume in NYUP's Literature and Psychoanalysis series, and has a big 70-page chapter on Lewis. Her cautionary remarks about Jeffrey Meyers's biography of Lewis are well made, though she is perhaps too kind to him as she has to spend a large chunk of the chapter altering his questionable emphases on the life of Lewis. Loewenstein's procedure is essentially to gallop through 12 of Lewis's many but little-read books, blending précis with comment. The psychoanalytical structure rarely rises above these foundations. The book is probably best used as a summary introduction to the textual manifestations of Lewis's anti-semitism. [M.D.]

Suzanne Raitt's *Vita and Virginia: The Work and Friendship of V. Sackville-West and Virginia Woolf* is a fascinating examination of the relationship, work, and ideas of these two writers. The preface situates the book in the context of theories of feminine and lesbian identity and narrative, and the introduction states the book's aim explicitly: to discuss Sackville-West's work in its own right; not merely as an influence on Woolf's oeuvre. Raitt stresses that for these women lesbianism and heterosexual marriage were complementary. She does not shy away from this as a potential problem for contemporary readers more used to essentialist notions of sexual identity as innate; neither does she avoid Sackville-West's rather dubious views about eugenic theory, and her fear of the reproductive dominance of the working class. The influence of such ideas on her early novels is fully discussed. This is only one of the ways in which Sackville-West's writing is situated in a specific, and sharply delineated social and cultural milieu: other chapters discuss her interest in female mystics and Catholicism; her withdrawal into the private pastoral idyll of Sissinghurst, and her interest in the maternal and its relationship with autobiography.

The book's discussion of Woolf's work is limited to an opening chapter on *Orlando* and a concluding one on *The Waves*. *Orlando* is discussed in the context of contemporary ideas about biography. Raitt argues that the Victorian idea of the biography as an account of the life of a great, exceptional man or woman was being replaced by a more Freudian model which suggested the similarity between people's psyches. The chapter on *The Waves* discusses the text as an examination of Woolf's fear of the dissolution of self without the support of other people or coherent narrative structures.

As well as being thoroughly and illuminatingly contextualized, the book is also theoretically astute. Sackville-West's biographies of female mystics, which stressed the integration between female mystical experience and everyday domestic details, are used to challenge Lacanian interpretations of female mysticism. In the chapter on *Orlando* Freud's theories of the importance of agency and control in the joke are used to suggest that the jokey tone and aims of *Orlando* are highly ambivalent. Raitt's book convincingly establishes that 'Woolf and Sackville-West [...] lived their sex as a coincidence and sometimes as a conflict of various and varying roles: wife, lesbian, writer. Femininity for them was not a stable condition, or a reliable constellation of qualities and behaviours. Rather, it was a site of continuing negotiation and adaptation.'

The collection of essays edited by Diane Gillespie, *The Multiple Muses of Virginia Woolf* discusses Woolf's interest in other artistic media and their effect on her writing. Gillespie points out that Woolf represented herself as a 'common viewer and listener', and was widely familiar with the other arts. Gillespie suggests that the book is, in part, a study of Woolf's circle and its members' views of the arts, and it also emphasizes the inter-connection between the arts which was characteristic of modernism. A number of the more interesting articles assess Woolf's ambivalent relationship with the formalist aesthetics of other Bloomsbury group members. Christopher Reed, in 'Through Formalism: Feminism and Virginia Woolf's Relation to Bloomsbury Aesthetics', argues that Woolf's view of formalism anticipates critical contemporary feminist views, which reject its 'penchant for hierarchization [...] the assumption of unchallengeable authority among critics, a model of isolated and antisocial creativity for artists, and a bias toward art that emphasizes size and brawn'. He argues that by paying attention to the dates of Woolf's texts and relating them to changes in formalist aesthetics it is possible to trace developments in her views. Her early enthusiasm (responsive to the idea that formalism could be supportive to feminist arguments because of its disinterested 'gaze') modified into a more doubtful attitude, more correctly termed 'post-formalist', which was influenced by her growing conviction that art could not be divorced from social and political issues. Panthea Reid Broughton, in 'The Blasphemy of Art: Fry's Aesthetics and Woolf's Non-"Literary" Stories' examines Woolf's pre-1910 juvenilia and post-1917 short stories in the context of Roger Fry's aesthetics, and Cheryl Mares connects Woolf's ambivalence about the work of Proust with her response to formalist aesthetics ('Reading Proust: Woolf and the Painter's Perspective'). Other articles in the collection examine Woolf's views on painting, photography, cinema, Russian ballet and music. Jane Fisher's '"Silent as the Grave": Painting, Narrative, and the Reader in *Night and Day* and *To the Lighthouse*' discusses painting versus prose narrative as ways of representing death in two of Woolf's novels. This is an interesting collection, although one feels that there is less of significance to be said about some media than others. Josephine Donovan also addresses the question of Woolf's aesthetics and her feminism in 'Everyday Use and Moments of Being: Toward a Nondominative Aesthetic' in *Aesthetics in Feminist Perspective*, edited by Hilde Hein and Carolyn Korsmeyer. She discusses the dominant and dominative formalism of western aesthetic theory, which divorces art from the real world, and reads Woolf's *A Room of One's Own* as an argument in favour of an alternative feminist nondominative aesthetic, apparent in her conception of truth and beauty as evidenced in random, illuminative moments in the everyday world. This aesthetic is aligned with Adorno's conceptualization of art as 'negative critique'.

S. P. Rosenbaum's edition of Woolf's *'Women and Fiction': The Manuscript Versions of 'A Room of One's Own'* (1992) is the most complete transcription of this central work. Based on his discovery of the manuscripts that eventually became *A Room of One's Own* in the Fitzwilliam Museum in Cambridge, and with additional material from the Monk's House papers at the University of Sussex, the volume traces the development of Woolf's text from its initial creation in the form of lectures to be delivered at Cambridge women's colleges, to a short article and finally to a book. The most interesting aspect is the way in which the manuscript is related to other projects she had either recently completed (*Orlando*) or was starting to write (*The Waves*), and the account in the introduction of the additions and deletions Woolf made at various stages. Rosenbaum argues that 'there is little in the manuscripts to suggest that Woolf is softening or censoring her text to make it more acceptable to male readers, as is sometimes claimed about her revisions'.

The introduction to the volume on *'Mrs Dalloway' and 'To the Lighthouse'* in Macmillan's New Casebook series, edited by Su Reid, places an emphasis on new ways of reading both novels as 'tightly and logically constructed', showing how they 'relate directly to important historical issues', and 'combine with Woolf's more polemical essays to say provocative things about the lives of women'. This attempt to construct a corrective view of Woolf replaces the clichéd response to her work which views it as vague, uncontrolled and baffling. Laudable in its aim to demolish patriarchal constructions of Woolf as a failed realist who lacked stamina, the introduction also has the knock-on effect of appearing to confirm traditional approaches centering on the authorial control of meaning and the importance of historical context. The choice of previously published work in the volume, however, includes a variety of approaches: some essays focus on the novels' narrative construction (David Lodge, John Mepham, J. Hillis Miller); some relate them to contemporary historical and philosophical issues (Jeremy Tambling, Gillian Beer); and others read the texts using feminist appropriations of psychoanalytic theory (Makikow Minow-Pinkney, Toril Moi and Margaret Homans on Lacan and Kristeva, Elizabeth Abel on Nancy Chodorow). Feminist approaches other than the psychoanalytic are also represented (Rachel Bowlby on different discourses and their construction of images of and roles for women).

Thomas C. Caramagno, in 'Suicide and the Illusion of Closure: Aging, Depression, and the Decision to Die' in *Aging and Gender in Literature: Studies in Creativity*, edited by Anne M. Wyatt-Brown and Janice Rossen, takes an anti-Freudian stance in seeking to explain the reasons for Woolf's suicide. He argues that her medical history of manic-depressive illness, coupled with the effects of the ageing process, may have influenced her decision, rather than any infantile trauma, and he suggests that we should re-evaluate her decision to die in the light of increased knowledge of the disease and the ageing process.

Journal articles have increasingly focused on *Orlando* this year. In 'Woolf, Carlyle, and the Writing of *Orlando*' (*ESC* 19.329–38), D. G. Mason discusses Woolf's treatment of historical and biographical narrative in *Orlando*. He compares her views on the possibility of discovering the 'truth' about one's subject with Carlyle's. Woolf was widely read in nineteenth-century biographies, and had a strong interest in Carlyle, who appeared to her to resemble her father. Mason suggests that both Woolf and Carlyle have a clear sense of the 'ultimate unknowability' of the subjects of their biographies, but both believed that the truth could be glimpsed in apparently irrelevant and insignificant moments of their subjects' lives. He compares Carlyle's method in such biographies as *Frederick the Great*, where he includes a multitude of material from different perspectives (some of it merely hearsay), with Woolf's approach in *Orlando*. He concludes that both biographers construct 'radial' rather than 'linear' biographies. This interest in biography is also apparent in Herbert Marder's 'The Biographer and the Angel' (*ASch* 62.221–31), a personal account of his impulse to write Virginia Woolf's biography, which is related to incidents in his own life. The article debates the purpose and function of biography for the biographer.

Nicola Thompson's 'Some Theories of One's Own: *Orlando* and the Novel' (*SNNTS* 25.306–17) examines the ways in which critics have sought to provide a Woolfian 'theory of the novel' despite Woolf's dislike of such theorization. She connects this desire to 'pin down' Woolf's views on fiction with the attempt to place *Orlando* generically. Thompson argues that 'Woolf does indeed have clearly formulated ideas on the novel, but ... they have been misunderstood and criticized because they do not conform to critical conventions'. She defines Woolf's philosophy of the novel as the evasion of concrete meanings and the encouragement of the readers' role in creating their own meaning. She examines the ways in which *Orlando* achieves this aim through its generic fluidity; its satire on masculine biographical and fictional conventions; its investigation of questions of style and language from a feminine perspective; and, more specifically, through the use of gaps and spaces; the posing of questions that remain unanswered; and the text's refusal of closure. In a fascinating article: 'The Other Side of the Looking Glass: Women's Fantasy Writing and Woolf's *Orlando*' (*Gramma* 1.137–53), Ruth Parkin-Gounelas relates *Orlando* to the genre of fantasy. In its resistance to closure and its incorporation of 'otherness', fantasy literature can be accurately understood in terms of Luce Irigaray's notion of mimicry or masquerade: an imitation of patriarchal discourse with a subversive surplus intention. Parkin-Gounelas discusses the half-teasing, ambivalent tone of the narrator of the text in particular detail in support of her argument.

Patricia Cramer, in 'Virginia Woolf's Matriarchal Family of Origins in *Between the Acts*' (*TCL* 39.166–84) examines Woolf's treatment of ritual and group/crowd dynamics in *Between the Acts*. She argues that Woolf was influenced by the work of Jane Harrison and Ruth Benedict who established matriarchal theories of group psychology. In this text, Woolf contrasts patriarchal and matriarchal group structures and their different psychological principles, and suggests the potentialities of matriarchal structures.

J. H. Stape's *E. M. Forster: Interviews and Recollections* is a compilation of memoirs of Forster which aims to provide a faithful account and avoid hagiography. The book is organized in a broadly chronological yet thematically coherent manner. There is a section on Forster as an individual and writer (which includes extracts from the diaries and letters of contemporaries); one including Forster's own comments on himself and his work; a section containing the impressions of friends and other writers; and a closing collection of portraits and obituaries. The book contains previously unpublished material; despite the editor's acknowledgement that there were difficulties in gathering and reproducing accounts, and the relative paucity of material covering the period 1901–14, a 'rounded' characterization of Forster is created. What emerges clearly, particularly in his later years, is an impression of a privileged, cloistered Cambridge world in which Forster appeared to have very little to do (a fact he himself acknowledged). One of the most amusing portraits is 'The Strangeness of E. M. Forster', in which Simon Raven comments on Forster's idleness, his reluctance to make decisions, and his personal ethics.

Malcolm Page's study of *Howards End* in Macmillan's The Critics Debate series uses its opening section to discuss the novel in terms of problems or difficulties which it may offer readers and critics, for example: 'Are there flaws of plot and characterisation?'; 'Can a feminist like Forster?'; 'Can a Marxist like Margaret?'. He also discusses the narrative technique, in 'Who is telling us the story?' and debates the ambiguities of the novel's ending and its 'mixed modes'. A potential problem arises due to the different levels of critical sophistication at which these difficulties in reading the novel operate. The section on flaws in plot and characterization assumes a fairly conventional approach to the novel as a perfect or imperfect work of art; the questions relating to Marxism and feminism require a more explicit framework, or approach to the novel. The issue of where we read *from* is not emphasized: at the end of the section on flaws of plot and characterization, Page writes: 'This section is written from within the convention that fictional characters are to be judged as "real people" ... Such an approach now tends to look old-fashioned; neither is it appropriate to all novels'. Issues like this needed fuller treatment. Two interesting recent journal articles relate the liberalism of *Howards End* to the ideas of Richard Rorty in an attempt to show that, rather than belonging to 'the fag-end of Victorian liberalism' as he claimed, Forster anticipated current trends in philosophical debate about the value and purpose of liberalism. In 'Private Gardens: Public Swamps: *Howards End* and the Revaluation of Liberal Guilt' (*Novel* [1992] 25.141–59), Daniel Born argues that the novel debates the future of liberalism through its preoccupation with houses and real estate, and its examination of the ways in which issues of property are entwined with personal relationships. This question is related to Rorty's view that 'self-creation' and social justice are incompatible. Born shows that Margaret Schlegel's views on this issue anticipate Rorty's, but that Forster critiques her lack of interest in the social. He concludes, in opposition to Rorty, that 'once liberalism abandons its traditional concern to integrate private and public modes of discourse [...] it becomes an intellectual game of diminished energy'. Brian May's 'Neoliberalism in Rorty and Forster' (*TCL* 39.185–207) also argues that Forster's liberalism in *Howards End* anticipates aspects of Rorty's work, particularly his concept of neoliberalism in *Contingency, Irony, and Solidarity*: a provisional, contingent, ironic practice which responds to 'a world of postliberal, anarchic ironies'. May suggests that Margaret Schlegel's reinscription of Leonard Bast's rather banal death as tragic is just such an ironic, provisional re-reading. He also establishes the connections between British Romanticism and neoliberalism. Jeane M. Olson's 'E. M. Forster's Prophetic Vision of the Modern Family in *Howards End*' (*TSLL* 35.347–62) is also part of this trend to find Forster's work almost 'predictive', in this instance in its creation of a radically new version of the family unit at the end of the novel: one which is egalitarian, inclusive and non-nuclear.

A Passage to India has also attracted attention this year. Wilfrid Koponen, in 'Krishna at the Garden Party: Crises of Faith in *A Passage to India*' (*IFR* 20.39–47), examines the novel's consistent undermining of public school values of friendship, love and creativity. 'Marabar: The Caves of Deconstruction' (*JNT* 23.127–35) by Robert Barratt argues that the Marabar caves serve as a 'topographical model of deconstruction' which undermines the belief-systems of all the characters in the novel. Chris Lane's 'Managing "The White Man's Burden": The Racial Imaginary of Forster's Colonial Narratives' (*Discourse* 15.93–129) analyses the complex analogies between sexual and racial difference in two of Forster's short stories, 'The Life to Come' (read as a 'supplement' to *A Passage to India*), and 'The Other Boat' (a 'supplement' to *Maurice*). The texts are examined as sites of sexual indeterminacy and colonial ambivalence. *Maurice* is also at the centre of Jon Harned's 'Becoming Gay in E. M. Forster's *Maurice*' (*PLL* 29.49–66), which discusses the use of the term 'homosexuality' in the novel in the context of other terminology of the period, arguing that the novel does not construct homosexuality as 'the essence of a timeless identity or ... as one of two mutually exclusive sexual categories', but rather, examines it as the product of various contemporary discourses about sexuality. [S.W.]

The Joyce world continued to wait in vain throughout 1993 for John Kidd's much-postponed new edition of *Ulysses*. Meanwhile Hans Walter Gabler finally published 'What *Ulysses* requires' (*PBSA* 87.187-248), his weighty reply to Kidd's 1988 attack on his edition. OUP offered an interesting alternative to the search for a 'definitive' *Ulysses* this year, by photographing the pages of the original 1922 edition, complete with misprints, and publishing them as a paperback. It is useful to have this historic document made more widely available, and while its reissue does not solve any of the textual problems facing Gabler and Kidd, it does foreground them in a fascinating way for the non-specialist reader. The text itself is presented without any editorial interference (except for the occasional restoration of broken type) but is supplemented with a wealth of background material, including a map, a list of the misprints, a publication history, and a set of very informative notes by Jeri Johnson. These additions may not be quite in the spirit of 1922, but the result is to make this the most attractive student edition currently available.

A Portrait of the Artist as a Young Man and 'The Dead' have also been published in new student editions with much additional material, as part of the 'Case Studies in Contemporary Criticism' series. The volume on 'The Dead' (published 1994) will be reviewed in next year's piece. The structure of these volumes, which are designed to 'provide college students with an *entrée* into the current critical and theoretical ferment in literary studies', is rather complicated. Besides the basic text and occasional explanatory notes, the editor of each volume (R. B. Kershner for *Portrait*) contributes two introductory essays, on the biographical and historical context and the critical history of the text; the Series Editor, Ross C. Murfin, provides a standard set of 'What is ...?' essays on Deconstruction, New Historicism, Feminist, Psychoanalytic and Reader-Response Criticism, plus an extensive Glossary of Terms; and five 'exemplary critics' supply essays on the text exemplifying each theory 'in praxis'. It is an interesting educational question whether this schematic approach is really a helpful way to introduce students to literary theory. Murfin's general outlines make it all seem much tidier than it can ever be 'in praxis' - and some of the contributors seem less than comfortable with their label. The volume is still a very useful package, however, and offers much more than an ordinary edition. Chester Anderson, the editor of the standard text, has provided a new corrected text - including the striking change that it is no longer a 'green wothe', but a more childlike '*geen* wothe', that Stephen sings about on the first page. In another *coup*, Norman Holland contributes what is claimed to be his first essay on Joyce. His robust confessional style is certainly refreshing: 'How can one take this seriously?' he demands of Stephen's last lines: '"Welcome, O life!" Give me a break!'.

Moving on to 'The Dead', John Huston's film version, which yields some intriguing perspectives on Joyce's text, is discussed in Frank Pilipp's 'Narrative Devices and Aesthetic Perception in Joyce's and Huston's "The Dead"' (*LFQ* 21.61-6). Earl G. Ingersoll raises the interesting question 'Who is Bartell D'Arcy, and why does he sing in both "The Dead" and *Ulysses*?' (*IUR* 23.ii.250-7). The answer seems to be that in both cases the tenor is associated with nostalgia, jealousy and imminent betrayal – recurring elements in Joyce's representation of sexuality.

Richard Peterson's *James Joyce Revisited* is a short survey of Joyce's work which claims to be written 'from the perspective of teaching'. It is not one of the better introductory guides, though, and there is very little evidence of this special interest. Much more promising is the MLA publication *Approaches to Teaching Joyce's* Ulysses, edited by Kathleen McCormick and Erwin R. Steinberg, in which 16 different American university teachers simply describe, in one chapter each, what they do in undergraduate classes on *Ulysses*. The result is a fascinating collection, full of insights and ideas: it would work quite well as an alternative book on *Ulysses* regardless of the teaching slant, but most of the essays are also admirably practical – listing or reproducing questions, handouts, worksheets etc., and not avoiding the basic issue of the considerable difficulty of the text for most students. It is particularly interesting to see how the authors of recent books on Joyce, such as Sheldon Brivic and Bonnie Kime Scott, apply their scholarship in the classroom. The one slightly depressing aspect of this book, from a British perspective, may simply be the amount of time the contributors seem able to devote to working through *Ulysses*; most allow for 20 or more contact hours, and there is not much encouragement here for the tutor attempting to 'do' Joyce in a week.

Four other book collections of essays by various Joyce specialists have appeared this year. *James Joyce: A Collection of Critical Essays*, edited by Mary Reynolds, is a useful selection of previously published work, mostly from the 1980s, and includes Jacques Derrida's often-cited essay 'Two Words for Joyce'. The basic premise of *Picking Up Airs: Hearing the Music in Joyce's Text*, edited by Ruth H. Bauerle, is that much remains to be discovered about the importance of music and musical allusions in Joyce's writing. Existing catalogues of allusions certainly haven't exhausted the texts, although occasionally they have exceeded them: Bauerle provides an Appendix listing 'Musical Delusions in *Finnegans Wake*' – apparent allusions which in fact pre-date the songs they refer to. The five substantial new essays which make up this book each explore a different musical context for Joyce's work: comedy, pantomime, music hall, opera and American popular music. In a nice touch, the book also includes words and music for four of the songs discussed – because, according to Bauerle, 'Joyceans love to sing'. According to Andrew Gibson, editor of *Reading Joyce's 'Circe'*, they also love to laugh. The collective experience of the London-based seminar group, whose work on *Ulysses* 15 this book represents, was that 'a huge monstrous gust of laughter sweeps right the way through the chapter' – though Gibson rather spoils the Dionysian effect of this by adding 'it is a complex laughter, and still in need of further analysis and contextualization'. The analysis in *Reading Joyce's 'Circe'* includes L. H. Platt's rather polemical reading of 'Circe' as a burlesque of Irish Literary Theatre, and R. G. Hampson on the relation of the published text to Joyce's early drafts. The shared aim of the essays is to consolidate what Andrew Gibson, in his very helpful introductory history, identifies as a recent second phase in the interpretation of 'Circe'. In the earlier 'humanist' phase, critics tended to reduce the phantasmagoric drama of the chapter to a series of hallucinations which the 'real' Bloom must be having. Later critics have abandoned this referential approach and explored 'Circe' as a prime site of decentred textuality which, by continually recycling material from the rest of the novel, ultimately subverts its apparent coherence as a narrative. This critical history of 'Circe' could be applied to Joyce studies generally, and is certainly reflected in the more wide-ranging collection, *Joyce: The Return of the Repressed*, edited by Susan Stanford Friedman. The contributors to this volume are described as 'working broadly and differently under the umbrella of psychoanalysis and poststructuralism'. As Friedman notes in her Introduction, Joyce's texts have proved 'ideally suited' to the recent acceleration of work of this kind: *Ulysses* and *Finnegans Wake*, especially, 'anticipate and perform with an increasingly dazzling display many basic tenets of recent critical theory'. The more accessible essays in this collection are those which draw on historical research to trace the workings of repression and return in the texts: Richard Pearce, for example, investigates the social history behind the song, 'Lilly Dale', that Stephen learns from his father. But the book also contains such formidable exercises in Derridean and Joycean word-play as Ellen Carol Jones's 'Textual Mater: Writing the Mother in Joyce': 'Like the children of *Finnegans Wake*, the artist would re-turn to the repressed, only to see "figurat-leavly" as figure, as symbol, the "whome" – womb, home, the (impossible) origin – of the "eternal geomater."' As Friedman suggests, the history of Joyce criticism can actually be read as a gradual transfer of interest from the 'Dedalean paternal' to the figure of the mother. Several more essays published elsewhere reflect and develop this theme, notably Mark Morrisson, 'Stephen Dedalus and the Ghost of the Mother'

(*MFS* 39.ii.345–68) and Marylu Hill, '"Amor Matris": Mother and Self in the Telemachiad Episode of *Ulysses*' (*TCL* 39.329–43).

JJQ published two special collections this year – a challenging 'Deleuze-Guattari Cluster' (*JJQ* 30.ii); and a double issue on the subject of 'Joyce and Advertising' (*JJQ* 30.iii–iv), guest-edited by Garry Leonard and Jennifer Wicke and dedicated to 'the primary assertion that advertising – and consumer discourse in general – constitutes a dynamic force every bit as influential on Joyce as, say, the works of Thomas Aquinas, Dante, Shakespeare, or Giordano Bruno'. The 15 essays in this collection (several of them illustrated) constitute a major new resource for this kind of approach to Joyce. They combine intensive theoretical discussion of the dynamics of advertising, commodity culture, subjectivity and pleasure, with interesting historical research – including a note by Suman Gupta on a 1934 Random House advertisement for *Ulysses* which advised readers: 'Do not let the critics confuse you. Ulysses is not difficult to read …' (861–868). An important supplement to this collection is Mark Wollaeger's illustrated article 'Posters, Modernism, Cosmopolitanism: *Ulysses* and World War I Recruiting Posters in Ireland' (*YJC* 6.ii.87–131), which uses the construction of colonial Ireland in a number of posters to highlight the way *Ulysses* works towards the opposite effect – 're-problematizing the category of Irishness and the very idea of national identity'.

Besides co-editing 'Joyce and Advertising', Garry Leonard has also contributed one of the more spectacular individual books on Joyce this year, *Reading* Dubliners *Again: A Lacanian Perspective*. Noting that *Dubliners* is still considered 'easy Joyce' and has not yet been thoroughly analysed in post-Freudian psychoanalytic terms, Leonard draws on Lacan to re-read the stories as 'an exploration of the mystery of consciousness that is both invigorating and unsettling for the reader'. What makes Leonard's own exploration so invigorating is his decision to devote a separate and self-contained chapter to each *Dubliners* story, and then to juxtapose segments of the Lacanian narrative with brilliant close readings of Joyce's text that discover meaning in the most unpromising details. The result is a most illuminating and valuable study, which doubles as a very helpful introduction to Lacan, and includes some useful reflections on the role of the teacher in the final chapter. Those who object to this prospect of 'easy Lacan' may prefer Sheldon Brivic's approach in *The Veil of Signs: Joyce, Lacan and Perception*, which is a more diffuse study of the 'veil of words' or 'tissue of signs' which Joyce's characters pass through in their looping Lacanian circuits of self and other. Brivic's central text is *Ulysses*, since at the climaxes of their visual careers 'Bloom and Stephen have experiences of passing through the veil, experiences that match Lacanian models for the formation of the subject'. But Brivic does not go in for extended close reading: his way of correlating Joyce and Lacan is to immerse the reader in uncertainty rather than attempt a clear explication, and his rather gnomic style makes few concessions to the reader who has not already come to terms with this kind of discourse.

Dubliners has generally been a popular subject this year. There have been several attempts to throw more light on the obscure relationship of the boy and the priest in 'The Sisters'. In 'Not "too much noise": Joyce's "The Sisters" in Irish Catholic Perspective' (*TCL* 39.306–28), Thomas Dilworth suggests that the dying priest wants to live on in the boy, and that both are guilty of simony in that both have an ulterior motive for their friendship. A. James Wohlpart sees the friendship in more positive terms in 'Laughing in the Confession-Box: Vows of

Silence in Joyce's "The Sisters"' (*JJQ* 30.iii.409–48): the priest encourages the boy to become a secular confessor – in other words, to write *Dubliners*. In 'The Stigma of Femininity in James Joyce's "Eveline" and "The Boarding House"' (*SSF* 30.501–10), Earl G. Ingersoll considers metaphor and metonymy in the stories as tropes corresponding to masculine and feminine, English and Irish: Eveline is represented as the ultimate 'feminized' subject, but in 'The Boarding House' Bob Doran is also feminized, suggesting that to lack 'the transformative power of metaphor' is a more general condition of all Dubliners. Each page of *Dubliners* text in John Wyse Jackson's and Bernard McGinley's *James Joyce's Dubliners: An Annotated Edition* is accompanied by a full page or more of background notes and illustrations. This is not quite the *deluxe* edition it seems, however. The notes are rather prescriptive, and the illustrations (all black-and-white) are not as lavish as the large format of the book suggests. In this respect, a useful companion volume would be David Pierce's *James Joyce's Ireland*, which offers a more sumptuous collection of photographs and other contextual material, and also includes a general survey of Joyce's life and work. Another useful companion to any work on *Dubliners* is Robert Scholes's *In Search of James Joyce*, a collection of Scholes's previously published essays which represents the different stages of his long engagement with Joyce – from textual scholarship, through a phase as 'hard-core semiotician', to a form of cultural materialism. The collection includes Scholes's early essays on the text of *Dubliners*, which resulted in the 'definitive' corrected 1967 edition. These are particularly timely, now that the end of pre-1941 copyright has encouraged several paperback publishers to revert to the less-than-definitive 1914 text. Jackson and McGinley have actually produced a new hybrid text for *James Joyce's Dubliners*, their most striking innovation being to restore Joyce's dashes to the *end* as well as the beginning of each paragraph containing direct speech. It is interesting to see this style in print for once, but difficult to agree with the editors that the effect is 'elegant and readable'.

Peter Costello's *James Joyce: The Years of Growth 1882–1915: A Biography*, is one of those books that constantly display a hostile attitude to Joyce scholarship: 'Although it contains a large amount of new material which will surprise the specialist, it is intended for the ordinary reader of James Joyce who enjoys his works, the common reader who is after all the true audience for literature'. What this means in practice is that Costello tends to limit his approach to identifying the originals for Joyce's fictional characters and narrating Joyce's life in terms borrowed from the fiction. But at the same time he clearly wants his work to be taken seriously by 'the specialist' – and it must be acknowledged that this is not just a digest of previous biographies, it does contain a substantial amount of new research, particularly into Joyce's family history. The two most important discoveries are that, contrary to what is suggested by *Portrait*, Joyce did not have his first sexual experience until after he had left school; and that 'Emma Clery' may have been based on one Mary Cleary, an intelligent and refined fellow-student who regarded Joyce with considerable distaste. These findings, if true, would seem to have some quite important implications for the way we read *Portrait*, but Costello doesn't pursue them, and elsewhere he continues to use the novel as a documentary source. The impressiveness of his research is also rather marred by his careless mishandling of more familiar details: Costello, for example, thinks it was a bicycle *lamp* found in 'An Encounter' rather than a bicycle pump. Any kind of reader, 'common' or otherwise, deserves better than this.

Costello's biography is quite readable, and will probably be useful for the occasional cross-reference, but it certainly doesn't inaugurate a new era in Joycean biography. Indeed, despite the constant drip of anti-Ellmann polemic in this book, the overall effect is to confirm the classic status of Richard Ellmann's *James Joyce*, which attracted several more studies in its own right this year. In 'On Literary Biography and Biografiends' (*NLH* 24.683–95), Suman Gupta uses Ellmann's work as the focus for a playful attempt to theorize literary biography as a 'reading situation' – one that differs from criticism inasmuch as it does not pretend to be a final statement but knows it is part of an indefinite process of reading and textualizing. In '"The Biography of the Century": Another Look at Richard Ellmann's *James Joyce*' (*Biography* 16.31–45), Lorraine Janzen Kooistra concedes that Ellmann wrote 'the century's greatest literary biography' but criticizes his 'hostility to psychological depiction' and suggests that he identified too closely with his subject. Michael Patrick Gillespie reveals more about a relatively new source of biographical data in '"Prying into the family life of a great man": A Survey of the Joyce/Leon papers at the National Library of Ireland' (*JJQ* 30.ii.277–94). This substantial collection of letters and other papers from the last decade of Joyce's life contains much new information about the composition and production of *Finnegans Wake*, and about Joyce's attitude to *Ulysses* – including which edition he regarded as the essential copytext. According to Gillespie, although they do not invalidate Ellmann's account, 'the letters have the cumulative effect of humanizing the view of Joyce that emerges'.

This year's work on Joyce has produced a number of interesting variations on the theme of 'Joyce and History'. James Fairhall's *James Joyce and the Question of History* is the richest in terms of historical research. Fairhall re-examines some of the standard topics in any contextual study – the fall of Parnell, for example, the municipal elections which figure in 'Ivy Day in the Committee Room', and the impact of the First World War on *Ulysses* – and provides some interesting new insights. His main concern, however, is not to locate Joyce in history but to read Joyce's works as 'a meditation on the nature of history and of Irish history in particular'. The test-case for his thesis is the treatment of the 1882 Phoenix Park murders in *Ulysses* and the unresolved question of whether, as Bloom wonders, the keeper of the shelter in 'Eumaeus' is or is not 'Skin-the-Goat' Fitzharris, the famous driver of the murderers' getaway vehicle. The ambiguous representation of this figure 'acts as a potential maieutic device ... making the reader a little uneasy through its subversion of traditional notions of history and fiction and even identity'. This is an original and stimulating start, but as Fairhall extends his analysis to the rest of Joyce's works it gradually develops into just one more reading of Joyce as poststructuralist – as Fairhall concludes: 'Joyce thus discovered the political potential of *jouissance* and *differance* long before deconstruction was a gleam in Derrida's eye. The playful, anarchical elusiveness of language threatens all fixed, hegemonic positions'. This is becoming a rather predictable conclusion: Gregory Castle arrives at a similar position in 'Ousted Possibilities: Critical Histories in James Joyce's *Ulysses*' (*TCL* 39.306–28). Albert Wachtel, on the other hand, is much less inclined to embrace the 'anarchical elusiveness of language'. In *The Cracked Lookingglass: James Joyce and the Nightmare of History*, Wachtel argues that 'having more things to say is less important than finding true things to say' and his concern is to show how certain 'truths' about what happens and has happened in Joyce's fiction can and should be established as controlling principles of interpretation. This is an unusually conservative approach for a recent book on Joyce – the emphasis is on lives rather than language – and Wachtel does not attempt to apply it to *Finnegans Wake*. But his analysis of the 'less problematic works', up to the first half of *Ulysses*, is quite impressive, and he produces some unusual results by concentrating less on symbolic correspondences and more on what he calls the 'actual base' of each narrative: 'why hunt for symbols until one understands events?'. The approach to 'history' is different again in John M. Warner's *Joyce's Grandfathers: Myth and History in Defoe, Smollett, Sterne and Joyce*. 'Myth' and 'History' are structural principles for Warner and equate to 'synchronic' and 'diachronic' – 'what is ever renewed and what is perpetually changing'. He sees *Ulysses* – the only Joyce work he discusses in detail – as a successful mediation of these two ways of seeing the world. But his most original point is that in this respect there is an 'affinity of form' between Joyce and the three eighteenth-century novelists who are thus recognized as his 'grandfathers': they also generate and explore the tensions between the two principles in ways that more 'homogeneous' writers do not. After the Introduction, the book consists of four fairly self-contained chapters – one on each 'grandfather' and a final one on Joyce, in which Warner shows himself every bit as brilliant a conjuror of detail as Garry Leonard or Bernard Benstock: at one point he infers his whole thesis from the words 'tea, wine and spirit merchant' in Bloom's Keyes advertisement. But the 'grandfather' idea remains undeveloped and somewhat misleading, and this is perhaps the one disappointing feature of the book. Warner constantly implies that Joyce was *conscious* of his relation to Defoe, Smollett and Sterne, and that he 'found' or 'learned' certain things from them. But he doesn't provide any evidence for this – except briefly in the case of Joyce's essay on Defoe – and one imagines it would actually be quite difficult to assemble much evidence of Joyce's interest in Smollett. The book works very well as a study of 'affinity' but doesn't develop into a thesis about filiation and, as such (to use Warner's own terms), it remains an exercise in myth rather than history. Jeffrey Segall's *Joyce in America* is a study of the different ways Joyce himself was mythologized by American critics in the 1920s and 1930s, and uses the reception of *Ulysses* to 'scrutinize a period in American cultural history when polemics dominated literary debate'. The different chapters sample Marxist, conservative, New and Catholic criticism, and Segall turns up some interesting quotations. The material is stretched rather thin in places, however, and Segall doesn't provide a very penetrating analysis of either Joyce or the different critical traditions sampled.

Two more general books which contain substantial sections on Joyce are David Scott Arnold, *Liminal Readings: Forms of Otherness in Melville, Joyce and Murdoch*, and David Trotter, *The English Novel in History 1895–1920*. *Liminal Readings* is an interdisciplinary study which draws on reader-response theory to analyse 'the reader's share in the narrative events of religion and literature'. In his section on Joyce, 'Epiphanic Otherness: *Ulysses*'s "Eumaeus" Episode and the Ambush of the Reader's Expectations', Arnold reviews the concept of 'epiphany' and suggests that it can be usefully applied to the last paragraph of 'Eumaeus', when the reader realizes that, despite the deliberately unpromising style of the chapter, the symbolic convergence of Bloom and Stephen has at last taken place. *Ulysses* is central to David Trotter's analysis of Modernism, and is the subject of two key chapters in *The English Novel in History*. He ends by identifying 'Penelope' as the perfect expression of Modernism's 'double helix' – deliberately 'lowering' the subject-matter of fiction, and deliberately raising its stylistic threshold so as to test to the limit the reader's powers of inference.

If Joyce and poststructuralism are 'ideally suited' to each other, H. G. Wells and poststructuralism does not seem such an obvious pairing. Sylvia Hardy has attempted it, however, and with some success, in 'H. G. Wells the Poststructuralist' (*Wellsian* 16.2–23). Hardy traces in Wells's writings a theory of language as both social fact and arbitrary signifying system, and sees *Tono-Bungay* particularly as characterized by 'a sceptical awareness of the power of language and narrative as a means of social control – and therefore a source of power – in a modern consumer-based society'. The advantage of this new perspective on Wells, for Wellsians, is that it implies a new kind of canonical status – the old 'modernist' kind having always been denied him. The logic of this traditional exclusion is analysed by Virginia Allen, in 'The Ethos of English Departments: Henry James and H. G. Wells, Continued' (*Extrapolation* 34.305–28). She sees it as symptomatic of a tendency to think in terms of given values ('ethos') rather than rhetorical analysis ('logos') within American English departments – but this polemical analysis has more to do with the status of science-fiction studies within the American curriculum than with Wells himself. Patrick Parrinder contributes an essay on new and old worlds in Wells's writing to *The Ends of the Earth*, the last volume in the series 'English Literature and the Wider World', edited by Simon Gatrell. Parrinder suggests that Wells was less interested in travelling to new worlds than in creating them on the site of old and familiar ones (in *The War of the Worlds* the Martians land in Woking): his most imaginative writing was inspired by a 'compound sense of otherness superimposed on Englishness, of an old world irresistibly giving way to a new'.

T. E. Lawrence believed that 'in the distant future' he would be 'appraised as a man of letters rather than a man of action'. His many biographers have tended to refute this, but in *Lawrence of Arabia, Strange Man of Letters: The Literary Criticism and Correspondence of T. E. Lawrence*, Harold Orlans has gone to considerable lengths to reconstitute Lawrence as (to quote his Introduction) 'booklover, writer, literary cognoscente'. Not only has Orlans hunted up all Lawrence's published criticism – mostly short reviews and introductions – for this volume, he has also gone through all the letters, extracting Lawrence's comments on different authors and literary topics and presenting them in encyclopaedic form, with helpful notes and additional information. Needless to say, despite all this effort the book does not reveal Lawrence to have been a great or even a particularly original critic. But the arrangement by subject does make it a fascinating volume to sample, and it should prove an invaluable aid to anyone working on Lawrence as a literary figure. Whether anyone else besides Orlans is actually engaged in such work is another matter. The last book I am aware of (not previously reviewed here) that devotes several chapters to Lawrence as a writer is *T. E. Lawrence: Soldier, Writer, Legend: New Essays*, edited by Jeffrey Meyers. This book also includes William Chace's 'T. E. Lawrence: The Uses of Heroism', which is a fascinating survey of the different constructions of Lawrence in biographies. Harold Orlans returns to this theme in 'The Many Lives of T. E. Lawrence: A Symposium' in *Biography* (16.224–48). Troubled by contradictory readings of Lawrence (was he 'a complete original' or 'a fake'?) Orlans puts a series of questions to six Lawrence biographers and reproduces their rather bad-tempered replies. Orlans himself then tries – and fails – to synthesize the different accounts, and concludes that if no one has succeeded in portraying 'the whole man', that may well be because 'he was not whole'.

Interest in Sylvia Townsend Warner continues to tick over. Bruce Knoll examines *Lolly Willowes*, her intriguing first novel about a favourite aunt who moves to a village in the Chilterns and becomes a witch, in '"An Existence Doled Out": Passive Resistance as a Dead End in Sylvia Townsend Warner's *Lolly Willowes*' (*TCL* 39.329–43) and sees it as working towards a form of assertiveness that lies between 'masculine' aggressiveness and 'feminine' passivity, but ultimately leads to separatism. It is an interesting analysis, but it becomes rather difficult to take seriously after Knoll refers to the Chilterns as 'mountains' which one has to travel 'long distances' to reach from London. J. Lawrence Mitchell provides a more general survey of the life and work in 'In Another Country: Sylvia Townsend Warner at Large', his contribution to *Writers of the Old School: British Novelists of the 1930s*, edited by Rosemary M. Colt and Janice Rossen. Besides studies of the more predictable names – Isherwood, Green, Greene and Waugh – this volume also contains Janice Rossen on 'Running Away from Home: Perpetual Transit in Elizabeth Bowen's Novels' and Judy Simons on 'The Torment of Loving: The Inter-War Novels of Rosamond Lehmann'. [R.S.]

(c) Individual Authors: Post-1945

Studies of postwar authors published in 1993 reveal a field pretty much unaffected by theory. This might be good news to conservative American educationalists (most of the material reviewed here is of US origin) concerned about the extinction of (their version of) value in literary studies, but it is also baffling to anyone who has recently thought about teaching contemporary literature to undergraduates or graduates. A sizeable portion of the books under review are narrowly conceived as introductory surveys of an author's output (whether other such books exist or not). They are notable for a lack of critical ambition, which may in part be the consequence of commissioning editors' rationing of words, but which confirms conclusions about last year's offerings: the idea of the academically respectable author lives on, despite everything we've learnt about what is possible in literary studies over the past 20 years. It is clear that Roland Barthes's polemic against the deified author (a fixture in theory readers, handbooks and histories) hasn't had much impact outside the classroom. Indeed, at least two writers of articles in 1993 deal with comparisons of writers to God, and many more invoke theological conceptions or categories. There are two cultures, and the English Association is neither trendy nor perverse in now issuing two versions of *Year's Work*.

Lawrence S. Friedman's *William Golding* takes an unexceptional stance. Opening with Golding's Nobel acceptance speech – the novel 'performs no less than the rescue and the preservation of the individuality and dignity of the single being' – Friedman outlines the career of 'an old fashioned Christian moralist'. The Second World War is presented, without qualification, as the event that 'exploded'(Friedman's word) Golding's (in his own words) 'liberal and naïve belief in the perfectibility of man', and presumably converted him to Augustinian tenets concerning original sin. (Subsequently, and in contradiction to the implied singularity of twentieth-century evil, his reaction is compared to Euripides's disillusion after the Peloponnesian War.) Golding's enterprise, according to Friedman, involves demarcating the limits of human reason, and offering a corrective to a diminished sense of the numinous. But this 'anti-modern' fable-making is explicated without sufficient investigation of the history, and historiography, that informs Golding's writing. The readings of individual novels are, however, efficient and clearly articulated, even if they contain few surprises. Moral/theological interpretations are embellished with some useful literary cross-referencing. For instance, Sartre surfaces in discussions of *Flies* and *Free Fall*. Eliot's *Four Quartets* provide a starting point for a reading of *Darkness Visible* in which Matty incarnates potential salvation in the moral waste land of sixties England. The account of Talbot's development as a 'man of feeling' on his passage to Australia draws on Coleridge, Melville and Conrad, as well as eighteenth-century epistolary models. There is nothing new about inserting Golding into an intertextual web; Friedman is less concerned however with Golding as a reviser of fictional archetypes than with allusion as a critical tool for implying the resonance of passages under discussion. He has written a consistently purposeful general account of Golding's novels which will prove useful to undergraduates in particular.

William Golding: The Sound of Silence (1991) is an eightieth-birthday tribute from Belgium, edited by Jeanne Delbaere. Twelve of the 18 essays are reprinted, the earliest from 1962, and the editor includes no less than seven articles by herself in order to stretch to coverage of the Golding oeuvre. Most of the contributions are formalist, thematic or motivic in focus. The two earliest pieces consider Golding updating or correcting the visions of Defoe and Ballantyne, from the perspective of a theology of the dark soul. Mark Adriaens offers a Jakobsonian analysis of 'Style in *The Inheritors*' which exhaustively describes the metonymic dimension of Golding's language; there is scope for developing this raw material into a more cohesive account of (i) epistemic conditions in the fictional world Golding has created, and (ii) the historical conclusions written into that world, in the shape of the New Men (discussed in the editor's essay on the novel). No less than three essays tackle *The Paper Men*, despite its portrayal of the artist's persecution by a literary researcher. Nadia D'Amelio discovers an allegory of the disintegration of Western Culture, a failure to hand down tradition (does the restoration of the authority of critical discourse follow from this reading?). Delbaere also detects a further stratum beneath the parody of academia, this time a metaphysical comedy in which Barclay is a 'poor caricature of the Ultimate Novelist' (the third *Paper Men* essay also opts for a supernatural thesis). By contrast, the marvellous trilogy gets rather perfunctory coverage. Overall, the collection lacks variety and any really substantial contributions to the study of Golding's work. Glorie Talbot, in 'Reading and Righting: Metafiction and Metaphysics in William Golding's *Darkness Visible*' (*TCL* 39.i.47–58) demonstrates her hypothesis about the novel's inscrutability by her own difficulties in bringing it to book (Willy Schreurs, in *The Sound of Silence*, insists the novel is to be understood in religious terms, lest it appear absurd). In the light of perceived 'metafictional tendencies', Talbot views the character Sophy as instantiating free will (authorial control is in question). However, there are problems with the analogical procedure of the argument (particularly as it issues in thoughts about human and divine authorship), and an authorial unease about the potentially reductive function of the category of the metafictional with regard to mystery and the spiritual. The elements of this essay do not come together. Unlike J. H. Stape's more suggestive use of the concept of metafiction in relation to Golding's trilogy (*YWES* 73.513), Talbot's efforts remain diffuse, and are trivialized by awful puns.

Elliott Malamet handles similar ideas more successfully in the unamusingly titled 'Penning the Police/Policing the Pen: The Case of Graham Greene's *The Heart of the Matter*' (*TCL* 39.iii.283–305). Malamet examines Greene's conflicting intentions ('entertainment'/'serious novel') by way of a useful analysis of the contradictions in the portrayal of Scobie. This argument makes more fruitful use of analogy than does Talbot's, because it bears more closely on an explicit interpretative crux, whether, on the one hand, the novel shows the destructive consequences of pity or whether, on the other, the reader exonerates Scobie. If, Malamet argues, Scobie is at once transparent to human surveillance and able to elude God, then he also eludes Greene, the novelist who has described his role as 'vaguely comparable to God's'. The author, like God, is a 'double agent', condemning and sustaining his characters, and it is the ambiguity of this role that permits the character to elude authorial control.

Christine de Vinne's 'Truth and Falsehood in the Metaphors of *A Burnt-Out Case*' (*ES* 74.445–50) is a less ambitious, and ultimately less helpful, consideration of the metaphoric tenor of allusions to childhood: 'in Greene's topography childhood corresponds with falsehood while adulthood symbolizes truth'. However, 'childlike' qualities become a catch-all motivation for a dualistic taxonomy of the characters in *A Burnt-Out Case*. The essay cannot say very much about what 'Greene's authentic message of life' might be. As so often with this kind of reading, all the attention is on distinguishing sheep from goats, and there is little meditation on what values are involved, or where they come from. *Conversations with Graham Greene*, edited by Henry Donaghy, reprints interviews with the novelist, the earliest being Julian Maclaren-Ross's from 1938 (extracted from *Memoirs of the Forties*). The best things in the volume are the pieces by Naipaul and Pritchett. For a writer as 'reluctant to be interviewed', there is a considerable amount of material, and Greene is remarkably explicit in discussing his fictions and his art. A number of the earlier interviews have been well trawled by critics and biographers, but it is useful to have them in one place, and to identify the contexts for Greene's pronouncements, if only to see how far his questioners are in thrall to various inflections of the Greene myth. The novelist supposedly revealed here is in fact firmly in control of these various opportunities to intervene in the discussion of his work.

Dale Salwak's substantial *Kingsley Amis: Modern Novelist* (1992), his third volume on the author, is part biography, part critical study. The book draws on Amis papers in the Huntington and the Humanities Research Centre at Austin to chart its subject's pre-*Lucky Jim* attempts at fiction. There is an unfinished collaboration written in the Army in Belgium (1944–5), and an effort called *The Legacy*, started at Oxford in 1941, finished on his return there, and rejected by 14 publishers by the time Larkin had successfully placed two novels. *The Legacy* contains the germ of a persistent Amis theme, wanting some things badly, but not wanting other things that go along with them, which dominates the early novels, and resurfaces in last year's pretty dreadful *You Can't Do Both*. Having got Amis as far as his 12-year tenure of a lectureship in English literature at Swansea, Salwak turns to a book-by-book account. He can be relied upon to provide accurate and insightful interpretations: the early Amis is 'a conventional moralist whose characters [...] fly in the face of that morality'. Salwak acknowledges that, at least early on, Amis's morality has more to do with novelistic conventions than with metaphysical convictions (to a certain extent, it is a rhetorical effect dependent on readers opting to side with narrator and protagonist against some comically exaggerated victimizer or fraud, and it appears as prejudice as soon as that sympathy fails). What we learn of Amis's life and opinions matches the studied animosity in his novels, which, like the 'comic pedantry' or the bathetic literalism of his style, is the source of comedy in both the author's 'angry' and right-wing incarnations. As a visiting fellow at Vanderbilt, in 1967, he upset his anti-war colleagues by speaking up for further increases in Western military strength in Vietnam. In the wake of the sixties, we are shown a Goldingesque Amis, despairing over 'human depravity'. The danger for Amis, as for his son Martin, is the possession of a stylistic facility that blinds readers, and sometimes authors, to the vacuity of what is being said. In claiming that the ever more serious Amis, with his increasingly depraved *dramatis personae*, is a writer 'for our difficult, changing times', Salwak commends his subject as the source of comic diversion, and as a 'spokesman'. The first judgement is uncontroversial, but there are many reasons for dissenting from the latter. This is a useful and informative book, very detailed in its narration of the practical dimensions of Amis's career as a writer, his reception and development. Amis emerges as a writer self-conscious of both his craft, and the shortcomings of some of his books (not obvious to anyone who thinks of Amis as repetitious). This will be the standard work on Amis for some time, and it deserves that status.

   Merritt Moseley's *Understanding Kingsley Amis* does in the end justify the slightly preposterous presupposition of its title. While Amis stands for common sense, decency and clarity, critics have condemned him to an 'overly narrow reception'. Moseley contends that mistakes arise when the author is confused with his creations. Thereafter, the book's recurrent critical strategy is claiming this to be heresy. This doesn't wear as thin as one might expect, but neither does Moseley win the argument against those who identify Amis with the schooled philistinism or the misogyny of his protagonists. After all, the real question lies with style and narration, and their implication as accessories to the positions adopted by Amis heroes. Moseley takes the career decade by decade, to show how Amis develops as humorist and moralist (compare John McDermott's *Kingsley Amis: An English Moralist* [1989]). Distinguishing the guy with 'decency' and 'integrity' from the 'bastards' quickly proves its limitations. Too often we are left with a statement about undecidability where this ought to be the starting point for discussion. Calling Amis a moralist doesn't actually take us very far. What needs to be decided is what Amis's judgements amount to, and this is something Moseley is reluctant to be positive about. The section on poetry and non-fiction is very thin, but elsewhere we are given a good sense of the generic variety of Amis's fictional output. Moseley doesn't get the recurring joke about N. A. Caton of Fortune Press, which must have been losing its capacity to delight insiders by the time *The Anti-Death League* was published in 1966, and this says something about his understanding of Amis. Moseley can show us a writer who 'takes a serious moral stance' only by dissociating him from the values and stances of his characters. But the constant in his fiction is opinionatedness, the use of the protagonist as mouthpiece or foil for an authorial monologue (Salwak refers to 'this narrating impressario') about drinking, money, and other people, especially women, but also younger people, older people and foreign people. Amis is entertaining, but it is advisable not to make him out to be serious without taking stock of the things he can be so daftly serious about.

   Cheryl Bove's *Understanding Iris Murdoch* comes from the same series, and is also committed to a certain kind of moral discourse. These *Understanding* books are conceived as primers in contemporary writing, preparation for 'more profitable literary experiences' on the part of students and 'good non-academic readers'. It is assumed that this need is met by telling readers what the books are about, rather than how they work, or discussing why they might be a challenging read in the first place. In this instance thematic coverage is achieved, in 60,000 words, by focusing on 12 novels and relegating the others to a pair of lumber-room chapters. The summaries are efficient, as befits the author of a *Character Index and Guide* to Murdoch's novels, but paraphrase does become rather formulaic. Bove's Murdoch is a philosophical novelist, so we begin with a helpful summary of the arguments about ethics and aesthetics in *The Sovereignty of Good* and other non-fictional work, including the 1953 book on Sartre that preceded *Under the Net*. The pages on that novel illustrate the strengths and weaknesses of Bove's approach: she can extract a proposition from her subject's narratives, but this is not, by her own account, what we should find there. Once Hugo Belfounder's 'moral worth' as a Wittgensteinian pacifist has been itemized, there is little scope for demonstrating Murdoch's interest in character, especially 'real, free characters'. The good (four other characters beside Hugo, in 24 novels, we are informed) are selfless, recognize others as separate from themselves, and intuit the interrelatedness of all things – these are the motifs that dominate Bove's interpretations. The interrelatedness of the Murdoch oeuvre is evidenced, therefore, by a reduction of narrative complexity to a recurring pattern. The trouble is that when moral philosophy is discussed in this way, it soon ceases to have much to do with the practical problems of how best to live, or with art's capacity to change consciousness, becoming instead a codification of norms and exemplars. The 'rich textures of actual experience' which are supposed to mark off this way of representing moral issues are lost to sight. If you did not believe in Murdoch's novels before reading this book, you are not going to be persuaded of their significance as explorations of the difficulties of the good life. But if you do, Bove supplies a functional inventory of her fictional output.

John J. Stinson takes on an even more daunting literary oeuvre in *Anthony Burgess Revisited*, Twayne's second shot at this writer (they issued the first book-length study, by DeVitis, in 1972). This is a helpfully conceived survey, opening with a biographical sketch and a good chapter on 'Style, Strategy and Themes' that establishes the terms in which the more detailed discussion of individual works is undertaken. Stinson's judgement, which he is not afraid to indulge, is reliable, adding a dimension to a format which can be bland and repetitive. He gives a good sense of the range of Burgess's output, his hobbyhorses, and some of the negative consequences of his prolificity. There is another good chapter on Burgess's dystopian texts, helpfully contrasting the weaknesses of *1985* and *The Wanting Seed* with the 'memorability' of *A Clockwork Orange*. Stinson's core concerns are Burgess's interest in myth, the idea of the creative use of conflict, and employing the Pelagian/Austinian polarity, elaborated in *1985*, as a framework for reading other works. Further chapters consider the fiction that derived from Burgess's Malayan experiences; novels about artists, creators and Prometheans, including the Enderby novels and experimental fictions like *MF* and *Napoleon Symphony*; the theme of a 'tepid, lukewarm' England; and later fiction, including *Earthly Powers*, where Stinson gives a balanced, suitably contextualized account of a novel which was viewed as an attempt to make a reputation. This is a well-written book, which sustains a high level of critical intelligence not at all usual in introductory studies of contemporary writers. While sympathetic to the breadth of his subject's ambition, Stinson does not give too much energy to the kind of advocacy of the neglected which is so often a feature of books of this kind; indeed, he is quite sanguine about the future reputation of an author whose polymathic productivity often counts against him.

Selected Essays on the Humor of Lawrence Durrell, edited by Betsy Nichols, Frank Kersnowski and James Nichols (all connected with the Lawrence Durrell Society), contains ten commissioned essays, designed to cover most of Durrell's prose writing. Candace Fertile notes, in a discussion of the *Alexandria Quartet*'s transvestite old salt, Scobie, that '[e]xplaining a joke is often the surest way to destroy any pleasure in it'. Her co-contributors have not found an answer to that dilemma. They go cheerfully about the task of presenting a Durrell who is for life, and against Modernist abstraction and angst. But this is not a cheering volume. Some of the pieces are terribly thin, such as the opening essay which pits Lawrence against his brother Gerald in their writings about Corfu, and throws in Prospero as tutelary spirit of their 'magic island'. Where substantial issues are raised, we lack substantial answers. James Nichols has Durrell taking time off from his Beckettian and Pinteresque characters in the Antrobus books, and having a 'laugh at life and its problems'. But the not unreasonable invocation of a rationalist eighteenth-century good humour gets lost amidst timeserving routines. It is hard to imagine an audience for a gathering of essays as inward looking and procedural as these, beyond Durrell's academic fan club.

The *Evelyn Waugh Newsletter and Studies* is also a publication for the converted, and for American keepers of the flame in particular. Between home-work-style essays on Waugh's characters, we learn that, to the chagrin of the author's 'scholarly' defenders, his last-but-one biographer cannot have liked Waugh, and was probably in it for the money. Fortunately, David Greene, in 'Waugh in Los Angeles' (*EWN* 27.i.3–5) can reveal that the present mayor of that third-world city is a big fan of the English novelist. *EWN* makes one dimension of postwar English fiction seem very important indeed, but this is not a view shared by major US journals in the field. In 1993, *Modern Fiction Studies*, edited at Purdue University, ran a special number on Tony Morrison (*MFS* 39.iii/iv) and another on 'Fiction from the Indian Subcontinent' (39.i). *Novel*, from Brown University, concentrated on African Literature (26.iii) and earlier fiction, and like *Studies in Short Fiction* did not include any work on postwar British narrative. *Studies in the Novel* (University of North Texas) did include work on Fowles and Waugh.

David Rothstein's '*Brideshead Revisited* and the Modern Historicization of Memory' (*SNNTS* 25.318–31) offers a new slant on a pretty conventional inter-pretation of Waugh's novel, pitting individual memory against the vortex of modern mass culture, in a world in which collective and traditional memory is dispersed, and maintained only in the individual's observance of ritual, or hallowing of 'memory sites'. Waugh's goal in *Brideshead* is described in terms of the fictional reconstruction of an aristocratic Catholic heritage in England, but Rothstein then argues for a broader reading, which centres on modern subjectivity and historical sensibility. Charles is viewed as a type of the modern individual; pre-Vatican II Catholicism, with its extreme choices, allows Waugh to express what is at stake for the reader in modern society. The religious motivations lose primacy when they are seen as inextricably bound up with questions about the preservation of identity.

The question of history is prominent in a number of articles on postwar authors. Graham Swift's *Waterland* is a wonderfully pregnant fictional meditation on story telling and the past, and ought to be a good subject for John Schad's 'The End of the End of History' (*MFS* 38.911–25). This is a very clever essay, which reveals Schad to be conversant, and engaged, with ideas from a number of theoretical camps, but one has to conclude that Swift found the better way of getting people to think about, and feel the significance of, these matters. Schad styles his piece an 'allegorical' exploration of postmodern theories of the end of history; in fact he has interesting things to say about 'Marxism's dependence upon the negations and paradoxes of theological discourse' and ends up invoking liberation theology. However, the essay is so unselfconscious about its practice of reading as to be untheoretical, and it doesn't contribute much to an appreciation of Swift. Lars Hartveit's 'The Imprint of Recorded Events in the Narrative Form of J. G. Farrell's *The Siege of Krishnapur*' (*ES* 74.451–64) takes a more empirical approach, but also fails to integrate its theoretical perspectives with the task of answering the questions it sets up. The topic is Farrell's use of documentary material, and the theory comes from Hayden White. Only at the very end does Hartveit's argument really bear fruit, when he analyses the Goldingesque reversal of perspective which has the General commanding the relieving forces comparing the besieged, who had got themselves 'in such a state', to untouchables. There is a good argument that Farrell himself offers an analysis of the process of legend formation, in which the strange is made familiar. Elsewhere, much attention is given to the use Farrell makes of materials relating to the Mutiny and the Great Exhibition. However, too much is left unresolved, particularly the point of invoking White's 'traces' of events.

The two most suggestive essays broaching history both approach the topic via literary history. Clement Hawes gets a long way with his piece on Rushdie, 'Leading History by the Nose: The Turn to the Eighteenth Century in *Midnight's Children*' (*MFS* 39.i.147–68). This is both a useful consideration of the connections between Rushdie and Sterne, and a sober reflection on the question of historiography in relation to the postcolonial. Hawes rejects crudely dichotomizing conceptions of 'imperialistic' history, in which the de-totalizing challenge of 'indigenous Indian modes' of historiography are celebrated. Rushdie avoids this kind of polarization, which can reinforce an East–West essentialism, by embarking on a 'nuanced' exploration of the fabrication of origins. The middle phase of the essay elaborates why *Tristram Shandy* figures as more than a symbol of Empire, spelling out the thematic and figural adjacencies of the two books — clocks and noses. There follows a closely argued account of the significance of Rushdie's Shandyism which discovers in Rushdie's interest in Sterne a focus on the beginning of the novel, and on a historical moment at which periodicity, canonicity and imperialism interpenetrated. Successively invoking Gauri Viswanathan's work on the institution of English literature in Indian education in the early nineteenth century, and Martin Bernal's revisionist history *Black Athena*, Hawes's line of thought becomes ever more speculative, but no less valuable. The supposed sychronicity of the invention of an 'original and continuous West' in the decades before and after 1800, and certain literary historical formations, is the jumping-off point for the contention that Rushdie resituates, rather than challenges, imperialist historiography (challenges, Hawes argues, often reinforce the opposed term). *Midnight's Children* is a multi-levelled attack on a rhetoric of self-legitimation which makes use of the trope of metalepsis, whereby effects are marshalled as causes. Hence Rushdie's interest in all those Sternean beginnings and genealogies, and Hawes's bold attempt to show why this fiction is more successful than 'glib postmodern attacks on the Enlightenment'. Diane Osland's juxtaposition of an early realist and a postmodernist in 'Loose Ends in *Roxana* and *The French Lieutenant's Woman*' (*SNNTS*, 25.381–96) has produced a fine essay in which a host of formal similarities are gathered up into a thoughtful account of how ethics and narratology might intersect. There are some subtle readings here, as well as incisive handling of the significance of characters' conduct and self-knowledge. Osland pinpoints the error of falling for the 'world as text' gambit: highly authored constructions may sometimes fiction-alize, i.e. falsify, but this doesn't mean that it is narrative constructions that fictionalize. There are many insights too about the relation between action, protagonists' awareness of their motives, and about reading plots that end over again.

Maya Slater's 'Problems When Time Moves Backwards: Martin Amis's *Time's Arrow*' (*English* 42.173) keeps its eye firmly on the ball, but as a consequence fails to register what kind of game is being played with it: there is none of the moral resonance of Osland's piece. Slater gets to her points by eschewing epistemology for close reading, and there are certainly initial advan-tages in this approach, as far as characterizing Amis's solutions go. For all its interest in the how, the essay is not forthcoming about why Amis should use such a narrative to address the Holocaust. The narration of a world in reverse turns readers into 'proof-readers of his novel', perhaps, like Slater, spotting what is inaccurate or implausible in terms of the rules of the game of challenging narrative techniques. But to what end Amis has 'deprived us of our ease of reading' and what this might have to do with Tod Friendly's repressing his memories, we are not told.

Kazuo Ishiguro (settled in Britain in 1960, a citizen since 1982) gives an interesting interview to American Allan Vorda in *Face to Face: Interviews with Contemporary Novelists*. *Remains of the Day* is top of the agenda, and its author speaks of his interest in the way words hide meaning, and his frustration at having created a parable (and a reworking of a myth of England) which readers insist on taking as a period historical fiction. Ishiguro has quite a lot to say about the new wave of the early eighties (Rushdie's Booker for *Midnight's Children* was the 'milestone'), and about the parochialism that it displaced – 'novels being written by middle-aged women for middle-aged middle-class women': the new genera-tion of novelists, accompanied by new generations of publishers and journalists, were non-Anglo-Saxons and 'straight' English writers using international set-tings. British English literature thus qualifies as a writing on the margins, while American novelists, who have claimed English language literature as their own since the war, produce parochial fiction that has a global interest. The logic of this argument might, ironically, explain why some of Ishiguro's readers mistake *Remains of the Day* for 'the world of Barbara Pym'.

Ishiguro, a product of Malcolm Bradbury's writing programme at the Univer-sity of East Anglia, is suspicious of the way the American creative writing industry gets novelists started. Anne Wyatt-Brown, who teaches 'Scholarly Writ-ing' at the University of Florida, feels that her subject in *Barbara Pym: A Critical Biography* is exemplary material for the study of the writer as 'aging person'. The author, who has placed Pym articles in *Journal of Aging Studies*, *Gerontologist* and *Human Values and Aging Newsletter*, has certainly lighted on a distinctive mode of engagement, and a timely one, too. As I write, David Sexton in the *Guardian* is damning Martin Amis: '*The Information* is not about a mid-life crisis

– it *is* a mid-life crisis'. Wyatt-Brown, who has also worked on Forster's interrupted career, makes much better use of the Bodleian's Pym archive than did Annette Weld in last year's *Barbara Pym and the Novel of Manners* (*YWES* 73.511), although she does get into a terrible mess with wartime chronology. Drawing suggestively on a diverse range of authorities (Winnicot, Norman Holland, Iser and Poulet succeed each other in a handful of pages), she narrates a psycho-literary biography in which fiction (published or in draft) dramatizes Pym's anxieties and fantasies. The narrative is in part motivated by what the author sees as a post-*A Very Private Eye* reappraisal of Pym's standing in the light of 'sometimes pathetic biographical facts', notably 'the discrepancy between the frivolity and sexual desperation evident in the private documents and the restraint of the novels'. That she is more interested in the former than the latter is manifest from the start – this is a case study in the careers of talented women, and an opportunity to '"value spinsterhood"'. As such, there is little in the way of new ideas towards textual interpretation, but Wyatt-Brown's overall strategy does yield a further angle on Pym's work. Maybe the issue of the 'assault on romantic conventions' can be decided in the light of the darker purposes revealed in this study, and the problems of growing old. In a chapter appositely entitled 'The Coming of Age', the rejection of *An Unsuitable Attachment* by Cape in 1963 and Pym's treatment for cancer in 1971 are viewed in terms of a transition to maturity which results in the bleakly brilliant *Quartet in Autumn* (1977), which Macmillan accepted shortly after the Cecil/Larkin puff in the *TLS*. Despite its partisan perspectives, and a presumptive narrative point of view, this book is oddly revelatory, and unlike a lot of Pym studies, permits one to entertain rereading her work.

Barbara Pym and Anita Brookner continue to be celebrated for their affiliations to (and disaffiliations from) the moral universe of pre-Victorian British fiction. Jean Kennard, in 'Barbara Pym and Romantic Love' (*CL* 34.i.44–60) covers much the same ground as Weld, but to even less effect. In having it both ways – Pym undermines the marriage plot and affirms small communities – Kennard ends up affirming little herself. Her conclusion that the reader takes away 'a sense of belonging to the world of Barbara Pym' confirms the absence of a critical thesis. The familiar diagnosis of a subversion of the tradition of romance resurfaces in Gisèle Marie Baxter's 'Clothes, Men and Books: Cultural Experiences and Identity in the Early Novels of Anita Brookner' (*English* 42.173.125–39). Again, the claim for a revisionary aesthetic is not located in any genuinely informative literary historical context, nor is it theorized in terms of gender, psychoanalysis or the sociology of texts. Baxter's approach looks more sophisticated than Kennard's, but it fails to make sufficiently explicit use of its speculative hypothesis about the relationship between literature and the broader culture. Basically, Brookner's novels are more than 'poignant yet dryly witty romantic novels'. They involve the manipulation of 'romance novel stereotypes' to demonstrate how idealized heroines might fare in contemporary England. The essay focuses on 'cultural experiences' – clothing, food, men hunting, and 'the application of literature to life' – the negotiation of which reveals tensions between impulses towards personal fulfilment and social integration. However, Brookner's protagonists are redeemed from popular romance stereotypes by virtue of a moral identity which, in marginalizing them, provides the ground for strength and self-awareness in recognizing that they are on the periphery. The discussion of the 'refunctioning' of the literary in her work (i.e. how Woolf, as a popular icon rather than any particular Woolf novel, operates as a subtext in *Hotel du Lac*) is one of the more interesting things in the essay, but this theme, as indeed that of Englishness, requires a more articulate formulation, and a more material context.

'J. G. Ballard's Empire of the Senses' (*PMLA* 108.519–32) finds Dennis Foster enlisting a pantheon of French intellectuals to unpack a very different fictional world. He contends that Ballard's later works, in particular *Empire of the Sun* and *Running Wild*, 'explain away' the earlier vision, by a failure to analyse the conduct of their child-protagonists. Foster makes a useful attempt to pin down just what it was Ballard had succeeded in doing in works like *Crash* (1973), by its author's account 'the first pornographic novel based on technology'. Ballard's diagnosis of 'the affective flaw in the heart of the late capitalist machine' is interpreted in terms of the displacement of the human into consumer culture and a world of perverse pleasure in submission to others' desires. However, the essay is less rhetorically successful over a longer range, and it does not completely convince as to how the relations between early and late Ballard can be construed along these lines. Granted that the origin of Ballard's 'vision of the modern world' may be deduced from Jim's love for technological violence in *Empire of the Sun*, the reader is still left wondering just what 'explain away' might mean in the context of hypotheses which presuppose the subject's disappearance or ephemerality.

In the US, Penn State Professor Christopher Claussen's bet that *The Color Purple* is taught in more English courses than the plays of Shakespeare was one of the less informed of some nasty claims made in the struggle over curriculum. The material facts of syllabus content and publishers' lists still get confused with that rather less tangible entity, the canon. In the mid-nineties, teachers in Britain who want to schedule writers like Jeanette Winterson and Angela Carter find it hard to stock the library shelves with secondary literature. Winterson and Carter, and the theoretical fields to which their work affiliates, attract massive interest from prospective research students, but we still await published scholarship in any bulk. Sally Munt's 1992 collection, *New Lesbian Criticism: Literary and Cultural Readings* includes Hillary Hinds's essay on *Oranges Are Not the Only Fruit*, which considers the novel's audience reach, and concludes that a text which transgresses so many barriers 'deserves all the critical attention […] it can get'. Carter is one of the writers featured in Robert Hosmer, ed., *Contemporary Women Writers: Narrative Strategies* (not seen), which also includes work on Byatt, Brookner and Susan Hill.

Some of the assumptions in the British debate over curricula and canons are defied by the persistent popularity of the totally unfashionable C. S. Lewis, who dubbed himself 'Old Western Man', but who isn't a favourite with exam setters either. 1993 saw the publication of two short book-length studies and a second research guide. In addition, Lewis was accorded the accolade of a reception anthology (as a critic) in 1992. *C. S. Lewis: A Reference Guide 1972–1988*, edited by Susan Lowenberg, updates the 1974 *Annotated Checklist* of writings about Lewis and his works. Much of this material is from the eight journals which are dedicated in whole or in part to Lewis's writings, in particular the *Chronicle of the Portland C. S. Lewis Society* (which ceased publication in 1984), and *The Bulletin of the New York C. S. Lewis Society*. Lowenberg gives substantial accounts of the ground covered by each of the 1,126 items included, but does not give much of a sense of where, intellectually, authors are coming from. Given the cultist and schismatic nature of the Lewis following, and material ranging from 'scholarly to pedestrian', it must have taken some restraint not to have done this. *Critical Essays on C. S. Lewis* (1992), edited by George Watson, features the kind of book production that flatters one's colleagues' lecture handouts. Someone failed to make a good job of photocopying from a bound-up *TLS*, resulting in an unreadable review of *Studies in Words*. The sloppy presentation severely weakens the claims of this series to give *The Critical Heritage*-style treatment to the reputations of major literary critics. With no annotation, and only a spare introduction, the volume risks condemning its contents back to the obscurity from which they have been lifted by its failure to make any sense of them to the user. Most of Watson's selections are contemporary reviews of *The Allegory of Love* (1936), *A Preface to Paradise Lost* (1942) and *English Literature in the Sixteenth Century* (1954). Of the five items that fall within Lowenberg's remit she has missed one – substantial remarks about Lewis's views on humanism in Emrys Jones's *The Origins of Shakespeare*. Oddly, Watson includes nothing on Lewis's *Experiment in Criticism*, an idiosyncratic book which has renewed life in the light of more recent theoretical trends. Neither of these volumes is a likely Christmas present for members of the Southern California C. S. Lewis Society, but their scholarly value is also unclear. It is one thing to aspire (whether rightly or wrongly) to neutrality in mediating the material history of a literary text, but surely those presenting the reception of a writer should intervene to analyse it? *Essays on C. S. Lewis and George MacDonald* (1991), edited by Cynthia Marshall, contains five lectures, two of which have already been published elsewhere. The contribution by the Lewis disciple Walter Hooper gives a good sense of the temper of debates within the Lewis industry in discussing the book *A Grief Observed*, and dismissing the idea of its author's alleged loss of faith in the wake of the death of Joy Gresham. Apart from the one piece focusing on MacDonald's children's novel *At the Back of the North Wind*, the rest of the volume takes a biographical and theological approach to Lewis.

Colin Manlove's *The Chronicles of Narnia: The Patterning of a Fantastic World* is a literary study of Lewis. Manlove is intriguingly self-conscious about the impropriety of such a venture, but this gesture is glossed by its context, a chapter on writings about the Narnia books which amounts to a generously worded testament of despair. His own book is good of its kind (Twayne seem to have a readership of High School instructors in mind, but the book would be useful on university courses on fantasy), especially in offering a way into studying Lewis's children's writing. Taking his cue from A. N. Wilson's account of Lewis bested by the Oxford philosopher Elizabeth Anscombe, Manlove presupposes an authorial turn from apologetics to mythmaking. The Narnia universe took shape according to the dictates of the form of the fairy tale, which, as Lewis saw it, was inflexibly hostile to 'all analysis, digression, reflections and "gas"'. Thus, in the composition of *The Lion, The Witch and the Wardrobe* (1950), and its successors, image gave rise to narrative embodying the numinous, and eschewing propositional argument. Manlove's treatment of the devices by which Lewis created an invented world within which to 'recreate Christian supernatural truth' is articulate and suggestive. He doesn't rest on his enthusiasm about these books, but is able to communicate a sense of their qualities, and their significance. This book is good enough, in fact, to demonstrate its contention that, for Lewis, myth had the capacity not only to get the reader to see, but to feel. Kath Filmer's *The Fiction of C. S. Lewis: Mask and Mirror* is a reassessment of Lewis in the light of a more secular and contemporary agenda, and intended as a reply to hagiographic appropriations of the '"Christian" message' of his work. Nevertheless, the study consciously stays within the conventions of biographical or authorial investigation. However, the claim that the conventionality of fiction provides the security for the 'paradoxical' revelation of 'the author's ideas, beliefs and intentions' is not established by the rest of the book (and given the conclusions about Lewis's 'consistency', the motives for such an approach are hard to see). Filmer's claim to fresh perspectives rests on her examination of Lewis as a political writer, and of his attitudes to women ('steadfastly condescending and deprecatory until the end' – not a promising subject). *That Hideous Strength*, a dystopic science fantasy of 1945, is discussed alongside Orwell's satire, and is the prime exhibit in the case for Lewis's 'active political consciousness'. Despite herself, Filmer does end up creating something of a 'trendy', 'new-age' Lewis for lack of a more incisive sense of what counts as a context in discussions of the political. This outline of his views on science, language and education is not going to convince many that Lewis is 'the consummate political thinker' who 'deserves a place beside that of his contemporary, George Orwell', but there is clearly a course to be charted in this direction.

Peter Wolfe has written books on Chandler, Hammett, Ross MacDonald and Le Carré, so we should be able to welcome his *Alarms and Epitaphs: The Art of Eric Ambler* as an informed treatment of a writer whose output since the 1930s has brought a critical dimension to genres – the detective novel, the spy story and the thriller – which have often domesticated the political within a narrow framework of good and evil. But this study suffers from poor editing. You would need to know your Ambler well to make sense of its organization, which is both hectic, despite the book's length and chronological sequence, and inexplicit. Wolfe contests Julian Symons's judgement favouring the Marxist Ambler's prewar fictions over those struggling to come to terms with cold war power blocs and late-capitalist multinationals. But he makes the additional point that, together with Greene's thirties Entertainments, these well-crafted and pacey fictions may well outlast their authors' 'more avowedly serious work'. *Alarms and Epitaphs* hums with suppressed critical energy; the duty of plot summary is frequently interrupted by imaginative leaps of comparative analysis and judgement. It could do more justice to its subject by filling us in on the competition, especially in the thirties, but this looks like being *the* book on Ambler for a while.

Finally, a volume worth noting from the Popular Press at Bowling Green State, which was missed last year: *Visions of War: World War II in Popular Literature and Culture*, edited by M. Paul Holsinger and Mary Anne Schofield. Among essays on poster art, advertising and cinema during the conflict, are a couple of pieces on contemporary fiction. Laura Hopke writes on 'a collective critique of the male military vision' in 'An Absence of Soldiers: Wartime Fiction by British Women'. Hopke, after examining work by E. M. Dellafield, Stella Gibbons, Pamela Frankau, Betty Miller, Elizabeth Bowen, posits the creation of 'a gallery of men who are [...] lacking' which 'question[s] a wartime code which enshrines men while relegating women'. Miller's work, reissued by Virago, is certainly worth reading, and reading in the light of this conclusion. Phyllis Lassner's article on Stevie Smith and Storm Jameson has no truck, however, with the view that 'women were besieged not only by the enemy but also by Allied propaganda'. This is an incisive and important account of Smith's and Jameson's fictional dealings with the fate of European Jews, in particular their several efforts to draw attention to anti-Semitism as a flaw in liberal ideology. Lassner's discussion of the complications in the notion of a just war is more productive than the search for wartime expressions of feminism. Work like this on the literature of the war years can also have a decisive role in identifying certain postwar frames of reference as myths. [M.R.]

2. Poetry

(a) Poetry 1900–50
My departure to the USA has not, I hope, lessened too drastically the coverage of material in this section, but those gaps which may be apparent shall be remedied in the next volume. I have to thank Dr Matthias Schubnell for his kind assistance in translating work in German, and the libraries of Incarnate Word College and Trinity University, both of San Antonio, Texas, for the provision of material for review.

Twentieth-Century Poetry: From Text to Context, edited by Peter Verdonk, is a series of essays approaching the discussion of individual poems through pragmatic literary stylistics, exploring the texts as dialogic structures only fully grasped within a larger social context. The book's aim is pedagogic, with chapters discussing individual poems by Hardy, Larkin, Hill, Heaney, Eliot and others in terms of how they may be read or taught, each one concluding with 'assignments' for its undergraduate readers. Whether or not the reader finds this approach helpful, it may have much to offer students uncertain of how to advance on texts amidst a barrage of theory, and for this reason it is to be welcomed.

Three articles interestingly approach less familiar areas of the poetry of the century's early years. Jay Losey writes on 'The Aesthetics of Exile: Wilde Transforming Dante in *Intentions* and *De Profundis*' (*ELT* 36.429–50). This describes Wilde's movement from the image of an exile 'destroying himself through bestial desire' to the reality of a damned soul as Victorian outcast in terms of the Dantesque references which articulate the theme. It is a movement involving the rejection of the aesthetic ideal of replacing life with art: only sorrow, as he says in the *Letters*, is 'the type and test of all great art', and Dante provides for Wilde the model of this transformation. Christopher Collard explores 'Gilbert Murray on Rudyard Kipling: An Unpublished Letter' (*N&Q* 40.63–4). The letter is to T. C. Snow, Murray's Oxford tutor, and confirms Murray's suspicions from the 1880s when he was asked by Kipling to write an epic poem with him: 'he is really not essentially a poet or artist but a narrow-minded moralist'.

Slightly later material is the subject of *Edwardian Poetry* by Kenneth Millard. There are separate discussions of Newbolt, Masefield, the Hardy of *The Dynasts*, Housman, Edward Thomas, Davidson and Brooke, which contain many individual felicities and are characterized by a desire to look afresh without the prejudices so often directed against many of these figures. Millard is at his best, perhaps, in the account of Edward Thomas, locating him alongside a specific kind of modernism in an exploration of the imperfections of language. Whether the book succeeds in its claim to see the writers as a homogeneous group is far less sure; but it certainly offers a valuable reappraisal of the individual figures. Thomas is also discussed with sensitivity in Peter McDonald's 'Rhyme and determination in Hopkins and Edward Thomas' (*EIC* 43.228–46). This is a fine and diverse essay which explores the whole nature of rhyme, not only in Thomas's balancing of self and technique but in a range of other poets too, revealing how the choice of rhyme words is dramatized and becomes a form in its own right in certain work by both Thomas and Hopkins, and suggesting the issues that this raises for poetic theory. Martha Bremser's 'The Voice of Solitude: The Children's Verse of Walter de la Mare' (*ChildL* 21.66–92) stresses the writer's notion that children experience directly through all the senses as the basis of the full range of feelings in his verse – although surely the child's awareness of the absurd has a part to play in their success, too? A. L. Rowse pleads for 'Justice for Robert Bridges' (*ContempR* 263.1531.86–92), opposing his poetic search for beauty against his medical experiences.

Much work has appeared on Hardy, aided largely by a special number of *CS*. Matt Simpson's 'Pomp and Circumstance – Hardy's "The Convergence of the Twain"' (*CS* 5.167–73) is a confused reading of the poem in the context of Hardy's relations with Emma: it pays tribute to the poem's skill, but its question 'is the poem all that consoling?' surely suggests a limited understanding of the text. John Schad is much more persuasive: 'Waiting in "Unhope": Negation in Hardy's Early Poetry' (*CS* 5.174–9) reappraises the poet's modernist negativity with reference to Derrida and Feuerbach, and looks closely at some of the most striking early poems. In 'Time's Laughingstocks and "English" Poetry' (*CS* 5.180–91) Peter Faulkner makes clear through some detailed readings that Hardy goes against not only 'convention and Edwardian taste' but also the ideal of Englishness much sought then. His conclusion is that Hardy is 'a disturbingly puzzled, sceptical, various, *modern* poet'. Similar ground is trodden by John Lucas in 'Hardy Among the Poets' (*CS* 5.192–201). This explores reactions to Hardy from Graves, Larkin, Donald Davie and others to show his range of influence and the ease with which we – and others – misread his Englishness. William W. Morgan considers 'Mr. Thomas Hardy Composing a Lyric' (*JEGP* 92.3.342–58). This examines the 'texture of intentions and choices' the poet had when writing 'Retty's Phases', 'Neutral Tones' and 'Afterwards'. In four stages – choosing content, planning form, drafting and revising – he suggests that we can find 'a strategy of reading that engages imaginatively with the process that brought the poem into being' which thus reveals 'the enigmatic human being'. I am not sure how much further this gets us. Finally, John Powell Ward has produced *Thomas Hardy's Poetry* in the Open Guides to Literature series for the Open University Press. This uses the familiar pattern of commentary, question and discussion and, while there is no doubt material which will aid insecure readers towards thinking about the poems, some of the questions seem extreme: 'Does it seem to you a little peculiar?' is one that leaps to mind. There is some reference to critical discussions, including work by J. Hillis Miller and Lacan, and doubtless it will be seized upon by students faltering around modular cultural studies courses, but overall I cannot help feeling that this is an opportunity lost rather than seized.

It is gratifying to note the continuing extension of readings of poetry of the First World War, of which Sharon Smulders's 'Feminism, Pacifism and the Ethics of War: The Politics and Poetics of Alice Meynell's War Verse' (*ELT* 36:2.159–77) is a good example. This details the shift from pacifism to complicity in war as an instrument of advancing feminism in the journey from 'Parentage' (1896) to 'A Father of Women' (1917). The former accepts the unwitting complicity of women in the patriarchal process that ensures war's continuance; the latter stresses 'equality of risk and responsibility' to show the value of women's contribution to public and artistic life. Also covering many other poems, this is an important article in exploring the political aesthetic of an overlooked and significant writer. Adrian Caesar's *Taking it Like a Man* has as its premise the idea that, far from being anathema, war was to the canonical poets of the war years an opportunity to release the sado-masochistic emotional confusion of the public school. In this context, idealized homosexuality is contrasted to its 'dirty' actuality which needs containment through flagellation and suffering, of which the supreme example is Christ on the cross. This is an idea which has no little persuasive force – but it is not one that sustains a complete book, and Caesar spends a lot of time recounting familiar biographical material and offering readings that are incomplete and insensitive. Of a wholly different order is Douglas Kerr's *Wilfred Owen's Voices: Language and Community*. Kerr looks at the range of registers in which Owen's poetry speaks, relating them to the maleness of his father, the powerful if not dominant influence of his mother and her artistic nature, the Church, and the linguistic polarities of the officers and the soldiers with whom he mixed in France. This is a powerful and intelligent study, using what it needs of the theory of heteroglossia to offer deep insights into the poetry. Not only is it a book which marks a new level of seriousness in Owen studies, it is one that reveals a great deal about the poignancy and stupidity of the English caste system's subtle shibboleths.

   YeA 10 contains the customary banquet of delights. 'Away' (3–32), by Deirdre Twomey, explores with gentle sympathy the place of Yeats's mother in his writings, particularly 'Away' and *Purgatory*, but also in her gift to him of a love of her country and 'the Unseen Life' by her passionate, wholly unintellectual love of Sligo and its folktales that 'Homer might have told'. Maria Tymoczko's 'Amateur Political Theatricals, *Tableaux Vivants*, and *Cathleen ni Houlihan*' (33–64) relocates Yeats's play in the context of popular theatre and politics, thus revealing the problems literary critics often find with it as elements of its generic identity. James Pethica writes of 'Contextualising the Lyric Moment: Yeats's "The Happy Townland" and the Abandoned Play *The Country of the Young*' (65–91), giving an account of the play's inception, providing a transcript of the text and showing how the associated poem is significantly changed by its publication in a collection of lyrics. Warwick Gould, the volume's editor, contributes 'No Right Poem ["I was going the road one day"]' (92–110). This discusses the 'optional verses' to the prose version of *The Hour-Glass*, arguing Lady Gregory's and George Yeats's part in their writing and revision to warn editors – especially Richard Finneran, whose revision Gould rejects – against the dangers of 'trying to create "poems" out of the "verses" in the plays'. Next comes 'Hawk and Butterfly: the Double Vision of *The Wild Swans at Coole* (1917, 1919)' by Ronald Schuchard (111–34), which contrasts the 'self-contempt that would make even Prufrock shudder' of the Cuala Press volume with the lunar confidence of the Macmillan one of the same title from two years later. Katharine Worth looks at '*The Words upon the Window-pane*: A Female Tragedy' (135–58), seeing women in control of the 'mystery of the imagination' as the key to the play. Wayne K. Chapman offers a masterly survey of ' "The Municipal Gallery Re-Visited" and its Writing' (159–87), complete with transcripts of textual variants and a full commentary. Peter Kuch edits ' "The Sunset of Fantasy" by AE' (188–203), there is a 'Forum on *A Vision*' by Colin McDowell (207–17), and Wayne K. Chapman and James Helyar write on 'P. S. O'Hegarty and the Yeats Collection at the University of Kansas' (221–38).

Shorter notes follow in the same volume. David Peters Corbett discusses 'T. Sturge Moore's "Do We or Do We Not, Know It?" and the writing of "Byzantium"' (241–9) to show the poet's struggle with spirituality and experience; Dennis Haskell explores '"Long-legged Fly and Yeats's Concept of Mind' (250–6); and K. Narayana Chandran writes on 'Yeats and Shakespeare: A Source for "The Great Day" in *King Lear* IV.vi.150–64' (257–8). A. Norman Jeffares writes an obituary of his fellow Yeats scholar Professor Barbara Hayley (259–60), R. A. Gilbert one of 'Ellic Howe (20 September 1920–28 September 1991)' (261–3), the pioneering researcher of the Golden Dawn. Reviews complete the volume, an outstanding contribution to the series.

Three other articles on Yeats were noted. Colin Graham's 'Hopkins, Yeats and the Death of Samuel Ferguson' (*N&Q* 40.493–4) suggests that Hopkins had read Yeats's obituary essay on the poet and antiquarian Samuel Ferguson, from echoes found in a letter from Hopkins to Coventry Patmore. 'Yeats and the Upanishads: An Introductory Note' by Shalini Sikka (*YER* 12.ii.56–60) chronicles Yeats's long journey towards the Upanishads and Vedantic thought, with examples of its presence in poems and letters. Finally, K. P. S. Jochum discusses 'Yeats' *Vision papers* and the Problem of Automatic Writing: A Review Essay' (*ELT* 36.3.323–36), in a lengthy and thoughtful review which raises issues concerning the complexity of the papers (see *YWES* 73.517) and what Jochum finds a puzzling and incomplete editorial philosophy. Finally, Nora A. McGuiness's *The Literary Universe of Jack B. Yeats* explores the fiction and drama of the poet's younger brother, better known as a painter, a valuable first survey which does much to add to the poet's cultural and familial context.

Work on Eliot is still profuse, and as diverse in approach as it is varied in quality. The man not the poet is the quest for Eda Howink in 'T. S Eliot: A Clinician's Perspective' (*YER* 12.i.27–30). The writer uses experience as a clinical social worker to range from Eliot's uncertainty with women in the early poems to *The Waste Land* and the letters to attempt insights into Eliot's 'silence' and Viv's 'oververbalization'. What is alarming here is not the superficiality of the readings, but the possible results of such a limited view applied to clinical social work. Other articles explore the critical writings. Noel Crook's 'A Lost T. S. Eliot Review Recovered' (*YER* 12.ii.44) is one that appeared in *The New Statesman* of 18 December 1915 and covered ten books on various aspects of Indian politics and economics. Gregory T. Dime's 'The Eliot Tradition in Criticism on "Metaphysical" Poetry' (*YER* 12.i.1–8) surveys critical work developing Eliot's approaches, particularly his stress on the conceit and the unified sensibility, from George Williamson's *The Donne Tradition* (1930: *YWES* 11.214–15) through Basil Willey and Cleanth Brooks to John Carey, and sees the tradition as one perpetuating '"romantic" precepts framed as observations on "metaphysical" verse'. In an article of considerable value in the history of critical debate, John N. Duvall discusses 'Eliot's Modernism and Brooks's New Criticism: Poetic and Religious Thinking' (*MQ* 46.i.23–37). He locates Brooks's reading of Eliot, and his advocacy of New Criticism, within varieties of Christianity, showing how Brooks shifts Eliot's stress on High Church Anglican community to the idealized democratic community of the American campus, taking in Fugitive and Agrarian positions on the way. The resultant faults in New Criticism were the privileging of texts that demonstrated 'organic unity' or celebrated the ideal community: as Duvall concludes, the apparent democracy of New Criticism rested on ideological assumptions 'only marginally hospitable to democracy'. More remote territory is travelled in 'Eliot's Chemical Analogy' (*N&Q* 40.67) by R. Sengupta, C. Laha and A. Nanda, which explains an error in Eliot's use of the analogy of oxygen and sulphur dioxide mixed in the presence of platinum to produce sulphurous acid, wherein 'the mind of the poet is the shred of platinum'. The product would be sulphur trioxide, not sulphurous acid. Glad we got that sorted out. M. A. R. Habib's '"Bergson Resartus" and T. S. Eliot's Manuscript' (*JHI* 54.2.255–76) studies Eliot's 1910–11 Harvard paper on Bergson to find three foci: the denial of Bergson's separation of consciousness and matter; a rejection of his prioritizing of time over space; and a rejection of his attempt to elide realism and idealism. This is closely argued, but the most valuable material for literary specialists lies in Habib's discussion of Bergson's influences on the poetry, most notably perhaps in the 'philosophy of integration' where past and present, sense and intellect, real and ideal are united. This is followed through briefly in a discussion of the 'integrative impulse' of thought and language in 'Prufrock', stressing its Romantic positions as opposed to the Classicism Eliot also espoused.

The poem itself is the subject of David A. Sanders's 'Heroic Mettle: Prufrock as Touchstone' (*YER* 12.ii.45–55), which sees the protagonist's name as a 'Proof-Rock' analogous to the Touchstone of Matthew Arnold, finding instances of heroic inversion, references to *Hamlet*, Guido, the Fool, Odysseus and finally to Arnold himself as a prophet, in an innovative and suggestive study. Nigel Alderman's '"Where Are the Eagles and the Trumpets?": The Strange Case of Eliot's Missing Quatrains' (*TCL* 39.ii.129–51) argues that the 1917–19 poems should be seen as a separate group, not a preparation for career or comment on marriage. In them Eliot espouses ideas revisited in the later work, explores topics covered in his critical writing, and develops the blend of exile and cosmopolitanism seen later: he also moves to the 'frigid intelligence' he praised in Wyndham Lewis. A detailed reading of possible significations of parts of 'Sweeney Erect' establishes the Quatrains as 'the works that made manifest the unstable nature of hermeneutical readings', the quality that has resulted in their comparative neglect. It is a valuable and provocative essay. 'Politics of Discourse in Eliot's "Portrait of a Lady"' by William Doreski (*YER* 12.i.9–15) sees the poem as one of Eliot's uses of a voice concessive yet controlling, with an ironic sense of community in the outdoor world set against inner Edwardian continuance reflecting the poet's sense of tradition and the individual talent. Mary Jean Gross and Dalton Gross write on 'T. S. Eliot's versatile countess: Observation on two additional references in the epigraph to "Burbank with a Baedeker: Bleistein with a Cigar"' (*ELN* 31.ii.56–9). The epigraph's final allusion quotes from Marston's *Entertainment of Alice, Dowager Countess of Derby*, and is an oblique link to the same writer's *The Insatiate Countess*, set in Venice. There may also be a reference to Countess Tarnowska who was involved in a sensational murder case in the century's early years, and of whom Eliot may have known. This, the authors argue, makes the epigraph complete and successful.

Sources of *The Waste Land* attracted their usual attention. George Monteiro's 'The (Black) Cock in Eliot's *Waste Land*' (*YER* 12.i.21–3) replaces traditional explanations of the animal as a reference to Peter's denial of Christ at cock-crow with the theory that it is a Portuguese symbol, the 'galo de Borcelos', or a punning reference to Jean Cocteau. James F. Loucks finds 'Another Link between Eliot and Tennyson: A "Shard" from *In Memoriam* in *The Waste Land*' (*YER* 12.i.24–6). Lines 329–30 of Eliot's poem echo lyric XXXIV of Tennyson's, in which 'a little patience' occurs in reference to death. The divergent tone of the two passages makes this an ironic echo or, as Loucks asserts, a deliberate reminiscence of subliminal effect on the reader. In 'A Note on Goldsmith in Eliot's *The Waste Land*' (*YER* 12.i.31), Brian Arkins comments on the exact nature of the reference to the songs in Chapter 24 of *The Vicar of Wakefield* in the 'Unreal City' seduction scene. Finally, to 'The Ending of *The Waste Land*' (*N&Q* 40.66–7), where J. A. Richardson points out that Eliot's statement in the poem's final note, stating that 'Shantih' is 'equivalent' to 'The Peace which passeth all understanding', refers to the blessing in the Anglican Communion service (*The Book of Common Prayer*), and not, as asserted by B. C. Southam in his *Student's Guide*, to Philippians 4:7.

Other essays raised larger issues about the same poem. In Stanley Sultan's 'Love as Death in *The Waste Land*' (*YER* 12.ii.38–44), the poem is seen as 'deploring human love become living death': in the drafts, Eliot writes '*about* love become death'. The argument is supple and offers the earlier versions as a necessary part of the later, which accepts them in contrapuntal fashion. Cynthia Olson Ho considers, in 'Savage Gods and Salvaged Time: Eliot's *Dry Salvages*' (*YER* 12.i.16–20), the varieties of savagery and salvage found in the 'Dry Salvages' section of *The Waste Land*. The salvages of time impel the narrator to call upon a Christian God, so that the processes of time are seen as the key. 'T. S. Eliot and D. H. Lawrence: The Relationship and Influence' is the title of a substantial article by John Zubizarreta (*ELN* 31.i.61–72). After listing critical attempts to show the writers' likenesses, it parallels the River Thames sequence of *The Waste Land* and Chapter XIII of *The Rainbow*, where Ursula's dreams of an historical Kingston-upon-Thames are later to dissolve into life at Ilkeston, a north-country version of Eliot's dispossessed city. This the writer links with a passage by Eliot in the *Criterion* which talks of a 'fine episode in the life of an elementary schoolmistress in *The Rainbow*' – though whether one can agree that the two passages are 'nearly identical in tone, content, meaning and verbal expression' is another matter. It reinforces, perhaps, Eliot's view of Lawrence wavering (as he said in a 1916 lecture) 'between dislike, exasperation, boredom, and admiration'. More convincing is A. James Wohlpart's 'The Sacrament of Penance in T. S. Eliot's "Journey of the Magi"' (*ELN* 30.i.55–61). This sees the tripartite structure of contrition, confession and satisfaction – making full – in the poem's three stanzas as a parallel to the questing of the soul as well as that of the Magi.

Sources of *Four Quartets* were also considered. In F. X. Roberts's 'A Source for T. S. Eliot's use of "elsewhere" in "East Coker"' (*ANQ* 6.i.24–5), the source is Gower's *Confessio Amantis*, which uses the word with the same sense of the life to come. James F. Loucks's 'Pater and Carlyle in Eliot's 'Little Gidding' (*N&Q* 40.500–2) finds the origin of the 'England and nowhere' topos in 'Goethe's American apothegm', 'America is here and now – here, or nowhere' discussed by Pater and Carlyle, and sees it as a resolution of Eliot's tension between America and England in favour of the latter. An interesting thought. K. Narayana Chandran examines '"Little Gidding" v: An Allusion to Vaughan's "On Sir Thomas Bodley's Library"' (*N&Q* 40.500). Eliot's 'Every poem an epitaph' echoes Vaughan's 'Every book is thy large epitaph': the opening of Vaughan's poem may also lie beneath Eliot's stress on the continued presence of the dead in the living through the influence of a library. Other articles looked at the *Quartets* with different issues in mind. 'The Evocative Power of T. S. Eliot's *Four Quartets*' (*YER* 12.ii.33–7) by David Finn is an account of the painter's 'thoughts and feelings' while producing 108 paintings based on the poem. It offers insights into a working method – but surely the paintings themselves, not the process of their production, are the more valid focus? In ' "Dancing around the bonfire": Tanz und Tod in T. S. Eliot's "East Coker" I' (in Franz Link, ed. *Tanz und Tod in Kunst und Literatur*), Klaus Weiss explores the unity of dance and death as thematic motifs, expressed primarily in figurative rather than abstract terms. 'Sentir sa pensée et penser son corps dans la poésie de T. S. Eliot' by Monique Lojkine-Morelec (in Bernard Brugière, ed. *Les figures du corps dans la littérature et la peinture anglaises et americaines de la renaissance à nos jours* [1991]) details the process by which body, feeling and thought elide throughout the poet's work, reaching its climax in the 'experience totale de la pensée faite corps et du corps devenu corps mystique' of 'Little Gidding'.

Rebuilding Babel: The Translations of W. H. Auden by Nirmal Dass is a study of a large body of work which, though largely overlooked by critics, was regarded as important by the poet himself. However, this is more than a simple survey. Firmly grounded in Derrida, Benjamin and other theorists, it argues a progression from the early translations, in which the original becomes raw material for transmutation, to the later work, in which a 'double articulation' results from a concern both for the original and for the new language. In the process it is a valuable discussion not only of Auden's work but of the nature of translation in general. Of three articles noted about Auden, the most important was David Pascoe's 'Auden and the Aesthetics of Detection' (*EIC* 43.33–58). This is a subtle and wide-ranging exploration of the uses the poet makes of the locations, rites and symbols of the classic detective story in poems, linking discussion of 'Detective Story', 'The Guilty Vicarage' and parts of the *New Year Letter* to passages of Freudian psychoanalysis. Most telling is the placing of this within the larger suffering of the thirties and forties, where there is guilt with neither the security of landscape nor the simple resolution offered by the detective story. The article goes beyond its declared subject to offer insight into the mindscapes of the age. 'An Early Gift to W. H. Auden' by Christopher J. P. Smith (*N&Q* 40.503) is a copy of *Prose Pieces and Poems* by Anthony Abbot, with an inscription from E. C. Tenterden, the mother of the book's author who died at the age of 19: Auden's involvement is not known. 'Lyric Suffering in Auden and Feldman' by Harold Schweizer (*ELN* 31.ii.66–75) draws parallels between Auden and the American Irving Feldman in their condemnation of the observant but detached bystander.

Peter McDonald's *Louis MacNeice: The Poet in his Contexts* attempts to move the poet out of the thirties enclave in which he is normally seen and place him within larger contexts: those of Irish poetry, the work of Yeats and the larger stream of British Modernism. In its inclusiveness it has much to offer in allowing us to arrive at a wider, and more balanced, view of the poet's achievement. Jem Poster's *The Thirties Poets* is, like Ward's study of Hardy, produced in the Open University's series of Open Guides, but that is the only resemblance it bears. Poster's approach is thoughtful and authoritative, ensuring that the reader is genuinely involved in complex readings not by facile questioning but by genuine discussion and exploration. Designed to be read with Robin Skelton's Penguin anthology, *Poetry of the Thirties*, this is an admirable critical approach which will be of value far beyond its intended readership.

Paul Volsik approaches 'Poèmes du corps/corps du poème dans l'oeuvre poétique de Dylan Thomas' (in Brugière). This perceptive article examines the ambivalence in the poet's attitude to his own body and those of others, especially women; the polarized images of the foetus and the cancerous growth; and the linguistic duality that results from these oppositions. Philip A. Lahey's 'Dylan Thomas: A Reappraisal' (CS 5.53–65) is largely a summary of recent critical approaches, but also looks at 'The force that through the green fuse' and 'Altarwise by owl-light'. It does little to resolve the split between biographical and textual approaches and its conclusion is facile: 'Poetic inspiration and dedicated craftsmanship are the qualities which shine through all that is most permanent in his achievement and testify to his gift as a truly lyrical poet'. If this is aimed at insecure undergraduates, I offer them my usual advice: read the poems and think about them.

(b)   Poetry – Post-1950

Arguably the year's most important and undoubtedly the most publicized and controversial contribution to the understanding of post-war British poetry was neither a learned article, a scholarly monograph nor an academic book, but rather a short, 14-page introduction to a popular poetry anthology. The anthology was, of course, *The New Poetry*, edited by Michael Hulse, David Kennedy and David Morley, who set out with the intention of showcasing work 'written by a generation of British and Irish writers who began writing or came to prominence in the 1980s and early 1990s', but who in the process, in the time-honoured tradition of such anthologies (Yeats's 1936 *Oxford Book of Modern Verse*, Alvarez's own 1962 *The New Poetry*, Motion and Morrison's 1982 *Penguin Book of Contemporary British Poetry*) offered a contentious assessment of the state of contemporary poetry. In their introduction to the anthology Hulse, Kennedy and Morley claim to have identified an over-arching tradition in recent poetry which derives from Ashbery, Auden, Elizabeth Bishop and Derek Mahon and whose distinguishing features include 'accessibility, democracy and responsiveness, humour and seriousness'. Furthermore, having identified this tradition, they feel confident to announce 'the beginning of the end of British poetry's tribal divisions and isolation, and a new cohesiveness'.

The New Poetry was significant not just for its accurate, or at least partly accurate, delineation of a hitherto unidentified poetic tradition (Ashbery, Auden and Bishop yes, but Mahon?), but also for the spirited debate it sparked off in the media about the nature and direction of post-war poetry, not a subject which usually fills column inches or airwaves (a comprehensive account of the controversies, debates and discussions aroused by the publication of the book can be found in '*The New Poetry*: A Symposium', *PoetryR* 83.ii.3–33). With its apparently contrary urges towards summary conclusiveness on the one hand and the championing of plurality and diversity on the other, the book was also indicative of a general tendency in 1990s' literary criticism towards a rather muddle-headed all-inclusiveness and the beginning of inevitable *fin de siècle* summings-up.

One example of the pre-millennial anxiety to put the record straight was Robert Hampson and Peter Barry's *New British Poetries: The Scope of the Possible*, whose allusive Poundian subtitle provides some indication of its own scope and bias, but which specifically concerns 'that area of poetic production that developed in the 1970s and 1980s in poetry readings, performances, and … small press and little magazine activity'. The book is divided into three sections, 'Mapping the Field', 'Poetics: Politics: Procedures' and 'Case Studies', each containing three essays, the most successful of which are, surprisingly, the most general: the late Eric Mottram's 'The British Poetry Revival, 1960–75', Fred D'Aguiar's 'Have You Been Here Long? Black Poetry in Britain' and Roger Ellis's 'Mapping the UK Little Magazine Field'.

Mottram's is a typically invigorating diatribe against the 'establishment restrictors' and 'agents of information and distribution' who, he claims, have prevented recent British *avant-garde* poetry from being published and popularized. With daemonic energy Mottram examines anthologies, magazines and the 'officially-sanctioned' British poetry institutions in an attempt to support his contention that those he terms 'poets of the Revival', (including Allen Fisher, Lee Harwood, Tom Raworth and Tom Pickard) have been systematically excluded by the poetry establishment and consequently ignored by the poetry-reading public. As ever, Mottram's rhetoric outstrips his argument, which would be more convincing if the alternative poetries that he promotes were not often deliberately, determinedly and quite happily marginal and marginalized. In his essay, in contrast, Fred D'Aguiar argues in more measured tones and with a range of historical reference (he begins with Phyllis Wheatley and ends with Amryl Johnson) that 'poets of a particular age, class, and locality, often have more in common in terms of their craft and themes, whatever racial differences may obtain, than poets of the same race who belong to a different generation and class and live at opposite ends of the country'. This is in itself hardly a novel claim but it leads D'Aguiar to his radical conclusion that work by black poets should therefore be seen as 'at the centre of what is happening in poetry in Britain'. Where Mottram is loudly argumentative and D'Aguiar is quietly irrefutable, Roger Ellis is fascinating and confused in his attempt to define the role and ambitions of Britain's numerous *avant-garde* poetry magazines, from *joe soap's canoe* to *Grosseteste Review*. Ellis's argument swerves between the abstract and the anecdotal, but his conclusion is surprisingly simple, if not actually simplistic: 'The point of the little magazine, potentially, is to teach us how not to "shut up". If a little magazine (to risk a pun) *realises* this, it has succeeded'.

Ellis's account was in fact superseded during the course of the year by Wolfgang Gortschacher's massive PhD-style *Little Magazine Profiles: The Little Magazines in Great Britain 1939–1993*, published by the University of Salzburg Press but available in Britain only by mail-order through Stride Publications. Unlike Ellis, Gortschacher attempts a comprehensive history of the little magazine in post-war Britain, providing a conceptual 'Phenomenology of the Little Magazine', an overview 'History of the Little Magazines 1939-1993' and a number of case studies, consisting of interviews with poetry magazine editors (including both the Michaels, Horovitz and Schmidt, Peter Dale, Kathleen Raine and William and Patricia Oxley) and detailed descriptive evaluations of several magazines. Gortschacher's prose style is at times strained and hard to follow, his conclusions occasionally wayward, and there do seem to be a number of factual errors, but for those wanting to put Mottram's accounts of the 'poetry wars' of the early 1970s in context or indeed for anyone wanting to know more about the recent history of the publication and reception of poetry in Britain, *Little Magazine Profiles* is an invaluable, if eccentric, reference guide.

A reference guide of an altogether different nature was Neil Corcoran's *English Poetry since 1940*, part of the much-praised Longman Literature in English Series. One reviewer accurately described Corcoran's book as 'half the book it could and should have been', an unfortunate state of affairs in part due to the nature of the Longman Series itself, which is designed as a comprehensive multi-volume student guide to literature in its 'historical and cultural contexts', a vague but ambitious aim which, as is the case with Corcoran's book, can lead to a foreshortening of argument in favour of mere summary and circumstantial detail. It does not help that Corcoran is deliberately uncontroversial in his approach and apologetic about his preferences: in his rather prissy introduction he lays claim to both a formalist and historicist methodology and makes the disclaimer that 'However much I insist on the diversity and plurality of my own narrative here, it is *my* narrative: the narrative, that is to say, of a white, middle-class male academic'.

The book does nevertheless contain a few shocks and surprises – there is a rare, fair-minded treatment of J. H. Prynne, for example, and a discussion of the much neglected poetry of Denise Riley – and Corcoran almost begins provocatively with his chapter titled 'Eliot or Auden', in which he measures the achievements of the two great poets and argues that they offer 'opposed models for other poets of the period', although he assiduously avoids concluding which model has proved the most popular (the answer, surely, is Auden's). Corcoran divides the post-Eliot and Auden period into decade-sized chunks, with sections titled 'From the Forties', 'From the Fifties', and so on, and he then groups poets together into themed, wittily-titled chapters ('Barbarians and Rhubarbarians: Douglas Dunn and Tony Harrison', 'A Pen Mislaid: Some Varieties of Women's Poetry'). He is undoubtedly at his best on the poetry written earlier in the period – he has an excellent chapter on David Jones and Basil Bunting – but he is also good when commenting in detail on any poem, which he tries to do for each poet under discussion, and even the short introductory overviews that preface each section are not without interest. It is, however, a book of lowered sights and patiently diminished expectations, or as Corcoran himself puts it, of 'hesitations, anxieties and provisionalities'; perhaps this is what makes it such a good introductory guide to post-war British poetry.

An overview which managed to be pluralist, partial and patrician all at the same time was Robert Crawford's *Identifying Poets: Self and Territory in Twentieth-Century Poetry*. The book is an extension of Crawford's project in *Devolving English Literature* (*YWES* 73.278, 528) and seeks to establish Scottish poetry as 'essential rather than peripheral to the development of poetry in the century now ending'. To this end, Crawford traces how a number of poets, particularly the Scots, MacDiarmid and Sorley Maclean, but also others including Les Murray, John Ashbery and Frank Kuppner create identities for themselves in their poetry 'which let them be identified with, re-state, and even renovate the identity of a particular territory'. Crawford argues that this process of identification is a central feature of modernity and that the notion of the 'identifying poet' is therefore a useful one, not least because 'The term "identifying poet" has about it none of the covert cultural imperialism that too easily attends words like "regional", "provincial", or even "national"'. He begins by making some rather grand theoretical claims that are not fully subsumed into his readings of particular poets, predicting, for example, that Mikhail Bakhtin 'will become the dominant, certainly the most attractive literary theorist of the 1990s' because his concept of 'dialogized heteroglossia' provides the key to understanding the 'crossings of territorial and linguistic boundaries' that characterize contemporary poetry (a prediction seemingly borne out by the evidence of Ian Gregson's modishly Bakhtinian piece, 'Your Voice Speaking in my Poems: Polyphony in Fleur

Adcock' [*English* 42.174. 239–51]). The close readings and the theory do not, however, come together convincingly until the final chapter, 'Home', in which Crawford examines the use of dialect and heteroglot language in work by numerous poets including Norman MacCaig, David Dabydeen, Peter Reading, Tom Leonard and Crawford's friend and collaborator, the brilliant young Dundonian W. N. Herbert. Crawford has become the panjandrum of English literary studies in Scotland and as those who are familiar with his earlier work will recognize and appreciate, he makes up for in lucidity, sympathy and range what he sometimes lacks in sophistication.

The same cannot be said for Linden Peach who, in his *Ancestral Lines: Culture and Identity in the Work of Six Contemporary Poets*, makes a similar point to Crawford, that 'Much of our most exciting poetry is being written away from the economic and cultural centre, at the geographical margins', and goes on to complain that this phenomenon 'has only been partly recognised by critics'. Peach attempts to fill the gap with his study of what he calls 'the tripartite theme of ancestry, culture and identity' in the work of six poets from the so-called 'geographical margins', but there is a sense throughout the book, particularly in the chapters on Heaney, Harrison and Dunn that he is fighting battles that have already been won. The book's one truly pioneering chapter, 'Igniting Pent Silences', examines the poetry of the English-language Welsh writers Gillian Clarke, Oliver Reynolds and Sally Roberts Jones. In bringing these poets to the attention of a wider audience, Peach does perform a valuable critical service.

An altogether more convincing plea for attention to the margins comes in Clair Wills's *Improprieties: Politics and Sexuality in Northern Irish Poetry* which, compared to Peach and even to Crawford, is almost ludicrously ambitious in its aims, claiming to attend to 'the relation between poetry and politics in contemporary Northern Ireland; the limits of Enlightenment and Romantic perspectives on Northern Irish culture; the role of myth in definitions of the political (with particular reference to the myth of the motherland); the division between public and private spheres of social activity, and the strategies adopted by women poets in order to combat its debilitating effects; the controversy over claims for the specificity of Irish cultural experience embedded in language and dialect; postmodern arguments about the nature of political violence'. And that's just Part I. In Part II Wills addresses these issues as they occur in works by Tom Paulin, Medbh McGuckian and Paul Muldoon. The 'impropriety' of the book's title refers to the experience 'of being inside and outside the project of modernity at the same time', an experience that Wills claims is common to Northern Irish poets. Again, in some respects this thesis reminds one of Crawford's notion of the Bakhtinian 'identifying poet' (clearly something of a catch-all), although Wills is in fact far more eclectic theoretically, a kind of feminist Eagletonian, sometimes afflicted with an irritating jargon. For all its pretensions the real achievement of the book is its careful attention to detail, with Wills particularly good at unravelling the entanglements of Paulin's politics and aesthetics and outstandingly good in her close readings of McGuckian – her analyses of the notoriously difficult poems in McGuckian's *The Flower Master*, *Venus and the Rain*, *On Ballycastle Beach* and *Marconi's Cottage* are exemplary, and in some cases (her explication of 'Venus and the Rain' for example) seem unsurpassable. Muldoon alone seems to escape her grasp, as he has escaped so many.

Generally, the year's round-ups and theoretical accounts, for all their efforts, were less impressive and less effective than those books and articles which directed attention to the work of individual poets, both the neglected and the notorious. Not the least impressive of these was *Roy Fuller: A Tribute*, edited by A. T. Tolley, fortuitously published to coincide with Fuller's posthumous *Last Poems*. The book is an odd mix of poems, essays and a disappointingly sketchy bibliography (which for scholarly purposes would need to be supplemented by Steven Escar Smith's checklist in *BB* [1990] 47.iii.163–6), but like any good tribute it amounts to more than the sum of its parts, and ultimately stands as powerful testimony to Fuller's achievements; certainly, it is the most substantial gathering of critical and appreciative work on Fuller since his death in 1991. The essays by Bernard Bergonzi, 'The Poet in Wartime', and Julian Symons, 'The Enterprise of St Mary's Bay', are predictably intelligent and entertaining, whilst Christopher Levenson is surprisingly readable in a much-needed essay on 'Roy Fuller and Syllabic Verse', and even Tolley himself, a critic renowned more for being thorough than for being inspiring, is interesting and illuminating on Fuller's manuscripts, in 'Fuller's Earth: Delving into the Notebooks'. None of the essays, however, quite achieve the descriptive accuracy of Peter Reading's short poem, 'For Roy Fuller', in which Reading successfully reconstructs the Fuller voice: *'Too much is wrong, Gibbonian undertones,/ schooling and bread and dress and manners,/ era's decline, Elgarian sadness'*. Would that all critical summaries could be so eloquent, and so brief.

Another old worthy who received much deserved critical attention was R. S. Thomas, with the year seeing the publication of the second edition of *Critical Writings on R. S. Thomas*, edited by Sandra Anstey (which added seven new essays to the original 1982 volume as well as an updated bibliography) and the publication of *The Page's Drift: R. S. Thomas at Eighty*, edited by M. Wynn Thomas. In his battling introduction, Wynn Thomas makes great claims for R. S. Thomas and condemns those critics who have subjected Thomas to 'critical condescension'. Unfortunately, some of the book's essayists substitute complacency for condescension, with Anne Stevenson and Helen Vendler the notable exceptions, both managing to combine criticism with enthusiasm in their outstanding essays on 'The Uses of Prytherch', in which Stevenson neatly summarizes Thomas's career, and 'R. S. Thomas and Painting', in which Vendler skilfully analyses and explains Thomas's painting-poems in his collections *Between Here and Now* and *Ingrowing Thoughts*.

Stevenson's own poetry undergoes scrutiny in a serious and celebratory essay, 'Better fame: the poetry of Anne Stevenson' (*PNR* 19.v.30–4), in which Chris McCully uses some simple linguistics to undo and unpack the mysteries of her verse: thus, he identifies in Stevenson's early work 'two presentational modes', 'the one lacking, or relatively lacking in finite (tensed) verbs, thus foregrounding nominal grouping, the other fully equipped with finite verbs, and thus discursive'. McCully is clearly something of an expert in prosody and the history and theory of language, but he wears his learning lightly and leads the reader gently through his discussion of 'modes' and 'clines' towards his profound conclusion that Stevenson's is 'a poetry that lies forever just out of reach of the feminism that might have tried (or might still try) to appropriate it'. It is prac crit as it should be writ.

The year's most welcome celebration had to be the bumper *IUR* Eavan Boland special issue (23.i), which, as well as the expected assortment of academic assessments, also contained wonderful anecdotal essays by Derek Mahon and Medbh McGuckian, a new long poem by Boland (the magnificent 'Anna Liffey'), an interview, and an extraordinarily long and thorough checklist compiled by Jody Allen-Randolph (which acted as a timely reminder that Boland is a polemicist and journalist as well as a poet, although one was reminded anyway during the course of the year by Boland's article 'The Serinette Principle: The Lyric in Contemporary Poetry' [*PNR* 19.iv.20–6]). The critical essays manage to hold their own, just, against the fascinating biographical and bibliographical material, by being carefully co-ordinated in approach, methodically covering each of Boland's collections in turn (Terence Brown on *The War Horse*, Mary O'Donnell and Sylvia Kelly on *In Her Own Image*, Patricia Boyle Haberstroh on *Night Feed*, Augustine Martin on *The Journey*, R. T. Smith on *Outside History*). Sadly, the underrating of Boland's work is of such long standing that it will take more than one worthy *festschrift* to make up for it.

Another triumphant, or at least triumphalist omnigatherum was *Liz Lochhead's Voices*, edited by Robert Crawford and Anne Varty, a further instalment in EdinUP's Modern Scottish Writers Series, whose backlist already includes authoritative studies of MacDiarmid, Edwin Morgan, Norman MacCaig, Iain Crichton Smith and Douglas Dunn. Crawford and Varty rightly claim that theirs is a significant contribution to the series not just because it is 'the first substantial study of Liz Lochhead's work' but also because it is 'one of the few books devoted to the work of a Scottish woman writer'. 'Writer' is a key word here, since the essays on Lochhead's plays are both more numerous and more interesting than the essays on her poetry, with only the indefatigable Crawford, on 'The Two-faced Language of Lochhead's Poetry', and Dorothy Porter McMillan on 'Liz Lochhead and the Ungentle Art of Clyping' managing to convey any real enthusiasm for Lochhead's verse. The saving grace, despite its modest disclaimer of incompleteness, is an excellent checklist by Hamish Whyte.

Any oversights or inadequacies hardly mattered, however, since evidence for the ascendancy of the Scots continued to pile up throughout the year, in Whyte's own short essay, '"Now you see it, now you don't"; The Love Poetry of Edwin Morgan' (*The Glasgow Review* 2.82–93), in Colin Nicholson's *Poem, Purpose and Place: Shaping Identity in Contemporary Scottish Verse*, a collection of interviews with 14 Scottish poets (including the venerable Naomi Mitchison), and also in the magazine *Agenda*, which began the year with a Tom Scott special double issue (30.iv–31.i.), much to be welcomed in the year which also saw the publication of Scott's *Collected Shorter Poems*, containing the full text of his magnificent *The Ship*, a poem not available since OUP's 1963 *The Ship and Ither Poems*. The Scott issue contains essays by Kathleen Raine, W. S. Milne, William Oxley and others, with Milne's panegyric perhaps the most extraordinary, full of wild praise for Scott's 'dirges, memorials, translations, epigrams, epistles, dramas, satires, essays, critical books, religious poems, marriage poems, epitaphs, classical visions, *Scottish poems*' and concluding with the extravagant assertion that 'After Hugh MacDiarmid, Tom Scott is probably the greatest poet (certainly the finest translator) in Scots this century'.

Agenda followed the successful Scott issue with a rather rag-bag effort entitled 'The Sixties Reconsidered' (31.ii), which contained workmanlike essays by Colin Falck ('From Sixties to Nineties') and Robert Richardson ('Concrete Poetry: An Assessment'), but was probably most remarkable for managing to bring Ian Hamilton and Michael Horovitz together between the same covers. 'Ian Hamilton in conversation with Peter Dale' provided a few interesting details about the history of Hamilton's infamous but influential magazine *The Review*, whilst Michael Horovitz's 'New Departures' degenerated into a rant against the 'monetarist millennium of stagnant hype conveyed via the Interdependent Fabber-Chatup n' Windon machinations of the Cranedrawn Moribreed (Craig Raine, Andrew Motion, B. Morrison, C. Reid & Sons plc)'. The most unusual contribution to what was anyway an eccentric issue was the essay by Patricia McCarthy entitled 'Three Poets: Anne Sexton, Penelope Palmer and Pauline Stainer', in which McCarthy argues that 'These three poets are all concerned with death – and life, with problematic relationships, with music, art and religion – and are all linked by the repeated use of red'.

Quirkiness continued in Andrew Thacker's 'Imagist travels in modernist space' (*Tpr* 7. 224–46), which was mainly concerned with some Imagist poems that, according to Thacker, illustrate 'early twentieth century visual relations as experienced on transport', but which in passing raised the interesting question of the meaning of the success of London Transport's 'Poems on the Underground' project. According to Thacker, the London Transport display 'points to the stress placed upon visual experience across the spaces of present-day urban life', but as one of the only sites in which the general public comes into contact with contemporary poetry, 'Poems on the Underground' could provide much more material for further study.

Aside from the fripperies and the fringes, the usual critical attentions were being paid to the great and the good. Michael Parker's stated aim in his *Seamus Heaney: The Making of the Poet* was 'to identify and analyse the biographical, literary, historical and political influences and experiences that have shaped the poetry of Seamus Heaney', and despite the occasional lapse into mere anecdote and gush he was entirely successful, dividing Heaney's career to date into six definite periods, 'A Good Anchor: Home and Education, 1939–61', 'Affinities, 1961–66', 'Pioneer, 1966–69', 'Exposure, 1969–75', 'Quickenings, 1975–84', 'Space, 1984–91', and working quickly and thoroughly through the major collections. The only worrying aspect of this otherwise admirable project is that it was another contribution to what is already a strong bias towards the historical and the biographical in criticisms of Heaney's work.

The same bias has always been apparent of course in criticism on Sylvia Plath, and Janice Markey's *A Journey into the Red Eye: The Poetry of Sylvia Plath – A Critique* continued the trend by taking a biographical and thematic approach to Plath's poetry (although with a nice nineties twist: Markey argues that Plath had a 'strong, humanist concern' for 'the preservation of all life' and was interested in the environment).

If anything, criticism on Geoffrey Hill has tended towards the other extreme, with critics eschewing the biographical for the purely technical, and in this respect Andrew Michael Roberts's essay 'Variation and False Relation in Geoffrey Hill's *Tenebrae*' (*EIC* 43.123–43) is good and typical of its kind. Roberts suggests analogies between certain musical devices and certain rhetorical structures in Hill's poetry, arguing, for example, that in the first part of *Tenebrae*, 'The Pentecost Castle', Hill's reliance upon 'recurrent unresolved ambiguity and paradox' deliberately resembles patterns of so-called musical 'variation' (defined by *The New Grove Dictionary of Music and Musicians* as 'a form in which successive statements of a theme are altered or presented in altered settings'), whilst in the second part of *Tenebrae*, 'Lachrimae or Seven teares figured in seven passionate Pavans' the puns and oxymorons are analogous to the musical trope of 'false relation' (defined by the *New Grove* as 'a chromatic contradiction between two notes of the same chord ... or in different parts of adjacent chords'). Such subtle analogymongering is never wholly convincing, as Roberts himself recognizes, but the approach does yield some valuable insights, particularly into Hill's use of paradox and pastiche.

Avril Horner's 'The "Intelligence at Bay": Ezra Pound and Geoffrey Hill' (*Paideuma* 22.i–ii.243–54) is a compacted and clod-hopping piece of work in comparison, pursuing the relatively straightforward argument that 'Hill's work should be seen, like that of David Jones and Basil Bunting, as a continuation of Pound's thought within the English tradition'. Horner uses Hill's poetry and prose to illustrate her main point that his 'sense of estrangement from the present moment' is, like Pound's, a position both of 'vulnerability' and of 'strength'. The essay prefers to tot up examples rather than making any attempt to explore or analyse them, but it is undoubtedly an original piece of work, since for some reason Hill's debt to Pound has until now remained uncharted territory.

A thoroughly well-ploughed area of critical investigation, in contrast, is Ted Hughes's reliance on myth and history, a subject turned over once again during the course of the year by David Gervais in 'Ted Hughes: An England Beneath England' (*English* 42.45–73). Gervais claims that 'England has not been enough' for Hughes and he demonstrates how in his poetry Hughes elides history into myth. Gervais concludes that 'There are things in England which are more than simply English and it is part of Hughes's achievement to have recognised this at a time when some English writers still assume that what is English is also universal'. Mohan G. Ramanan argues the complete opposite in his essay, '"The voice of authority": A Theme in Contemporary English Poetry' (*CS* 5.i.34–44), grouping Hughes together with Kingsley Amis, Philip Larkin, Donald Davie, Charles Tomlinson and Heaney and accusing them all of glossing over 'the divisions in class-ridden British society by pretending that things are just the same as they were' and accusing Hughes in particular of attempting 'to impose, through violence, and the masculine energy of his rhythms, a myth about England'. Gervais has the better of the argument, but this is a debate, one feels, that will run and run.

Finally, as if to reassure those who might be doubting that contemporary poetry can deal with matters of real substance and consequence, the publication of *Klaonica: Poems for Bosnia*, edited by Ken Smith and Judi Benson, stimulated a vigorous debate in *PoetryR* (see, for example, 83.iv.44–5) about poetry's public role. The last word should go to Smith: 'I hoped to challenge the powerlessness most of us are encouraged to feel, and to demonstrate that poetry can have a practical use when directed to a particular end. That merely. The result was *Klaonica*, for better or for worse, and funds raised for *Feed the Children*'s work in that part of the world. I rest my case. To hell with political correctness'.

3. Drama

This section has two categories: (a) General Studies; (b) Individual Authors, in alphabetical order. Coverage of film and television is confined to works by writers with a substantial theatrical reputation. An author who is considered in a general work and is the subject of an individual study may appear in both sections. *MD* (36) should be consulted for Linda Corman and Charles A. Carpenter's annual bibliography, and *LTR* for reprints of reviews of current London productions.

(a)   General Studies
The New Woman and Her Sisters: Feminism and Theatre 1850–1914, edited by
Viv Gardner and Susan Rutherford, is a very significant contribution to our
understanding of some of the cross currents in the representation of women in
theatre in the early years of the century. The essays cover a wide range of topics
(including female singers, dare-devils, and female Hamlets) but those of particular relevance to this section include Gardner's effective delineation of the whole
subject in the introduction, Sheila Stowell's 'Drama as a Trade: Cicely Hamilton's *Diana of Dobson's*', which is to be found in extended form in Stowell's own
A Stage of Their Own (*YWES* 73.539), Elaine Aston's enlightening 'The "New
Woman" at Manchester's Gaiety Theatre', which examines the plays presented
under Annie Horniman's management in terms of their subject matter and their
reception, and Christine Dymkowski's 'Entertaining Ideas: Edy Craig and the
Pioneer Players' which skilfully uses their first production in 1911 as an index to
a whole range of contemporary attitudes to the 'New Woman'.

It is always particularly welcome when a gap in our knowledge is filled and
Steve Nicholson's 'Theatrical Pageants in the Second World War' (*TRI* 18.186–
96) is an exemplary account of how pro-Soviet pageants deriving from the
traditions of the Workers' Theatre Movement, Unity, and Theatre of Action, were
at once promoted but also limited in scope by the British government during the
war. This is a fascinating illustrated account, centring on the Louis MacNeice
scripted pageant *Salute to the Red Army* (1943). Many of the issues which arise
here are considered in the context of developments some 40 years later in Baz
Kershaw's two linked pieces in *NTQ* on aspects of the relationship between
funding and artistic activity. In 'Poaching in Thatcherland: A Case of Radical
Community Theatre' (34. 121–33) he uses a case study of the company EMMA
to investigate what Terry Eagleton has called the 'performative contradictions'
which emerge when 'an oppositional cultural formation struggles to muster a
coherent response to intensified hegemonic domination'. In the second essay,
'Building an Unstable Pyramid: The Fragmentation of British Alternative Theatre' (*NTQ* 36.341–56) he extends this account through a comparative analysis of
a small-scale 'reminiscence theatre' group and the better known Joint Stock. This
is an important discussion of the industrial and institutional parameters of
alternative theatre productions in the seventies and eighties. The problem, as he
puts it, was that 'the facilitative functions of state funding were the positive side
of a bureaucratic process which was increasingly also about cultural annexation
and control' and 'the image of a harmonious nationally co-ordinated funding
system for the arts was constructed in the face of acute conflicts between regional
and national interests'. This meant that when the government changed in 1979,
the structures were already in place for the decimation of companies that followed. As I know, from personal experience with the Foco Novo Company, this
account is only too accurate.

Also of interest in *NTQ*, and reflecting its eclectic interests, are Geraldine
Cousin's useful account of the Footsbarn Theatre Company, 'Footsbarn: From a
Tribal *Macbeth* to an Intercultural *Dream*' (33.16–30), Nina Rapi's brief medi-
tations on her own work and plays by Sarah Daniels, Holly Hughes, Caroline
Griffin and Maro Green, and Jackie Kay under the title 'Hide and Seek: The
Search for a Lesbian Theatre Aesthetic' (34.147–58), Christine Hardy's informa-
tive 'Keen Edge in Sheffield: Towards a Popular Political Theatre and Cabaret'
(35.233–45), and Graham Ley's careful 'The Rhetoric of Theory: The Role of
Metaphor in [Peter] Brook's *The Empty Space*' (35.246–54).

There are a number of books on aspects of contemporary drama. James Acheson has edited a collection of new introductory essays to 15 modern dramatists under the title *British and Irish Drama since 1960*. All the essays – on Howard Barker, Samuel Beckett, Edward Bond, Howard Brenton, Caryl Churchill, Brian Friel, Pam Gems, David Hare, Tony Harrison, Tom Murphy, Peter Nichols, Harold Pinter, Peter Shaffer, Tom Stoppard, and Timberlake Wertenbaker – offer useful introductions to their work, while John Fletcher takes the most provocative position in his essay on Pinter with his suggestion that Vivien Merchant may have been as much Pinter's muse as his wife. Michelene Wandor's short *Drama Today: A Critical Guide to British Drama 1970–1990* suffers from attempting to balance too many competing demands in a brief compass. As always, she has interesting things to say about the socio-political contexts in which the theatrical activity she covers was created but her discussions of works by 16 dramatists and one company in some 50 pages are too truncated to offer more than the sketchiest introductions to their work.

One notable feature of Wandor's work has always been the attention she pays to women in theatre, and her pioneering work on contemporary British drama is gradually being supplemented by such works as Lizbeth Goodman's *Contemporary Feminist Theatres* (and her 'Feminist Theatre in Britain: A Survey and a Prospect', *NTQ* 33.66–84) and my own and Margaret Llewellyn-Jones's *British and Irish Women Dramatists Since 1958: A Critical Handbook*. Goodman has based her work on extensive surveys and interviews with practitioners and covers both organizational and aesthetic issues since 1968; Griffiths and Llewellyn-Jones cover a longer time span and pay separate attention to Ireland, Wales and Scotland with the help of their contributors (April de Angelis, Rose Collis, Susan Croft, Anna McMullan, Susan Triesman, and Lib Taylor). Both works have been recognized as significant contributions to recording and analysing the work of women in theatre. George W. Brandt has edited a collection of essays on *British Television Drama in the 1980s* which deals admirably with some of the key productions of the period. Dramatists with a substantial stage output whose television work is considered here include Alan Bennett, Alan Bleasdale, Charles Wood, Mike Leigh, John Byrne, and A. E. Whitehead.

There are also some significant contributions to the study of such topics as the thriller, adaptation for stage and screen, and staging the fantastic. In *Deathtraps: The Postmodern Comedy Thriller*, Marvin Carlson has produced a multivalent study of not only his title subject but the whole stage thriller genre, which has been little considered in academic criticism. Fully informed by contemporary critical theory, Carlson is able to delineate his territory and analyse its conventions and generic expectations with great skill. From the point of view of this section of *YWES*, the book's one organizational limitation is that the author does not always indicate whether he is dealing with British or American plays. This links to my other reservation that Carlson may not have paid sufficient attention to the cultural differences between the British and American manifestations of the genre. Nevertheless, this is an impressive and illuminating study which rescues Anthony Shaffer and Francis Durbridge in particular from the critical limbo to which they are often confined. Carlson's essay 'Is There a Real Inspector Hound? Mousetraps, Deathtraps, and the Disappearing Detective' (*MD* 36.431–42) complements his book.

Novel Images: Literature in Performance, a collection of essays on adaptations for stage and screen edited by Peter Reynolds, includes several essays on specific authors which are discussed below; Christopher Innes's 'Adapting Dickens to the Modern Eye' includes a brief discussion of David Edgar's version of *Nicholas Nickleby*. Patrick D. Murphy's wide ranging collection of essays *Staging the Impossible: The Fantastic Mode in Modern Drama* includes an insightful introduction by Murphy himself and some general essays on the whole issue of the fantastic in modern drama, and an annotated select bibliography of science fiction plays, Susan Taylor Jacobs's 'When Formula Seizes Form: Oscar Wilde's Comedies' and Lance Olsen's 'Beckett and the Horrific'.

Theoretically focused studies include Iain Mackintosh's *Architecture, Actor and Audience*, an important contribution to our understanding of how theatres work as playing spaces, written by an author whose own role in the creation of actual theatre buildings has been highly significant. Contributors to Julian Hilton's collection of essays on *New Directions in Theatre*, a significant contribution to the theoretical debates about the nature of theatre studies, include Denis Calandra and Patrice Pavis, while topics considered include Carnival, Hermeneutics, the aesthetics of Reception, Catharsis, and technology.

Essays on Irish drama include Jochen Achilles's 'Religious Risk in Contemporary Irish Drama' (*Éire* 28.iii.116–28). This is a thoughtful account of plays by Thomas Murphy, Thomas Kilroy, Brian Friel and Frank McGuinness, which leads him to the conclusion that 'The more precarious and paradoxical the relationship between the world and its potential redemption appears, the more original, fresh, and brilliant the artistic responses of Irish playwrights seem to become, thus transforming an ossified religious tradition into a living and personal faith'. Maria R. DiCenzo's 'Charabanc Theatre Company: Placing Women Center-Stage in Northern Ireland' (*TJ* 45.175–84) is an important exposition of the work of an innovative company that has never been given the recognition its work deserves.

Two general essays do not fit in elsewhere very easily. Marybeth Inverso's '*Der Straf-block*: Performance and Execution in Barnes, Griffiths, and Wertenbaker' (*MD* 36.420–30) notes the presence of punishment, executions and threats of executions in *Laughter, Red Noses, Comedians*, and *Our Country's Good* but does not develop a significant analysis from her observations. In 'Three recent versions of the *Bacchae*' (*TD* 15.217–28), Elizabeth Hale Winkler examines Maureen Duffy's *Rites*, Caryl Churchill and David Lan's *A Mouthful of Birds* and Wole Soyinka's *The Bacchae of Euripides*. Her discussion of Maureen Duffy's relatively neglected play is particularly welcome and illuminating.

Hersh Zeifman and Cynthia Zimmerman have selected 21 essays previously printed in *MD* in *Contemporary British Drama, 1970–90*. Writers covered include Harold Pinter, Peter Shaffer, Edward Bond, Alan Ayckbourn, Christopher Hampton, David Storey, Tom Stoppard, Simon Gray, Trevor Griffiths, Caryl Churchill and Howard Brenton. There are also more general essays on aspects of socialist drama and television drama as well as a select bibliography. Perhaps the most interesting aspect of the volume is the introduction, in which Zeifman draws attention to the fact that the editors of *MD* had never had a submission on the work of Howard Barker, nor many on recent women dramatists except for Churchill; an interesting example of canon formation in operation.

I have not seen J. P. Wearing's *The London Stage 1950–59* (Scarecrow), but if it is anything like the quality of its predecessors it will be an indispensable research tool.

(b) Individual Authors

J. R. Ackerley remains an unfamiliar name, so John M. Clum's ' "Myself of Course": J. R. Ackerley and Self-Dramatization' (*Theater* 24.76–87) is a pertinent account of how the concerns of his play *The Prisoners of War* (1925), claimed as the century's first gay play, intertwine with his self dramatization through autobiography.

It is becoming increasingly difficult to create hard and fast rules about the placing of dramatists within this section, as the case of Karim Alrawi demonstrates. Susan Carlson's 'Collaboration, Identity, and Cultural Difference: Karim Alrawi's Theatre of Engagement' (*TJ* 45.155–73) is an informative account of the work of this Egyptian-born, sometimes English domiciled dramatist who was active with Joint Stock in its last years. The essay is full of significant information about both the last years of Joint Stock that complements Baz Kershaw's account, and about Alrawi's subsequent career in Egypt and the USA.

Linda Fitzsimmons's 'Typewriters Enchained: The work of Elizabeth Baker' (Gardner and Rutherford) is an explicatory account of a neglected dramatist, exploring the feminist focus of her work with a particular concentration on *Chains*. Fitzsimmons's work complements Rudolf Weiss's (*YWES* 71.518) and Stowell's in *A Stage of Their Own* (*YWES* 73.539), although neither Stowell nor Fitzsimmons seems to be aware of Weiss's essay.

Critics continue to display little interest in Edward Bond, so Jenny S. Spencer's *Dramatic Strategies in the Plays of Edward Bond* is particularly welcome. Spencer has always been an acute critic of Bond and her book explores his work up to *The War Plays*. She includes some informative material on the reception of the plays' original productions but her greatest strength lies in her capacity to tease out the nuances of his dramatic practice in a sustained and coherent reading. Her final words sum up the dilemma with Bond very well: 'Whether Bond's plays will provide a productive model [...] for a younger generation of politically committed artists, or whether they will remain no more than an illustration of the historical contradictions they embody, is important work for future audiences to decide'. At this moment it seems doubtful if those audiences will be found in the professional theatres of Great Britain.

Howard Brenton and Tariq Ali seem to have really annoyed Carl Caulfield by not writing the play about Perestroika and Glasnost that he thinks they should have written. In '*Moscow Gold* and Reassessing History' (*MD* 36.490–8) he berates them for all manner of shortcomings before concluding that 'In its historical and dramatic inadequacies, *Moscow Gold* reflects a continuing need for the British left to rise to the challenge of *glasnost* and move beyond naïve and schematic Marxist analytical frameworks'. This seems a rather inadequate account of the play.

Interest in Caryl Churchill remains strong. Amelia Howe Kritzer suggests in 'Madness and Political Change in the Plays of Caryl Churchill' (*TD* 15.203–16) that 'Madness is shown as a means through which one may throw off the oppressive blinders kept in place by patriarchal social structures and for once experience a new way of seeing not controlled by social conditioning. Through altered states of consciousness one may find the possibility of alternative political states'. This thesis is successfully pursued in useful analyses not only of the familiar *Softcops* and *A Mouthful of Birds* but also of the less well known *Lovesick*, *Schreber's Nervous Illness*, and *The Hospital at the Time of the Revolution*. In 'Caryl Churchill's *Mad Forest*: A Polyphonic Study of Southeastern Europe' (*MD* 36.499–511), Tony Mitchell compares Churchill's play incisively to other attempts to dramatize events in Eastern Europe, such as David Edgar's *The Shape of the Table*, Howard Brenton and Tariq Ali's *Moscow Gold*, and Brenton's *Berlin Bertie*. He persuasively suggests that '*Mad Forest* eschews the "master narratives" of totalizing social-realist paradigms on the one hand and epic pageantry on the other for an open-ended, quasi-cinematic series of cryptic vignettes portraying everyday life in Romania'.

Two contrasting essays on T. S. Eliot in *MD* 36 offer implicitly contradictory readings: in 'Sweeney, Beckett, and the "Marina Figure" in Eliot's Modern Plays' (569–77), Ernest G. Griffin establishes a contrast between the Sweeney and Thomas Beckett figures and traces the emergence of a redemptive figure like Marina in *Pericles*; Laura Severin's much more incisive 'Cutting Philomela's Tongue: *The Cocktail Party*'s Cure for a Disorderly World' (396–408) explores Eliot's attitudes to gender. She suggests that only in this play does it become completely clear 'that Eliot's hierarchical goals extend to gender as well as class' and that it is his most sinister work 'in its war on the educated middle class woman, that "modern woman" whose departure from the home threatened the exclusive rights of such male public spheres as the literary world'. This is an exemplary introduction to a complex issue that demands further examination across Eliot's work.

Graham Holderness picks over some of the issues arising from Christopher Hampton's adaptations of *Les Liaisons Dangereuses* for theatre and film in 'Dangerous Les's Liaisons' (Reynolds). Unusually for this critic, the argument never takes flight and the whole essay remains at the level of prefatory remarks to a potentially interesting discussion.

David Hare gets an easy ride in Georg Gaston's interview (*TJ* 45.214–25). Hare seldom gives interviews so this is an important event. Although the questions cover most of Hare's work and sometimes elicit some interesting points, the interviewer seems very reluctant to press Hare hard on any of the problematic elements in his work.

The generally neglected Deborah Levy benefits from an interview conducted by Irini Charitou who follows it with a very brief introduction to three of her plays (*NTQ* 35.225–9 and 230–2). There is not much room to do more than acknowledge the writer's existence, but it is better than nothing.

Jan McDonald's account of Liz Lochhead's *Dracula* in ' "The Devil is beautiful": *Dracula*: Freudian novel and feminist drama' (Reynolds) offers a nicely judged reading of the ways in which Lochhead opens up the Bram Stoker original and appropriates it for feminism. Readers unfamiliar with the play may find the analysis hard to follow at times, and the discussion might have benefited from a reference to Lochhead's reappropriation of Frankenstein elsewhere.

I have not seen 'Orpheus Descending: Frank McGuinness's *Someone Who'll Watch Over Me*' (*JIL* 23.197–201).

In 'The Theatre of Thomas Murphy and Federico Garcia Lorca' (*MD* 36.481–9), José Lanters traces elements of similarity in the themes and stagecraft of the two writers, following Murphy's own claim that Lorca is his favourite playwright.

I have not seen Bernice Schrank's 'Pastoralism and Progress in O'Casey's *Purple Dust*' (*JIL* 23.236–49).

It is always good to see a challenge to John Lahr's domination of the Orton industry such as Randall S. Nakayama's 'Domesticating Mr Orton' (*TJ* 45.185–95). Nakayama challenges Lahr's conception of Orton's Oedipal shaping, claiming that Orton created 'subversive communities that stand as self-consciously created alternatives to the bourgeois norm of the nuclear family rather than neurotic repetitions of it'. It is a useful supplement to Alan Sinfield's essay (*YWES* 71.523) and Simon Shepherd's book (*YWES* 70.564), but it certainly does not replace them.

Pinter at Sixty, a collection of essays edited by Katherine H. Burkman and John L. Kundert-Gibbs, is distinguished by a number of comparative analyses of Pinter and other writers, essays on his work for television and film, and some allusive free associative streams of consciousness on Pinterian pretexts. Many of the essays circle round Pinter's new found overt politicization, trying to discover a formulation that will offer some kind of coherent explanation of the apparent disjunction between his earlier and less explicit concern with the machineries of power and his later dramatization of totalitarianism. There are, appropriately, two subtexts to the discussion: one, scarcely discernible is the concern that a (politically useful) binary opposition in which Pinter (like Stoppard) could be held up as a positive term in contrast to a group of politically committed dramatists such as Edgar and Brenton will no longer hold water; the second is that the latest plays may not be as good as the earlier ones. Carey Perloff, whose 'Pinter in Rehearsal: From *The Birthday Party* to *Mountain Language*' is a gold mine of useful insights into rehearsal processes and Pinter's own approach to theatre, puts the case diplomatically in her account of hearing Pinter express himself as a 'born-again political activist': 'it is disconcerting to hear these kinds of views expressed by a writer who has until recently so assiduously concealed his personal beliefs beneath a complex web of language. And I am not convinced that *Mountain Language* is a better play for expressing his sentiments so boldly'. It is probably significant that she played the later play as a prelude to the earlier one, offering her audiences a political context within which the less overtly political play could be read. Although the quality of the essays is variable, the comparative emphasis and the first-hand accounts of working with Pinter in the theatre and in television make this a significant if not essential contribution to Pinter studies.

'Stephen Poliakoff's Drama for the Post-Scientific Age' (*TJ* 45.197–211) by Matthew Martin is an exploration of the thesis that Poliakoff's themes have remained constant throughout his work and that 'the quirky, volatile Urban canyon plays expressed them better, certainly with greater passion and energy'. The case is argued convincingly across a number of plays, with particular reference to the growing schematization of his work.

I have seen two rather different essays on George Bernard Shaw this year. Jill Davis's 'The New Woman and the New Life' (Gardner and Rutherford) offers a subtle, important, and persuasive reading of some of the tensions around the whole concept of the 'New Woman', focused on Shaw because of his dominant cultural standing in the period. With incisive references to *Mrs Warren's Profession*, *Man and Superman*, and *Getting Married*, Davis convincingly shows how Shaw combined 'progressive ideas and patriarchal reaction' so that his representations of women are not only 'deeply ambiguous ... but [also] cyphers for a psychic strategy to achieve and protect masculinity'. On the other hand, Frederic Berg's 'Bernard Shaw's *The Simpleton of the Unexpected Isles*: A New Approach' (*MD* 36.538–46) is a brave but not wholly successful attempt to redeem the play from critical condemnation by relocating it as Shaw's exploration of his own psychology.

Peter N. Chetta's 'Multiplicities of Illusion in Tom Stoppard's Plays'

(Murphy) is a routine account of *Rosencrantz and Guildenstern* and (very briefly) *Travesties*.

In 'The Dialectics of Space in Synge's *The Shadow of the Glen*' (*MD* 36.409–19), Aspasia Velissariou competently pursues the well-established staying versus leaving conflict through a discussion of the structural antithesis of the opposition between mimetic and diegetic space. Jane Duke Elkins also takes another established line of inquiry further with her examination of '"Cute Thinking Woman": The Language of Synge's Female Vagrants' (*Éire* 28.iv.86–99), concluding, perhaps unsurprisingly, that the vagrant women 'rely on imaginative language, both poetic and dramatic, in order to survive'.

C. P. Taylor continues to attract so little attention that essays on his work continue to operate largely at an expository level. Susan Friesner's 'Travails of a Naked Typist: The Plays of C. P. Taylor' (*NTQ* 33.44–58) is no exception to this rule but her summing up also indicates incidentally why he may not attract critical analysis: he was 'a profoundly serious writer who frequently chose to express his most passionate personal, social, and political preoccupations not as tragedy but as farce'.

Timberlake Wertenbaker is now the centre of considerable interest. Susan Carlson's 'Issues of Identity, Nationality, and Performance: The Reception of Two Plays by Timberlake Wertenbaker' (*NTQ* 35.267–89) is a very thoroughly researched and important analysis of how *The Love of the Nightingale* and *Our Country's Good* were received critically in Britain, Australia, Canada and the USA. It is an excellent example of the benefits of a genuinely comparative criticism that illuminates the plays, the productions, and the cultural horizons of the different audiences. In the original British production, for example, the aborigine remained an underwritten and unfocused aspect of the play; in the Melbourne production, the aboriginal actor Tom Lewis played musical interludes between the scenes on a didgeridoo, thus reinstating an element from the novel and refocusing the production. Similarly, in the original British production, the audience shared the actors' viewpoint in the final scenes as they prepared to present the Farquhar play, looking over their shoulders towards the imagined auditorium beyond; in Melbourne and in Canada the actors faced the real audience in these scenes, identifying the real audience with the ruling classes of the play. As its title perhaps indicates, Jim Davis's essay on *Our Country's Good* ('A Play for England: The Royal Court Adapts *The Playmaker*' [Reynolds]) is somewhat constricted by the format of the volume on stage and film adaptation in which it appears. It offers a clear account of the differences between the play and Thomas Keneally's novel on which it is based, makes some relevant points about why certain choices may have been made, and is good on the way the 'token aboriginal' in the play fails to compensate for the absence of a whole strand in the novel. Esther Beth Sullivan's 'Hailing Ideology, Acting in the Horizon and Reading between Plays by Timberlake Wertenbaker' (*TJ* 45.139–54) tackles *Our Country's Good*, *The Grace of Mary Traverse*, and *Three Birds Alighting on a Field*, suggesting that the plays function to keep alive the debates they have pursued, despite their final episodes which seem to be 'a facile resolution to the complexities and contradictions of the debates that have been acted out'. While the stress on the importance of process is valuable, I find some of the readings rather forced: the governor and Ralph did not come over as 'absolutely sympathetic' in the Royal Court production of *Our Country's Good* and, as Carlson demonstrates, its initial reception was not 'overwhelmingly positive'; similarly, the final scenes of the Royal Court productions of *The Grace of Mary Traverse*, and *Three Birds Alighting on a Field* were by no means unironic. Frederick S. Lapisardi offers an interesting first-hand account of 'A Task most Difficult: Staging Yeats's Mystical Dramas at the Abbey' (Murphy) with reference to productions he was involved in the early 1990s, while Robert Tracy concludes that the real hero of Yeats's version of *Oedipus* is language itself ('"Intelligible on the Blasket Islands"; Yeats's *King Oedipus*, 1926', *Éire* 28.ii.116–28).

Books Reviewed

Acheson, James, ed. *British and Irish Drama since 1960*. Macmillan. pp. x + 230. ISBN 0 333 53259 7.

Anstey, Sandra, ed. *Critical Writings on R. S. Thomas*. Seren Books, (1992). pp. 235. £12.95. ISBN 1 85411 062 4.

Arnold, David Scott. *Liminal Readings: Forms of Otherness in Melville, Joyce and Murdoch*. Studies in Literature and Religion. Macmillan. pp. 161. £37.50. ISBN 0 333 55566 X.

Bauerle, Ruth H., ed. *Picking Up Airs: Hearing the Music in Joyce's Text*. UIllP. pp. 220. $32.50. ISBN 0 252 01984 9.

Bergonzi, Bernard. *Wartime and Aftermath: English Literature and its Background 1939–1960*. OPUS: English Literature and its Background. OUP. pp. vii + 230. pb £7.99. ISBN 0 19 289222 3.

Bloom, Clive, ed. *Literature and Culture in Modern Britain. Volume One:1900–1929*. Longman. pp. xviii + 250. hb £30, pb £11.99. ISBN 0 582 07549 1, 0 582 07548 3.

Booker, M. Keith. *Literature and Domination*. UFlorP. pp. x + 188. £22.50. ISBN 0 8130 1195 7.

Bove, Cheryl K. *Understanding Iris Murdoch*. USCP. pp. 216. $29.95. ISBN 0 87249 876 X.

Bracco, Rosa Maria. *Merchants of Hope: British Middlebrow Writers and the First World War, 1919–1939*. Berg. pp. ix + 210. £25. ISBN 0 85496 706 0.

Brandt, George W., ed. *British Television Drama in the 1980s*. CUP. pp. xix + 283. ISBN 0 521 41726 0, 0 521 4273 1.

Brivic, Sheldon. *The Veil of Signs: Joyce, Lacan and Perception*. UIllP. (1991). pp. 224. pb $10.95. ISBN 0 252 06159 4.

Brugière, Bernard, ed. *Les Figures du Corps dans la Litterature et la Peinture Anglaises et Americaines de la Renaissance a nos Jours*. Sorbonne (1991). pp. 352. pb. ISBN 2 85944 203 0.

Buckley, Margaret, and Brian Buckley. *Challenge and Renewal: Lawrence and the Thematic Novel*. Chrysalis Press. pp. 150. pb £12.00. ISBN 1 897765 02 9.

Bukataman, Scott. *Terminal Identity: The Virtual Subject in Postmodern Science Fiction*. AUPG. pp. xii + 404. pb £15.95. ISBN 0 8223 1340 5.

Burkman, Katherine H., and John L. Kundert-Gibbs, eds. *Pinter at Sixty*. IndUP. pp. xvii + 219. ISBN 0 253 34499 9.

Caesar, Adrian. *Taking it Like a Man: Suffering, Sexuality and the War Poets: Brooke, Sassoon, Owen, Graves*. ManUP. pp. 246. £35. ISBN 0 7190 3834 0.

Carlson, Marvin. *Deathtraps: The Postmodern Comedy Thriller*. IndUP. pp. 212. £11.99. ISBN 0 253 20826 2.

Chavkin, Allan, ed. *English Romanticism and Modern Fiction: A Collection of Critical Essays*. AMS. pp. 205. £37.50. ISBN 0 404 61591 0.

Cheyette, Brian. *Constructions of 'the Jew' in English Literature and Society: Racial Representations, 1875–1945*. CUP. pp. xvi + 301. hb £35.00. ISBN 0 521 44355 5.

Colt, Rosemary M., and Janice Rossen, eds. *Writers of the Old School: British Novelists of the 1930s*. Macmillan (1992). pp. 209. £40. ISBN 0 333 53267 8.

Corcoran, Neil. *English Poetry since 1940*, Longman. pp xvii + 308. pb £13.99. ISBN 0 582 00322 9.

Costello, Peter. *James Joyce: The Years of Growth 1882–1915*. KC (1992). pp. 374. £40. ISBN 1 85626 053 4.

Crawford, Robert. *Identifying Poets: Self and Territory in Twentieth-Century Poetry*. EdinUP. pp viii + 191. £25. ISBN 0 7486 0409 X.

Crawford, Robert, and Anne Varty, eds. *Liz Lochhead's Voices*. Modern Scottish Writers Series. EdinUP. pp x + 198. pb £14.95. ISBN 0 7486 0406 5.

Dass, Nirmal. *Rebuilding Babel: The Translations of W. H. Auden*. Rodopi. pp. 196. ISBN 90 5183 405 5.

Day, Gary, ed. *The British Critical Tradition: a Re-evaluation*. Insights. Macmillan. pp. 257. ISBN 0 333 53275 9.

Delbaere, Jeanne, ed. *William Golding: The Sound of Silence: A Belgian Tribute on his Eightieth Birthday*. ULiège Language and Literature (1991). pp. 195. pb 950F. ISBN 2 87233 011 9.

Donaghy, Henry, ed. *Conversations with Graham Greene*. UMP (1992). pp. 185. ISBN 0 87805 550 9.

Ellman, Maud. *The Hunger Artists: Starving, Writing and Imprisonment*. Virago. pp. ix + 136. pb. £7.99. ISBN 1 85381 675 2.

Fairhall, James. *James Joyce and the Question of History*. CUP. pp. 290. £35. ISBN 0 521 40292 1.

Feinstein, Elaine. *Lawrence's Women: The Intimate Life of D. H. Lawrence*. HC. pp. 275. £18. ISBN 0 00 215364 5.

Fernihough, Anne. *D. H. Lawrence: Aesthetics and Ideology*. Clarendon. pp. 211. £25. ISBN 0 19 811235 1.

Filmer, Kath. *The Fiction of C. S. Lewis: Mask and Mirror*. Macmillan. pp. 153. £40. ISBN 0 312 08667 9.

Foshay, Toby Avard. *Wyndham Lewis and the Avant-Garde*. McG-QUP (1992). pp. x + 177. $34.95. ISBN 0 7735 0916 X.

Friedman, Lawrence S. *William Golding*. Continuum. pp. 195. $19.95. ISBN 0 8264 0564 9.

Friedman, Susan Stanford, ed. *Joyce: The Return of the Repressed*. CornUP. pp. 314. pb $18.65. ISBN 0 8014 8073 6.

Gardner, Viv, and Susan Rutherford, eds. *The New Woman and Her Sisters: Feminism and Theatre 1850–1914*. Harvester (1992). pp. xxi + 238. pb £12.99. ISBN 0 7108 1380 5.

Gatrell, Simon, ed. *1876–1918: The Ends of the Earth. English Literature and the Wider World 4*. AshfieldP, 1992. pp. 257. £38.50. ISBN 0 948660 11 2.

Gervais, David. *Literary Englands: Versions of 'Englishness' in Modern Writing*. CUP. pp. xvi + 280. £30. ISBN 0 521 44338 5.

Gibson, Andrew, ed. *Reading Joyce's 'Circe'*. European Joyce Studies. Rodopi. pp. 280. pb $47.00. ISBN 90 5183 546 9.

Gillespie, Diane F., ed. *The Multiple Muses of Virginia Woolf*. UMissP. pp. 273.

£33.95. ISBN 0 8262 0882 7.

Goldman, Dorothy, ed. *Women and World War 1: The Written Response*. Insights. Macmillan. pp. xiv + 211. pb £13.99. ISBN 0 333 51310 X.

Goodman, Lizbeth. *Contemporary Feminist Theatres*. Routledge. pp. xii + 313. £11.99. ISBN 0 415 07306 5.

Gortschacher, Wolfgang. *Little Magazine Profiles: The Little Magazines in Great Britain 1939–1993*. USalz. pp. ii + 751. pb £17.50. ISBN 3 7052 06087.

Griffiths, Trevor R., and Margaret Llewellyn-Jones, eds. *British and Irish Women Dramatists Since 1958: A Critical Handbook*. OpenUP. pp. viii + 193. ISBN 0 335 09603 4, 0335 09602 6.

Hampson, Robert, and Peter Barry, eds. *New British Poetries: The Scope of the Possible*, ManUP. pp. viii + 247. £35. ISBN 0 7190 3485 X.

Hein, Hilde, and Carolyn Korsmeyer, eds. *Aesthetics in Feminist Perspective*. IUP. pp. 252. pb £12.99. ISBN 0 253 32861 6.

Hilton, Enid Hopkin. *More Than One Life: A Nottinghamshire Childhood with D. H. Lawrence*. Sutton. pp. 150. £12.99. ISBN 0 7509 0314 7.

Hilton, Julian, ed. *New Directions in Theatre*. Macmillan. pp. viii + 184. hb £35, pb £10.99. ISBN 0 333 392914, 0 333 392922.

Holsinger, M. Paul, and Mary Anne Schofield, eds. *Visions of War: World War II in Popular Literature and Culture*. BGUP. pp. 203. pb $15.95. ISBN 0 87972 556 7.

Hughes, Helen. *The Historical Romance*. Popular Fictions. Routledge. pp. ix + 165. £35. ISBN 0 415 05812 0.

Hulse, Michael, David Kennedy, and David Morley. *The New Poetry*. Bloodaxe. pp. 352. pb £7.95. ISBN 1 85224 244 2.

Ian, Marcia. *Remembering the Phallic Mother: Psychoanalysis, Modernism, and the Fetish*. CornUP. pp. xiii + 241. £23.50. ISBN 0 8014 2637 5.

Ingle, Stephen. *George Orwell: A Political Life*. ManUP Lives of the Left. pp. 146. ISBN 0 7190 3233 4.

Ingram, Angela, and Daphne Patai, eds. *Rediscovering Forgotten Radicals: British Women Writers 1889–1939*. UNCP. pp. viii + 319. hb $49.50, pb $19.74. ISBN 0 8078 2087 3, 0 8078 4414 4.

Jackson, John Wyse, and Bernard McGinley. *James Joyce's Dubliners: An Annotated Edition*. Sinclair-Stevenson. pp. 200. £25. ISBN 1 85619 120 6.

Joyce, James. *Ulysses*, ed. Jeri Johnson. WC. OUP. pp. 980. pb £6.99. ISBN 0 19 282866 5.

Kemp, Sandra, and Paola Bono, eds. *The Lonely Mirror: Italian Perspectives on Feminist Theory*. Routledge. pp. 251. ISBN 0 415 03777 8.

Kerr, Douglas. *Wilfred Owen's Voices: Language and Community*. Clarendon. pp. 346. £35. ISBN 0 19 812370 1.

Kershner, R. B., ed. *James Joyce, A Portrait of the Artist as a Young Man: Complete, Authoritative Text with Biographical and Historical Contexts, Critical History, and Essays from Five Contemporary Critical Perspectives*. Macmillan. pp. 404. pb £6.99. ISBN 0 333 59490 8.

Lawrence, D. H. *Lady Chatterley's Lover; A Propos of 'Lady Chatterley's Lover'*, ed. Michael Squires. CUP. pp. 462. £55. ISBN 0 521 22266 4.

—— *The Rainbow*, ed. by Jan Hewitt. Dent. pp. 500. pb £5.99. ISBN 0 460 87323 7.

—— *Selected Poems*, ed. Jan Todd. OUP Student Texts. pp. 184. pb £5.95. ISBN 0 19 831962 2.

—— *Women in Love*, ed. Linda Ruth Williams. Dent. pp. 545. pb £5.99. ISBN 0 460 87322 9.

Leonard, Garry. *Reading* Dubliners *Again: A Lacanian Perspective*. SyracuseUP Irish Studies. pp. 376. pb $18.95. ISBN 0 8156 2600 2.

Lilly, Mark. *Gay Men's Literature in the Twentieth Century*. Macmillan. pp. xv + 233. pb £10. ISBN 0 333 49436 9.

Link, Franz, ed. *Tanz und Tod in Kunst und Literatur*. D&H. pp. 672. pb DM 138. ISBN 3 428 07512 9.

Lowenberg, Susan, ed. *C. S. Lewis: A Reference Guide 1972–1988*. Hall. pp. 304. £40.50. ISBN 0 8161 1846 9.

Loewenstein, Andrea Freud. *Loathsome Jews and Engulfing Women: Metaphors of Projection in the Works of Wyndham Lewis, Charles Williams, and Graham Greene*. NYUP. pp. 384. ISBN 0 8147 5063 X.

Mackintosh, Iain. *Architecture, Actor and Audience*. Routledge. pp. vii + 184. £12.99. ISBN 0 415 03183 4.

McAleer, Joseph. *Popular Reading and Publishing in Britain 1914–1950*. Oxford Historical Monographs. OUP (1992). pp. xiii + 284. £35. ISBN 0 19 820329 2.

McCormick, Kathleen, and Erwin R. Steinberg, eds. *Approaches to Teaching Joyce's* Ulysses. MLA. pp. 178. pb $19.75. ISBN 0 87352 712 7.

McDonald, Gail. *Learning to be Modern: Pound, Eliot, and the American University*. Clarendon. pp. xii + 241.

McDonald, Peter. *Louis MacNeice: The Poet in his Contexts*. Clarendon. pp. 242. £30. ISBN 0 19 911766 3.

McGuiness, Nora A. *The Literary Universe of Jack B. Yeats*. CUAP (1992). pp. xvi + 288. £41.50. ISBN 0 8132 1737 1.

Manlove, Colin. *The Chronicles of Narnia: The Patterning of a Fantastic World*. Twayne's Masterwork Series. Twayne. pp. 136. pb £6.95. ISBN 0 8057 8801 8.

Markey, Janice. *A Journey into the Red Eye: The Poetry of Sylvia Plath – a Critique*. WP. pp. 216. pb £7.99. ISBN 0 7043 4316 9.

Marshall, Cynthia, ed. *Essays on C. S. Lewis and George Macdonald: Truth, Fiction and the Power of Imagination*. Studies in British Literature, vol. 11. Mellen (1991). pp. 114. $59.95. ISBN 0 88946 494 4.

Meyers, Jeffrey, ed. *T. E. Lawrence: Soldier, Writer, Legend: New Essays*. Macmillan (1989). pp. 220. ISBN 0 333 44036 6.

Millard, Kenneth. *Edwardian Poetry*. Clarendon (1991). pp. 200. £27.50. ISBN 0 19 812225 X.

Monk, Leland. *Standard Deviations: Chance and the Modern British Novel*. StanfordUP. pp. 199. ISBN 0 8047 2174 2.

Morgan, W. John, and Peter Preston, eds. *Raymond Williams: Politics, Education, Letters*. Macmillan. pp. x + 215. hb £42.50. ISBN 0 333 48587 4.

Moseley, Merritt. *Understanding Kingsley Amis*. USCP. pp. 192. hb $29.95. ISBN 0 87249 861 1.

Munt, Sally, ed. *New Lesbian Criticism: Literary and Cultural Readings*. Between Men–Between Women Series. ColUP (1992). pp. 207. $40.00. ISBN 0 231 08018 2.

Murphy, Patrick D., ed. *Staging the Impossible: The Fantastic Mode in Modern Drama*. Greenwood. pp. viii + 245. £44.95. ISBN 0 313 27270 0.

Nichols, Betsy, Frank Kersnowski, and James Nichols, eds. *Selected Essays on the Humor of Lawrence Durrell*. ELS Monograph Series, no. 60. pp. 132. ISBN 0 920604 72 2.

Nicholson, Colin. *Poem, Purpose and Place: Shaping Identity in Contemporary Scottish Verse*. Polygon. pp. xxii + 254. £11.95. ISBN 0 7486 6138 7.

Orlans, Harold, ed. *Lawrence of Arabia, Strange Man of Letters: The Literary Criticism and Correspondence of T. E. Lawrence*. AUP. pp. 334. £36.50. ISBN 0 8386 3508 3.

Page, Malcolm, ed. *'Howards End': An Introduction to the Variety of Criticism*. The Critics Debate. Macmillan. pp. 102. ISBN 0 333 48848 2, 0 333 48849 0.

Parker, Michael. *Seamus Heaney: The Making of the Poet*. Macmillan. pp. xi + 294. £25. ISBN 0 333 47181 4.

Peach, Linden. *Ancestral Lines: Culture and Identity in the Work of Six Contemporary Poets*. Seren Books. pp. 175. £14.95. ISBN 1 85411 061 6.

Peterson, Richard E. *James Joyce Revisited*. TEAS. Twayne (1992). pp. 131. ISBN 0 805 77016 X.

Pierce, David. *James Joyce's Ireland*. YaleUP. pp. 239. £19.95. ISBN 0 300 05055 0.

Poplawski, Paul. *Promptings of Desire: Creativity and the Religious Impulse in the Works of D. H. Lawrence*. Greenwood. pp. 210. £45.50. ISBN 0 313 28789 9.

Poster, Jem. *The Thirties Poets*. Open Guides to Literature. OpenUP. pp. 102. hb £30, pb £8.99. ISBN 0 335 09664 6, 0 335 09663 8.

Raitt, Suzanne. *Vita and Virginia: The Work and Friendship of V. Sackville-West and Virginia Woolf*. Clarendon. pp. 195. ISBN 0 19 811249 1, 0 19 812277 2.

Reid, Su, ed. *'Mrs Dalloway' and 'To the Lighthouse': Contemporary Critical Essays*. New Casebooks. Macmillan. pp. 168. pb £9.50. ISBN 0 333 54141 3, 0 333 54142 3.

Reilly, Jim. *Shadowtime: History and Representation in Hardy, Conrad and George Eliot*. Routledge. pp. 185. £30. ISBN 0 415 08597 7.

Reynolds, Mary T., ed. *James Joyce: A Collection of Critical Essays*. S&S. pp. 238. pb $12.95. ISBN 0 13 512211 2.

Reynolds, Peter, ed. *Novel Images: Literature in Performance*. Routledge. pp. ix + 208. ISBN 0 415 09103 9.

Rosenbaum, S. P., ed. *A Bloomsbury Group Reader*. Blackwell. pp. xii + 428. hb £40.00, pb £14.99. ISBN 0 631 17318 8, 0 631 19059 7.

Rossen, Janice. *The University in Modern Fiction: When Power is Academic*. Macmillan. pp. viii + 202. £35. ISBN 0 333 47182 2.

Salwak, Dale. *Kingsley Amis: Modern Novelist*. Harvester. pp. 302. £24.99. ISBN 0 7450 1096 2.

Sagar, Keith, and James T. Boulton, eds. *The Letters of D. H. Lawrence*, vol. VII. CUP. pp. 683. £60. ISBN 0 521 23116 7.

Said, Edward. *Culture and Imperialism*. C&W. pp. 444. ISBN 0 7011 3808 4.

Scholes, Robert. *In Search of James Joyce*. UIllP (1992). pp. 215. pb $12.95. ISBN 0 252 06245 0.

Segall, Jeffrey. *Joyce in America: Cultural Politics and the Trials of Ulysses*. UCalP. pp. 208. hb £20. ISBN 0 520 07746 6.

Shaffer, Brian W. *The Blinding Torch: Modern British Fiction and the Discourse of Civilization*. UMassP. pp. xii + 208. £26.95. ISBN 0 87023 831 0.

Sherry, Vincent. *Ezra Pound, Wyndham Lewis, and Radical Modernism*. OUP. pp. xi + 228. £35. ISBN 0 19 507693 1.

Spencer, Jenny S. *Dramatic Strategies in the Plays of Edward Bond*. CUP (1992). pp. xv + 270. £30. ISBN 0 521 39304 3.

Stape, J. H., ed. *E. M. Forster: Interviews and Recollections*. St Martins. pp. 235. ISBN 0 333 57083 9.

Stinson, John J. *Anthony Burgess Revisited*. TEAS. Twayne (1991). pp. 165. hb £14.95. ISBN 0 8057 7000 3.

Taylor, D. J. *After the War: The Novel and English Society since 1945*. C&W. pp. xxvi + 310. £17.99. ISBN 0 7011 3769 X.

Thomas, M. Wynn, ed. *The Page's Drift: R. S. Thomas at Eighty*. Seren Books. pp. 232. pb. £8.95. ISBN 1 85411 100 0.

Tolley, A. T., ed. *Roy Fuller: A Tribute*. CarletonUP. pp. 124. £19.95. ISBN 0 88629 210 7.

Trotter, David. *The English Novel in History 1895–1920*. Routledge. pp. 337. pb £10.99. ISBN 0 415 01502 2.

Turner, Martha A. *Mechanism and the Novel: Science in the Narrative Process*. CUP. pp. xi + 199. £30. ISBN 0 521 44339 3.

Verdonk, Peter. *Twentieth-Century Poetry: From Text to Context*. Interface. Routledge. pp. 194. hb £35, pb. £10.99. ISBN 0 415 05862 7, 0 415 05863 5.

Vorda, Allan, ed. *Face to Face: Interviews with Contemporary Novelists*. RiceUP. pp. 235. $14.95. ISBN 0 89263 322 0.

Wachtel, Albert. *The Cracked Lookingglass: James Joyce and the Nightmare of History*. AUP (1992). pp. 172. £27.50. ISBN 0 9456 3627 X.

Wandor, Michelene. *Drama Today: A Critical Guide to British Drama 1970–1990*. Longman with the British Council. pp. x + 82. £5.99. ISBN 0 582 06061 3.

Ward, John Powell. *Thomas Hardy's Poetry*. Open Guides to Literature. OpenUP. pp. 112. hb £30. pb £8.99. ISBN 0 335 09991 2, 0 335 09990 4.

Warner, John M. *Joyce's Grandfathers: Myth and History in Defoe, Smollett, Sterne and Joyce*. UGeoP. pp. 193. £31.50. ISBN 0 8203 1495 1.

Watson, George, ed. *Critical Essays on C. S. Lewis*. Scolar Critical Thought Series: 1 (1992). pp. 284. ISBN 0 85957 853 9.

Watts, Cedric. *A Preface to Conrad*. Longman Preface Books. Longman, 2nd edn. pp. 288. pb £10.99. ISBN 0 582 08883 6.

Welch, Robert. *Changing States: Transformations in Modern Irish Writing*. Routledge. pp. xii + 307. hb £35, pb 12.99. ISBN 0 415 08666 3, 0 415 09361 9.

White, Andrea. *Joseph Conrad and the Adventure Tradition: Constructing and Deconstructing the Imperial Subject*. CUP. pp. 233. £32.50. ISBN 0 521 41606 X.

Williams, Linda Ruth. *Sex in the Head: Visions of Femininity and Film in D. H. Lawrence*. HW. pp. 178. pb £12.95. ISBN 0 7450 1331 7.

Wills, Clair. *Improprieties: Politics and Sexuality in Northern Irish Poetry*. Clarendon. pp vi + 263. £11.95. ISBN 0 19 818239 2.

Wolfe, Peter. *Alarms and Epitaphs: The Art of Eric Ambler*. BGUP. pp. 230. ISBN 0 87972 603 2.

Woolf, Virginia. *Women and Fiction: The Manuscript Versions of 'A Room of One's Own'*. Trans. and ed. S. P. Rosenbaum. Shakespeare Head Press edition of Virginia Woolf. Blackwell. 1992. pp. 215. £37.50. ISBN 0 631 18037 0.

Wyatt-Brown, Anne M., *Barbara Pym: A Critical Biography*. UMissP. pp. 210. ISBN 0 8262 0820 7.

Wyatt-Brown, Anne M. and Janice Rossen, eds. *Aging and Gender in Literature: Studies in Creativity*. Feminist Issues. UPVirginia. pp. 375. ISBN 0 8139 1431 0.

Zeifman, Hersh, and Cynthia Zimmerman, eds. *Contemporary British Drama, 1970–90: Essays from 'Modern Drama'*. Macmillan. pp. xiii + 348. £40. ISBN 0 333 49114 9.

Zurbrugg, Nicholas. *The Parameters of Postmodernism*. Routledge. pp. xvi + 183. pb £11.99. ISBN 0 415 10562 5.

XV

American Literature to 1900

HENRY CLARIDGE, KEVIN MCCARRON and JANET BEER GOODWYN

This chapter has the following sections: 1. General; 2. American Literature to 1830; 3. American Literature 1830 to 1865; 4. American Literature 1865 to 1900. Sections 1 and 2 are by Henry Claridge, section 3 is by Kevin McCarron and section 4 is by Janet Beer Goodwyn.

1. General

Current bibliographical listings for the field and the period continue to be available quarterly in *AL* and annually in *MLAIB*. *AmLS* for 1991, under the editorship of David Nordloh, offers the now customary thoroughness and serviceableness in its coverage of criticism and scholarship. Louis Owens, who edited *AmLS* for 1990, has, we are told, decided to resign from his 'alternating editorship' and will be replaced by Gary Scharnhorst of the University of New Mexico who has done an exemplary job in past sections of *AmLS*, notably, in recent years, on '19th century Literature' and 'Fiction: The 1930s to the 1960s'. David Nordloh, however, will edit *AmLS: 1992* and will, no doubt, acquit himself as admirably as he has done here. Inevitably, there have been changes to the 'cast' of contributors although there is little point my enumerating them here; a pity, however, to see that Michel Gresset has resigned from his coverage of 'French Contributions' and, unfortunately, no one has yet been found to replace him, although East European, German, Italian, Japanese and Scandinavian contributions are thoroughly accounted for.

As with my contribution for last year, this year's task has been made difficult by my having received only a fraction of what I have ordered. Again, there are a number of works published this year which will have to wait until next year for my review.

Those interested in the recent agitation about the 'canon' of American literature and the attendant, and sometimes considerable, problems of putting together 'representative' anthologies of American literature, given the elasticity of the contemporary sense of 'representative', will find the contributors to the 'Forum' in the June issue of *AL* addressing these and other related issues. Most of the pieces here are brief but the essays by Paul Lauter 'On Revising the *Heath Anthology of American Literature*' (*AL* 65.327–30) and Jay Fliegelman's

'Anthologizing the Situation of American Literature' (*AL* 62.334–8), in particular, make cogent and informed points about both the many virtues of anthologies and their (arguably necessary) evils.

Hot on the heels of *The Columbia History of the American Novel* (*YWES* 72.422–3) comes *The Columbia History of American Poetry* edited by Jay Parini. At something in excess of 900 pages this volume draws together 30 individually authored essays covering American poetry from the writings of Anne Bradstreet and Edward Taylor to those of Philip Levine and James Wright. The great temptation for any reviewer with books of this magnitude is to quickly skim through the index looking at the names of those covered and, more importantly, looking for those omitted. I'm afraid to say I couldn't resist the temptation and was pleasantly surprised to find that many of the more contemporary poets one might confidently expect to not get a mention are, indeed, there, although it has to be said that 'mention' is the operative word: Rita Dove and Jorie Graham, for example, two considerable younger poets, are only very briefly noted, the latter in a list of contemporaries writing in what might be called the 'Wallace Stevens tradition'. It is, however, unfair to assess the worth of such an enterprise as this on the basis of its consideration of those who are writing today. Literary histories are, after all, *histories* and one might reasonably expect them to have most to offer in their account of those reputations which are established and around which a body of criticism and scholarship has emerged. Here *The Columbia History of American Poetry* is conventional in its assessment of those poets who are, unquestionably, major figures and most of them are given a chapter, or part of a chapter, to themselves: Longfellow, Dickinson, Whitman, Poe, Frost, Pound, Eliot, Stevens, Williams, Hart Crane, Berryman, Ashbery. Who is missing from this impressive canon? Well, Robert Lowell will spring immediately to mind, although he is dealt with at some length in Diane Wood Middlebrook's intelligent assessment of 'confessional poetry'. Some might offer Sylvia Plath's name; she, too, gets two pages in Middlebrook's chapter. But there are a number of American poets who, while being first and foremost novelists (and in some cases *great* novelists), are given only the most cursory consideration as writers of verse: Stephen Crane gets only one mention, and for *The Red Badge of Courage*, in John McWilliams's excellent essay on 'The Epic in the Nineteenth Century'; Melville gets some five pages in the same essay but, primarily, through McWilliams's analysis of the 'poetry' in *Moby-Dick*, and his long poem *Clarel* merits only one mention in the whole volume (again, in McWilliams's essay); no mention is made of Sherwood Anderson's poetry (admittedly, it's rather bad) and that of Faulkner and Hemingway is ignored. Some poets whom we would naturally expect to be dealt with seem to have evaded the contributors altogether (no reference at all to Philip Freneau and Frederick Goddard Tuckerman) while William Cullen Bryant merits only three sentences, largely by way of his relationship with other poets. Some, of course, might want to make a case (and it's not capricious) for songwriters such as Bob Dylan, Cole Porter or Jim Morrison as poets: none of them gets a mention here. This isn't therefore, strictly speaking, a *history*; it is a series of essays on American poetry, following, roughly, a chronological path, that has been shaped into something that seeks to resemble a history, and the strengths of the volume are, it seems to me, to be found in those chapters that bring together poets in challenging and intriguing contexts, notably Jeanne Larsen's chapter on 'Lowell, Teasdale, Wylie, Millay, and Bogan', or try to assess an established reputation in a new way, and here Dana Gioia's chapter, 'Longfellow in the

Aftermath of Modernism', is strikingly perceptive. Other intelligent and work-manlike assessments include Lawrence Buell on 'The Transcendentalist Poets', William Pritchard on T. S. Eliot and Lynn Keller on 'The Twentieth-Century Long Poem'. A mixed bag, overall, one would have to conclude, and somewhat sparsely annotated ('Further Reading' is appended to each chapter but, beyond this, there are no bibliographies or biographical *resumés* for each of the major poets discussed).

Two books published this year, one a single-author volume, the other a collection of essays, have much in common and I shall endeavour to treat them comparatively. We have come to expect a high standard of criticism and scholar-ship from Richard H. Brodhead and those who consult *Cultures of Letters: Scenes of Reading and Writing in Nineteenth-Century America* will find this high standard maintained. Like Brodhead's earlier *The School of Hawthorne* (*YWES* 70.581), this is socio-historical criticism which seeks to explore the interplay between a middle-class domestic culture of letters, popular literary culture, 'high' culture, and the newly emancipated world of black writing and black education; these contexts Brodhead calls 'scenes of writing' and his argument is that 'writing has been envisioned and practiced in many different ways in America – ways neither wholly self-invented nor merely dictated from without but realized from among the possibilities set in different cultural situations'. It is the very socio-historical perspective that gives such a latitude to Brodhead's concerns here: the first chapter, 'Sparing the Rod: Discipline and Fiction in Antebellum America', for instance, mixes together the issues of corporal punish-ment in schools, the whipping of slaves in the South and the abolition of flogging in the American Navy with critical readings of novels such as Lydia Sigourney's *Letters to Mothers* (1839), Susan Warner's *The Wide, Wide World* (1850), and Harriet Beecher Stowe's *Uncle Tom's Cabin* (1852) into a heady, but frequently fascinating, brew. Later chapters explore regional fiction, 'women's literary work space' (largely through a consideration of Sarah Orne Jewett), and Charles W. Chesnutt's 'historical renegotiation of the relation of members of his race *to* writing as a cultural activity'. *Readers in History: Nineteenth-Century American Literature and the Contexts of Response*, edited by James L. Machor, gathers together 12 essays (I am including Machor's introductory essay which usefully summarizes the 11 remaining essays) that collectively address 'the nature, goals, and implications of examining reading as a historical act'. Machor's contributors employ a variety of critical perspectives: Steven Mailloux in 'Misreading as a Historical Act: Cultural Rhetoric, Bible Politics, and Fuller's 1845 Review of Douglass's *Narrative*' examines what he calls 'the rhetorical history of Fuller's interpretation' of Frederick Douglass's autobiography, arguing that a 'Bible politics of interpretation' is historically situated in Margaret Fuller's response; John Carlos Rowe's 'Swept Away: Henry James, Margaret Fuller, and "The Last of the Valerii"' follows Mailloux's essay, for here it is Margaret Fuller who is being 'responded' to, Rowe arguing that Henry James's reading of the Fuller 'legend' informs a story that is 'full of the Margaret-ghost'; Margaret Fuller surfaces again in Christina Zwarg's 'Reading before Marx: Margaret Fuller and *The New-York Daily Tribune*' where she seeks to understand Fuller's 'theory of reading' through her contributions to the New York newspaper; Robert Daly writes on 'Cooper's Allegories of Reading and "the Wreck of the Past"' (my remarks on this essay are offered in a later section of this chapter); in 'The Address of *The Scarlet Letter*' Stephen Railton examines how Hawthorne might have conceptualized his audience, although he concedes that there is 'an aboriginal audience' inscribed into the text, that 'crowd of spectators' at the beginning of the novel being understood as 'Hawthorne's acknowledgement of the point that the audience precedes the text'; Willis Buckingham offers an instructive summary of the early critical reactions to the 1890 edition of Emily Dickinson's poems in 'Poetry Readers and Reading in the 1890s: Emily Dickinson's First Reception', and in *Uncle Tom's Cabin* and Antebellum Black Response' Marva Banks explores the critical responses of black readers to Stowe's influential novel, arguing that the 'racial ambivalence' of the novel is a consequence of the fact that 'Stowe was as much influenced by her race, moment, and milieu when she created *Uncle Tom's Cabin* as the black readers who responded to it were affected by theirs'.

Other essays in Machor's collection (including the editor's own) are more generally theoretical in character, notably Wai Chee Dimock's 'Feminism, New Historicism, and the Reader' (a revised version of her earlier article for *American Literature* in the December 1991 issue) which tries to construct a very large theory of contextualized reading on a very small foundation, Charlotte Perkins Gilman's story 'The Yellow Wallpaper'. This collection could not justifiably be accused of pursuing the theoretical at the expense of those very things that might be theorized about, as my account of some of the articles therein will indicate, but a kind of unstated belief in the primacy of theory governs, more or less, every contribution. One must concede to Machor his recognition of this fact, for in his introduction he takes issue with Stanley Fish's argument that the claims of theory should, in Machor's words, 'be declared irrelevant if any truly consequential work, such as the investigation of the past, is to proceed' by dismissing 'the attendant claim that the principle of the historical textuality of all discourse has no consequences for practice itself'. In other words, all practice is theoretically grounded.

Frontier Gothic: Terror and Wonder at the Frontier in American Literature, edited by David Mogen, Scott P. Sanders and Joanne B. Karpinski is a rather different kettle of fish. Most of the essays here address the place of the gothic in writings about the American wilderness through both canonical and non-canonical texts: Stephen Mainville writes on 'Language and the Void: Gothic Landscapes in the Frontiers of Edgar Allan Poe' while David Mogen locates H. P. Lovecraft's American gothicism within a tradition of American historical fiction, notably that of Hawthorne, although here one might question his use of the word 'historical', in his valuable essay, 'Wilderness, Metamorphosis, and Millennium: Gothic Apocalypse from the Puritans to the Cyberpunks'. One intriguing feature of this collection is the contributors' interest in tracing continuities between gothic origins (for example in Charles Brockden Brown) and later twentieth-century manifestations of 'wilderness gothic' in writers such as Flannery O'Connor and Sam Shepard. Although there is some unevenness in the quality of the contributions, the editors are to be congratulated for having brought together a volume of essays on an important but neglected subject.

Studies in the American Renaissance: 1993, under the editorship of Joel Myerson, once again draws together a body of essentially scholarly essays on this important phase of American literary history. Two recently discovered letters of James Fenimore Cooper to a family friend (found in a bequest to Hartwick College) are published for the first time in an essay by Alan Taylor, and 'A Calendar of the Letters of Mary Moody Emerson' (Ralph Waldo Emerson was her nephew) is presented in an essay by Nancy Craig Simmons. William Cullen Bryant II writes on 'Bryant and Poe: A Reacquaintance' and offers a brief account of Poe's attitudes to Bryant's verse while James M. Hutchisson explores the possibility that Anna Cora Mowatt modelled her dramatic character T. Tennyson Twinkle in her 1845 comedy *Fashion; or, Life in New York* on Edgar Allan Poe.

Also to be noted is the reappearance in paperback (now in a Penguin edition) of the two volumes on American literature edited by the late Marcus Cunliffe, *American Literature to 1900* and *American Literature Since 1900*, which were previously published as part of the Sphere History of Literature series in 1975; these volumes incorporate the revisions and enlargements Cunliffe made for the 1987 Sphere edition and have very good bibliographies, both of individual authors and general topics.

2. American Literature to 1830

There has been a good deal of valuable scholarship this year on seventeenth-century writers, notably in the pages of *EAL*, now under the exemplary editorship of Philip F. Gura; I shall return to this in due course. First of all, two connected essays in *AmLH* address broad questions of a theoretical and methodological nature: William C. Spengemann in 'Early American Literature and the Project of Literary History' (*AmLH* 5.512–41), an article adapted from his forthcoming book, *A New World of Words: Redefining Early American Literature*, extends and enlarges arguments he puts forward in *A Mirror for Americanists: Reflections on the Idea of American Literature* (see *YWES* 71.533–4), particularly his belief that the study of early American literature has been seriously distorted by an over-emphasis on writings from the British colonies and what he calls the 'disfiguring context of American nationalism'; in 'Rehistoricizing Early American Literature' (*AmLH* 5.542–63), David S. Shields in effect 'replies' to Spengemann's article, although his review also takes in the positions of other recent scholars of early American writings, notably Michael P. Kramer and Michael Warner, and the whole essay offers a valuable conspectus of recent work in the field. A contribution towards an 'historicizing' of the place of violence in early New England is offered by James Schramer and Timothy Sweet in 'Violence and the Body Politic in Seventeenth-Century New England' (*ArQ* 48.1–32), an article from 1992 that analyses the 'Puritans' rhetoric of rationalization, focusing on the ideology represented by the figure of the 'body politic', and shows how 'during crises in seventeenth-century New England, the distinct discourses of salvation and politics interpenetrated, with the effect of legitimating political repression or violence'.

Stephen Carl Arch seeks to further the revaluation of Edward Johnson in his 'The Edifying History of Edward Johnson's *Wonder-Working Providence*' (*EAL* 28.42–59) where he argues that Johnson's work has a 'narrative structure hitherto unnoticed by critics', one which is 'part of a larger tropology of "edification" which pervades the narrative' and points to the place of Johnson's project in the 'larger cultural configuration being undertaken in New England in the late 1640s and 1650s'. A somewhat later New England writer, Benjamin Tompson, finds his poems on King Philip's War read as experiments in 'verse history' in Jane Donahue Eberwein's '"Harvardine Quil": Benjamin Tompson's Poems on Philip's War' (*EAL* 28.1–20), her account pointing interestingly to affinities –

although, unfortunately, undeveloped in her essay – with Anne Bradstreet's 'Foure Monarchies' and Edward Taylor's 'Metrical History of Christianity'. Three essays on Edward Taylor in *EAL* are worthy of note: in ' "Both Great and Small": Adult Proportion and Divine Scale in Edward Taylor's "Preface" and *The New England Primer*' (*EAL* 28.120–32) Elisa New looks at the 'Preface' to *God's Determinations* in a context established by *The New England Primer* and Puritan conceptions of childhood innocence and child psychology, concluding that 'Taylor's poem, like the *Primer*, collapses child into adult to apprise them together of the insignificance of human scale with its developmental gradations'; *God's Determinations* is also the centre of interest for Carol M. Bensick in her article 'Preaching to the Choir: Some Achievements and Shortcomings of Taylor's *God's Determinations*' (*EAL* 28.133–47) where she advances the arguments of John Gatta in *Gracious Laughter* (1989) by suggesting that Taylor's poem 'goes beyond merely showing that Puritanism didn't approve, let alone mandate, gloom' and that 'gloom is actually a Puritan dysfunction', the poet proffering cures for 'morbid subjectivity'; and in 'Evidence of Medicinal Cannibalism in Puritan New England: "Mummy" and Related Remedies in Edward Taylor's "Dispensatory" ' (*EAL* 28.185–221), Karen Gordon-Grube writes at length about Taylor's work as the town physician of the frontier settlement of Westfield and the evidence from his 'Dispensatory' that 'he participated in the vogue of medicinal cannibalism', approving of the 'ingestion of "mummy", which was medicinally prepared human flesh': her essay (which contains, it might be noted, a very useful list of works cited) is more history of medicine than literary criticism but its scholarly value is considerable. Also on Taylor, Linda Munk in 'Edward Taylor: Typology and Puritanism' (*HEI* 17.85–93) returns us to some of the more well-trodden paths of Puritan scholarship in her analysis of the relationship between typology and the rhetorical structures of the sermon in Taylor's work.

Mary Rowlandson's *Narrative of the Captivity* continues to attract a good deal of intelligent critical and scholarly attention. Two essays in *EAL* help further our understanding of this important work: Michelle Burnham in 'The Journey Between: Liminality and Dialogism in Mary White Rowlandson's Captivity Narrative' (*EAL* 28.60–75) subjects the narrative to an analysis that draws on recent scholarship of Rowlandson, Bakhtinian narratological theory and Victor Turner's concept of 'liminality' in an attempt to show that the narrative is a 'text which documents a cross-cultural interaction and mixes the several languages which engage in or result from that interaction, including the discourse of an orthodox Puritan woman and minister's wife, the discourse of that Puritan woman undergoing the process of acculturation, and conversations between that woman and individual Indians who speak an entirely different language'; the notion of Rowlandson as a woman author and 'a gendered and political subject' is at the centre of Lisa Logan's 'Mary Rowlandson's Captivity and the "Place" of the Woman Subject' (*EAL* 28.255–77) where the text is construed as 'a model for the issues American women struggle with when, as subjects, they enter the area of representation', although whether such a formulation is adequate to the palpable trials Rowlandson confronted during her captivity is another matter. Also on Rowlandson, Julia Stern's 'To Represent Afflicted Time: Mourning as Historiography' (*AmLH* 5.378–88) is a long review of Mitchell Breitwieser's *American Puritanism and the Defense of Mourning* (1990) which addresses many of the historiographical and interpretative problems that arise in readings of

Rowlandson. The most substantial work on Cotton Mather this year is Christopher Felker's *Reinventing Cotton Mather in the American Renaissance: Magnalia Christi Americana in Hawthorne, Stowe, and Stoddard* which seeks to demonstrate 'the importance of a Puritan political sentiment that advanced the desire of several American Renaissance writers to address the implications of democracy'. Felker's point of departure is the American publication of the *Magnalia* in 1820 and the ensuing responses to it of three writers, two of whom are considerably better known than the third: Nathaniel Hawthorne, Harriet Beecher Stowe and Elizabeth Stoddard. The opening chapters establish a context for Felker's readings of these three figures: Chapter 1 is largely historical in that it considers 'Mather's political and rhetorical involvements in New England during the period between charters (1684–91)' whilst Chapter 2 explores the 1820 edition by Thomas Robbins of the *Magnalia* and its contribution to the 'cultural moment of self-definition in the writing of Hawthorne, Stowe, and Stoddard', and it is here that one begins to see Felker's thesis taking shape for the responses to the *Magnalia* are located in what Felker, along with others, sees as a *locus classicus* in American literary history, a point in time when a nativist culture emerges against the background of a 'democratic readership'. Separate chapters are given to the various ways in which works by Hawthorne, Stowe and Stoddard 'interrogate' Robbins's issue of *Magnalia*: the reading of Hawthorne's use of Mather seeks 'to show how Mather and Hawthorne, working as fundamentally ironic historians, inscribed traces of Puritanism's legacy within a cultural poetics organized around object-choices and object-investments'; Stowe's *The Minister's Wooing* (1859) is construed as a novel which re-enacts the preoccupations with the 'exemplaristic personality' found in the *Magnalia*; and Elizabeth Stoddard's novel *The Morgesons* (1862) reveals, Felker argues, Stoddard's debt to Mather in its 'intersection of nineteenth-century circumstances with seventeenth-century phenomena', particularly in its ethnographic character and its interest in spectral phenomena. Felker's study works partly from arguments of influence, partly from arguments of affinity, and the dividing lines between these types of argument are not entirely perspicuous, so much so that one is occasionally confused about the kind of case he is offering. But this remains an important contribution to scholarship, enlarging both our understanding of Mather and our understanding of some nineteenth-century responses to the Puritan legacy. Also relevant to Cotton Mather, Constance Post's 'Old World Order in the New: John Eliot and "Praying Indians" in Cotton Mather's *Magnalia Christi Americana*' (*NEQ* 66.416–33) addresses the issue of Christian prayer amongst Native Americans in the seventeenth century. Dana D. Nelson's 'Economies of Morality and Power: Reading "Race" in Two Colonial Texts' in Frank Shuffleton's collection of essays, *A Mixed Race: Ethnicity in Early America*, which deals, in part, with Mather has yet to be received and will, hopefully, be dealt with next year. A more traditional sense of 'economy' is at work in Peter A. Davis's 'Puritan Mercantilism and the Politics of Anti-Theatrical Legislation in Colonial America' from Ron Engle's and Tice L. Miller's collection of essays, *The American Stage: Social and Economic Issues from the Colonial Period to the Present*, where Davis argues that business interests and anti-British sentiments are more important than religious reasons for anti-theatrical legislation in British America.

In my consideration of work on the eighteenth century, pride of place must go to Larzer Ziff's *Writing in the New Nation: Prose, Print, and Politics in the Early United States* (1991). Ziff's concern is 'the relation of literature to society in the first decades of United States history, a relation that was conceptualized by some as one between the republic of letters and the new republic'. Ziff proposes that 'print culture and American political culture were twins born from the same conditions and dependent upon one another for their well-being', so much so that to 'pursue this argument is to trace the ways in which literary paralleled political representation and how both in turn related to a shift in the economic sphere from real to personal – or represented – property'. The evidence adduced to support this thesis is taken largely from the major figures in colonial American literature – Edwards, Crèvecoeur, Bartram, Franklin, Jefferson – but Ziff is so widely read in the period that some of his 'asides' about minor figures carry a weight of authority and intelligence few other scholars can match. Throughout the study, literature is construed as something other than '*belles lettres*' and this freedom from the constraints of treating only imaginative literature enables Ziff to describe some intriguing 'debates', notably his 'pairing' of Jefferson with Timothy Dwight, the latter's *Travels in New England and New York* being seen as an important articulation, in a revolutionary climate, of the present's continuity with, rather than severance from, the past. The concluding chapter, 'Wild Usages', takes the argument on into the nineteenth century with Cooper and Melville offered as instances of writers 'who sought to open their culture to the redeeming influence of American nature and the people who inhabited it'. This is a relatively short book (about 200 pages) but it is an indispensable study for those interested in exploring the continuities between colonial and republican writing.

Some of the minor figures in eighteenth-century literature have received critical attention this year. Ann Eliza Bleecker (1752–83), a poet who rarely, if ever, finds her way into the anthologies and whose work lacks a modern, scholarly edition, is discussed in Allison Giffen's '"Till Grief Melodious Grow": The Poems and Letters of Ann Eliza Bleecker' (*EAL* 28.222–41), an article that concerns itself, centrally, with the poems Bleecker wrote mourning the loss of her young daughter, Abella, and which Giffen reads in the light of 'the dynamic between generic expectation and the particularities of her experience as a grieving mother'; she tries to protect Bleecker from 'the disparaging and totalizing use of the label "poetess"', and speaks of her work as 'diverse and sophisticated', although from what one sees quoted in the article there is little to suggest that Bleecker ever transcends a very minor key of eighteenth-century elegiac convention. A further essay on Bleecker, Julie Ellison's 'Race and Sensibility in the Early Republic: Anne Eliza Bleecker and Sarah Wentworth Morton' (*AL* 65.445–74), seeks 'to map the literary history of emotional politics' by examining Bleecker's poems and Morton's long narrative poem *Ouabi* in the light of 'sentimental treatments of race and the development of women's poetry'. Another minor figure, Hannah Adams, sometimes referred to as America's first professional woman writer, as Michael W. Vella notes in the introductory paragraph to his 'Theology, Genre, and Gender: the Precarious Place of Hannah Adams in American Literary History' (*EAL* 28.21–41), has suffered from a fairly precipitous decline in the estimation of her importance to American letters, one that Vella seeks to redress in an interesting historical account which argues that her position is a consequence of 'our concept of a literary text, and by extension our literary history itself', which 'marginalizes more than it enfranchises, and this to the detriment of our understanding of American literary history and woman's place within it'.

Two important volumes of essays devoted, wholly or in part, to Benjamin Franklin have been published this year, though neither, unfortunately, has been seen by this reviewer and both will have to wait until next year for review: J. A. Leo Lemay's *Reappraising Benjamin Franklin: A Bicentennial Perspective* (UDelP), and Barbara S. Oberg and Harry S. Stout's *Benjamin Franklin, Jonathan Edwards, and the Representation of American Culture* (OUP). In 'The Board of Trade's "*cruel* Sarcasm": A Neglected Franklin Source' (*EAL* 28.171–6), Kevin J. Hayes shows how a Board of Trade report of 5 December 1746 to the Privy Council was Franklin's source for the phrase 'the improvement and well-peopling of the colonies', found in works such as 'Rattle-Snakes for Felons', 'An Edict by the King of Prussia' and 'Causes of American Discontents Before 1778', the phrase being used by him 'to express his indignation with British attitudes toward America'.

Two essays on Crèvecoeur have been seen this year, both in *EAL*: in 'Crèvecoeur and the Politics of Authorship in Republican America' (*EAL* 28.91–119) Grantland S. Rice reads *Letters from an American Farmer* as an 'epistolary novel', one shaped by Crèvecoeur's familiarity with 'Abbe Raynal's nascent theory of civilizational decline in which a European mode of exploitative speculation succeeds in displacing an idealized portrait of New World agrarianism', his argument opening up broader questions concerning 'the assumptions and fallacies of Republican print culture'; Anna Carew-Miller in 'The Language of Domesticity in Crèvecoeur's *Letters from an American Farmer*' (*EAL* 28.242–54) reads the *Letters* as an articulation of central cultural myths of America, particularly, 'the myth that a man's relationship with the land confirms his masculinity and dignity as a citizen', and the conclusion of her essay seeks to show how Crèvecoeur's own life reflects an 'anxiety about man's domestic role and search for masculine work'; both essays, it might be noted, contain useful lists of 'Works Cited' that will be of benefit to Crèvecoeur scholars.

Jay Fliegelman's *Declaring Independence: Jefferson, Natural Language, and the Culture of Performance* is a book that merits some comparison with Thomas Gustafson's *Representative Words: Politics, Literature, and the American Language, 1776–1865*, reviewed in these pages last year (*YWES* 73.550). Fliegelman's intention is squarely stated in his introduction: 'In *Declaring Independence* I seek to recover yet another lost world, one that makes possible a new way of understanding the *Declaration*, specifically, and Jefferson and late eighteenth-century American culture more generally. That lost world is the world of eighteenth-century theories and practices of rhetoric, the classically derived art of persuasive communication that prescribed the codes and character of public speaking in England and America.' Rhetoric, therefore, becomes as much a matter of oratory as it is of grammar and syntax, and in Fliegelman's hands rhetoric becomes 'performative' and independence 'something that is rhetorically performed'. The early chapters of this study are, therefore, assiduously preoccupied with performative acts, notably Fliegelman's attempt to recover the pauses, rhythms and nuances of Jefferson's oral delivery of the Declaration; some of this is presented in tabular or diagrammatic form and throughout the book there is an intriguing use of visual, illustrative commentary. Later chapters enlarge the discussion with considerations of the growth of the American theatre in the late eighteenth century, the oratory of Patrick Henry, and a literary-philosophical discussion of the problem of plagiarism (which arises from Fliegelman's interest in John Adams's charge that in Jefferson's *Declaration* 'there is not an idea in it, but what had been hackneyed in Congress for two years before'). Reading this book one occasionally gets the sense that rather discrete materials are being forced to cohere, somewhat against their will, and so little is made of the profound political consequences of the *Declaration of Independence* that one wonders if Fliegelman has been reading the same text as the rest of us. In a characteristically postmodernist way, however, 'text' is construed as a rather slippery term. The localized insights are frequently penetrating and perceptive, even if the whole somehow fails to convince. StanfordUP, it must be added, is to be congratulated on a handsome publication (here in paperback form; I haven't seen the hardback).

ECS devotes the whole of its summer issue to work on Jefferson, although most of the articles here are of an historical character. George Alan Davy, however, in 'Argumentation and Unified Structure in *Notes on the State of Virginia*' (*ECS* 26.581–93) suggests that the *Notes* are 'not independent digressions in a book designed to provide information for immediate practical use by the French government' but are, rather, structurally arranged to 'provide a starting point for arguments in which Jefferson presents his controversial vision of America and its future'; and in 'Jefferson, Poe, and Ossian' (*ECS* 26.627–34), Jack McLaughlin seeks to establish an affinity between Jefferson and Poe, despite the latter's indifference to politics, by pointing to their common admiration of Ossian and their shared 'belief in and dedication to quantification, classification, and analysis' (some readers will, no doubt, find the affinity a little strained). Also on Jefferson's reading of Ossian we have Paul J. Gategno's brief note ' "The Source of Daily and Exalted Pleasure": Jefferson Reads the Poems of Ossian' (*SVEC* 305.1385–6) which reminds us of Jefferson's enthusiasm for *The Poems of Ossian*, and in the same volume of *SVEC* John Stephen Martin in 'Jefferson, Democracy, and Commonsense Rhetoric' (*SVEC* 305.1382–5) briefly discusses what he calls Jefferson's 'rhetorical pragmatics' and its relationship to democratic theory and practice.

Work on late eighteenth-century fiction is largely concerned with Charles Brockden Brown and Susanna Rowson. Elizabeth Jane Wall Hinds's 'Charles Brockden Brown and the Frontiers of Discourse' in *Frontier Gothic* (see my general comments on this above) examines the place of the frontier in Brown's fiction, seeing the 'frontier' as much a metaphorical place as a literal one: 'Brown's novels take place at the frontier of prose narrative, beyond narrative conventions of causality and motivation'. In 'Rhapsodist in the Wilderness: Brown's Romantic Quest in *Edgar Huntly*' (*SAF* 21.171–90), Steve Hamelman draws connections between Brown's treatment of the quest in *Edgar Huntly* and the posthumously published *The Rhapsodist*. Carroll Smith-Rosenberg in 'Subject Female: Authorizing American Identity' (*AmLH* 5.481–511) invites us to see a kind of antiphonal relationship between *Edgar Huntly* and Rowson's *Reuben and Rachel; or Tales of Old Times* published in 1798, the year before Brown's novel appeared. The argument of her essay turns, in part, on matters of audience, for while both authors 'focused on scenes of American Indian/Euro-American warfare', Rowson, unlike Brown, 'chose as her audience not generic Americans, but Euro-American women', although both, in her analysis, 'through their explanations' became 'part of the process by which Britons, resident for generations in North America, invented themselves subjects of and subjects to a new American constitution'. This essay contains much intelligent commentary, both on the novels discussed and early treatments of Indian captivity, notably that of Mary Rowlandson, and, more generally, on what the author calls 'the complex processes that instituted *Homo Americanus*', or what we might call the creation of an American sensibility. Another essay from Julia Stern, 'Working Through the Frame: *Charlotte Temple* and the Poetics of Maternal Melancholia' (*ArQ* 49.1–32), reads Rowson's most famous novel from a perspective that sees Charlotte's fatal melancholia as a kind of 'poetics' of motherhood, although the emphases in this essay seem somewhat at odds with Rowson's rhetoric in her novel.

Two review articles in *AmLH* deserve brief mention: Philip Gould's 'Virtue, Ideology and the American Revolution: The Legacy of the Republican Synthesis' (*AmLH* 5.564–77) intelligently summarizes some of the recent work on the political culture of the American Revolution, while Jeffrey H. Richards in 'Religion, Race, Literature, and Eighteenth-Century America' (*AmLH* 5.578–87) does the same for recent work on eighteenth-century religion.

My second year of covering work on James Fenimore Cooper sees two important book-length additions to the criticism, one a collection of essays, the other a monograph. *James Fenimore Cooper: New Historical and Literary Contexts*, edited by W. M. Verhoeven, brings together 12 newly commissioned essays on Cooper, with an introduction from the editor which presents a useful overview of the growth and development of the criticism. The essays themselves range quite widely in critical approach: George Dekker rehearses arguments about the 'American Romance Tradition' that will be familiar to those who know his *The American Historical Romance* (*YWES* 68.573–4); A. Robert Lee in 'Making History, Making Fiction: Cooper's *The Spy*' reads the novel both contextually and critically, seeing it as, in part, fictionalized history, an 'impersonation', as he puts it, with its own masquerades and self-inventions; 'Property, Marriage, Women, and Fenimore Cooper's First Fictions' by Robert Lawson-Peebles relates the early fictions to a discussion of questions of property, marriage and the status of women; the editor's chapter, 'Neutralizing the Land: The Myth of Authority, and the Authority of Myth in Fenimore Cooper's *The Spy*', sees the 'neutral ground' of Cooper's landscapes as 'an active, creative instrument – that is, the neutral ground is not so much morally and ideologically neutral, as morally and ideologically *neutralizing*'; John McWilliams in 'Revolt in Massachusetts: The Midnight March of Lionel Lincoln' reads Cooper's novel historically, restoring *Lionel Lincoln* to 'its due importance in creating Revolutionary history for the new Republic', and, like so much of what McWilliams writes, this essay is consistently informed and intelligent; *The Last of the Mohicans*, arguably the most re-readable of the Leatherstocking novels, is discussed for its stylistic qualities in Donald A. Ringe's 'Mode and Meaning in *The Last of the Mohicans*', and his essay is valuable for his sensitivity to what he calls 'Cooper's modes of expression'; Susan Scheckel's essay on *The Pioneers*, '"In the Land of His Fathers": Cooper, Land Rights, and the Legitimation of American National Identity', addresses some of the central questions that arise in any account of this novel, particularly those of inheritance, Indian rights and 'the Euro-American claims to the land once possessed by Native Americans', and while she rehearses some conventional critical and historical positions her essay has much to commend it; a different way of looking at how Cooper contributed (perhaps unwittingly) to the American sense of national identity surfaces in John G. Cawelti's 'Cooper and the Frontier Myth and Anti-Myth', but those familiar with the criticism of Cooper will find this rather abbreviated essay covering much familiar territory in its account of the nature of the American myth (and, indeed, its anti-mythical properties).

Cooper and Thomas Pynchon may not seem the most obvious of American literary 'pairings' but Jan Bakker's 'From Leatherstocking to Rocketman: Cooper's Leatherstocking Tales and Pynchon's *Gravity's Rainbow* Reconsidered' explores the affinities between these two writers in ways which, while occasionally simplistic (especially so in respect of Pynchon's novel), might well suggest similar lines of enquiry for other scholars; Richard D. Rust returns us to what might be called first-order questions of art in his reading of *The Pathfinder*, 'On the Trail of a Craftsman: The Art of *The Pathfinder*', and, like Donald A. Ringe's essay, this gives us an intelligent account of those purely literary qualities that nineteenth-century readers, notably Balzac, saw in Cooper's fiction; Theo D'Haen's 'Dis-placing *Satanstoe*' takes us on to the Littlepage trilogy of which *Satanstoe* forms the first part and reads the novel in the light of what he calls 'the clash between the marriage and linguistic ecologies presented' there; the concluding essay by Charles H. Adams, 'Uniformity and Progress: The Natural History of *The Crater*', is particularly welcome for its discussion of this largely neglected late work, Adams relating it intelligently to developments in nineteenth-century geology, notably the publication of Sir Charles Lyell's *Principles of Geology*, and arguing that both Cooper and Lyell write 'in opposition to a conception of history that is linear' while simultaneously suggesting that Cooper 'found in Lyell's work a scientific articulation of the same sense of permanence underlying change that he sought to define in all of his works, but especially in his later novels'. Inevitably with any collection of this kind there are strengths and weaknesses but the former outweigh the latter and even the most hardened of Cooper scholars will find something of interest here. Regrettably, there is neither a general bibliography nor an index, although the footnotes occasionally provide suggestions for further reading

Donald Darnell's intentions in *James Fenimore Cooper: Novelist of Manners* are unambiguously established in his very first sentence: 'This work undertakes a study of James Fenimore Cooper as a novelist of manners, a subject long neglected or afforded only scant attention by modern scholars.' Darnell is right to suggest that those critics who have turned their attentions to Cooper in recent years have been neglectful of this important aspect of his fiction (as the emphasis in Verhoeven's collection will, to some extent, testify) and his intentions are, in part, realized by his reminding us of Cooper's affinities with Jane Austen (although he also shows us how he is distanced from her) and earlier eighteenth-century fictional moralists. Darnell's argument rests on three central propositions: that Cooper is serious and didactic, that the theme of manners is central to his canon, and that Cooper's upper-class characters perform an important thematic role in his novels, despite what we might say about the stiltedness of his portrayal of them. He pursues this argument through the discussion of 15 of Cooper's novels, giving roughly equal weight to Leatherstocking and non-Leatherstocking fictions, and, indeed, as one might expect, his critical approach tends to work better with those texts which are the less preoccupied with life at the furthermost extension of the frontier, notably *Precaution, Homeward Bound* and the Littlepage trilogy. Darnell's method is chronological and this allows him to explore the changing pattern of Cooper's depiction of American manners both in relation to historical change and the circumstances of his personal life. Despite the brevity (124 pages plus notes and bibliography) and the occasional clumsiness of the prose this is an intelligent book and a welcome addition to the Cooper bibliography.

Not all the article material on Cooper this year has been available for my review and I shall make every effort to catch up with the more important essays that have eluded my reaches next year. Those wanting an informed overview of the current state of Cooper criticism and scholarship could do little better than look at James D. Wallace's 'Leatherstocking and His Author' (*AmLH* 5.700–14) which covers both primary and critical texts in a valuable review-essay that seeks to address what Wallace sees as the 'marginal' place Cooper occupies 'in the shifting canons of American literature', although whether those who have recently written on Cooper, such as Darnell or Verhoeven whom I have discussed above, see him as a 'marginal' figure is another matter. Of equal value as a review essay is Wayne Franklin's' Cooper Redivivus' (*ESQ* 39.49–75), although this is concerned exclusively with the volumes that have appeared, at the time of writing, in The Writings of James Fenimore Cooper series under the auspices of SUNYP at Albany; the essay is chiefly bibliographical and textual in character, Franklin welcoming the SUNYP edition because 'it gives us access into the heart of Cooper's creativity'. Robert Daly's 'Cooper's Allegories of Reading and "The Wreck of the Past"' in James Machor's *Readers in History* (see above) analyses Cooper's critical standing in the light of New Historicist theory, and seeks to expand our view of the reading of Cooper, 'to consider how other readers read him before Twain and how recent developments in literary theory might offer us new ways of reading him now'. These 'new ways' are bound up with epistemological, rather than historical or mythical, questions and with the methods by which Cooper cultivated a community of readers for American fiction that was attentive to 'an America that was culturally various and vocally polyphonic'. Two essays explore *The Last of the Mohicans* through cinematic and televisual contexts: Martin Barker in 'First and Last Mohicans' (*Sight and Sound* 3.viii.26–9) explores the persistence of cinematic and televisual interest in the novel and, in particular, offers a critical account of Daniel Mann's 1992 film adaptation, arguing that it 'celebrates cultural pluralism, but depoliticises racial politics'; in 'Agent Cooper's Errand in the Wilderness: *Twin Peaks* and American Mythology' (*LFQ* 21.287–94) Michael Carroll rather more fancifully invokes recent American TV shows (here, of course, David Lynch's *Twin Peaks*) to suggest a correspondence between Cooper's hero and (one assumes coincidentally named) Dale Cooper in Lynch's programme. Last year I neglected to cover Scott Michaelsen's 'Cooper's *Monikins*: Contracts, Construction, and Chaos' (*ArQ* 48.1–26); so herewith I make amends for my oversight: Michaelsen defends Cooper's 1835 novel against charges that large parts of it are 'dull' and 'exasperating' (large parts of many of Cooper's novels could be so criticized) by suggesting that Cooper is 'practicing satire of a type that enacts certain problematics of construction, or interpretation, in order to criticize the relatively new and shifting canons of interpretation' and he suggests that the rejection of *The Monikins* by contemporary readers 'reflects, in part, the impossibility of finding a voice in Jacksonian America distinct from the one that spoke through the parties', although the more sceptical reader might see this as a rather sophisticated way of trying to turn Cooper's failings into assets. Finally, I referred above in my review of *Readers in History: Nineteenth-Century American Literature and the Contexts of Response* to Robert Daly's 'Allegories of Reading and "The Wreck of the Past"': here Daly addresses the ways in which we might 'expand our view of the reading of Cooper, to consider how other readers read him before Twain and how recent developments in literary theory might offer us new ways of reading him now'.

Again, this essay spends far too much time pursuing endless and intractable theoretical debates about reading, invoking, as it does so, fashionable theorists of the act of reading – Pierre Bourdieu, Hans Robert Jauss, Wolfgang Iser, Eric Sundquist, amongst others – and far too little time saying anything about reading Cooper's novels. When it does engage with primary works the critical responses are little more than commonplaces disguised in theoretical obfuscations: it is time, we are told, 'to read Cooper again, less as a maker of timeless American myth than as a historian of American epistemologies, a writer who attracted an enormous community of readers, then lost some of them in trying to alter the way they read'; again, as with Scott Michaelsen's essays, Cooper's faults (and he has many) are not his own but those of his readers.

3.   American Literature 1830 to 1865

Although it is rather disconcerting to read in the preface to a book of nearly 700 pages, *The Correspondence of Washington Allston*, that 'Allston was not a great letter writer,' this book, edited by Nathalia Wright, was certainly the most enjoyable received this year. Wright brings together here all known letters by and to Allston (1779–1843) and in her introduction she is informative on his general place in American culture, noting that he was the first major American artist, trained in both England and Italy, and that he not only produced important paintings in several genres, but also explored sculpture and architecture, as well as publishing poetry and art criticism. Wright can be a rather dogmatic critic when she considers art and literature, writing, for example, that the evocations of serenity, which she sees as characterizing Allston's most original work, 'arise from transcendence rather than from a resolution of conflict, the hallmark of the greatest art'. Equally, however, she can be persuasively perceptive, as when she accounts for the success of Allston's *The Dead Man Restored to Life by Touching the Bones of the Prophet Elisha* (1814) by pointing out that it brings together three of the major elements in Allston's work: biblical subject matter, the miraculous, and ideal figures after the example of Michelangelo. Wright is surely correct in her view that Allston was not a great letter writer, but there are a number of pleasures to be taken from this book. As we might expect, the letters are interesting on the subject of painting, and particularly on the vexed issue of verisimilitude, and they also contain Allston's accounts of the composition of his most famous paintings, including *Rising of a Thunderstorm at Sea*, *The Dead Man Restored . . .* and *Belshazzar's Feast*, as well as offering trenchant criticisms of a number of English and European artists, including West, Opie and Fuseli. Allston corresponded with many of the leading figures of the day: Wordsworth, Longfellow, Channing, Washington Irving, and Elizabeth Peabody and yet many of his most interesting letters are written to the less celebrated. The book has an excellent bibliography, a very useful biographical outline of Allston's life and work, and several very helpful appendices, including one on Allston's reading.

Although there were, as usual, a large number of books devoted to single authors, particularly Hawthorne and Melville, the year also saw the publication of several texts which surveyed large swathes of American history, culture and literature. Sacvan Bercovitch, in *The Rites of Assent: Transformation in the Symbolic Construction of America*, is interested primarily in what he refers to as 'the rhetoric of consensus'. Bercovitch suggests that the myth of America eliminated the very issue of transgression; from being a dividing line, the 'frontier' actually became a synonym for progress. He writes that all the major writers of the American Renaissance participated in this rhetoric of consensus: 'None of our classic writers conceived of imaginative perspectives radically other than those implicit in the vision of America. Their works are characterized by an unmediated relation between the facts of American life and the ideals of liberal free enterprise.' In three separate chapters Bercovitch then considers *The Scarlet Letter*, *Pierre* and several extracts from Emerson's journals. Throughout his evaluation of *The Scarlet Letter* Bercovitch stresses that text and context are reciprocal, and that the novel gathers its extraordinary aesthetic power from its relationship to American culture. Bercovitch's emphasis in the section on *Pierre* is less culturally orientated, although he writes informatively on the changing literary marketplace of antebellum America, and he suggests of Melville's novel that it can be read as parody turned against itself, as a satire of the comic pretensions of the parodic mode. Bercovitch selects two passages from Emerson's journals for close analysis, and links Emerson's writing with *The Scarlet Letter* by arguing that political norms are inscribed in aesthetic judgement and therefore inherent in the process of interpretation. He concludes his highly readable, provocative book by returning to the issue of the 'oppositional', noting that an older consensus privileged the subversive: duplicity in Hawthorne, protest in Thoreau, marginality in Poe, antinomianism in Emerson, and asking a question that has considerable resonance for readers of nineteenth-century American literature – how can an antagonistic literature be considered culturally representative?

Nicholas K. Bromell, in *By the Sweat of the Brow: Literature and Labour in Antebellum America*, similarly covers a very large area in an attempt to uncover the ways in which antebellum writers participated in the broad cultural contestation of the meaning of work. Bromell suggests that during this period work was understood primarily by way of a distinction between manual and mental labour, which in turn rested upon an assumed dichotomy of mind (and soul) and body. He argues throughout the book that writing, too, must be seen as a form of work and that the work of writing and the work which writing represents are always engaged in a dialectical, mutually constituting relation. He moves smoothly between the analysis of literary texts and close readings of extracts from the 'work' of public figures like Horace Greely and William Ellery Channing (whose writings are referred to in a strikingly large number of the critical texts received this year, perhaps indicating the way in which 'text and context' are indeed becoming inseparable for critics of nineteenth-century American literature). His use of painters and painting, particularly William Sidney Mount's *Farmers Nooning* (1836), is also a feature he shares with a considerable number of critics writing this year, and is indicative of, presumably, an increasing awareness of cultural reciprocity in the art of the time. The early part of Bromell's book focuses upon *Redburn*, *The Blithedale Romance* and *A Week on the Concord and Merrimack Rivers*, and he writes particularly well on Melville's 'The Paradise of Bachelors, The Tartarus of Maids' and Hawthorne's 'The Arts of the Beautiful', 'The Birth-mark' and 'Drowne's Wooden Image', noting of the latter stories that they demonstrate Hawthorne's ironic use of birth and generation as a trope for artistic production. He uses this observation as a way of moving into the next part of his book, which considers Catharine Maria Sedgwick's *A New England Tale*, Susan Warner's *The Wide, Wide World*, and Rebecca Harding Davis's *Life in the Iron Mills* and then links the female experience of work to the issue of slavery, discussing, in particular, *Uncle Tom's Cabin* and *Narrative of the Life of Frederick Douglass*. He concludes this excellent book with an evaluation of *Walden*, noting of Thoreau that work is the central concern of both the books he published in his lifetime, and suggesting that the critique of work found in *Walden* derives much of its power from being grounded in the two ideologies it would subvert: an ethic that ascribes spiritual value to work and a theory of political economy that values work above all other activities.

Elisa New's *The Regenerate Lyric: Theology and Innovation in American Poetry* is a bold, revisionist book which also covers a large historical period, in her case from Emerson to Robert Lowell. New subverts the view that Emerson overthrew New England religious orthodoxy and founded a poetical tradition that essentially renounced that orthodoxy in favour of a secular Romanticism. New's primary concern, at least initially, is to persuade her readers that in the years between the Unitarian controversy of the early nineteenth century and the rise of Neo-Orthodoxy a century later, the orthodoxy Emerson is believed to have displaced actually appears consistently throughout American poetry. She writes at times with a disarming and refreshing frankness: 'With a few notable exceptions, Emerson's poems are unnervingly undistinguished', and she uses Frost's work, in particular, to illustrate the later poet's superior gifts. She is illuminating on Dickinson, Crane and Lowell, but it is the chapter on Whitman that is especially memorable. Overall, New suggests that much of Whitman's work remediates Emersonian duality through a lyric regeneracy, noting of the last lines of 'The Sleepers', for example, that rather than claiming the freedom *from* the Fall that Emerson had asked why we might not enjoy, Whitman's poem claims its freedom *in* the Fall.

In *Washington Irving: The Critical Reaction*, edited by James Tuttleton, sixteen writers offer a comprehensive survey of Irving's *oeuvre*. There are several pieces of his most famous short stories and, in an essay called 'Rip and Ichabod', Terrence Martin perceptively notes that Irving writes as if his settings had antiquity, as if America had a past. This collection contains a number of similarly interesting and suggestive readings of Irving's work. Philip Young argues in 'Rip Van Winkle' that the protagonist presents a near-perfect image of the way in which a large part of the world views Americans: 'likable enough, up to a point, but essentially immature, self-centred, careless, and above all, and perhaps dangerously, innocent'. Tuttleton himself suggests, in 'Style and Fame: *The Sketch Book*', that Irving's skill as a story-teller lies in his ability to merge the archetypal and the individualized, and in a second essay he argues that Irving's historical work *The Companion of Columbus* manifests a virtual postmodern fusion of multiple genres. Inevitably, perhaps, not all the essays are quite as stimulating – Mary W. Bowden's appraisal of *Bracebridge Hall*, for example, is long on plot and short on analysis. There is, overall, more space devoted to Irving as biographer than there is to him as story-teller and several of the essays, including John H. McElroy's 'The Life of Christopher Columbus', Earl N. Habert's The Conquest of Granada' and Andrew B. Myer's 'The Life of George Washington', are impressively informative about this aspect of the work of an early American writer who persisted in seeing himself as a *dilettante*, and whose collected writings amount to 30 volumes. In 'Oblique and Ordinary: Stanley Cavell's Engagement of Emerson' (*ALH* 5.172–92), Stephen Melville suggests that what Cavell particularly values in Emerson's work is his way of seeing or feeling in scepticism something other than what scepticism explicitly claims for itself. Like Kant and Wittgenstein, Melville argues, Emerson is always willing to see that this disappointment is serious and, in a certain sense, indefeasible.

Richard Grusin, in 'Thoreau, Extravagance, and the Economy of Nature' (*ALH* 5.30–41), is particularly interested in the way in which *Walden* is obviously informed by the capitalist ideology of antebellum America. However, Grusin argues, Thoreau's understanding of 'nature's economy' operates according to a logic antithetical both to the classical economic tradition of capitalism and to its Marxist critique. He notes that the economy Thoreau practised at Walden Pond constituted not an economy of simplicity but one of extravagance, and he writes of 'Autumnal Tints' that in emphasizing the aesthetic value of these autumnal tints: 'Thoreau initiates the rhetorical contrast between market and symbolic economies that informs the essay'. In 'A Response to Walden' (*JAmS* 27.237–48), Jim Lewis draws a distinction between 'consumers' of texts and 'collaborators'. Thoreau expects reciprocity, an exchange of purpose between reader and writer. Lewis links Walden Pond with Thoreau's journal and suggests that the pond is nature's journal, recording and reflecting change. In *New Essays on Walden*, edited by Robert F. Sayre, Lawrence Buell's 'Henry Thoreau Enters the American Canon' reminds us that, with the possible exception of Poe, Thoreau is the first case of an American author initially considered second rate to be 'officially' promoted to canonical status. Buell argues that the vicissitudes of Thoreau's reputation allow us to glimpse the whole American canon in the process of formation and he is extremely informative on the role publishers such as Horace Greely, James T. Fields and George Mifflin played in the construction and maintenance of this reputation. Anne LaBastille's 'Fishing in the Sky' is an account of the influence *Walden* has had on her life, as a woman, an ecologist, a writer and a log cabin dweller. Although the essay adds little to our understanding of *Walden*, LaBastille's defiantly informal style of writing ('Guess I've finally grown into *Walden*') could appeal to those Thoreau enthusiasts who find literary criticism tedious or threatening. Michael R. Fischer's '*Walden* and the Politics of Contemporary Literary Theory' uses the writings of Stanley Cavell, Wittgenstein and ordinary-language philosophy in general to investigate the conflict that emerges between Thoreau's historical 'situatedness' and his universal claims. In 'The Crosscurrents of *Walden's* Pastoral', H. Daniel Peck places *Walden* against George Inness's paintings *The Lackawanna Valley* and *On the Delaware River* (reproduced here) to consider the ways in which Thoreau never allows himself the resolution of conflict which is central to Inness's vision of the pastoral.

On Poe: The Best from American Literature, edited by Louis J. Budd and Edwin H. Cady, contains 17 articles, all of which were originally published in 1930 and the last of them was published in 1987. There are, however, no articles from the 1940s and no explanation for this omission in the very brief introduction to the book. It would have been useful to have had the editors' thoughts on what, presumably, was a decline in Poe's reputation during this decade. All other periods are well represented, especially the 1930s, and it is interesting to see how, over a period of more than 50 years, literary criticism, not just Poe studies, has changed. Many of the earlier essays, such as Edward Hungerford's 'Poe and Phrenology' (1930), Ernest Marchand's 'Poe as Social Critic' (1934), and William F. Friedman's 'Edgar Allan Poe, Cryptographer' (1936) are preoccupied with factual matters and predicated on the assumption there is a 'right reading' of a Poe story. Many of the critical observations now seem those of an age as far removed from us as Hawthorne's Salem. Yvor Winters writes, for example, in

'Edgar Allan Poe: A Crisis in the History of American Obscurantism' (1937), after quoting from Poe's poetry: 'This is an art to delight the soul of a servant girl; it is a matter for astonishment that mature men can take this kind of thing seriously.' It says much about literary fashion that virtually all of the most stimulating articles collected here were published after 1960: Emerson R. Marks's 'Poe as Literary Theorist: A Reappraisal' (1961), Jules Zanger's 'Poe and the Theme of Forbidden Knowledge' (1978), and J. A. Leo Lemay's 'The Psychology of "The Murders in the Rue Morgue"' (1982). Perhaps the finest essay in the book is the last one: Cynthia S. Jordan's 'Poe's Re-Vision: The Recovery of the Second Story' (1987), in which Jordan links Poe's victimized women with Hawthorne's, and then notes of Poe's detective stories that they constitute a 'new narrative form that critiques male-authored interpretive paradigms which fail to do justice for women'.

The Critical Response to Nathaniel Hawthorne's 'The Scarlet Letter', edited by Gary Scharnhorst, furthers this year's preoccupation with the ways in which literary canons are constructed. As is also consistent with much critical work in this period of American literature this year, Scharnhorst draws the reader's attention to the large part played by the Boston publishing firm of Ticknor, Reed and Fields in the emergence of The Scarlet Letter as an American classic. The book is divided into six chapters: 'Background and Composition History', 'Contemporary American Reception', 'Early British Reception', 'The Growth of Hawthorne's Posthumous Reputation', 'Modern Criticism', and 'The Scarlet Letter on Stage and Screen', and there is much of interest in all of them. The first chapter contains contemporary reviews from publications as diverse as Literary World, the Boston Advertiser, Universalist Quarterly and the Southern Literary Review, and, rather surprisingly, many of the reviews are warmly enthusiastic. The account of the book's reception in England is informative and there are laudatory reviews from Trollope and James. In the chapter which deals with Hawthorne's posthumous reputation, W. D. Howells makes a particularly telling observation when he notes that while Europeans had assumed 'the genuine American fiction' would be aesthetically responsive to America's vast spaces: 'when it came, the American fiction which owed nothing to English models differed from English fiction in nothing so much as its greater refinement, its subtler beauty, and its delicate perfection of form'. The section on modern criticism begins somewhat arbitrarily in 1939 and contains some of the best-known and deservedly celebrated pieces on The Scarlet Letter since that time, including Nina Baym's 'Passion and Authority in The Scarlet Letter' and Elizabeth Aycock Hoffman's 'Political Power in The Scarlet Letter'. Millicent Bell, the editor of New Essays on Hawthorne's Major Tales, also lays great stress on the changing literary market of the 1830s and 1840s, and notes that the emergence of a more competitive publishing industry dedicated to making use of native authors turned Hawthorne's fortunes. Indeed, Bell is so eager to stress the power of cultural forces in the construction of a national literature that she becomes uneasy when considering the role of the individual author, conceding only this, for example, near the end of her introduction: 'Although writers do, in some sense, speak out of the personal'. Bell places Hawthorne's writing in the context of contemporary audience expectation and surveys the history of critical responses to his stories from the date of publication to our own time. There are six essays in the book and it makes an impressive addition to Hawthorne studies. Michael Colacurcio focuses primarily upon 'Roger Malvin's Burial' and 'Young

Goodman Brown' to argue that doubt becomes the source of, and even participates in, the nature of faith in Hawthorne's stories; Carol M. Bensick subjects 'Rappaccini's Daughter' to a close analysis in order to re-allegorize one of Hawthorne's most problematic stories; Rita K. Gollin uses 'Ethan Brand' as an exemplary text to argue that the large number of Hawthorne's stories which feature excursion and return need to be read symbolically; David Leverez places 'My Kinsman, Major Molineux', 'The Celestial Railroad' and 'Earth's Holocaust' against Dante and contemporary hermeneutic theory; and Edgar A. Dryden focuses on 'The Minister's Black Veil' to argue that for Hawthorne the generic mark of the parable is not so much the sign of an aesthetic and/or historical category as it is an epitaphic inscription that becomes a figure for story. In 'What Happened to Hawthorne? Metaphor Versus Narrative in the Unfinished Romances' (*Raritan* 4.xii.94–108), James Barszcz argues that the fictions known now as *The Elixir of Life Manuscripts* and *The American Claimant Manuscripts*, which Hawthorne never put into publishable form, do not mark, as is often argued, the final deterioration of Hawthorne's imaginative powers. Instead, Barszcz suggests, in these later texts the activity of metaphor-making functions as theme and technique, and Hawthorne's tropes are solely in the service of troping, and not of an oration or a narration that might justify troping. In 'The Two Lives of Franklin Pierce: Hawthorne, Political Culture, and the Literary Market' (*ALH* 5.203–30) Scott E. Casper continues the year's fascination with publishing. His superbly researched article examines the 'Battle of the Books' between Hawthorne's biography of Pierce and David W. Bartlett's, and he evaluates the use of the production, advertising and distribution tools of the newly national literary market. Lesley Ginsbery, in '"The Willing Captive": Narrative Seduction and the Ideology of Love in Hawthorne's *A Wonder Book for Girls and Boys*' (*AL* 65.255–73) emphatically argues that *A Wonder Book* is inextricably linked to the culture in which it was produced. She notes that fears of fragmentation and disunion haunted the discourse of the period and suggests that Hawthorne's text invokes contemporary attempts to mollify the demands of 'various unfree or half free peoples' through the refashioning of a cultural myth based on the myth of the willing captive. G. R. Thompson, in *The Art of Authorial Persuasion: Hawthorne's Provincial Tales*, considers an issue which also preoccupies Millicent Bell: Thompson wishes to know, as does Bell, when Hawthorne speaks *in propria persona*. His declared focus is 'the figured authorial self of Hawthorne's works' and in a succession of chapters with titles like 'Narratological Transaction and Dialogical Framing' and 'Negative Closure and Negative Epiphany' Thompson builds an extremely persuasive argument, demonstrating the ways in which Hawthorne deliberately constructs sentimental narratives only to deconstruct them, just as he weaves and unravels versions of American historical myths. The writings of Bakhtin, Foucault, Derrida and Lyotard are used to further the argument rather than to show the author's reading and Thompson himself, despite the complexity of his thesis, is nearly always readable. Throughout the book there is what amounts to a double narrative: an explication of Hawthorne's stories and a simultaneous interrogation of previous critical opinion, and this aspect of the book is done particularly well. Eric Fretz also draws heavily on Bakhtin for his article 'Stylized Procession and the Carnivalesque in Nathaniel Hawthorne's Fiction: A Selected Sampling' (*NHR* 19.11–17), and in the same issue Carol M. Bensick considers Hawthorne's relationship to Bunyan's writing (1–10), while Raymond Benoit constructs a

Jungian reading of 'Young Goodman Brown' (18–21). Finally, Buford Jones and Stanley Blair offer a very comprehensive 'Current Hawthorne Bibliography' (22–43), which even includes dissertations. In the autumn edition of the *Review*, Will and Mimosa Stephenson argue for the influence of John Gibson Lockhart's *Adam Blair* upon Hawthorne's best-known novel, going so far as to say: 'a careful reading of *Adam Blair* sheds such a light on *The Scarlet Letter* that it seems likely Hawthorne wrote in active dialogue with it' (*NHR* 19.1–10). In the same issue, John L. Idol, Jr. and Sterling Eisiminger consider various early performances of *The Scarlet Letter* as opera (11–16), and John K. Hale, in 'The Serpentine Staff in "Young Goodman Brown"' (17–18) draws on the Biblical book of Exodus to suggest that the staff used by Goodman Brown's companion should not be seen as a symbolic phallus but instead as an object linked with the opponents of Moses and the God of Israel.

Although last year Hawthorne was the dominant figure in the period, this year the honour goes to Melville. 1993 saw the publication of Lynn Horth's edition of Melville's *Correspondence*, which is volume 14 in the Northwestern-Newberry edition of *The Writings of Herman Melville*. In this superbly edited book, Horth presents 313 letters written by Melville and, for the first time, in a separate sequence, 88 letters written to him. Because Melville habitually destroyed letters he received, and someone, probably his daughter, destroyed the numerous letters he wrote to his wife, 542 editorial entries are chronologically interspersed with letters both by and to Melville, for which no full text has been located but for which some evidence survives. Virtually all of the letters written by Melville will be of interest to Melville scholars; the volume contains, for example, his extraordinary imprudent letter to John Murray of 25 March 1848, in which he writes, in reply to a request for documentary evidence of his travels: 'I will give no evidence – Truth is mighty & will prevail – & shall & must', and there is also the full text of his famous letter to Hawthorne, written in April 1851, where he writes: 'There is a grand truth about Nathaniel Hawthorne. He says NO! in thunder, but the Devil himself cannot make him say *yes*.' The letters written to Melville are, generally, of less interest, but the final letter in the volume is, with hindsight, deeply ironic – it is a request from Havelock Ellis for biographical details and contains this poignant comment: 'At present your books are, practically, not before the public at all in this country.' Although Richard Dean Smith's *Melville's Science: 'Devilish Tantalization of the Gods!'* attempts to show the influence of developing scientific thought on Melville's work, the book relies too much on supposition and speculation and too little on evidence. There are far too many sentences in the book of this type: 'Another source of scientific information he probably used was the forty-volume, *The Naturalist Library*, edited by William Jardine.' Smith is certainly knowledgeable about science, under whose aegis he includes philosophy, but knows little about the literary criticism written on Melville, writing, for example, in his section on *Moby-Dick*: 'the two short sections at the beginning of the book which examine the origin of the word "whale" are often overlooked'. Overall, the book is hugely informative, but rarely about Melville. Stanton Garner's *The Civil War World of Herman Melville* furthers the great interest in painting shown by critical writers this year in his discussion of the impact upon Melville of the work of Elihu Vedder, which he saw at the National Academy of Design Exhibition in June of 1865 and which, Garner suggests, prompted Melville to write poetry on the subject of slavery. Garner's book offers itself as both an account of the life of Melville during the Civil War and as a study of Melville's collection of poems, *Battle Pieces*, written during the war and published in 1866. In fact, the book is more a history of the Civil War, in which Melville plays a small part, with readings of Melville's individual poems, always read as historically occasioned, functioning as a *leitmotif.* Garner makes great claims for Melville as a poet: '*Battle Pieces* is the maiden offering of an important new American poet', likening the work to *Leaves of Grass* and to the poems of Emily Dickinson, but he never subjects the poems to a sufficiently technical analysis to substantiate this belief. In *Closet Writing/Gay Reading: The Case of Melville's Pierre*, James Creech also considers the influence of painting, in his case the 'chair portrait' of Pierre's father, which, Creech plausibly argues, Melville based on a real portrait of Allan Melville, painted in 1810 by John Reubens Smith. Creech begins his interesting, if rather belligerent, book by arguing against Barbara Johnson's 'Melville's Fist: The Execution of *Billy Budd*' (1980), for purging Melville's text of its homosexual content, and he then uses Eve Kosofsky Sedgwick's *Epistemology of the Closet* to read *Pierre* as a classic example of 'writing from the closet'. The book is impressively researched and well written but, at times, speculation is allowed to assist in the construction of his argument, as when he writes of Melville's time at sea: 'where he experienced – certainly second hand, perhaps indeed as participant – sexual relations between men'. Creech has little patience with critics who do not privilege homosexual readings: 'Only wilful denials can purge Melville's novels of the yearning gazes and subtle glancings of homoerotic sexuality.' His impatience and intolerance lead him, at times, into making statements about other scholars which are, surely, quite unacceptable, as when he refers to 'the rantings of a homophobic buffoon like Edward Dahlberg'. Overall, however, Creech deciphers Pierre's 'encrypted erotics' with energy and skill, and his argument that Melville's apparent tale of incest is 'really a homosexual novel in disguise' is provocative and persuasive. In *Melville and the Politics of Identity: From King Lear to Moby-Dick*, Julian Markels takes as his point of departure the scholarly tradition that sees in *King Lear* a dramatization of the transition from feudal to bourgeois culture, and he shows how Melville takes up the 'ideologically unfinished business' of Shakespeare's play to dramatize in *Moby-Dick* a distinctive American tension between private competition and mutual responsibility within bourgeois individualism. Markels writes with assurance on the theories of both Locke and Hobbes and the ways in which the ideological conflicts their work embodies are traceable in the tensions within *Moby-Dick*. However, he also uses the work of more contemporary writers, and while his book is preoccupied throughout with questions of ideology he uses the word not in the older Marxist sense of 'false consciousness', but in the neo-Marxist sense of historically created and inescapable consciousness most often associated with the writings of Althusser and Gramsci. Markels gives a comprehensive account of Shakespeare performances and editions of his plays available in America by the time Melville began work on *Moby-Dick*, and the book's appendix contains Markels's summary of the 491 markings Melville made in the seven-volume edition of Shakespeare's plays that he acquired in 1849. Although Markels notes that a number of the markings show that Melville was impressed by Shakespeare's images of congruence between appearance and reality, he also, perhaps surprisingly to some of Melville's readers, notes that many of the passages Melville marked were simply comic. There is little that is comic in Stan Goldman's *Melville's Protest Theism: The Hidden and Silent God in Clarel*, perhaps the best of the books received on Melville this year. This, the first book-length study to appear in 20 years, offers a close analysis of Melville's 20,000 line poem *Clarel: A Poem and Pilgrimage in the Holy Land*, published in 1891. Goldman suggests that the narrative design, characters and cantos of *Clarel* can be viewed as gnostic pilgrimage quest for insight, and that the 'hidden God' of *Clarel* is the same God found in the Hebrew Bible. He notes, for example, that a quarter of the poem's lines are questions and argues that many stem from the Biblical genre of the lament. Goldman devotes considerable time to an analysis of the multiplicity of voices within *Clarel*, and he eloquently rejects the conventional critique of the poem: that there is an irreconcilable disjunction between the despair of the poem itself and the optimism of the Epilogue, by writing: 'The Epilogue is the result of a twenty-thousand line pluralistic theological hunt that finds ... despair *and* hope in a theological interrelationship'. Condy Weinstein, in 'The Calm Before The Storm: Laboring Through *Mardi*' (*AL* 65.239–53), like a number of critics this year, is interested in the notion of 'work', as the pun in her title indicates. Weinstein gives a concise and informative survey of the ways in which the development of the work ethic was promoted in early nineteenth-century America by men such as William Ellery Channing, Horace Greely and Thomas Skidmore, before suggesting that in *Mardi* Melville investigates market forces, labour and consumption while simultaneously calling attention to the book itself as the product of hard labour by including an allegory about his own making of the novel. Andrew Delbanco, in 'Melville's Sacramental Style' (*Raritan* 3.xii.69–91), focuses on the role of language in Melville's 'sea fiction', and argues that throughout this specific body of work Melville is in flight from the oppressive totality of language. He suggests that Melville's instinct is always to deprive language of its air of authority by disrupting it at every level, and acknowledges the difficulty of Melville's task by concluding his analysis with an appraisal of *Billy Budd*, a story in which 'speechlessness leads to death'.

Whitman received considerably less attention this year than he did last year, but, as if to compensate, Joel Myerson's 1,097-page *Walt Whitman: A Descriptive Bibliography* was published in the Pittsburg Series in Bibliography. This extraordinary work of scholarship documents all the collected works of Whitman up to 1991: the numerous editions, reprintings and re-arrangings of *Leaves of Grass*, individually published poems, magazine and newspaper articles, broadsides, circulars, advertisements and other prose works. An index shows the publishing history of the poems in *Leaves of Grass*, and there is also an extremely useful bibliography of works about America's most celebrated book of poetry. The chapter entitled 'First Appearance Contribution to Magazines and Newspapers' is probably the most interesting section, running to several hundred pages and showing the quite astonishing range of Whitman's subject matter. This is obviously a highly specialized publication, but it is one that will prove invaluable to Whitman scholars. This is an observation unlikely to be applied to *Singing With Whitman's Thrush: Itineraries of the Aesthetic*, by Frederic Will. The title is misleading: Will spends only a few pages discussing 'When Lilacs Last in the Dooryard Bloomed' and he does this in a manner which is quirky, to say the least: 'Whitman and I read each other by details, staccato runs at each other, an embrace, a fuck, withdrawals, and contempt.' The rest of the book, which although full of quotations from other writers has no annotation, contains extracts from Will's letters to his family, extracts from what can only be assumed to be his own fiction, and his comically obsessive musings on classifying his books. His own book is totally unclassifiable. *Walt Whitman*, by Bettina L. Knapp, is published in the Literature and Life: American Writers series and is, appropriately enough, divided into two sections: Life and Work. There is occasionally some archness in Knapp's writing; the young Whitman is referred to as an 'open and winsome lad', but she moves her story along briskly – by page 4 Whitman is already working on the *Long Island Star*. She writes particularly well on Whitman's passion for music and the influence this had on his poetry, his relationship with Emerson, and his homosexuality. When discussing the work, Knapp is equally lively and readable. She focuses on *Leaves of Grass* but does not neglect Whitman's other poems. Her critical perspective is indebted to psychoanalysis and she devotes a considerable amount of space to 'The Sleepers', writing of it that it shows 'the poet leading the reader into the heart of his own oedipal narcissistic dramas'.

4. American Literature 1865 to 1900

Martha Banta's weighty study, *Taylored Lives: Narrative Productions in the Age of Taylor, Veblen and Ford*, conducts an exploration of the effect of 'Scientific Management', as constructed by Frederick Winslow Taylor, upon American culture. The permeation of the cause of efficiency into every kind of narrative is interrogated on two levels here: the first treats Taylorism as reflected in narratives which either defend or deny that the secret to all mythologies and everything else has been discovered, and the second examines narratives which reflect what Banta calls 'the constant tension between containment and resistance' to the idea that there can ever be a single answer or method, especially as it appears in socio-literary theory. One of the writers who absorbs her attention is Henry James, whose fictions, described as unmanly by Theodore Roosevelt, concern themselves with 'the unholy alliance of barbarous instincts of acquisition and rationalist managerial practices'. Others include Richard Harding Davis, working in narratives which 'define war as romance and as business enterprise'. Henry Adams, whose *Education* is described as 'a story about helplessness and impotence', and Charlotte Perkins Gilman, with her devastating critique of the 'home as heaven' myth. Banta's work is interdisciplinary in the best and most productive sense of the word and ranges between Buster Keaton's silent decimation of the mail-order catalogue dream-home in *One Week* (1920) and Dreiser's *American Tragedy* read with its 'unfamilied characters "adrift" in an interlocking series of management cultures, with no way out'. Not least of Banta's achievements here is the magnificent bibliography and survey of the period, its theorists and practitioners.

Michael Davitt Bell's *The Problem of American Realism: Studies in the Cultural History of a Literary Idea* begins, as any such study must, with the vexed question of definition when considering American realism, and does not neglect all those who have grappled with its toils as artists or critics. Bell proceeds systematically through a consideration of those writers who have 'embraced' or 'resisted' the terms of engagement apparently offered by realism or naturalism and who are in the forefront of any formulation of the genre in its American manifestations. The first part of the book groups Howells, James and Twain together, acknowledging the strains in setting up this particular *ménage à trois* but nevertheless working with the tensions productively; the first chapter treats Howells, concentrating on his work as disseminator of literary realism in his essays, specifically the 1891 collection *Criticism and Fiction*; the second and third then contextualize the fiction of Mark Twain and Henry James within the tenets of Howellsian realism. The second part again brings forward a familiar triumvirate, Norris, Crane and Dreiser, and here Bell begins with Norris as the most vocal of the three in public pronouncement of the merits of literary naturalism proceeding to a discussion of an 'apparent *stylistic* affiliation with naturalist conventions' in tense relationship with a concomitant lack of 'affiliation with naturalist *thinking*' in the work of Crane and Dreiser. The final part of the book, 'A "Woman's Place" in American Realism: Sarah Orne Jewett', as clear, well-organized and illuminating as the preceding 'case studies on the influence of realist thinking', concentrates on the connections between local colour and the larger proposition of 'American realism' as it is realized in a range of Jewett's writing.

Cultures of Letters: Scenes of Reading and Writing in Nineteenth-Century America by Richard Brodhead is, as he announces in his opening sentence, 'a book about communities', but communities which have distinct identities and which constitute 'writing worlds' whose overlappings as well as differences are productive of meaning. In his first chapter, 'Sparing the Rod: Discipline and Fiction in Antebellum America', Brodhead provides a way into a number of works through corporal punishment, with whipping scenes predicated as 'endemic to antebellum educational writing' even in so perverse a form as Bronson Alcott's insistence that his pupils whip *him* 'hard' for their infractions of discipline, and culminating with discussion of Susan Warner's *The Wide, Wide World* as 'the most impressive recognition of discipline through love as a culture-specific historical formation'. Other chapters treat: 'Veiled Ladies', approached through Hawthorne's Priscilla, at a moment in the culture when women who entertained the public, in one form or another, 'emerged into mass visibility'; 'Starting Out in the 1860s', a study of Louisa May Alcott which has her 'reactivate a philosophy of disciplinary intimacy little changed from its classic articulations in the 1840s and 1850s'; and 'The Reading of Regions' which examines regionalism as providing an entry point into the profession of authorship and redefines it as genre by positioning it in 'a literary culture projected toward an American upper class coming together as a social entity in the later nineteenth century'. This latter discussion enables Brodhead in his characteristically level and lucid manner to bring the work of Jewett and Chestnutt back into the context of a wider audience in the final two chapters. It is particularly instructive to read Brodhead in tandem with the critics who are involved in the vital journeywork of reclaiming the work of writers such as these; he reminds us that we can have a delimiting effect if we focus too narrowly, performing vital service to the culture of letters by fulfilling brilliantly his promise to 'reroute theoretical discussions into particular historical instances, to the end of letting history qualify theory'.

By the Sweat of the Brow: Literature and Labor in Antebellum America by Nicholas K. Bromell is, like Martha Banta, concerned with the 'professionalization' of life in America, with the form and function of work, and seeks to show the way that a range of pre-Civil War writers represented, challenged and reflected labour in their writing. Bromell points first to the culture's apparent reluctance to show itself at work and then to the actual evidence of both practice and theory in the construction of ideas of work, although as he says, 'during the antebellum period work was understood primarily by way of a distinction between manual and mental labor'. Melville's *Redburn* is read as a dual narrative about two kinds of work, the physical which bestows adult certainties of wisdom and sexual maturity, and the artistic which undoes those certainties through the discovery of the unreliability of language and modes of representation. Thoreau's writing, however, in *A Week on the Concord and Merrimack Rivers*, is distinguished from Melville's model of work as developing the erotic in the worker by being shown to be concerned with the problem of distinguishing 'work and desire'. Bromell links Hawthorne with Rebecca Harding Davis by demonstrating their contiguity on 'questions about artistic practice with concerns about gender identity and class politics', but divergence on the outcome of such concerns, with Hawthorne making mental labour masculine and manual labour female, whilst Davis is concerned to forge a connection between writing and manual labour, thus feminizing both. Harriet Beecher Stowe's writing is considered within the framework of maternal labour and, in the most compelling of the discussions of individual authors here, Frederick Douglass's *Narrative* is used as a means of focusing upon the questions which arise from the relationship between slave-labour and work, indeed whether slavery is the 'ontological opposite of work' and, as with Douglass's insistence on the significance of the slave-song as expressive of misery rather than pleasure, that work here cannot be recognized as such because the nature of slavery precludes the exercise of free will that makes work work.

Frances Smith Foster's *Written By Herself: Literary Production by African-American Women, 1746–1892* adds a good deal to our knowledge of the conditions of textual production by Afro-American women before and after abolition. Early in the book, Foster makes the claim that 'the story of the African American woman is the quintessential enactment of the New World being, combining the religious faith of the Puritans and the Protestant evangelists with the Common Sense approach to social betterment of Paine, Jefferson, Franklin, and Lincoln', and she does manage to combine analysis of the individual writers in their particular American context with a demonstration of how they managed to transcend its limitations. Foster begins her discussion of individual writers with Lucy Terry Prince and Phillis Wheatley, the former's poem 'Bar's Fight', being an account of an Indian attack in Deerfield, Massachusetts in 1746. She moves through the severely circumscribed writings of black women during the Revolutionary period, limited to petitioning for freedom or better treatment but organized enough to establish the 'Colored Female Religious and Moral Society of Salem' in 1818, to the publication of a large number of books – mainly memoirs – in the 1830s. Subsequent chapters focus on Jarena Lee, her 'Religious Experiences, Life and Journal', Harriet Jacobs, Elizabeth Keckley, Frances Ellen Watkins Harper and Octavia Victoria Rogers Albert and concludes with a consideration of the political influence of Anna Julia Cooper, to whom the last words of the study are given in 'consecration' of the rich variety of African-American women's achievements, a variety to which Foster does ample justice.

The three editors, David Mogen, Scott P. Sanders and Joanne B. Karpinski, of *Frontier Gothic: Terror and Wonder at the Frontier in American Literature*, write a joint introduction and have individual essays amongst the 13 here collected. The introduction provides both definition of and insight into the territory of the title and the cultural baggage of both *Frontier* and *Gothic* is examined for what it contains: 'American frontier gothic literature derives from this conflict between the inscripted history of civilization and the history of the other, somehow immanent in the landscape of the frontier.' The author-centred essays in the collection include work on 'Charles Brockden Brown and Frontiers of Discourse', where Jane Wall Hinds links the figurative with the geographical in discussion of the gothic frontier in *Edgar Huntly, Arthur Mervyn, Wieland* and *Ormond*; Joanne Karpinski examines the work of Jewett and Freeman to illustrate how women writing as local colourists 'incorporated gothic motifs into their honestly observed depiction of the female-dominated communities of post-Civil War New England', and Stephen Mainville locates Edgar Allan Poe's frontier drama in interior space predicated only as a 'lexical frontier'. The volume also contains a welcome reprinting of Charlotte Perkins Gilman's story, 'The Giant Wistaria', alongside an essay by Gary Scharnhorst which considers the experimental nature of the narrative and its relationship to both the 'The Yellow Wallpaper' and Gilman's personal life. There are also essays on the various topographies of gothic, metaphorical, temporal and geographical; the collection as a whole ranges widely and inclusively through what the editors describe as the 'positive and negative forces ... entwined in the pluralism that is at the heart of the American experience'.

Femininity to Feminism: Women and Literature in the Nineteenth Century (1992) by Susan Rubinow Gorsky conducts a survey of the way in which women are portrayed in nineteenth-century British and American fiction written by both men and women. Gorsky's subject is so huge that individual texts are merely mentioned as contributing to a picture of 'Death and Dying', wherein 'Accidents occur more frequently in literature than in reality', 'Husbands and Wives', 'A Genteel Education for Girls' and numerous other categories. This study might serve a bibliographical purpose for students seeking to identify texts by basic theme but adds little to our understanding of either period or author.

The Theory and Practice of American Literary Naturalism by Donald Pizer, collects together essays and reviews he has written over the last 30 years which treat the full range and extent of nineteenth- and twentieth-century American naturalism. There are two new pieces in the volume, Pizer's introduction, in which he gives an account of his beginnings and development in the study of American naturalism and testifies to his eternal vigilance against 'the incubus of determinism', and an essay on William Kennedy's *Ironweed*. The collection bears witness to the range and divergence of American naturalism and the writers treated here, alongside the obvious Norris, Crane and Dreiser, include Wharton, Farrell, Oates and Mailer. Pizer's work is so central to any understanding of the complexities of American naturalism that, despite the familiarity of some of the essays collected here, this volume is indispensable.

Eric J. Sundquist's *To Wake the Nations: Race in the Making of American Literature* is a book whose thesis is movingly prefigured in its epigraph from W. E. B. Du Bois: 'Would America have been America without her Negro people?' as it argues for a literary canon which more closely reflects the different – both contradictory and complementary – ethnicities of its constituent parts in the period 1830–1920. In this enterprise Sundquist seeks to problematize the canon, not to exclude Melville and Twain but to engage with the difficulties of reading *Benito Cereno* and *Pudd'nhead Wilson* in conjunction with Nat Turner's *Confessions* and Martin Delany's *Blake; or the Huts of America*, to place Charles Chesnutt and W. E. B. Du Bois as practitioners of 'alternating sounds', that is, their incorporation of those social conditions which distinguish white and black American experience into a literature that 'forms part of the text's own cultural strategy'. The first part of this book treats the antebellum period with slavery and revolution as the key issues in an enterprise which revisits the founding principles of the nation and the conditions of their betrayal and emphasizes the rights of Turner, Douglass and Delany to be included among the key documents in 'a proper conceptualisation of the renaissance'. The second part, 'The Color Line', concerns chiefly Mark Twain and Charles Chestnutt but devotes the most attention to the latter, articulated by Sundquist as a seminal figure negotiating his way along a number of fine lines or 'cakewalks' in both his professions – attorney and writer; *The Marrow of Tradition*, Chestnutt's fictionalized account of the race riots in Wilmington, North Carolina, is celebrated as an 'anatomy of the racial politics of the nation' as well as a portrait of the cultural complexities adhering to the position of the 'New Negro' of the twentieth century. Sundquist ends with W. E. B. Du Bois, contextualizing his work in the Black spiritual, Pan-Africanism and using Du Bois to provide a methodology with which to achieve an overview of African-American culture, a task admirably and powerfully executed in this indispensable study.

The unacknowledged texts of the American Renaissance also provide a focus for *The (Other) American Traditions: Nineteenth Century Women Writers*, edited by Joyce W. Warren and divided into two parts: 'The Writers' and 'The Traditions', categorizations which challenge – in both cases – the old-established canon with alternative versions of the dominant ideological and sociological constructs of nineteenth-century America. The central focus of Warren's introduction is the re-orientation of critical focus away from 'the myth of American individualism, which has come to form the basis of American thought' and towards those writers whose subjects and perspectives are those of the under-represented in society and she provides a very useful survey of writers whom she groups as writers of seduction, frontier, domestic and local colour novels. The first essay in the collection is Jane Tompkins's 'Susanna Rowson, Father of the American Novel' which sets the pattern for the whole volume of rigorous inquisition of the assumptions which continue to govern our literary judgements. Carol Singley takes this approach in her treatment of Catharine Maria Sedgwick's *Hope Leslie*, and Nina Baym in 'Reinventing Lydia Sigourney' concludes with a suggestive paradox – that 'a writer with so obviously public a program should come down to us as the most private and domesticated of antebellum women authors suggests the need to look again at the scope of antebellum women's writing'. Other writers scrutinized in the first part include Fanny Fern, Harriet Jacobs, Harriet Beecher Stowe, Harriet Wilson and Frances Harper. The 'Traditions' half of the book includes thematic as well as genre study of fiction by women and ranges widely and provocatively among well and lesser known writers of the nineteenth century before concluding with Susan Harris's call 'to construct evaluative criteria' by which to judge such writers, and Paul Lauter's practical piece on pedagogical strategies for incorporation of obscure works in the curriculum by pairing them with canonical male writers. Another writer in the process of being reclaimed for serious academic study is Louisa May Alcott. Madeleine B. Stern and Daniel Shealy have edited and introduced a new collection of nine recently rediscovered stories, *From Jo March's Attic: Stories of Intrigue and Suspense*. Stern's introduction provides details of the magazines which published the stories, biographical information and critical commentary on the stories with Shealy supplying a bibliography of all located Alcott thrillers.

There is much activity in Dickinson criticism at the moment, particularly among feminist critics. Martha Nell Smith in *Rowing in Eden: Rereading Emily*

Dickinson (1992) asks us to reconsider our preconceptions of what constitutes publication or, indeed, text, and whether Dickinson's refusal of one kind of publication was contiguous with the self-publication of her poetry in her letters. In order to re-read Dickinson, Smith goes to the manuscripts and is therefore in continuous dialogue with the massive editorial intervention of ages, especially as regards the received wisdom on the 'Master Letters' and on the extent of Susan Dickinson's intervention in the textual as well as sexual substance of Dickinson's verse. Smith uses the metaphor of 'rowing' in order both to interrogate the poetry and to remind readers that 'reading is dialogic drama, always a matter of editing, of choosing what to privilege, what to subordinate' and she performs detailed exegeses of the fascicles whereby they reveal new patternings and readings. Alternative recipients/addressees for the letters are posited in order to unfix what might otherwise be constructed as critical certainties fed by (auto)biographical interpretations; Smith seeks to realign, as she says, not invalidate other readings and, indeed, opens all manner of routes into the writings. The final chapter of Smith's rewardingly complicated and complicating study of Dickinson's writing looks at Susan Dickinson's obituary for her sister-in-law and emphasizes as primary the relationship between the two women, with Susan as the paradigmatic participatory reader at work in Dickinson's texts. Smith, along with Suzanne Juhasz and Cristanne Miller, is co-author of *Comic Power in Emily Dickinson*, a volume to confute both assertions of feminism as humourless and Emily Dickinson's verse as irredeemably tragic in style and content. In their introduction the three survey the critical and biographical work which has gone to make up the portrait of Dickinson as *tragedienne* in order to make the point that such a one-dimensional view of the poet 'edits out the wry, the witty, the playful, the tough, the challenging, the successful Dickinson' and go on, in their respective chapters, to examine not only comedy but parody, teasing, visual and verbal cartoons, satire and the grotesque. It falls to Suzanne Juhasz to negotiate 'The Big Tease', working with two definitions of teasing in order to show Dickinson poking fun at established norms whilst also looking at the sexual implications of the verse, endlessly promising whilst yet deferring – as exemplified by 'Come slowly – Eden!' – both forms of tease, however, creating 'the space of the poem, positioned between the mind of the poet and the culture she questions'. Martha Nell Smith delivers 'The Poet as Cartoonist' in which the poet's transactions with her community through the cartoonist's art are scrutinized alongside the wider cultural context of her drawings and writings, directing Dickinson's pictorial as well as written productions towards the argument which fuels *Rowing in Eden*: 'by manufacturing her own books and cartoons and controlling her final copy, Dickinson was neither limited to poetic forms ... critical wisdom ... nor to poetic subjects'. 'The Humor of Excess' is Cristanne Miller's means of access to the grotesque, the extreme in the verse which approximates the 'loss of control, the rush toward chaos that occurs at moments of great intensity', and in many ways her chapter is the consummation of the entire project in its serious treatment of the disruptive quality of Dickinson's work and working practices and their concomitant comedic possibilities.

Emily Dickinson: Woman of Letters is a collection of poems written by the editor of the volume in response to and incorporating lines from Dickinson's letters; also contained within Lewis Turco's collection are essays by four critics writing on various aspects of Dickinson's letters. The first of these essays, by Jeanne Holland, '"Knock with tremor": When Daughters Revise "Dear Father"' examines in detail the draft of the poem cited in the title in the context of its 'negotiation of patriarchal authority' and includes a discussion of Cynthia Griffin Wolff's analysis of the courtship of Dickinson's parents through their correspondence in substantiation of the reading of the draft with its tantalizing empty letter – 'Dear Father – Emily' on the reverse. Ellen Louise Hart, in 'The Encoding of Homoerotic Desire: Emily Dickinson's Letters and Poems to Susan Dickinson, 1850–1889', reads both poetry and letters written to Susan as they demonstrate the vicissitudes of the friendship but also, crucially, the unswerving constancy of Dickinson's love for her sister-in-law. Like Martha Nell Smith, Hart points to the omission of discussion of Dickinson's erotic desire for Susan from the work of other critics and seeks to insert the poem 'Morning', or Letter 921, written around 1884, into the heart of a Dickinson canon as a means towards interpretation; certainly its lines reverberate with an endlessly expectant love. David W. Hill in 'Words Doing: Dickinson's Language as Autonomous Action' considers language as event in the letters and selected poems, and in the final essay Marta Werner responds impressionistically to the 'Master Letters'.

Fanny Fern: An Independent Woman (1992) by Joyce W. Warren provides comprehensive and enthusiastic coverage of the life and works of Sarah Payson Willis Parton or Fanny Fern, as she became known to her readers, among whom featured an enthusiastic Hawthorne: 'I have since been reading "Ruth Hall" and I must say I enjoyed it a good deal. The woman writes as if the devil was in her.' Fern was born in 1811 in Portland, Maine, the fifth of the nine children of Nathaniel and Hannah Willis; soon after her birth the family moved to Boston and at 16 Fern went to school at the Hartford Female Seminary, run by Catharine Beecher, who was providing what was probably the best education on offer to girls at that time. Warren is a biographer partial to her subject but this is part of the appeal of the volume as she takes us from the oppressive Calvinism – wielded by her father – of her childhood to the financial and emotional crises of Fern's adult life and the circumstances in which she began her work. Fern's three marriages, her friendships, her children and, above all, her professional life – Fern was the first woman newspaper columnist in America – are amply covered here and of particular note is Warren's discussion of the often controversial subjects of her journalism and also of her 1854 novel, *Ruth Hall*.

Nancy A. Walker takes considerable care to do justice to Fern's journalism in her study of *Fanny Fern* for the TUSAS, and also to her writing for children, arguing that through these works she reached and influenced large audiences and that, for this reason, they are likely to provide a comprehensive picture of the matters important in the lives of American readers of the 1850s and 1860s. The role which Fanny Fern played in the culturally resonant evolution of the American newspaper column is seriously treated and the collected articles published as *Fern Leaves* in 1853 are examined in some detail. The critical reception given to *Ruth Hall* at the time of publication, in all its vitriol, forms a part of Walker's thorough discussion of the novel and subsequent chapters deal with Fern's little discussed second novel, *Rose Clark*, and her collections of stories for children.

Continuing the theme of why women write, 'Mary Wilkins Freeman and the Taste of Necessity' by Virginia L. Blum (*AL* 65.69–94) begins with Nina Baym's assertions that we oversimplify when we prescribe economic necessity as the driving force behind women writing in the nineteenth century and goes on to describe Freeman as a 'transitional' figure – the woman writer mediating between ideas of 'art for profit and art for art's sake' in terms of both her own status as artist and of her subject matter, particularly in her representations of food and eating.

Margaret Fuller: Writing a Woman's Life by Donna Dickenson claims Fuller as '*the* emblematic woman of her time' and begins her study of the life and works with an account of the manner in which they were treated after her death. The three editors of her memoirs, Ralph Waldo Emerson, James Freeman Clarke and William Henry Channing, began, as Dickenson says, 'the process of mythologising Fuller into obscurity after her death', a cause taken up by Nathaniel Hawthorne and Henry James at subsequent points. From the conditions which shaped her posthumous reputation, Dickenson then moves on to Fuller's childhood and early education, comparing her along the way with other women writers like Emily Dickinson and drawing on the work of Carol Gilligan and Nancy Chodorow in order to construct a reading of 'female development and identity differentiation'. The variety of Fuller's writing is treated here and Dickenson works in new and thorough ways with the restored versions of Fuller's letters as well as with the published works. Mary E. Wood, in '"With Ready Eye": Margaret Fuller and Lesbianism in Nineteenth Century American Literature' (*AL* 65.1–18), also locates an unfamiliar Margaret Fuller as she interrogates the writing for its capacity to 'reveal the ways that heterosexuality struggled to assert itself in nineteenth-century American discourse against women's desire for each other'.

Charlotte Perkins Gilman is one of the women writers examined in Diane Price Herndl's account of *Invalid Women: Figuring Feminine Illness in American Fiction and Culture, 1840–1940*. She compares 'The Yellow Wallpaper' with Wharton's *The House of Mirth* in order to show how both writers 'portray seriously "sick" societies in which social and sexual oppression makes women ill', an argument which is representative of the larger thesis of the book which moves between the medical theories of mid-nineteenth-century America and its literature and, specifically, its representations of women as invalid.

On Howells: The Best from American Literature edited, inevitably, by Edwin H. Cady and Louis J. Budd, reprints essays written between 1942 and 1977 which offer a serious look at *The Rise of Silas Lapham* and *A Boy's Town* and, among other treatments of lesser-known fiction, reprints William L. Andrews, from 1976, on 'William Dean Howells and Charles W. Chestnutt: Criticism and Race Fiction in the Age of Booker T. Washington'.

The collection *Anxious Power: Reading, Writing and Ambivalence in Narrative by Women*, edited by Carol J. Singley and Susan Elizabeth Sweeney, contains an essay on 'Power and Resistance in Harriet Jacobs' *Incidents in the Life of a Slave Girl*' by Debra Humphrey. Using the work of Foucault to conduct an analysis of power structures in Jacobs's text, Humphrey relocates and problematizes both the genre of the *Narrative* and the sites of authority which are variously 'appropriated and redefined'.

Among the large number of significant studies of Henry James published in 1993 is Ian F. A. Bell's '*Washington Square': Styles of Money*, which provides the kind of thorough coverage of the novel to be expected from the Twayne's Masterwork Studies series with immediate attention paid to the 'Historical Context', 'The Importance of the Work', and the 'Critical Reception' before getting down to the real business in 'A Reading'. Bell, however, takes us straight back into the context of the novel with his straightforward declaration: '*Washington Square* is about history, about the ways in which economics and commercial practices structure human relationships, and about the ways in which history may be represented in fictional forms.' Bell problematizes this argument in a number of ways, not least of which treats the different uses to which James put the examples of Hawthorne and Balzac in their respective identifications with 'latitude' and 'fact' in order to reach the point where the text can be read 'as it conjures away the conventions of realism'. Bell pays close and illuminating attention to the topography of the novel, to the connections between the decade of its composition and the decades of its setting, to the 'debates about "soft" and "hard" money, paper and coin', and to the emergence of corporate America, but he also focuses intently on the language in which these thematic strains emerge. Morris Townsend comes out of Bell's reading of the novel a rehabilitated character, a victim of the 'period's transformations as he struggles within its simultaneous promise of economic amelioration and damnation of those whom its accelerations leave behind', whilst manners and the means and ends of self-representation are further interrogated in comparison with *The Europeans*.

Subjects covered in *HJR* 14.ii. range between an essay describing Mrs Chichester, the woman to whom Henry James Senior paid tribute as having been instrumental in directing him towards Swedenborg (132–40) by Jacqueline Latham, through 'Milly Theale's London' (215–22) by Chris Brown, to a discussion of the BBC video adaptation of *The Portrait of a Lady* by Anthony J. Mazzalla (179–87). Other notable contributions include Jonathan Freedman on 'Trilling, James and the Uses of Cultural Criticism' (141–50) where the identity of the 'international intellectual' or 'urbane insider-outsider' fashioned by James is shown as taken up and assimilated by Lionel Trilling; and Suzi Naiburg on 'Archaic Depths in Henry James's "The Last of the Valerii"' (151–65). Martha Banta opens *HJR* 14.iii. with 'From "Harry Jim" to "Saint James" in *Life Magazine* (1883–1916): Twitting the Author; Prompting the Public' (237–56), an account of the changing relationship between the editors of the magazine and the literary scene as expressed in their treatment, in both words and pictures, of James. Hershel Parker writes 'Deconstructing *The Art of the Novel* and Liberating James's Prefaces' (284–307) in which he provides a history of critical dealings with the text which treat it as 'an authorially controlled artifact' and subsequently – and literally – performs a 'deconstruction' of the text so that it represents the order of composition and thereby presents itself for consideration in terms of the '"development" of James's critical ideas from one preface to another'. Also in this issue is an essay on 'Henry James's Letters to Jessie Allen' by Rosella Mamoli Zorzi (273–83), which brings to light a 'Venice story' in addition to the opportunity to look briefly at the language and terms of reference of this particular friendship.

Following his 1990 *The French Side of Henry James*, Edwin Sill Fussell has now produced *The Catholic Side of Henry James* in which he declares loud and clear that he is not performing some belated act of conversion upon the man or his works but is challenging the unremittingly secular nature of the Jamesian interpretative endeavour in order to engage with what James himself called 'the aesthetics of religion' as they intersect with the wider literary enterprise of the American nation, artists and readers alike. As James has it in *The American*, '"I'm not a real Catholic, but I want to buy it."' Fussell goes some way towards articulating the dual nature of attraction and repulsion expressed by a wide range of American writers from Lydia Maria Childs and Catharine Maria Sedgwick to William Dean Howells and Nathaniel Hawthorne, setting James in both secular and spiritual context as a self-reflexive member of family and nation 'Belonging as we do to the profane and Protestant half of society'. Fussell charts, in both calendar and discursive form, James's 'Chief Items of Catholic Interest', ranging between reviews, essays, stories, novels and plays, a discussion of *Guy Domville* forming an important part of the penultimate chapter alongside 'De Grey: A Romance' and *The Golden Bowl*, where he finds that the 'Roman Catholic *ménage* serves the aesthetic purpose of defining and delimiting a literary space'. Among the texts he delineates as narratives of Catholic conversion is *The Turn of the Screw*, upon which he performs an ingenious reading which expresses 'the horror of Roman Catholic conversion from a Protestant point of view so excessive as to be psychopathic'. The context of James's explorations of the Catholic in the whole range of his writing is conscientiously treated in Fussell's study, but the chief pleasure here is in the insights his approach allows him into the structural as well as the thematic *Side* of Henry James.

New Essays on 'Daisy Miller' and 'The Turn of the Screw', edited by Vivian R. Pollak, has two essays on each book and a substantial introduction by the editor which offers readings of both texts in the light of the particular conditions of life in the James clan and, appropriately in a volume that has for its subject the definitive Jamesian stories of the American girl and the English governess, considerable attention is paid to the conditions of existence for Alice James in such a family. In the first essay, '*Daisy Miller*: Dynamics of an Enigma', Kenneth Graham centres Daisy as 'unknowable' in his argument in order to navigate a way between critical readings rooted either in the moral or psychological imperative or the narratological argument, in a manner which will foreground irresolution. Robert Weisbuch gives a sprightly account of Daisy in which her perpetual motion ('If I didn't walk I should expire') is ultimately pinioned by Winterbourne's imprisonment in gender in 'Winterbourne and the Doom of Manhood in *Daisy Miller*'. Millicent Bell, in 'Class, Sex and the Victorian Governess: James's *The Turn of the Screw*', places James's narrative firmly in the context of the governess novel of the 1840s and beyond so as to confute 'generic expectations' about the outcome of the story, yet also to utilize the doubleness attendant upon the figure of the governess: 'as a defender of innocence and conserver of morality' but also 'as a problematic person whose situation inspires the fear that she will menace the definition of class and gender'. The final essay, 'In the "Other House" of Fiction: Writing, Authority, and Femininity in *The Turn of the Screw*', David McWhirter describes the text as terrorizing its readers with its ambiguities, with its shifty sliding between genres in order to avoid categorization as ghost story or psychological drama so as to 'express the experience of in-betweenness for which our language and culture, and all the genres of genre they entail, possess no adequate terms'.

Thomas Strychacz, in *Modernism, Mass Culture and Professionalism*, devotes two chapters to the work of Henry James; the other writers considered are Theodore Dreiser, John Dos Passos and Nathanael West, and all are read in terms of their attempts to find appropriate forms in which to express the twentieth century whilst distinguishing themselves as practitioners of a literature which is distinct from mass culture. *The Reverberator* and *The Sacred Fount* are both scrutinized for their accommodations with mass culture; the former is construed as setting off a 'debate between literary and non-literary principles', whilst the latter expresses, via the image of the 'newspaper-man kicked out' but re-entering through the back-door, a representative of the forces of mass communication which haunt 'the magisterial complexity of the narrative and language of the "palace of thought"' in the Jamesian novel.

Henry James and the Lust of the Eyes: Thirteen Artists in His Work by Adeline Tintner continues this critic's exploration of the who's who, what, where and when in the writing of James and the book is, in many ways, an appendix to *The Museum World of Henry James* (1986). The 12 brief, tightly focused chapters of the book discuss selected texts and related paintings and they are followed by nearly 100 pages of black and white reproductions of works of art and a few assorted bits of James memorabilia. Tintner begins her intertextual attributions with the 1883 story 'The Siege of London' in order to demonstrate that 'the form of the story is ... created by the picture', the picture in question being Thomas Couture's *The Romans of the Decadence*. Other works by James which Tintner ruthlessly interrogates for their allusions to visual artists are *The Reverberator*, 'A London Life', 'The Chaperon', *The Ambassadors*, 'The Private Life', as well as the more predictable *Tragic Muse, The Wings of the Dove* and *Roderick Hudson*. *Black and White Strangers: Race and American Literary Realism* by Kenneth W. Warren takes Henry James out of the largely European cultural context visited and revisited in Adeline Tintner's work and positions him squarely in *The American Scene*, a text here fruitfully scrutinized in tandem with *The Souls of Black Folks* and *Iola Leroy*. Warren draws James into unfamiliar critical territory by engaging with the writer's 'effort to locate aesthetic freedom within some framework mimetic of social relations', and, early in his study, states loud and clear that his thesis is based on the premise 'that concerns about "race" may structure our American texts, even when those texts are not "about" race in any substantive way'. Building on the line of enquiry called for by Toni Morrison in her seminal essay 'Unspeakable Things Unspoken: The Afro-American Presence in American Literature' (1989), Warren aims to rethink the culture in terms of all its constituent parts as active in formation of both the political and the aesthetic. He puts his writers – and especially James and Howells – in the context of the post-Reconstruction erosion of black civil rights in order to establish the particular contingencies of such a reformulation of the democracy as major contributory factors in the 'realistic novel's focus on the importance and fragility of the social order'. Warren's discussion of the political and literary culture in the last decades of the nineteenth century also extends to consideration of the role of the *Century* magazine, a comparison between *Uncle Tom's Cabin* and *The Bostonians* so as to scrutinize 'realism's critique of sentimentalism', and concludes with some consideration of Afro-American literary criticism and theory.

Five novels structure the course of the argument in Merle A. Williams's study *Henry James and the Philosophical Novel: Being and Seeing*, which is shaped by James's position in relation to the philosophical ideas of his brother, William, his father, Henry Senior and the work of Maurice Merleau-Ponty. Pursuing the line, as he says, of 'story-telling as a mode of philosophical enquiry' Williams takes the primary concerns of phenomenology and places them alongside the narratives to demonstrate that 'the rigour and comprehensiveness of their design embodies a series of searching investigations into problems of subjectivity, truth and social intercourse'. *What Maisie Knew,* the first novel under discussion here, is viewed as a text which rewrites and reorders 'established modes of seeing and judging' whilst *The Ambassadors* reveals Strether's quest for the style which will enable him 'to achieve a fully integrated structure of vision'. Williams also looks in detail at *The Wings of the Dove* and *The Spoils of Poynton*, the latter exegeticized as a text with a correlative in a mathematical problem, showing 'its "workings" from the first step to the conclusion'. The study climaxes with an appropriately densely figured interpretation of *The Golden Bowl* where the 'maximum of hermeneutic sophistication' in the Master is matched by his hierophant. Williams is one of the guest editors, with Karen Scherzinger, of a Henry James Special Issue of *ESA* (36.ii.) which celebrates James 150 years after his birth. The opening essay, 'James Under Stress' (5–19) by Kenneth Graham, looks at the year 1893, James's fiftieth, a year in which he wrote only one story, 'The Middle Years' and which can be seen, with the help of the autobiographical texts, as a 'climacteric'. Both the editors of the volume take theoretical approaches with Scherzinger examining 'Henry James, Jacques Lacan and the Purloined Spoils' (31–41) and Williams, reading *The Europeans,* invokes both William James and Jacques Derrida in order to find 'Traces of James's Later Manner' (21–9).

The work of Harriet Beecher Stowe features in an essay entitled 'Eva's Curl' in Susan Wolstenholme's *Gothic (Re)visions: Writing Women as Readers*. Wolstenholme begins with Freud's work 'A Child Is Being Beaten' as means of entry into the text and the fetishization of little Eva, but moves on to consider it as 'protest novel' as well as gothic where 'Stowe's use of Gothic conventions casts light on the novel's status as a feminist tract'.

Shelley Fisher Fishkin's book, *Was Huck Black? Mark Twain and African-American Voices*, questions the received wisdom on the whiteness of the models and antecedents of Twain's *Huckleberry Finn*, seeking to exegeticize the Afro-American presence in the novel and thus re-orient both our reading of the text and its position in the literary culture of America. This study situates Twain in a profoundly multi-cultural society, and also takes us beyond the gilded age into the sphere of Twain's influence upon black writers of the twentieth century. There are difficulties attached to Fishkin's undertaking here and they are acknowledged obliquely in the emphatic nature of some of the writing. Every time that she wants us to take 'particular notice', as Huck would say, she italicizes her prose and when she points to the omission of certain of Twain's publications from general discussion of his work she writes: ' *"Sociable Jimmy" takes the place of honor as the first piece Twain published that is dominated by the voice of a child'*. This is characteristic of the book in various ways for whilst Fishkin has interesting things to say about possible models for Twain's vernacular it is so transparently *worthy* and *honourable* in its intentions that it makes one *impatient* with its *assumptions* and *conjectures.* Fishkin does, however, assemble – to some effect – analyses of language and syntax that have been carried out on Huck's speech and provides an extensive and impressive bibliography.

Sander L. Gilman in 'Mark Twain and the Diseases of the Jews' (*AL* 65.95–115) notes that Twain was as contradictory in his views about the Jews as he was on other subjects and whilst these views found public expression in a late essay, 'Concerning the Jews' (1898), there are earlier images of the Jew in his writing – specifically *The Innocents Abroad* – which bear comparison with 'the various racial models of the diseased Jew which existed in European and American thought through the nineteenth century'.

The collection of essays, *Satire or Evasion? Black Perspectives on 'Huckleberry Finn'* (1992) edited by James S. Leonard, Thomas Tenney and Thadious M. Davis has a range of diverse responses to the text; rehabilitation is not the aim here but close examination of the novel in the variousness of both historical and contemporary readings. Leonard and Tenney introduce the volume in the context of controversy old and new and spend a good deal of time addressing the contingencies of the negative aspects of both nineteenth- and twentieth-century cultural contexts to get at the text itself and also to make the point that 'thematic energy works on the central characters to disrupt stereotypes both black and white'. The editors demonstrate the fact that there can be no single reading, no unity of interpretation of this text among black critics any more than there can be among white. The diversity of opinions and reactions is one of the most exciting things about this collection which ranges between John H. Wallace: 'The *Adventures of Huckleberry Finn*, by Mark Twain, is the most grotesque example of racist trash ever written' in the essay which opens the collection, to Charles H. Nilon's inclusive discussion of 'The Ending of *Huckleberry Finn* "Freeing the Free Negro"' which productively and positively locates the book in its historical context and also accommodates the influence that George Washington Cable might have had upon Twain in the writing of the novel. This collection reverberates with both emotion and intelligence and in itself is true to the spirit with which William Dean Howells exhorted us to read Twain, here quoted by Charles H. Nichols: 'I warn the reader that if he leaves out of the account an indignant sense of right and wrong, a scorn of all affectation and pretense, an ardent hate of meanness and injustice, he will come infinitely short of knowing Mark Twain'.

Critical Essays on 'The Adventures of Tom Sawyer' edited by Gary Scharnhorst is divided into two sections; the first deals with the contemporary response to the novel and the second critical essays written between 1961 and 1993. Scharnhorst's introduction charts the role that commercial considerations played in the change between Twain's statement in 1875, after completing the manuscript, that it was '*not* a boy's book, at all. It will only be read by adults. It is only written for adults', and the preface of the American edition in which he claims: 'my book is intended mainly for the entertainment of boys and girls'. Scharnhorst puts the book in its wider cultural context, taking in a number of celebrity manipulators of Tom Sawyer's potential as American icon from Norman Rockwell through Frank Capra to Walt Disney and its simultaneous rejection by New Critics on the grounds of its failure to meet any coherent aesthetic principles. This collection picks *Tom Sawyer* criticism up in the early 1960s when the combination of close scholarly attention to the manuscript of the novel and the interdisciplinary or historicist approach opened new areas for discussion. Scharnhorst includes those essays which he regards as charting and also defining the trends in *Tom Sawyer* criticism, like James M. Cox on 'Myth and Reality in *The Adventures of Tom Sawyer*' and Judith Fetterley on 'The Sanctioned Rebel', and also illustrates the production of new critical approaches from old categorizations, like Fred See's Lacanian 'Tom Sawyer and Children's Literature'. The only new essay is the final one, 'Undoing Romance: The Contest for Narrative Authority in *The Adventures of Tom Sawyer*' by Henry B. Wonham which addresses itself both to Twain's indecision about the book's intended audience and whether it was satire or romance, concluding, with a degree of inevitability, that the uncertainty allowed 'Twain to question the method of his novel as he writes it'. This essay then immediately reappears in Wonham's single authored book, *Mark Twain and the Art of the Tall Tale*, where it forms part of an argument which has Twain playing a number of rhetorical games with his readers in his use and abuse of narrative conventions. Wonham devotes the introduction and first chapter to the tall tale which, he says, 'with its mutable form and its rhetorical pattern of interpretive challenge and response, offered [Twain] a means of dramatizing the interaction of voices without pretending to have resolved them into a single, unified voice'. In the chapters dedicated to *The Innocents Abroad*, *Roughing It*, 'Old Times on the Mississippi', *Tom Sawyer* and *Huckleberry Finn*, Wonham deploys the tall tale in a variety of inventive strategies, not least of which is to mark out some kind of common language which kept current 'the possibility of a viable oral community'. After publication of *Huckleberry Finn*, however, comes the effect which he describes under the title of 'The Eclipse of Humor', where satire replaces humour as the driving force behind the 'subversive project' of his writing in texts like *Pudd'nhead Wilson*.

An essay on *Pudd'nhead Wilson* features in Arnold Weinstein's book, *Nobody's Home: Speech, Self, and Place in American Fiction from Hawthorne to DeLillo*. Here Weinstein makes the central thrust of his study an examination of free speech informing national identity in America as it signifies either the unreal or fictive self as well as the subject 'who is denied status or selfhood by the culture'. Paired with *Pudd'nhead Wilson* on the basis of their shared concern with disguise, with locating a 'way out, a writerly way of breaking the prison' is Stowe's *Uncle Tom's Cabin* which is read in illuminating detail as firmly within both the literary and the American tradition of treating the ruptured family, placing the role of art foremost in the processes of reunion and reunification. Weinstein's argument is thematic and so ranges between Hawthorne and Melville to Morrison and DeLillo, establishing lively and cogent readings of individual texts. His use of *Uncle Tom's Cabin* as providing a context for *Beloved* is particularly interesting on the 'dis-membering and re-membering of the human family'.

The 19 essays in the collection *Wretched Exotic: Essays on Edith Wharton in Europe* derive from the 1991 international literary conference, 'Edith Wharton in Paris', and the expatriation of Edith Wharton, in its personal and literary effects, is the centre of interest here. The volume editors, Katherine Joslin and Alan Price, provide an introduction to Wharton's life, to the topics under discussion and an essay apiece. Joslin opens with Wharton's infamous description of herself and her 'class' – '*we* are none of us Americans, we don't think or feel as the Americans do, we are the wretched exotics produced in a European glass-house, the most déplacé & useless class on earth!', and the contributors to the collection take Wharton's self-confessed displacement from topographical certainty as their creed here. As Millicent Bell explains, nothing could indicate more the state of Americanness than the desire to live in Europe and so Wharton's nationality is, in this inversion, reinforced by the essayists who explore the business of her expatriation in all its complications and convolutions. Other notable contributors are Kristin Olson Lauer, with her account of the perennial themes and concerns of reviewers in 'Can France Survive This Defender? Contemporary American Reaction to Wharton's Expatriation'; Susan Goodman on 'Edith Wharton's Inner Circle'; Judith L. Sensibar in '"Behind the Lines" in Edith Wharton's *A Son at the Front*', declaring for Wharton as modernist; and Carol Wershoven bringing new insights to Wharton's neglected novels of the 1920s and 1930s.

Anxious Power: Reading, Writing and Ambivalence in Narrative by Women includes an essay by Carol J. Singley and Susan Elizabeth Sweeney, the editors of the volume, on 'Forbidden Reading and Ghostly Writing in Edith Wharton's "Pomegranate Seed"'. The authors here use Wharton's tale to illustrate the contingencies of 'anxious power' itself through the relationship between supernature and realism and the expression of ambivalence towards both the production and consumption of the written text, in this case, as so often in Wharton's fiction, a letter.

An essay on *The House of Mirth* is included in *Gothic (Re)visions: Writing Women as Readers* by Susan Wolstenholme and exegeticizes the *Tableaux Vivants* episode of the novel as part of a wider thesis which looks at 'the moments where women writers write their writing acts into their texts', here particularly as it delineates Wharton as influenced by the British tradition of romance, by George Eliot and Charlotte Brontë.

Books Reviewed

Alcott, Louisa May. *From Jo March's Attic: Stories of Intrigue and Suspense.* Ed. Madeliene Stern and Daniel Shealy. NortheasternU. pp. 160. £20.95 ($21.95). ISBN 1 555 53177 6.

Banta, Martha. *Taylored Lives: Narrative Productions in the Age of Taylor, Veblen and Ford.* UChicP. pp. 464. £27.95 ($34.95). ISBN 0 226 03701 1.

Bell, Ian F. A. *'Washington Square': Styles of Money.* Masterworks Series. Macmillan. pp. 193. £16.95, pb £10.95. ISBN 0 805 78359 8, 0 805 78596 5.

Bell, Michael Davitt. *The Problem of American Realism: Studies in the Cultural History of a Literary Idea.* UChicP. pp. 256. $21.95. ISBN 0 226 04201 4.

Bell, Millicent, ed. *New Essays on Hawthorne's Major Tales.* CUP. pp. 155. pb $8.95. ISBN 0 521 42868 8.

Bercovitch, Sacvan. *The Rites of Assent: Transformations in the Symbolic Construction of America.* Routledge. pp. 424. pb £11.99. ISBN 0 415 90015 8.

Brodhead, Richard. *Cultures of Letters: Scenes of Reading and Writing in Nineteenth-Century America.* UChicP. pp. 245. £23.95. ISBN 0 226 07525 7.

Bromell, Nicholas. *By the Sweat of the Brow: Literature and Labor in Antebellum America.* UChicP. pp. 278. $40.00. ISBN 0 226 07554 0.

Budd, Louis and Edwin H. Cady, eds. *On Poe: The Best from American Literature.* DukeUP. pp. 272. $35.00. ISBN 0 822 31311 1.

Cady, Edwin H., and Louis J. Budd, eds. *On Howells: The Best from American Literature.* DukeUP. pp. 288. £32.25. ISBN 0 822 31300 6.

Creech, James. *Closet Writing/Gay Reading: The Case of Melville's Pierre.* UChicP. pp. 219. pb $14.95. ISBN 0 226 12022 8.

Cunliffe, Marcus. ed. *The Pelican History of Literature: American Literature to 1900.* Penguin. pp. 400. pb £6.99. ISBN 0 14 017758 2.

——, ed. *The Pelican History of Literature: American Literature Since 1900.* Penguin. pp. 489. pb £6.99. ISBN 0 14 017759 0.

Darnell, Donald. *James Fenimore Cooper: Novelist of Manners.* AUP. pp. 142. £25. ISBN 0 87413 487 0.

Dickenson, Donna. *Margaret Fuller: Writing a Woman's Life.* St Martin's. pp. 244. $35. ISBN 0 312 09145 1.

Engle, Ron, and Tice L. Miller, eds. *The American Stage: Social and Economic Issues from the Colonial Period to the Present.* CUP. pp. 320. £40.00. ISBN 0 521 41238 2.

Felker, Christopher. *Reinventing Cotton Mather in the American Renaissance: Magnalia Christi Americana in Hawthorne, Stowe, and Stoddard.* NortheasternU. pp. 309. $42.95. ISBN 1 55553 17 3.

Fishkin, Shelley Fisher. *Was Huck Black? Mark Twain and African-American Voices.* OUP. pp. 288. $25. ISBN 0 19 502214 1.

Fliegelman, Jay. *Declaring Independence: Jefferson, Natural Language, and the Culture of Performance.* StanfordUP. pp. 268. hb £27.95, pb 9.95. ISBN 0 8047 2075 4, 0 8047 2076 2.

Foster, Frances Smith. *Written by Herself: Literary Production by African-American Women, 1746–1892.* Blacks in the Diaspora. IndUP. pp. 240. hb £30, pb £12.95. ISBN 0 253 32409 2, 0 253 20786 X.

Fussell, Edwin Sill. *The Catholic Side of Henry James.* Cambridge Studies in American Literature and Culture No. 61. CUP. pp. 208. £35 ($54.95). ISBN 0 521 43202 2.

Garner, Stanton. *The Civil War World of Herman Melville.* UKanP. pp. 544. $60.00. ISBN 0 7006 0602 5.

Goldman, Stan. *Melville's Protest Theism: The Hidden and Silent God in Clarel.* NIUP. pp. 202. $27.00. ISBN 0 87580 174 9.

Gorsky, Susan Rubinow. *Femininity to Feminism: Women and Literature in the Nineteenth Century.* Women and Literature. Macmillan. pp. 300. hb $22.95, pb $13.95. ISBN 0 805 78975 8, 0 805 78978 2.

Herndl, Diane Price. *Invalid Women: Figuring Feminine Illness in American Fiction and Culture, 1840–1940.* UNCP. pp. 270. $32.50. ISBN 0 807 82103 9.

Horth, Lynn, ed. *The Writings of Herman Melville: Correspondence.* NorthwesternUP and The Newberry Library. pp. 923. $29.95. ISBN 0 8101 0995 6.

Joslin, Katherine, and Alan Price. *Wretched Exotic: Essays on Edith Wharton in Europe.* American University Studies: American Literature Series XXIV, Vol. 53. Lang. pp. 418. $48.95. ISBN 0 820 42223 1.

Juhasz, Suzanne, Cristanne Miller, and Martha Nell Smith. *Comic Power in Emily Dickinson.* UTexP. pp. 184. $27.50. ISBN 0 292 74029 8.

Knapp, Bettina. *Walt Whitman.* Continuum. pp. 240. $25.00. ISBN 0 8264 0566 5.

Leonard, James S., Thomas Tenney, and Thadious M. Davis. *Satire or Evasion? Black Perspectives on 'Huckleberry Finn'.* DukeUP (1991). pp. 288. $45. ISBN 0 822 31163 1.

Machor, James L., ed. *Readers in History: Nineteenth-Century American Literature and the Contexts of Response.* JHUP. pp. 285. pb £13. ISBN 0 8018 4437 1.

Markels, Julian. *Melville and the Politics of Identity: From King Lear to Moby-Dick.* UIllP. pp. 165. $13.95. ISBN 0 252 06302 3.

Mogen, David, Scott P. Sanders, and Joanne B. Karpinski, eds. *Frontier Gothic: Terror and Wonder at the Frontier in American Literature.* AUP. pp. 206. £33.50. ISBN 0 8386 3489 3.

Myerson, Joel, ed. *Studies in the American Renaissance: 1993.* UPVirginia. pp. 380. £35.95. ISBN 0 8139 1453 1.

——. *Walt Whitman: A Descriptive Bibliography.* UPittP. pp. 1,097. $250. ISBN 0 8229 3739 5.

New, Elisa. *The Regenerate Lyric: Theology and Innovation in American Poetry.* CUP. pp. 280. $54.95. ISBN 0 521 43021 6.

Nordloh, David J., ed. *American Literary Scholarship: An Annual, 1991.* DukeUP. pp. 519. $43. ISBN 0 8223 1315 4.

Parini, Jay, ed. *The Columbia History of American Poetry.* ColUP. pp. 894. $59.95. ISBN 0 231 07836 6.

Pizer, Donald. *The Theory and Practice of American Literary Naturalism.* SIUP. pp. 272. $32.50. ISBN 0 809 31847 4.

Pollak, Vivian R. *New Essays on 'Daisy Miller' and 'The Turn of the Screw'.* The American Novel Series. CUP. pp. 210. $29.95. ISBN 0 521 41673 6.

Sayre, Robert, ed. *New Essays on Walden*. CUP. pp. 118. $10.95. ISBN 0 521 42482 8.

Scharnhorst, Gary, ed. *Critical Essays on 'The Adventures of Tom Sawyer'*. Critical Essays on American Literature Series. Hall. pp. 264. $45. ISBN 0 816 17320 6.

——, ed. *The Critical Response to Nathaniel Hawthorne's 'The Scarlet Letter'*. Greenwood (1992). pp. 268. £44.95. ISBN 0 313 27599 8.

Singley, Carol J., and Susan Elizabeth Sweeney, eds. *Anxious Power: Reading, Writing and Ambivalence in Narrative by Women*. SUNYP. pp. 400. hb $59.50, pb $19.95. ISBN 0 791 41389 6, 0 791 41390 X.

Smith, Martha Nell. *Rowing in Eden: Rereading Emily Dickinson*. UTexP. pp. 300. hb $35, pb $15.95. ISBN 0 292 72084 X, 0 292 77666 7.

Smith, Richard. *Melville's Science: 'Devilish Tantalization of the Gods!'*. Garland. pp. 340. $57. 0 8153 1308 X.

Strychacz, Thomas. *Modernism, Mass Culture and Professionalism*. Cambridge Studies in American Literature and Culture No. 65. CUP. pp. 272. £37.50. ISBN 0 521 44079 3.

Sundquist, Eric J. *To Wake the Nations: Race in the Making of American Literature*. HarvardUP. pp. 720. $23.95. ISBN 0 674 89330 1.

Thompson. G. *The Art of Authorial Presence: Hawthorne's Provincial Tales*. DukeUP. pp. 320. $18.95. ISBN 0 8223 1321 9.

Tintner, Adeline. *Henry James and the Lust of the Eyes: Thirteen Artists in His Work*. LSUP (1992). pp. 328. $32.50. ISBN 0 8071 1752 8.

Turco, Lewis. *Emily Dickinson, Woman of Letters: Poems and Centos from Lines in Emily Dickinson's Letters*. SUNYP. pp. 164. hb $49.50, pb $16.95. ISBN 0 791 41417 5, 0 791 41418 3.

Tuttleton, James, ed. *Washington Irving: The Critical Reaction*. AMS. pp. 245. $39.50. ISBN 0 404 61490 6.

Verhoeven, W. M., ed. *James Fenimore Cooper: New Historical and Literary Contexts*. Rodopi. pp. 217. np. ISBN 90 5183 360 1.

Walker, Nancy A. *Fanny Fern*. Twayne. pp. 150. $21.95. ISBN 0 805 73981 5.

Warren, Joyce W. *Fanny Fern: An Independent Woman*. RutgersUP (1992). pp. 380. £21. ISBN 0 813 51763 X.

——. *The (Other) American Traditions: Nineteenth-Century Women Writers*. RutgersUP. pp. 380. hb $45, pb $15. ISBN 0 813 51910 1.

Warren, Kenneth W. *Black and White Strangers: Race and American Literary Realism*. UChicP. pp. 168. hb $27.50, pb $10.95. ISBN 0 226 87384 6.

Weinstein, Arnold. *Nobody's Home: Speech, Self, and Place in American Fiction from Hawthorne to DeLillo*. OUP. pp. 368. $19.95. ISBN 0 19 508022 X.

Will, Frederic. *Singing With Whitman's Thrush: Itineraries of the Aesthetic*. Mellen. pp. 202. $39.95. ISBN 0 7734 3046 6.

Williams, Merle A. *Henry James and the Philosophical Novel: Being and Seeing*. CUP. pp. 276. £35 ($44.95). ISBN 0 521 43110 7.

Wolstenholme, Susan. *Gothic (Re)Visions. Writing Women as Readers*. SUNY Series on Feminist Criticism and Theory. SUNYP. pp. 224. $59.50. ISBN 0 791 41219 9.

Wonham, Henry B. *Mark Twain and the Art of the Tall Tale*. OUP. pp. 224. £25 ($35). ISBN 0 19 507801 2.

Wright, Nathalia, ed. *The Correspondence of Washington Allston*. UPKen. pp. 682. $75.00. ISBN 0 8131 1708 9.

Ziff, Larzer. *Writing in the New Nation: Prose, Print, and Politics in the Early United States*. YaleUP. pp. 209. $25. ISBN 0 300 05040 2.

XVI

American Literature: The Twentieth Century

PETER VERNON and STEVEN PRICE

This chapter has two sections: 1. Fiction Since 1945; 2. Drama. Section 1 is by Peter Vernon and section 2 is by Steven Price.

1. Fiction Since 1945

(a) General

Arthur M. Saltzman's new book, *The Novel in the Balance*, considers concepts of balance and examines narrative tactics of consolidation in the work of a number of important postmodern writers. The book draws useful distinctions between modernism and postmodernism. The opening chapter compares and contrasts John Hawkes's *Second Skin* and Marilynne Robinson's *Housekeeping*: both authors are found to have a non-authoritarian vision and make evident the tensions and inconsistencies within their works. Next, *Lives of the Poets: Six Stories and a Novella* by E. L. Doctorow and *The Things They Carried* by Tim O'Brien are considered as story cycles; the features examined are the ways in which the stories either oppose each other or blend together. Saltzman goes on to look at 'play' in Robert Coover's *The Universal Baseball Association* and Paul Auster's *The Music of Chance*. In Coover one finds a 'reliable yet fluid artifice of an eternal game'; in Auster, however, chaos theory is more in evidence, so that 'while randomness (chance) pervades the world of protagonist Jim Nashe, a decorum (music) lies at the core'. The next comparison is between Don DeLillo's *Ratner's Star* and Joseph McElroy's *Plus*: both authors are concerned with the 'appeal and the fallibility of systems of thought themselves'. The tension between linguistic reach and grasp is the crisis that spurs both novels. In *Prisoner's Dilemma* by Richard Powers and *The MacGuffin* by Stanley Elkin something is saved through the writing itself. *Ceremony* by Leslie Marmon Silko and *Middle Passage* by Charles Johnson shows that the claims to pure racial and cultural legacies are false. Finally, Saltzman considers the boundaries between story and novel by looking at Alf MacLochlainn's *Out of Focus*, Nicholson Baker's *The Mezzanine*, Charles Simmons's *Wrinkles*, Renata Adler's *Speedboat*, Stephen

Dixon's *Work* and Ronald Sukenick's *The Endless Ghost Story*. This is a book of massive learning and anyone working on the contemporary American novel will benefit from its fine insights. Unfortunately, Saltzman does not wear his learning lightly: rather than a picker-up of learning's crumbs, he is an industrial digger in the mines of literature. Every chapter, each section of every chapter, is prefaced by quotation; scarcely a paragraph or sentence is left to speak for itself, thus the argument is attenuated, as analogy and comparison proliferate. A discussion of *Housekeeping*, for example, leads him to Wordsworth's 'Mutability', we find another parallel in *To the Lighthouse*, from whence we move briskly to 'The Garden' and are finally spewed up with the biblical flood. Why not Spenser, Shelley and *The Epic of Gilgamesh* one wonders? In so Babeling his book, Saltzman does his readers and himself a disservice: to discuss postmodern texts it is not necessary to produce, oneself, a criticism in which everything is likened to everything else so that, ultimately, nothing has significant relief.

In contrast to Saltzman, Stephen Matterson in 'Why Not Say What Happened? E. L. Doctorow's *Lives of the Poets*' (*Crit* 34.113–25) considers the book in light of the rest of Doctorow's work. Although *Lives of the Poets* is an oddity in Doctorow's work, none the less it illuminates and adds much to our understanding of the other novels. *Lives of the Poets* may exemplify Eliot's point in 'Tradition and the Individual Talent', in that after reading it our understanding of Doctorow's other work is altered; particularly since here Doctorow asks fundamental questions about the nature and function of the writer which he had only touched on previously. In 'Ventriloquists' Conversations: The Struggle for Gender Dialogue in E. L. Doctorow and Philip Roth' (*ConL* 34.512–37), Marshal Bruce Gentry states that gender politics is a crucial issue in contemporary American Jewish Literature. An historical opposition between feminism and Judaism presents Roth and Doctorow with problems, in that they want to be both Jewish *and* Contemporary Americans. In both writers, anger is released towards a woman in order for her to tell her story; although Gentry is worried by this, he still argues that both writers have been engaged for a long time in an attempt to express the perspectives of women. Meanwhile, Marjorie Perloff in 'Postmodernism: *Fin de Siècle*: The Prospects for Openness in a Decade of Closure' (*Crit* 35.161–91), gives a useful survey of the last 20 years of the postmodern debate beginning in 1972 with *boundary 2 (An International Journal of Postmodern Literature)*, and points out just how far the debate has moved on from questions of who should inherit the mantle of the great moderns. Indeed, can the same term be used to refer to Olsen and the poetry of the 1960s and the writing of the 1990s? Perhaps our post-post days prefigure a term we have yet to invent.

Two useful articles on Coover have appeared which fit in well with Saltzman's thesis. Richard Walsh in 'Narrative Inscription, History and the Reader in Robert Coover's *The Public Burning*' (*SNNTS* 25.332–46), shows that Coover has always been interested in the ways our various explanatory narratives impose on the truth of experience. This was abstract and metafictional in *Pricksongs and Descants* (1969), and given hard political edge in *The Public Burning* (1977), where recent American history entered his book to the extent that the final editing was performed under pressure from lawyers at Viking. Meanwhile Pierre Joris, 'Coover's Apoplectic Apocalypse or 'Purviews of Cunning Abstractions' (*Crit* 34.220–31), considers *A Night at the Movies* and *Pricksongs and Descants* as Möbius strip strategies in which observer and observed, viewer and viewed, inside and outside are continuously switched; thus the boundaries of fiction and reality are seen as porous.

Storming the Reality Studio: A Casebook of Cyberpunk and Postmodern Science Fiction, edited by Larry McCaffery, is a casebook dedicated to that heady mix of violence, sex and science-fiction known as cyberpunk. With contributions by Ballard, Burroughs, DeLillo, Gibson, Jaffe, Pynchon and Sterling, plus many more in the fiction section; and, amongst others, Baudrillard, Csicsery-Ronay, Jr, Derrida, Hollinger, Jameson and Lyotard in the criticism section; this is a useful and necessary introduction to a new wave of writing. The term 'cyberpunk' was apparently coined to describe William Gibson's *Neuromancer* (1984), and the style was later defined as being 'harder, faster, greater and louder'. Than what? One wishes to ask, and of course the answer comes back – to everything that has been written before. That this is a somewhat arrogant proposition should not need emphasizing. One of the commentators (Csicsery-Ronay, Jr) suggests that cyberpunk is the apotheosis of postmodernism in that it negates manners, history, philosophy and anything to do with cultural memory, and, on the other hand, it is about power 'and the grace of Hip'; nature has been replaced by virtual reality and what we find is a future world construct 'that is as remote from the "lessons of history" as the present mix-up is from the pitiful science fiction fantasies of the past that tried to imagine us'. The statement is revealing in two ways: first, the adolescent arrogance that cannot imagine that previous generations can have had the same thoughts and goals and desires (whose expression 'one cannot hope to emulate' as T. S. Eliot wrote, and Donne, too, was here before in *The Anniversaries* 'when new philosophy put all in doubt'); secondly, the unconscious looking back to a norm, to a golden age of nature when things were right, from the stand-point of this 'present mix-up'. The insistence on the new, whilst holding a nostalgia for the past, is a contradiction that seems hardly to be mentioned, but is endemic in nearly all the pieces extracted. For example: 'He was gazing on this world before its rot, an image of the past, projected on false doors that could never open' (Bruce Sterling). McCaffery does make a nod in this direction early on but makes no attempt to resolve the contradiction.

For McCaffery the postmodern can best be understood by examining technological change, and thus the book is dedicated to the interaction between genre science-fiction and the literary *avant-garde*. The argument, such as it is, comes from Baudrillard, Jameson et al., and runs as follows: technological advances have meant that people can interface with machines, recreate experience, fulfil desires etc. – this is Baudrillard's 'precession of the simulacra'. Thus cyberspace has become so integrated in our daily lives that the images often seem more 'real' (real always takes inverted commas), more 'substantial' more 'natural' than reality and have overtaken reality. We now have a desert of the real (Borges *via* Baudrillard) in which people are consuming themselves in the form of images and abstractions through which their desires and identities are replicated and sold back to them as products. According to McCaffery, the whole technological advance, genetic engineering, information technology, virtual reality are not dealt with by mainstream 'realistic' writers, not only because of the specialized knowledge required, but also because these concepts challenge 'the normative bedrocks upon which the fantasies of "realism" are grounded'. McCaffery does not tell us who he is thinking of in terms of these mainstream realistic writers – Jeffrey Archer and Barbara Cartland perhaps? Which raises a larger question of methodology: the criteria for selection never seem to be mentioned; this is even more apparent in the bibliography where who's in and who's out seems whimsical to say the least. Cyberpunk, McCaffery states, has a particular aesthetic within the postmodern condition because it presents an 'intense, vital and often darkly humorous vision of the world space of multinational capitalism'. Which would seem to imply that these authors are fighting some lone battle against the unidentified and amorphous multinationals who are mystified into this moment's mythological enemy, thus replacing the Yellow Peril and the Jews. The cyberpunk authors, we are informed, in their battle against big business, move seamlessly through the realms of hard science and pop culture, chaos theory and Madonna, Arthur Rimbaud and Arnold Schwarzenegger etc. But how trendy all this is; so *commercial*: what joins these movements and figures together is *sales* and I would not exclude *Storming the Reality Studio* from that goal.

For all its modish flashiness, this is nevertheless a useful introduction to an interesting and entertaining group of writers who deserve to have more thought and less enthusiasm expended on them. The opening section 'Cyberpunk 101: A Schematic Guide to *Storming the Reality Studio*' presents the reader with a series of quirky, knowing paragraphs on texts as diverse as *Frankenstein* (inaccurate and trivial), *The Big Sleep* ('Chandler's polychromatic prose style and vision of the knight-errant detective has influenced more than one cyberpunk'), *Crash* ('like approaching orgasm with Jayne Mansfield just before Fatal Impact') and *The Crying of Lot 49* (wrong-headed, and why nothing on *V.* which has been much more influential on cyberpunk with its central theme of the interaction of man/woman and machine?). The selection of prose and poetry is always going to be controversial, but on the whole McCaffery has given us a representative group of readings – although one might have expected to find some Vonnegut. However, the selection of criticism, theoretical discussion and analysis is excellent and the book is worthwhile for this alone. But the critical apparatus leaves a lot to be desired: what has guided the choice of inclusion in the bibliography (Hegel, Marx, Sade, Faulkner), and exclusion (Vonnegut, Derrida – who is actually one of the contributors, Prigogine and Gleick)? The selection of films seems to serve no function whatever, so brief and arbitrary as it is. Given that this is a groundbreaking book on an immensely popular subject one can only hope that in future editions some of these problems may be addressed.

The interest in cyberpunk is continued in George Slusser and Tom Shippey (editors), *Fiction 2000: Cyberpunk and the Future of Narrative*, a series of papers delivered at Leeds in 1989. Many of the contributors are common to *Storming the Reality Studio*, and much of the material, especially *Neuromancer,* is just a rehash. Part I attempts to put cyberpunk in perspective with articles by Csicsery-Ronay, Jr on the appropriation of the future by the present, and George Slusser on what he calls 'the Frankenstein barrier', in which Victor Frankenstein loses all claim to the future by refusing to create a bride for the monster. This is true enough, but the complexities of Frankenstein's motives are forgotten and therefore one of the central debates in the novel: the dual claims of 'masculine' science vs. the feminine principle is lost. Slusser naively asks why does Walton 'turn back toward the myth of the warm place at the heart of these frozen wastes?'. As any reader of *Frankenstein* knows, he doesn't: Walton starts off with this myth and then rejects it to return *home* to England and womankind for a number of reasons: two of the most important being the warning of Frankenstein not to overgo; and the blandishments of the crew who are understandably mutinous. Slusser could have profited from the mass of recent criticism on *Frankenstein*.

However, in resurrecting J. D. Bernal, 'The World, The Flesh and The Devil: An Inquiry into the Future of the Three Enemies of the Rational Soul' (1929), and considering Bernal's 'dimorphic' evolution (the 'good' part of humanity will transcend itself and reach for the stars; the 'bad' part will remain behind in custody to the former and will become a 'well-tended zoo'), Slusser begins to ask some important questions. Although the assumption that the good, transcending part of humanity will necessarily be benevolent is not questioned. It is also irritating to find no reference to Bernal in the notes.

Part II examines questions of tradition in cyberpunk and science fiction. Paul Alkon considers 'Deus Ex Machina in William Gibson's Cyberpunk Trilogy' and goes all the way back to Félix Bodin's *Le Roman de L'avenir* (1834) which provided the first poetics of futuristic fiction. Gary Westfahl usefully examines the central paradox in cyberpunk fiction (the sense of continuity of cyberpunk within a tradition of SF vs. the claims cyberpunk makes for being radically new and different), in '"The Gernsback Continuum": William Gibson in the Context of Science Fiction'. The essay is valuable for the trenchant manner in which Westfahl dismisses the superficial claims of Sterling et al. for the radical newness of cyberpunk. The argument is continued in Carol McGuirk's 'The "New" Romancers: Science Fiction Innovators from Gernsback to Gibson', which is also valuable for the use she makes of Bakhtin's studies on the novel endlessly renewing itself in parody and polyphony. Although the breadth and depth of Bakhtin's thought makes much of the debate on cyberpunk look like an argument on total immersion vs. sprinkling in the question of baptism.

Part III considers cyberpunk and postmodernism: John Huntington, Lance Olsen and Brooks Landon variously, and learnedly, examine Gibson's work from a more engaged viewpoint (Bourdieu, Peter Brooks, Raymond Williams etc.); 'science fiction tells us nothing about our future and everything about our present' (Olsen) – a position fiercely refuted by Stirling, quoted in interview. Landon, in one of the most thoughtful papers, considers the larger question of memory and forgetting and goes way beyond *Neuromancer* in his discussion of computers and 'our amnesiac society' – Barthes's concept of *oublie* might have been useful to him here.

Part IV deals with the cyberpunk canon (which might be regarded as an oxymoronic term): John Christie argues for discontinuity in reading Gibson's trilogy – they 'constitute a diversity, not a unity'. Robert Donahoo and Chuck Etheridge examine the figure of the 'Good' Anarchist in the works of Lewis Shiner where anarchy is seen 'as a cleansing force necessary for the destruction of decaying social structures'. Francis Bonner looks at cyberpunk in film and TV and comes to the rather surprising conclusion that it is probably not worth talking of either medium in terms of cyberpunk; this position is contradicted by a number of essays in *Storming the Reality Studio*. Tom Shippey writes wittily of 'semiotic ghosts' (bits of deep cultural imagery that have split off and taken on a life of their own), in the works of Bruce Sterling and Gibson.

Finally, Part V is entitled 'The New Metaphoricity: The Future of Fiction' – a somewhat overstated claim. Gregory Benford in a brief, thoughtful polemic argues for more thought in the genre and less energy in surface effects; he challenges critics to work out new methods of dealing with fantastic literature that do not rely on old habits of mind. Ruth Curl looks at the metaphor of the computer in *Neuromancer* and Benford's *Great Sky River* which, she argues, are used in significantly different ways: Gibson uses the computer as an ontological metaphor, in which the tenor controls the vehicle; whereas Benford perceives metaphor more epistemologically (I think the real question has yet to be addressed – when can we move beyond the dead weight of the metaphor to a more productive metonymy?). In an essay that ranges from Pythagoras and Eudoxus (who, I was glad to learn, discovered irrational numbers), to Norbert Wiener and beyond, David Porush examines, with panache and optimism, the central problem of AI, which, he believes, will emerge, not through complications but complexity: 'through a cybernetics in which the observer and the observed lock in a self-conscious loop of growing organization and complexity: in short, a postmodern text'. Eric S. Rabkin returns to *Frankenstein* and examines the workings of science as a pretext in the invention of fictions; he analyses with penetration the figure of oxymoron in helping us go beyond the reach of human sense. The workings and questionings of the conference are summed up in a discussion reported by Terri Frongia and Alida Allison. *Fiction 2000* and *Storming the Reality Studio* are probably all one needs to know about cyberpunk and the postmodern condition of narrative.

Edited by N. Katherine Hayles, *Chaos and Order: Complex Dynamics in Literature and Science* has rather more science than literature about it, but it is an important book for anyone working in postmodern literature. Hayles's introduction begins with the standard view that order can be classified while disorder has been seen as chaos. She moves on to the contemporary view that chaos is seen as exceptionally complex information which is beginning to be described as the science of chaos. Although the term 'chaos' has apparently lost cast with professional scientists after James Gleick and is now a sign that the user is a dilettante, nevertheless Hayles maintains the term because of its ambiguity. Chaos has traditionally been seen as a negative force against which order must fight, but the science of chaos has put into question western assumptions: thus another possibility to order is 'not-order' rather than anti-order. The science of chaos is not opposed to normal science, it *is* normal science, tested and evaluated in precisely the same terms as traditional experiments. The result, according to Hayles, is therefore not a simple evolution in which a new view replaces an old, but rather a 'set of negotiations at multiple sites' among those who work in this field. This book aims to treat 'chaos both as a subject of scientific inquiry and a crossroads where various paths within the culture converge'. Therefore, Hayles argues, it is high time that scientists realize that language cannot be seen as purely instrumental. From the work of Barthes, Beer, McClosky, Latour and others, we arrive at what literary scholars have known for a long time: when 'discovery is communicated through language, it is also constituted by language'. Thus the science of chaos is not peculiar: it is merely another sign of the postmodern condition, and is not the originator of 'chaotics' (i.e. the attitude to chaos within the culture). Of course, much of this is obvious and has been known since the Greeks put forward Apollo and Dionysus as two different kinds of wisdom. Perhaps the one lacuna in the quite exceptional scholarship in this volume is the way in which writers have in some ways predicted many of these ideas: for example, we read 'To some extent, we see what we are taught to see', well, yes, and Coleridge said the same thing in *Biographia Literaria* nearly 200 years ago. Using recursive symmetry – the replication of symmetries which allows for asymmetries and unpredictabilities – Hayles can tie chaos theory into the postmodern condition of fragmentation, rupture, discontinuity, iteration, self-reflexivity etc. The science of chaos now has two branches which can, roughly, be explained as 'the order hidden within chaotic systems' emphasized by Gleick and 'the order that arises out of chaotic systems' emphasized by Prigogine and others. Both branches have influence on the cultural realm, but the latter is seen as having a self-organizing principle which operates against traditional thermodynamics and envisions a universe that is renewing itself towards increasing complexity rather than death.

As one might expect Pynchon, DeLillo, Borges, Barthes and Derrida figure largely in the volume; but then so do Eliot, Ruskin and Hardy. However, the major influence would seem to be that of Ilya Prigogine and Isabelle Stengers, whose theories inform most of these essays. Despite the argument that traditional studies in science and literature have evinced a somewhat sterile pattern that needs challenging (1. scientific theory explained; 2. parallels constructed between it and the literary text; 3. QED), the majority of essays collected here privilege science over literature in precisely the traditional way. It might have been interesting to argue, as I suggested above, some of the ways in which literature has predicted scientific theory: the Romantics and relativity, the Victorians and psychology. The essays in this volume are collected under three sections: I 'Chaos More than Metaphor' is theoretical; II 'Order Revisioning Form' reinterprets past literatures, thus Ruskin (and Turner) share an insight with the science of chaos which is that spatial forms are interpretations of temporal flows; III 'Chaos and Order: Probing the Limits' which has essays on Borges, Lem, and Michel Serres compared with Thomas Pynchon.

In William Paulson's challenging essay 'Literature, Complexity, Interdisciplinarity' we get quite a lot of complexity, some interdisciplinarity, but, so far as I can see, no literature – or rather, no literary text. What we find are theoretical statements about literature that are finally not very helpful. Thus rhetorical figures 'pose fundamental problems of decidability preventing texts from being fully decoded by unambiguous, grammar-like procedures'. Indeed, one would hope so, otherwise literature would be reduced to *Postman Pat*. But Paulson goes further: utilizing information theory, he continues by saying that whatever is not immediately decodable in the literary text functions as noise. No matter how carefully this is hedged about (and Paulson is a careful scholar), this seems wrong-headed. Take a line, any line, say: 'Black milk of daybreak we drink you at nightfall'. Even though I must have read this line more than 50 times I still do not know what the words mean in an unambiguous way, but that they do mean, and have the potential for meaning, that they are *not* noise, is sure. T. S. Eliot, we might recall, makes much the same point in the great essay on 'Dante' '... genuine poetry can communicate before it is understood'.

In 'Negentropy, Noise and Emancipatory Thought' Eric Charles White interestingly compares Michel Serres with Thomas Pynchon. In both writers, the characters reach impasse; in attempting to project a world, to see the piston move on the Nefastis Machine, we find ourselves, like Oedipa, caught in a double-bind. The essay ends, aptly, with a more traditional view of entropy: '... the activity of making sense by way of recourse to chaos, noise and chance circumstance is an interminable task because power, like desire, is protean and omnipresent'. This is a challenging, thought-provoking book which I think will be essential reading for anyone trying to understand the postmodern world.

In *Voix Ethniques* and *Voix et Langages aux Etats-Unis* two research groups in France discuss the difficulties of discovering and expressing different minority voices. In *Voix Ethniques* Michel Fabre finds in the work of John F. Matheus a remarkable treatment of ethnic differences which deal with both cooperation and conflict within the American mosaic. Jacqueline Berben discusses John Wideman's recent fiction, while Dwight Hopkins looks at the voices of poor African–American women in the novels of Toni Morrison. Meanwhile *Voix et Langages aux Etats-Unis* presents papers on the voice of Africa in John Updike's *The Coup*, a fine discussion of voice and language in *Rabbit At Rest* which concludes with Updike achieving a 'tenuous balance between death and triumph', and a useful essay on the voices of solitude and memory in Paul Auster's *The Invention of Solitude*. Charles Holdefer reappraises Henry Miller and discovers in his writing the voice of an early postmodern. Holdefer compares Orwell's engagement with Miller's passivity and then goes on to look at the attitude of Salman Rushdie who makes explicit use of Orwell's criticism of Miller. Holdefer concludes that Orwell's 'Inside the Whale' (1940) was a prescient criticism and that Miller's passive stance inside the whale of history allowed him to record accurately the horror of events.

Temperamental Journeys: Essays on the Modern Literature of Travel, edited by Michael Kowalewski, is an interesting collection of essays on the modern literature of travel. Since there is, apparently, no accessible general bibliography of travel writing in either the USA or Britain, the editor has provided a very useful chronology and bibliography from 1900 to 1991, together with a listing of works from Australia to Wales, and the book will probably be used more as a reference work rather than for the collection of essays. Travel writing, especially American travel writing, has received very little criticism; it has been seen as on the margins of literature, not part of the canon. Kowalewski believes this is because of the commodification of travel and because travel literature in some ways has been seen as an adolescent escape: 'All I wanted was to go somewheres' as Huck Finn says. Kowalewski, however, argues that many travel narratives are literature, and that travel literature is still being written despite the dire warnings of Evelyn Waugh and Forster that the genre is dead. Travel writing involves border crossings which are both literal and figurative; as a genre it is something of a mixed bag which joins narrative and discursive writing. As Jonathan Raban has pointed out, 'factual' material is used to authenticate what is really fiction, while the wildest fiction takes on the status of facts. The Claude glass of the eighteenth century has become internalized by modern travel writers, but the modern writers 'seem more aware of their own perceptual restrictions'. This seems to me dubious and somewhat patronizing of past 'Picturesque' writing, indeed almost a colonization of a past view of life which might be seen as unpolitically correct as the cultural chauvinism against which Kowalewski inveighs. Many of the articles printed have appeared before and mostly date from the 1980s and cover travel writing from Chateaubriand to Olson, from Baedecker to Spender and Hockney.

William Least Heat-Moon, the author of *Blue Highways* (1982), explains how he is researching his new book on a single county in East Central Kansas, which sounds as unpromising a project as it is possible to find. However, Heat-Moon points out that it is just the preconceptions of Kansas that he wants to uncover: to move both centrifugally and centripetally, away from self and back to self, a strategy which he finds in that neglected masterpiece *Let Us Now Praise Famous Men*. Mary Morris writes about the particular interests and problems faced by women travellers, while Rockwell Gray finds in New York and Chicago the same relationship to space as Nick Carraway in *The Great Gatsby*, and gains fresh insights from Whitman. Terry Caesar in 'Romancing the Facts in American Travel Writing' mostly treats texts from pre-1945, but he has a fine analysis of

S. J. Perelman's *Westward Ha! or Around the World in Eighty Clichés* (1947), which has Perelman at his acerbic best finding Macao 'slightly less exciting than a rainy Sunday evening in Rochester'. Elton Glaser looks at 'Paul Theroux and the Poetry of Departures' in which he claims for Theroux the position of 'departure point' for anyone interested in establishing, for travel literature, an important place in the canon. John McPhee's work, mostly centred around New Jersey, is examined by David Espey who finds McPhee closer in spirit to Thoreau than Theroux on the grounds that McPhee stays closer to home; although he is very well aware of the distinction between home and non-home. He fulfils Thoreau's aims of celebrating the natural beauty of wilderness. Joan Didion's work is usefully abstracted by Mark Z. Muggli as an exploration of the definition of place and the people who live there. Muggli finds in Didion's fiction and non-fiction the same obsessions: objects, landscapes, weather, place names and epiphanic moments of local colour. *A Book of Common Prayer* (1977) and *Democracy* (1984) are seen to be vitally interconnected to her travel writing in that they expose the fiction writing process by focusing on the accurate re-creation of character meeting place, and the unease and doubt generated in the attempt to re-create empirical reality. In 'More Names on Inscription Rock: Travel Writers on the Great Plains in the Eighties' Nancy Cook looks at Dayton Duncan's *Out West* (1987) and Ian Frazier's *Great Plains* (1989). Whereas Frazier celebrates the myth of the great plains – 'the Lodge of Crazy Horse', Duncan, more aware, perceives that all travellers leave a mark: the great plains are not so much a blank sheet as a palimpsest. In some ways this is a pioneering collection, and as such deserves high praise. However, the reader negotiating its considerable spaces might have been afforded an index as guide, and the editor who decided not to give page numbers to the many hundreds of quotations deserves some dreadful frontier fate.

M. Paul Holsinger and Mary Anne Schofield (editors), *Visions of War: World War II in Popular Culture*, as its title indicates, deals more with cultural studies than with literature. However, there are two papers worth noting for this chapter. Sally E. Perry, 'Learning to Fight the Nazis: The Education of Upton Sinclair's Lanny Budd', surveys the progress of Lanny through the 11-volume *World's End* series of novels begun in 1940 and ending with *The Return of Lanny Budd* (1953). Sinclair was a chronicler who perceived his art as serving a cause: initially the cause was socialism, but it gradually turned into nationalistic anti-communism. The point of Sinclair's realism is made succinctly with a quotation from a letter G. B. Shaw wrote to Sinclair in 1941: 'When people ask me what has happened in my long life time, I do not refer them to the newspaper files and to the authorities, but to your novels'. Lanny Budd is the illegitimate son of an American arms dealer, who lives with his mother near Cannes, and is thus, at the beginning of the cycle, removed from the American political scene. Sinclair makes Lanny gradually mature into political awareness as he becomes a double agent and Roosevelt's personal spy; but by the time this occurs the novels have become overt political propaganda. In the final two volumes of the series *O Shepherd Speak!* (1949) and *The Return of Lanny Budd* (1953), the idealistic Lanny has turned into a jingoistic Cold War warrior. Sinclair actually sent the last volume to J. Edgar Hoover writing: 'This volume is concerned with the Communists and their whole bag of clever tricks'. The article does not go much beyond description, but serves the useful function of reminding us of Sinclair's achievement.

Robert L. McLaughlin in 'I. G. Farben's Synthetic War Crimes and Thomas Pynchon's *Gravity's Rainbow*' (*GR*) looks at the history of the international cartel known as *interessan gemeinschaft* (fellowship of interest) *Farbenindustrie*, who from 1900 onward dominated the world chemical industry having forged deals with, amongst others, Dutch Shell, ICI, Ford, Sterling Drug, and, most importantly, with Standard Oil. The article is both fascinating and horrifying on Farben: the deals struck; the establishment of its own concentration camp, Monowitz (where, we might remember, Primo Levi was imprisoned), close to its enormous synthetic fuel and rubber plant. The plant was created in 1941, adjacent to Auschwitz, Birkenau, whose prisoners Farben had used at first, but it was felt too much time was lost on the trek to and from the work site. As McLaughlin quotes from Joseph Borkin, I. G. Farben went way beyond the 'conventional economics of slavery' by considering the slaves themselves as consumable raw material: once their energy was used up, they could be recycled into gold, mattresses and soap. There is some interest on the level of plot to *Gravity's Rainbow*, particularly with regard to Kekulé's dream of the great snake (*GR*, 412), but it is a pity that careless proofreading should print 'faction' for 'fraction' for this subtly alters Pynchon's careful sentence. However, the detailed analysis of Slothrop's conditioning by Laszlo Jampf, the way in which individuals are turned into objects, the mass murder of whole groups of people, and, finally, the point that I. G. Farben's methods are not particular to Farben, nor to Germany; but, because of cartels, and the way big business works, are global; that, most frighteningly, we are also the products of I. G. Farben's world view: all of this is brought out well in the article.

The literature of the Vietnam War is well covered in *Fourteen Landing Zones* edited by Philip K. Jason. With essays by various contributors on, amongst others, Joan Didion's *Democracy*, Bobbie Ann Mason's *In Country*, John Clark Pratt's *The Laotian Fragments*, Larry Heinemann's *Close Quarters,* as well as numerous references to the work of Philip Caputo and Michael Herr's *Dispatches*. The book deals with descriptions of very ugly material: torture, rape, indiscriminate atrocities, and one needs a strong stomach to read chapters entitled 'Humping the Boonies' and 'She's a Pretty Woman ... for a Gook'. While there are useful analyses of the influence of *Heart of Darkness* and *Catch-22* on Vietnam War literature, what is conspicuously missing is the growing body of work emerging from Vietnam and Cambodia. The only oriental perspective comes from an article on the Vietnam novels of Takeshi Kaiko – a Japanese war correspondent during the 'conflict'. By omitting the work of Bao Ninh, Pham Thi Hoài, Nguyên Huy Thiêp, to name but three, this collection creates an uneasy feeling that the ignorance, and brutality which so marked the Vietnam War is being continued by the insular view of occidental critics of this genre. (Although a more pragmatic reason for the omissions might be that these authors are more readily available in French.) Nevertheless, the views of the American experience analysed here: the jungle seen as 'Indian Country'; the experience of war seen as a Hollywood movie; the war seen as sexy (Herr's 'It was the feeling you'd had when you were ... undressing a girl for the first time' is quoted twice with relish); the equation of sex, war and death; all this makes *Fourteen Landing Zones* a useful starting point for anyone researching Vietnam War Literature.

Joanna Price, 'Remembering Vietnam: Subjectivity and Mourning in American New Realist Writing' (*JAmS* 27.173–86), fits Jayne Anne Phillip's *Machine Dreams* and Bobbie Ann Mason's *In Country* into a genre of New Realism or

Dirty Realism (as announced in *Granta* 8), where women acquire adulthood in contemporary America by mourning a brother or father lost in Vietnam.

From the Vietnam War, we move one step nearer Armageddon with Nancy Anisfield (editor), *The Nightmare Considered: Critical Essays in Nuclear War Literature*. As Anisfield points out in her introduction, with the Berlin Wall down, and worldwide nuclear freeze, it may seem pessimistic and counter-productive to argue for the necessity of nuclear studies. Nevertheless, apart from necessary classification work, the analysis of horrifying oxymorons ('peace-keeper missiles', 'star-wars defence' etc.), there is a continuing outpouring of post-holocaust novels – which may seem paradoxical given the diminished threat of nuclear war. The book begins with a series of essays on general issues: H. Bruce Franklin surveys apocalyptic literature and interestingly relates it to the Truman presidency; Jaqueline R. Smetak writes of 'Sex and Death in Nuclear Holocaust Literature of the 1950s' which has some useful analysis of Vonnegut; in 'The Days After Tomorrow: Novelists at Armageddon', Michael Norris and Louise Erdrich reconsider Paul Auster, Ursula K. LeGuin and Vonnegut amongst others, pointing out that a blacker view existed in the 1950s which was replaced with a kind of wish-fulfilment expressing salvation through a drastic reorganiza-tion of the species; heavy on theory and shorter on novels, William J. Scheick 'Post-Nuclear Holocaust Re-Minding' presents the paradox that the nuclear-holocaust novelist cannot win – if he is wrong then the book will 'die' in the future, if he is right it will also 'die' in the future. That the argument is specious, since it takes no account of quality, should not need pointing out. Part II analyses specific texts: Vonnegut's novels are considered in two useful articles by Tom Hearon and Jerome Klinkowitz; Paul Brians makes some clear connections between the works of Judith Merril, Helen Clarkson and Carol Amen, the works are seen to be connected in complex structural ways as well as by gender; Jack Branscomb looks at Russell Hoban's dark vision expressed in *Pilgermann* and *Ridley Walker*. However, some more comment on Hoban's use of debased English reflecting the debased environment would have been welcome, for in truth there is more clockwork than orange about it. All in all this is a useful introduction to some of the dystopic literature emerging from America in the contemporary period.

William Lavender in 'The Novel of Critical Engagement: Paul Auster's *City of Glass*', (*ConL* 34. 219–39), writes that *City of Glass*, like the others in *New York Trilogy*, is a detective story. Lavender argues that Auster goes beyond Todorov and Peter Brooks's *Reading for the Plot*, in that *City of Glass* is an allegory for fiction in general, it partakes of a specific metafictional tradition, and is itself a deconstruction which falls apart as it progresses. The novel is seen to be working out how many normally assigned qualities of the novel can be wrecked whilst still remaining identifiable as a novel: e.g. the mystery is aban-doned when it is most profligate of potential solutions; one character, Stillman Sr, keeps popping up with no memory of what has happened to him previously in the fiction; the third person narrator is junked for an enigmatic 'I' two pages before the end. Subtle analysis of narrativity in Auster's novels is based on the models of Genette and Seymore Chatman. The article makes high claims for Auster's novel of engagement clearing a temporary space where representation can close with politics and society and be equal to the task.

The 16 short papers collected by J. L. Plakkoottam and P. K. Sinha under the title of *Literature and Politics in Twentieth Century America*, testify to a continuing interest in contemporary American culture in India. M. Glen Johnson opens with an ambitious paper entitled 'Literature and Politics', and takes to task literary critics who write about very few political novels, whereas, he says, political scientists write about very many novels. This seems to miss the obvious point that if you survey 81 novels in 95 pages (one of his examples) you cannot be said to be engaged in literary criticism at all, and it makes somewhat ironic his plaintive conclusion that no political scientists took part in the seminar. P. P. Raveendram gallops through reader-response theory, while P. Agnihotri writes interestingly of the politics of pedagogy. V. M. Madge rightly castigates simplistic categorizations of T. S. Eliot and argues for a new look at Eliot's social criticism. In S. Sen's intemperate analysis of 'The Relationship of the African–American movement with Marxism' it is surprising to find no reference to *Invisible Man* since Ellison exploded the Marxist lure more than 40 years ago. N. K. Ghosh considers Maxwell Anderson's two plays on the Sacco-Vanzetti case, and Leena Prachand writes of gender in Eugene O'Neill, concluding with O'Neill deliberately taking an anti-feminist stand. R. S. Nanda in 'Saul Bellow and the Rejection of Modernist Ideology' writes elegantly of Bellow targeting 'the twin cults of nihilism and irrationalism'. Of course India has resource problems, but it is a shame that this book is not more up to date – almost nothing published in the last 15 years is referred to.

Crossing Borders: American Literature and Other Artistic Media edited by Jadwiga Maszewska is a collection of papers from the University of Lodz. Jerzy Durczak looks at language in two recent multicultural autobiographies (Richard Rodriguez's *Hunger of Memory* and Eva Hoffman's *Lost in Translation*) and comes to the unsurprising conclusion that the autobiographical mode helps the immigrant voice order confusing experience. Krzysztof Andrzejczak writes interestingly of Roth's superficial, detached treatment of Kafka and Czechoslovakia. Andrzejczak points out the progression in Roth's work towards a closer parallel to Kafka the artist. (The essay would have gained if Kafka had been read himself, rather than always seen through the prism of Roth.) Mark Shechner in 'American Realism, American Film' concludes that the new realism of the 1990s is a vast improvement over the postmodern works of Coover, Gaddis, Gass, Hawkes and Pynchon which have been fostered by the Academy. This new realism is an Age of Silver 'family-heirloom sterling silver'. His rationale for this judgement on Tom Wolfe, Richard Ford, E. L. Doctorow, John Casey et al., is the way in which two forces operate: market factors and film, the latter being by far the most potent. In 'Crossing Borders: Thematics of Sexcess, Intellectuals and Hybris' John Michael draws on Emerson's views of hubris and success. The paper shows how 'Risky Business' rewrites the moral map of middle America as the hero is rewarded for his forays into pimping; while 'Pretty Woman' rewrites the 'Horatio Alger' plot for the postmodern 1980s. On the whole this collection contains some useful essays, brought together by the common themes of borders and transgression, which shows that contemporary American fiction is a flourishing field of study in Poland today.

The subject of borders is continued in *Frontier Gothic: Terror and Wonder at the Frontier in American Literature* edited by David Mogen et al. This collection of 13 essays examines the gothic tradition within frontier writing; the frontier subject being defined as 'the imaginative border between the known and the unknown'. At the centre of the indigenous frontier story is an encounter with the wilderness which is 'charged with paradox and emotional ambivalence'. Unfortunately there is no reference to the work of Francis Jennings who, in *The Invasion of America* (1975), pointed out that Europeans did not find a wilderness in America, they created one. Lawrence, of course had made much the same point, more poetically, in *Studies in Classical American Literature* (1923). Mogen et al. do invoke Lawrence in their introduction, and there are some references to Lawrence in the essays (regrettably not all of them indexed). In the introduction, however, Lawrence's elegant prose is transformed out of recognition by statements like: 'D. H. Lawrence, who proclaimed that the most eloquent American art works express an agonizing transformation of consciousness portrayed as an ongoing wilderness experience'. Lawrence wrote of many things in *Studies*: he wrote of the soul of man being a dark forest, he wrote of the Hercynian wood that scared the Romans so, and, perhaps most memorably, he wrote of 'A new world, a world of the Noble Savage and Pristine Nature and Paradisal Simplicity and all that gorgeousness that flows out of the unsullied fount of the ink-bottle'! What he certainly did not do was write about 'an ongoing wilderness experience'. By this token, I suppose, old Count Leo might have been involved with an ongoing digit in the balance situation. However, if we can ignore the rebarbative style of the introduction, there is value in a number of the contributions which cover American gothic literature from Melville and Hawthorne down to Cyberpunk. In 'Rural Gothic: The Sublime Rhetoric of Flannery O'Connor', Ronald Schleifer usefully reminds us of O'Connor's statement on the South: 'While the South is hardly Christ-centered it is most certainly Christ-haunted'. Drawing on the work of Todorov and Fiedler, Schleifer is particularly good on O'Connor's language: 'O'Connor creates the rhetorical *effect* of godly presence by narrating in a language that implies its own transparence'. Schleifer concludes that the rural Southern frontier enables O'Connor to present a stranger who may have supernatural attributes: 'Jesus, the Devil, the Holy Ghost'. Meanwhile, James K. Folsom in 'Gothicism in the Western Novel' looks at a number of Westerns, including Alan LeMay's *The Searchers*, and determines that the fascination with western gothicism is due to the transmutation of the colourful aspects of American culture into 'material more suited for the examination of interior states of mind'. David Mogen, in his essay on 'Wilderness, Metamorphosis and Millennium', covers literature from the Puritans to Cyberpunk and makes the valuable point that there is frequently a gothic element in the American pastoral, just as there is often a pastoral element in works like *The Scarlet Letter* whose primary effect is gothic. In this volume, which is a useful starting point for anyone interested in the American gothic, there are also studies of Brockden Brown, Cooper, Hawthorne, Poe and Melville amongst others.

In *The Literature of Emigration and Exile* edited by James Whitlark and Wendell Aycock we have a collection of essays which look at emigration, exile, ostracism etc. in comparative literature. Criticizing Eagleton's *Exiles and Emigrés* as being chauvinist and Seidel's *Exile and the Narrative Imagination* as being parochial, Whitlark, in the introduction, makes a strong case for a comparative approach to this theme. From Ovid and the Psalms, the editor argues that the ancient world saw exile as catastrophe – thus all mundane existence is seen as an exile from Paradise. Petrarch, however, regarded man as lazy and soft '*desidiosus ac mollis*' for not leaving home at some point, nevertheless he was only at home in books and saw his life as an arduous pilgrimage towards a heavenly Jerusalem. Whitlark goes on to ask whether suffering in exile is essentially more masculine than feminine. These premises and questions are worked out in a number of valuable essays which are unfortunately beyond the scope of this chapter. However, of particular interest to readers of Maxine Hong Kingston is Shu-mei Shih's article on exile and intertextuality in *China Men*. Shih points out that some women have adapted smoothly to exile, because they were already used to second-class status whereas Chinese male *émigrés* had to learn something new: a gender reversal. Sexism sees the feminine as second-class, and American racism imposes that negative quality on China Men (Chinese American males as pioneers, rather than 'Chinamen' a racist epithet). Shih points out that 'Kingston writes of the various contributions China Men made to the welfare of the country that denied them, and how their blood and sweat enriched the American soil'. Kingston, then, is in accord with Kristeva's view that 'marginality is not a matter of essence, but one of positionality in a given society'. Shih shows how Kingston subtly points out both racism and sexism by counterpointing her main narrative with intertexts from traditional Chinese stories. Thus, Tang Ao is banished to a world dominated by women; whereas 'The Ghostmate' and 'The Father from China' consider 'exile on the level of personal desire' (in the Chinese language 'ghost' often means foreigner). The rewriting of the traditional Chinese tale by Kingston thus points out the frustration of Chinese men who were both prevented from bringing Chinese women with them and from marrying non-Chinese women. In contrast to the works of Kingston, Frank Dietz examines the exile motif in the science fiction novels of Ursula K. LeGuin. For LeGuin, Utopia is always in the process of becoming, it is never a stasis. A crucial figure in her work is that of the expatriate because he acts out the transition from the static Utopian laws to the ever-present Utopian horizon. Dietz claims that LeGuin's later work is unique because of the way in which meta-utopian elements dominate. Meanwhile, Jefferson Fay considers self-exile and self-destruction in the novels of Jay McInerney. In *Bright Lights, Big City* (1984), *Ransom* (1985), and *Story of My Life* (1988), in which expatriation is seen as an underlying metaphor for alienation, Fay concentrates on McInerney's treatment of television and tabloids. The horrors displayed and written take over all traditional values, thus McInerney's characters cannot respond to failure and therefore abandon family and cultural relationships. This is a fine collection of essays on an interesting subject.

(b)   Individual Authors

Nicholas Birns in 'Beyond Metafiction: Placing John Barth' (*ArQ* 49.ii.113–36), writes that although Barth is consistently labelled a metafictionist, nevertheless his novels are full of sympathetic and memorable characters. Metafiction, according to Birns, appeals simultaneously to the puerile and the retrogressive reader. Barth shows that fictional self-reference and historical rhetoric do not exclude each other as the idealists of metafiction have maintained.

In 'Father-Murder and Father Resne: The Post-Freudian Allegories of Donald Barthelme' (*ConL* 34.182–203), Michael Zeitlin attempts to move beyond questions of form (Barthelme is normally seen as an epitome of American postmodernism who privileges the signifier over the signified), to see if we can celebrate the 'structural function' of the sign and locate Barthelme's narrative experiments within a cultural context. The article concentrates on *The Dead Father* and 'Views of My Father Weeping' which are illuminated by subtle readings of Freud.

L. H. Goldman et al. (editors), *Saul Bellow: A Mosaic* is a collection of papers given at Haifa in 1987, which seem to have taken an unconscionable time to reach the press. Bellow has often stated that he is not a Jewish-American writer, but an American writer who happens to be Jewish. For Goldman this is 'an absurd word play'; in his essay 'The Jewish Perspective of Saul Bellow' he finds Bellow's Jewish heritage pervasive in the novels: both consciously, in the choice of material, characters, themes etc., and unconsciously, in the general philosophy that permeates Bellow's work. To define this philosophy Goldman borrows Leo Baeck's term 'ethical optimism' and he relates Bellow's humanism to his concerns about Romanticism which, in an extreme form, can result in Nazism. Romanticism is seen to be essentially anti-humanistic since it views life in terms of the individual fulfilling his own desires and ambitions as freely as he can, and thus rejecting the group, community life. 'All Bellow's protagonists', writes Goldman, 'are social creatures who consider solitude anathema'. The 'quality' of Bellow's Jewishness is incontrovertible and is everywhere manifest in his early depiction of anti-semitism, his sensitivity to global injustices and his continued assaults on Nazi philosophy. Amos Oz in 'Mr. Sammler and Hannah Arendt's Banality' writes passionately on the superficiality of Arendt's 'banality of evil' which is as Ussher Arkin, Sammler and behind them Bellow say, nothing but Weimar *Schmaltz* — the image of evil in the eyes of the sentimental good. Daniel Waldon also writes of Bellow's Jewishness and perceives in his work a development from existentialism to a reintegration in society for the character. Both Oz and Waldon are concerned with engagement and responsibility: these ideas are taken further in a stimulating article by Ada Aharoni who states that Bellow has created a new art form 'engaged introspective fiction', which 'registers the pulse of a responsible modern consciousness'. Daniel Fuchs analyses the Bellow/Grass confrontation at the 1986 PEN Conference: his conclusion is that Grass does not seem to have read Bellow very carefully, and has got Eastern Europe all wrong. Bellow cautions against 'the stampeding of writers into political boxes', and Fuchs states that the heart of the confrontation is 'the vexed question of the relationship between truth and power, vision and action'.

Alan Lelchuk reflects on Bellow's style in 'What Kind of Day Did You Have?': it is a controlled style, heavily textured, to be digested slowly. Lelchuk is surely right to underline Bellow's 40-year achievement in evoking American reality; he describes Bellow's effort as a 'fight through the ingenious maze of distractions and camouflage constructed by the culture'. Marianne M. Friedrich looks at two short stories that, unusually for Bellow, have women protagonists: 'Dora' and 'Leaving the Yellow House'. In 'Dora' Bellow both uses and challenges Freud's view expressed in 'Dora: An Analysis of a Case of Hysteria'. Bellow's Dora transcends the case history; although lonely she has the strength to survive. 'Leaving the Yellow House' marks a crucial change in Bellow's style between the writing of *Augie March* and *Herzog*. In this short story Bellow utilizes an inner voice which signals a move to mimetic fiction. The story was influenced by Bergson and Proust in that Bellow turns 'the two basic principles of Bergson's philosophy — motion and duration — into aesthetic categories of narration. However, while Bellow uses Proust as a point of contact, his concepts of self and interior time differ radically from Proust. Mark Weinstein considers Bellow's endings and finds them a 'kind of genre in themselves'. While Bellow's narratives suggest life, his artistic closures suggest art. The endings have shared characteristics, offer revealing commentaries on each other, and finally 'suggest that all of Bellow's major novels are comedies about death'.

Gloria Cronin, meanwhile, studies misogyny in *Mr. Sammler's Planet*: in the character of Sammler 'converge the misanthropic and misogynistic Western intellectual traditions of the Greek, Roman, Jewish, Christian, and modern literary cultures'. Perhaps she has a point, but in my experience of modern literary cultures they are just as likely to be misoneist as misogynist. Cronin continues with a subtle argument and shows that the character of Sammler is a careful construction; she dissects the 'vital working space' – the gap, in which Bellow criticizes 'interprets, and even deconstructs his own intellectual acculturation'. Jonathan Wilson takes a new look at Bellow's characters, particularly Moses Herzog, and takes issue with those critics who have found the character more presence than person. Wilson argues that Herzog is very much 'there' as a character – but in uncompromisingly postmodern terms: which is to say that he is constantly re-creating himself as a kind of con man, a performer. Andrew Gordon takes the idea of performance further in considering theatre and role-playing in Bellow's novels. He plays with the terms 'good acting' and 'bad acting' as signifying both performance and morality. Harold Fisch points out Bellow's debt to Kafka, despite their completely different approaches to language: Kafka symbolic, Bellow realistic. In the same vein, Edward Bloomberg shows how *Henderson the Rain King* echoes Pascal's concern with individual experience, as opposed to abstract theory, about the meaninglessness of existence. Bellow here and elsewhere shows himself to be 'a superior Pascalisant'.

Saul Bellow: A Mosaic ends with Bellow's 'Summations' which originated as a lecture at Haifa (1986), and was revised for Bennington (1987). 'Only the purest human consciousness, art consciousness, can see us through this time of nihilism', Bellow concludes, in almost Paterian, apocalyptic terms. 'Summations', evidently, is essential reading for anyone interested in Bellow's work. On the whole the essays are of a high standard, although the introduction could have done with more careful proofreading, and it is a shame that such a valuable collection of essays should have taken so long to be published.

Elaine B. Safer, 'From Poem to Cartoon in Saul Bellow's *More Die of Heartbreak*' (*Crit* 34.203–19), points out Bellow's critical attitude to much modern thought, Bellow's mode here and elsewhere being a coruscating irony. Sanford Pinsker, 'Imagining American Reality' (*SoR* 29.767–81), argues cogently that Bellow, Roth, Updike and others are writing against the grain of post-structuralist jargon and literature. Pinsker asserts that New Realism will 'last' while the flashy experiments in metafiction will not. If only things were so straightforward!

Most books are written, some are researched, but Michelle Green's book on Paul Bowles, *The Dream at the End of the World*, was four years 'aborning'. Centring her story on Paul and Jane Bowles, Green writes of the gossipy, sordid world of Tangier after the war. William [Burroughs], Allen [Ginsberg], Truman [Capote] flit in and out of the pages, as do their catamites and servants. The political and social climate is sketched in from time to time. There is some plot outline of some of the works, but no literary analysis or judgement is made. For example '*Up Above the World* would echo the themes that he explored in *Let It Come Down* and *The Sheltering Sky*'; this is about the limit of the argument. From the notes, it is clear that a lot of work has gone into the book, and it is a pity that a potentially interesting story should lose itself in gossip. The volume is handsomely produced and fully indexed; along with the recently published letters, it should prove a useful starting point for any serious criticism of Bowles's life and work.

In *Reading Raymond Carver*, Randolph Paul Runyon has written quite a useful introduction to the short stories, but it is a book that does not fulfil the claims made for it in the introduction. Having briefly considered 'minimalism' and decided Carver does not fit that genre – he 'is in fact a self-reflexive metafictional writer' – Runyon goes on to say that he has found no study that focuses 'in quite the way I intend to here on the importance of the *order* in which stories appear'. In fact most undergraduate essays on *The Dubliners* make a point of discussing the order of the stories: obviously there are thematic, verbal, rhetorical continuities and self-reflections between any collection of short stories. What Runyon does is pick up what he considers significant items: themes, phrases, images, whatever and proceeds mechanically to link the stories together. Thus, the last words of 'Are You a Doctor?' are 'You don't sound like yourself'. These announce the plot of the next story 'The Father' where we have a question as to who or what selfhood the father holds, and the next story 'Nobody Said Anything' is linked to what has gone before when a son overhears *his* father arguing in the kitchen. And so on. Apart from the pedestrian nature of this analysis (two to three pages devoted to each story, the first few sentences of each discussion linking backwards to the previous discussion repetitively), the 'argument' is contingent. By what criteria are these links made? What methodology informs the selection of one phrase or concept rather than another? What happens to the argument when the stories change their order as in Carver's final selection, *Where I'm Calling From*? What happens when characters change roles as in 'What's in Alaska?'? The lack of methodology means that, in fact, one could prove anything. For example, in 'Nobody Said Anything' we find a green woman and a green fish, the story is followed by 'Sixty Acres' which are certainly green, we then find green M and M's being the favourite in 'What's in Alaska?' Ergo: Carver has a powerful ecological sub-text running through his stories. In his urge to crack codes and fix answers Runyon tends to ignore the openness, the beauty, mystery and the sometimes heart-piercing force of the period placed exactly right, to which Carver refers in his introduction to *Where I'm Calling From*. In 'Night School' two women make a 'mildly sexual proposal' to the unnamed narrator and want him to drive them to Patterson (their nightschool professor) to carry on partying. Well, maybe, but there are other much darker interpretations one could give – this is schooling in *night*, and it does not help much for Professor Runyon to tell us 'This is a puzzling story, with the slightest of plots. It doesn't exactly go anywhere, but then neither does its protagonist'. Nor, I fear, does Professor Runyon.

Frank Lentricchia has edited a book, *Introducing Don DeLillo*, which amply fulfils its title; the second printing shows how popular DeLillo has become as well as proving the use of this volume. Lentricchia opens with a brief survey: DeLillo is a novelist of ideas, a difficult novelist, someone who experiments with literary conventions, who yokes 'together terror and wild humor as the essential tone of contemporary America'. DeLillo, Didion, Morrison, Ozick and Mailer are contrasted to New Regionalists such as Carver, Tyler, Welty et al., in that the former group look beyond the individual for an explanation of America: they are authors who 'invent in order to intervene'. (Lentricchia, quite unnecessarily, overstates his case against Carver et al.: 'fiction all but labeled "No expense of intellect required. To be applied in external crises of the heart only"'.) However, he usefully reminds us of the campaign against DeLillo by the American right-wing media, who believe that America is good and only individuals go astray (that this is essentially Christian dogma goes unmentioned). DeLillo's novels, Lentricchia states, are a fundamental critique of American society, they are novels which give an experience of overwhelming cultural density and they are politically outrageous because of their historical rigour (though DeLillo has stated categorically that he has not attempted a systematic exploration of the American experience). Lentricchia next prints 'Opposites' Chapter 10 from *Ratner's Star* which shows DeLillo at his most baroque, with playful deconstructions and *malentendus* (guilt = kilt). Anthony DeCurtis prints an extended version of the *Rolling Stone* interview (1988), following the publication of *Libra*. DeLillo comes across very much as his own, private, person: 'I'm just not a public man. I'd rather write my books in private and then send them out into the world to discover their own public life.' De Curtis labels DeLillo as a 'modern-day Kurtz, a literary explorer of the heart of darkness', which seems like complete nonsense. DeLillo, from this interview, is marked by restraint, care, modesty and, above all, responsibility to his art. As Aaron rightly says he promises but he holds back. DeLillo seems to flirt with mysticism in searching for solutions, but he has faith in fiction, because the fiction provides a redemptive truth, which consoles one from despair – in this, at least, DeLillo might come close to Marlow, if not Conrad.

Daniel Aaron provides readers with some notions on 'How to Read Don DeLillo' – the title sounds prescriptive, but the essay is not. Written almost in note form, Aaron jots down a few key concepts: Catastrophe, Conspiracy, Landscape, America etc., and then dedicates three pages to *Libra* using the same headline format: Technology and Human Values, Language and Secrecy, the Aesthetics of Conspiracy. The writer is like the conspirator cutting through the Jamesian 'clumsy life' or what DeLillo calls 'the daily jostle' to find the pre-established design beneath; this is a clear and thoughtful article. Hal Crowther goes way over the top in 'Clinging to the Rock: A Novelist's Choices in the New Mediocracy', in which he defends DeLillo against the diatribes of such as George Will ('of Himalayan self-importance') and his 'coreligionist' Jonathan Yardley ('one of those eager egos of letters'), both of whom use the language of 'pre-perestroika *Izvestia*'. Crowther inveighs, ponderously, against the American media but does not say a lot about DeLillo. However, his essay raises the one problem with *Introducing Don DeLillo*: the book could have benefited from a more dialectical approach. By all accounts the anti-DeLillo criticism quoted in this work is crass and silly (to put it at its kindest), but it would have been instructive to read an article that engaged, intelligently, with some of the issues on the relation between fact and fiction which seem to lie behind the diatribes of Will, Yardley et al. John A. McClure writes of 'Postmodern Romance: Don DeLillo and the Age of Conspiracy' where the novels, like Conrad's, are seen to reproduce 'the excitements of popular romance and to reject them as unworthy'; ultimately the romance deconstructs and leads to a deeper sense of mystery. Eugene Goodheart speculates on Don DeLillo's characters who speak with intelligence and fluency, but are disembodied, indistinguishable and lack a sense of self. His characters in fact are two-dimensional film images which reflect our apocalyptic age of TV watchers who 'shape their conduct by the coded messages and images of the medium'. Anthony DeCurtis considers the notion of 'product' in *Great Jones Street* and perceives that the buying and selling of products (which means everything), is what makes the world turn – this seems a somewhat banal conclusion to reach on this hilarious Pynchonesque novel. Charles Molesworth in

'Don DeLillo's Perfect Starry Night' examines structure, identity, the superabundance of technology etc. and considers ways in which DeLillo searches for explanation. By its very nature explanation is going to be ambiguous; thus, at the end of *Ratner's Star*, Billy Twillig is both half-illuminated and half-obscured by 'the shadow bands that precede total solar eclipse'. Billy, as Molesworth says, 'seems perfectly poised between some mystical enlightenment and some final nightmare'.

Dennis A. Foster muses on the trigramaton CIA and the tetragramaton YHWH and considers the search for rational being in *The Names* – a rationality which is countered by a truth which lies beyond or behind language. As one of the lunatic cultists says: 'I want to get at a use of language that functions without symbolic representation'. The search is, of course, for God, but in *The Names* God has been replaced by institutions. John Frow writes some useful notes to *White Noise* which question the nature of the 'real' in this work. Given that the central mediating agency in the world is TV, then 'everything' is product and relates to the market place. In considering the world of the supermarket, Frow utilizes Baudrillard's melancholic vision (once there was a referent, now it's gone), which is countered by DeLeuze who finds no sense of loss in the simulacrum, since every original is itself a copy. Finally, Lentricchia considers *Libra* as a postmodern critique: De Lillo's American tragedy is much more Oswald's than Kennedy's. Both Kennedy and Oswald are products of the dream factory, but unlike J.F.K., Oswald is the genuine American article. *Introducing Don DeLillo* is indexed, but has no list of works cited. It will be essential reading for anyone interested in DeLillo and the postmodern novel.

Thomas Carmichael, 'Lee Harvey Oswald and the Postmodern Subject: History and Intertextuality in Don DeLillo's *Libra*, *The Names,* and *Mao II*' (*ConL* 34.204–18), points out that DeLillo's fiction fully participates in Hayden White's contention that there is no history without a metahistory and Linda Hutcheon's 'historiographic metafiction'. He goes on to suggest that the supposedly stable world view of the prior text in DeLillo's work, is subverted by DeLillo so that the prior text is representative of the instability his fiction portrays. The intertextual relationship in DeLillo's work is one of 'incontestable dissemination, of endless trace and *différance*'.

Two useful articles on William Gass have appeared: 'A Conversation with William H. Gass' by Marc Chénetier (*RFEA* 51.89–94) and Claire Maniez , 'The World Within the Words of William H. Gass's "In the Heart of the Heart of the Country"' (*EA* 45.i.27–37). Chénetier poses a series of questions which prompts Gass to respond on the structure of sentences in 'The Pederson Kid', his abiding interest in architecture, the influence of Stevens's 'The Snow Man', voyeurism, his attitude to and experiment with narrative voice, his imaginary political party 'The Party of Disappointed People', the influence of Rilke on his refusal to accept straight referentiality (not a matter of imitating reality but of adding something to the world), learning through defamiliarization and much else. There is almost no sense of debate in the interview, as though Chénetier is asking the questions that Gass wants to be asked. The piece could have done with better proofreading, but nevertheless this interview is sure to be a valuable source of Gass's views for some time to come. Drawing heavily on a previous interview between Gass and Thomas Le Clair, Maniez proceeds to analyse the structure of 'The World Within the Words' in Gass's story which she brings back to an original title 'In the Country of the Heart of the Heart' which reinforces the circular structure of the story. The article is particularly useful for the detailed connections made in her schema between key words and concepts.

Sharon Davie, 'Free Mules, Talking Buzzards, and Cracked Plates: The Politics of Dislocation in *Their Eyes Were Watching God*' (*PMLA* 108.446–59), writes that Zora Neale Hurston's novel is profoundly political in its undermining of hierarchy. Drawing on Kristeva and Gates, Jr, Davie points out that 'the novel confronts the complexities of racism and sexism while undercutting a belief in any monological understanding of person or politics, text or nation'.

Denise Heinze in *The Dilemma of 'Double-Consciousness': Toni Morrison's Novels* begins by briefly surveying Morrison's literary reception in America. This is a move which has taken her from a double marginal status as a black woman to that of canonical writer. Heinze then goes on to inquire if Morrison's novels work in the same way as the ghost in *Beloved* which haunts and torments the guilty conscience of America. Whereas most writers canonized in America have created or perpetuated myth, Morrison in contrast is seen as a 'mythbasher' who in each of her works 'launders one American ideal after another'. Criticism has been levelled at the way minority group literature has been utilized by the establishment, and Heinze shows herself to be politically naive by asking how Morrison can be regarded as canonical if her works constantly undermine the values and codes of authority? Like the jester in a medieval court, sophisticated authority has always tolerated the safety-net of criticism. Thus, of course, Morrison can bash myths and be canonical simultaneously. Heinze's answer to her dilemma gives the title to the book and lies in Du Bois's formulation of double-consciousness, in which an individual is representative of, and immersed in, two distinct ways of life, and which, in the case of African–Americans, may not be resolved. Whatever theory lies behind this seems to be supplied by Gates, Jr (out of Bakhtin) and is not terribly convincing: 'black formal repetition always repeats with a difference, a black difference that manifests itself in specific language use', but exactly the same would be true if one were to replace 'black' with 'white'. Morrison's political involvement and aesthetic endeavour is carefully examined and two reasons are found to account for her canonization: first, her ability to manipulate her insider/outsider status with the literary establishment; and, secondly, her recognition that her double-consciousness can never be integrated into a single vision. Heinze accurately notes that Morrison's own career has transcended the permanent condition of double-consciousness which affects her characters.

Heinze's introduction is followed by four chapters of fine analysis. The first deals with Morrison's aesthetic, where romantic love and physical beauty are seen as the most destructive ideas in human thought: the black aesthetic has moved from an overtly political stance to re-create art in the beauty of the black experience; but, paradoxically, the concept that 'black is beautiful' is seen as a white idea turned inside out, and therefore still a white idea. Morrison is seen attempting to overcome a white aesthetic and move towards a spiritual love between people which is a prerequisite to communal love. Second, Heinze deals with Morrison's treatment of the black family which is the most complicated and controversial manifestation of Morrison's double-consciousness. Throughout her work, Morrison is seen to be dissecting the nuclear family where unity cannot be maintained. Her most scathing criticism is centred on black families who seem to have successfully integrated into middle-class respectability. With *Beloved* and *Jazz* the 'family' is deconstructed into an individual awareness that family is not a geographical and spatial construct united by blood ties, but a collective consciousness of caring that will grow into a 'universal family'. Third, Morrison's social dialectic is examined and seems the weakest of the chapters because of rather too much dubious social theorizing. Nevertheless, valuable points are made about Morrison's criticism of value systems becoming institutionalized, and that Morrison's deinstitutionalization is not necessarily an argument for primitivism (a charge sometimes levelled against Morrison), but rather a return to an organic natural wholeness of the community. The journey South, the return to roots, is a journey of immersion into the deeper recesses of black consciousness and another attempt to resolve the double-consciousness. Finally, in 'The Metaphysical Argument for the Supernatural', Heinze perceives the highly negative impact of double-consciousness on the black community. Morrison is seen to negotiate divisiveness through fantasy. Using Kathryn Hume's *Fantasy and Mimesis* as a theoretical base, Heinze shows how Morrison collapses fantasy and mimesis in the same work. Hume's categories of fiction are not very helpful, but Morrison's reconstruction of the black community, which has been invisible and unreal to mainstream society, is therefore seen to be a defamiliarization of the mimetic. This is best seen in *Jazz* where Heinze comes to the conclusion that in this novel Morrison rejects attempts at resolution or transcendence of the double-consciousness and instead invokes reader responsibility in a love affair between the book and the reader. *The Dilemma of 'Double-Consciousness'* began life as a doctoral thesis, but there is little of that rebarbative form in the work: on the contrary, this is a fine, sensitive, well-written introduction to Morrison's novels despite the naiveté of some of the political argument.

Heinze's conclusions on the collective unconsciousness are supported by Patrick Bryce Bjork's *The Novels of Toni Morrison: The Search for Self and Place Within the Community*. Bjork begins with the statement that 'The search for self and place is an on-going phenomenon in American discourse' (of course it was, is and will be in almost all discourse). Given that search for self and place is manifest most strongly in the national literature, Bjork goes on to argue that Morrison's identity and place are found in community, not in the transcendence of society, nor in the search for a single private self. That the search for a single private self is essentially a white *male* stereotype – lone American women are not that highly regarded – could have been examined further. As we have seen from Heinze's book, the finding of self in community is predominantly a black experience in America. Bjork usefully quotes Morrison's 'City Limits, Village Values': 'When a character defies a village law or shows contempt for its values, it may be seen as a triumph to white readers, while Blacks may see it as an outrage'. The book opens with two introductory chapters: the first gives a short history of the African–American novel from *Clotell* (1853) by William Wells Brown and Francis E. W. Harper's *Iola LeRoy* (1892), the first published novel by a black woman, both of which have as protagonists the figure of a 'tragic mulatta' – the most stereotypical figure in black Reconstruction literature. The second chapter considers the role of black women in the community and shows how these roles have been incorporated into African–American narratives. The overall purpose of the book would seem, therefore, to verge on the sociological; it is to trace the emergence and presence of critical and cultural values in black American literature and show how these have influenced contemporary black women writers (in fact, he only deals with Hurston and Morrison). Bjork continues with individual chapters on *The Bluest Eye* (Selfhood and the Community); *Sula* (The Contradictions of Self and Place); *Song of Solomon* (Reality and Mythos within the Community); *Tar Baby* (The Presence and Absence of Self and Place); and *Beloved* (The Paradox of a Past and Present Self and Place). There is a brief conclusion which points out that each character is unable to realize selfhood because they have been warped by communal experience, but, at the same time, through memory, story, dream and song 'each of Morrison's narratives continually focuses beyond the isolated, dystopian self and toward the potentialities of a desired, collective self'. The book contains a useful list of works cited – though regrettably no index; the analysis is competent, though not very subtle; the separate chapters devoted to individual works means that there is little synthesis; nevertheless, the undergraduate student could find this a useful starting place for work on Morrison's novels.

In the year when Morrison won the Nobel Prize for literature it is not surprising to find so much scholarship devoted to her work. *MFS* 39.iii and iv, edited by Nancy J. Peterson, is a double issue of some 400 pages on Toni Morrison. Peterson begins by examining the difficulties in canonizing Morrison. Section I is entitled 'Multicultural Morrison' and has papers by Barbara T. Christian, 'Layered Rhythms: Virginia Woolf and Toni Morrison'; Richard C. Moreland on the interconnections between *Huckleberry Finn* and *Beloved* (Morrison's novel is taking up again and reimagining 'the American Romance'); and Caroline M. Woidat, 'Talking Back to Schoolteacher: Morrison's Confrontation with Hawthorne in *Beloved*' (Morrison's Sethe is something of a black Hester Prynne, but one that subverts Hawthorne's text). Section II 'Nihilism and the Novel' contains papers by Linda Krumholz, 'Dead Teachers: Rituals of Manhood and Rituals of Reading in *Song of Solomon*' (the politics of pedagogy treated as both theme and form – the reader's initiation parallels that of Milkman's); Deborah Guth, 'A Blessing and a Burden: The Relation to the Past in *Sula*, *Song of Solomon* and *Beloved*' (one of the most absorbing issues in Morrison's work is the multifaceted, problematic relationship of the present to the past – 'the search for self-definition and understanding of what the past is about – interact constantly throughout her work'); Judlyn S. Ryan, 'Contested Visions/Double Vision in *Tar Baby*' ('Morrison's fiction displays an extensive concern with the erasure of African cultural consciousness and cultural history, and the persisting cultural illness which this erasure precipitates'); Dorothea Drummond Mbalia, 'Women Who Run with Wild: The Need for Sisterhoods in *Jazz*' (almost impossible to separate theme – 'we are all connected as African people' – from structure in *Jazz*. The narrator affects, and is affected by, the story she tells).

'The Tower of Babel', Section III, contains essays by Terry Otten, 'Horrific Love in Toni Morrison's Fiction' (Morrison inverts conventional moral categories, thus monstrous deeds can become expressions of compassion); Jennifer FitzGerald, 'Selfhood and Community: Psychoanalysis and Discourse in *Beloved*' (reads the novel through 'various discourses, including the repressed pre-Oedipal discourse triggered as each character confronts a psychic trauma'); Raphael Pérez-Torres, 'Knitting and Knotting the Narrative Thread – *Beloved* as Postmodern Novel' (presence emerges from absence, identity emerges from exploitation, *Beloved* creates aesthetic identity 'by playing against and through the cultural field of postmodernism'); James Phelan, 'Toward a Rhetorical Reader-Response Criticism: The Difficult, the Stubborn, and the Ending of *Beloved*' (somewhat quirky, experimental and hesitant, an attempt to use and show the limits of reader-response criticism – finally *Beloved* resists such criticism). Section IV 'The Vitality of Language' is, curiously, the shortest: Eusebio L. Rodrigues, 'Experiencing *Jazz*' (the novel's appeal is beyond logic, it offers a powerful experience but does not insist on definite meanings – the essay is written from a deep knowledge of music and jazz); Dwight A. McBride, 'Speaking the Unspeakable: On Toni Morrison, African American Intellectuals and the uses of Essentialist Rhetoric' (a thoughtful and provocative reading of Morrison's 'Unspeakable Things Unspoken: The Afro-American Presence in American Literature'). Finally, Section V presents three useful research tools: Malin LaVon Walther, 'And *All* of the Interests are Vested: Canon-Building in Recent Morrison Criticism'; Debbie Mix, 'Toni Morrison: A Selected Bibliography' (which nevertheless runs to some 22 pages); and, a fine piece of research, P. Jane Splawn, 'A Selective Annotated Bibliography'. This double issue is obviously essential reading for Morrison scholars and anyone interested in African American Studies. *MFS* are to be congratulated for making such a wealth of material available at such a reasonable price.

Jean Wyatt, 'Giving Body to the World: The Maternal Symbolic in Toni Morrison's *Beloved*' (*PMLA* 108.474–88), writes that in *Beloved* Morrison expresses various types of experience – childbirth and nursing from a mother's perspective, the desires of a pre-verbal infant, the sufferings of those destroyed by slavery – which cultural narratives usually omit. The expression of these experiences disrupts language in the 'telling' of the 'unspeakable' story of Sethe's infanticide which distorts discursive structures, and challenges Lacan's assumptions about language and language users.

In *Nabokov's Art of Memory and European Modernism* John Burt Foster, Jr sets himself the ambitious task of examining the role of memory in Nabokov's work, and further, considering Nabokov in relation to Proust and Bergson in France, Freud and Mann in the German-speaking world, and Joyce and Eliot in the English-speaking world. It may be said at once that this comparative study succeeds triumphantly. Foster wisely omits various Russian and Slavic influences as having already been well researched, and explores the possibilities of 'cultural biography' in which he subordinates Nabokov's life to his writings, and emphasizes how Nabokov's art of memory intersects with high European modernism. The basic enterprise of the book is to study Nabokov's life and achievements as they unfold within a specific cultural context. Foster makes the point that Nabokov's European background has been, to a certain extent, forgotten in studies of the 'Russian Nabokov' and the 'American Nabokov'. However, Foster writes, Nabokov's development from 1925 to 1950 connects essentially with broad issues of European culture. Foster rightly points out how ideally Nabokov is placed in time, space and language to provide new insights into European modernism. This he achieves by subtly teasing out Nabokov's interests in time and the mnemonic image and the Proustian issues of reinterpreted past, of fiction and autobiography, of voluntary memory and retrospective emotion in Nabokov's work. Though Foster explicitly states that his title does not reflect Frances Yates's, *The Art of Memory*, nevertheless when he describes Nabokov continually desiring to be modern, but at the same time irresistibly urged to remember his past, we cannot but be reminded of the oscillation backwards and forwards expressed at the beginning of Yates's work.

The book begins with a brilliant discussion of early works, particularly *Mary* and *The Gift*, the various interactions with *Speak Memory*, and autobiographical treatments of the same event in sketches like 'Tamara': Foster shows that Nabokov's early discovery of synesthesia with a simple spontaneous verbal-visual correspondence, leads ultimately to the mnemonic image which is 'the crowning achievement of the mature writer who intentionally strives for halluci-natory recall'. These early works also contain two motifs – his mother's jewels and rainbow-coloured windows – to which Nabokov returned time and again, and which inform his two master narratives: 'the Swiss governess' reading Dumas; and 'the summer of love' begun in the pavilion with its rainbow-coloured glass. These master narratives show that *Mary* and 'Mademoiselle O' are key transi-tions in Nabokov's work: as the remembered event is first seen poetically, then in fiction, then in autobiography, then possibly in fiction again with the use of a real love letter as the genres collapse into one another. The emerging art of memory is seen to be a central issue from *Laughter in the Dark* through *Speak Memory* to *Pale Fire*. In considering the currents of European modernism, Foster shows how Nabokov works within the tradition of Flaubert, Proust and Bergson, rejecting Freud's psychoanalytic concepts of sexuality, and the Anglo-American tradition of modernism (particularly Eliot – not quite first rate, and Pound – definitely second rate), the Gallic influence enables Nabokov to place *Ulysses* as the key text of high modernism. *Nabokov's Art of Memory* addresses itself to important biographical questions, considers the way Bakhtin and others view intertextuality and how this is vitally important for Nabokov's work, and finally gives a masterly reading of Nabokov's writings and their assumptions and reflections of modernism as a concept; this is an excellent book which should be read by anyone interested in Nabokov and cultural history.

Maurice Couturier, 'Nabokov in Postmodern Land' (*Crit* 34.247–60), points out that Nabokov's English novels, like Barthelme's, are text oriented, they thus project an as yet unheard of reality and only indirectly induce us to reassess the basis and functioning of our world. Nabokov is therefore contrasted to Coover, Gass, Pynchon etc., who realized that the old consensus had to be exploded, although their novels are mostly reality oriented. The article gives a useful, although controversial, survey of Nabokov's work set into the general chronology of pre-postmodernism and postmodernism from 1955 (*Lolita*, Paris edition) to 1985 (DeLillo's *White Noise*). *Lolita*, *Pale Fire* and *Ada* are, in Couturier's view, archetypal postmodern novels, since there is in them nothing beyond the text. In 'Nabokoviana' (*RFEA* 58.411–20), Couturier provides a useful summary of Nabokov criticism in France at the point when almost everything has been translated and Gallimard has decided to create a Pléiade edition. The article includes an excellent bibliography.

Anaïs (1993) is the eleventh annual volume dedicated to the work of Anaïs Nin. 'Return to Louveciennes' gives some pages from Nin's original diary from June and July 1935, on the eve of her first publications. The writing is hectic: 'Paris is like a second-rate fair. Shoddy. Everything is askew and small. There is no wind. They say it has charm. But I smell the decomposure.' Nin makes explicit her dependence on and involvement with the diary: an involvement that would cause discord with various lovers and psychoanalysts in her life. 'I am gifted for the diary and nothing else.' Suzanne Nalbantian writes of Nin's alchemical view of art which heightened personal experience and turned it into metaphor. Taking *The House of Incest* (1936), Nin's first published novel with its false window and imaginary room, Nalbantian points out that this imaginary space is based on the house at Louveciennes, although in the novel the narrator seeks a room without a window – a fortress of incestuous love. The metaphor will be replaced in her later work by the image of a labyrinth. In contrast, Wendy M. DuBow points out Nin's discontinuities in reading *The Diaries*, which express 'a belief in an essential self and an essential femaleness', but the female self is at war with her artistic self. *The Diaries* suggest that only the readers of the diary can truly know her, but DuBow, rightly, points out how problematic this assumption is. The argument is particularly convincing when considering Nin's decision to write in the present tense as though to suggest that her writing life and her living life were simultaneous, but then suddenly switching to an impersonal third-person narrator, which points out the impossibility of the text as transparent record. The writer of the diary gains power over the psychoanalysts Allendy and Rank, and 'contrary to what diary-readers often expect, the narrator's elusiveness and role-playing leave the reader less powerful than the narrator in this exchange'. The narrator's control is never more manifest than in the pregnancy episode of volume I: no father is mentioned, the child is stillborn, only few references to the pregnancy occur very late on, thus great swathes of the diary must have been written when she was pregnant but the diary makes no mention of the fact. The omissions, DuBow writes, are provocative from a feminist point of view – one might argue they are provocative from any point of view. Jean Fauchette's fine introduction to Nin's work, first published in *Two Cities* (1959), is translated by Gunther Stuhlmann, and current issues in Nin criticism are addressed by Philip K. Jason. This finely produced little book will be of interest to anyone concerned with Nin and her circle.

Anthony Di Renzo in *American Gargoyles* has written a useful and original work on Flannery O'Conner, although not as original nor as useful as he and the dust-jacket would have us believe – it is surely not true to say that the grotesque has been overlooked in studies of O'Conner. Di Renzo's strength is to remind us of the world of medieval art and find in those grotesque representations a duality which he rightly sees connected to O'Conner's world-view. Beginning, nicely, with Bernard of Clairvaux denouncing the gargoyles on his cloister walls: *deformis formositas, formosa deformitas* – hideously beautiful, beautifully hideous, Di Renzo then continues, using Derrida and the *pharmakon*, the scapegoat who cures, but who represents evil: both 'Alarming and calming. Sacred and accursed'. Di Renzo's basic point is that there is a profound connection between medieval gargoyles and the comic creations of Flannery O'Conner, which is based on 'a demonic topsy-turviness', a belief that the old gods are still with us. Grotesque art expresses the repressed and is itself transgressive. Its chief technique, and here Di Renzo is drawing on Bakhtin, is the degradation of high spiritual ideals; but this transgression and degradation can serve a positive end: the ultimate purpose of the grotesque is therapeutic, it is comic shock treatment into rebirth, into new insight. Di Renzo's otherwise excellent introduction is sometimes marred by hasty generalizations: thus, 'Like all comic forms, the grotesque is a descent into the concrete, the material'. In terms of Dante, Shakespeare, Milton, not to mention Jane Austen and Oscar Wilde, this needs a lot more argument before it is acceptable.

The first chapter proposes that the roots of O'Conner's grotesque fiction are located in medieval folk art. In the second, Di Renzo sees the figure of Christ as the ideal which lies behind O'Conner's special brand of satire. Third, he goes on to argue for O'Conner's unusual treatment of the human body which he examines in relation to medieval fabliaux. The fourth chapter looks at the interplay between the saintly and the demonic in O'Conner's work: good and evil are both seen as grotesque because both are in the process of becoming, they are both under construction. The final chapter continues the dialectic between the sacred and the grotesque in a study of the carnival. Here Di Renzo deals with a symbolic grotesque within O'Conner's dances with death and apocalyptic vision – Judgement Day is a comic Mardi Gras.

Despite Di Renzo's undoubted achievement there are two major problems with the book. One, he has an oddly appropriative attitude to his subject and the world: thus he seems to have been led to O'Conner and gargoyles by nothing less than the divine hand of providence; and to describe Italy (which coined the term grotesque) in terms of 'my mother's Sicily', 'my father's Abruzzi', 'my uncle's Rome' seems more than ordinarily solipsistic. This attitude, inevitably, affects the argument. Although Di Renzo has justly pointed out the dual function of the grotesque, his argument all too often falls into the Manichean: his particular *bêtes noires* being Martha Stephens, Harold Bloom and John Hawkes who get ritually bashed every ten pages or so (whereas these critics, particularly Stephens's insights into O'Conner and *Everyman*, look remarkably similar to his own); while, on the other hand, authority figures such as 'the noted depth psychologist', 'the noted medievalist' etc. are wheeled on whenever he feels the need. This approach to criticism means that, all too often, the analysis of the text remains univocal, and lacks the complex, subtle duality he has early established and only sometimes remembers. Thus in *Wise Blood* the penitential death of Hazel Motes 'leaves us unmoved', 'the comedy in this scene is sly and arch, but it is almost too clever for its own good'. At moments like this Di Renzo relies on assertion, not analysis; early on he writes: 'I will stick to the immediate surface of her work', that is, regrettably, all too often true. The second problem is that Di Renzo mixes categories to such an extent that logic escapes him: the artist, the fiction, the characters in the fiction all have the same ontological status. So Adelmo's marginalia in *The Name of the Rose* is the *same* religious satire as Flannery O'Conner's; *Wise Blood* is like Bosch's comic nightmares, but then it is also like Goya's *Caprichos*; in 'A Late Encounter with the Enemy' one of the characters, General Sash, is senile, this leads Di Renzo into a differentiation between Flannery O'Conner and other Southern writers on the grounds that they rely on an 'aesthetic of memory' to inform their works. In an otherwise good and learned book this illogic is disturbing. There are occasional misprints, but the index and bibliography are excellent and all in all Di Renzo has taken the first step in a fundamental reappraisal of Flannery O'Conner.

Ann Reuman, 'Revolting Fictions: Flannery O'Conner's Letter to her Mother' (*PLL* 29.197–214), points out that O'Conner's later short stories suggest a mother/daughter relationship which was deeply troubled and complex and which has a significant bearing on O'Conner's later writing. Although this is a somewhat circular argument, nevertheless useful connections are drawn from Kafka's *Letter to His Father* and 'Good Country People' and other stories, which reveals O'Conner's 'sense of entrapment, impotence, and frustration in the face of her mother's willful blindness'. Rebecca K. Rowley, 'Individuation and Religious Experience: A Jungian Approach to O'Conner's "Revelation"' (*SLJ* 25.92–102), writes that O'Conner read and was deeply influenced by Jung's work and this shows in many of her stories, particularly 'Revelation' where she utilizes Jung's comments on the reality and pervasiveness of the shadow which is worked out in the relationship between Mary Grace and Mrs Turpin.

Elaine M. Kauver's 'An Interview with Cynthia Ozick' (*ConL* 34. 359), presents a lengthy discussion on the basic distinction, in Ozick's mind and work, between what it is to be Jewish and what it is to be a writer: to be a Jew is continuously to say no to the parade of the world and the 'group-think agenda of multiculturalism'; while to be a writer is to plunge into the parade of Vanity Fair. The interview ranges widely on contemporary Jewish writers and writing, and will be essential reading for anyone interested in Ozick's work.

Hanjo Berressem's *Pynchon's Poetics: Interfacing Theory and Text* is a thoughtful, careful analysis of Pynchon's fiction from *V.* to *Vineland*. In the introduction, Berressem briefly surveys the theories of Lacan, Derrida, Foucault, Baudrillard et al. and points out that they 'are not competitors but components in a complex grid of complementary systems'. Post-structural theorists, Berressem argues, far from excluding notions of subjectivity, have reinvested subjectivity with vigour and great complexity. Modern critics have also pointed out the textualization of the world which has the effect of radically emancipating the signifier from the signified. Berressem concentrates on certain key passages (Pynchon would call them 'nodes') in the text, in which the poetics can unfold, and, by being selective in the analysis, he has the advantage of working as close to the signifier as possible. Part I of the book is composed of three interesting chapters on Lacan (the Text of the Subject); Derrida (the Subject of the Text); and Baudrillard (the Subject in the Text). Part II gives a series of close readings of 'V. in Love', Chapter XIV of *V.*; *The Crying of Lot 49*; the Kirghiz Light episode from *Gravity's Rainbow* (*GR* 336–59); the final chapter is on *Vineland* and concentrates on the fatal complicity between subjectivity, power and language. The three short opening chapters lay out Berressem's theoretical framework of Lacanian psychoanalysis, Derridean deconstruction, and Baudrillard's theory of simulation. Of these Baudrillard is seen as the most powerful because Lacan and Derrida base their theories on a specific view of the structure of language, whereas 'Baudrillard aims at a fundamental critique of this very structure and its effects on the subject in sociopolitical space'. The chapters on Pynchon which follow are exceptionally good analyses of certain key topics such as Pynchon's rhetorical deconstruction of psychoanalysis, his breakup of the network of signifiers, his treatment of language as a simulation machine, the subject's relation to networks of social conditioning and control, and its dissolution.

Because *V.*, *Lot 49*, and, particularly, *Gravity's Rainbow* have an enormous body of work on them already I should like to consider Berressem's treatment of *Vineland*, in which he takes issue with the common critical assumption that, in his latest novel, Pynchon has taken a step backwards. Berressem considers *Vineland* the most Lacanian of Pynchon's books: it is seen as the first work of Pynchon's late period, and it is a step forward in the sense that it is simpler, less abstract and thus more grounded in human reality. That *Vineland* has been seen as a step backward is not surprising given that 'Cyberpunk' is the latest literary fashion; and that the novel is retrospective, both in the sense of an era which reunites characters who have been out of touch, but also in the sense that it reunites characters from other Pynchon novels, for example Takeshi from *Gravity's Rainbow* and Mucho Maas from *Lot 49*. Even more than the other novels, *Vineland* builds TV into the interface between reality and simulation, which ultimately becomes the interface between life and death. *Vineland*, for Berressem, is a book that analyses power, particularly the complicity between the subject and power. Although there is rather too much of Lacan's matheme of 'four discourses' of master, knowledge, hysteric and analyst, this is, nevertheless, a fine analysis of Pynchon's latest, most controversial novel. *Pynchon's Poetics* is a masterly study of some of America's most complex narratives.

William Gleason, 'Postmodern Labyrinths of *Lot 49*' (*Crit* 34.83–97) is a somewhat over-polemical article which takes issue with Jameson et al. who argue that *The Crying of Lot 49* is mere play. However, Gleason usefully shows various possibilities of the metaphor of labyrinth in reading Pynchon's *Lot 49*, where literal and symbolic labyrinths interpenetrate the novel as Oedipa Maas follows the labyrinth of Inverarity's will (Gleason points out that Maas is Afrikaans for 'mesh' and thus the name itself invokes ancient myth and encodes labyrinth). The article comes to the unsurprising conclusion that language lies at the root of the topics discussed: symbolic landscape, narrative design and sexual dynamics. Nevertheless, Gleason is surely right to argue for Pynchon's social awareness, and the trenchant criticism in the novel which goes far beyond mere play. Ronald W. Cooley, 'The Hothouse or the Street: Imperialism and Narrative in Pynchon's *V*' (*MFS* 39.307–25), states that all Pynchon's novels examine power structures which influence our lives, but they refuse to rest on equilibrium or system, which might simply replace the power structures they were attempting to subvert. Pynchon's narrative strategies are as diffuse, discontinuous and contradictory as the machinations of power. However, it is in *V.* that Pynchon identifies the power with imperialism. Cooley discovers a kind of failure in *V.* in that it looks for narrative closure with the projected reconciliation of Paola and Pappy Hod. Of course this misses the point entirely: neither of the two narrative strands end in resolution – the resolution lies outside the book with Suez, the final nail in the coffin of the British Empire.

Jay Boyer has written a useful introduction to the work of Ishmael Reed concluding that, like Ellison, Reed writes novels that celebrate life. After a brief biographical introduction (Reed has been teaching at Berkeley for the last 20 years and edited *Calafia: The California Poetry*), Boyer sets out Reed's main preoccupations: the figure of the cowboy to express the disparity between the promise of America and its realities; the loss of the American Dream and the takeover of America by ultra right-wing values; the position of blacks who are denied American acceptance. To express these dilemmas Reed uses 'Hoodoo' (myth, the occult, Caribbean magic). In *Mumbo Jumbo* (1972), for example, Reed rewrites the Osiris legend with Osiris a black fertility bull god, while his brother Set is a white cannibal killer. Set's victory over Osiris gives rise to Judaeo-Christianity and the supremacy of whites over blacks. Situated in 1920s' America the book is a kind of detective story in which the protagonist, wonderfully named Papa LaBas, searches for Osiris's lost text; in his search he comes across the 'Jes Grew' (Just Grew? = organic, natural life), which is manifested in the Jazz Age – in a sense Reed's novels are both jazzy *and* metafictional. Boyer briefly considers Reed's essays and poetry and then proceeds to survey Reed's eight novels which he perceives as fitting comfortably into traditional forms: *The Free-Lance Pallbearers* and *Reckless Eyeballing* are *Bildungsromans*; *Mumbo Jumbo* and *The Last Days of Louisiana Red* are detective stories etc. Reed has frequently been accused of misogyny and of portraying black men as the victims of matriarchy; but Boyer hedges his bets on these controversial issues. *Ishmael Reed* has no pretensions to theory and is written for someone coming to Reed's work for the first time; with its clear exposition and useful bibliography it fulfils its aims well.

Kathryn Hume's 'Ishmael Reed and the Problematics of Control' (*PMLA* 108.506–18) draws on Foucault and shows that Reed, like Pynchon, Mailer,

Burroughs and Acker, has produced violent satires on the exercise of power in America. But Reed is more successful than the others in suggesting an answer to the problematics of control. However, the message emerges only from a reading of all the novels together: individually they are disparate, but together they can be seen to offer an alternative vision of social structure which is more stoic and epicurean than might at first appear. Richard Hardack's 'Swing to the White, Back to the Black: "Sourcery" in Ishmael Reed's *Mumbo Jumbo*' (*ArQ* 49.iv.117–38) writes that Reed has been classified in many ways, but in fact he is a hybrid stylist, and not likely to be considered a traditional writer in any genre. Reed seems unable to decide whether he is Pan-African or Pan-American, his myth of origins has tragic implications since he can find himself neither in the Black Renaissance nor the American Renaissance (each of which parodies the other). In *Mumbo Jumbo*, using Emerson's rhetorical strategies, 'Jes Grew' is not so much the voice of Black culture, so much as a form of American transcendentalism. Thus Reed passes off a White transcendental vision of Pan as Black, since the figure was stolen property to begin with.

John Neary, in *Something and Nothingness: The Fiction of John Updike and John Fowles*, has produced a work that might have looked like a good idea, but does not quite succeed – this is despite some acute observations on Updike. Neary begins with two methods for the apprehension of God: the apophatic, *via negativa*, which points to the mystery of God lying behind language and all things (God is not this); and the kataphatic, *via affirmativa*, in which God is apprehended in everything (God is in this, that, *and* the other). Fowles, classified as postmodern, metafictional and experimental fits into the apophatic; whilst Updike, classified as a social realist, fits into the kataphatic. Neary claims that he is, ultimately, 'comparing the writers' presentations of philosophical/aesthetic visions that have decided, though decidedly different, existentialist and theological foundations'. In order to perform this exercise he compares several pairs of similar novels. Thus Chapters 2 and 3 consider *The Collector* and *Rabbit Run* respectively; while Chapter 4, the philosophical heart of the book, examines Fowles and Updike's biographical and philosophical orientation. Neary points out that Fowles's *The Tree* (1979), and Updike's 'The Dogwood Tree' (1965) 'uncannily' use the same image of the 'key romantic, organicist image – the tree ... like their fictions, the persons of these writers are mirror images: they are polar opposites, with opposing world views, and yet they confront each other with remarkably similar features'. The problems here are obvious: Neary allows no critical distance, there is no problematic, the writing Fowles *is* Fowles, the storytelling Updike *is* Updike; mirror images are scarcely the same as polar opposites; and far from being 'uncanny' the use of tree imagery in terms of youth, process, presence and absence etc. seems to me archetypal (the discussion on presence in absence could have benefited from a reading of Yves Bonnefoy's immensely stimulating *Arrière Pays*). Chapter 5 compares *The Centaur* and *The Magus* as *Bildungsroman* informed by Greek mythology. Neary suggests that while the Rabbit books contain some of Updike's theological ideas, *The Centaur* presents a human encounter with Levinas's '*absolutely other*' or Karl Barth's 'Wholly Other' in phenomenological rather than theological terms. Chapter 6 looks at *Couples* and *The French Lieutenant's Woman* as novels that use sex to deconstruct nineteenth-century fictional conventions. While Neary may have a point about *The French Lieutenant's Woman* (in which there is very little sex), he falls into banality when writing about Updike. After a lengthy quotation of Piet's explicit, joyful cunnilingus with Angela, we read that such a passage could hardly have been written by a George Eliot let alone a Charles Dickens. Well, indeed not! Poor Mr Casaubon, even poorer Dorothea (although Will Ladislaw might have got a lick in). Neary tries to link the treatment of location of both Tarbox and Middlemarch, but this is to do an injustice to both *Middlemarch* and *Couples*: there may be an argument for Tarbox being the protagonist of *Couples*, although its status is more that of Peyton Place, however it is certainly not 'anatomized' in the same way as provincial society in *Middlemarch*. Tarbox on the eve of the Kennedy assassination is *radically* different from Loamshire on the eve of the First Reform Act. Neary is much more successful with his references to Denis de Rougemont's *Love in the Western World*, and his distinctions between passion and love. The final chapter considers *Roger's Version* and *S.* together with Fowles's *Mantissa* and *A Maggot*; Neary perceives them as experimental texts that look directly at the issue of religion, and in which the authors almost reverse their positions with the two *via*. Although the book places the various novels on too procrustean a bed, nevertheless Neary is an acute analyst of contemporary fiction who usefully points out Updike's debt to Kierkegaard in his narrative use of repetition founded on a Christian belief in presence rather than absence.

At the time *Frank Waters: Man and Mystic*, edited by Vine Deloria Jr was published, Waters was over 90 years old and still active in 'deep ecology'. His writing career runs over 60 years and, with a face almost as weatherbeaten as the Taos mountain, he is clearly a charismatic figure. Waters is best known as a regional novelist, but this book attempts to celebrate the life and work by making more universal claims for him: the claims do not stand because they are over-stated; although this is not to denigrate Waters's considerable achievement. As Bobby Bridger rightly says in 'Frank Waters: Becoming Indigenous', 17 of his 25 books have never been out of print including his classics *The Man Who Killed the Deer* (1942) and *Masked Gods* (1950), and he is rightly praised for his interest in Native American culture and various ecological issues. The book has two sections: 'The Memories' and 'The Commentaries'. There is far too much memory in 'The Commentaries', whereas 'The Memories' are full of New Age gibberish: 'At the base of the Taos mountain I saw a group of glowing amethyst pyramids. I counted seven pyramids in all. There was a green aura on the peak closest to the Pueblo.' 'The Memories' are also marked by an unconscious humour: 'Frank has lost three human projections of his anima. "When I finally looked up from my typewriter, three of my wives were gone for good", he says with a woeful shake of his head.' This is reported by his fourth wife – apparently four is a lucky number for Frank Waters. In 'The Commentaries' T. N. Luther provides a useful annotated bibliography with some indication of prices collectors might expect to pay – up to $200 for *The Man Who Killed the Deer*. Stephen Wall finds it very hard to put into words the feelings evoked from reading Waters's words, but has a go anyway. He argues that Waters's strong connections with the Taos mountain, the Rio Grande Southwest etc. have restricted Waters's fame beyond this area. But then argues that only those who share this connectedness with the place can really appreciate the work. Relying on F. L. Lucas, *Style* (1955, 1974), Alexander Ball has some 'Observations on the Style of Frank Waters'. Some of Waters's prose is quoted and over-praised – better than Hardy, more like Flaubert, Waters and Hardy better than Hemingway – but the basis for these 'appreciations' lack all rigour. Charles Adams usefully details Waters's continu-ing defence of American Sacred Spaces, while Thomas J. Lyon says that he will be teaching *The Man Who Killed the Deer* for the twenty-sixth time this autumn – it must be almost time to change the text. Throughout this book there is a special pleading, sometimes reaching hagiography, as though Waters's words were beyond the reach of critics. Lyon makes the point more cogently than most: he expresses 'the instinctive feeling that the map (the criticism, that is) was not the territory. Critics and scholars speak, almost inevitably, from the tamed world, most of the time'. Not if they are any good they don't. Will Blevins in his 'Tribute to *The Man Who Killed the Deer*' comes closest to some kind of critical appreciation of the way Waters uses words, but then relapses into emotional description: 'I am powerfully struck, and humbled, by the subtlety, the power, and daring of this use of language.' Given the sterility of much contemporary critical writing, one is partly sympathetic to this straightforward emotionalism. However, Frank Waters's novels richly deserve a critical reappraisal; it is a pity they do not receive it in this volume.

SoQ 32.i. is a special issue on Eudora Welty edited by Stephen Young. It opens with four short papers and a round table discussion by scholars from the Gorky Institute in Moscow. Alexandr Vaschenko writes of the function of folklore in Welty's stories pointing out the influence of Greek and Celtic mythology on *The Golden Apples*, and the way in which *The Wide Net* and *The Robber Bridegroom* create legendary time and space with the Natchez Trace which enters our consciousness as an aesthetic symbol. Ekaterina Stetsenko, after writing of the two main strands of American autobiography (the ecclesiastical/spiritual and the secular), turns her attention to Welty's *One Writer's Beginnings*, which is exceptional in that it pushes historical and political problems into the background. Welty learned to write, as she insists all Southern writers learned to write, in three movements: 'Listening'; 'Learning to See'; and 'Finding a Voice'. She has a strong physical feeling for the accordance of a subject with its word equivalent: thus the word 'moon' is round as a grape in her mouth; and her abiding interest in photography has 'taught her to fix visual images and then to hold transient life in words'. Natalia Yakimenko finds Welty using almost the same idea as Bakhtin's formulation of *chronotop* (*chronos* + *topos*), in her essays *The Eye of the Story*. In particular, the *idyllic chronotop* (time seen through space and place viewed over time) is seen as an active shaping force in *Delta Wedding*. While linear time was ruled by the timeless in the idyll in *Delta Wedding*, Aleksei Zverev, in contrast, looks at *Losing Battles* in a historical context: the depiction of the thirties; but informed by the sixties which is seen as the last period when the prevailing view of humanity was historical. In *Losing Battles*, as in other Welty novels, there are values beyond those of individual fulfilment; they are the values of the clan, 'the home ties'; it may be, Zverev suggests, the last time such claims can be made. The round table discussion makes some interesting points on Welty's reputation and publishing history in Russia, and on certain similarities between Russian and Southern Literature. The volume also contains valuable articles on 'Moon Lake', the central story of *Golden Apples*, by Marrilyn Arnold; the Altering/Alterity of History in *The Robber Bridegroom*, by Deborah Wilson; a reconsideration of 'Why I Live at the P.O.' by Axel Nissen; and an article, finely illustrated with Welty's photographs, entitled 'Images of the Depression in the Fiction of Eudora Welty' by Ruth D. Weston. *SoQ* have made a valuable contribution to Welty scholarship with the essays collected here.

Eben E. Bass, 'The Languages of *Losing Battles*' (*SAF* 21.67–82), considers the way written and spoken language complement and compete with each other in Welty's *Losing Battles*. The language of print, and writing and print, are seen as a centrifugal force moving outwards to abstraction, whilst spoken language is seen as centripetal, gathering the family together. The problem that Welty's oral language is, of course, written in the novel, is not addressed. Meanwhile, Gina D. Peterman, '*A Curtain of Green*: Eudora Welty's Auspicious Beginning' (*MissQ* 46.i.91–114), provides a useful analysis of the difficulties encountered, and overcome, in the publication of Welty's first collection. Peterman is good on the economics, the supporters (Ford and Porter), the enemies (all editors, with the exception of Doubleday), she is less good on critical analysis. Claudine Verlay, 'Les Metamorphoses du texte et les avatars de la circularité dans "The Whole World Knows" de E. Welty' (*RFEA* 56.193–204) is a fine article which points out the fragmented, chaotic narrative of 'The Whole World Knows'. The centripetal closure of the narrative opposes the centrifugal dynamics of a revelation impossible to utter.

2. Drama

(a) General

Undoubtedly the publishing event of the year in this field was the appearance of the *Cambridge Guide to American Theatre*, which the editors, Don B. Wilmeth and Tice L. Miller, modestly describe as a 'spinoff' from Martin Banham's *Cambridge Guide to World Theatre*. Wilmeth and Miller have assembled an imposing panel (Banham, Marvin Carlson, Jill Dolan, Spencer Golub, Errol G. Hill, Philip Kolin, Brenda Murphy, Laurence Senelick and Louis Scheaffer are just a few of the distinguished contributors) to produce an encyclopaedia of some 2,300 entries supplemented by 170 black-and-white illustrations. The shorter entries offer the expected concise accounts of plays and playwrights, plus a wealth of additional information including suggestions for further reading. The reader will also find an excellent, 20-page introductory historical survey by Wilmeth and C. Lee Jenner, along with no fewer than 100 'topical entries' which explore in more detail subjects as diverse as AIDS, criticism, censorship, magic (a delightful entry by professional magician and actor Ricky Jay), the minstrel show, nudity, the Wild West exhibition; the list goes on, with entries addictively cross-referenced. The *Cambridge Guide*'s remarkable range, extremely high standards of scholarship and presentation, and lavish pictorial record ensure that it will become the standard reference work, comfortably superseding the comparatively limited *Oxford Companion to American Theatre* (the second edition of which was reviewed in *YWES* 73.613).

Some of those writing for the *Guide* belong to another reassuringly impressive team of scholars (Linda Ben-Zvi, C. W. E. Bigsby, John Russell Brown, Christopher Innes, Helene Keyssar, Bruce King, J. L. Styan, Peter Thomson, etc.) compiled to produce the fifth edition of Gale Research's *Contemporary Dramatists* under the editorship of K. A. Berney, which provides very full bibliographical and introductory critical material on around 450 living English-language playwrights. Each entry contains a biography, a complete list of published and/or produced works, and a signed essay, usually of several hundred words or more, which tends to be more critically oriented than is often the case with reference works. There are no cross-references or illustrations, and the overriding aim is clearly to provide scholars with the necessary materials to research a given writer in greater depth. A particularly helpful feature in this regard is that some entries contain information as to the whereabouts of manuscript collections. The book is too expensive to find itself on many shelves, but should be a required purchase for university libraries.

Two American critics published collections of their shorter pieces of theatre writing. Jonathan Kalb has brought together in *Free Admissions: Collected Theater Writings* a range of material written and mostly published between 1984 and 1992. Much of the book is preoccupied with Germany in the transitional period prior to unification, and for Kalb 'somewhere between the cerebralism of the German theater and the anti-intellectualism of the American theater is a benign middle ground for both cultures, though doubtless not the same one'. Several pieces consider Beckett, who consented to an interview with Kalb in 1986 which is reprinted here, and on whom Kalb has written at length in *Beckett in Performance* (CUP, 1989). Kalb's deliberately untheoretical style is directly related to the anti-authoritarian stance of his assault on the *auteur* director, and perhaps owes something to the fact that much of his work might be loosely termed journalism (he is theatre critic for the *Village Voice*), albeit a journalism with a critical weight rarely encountered in his fellow-reviewers. His opposition to theory as it is conventionally practised is incomparably more astute than the ostensibly similar position of Bert Cardullo, who has published a collection of his essays, notes and reviews in *Theatrical Reflections: Notes on the Form and Practice of Drama* (1992). Cardullo prefaces the collection with the observation that his preoccupations are 'not theoretical', but are instead concerned with 'analysis of character, action, language, and setting that can be translated into concepts for theatrical production'. Inevitably, in essay after essay Cardullo falls headlong into the trap he has set himself by assuming that his concerns and methodology (a drearily old-fashioned close reading) are free of both theory and ideology, and therefore somehow more clear-sighted than the analyses of those who are more critically aware of their own ideological situation. So, for example, just four pages into the first article, an account of 'Birth and Death in *A Streetcar Named Desire*', Cardullo maps out a whole set of startlingly naive assumptions: that the 'problem' with analyses by, among others, 'the Russian Marxists, and the feminists', is that they ignore 'the *human* element in the play', since Blanche and Stanley 'are human beings *first*'; that Cardullo's own method 'is formalistic, which is to say that it depends on formal considerations and organic connections within the work of art itself, not on a theoretical framework imposed on the art object from without'; that such frameworks are guilty of 'ignoring the text, by eschewing close analysis'; and that his own reading 'gains what authority it possesses from its thoroughness, not from any ideological conviction behind it. I unabashedly declare that I have no ideological axe to grind – unless one considers humanism an ideology ... I suffer, then, from what could be called the aesthetic bias: the compulsion to treat works of art as *works of art*'. The prosecution could safely rest at this point, but it is worth noting that the reason why this book is not just pompous, naive and ignorant but actively offensive is that Cardullo seems to think that any critics who have bothered to become theoretically informed are condemned thereafter to spend their lives wandering around with their eyes shut.

The theatre writings of a major American critic have been selected, edited and introduced by Brenda Murphy in *A Realist in the American Theatre: Selected Drama Criticism of William Dean Howells*, which brings together 29 essays written for magazines between 1875 and 1919 by a man accurately described by Murphy as 'one of America's best-known literary critics, and one of its least-known drama critics'. In her characteristically lucid introduction, Murphy argues for the influence of Howells as both critic and chronicler of a period in which his championing of realism engaged some of the central concerns of both American and European drama. From an early preference for American plays, Howells by the turn of the century had moved towards conceding the superiority of contemporary British dramatists on the grounds that their plays exposed the complicity of society in the life of the individual, whereas '[i]n Howells's view, American drama at its best was psychological, not sociological'. Ibsen took drama further still, by writing plays which, in Howells's words, sought 'a solution in the conscience of the spectator for the future rather than the present; it is not an isolated case; it does not demand what he would do or would have done, in a given event; and this is what makes the difference between him and the modern English playwrights'. Murphy, then, has recovered a collection of essays which not only provide a valuable contemporary analysis of the tensions between morality, form and society in the drama of this period, but in particular offer an arguably stronger, if less extensive, defence of Ibsen than the much better-known Shavian misreading.

Howells displayed a preference for text over performance, but this was in large part because he rightly considered American theatre as business, with the profit motive and the effects of syndication conspiring to banish the innovative and controversial play from the mainstream American stage. As Murphy notes, in this respect he was remarkably prescient, as Bernard Rosenberg and Ernest Harburg's *The Broadway Musical: Collaboration in Commerce and Art* shows. This lavishly illustrated account of the rise, fall and survival of the genre is a documentary rather than critical record, drawing on extensive interviews and a welter of statistical evidence (in the text as well as in the numerous appendices), but largely eschewing evaluation. The survey falls into three parts: the financing of Broadway musical theatre; the structuring of the workforce, examining the interactive relationships between executives and staff in the production; and the creative conflicts within the artistic team. The authors' diligent research sits a little uneasily alongside their sometimes bland commentary, but this is a very informative account of the business structure of Broadway which has a significance beyond its immediate subject, and although much of the material is genre-specific its account of the effects of capital and syndication show how right Howells was to call in 1916 for alternative forms of theatre funding.

Marvin Carlson's *Deathtraps: The Postmodern Comedy Thriller* examines those forms of drama which offer a sceptical subversion of the positivistic conventions of detection. Something similar, of course, has happened in post-war prose fiction, in the work of Borges, Eco and Auster, for instance, and as Carlson's subtitle might suggest, the possibilities for this kind of subversion in the theatre appear comparatively limited. His argument for a specifically theatrical double-coding is based in part on the tension between the closure of the dramatic text and the self-reflexivity of performance: the stage scene, for example, can create the illusion of authenticity which may subsequently be exposed as a ludic frame, while performance can generate energies beyond authorial control. What emerges, however, is that the success of these works comes to depend almost exclusively on the subversion of audience expectations; and since this ironic self-regard is now built in to that horizon of expectations the plays ultimately seem somewhat impoverished in comparison to many postmodern detective novels. Carlson's is a well-informed and judicious analysis, offering detailed discussion of a range of plays (by Anthony Shaffer, Ira Levin, Nick Hall, Terence Feely and Rupert Holmes, for instance) some of which perhaps receive less than their due in most critical surveys of the contemporary theatre, but the book is likely to appeal primarily to those who are already addicts of this kind of drama.

James S. Moy's *Marginal Sights: Staging the Chinese in America* contains ten essays exploring various Euro-American strategies for the construction and containment of Chinese identity. Beginning with two forms of the gaze in the nineteenth century, the serial (the non-narrative, panoptic museum or circus show, for instance) and the voyeuristic (associated with literary realism), Moy moves through the history of twentieth-century representations to argue that such recent works as David Henry Hwang's *M. Butterfly* and Philip Kan Gotonda's *Yankee Dawg You Die* are still trapped by commercial considerations into producing 'authenticated stereotypes'. In between he examines such plays as Bret Harte and Mark Twain's *Ah Sin*, Henry Grimm's *The Chinese Must Go* and O'Neill's *Marco Millions*, Arnold Genthe's turn-of-the-century photographs of Chinatown, anthropological exhibitions and today's popular representations in cinema and on television. The book explores the historical contexts of Chinese stereotypes, moving through the strategies whereby Chinese America is marginalized or rendered invisible to the 'containment fields' of the ghetto and the still current spectacle of the dead or dying Asian in popular media, before arriving at today's 'strategy of exhaustion, in which the victims – in spite of their best intentions and their complaints that their representations have been disfigured by Anglo-America – remain victims'. Moy's closing suggestion that Asian America can learn from W. E. B. Du Bois's call in 1926 for an African–American theatre about, by, for and near its own people might helpfully be considered alongside Rena Fraden's excellent *Blueprints for a Black American Theatre 1935–1939* (CUP, 1994; to be reviewed in *YWES* 75), which contrasts Du Bois's separatism with the ideas of such writers as Alain Locke and, more recently, Cornel West. *Marginal Sights* is a superbly written and well-illustrated account, an excellent contribution to current thinking on orientalism which seemingly effortlessly incorporates poststructuralist methodologies within a compelling historical framework. Moy's discussion of the problem of the 'authentic' remains contestable, however, and is indeed directly challenged by Karen Shimakawa in '"Who's to Say?": Or, Making Space for Gender and Ethnicity in *M. Butterfly*' (*TJ* 45.349–62). Perhaps unfairly criticizing Moy as someone searching for a 'clearly-delineated role model' in this play, Shimakawa argues that Baudrillard's postmodern 'ecstasy of communication', which erases distinctions between the public and the private space, merely describes ordinary lived experience for those without authority, and goes on to explore how Hwang's character of Song lives actively within this ecstasy, resisting but also creating perceptions of boundary and gender.

A less heated subject is engaged in Marianthe Colakis's very brief account of *The Classics in the American Theater of the 1960s and Early 1970s*. Specifically, the book considers how classical literature (predominantly the tragic dramas of ancient Greece) were reinterpreted and transformed by American playwrights according to their contemporary concerns. Jack Richardson's *The Prodigal* finds in the House of Atreus a modern theme of individual rebellion against conformity;

David Rabe exploits the same mythic family in *The Orphan*, which prefigures his Vietnam plays, and similarly Daniel C. Gerould's *Candaules, Commissioner* had previously commented on Vietnam by way of an incident in Herodotus; Robert Lowell's *Prometheus Bound* and Archibald MacLeish's *Herakles* are framed by the possibility of global annihilation; and theatre collectives advocated political activism and revolution in such pieces as the Performance Group's *Dionysus in '69* and the Living Theatre's *Antigone*. Some of this material, especially that concerning the theatre groups, has been treated more interestingly and extensively elsewhere, and there is little in Colakis's book, either in scholarship or argument, which is likely to make it indispensable even to those for whom this subject represents more than a footnote to the American drama of this period.

(b)   Individual Authors

As ever, there was a healthy crop of publications on Eugene O'Neill, despite the fact that *EONR* has got slightly behind schedule. The only number to appear in 1993 was nominally the autumn 1992 issue (16.ii), which as usual contained a number of pieces of scholarly and archival research. Donald Gallup has edited and provided an introduction to ' "Greed of the Meek": O'Neill's Scenario for Act One of the First Play of His Eight-Play Cycle' (5–11); Madeline C. Smith and Richard Eaton provide a running commentary linking 13 letters of the period 1925–1936 from the playwright to his editor and friend Manuel Komroff (13–28); and Edward L. Shaughnessy continues his biographical investigations with a piece on 'Ella O'Neill and the Imprint of Faith' (29–43). Frank R. Cunningham's 'Eugene O'Neill in Our Time: Overcoming Student Resistance' (45–55) is derived from a conference paper which considers the difficulties and opportunities in teaching O'Neill in the classroom. The issue also contains two critical-interpretive pieces: David Aaron Murray's 'O'Neill's Transvaluation of Pessimism in *The Iceman Cometh*' (73–79) rightly emphasizes the Nietzschean 'strong pessimism' which informs O'Neill's work, in place of the parody of nihilism to which both playwright and philosopher are so commonly reduced, while Stephen A. Black's 'Reality and Its Vicissitudes: The Problem of Understanding in *Long Day's Journey Into Night*' (57–72) explores the same Nietzschean influence, along with that of Freud and others, in seeking to extract the play from its biographical contexts and to reinscribe it within the forms of modern tragedy. Black has also edited the *File on O'Neill*, which like all the volumes in Methuen's *Writer-Files* series contains a wealth of useful information in a very compact form. Not surprisingly, with such a prolific playwright this compactness, and indeed the series format in general, proves to be something of a problem. With only 96 pages at his disposal Black has properly focused attention on earlier reviews at the expense of more recent revivals, but inevitably there is still a sketchiness about the survey of the plays, while O'Neill's comments on his work are squeezed into five pages. It's a shame that a longer volume could not have been compiled, but this is still a remarkable feat of condensation.

Travis Bogard, one of the most eminent of O'Neillians, published two further volumes on the dramatist. '*From the Silence of Tao House*': *Essays About Eugene and Carlotta O'Neill and the Tao House Plays* is a collection of Bogard's occasional writings such as conference papers, programme notes, introductions to radio broadcasts of the plays, and entries in reference works. It is, in fact, an occasional book, published to raise funds for the Californian residence at which

O'Neill composed many of his plays, but despite its modest origins and intent this collection contains several items of interest, and although much of the material is familiar it is all very readable and well presented. Elsewhere, Bogard's characteristically rigorous scholarship has unearthed the words and music to all but three of the 70-odd songs featured in the plays. *The Eugene O'Neill Songbook* provides good evidence for Bogard's surprising observation that 'it is probable that O'Neill used song to enhance the action of his plays more than any dramatist since Shakespeare'. The foreword gives an overview of the importance of music in O'Neill's life, and Bogard also comments on the significance of each song in its context within the play. While this collection will, of course, be of greatest interest to directors and actors, it also has obvious relevance for critics and scholars.

Conversations with Thornton Wilder, edited by Jackson R. Bryer, appears in UPMissip's valuable Literary Conversations series, and brings together in chronological order some 24 interviews with Wilder conducted between 1929 and 1975, including translations of some pieces previously available only in German or French. As with other titles in the series, the interviews are reprinted uncut and in their original form, which results in some repetition of biographical material from article to article, and, in one or two cases, preserves some rather tiresome journalistic asides. It's also a little disappointing that Wilder's interrogators are so reverential throughout, and no one should come to this collection expecting personal revelation, or even intellectual debate. But Wilder was, as Bryer notes in the introduction, 'a great conversationalist', pithy and epigrammatic, with a huge range; and although his ideas on theatre are neither profoundly original nor unavailable elsewhere – indeed, all the significant insights here are present in more condensed form in 'Some Thoughts on Playwriting', Wilder's essay of 1949 – the exposition throughout is easy, lucid and witty, as befits a writer who accurately described himself as 'a fabulist, not a critic'.

In '"Through Soundproof Glass": The Prison of Self-Consciousness in *The Glass Menagerie*' (*MD* 36.529–37), Eric P. Levy provides a close reading of the recurrent references to mirrors in Tennessee Williams's play, although this is one case where a knowledge of Lacan would definitely have furthered the discussion. Philip C. Kolin, for whom it was a bumper year, published a number of short pieces on this playwright: 'The Existential Nightmare in Tennessee Williams's *The Chalky White Substance*' (*NConL* 23.8–11) considers this recently published late play to be a Beckettian 'anti-parable' and 'Williams's bleakest work'; with Auxiliadora Arana, Kolin conducted 'An Interview with Wolf Ruvinskis: The First Mexican Stanley Kowalski' (*LATR* Spring 1993, 159–65); and a note, 'Tennessee Williams Sends His Autobiography to Mexico' (*MissQ* 46.255–6), reveals that a Spanish translation of his short autobiographical piece, 'Facts About Me', appeared in a review of the first Mexican production of *Streetcar* in 1948.

A special issue of *SAD* (8.ii), which Kolin co-edits, was largely devoted to Williams. John L. Gronbeck-Tedesco's 'Absence and the Actor's Body: Marlon Brando's Performance in *A Streetcar Named Desire* on Stage and in Film' (115–26) uses (disappointingly unreproduced) photographic and video records of the performances to argue that they 'position the play as an allegory of post-war America – an allegory that focuses on changing domestic relationships between men and women', for example in the way Brando and Kazan organized Stanley's role around the text's intermittent allusions to a military background. Several

598   AMERICAN LITERATURE: THE TWENTIETH CENTURY

pieces in this issue consider various perceptions of Williams's work outside
America. The reception of his plays in Poland and Russia is considered respec-
tively in Anna Kay France's interview with the director and scholar Kazimierz
Braun (189–99) and Philip C. Kolin and Colby H. Cullman's interview with the
Russian scholar Maya Koreneva (201–13), while Zhu Lian Qun has compiled a
bibliography of Williams criticism in China from 1975–92 (214–16). Laurilyn J.
Harris writes on '*Menagerie* in Manila and Other Cross-Cultural Affinities: The
Relevance of the Plays of Tennessee Williams on the Filipino Stage' (163–74),
and the same play is the subject of Laura Morrow and Edward Morrow's
'Humpty-Dumpty Lives!: Complexity Theory as an Alternative to the Omelet
Scenario in *The Glass Menagerie*' (127–39), one of several recent essays which
utilize developments in scientific theory, in this case complexity and chaos
theory, to explore the relativistic universe of the modern stage (see also the same
authors' piece on *Streetcar* and Gary Grant's discussion of Shepard, below). In
all of these cases the authors fail to demonstrate convincingly that there is a
necessary correlation between the scientific paradigm and the dramatic or performance text, although we can expect more sustained efforts to this end in the
near future. Finally in this issue, Kolin himself gives an alternative reading of the
much-criticized character of Chicken Ravenstock in 'Sleeping with Caliban: The
Politics of Race in Tennessee Williams's *Kingdom of Earth*' (140–62).

Kolin was the editor of yet another collection, *Confronting Tennessee
Williams's 'A Streetcar Named Desire': Essays in Critical Pluralism*, to which
he also contributed a helpful introduction, 'Reflections on/of *A Streetcar Named
Desire*', which surveys recent approaches to the play in theatre and in criticism.
As the subtitle suggests, the book goes out of its way to foreground critical theory,
in a way which implies an unstated recognition (noted recently by C. W. E.
Bigsby and others) that students of American drama came rather late to this
particular party. A significant number of the essays therefore contain quite
lengthy summaries of the particular theories on which their authors have drawn,
although many of these approaches are already familiar: this is the case, for
example, with William Kleb's 'Marginalia: *Streetcar*, Williams, and Foucault',
which relates the presentation of confinement and transgression in the play to
Foucault's theories of power-knowledge (especially in *The History of Sexuality*),
but is more suggestive in noting the more contemporaneous connection with
Kinsey; June Schlueter's '"We've Had This Date With Each Other From the
Beginning": Reading Toward Closure in *A Streetcar Named Desire*' (reception
and reader-response theories, specifically those of Iser and Jauss); and Mark
Royden Winchell's 'The Myth is the Message, or Why *Streetcar* Keeps Running',
an unconvincingly provocative Fiedlerian account of Blanche as wrecker of 'a
patriarchal vision of home as Heaven'. A more subtle reading of Blanche is
provided by Laurilyn J. Harris, whose 'Perceptual Conflict and the Perversion of
Creativity in *A Streetcar Named Desire*' exploits some relatively unfamiliar
theories of perception in pursuing a number of important points, including the
argument that Blanche becomes complicitous in the stereotyping of herself by
others, and that in each of her lovers she attempts to find again her relationship
with Allan Grey.

In 'The White Goddess, Ethnicity, and the Politics of Desire', Lionel Kelly
notes that, *pace* Williams, there is a distinctly *un*easy mingling of races in the
play, and argues persuasively that *Streetcar* contains both a problematic realism
in its presentation of history and ethnicity, and a mythic exploration of sexuality

in the figure of Blanche, who can be seen as a 'secularized version' of Robert Graves's White Goddess. Some related issues are considered from a very different angle in Robert Bray's wide-ranging Marxist account of property and desire in '*A Streetcar Named Desire*: The Political and Historical Subtext', while W. Kenneth Holditch's 'The Broken World: Romanticism, Realism, Naturalism in *A Streetcar Named Desire*' places Williams's play in its Southern literary context alongside Chopin's *The Awakening* and Faulkner's *The Wild Palms*. The range of possible approaches to history, ideology and intertextuality in these essays alone must cast some doubt on the applicability of the Chaos and Antichaos theories in Laura Morrow and Edward Morrow's 'The Ontological Potentialities of Antichaos and Adaptation in *A Streetcar Named Desire*'. Their supposedly scientific, 'holistic' approach seems to me to operate according to the same principles of self-definition and exclusion as the 'partial and sentimental' theories they reject: so, for example, they argue that their method should enable them 'to assess the degree of determinism' informing the characters, but make all kinds of assumptions about authorship and art ('fine playwrights like Williams perceive intuitively that the interaction between a few apparently simple characters can generate a complex and compelling work of art'), and about the literary text's conformity to their reading of systems in finally asserting that 'the fates of the characters are predestined, predestined not by fate but by a combination of their inherited psychological make-up and the values to which they are exposed in their basins of attraction'.

Other essays take a productively pluralistic approach. Herbert Blau's 'Readymade Desire' succinctly places the work in relation both to Williams's early political radicalism and to the self-conscious pop culture of postmodernism, while Calvin Bedient's major studies of modern poetry seem to inform the style of his complex and allusive 'There Are Lives that Desire Does Not Sustain', which blends Kristeva, Baudrillard, psychoanalysis and myth in reading the play as a 'powerful work of mourning' in which 'Williams is suspended between wanting to forgive his mother ... and wanting to uproot her from his psyche'. More traditional scholarly approaches are also well represented. Philip C. Kolin's 'Eunice Hubbell and the Feminist Thematics of *A Streetcar Named Desire*' traces a number of 'feminine' themes and motifs in the play by way of this often neglected character; Jürgen C. Wolter gives a sophisticated analysis of 'The Cultural Context of *A Streetcar Named Desire* in Germany'; and Gene D. Phillips provides a detailed account of an obligatory topic in '*A Streetcar Named Desire*: Play and Film'. This book is the first collection of original essays devoted to the play, and demonstrates throughout a consistently high standard of scholarship, editing and critical thought.

Donald P. Costello reinvents the wheel in 'Arthur Miller's Circles of Responsibility: A View from the Bridge and Beyond' (*MD* 36.443–53), which not surprisingly discovers in Miller's plays a concentric series with the self at the middle surrounded by family, society and universe/fate/God. Miller had recently been the subject of some major studies, possibly stimulated by the celebration of his 75th birthday in 1990, but as critics took time out from his work, attention returned to Edward Albee, whose plays, by contrast, appeared to have dropped almost completely from critical view. Albee's career is re-evaluated in an important special issue of *AmDram* (2.ii), which also contains 'The Hamlet Machine' (100–3), a short scene from a new, unpublished play called *Fragments*. Two essays focus in differing ways on aspects of performance. In '*All Over*: Defeating the Expectations of the "Well-Made" Play' (12–31), Andrew B. Harris uses his expert knowledge of Broadway theatre to argue that in this play's first production in 1971, the size of the theatre and the rhetorical style of the delivery gave the wrong signals to its audience and contributed to its failure. Rakesh H. Solomon kept notebooks detailing Albee's revisions and directing methods for his 1978 production of *Fam and Yam* and *The Sandbox*, and has now written up an account in 'Crafting Script into Performance: Edward Albee in Rehearsal' (76–99). Robert M. Post writes on 'Salvation or Damnation?: Death in the Plays of Edward Albee' (32–49), which considers both literal deaths and those which are figurative, in the sense that characters often intuit a kind of death-in-life. Finally, two essays deal in radically different ways with questions of dialogism and monologism. Deborah R. Geis's 'Staging Hypereloquence: Edward Albee and the Monologic Voice' (1–11), although a little dry, establishes a good case for the claim that 'Albee's paradoxical renderings of the monological and the dialogical bring him considerably closer than Williams and Miller to a postmodernist appreciation for gameplaying, fragmentation, and refusal of coherence'; but the most ambitious piece in the collection is Jerre Collins and Raymond J. Wilson III's 'Albee's *Who's Afraid of Virginia Woolf?*: The Issue of Originality' (50–75). Beginning with a summary of some important sources, the authors go on to argue that despite the implications of some theories of intertextuality, there are nevertheless four mechanisms by which a play's 'originality' becomes perceptible: aura (a rather problematic variation on Benjamin's term for the quality of uniqueness effaced in mass reproduction, now described by Collins and Wilson as 'an intentional structure, both emotional and cognitive, to which the viewer-reader of a work of art responds'); frame (we are referred to Eco's common, intertextual and genre frames); 'rule-governed deformation' (according to Ricoeur, 'the axis around which the various changes of paradigm through application are arranged', under which heading Collins and Wilson consider various compressions and changes in context from the play's sources); and 'reply or intertextual dialogism', which follows some of Bakhtin's ideas regarding the interaction of author and reader. Although the essay elides a number of important generic distinctions in arguing for the operation of these mechanisms in theatre and drama, it is nevertheless a stimulating attempt to breathe new life into a genuinely problematic debate.

The playwright who received by far the greatest attention, comfortably eclipsing even O'Neill, was Sam Shepard, who until recently had been the subject of many essays but very few critical books. Several have now appeared, but none of the single-authored volumes in this year's survey does him justice. His remarkably varied career can seldom have been made to appear so dull as it is in Martin Tucker's *Sam Shepard*: lengthy plot summaries, and the reduction of the plays to more-or-less coded accounts of Shepard's relationship with his father, are hardly the most interesting or helpful ways of approaching this playwright, but time and again Tucker sees the plays as little more than variants on the same boring themes, while there is little feeling here for the vitality of Shepard's experiments in form, medium, language and gesture. Sloppy editing has made a dull book positively bad. The text is riddled with misprints, while the concluding chapter of 'Notes' is almost comical: unable to persuade Shepard or his friends to talk, Tucker offers instead a selection of dreary items of gossip he picked up from minor acquaintances. Those looking for an introduction to this dramatist should turn instead to David J. DeRose's excellent *Sam Shepard* (*YWES* 73.628).

The German publisher Lang issued two books on Shepard. Of these, Carol Benet's *Sam Shepard on the German Stage: Critics, Politics, Myths* may be of interest within a rather specialized field, but otherwise has little to recommend it. Benet outlines the history of German productions of Shepard's plays, and discusses the linguistic and conceptual problems of translation before considering how an audience and its expectations were created by the programmes accompanying 11 different productions, and by additional materials and information disseminated by German agents and publicists. A chapter on politics and German reception is really little more than an account of a local skirmish in theatre circles occasioned by differing responses to Ulrike Meinhof, while the discussion of American myth perhaps not surprisingly discovers a certain amount of misunderstanding on the part of German audiences. Although there's a lot of information in this book, it's hard to find much of it interesting or useful: the discussion of publicity is rather banal, that of myth and politics rather superficial. Benet really has no theory of reception, and indeed signals her avoidance of it by stating that 'new dramatic criticism is only in its infancy', which may have been the case in the early 1980s, when the books Benet cites in support of this statement were written, but is not the case now. Benet claims instead that 'I merely try to objectively relate what did occur and the Germans' reaction to it', but in the absence of a theory she often writes awkwardly about 'the Germans' as if they formed a homogeneous group.

In *True Lies: The Architecture of the Fantastic in the Plays of Sam Shepard*, Jim McGhee follows Eric Rabkin and Tzvetan Todorov in regarding the fantastic as an unexpected reversal of the perspectives established earlier within a text or play, so causing the reader or spectator to hesitate between a realistic and a supernatural explanation of events. Unfortunately, this promising framework becomes constricting instead of enabling, leading to a disappointingly schematic and curiously statistical approach. McGhee devotes a chapter each to the one-, two- and three-act plays, followed by a chapter each on character, themes, and staging. Most of the material in the final chapter, which relates the plays to Shepard's life, is very well-known, although the account of the writing process as Shepard has described it remains very interesting and offers a somewhat more productive way into the plays than McGhee's methodology throughout the preceding chapters, which seems to depend heavily on the use of a pocket calculator. There is an almost oxymoronic discrepancy between the insistence on the fantastic dimension of Shepard's writing and the numbingly prosaic fashion in which it is discussed; at the start of the section on character, for instance, McGhee takes 30 plays, adds up the number of speaking parts, and then estimates their average age to be 28. Maybe this book is intended to provide a kind of objectivity for the very predictable conclusions it draws about Shepard's work, but that aside, it's hard to see the point.

Elsewhere there was some excellent criticism of Shepard. He is one of the ten representative writers considered in David Wyatt's *Out of the Sixties: Storytelling and the Vietnam Generation*, which like many books before focuses on the family as 'the site where socialization and privacy intersect', but here the interest is in what this tension means for a particular generation, one formed, according to Wyatt, by six 'causes or determinants': the traumatic event (Vietnam); the dissenter as mentor (of whom there are many); demography; the bracketing of the decade by affluence at one end and economic contraction at the other; the university as the common space for active participation; and, more vaguely, the sense of a common effort or test. This range means that the ten essays (on an equally disparate group of artists: George Lucas, Bruce Springsteen, Sam Shepard, Ann Beattie, Sue Miller, Ethan Mordden, Alice Walker, Gregory Orr, Louise Glück and Michael Herr) do not really cohere in quite the way the title might suggest, but this is not at all to the book's detriment and in fact allows Wyatt to develop a kind of intratextual dialogue between the ten without becoming over-schematic. Consequently, while in isolation the view of Shepard's plays is fairly familiar (the compulsion to performance is overdetermined, a sign of the craving for love, maleness, recognition etc.), the subtlety and density of the ways in which this view is qualified and deepened only emerges in the context of the book as a whole. In particular, Wyatt's perception that Shepard seems to be tiring of this compulsion to performance (especially in relation to masculinity) while recognizing that 'to give up performance ... is also to risk being unmanned' touches on the predominant concerns not only of this book but of recent critical views of this playwright.

For example, Leonard Wilcox, who some years ago wrote a fine article on *The Tooth of Crime* as an allegory of the eclipse of modernism by postmodernism, has edited *Rereading Shepard: Contemporary Critical Essays on the Plays of Sam Shepard*, many of which, like Wilcox's own 'The Desert and the City: *Operation Sidewinder* and Shepard's Postmodern Allegory', Sheila Rabillard's excellent critique of the authorial function in 'Shepard's Challenge to Modernist Myths of Origin and Originality: *Angel City*', and Ann Wilson's illuminating discussion of the interviewee in 'True Stories: Reading the Autobiographic in *Cowboy Mouth*, "True Dylan" and *Buried Child*', in some way engage this postmodern, post-structuralist and undoubtedly accurate view of Shepard as a writer who simultaneously celebrates and problematizes notions of origin, authenticity and authorship. Two essays in the collection rehearse arguments explored in greater depth in book-length studies by their authors: David DeRose's contention in 'A Kind of Cavorting: Superpresence and Shepard's Family Dramas' that the later, more conventionally structured plays represent a retrograde movement away from the experimentalism of his earlier pieces repeats one of the major lines of argument in his monograph on Shepard for Twayne, while Ann C. Hall's Lacanian analysis in 'Speaking Without Words: The Myth of Masculine Autonomy in Sam Shepard's *Fool for Love*' complements the view of the playwright she develops in her book on O'Neill, Pinter and Shepard (reviewed below). Hall's belief that the figure of May in this play in some ways resists the patriarchal system is challenged by Susan Bennett (in 'When a Woman Looks: The "Other" Audience of Shepard's Plays'), who argues that such resistance can be located instead in the projection of a less exclusively male gaze in *A Lie of the Mind*; indeed, in '"I Smash the Tools of My Captivity": The Feminine in Sam Shepard's *A Lie of the Mind*' Jane Ann Crum goes so far as to suggest that in this play 'Shepard embraces the feminine'. It is remarkable how consistently the most interesting debates in this volume revolve around these late plays: DeRose, for example, unlike both Bennett and Crum dismisses *A Lie of the Mind* as a play which 'den[ies] theatrical form and presentation any role whatsoever in the expression of theme', while on the contrary Felicia Hardison Londré, in pursuing her fascinating account (in 'A Motel of the Mind: *Fool for Love* and *A Lie of the Mind*') of Shepard's motel rooms as milieux 'closer to the neoclassical antechamber than to the middle-class living room' which 'reify a transitory state between dream and waking', argues that 'Shepard's motel rooms are occupied by a character or characters whose perceptions – like those of a Strindbergian artist-dreamer – shape, and perhaps distort, the reality offered to the audience'. The comparison to Strindberg relates Londré's argument to Sherrill Grace's 'Lighting Out the Territory Within: Field Notes on Shepard's Expressionist Vision', which argues for an expressionist dimension to the late plays which captures the postmodern confrontation of linguistic construction and expressive essence to which this book calls attention again and again. Collectively, the articles by DeRose, Bennett, Grace, Crum and Londré represent the best discussion yet of the late family dramas, and are helpfully preceded by Charles R. Lyons's contextualizing piece on 'Shepard's Family Trilogy and the Conventions of Modern Realism'. By contrast, the book is a bit lightweight on the earlier plays.

MD devoted a special issue (36.i) to contemporary American drama, with a special emphasis on Shepard, whose interview with Carol Rosen (1–11) is excerpted from her forthcoming book on the playwright. The conversation ranges over largely familiar territory (his views on directing, acting, the attempt to embrace 'the female part of one's self as a man', his dislike of closed endings), touching on many phases of his career but finally offering little that's new beyond his reaffirmation of a commitment to writing. Nevertheless, the interview does frame the collection in illuminating ways. A fairly early play which the dramatist now understandably considers 'dated' is the subject of a challenging reinterpretation by Gregory W. Lanier, whose 'The Killer's Ancient Mask: Unity and Dualism in Shepard's *The Tooth of Crime*' (48–60) exploits René Girard's work on blood sacrifice to suggest that Hoss and Crow are brought into tragic conflict not through their difference but through their sameness, the younger man's destiny being 'to enter into the sacrificial pattern by donning the ancient mask and assuming the role of sacrificer'. Leonard Wilcox repeats, with variations, his by now familiar argument concerning modernism and postmodernism in 'West's *The Day of the Locust* and Shepard's *Angel City*: Refiguring L. A. *Noir*' (61–75), the argument here being somewhat undermined by Shepard's laconic observations in the Rosen interview that 'they've been singing that song [about Hollywood's exploitation of the artist] forever', and that West's novel 'says the whole thing about Hollywood'.

Quite a lot of these essays are disappointing. In the final analysis Gary Grant's 'Shifting the Paradigm: Shepard, Myth, and the Transformation of Consciousness' (120–30) amounts to a redescription of Shepard's plays in terms of Kuhnian paradigm shifts, specifically from Newtonian to Eisensteinian interpretations of the universe. These analogies between scientific and dramatic paradigms have been drawn many times before (e.g. by Robert Brustein and even Clive James: see the discussions of Tennessee Williams by Laura and Edward Morrow, above), and in the case of this essay do not appear to me to add much to our understanding of Shepard, although Grant makes some interesting local observations. Henry I. Schvey's 'A Worm in the Wood: The Father–Son Relationship in the Plays of Sam Shepard' (12–26) is a rather bland introduction to a very familiar topic, while Jeffrey D. Hoeper's 'Cain, Canaanites, and Philistines in Sam Shepard's *True West*' (76–72) becomes so strained in attempting to relate the play to an alleged Biblical paradigm that Hoeper is led to the bizarre conclusion that in *True West* 'mothers and fathers, as well as matriarchy and patriarchy, are equally irrelevant to modern life'. Steven Putzel's 'An American Cowboy on the English Fringe: Sam Shepard's London Audience' (131–46) argues much more convincingly that in the plays of his London period the dramatist experimented with the effects of theatrical and national stereotypes on his British audience. On the other hand, in view of the subtlety of more recent feminist responses to Shepard and exemplified here in Janet V. Haedicke's essay (see below), Susanne Willadt's assertions in 'States of War in Sam Shepard's *States of Shock*' (147–66) not only that 'Shepard has finally become a victim of his most prominent personal and artistic obsession: his fascination with machismo and with the "mystery" he finds *solely* in relationships between men', but that 'in all of his plays that dramatize a father–son conflict, Shepard's sympathies lie *solely* on the side of the son' (my italics both times; on this latter point, contrast Lanier) seem highly questionable.

Indeed, if there has been any definable recent change in the direction of studies of contemporary American drama, it has been away from the routine confrontation of feminist theory and male playwrights and towards a more problematic but also more fruitful *rapprochement*. For example, in '"A Population [and Theater] at Risk": Battered Women in Henley's *Crimes of the Heart* and Shepard's *A Lie of the Mind*', published in the same issue of *MD* (83–95) as Willadt's piece, Janet V. Haedicke argues that unlike the Nietzschean slave morality expressed by Henley's women, the more postmodernist Shepard 'consistently dramatizes the urgency of a move beyond *ressentiment* in his plays, which denaturalize rather than revalidate individualism and the traditional family', and so 'increasingly offers that "Democratic political space" essential for feminism'. (It should be noted that Alan Clarke Shepard's 'Aborted Rage in Beth Henley's Women' (*MD* 36.96–108) presents a less conservative Henley, although his closing observation that 'osmotically the heroines have absorbed some of the energies of the feminist movement, and in their own ways, they grope towards liberty' hardly inspires confidence.) Colby H. Kullman takes a different tack and considers 'Beth Henley's Marginalized Heroines' (*SAD* 8.21–8) as figures carving out an identity for themselves against the backdrop of a garish Southern pop culture.

This is perhaps the place to mention Ann C. Hall's '*A Kind of Alaska*': *Women in the Plays of O'Neill, Pinter, and Shepard*. Hall begins with an introductory guide to Lacan and Irigaray, whose work she exploits to provide a feminist, psychoanalytical reading of plays which 'expose the process by which patriarchy attempts to oppress women'. This rather stark description is offered in resistance to the assumption that male playwrights cannot create 'real' female characters; Hall argues instead that the women in the mature dramas of these writers resist incorporation into the strategies of stereotyping by which patriarchy attempts to complete itself. Those already familiar with the theoretical basis of this discussion will probably find many of Hall's readings somewhat predictable, although some of the distinctions between the playwrights are helpful: O'Neill, perhaps surprisingly, reveals a 'sympathy towards women's rights ... while Pinter repeatedly defends his female characters against male-biased critics who oppose female characterization that violates traditional expectations', but like Haedicke, Hall is acutely conscious that 'for many feminists, Sam Shepard symbolizes the dramatic backlash to these feminist cultural and political gains', and bases her defence of Shepard on a discussion of the various ways in which the women in his plays express a resistance to the male gaze.

The increasing volume of work on David Mamet confirms that he, like Shepard, is now very much part of the established canon. In *Mamet, Bakhtin, and the Dramatic: The Demotic as a Variable of Addressivity*, Ilkka Joki gives a Bakhtinian sociopolitical analysis of 'addressivity', in other words, of the relation of the dramatic text or performance to its addressees. Joki has chosen to concentrate on Mamet, firstly because he has written works in all the major dramatic media (radio, television and cinema as well as theatre) and, secondly, because the prevalence of 'demotic' or popular speech in his work allows Joki to explore how this speech varies from work to work in accordance with the envisaged addressees of each medium. This sounds fine, and although the book retains the over-schematic structure of the doctoral thesis from which it is evidently derived (and therefore begins with a skippable survey of journalistic responses to Mamet which not surprisingly finds inadequacies in them), there is much of value here, particularly in the third chapter's critical condensation of current responses to Bakhtin's curious insistence on the necessary monologism of drama, but also in local sections on aspects of Mamet's work, and in the detailed cross-referencing. The problems with Joki's study lie in its foundation on some questionable assumptions: that there can ever be a truly 'monologic' utterance, let alone text (a problem in Bakhtin studies which needs to be addressed more fully here, if only to be dismissed), and that 'demotic' and 'ordinary language' are terms sufficiently definable to function as controls in a linguistic analysis. See also Steven Price's '"Accursed Progenitor": Samuel Beckett, David Mamet, and the Problem of Influence', in Marius Buning and Lois Oppenheim's *Beckett in the 1990s* (77–85).

Gay Brewer's *David Mamet and Film: Illusion/Disillusion in a Wounded Land* is the first book-length discussion of Mamet's work as screenwriter and director. In some respects this lucid and accessible account, which also explores the cinematic techniques of some of the later plays, resembles Anne Dean's *David Mamet: Language as Dramatic Action* (AUP, 1990). Like Dean, Brewer offers a detailed analysis of theme, language and imagery in a restricted number of works, with limited comparison to other writers but full cross-references to a wide range of other writings by and about the author, while tending to avoid theoretical engagement (his account of Mamet's directorial style, for instance, is almost wholly drawn from Mamet's own *On Directing Film*, and some other critical approaches are summarily dismissed as 'shibboleths'). Brewer's critical proximity to his subject at times suggests a careful avoidance of some of the more provocative sides of Mamet's work, but the aim here is not so much to enter into debate as to elucidate subtleties of nuance and texture. Here the book is very successful indeed, drawing on both internal evidence and the evidence of other works, including numerous drafts, to bring to light many of the submerged themes and ideas in the finished scripts and films. Brewer's style is sympathetic, elegant and engaging, the analyses subtle and cogent, and the book as a whole is a valuable study of what is sure to become a hotly contested body of work.

Less impressive were the two essays on Mamet which appeared in *MD*. It's hard to imagine that anyone who has actually read Thomas Morton's play of 1800 will swallow Tony J. Stafford's contention in '*Speed-the-Plow* and *Speed-the-Plough*: The Work of the Earth' (*MD* 36.38–47) that these texts are meaningfully related: the only connection is that they're both in some way about work, which is hardly surprising since that's what the titles refer to. Equally unconvincing is David Skeele's 'The Devil and David Mamet: *Sexual Perversity in Chicago* as Homiletic Tragedy' (*MD* 36.512–18), which in order to hammer this play into a medieval matrix not only has to turn cartwheels to describe Danny as 'the Humanum Genus figure', Bernie as the Vice, and Deborah as 'a force of virtue', but also has to forget the existence of a fourth character, Joan, who doesn't fit into this scheme in any way whatsoever, and therefore isn't mentioned.

David Rabe is compared to Mamet in David Radavich's 'Collapsing Male Myths: Rabe's Tragicomic *Hurlyburly*' (*AmDram* 3.i.1–16), which argues that Rabe's presentation of heterosexual and homosocial relationships is sufficiently stylized to open up an ironic space between play and author, a space which Mamet's work tends to eclipse. Different approaches to the same question are explored in a number of essays in *David Rabe: A Casebook*, a generally excellent collection of original essays edited by Toby Silverman Zinman which appears in Garland's valuable Casebook series. Not surprisingly, the book focuses on the two questions most commonly raised in connection with Rabe: his relation to realism, and the centrality in his work of the American experience of Vietnam. Zinman conducted a lengthy interview with the playwright, extracts from which appear both at the beginning and, helpfully, throughout the collection as material prefatory to the critical discussions of diverse plays and topics. Inevitably, some of the articles are less arresting than others: Jacqueline Christman's 'Neglected But Still Family: *The Orphan*' is a somewhat descriptive and critically dull comparison of this play to its source in the *Oresteia* (on which see also Colakis, reviewed in the general section above); James J. Christy's 'Remembering *Bones*' is an interesting but largely anecdotal account of developments in the writing and production of the play that became *Sticks and Bones*; and Jennifer McMillion's 'The Cult of Male Identity in *Goose and Tomtom*' sees this unsuccessful work as 'a thematic blueprint for the more realistic plays', but otherwise finds little to add to the critical debate around this well-worn topic. The reader of Robert Scanlan's 'Fighting Saints: The Idea of *Hurlyburly*' needs to take on board Scanlan's warning that 'I approach with the practicality of a working dramaturg and director', since otherwise the article's deliberately perverse range of approaches to the play (via testosterone, Hollywood, and *De Divinis Nominibus*) can seem wilfully irrelevant. Scanlan's important point is not simply that a director can make productive use of such seeming serendipity, but that Rabe's own 'semi-accidental correlation with a theory of Jung's concerning the Self as King and its "shadow" figured as a beggar' is no more legitimate than Scanlan's, and that '[h]ad Rabe stumbled across a different context for explaining (or understanding) his play, perhaps a different set of revisions would have ensued'.

Several essays explore the ways in which Rabe's plays diverge from the depth psychology of the realism with which he is conventionally associated: Howard Stein, in the course of his argument in 'The Lost People in David Rabe's Plays' that Rabe represents the 'lapsed Catholic' sensibility which on the contemporary stage has come to replace the 'Jewish sensibility' of Miller's generation, finds that 'Rabe's surreal writing, his sense of irony, and his genuine poetic sensibility' distance him from social realism; Zinman herself very productively relates Rabe's characters to Roy Lichtenstein's huge pop-art canvases in 'What's Wrong With This Picture?: David Rabe's Comic-Strip Plays', while in an analogous comparison Lindsay Davies, in 'Watching the Box: TV on Stage in *Sticks and Bones*', notes that staging subverts the sitcom model Rabe deploys; and Stephen Watt's excellent 'In Mass Culture's Image: The Subject of (in) Rabe's Boom Boom Rooms' further extends the analysis of the 'tension ... between psychologically or psychoanalytically deep models of identity or selfhood and a flattened model of subjectivity in which popular cultural messages construct and thereby contain the subject', although in grounding the discussion in Baudrillard's theories of the postmodern Watt is at times in danger of bringing the sledgehammer too close to the nut. In another outstanding essay, 'Gender and History in

Hurlyburly: A Feminist Response', Janelle Reinelt exposes a double bind: on the one hand, despite the various 'marked representations' by which Rabe appears to offer a critique of the masculine culture of the play, the effects of repetition, fragmentation and a certain resignation of response actually reinforce it; and on the other hand, the play's simultaneous reinstatement of aspects of the traditional, linear, realistic narrative brings with it the presumption of objectivity, and in so doing 'the original criticisms of negative representations of women come back with a vengeance'.

Of those articles which explore the influence of Vietnam, Deborah R. Geis's '"Fighting to Get Down, Thinking It Was Up": A Narratological Reading of *The Basic Training of Pavlo Hummel*' illustrates again the characteristic strengths and weaknesses of this critic's formalist approach to drama; Martin Novelli's 'Spiking the Vietnam Film "Canon": David Rabe and *Casualties of War*' compares the unpublished script to Brian DePalma's completed film to demonstrate convincingly that the film failed because of the director and not the writer; and N. Bradley Christie unashamedly pronounces Rabe 'Still a Vietnam Playwright After All these Years', powerfully argues for the simultaneous centrality and denial of Vietnam in American literature, and consequently has important things to say about contemporary canon formation.

I conclude with a round-up of dramatists who received less extensive critical attention than those discussed above. *SAD* 8.i contained wide-ranging interviews with three playwrights. Ted Shine (interviewed by Whitney J. Leblanc, 29–43) gives an overview of his career and of black American theatre; Karen Malpede's comments on political and feminist theatre (interview by Richard E. Kramer, 44–60) represent a detailed contribution to a still-developing critical debate; while the interview with Mark Medoff by Mimi Gladstein (61–83) is particularly interesting for Medoff's account of Hollywood and what it did to *Children of a Lesser God*.

A number of essays argued for a more critical appreciation than that to which their subjects are generally treated. Joan T. Hamilton's 'Visible Power and Invisible Men in Clare Booth's *The Women*' (*AmDram* 3.i.31–53) uses a familiar but still effective Foucauldian discourse analysis to show that the play's apparently conventional formal comedic frame fails to contain a disruptive feminine desire. Tony J. Stafford's '"Gray Eyes is Glass": Image and Theme in *The Member of the Wedding*' (*AmDram* 3.1.54–66) traces the persistent references to gazing eyes in Carson McCullers's dramatization of her novel to her 'sense of alienation from an indifferent God'; this, and Stafford's cross-reference to Berkeley, suggest that an interesting comparison could have been made to Beckett. Charles S. Watson's 'Beyond the Commercial Media: Horton Foote's Procession of Defeated Men' (*SAD* 8.175–87) briefly but helpfully compares Foote to Wilder and Inge to suggest that Foote's later plays contain a darker vision than the more homely plays for which he has sometimes been critically dismissed. June Schlueter's 'Ways of Seeing in Donald Margulies' *Sight Unseen*' (*SAD* 8.3–11) is offered by way of an introduction to this Obie Award-winning playwright.

Finally, some very miscellaneous pieces in no particular order. A little-known Federal Theatre Project play by Orrie Lashin and Milo Hastings is described in some detail by Michael M. O'Hara in '*Class of '29* and the American Dream' (*AmDram* 3.i.17–30). Rosette C. Lamont argues in 'Tina Howe's Secret Surrealism: Walking a Tightrope' (*MD* 36.27–37) that the comparative conservatism of

Howe's later work veils a more subversive surrealism which she abandoned in its overt form after hostile critical reaction to her earlier plays. Surprisingly little was published on Adrienne Kennedy, but Philip C. Kolin introduced a 'Photo Essay' of 'The Adrienne Kennedy Festival at the Great Lakes Theater Festival' (*SAD* 8.85–94). The photographs concentrate on the première of *Ohio State Murders* which was staged at this event. In '*Lips Together, Teeth Apart*: Another Version of Pastoral' (*MD* 36.547–55), Benilde Montgomery argues that Terence McNally's play invokes the communal world of pastoral only to question its effectiveness in the era of AIDS. In 'Jessie and Thelma Revisited: Marsha Norman's Conceptual Challenge in '*night, Mother*' (*MD* 36.109–19), William W. Demastes argues that this is 'essentially a realist play that challenges realist assumptions, that is, naturalist or "classic realist" assumptions', a contention which hardly prepares one for the stunning conclusion that 'Norman has commissioned the realist form to present perhaps the most radical vision of experience in human history'. Jean-Claude van Itallie's short essay 'On Laughter' (*AmDram* 3.i.87–91) accompanies an excellent piece by Gene A. Plunka on 'McLuhan, Perfect People, and the Media Plays of Jean-Claude van Itallie' (67–86), which shows how the contemporaneous ideas of the two writers were brought into dramatic focus by Joseph Chaikin's Open Theater in the 1960s. Mark Royden Winchell's essay on 'Rod Serling's *Requiem for a Heavyweight*: A Drama for Its Time' (*SAD* 8.13–20) is particularly interesting for its necessarily fleeting contextualization of this 1956 piece in relation to the televisual medium for which it was written.

Books Reviewed

Anisfield, Nancy, ed. *The Nightmare Considered: Critical Essays on Nuclear War Literature.* BGUP. pp. 201. pb $18.95. ISBN 0 87972 530 3.

Benet, Carol. *Sam Shepard on the German Stage: Critics, Politics, Myths.* American University Studies. Lang. pp. 222. £29. ISBN 0 8204 1624 X.

Berney, K. A., ed. *Contemporary Dramatists.* Contemporary Writers of the English Language. 5th edn. St James. pp. 843. £97.50. ISBN 1 55862 185 7.

Berressem, Hanjo. *Pynchon's Poetics: Interfacing Theory and Text.* UIllP. pp. 273. pb. $15.95. ISBN 0 252 06248 5.

Bjork, Patrick Bryce. *The Novels of Toni Morrison: The Search for Self and Place Within the Community.* Lang. pp. 172. pb FF168. ISBN 0 8204 2569 9.

Black, Stephen. *File on O'Neill.* Writer-Files. Methuen. pp. 96. £6.99. ISBN 0 413 66330 2.

Bogard, Travis. *The Eugene O'Neill Songbook.* East Bay. pp. 249. $49.95. ISBN 0 930 99703 4.

——. '*From the Silence of Tao House*': *Essays About Eugene and Carlotta O'Neill and the Tao House Plays.* EONF. pp. 198. hb $125, pb $24.95. ISBN 0 963 72150 X, 0 963 72151 8.

Boyer, Jay. *Ishmael Reed.* Western Writers Series No. 110. BoiseSUP. pp. 52. $3.95. ISBN 0 884 30109 5.

Brewer, Gay. *David Mamet and Film: Illusion/Disillusion in a Wounded Land.* McFarland. pp. 211. $27.50. ISBN 0 899 50834 0.

Bryer, Jackson R., ed. *Conversations with Thornton Wilder.* Literary Conversations. UPMissip (1992). pp. 130. hb $32.50, pb $14.95. ISBN 0 878 05513 4, 0 878 05514 2.

Buning, Marius, and Lois Oppenheim, eds. *Beckett in the 1990s: Selected Papers from the Second International Beckett Symposium, Held in The Hague, 8–12 April, 1992*. Rodopi. pp. 367. £20. ISBN 9 051 83566 3.

Cardullo, Bert. *Theatrical Reflections: Notes on the Form and Practice of Drama*. Lang. (1992). pp. 276. £33. ISBN 0 820 41935 4.

Carlson, Marvin. *Deathtraps: The Postmodern Comedy Thriller*. IndUP. pp. 212. hb £27.50, pb £11.99. ISBN 0 253 31305 8, 0 253 20826 2. ·

Colakis, Marianthe. *The Classics in the American Theater of the 1960s and Early 1970s*. UPA. pp. 96. $34.50. ISBN 0 819 18972 3.

Deloria Jr, Vine, ed. *Frank Waters: Man and Mystic*. Swallow/OhioUP. pp. 249. pb £15.60. ISBN 0 8040 0979 1.

Di Renzo, Anthony. *American Gargoyles: Flannery O'Conner and the Medieval Grotesque*. SIUP. pp. 250. $34.95. ISBN 0 809 31848 2.

Foster Jr, John Burt. *Nabokov's Art of Memory and European Modernism*. PrincetonUP. pp. 260. ISBN 0 691 06971 9.

Goldman, L. H., Gloria L. Cronin, and Ada Aharoni, eds. *Saul Bellow: A Mosaic*. Lang. pp. 209. FF262. ISBN 0 820 41572 3.

Green, Michelle. *The Dream at the End of the World: Paul Bowles and the Literary Renegades in Tangier*. Bloomsbury. pp. 381. £19.99. ISBN 0 747 50524 1.

Groupe de Recherches Anglo-Américaines de Tours. *Voix Ethniques, Ethnic Voices*. UTours. pp.141. FF120. ISSN 0997 4970.

Groupe de Recherche et d'Etudes Nord-Américaines. *Voix et Langages aux Etats-Unis*. UProvence. Tome 2. pp. 276. FF160. ISBN 2 853 99331 0.

Hall, Ann C. *'A Kind of Alaska': Women in the Plays of O'Neill, Pinter, and Shepard*. SIUP. pp. 146. $34.95. ISBN 0 809 31877 6.

Hayles, N. Katherine, ed. *Chaos and Order: Complex Dynamics in Literature and Science*. UChicP. pp. 308. pb $14.95. ISBN 0 226 32144 4.

Heinze, Denise. *The Dilemma of 'Double-Consciousness': Toni Morrison's Novels*. UGeoP. pp. 209. pb $35.00. ISBN 0 820 31685 7.

Holsinger, M. Paul, and Mary Anne Schofield, eds. *Visions of War: World War II in Popular Literature and Culture*. BGUP. pp. 203. hb $39.95, pb $15.95. ISBN 0 879 72555 9, 0 879 72556 7.

Jason, Philip K., ed. *Fourteen Landing Zones: Approaches to Vietnam War Literature*. UIowaP. pp. 250. hb $35.95, pb $15.95. ISBN 0 877 45314 4, 0 877 45315 2.

Joki, Ilkka. *Mamet, Bakhtin, and the Dramatic: The Demotic as a Variable of Addressivity*. Åbo. pp. 233. FIM180. ISBN 9 529 61640 6.

Kalb, Jonathan. *Free Admissions: Collected Theater Writings*. Limelight. pp. 218. $18. ISBN 0 879 10168 7.

Kolin, Philip C. ed. *Confronting Tennessee Williams's 'A Streetcar Named Desire': Essays in Critical Pluralism*. Contributions in Drama and Theatre Studies 50. Greenwood. pp. 255. $47.95. ISBN 0 313 26681 6.

Kowalewski, Michael. *Temperamental Journeys: Essays on the Modern Literature of Travel*. UGeoP. pp. 359. hb $45.00, pb $20.00. ISBN 0 820 31431 5.

Lentricchia, Frank, ed. *Introducing Don DeLillo*. DukeUP. pp. 221. pb £11.95. ISBN 0 822 31144 5.

McCaffery, Larry, ed. *Storming the Reality Studio: A Casebook of Cyberpunk and Postmodern Science Fiction*. DukeUP (1991). pp. 405. hb £47.50, pb £19.95. ISBN 0 822 31158 5, 0 822 31168 2.

McGhee, Jim. *True Lies: The Architecture of the Fantastic in the Plays of Sam Shepard*. American University Studies. Lang. pp. 224. £28. ISBN 0 820 42052 2.

Maszewska, Jadwiga, ed. *Crossing Borders: American Literature and Other Artistic Media*. ULodz, Polish Scientific Publishers. pp. 89. ISBN 8 301 10996 3.

Mogen, David, Scott P Sanders, and Joanne B. Karpinski, eds. *Frontier Gothic: Terror and Wonder at the Frontier in American Literature*. AUP. pp. 206. £33.50. ISBN 0 838 63489 3.

Moy, James S. *Marginal Sights: Staging the Chinese in America*. Studies in Theatre History and Culture. UIowaP. pp.158. hb $29.95, pb $12.95. ISBN 0 877 45427 2, 0 877 45448 5.

Murphy, Brenda, ed. *A Realist in the American Theatre: Selected Drama Criticism of William Dean Howells*. OhioUP (1992). pp. 244. £34.20. ISBN 0 821 41036 9.

Neary, John. *Something and Nothingness: The Fiction of John Updike and John Fowles*. SIUP. pp. 233. $24.95. ISBN 0 809 31742 7.

Plakkoottam, J. L., and P. K. Sinha, eds. *Literature and Politics in Twentieth Century America*. Seminar Proceedings Series 1 (Gen. Ed. M. Glen Johnson). American Studies Research Centre. Hyderabad 500 007, India. pp. 115. Rs. 100, $10. ISBN 8 185 84811 4.

Rosenberg, Bernard, and Ernest Harburg. *The Broadway Musical: Collaboration in Commerce and Art*. NYUP. pp. 356. $39.95. ISBN 0 814 77433 4.

Runyon, Randolph Paul. *Reading Raymond Carver*. SyracuseUP. pp. 226. hb $24.95, pb $15.50. ISBN 0 815 62563 4, 0 815 62631 2.

Tucker, Martin. *Sam Shepard*. Literature and Life: American Writers. Continuum (1992). pp. 179. £15.95. ISBN 0 826 40549 5.

Saltzman, Arthur M. *The Novel in the Balance*. USCP. pp. 188. $22.95. ISBN 0 87249 960 X.

Slusser, George, and Tom Shippey, eds. *Fiction 2000: Cyberpunk and the Future of Narrative*. UGeoP. pp. 303. ISBN 0 820 31449 8.

Whitlark, James, and Wendell Aycock, eds. *The Literature of Emigration and Exile*. Texas TechUP. pp. 186. ISBN 0 896 72263 5.

Wilcox, Leonard, ed. *Rereading Shepard: Contemporary Critical Essays on the Plays of Sam Shepard*. St Martin's, Macmillan (1992). pp. 229. £42.50. ISBN 0 333 53849 8.

Wilmeth, Don B., and Tice L. Miller, eds. *Cambridge Guide to American Theatre*. CUP. pp. 547. £35. ISBN 0 521 40134 8.

Wyatt, David. *Out of the Sixties: Storytelling and the Vietnam Generation*. Cambridge Studies in American Literature and Culture. CUP. pp. 228. hb £35, pb £10.95. ISBN 0 521 44151 X, 0 521 44689 9.

Zinman, Toby Silverman, ed. *David Rabe: A Casebook*. Casebooks on Modern Dramatists. Garland (1991). pp. 238. $38. ISBN 0 824 07079 8.

XVII

New Literatures in English

FEMI ABODUNRIN, BRIAN KIERNAN, EVA-MARIE KRÖLLER,
PAULA BURNETT, PHILLIP LANGRAN and CAROLE DURIX

This chapter has six sections: 1. Africa by Femi Abodunrin; 2. Australia by Brian Kiernan; 3. Canada by Eva-Marie Kröller; 4. The Caribbean (for 1992 and 1993) by Paula Burnett; 5. India by Phillip Langran; 6. New Zealand and the South Pacific by Carole Durix.

1. Africa

(a) General

In 1993 special issues of journals included *Commonwealth* 16 on 'Prizes and the New Literatures in English'; *Matatu* 11 on 'African Literatures in the Eighties'; *Twentieth Century Literature* on Athol Fugard; *RAL* 24.ii on 'Oral literature in Francophone Africa' and 24.iv, a special issue in 'Memory of Josephat Bekunuru Kubayanda'.

Carole and Jean-Pierre Durix's *An Introduction to the New Literatures in English* introduces the general reader to the cultural and political factors underlying the preoccupation of the postcolonial writer. The authors seek to contextualize the colonizer's adventurism by placing colonialism at the centre of a phenomenon which has resulted in 'a total population of about 1.3 billion' inhabiting Africa, Australia, New Zealand, the South Pacific, the Indian subcontinent, Canada and the Caribbean being labelled as postcolonial societies. Thus, 'the New Literatures', according to the authors, 'are all marked by the history of colonization which has meant the imposition of one culture, which is presented as superior, on those of the conquered countries'.

Surveys of African literature(s) in European languages along historical lines are beginning to trickle in. Titles such as *Matatu*'s 'African Literatures in the Eighties', and *A History of Twentieth-Century African Literatures*, edited by Owomoyela and others, herald a period of reflection over developments in the field and the sociocultural and political factors mediating them. With justification, Owomoyela claims his volume has an advantage over most 'in its assemblage of eminent scholars who together provide a full coverage of the entire subject with uniform depth and assurance, and in its emphasis on the historical dimension, which contextualizes the various developments in African writing so far'.

Similarly, Frank Schulze-Engler's 'Discourses of Arrested Modernization: African Literary Theory in the 1980s' (*Matatu* 11.9–26) opens *Matatu*'s coverage of developments in African Literatures in the eighties, and reflects on a decade which was an historical watershed in that continent's relationship with the rest of the world. To begin with, the anti-colonial struggle that brought about political independence for many African states in the 1960s has run into varied and diverse but deepening crises, and the upbeat mood of post-independence Africa has been replaced by neo-colonial disillusionment. 'The stasis of the waiting room', Schulze-Engler suggests, is one way of viewing the contemporary African situation. However, the collapse of the old African structures and the near absence or sheer inadequacies of the new ones seeking to replace them merely problematize further Schulze-Engler's 'Discourse of Arrested Modernization' as they characterize postcolonial reality.

If 'the greatest influence colonial rule had on Africa was a linguistic and therefore cultural one', as Robert Cancel suggests in 'African-Language Literatures: Perspectives on Culture and Identity' (in Owomoyela), then the age-old conflict appears to be one still largely bestriding the modern and the traditional. In this sense, adequate effort to conceptualize further the problematic terms 'traditionalism' and 'modernism' could be said to have been made by the trio of Erhard Reckwitz, Lucia Vennarini and Cornelia Wegener in their editorial to yet another reflective work, *The African Past and Contemporary Culture*, a volume of essays on Africa delivered at the Annual Conference of the Association for the Study of the New Literatures in English. Having acknowledged their false start in setting up a rather simplistic binary opposition between tradition and modernity, by equating the former with backwardness and the latter with progress, Reckwitz et al. move swiftly to incorporate the (Derridean) poststructuralist notion that seeks to deconstruct all 'violent hierarchies'. Ostensibly, the editors, confessing to being wizened by the conferees' critical/creative angst, have seen how a vigorous encounter with the two terms could lead to a *regressus in infinitum*, resulting in 'a complete relativization of either concept, thus requiring the opposition to be recontextualized time and again'. Breyten Breytenbach's keynote address, entitled 'The Shattered Dream', and Kenneth Parker's 'Traditionalism Versus Modernism: Culture, Ideology, Writing', which employ the contrasting viewpoints of the creative writer and the critic respectively, continue the task of illuminating the binary opposition between the traditional and the modern. For Parker, the philosophical problem of what might be contained by each of these two terms, conjures up accusations of dysformation, and raises/ silences questions of the specific ideological baggage both are capable of carrying, depending on who is handling them. Equating Africa with traditionalism and modernism with Europe (or, at least, identifying Europe as its harbinger) on the other hand, merely complements the lyricism of Breytenbach's title: 'modernism is not the dream but the shattering of a dream'. Seen from this peculiar postcolonial perspective, Breytenbach argues that colonialism is the tradition and the purported privileges accruing from the colonial enterprise, packaged and presented as modernism, are what we ought to see as 'the product of modernism applied to protect traditional interest'.

Criss-crossing the versatile and sometimes the facile, 'the field of applied theory' in Africa, according to Schulze-Engler, has remained a remarkably pluralist one 'where different perspectives continued to confront each other publicly, and thus the cultural nationalist claim to represent "Africanness" (as against other theoretical perspectives) has been criticized and rejected in a long-drawn and often heated debate that has extended far beyond a confrontation of "Western academics" and "African practitioners"'. An integral aspect of this pluralism and often heated debate includes the growing confidence of feminist aesthetics and cultural theory in African writing. This is described by James Booth in 'Sexual Politics in the Fiction of Ama Ata Aidoo' (*Commonwealth* 16.80–96) as 'a new agenda being set in African literary criticism'. The titles this year are suggestive and they follow the same pattern of reflection over developments in the field. In this regard, Anne Adams's 'Claiming Her Authority From Life: Twenty Years of African Women's Literary Criticism' (*Matatu* 11.155–72), and Carole Boyce Davies and Elaine Savory Fido's 'African Women Writer: Towards a Literary History' (in Owomoyela) both complement what we might (following James Gibbs), refer to as Ali Mazrui's 'Larsony with a difference' in 'The Black Woman and the Problem of Gender: An African Perspective' (*RAL* 24.i.87–104), which engenders Omolara Ogundipe-Leslie's swift rejoinder, 'Beyond Hearsay and Academic Journalism: The Black Woman and Ali Mazrui' (*RAL* 24.i.105–12). Identifying with feminist politics, making the necessary links between gender, location and writing on the one hand, and defining these conceptual terms within African contexts on the other, are some of the critical issues energizing the field of feminist discourse today. The duo of Davies and Fido quote Ogundipe's formulation that 'the female writer should be committed in three ways: as a writer, as a woman and as a third world person; and her womanhood is implicated in all three' to underscore one paradigm. Itself a revision of the cautious stance of some of her contemporaries on the issue of feminist politics, Ogundipe-Leslie's formulation critiques this largely divisive issue, which, like the search for oral origins in African writing, often takes the form of a quest for African authenticity. In her polemical aside with the eminent political scientist Ali Mazrui in the pages of *RAL*, Ogundipe-Leslie concedes that even though rites of initiation into gender studies need not be biologically constructed, the would-be gender scholar 'must want or try to become a cultural insider through the various means possible: doing the enlightening and enabling research; showing capacity for empathy; understanding, if not taking the perspectives of one's research subjects; testing the knowledge gained with those who live the culture; living the culture; and learning the relevant languages'.

Equally steeped in controversy is the issue of 'Orality in African Literatures'. Isidore Okpewho's *African Oral Literature: Backgrounds, Character, and Continuity* is a giant effort aimed at resolving some of these debates. Described variously as *oral literature, orature, traditional literature, folk literature* or *folklore*, the field has emerged as a subject of comparative study for scholars interested in the ways the various techniques and elements of oral literature combine to influence, refine or dilate our cultural, aesthetic and even ideological perception of written literature. In *African Novels and the Question of Orality*, Eileen Julien argues, in part, that the practical and theoretical issue raised by the question of orality 'is no longer the extent to which the African novel is derivative of oral traditions, but rather the extent to which such references hold the means of imaginative solutions to problems of aesthetic and ideological dimensions'. Seen from this open-ended approach, writers, according to Julien, could then be regarded as thinking architects rather than prisoners of a cultural heritage. A special issue of *RAL* was also devoted to oral literature. The volume, according to the guest editor, Lilyan Kesteloot, was 'planned to present to anglophone scholars a significant sampling of the work being done in francophone African universities'.

Yet, this catalogue of controversial issues relating to African Literatures could be deemed incomplete without a look at the other question to which *Commonwealth* devoted a special issue (16): 'Prizes and the New Literatures in English'. While Ezenwa Ohaeto's 'Reflections and Reactions: Literature and Wole Soyinka's Nobel Prize in Nigeria' (21–7) examines some of the sociocultural and political questions raised by the award of this coveted prize to its first African recipient, it is Paula Burnett's 'Hegemony or Pluralism? The Literary Prize and the Post-Colonial Project in the Caribbean' (1–20) that responds, in practical and theoretical terms, to the canonizing and universalizing notions the prizes portray. Rightly or wrongly, they are perceived in certain parts of the world as yet another indication of age-old western hegemony or colonizing spirit, 'of which the Nobel institution is a part and America the centre'. Moreover, a rigorous theory of literary production would not fail to encapsulate reasons for the disquiet raised by the prizes in certain quarters in an age in which, according to Hans Zell's 'Publishing in Africa: The Crisis and the Challenge' (in Owomoyela) 'much of Africa has become a bookless society', which 'has meant that young writers and scholars are finding it difficult to place their works'. The matter might not be quite so bad, according to Burnett, if the prizes lead to pluralism rather than reinforce old stereotypes, or in Achebe's words turn literature into a 'heavyweight championship'. In 'Desert Gold: Irrigation Schemes for Ending the Book Drought' (*Matatu* 11.27–38), Bernth Lindfors observes that, while the 1980s could be regarded as a decade of glory for African literature, the rich rewards which accompanied this glory, such as prestigious professorships, honorary degrees, and even the Nobel prize for literature, were not felt within Africa itself: 'the gold simply didn't trickle down to the younger writers who stayed at home and carried on their work without much fanfare or encouragement from outside agencies'.

(b) West Africa

Jonathan Peters's 'English-Language Fiction from West Africa' (in Owomoyela), employing the retrospective insight of the chronicler, is a compendium which anyone interested in the linear history of West African fiction in the English Language will find useful. Besides its bibliographical detail, covering all the major works of fiction and their accompanying criticism, Peters's study is a welcome attempt to put in context developments within the West African subcontinent, which Eileen Julien has defined in Bakhtinian terms as that genre which is, after all, always 'in the making'. The study encapsulates what it describes as the three 'Waves of West African Writing, dictated by developments more in Nigeria than in the other countries'. The first wave of writing, terminating at 1964, spans the earliest attempts by Africans to venture into writing as an élitist practice, and culminates in the period of conscious rewriting/revising the European notion of the 'white man's burden' or an imposition placed on them from the outside instead of as a 'deliberate program of worldwide imperialism'. The second wave, starting from 1965, is equally characterized by the tension in Nigerian politics, and lasted until about 1976, 'when the cycle of war novels subsided; and in the third, from about 1976 to 1988, newer writers began to publish works in which the colonial themes continued during the second phase all but completely disappeared'. Servanne Woodland's 'Francophone-Language Fiction' (in Owomoyela) supplies critical insights into developments on the other side of the (colonial) linguistic divide, and, like Peters, concludes that 'just as English- French-speaking West Africa as a region has far exceeded other regions in literary production'. Russel G. Hamilton's 'Portuguese-Language Literature', on the other hand, blames the relative obscurity of the Lusophone writer on the largely 'Anglocentric and Francocentric Africanist universe', even though 'the Portuguese have had the longest, most sustained European presence in Africa'. The equally penetrating insights of Thomas Knipp's 'English-Language Poetry', and Ndukaku Amankulor's 'English-Language Drama and Theatre', among others, underscore the overall importance of the essays in *A History of Twentieth-Century African Literatures*.

Once described as a useful barometer for measuring the continent's intellectual development, and having had his high-profile raised even higher by the Nobel prize, Wole Soyinka continues to attract attention from critics. A lengthy 'Conversation(s) with Wole' (in *Commonwealth* 16.1–42) finds the Nobel laureate engaged in an unusual exercise, allowing himself to be interrogated widely on many aspects of his writing by students in France, most especially on his extravagant play, *A Dance of the Forests*, which had been selected for the *Agregation* in Paris. The play itself has been described by Neloufer de Mel, in an engaging essay entitled 'Myth as History: Wole Soyinka's *A Dance of the Forests*' (*Wasafiri* 18.27–33), as marking 'a watershed in Soyinka's dramatic canon not only because it is his first major work, but more importantly for being an inaugural work which, despite its marginalizing by criticism on the grounds of incomprehensibility, carries with remarkable clarity metaphors that Soyinka was to elaborate throughout his oeuvre'. The sessions, first at the Sorbonne Nouvelle, and then at the University of Tours, complement Mary David's previously unpublished 1985 'Interview with Wole Soyinka' (*Wasafiri* 18.22–7), and together should provide critics of Soyinka's work with adequate resources to validate their numerous claims on issues ranging from the writer's theoretical and dramaturgical concerns and the logicality of their conception, to Soyinka's much discussed African/Yoruba aesthetics, and matters equally contemporaneous with developments in African Literature, such as the language issue.

Derek Wright's *Wole Soyinka Revisited* is a book-length study focusing on many aspects of the issues highlighted above. Problematizing Soyinka's hybridized creative articulation of the Yoruba Worldview and his highly idiosyncratic and selective translation of myth into a private religion of essences, for example, Wright observes that 'if Soyinka has fallen victim to radical historicist criticism, it must be conceded that he has to some extent invited such criticism by his somewhat erratic attempts to remove Ogun from the purely conceptual realm of essence and give him some practical application or analogue in the contemporary world'. One such radical historicist criticism can be found in Adebayo Williams's 'Ritual and the Political Unconscious: The Case of *Death and The King's Horseman*' (*RAL* 24.i.67–79). Williams argues that only a dialogized interface between the communal *langue* and the author's *parole* could unravel the deeper ideological necessity behind the ritual in *Death and the King's Horseman*, for example, or reveal 'the political reality behind both the social text itself and the playwright's textualization of it in his play'. The impending ritual suicide of

Elesin or the King's Horseman, according to Williams, takes on a major historical and political burden 'precisely because his suicide is supposed to compel respect for the integrity and inviolability of a besieged culture'. As a mode of discourse that inserts itself between the gaps in colonial narratives with a view to exploding their internal contradictions, Williams chastises some of his radical colleagues for failing to see the 'utopian dimension of the Elesin ritual' and consequently why the playwright himself could be viewed as 'an unabashed horseman ("Elesin" in the Yoruba language) of a besieged culture, fighting a desperate battle against the cultural "other"'. Urging all genuinely revolutionary postcolonial discourses to smuggle themselves into this gap, one of the primary conclusions of Williams's essay is that like all such 'mythicization of historical events' and 'deployment of ritual in a desperate cultural offensive', the essential Soyinka 'demonstrates how all master narratives [...] are dogged by a political unconscious which derives from the logic of their own insertion into the historical process'.

From a slightly divergent viewpoint, Obi Maduakor's 'Myth and Mysticism in Gabriel Okara's *The Voice*' (*Commonwealth* 16.58–65) argues a place for Okara's novel in the realm of the mystical and the mythological. Okara's formalistic experimentation, often perceived as unparalleled in the annals of African fiction, is described by Jonathan Peters as a landmark creative articulation, and one that fittingly brings to an end the first wave of fiction writing in English by West African writers. However, Maduakor remarks that the novel has not only been praised for the wrong reasons, but argues with conviction that 'if the novel were simply a parable of post-independence disillusionment, one would not be so easily overwhelmed by its haunting magic'. Also, in 'Sexual Politics in the Fiction of Ama Ata Aidoo' (*Commonwealth* 16.80–90), James Booth contends that an overview of Aidoo's writing and its critical reception would reveal that 'Aidoo does not generally attract the enthusiasm evoked among critics and students by her contemporaries, Armah, Soyinka, Ngugi and Achebe'. Aidoo's distinctive literary profile, which is often 'allied to an adventurous but controlled narrative technique', should, according to Booth, 'serve to place Aidoo's work on an equal footing with that of her male counterparts'.

Frank Schulze-Engler's 'Chinua Achebe and the Politics of Civil Society in Modern African Literature' and Eckhard Breitinger's 'Writers and Censors – *Le Scribe et le Prince*: Observations on the Cultural Milieu in Cameroon' (both in Reckwitz), encapsulate the twin evils of censorship and political repression, two phenomena which are coterminous with the postcolonial situation in many parts of Africa. While Schulze-Engler cites Patrick Chabal's observation that 'African intellectuals [...] have in no way been able to transcend the epistemic gulf between the state and society' to underscore one paradigm, Breitinger offers an equally pertinent observation: 'The French journalist Jacques Tillier is reported to have received roughly ten thousand dollars a month for placing friendly articles in the French Press' for and on behalf of the Cameroonian President, Paul Biya. The political élites, the two critics agree, are ultimately to blame for the breakdown in civil society in many African states, while they recognize the positive contribution writers like Achebe, Mongo Beti, Bole Butake, Nuruddin Farah and many others have made to overcome the not-too-understandable conceptual logic of the postcolonial state. Achebe's *Anthills of the Savannah*, for example, is described in Eustace Palmer's 'West African Literature in the 1980s' (*Matatu* 11.61–84) as 'a severe indictment of what Achebe sees as Nigeria's contemporary malaise'. Meanwhile, in 'The Eighties and the Return to Oral Cadences in Nigerian Poetry' (*Matatu* 11.85–105), Nwachukwu-Agbada describes a period when political and social views of their society are articulated by post-war poets in bold relief as one in which 'proverbs, tongue-twisters, riddles, communal traditions, even folktales in snippety forms are built into poetic lines, certainly with the intention of Africanizing poetic mediation'.

(c) East and Central Africa

Arlene A. Elder's 'English-Language Fiction from East Africa' (in Owomoyela) begins with the following 1976 summation on East African Literature by Bernth Lindfors: 'twenty years ago East Africa was considered a literary desert' – a deficiency which the Ugandan writer Taban lo Liyong made public in 1965 when he raised the controversial question that forms the title of his article 'Can We Correct Literary Barrenness in East Africa?' However, by 1976, over a decade of vigorous creativity had galvanized the literary desert that used to be East Africa into a beehive of literary activities. Many reasons account for the late start. Elder attributes the relative lateness of East African colonization as chief among these factors, while noting that at its inception, unlike its West African counterpart, traditional orature had little impact on the emergent writing from East Africa, or at least not as much as the marked influences of the university colleges established by the British. Also, having run the whole gamut of anthropological and autobiographical writing, East Africa, according to Elder, could not have produced its own Tutuola as a result of a sanctified approach to the English language. The near absence of a creole or pidgin might have inhibited early growth, but a combination of three factors – namely colonial and postcolonial education, the establishment of publishing houses, and pre- and post-independence politics in East Africa – had, by the mid-1970s, produced a tremendous growth of artistic vitality such that 'the Kenyan Ngugi wa Thiong'o had achieved both a local and an international stature comparable to that of Achebe or Soyinka'.

Francis Imbuga's 'East African Literature in the 1980s' (*Matatu* 11.121–35) complements Elder's retrospective insights, and identifies the major step in the development of East African Literature as that taken by Ngugi when he published *Weep Not, Child* (1964) and *The River Between* (1965), 'both historical novels treating representative experiences by mainly the Kikuyu during colonial times, just before Kenya's attainment of political independence'. However, East Africa's literary history in the 1980s, according to Imbuga, 'will be remembered for the upsurge of creativity in four major literary genres: drama, popular literature, children's literature and orature'. While growth in these genres could be attributed to the emergence of a post-Ngugi group of younger writers, the pace had been set by the older Ngugi, whose creative experimentation as co-author of a play in Gikuyu with Ngugi wa Mirii and the villagers of Limuru in 1978 criss-crossed not just the dramatic, but also the popular and oral genres. The experiment, widely believed to be the reason for Ngugi's detention for almost a year in Kamiti Maximum Security Prison soon after the ban on the play, has since been followed by many others. This language shift in Ngugi's career, and what it signifies for writing in East Africa, according to Elder, echoes 'Okot p'Bitek's comment in 1976 [and] seems eerily prophetic of this situation: writers in East Africa are becoming timid because they know the hawk is flying overhead. They know there is detention and imprisonment awaiting us and I think this is discouraging people from commenting on certain political matters that are going on in all East African countries.'

Taban lo Liyong's 'On Translating the "Untranslated": Chapter 14 of *Wer pa Lawino* by Okot p'Bitek' (*RAL* 24.iii.87–92) returns to the premise of p'Bitek's *magnum opus*, a poetic experiment almost unparalleled in the annals of African poetry. However, as lo Liyong reveals, the renowned Ugandan/East African epic, *Song of Lawino*, 'had been composed as *Wer pa Lawino* over a period of time – at least twelve years – and it had benefitted from the contribution of many friends and relatives'. What English language readers got in *Song of Lawino*, according to lo Liyong, was a diluted version of the Acholi original *Wer pa Lawino*, for which p'Bitek did not even bother to translate the chapter (14) that resolved the major themes of the *Song*. In reality, p'Bitek 'did not translate *Wer pa Lawino* into *Song of Lawino*. He wrote two books: *Wer pa Lawino* (a very deep, philosophical book in Acholi; a book of morals, religion, anthropology, and wisdom) and a second light book, *Song of Lawino*. In *Song of Lawino*, Okot the jester – the cultural critic of the whiteman, the whitewoman, and their African imitators – is in the fore. Whatever was striking, dramatic, and sarcastic was highlighted, and by the same token, whatever was more philosophical and deeper was suppressed or left out.'

In 'Allegorical Names as a Means of Conscientization in the Work of Ngugi wa Thiong'o' (in Reckwitz), Herta Meyer conceptualizes Ngugi's indebtedness to onomastic possibilities as a means of settling partisan issues in novelistic characters. From *A Grain of Wheat* (1967), through *Petals of Blood* (1977), and *Devil on the Cross* (1982) to *Matigari* (1989), place names, names of institutions, and even vehicle names, according to Meyer, can have political components. Thus, while the allegorical names that are central to traditional culture supply Ngugi's novels with their African flavour/referent, the foreign ones are made to epitomize class differentiation/membership: 'A case in point is [*sic*] Rev. Kamau in *Petals of Blood*, who calls himself Jerrod Brown when in town, i.e. with the ruling élites. Others shed their English names in order to appear as a man of the people like Nderi wa Riera, the MP for Ilmorog.'

In the introduction to the 1993 edition of Margaret Laurence's renowned *A Tree for Poverty: Somali Poetry and Prose* (first published in 1954), Donez Xiques acknowledged that when Laurence died in Canada in January 1987 she left behind a significant literary legacy. *A Tree for Poverty* is not just 'the first English translation of the rich and complex oral literature of Somalia', but as Laurence's first published book in a long and distinguished career was also one of the first products of what Laurence later referred to as 'a seven years love affair with a continent'. Laurence's comments on approximately ten different types of Somali poetry, translations of 30 poems, and paraphrases of 36 tales that are either Somali or Arabic in origin, according to Xiques, 'offer to English readers texts that convey an authentic sense of the beauty of Somali poetry'.

(d) Southern Africa

The Republic of South Africa's transformation from 'the pariah' among nations to 'the doyen' of Africa (an accolade still fiercely contested by Nigeria in political and, possibly, as the coming years might reveal, literary terms) has raised literary activities to unprecedented heights in the former apartheid enclave. Historically speaking, literary activity in African languages in South Africa is on a par with the foremost in other parts of East, Central and West Africa, and as Robert Cancel observes in 'African-Language Literatures' (in Owomoyela) as far back as 1823 'when a small press was introduced, the Ngqika was launched as the future "standard" form of Xhosa literature, in much the same way that the Oyo dialect became the model for Yoruba writing'. However, as writers and critics move to encapsulate the politics and poetics of post-apartheid South Africa in practical and theoretical terms, the sheer volume of both creative and critical writing in 1993 alone almost equalled that of the rest of the continent put together, in ways that transcend what the space allocated for the entire region of Southern Africa in the *YWES* can hope to do justice to.

Perhaps a good point to start is with the works that put in context the historical reality behind the present frenzy of literary activities. John F. Povey's 'English-Language Fiction from South Africa' (in Owomoyela) and Ursula Barnett's 'South African Literature of the Eighties' (*Matatu* 11.139–53) supply some of these historical paradigms. It has often been perceived as difficult, if not impossible, to separate the political motives behind much South African writing from its literariness. This point of divergence is described by Povey as the clearly observable contrasting tones and styles of writers of the different races:

> White writers, determined to scarify an intolerable regime, brilliantly employ a range of subtle devices that allow them to explore in fearsome sarcasm the metaphysical absurdity of the system and the inconceivable crimes it generates. Black writers speak more directly, preferring to oblique reference an exact and pungent description of the atrocities that make up the daily circumstances of their lives. This distinction is more than technical, since it touches on a very arguable issue in conveying reality: what is the function of artistic construct and what is the appropriate formal stance of a writer in time of political oppression? Blacks sometimes express scorn at formal technique, dismissing skilful devices as artificial, even frivolous in a situation that to them requires only vehement condemnation. White writers consider that literary technique itself is part of the means by which they forge their moral stance and guide readers to a deeper comprehension of the situation.

The *modus operandi* of both sides of the political divide, although arguably balanced, merely reveal another aspect of the symbiotic relationship between literature and politics. If, as Ursula Barnett observes, it took a couple of years for the politically stupefying experiences of 1976 to erupt into literature, it is often the case that the effects of a literary landmark such as the 1987 launch of COSAW (the Congress of South African Writers), which unlike previous associations attracted membership from a wide field of political affiliations because of its non-racial constitution, would also take a few years to sink into the body politic. It can also be argued that more than literary or political fortune or coincidence is at work. One of the ways in which literature and politics are equally capable of fragmenting one another is observed by Povey: 'By about 1970, the increasing degeneration of the political situation finally brought forth condemnation from several Afrikaner writers who for the first time exhibited an urgent, liberal conscience not commonly associated with their kind'.

The resultant 'stasis of the waiting room', to appropriate Schulze-Engler's phrase, is only transcended when literature and politics have moved in the same direction once again, and this movement approximates the contemporary scene, which gives the editors of an important journal like *Current Writing: Text and Perception in Southern Africa* the joyous but hardly uncritical opportunity to describe South Africa as 'a country that is at last experiencing rapid change'. Appropriately, during the year under review a special issue of *Current Writing* (5.ii.) is devoted to critical evaluations, in theoretical terms, of this exuberant affirmation. Problematizing South Africa's postcoloniality, in his introduction to the volume of essays, David Attwell observes that 'if we understand postcoloniality as referring to an historical and cultural condition, one in which the legacies of colonialism have yet to be transcended, then South Africans are hardly in a position to decline the term'. Contrasting the hegemony of the polysystem theory with the postcolonial in 'In/Articulation: Polysystem Theory, Postcolonial Discourse Theory, and South Africa's Literary Historiography' (*CW* 5.ii.25–43), Louise Shabat Bethlehem argues that while a variant of the polysystem has been adopted by Afrikaans academics, and is therefore somewhat institutionalized, 'it is precisely postcolonial discourse theory's struggle for institutionalization in the South African academy which complicates its use'. Unlike Leon de Kock's equally suggestive 'Postcolonial Analysis and the Question of Critical Disablement' (*CW* 5.ii.44–69), although it is written from a position more sympathetic towards discourses of postcoloniality, Bethlehem's well-argued essay betrays an insufficient grasp of the primary concerns of postcolonial discourse theory, and it cannot be said to have compared like with like in counterposing the polysystem with the postcolonial.

However, as Attwell observes further, because the proliferation of theories on the contemporary South African terrain transcend what would pass as mere rhetorical strategies elsewhere, South Africa will continue to be seen for some time 'as a crucible wherein many of the questions being addressed elsewhere burn with unusual intensity'. According to Dennis Brutus, 'there will always be in the ranks of those who create, those who are acutely sensitive to any attempt to place fresh shackles on their energies and ideas: the creative writer will continue to insist on creative freedom in a new South Africa'. However, the altruism of Brutus's other observation in his 'Literature and Change in South Africa' (*RAL* 24.iii.101–4) is equally pertinent and must be recognized as such on each side of the political and ideological divide, most especially by those who possess the wherewithal to ensure equal access to relevant materials: 'As a result of research I was able to compile a list of over 200 books useful in the field of African literature which were not in the library, either uncatalogued or not physically present, and was able to recommend purchases to the English Department and the University library'. Craig MacKenzie's 'Literary Research in South Africa: The Case of the National English Literary Museum' (*RAL* 24.iii.105–12) and the publicity it gives, not only to the wealth of materials, but also to the activities at the NELM, shows that efforts are under way to remove the constraints that lack of materials could pose to literary research in South Africa. NELM, according to MacKenzie, 'has the distinction of being the only institution that collects exclusively South African literary manuscripts: its brief is at once narrow (South African) and specialized (literary)'.

In two important respects, it is also significant that Jack Barbera subtitles his introduction to *Twentieth Century Literature*'s Athol Fugard Issue, 'Fugard,

Women and Politics' (39.iv.). Firstly, the introduction foregrounds Barbera's claim that Fugard has always acknowledged the fact that his life has been 'sustained by women'. The implication of this admission, as Barbera observes further, is readily observable in 'a number of vital roles for women in Fugard's plays: Hester in *Hello and Goodbye*, Milly in *People Are Living There*, Lena in *Boesman and Lena*, Frieda in *Statements After an Arrest Under the Immorality Act*, Elsa and Helen in *The Road to Mecca*, and even the down-to-earth Praskovya in *A Place with the Pigs*'. Secondly, and perhaps more importantly, Fugard's acknowledgement is itself paradigmatic of the feminist agenda as an integral aspect of the new South Africa's field of cultural theorizing. Fugard himself has written a tentative manifesto of what we might expect:

> I think in the new South Africa, women are going to have an infinitely more creative role [...] Young white women — I've met them, and there's no way that they are going to take from their peers and from their equals the nonsense that their fathers and their uncles are handing out. And the same is true in terms of black South Africans, African, Coloured and Indian, whatever you'd like to think of — since those Soweto boycotts, gender has not been a significant factor. And hand in hand with [...] the breaking down of race, has got to be the gender barrier. It has been there as viciously in black society as it has been in white. I know some of my black friends outdo my white friends in male chauvinism. But I think the people at the top of the political movements realize ... women have got to be recognized as an equal force ('Fugard's Treaty').

The volume brings together prominent critics such as Dennis Walder, Graig McLuckie, and Mary Benson, South African writers such as André Brink, actors and actresses in Fugardian theatre, one of the women 'who have sustained Fugard's life', Sheila Fugard, discussing 'The Apprenticeship Years', and last but not least, Fugard himself explaining 'Some Problems of a Playwright from South Africa'. An abiding theme concerns the question of Fugard's relevance in the new South Africa. Again, according to Barbera, Fugard himself, in his talk at New York University in 1990, expressed his frustration at being asked if his plays are not out of date, and what he would do for subject matter when apartheid is abolished. Such questions arise, he said, from the false perception that he is in a very narrow sense a political playwright'.

The return to South Africa of the veteran anti-apartheid campaigner and epic poet Mazisi Kunene after 34 years in exile is described by his compatriot, Ntongela Masilela, in his 'The Return of Mazisi Kunene to South Africa: The End of an Intellectual Chapter in Our Literary History' (*Ufahamu* 21.iii.7–15) as one which would 'help to resituate the indigenous literatures in their proper place in our cultural history'. Kunene's return is a cultural if not a political landmark and at the same time one which, according to Masilela, portends a brighter future for the indigenous literatures, once emasculated by modern South African national literature in the English language.

Although *The African Past and Contemporary Culture*, edited by Reckwitz et al., purportedly covers the entire African continent, only seven out of the 18 essays are not pre-eminently focused on different aspects of South African writing. The scope of the essays is impressive, ranging from Gareth Cornwell's 'Colonial Discourse and Culture in South Africa', to Kathrin Wagner's 'The "Conspiracy Against Keeping Apart": Some Images of Blacks in Nadine Gordimer's Novels', to Eva Hunter's 'Tradition and Change in Lauretta Ngcobo's *And They Didn't Die*', and Hans-Christoph Hummel's 'Unintentional Writers for Posterity: A Glimpse at the Graham's Town Series', to mention just a few.

Nobantu Rasebotsa's '*Maru* and Bessie Head's Place in Botswana' (*CW* 5.i.25–35) and Flora Veit-Wild's 'Dances with *Bones*: Hove's Romanticized Africa' (*RAL* 24.iii.5–12) move beyond the confines of South Africa's cultural/national space and articulate cultural issues in other parts of the subcontinent. In the former, Rasebotsa's attempt to locate Bessie Head in her several worlds – those of South Africa, of Botswana and of *Maru* – leads to an examination of the way Head seeks to resolve the multiplicity inherent in her identity. However, this multi-heritage, both ascribed and inscribed, and the mode of its reflection in Head's writing are not unproblematic: since Head never spoke Setswana and lived most of her life in social and cultural isolation in Botswana, Maru's character, cultivated as it is in traditional values and Western romantic ideas, according to Rasebotsa, becomes merely a fusion of the author's 'own spiritual values, and Botswana's traditional modes of belief'. Similarly, after his emergence as a major poetic observer of the war of liberation, and with the publication of his award-winning novel, *Bones*, Chenjerai Hove, according to Flora Veit-Wild, 'holds an important place in Zimbabwe's post-independence literary scene'. Above all, Veit-Wild sees *Bones* as 'a faithful embodiment of Hove's literary manifesto' which includes among other things 'the writer's immense responsibility of persuading the world to listen to the many cries of Africa'.

(e)   North Africa

Mireille Rosello's 'The "Beur Nation": Toward a Theory of Departenance' (*RAL* 24.iii.13–24) defines the term 'Beur' as referring to 'second and third generation North African (particularly Algerian) immigrants in France'. Rosello's well-conceived and vigorously argued essay analyses 'Beur' culture using examples of discourses from apparently different perspectives (the media, sociology and fiction) or 'disciplines (written or visual) that present themselves as analyses of Beur culture'. All three forms of discourse, according to Rosello, 'are based on the same assumption – on the notion that the "Beurs" are half French and half Arab, or that they exist existentially between France and the Maghreb'.

However, neither the manichaean space of media discourses, nor the statistics-laden sociological theses, in spite of their pleas for legitimacy and authenticity, transcend what Rosello describes as 'the simplistic opposition between Africa and France', most especially when 'the France-Maghreb opposition is replicated (or subdivided into) oppositions between modernity and tradition', among other conflict-lacking syntheses. Even though Rosello does not claim that it is more 'real' than the others, an exploration of the 'Beur' novelistic space reveals modes of discourse that do not presuppose a monolithic audience comprised mainly of 'native Frenchmen', and do not focus pre-eminently upon the need to choose between 'North Africa' and 'France' or 'seek an harmonious synthesis between two cultures; on the contrary, by placing the emphasis on other sorts of questions, they suggest possible new ways of looking at culture and "belonging"'. Besides offering themselves as interpretable constructs, the novelistic modes of discourse lead to creative articulation of speaking subjects who control their own itineraries, or characters such as the young 'run-aways' of *Carnets de Sherazade* and *Georgette!*, who are not circumscribed by the two poles (France and North Africa) that supposedly define 'Beur' geography.

2. Australia

This section is divided into three sub-sections: (a) General (books, articles and bibliographies); (b) Individual Authors: 1789–1920 (books, articles and bibliographies on); (c) Individual Authors: Post-1920 (books, articles and bibliographies on).

(a) General

Three general review articles criticize different aspects of the cultural context in which Australian literary studies are appearing. Peter Pierce's 'Australian Literature Since Patrick White' in the Australian issue of *WLT* (67.iii.515–18) castigates 'the restless, envious, modish cultural climate' which in relentless pursuit of 'experimental, self-referential, postmodern fiction' leads critics to exaggerated claims on behalf of writers such as Mark Henshaw or Gerald Murnane at the expense of others with long-established careers, and he savages both publishers and critics for their lack of discrimination. He quotes approvingly Les Murray's assertion that 'publishers to ten multinationals indifferently bring out good and bad Australian literary books and scarcely bother to market them because the Literature Board pays for them anyway'. As for the critics, too many writers have been uncritically praised (among them Elizabeth Jolley) and 'obliged exercises in spurious guilt' have meant that Aboriginal writers, among them Oodgeroo and Mudrooroo, 'have suffered from suspension of critical judgement of their work'. His conclusion is that 'writers who have mastered their craft find themselves jostled aside by one-book wonders ....Those of the few who have enjoyed commercial success – a handful of novelists, Williamson among playwrights – find that their other, ambiguous rewards include critical suspicion and envy. A terrible want of generosity obtains.' While Pierce hardly redresses the want of generosity complained of, he brings back, with a vengeance, the discrimination he claims is lacking in the current critical climate.

Ken Stewart's 'Australian Criticism in "Transition"' (*ALS* 16.100–5) traces the absorption of deconstructionist, feminist and postcolonial theories, which he sees as having produced a broad division between 'modern' academic criticism and 'traditional' or 'general' reviewing. His article registers the interests in gender, race and ethnicity, and in the processes of social construction generally, apparent in much of the criticism that appeared during 1993. However, given that these interests are widely shared beyond the academies, are indeed reflected in the domestic political agenda, and given also that most 'general' reviewers today are academics, the division he postulates seems exaggerated. One indication of how poststructuralist interests are no longer academically rarefied, but have permeated the undergraduate and senior secondary syllabus, is Ian Saunders's *Open Texts, Partial Maps: A Literary Theory Handbook*, an engagingly presented primer which discusses, and cross-refers, 32 key concepts from 'Agency' to 'Truth', and illustrates them with examples that include the local, so assisting the naturalization of what was once considered 'foreign'. (Unaccountably though, 'Postcolonial', an area of contemporary theory in which Australian critics could claim some pre-eminence, is omitted.) Other indications are contained in contributions to series aimed at this educational market; e.g., OUPAus's Horizon series of monographs on senior secondary school texts, which are intended, in the General Editor's words, to be 'informed by recent trends in criticism and scholarship'. UMelb's new Interpretations series of 'clearly written and up-to-date introductions to recent theories and critical practices in the humanities and social sciences' appears to be directed as much to postgraduates as to undergraduates. While the first titles seem belated attempts to explain developments in 'the new humanities' that happened elsewhere and long ago (Foucault, cultural materialism etc.), Wenche Ommundsen's *Metafictions?*, an enquiry into the relationships between self-reflexiveness, metafiction and the postmodern, discusses Australian as well as international examples of these modes; in doing so she provides original and incisive observations on works by Carey, Bail and Grenville.

The third review article, Susan Lever's 'The Cult of the Author' (*ALS* 16.229–33), considers the implications for research in this pattern of publishing for the educational market. Her regret is not at the preponderance of theoretical discourse in the academies but that the smallness of the local market, dominated by both the secondary school curricula and multinational publishers, forces critics into a conservative and untheoretical role. As a result, she claims, only two kinds of critical books are currently appearing: collections of essays by various hands (such as those Stewart reviews in his article) and the author-centred studies she is reviewing, which include titles in OUPAus's Australian Writers and UQP's Studies in Australian Literature series. These she sees as emphasizing relationships between the author's life and work at the expense of the relationships between that work and other 'cultural formations'. The latter would have to include the universities, and they invite another set of general observations to join the above attempts to characterize the current critical climate. Today, Departments of 'English' (if that nomenclature is employed at all) are more likely to be departments of 'Communications/Cultural/Media Studies' than of 'Literature and Language'. But while traditional 'English' literary courses have shrunk, or were never introduced into newer institutions, Australian literature has expanded as a field for study and research. It has been recontextualized by theoretical interests and within cross-disciplinary formations like Australian Studies, Aboriginal Studies and (still the most productive) Women's Studies. This recontextualizing of earlier literature and recognition of diverse components within the contemporary literary culture is strongly reflected in the work under review, which – to hazard another generalization – is characterized most of all by impulses for revision.

The most frequent target, and starting point, for revisionist readings, whether feminist, Aboriginal, multicultural, gay – or the time-honoured anti-nationalist – continues to be 'the Australian legend', 'bush legend', or 'legend of the Nineties'. Perhaps John Barnes had his tongue in cheek, or was being wishful, when he wrote in 'On Misreading *Such is Life*' that the legend has by now been 'well and truly deconstructed'(*Westerly* 38.iii.38–49); instead it is hastily re-erected, in an increasingly ramshackle fashion, before each enthusiastic new demolition begins. In his introduction to *The Penguin Book of 19th Century* [*sic*] *Australian*

Literature, Michael Ackland declares his intention to reinscribe women in the record of 'the conceptual shaping of white Australia', because he sees them as having been excluded since the 1920s by 'the elevation of bush, democratic, egalitarian concerns associated with Henry Lawson and the *Bulletin*, into hallmarks of the national literary tradition'. Ackland helps redress this historic wrong by providing exceedingly generous representation to Ada Cambridge, although glaringly he leaves out Joseph Furphy. (Like the Brennan poems Ackland includes, but which were not published until 1913, *Such is Life* (1903) was written in the late nineteenth century; perhaps Furphy is being punished for mocking women's romances à l'Ouida?) This considerable omission apart, the editor can fairly claim that he has included selections 'which most readers would recognize as part of their cultural heritage', along with less familiar writings 'made accessible by recent scholarship [including Ackland's own] and innovative publishing ventures'; however, some inclusions, such as Harpur's 'Note to "A Wanton"', are mystifyingly trivial. The selections are arranged under the headings of 'The Challenge of a New Landscape', 'The Burden of the Past', 'Renegotiating Sexual Roles', 'The Quest for Fulfilment', and 'Existential Anxieties', but as they are neither dated in the table of contexts or the text, nor chronologically ordered under these headings, the reader has to consult the notes to discover when a piece was written or published. Despite Ackland's pains in his introduction to dispel notions of a *Zeitgeist*, this chronological vagueness has the effect of obscuring the changes that occurred over more than a century as the colonies moved from early settlement to nationhood.

The reinscription of women in literary cultural history, an already well-established enterprise, generated a considerable proportion of the most stimulating criticism of the year. As its sub-title indicates, *Debutante Nation: Feminism Contests the 1890s*, edited by Susan Magarey, Sue Rowley and Susan Sheridan, tackles the 'masculinist' legend head-on. Conveniently, it reprints Marilyn Lake's 'The Politics of Respectability' (originally published in *Australian Historical Studies* in 1986), which proposes the gendering of history – specifically what Lake sees as the contest between women and men for control of the national culture in the 1890s – and deconstruction of the 'masculinism' propagated by the *Bulletin* as a political ideology. While Lake's essay has proved seminal, not only for contributors to this volume but also others writing during this year, John Docker, in his chapter 'The Feminist Legend: A New Historicism?', exposes the selectiveness, and reductiveness, of Lake's literary evidence, and argues that essentially she has substituted another 'monistic', if feminist, legend for the masculinist one under attack. Another wide-ranging essay concludes the collection: Kay Schaffer's 'Henry Lawson, the Drover's Wife and the Critics', which traces the figure of Lawson's character from his story through those by more recent, and parodic, writers as a means of enquiring into the ever-shifting nature of the quest for defining the 'national identity'. Between are essays demonstrating how contemporary interests in the relationships between gender and genre can inform a 'new' literary history and generate interest in often forgotten texts.

The feminist revisionist concerns of *Debutante Nation* are well complemented by the essays in *The Time to Write: Australian Women Writers 1890–1930*, edited by Kay Ferres. This is a more than usually cohesive collection because, while the dozen contributors consider individual authors and texts to provide a good survey of major figures in the period, the reader gains a strong sense of what the editor calls 'an alternative myth to mateship' emerging thematically from the book as a whole. Particularly noteworthy as conceptually critical contributions to feminist revisionist history are those by Joy Hooton, Susan Martin, Kerry M. White and Ferres herself. Hooton's 'Mary Fullerton: Pioneering and Feminism' disputes contemporary assumptions that earlier women writers must have experienced an antagonism between their own feminism and the romantic 'masculinist' myth. She instances Miles Franklin, who embraced many of the myth's values: 'physical freedom, egalitarianism, independence and solidarity, especially when invested with the distinctive mystique of the bush landscape and loosely associated with the inspiring history of pioneering'. Hooton sees Mary Fullerton, poet and close friend of Franklin, as having been more successful in reconciling these values with feminism. (Fullerton is also the subject of an article not seen: Sylvia Martin's 'Rethinking Passionate Friendships' (*Women's History Review* 2.iii.395–406).) Susan Martin's 'Relative Correspondence: Franklin's *My Brilliant Career* and the Influence of Nineteenth-Century Australian Women's Writing' argues that in rewriting the nineteenth-century romance about growing up in rural Australia, Franklin, Richardson and Baynton were wanting to identify with 'serious' male writers, and that their success helped elide the 'female' tradition of romance in the minds of later generations of readers. Related to both the above essays is Kerry M. White's 'The Real Australian Girl?: Some Post-Federation Writers for Girls', an insightful re-reading of Ethel Turner's and Mary Grant Bruce's children's books, which observes that 'one of the ironies of the Australian girl in literature was that the special childhood freedoms deemed the privilege of all Australian children served to later emphasize the restrictions of womanhood'. The editor's own essay, 'Rewriting Desire: Rosa Praed, Theosophy and the Sex Problem' is, like her article on Praed referred to below, an imaginative example of 'new historicist' contextualizing and interpretation. In all, *The Time to Write* is the strongest collection of essays this year.

Recuperation of the 'lost tradition' of women's writing through reprints continues. As well as representing women, and writers of romance, heavily in his Penguin anthology, Michael Ackland has edited a selection of Tasma's short fiction under the confusing title *A Sydney Sovereign* (confusing because it is similar to the title of an 1890 collection of this writer's work). Mulini Press, which specializes in reprinting nineteenth-century works, republished Rosa Praed's *The Bond of Wedlock* (1889) and Ellen Davitt's *Force and Fraud: A Tale of the Bush* (1865). In her introduction to the Praed, Elizabeth Webby notes that it was the author's eleventh novel, originally subtitled 'A Tale of London Life', and was successfully adapted for the English stage; it is also the subject of Kay Ferres's other essay on Praed, 'Women Making a Spectacle of Themselves: Rosa Praed's *Ariane*, Melodrama, and Marriage Reform' (*ADS* 23.56–64), which considers the stage version within the context of controversies in England at that time. Lucy Sussex's introduction to Davitt's novel, which had not been republished since it first appeared as the lead serial in the first issue of the *Australian Journal*, proves considerably more interesting than the wooden and sketchy tale. Sussex has established that Davitt was Trollope's sister-in-law, and she argues for the text's historical interest as an early example of the murder mystery which anticipates what is usually regarded as Wilkie Collins's innovative plot in *The Moonstone* (1868). (Also published by Mulini Press, in 1992, was John Lang's *Lucy Cooper: An Australian Tale*, edited by Victor Crittenden. Published anonymously as a serial in 1848, this is its first appearance in book form.) Louise Mack's *The World is Round* (1896) – which, *pace* current conventional wisdom, was one of numerous texts by women hailed by arch-patriarch A. G. Stephens in the *Bulletin* of the 1890s – has been reprinted with an introduction by Nancy Phelan, Mack's biographer. Phelan does not bother to pretend to the slightest interest in what she sees as an irredeemably patriarchal and imperialistic text. Susan Martin provides a most individual, if unhelpful, introduction to a reprint of Henry Kingsley's *The Recollections of Geoffry Hamlyn (1859)*. Calculatedly written against the grain of current mainstream revisions to literary history are Michael Wilding's Townsville lectures, *The Radical Tradition: Lawson, Furphy, Stead*. His position is that recent theorizing, like the old New Criticism, has depoliticized these writers and their works; and he reads them anew, and closely, against the international contexts of socialist thought and writing. Most provocative is his argument that *Such is Life* should be read with the original but now fragmented text in mind to recover Furphy's positive socialist vision.

Revisionist intentions characterize three major anthologies this year. In their introduction to *The Penguin Book of Australian Ballads*, Philip Butterss and Elizabeth Webby state that their selection is intended to replace Russel Ward's (1964) collection of the same title and that, while they retain much from that standard work, they have been guided in their selection by consciousness of readers' interests today in the historical construction of gender and race, and in 'diversity, difference and dialogue'. They seek to diversify the 'radical nationalist' view (attributed to Ward, among others), which they claim has distorted the 1890s since the 1950s, by reprinting forgotten newspaper verses, many by women, which answer to the preoccupations of the 1990s, although whether these were 'ballads' popular in their time is not established. A scholarly *coup* is their discovery that a Queensland newspaper in the 1890s was a major source for 'Banjo' Paterson's *Old Bush Songs* (1905), information not found in Roderick's biography (reviewed under individual authors below). However, neither in Butterss and Webby's introduction nor Roderick's biography is it noted that Paterson opened his collection with two untranslated Aboriginal songs – one of those irritating if petty details which interfere with the best intentions to correct the ideological blindness of the past.

In her introduction to *The Oxford Book of Australian Love Poems*, Jennifer Strauss expresses surprise at having found so many examples to select from, because the ways in which 'a national poetry' has been constructed had led her to expect many fewer. Given the centrality of love as a poetic subject – Eros as unifier and destroyer, in Strauss's own terms – one is rather surprised by her surprise. For the reader, however, this anthology is characterized more by an impression of the editor's dutiful representation over time and across genders and ethnic groupings. (Not seen is Strauss's 'Within the Bounds of Feminine Sensibility: The Poetry of Rosemary Dobson, Gwen Harwood, and Judith Wright' in Shiela Roberts and Yvonne Pacheco Trevis (eds), *Still the Frame Holds: Essays on Women Poets and Writers* [publisher unknown]). In comparison with Strauss's anthology, Robert Dessaix's *Australian Gay and Lesbian Writing*, also from Oxford (but that is not declared in its title), does surprise by presenting a whole new dimension to Australian writing. Dessaix's intentions are not to win wider recognition for minority homosexual writers, nor to claim as homosexual a considerable number of major figures – among them White, Porter, Harwood, Jolley, Garner, Malouf, Moorhouse – but to delineate a substantial strand in mainstream writing, whether by homosexuals or not. What could be termed the 'queerness' of the writing rather than its authors' proclivities has determined inclusion in this impressive selection which convincingly demonstrates its editor's observation that 'sexuality itself has become a leading theme in Australian fiction, poetry and drama, to the point where some writers have made literary careers writing about nothing else'.

A major contribution to the now internationally well-established area of postcolonial literary studies is *Decolonising Fictions* by Canadian critic Diana Brydon and Helen Tiffin, one of the authors of *The Empire Writes Back*. An impressively independent contribution to theory, not least because it is conscious of theory's 'Eurocentric' provenance and potential to be another hegemony, this is at the same time a 'how to' manual for subverting imperialism in the classroom. The authors' stated purposes are to explore possibilities of *comparative* readings of texts which they see as, at best, colonized within the Anglocentric canon, and to accommodate the poststructuralist within the postcolonial context. The Australian texts chosen for these readings (and, in different chapters, compared with both Canadian and West Indian texts) are White's *A Fringe of Leaves* and Stow's *Visitants*. Through these close, although very theoretically informed discussions, *Decolonising Fictions* complements *The Empire Writes Back*, and deserves to enjoy a similar international success; however, no doubt on principle, it has been published not by a multinational but by a small press associated with *Kunapipi*. The production is attractive, but the endnotes to the Australian section have been lost in the setting.

John McLaren's *New Pacific Literatures: Culture and Environment in the European Pacific* is another major contribution to this area, even though he finds 'postcolonial' too limiting a term to describe 'the function of literature in the societies which now occupy the territories of the old European empires'. McLaren begins by outlining the European conquest, and imaginative possession, of new worlds, including Africa, and moves chronologically towards accounting for the current diversity of settler and indigenous literatures around the Pacific. The conception is boldly ambitious and, if this summary might suggest some sketchiness and questionably easy generalization, overall the ambition is justified by the author's obviously intimate and thoughtful acquaintance with an extraordinary range of texts. *Culture and Imperialism* might have been an alternative title, if that had not been pre-empted; but in its comprehensiveness, coherence and clarity, McLaren's study compares very favourably with the much-touted miscellany of essays with that title. In connection with this unkind observation, it is worth noting that *New Pacific Literatures* is published in the United States – where postcolonial studies are a growth area – and that, probably to the surprise of theorists there, McLaren properly includes American among the new or postcolonial literatures (although he is not at his strongest in discussing it). *Westerly Looks to Asia*, a selection of poetry, fiction and essays from that journal between 1956 and 1992, edited by Bruce Bennett, Peter Cowan, Denis Haskell and Susan Miller, indicates that literary interest in the Pacific region has long been established.

While interests in gender, multiculturalism and Aboriginality are pursued more often in articles than in books this year, their pervasiveness is indicated in two major publications on children's literature. *The Oxford Companion to Australian Children's Literature*, edited by 'Immigrants' (and 'Italians', etc.), 'Girls' and 'Boys', as well as authors and titles. Like the revised and updated paperback edition of Peter Pierce's *The Oxford Literary Guide to Australia* and OUPAus's Companions – which now include Gwenda Davey and Graham Seal's

The Oxford Companion to Australian Folklore – this is immediately an indispensable reference. The contemporary agenda it reflects is apparent also in H. M. Saxby's *The Proof of the Puddin': Australian Children's Literature 1970–1990*, which updates the information in his two-volume history of Australian children's literature 1841–1970 (1969; 1971) – and Saxby estimates that as many volumes have been published since 1970 as before. From the table of contents it appears a jumble of different categories: targeted age groups, genres and issues (Aboriginals, conservation, multiculturalism), but the author, whose introduction offers observations on the world that contemporary children's literature reflects, presents it as a reference work and advises users to consult the indexes (to titles/authors, editors/illustrators and photographers/subjects) rather than attempt to read it as a further volume in his history.

Two books which, quite differently, extend the range of Australian literary studies this year are Fiona Capp's *Writers Defiled* and Sue Woolfe and Kate Grenville's *Making Stories: How Ten Australian Novels Were Written*. *Writers Defiled* is a study of the security surveillance of authors and intellectuals from 1920 to 1960 and documents a significant aspect of the cultural context, especially in the decades immediately following the Second World War. Among those writers whose dossiers Capp has inspected under Freedom of Information legislation are Manning Clark, Jean Devanney, Frank Hardy, Dorothy Hewett, Alan Marshall, Stephen Murray-Smith, Vance Palmer, Katherine Susannah Prichard and Judah Waten, and among institutions the New Theatre. Capp reads these dossiers imaginatively, analysing the spies' stumbling attempts to construct their surveillance reports according to the conventions of genre fiction. *Making Stories* contains interviews with nine of the ten writers represented, and extracts from their notes and drafts (with facsimile illustrations) for comparison with an extract from a published version of their work. As well as Woolfe and Grenville themselves, the writers are Jessica Anderson, Peter Carey, Helen Garner, David Ireland, Elizabeth Jolley, Thomas Keneally and Finola Moorhead. While there is no interview with Patrick White, an extract from his only extant novel manuscript is included. Intended for classroom use (with teacher's notes appended), *Making Stories* could serve to introduce elements of textual criticism in a refreshingly practical and intrinsically interesting way.

For drama scholars the most important book in their area this year is likely to be *The Campbell Howard Annotated Index of Australian Plays 1920–1955*, edited by Jack Bedson and Julian Croft. While a checklist of the 300, largely unpublished plays in the Campbell Howard Collection held by the Dixon Library at UNE was published in 1968, this omitted the collector's (and others') annotations and synopses, which are provided by Bedson and Croft together with the location of the manuscripts (not all are held in the Dixon). The editors point out that the collection, to which they have added, represents perhaps only half the plays published or performed by reputable companies within the period (which they have stretched to include other plays by authors whose main work falls within that period). They hope to fulfil Howard's ultimate goal of a complete guide to works published or performed; they present this edition as research in progress, eventually to be updated electronically and made available on disk. An indication of the importance of the Collection as a database for researchers is given by Susan Pfisterer-Smith's 'Playing With the Past: A Feminist Deconstruction of Australian Theatre Historiography' (*ADS* 23.8–22), which finds that more than half the plays it includes were written by women, and that their favourite subject was women – which leads her to pose a number of questions for future research.

Shakespeare's Books, edited by Philip Mead and Marion Campbell, is a collection of papers from a conference on the institutionalization of Shakespeare, and the first in a new series of monographs on Literary and Cultural Studies from the English Department, University of Melbourne. In passing, it contains much interesting, if miscellaneous, theatrical history, as well as Mead's engaging meditation on inter-textuality/sexuality, 'Reversible Empires: Melville/Shakespeare/Furphy'. Issued in a limited edition, and printed in a nostalgic sepia on vanilla paper, *The Story of the Theatre Royal* by 'Ian Bevan' (Ian Archibald Winchcombe), is an antiquarian's stage-struck account of the country's oldest theatre (although its sites have changed frequently since 1833). While the author has been criticized for raiding the researches of others, the result can be recommended to the non-specialist as providing an entertaining introductory 'slice' through not only Sydney's but also Australia's theatrical history, rich in anecdotes, gossip and records of box-office receipts. Also richly anecdotal is John Sumner's *Recollections at Play: A Life in Australian Theatre*. The foundation director (in 1953) of the Melbourne Theatre Company, which became the largest in the country and first produced *Summer of the Seventeenth Doll*, Sumner provides in passing a valuable account for future theatre historians of his involvements with the development of local drama following his company. Such historians will be aware that opposition to the MTC, and Sumner, was a common cause for 'alternative' playwrights and performers in the early 1970s. Peta Tait's *Original Women's Theatre: The Melbourne Women's Theatre Group 1974–77* presents some useful research into an alternative within the alternative at that time. Unfortunately, it assumes too much knowledge (e.g., what the APG was) and is not organized to provide the uninitiated with a clear chronological sense of the developments it traces; given the dearth of material in this area, this is a missed opportunity, but it is valuable nevertheless for Tait's analyses of the kind of ideological positions these writers were taking up and the check-list of productions. Contemporary alternative or fringe theatre is touched on by Maria Shevtsova in her *Theatre and Cultural Interaction*, which surveys audience responses to some local productions of European classics and contains interviews with Italo-Australian actresses. The revised edition of Elizabeth Webby's *Modern Australian Plays*, in OUPAus's Horizon series, adds a consideration of Jack Davis's 'The First Born Trilogy', the most impressive achievement by an Aboriginal playwright to date.

The major publication in language studies this year is Gary Simes's *A Dictionary of Australian Underworld Slang*, which conflates, with commentary and illustrative quotation, two glossaries of underworld slang compiled by prisoners in the 1940s and 1950s (one of them consulted by novelist Kylie Tennant), and has a lengthy introduction tracing the literature and lexicography of crime from the Middle Ages on. This is a rare, indeed lavish, example of scholarly publishing from an Australian press today. The range of Australian language studies is exemplified in *The Languages of Australia*, edited by Gerhard Schulz from papers delivered – some by opinionated amateurs, most by specialists – at an Australian Academy of the Humanities symposium in 1992.

A major bibliographical project is Kay Walsh and Joy Hooton's *Australian Autobiographical Narratives: An Annotated Bibliography*. The first volume provides a comprehensive guide to published autobiographical writing dealing with life in Australia up to 1850. Entries, alphabetical by author, summarize the texts, and there are indexes to personal names, places and subjects in these texts – but not necessarily in the summaries provided. Carol Mills and June Dietrich's *Melbourne Review Index: 1876–1885* is a welcome author and subject guide to a journal modelled on the *Fortnightly Review* that attracted many of the colonial *literati* and reflected their wide-ranging intellectual interests (it was modestly subtitled 'A Quarterly Publication Devoted to Philosophy, Theology, Science, Art, Politics and Belles-lettres'). Acquaintance with the *Review*'s contents, if only through this bibliography, might help moderate the current frenzy for *Bulletin*-bashing. Except that the *JCL* Bibliography for 1992 has not yet appeared, serial bibliographies remain the same as in recent years: the monthly and annually cumulated *Australian National Bibliography*, Thorpe's bi-monthly *Guide to New Australian Books*, the annual *ALS* bibliography of studies in Australian literature, and *Antipodes*' annual bibliography of Australian literature and criticism published in North America. The *ALS* remains the most useful in the field, although it suffers from limiting itself, and hence its record of local reception, to only three metropolitan Australian dailies, even though it continues to list selectively English and American serials (the latter now comprehensively covered by *Antipodes*). Extension of the deadline for contributions to *YWES* means that reference now is to the current instead of the previous year's *ALS* bibliography.

In some of the journals still identified as literary because of their verse and fiction content, the critical essay has been almost completely replaced by cultural critique (the best, or worst, examples in this respect are *Meanjin* and *Meridian*); in others it has been replaced by interviews with authors. Compensating for this, journals not identified as primarily literary (like *Hecate*) are attracting outstanding critical contributions, and there is an increasing number of European and North American journals with interests in Australian writing. Among general articles in the journals, Susan Magarey's 'The Feminist History Group Goes to the Berks' (*Hecate* 19.i.36–57) is a delightfully entertaining but simultaneously insightful engagement with what is the underlying theme of so many other discussions, which Magarey herself describes as the 'linguistic turn' taken by historians and the turn to 'new historicism' taken by literary critics. These she dramatizes through the papers she has her three delegates present to an international feminist history conference. The first compares the 'authenticity' of Miles Franklin's *Some Everyday Folk and Dawn* (1909) with that of the Parliamentary record of the passing of the South Australian suffrage bill, to bother the distinction between historical fact and fiction. The second paper discusses the exchanges that followed the appearance of Marilyn Lake's 'The Politics of Respectability' as examples of 'the ways in which historians are reading each other these days'. The third uses examples of medical advice to males and females in the 1890s to deconstruct the discourses of sexuality in this period. While her delegates might not be concerned exclusively with literary texts, Magarey presents, with an appropriately postmodern playfulness, some of the basic deconstructive procedures employed in much contemporary criticism. An instance of the linguistic, or poststructuralist, turn taken by historians is provided by Bain Attwood's 'Portrait of an Aboriginal as Artist: Sally Morgan and the Construction of Aboriginality' (*AHS* (1992) 99.302–18), which attracted responses in this year's issues over the problematical concept of 'identity', including Tim Rowse's 'Sally Morgan's Kaftan' (100.465–8). A perfect instance of criticism's new interest in history is Alison Bartlett's 'Other Stories: The Representation of History in Recent Fiction by Australian Women Writers' (*Southerly* 53.i.165–80) which shows how, in novels by Jean Bedford, Kate Grenville and Janine Bourke, 'the boundaries between history, literature and theory are indeed porous'.

The extent to which postcolonial theory should influence perceptions of Australian writing was discussed by a panel at the 1992 Association for the Study of Australian Literature's conference (*ACS* (1992) 10.ii.111–59). While most contributors gave instances of how postcolonial consciousness affected their reading practices, Bill Ashcroft addressed what he saw as 'The Present Crisis in Australian Literary Studies' (147–52): that because 'nation' was such a contested term, to be locked into it by concentrating on local writing in isolation could bring about vulnerability to imperialist postmodern theorizing. Like other speakers on the panel (and like Brydon and Tiffin, and McLaren, in their books), Ashcroft was calling more generally for comparativist approaches within postcolonial literatures. A glance at the titles of journal articles this year, both general and on individual authors, will reveal that such a call is belated. Comparative readings (especially with Canadian and New Zealand texts) are frequent, and fears of either Eurocentric theoretical hegemony or nationalistic self-congratulation seem unduly alarmist. Bruce Bennett's 'Short Fiction and the Canon: Australia and Canada' (*Antipodes* 7.ii.109–14), which is only nominally about short fiction, makes the observation that 'the formerly exclusive preoccupation of Australians and Canadians with defining themselves against their colonial masters has diversified in recent years in a process of reorientation towards the countries of the Asia–Pacific region' and predicts these new international affiliations will 're-orient the direction of national canon-formation over the next decade'. Bennett's own role in pioneering these 'new affiliations' is indicated by the special issue of *Westerly* (38.iv), 'Crossing the Water; Asia and Australia', which includes Koh Tai Ann's '"Crossing that little bridge into Asia ...": Australian Fiction Set in Southeast Asia' (20–32); Rob Blaber''s 'Australian Travel Writing About Asia in the 20s and 30s'(46–57); Ouyang Yu's study of the shifting representation of the Chinese in popular fiction during this century, 'Charles Cooper and the Representation of the Chinese in Australian Fictions' (65–73); and Graham Huggan's 'Transformation of the Tourist Gaze: India in Recent Australian Fiction' (83–9). Huggan also writes on 'The World, the Text, and the Tourist: Murray Bail, Inez Baranay, Gerard Lee' in *ALS* (16.168–78); and Ouyang Yu on representations of the Chinese from 1888 to 1988 in 'All the Lower Orders' (*Kunapipi* 15.iii.21–34).

Consideration of Aboriginal writing has this year focused preponderantly on Mudrooroo, but J. J. Healy's 'Ethnogenesis, the State and the Beginnings of Aboriginal Literature in Australia' (*ANZSC* (1992) 8.1–17) provides a most general, indeed abstracted, discussion of the contemporary situation. His term 'ethnogenesis' is intended to register 'the beginning of a renewed sense of group identity in which the roots of past histories are explored as a frame for present struggles and future prospects', and accordingly Aboriginal literature is identified as 'a functional, instrumental, political literature, a reflexive performative set of utterances ... a discursive field of private and public reflection, taking place as an activity of constant negotiation'. Ivor Indyk's 'Pastoral and Priority' offers a thematic and historical survey of the Aboriginal in Australian 'pastoral' (*NLH* 24.837–55) from early colonial poetry, through modern fiction to recent writing by Aboriginals. In the Australian issue of *WLT* Ken Gelder's 'The Politics of the

Sacred' (67.iii.499–504) considers the practical difficulty for non-Aborigines of interpreting some recently published Aboriginal narratives, including Ruby Langford Ginibi's *Don't Take Your Love to Town*. 'A Word with the Natives: Dialogic Encounters in Journals of Australian Exploration' (*ANZSC* (1992) 8.71–84) by Simon Ryan is an imaginative theorized reading of explorers' accounts of the information they received, or failed to receive, from indigenes, finding that 'the journals themselves construct a quite different story ... of the complexities of cultural communication'.

Robert Zeller's 'News from Australia: Journalism, Fiction and Criminality in the Early Australian Novel' considers the hybrid 'non-fictional' forms of *Settlers and Convicts*, *Tales of the Colonies*, *Ralph Rashleigh* and *Quintus Servinton* and the ideologies they are subsumed under (*Antipodes* 7.51–8). Crime fiction from John Lang's *The Forger's Wife* (1855) to the present is the subject of Stephen Knight, 'The Vanishing Policeman: Patterns of Control in Australian Crime Fiction' (*AuS* 7.109–22), which seeks to distinguish Australian examples of the genre from English and American in terms of historical differences in attitude towards police; and in 'A Blood Spot on the Map' (*ACH* 12.145–59) he writes on 'place and displacement' in local crime fiction. Speculative fiction is surveyed in H. M. Doyle's 'Australian Literary Utopias – 1920–1950' (*AuFL* 8.69–76), which brings to light some forgotten titles, as do Robert Dixon and Gillian Whitlock in their contributions, respectively, to *Debutante Nation* and *The Time to Write*, 'The New Woman and the Coming Man: Gender and Genre in the "Lost-Race" Romance' and '1901/1933: From Eutopia to Dystopia'. Another genre is sweepingly entertained in Gerry Turcotte, 'Footnotes to an Australian Gothic Script' (*Antipodes* 7.127–34) which ranges suggestively over literature, architecture and design from the colonial period to the present.

Christopher Lee's 'The Australian Girl Catches the First Feminist Wave' (*Hecate* 19.i.124–33) on Catherine Martin and 'Women, Romance, and the Nation: The Reception of Catherine Martin's *An Australian Girl*' (*AuFS* 17.67–80) contributes to the feminist revisionist project of recuperating 'colonial romances' by women, which are assumed to have been suppressed in the interest of furthering a masculinist construction of the nation; however, this widespread assumption of a local patriarchal conspiracy against these authors leaves out of account the international swing in critical preferences against romance and towards realism in the later nineteenth century. Also anti-nationalist in its impetus is Adrian Mitchell's 'Edwardians and Others: A Forgotten Age in Australian Literary History' (*ANZSC* (1992) 7.1–9) which freshly and persuasively argues for recognition of the post-Federation era, in which nationalism was subsumed in 'the greater idea of God, King and Country', as equally and continuingly an influential part of the cultural past as the legendary 1890s and the *Bulletin*. The polemics of a later period are revisited by David Carter in 'Paris, Moscow, Melbourne: Some Avant-garde Australian Little Magazines, 1930–1934' (*ALS* 16.57–66). Analysing *Stream*, *Strife*, *Proletariat* and *Masses*, he argues that the Depression forced modernists and communists to find common cause. Post-Second World War proletarian writing is discussed by Ian Syson in '"The Problem Was Finding the Time": Working Class Women's Writing in Australasia' (*Hecate* 19.ii.65–84), which considers novels by Betty Collins and Jean Devanney in some detail and ranges more widely to suggest that, as well as 'a room of one's own', the experience of work is necessary for indigenous and immigrant writers, male as well as female. Syson also relates his personal encounters (as a PhD student) with conflicts between liberal humanist and poststructuralist academics in 'Approaches to Working Class Literature: Towards a Point of Departure' in *Overland* (133.62–73), and contributes 'Towards a Poetics of Working Class Writing' to *SoRA* (26.i.86–100).

Intersecting with this revival of interest in proletarian writing is Roslyn Pesman Cooper's survey 'Italian Immigrants in Australian Fiction 1900–1950' (*ALS* 16.67–78). The late D. R. Burns's '"Visionary Monsters" Versus "Contained Accounts": Self Contradiction in Australian Fiction Since 1960' (*Southerly* 53.ii.146–53) parades an impatience with 'Gallic Phallic' criticism and seeks to discover appropriately local terms for discussing uniquely Australian writing; hence 'visionary monsters' for works by White, Herbert and others who seek to reject suburban Australian experience, but are obliged to engage with it, and 'contained accounts' for those by Jessica Anderson, Drewe, Garner, Moorhouse and others who seek to embrace it but are aware of its limitations. Burns's tongue-in-cheek manner suggests that he is less intent on postulating a new theory himself as on setting a practical cat among the theoretical pigeons by reminding them that Australian fiction has a frame of specific social reference. Well informed theoretically, Colleen Keane in 'New Fictions, Old Fictions: Postmodernism and Gender in Some Recent Australian Fiction' (*Meanjin* 50.i.195–206) pulls no punches in distinguishing between cultural and textual radicalism, and in seeing postmodern fictions by David Brooks, Mark Henshaw, David Ireland and Gerard Windsor (she makes an exception of Rod Jones) as conservative in their representations of the female as Other. This is a sharply argued reminder that while feminist, like postcolonial, critics embrace poststructuralist theory when congenial, their concerns are ultimately with actuality rather than textuality.

Examples of the general articles which compare themes in Australian and Canadian writing are Thomas E. Tausky's 'Old Ghosts in New Countries: Memory and Renewal in Canadian and Australian Fiction of the Holocaust' (*Antipodes* 7.115–22) and Rachel Felday Brenner's 'Excavating the Self in Canadian & Australian Auto/fictional Writing' (*ANZSC* (1992) 7.63–79), both by Canadian critics. Other comparative essays, especially of Australian and New Zealand writers, will be noted in the sections on individual authors; but Lawrence Bourke's 'Maori and Aboriginal Literature in Australian and New Zealand Poetry Anthologies: Some Problems and Perspectives' (*NLitsR* 25.23–36) aptly makes the general point that 'Comparative literature in Australia and New Zealand begins at home', with awareness of indigenous traditions.

General articles on poetry range from the colonial period to the present, as does Horst Priessnitz's checklist 'Sonnet Sequences in Australia (1832–1990)' (*ALS* 16.218–28) which is usefully indexed by topic. Adrian Mitchell's 'Writing Up a Storm: Natural Strife and Charles Harpur' (*Southerly* 53.ii.90–113) traces the influence of Thompson's 'Summer' on Harpur's 'A Storm in the Mountains'; his wider point is that if colonial poetry is to be recuperated it needs to be read in its own terms, its conscious imitativeness recognized. Imitativeness is also the subject of Diane Fahey's 'Greek Mythology in Modern Australian Poetry' (*Southerly* 53.i.5–29) which ranges widely over the poetry of the past 40 years to argue that with multiculturalism, and the emergence of Australian poets like Dimitri Tsalamous, 'Europe' has now become a cultural source without its earlier associations with Eurocentric dominance. In 'After Poetry 16, a Quarterly Account of Recent Poetry' (*Overland* 130.61–6), Graham Rowlands begins promisingly by asking if critical theory leads to consideration of what actual poems are doing, but soon loses sight of this question in his discussion of a clutch of collections. In 'After Poetry 17' (*Overland* 131.42–8), Kevin Hart prefers to discuss theory, French philosophers of the 'unknown' he has been reading, than the collections nominally under review. Hart also contributes 'Open, Mixed and Moving: Recent Australian Poetry' to the Australian issue of *WLT* (67.iii.482–8), discussing Murray, Harwood, Dobson, Riddell, Forbes and Malouf. Fortunately, Adamson and Tranter, glaring omissions from Hart's list, are represented by poems elsewhere in the issue.

This issue of *WLT* also contains 'Developments in Recent Australian Drama' (489–93) by Peter Fitzpatrick and Helen Thomson. The dominant playwrights are acknowledged to be Williamson, Nowra and Sewell – each of whom has made unexpected moves recently – but the survey is more concerned to desiderate greater difference and diversity through more Aboriginal and migrant plays, and the note of regret that 'the feminist agenda' is still in Dorothy Hewett's hands is poignant. The situation of Aboriginal theatre and the theoretical issues it raises are outlined from a North American perspective in Kelly Rowett's 'Approaches to Aboriginal Drama' (*Antipodes* 7.27–32). In 'Melodrama, an Australian Pantomime, and the Construction of Colonial History' (*JAS* 38.51–61), Veronica Kelly argues for the study of the popular, 'consensual' form of pantomime in the reconstruction of past ideological contests over such terms as 'Australian', 'British' and 'colonial', and in 'Orientalism in Early Australian Theatre' (*NLitsR* 26.32–42) she extends her postcolonial interests to 'orientalist' spectacles like Oscar Asche's *Chu Chin Chow* and, consistently enough, discovers carnivalesque hybridity. In *Voices* (3.iii.21–37) Stephen Alomes's 'The Search for a National Theatre' surveys, and interrogates, various phases in the pursuit of this elusive notion and suggests that it has now been achieved in the work of a variety of theatre practitioners; and Katharine Brisbane's 'Investing in Authors: A History of Currency Press' (38–50) summarizes the development of this small independent family firm into the country's major theatrical publisher.

(b) Individual Authors: 1789–1920

Against the grain of sweeping theoretical revisionism observed above, some earlier writers, males among them, have been the subject of substantial scholarly attention. Russell McDougall's *Henry Kendall: The Muse of Australia* (1992) collects fugitive writings by this poet, together with both previously published and new studies of his life and work; and Michael Ackland's *Henry Kendall* in UQP's Australian Authors series makes a representative selection of the poetry, prose and correspondence readily available. Together, these collections invite a fuller appraisal of Kendall than that encouraged by his earlier and simplistic reputation as a proto-nationalist. Ackland's 'A Moral Code: Meditation and Action in the Verse of Adam Lindsay Gordon' (*Westerly* 38.ii.53–65) reconsiders this much-anthologized example of 'healthy action verse', finding in it a deep-seated cultural pessimism that pervades Gordon's oeuvre. Barbara Holloway's delightfully titled 'What Made the Sick Stockrider Sick? The Function of Horses and Fever in A. L. Gordon's "The Sick Stockrider"' (*Westerly* 38.i.35–42) ingeniously re-reads the poem as an assertion of British male domination. No such attempt at interpretative ingenuity marks Colin Roderick's *Banjo Paterson: Poet by Accident*, a biography of the most popular of the riding rhymers; in fact, there is little discussion of his verse at all. Although, at well under 300 pages, the mere shadow of Roderick's biography of Lawson, this displays the same Gradgrindian conception of the biographer's tasks: a zest for genealogy and the hope of finding there the determinants of the subject's personality, or fatal flaw, and a commitment to clearing away myths and misconceptions to get to the facts. For Roderick, the facts that Paterson came from a line of military men but suffered a deformity to his arm in infancy made him a poet by accident; and he sees Paterson's simple, 'pious' values (war and sport) as having been distorted by those who know only his most familiar ballads and want to enlist him into the nationalist camp. Richard Hall's introduction to his selection *Banjo Paterson: His Poetry and Prose* provides a well-researched biographical sketch. While the verse of 'poet militant' Bernard O'Dowd has most often been referred to derisively, John Docker's 'Politics and Poetics: Bernard O'Dowd's *Dawnward?* and Nineteenth-Century Chartist Poetry' (*Southerly* 53.ii.13–33) argues for its reappraisal within an international tradition, and the problematical genre, of radical verse. In its concern to return the texts to their appropriate political and literary contexts, Docker's fine essay, like Wilding's *The Radical Tradition*, represents a scholarly revisionism that is far removed from the current fashion for historically uninformed 'deconstructions' of writers associated with turn-of-the-century nationalism.

The special issue of *JNZL* (10 (1992)) on immigrant and emigrant writers contains 'David McKee Wright, Moarilander' (35–54) by Michael Sharkey, who is working on a biography of Wright, poet and *Bulletin* Red Page editor from during the Great War to 1926. Sharkey here details the years 1887–1910, which the youthful Wright spent in New Zealand writing and publishing prolifically. A substantial contribution to literary history is Jill Roe's *My Congenials: Miles Franklin and Friends in Letters*, two volumes selected from Franklin's voluminous correspondence with friends and literary colleagues. With the latter, Roe's selection deliberately complements Carole Ferrier's *As Good As a Yarn with You* (*YWES* 73.669–70) which contains the correspondence among Franklin, Prichard, Devanney and other left-wing women writers. While Roe's volumes lack the editorial apparatus of Ferrier's, each section is well introduced and the index is comprehensive. Articles of literary historical interest include: Margaret Bradstock's 'Mary Gaunt in China' (*Southerly* 53.iii.151–60), about the novelist and travel writer who was one of the first women admitted to the University of Melbourne – her novel *Kirkham's Find* is the subject of Dorothy Jones's essay 'Water, Gold and Honey' in *Debutante Nation* – and Gillian Whitlock's ' "A Most Improper Desire": Mary Gaunt's Journey to Jamaica' in *Kunapipi* (15.iii.86–95); Leigh Dale's 'Walter Murdoch: "A Humble Protest"?' (*ALS* 16.179–89) about the essayist and editor of the first *Oxford Book of Australian Verse*; and Lesley Heath's 'John Le Gay Brereton: The University, and Australian Literature' (*N&F* 31.3–7) about the Renaissance scholar, poet, and friend of many writers including Henry Lawson.

Among prose writers, Lawson continues to provide deconstructionists with their stereotype of nationalist and masculinist values. Phillip O'Neil's 'Aborigines and Women in Lawson's "The Bush Undertaker" '(ANZSC 8.59–70) is a Lacanian reading of this story which seizes on these absences 'to explore the repression of aborigines and women during the construction of what has been called a distinct Australian identity'. Christopher Lee's contribution to the ASAL forum on post-colonialism, 'The National Myth and the Stereotype: "The Bush

Undertaker" Goes to the Bhaba'(*ACS* 2.136–41), is equally unforgiving in its theoretical approach to what, after all, is a blackly humorous version of the magazine Christmas tale, and which can hardly, or convincingly, bear the burden of representation, and guilt, imposed on it. Henry Handel Richardson, on the other hand, is being recuperated through gendered readings: Hanne K. Bock's 'Her Own Room' in *The Time to Write*, Catherine Pratt's '"What Had She to Do with Angles?" Gender and Narrative in *The Fortunes of Richard Mahony*' (*ALS* 16.152–60), Delys Bird's 'Woman-as-Artist/Woman-as-Mother: Traversing the Dichotomies' (ANZSC (1992) 7.10–19), and Mandy Dyson's '"Those Marvellous Perhapses" [*sic*]: Form and the Feminine in *The Getting of Wisdom*' (*LiNQ* 20.ii.83–8).

(c) Individual Authors: Post-1920

The modern writer who has attracted by far the most scholarly and critical attention this year is Christina Stead. Justifiably, Hazel Rowley's *Christina Stead: A Biography* has been compared with David Marr's *Patrick White*, both for the magnitude of her subject and her achievement in combining thorough research with narrative skill. Rowley integrates masses of personal, professional and political detail into her well-unified account of Stead's long life in many countries, and uses the fiction as biographical evidence with critical tact. Very much a *literary* biography, it is full of such details as Stead's reading and its influences upon her, the real-life models for her characters and her theories about fiction, her working methods and relationships with publishers, as well as her critical reception. Destined to be a cornerstone for the rapidly expanding field of Stead studies, *Christina Stead* is also a major contribution to the similarly widening field of Australian literary biography. (In this connection, mention should also be made of *Noel Counihan: Artist and Revolutionary* by the pre-eminent art historian Bernard Smith. While this is not the biography of a writer, it contains much information on the ideological disputes that affected many artists of all kinds, particularly because of Counihan's life-long but troubled friendship with novelist Judah Waten.)

Southerly 53.iv. contains eight articles on Stead, some given as papers at a conference on her work. Margaret Harris's 'A Note on Christina Stead in 1993' (161–5) outlines the effect that new reading interests in gender and feminism have had on Stead studies. While undeniably stimulating, these interests prove to be problematical for a number of the contributors. Kate Lilley's 'The New Curiosity Shop: Marketing Genre and Feminity in Stead's *Miss Herbert (The Suburban Wife)*' (5–12) finds 'anti-feminist and homophobic ethics' pervading this novel. Virginia Blain in '*A Little Tea and Little Chat*: Decadent Pleasures and the Pleasures of Decadence' (20–35) argues, à la Barthes, that we might be guilty of reading Stead too solemnly, as either a naturalist or a moral satirist, and refusing to acknowledge the 'more devious (and deviant) pleasures' she offers. Susan Sheridan's 'Re-Reading Christina Stead' (42–6) pursues a similar concern by considering the difficulty of establishing the 'critical distance' in Stead's writing. Not unrelated in its stylistic interests is Wendy Woodward's 'Concealed Invitations: The Use of Metaphor in Some of Christina Stead's Novels'(80–95). This breaks new ground by arguing not only that Stead conveys the sexuality of her female characters through the metaphoric rather than the metonymic mode but also, against the author's explicit denials, that 'those metaphors which are metaphysical suggest an unconscious desire for a realm of transcendence or a place elsewhere'.

In comparison with Stead, Patrick White – for many years the writer most discussed, nationally and internationally – has attracted little attention in the journals. Perhaps with this in mind, Robert Ross's 'Patrick White and Multitextuality', in the first issue of the *Journal of Commonwealth and Postcolonial Studies* (1.i.70–2) outlines aspects of this writer's fiction that answer to current theoretical interests. J. A. Wainwright's '"The Real Voss as Opposed to the Actual Leichhardt": Biography, Art, and Patrick White' (*Antipodes* 7.139–41) seems unhappy about David Marr's references to White's characters in his biography, although I did not find it clear why. Joan L. Dolphin's 'The Rhetoric of Painting in Patrick White's Novels' (*Ariel* 24.iii.33–51) demonstrates that there is still much to be considered in this writer's work. While White's colour symbolism and artist-characters have been discussed frequently, and separately, this article is original in bringing them together, and illuminating in showing how colour, texture and light are used to create an appropriately 'painterly' linguistic medium. Although articles on White may be fewer, Mark Williams's volume on this author in Macmillan's Modern Novelists series is an excellent example of how, *pace* Susan Lever, a study addressed to 'the general reader' can also offer fresh insights and perspectives to 'specialists', who should find his comparisons of White with Malcolm Lowry and Janet Frame, and his contrasting of them to their contemporaries among English novelists, an enlightening application of a postcolonial perspective.

The publication in 1983 of a 'restored' version of Barnard Eldershaw's *Tomorrow and Tomorrow and Tomorrow* was hailed as a major step in the reconstitution of a 'repressed' tradition of writing by women. In a fascinating amalgam of scholarly and theoretical enquiry, 'The Texts of *Tomorrow and Tomorrow and Tomorrow*: Author, Agent, History' (*SoRA* 26.ii.239–61), Ian Saunders argues that the text has not been restored at all, that it was never officially censored to the extent claimed, and that its 'authenticity' – a concept with which the novel itself engages – remains problematical.

In *A Gallop of Fire: Katherine Susannah Prichard: On Guard for Humanity: A Study of Creative Personality*, Jack Beasley seeks to rescue his subject from the misappropriations of contemporary feminist revisionists and reassert her preeminence in the 'militant democratic' realist tradition that he claimed for her in his *Rage for Life* (1965), but essentially this adds little that is new to that earlier study. Sandra Burchill's essay 'Katharine Susannah Prichard: "She Did What She Could"' in *The Time to Write* (edited by Ferres) provides a succinct account of Prichard's political involvements, including feminism, and their relationships to her writing.

On its appearance, Mary Lord's 'sensational' revelations that Hal Porter was not only a paedophile but had seduced her son, in her *Hal Porter: Man of Many Parts*, distracted attention from its merits as both the first biography of a writer once held by many to be superior to Patrick White and as a formally original contribution to the growing field of literary biography. Beginning with 'A Declaration of Bias', Lord blends personal reminiscence with her account of the numerous roles Porter played. While, engagingly but at times repetitiously, she departs from conventional 'impersonal' or 'objective' chronological presentation, she provides much hitherto unknown information on Porter's long career. (Not seen is Joan Newman, 'Hal Porter's Australian Autobiography: *The Watcher on the Cast-Iron Balcony*', *Auto-Biography Studies* (8.i.91–101).)

Valuable biographical information is also provided by Anita Segerberg in 'Strangled by a Bad Tradition? The Work of Eve Langley' (*JNZL* (1992) 10.55–73). Australian-born Langley lived from 1932–60 in New Zealand but her name has all but disappeared from recent accounts of that country's literature. While Segerberg sees Langley as having been marginalized as a woman writer she also makes the same point as other contributors to this special issue of the journal: that the construction of a national tradition worked against those writers not native-born. In 'Body in the Vault' (*ALS* 16.50–6), Lucy Frost writes on Langley's unpublished novels. Julie Lewis's 'The Modernist Impulse: Peter Cowan's Early Fiction' (*Overland* 131.58–64) uses biographical information to situate her subject informatively into the literary context of the 1930s and 1940s. Also of biographical and cultural historical interest is Nancy Tischler's 'Bruce Sutherland and Images of Australia' (*Antipodes* 7.135–8), an account of the first professor of Australian Literature anywhere, who introduced the subject in 1942 – at Penn State!

For poetry, 1993 was Ern Malley's year. In *The Ern Malley Affair* Michael Heyward presents the definitive critical biography of the poet who never existed, except textually, but who took on a life of his own internationally. The story of how James McAuley and Harold Stewart perpetrated what is widely regarded as the literary hoax of the century has often been told, more cursorily than tendentiously – and Ern's *The Darkening Ecliptic* (1944), which has been in print continuously over the past 30 years, was reissued this year with a new introduction by Albert Tucker, under the imposing title *Collected Verse*. As well as being entertaining, Heyward's account is a fine literary historical discussion of 'the definitive moment in Australian modernism' and of 'the only genuinely avant-garde writer in a country which has never sponsored a literary revolution'. His analyses of the parodies, which in so many ways exceeded the perpetrators' intentions, make this also an engaging critical study. Of related interest are D. C. McLaughlin's 'McAuley in Malley's "Dürer: Innsbruck, 1495"' (*Westerly* 38.i.59–62), and surrealist painter James Gleeson's *Selected Poems*. The latter, written between 1938 and 1943, and first published in *Angry Penguins* and other avant-garde magazines of that time, would presumably be among the models Ern studied.

Sir Herbert Read played a part in promoting the reputations of both Ern Malley and Francis Webb. James Paull's 'The Thematic of History in Francis Webb's Poetry' (*NLitsR* 26.58–67), noting that the high claims made for Webb's poetry have not been grounded in any detailed consideration of its 'textual operations', brings post-colonial consciousness to bear illuminatingly on the explorer poems; and in *Southerly* (53.iii.54–62) Patricia Excell publishes and comments on a 'lost' poem by Webb, 'Before Two Girls'. Max Richards's 'William Hart Smith (1911–1990): Poet of Two Countries' (*JNZL* 10.74–91) argues that, by virtue of the poems written out of his experience of a number of long periods in New Zealand, Hart Smith was as much a poet of that country as of Australia; and, with his sympathy for the Aborigines and the Maoris, a Jindyworobak of both countries. A superior example of what comparative readings can contribute to awareness, this article valuably situates the long-derided Jindyworobak movement within the international context of poetry at that time. In his well-researched 'Making the Crossing: Douglas Stewart the Expatriate Patriot' (*Southerly* 53.ii.40–53) Lawrence Bourke adds to awareness of the complexities in the relationships between New Zealand and Australian writing by arguing that Stewart, having been excluded by modernists in New Zealand, reacted by cultivating Australian 'nationalism' when he became literary editor of the *Bulletin*.

The contemporary writer to have attracted most critical interest is Mudrooroo (formerly Colin Johnson, then Mudrooroo Narogin), who this year published a novel, *The Kwinkan*, and contributions to *The Mudrooroo/Müller Project* (to be noted below with drama). Adam Shoemaker's *Mudrooroo: A Critical Study* is the first monograph on his work. It provides an up-to-date and enthusiastic survey which sees Mudrooroo as a playful 'confidence trickster'; generous quotation from his writings enables the reader to ponder the subtleties Shoemaker finds in them. Shoemaker has an interview with Mudrooroo in *Island*, 'It's the Quest which Matters' (55.38–44) and this issue also contains Helen Daniel's 'Mudrooroo's Shadow Boxing' (44–7), a thoughtful overview which sees each new work by this author as 'at once self-contained and yet collaborating with an earlier work, at once intent on new purposes and contesting old ones'. Margery Fee, in 'The Signifying Writer and the Ghost Reader: Mudrooroo's *Master of the Ghost Dreaming* and *Writing From the Fringe*' (*ANZSC* (1992) 8.18–32) engages with the issue of Aboriginality, as addressed in Mudrooroo's theoretical text *Writing From the Fringe* (1990) – which seems to posit an essential Aboriginal identity – but her consideration of the novel argues that instead it enacts 'an active process of transformation, resistance and renewal'. In Janine Little's 'A Conversation with Mudrooroo' (*Hecate* 19.i.143–54), Mudrooroo discusses more generally the effects of publication on black writing as well as his own work. *Westerly* (38.iii.71–8) contains Jodie Brown's comparative study 'Mudrooroo's *Doctor Whooreddy's Prescription for Enduring the End of the World* and Robert Drewe's *The Savage Crows*'.

The most popular of Aboriginal poets was Oodgeroo, who first published as Kath Walker, and Geoff Page's commemorative note, 'The Poetry of Oodgeroo' (*Island* 57.4–5), suggests that, while poetry and politics were indivisible for her and her black audience, her verse contains sufficient complexity to continue to appeal to a wider audience. In *ALS*, Tim Rowse discusses 'The Aboriginal Subject in Autobiography: Ruby Langford's *Don't Take Your Love to Town*' (16.14–28), and Janine Little the short stories of Archie Weller in '"Deadly" Work' (16.190–9).

Like Mark Williams's *Patrick White*, two new titles in OUPAus's Australian Writers series demonstrate how theoretical sophistication need not be at the expense of clarity. Ivor Indyk's *David Malouf* elegantly combines an interest in the 'gendering' of this writer's work – poetry and writing for the stage as well as fiction – with close stylistic discussion. The theme of masculine, specifically homosexual, desire is discussed in relation to Malouf's employment of pastoral and epic modes, his being seen as more successful with the former. (Unseen is Marianthe Colakis, 'David Malouf's and Derek Mahon's Visions of Ovid in Exile', *CML* (13.iii.229–39)). Imre Salusinszky's *Gerald Murnane* sees this writer's fiction as paralleling, chronologically but independently, the concerns of Derridean deconstruction – and manages to argue this with 'the general reader', or at least with the reader of Murnane's fiction but not philosophy, in mind. Salusinszky's comprehensive *Gerald Murnane: An Annotated Bibliography* is a model of its kind, even reprinting Murnane's few published verses.

In *Helplessly Tangled in Female Arms and Legs: Elizabeth Jolley's Fiction* in UQP's Studies in Australian Literature, Paul Salzman explicitly sets out to avoid presenting the work of this popular, playful, but enigmatic writer as either a 'disruptive postmodernist' or a 'life-enhancing creator of characters in search of selves' – the polarizing tendencies which have attended the reception of her work. Eschewing such 'monological criticism', he considers Jolley's representation of Women (finding she depicts women instead); the themes of migration, home and exile; her narrative procedures; the role of memory; and 'Inside/Outside Families'. Salzman provides, if not a clearly synthesised argument, a useful critique of Jolley's reception; and his discussion of her use of memory as a structural device throughout her oeuvre is insightful (if open to the charge of being unfashionably traditional). By comparison, articles on Jolley suggest that the interpretative difficulties her texts pose are best avoided by writing about something else. In their outstandingly titled 'Aristophanic Love-Dyads: Community, Communion, and Cherishing in Elizabeth Jolley's Fiction', Barbara Milech and Brian Dibble (*Antipodes* 7.3–10) employ the 'borderline-narcissist' syndrome to categorize Jolley's characters and their concerns with love; and in the same issue Shirley Paolini's 'Narrative Strategies in Elizabeth Jolley's *The Well* and African Folktales'(11–13) draws attention to the unilluminating coincidence that both Jolley's novel and the oral tales have open endings.

Like Salzman with Jolley, Ken Gelder engages with a challenging subject in his *Atomic Fiction: The Novels of David Ireland*, also in UQP's Studies in Australian Literature series. His title and introduction emphasize the structure of Ireland's fiction: 'a myriad of "situations" (or they might be called events, or moments) are [*sic*] triggered off and channelled through a constellation of characters, to produce a narrative that at one level ... is irreducible' – which might suggest a Sisyphean endeavour. Perhaps, though, this is the model for his own critical practice: with the assistance of moments from Marx, Nietzsche and Freud, Foucault, Kristeva, Deleuze and Guattari he manages to reach a conclusion which perceives an irreducible standoff between optimistic humanism and a pessimistic anti-humanism throughout Ireland's work.

Edited by Richard Rossiter and Lyn Jacobs, *Reading Tim Winton* is the first monograph devoted to this writer. It appears in a series sponsored by the Association for the Study of Australian Literature and intended for students. As such it provides a range of useful introductory articles, a bibliography, and study questions. Rossiter criticizes Winton's books for children in 'Speaking to Adults, Speaking to Children: Tim Winton's *Cloudstreet* and *Lockie Leonard, Human Torpedo*' (*Southerly* 53.iii.92–9). In 'Thea Astley's Long Struggle with the Language of Fiction' (*WLT* 67.iii.505–9), Robert L. Ross engagingly seeks to win Astley a wider audience by stressing her quirky individuality (an individuality which he sees as of a recognizably Australian kind) and her humour and seriousness. Elizabeth Perkins's 'Hacking at Tropical Undergrowth: Exploration in Thea Astley's North Queensland', primarily a discussion of *Vanishing Points*, appears in the special issue of *Outrider* (10.i–ii.377–86), which has been issued as a book, *Queensland: Words and All*.

In *WLT* 67.iii, Paul Kane writes on 'Postcolonial/Postmodern: Australian Literature and Peter Carey' (519–22); and in *ALS* 16 Graeme Turner's 'Nationalising the Author: The Celebrity of Peter Carey' (131–9), considers the role of the media in constructing this writer's local reputation. In 'Koka-Kola Kulture' (*Southwest Review* 78.ii.231–44), Don Graham offers US readers some observations on the Americanization of Australian culture, particularly literary culture, and elaborates its effects on the fiction of Frank Moorhouse and Michael Wilding.

A writer referred to with increasing frequency in general discussions is Kate Grenville, who receives detailed attention in Wendy Goulson's 'Herstory's Re/vision of History: Women's Narrative Subverts History in Kate Grenville's *Joan Makes History*' (*ANZSC* (1992) 7.20–7), and in Susan Midalia's 'Re-writing Woman: Genre Politics and Female Identity in Kate Grenville's *Dreamhouse*' (*ALS* 16.30–7). While Grenville's novels overdetermine feminist readings, those of the prolific, entertaining but quirkily individual David Foster are difficult to fit so neatly under any contemporary critical template: in 'Boundary Crossing: The Novels of David Foster' (*ALS* 16.38–49), Narelle Shaw provides a thoughtful overview of his fiction which sees the recurring trope of the Fall as the key to its structure, concerns and comic mode. *Overland* 133 focuses on science fiction, and Judith Raphael Buckrich writes on 'George Turner – One of Australia's Best Kept Secrets'(24–30), providing what she calls 'a little potted history' of this internationally published and recognized writer, who is little known in Australia, except for his winning the Miles Franklin prize in 1962.

More than usual interest in an edition of recent verse has been taken in John Tranter's *Martin Johnston: Selected Poems and Prose*. As a poet, Johnston (1947–90) had been associated with the 'generation of '68'; the appearance of this selection of his varied writings in the 'multicultural' 1990s invites some adjustment to perceptions of that earlier period. Educated partly in Greece (as son of the writers George Johnston and Charmian Clift), and a translator of Greek poets, the erudite and witty Johnston displays a far wider range of interests and influences than the American ones usually attributed to his generation of 'new' poets. Tranter deserves to be complimented for his imaginativeness and editorial expertise in making available this selection from Johnston's scattered publications and manuscripts; it is one of the year's more significant contributions to scholarship. The editor is himself the subject of one of the year's most illuminating critical essays: Alan Urqhart's 'Hacking at the Pattern: Post-Romantic Consciousness in the Poetry of John Tranter' (*Southerly* 53.iii.12–29). While Tranter's verse has been highly acclaimed, and a shift towards greater accessibility observed in his recent collections, there has been little critical engagement with it, merely vaguely explanatory gesturings towards 'postmodernism' and 'post-structuralism'. Urqhart's philosophical disposition enables him to distinguish insightfully between Tranter's postmodern manner and his ironic distance from poststructuralist negativity. He sees the poetry as filled with desire for what the poet knows cannot be – 'romantic gush', grand narratives, wholeness – yet which, like an unrequited lover, he is doomed to pursue.

Jenny Digby in 'Representations of Female Identity in the Poetry of Dorothy Hewett' (*Southerly* 53.ii.167–89), is also illuminating in her application of feminist theories of autobiography to argue that Hewett's derogated 'confessional' themes are critical engagements with social constructs of the female. Lawrence Bourke's 'A Place in History: *The Ash Range*, Landscape and Identity' (*Westerly* 38.i.17–24) emphasizes the (undeniable) regional rather than national character of Duggan's 'epic', and claims therefore that it is a departure from the tradition of perceiving national identity through landscape – a conclusion which presupposes that the possibility of there being regional traditions had never previously been entertained.

The Mudrooroo/Müller Project: A Theatrical Casebook edited by Gerhard Fischer in collaboration with Paul Behrendt and Brian Syron contains the text of Heiner Müller's play *The Commission – Memory of a Revolution* and

Mudrooroo's rehearsal play *The Aboriginal Protesters Confront the Declaration of the Australian Republic on 26 January 2001 with the Production of 'The Commission' by Heiner Müller*, which 'hijacks' Müller's text. This, together with an account of its workshopping, provides a valuable case study of Aboriginal drama. The only book on a contemporary playwright this year is a collection of articles on *John Romeril* edited by Gareth Griffiths for Rodopi's Australian Playwright's series. This has a high proportion of contributions specially commissioned from the playwright's collaborators because, while Romeril has been a prominent figure in theatre since the 'New Wave' of the late 1960s, the performance-oriented nature of much of his work has not encouraged much critical discussion of his texts. The result is very much a miscellany but one with historical and bibliographical value for scholars. In the journals, articles on particular plays and playwrights are sparse, perhaps because of a perceived need to 'theorize' drama studies. Alma De Groen has attracted most attention, especially for her *The Rivers of China*, the play discussed by Helen Gilbert in 'The Catherine Wheel: Travel, Exile and the (Post) Colonial Woman' (*Southerly* 52.ii.58–77), and by Jeni-Rose Hall in 'Language as an Instrument of Transformation in De Groen's *The Rivers of China*' (*LiNQ* 20.i.26–35); Carolyn Pickett writes on 'Reality, Realism and a Place to Write in Alma De Groen's *Vocations*' (*ADS* 22.63–72). A welcome awareness of the need to discuss playscripts in terms of their theatricality as well as their (theorized) themes is shown by Paul Makeham in 'Framing the Landscape: Prichard's *Pioneers* and Esson's *The Drovers*' (*ADS* 23.121–34); while he is alert to the thematic, or ideological, implications of these plays' settings, he takes the appropriate further step of considering how these would be realized on stage.

Despite the pessimistic surveys quoted by way of introduction, much thoughtful criticism and valuable scholarship (sometimes the two together) appeared during this year in both books and journals. 'Theory', of various kinds, stimulated much of the best, if also – as could only be expected, given its pervasiveness – some of the worst. Feminist, multicultural, and postcolonial interests (which share a post-structuralist awareness) have so recontextualized Australian literary studies that they now constitute the dominant discourse, not, as some of their proponents still imply, a set of Anglo-Celtic patriarchal assumptions overdue for deconstruction. Beneath such revisionist rhetoric, substantial investigation and reappraisal continues to take place across the span of Australian writing from the early colonial period to the present, especially with fiction and poetry.

3. Canada

(a) General

The recent proliferation of literary theories has spawned several useful reference works which include commentary on Canadian criticism. *The Johns Hopkins Guide to Literary Theory and Criticism*, edited by Michael Groeden and Martin Kreiswirth, contains essays on leading figures and concepts, generous in length and allowing for a good overview of contexts, complexities, and problems, as well as a bibliography. The Canadianist will find entries on Canadian theory and criticism useful, as well as articles on Northrop Frye and Marshall McLuhan. In its determined effort to move away from Eurocentric theory the volume also discusses theory from Africa, Australia, the Caribbean, China, India, Japan and elsewhere. *The Encyclopedia of Contemporary Literary Theory: Approaches, Scholars, Terms*, edited by Irena R. Makaryk, also features material relevant to Canadian Studies. Apart from the obligatory entries on Frye and McLuhan, the essays on post-colonial theory, feminist criticism and ideological criticism are noteworthy. Alvin A. Lee's entry on Frye does not, however, discuss the scholar's impact on Canadian criticism and literary history. Two essays published elsewhere fill at least part of the gap by looking at Frye's 'Conclusion to the Literary History of Canada'. In '"A Quest for a Peaceable Kingdom": The Narrative in Northrop Frye's Conclusion to the Literary History of Canada' (*PMLA* 108.283–93), Robert Lecker analyses Frye's famous (and controversial) essay as a rewriting of the romantic quest, arguing that instead of compulsively leading to thematic criticism, Frye's narrative creates an 'idea of Canada, a metaphoric conception that is transhistorical, autonomous, and distinctly literary before it is cultural'. While Lecker's essay is little concerned with the historical circumstances that produced Carl Klinck's *Literary History of Canada*, and Frye's role in it, Sandra Djwa's contribution to a special edition of *English Studies in Canada* devoted to Frye (*ESC* 19.ii.133–49) provides a great deal of detail, situating the project in Canadian criticism in general and Frye's oeuvre in particular. Drawing on archival materials, Djwa documents the ideological and practical implications of charting a literature as well as outlining Frye's considerable influence on all aspects of the project.

In general, Canadian criticism in all its manifestations appears to have become a subject of investigation. Frank Davey's 'English–Canadian Literature Periodicals: Text, Personality and Dissent' (*OL* 8.5–6.67–78) is somewhat marred by a subtext of professional rivalries, whereas Margery Fee provides a virtuoso overview over institutional developments and academic tropes in 'Canadian Literature and English Studies in the Canadian University' (*ECW* 48.20–40). Like Djwa, Fee draws on extensive historical and archival documentation to correct several myths about the teaching of Canadian literature, arguing that it was neither as neglected prior to the 1960s nor as emphasized from then on as is commonly believed. Fee's essay provides an important addition to Paul Litt's excellent *The Muses, the Masses, and the Massey Commission*, which reads like a sequel to Maria Tippett's earlier *Making Culture: English–Canadian Institutions and the Arts Before the Massey Commission*. Litt analyses Massey's Arnoldian aspirations in wanting to uphold high culture against the onslaught of American popular culture, and he is very good at describing the interpersonal dynamics among the members of the commission who shaped this influential report.

Neither *The Johns Hopkins Guide to Literary Theory and Criticism* nor *The Encyclopedia of Contemporary Literary Theory: Approaches, Scholars, Terms* devotes a special entry to the Toronto critic Linda Hutcheon. Given the number of her publications and her considerable influence on the study of postmodernism in general and of historiographic metafiction, this is a serious omission. Instead, a small critical cottage industry has sprung up around her. Colleagues and graduate students alike hasten to publish articles and reviews pointing out the error of her ways and committing not dissimilar ones in the process. The most polemical of these recent attacks, which generally focus on Hutcheon's allegedly apolitical analysis of postmodernism, is Diana Brydon and Janice Kulyk Keefer's joint review of Hutcheon's 1991 *Splitting Images: Contemporary Canadian*

Ironies (ECW 48.41–7). Without acknowledging that this is surely true of any coherent critical approach, Brydon and Keefer assert that 'Hutcheon and the students whom she forms may inadvertently create countercanons that prove as restrictive and tendentious as the traditional CanLit canon', while David Leahy's analysis of Hutcheon's readings of Cohen and Aquin (SCL 18.ii.27–42) deploys a sophisticated critical apparatus to formulate a criticism which could have been more briefly stated, namely that Hutcheon's linkage of metafictional strategies with political activism, although now expressed with less certainty than at the beginning of her career, remains idealistic.

Warren Tallman's *In the Midst: Writings 1962–1992* makes for an eccentric but inspiring 'Notes From the Underground'. Among the less original inclusions are Tallman's generous but somewhat repetitive endorsements of the poets originally associated with *TISH*, the legendary early 1960s poetry magazine published in Vancouver; on these occasions the book becomes something of an indulgent family album, an impression supported by the many casual photographs scattered throughout the book. However, the book also contains some of the most scathing indictments of Canadian nationalism in existence, largely in response to Robin Matthews's continued feud against the *TISH* poets as purveyors of 'American imperialism'. There is also a delirious 'Treatise on Alcohol' which provides a delicious antidote to the measured prose of a George Woodcock. The 1960s Vancouver scene and other locales associated with the Canadian avant-garde are evoked in Eva-Marie Kröller's *George Bowering: Bright Circles of Colour*, which traces the writer's career through its various stages on the west coast, in Calgary, London and Montreal, and the artistic communities he encountered there. Focusing on the interrelations of literature and the arts in Bowering's oeuvre, the book offers an interdisciplinary discussion of a seminal period in Canadian contemporary culture. Tom Marshall's *Multiple Exposures, Promised Lands: Essays on Canadian Poetry and Fiction* stitches together occasional pieces on Klein, Pratt, Layton, Purdy, Cohen, Leacock, Callaghan, Richler and others published over a period of 20 years or so. For sustained analyses of these authors readers will, however, have to go elsewhere. This is a pity, for sometimes Marshall covers material well worth the effort, such as Layton's response to Elspeth Cameron's controversial biography of him.

Caroline Bayard attempts a broader historical perspective in *100 Years of Critical Solitudes: Canadian and Québécois Criticism from the 1880s to the 1980s*, a collection of essays pairing off the insights of Anglo-Canadian and Québécois critics on such topics as historical, formalist, thematic, and feminist criticism. Some of the material discussed has been well rehearsed elsewhere, but a collection giving equal weight to francophone critics and their anglophone colleagues is so rare that any effort in this area will be welcome. Another enterprise which includes work on both languages is *Challenges, Projects, Texts: Canadian Editing*, edited by John Lennox and Janet M. Paterson. The collection, based on a 1989 conference at the University of Toronto, and meticulously edited as befits its subject, contains essays on editorial problems posed by the works of writers such as Aquin, Lowry, Klein and McCulloch. A discussion of editorial complexities also prefaces *Letters of Love and Duty*, edited by Carl Ballstadt, Elizabeth Hopkins and Michael Peterman, a collection of the correspondence of Susanna and John Moodie, which will be welcome news to anyone interested in this intriguing pair.

The unfortunate title of *A Few Acres of Snow: Literary and Artistic Images of*

Canada, edited by Paul Simpson-Housley and Glen Norcliffe, does not reflect the specific focus of the book or give an indication of the broad spectrum of its offerings. The volume explores the relevance of geography to literature, emphasizing the 'humanistic approach to geography [which] argues that art and literature, among other forms of cultural expression, may foster a more acute sense of place and region than conventional description'. Based on a 1987 conference, these essays cover both well-travelled and less-visited ground: in addition to comments on *Anne of Green Gables* and the tourism generated by it, on the tension between urban and pastoral landscapes in Gabrielle Roy's oeuvre, F. P. Grove's prairie landscapes and Malcolm Lowry's British Columbia, there is also work on Japanese–Canadian poetry, on Elizabeth Bishop's Nova Scotian roots, and a comparative analysis of Swedish and Canadian Maritime landscapes. Using an interdisciplinary perspective, the book will be of great interest to instructors of, and scholars in, Canadian Studies. L. M. Montgomery continues to attract attention that goes well beyond analysing the regionalist charm of *Anne of Green Gables*. A recent addition to the ever-growing list of books on the author is Elizabeth Rollins Epperley's *The Fragrance of Sweet-grass: L. M. Montgomery's Heroines and the Pursuit of Romance*.

W. F. Keith's *Literary Images of Ontario* is part of the Ontario Historical Studies series, a 31-volume project 'covering many aspects of the life and work of [Ontario] from its foundation in 1791 to our own time'. The book presents an overview of representations of the Province, ranging from explorers' narratives to contemporary literature. While the book is useful to the uninitiated reader seeking such an overview, the specialist will be troubled by the absence of definition (Keith's approach to regionalism is never adequately explained) and a casual, even journalistic, approach to literary analysis. The coverage tends strongly towards the Anglo-Saxon component of Ontario, while the ethnic communities are introduced as something of an afterthought, filling in, as do F. G. Paci's novels, 'a bothersome gap'. Ondaatje's *In the Skin of a Lion* warrants one brief sentence. *Vancouver and Its Regions*, a collection edited by UBC geographers Graeme Wynn and Timothy Oke, dwells on the city's geographical location and the qualities generated by it, but the book will still be useful to a literary critic not only in order to verify local references with which she may be unfamiliar, but also to appreciate the often inspiring cross-fertilization of geography and literature, a relationship which becomes especially apparent in Derek Gregory's delightful 'epilogue'. A very important collection is *Vancouver Anthology: The Institutional Politics of Art*, edited by Stan Douglas, which, in addition to covering various aspects of Vancouver avant-garde culture, includes Marcia Crosby's 'Construction of the Imaginary Indian'. The essay, which is on its way to becoming one of the most frequently cited pieces of criticism in Canadian Native Studies, presents a critique of George Bowering's novel *Burning Water* from a Native perspective. A somewhat more casual work is *Vancouver Forum 1: Old Powers–New Forces*, edited by Max Wyman. Several of the contributors tend towards the journalistic, but lawyer and novelist Leslie Hall Pinder's piece on Native land claims is well worth reading. The questions of region and of cultural barriers inform *Silence Made Visible: Howard O'Hagan and Tay John*, edited by Margery Fee, which assembles a great deal of useful information on a much neglected writer, including an interview with the writer, a detailed bibliography, previously unpublished materials from the Howard O'Hagan papers at the University of Victoria, and several good articles. Particularly noteworthy is Fee's investigation into the processes of literary canonization, in a piece comparing O'Hagan's reputation with that of Malcolm Lowry.

Multiculturalism and ethnicity continue to be among the most controversial issues in Canadian literature: the jurors of the newly created Giller Prize belligerently announced that they were not prepared to make 'political correctness', including ethnic affiliation, one of their criteria (implying that the venerable Governor General's Award had long been hampered by such considerations), only to be accused, in their turn, of falling into the same trap when the Giller finalists included two non-white authors. Over the past few years, the Writer's Union of Canada has been rocked by racial dissent, culminating in its 1994 'Writing Thru Race' conference, at which white participants were excluded from some of the sessions. Myrna Kostash, president of the Writer's Union of Canada through much of its most embattled time, has written *Bloodlines: A Journey into Eastern Europe*, a memoir of her travels throughout the 1980s in Eastern-bloc countries, including her ancestral Ukraine. Not a piece of literary criticism, the book still reads as a poignant commentary on, and allegory of, the Canadian situation. Its formal sophistication places it well ahead of Eva Hoffman's *Exit into History* which deals with a similar subject matter. Some of the most intense debates over Canadian multiculturalism have been documented in alternative publications such as *Borderlands*, *This Magazine* and *FUSE*, all of which often respond more quickly and more polemically to controversial topics than do mainstream publications. The coverage in *FUSE* of the debates surrounding the Royal Ontario Museum's exhibit, 'Into the Heart of Africa', comes to mind, as do its articles on the controversial stagings of *Show Boat* and *Miss Saigon* in Toronto.

Virtually all of the essays in *Double-Talking: Essays on Verbal and Visual Ironies in Contemporary Canadian Art and Literature*, edited by Linda Hutcheon, are concerned with traditionally marginalized aspects of Canadian culture. Arun Mukherjee deals with 'Ironies of Colour in the Great White North: The Discursive Strategies of Some Hyphenated Canadians', drawing out revisions, from a Native and other perspectives, of presumably pan-Canadian symbols such as Canada Day and the national anthem, but she generalizes when she avers that 'we do not hear white Canadian literary theorists or artists quoting Derek Walcott or Franz Fanon, C. L. R. James or Aimé Césaire'. Similarly, Marina Jones is not quite accurate in classifying Expo's 'Indians of Canada Pavilion' as 'a pat symbolic gesture', as the pavilion was in fact a native-run and highly complex construct ironizing several of the other pavilions surrounding it, but her work on 'found poems' is still original and thought-provoking. Probably the most important recent book on racism in Canada is M. Nourbese Philips's *Frontiers: Essays and Writings on Racism and Culture 1984–1992*. The book is particularly valuable for its response to the controversy surrounding the 'Into the Heart of Africa' exhibition, and for its detailed documentation of the incidents at the 1990 P.E.N. conference in Toronto, when Nourbese Philips and others accused organizers of failing to encourage adequate ethnic representation. The book contains the author's views on writers such as Alice Walker and Neil Bisoondath, both of whom Nourbese Philips considers insufficiently committed to the cause of people of colour. Julia V. Emberley's *Thresholds of Difference: Feminist Critique, Native Women's Writings, Postcolonial Theory* is an important but also problematic book which, despite the author's protestations to the contrary, may well confirm some of Mukherjee's suspicions about the preponderance of European theory in postcolonial criticism. Following the postmodern assumption that the critic may be both deconstructor of, and accomplice in, the patriarchal/hegemonic/etc. system, Emberley characterizes her procedure as 'blithely following the lines of expectations, occasionally fighting for a leading role as a rebellious feminist with a strong, however undirected, desire to threaten the master narrative of the bourgeois colonial woman', before subjecting her material to an investigation which at times almost parodically imitates the master narrative not only of the bourgeois colonial woman but the much maligned patriarchal academy as well: the book is written in highly abstract, sometimes impenetrable prose, and the cross-fertilization of various discourses announced in the introduction never quite happens. The short section on Beatrice Culleton's *In Search of April Raintree*, for instance, bristles with references to Kristeva and Bakhtin without so much as a trace of irony, and the conclusion of the chapter solemnly intones, 'Setting aside difference instead of effacing the irreducibility of difference produces a configuration of political praxis that involves a process of articulation'.

(b)   Fiction

The series 'Theory/Culture', launched by the University of Toronto Press, which already includes such notable works on Canadian literature as Smaro Kamboureli's *On The Edge of Genre: The Contemporary Canadian Long Poem* and Sylvia Söderlind's *Margin/Alias: Language and Colonization in Canadian and Québécois Fiction*, has now also published Martin Kuester's *Framing Truths: Parodic Structures in Contemporary English–Canadian Historical Novels*. Concentrating on the works of three contemporary authors (Findley, Bowering, Atwood), the book contains a substantial chapter commenting on parody in Richardson, Grove and Buckler. This historical spread allows Kuester to draw some very startling connections, most notably the one between Buckler and Bowering's *A Short Sad Book*, a complex work generally neglected in Canadian criticism. Relying strongly on Linda Hutcheon's theory of parody, *Framing Truths* is still distinguished by its broad consideration of previous discussions of parody; its comprehensive and informed knowledge of literary history, both Canadian and European; and its conscientious attention to the texts. Readers in search of the Orwellian intertext in *The Handmaid's Tale* will find an attentive reading of one here, together with an analysis of Pound's 'Hugh Selwyn Mauberly' through Findley, and of Coleridge's 'Ancient Mariner' through Bowering. Kuester's book is based on a dissertation, and the strutting of background knowledge endemic to the genre is sometimes visible. However, the conversion to a book has been more successful than in Karen Smythe's *Figuring Grief: Gallant, Munro, and the Poetics of Elegy*, which tends to smother two of Canada's most accomplished stylists in bookish prose.

   Essays on Life Writing: From Genre to Critical Practice, edited by Marlene Kadar, also a volume in the 'Theory/Culture' series, contains some lively work on the fictional and factual interstices of life-writing, both from the point of view of theoretical sophistication and practical application. Admirers of Marian Engel's work will, for instance, find new material in Christl Verduyn's introduction to Engel's archival *Cahiers* and notebooks here. The most harrowing and formally challenging piece comes from Janice Williamson, who combines a reading of Danica's *Don't: A Woman's Word* with personal experience. The book also contains work on Anna Jameson, Elizabeth Smart, Nicole Brossard and Margaret Atwood, as well as a selection of non-Canadian writers.

Nineteenth-century fiction in both English and French is the topic of Steven Tötösy de Zepetnek's *The Social Dimensions of Fiction: On the Rhetoric and Function of Prefacing Novels in the Nineteenth-Century Canadas*. The book, which comes with useful bibliographies, but a very poorly produced index, classifies prefaces according to a detailed taxonomy considering, among other criteria, their intended purpose as acknowledgement, apology, criticism, dedication, explanation. Based on a doctoral dissertation, *The Social Dimensions* demonstrates once again the commitment of the University of Alberta's Research Institute of Comparative Literature to polysystem theory, an approach in which the social functions of literature are sometimes overwhelmed by the categories developed to demonstrate them.

Among Canadian novelists, Margaret Atwood continues to attract the lion's share of critical attention. Noteworthy essays include Sandra Tomc's reading (*CL* 138/139.73–87) of Atwood's *The Handmaid's Tale* as nationalist allegory. Her approach is one of the few plausible interpretations to date of Offred's somewhat unconvincing feminism. Jonathan Bignell shares some of Tomc's concerns in 'Lost Messages: *The Handmaid's Tale*, Novel and Film' (*BJCS* 8.i.71–84), where he concludes that the absence of a 'legitimate master-discourse' is 'distinctly Canadian'. Jessie Givner provides an extended footnote on 'Names, Faces and Signatures in Margaret Atwood's *Cat's Eye* and *The Handmaid's Tale*' (*CL* 133.56–75), and Joseph Andriano reads 'The *Handmaid's Tale* as Scrabble Game' (*ECW* 48.(Winter 1992–93).89–96) by paying detailed attention to the many ways in which the narrator linguistically undercuts Gilead's power structures. R. D. Lane links *Cat's Eye* to its Shakespearean sources in 'Cordelia's "Nothing": The Character of Cordelia and Margaret Atwood's *Cat's Eye*' (*ECW* 48.(Winter 1992–93).73–88). The construction of female identity in a world offering contradictory messages of freedom and entrapment is the subject of Stephen Ahern's '"Meat Like You Like It": The Production of Identity in Atwood's Cat's Eye' (*CL* 137.(Summer 1993).8–17). J. Brooks Bouson's *Brutal Choreographies: Oppositional Strategies and Narrative Design in the Novels of Margaret Atwood* purports 'to provide a critical reading of Atwood's novels and to read her work with [the author's] feet planted firmly on the ground'. This is indeed a commonsensical approach to Atwood's major fictions, giving a detailed reading of existing criticism and presenting as plausible an account of her major thematic and structural concerns as any. The book does not cover new ground, but readers wishing a good introduction or a refresher course will be well served. The only other writer to attract as much attention as Atwood, if not more, is Malcolm Lowry. The ever-growing industry around him has been enriched by Cynthia Sugars's edition of *The Letters of Conrad Aiken and Malcolm Lowry 1929–1954*, by *Swinging in the Maelstrom: New Perspectives on Malcolm Lowry*, edited by Sherrill Grace and *The Collected Poetry of Malcolm Lowry*, edited by Kathleen Scherf. Scherf also edits the journal *Studies in Canadian Literature*, and virtually every issue carries an essay on Lowry.

New publications on multiculturalism have been discussed in the 'general' section, and they will provide good background to the increasing amount of criticism on ethnic writers. Ajay Heble's '"A Foreign Presence in the Stall": Towards a Poetics of Cultural Hybridity in Rohinton Mistry's Migration Stories' (*CL* 137.(Summer 1993).51–61) aptly summarizes its subject in its title. Following a sophisticated typology of 'cultural hybridity', Heble suggests that authors like Mistry, Highway and Kogawa create 'the necessity of moving beyond a nationalist critical methodology'. Douglas Barbour's book on Michael Ondaatje for TWAS provides a cogent overview of the author's work, only the second such undertaking after Leslie Mundwiler's 1984 study. In a careful reading of Ondaatje's poetry and fiction, Barbour argues that the author has moved from modernism to postmodernism and finally postcolonialism, investing his most recent fiction with a political agenda he previously rejected.

(c) Poetry and Drama
The Tightrope Walker: Autobiographic Writings of Anne Wilkinson, edited by Joan Coldwall, has a photo of Wilkinson which makes her look eerily like Elizabeth Smart. The affinity, in this collection of journals, poems, and autobiographical writing, with Smart, Sexton and Plath, is apparent throughout: like these writers, Wilkinson strove to reconcile the demands of her creativity with those of her marriage and children, and although her story is not as tragic as Plath's or Sexton's, the strains were still insurmountable. The book is equally important for students of Canadian poetry and of women's life-writing.

Few Canadian poets have inspired as much affection and respect as the late bp nichol. Irene Niechoda's *A Sourcery for Books 1 and 2 of bp nichol's The Martyrology* presents a formidably researched exegesis, documenting nichol's inspiration by comic book imagery as much as his reliance on medieval book illumination. Doug Barbour contributes an entry on bp nichol to volume 8 of *ECW's Canadian Writers and Their Works* (Poetry) series, as well as a piece on Daphne Marlatt. These are substantial and sensitive introductions; Karl Jirgen's contribution on bill bissett is also noteworthy, although not quite as balanced, and Nell Waldman competently introduces Michael Ondaatje. John Harris's piece on Bowering stops with his 1988 publications, that is four years before this appreciation appeared, and therefore has limited usefulness. Volume 10 in the same series provides introductions to Leonard Cohen (by Linda Hutcheon), Eli Mandel (by Dennis Cooley), John Newlove (by John Barbour) and Joe Rosenblatt (by Ed Jewinski). A particularly attentive and differentiated reading of Robert Kroetsch's poetry comes from Ann Munton. George Woodcock's introductions to this and previous volumes have been collected in George Woodcock's *Introduction to Canadian Poetry*, because both he and editors Jack David, Robert Lecker, and Ellen Quigley realized that they 'were in fact developing a personal view of Canadian writing that was worth pursuing for its own sake' and that is sometimes, as Woodcock points out, in contrapuntal relation to the essays it introduces. Munton's essay on Kroetsch, for instance, 'enlarges greatly on [the theoretical] aspect of his writing and thinking – so greatly that I need hardly say any more, particularly since I feel that critical theory can bear only obliquely on the work of literature'.

One of Woodcock's subjects, Eli Mandel, receives a careful reading in Andrew Stubbs's *Myth Origins Magic: The Study of Form in Eli Mandel's Writing*, although one would have wished for a more detailed placement of Mandel's work in contemporary poetry. By contrast, the special issue of *Essays on Canadian Writing* on Al Purdy (49), guest-edited by Louis K. MacKendrick, richly explores Purdy's connections to other Canadian poets and to the international scene. bp nichol and Bronwen Wallace document the impact of his poetic voice on their own work; Peter Stevens links Purdy's poem 'The Cariboo Horses' to A. Alvarez's *The New Poetry*; Sam Solecki explores D. H. Lawrence's influence on Purdy and Layton. There are also a foto-album and various pieces by Purdy himself. *Inside the Poem*, edited by William H. New, a *Festschrift* marking the retirement of UBC scholar Don Stephens, is divided into four sections, including texts, discussion of texts, new poems and an affectionate epilogue by novelist David Watmough. The section containing 'discussion of texts' assembles brief analyses of a wide array of Canadian poems, ranging from Atwood's 'Notes Towards a Poem', Avison's 'Just Left or The Night Margaret Laurence Died', and Birney's 'David', to Phyllis Webb's 'Krakatoa' and 'Spiritual Storm', P. K. Page's 'Portrait of Marina', and F. R. Scott's 'Audacity'. Contributors include established critics Frank Davey, Elspeth Cameron, Laurie Ricou, George Woodcock, Clara Thomas, Sandra Djwa, and newcomers like Tom Hastings, Manina Jones, and Nathalie Cooke. Approaches vary from a brief source study, such as Cameron's comparison of 'David' with the epic 'Song of Roland', to a rather stern post-colonial reading of 'The Bear on Delhi Road' by Tom Hastings, from Ricou and Bringhurst's dialogic 'Sunday Morning' to Christine Somerville's shrewd reading of an elegiac poem by Avison. In some of its more polished pieces, the book demonstrates that close reading remains a valuable critical option.

Post-Colonial English Drama: Commonwealth Drama Since 1960, edited by Bruce King, features three essays on Canadian drama. An overview by Eugene Benson is complemented by pieces focusing on George F. Walker by Chris Johnson and on Sharon Pollock and Judith Thompson by Diane Bessai. The book offers valuable introductions to the novice in Canadian drama. Native theatre attracts considerable critical attention. Helen Hoy's '"When You Admit You're a Thief, Then You Can Be Honourable": Native/Non-Native Collaboration in the Book of Jessica' (*CL* 136.24–39) will be compulsory reading for anyone interested in Native Studies, presenting a white academic's astute analysis of, and moving testimony to, the increasing difficulties involved in working in this field. Marc Maufort analyses Thomson Highway's work in 'Recognizing Difference in Canadian Drama: Thomson Highway's Poetic Realism' (*BJCS* 8.ii.230–40), comparing it to George Ryga's plays, with which it shares the influence of German expressionism. However, Highway also transcends Ryga's distanced reading by evoking 'deep emotional resonances' not available to the older author.

4.   The Caribbean

This section is divided into four sub-sections: (a) General; (b) Fiction; (c) Poetry; and (d) Drama.

(a)   General

The award of the first Nobel Prize to an anglophone Caribbean writer marks a particular sort of arrival (some would say one of dubious value) in the region's literature. The tiny population, of some four million people, has produced an exceptional community of writers in the last half century who between them have made a disproportionate contribution to the literature of the world. The 1992 Nobel award to Derek Walcott occasioned also his important articulation of a Caribbean aesthetic – the culmination of his life-long meditation on the topic – in his inaugural lecture, published under the title *The Antilles: Fragments of Epic*

Memory. He repudiates both the tragic and the romantic view of the region as seen by outsiders with equal distaste, preferring to see it as transcending a history of fragmentation and loss through the power of its natural beauty and of its people's creative response. The essay deserves to become a classic of Caribbean literature in its own right. As well as being published by Faber, it is reprinted in *WLT* 67.ii, along with a tribute from Stephen Breslow, who asserts, 'If we are entering an era in which multiculturalism is our central ideology, Derek Walcott must be acclaimed as one of our greatest cultural leaders [...] We may detect in Walcott's microcosmic Caribbean a paradigm for the most tolerant, mutually enriching coexistence of all the world's voices'. The meaning of the selection of Walcott for the Nobel and of Naipaul as the recipient of the first British Literature Prize is explored in Paula Burnett's 'Hegemony or Pluralism? The Literary Prize and the Post-Colonial Project in the Caribbean' (*Commonwealth* 16.i). The media response to these events is examined internationally and found to exhibit marked differences reflecting national cultural biases.

Likely to stand as the most important scholarly work in the field for a decade, not just a year, is Anne Walmsley's study *The Caribbean Artists Movement 1966–1972*. Subtitled 'A Literary and Cultural History' it provides in rivetingly readable form a hugely important record of a neglected community's acquisition of faith in its own difference. The early discussions as to whether there was or could be or should be a Caribbean aesthetic are salutary reminders, a quarter of a century later, of what a knife-edge there is between happening and not happening. Not that Caribbean literature would not have happened if there had been no CAM: a number of novelists were established before it began and, its now most well-known figures, Derek Walcott and V. S. Naipaul, were never directly involved in it, Walcott primarily because he chose to remain (for decades) in the Caribbean, Naipaul because he preferred a solitary role. But the direction of the work – of those both inside CAM and outside it – might have been very different without it. What Walmsley's account reveals so powerfully is on the one hand the almost oblique internal growth towards self-realization, and, on the other, the chancy negotiations with the wider cultural world, which could so often and so easily have turned out differently.

The central paradox is of course that this self-construction through an aesthetic happened among those working not in the region itself but in London. Ironically, this enables the particular difficulties of a colonial culture in securing access to such necessary realms as publishing to emerge with poignant clarity. In the words of John La Rose in 1969, they were 'a people of exile, living in the permanence of tragedy and dispossessed hope' but 'exporting ourselves from hopelessness into hope [...] Exile paid its premium in self-awareness'. Such a concept of 'exile' went beyond the specific condition of those whom Selvon immortalized as 'lonely Londoners': it was a symbolic condition of all Caribbean people, but given particular immediacy in metropolitan centres such as London. The secondary paradox was that artists with every historical reason for a sceptical approach to power and centrism, coming themselves from scattered and proudly distinct communities, were attempting to organize themselves into a movement. As Salkey said in 1972, CAM in its refusal of formality had 'an almost mirage-like structure. The only thing we've ever planned is that we look as if we're disappearing. You know why? Our history has been full of authoritarians. But the work gets done'. Despite doubts and difficulties, the work did indeed 'get done'; reading this book prompts the wish that some of the early papers on the nature of a Caribbean aesthetic, all by important writers and critics, could be printed in their entirety for those who would like to go beyond the well-chosen quotations and judicious summaries which the book offers, and we may wish that we had been present at such seminal occasions as Brathwaite's 1967 reading at the Jeanetta Cochrane Theatre of *Rights of Passage*.

Some of the incidental details are unforgettable: Wilson Harris's first manuscript being refused by the first six readers Charles Monteith of Faber put it to, but Andrew Salkey, the seventh, waking them up to what they were on the point of missing; or Brathwaite being given the Gikuyu name Kamau by Ngugi's grandmother. Far from being a rather dry account of events of specialist interest only, Walmsley continually surprises with the immediacy of her still valent details, and makes a coherent and fluent narrative out of an ocean of material which might have drowned a lesser scholar. She does not confine herself to the central CAM narrative: her introductory chapter alone, summarizing the pre-CAM Caribbean cultural experience in Britain from the 1930s to the 1960s, offers a new and valuable account, and her later sections on the wider context provide compelling insights into the interactions with political and cultural activity in a range of connected communities at a time of great historical importance.

This is a book which no one interested in Caribbean culture should be without. It is a great testimony, first, to the vision of the Brathwaites, who ensured from the outset that full records were kept, including the laborious tape-recording on a heavy reel-to-reel machine of most CAM sessions; second, to Anne Walmsley's industry and skill in using the archive and her own painstaking research, including almost 90 interviews with those concerned (she refers to her own involvement in CAM in the third person); and third, to publishers New Beacon Books, in the persons of John La Rose and Sarah White, founder members of CAM and long-standing catalysts of Caribbean culture, who have produced a handsome, accurate, and beautifully illustrated book, including full colour plates of Caribbean artists' work and miniature marginal illustrations throughout which bring the narrative vividly to life. Although it is in some ways a matter for surprise that CAM itself lasted for as few years as it did, given its impact, it is none the less excitingly apparent that its work goes on in all sorts of diverse ways, of which the book itself is an instance. There could be no more appropriate publisher for such a study; the only worry is that because it is a small press, it may not reach as wide a readership as it should. The hope must be, however, that it will gradually disseminate itself as a classic, to New Beacon's and hence Caribbean publishing's long-term benefit, as Walter Rodney's *How Europe Underdeveloped America* has done for fellow London small press, Bogle L'Ouverture. Much of the book's poignancy derives from the painstakingly detailed picture it builds up of the means whereby complex and multiple cultural events and exchanges can come about. It provides constant reminders of the difficulties faced by marginalized communities in getting published or finding a platform – to reach their own communities, let alone for wider contact. It raises an acute awareness of the fragility of their cultures' survival and growth.

In *The Repeating Island: The Caribbean and the Postmodern Perspective* Antonio Benitez-Rojo undertakes a very different project. As a Cuban novelist working now in the USA, and an inheritor of the modern hispanophone and francophone intellectual tradition, he applies chaos theory to the Caribbean cultural experience, which he describes as 'a soup of signs'. The theoretical model, however, is one which identifies order as central to chaos: 'a given region's flight of textual signifiers is neither wholly disorganized nor absolutely unpredictable'. The repeating island of his title illustrates a way of organizing the 'soup' concept; the essential feature is that of difference within sameness, 'where every repetition is a practice that necessarily entails a difference and a step toward nothingness', as in entropy theory. Benitez-Rojo's two organizing signs are the Fleet and the Plantation, which he deploys to account for the variety and the sameness of the Caribbean cultural phenomenon. With great erudition and imaginative force he investigates a range of texts, both fictional and non-fictional, from the sixteenth century to the present, to establish his overall historical thesis that it is the date of the introduction of a plantation economy, and its duration, that has determined the precise degree to which African cultural signifiers have survived in the New World syncretist 'soup'. His reading of Caribbean culture might be characterized as romantic: 'the Caribbean is not an apocalyptic world; it is not a phallic world in pursuit of the vertical desires of ejaculation and castration. The notion of the apocalypse is not important within the culture of the Caribbean. The choices of all or nothing, for or against, honor or blood have little to do with the culture of the Caribbean. These are ideological positions articulated in Europe.' This thesis is contextualized by his autobiographical experience as a child, evacuated from Havana for fear of nuclear strike at the time of what the West has come to call the Cuban missile crisis. Paradoxically, for all its theoretical transcendence of specifics and deconstruction of authorial positions, the book's strength is its authority, the sense it creates that the writer knows what he is talking about. He approaches his subject from an insider position which qualifies him to evaluate, although the intellectual matrix he applies is one associated with European hegemony and therefore likely to be rejected by some other insiders.

He distinguishes 'terrestrial' cultures from those he calls 'aquatic', such as those of the Greek and Caribbean 'meta-archipelagoes' whose culture is feminine Other to those dominated by the law of the Father. Their societies, the 'Peoples of the Sea', exhibit the 'repeating island' syndrome, as they 'proliferate incessantly while differentiating themselves from one another, travelling together toward the infinite' – their culture being 'a chaos that returns, a detour without a purpose, a continual flow of paradoxes'. But the postmodern premise of undifferentiated replication – of the 'feedback machine' – is rejected in Benitez-Rojo's model. What intervenes is the 'mystic or magical [...] loam of the civilizations that contributed to the formation of Caribbean culture'. The result is that the Caribbean text undergoes a 'metonymic displacement toward scenic, ritual and mythological forms', to become typically 'excessive, dense, uncanny, asymmetrical, entropic, hermetic'.

This hermeneutic is delivered through compelling readings of texts from Las Casas to Wilson Harris, supported by a wealth of knowledge from a range of disciplines. Although Benitez-Rojo may be something of a polymath, it is not necessary to be on his philosophical level to be stimulated and enriched by his arguments. Although his reading of Harris's *Palace of the Peacock* is indebted to Gilkes, as he acknowledges, he develops it according to concerns of his own, and for those less versed in hispanophone literature the readings of Guillen, Ortiz and Carpentier will be mind-stretching. In addition, his deconstruction of the various cultural phenomena arising from the Plantation enables a more profound understanding of Caribbeanness in general to emerge, in all its variety. This is a study which is likely to have far-reaching influence in Caribbean studies, and is a reminder of the limitations imposed by the linguistic compartmentalization of the region and its intellectuals. Benitez-Rojo's thesis meshes with Walcott's Nobel lecture. Both are writers first and critics second, and a comment of Benitez-Rojo's could have been written about Walcott: 'Antilleans tend to roam the entire world in search of the centres of their Caribbeanness'.

Kenyan critic Simon Gikandi, now working out of the American academy, follows in the footsteps of Ngugi in bringing an African vantage point to bear on Caribbean literature. He too offers a book which sets out a Caribbean hermeneutics but it is very different from Benitez-Rojo's. His is a revisionary project: he wishes to counter the antipathy to modernism amongst the anglophone Third World academy. He aligns himself with Paul Gilroy in his assertions that the black contribution has been central to the construction of the modern West – that, however, is not the same thing as modernism. Gikandi titles his work *Writing in Limbo: Modernism and Caribbean Literature*, which is misleading, as it does not focus on modernism and Caribbean literature, but on various concepts of modernity. If anything, its long title might more usefully have referred to history than modernism, because the theme of history and the fictional text's relation to it is much more central to its discussion than what is normally understood by modernism. Gikandi distances his argument from what he terms 'high modernism', preferring to begin by locating the start of the modern at the point of the Columbian intervention in the Americas. The texts on which he focuses are, however, drawn from the second half of the twentieth century, and are all prose works, and all novels except for C. L. R. James's *Beyond a Boundary* – a bias which he does not attempt to justify. More unsettlingly he avoids those texts which might spring to mind as being examples of Caribbean modernism – Rhys or Harris or Lovelace, for example – to concentrate on readings of Lamming, Selvon, and a group of women novelists – Marshall, Collins, Edgell and Cliff. His exception is Carpentier, who comes more naturally under a modernist label. As his chapters unfold, his academically suspect switching of terms such as 'modern', 'modernity' and 'modernism' becomes irritating, and undermines what he has to say.

His practice of constant citation of 'authorities' also becomes an irritant; he seems to stalk his theoretical argument, taking cover like a huntsman behind the rocks of others' statements. He takes careful bearings between Caribbean and metropolitan criticism, presumably hoping to allay Southern suspicion of Northern neo-colonial hegemony and to draw Northern critics into an acknowledgement that the Southern academy, scandalously marginalized, has an important contribution to make – both of which are, of course, worthwhile objectives. It is a pity, however, that because of the sheer frequency of these external references, the reader is left with a sense of a hollow centre – as if Gikandi has stalked so well he is almost invisible. Intertextuality in criticism can in such circumstances end by being disabling rather than empowering.

This is particularly a pity as it detracts from what is the book's strength, the detailed reading of the chosen works, where Gikandi is unfailingly interesting and frequently persuasive. He pitches his critique at a sophisticated and well-informed level, and provides some passages which could be useful in educational contexts as models of current theory in action. He is equally at home with Foucault and Fanon, and gives, for example, a brilliant excursus into Bakhtinian carnival theory in relation to Paule Marshall's work. But the attempt to recuperate Collins and Cliff to modernism becomes fussy and obsessive, obscuring really cogent analysis of, for instance, their language and narrative strategy. Also, as the chapters unfold, it is the invisibility of the postmodern which becomes more and more conspicuous. Eventually, near the end, a reference to postmodernism is slipped in, and then, right at the end, addressed. But really, Gikandi should have established his parameters much more clearly at the outset. If he had given an account of his eschewal of the postmodern as hermeneutic, his whole project in relation to the modern would have been much more convincing. As it is, he founders on the rocks concealed by his false bearings, which is regrettable, as his is an original intellect of a wide reach, with the courage to challenge conventions and prejudices and the imagination to pioneer new and valuable ways of reading and discussing texts.

There is a profound difference between an outsider's view of a culture and that of an insider who has agonized over a society's dilemmas and lived its crises. The definition of a Caribbean aesthetic has been the lifelong project of the region's most penetrating literary critic and scholar, Gordon Rohlehr. His monumental studies of Brathwaite's poetry and of calypso are now joined by a collection of diverse writings of cultural analysis. Published in two volumes, *My Strangled City* includes 12 essays from the 1970s, while *The Shape of That Hurt* gathers essays from 1981–92, most of them from the mid-1980s. Most of the contents have been published elsewhere, although the texts of several hitherto unpublished addresses are also included, but in that they tend to have been published in journals such as *Tapia*, *Bim* and *Trinidad and Tobago Review* which are not readily accessible outside the Caribbean (or inside it, for that matter), and as some were given serial publication initially, their collection in paperback should enable a much wider readership to engage with Rohlehr's work. He is unfailingly acute and interesting, bringing his wide knowledge and sensitive intelligence to bear on a range of topics both literary and social. What emerges from this collection of assorted work is 'the balance of negativity and affirmation which we bring to our historical moment', an 'identification of the shapes which have emerged out of the apocalyptic process through which the Caribbean has been engendered'. His prefaces make clear the cost of creative engagement with what he calls the 'Caribbean vortex' in which he has spent his life; in the early nineties he is beset by weariness and depression as 'my Caribbean drifts blindly towards atrocity and anguish'. History still haunts the region, he says, as 'a duppy, a malign, unburied and unplaced spirit of time past', which only the artist can lay to rest. The volumes are 'a requiem for two decades'; with the wit that shows he has not yet given up the struggle he wishes 'May these two decades of ferment, farce and phenomenal unchange, fold up, fade out and sink to rest'. Yet, as the essays repeatedly demonstrate, the story of the region's art miraculously transcends the continuing tragedy of its history.

Roots, a collection of literary essays by Kamau Brathwaite, originally published in 1986 by Casa de las Americas, has been usefully reissued by the University of Michigan Press. Chronologically arranged, it collects eight thoughtful and accessible essays dating from 1957 to 1979, many of them written for oral delivery and therefore using a relaxed, informal style. It includes such classics as 'Roots', 'Jazz and the West Indian Novel' and 'The African Presence in Caribbean Literature', as well as the original version of 'History of the Voice'. The volume is full of delights, such as an essay on Mais, and Brathwaite's wide-ranging humanity as a literary commentator, evaluating the early talent of

Naipaul and patting Walcott on the back for his first extended use of Nation Language in 'The Schooner *Flight*'.

Another kind of anthology which may have escaped notice is John Murray's *The Islands and the Sea* which offers, it says, 'five centuries of nature writing from the Caribbean'. This is a fascinating assembly of almost 50 texts from a Columbus letter to Jamaica Kincaid. Arranged chronologically in three sections, the last and biggest covering the period since 1800 (which might have been better divided between nineteenth- and twentieth-century groups), it has some translated material, such as that from las Casas and von Humboldt, but the great majority is in its original form. Raleigh, Sloane, Darwin and Defoe rub shoulders here with Harriet Beecher Stowe and Hemingway as well as Naipaul and Walcott. Murray provides an excellent introduction and prefatory notes to each passage which give exactly the information needed, as well as a useful bibliography. It would have been possible to make a different book on the same theme by drawing exclusively from Caribbean literature, but the textual eclecticism of Murray's selection is part of its charm in that it illuminates the historical importance of key texts in determining hegemonic – and later resisting – perceptions of the region. This is a handsome book, well illustrated in black and white, and one which anyone who has loved the region will find of enduring appeal.

That the community of Caribbean writers is an etiolating phenomenon is thankfully attested by the new talent celebrated in a special issue of *ArielE*, 'New Voices in Caribbean Literature' (24.i). Women writers such as Olive Senior, Pauline Melville, Michelle Cliff, Merle Collins and Opal Palmer Adisa are introduced through recent work, alongside new fiction from some male writers. David Dabydeen's wry inversion of Conrad's *Heart of Darkness*, *The Intended* is given a first critique by Margery Fee, and Robert Antoni's acclaimed novel *Divina Trace* is reviewed by John Hawley. Keith Ellis offers an essay on 'Images of Sugar in Caribbean Poetry', an intriguing subject which could be developed at greater length, and Fred D'Aguiar, now a novelist as well as a poet, is interviewed by Frank Birbalsingh.

Other interviews which are of interest are Stewart Brown's discussion with Willie Chen about what it means to be a Chinese Caribbean person and writer (*JWIL* 5.1–2), and Luigi Sampietro's two-part post-*Omeros* interview with Derek Walcott (*Caribana* 2.3). Daryl Cumber Dance provides a whole book of interviews in *New World Adams: Conversations With Contemporary West Indian Writers*, among them Walcott, but this is speaking with a late seventies voice. All of the interviews were conducted in 1979–80, which gives the book a curiously dated feeling. The list of interviewees, for a start, includes names like Orlando Patterson, Jan Carew and Vic Reid, and others who have somehow dropped from view. Some of the big names are here – Louise Bennett, Martin Carter, Wilson Harris, C. L. R. James, George Lamming, Earl Lovelace, Mervyn Morris and Dennis Scott – but seeing Anthony McNeill's name makes one wonder what has happened to him as a writer, then of such promise. Names which must have been new in 1979 have since become familiar, such as Pam Mordecai and Velma Pollard (who are interviewed together), but some who should have been here are omitted: Dance notes cryptically that Brathwaite and Salkey both withheld permission for publication of the interviews they gave her. It is a pity that the book did not appear when the interviews were young, and it is sad to note how many of those interviewed are now dead. This was an important generation of founders, but its successors can also provide interesting dialogue: a follow-up volume covering today's writers would paradoxically enhance rather than detract from the status of this belated pioneer.

Bernth Lindfors and Reinhard Sander have added substantially to the genus of library reference tomes with their twin-volume heavies *Twentieth Century Caribbean and Black African Writers*. A series introduction describes the entries as 'career biographies, tracing the development of the author's canon and evolution of his reputation'. Unfortunately, the masculine term is accurate, as only two women make it into the august ranks of the 24 anglophone Caribbean writers covered, the 'odd couple' of Louise Bennett and Jean Rhys. Selections for such listings will never please everyone, and certainly the men included range from the obvious big names to some whom it is good to see getting serious attention, in some cases for the first time. In the main those who know their subject well have been enlisted to write the articles; it is good to see Durix on Harris, Hamner on Walcott, Paquet on Lamming, Thieme on Naipaul, and so on, while it is Brathwaite himself who is given the topic of Roger Mais. Each entry lists publications, usually divided between fiction and nonfiction where appropriate, but Thieme wisely dodges the issue by just classing all Naipaul's as 'Books'. There is then a biographical and critical essay, the length of which reflects the output of the author and his importance, with Walcott and Naipaul getting quite substantial reviews. After the essay come lists of interviews, and such matters as bibliographies and biographies, followed by a section headed 'References', which appears to be a critical bibliography which in some cases includes monographs but in others seems confined to journal articles. Hamner, for instance, mentions Stewart Brown's *The Art of Derek Walcott* under the bibliography heading, but not in the critical section; nor does he mention his own Walcott monograph, which is a pity.

The division of the authors between the two volumes, which were published separately, is also mysterious. The first volume includes writers from Guyana, St Lucia and Dominica; the second has those from Barbados and Trinidad and Tobago; but Jamaican writers are scattered across both. The editors provide a general introduction which marvels at the range and quality of Caribbean writing from so small a population, and asserts that the fiction of Lamming, Harris and Naipaul 'remains unsurpassed by any other trio of postcolonial novelists writing in the English language'. They plan, thankfully, a third volume which will round up 'some of the younger writers who have earned reputations for themselves in recent years', as well as 'several significant older authors' for whom there was no space in the first two volumes, and they recognize that as the body of literature continues to grow, a dictionary of literary biography in the future may need a volume per country. For the time being, we can only hope that the third volume will find space for seniors such as Allfrey and Marson as well as the next generation of fine women writers, who are legion.

Intended more as a primary reader than a reference work, Jean-Pierre and Carole Durix's *An Introduction to the New Literatures in English* is divided into six sections, the Caribbean being the last. Texts by Brathwaite, Harris, Lamming, Lovelace, Naipaul, Selvon and Walcott are offered alongside support material, contextualizing the writing historically and geographically. Its publication in France by the editors of *Commonwealth* is a reminder of the important contribution made by scholars based in continental Europe to postcolonial studies in English.

An interesting approach to the intertextuality of national literatures within the postcolonial is Diana Brydon and Helen Tiffin's *Decolonising Fictions*, which from an Australian base looks also at West Indian and Canadian literature. The contents page bills a chapter titled 'West Indian Literature', but this proves to be misleading, as the chapter itself bears the label 'West Indian Literature and the Australian Comparison'. Points about the core texts of imperialism, such as *Robinson Crusoe* and *Heart of Darkness* are related to colonial education systems involving such classroom familiars as the Royal Readers, but it is in subsequent chapters that the reader will find illuminating analyses of Caribbean literary texts, with Lamming's *Natives of my Person* read against White's *A Fringe of Leaves*, and Naipaul's *Guerrillas* and Rhys's *Wide Sargasso Sea* put in the context of Stow's *Visitants*. The range and internationally intertextual approach of this study open inviting avenues for further stimulating exploration on a similar principle.

Lizabeth Paravisini-Gebert and Olga Torres-Seda have made a fine contribution to the anglophone Caribbean's bibliographical scholarship with their *Caribbean Women Novelists: An Annotated Critical Bibliography*. Brenda Berrian with associate editor Aart Broek laid a substantial foundation with their *Bibliography of Women Writers from the Caribbean (1831–1986)* in 1989, which was pan-Caribbean and without annotation. The closer focus of the new volume enables really substantial annotation to enrich the factual listings, and the production is first-rate, unlike the earlier book which looked like a typescript and was visually hard to use. It is a huge task, carried through with great scholarliness, thoroughness and accuracy – and, of course, not only by two people. The list of acknowledgements includes support from many, not only devoted research assistants and librarians, but fellow academics such as Pierrette Frickey, who 'generously shared her unpublished bibliography on Caribbean women writers'.

After a bibliography of general criticism (a substantial list which brings home how much has been achieved in a decade), and list of bibliographies, novelists in all the region's languages are listed in a single alphabetical sequence, which gives striking reality to the notion of a pan-Caribbean cultural group. At the end are indices to authors by country, to novels and to critics, and even an index of themes and key words. Here Ana Velez of Puerto Rico is followed by Bea Vianen of Surinam, Myriam Warner-Vieyra of Guadeloupe, Joanna Werners of Surinam, Jeanne Wilson of Jamaica and England, and Sylvia Wynter of Jamaica. Both primary and secondary material is annotated, with novels, poetry, drama and nonfiction listed, as well as excerpts, translations, children's literature, recordings and broadcasts, criticism and reviews. How fascinating it is to find that *Wide Sargasso Sea* has been translated into Danish, Finnish, Norwegian, French, Hungarian, Italian, Polish, Czech, Dutch, Spanish, German and even Japanese. Rhys's critical bibliography takes up 36 pages, followed by eight pages of reviews, and will be invaluable as a means of identifying the critical work most pertinent to one's line of inquiry. How many of us were aware, for instance, of a monograph by Kamau Brathwaite from 1974, in which he argues against regarding *Wide Sargasso Sea* as West Indian literature at all, because white creoles do not sufficiently identify or cannot be identified with, in his words, 'the spiritual world on this side of the Sargasso Sea'?

Writers such as Grace Nichols, who have written one novel but a lot of poetry, end up with what is essentially a poetry bibliography, and even those who are firmly centred on prose but have written the occasional poem, such as Jean Rhys, have their poetry carefully tagged by the editors. All it does is make the reader hanker for an equivalent bibliography for poetry, and for drama – and not just for the women, either.

(b) Fiction

Margaret Paul Joseph pitches her book, *Caliban in Exile: The Outsider in Caribbean Fiction*, at a rather different level. She felt, she writes, 'no compulsion to mount the esoteric soapbox' and aims to 'reach not a select few, but as many people as I can'. She targets particularly the USA, where she says awareness of postcolonial literature, outside the academy, is 'minimal' – a thought-provoking claim, and one which is silent on the way in which American literature, and black American literature in particular, are necessarily also postcolonial. The book's organizing concept is that of exile, yoked to the notion of displacement symbolized by Caliban.

The opening chapter is a useful although rather superficial summary of the reworkings of *The Tempest* through which the postcolonial appropriation of Caliban as archetype has been established. Joseph then goes on to readings of Jean Rhys, Lamming and Selvon, with the objective of demonstrating how 'Rhys's quivering web of anguished alienation, Lamming's psychedelic flashes of violence, and Selvon's tragi-comic irony are their various responses to the experience of living as Outsiders in England'. For the purposes of the study she appropriates the name 'Caliban' to her particular project: 'I shall use the name Caliban as a symbol of the West Indian, as both author and character and as both man and woman.' Her thesis is to resist the perception of physical and cultural displacement as negative by positing the triumph of Caliban through art: 'Possession of a heritage can result in one's taking it for granted. Leaving it makes one aware of loss. Transcending it implies an act of will from which something new can be born.' Caliban transcends his loss crucially in his deployment of language: 'The very articulation of his experience in Prospero's language shows the conversion of Caliban's "curse" into his triumphant paean.'

The resultant 'therapeutic effect' has to be, however, only part of the story, and the other half, which is to do with physical restoration alongside the cultural recuperation, is hardly addressed by Joseph. Her conclusion in identifying what she calls a 'new kind of victimization', that of being made an outsider in one's own country because of class rather than race, seems both naïve and seriously misleading: it is not clear how class can be categorized as 'new'; if what is meant is that for established racial minorities within metropolitan countries the grounds of discrimination and oppression have shifted from race to class, a grave mistake is being made. At the time of the publication of *Omeros*, which Joseph introduces as her final example of the possibility of a new era, race is, if anything, *more* important as a category of cultural and economic exclusion than it was at the time of publication of Lamming's *The Emigrants*, not less. Using Arnold Toynbee to support her syncretist argument, she anticipates a future in which the Caliban myth would be superseded, as Caribbean writers move 'out of otherness and exile into Miranda's brave new world'. The neatness of this, depending as it does on a construction of certain key texts of the 'middle' period of Caribbean literature as negative, in order to suggest an alternative positive position, is suspect. The 'X' factor, which, as a resisting nomenclature, Joseph reminds us, comes from Cesaire's vision of *The Tempest*, is Shakespeare's irony – a device well understood by Walcott and Brathwaite, whose optimism she wants to see replicated in the novel; but the full paradox of that optimism, its framing within a tragic present and the possibility of a tragic future, is something she seems to miss.

Joseph's reading of the chosen works is, however, clear and generally illuminating. She is in touch with recent criticism (she relates, for instance, Spivak's comments on Narcissus and imperialism to *Wide Sargasso Sea*), but there is such reductionism involved in her fleeting allusions that they are of limited value. In addition, her style is at times simplistic, and even precious: 'I shall now allow myself the liberty of linking ...', for instance. None the less, although the book attends to a phase of Caribbean literature which is, as it acknowledges, already in part superseded, Joseph's study will make a useful addition to school and college libraries, and should, as it aims to, 'increase the enjoyment of Caribbean fiction for those who already know it and ... introduce it to those who do not'.

Also collecting various texts from recent decades, like the Brathwaite and Rohlehr volumes mentioned above, is *Conversations: George Lamming; Essays, Addresses and Interviews 1953–1990*, edited by Richard Drayton and Andaiye. Lamming's fictional output has been of great historical moment, although small, but because he was prominent right at the start of the post-war Caribbean literary renaissance there has been a tendency for him to be associated exclusively with that early period. His most recent novels now being 20 years old, and his next being imminent, it is illuminating to see his other modes of engagement with the power of language in the intervening years. Divided into five sections, each prefaced with a passage from Lamming's fiction, these texts – some written for publication, others for oral delivery, as well as interviews – reveal Lamming to be active in the region's politics and its critical self-assessment. For instance, at the 1983 crisis of the US invasion of Grenada he is revealed to have spoken passionately and persuasively at the Barbados campus of the University of the West Indies against the deportation of the editor of *Caribbean Contact*, who had criticized the Barbadian government's complicity in the American intervention. Lamming, ever the master of language, pointed the students to the choice between the heroic road of resistance to imperialism or 'the other tradition which leads down the defeated tracks of the Black plantation mongrel'. It is some of the short pieces like this which have the most impact. They present a picture of Lamming, who left London to return to the Caribbean in the early 1970s, engaging with all his formidable intelligence and imagination in Caribbean political and cultural reality. The interviews are valuable for the way they illuminate his fiction, and his own literary criticism is perceptive, although it now conveys a distinct sense of period, as in 'Caribbean Literature: The Black Rock of Africa'. The editors recall that Lamming was a catalyst of African fiction in English through his influence, particularly on Ngugi, and Lamming himself reminds us of how independently of black US fiction the fiction of the Caribbean emerged in those early years. But what the volume as a whole does is to remind us of the humility of the committed writer, aware that the creation of fiction is only one of several roads to a better future. Lamming is an Africanist and a regionalist of the left who attributes the failures of political will to the Caribbean's fragmentation. In the most recent essays he calls on the intellectual worker for 'an almost evangelical role on behalf of an authentic integration of the region': 'A genuine national identity will only be experienced when there is a liberated regional Caribbean of one people, and an environment is created in which we may be able to say: "here man is truly man, and the world he lives in is a human place."' In his speech for the funeral of C. L. R. James in 1989 he identified James as such an evangelist, one who 'laid, for us in the region, the foundations of a native intellectual tradition, and set the highest standards of political morality'. As his editors point out, Lamming thinks the language of the political speech 'incapable of the same layers of meaning and feeling as the language of his novels', but that does not prevent this collection providing an emotive image of a life of commitment.

Lamming's use of spirituality as a trope through which to explore the socio-political question of identity is Gordon Rohlehr's topic in 'Possession as Metaphor in Lamming's *Season of Adventure*' (*JWIL* 5.1–2). Rohlehr, always interesting, offers a compelling reading of the novel, and locates Lamming as novelist 'somewhere between Naipaul and Harris in his approach to realism; his fictionalizing of fact, his bent towards allegory and metaphorical situation'. He takes the dialogue between the living and the dead, with its concern for confession, reparation and healing, as a metaphor for what is needed in international politics – 'a central feature of the humanization of historical process'. Yet Rohlehr's discussion of the possession motif, for all its sympathetic tone, is couched in what some would see as a denial of its crux, in that he represents it as an internal phenomenon of the psyche rather than external spirituality: 'The loa reside within the consciousness and seek release by means of the music and the dance; even though such release of the loa from the depths of the consciousness often appears to be a visitation or entry from outside the consciousness'. It is easy, reading Rohlehr here, to forget that he is talking about literature, not life. A particular sort of intellectual gymnastics seems to come into play when marxism meets mysticism.

Although C. L. R. James wrote only one novel, *Minty Alley*, his numerous writings established him as a prose stylist of a spare elegance as well as a great political philosopher. A generation older than fellow Trinidadian V. S. Naipaul, he too began from an ambivalent attitude to his birthplace, as the editors of *C. L. R. James's Caribbean* remind us. However, unlike Naipaul, James's assertion that 'the populations in the British West Indies have no native civilization at all' was given a generous response and was not allowed to obscure his outstanding contribution to the cultural life of the region. Paget Henry and Paul Buhle have assembled from some eminent contributors interviews and essays to give an overview of James's achievement, but the volume is strangely disappointing. The biographical chapters are weakened by a tendency to awe, and the political chapters, which, among other things, apply Jamesian ideas to the history of the left in Trinidad and Antigua, while they are of politico-historical interest, are not sufficiently related to James himself – a factor the editors may have been aware of in deciding to attach 'C. L. R. James and ...' to what feels like the real title of the chapters, such as 'Caribbean Economic Tradition' or 'Trinidadian Nationalism'. The double bind is that while hostility to the cult of personality may be central to the marxist praxis, none the less if it is legitimate for a collection of essays to focus on one undoubtedly great man then he should truly be the focus of the volume. The section entitled 'Textual Explorations' is particularly frustrating. The chapter by the editors themselves on 'Caliban as Deconstructionist: C. L. R. James and Post-Colonial Discourse' exhibits the core problem. It attempts a potted introduction to postcolonial theory, which is shallow and unnecessary, and then, when it does get down to discussing James's texts, passes rapidly over the fiction to settle on the polemical writing, with which it seems the editors are more comfortable. The dubious phrase 'narrative photography' is applied to the fiction, which is left behind with the remark, 'as his writing became more politically engaged, fiction slowly gave way to political critique via biography', leaving the crucially interesting shift away from fiction entirely without analysis. There are gems here, however: an interview with James himself, one with Lamming about James, and some previously unpublished letters by James written in his forties and wooing the woman who was to become his second wife with a quaintly formal autobiography of great charm. On the scholarly front, honours go to Sylvia Wynter who manages to capture James's elusive poetic in an imaginative and penetrating essay. Her critique, which relates James's fiction to his overall discursive project and relates that to the region and the world, makes an important contribution to Caribbean literary studies. She ends by adapting James's evaluation of W. G. Grace to himself, but where 'Grace embodied a national process, James embodies an entire world historical process. And so, too, does his poiesis. With its ease and certainty of phrase, its refusal at whatever price to fake the game, it establishes the new identity of Caliban. The region is not only new. It evokes a shared "Ah!" of recognition and delight.' It is a pity that some of the other contributors felt their political seriousness required a didactic stiffness. As Wynter shows, and as James understood, the real trick is to be creatively serious.

Quick to point out that he is not a critic, Wilson Harris has spoken of his own critical pronouncements as 'a long, extended footnote to my fiction'. In fact, as the latest addition to his non-fictional works, such as the 1983 volume, *The Womb of Space*, makes plain, his critical views are relevant not just to his own writing, but to the whole project of art. In *The Radical Imagination* he engages in an illuminating way with human creativity in a wide range of historical and social contexts, characteristically linking with an acrobat's suppleness the language arts with the plastic, prehistory with the present, the popular with the esoteric. He refuses the scientific tendency to create divisions by classification, a tendency which is now colonizing the humanities, preferring to draw attention to the miracle of bridges rather than the given of gulfs. Collections of his critical utterances, such as this, therefore have a dynamic relevance to modern thought of all kinds, since he resists a dominant philosophy and posits an alternative way of perceiving the world, in which the human imagination is the key to the possibility of regeneration.

A 1990 interview was recorded at his Essex home in Chelmsford, and this is flanked by the edited texts of lectures given in Cambridge in 1989 and 1990, and in Liège in 1991. The editors, Alan Riach and Mark Williams, point out in a preface which helpfully introduces Harris's concerns to newcomers that they have worked from sound recordings of the events concerned but have not attempted a literal transcription, although they hope to have retained an orality of tone. Their intention was to 'produce a text which reflected the intricate spiralling of Harris's thought and the interconnecting nature of his logic, which continually reiterates and revises itself', an objective which would seem to be best served by sticking to his actual words. This raises some worries as to the extent of the editing, and undermines confidence that any of the printed text represents precisely what Harris said, although for those who have listened to Harris, the versions given ring 'true' in that they can be readily imagined in his delivery.

The interview with the Scottish poet Alan Riach introduces a discussion of the worldwide Scottish presence within the growth of the English language under empire. Harris suggests that Scotland may offer a more interesting microcosm of Europe than England does, and says, 'I often wonder if the Scottish ethos has not actually permeated the Imperial ethos, because Calvinism was so involved in Imperialism', and identifies 'a peculiar resemblance between Scotland and Guyana'. There is a tendency to forget, he says, the 'traditions which nourish English literature which come out of Scotland, out of Wales, and out of Ireland', and explores this 'complicated reality' through the idea of 'creative schizophrenia' which Michael Gilkes develops in relation to colonial literature.

It would be easy to categorize Harris as a Jungian, but his own comments problematize any glib connections. He had developed independently his own views of the universal unconscious before reading Jung, and states, 'Jung never influenced me, but I had a dialogue with him'. His account of his own creative process demonstrates his openness to the mythical in meaning; as he revised his drafts he would find 'images that seemed to have been planted by another hand', which were both particular, personal, and, because they came out of the unconscious, universal: 'In other words, what is native, what is profoundly native, relates to what is profoundly universal'. Prefiguring the wisdoms of modern critical theory, he sees his own role as agent rather than creator: 'there are strange elements that remain in the text which you cannot properly see ... You cannot *exhaust* the text'.

Harris comments not only on his own work, but on Jean Rhys, Erna Brodber, Pauline Melville and other Caribbean writers and artists (a colour illustration of Aubrey Williams's painting 'Olmec Maya – Night and the Olmec' is included), as well as Homer, Dante, Goethe et al. He is equally at home with the classical and the German philosophers, with the myths of Asia or pre-Columbian America. His own heritage is plural – he is partly of Arawak descent – and he celebrates with conviction the creative potential of cross-culturality, but rejects the current critical orthodoxy which would repudiate all universalism as a form of Eurocentrism. In postcolonial cultures the 'native' archetypes are, he argues, 'all overlaid by European skeletons and archetypes [...] You will never activate them unless you activate the so-called "European" archetypes as well. They are locked together [...] cross-culturalism can no longer be evaded because the whole world has been built on it for centuries.' Those concerned with cultural values and cultural processes, and the theorizing of the aesthetic, cannot afford to ignore what Wilson Harris has to say.

Harris's essay, 'The Fabric of the Imagination', delivered in 1989 at the silver jubilee conference of the Association for Commonwealth Literature and Language Studies (ACLALS) at the University of Kent, is published in *From Commonwealth to Post-Colonial*, edited by Anna Rutherford. He begins by celebrating his inherited language, saying, 'I am not at all engaged in a politics of protest against the language of the so-called imperialist master', identifying instead 'the supreme blessing of a language I genuinely love'. Touching on Poe, Melville, James Hogg and Randolph Stow, as well as his own novel *Carnival*, he addresses the question of the Other. Chaos theory is a development he welcomes; it validates, he asserts, his own idea of 'a thread that may sustain us to cope with an abysmal otherness whom and which we dread but which may also bring resources to alter or change the fabric of the imagination in the direction of a therapeutic, ceaselessly unfinished genesis'. He concludes with a broadside aimed at postmodernism: 'A post-modernism that is bereft of depth or of an appreciation of the life of the intuitive imagination is but a game for a dictatorship of technologies aligned to sophistry and nihilism. Cross-culturalism needs to breach nihilism. I repeat, CROSS-CULTURALISM NEEDS TO BREACH NIHILISM.' Harris, as always, demonstrates how central the Caribbean aesthetic project is to the modern project as a whole.

Barbara Webb also focuses on Harris in her valuable study *Myth and History in Caribbean Fiction*. Taking one writer from each of the main language communities of the region – Carpentier and Glissant are the other two – she collapses the difference between myth and history, referring back to Vico for the idea of myth as 'both a form of historical knowledge and a method of historical inquiry'. The book is divided into three sections entitled 'Myth as a Historical Mode: Lo Real Maravilloso Americano', 'The Problematic Quest for Origins' and 'Myth and History: The Dialectics of Culture'. Works by all three writers are examined under each heading; Harris's *The Secret Ladder*, *Palace of the Peacock*, *Tumatumari* and *Black Marsden* are all given detailed and stimulating analysis. Webb's conclusion is that Harris 'always establishes a negative correlation between myth and history' in order to '*subvert* the role of history'. For him 'myth or the mythic imagination is tantamount to deliverance from the alienating effects of the historical process', which brings him into alignment with Carpentier and Glissant, as they all affirm 'the creative potential of the future in the roots of the past'. The particular value of the book for readers familiar with the anglophone Caribbean lies in its juxtaposition of important hispanophone and francophone texts (discussed in English with the originals in the notes) with Harris's. It is a pity that so few critical studies cross the linguistic divides, preventing the further fragmentation of a geographically fragmented region. Webb's book should be read as much for its absorbing introduction to Carpentier and Glissant as for its critique of Harris. The writers themselves have long paid attention to what artists in other language groups are producing. It is time that more anglophone readers did likewise.

It is a feeling of pathos which emerges most strongly from Tyrone Tillery's biography of Claude McKay. McKay crossed many geopolitical boundaries in his life, but according to Tillery had one great task, his search for identity. The work's long title is *Claude McKay. A Black Poet's Struggle for Identity*, but despite this definition of him in terms of his poetry, he appears here under the 'Novel' heading partly because he is best known as a novelist, but chiefly because Tillery himself is on surer ground when dealing with McKay the novelist. The early part of the book, about McKay's early life in Jamaica, when he was exclusively a poet, displays some alarming misconceptions. He writes of the Jamaican peasant belief that 'natural catastrophes were caused by the Obi or Obeah, a West African god'; and he repeats more than once the errors that the Jamaican medal is the Silver Mulgrave (not Musgrave), and that Tom Redcam's real name was 'MacDermont' (not MacDermot — the whole rationale of the pen-name, a reversal of the real name, is lost). Other elements are worrying in a different way: Tillery's claim, for instance, that McKay's 'artistic creativity and intellectual independence set him apart from most of his fellow Jamaicans' reveals more about Tillery than McKay. None the less, there are tantalizing glimpses of new research even in the Jamaican part of the book. How many are aware, for example, of a 1911 *Gleaner* piece in which G. B. Shaw, visiting Jamaica, said 'what is wrong here is that you produce a sort of man who is only a colonial' and went on to call for the development of specifically Jamaican culture — but this is just adduced uncritically as a footnote to Tillery's generalized point as to the 'difficulty of native Jamaicans to develop and preserve a distinctly Jamaican culture'.

At the outset, Tillery repeats the traditional description of McKay as a Jamaican Robert Burns, but hardly considers the implications of this, or the way in which McKay's early writing was an attempt to establish a distinct Jamaican poetics. He seems more interested in the role of white patronage than in McKay's bisexual vulnerability, which he introduces rather coyly, as if under plain cover. Much of the writing in the early part of the book seems naïve or tentative, but later on, in the sections dealing with McKay's relationship to other black intellectuals of the Harlem Renaissance, and with black America generally, Tillery gets into his stride and writes with energy and understanding of the difficulties, both subtle and crude, a West Indian in New York in the first half of this century had to face. His analysis of McKay's racial dilemmas is illuminating, but he seems insufficiently alive to the role of his sexual dilemmas in complicating them. The critical commentaries are useful, although they often stop short of the really interesting questions: he notes, for example, the way Squire Gensir in *Banana Bottom* is modelled on Walter Jekyll, his early patron, but does not consider the consequent implications for the fictional gender of Bita, who parallels McKay's position; and he nowhere addresses with any seriousness the central question of McKay's use of language.

Tillery's book does, however, paint a convincing and disturbing picture of a society in crisis. McKay's self-distantiation from African Americans became neurotic. Tillery acknowledges his feelings as 'tortured, at best ambivalent', but fails fully to unpack the cultural load McKay trailed, although he does recuperate him to the wider story in his conclusion that he was an 'extreme manifestation' of the black American tragedy. The dimensions of that shared tragedy are evident in some of the primary material Tillery here makes public, which in the end is his book's strength (for instance, the comment by Max Eastman, publisher and McKay's editor, in a 1948 letter to his wife on hearing of his death: 'It is sad to think of McKay, but he really stopped living ten years ago. Too bad, for he had such good brains and so much charm. Perhaps we should have kept him as a cook or a maid').

McKay is also the subject of a collection of papers from a conference on 'Claude McKay, the Harlem Renaissance and Caribbean Literature' organized by Anniah Gowda at Mysore in 1990 to commemorate the centenary of his birth. Edited by A. L. McLeod, *Claude McKay: Centennial Studies* embraces topics such as male bonding, cultural dualism, his ideal woman and his African experience, and brings in Selvon, Reid, Toomer, Zora Neale Hurston and Gandhi for comparison. Carl Pedersen argues provocatively that McKay was the 'true inventor of negritude', but as is perhaps inevitable with collections of this kind a rather patchy image of the man emerges and the quality of the essays is uneven. This is a book for aficionados who will pick it over discriminatingly rather than for readers new to McKay.

Once again it is Naipaul studies that have dominated the field of the novel, however. One of the most finely argued and interesting accounts to emerge for some time is that by Sara Suleri in her book, *The Rhetoric of English India*. Although only a chapter is devoted to Naipaul, Suleri goes beyond his connections with India to give in little a reading of his whole project as a writer. Speaking of his 'uncanny ability to map the complicity between postcolonial history and its imperial past' she calls for an end to the carping about Naipaul, which she sees as reductionist, and a re-engagement with the subtle strategies of the texts themselves. Between her critique's two poles of canonicity and the body, Suleri locates Naipaul's writings as a nervous agitation in the middle. Her analysis of *An Area of Darkness* introduces concepts developed later: 'its language embodies two vital junctures in a consciousness peculiarly situated between colonial and postcolonial worlds: on the one hand, its revision of the literary represents a defetishization of the canonical authority of the British; on the other, it is prepared to address the possibility that the only alternative location left to its narrative is the obsolete fetish of the colonial body'. Taking up the metaphor of the body which is invisible because of its ubiquity – the Naipaul who expresses his dismay at his own invisibility in India, and the omnipresent, disregarded, public defecators in India whom Naipaul likens interestingly to Rodin's sculpture *The Thinker* – Suleri develops some thought-provoking readings. Her comments on *The Enigma of Arrival* in particular make a valuable contribution to a critical canon which had seemed to be settling into a half-reasoned antipathy. She uses the evacuation metaphor in relation to the entropic patterns of the narrative, and perceptively identifies its aporia. In discussing Naipaul's relationship with his father and younger brother, Shiva, whose death *The Enigma of Arrival* commemorates, she rightly identifies repression, the unspoken, and displacement, but seems unaware that *A House for Mr Biswas* is an early fictional 'writing out' of his relationship with his father. In the end she returns to the autobiographical drive in Naipaul's writing, evident in his travel writing as much as in his fiction, ridden by his 'perception of the writer's guilty involvement in the construction of his own plots'. Importantly, she identifies the unique predicament of writers of Naipaul's generation, who have straddled colonial and postcolonial worlds and therefore inherit a problematic which younger writers do not share and tend to dismiss: 'His nervously intelligent anticipation of the obsolescence of his discourse [...] causes his narratives to function as those peculiar paradigms that proffer themselves to the world as though they must be paradigmatic, begging an urgent reading before the context of that urgency has been elaborated'. The 'ideological ambivalence' which results is, Suleri insists, both symptom and strategy, the only course for such a writer (a player whose goalposts have been moved in the middle of the game has only one defence, that of moving them himself). Her assertion is that Naipaul's narratives deserve a reading in the light of that knowledge.

Rob Nixon's monograph on Naipaul is firmly of the other camp, and engages at the outset with Suleri and other attempts to recuperate for Naipaul a sympathetic reading. His rather clumsily entitled *London Calling: V. S. Naipaul, Postcolonial Mandarin* (clumsy also in the frequency of literal errors, not expected from OUP) begins by asserting 'we should avoid the error of viewing Naipaul simply as a writer', a claim which if it were not so serious would be laughable. It is apparent from what follows that 'writer' means something like 'novelist' in the first instance: 'His prestige as a novelist has surely assisted him in sustaining his high profile as an interpreter of the postcolonial world', writes Nixon, who goes on to characterize him as a 'mandarin ... an "expert"', and devotes his study to Naipaul's nonfiction works, which he attacks for their ideology – or supposed lack of it – and for their cumulative, negative representations and presumptions. His discussions therefore start from a hostile premise, and a partial survey. That said, Nixon's analysis is intelligent, perceptive and well-grounded, a paradox which is more frequently evident in literary studies than tends to be acknowledged.

Conrad is a writer whose critical reception – partialities, confusions and all – closely mirrors Naipaul's; between them they present perhaps an object lesson in the pitfalls of irony as creative strategy. In fact, one of the most valuable parts of Nixon's discussion is his chapter on *Heart of Darkness* and its canonical revisions, from Graham Greene to Francis Ford Coppola and Walcott. But his examination of Naipaul's nonfiction account of his up-river journey to Mobutu's kingdom badly needs an accompanying reading of the fiction which grew out of it, *A Bend in the River*. What Nixon's project does is to confirm how virtually impossible it is to separate the 'nonfiction' Naipaul from the 'fiction' writer. The modern understanding of such categories should surely lead to a more sophisticated approach – a sophistication which Naipaul himself exemplifies in his firm statement on the cover of *The Enigma of Arrival*, which presents a quasi-autobiographical narrative, that it is a novel. In spite of this, Nixon includes *The Enigma of Arrival* for extended attention, and ends by criticizing it for what it is not: 'Naipaul's angle, ingenious yet perverse, screens out the violent decrepitude of London and Birmingham's inner cities as well as the monumental industrial collapse of the rusting north, all regions where he could not have nurtured the sensation of his "oddity" or mused with delicate melancholy on the England of Roman conquerors and Camelot.' Aside from the absurdity of indicting a fiction for being itself and not a different fiction, this seems entirely to miss the point of the use of the residually feudal, decaying 'home counties' as mythic signifier, on which the meaning of the whole text is constructed. Nixon does soften towards Naipaul's more recent work, as bearing some evidence of mellowing towards the positive – in *A Turn in the South*, for instance.

For all the irritations of Nixon's attitudinizing, much of his book succeeds in uncovering the specific problematic of Naipaul's personal life, out of which, of course, he writes. At its best it offers insights such as the following: 'His determined disowning of a past that had injured him resulted in a lifelong sensation of severance that he dubiously portrayed as "homelessness". It is only in these later works that he finds the forms of forgiveness – both literary and emotional – that would allow him to reintegrate the perpetual present of elected abandonment into unbroken narrative. This restitution of the past lies at the very heart of his late-middle-aged inquiry into the enigma of arrival.' Nixon might have been better advised to write a biography, for although he rightly identifies a shallowness of critical response to the nonfiction, what he fails to address is the shallowness of the essential distinction between fiction and nonfiction in the first place.

Bruce King, in his *V. S. Naipaul*, takes on virtually the whole of Naipaul's substantial output of fiction, nonfiction and something in between in eight short chapters. The only work he does not examine in any detail is Naipaul's hottest potato, *Among the Believers: An Islamic Journey*. King's style is direct and uncomplicated. He is informative and generally shrewd in his literary judgements, which makes this a useful work of first resort for non-advanced students, although it deals rather too rapidly and shallowly with much of the material to be of more academic value. None the less there are some fascinating snippets of information here, such as that Naipaul played Hounakin in a London production of Walcott's *The Sea at Dauphin* in the fifties. (Other details are inaccurate. King claims that for Trinidadians there was no local university until 1970, when – although it was scandalous that the British did not set up a university in the region sooner, when the Spanish had established universities in their empire back in the sixteenth century – the University College of the West Indies was founded in 1948.) King's judgements are incisive and usually perceptive; sometimes provocative, they are likely to stimulate thought and debate even among those who disagree. Statements such as his summary of *A Bend in the River* as 'perhaps the last modernist epic, using Africa as a symbolic wasteland for the collapse of a universal European order' are sweeping and contentious, but they at least kindle a reaction.

Renzo Crivelli's study of Naipaul's *Enigma of Arrival* employs the de Chirico painting referred to in its title to bring out the metaphysical quality of the novel. In his essay, 'The Paradox of Arrival: Naipaul and De Chirico' (*Caribana* 3) he develops the idea of death as the arrival from which there is no possibility of further departure, applying this to oneiric concepts of time and space. He explores Naipaul's need of mobility and his dread of immobility to perceive a myth of eternal return, of 'a vital circularity, emblem of eternal mystery, not unlike the ancient enclosure of Stonehenge'. For Crivelli this suggests a Yeatsian concept of myth (not often mentioned in the same breath as Naipaul) – of 'a universal reservoir of images in which symbolic systems and cultures that are very different in themselves co-penetrate and become integrated to the point of giving shape to a clear, hermeneutic objective'. Historic time, while certainly problematized by prehistoric and mythic time in the novel, is not perhaps as subordinate as Crivelli would make it, and when he writes of Trinidad's '"indentured labourers" who from time immemorial were employed, under barbarous conditions, in the plantations', he seems to be conflating two quite distinct historic periods and social practices. Nevertheless, his thesis that the geographical journeys are here replaced by 'a new cognitive model: the interior journey' leads him to the thought-provoking insight that Naipaul's arrival is to his 'writing self', which 'arrives, after painful symbolic sedimentations, at the act of composition within a unique system of images and mythological references which proceed from a variety of cultures'. Such comment is a reminder that Caribbean writers are so often questing above all for an aesthetic synthesis.

Women novelists of the region are well served by two studies which demonstrate original and scholarly approaches. Evelyn O'Callaghan's *Woman Version: Theoretical Approaches to West Indian Fiction by Women* takes the figure of the dub version as its trope, tracing it through six heterogeneous chapters which between them give illuminating readings of most of the well-known Caribbean novels by women as well as some less well-known. O'Callaghan picks over others' critical ideas like a magpie, to use them at will in the service of her own overarching conceptual design (which it would be inappropriate to call a master trope). There is charm in her dub metaphor, with all of its implications of versatility and variety, to explore what she plainly sees as a distinctively plural body of texts. She is, of course, also aware of the hostility, among the region's academy, to Northern critical appropriation of the South – its ideological colonization by Western ideas. Yet she refuses to take a monadic oppositional stance. Instead she uses what she wishes when she will, in an eclecticism which is in keeping with her ideology – a policy of 'unapologetic indigenizing appropriation' combining 'methodological heterogeneity *and* ideological commonality while refusing to be ultimately formalized, boxed, labelled under any one "ism"'. The writing, she argues, has a distinctive 'creole ethos', including a range of voices, rather than using speaking from the 'margins' as a means of silencing that which had been centred. The primary bibliography – in itself a fascinating document – lists over 40 female writers, ranging from little-known early novelists (the mid-nineteenth century Mrs Henry Lynch is here, for example, with her three novels, as well as the earlier diarist Lady Nugent), to recently published new talents, such as Elean Thomas and Alecia McKenzie. The critical bibliography is also likely to prove extremely helpful for any students in the field. While, however, she is alive to theory in a constantly organic and stimulating way, O'Callaghan is at pains to stress that in this book 'literary works come first'. She gives such writers as

Brodber, Cliff, Edgell, Hodge, Kincaid, Marshall, Nichols, Rhys and Senior penetrating analysis, which consistently registers the plural intricacies of textuality without becoming obscure or alienating.

Moira Ferguson also offers a fascinating study, which shows how illuminating the drawing of imaginative connections between texts disparate in period and genre can be. Her *Colonialism and Gender Relations from Mary Wollstonecraft to Jamaica Kincaid: East Caribbean Connections* takes the geographical location of the lesser Antilles as its impetus for mapping a web of parallels and differences between a chain of texts, linked by their relationship to history. Ferguson traces the grounding of Wollstonecraft's polemic in philosophical discourse and, while acknowledging her as a pioneer, pinpoints the ambivalence of her position: 'contradiction emerges as a major textual coherence, problem solving beyond reach'. Ferguson goes on to give an absorbing introduction to the Hart sisters, African–Caribbean women in Antigua who in the early years of the nineteenth century wrote a history of Methodism (in the archive of London University's School of Oriental and African Studies) and engaged in abolitionist discourse. Jane Austen is Ferguson's next topic, with *Mansfield Park*, but she argues that it is only the Hart sisters who 'realize how extensively their society constructs them within its dominative hierarchy'. The book then jumps to Jean Rhys's fictional recreation of the post-emancipation period in *Wide Sargasso Sea*. In one of the most original and perceptive contributions to Rhys scholarship for years, Ferguson acknowledges Rhys's ambivalence as both pioneer and conservative: 'From a class, race, and gendered perspective, [she] cannot allow the implied victors of the text to be articulated as victors.' It is to Jamaica Kincaid that Ferguson then looks for the end-point of her argument. In a critique of *Annie John* and *A Small Place* she pinpoints Kincaid's resolutely 'oppositional voice, regardless of consequences', seeing her as enacting 'a politics of engagement, of political exhortation to others to take up cudgels for a future, richer self-determination'. The clarity of Ferguson's analysis and the originality of her scholarship make this an important book.

Followers of Jean Rhys studies will find a number of articles to chew over. Teresa O'Connor gives a tantalizing glimpse in 'Jean Rhys, Paul Theroux and the Imperial Road' (*TCL* 38.iv) of a Rhys story which was never published because it was considered to be, in the terms of a manuscript sale catalogue at the time, 'too anti-negro in tone'. The story, 'The Imperial Road', is alluded to by Theroux, its title of course having a nice irony, as O'Connor's title suggests. Reading her article (or Elaine Campbell's on the subject in *JCL* for 1979) prompts a desire to see precisely what Rhys wrote, without having to trek to the Rhys archive in Tulsa, Oklahoma (which also has the Naipaul archive) to read it. Rhys's complex racial attitudes are also behind Maria Olaussen's 'Jean Rhys's Construction of Blackness as Escape from White Femininity in *Wide Sargasso Sea*' (*ArielE* 24.ii) which goes over some familiar ground without adding a great deal. Thorunn Lonsdale takes on the subject of 'The Female Child in the Fiction of Jean Rhys' (*Commonwealth* 15.i), which pins the Rhys heroine's quest for male partners on the absence of the mother–daughter dyad in the representation of her childhood, reading the male–female relationships as doomed in part because they are mother–daughter surrogates.

The childhood theme is developed further in relation to Caribbean women novelists by Mary Condé. Her 'Unlikely Stories: Children's Invented Worlds in Caribbean Women's Fiction' (*Commonwealth* 15.i) touches on a wide range of texts by Gilroy, Melville, Allfrey, Goodison, Hodge, Senior, Shinebourne, Nichols, Collins, Edgell, Kincaid and Marshall, as well as the old favourite, Rhys. This risks the low impact of the scattershot tactic, but Elaine Campbell restricts herself to four writers. Her 'The Theme of Madness in Four African and Caribbean Novels by Women' (*CNIE* 6.i–ii) addresses, predictably, *Wide Sargasso Sea* yet again, but sets it interestingly against novels by Bessie Head, Myriam Warner-Vieyra and Doris Lessing. She questions whether the trope of madness will continue to be used by women writers to 'express outraged justice [...] The theme of madness may already be yielding to new portraits of strong women who prevail in spite of injustices suffered'. Both Joyce Walker-Johnson and Catherine Nelson-McDermott choose Brodber's *Myal* as their subject. In '*Myal*: Text and Context' (*JWIL* 5.i–ii) Walker-Johnson looks at the sociology of attitudes to illness and healing, and in arguing that the novel tells 'the submerged half of history', concludes that it shows how print culture, 'originally the cause of the individual's and the society's separation from self, can be used to correct images of the people and the society'. Nelson-McDermott too, in her 'Myal-ing Criticism: Beyond Colonizing Dialectics' (*ArielE* 24.iv), begins with sociology, and reads the text through the trope of spirit-thievery, to show how it 'enacts a myal process upon colonialist education systems and notions of community and identity, as well as upon critical dichotomies, by offering the reader alternative methods of perceiving'. Brodber's texts seem to be laying the foundation of a critical industry. A very different writer is Joan Riley, who may not excite women critics in quite the same way but has a huge popular following. Aamer Hussein's interview with her (*Wasafiri* 17) adds new, accessible dimensions to help students engage with her creative project.

Finally, as a reminder of the increasing exchanges between the region's various language communities, and the growing sense of an emerging pan-Caribbean aesthetic which the compass of the works by Benitez-Rojo and Webb reinforces, Gaudeloupe's Maryse Condé is the subject of a special collection of critical essays, in English (*WLT* 67.iv).

(c) Poetry

The vigorous inventiveness and rapidly shifting social interaction of the oral tradition are given a fresh perspective in Rudolph Ottley's book *Women in Calypso*. It presents profiles of and interviews with 15 female calypsonians who came to prominence between 1964 and 1991, and usefully interleaves these not only with photographs but also with the texts of a handful of calypsoes. Ottley briefly acknowledges the male chauvinism typical of the calypso tradition and recommends Rohlehr's study for fuller discussion, but, unsophisticated though his presentation is, a poignant picture is gradually built up of the revolution women have effected in calypso. In the words of Easlyn Orr, 'The sky is the limit / We rising, we rising, we women rising'. Ottley speaks of an 'avalanche' of women into the calypso arena during the late 1970s and the 1980s, but there seems nothing cold about it; as Calypso Rose sings, 'Is people like rain, jammin Port of Spain, / Marine Square hot, Frederick Street hot, / Charlotte Street hot, so I can't stop'. Joslynne Sealey's foreword attributes to the women the 'more sensitive and nurturing calypsoes dealing with social problems, nation building, advice to the youth and personal relationships', a claim which would have been better substantiated if more of the lyrics had been included. It is Drupatee in particular who symbolizes the forward-looking nature of the women's creativity. As the first person of East Indian descent to compete in what has been an African-dominated cultural arena, and as a woman in a heavily male-dominated field, it is appropriate that she should sing of intercultural optimism: 'For the music of the steeldrum from Laventille / Cannot help but mix with the rhythm from Caroni / For it's the symbol of how much we come of age / It's a brand new stage'. A locally published book such as this is a frustrating reminder of how difficult it is for outsiders to be in touch with popular culture and unfolding oral traditions. Those who have read the few books there are and would like to know more need a plane ticket to Port of Spain.

The oral tradition is also Isabella Maria Zoppi's subject in 'Michael Smith: From Myth to History' (*Caribana* 3). The tragic cutting short of Smith's young life raises urgent questions as to how we relate to performance poetry when the performer is no longer with us. Zoppi draws on recordings as well as print versions of Smith's work, and his own discourse about his art, to give a thoughtful and useful introduction to this 'visionary poet'.

Anthony Kellman's anthology *Crossing Water*, billed as contemporary poetry of the English-speaking Caribbean, presents 37 poets, 12 of them women, through recent work. Kellman gives them roughly equal space and is not afraid to offer longer poems, such as David Dabydeen's 'Coolie Odyssey', rather than the short ones typical of anthologies. Walcott and Brathwaite are here, and Scott and Seymour are honoured posthumously with publication of some of their final work, Scott reminding us once again what a major poet he was. His 'Beesong', taken from his last collection, *Strategies*, published in 1989, deserves to become well-known and cherished. The poets are arranged alphabetically, which puts Brathwaite near the beginning and Walcott at the end. Between them is a selection of poets which introduces some new names but is far from representative. Kellman, a Barbadian living in America, has a reasonable selection of poetic voices emanating from the Caribbean (particularly Guyana) and North America, but is light on those writing in Europe and unaccountably omits such significant poets as the firmly Jamaica-based Mervyn Morris and the firmly Guyanese Martin Carter. Obviously a book of some 200 pages has to be selective, but the quality of some of the poets included does not merit such exclusions. Such editorial decisions would have had a clear remit if the volume had been billed as a 'new voices' anthology, but the inclusion of the older generation, specifically the inclusion of the two 'big name' poets, Brathwaite and Walcott, suggests an intention to be representative. Kellman's introduction distinguishes First Generation, Mid-Generation and New Generation poets (the latter offering equivalent talents to the young Walcott and Brathwaite), speaks of a renaissance, and sees the ever-growing band of diaspora poets, in flight from the region's 'political corruption and disorder', as not negative but 'an opportunity for a revision of the self and of history and the Caribbean person's position in world civilization'. While the upbeat tone is a welcome change from some of the negative modelling of displacement, concepts such as 'world civilization' could do with a little analysis. Kellman predicts that the poetry 'will increasingly suggest the public plain from a private, more interior point of view [...] although the "Rhythmn" [*sic*] poets, in the tradition of the calypsonian, will continue their important political and educational role'. Among the fine poems here are some with a strongly oral voice: Sybil Maundy's 'Football Monologue' is a telling addition to a long-established genre and is a reminder of how cultural patterns change – though there is also a cricket poem from Krishna Samaroo. It is good to see the East Indian voices coming through in poetry as well as prose, and the volume is particularly welcome for giving a full-page portrait of its poets, although fuller biographical information would have made it of greater educational use. Foot-notes are supplied to only a small handful of references which will be unfamiliar to outsiders, when more comprehensive footnoting would have aided a wider readership. But above all the volume should be praised for bringing forward some little known significant voices, such as Brian Chan and Rachel Manley, and showing important poets already on the map such as Claire Harris and Kendel Hippolyte, going from strength to startling strength.

Ian McDonald and Stewart Brown, who edit Heinemann's new anthology *Caribbean Poetry*, give a much wider-ranging and more reliably representative selection, with 60 poets represented. Again the emphasis is on recent work (although not so recent as to exclude Victor Questel or Michael Smith, who died in 1982 and 1983 respectively), and again the arrangement is alphabetical. The choice of poems is well judged, with an eye to the variety of a poet's work as well as to the effective individual poem. The editors say their brief was to select 'simply the best', which as they rightly point out is not simple at all. But they have done a fine job in sketching in the variety of shapes and colours – and, yes, the sheer quality – of the anglophone writing of Caribbean people today. Those who read in the introduction of the editors' 'conviction that West Indian poetry is one of the real growing points of contemporary writing' may close the book at Walcott, well satisfied that this is no idle boast. They say they have 'avoided the standard anthology pieces', but it is interesting that new 'standards' seem to be emerging, including some unforgettable, almost epigrammatic poems, such as Agard's 'Pan Recipe', Carter's 'Bent', Escoffery's 'After The Fall', Nichols's 'Epilogue', Scott's 'Epitaph' and Salkey's 'A Song For England'. With such memorable longer poems as Markham's 'Don't Talk To Me About Bread' and Keens-Douglas's 'Wukhand', they as well as several others can all be found in the Penguin anthology too. There are also some agreeable surprises here: new work from Wayne Brown, for instance, after a long silence, and a good clutch of the fine women poets who have come to the fore since the Penguin selection was made a decade ago. However, the editors controversially omit many of the oral poets, such as Mutabaruka and Malik, on the grounds that however powerful in performance their work 'often seems so thin *as text* that to include them in this anthology would be to do [it] a dis-service'. Perhaps the Penguin anthology's oral poetry section demonstrates that there is in fact no shortage of work designed primarily for performance which can also leap into life off the page (I should, of course, declare an interest in this discussion). If McDonald and Brown could have given more than the very occasional footnote – terms such as 'liming', for instance, are obscure to non-Trinidadians – they do give short and helpful biographical and bibliographical notes at the end of the book, although from the incomplete birth dates given, it appears that Fred D'Aguiar, born in 1960, may again be the youngest poet, as he was in the Penguin anthology. It is reassuring to see, none the less, from this often new work, that the anglophone Caribbean community worldwide is still producing so much strong and supple writing, and that its so-called renaissance is an on-going phenomenon, 'win'ing' on.

J. Edward Chamberlin takes a phrase of Derek Walcott's as the title for his study of poetry and the West Indies, *Come Back To Me My Language*. It is an ambitious book, constructed not chronologically or geographically or poet by poet, but under conceptual headings. Each chapter bears a quotation from the poetry as its title, and introduces a theme, supported by informative background material, and explored through a scattering of critical readings of individual works by a range of poets, amongst whom Chamberlin keeps reverting to Walcott. Chamberlin writes with an engaging verve and openness of style, which means that passages such as his introduction to the Columbus encounter could be usefully excerpted for use as a class text with inexperienced students. It also means, however, that there is a certain loss of focus, as the narrative of each chapter flits from one half-read poem to another. There is always a difficulty in knowing where to draw the line in critical publications between the reading which is complete, but so detailed that it becomes alienating as a text (partly because it inevitably seems prescriptive, however much this is disclaimed), and the allusive generalized comment which is referenced to individual works or exemplary short quotation, but which assumes a certain given as to its overall validity. Chamberlin's quotations are, for a book of academic criticism, substantial, quite large chunks of poems being incorporated in the text. On the one hand, this is admirable in that it enables those who do not have at their elbow a comprehensive collection of slim volumes of modern poetry from the region, to at least engage with (parts of) the texts under discussion. However, for what I imagine are logistical reasons, having introduced these chunky quotations, Chamberlin tends to offer a critical evaluation which is either not incontestably manifest from the passage or is swamped by a whole range of other responses which the passage seems to cry out to have discussed. As an academic study this makes it unsatisfactory. Unfortunately, it does not work as a teaching text either (as if each quotation were to be used as a point of departure for group discussion), since the fact that most quotations, although chunky, are not in fact whole poems, would make it essential for an extensive accompanying file of entire poems to be provided. That said, this is an engaging and useful book which takes the study of West Indian poetry on from the short introductions to anthologies and the scattered essays which have been the norm since Lloyd Brown's impressive and still useful *West Indian Poetry*, first published in 1978. A comparison with Brown's structure, however, serves to reinforce the sense that Chamberlin's book would have benefited from a clearer format.

His chapter bearing the same title as the book, for instance, revisits Walcott's 'Sainte Lucie' as the point 'where contemporary West Indian poetry begins, not so much with this poem alone as with the distinctive ambitions it represents ... [Walcott] is asking for a return of original power: the power to bring things into being by naming them; and the power to convey their presence to others'. The chapter, 40 pages long, begins with Naipaul, Brathwaite and Agard, touches on Bakhtin and Jakobson, goes on to Goodison and Merle Hodge, juxtaposes Macaulay, Arnold and Joyce with A. J. Seymour, Philip Sherlock and Sam Selvon, brings in the linguists Cassidy and LePage as well as the OED's Murray, and gives critiques of poems by poets as diverse as Merle Collins, Claude McKay, Martin Carter, Louise Bennett, Evan Jones, Bruce St John, Bongo Jerry, Mervyn Morris and Eric Roach. What emerges is an exploration of the language choices available to the regions' poets, which is both helpful and yet frustrating, as it tends to gallop over its wide territory. Perhaps this is a book to dip into, rather than to read right through, particularly for those who already know a bit about the poetry, for Chamberlin has the gift of encapsulating some keystone ideas with simple clarity. He writes, for instance, of Mervyn Morris's 'Valley Prince', a portrait of Don Drummond the trombonist, that it is 'about a figure who belongs to his place and time the way William Wordsworth's Leech Gatherer did, or Evan Jones's Banana Man, or Lorna Goodison's Guinea Woman, a figure whose identity is both unique and universal, neither straight nor standard but simply and enduringly West Indian'. Chamberlin can be irritatingly naïve (as in his painting analogy on p. 220), but at his best he is both perceptive and memorable.

If Walcott is the presiding genius of Chamberlin's book, it might be fair to characterize Rei Terada's relationship to him in *Derek Walcott's Poetry: American Mimicry* as Jacob wrestling with the angel. Her intelligent, intricate and endlessly inventive attempt to – it has to be said – subdue him to postmodernism somehow ends with a distinct sense that postmodernism's hip is out of joint. It is not difficult, however, to be glad that the attempt was made. Terada's study takes Walcott scholarship on by leaps and bounds, something she is aware of, speculating disarmingly that 'following books [...] will lay the groundwork for this one. Until then, a moment or two out of sequence never hurt anybody.' It is through the particularity of her response and her willingness to use quasi-poetic language that Terada is most illuminating. She writes for instance of some early Crusoe poems as seeming to 'fight their own attraction to culture, throwing the bottle out and watching it return', and characterizes Walcott later as 'a magpie poet'. She has the great gift of modulating her engagement in theoretical abstractions with returns to touch base through the immediacy of imagery; her figure for Walcott's project applies equally to her own: 'As one reads Walcott's poems the particular continually produces the universal, like an everlasting handkerchief from a magician's sleeve'. The conjuring simile is apt, as is its realization in a skein of cloth, as there is something anansi-like in Terada's weaving of her, at times, tenuous argument, which hopes to trap Walcott but in the end fails. Postmodernism does not offer a rhetoric large enough to enclose Walcott's poetry and ends up being itself enclosed. The whole project, in fact, smacks significantly of ideological appropriation – of the kind of intellectual neocolonialism – which the South rightly abhors.

Terada's subtitle is an indicator of the problem. Although she explains that she uses 'American' in its widest sense to embrace all the Americas, and that she distinguishes mimicry from mimesis, the latter, defined as 'the representation of reality', as against the former's 'the representation of a representation, a repetition of something itself repetitious', her definition does not shed the pejorative connotations of 'mimicry' but paradoxically reinforces them. It comes down to the question of the new. Postmodernism, to which Terada adheres like a limpet, if it has a single distinguishing feature, has introduced the idea of the non-existence of the new. Walcott, she argues, understands the inevitable referentiality of language, and she asserts some sensible things: 'each language [...] must finally be viewed as a creole [...] for creolization is the very model of language formation'. Yet this is developed in a way which undercuts its real force: 'creoles, like poetic language, can therefore be seen as language building as though towards a lost unity – piecing together the Tower of Babel – instead of as language degenerating. Poems like "The Schooner *Flight*" emphasize, however, that this construction can never be other than incomplete'. The introduction of the monadic and of the irretrievable here seems altogether awry, destroying what had been a valuable insight. It seems impossible for academics such as Terada to acknowledge the reality of the hope which a poet such as Walcott (and he is not alone) holds out – that cultural creolization is indeed a way of breaking out of the locked spiral of historical determinism.

Terada does not pretend to exhaustiveness. She acknowledges less attention to *Sea Grapes*, *Another Life* and *Midsummer* because they are not as germane to her argument, and admits to a troubleshooting strategy: 'If it's not a problem, I don't mention it (though that doesn't mean that if it is a problem, I do mention it)'. Part of the charm of what she does offer is this going straight for the crux – the intertextuality and the relationship between art and the world. She clearly admires Walcott as poet, although it is disturbing to find her dismissive footnote that she declines to address the drama 'for aesthetic rather than thematic reasons'. The essential arrogance of her stance is clear. Towards the end she perhaps nervously introduces the question of modernism, which her focus on postmodernism has obscured, and bows out, acknowledging both that 'It may be typical of Postmodernism to lose itself in the perspectivism of which it is so fond' and that 'if Postmodern poetry characteristically inhabits and describes the circulation of these perspectives, Walcott's metaphorization of himself as the figure of the contemporary American poet will be difficult to assail'. To shift my opening figure to a related one: in the words of Martin Carter, 'Laocoon, for all the snakes, struggled well'. Terada makes one long for other books of a similar seriousness to wrestle with, and is a reminder that, for all the long list of criticism, Walcott study is still, in a sense, in its swaddling clothes.

Robert Hamner's selection of *Critical Perspectives on Derek Walcott* collects between one set of covers a range of material which would otherwise be quite difficult to assemble, and is for that reason very welcome. But it is also disappointing in that some of the material selected seems less likely to represent a first choice of the wealth of reviews and criticism now available than that which came within the range of a rather limited budget. It is, however, good to see more than a smattering of Caribbean critics, including Rohlehr, Figueroa, Baugh, McWatt and Morris, as well as early classics such as Frank Collymore and Harold Simmons's review of Walcott's first collection of poetry, *Twenty-five Poems*, which contains the prophetic words, 'This poet has lit a beacon that will shine far beyond the horizon of the Caribbean'. It is the first section, however, which is the most valuable, collecting as it does a number of Walcott's own nonfiction pieces, including a handful of Trinidad *Guardian* reviews from the sixties. These provide fascinating glimpses of the interaction between budding writers who were to have such signal careers – such as the stripling Naipaul and the youthful Brathwaite. The gem here, however, is the important, previously unpublished lecture delivered at the University of the West Indies in Trinidad in the sixties, 'The Figure of Crusoe'. In addition, the essays entitled 'Leaving School', part of a series run in the *London Magazine* by Alan Ross, also in the sixties, and the more recent, illuminating 'The Caribbean – Culture or Mimicry?' give precious insight into the origins and objectives of Walcott's aesthetic project. Interviews by Anthony Milne and Edward Hirsch round off the section. The collected essays planned by Farrar Straus and Giroux should, however, be able to provide a thorough handbook to Walcott's art, which this section can only map very sketchily.

The rest of the book is called Part II, and is divided into four chronological sections which borrow the titles of the books of *Another Life* – although in so doing they alter their resonance. In the poem they relate to events before 1973, whereas as section headings here they bring us up to date. It is not helpful, for instance, to have a section titled '"Homage to Gregorias" 1970–79', in which only Edward Baugh has anything to say about painting and Dunstan St Omer, 'Gregorias' in the poem. The decade-based chronology assembles writings on both the poetry and the drama, which gives a fruitful sense of the multifaceted nature of Walcott's work at all points in his career, something which is often absent from critical works which focus on either poetry or drama to the exclusion of the other. However, most of the items are reviews, and not all of them are memorable. The collection as a whole underscores the need for a volume collecting substantial critical essays. There are a few here, among them Patricia Ismond's well-known 'Walcott versus Brathwaite', which laid down a simplistic and (to both poets) unhelpful binary opposition which would have been better forgotten than given a new lease of life in fresh covers. And the cover is indeed fresh – a portrait of a long-haired, seventies Walcott in an exotic carnival costume. The book is worth getting for that alone.

There are a number of essays on different aspects of Walcott's poetry (his drama is considered below). It is always of interest to see what one poet makes of another. Fred D'Aguiar may be drawn to Walcott's *Castaway* and *Another Life* because they were begun in his mid-thirties, the age of D'Aguiar now. In 'Adam's Other Garden: Derek Walcott's Exploration of the Creative Imagination' (*Caribana* 3) he charts Walcott's turning away from history towards myth and nature; nothing new, perhaps, but traced through in an individual way. Russell McDougall offers a meditation on a single poem in 'Music, Body, and the Torture of Articulation in Derek Walcott's "Sainte Lucie"' (*ArielE* 23.ii). Reading the poem as a 'drama of consciousness', he relates it to Ellison's *Invisible Man* through a jazz metaphor. Julie Minkler, on the other hand, addresses Walcott's recent epic *Omeros*, which she relates to Shakespeare's *Tempest* in a rather strained analogy. In 'Helen's Calibans: A Study of Gender Hierarchy in Derek Walcott's *Omeros*' (*WLT* 67.ii) she gives a mythic reading of the poem, identifying its importance in gender terms as one which centres Helen as a figure of Caliban's Woman, the 'female creative force that propagates, procreates, and builds upon her own mental capabilities, without man's or "god's" intervention'. Minkler is interesting even when she is not wholly persuasive, and has the merit of being alive to the endlessly punning playfulness of Walcott.

As well as all the serious scholarship on Walcott, Longman has now issued a York Notes on his *Selected Poems*. Loreto Todd provides useful information for inexperienced students on a selection of 35 poems from Walcott's first six collections of poetry. Expectations that the selection will match Wayne Brown's choice in Heinemann's *Selected Poems* are cheated, however, although there is some overlap. From the most recent collection *The Star-Apple Kingdom*, for instance, Brown has 'Sabbaths WI', 'The Forest of Europe' and the eleventh section of 'The Schooner *Flight*', while Todd comments on section five as well as eleven, and puts 'The Saddhu of Couva' alongside 'Sabbaths WI'. So slight is the scale of his notes that from *Sea Grapes* he selects only three poems, where Brown has ten. So narrow is the space available that he can do little more than headline areas of concern and help with background details. He says he has used three main sources, the Wayne Brown, Stewart Brown's anthology *Caribbean Poetry Now* and Paula Burnett's *Caribbean Verse*, but it might have made better sense for Longman to have swallowed their pride and asked Todd to stick to poems in the Heinemann selection. The scale of Walcott's work, not to mention its range and complexity, make it ever more difficult to address usefully in less than a tome, and this slim volume, while it will have its value for those new to Walcott, fails to address anything from the last 15 years of his prodigious poetic output, which is a pity as some of it – much of *Midsummer*, for example – is among his most accessible work. If Todd had stayed with the Wayne Brown, to end in 1979 would at least have had a rationale; as it is, it is indefensible.

It is good that Walcott is now being taught widely and at a number of different levels, but there are many other Caribbean poets who perhaps lend themselves better than much of his work does to classroom study. One such is Mervyn Morris, a deceptively simple poet whose gem-like poems are beautifully crafted and have luminous depths. In 'Behind the Poems' (*JWIL* 5.i–ii) he provides an extremely useful study guide by giving the background to and an account of the genesis of some of his best-known and best-loved poems. This has a value and a validity which Todd's rather haphazard commercial venture lacks. Armed with the New Beacon-published poems and a copy of this essay – the text of a paper given at the Tenth Conference on West Indian Literature in Trinidad in 1991 – poetry-loving teachers everywhere can offer a really stimulating experience to their students.

(d) Drama
Two drama anthologies have incorporated plays by Caribbean writers. *Cross-winds: An Anthology of Black Dramatists in the Diaspora*, edited by William Branch, reprints Walcott's *Pantomime*, which wittily inverts the Crusoe–Friday paradigm in modern-day Tobago, and Edgar White's 1983 play, *Lament for Rastafari*, which narrates a symbolic journey from Jamaica to England and then on to New York. Branch provides a useful general introduction to African theatre worldwide, but his use of the term 'diaspora' is idiosyncratic: it would not normally suggest the inclusion of, for example, Soyinka's *Death and the King's Horseman* or the South African drama *Woza Albert*, which are very much African plays, although they may have been staged elsewhere.

In *Six Plays by Black and Asian Women Writers* Kadija George offers dramas reflecting the pluralism of British society today, including Winsome Pinnock's *A Hero's Welcome*, and Trish Cooke's *Running Dream*. The volume opens with a series of very short essays by a number of women and an interview with Yvonne Brewster, who laments the fact that as a director in Britain she is still up against those who can accept black people as 'good runners, singers, boxers and dancers, but not good thinkers'. Bernardine Evaristo traces the story of the first black women's theatre company in Britain, and Valerie Small gives a useful introduction to 'The Importance of Oral Tradition to Black Theatre', asking some pertinent questions about what is meant by Black Theatre: does it encompass Shakespeare played by a black cast, for instance, or is it confined to the content of a play? Although she does not provide answers, she does map out the concerns.

On the critical front, Bruce King has edited a global selection of essays on *Post-Colonial English Drama: Commonwealth Drama Since 1960*, which offers introductions to the regions' drama. In his introduction, King uses Walcott as an exemplar of the kind of versatility which went into the early Commonwealth theatre, where a dramatist often 'founded a theatre group, wrote, directed and acted in the plays, and even functioned as publicist, money-raiser, reviewer, and producer'. The regional surveys conclude with a section on the West Indies, with Pierrette Frickey's essay on 'Jamaica and Trinidad', and Renu Juneja's on 'Derek

Walcott'. The headings immediately raise concerns about omissions. What about the rest, Guyana, for instance? Michael Gilkes's *Couvade* is an important play. And is it appropriate to focus on St Lucia's Derek Walcott to the exclusion of his twin brother, Roderick, also a playwright?

Frickey's opening premise of the need for an indigenous drama starts from the extraordinary fact that in Jamaica, in 1914, 14 Shakespeare plays were performed in 20 days. She goes on to point out the crucial importance of the extra-mural department of the University of the West Indies in those early years in fostering writing talent as well as performance. The chapter covers Errol Hill, Trevor Rhone, Mustapha Matura, Dennis Scott, Earl Lovelace and Sistren, the Jamaican women's theatre collective, with each given a short biographical and critical introduction, stimulating and informative. The death of Dennis Scott (according to Frickey a 'possible rival to Derek Walcott because of his talent as poet and playwright') is a reminder that these are a generation of founders, to whom the coming writers will owe a great deal. There is a sense that for most the peak of their activity is over, but some are still producing. The book was just too soon to include Matura's fine play *The Coup* which was premiered at London's National Theatre in 1991. The bibliography of plays and criticism at the end of the chapter is particularly useful; the scale of some of the listings is impressive, with, for example, 14 plays by Errol Hill alone, although none since 1970.

Juneja's chapter on Walcott's drama is long and eccentrically organized (she begins for example with *The Last Carnival* and goes back to earlier plays), but provides a wide-ranging and generally perceptive introduction to the best-known plays, those published in the four collections. She mentions briefly Walcott's first play, *Henri Christophe*, but says nothing about either *Harry Dernier* or his epic drama *Drums and Colours*, commissioned in 1958 for the inauguration of the West Indies Federation. Recent published plays, such as *The Odyssey*, and unpublished ones such as *Viva Detroit!* and *The Ghost Dance* are outside the essay's compass, but even so, the short critiques of each play add up to something of a marathon chapter, which could have done with a sharper overall argument. None the less, its contextualization of the critical analysis in Walcott's thinking, as expressed in his parallel account of his aesthetic project in various essays and interviews, means that the piece provides a useful grounding for those embarking on Walcott studies. There are some misapprehensions and overstatements which undermine its authority, however. Excepting only *The Joker of Seville*, Juneja makes claims that 'as a poet he sometimes leaves the West Indian terrain, but never so as a dramatist', and that first performances of the plays have been 'invariably' in the Caribbean – which are nearly true but not quite. There seems to be some confusion over the meaning of 'French Creole', which Walcott uses in the traditional way to refer to the island-born white planter class, and Juneja's reference to Walcott's avoidance of what she calls the 'extreme' of 'gross overuse of dialect to the point of incomprehension' betrays a blinkered centrism which an editor worth his salt would have excised. Terms such as 'gross' and 'overuse' are offensive, and the phrase masks alarming assumptions as to the status of those whose 'incomprehension' is being privileged over others' comprehension – those whose vernacular language is here being, yet again, marginalized. It may be accurate to say that Walcott steers a judicious path between vernacular and standard polarities in the interests of accessibility, but it is not acceptable – particularly in a serious book of this kind – for such a statement to be couched in terms which assume that the vernacular extremity of the creole continuum is negative, and not a fit language for cultural expression.

Juneja ends rather surprisingly with a brief note on *Omeros* in which, she says, 'the playwright and poet come together in creating a narrative poem with characters as alive and vibrant as in any play' – which is a fair point, but could lead, on this principle of inclusion, to volumes of drama criticism getting very bogged down in the quasi-dramatic aspects of other kinds of text. It is, however, in keeping with the essay's urge to present a discursive overview of Walcott's whole project as a writer rather than a limited sequential analysis of individual dramatic works *in vacuo*, which is, if anything, its strength. And she leaves us with the gem of information that 'Homeros' means 'hostage', applying it neatly to Walcott's project to 'remember the past without becoming hostage to it'. The essay is a reminder that Walcott's drama offers students a way in to his work which is just as stimulating as the poetry – which *is* poetry, most of it – without the allusiveness and intellectual athleticism which the less experienced find off-putting in some of the verse. The plays are extremely sophisticated, but they are also accessible and, quite simply, fun; the poems are frequently witty, but those who are struggling to make sense of them, sadly, often miss the humour. Along with the drama essays in Stewart Brown's *The Art of Derek Walcott*, Juneja's 10,000-word marathon should prove a useful study aid for Walcott's plays.

Juneja takes further her engagement with the region's drama with a welcome article on Dennis Scott's *An Echo in the Bone* (*ArielE* 23.i). Contextualizing the ritual aspects of the drama by reference to Beckwith, Bastide and Alex Haley, she examines its relationship to time, seeing Scott as 'violating the tyranny of chronological memory', and concluding: 'It may be necessary to possess the past in order to function in the present but it is equally necessary not to become possessed by the past'. The essay is a good example of how to stimulate interest in those who do not know a work, as well as those already familiar with it.

The peak of Mustapha Matura's activity as a dramatist came in the next decade after Scott's. Sandra Pouchet Paquet gives a Bakhtinian critique of his Synge intertext in 'Mustapha Matura's *Playboy of the West Indies*: A Carnival Discourse on Imitation and Originality' (*JWIL* 5.i–ii). She begins with a discussion of imitation and assimilation which assumes Walcott and Naipaul as binary oppositions in a way which is actually misleading as to both their positions, but moves on to an effective reading of Matura's play as both carnival art, in the Bakhtinian as well as the Trinidadian sense, and theatre art: 'a drama of imitation and transformation from which indigenous culture emerges refreshed and strengthened'. She ends by arguing that the senior generations' *angst* over identity is here resolved into something 'grotesque and derisive, yet joyous and celebratory', like Port of Spain's carnival.

An intertextual drama of a very different kind is addressed by Robert Hamner in '*The Odyssey*: Derek Walcott's Dramatization of Homer's *Odyssey*' (*ArielE* 24.iv). Responding to the text, and not the production by the Royal Shakespeare Company which commissioned the play (although he mentions reports of it), Hamner goes through the play in a rather descriptive way, concluding that it is a 'fitting complement to Walcott's 1990 rewriting of the venerable epic genre'. It is Hamner too who connects three dramatic explorations of the life of Henri Christophe, the post-revolution Haitian leader. In 'Dramatizing the New World's African King: O'Neill, Walcott and Césaire on Christophe' (*JWIL* 5.i–ii) he examines the differences and similarities between O'Neill's *The Emperor Jones*, Césaire's *La Tragédie du Roi Christophe* and Walcott's *Henri Christophe* which precedes the Césaire, written in 1950 when he was 20 years old. O'Neill's one-act drama from 1920 was, Hamner argues, progressive for its time but limited by stereotypes, while Walcott's use of a Jacobean tone smacks of 'the very cultural imperialism that enslaved Christophe to European models'. Césaire's play brings 'the enigma of Christophe full circle', with the protagonist as a kind of demiurge, mirrored in the life of the dramatist. Hamner concludes that while O'Neill brought the story to mainstream theatre, it is Walcott and Césaire who exploit its 'tragic example, the dangerous implications for black consciousness and for the political aspirations of the entire Third World'. There may be rejoinders one could make to this, but the essay maps some thought-provoking connections, and is a reminder once again of the early contribution Walcott made to the development of the region's literature. It is something of a surprise to think of him, in this context, as in a sense 'senior' to that grand old man, Césaire.

The dominance of the region's prose fiction as the object of critical attention has been long due for relaxation; the drama, which tends to be so little known (as well as the relatively well-known phenomenon of the poetry) can offer fresh pastures, as Juneja, Paquet and Hamner have evidently realized. An interview with two members of the Sistren collective (*ArielE* 23.i) is a reminder of the endlessly fascinating process of drama, which is not just text, not just performance, but a continual creative exchange between life and art. It is salutary to realize that Sistren has kept going, against the odds, since 1977 and has refused to compromise its principles. As Pauline Crawford puts it when considering the lure of sensationalism as audience bait, with its corollary of negative portrayals of women, 'Since 1977, we have not moved from the line where we are. Who are going to be the role models? Sometimes we have to jolt ourselves to say well, look, yes we're not making the money for the productions and if we were to shift a little, it would bring in more. But we won't shift.' Our increasingly compromised times can learn from such a statement of faith.

5. India

This section is divided into two sub-sections: (a) General, Poetry and Drama; and (b) Fiction.

(a) General, Poetry and Drama

'Indian Literature in English' has long been recognized as a problematic term, and recent developments in theory and practice often militate against attempts to offer a simple demarcation of this area of study. The Indian diaspora alone problematizes definition, and trends towards the comparative study of texts written in English and indigenous language texts, particularly in English translation, further complicate a survey of the field. Moreover, the emphasis in some academic quarters on cultural as opposed to literary studies means that a number of recent critical works stress the hybrid and overlapping nature of the postcolonial world. This general section therefore attempts to take account of the shifting nature of the field.

For bibliographical information Shyamala A. Narayan's entry on India (*JCL* 28.iii.45–68) is as thorough as ever. The introduction reviews creative writing, noting that no new drama was published in 1992. The accompanying bibliography is an indispensable source, particularly for details of work published in India.

Reworlding: The Literature of the Indian Diaspora (1992), edited by Emmanuel S. Nelson, is a collection of 14 informative essays which discuss writing from the major areas of the Indian diaspora: the South Pacific, the Caribbean, Singapore, Britain, the United States, Canada and Africa. In his introduction, Nelson suggests that the diasporic paradigm enables a global (rather than merely national or regional) approach, allowing us 'to grasp more fully the unresolved tensions in the diasporic consciousness that shape those texts as well as the ethnohistorical significance of those texts'. This approach also allows for some comparative analysis; see, for example, K. Chellappan's 'Voice in Exile: "Journey" in Raja Rao and V. S. Naipaul', and C. L. Chua's 'Passages from India: Migrating to America in the Fiction of V. S. Naipaul and Bharati Mukherjee'. Craig Tapping's 'South Asia/North America: New Dwellings and the Past' demonstrates something of the intriguing scope of the paradigm by looking at the work of a disparate group of writers (Ved Mehta, Rohinton Mistry, Bharati Mukherjee, Suniti Namjoshi, Michael Ondaatje, Vikram Seth and Sara Suleri) who are united by their historical situation, and 'who variously emplot their relation to the partition of the Indian subcontinent [...] the consequent political histories of newly created nations and nationalities which they have variously left, and the construction ... of even newer identities in the countries to which they have emigrated'. Whilst the collection is dominated by fiction studies, there is some examination of other genres in, for example, Tapping's analysis of autobiography, and Lawrence Needham's '"The Sorrows of a Broken Time": Agha Shahid Ali and the Poetry of Loss and Recovery'. Naipaul's work is especially prominent, as is that of Rushdie, whose novels are considered in Anuradha Dingwaney's 'Author(iz)ing *Midnight's Children* and *Shame*: Salman Rushdie's Constructions of Authority' and Vijay Lakshmi's 'Rushdie's Fiction: The World Beyond the Looking Glass'. Also worth noting in the present context is Hena Ahmad's 'Kamala Markandaya and the Indian Immigrant Experience in Britain'. On the whole, this is a stimulating collection that extends the frames of reference for the study of Indian writing in English.

An Introduction to the New Literatures in English, by Jean-Pierre and Carole Durix creditably performs the difficult task of surveying Indian writing in English in a very short chapter. There are inevitable omissions, but the authors manage to outline many key areas, including 'Tradition and the Rise of Anglophone Literature', 'The Poetic Tradition', 'Women Novelists', and 'Metafiction', whilst giving useful introductions to the work of Mulk Raj Anand, Raja Rao, R. K. Narayan, Anita Desai and Salman Rushdie. Clearly orientated to the teaching of New Literatures, the volume includes some useful extracts from the writers' work, and some sample questions for students.

G. N. Devy's 'Indian Literature in English Translation: An Introduction' (*JCL* 28:i.123–38) suggests that 'Indian Literature in English Translation (ILET) is rapidly becoming an indispensable component of literary and cultural studies in India'. He links this to a number of sociological changes such as the spread of education and the undermining of traditional language loyalties, whilst also noting that in English studies generally there is a movement away from the 'romantic notion of homogeneity among various Anglophone post-colonial litera-tures' to an awareness of Indian–English literature as 'an integral part of the mosaic of Indian literatures rather than as a part of the lame-duck group of literatures in English'. Devy gives a good survey of the history of ILET over the past 200 years, as well as a more detailed introduction to a selection of works in

Marathi. The article is persuasively argued and full of useful bibliographical information. In the light of Devy's assertions it is also worth noting the launch this year of the Heinemann Asian Writers series, which offers six works of fiction in English translation: *Quartet* by Rabindranath Tagore, *The One Who Did Not Ask* by Altaf Fatima, *Water* by Ashokamitran, *The Fire Sacrifice* by Susham Bedi, *Scavenger's Son* by T. Sivasankara Pillai and *Janani* by Shaukat Osman.

Susie Tharu and K. Lalita are among those critics and scholars singled out by Devy for special praise. Their *Women Writing in India: 600 B.C. to the Present: Volume II: The Twentieth Century*, is one of the year's major publishing events. Together with Volume I, this project makes available an impressive range of writing, chiefly in translation, from the past two and a half thousand years. The title of the second volume is slightly misleading: all of the writers included were born this century, but the selections themselves are drawn from the 1940s onwards (picking up where the last volume left off). Whilst acknowledging, in the preface, some important omissions (including, for example, writing in Punjabi, Rajasthani, Kashmiri and Sindhi), the editors have nevertheless produced an excellent anthology of writing in English translation that includes prose fiction, poetry, drama and other genres. Tharu and Lalita go to great lengths to clarify the theoretical context of their project. The introduction offers a survey of chiefly American feminist approaches to the recovery of women's voices in literary studies, whilst expressing concern regarding the dangers of applying western theories to Indian women's writing, specifically in adopting a universalizing, essentialist view that fails to account for the particularities of class, caste, race and imperialism. They then offer a lengthy essay entitled 'Women Writing the Nation', which is at pains to locate the texts (and, indeed, the whole project) in a specifically Indian context, and to demonstrate their relevance to cultural studies by including, for example, an outline of post-Independence political history. In short, the texts are very firmly placed. The unfortunate side-effect of this mass of critical comment, together with substantial biographical and critical headnotes, is that space for the writings themselves is rather limited. The reader is presented with some often frustratingly brief extracts and short pieces. One is left wondering why these hitherto marginalized voices are not allowed fuller expression. Nevertheless, the project as a whole has clearly energized a debate that not only addresses the triple marginalization of Indian women writing in indigenous languages, but also questions the very construction of literary studies as an academic discipline.

The critical impact of *Women Writing in India* is apparent in Rajeswari Sunder Rajan's *Real and Imagined Women:Gender, Culture and Postcolonialism*. Whilst praising the 'stupendous research, scholarship and critical energy' of Tharu and Lalita's work, Sunder Rajan is critical of the opposition that the editors, in their critical commentary, maintain between the political and the aesthetic. She quotes at length from her own review of Volume I as a starting point for her enquiry into postcolonial feminist issues with special reference to India. The review itself is a cogent appraisal of Tharu and Lalita's critical stance and methodology, and particularly their celebration of resistance. Sunder Rajan feels that 'it is time for a judicious review of the politics of women's writing — one which recognizes that it is not always resistant, and which historicizes its conformism scrupulously'. The essays that follow 'attempt to map the space of the postcolonial female subject' through an examination of a wide range of texts including film, journalism and prose fiction. The results are often striking; in a chapter entitled 'Life After Rape: Narrative, Rape and Feminism', a short story in Tamil ('Prison', by Anuradha Ramanan) is chosen as 'a model against which the master-texts of "first world" literature [in this case, *Clarissa* and *A Passage to India*] and their criticism can be measured'. Sunder Rajan also makes excellent use of the comparative method in a chapter on 'Gender, Leadership and Representation: The "case" of Indira Gandhi', analysing O. V. Vijayan's Malayalam story, 'The Foetus', and Salman Rushdie's *Midnight's Children* to examine representations of Indira Gandhi during the Emergency.

Prominent within the school of critics and theorists whose work tends to be labelled 'cultural studies' is Gayatri Chakravorty Spivak. *Outside in the Teaching Machine* is a demanding, densely written and wide-ranging study of gender, postcolonialism, multiculturalism and the uses of contemporary theory. Some idea of Spivak's co-ordinates may be gleaned from the following statement: 'Mahasweta Devi is as unusual within the Bengali literary tradition as Foucault or Derrida within the philosophical or political mainstream in France. She is not representative of Third World feminism.' Once again, the study of indigenous language texts (in this case, through detailed discussion of the work of Mahasweta Devi, widely felt to be the most significant contemporary Bengali novelist) promotes a recasting of critical perspectives. Perhaps unsurprisingly, the English language writer who receives Spivak's most detailed attention is Salman Rushdie. In a chapter entitled 'Reading *The Satanic Verses*' she moves out from 'the impossible: a reading of *The Satanic Verses* as if nothing has happened since late 1988', to a consideration of the cultural politics of the 'Rushdie affair'.

Given the proliferation of writing informed by and extending contemporary theory in relation to postcolonial issues, *Colonial Discourse and Post-Colonial Theory: A Reader* is a timely and invaluable collection. The editors, Patrick Williams and Laura Chrisman, supply a cogent general introduction to the field and succinct summaries of the individual perspectives. Indian themes and writers are well represented. Spivak's influential piece 'Can the Subaltern Speak?' is usefully reprinted, together with essays from, among others, Homi K. Bhabha and Aijaz Ahmad. There is a liberal sprinkling of references to Rushdie throughout the collection.

Raj Nostalgia: Some Literary and Critical Implications (1992), edited by Annie Greet, Syd Harrex and Susan Hosking, offers an interesting grouping of pieces, of which the centrepiece is Salman Rushdie's celebrated attack on 'Raj Nostalgia' and the separation of politics and art, 'Outside the Whale'. The range is wide, including a contribution from Nayantara Sahgal, 'An Indian Family, A Struggle for Freedom', which consists of modified extracts from her 1956 memoirs, *Prison and Chocolate Cake*, and a rather slight and inconclusive piece by R. K. Narayan, 'After the Raj'. Syd Harrex supplies a useful historical and literary contextualization of some key figures and texts in Indian writing in English from Rammohun Roy to Rushdie in the opening essay, 'Introductions'. He also gives a stimulating comparative analysis of British and Indian fiction in 'The Game and the Goal: Kipling, Forster, and the Indian English Novel', which includes some consideration of the work of R. K. Narayan, Raja Rao and G. V. Desani. Narayan also features in S. Nagarajan's 'The Englishman as a Teacher of English Literature Abroad', which looks at The Bachelor of Arts and the work of Edward Thompson. The whole volume testifies to the value of the comparative method by bringing together Indian, Australian and British perspectives on many aspects of the imperial encounter.

Enormously influential in the broad field of cultural/postcolonial studies is the work of Edward W. Said. *Culture and Imperialism* is a refreshingly accessible and very extensive analysis of the links between European culture and imperial practice, and their implications for the postcolonial world. Said insists on a philosophy of interconnectedness: 'No one today is purely one thing. Labels like Indian, or woman, or Muslim, or American are no more than starting points, which if followed into actual experience for only a moment are quickly left behind [...] Survival in fact is about the connections between things.' Salman Rushdie once again provides a point of reference, and whilst there is no sustained analysis of individual works, Said does refer to *The Satanic Verses* and some of its consequences, as well as *Midnight's Children* and the essay 'Outside the Whale'. His work is also notable, in the present context, for the way in which it promotes the practice of reading earlier canonical works, such as *Kim*, alongside contemporary postcolonial texts.

Sudhakar Marathe, Mohan Ramanan, and Robert Bellarmine are the editors of *Provocations: The Teaching of English Literature in India*, an extensive collection of papers from the 1991 TELI seminar at Hyderabad. These offer a vigorous discussion of the perceived 'crisis' in English studies in India, and include some refreshingly pragmatic approaches to the postgraduate classroom situation. The editors' introduction is interestingly opposed to the use of 'the latest theories imported from the Anglo-American academy and from France' which seek to 'use English departments to get rid of English altogether', and the tone of the volume as a whole is cautiously optimistic about the future of English Studies in India. Perhaps the most notable contribution is Meenakshi Mukherjee's 'Certain Long-Simmering Questions', which considers the shifting theoretical and practical issues with considerable clarity, suggesting that 'there is a growing awareness that English teaching in India cannot be re-examined without correlating the literary text that is taught in the classroom with the social text in which the teacher and the taught live'.

The text of the Arthur Ravenscroft Memorial Lecture, given this year by Nayantara Sahgal, is published in *JCL* (28:i.3–15). 'Some Thoughts on the Puzzle of Identity' sees the novelist in combative mood, stressing that the essence of her own 'cherished sense of Indianness' is its 'ethnic and religious diversity, and its cultural plurality', and resisting the imposition of Western modes of thought and practice on India. Of her own novels she says, 'I don't write about caste, joint family, or picturesque ethnicity. I'm more interested in trying to trace in human terms the implications of what happens to us politically [and] the ideas and behaviour that religion breeds in us'.

Vikram Seth is fast becoming recognized as the 'renaissance man' of Indian literature in English. *PoetryR* (83:ii.56–9) includes an interview from 1986 which chiefly concerns his views on poetry and his novel in verse, *The Golden Gate*. Seth's facility for working in a variety of genres, his interest in translation and his cosmopolitan experience make him difficult to categorize, but he nevertheless considers India to be 'home', and describes himself as 'foremost an Indian writer'. He also ruminates briefly on 'a solid Victorian-type novel set in India', and states that 'eventually, what critics say is entirely irrelevant'.

PoetryR (83:iii.77) includes a tribute to A. K. Ramanujan by Bruce King. Ramanujan's death means that we have lost not only a major poet but also a fine translator. *PoetryR* (83:i) is a special issue; subtitled 'In Search of Kavita: Poetry from the Indian Subcontinent and Beyond', it offers an excellent survey of the current state of Indian poetry, chiefly written in English, but with a few translated works. The range is pleasingly wide; a generous selection of poems from established names such as Eunice de Souza, Keki Daruwalla, Kamala Das and Jayanta Mahapatra is presented together with work by many of the younger talents. There are some interesting surveys of Bengali poetry and of the 'new generation' of English language poets, the latter including a brief consideration of the diaspora in its widest sense. The numerous book reviews and articles also contain much useful bibliographical information.

There has been a familiar lack of drama criticism this year, but Routledge's publication of Rustom Bharucha's *Theatre and the World: Performance and the Politics of Culture* (originally published in 1990) makes this stimulating critique of intercultural theatre more readily available. M. N. Sundararaman's 'Tradition and Modernity in Indian English Drama' (*JIWE* 21:i.1–13) is also worth noting as a brief examination of some recent drama in relation to Indian classical and western influences.

(b) Fiction

Given the problems of categorization mentioned in the general section of this review, readers should also refer to that section for works that include discussion of Indian fiction in English. This section will review books and articles more specifically and exclusively concerned with the Indian novel and short story in English.

Chitra Sankaran's *The Myth Connection: The Use of Hindu Mythology in Some Novels of Raja Rao and R. K. Narayan* demonstrates that useful and illuminating work can still be produced in the more 'traditional' author-centred mode of criticism. Sankaran takes six novels by Rao and Narayan (*Kanthapura*, *The Man-Eater of Malgudi*, *The Serpent and the Rope*, *Mr Sampath*, *The Cat and Shakespeare* and *The Guide*) and locates them very clearly in the context of Hindu mythology and philosophy. Her introduction gives a useful summary of the importance of myth in Hindu narrative, and the following chapters, whilst mainly devoted to individual works, supply excellent specific and comparative insights into novels that might be thought to have been exhausted in critical terms. Analysis of Rao's work in such a context could become especially obscure, but Sankaran clearly delineates the Hindu philosophical underpinning of his novels without oversimplifying the complex range of references on which they depend. The chapters on Narayan are especially good, making apparent the specifically Hindu cultural context of his work, and ably demonstrating the influence of indigenous models on his narrative technique.

Modern Fiction Studies (39:i) devotes a special issue to 'Fiction of the Indian Subcontinent'. Aparajita Sagar's introduction stresses 'the need to position South Asian fiction and our readings beyond literary criticism and in the contested and interdisciplinary ground of cultural studies'. Most of the essays focus on one or two novels, in many cases offering critical revisions of some much-discussed texts; for example, Teresa Hubel's 'Charting the Anger of Indian Women Through Narayan's Savitri', looks at R. K. Narayan's *The Dark Room* in the light of the 1930s women's movement in India, whilst Alpana Sharma Knippling's 'R. K. Narayan, Raja Rao and Modern English Discourse in Colonial India' examines *The English Teacher* and *Kanthapura* from a Foucauldian perspective. A reasonable range of women's writing is considered; Geetha Ramanathan's

'Sexual Violence/Textual Violence: Desai's *Fire on the Mountain* and Shirazi's *Javady Alley*' draws parallels between these Indian and Iranian texts; Anuradha Dingwaney Needham's 'Multiple Forms of (National) Belonging: Attia Hosain's *Sunlight on a Broken Column*' renews interest in a novel that, as a 'narrative of nation', pre-dates Rushdie's more celebrated *Midnight's Children* by two decades; and Rajeswari Sunder Rajan's 'The Feminist Plot and the Nationalist Allegory: Home and the World in Two Indian Women's Novels in English' examines Sashi Deshpande's *That Long Silence* and Nina Sabal's *Yatra* (*The Journey*). The inclusion of a piece on Rushdie is almost inevitable in the context of this special issue and its theoretical concerns; Clement Hawes, in 'Leading History by the Nose: The Turn to the Eighteenth Century in *Midnight's Children*' offers an absorbing discussion, prompted by the complex intertextual relationship between Rushdie's novel and *Tristram Shandy*. Finally, Nivedita Bagchi's 'The Process of Validation in Relation to Materiality and Historical Reconstruction in Amitav Ghosh's *The Shadow Lines*' examines a fascinatingly convoluted narrative which 'undermine[s] the West's craving for validity, chronology, and order by taking recourse in a language that undermines the concept of chronology itself'.

Catherine Cundy's 'Rushdie's Women' (*Wasafiri* 18.13–17) gives a cogent account of the continuing and now ingrained tendency to 'demonize the female' in all of his novels, further suggesting that there is a contradiction between Rushdie's 'non-fictional espousals of the cause of women and his fictional representations of them'. In '"The Gardener of Stories": Salman Rushdie's *Haroun and the Sea of Stories*' (*JCL* 28:i.114–22), Jean-Pierre Durix offers a fairly extensive commentary on Rushdie's recent novel that locates it in relation to its hybrid range of reference: 'the novel becomes a library of world literatures, a combination of high-brow and popular culture, of adult and children's fiction, an unusual synthesis of varied cultural sources'. Durix also explores some of the ways in which *Haroun and the Sea of Stories* reflects the writer's personal situation.

Subhendu Mund's 'Towards the Horizon: A Study of the Early Indian English Novelist's Use of Language' (*Wasafiri* 18:45–8) looks at some of the ways in which nineteenth-century Indian novelists developed their own idiom 'to present typical Indian situations and experiences', and suggests that this formed a legacy for 'the next generations of Tagore, Raja Rao, Anand and Amitav Ghosh'. Amin Malak's 'The Shahrazadic Tradition: Rohinton Mistry's *Such a Long Journey* and the Art of Storytelling' (*JCL* 28:ii.108–18) is chiefly concerned with enumerating 'the salient features of storytelling that have bearing on our reading of *Such a Long Journey*'. The discussion that follows offers some illustrations of the nature of oral narrative in general, but there is relatively little sustained analysis of Mistry's novel. Finally, Michel Pousse's 'R. K. Narayan: Confronting the Man and his Manuscripts' (*CE&S* 16:i.49–62) discusses the collection of papers held by the University of Boston.

6.   New Zealand and the South Pacific

This section is divided into the following sub-sections: 1. New Zealand: (a) General Studies; (b) Fiction; (c) Poetry; (d) Drama and Theatre; and (2) The South Pacific.

1. New Zealand

(a) General Studies

The New Zealand section of the *JCL* Annual Bibliography of Commonwealth Literature 1991 (*JCL* 28.ii (1992).72–92), compiled by John Thomson, includes entries from the South Pacific islands this year, but has no introductory article. The review journal *New Zealand Books* is now in its second year and provides an excellent account of the most notable book publications. It has the format of the *TLS* but is only concerned with New Zealand. Review articles are commissioned and the choice is varied – novels, poetry, anthologies, criticism as well as reference books. The journal also publishes a little poetry and opens out its focus onto comments on literary events and a general view of the arts in New Zealand. The *CRNLE Reviews Journal* from Flinders University, South Australia, devoted its first issue this year to New Zealand Literature; apart from the usual review articles, a considerable number of contributions give a more extensive view of the field – these are accounted for in the appropriate sections of this article.

Heather Murray in 'Celebrating Our Writers: 1936, 1951' (*JNZL* 10.99–114) gives a detailed overview of the events of 'Author's Week' in 1936. This year was an initial turning-point in the history of New Zealand literature, for it installed the up-coming writers centred around the *Phoenix* magazine in positions of power which enabled them to demote the former established colonial writers. In 1936, many women were recognized for the quality of their writing but, under the regime of the Phoenix group, by 1951, they had largely been reduced to silence. Murray goes on to review the varying literary and political arguments put forward in different newspaper articles of the time. In 'Splitting the Golden Arrow: Immigrants, Emigrants and Exiles' (*JNZL* 10.3–8) Alan Riach examines the implications of the 'melting pot' in a multi-cultural nation; although exclusion from the various appurtenances occurs, Riach illustrates that those writings which survive are enriched linguistically and culturally, thus earning a double place in the literary posterity of both the country of origin and the immigrant's adopted homeland.

Basing her remarks on the correspondence and writings of Mary Taylor and Charlotte Brontë, Jane Stafford in ' "Remote must be the shores": Mary Taylor, Charlotte Brontë and the Colonial Experience' (*JNZL* 10.8–15) is particularly concerned with the '*décalage*' between the colonial experience as recounted in the letters (with the self-imposed constraints of the genre) of Mary Taylor and the transformation of the information into fiction within the constraints and environment of colonial Britain by Charlotte Brontë. Brontë places in her fiction descriptions of situations that she can hardly apprehend, while Taylor has to use her literary experience in order to convey some idea of the strangeness of her new abode.

Lydia Wevers's 'Big Picture, Short Text: New Zealand Short Fiction in the 1990s' (*CRNLE* 1.49–55) looks in particular at the tremendous variety of attitudes in short stories by Manhire, Te Awekotuku, Wells, Delahunty, Cranna and Lloyd Jones. Wevers believes that, while New Zealand short fiction has in the past 'contributed rather more to the perceived homogenization of a national culture than to its proliferation of difference', recent collections of short stories are more concerned with dismantling stereotypes that are to be found in national history. If readers recognize the familiar, they are also aware of the inexplicable in these texts. Wevers concludes that 'it is precisely this sense of the movement and instability of cultural identity that short fiction exploits'.

(b)   Fiction

In his very perceptive and analytical article, 'Gender and the Politics of Tradition: Alan Duff's *Once Were Warriors*' (*Kunapipi* 15.ii.57–67), Nicholas Thomas starts from the premise that, while indigenous cultures are widely legitimized and celebrated, this image fits uneasily into the present-day urban, unemployed reality of the Maori. He argues that the 'primitive' is preferred to the 'modern' so that the phrase 'modern indigenous' tends to become a contradiction in terms. In these circumstances how can the contemporary modern indigenous writer convey present realities without being excessively negative? Duff's *Once Were Warriors* powerfully and uncompromisingly depicts Maori life today, while simultaneously evoking a heroic past. Thomas maintains that, by pushing the negative view of present day Maori society, Duff 'makes the operation of anti-idealization visible', thus opening up the possibility of reappropriating the past without falling into the trap of archaism. Thomas concludes that this novel is an initial step out of the straitjacket of post-colonial discourse on indigenous society but fails to proceed beyond negation.

Perhaps the most important literary criticism event in New Zealand in 1993 was the publication in the *Journal of New Zealand Literature* of the papers delivered at the inaugural conference of the Association of New Zealand Literature (ANZL) devoted to the work of Janet Frame, and held in August 1992. This issue illustrates the continuing interest in Frame's writing and will constitute another indispensable volume for Frame scholars. Patrick Evans gave the formal address at the Conference dinner in which he underlined the initial reasons that lie behind Janet Frame's self-effacement – the difficulties of her early life both at home and in medical institutions, and her emergence as a writer at a time when the literary establishment was essentially male and unused to radical, innovative writing. Despite these adversities, Frame's writing firmly established itself. In 'The Case of the Disappearing Author' (*JNZL* 11.11–20), Evans goes on to analyse how Frame's self-effacement is counterbalanced by a strong need to belong within society; her resistance to outside encounters is driven by a need to survive the onslaughts of realism and criticism. The result is a writing technique that is deliberately severed from reality and which provides space for the reader to bring his personal contribution to the text: 'The very act of disappearance [that] enables her to write at all draws our attention to the fact that she has withdrawn.'

Susan Ash uses the theory whereby Bakhtin differentiates the epic from the novel by the epic's use of 'an absolute past' and of 'the absolute distanced image' as a basis for her excellent article ' "The Absolute, Distanced Image": Janet Frame's Autobiography' (*JNZL* 11.21–40). Ash analyses the conflation of the time of the story with the time of narration as well as of Frame's various comments on her work in later interviews. Ash then outlines the methods by which Frame, the writer, separates herself from Frame, the subject of the auto-biography, and again further distances the narrative in her comments on her work in a later interview published in *Landfall*. In her comparison of Frame's accounts of her stay in a mental hospital at Seacliff in *Scented Gardens for the Blind* and the autobiography, Ash underlines that the time/space element of the novel is 'continuous with no fixed border(s)' whereas in the autobiography these elements are separated and distinctly distanced in the past. Consequently, this critic believes that 'the narration of consciousness in the autobiographies constitutes Frame herself as "absolute distanced image", which helps to install and maximize the absolute epic distance between the reader and the autobiography's "hero"'. Ash concludes first that the autobiography seals off the reader's direct response by the deployment of narrative strategies to isolate the subject Frame from the present writer. Her final comments on Frame's difficulty to exist in a male-oriented world are far less convincing.

Gina Mercer's '"A Simple Everyday Glass": The Autobiographies of Janet Frame' (*JNZL* 11.41–8) is a descriptive article confronting the impressions the reader has formed of the writer with the image that Frame has inscribed in the autobiographies. Indicating that the autobiographies seem much less complicated than the novels, Mercer expresses her preference for the fiction but nevertheless distances herself from those male critics who have discerned lacks and lacunae in the autobiographies. In '*A State of Siege*: The Sociable Janet Frame' (*JNZL* 11.49–58) Ruth Brown examines conflicting ways of seeing. Taking *A State of Siege* as a focal point, Brown traces the development of the idea that society, with all its material comfort, provides a 'false' way of seeing; she, however, challenges some artists' construction of the artist as a 'man alone' within society, for the heroine of the novel, Malfred Signal, fails to find any specific artistic vision in her isolation. The heroine's death would, according to Brown, signify a transcendent status for the artist who, within society, endeavours to construct meaning out of chaos.

Judith Dell Panny also explores the vision and creativity of an artist in 'A Hidden Dimension in Janet Frame's Fiction' (*JNZL* 11.59–70). She maintains that, in Frame's fiction, there is 'a carefully ordered allegorical pattern that has been deliberately concealed' and that 'its moral purpose is to encourage a reassessment and questioning of codes and values that have long been taken for granted'. She compares the imagery of *Intensive Care* with the motif of father–daughter incest in Milton's *Paradise Lost*. In her article, 'Powers of Speech and Silence' (*JNZL* 11.71–88), Tessa Barringer uses the theories of Julia Kristeva to elucidate the positioning of the characters in relation to the oedipal triangle in *Scented Gardens for the Blind*. In this novel, the central character has refused to assume her place in society by a rejection of speech. Her return to society must involve language, but the words she utters at the conclusion of the novel remain ambivalent and disturbing.

Using Freudian dream theory and Kristeva's definition of abjection, Howard McNaughton studies the varying aspects of textuality and subjectivity in the narrative construction of *Owls Do Cry* in 'Abjection, Melancholy, and the End Note: The Epilogue to *Owls Do Cry*' (*JNZL* 11.89–105). He perceptively examines the way in which the characters textualize themselves and are textualized by others. Contesting the claim that the italicized passages run parallel with Daphne and that the Epilogue represents a wider implication of the novel, McNaughton suggests that this final section of the novel may be considered as end-notes, in which case 'questioning the textual status of the Epilogue in this way asks whether it constitutes part of the body of the novel proper, and whether it is an authenticating – or voiding – appendage'. In 'A Ventriloquist in the House of Replicas: A Reading of *The Carpathians*' (*JNZL* 11.106–13), Valerie Sutherland also claims that the exploration of language, narrative voice and the function of writing in *The Carpathians* returns to Frame's initial forms of language and meaning. Although the novel explores the upheaval of notions of time and space, the essential issue is how one is to maintain or develop a sense of identity within such a context, and this in turn raises the fundamental question of language and its use by the individual.

In her article 'Post-modernism or Post-colonialism? Fictive Strategies in *Living in the Maniototo* and *The Carpathians*' (*JNZL* 11.114–31), Janet Wilson links Frame's fictive strategies to post-colonialism and post-modernism. As Frame dissimulates, displaces, decentres the narrative and subjective structures, she highlights that 'the truth behind the deception that language perpetrates is discoverable only by those who are on the margins'. This technique of displacement is, according to Wilson, a central motif in post-colonial writing. Ken Bragen views Frame's writing from the standpoint of reader and psychiatrist. In 'Survival after the Cold Touch of Death: The Resurrection Theme in the Writing of Janet Frame' (*JNZL* 11.132–43) he examines the reasons why Frame has been able to transcend the pains of bereavement and to spectacularly overcome the trauma of the years she spent in mental institutions. He posits that it is in the exceptional interior strength of her imagination that was so carefully nurtured in childhood that the answer is to be found. Furthermore, Bragen maintains that Frame's success in confounding death and her subsequent renewal has structured her perception of life and given it renewed vigour. Eve Scopes develops similar ideas in 'Re-visioning *Daughter Buffalo*' (*JNZL* 11.144–51).

In her article on 'Janet Frame and *The Tempest*' (*JNZL* 11.152–71), Diane Caney explores Frame's debt to Shakespeare. In her study of the autobiographies she highlights the images of storm and sea which, for both writers, indicate the states of the mind which refuse to be subordinate to the rational. Caney sees in Prospero's exile on an island a parallel to the exile experienced by Frame in the forties in New Zealand where she in no way fitted in with the conformist society. Alison Lambert in 'Coverups and Exposure: Art and Ideology in *The Carpathians*' (*JNZL* 11.172–7) discusses the relationship between art, ideology and politics in this novel and points not only to the critical elements included in the work by the author but also to the space provided for the reader to actively engage in the production of meaning. Jennifer Lawn refers to Michel Foucault's ideas on the function of discipline in the normalizing process. In 'Docile Bodies: Normalization and the Asylum in *Owls Do Cry*' (*JNZL* 11.178–87) Lawn analyses the result of Daphne's resistance to institutional discipline and illustrates Frame's own refusal to submit to the diagnosis of madness.

Lidia Conetti's 'Janet Frame, the Little Child in Us' (*JNZL* 11.188–92) deals specifically with childhood and the complications of understanding language. Conetti has translated the autobiographies into Italian and explains the immense difficulty of rendering such plays on words as 'Is-land' and 'I-land'. In the final article of this special issue, 'What Does "Janet Frame" Mean?' (*JNZL* 11.193–205), Vanessa Finney discusses the existence of a local Frame folklore in New Zealand which has resulted in a greater popularity in New Zealand, where Frame's life took shape, for the autobiographies. Finney also observes that a measure of Janet Frame's 'greatness' is the way in which different strata of the literary population have adopted her writing and fitted it into such categories as 'women's literature', 'post-modernist literature' or 'post-colonial writing'.

Ruth Brown in 'The Rainbirds – And Other Dunedins' (*JNZL* 10.115–25 (1992)) explains that, although Janet Frame in *The Rainbirds* offers an apparently very provincial representation of Dunedin, where the artist feels ostracized by a determinedly unimaginative audience, she is, in fact, subverting her own provincialism because the reader is shown that there is absolutely no reason to accept the writer's version of the situation. Indeed 'conformity to any given formula is shown to be restrictive'. Ruth Brown's somewhat circuitous argument also underlines Frame's insistence on an apolitical spiritual deficiency supposedly present in the provincial city, a vision which reinforces the status quo, diverting the reader's attention from real solutions to the problems faced by people. Howard McNaughton's 'Fraying the Edge of an Alphabet' (*SPAN* 36.i.131–43) deals with the transformation of physical spaces into written spaces and vice versa in Janet Frame's *The Edge of the Alphabet*. For McNaughton, the structure of the novel can be seen 'as reflexive condensation in which Frame's fiction is subsumed by an anthropological metafiction bearing on colonial discourse itself'. Applying the theories of De Certeau and Kristeva, McNaughton traces the contradictory development of characterization. Toby's body is shown to be no more than a void, a mirror on to which other identities are projected; but the mirror distorts, contracts and reflects new perspectives that are difficult to verbalize. Susie O'Brien in ' "Little Ole Noo Zealand": Representations of NZ–US Relations in Janet Frame's *The Carpathians*' (*Kunapipi* 15.i.94–102) examines how the practices of writers and critics engender similar reactions to those of the voyeurism of tourism. Following a detailed analysis of the attitudes of the protagonist Mattina in *The Carpathians*, O'Brien concludes that the researcher/critic ultimately uses his material to consolidate his own 'authentic' position at home rather than explore the otherness of his subject on the other side of the Pacific.

Miriam Fuchs's excellent 'Reading towards the Indigenous South Pacific: Patricia Grace's *Potiki*, A Case Study' (*SPAN* 36.ii.566–83) uses Gérard Genette's literary theories to highlight the indigenous nature of speech and communication in Grace's apparently simple narrative. In her exhaustive examination of the varied and varying time sequences Fuchs brings out the underlying text and centralizes the character of Toko in a way that other more superficial critiques have never perceived. Such a study should convince many critics who have put aside Genette for more modern literary theories to reconsider their choice for Fuchs's article, which is devoid of jargon, clarifies the complex shadowy areas of *Potiki* and, with its illuminating qualities, invites the reader to re-read both Grace and Genette. Elisabeth Köster's 'Oral and Literacy Patterns in the Novels of Patricia Grace' (*ANZSC* 10.87–105) is a very thorough exploration of the complementarity of orality and literacy both as subject and as a means of communication in *Mutuwhenua*, *Potiki* and *Cousins*. Köster competently illustrates that Grace's accomplishment is 'to confront differences between orality and literacy, between Maori and Pakeha, between old and new [...] while celebrating the power of language to communicate alterities without replicating their exclusive oppositions'.

In contrast, Jane McRae's 'Patricia Grace and Complete Communication' (*ANZSC* 10.66–86) underlines the importance that Grace attaches to full and meaningful communication and the moral obligations that this precept raises for the writer and, in particular, for the Maori writer in bi-cultural New Zealand. McRae tends to view Grace's concept of communication in fusional terms. While this article examines in detail all forms of communication or lack of communication in Grace's writing and supplies the wide-ranging opinions of critics and philosophers, its weakness lies in its lack of argumentation which could lead to a conclusion not only of Grace's ideas but also of her methods of achieving the expression of these in her fictional works. McRae's 'The Maori Voice' (*CRNLE* 1.1–12) is an interview with Patricia Grace which was first published in Elizabeth Alley and Mark Williams (eds), *In the Same Room: Conversations with New Zealand Writers* (see *YWES* 73.688–9).

Roger Robinson's very perceptive and informative article '"The Strands of Life and Self": the Oral Prose of Patricia Grace' (*CRNLE* 1.13–27) analyses the unique quality of Grace's art of bringing Maoridom to the fore within writing intended for the English-speaking public. By developing the verbal mastery of her characters as the narrative progresses Grace 'shows how language can wrest power from the privileged, inflict discomfiture, and restore identity and purpose to the repressed'. By including skilfully inverted word order, typical of Maori oratory, Grace disturbs the unaware reader. By refusing to provide translations of Maori expressions included in her texts, she excludes the uninitiated at crucial moments of the narrative – 'The English reader suddenly loses the privilege of that language. It is a cunning stroke of disempowerment'. The reader is also excluded from the imagining of Maori rituals that Grace subtly evokes in her texts. Finally, Robinson illustrates the fact that this writer, by her inclusion of Maori names and her meticulous attention to rhythm and cadence, constructs an environment that pulsates with the indigenous life that runs through it. In short, Patricia Grace's greatest achievement is 'to adapt fiction in English to Maori forms, rather than the other way round'.

In '"Fitted to His Own Web of Music": Art as Renaming in *the bone people* (sic)' (*ANZSC* 10.106–20) Christine Hamlin explores the theory that post-colonial artists have to unname their world before they can recreate it in an art form. It is the void created by the unnaming that stimulates artistic expression which enables the artist to articulate and connect 'their private reimagining of self and place'. Hamlin examines in detail the interconnections between the three characters of *the bone people*, and by so doing throws light on the various roles of the artists that Keri Hulme puts into play: they reject absolutes, society's rigid conventions, strict polarities and accepted definitions. These sterilizing features in the world of the protagonists are to be replaced, according to Hulme, by a renewed look at society, by emotions or artistic intuition, by connection. Hulme uses the images of mirror and windows to create an area of flux and reflection between characters and places which enables them to define their past, their present and their future.

Andrew Peek's 'An Interview with Keri Hulme' (*NLitsR* 20.(Winter South 1990).1–11) concentrates on her multifarious origins. This is particularly enlightening after the many controversies over her affiliations. Hulme clearly acknowledges her multicultural origins and her firm attachment to varying aspects of each; she feels particularly close to her Scots and Maori heritages since they provide traditional tales that have been transmitted over the generations. These provide material for a writer who values people because, for Hulme, they define the time, place and circumstance of reality by their very recognition of these elements. Time is all-englobing: 'We see the past before us; Our word for the past is mua, the time's in front of you. And the word for the future is muri, time's behind you and you go backwards into the future.' In 'Grounding Post-colonial Fictions: Cultural Constituencies, Cultural Credentials and Uncanny Questions of Authority' (*SPAN* 36.i.100–12) Chris Prentice uses the examples of Wongar and Keri Hulme as illustrations in his discussion of the effects of assumed identities and adopted appurtenances to social groups on readers' attitudes to Otherness in post-colonial contexts. Both Australia and New Zealand are facing the question of bi- or multi-culturalism in a post-colonial context and the shifting borders of identity have and will cause heated arguments in both political and literary contexts. Prentice argues that it is precisely out of this uneasiness in situating the self and other, and the ensuing struggle that formulates a new 'authentic' (post)-colonial voice which 'can allow room for negotiations of identity and subjectivity in ways which acknowledge the impact of history on tradition, and tradition on history, but still hear expressions of difference for the contemporary moment'.

Witi Ihimaera: A Changing Vision by Umelo Ojinmah, is basically an adaptation of a PhD thesis which compares the works of Ihimaera and Chinua Achebe. The enterprise as such was valuable since one is often struck by the similarity of outlook of the two writers: both are or were at some time 'ancestor-worshippers' and both have had to adapt their vision to a changing world. Both have also worked within the 'culture-clash' framework. Ojinmah's book is basically about Ihimaera's changing political standpoint. It traces his evolution from the pastoral represented by *Pounamu Pounamu* through to the transitional period of *The New Net Goes Fishing*, in which the concern is with the bewilderment of the recently urbanized Maori, to the more recent radicalization of *The Matriarch* in which the author revisions history from a Maori point of view. Ojinmah also accounts for the recent more 'feminist' orientation of *The Whale Rider*, a novel in which myth and ecology merge. As a political examination of Ihimaera's fiction, the book rightly traces the changes in the author's idea of biculturalism, from what has been called by some an 'Uncle Tom' attitude to the more recent militant stance which still makes room for cohabitation with the Pakeha provided that disputes are properly settled.

Ojinmah's conception of the artist as an involved person is strongly marked by the Nigerian origins of the critic, who comes from a country where corruption and political violence have been rife for decades. For him, therefore, the writer must be the conscience of the nation. This politically correct attitude has its limits when one deals with art: his study, while detailed on the political front, seriously lacks in an examination of the artistic strategies used by the author. His arguments are substantiated by pertinent quotations from interviews, articles by the writer, and his fiction; it is regrettable, however, that the quotations are insufficiently placed within their context and that those from Ihimaera's fiction are frequently used to justify the author's personal opinions with no acknowledgement of the distancing that an artist inserts between life and fiction. After Richard Corballis and Simon Garrett's very compact and remarkably perceptive *Introducing Witi Ihimaera*, this could have been a welcome development, and it partly fulfils its promises. But, given the scope of this study, it fails to show the wealth and complexities of Ihimaera's artistry. There is still room for further studies on this fascinating novelist, who has recently rediscovered the pleasures of writing fiction after a period of doubting. Cathe Giffuni contributes another version of her 'Witi Ihimaera: Bibliography' (*NLitsR* 20.(Winter South 1990).53–63) that appeared in *ANZSC* 4. The work remains incomplete and the selection criteria mysterious; why, when she includes Richard Corballis and Simon Garrett's *Introducing Ihimaera* (1984), does she not include elements of their excellent select bibliography?

Katarina Baclinger's gender-orientated analysis in 'New Light on Mansfield's "Sun and Moon"' (*CRNLE* 1.114–25) is far from convincing; comparing the letters and journal with different aspects of this short story, Baclinger elaborates a theory that the doubling of characters and character/narrator may be explained by a gender dichotomy. Indeed, she claims that 'Mansfield begins her story with symbolism that oscillates between an obvious Freudian representation of dichotomous heterosexual gender and a hidden representation of bisexual gender'.

(c)   Poetry
Alan Loney's 'The Influence of American Poetry of Contemporary Poetic Practice in New Zealand' (*JNZL* 10.92–7) is part of a lecture given at the University of Auckland in 1986 during the 12th Australia and New Zealand American Studies Association Conference. Although not a 'practising' poet at the time, Loney indicates that his transfer from reading poetry as an inspiration to reading theory was beneficial to his writing, and that absorbing influences from elsewhere contributes to the development of creative artists. In her overview 'Playfulness and Politics: New Zealand Poetry 1987–1990' (*ANZSC* 10.121–33), Emma Neale singles out the element of gaming in the poetry she has chosen to examine. Neale has had to reduce her selection from over 60 works published in this three-year period; she nevertheless manages to briefly analyse the work of such poets as Curnow, O'Brien, Stead, Sullivan, Tuwhare and Wedde and the poetesses Hawken, French, McAlpine, McQueen and Smither, thus providing a range of approaches: Hawken is the outsider writing from New York, Wedde the self-conscious linguist, McAlpine the dedicated feminist. O'Brien chooses to join his line drawings to his writing. Tuwhare explores Maoridom and politics with great sensitivity and variety. Smither advances by repetition and variation while Wyston Curnow prefers the graphic set-out of words on a page. Vincent Sullivan is interested in combining the Maori language with English in his poems. C. K. Stead's commissioned work, *Voices*, documents the chronology of New Zealand's plural society. Finally, Kevin Ireland's *Tiberius at the Beehive* is an openly political statement urging the people of New Zealand to fulfil their civic duties. Neale concludes that, while a void in political awareness seems to exist in the public, the arts seem 'to be thoroughly engaged in debate and confrontation'.

Alan Riach argues, in 'James Baxter and the Dialect of the Tribe' (*NLitsR* 20.(Winter South 1990).12–18) that, while much has been written about this poet and his place in literary history, he seems to exert little influence on the contemporary. For Riach, this appears as an erroneous conception because, although Baxter opted out of what he conceived to be the bourgeois paths of the intellectuals to write poetry about, but also for, the people of New Zealand, this writer should be considered as more than a poet of his time; he is a man whose writing was to be shared by his contemporary readers as well as those of today.

In 'Allen Curnow, Memory, and the Avro 504K4' (*CRNLE* 1.90–102), Michael Hulse is interested in Curnow's philosophy of memory. He alludes to the changing points of view in such poems as 'The Pug-mill' where the onlooking child shifts to become the poet – it is a shift where the memory referred to as a detached reflection becomes a reliving of the experience. The memory of the past 'exists in a present tense continuum; [...] it defeats time'. This process enables the poet to closely confront and analyse memories that were and continue to be modelled by the polarities of belief and doubt or the metaphysical and empirical. This process leads to a phenomenon beyond reality where the poet transforms memory to enact a real presence that may be termed religious.

Having noted French's refusal to be categorized in spite of her obvious familiarity with feminist politics and theories, Jane Stafford in 'French Fishes: Evasions and Tensions in the Poetry of Anne French' (*CRNLE* 1.77–81) goes on to compare this poet's positioning and the techniques she employs in order to evade such classification in her writing. French exploits the innate ambiguities of her subject matter to destabilize the conventional descriptive discourse that she uses; she avoids direct involvement in the issues she discusses by her self-mocking tone and the use of an implied female observer who is other than the narrator; she structures the tension of her poems by contrasting the inner power of the subject of her lines with the 'puppeteer role' she, as author, has assumed. The discipline and control of these poems is, according to Stafford, admirable; the danger is that the self-conscious effacement may lead to the disappearance of that individual and multifarious voice of Anne French's poetry.

In a long overview (a detailed bibliography is included), 'Rob Jackaman: An Introduction to Poetry and the Poet' (*JNZL* 10.16–34), Alistair Paterson attempts to rehabilitate Jackaman, who emigrated to New Zealand to improve his literary knowledge and to learn the craft of poetry with C. K. Stead. Despite an impressive output, Jackaman still has to gain recognition in New Zealand, although he is already widely published abroad; Paterson believes that his latest longer poems are likely to give him a long-earned place in New Zealand poetry anthologies. In '"Strangled by a Bad Tradition"? The Work of Eve Langley', an article which also includes a bibliography (*JNZL* 10.55–73), Anita Segerberg deals with Langley's fiction and poetry. She argues that the factors of gender, timing and changing literary traditions in the male dominated literary scene of New Zealand in the late thirties and early forties all contributed to the demise of this Australian-born woman writer. Confusion of gender in her writing and in her private life was an attempt to escape the restrictive fields left open to the female writer. Other female writers used similar subterfuges to conceal their feminine identity in the thirties, but Langley's transvestism was finally to lead her to a psychiatric hospital. Langley's poetry suffered from the in-fighting of the dominant male poets who, seeking a national identity, rejected Georgian writing. Finally, she was a victim of the fact that, being born out of the country, she was never really integrated into the New Zealand literary scene.

This was also the case of William Hart-Smith who, according to Max Richards, introduced American modernism into both Australian and New Zealand poetry. In his article 'William Hart-Smith (1911–1990): Poet of Two Countries' (*JNZL* 10.74–91), Richards gives an account of the development of Hart-Smith's art, emphasizing his concern for the usurped brown inhabitants of the two countries, the patterns of nature and their influence on the patterns of his writing, and the gradual development of minimalism in Hart-Smith's poetry, which reduces his concerns to expressions of essence rather than epic declarations.

Michael Sharkey's 'David McKee Wright, Maorilander' (*JNZL* 10.35–55) is a biographical account which traces the poet's origins in Ireland and his life, which was divided between poetry and religion, in both Australia and New Zealand.

(d) Drama and Theatre
In 'Confronting History: The Abandonment of Mother England in Contemporary New Zealand Literature' (*NLitsR 19*.(Summer South 1990).4–13), Philip Mann

examines the current change of direction in theatre which follows the transformation of New Zealand attitudes to the mother country during the seventies. When
Great Britain chose to integrate with Europe, New Zealand realized that it would
increasingly have to face the world without the support of its former colonizer;
consequently, adherence to empire and its institutions weakened. For Maurice
Shadbolt, this distancing of New Zealand from 'home' began much earlier, at
Gallipoli, during the Second World War. His play, *Once on Chunuk Bair* (1981),
while giving an account of the taking of Chunuk Bair, illustrates how the Kiwis
were forced to be independent, for no British troops came to their aid in times of
danger, even though it was Britain's war. The 1970s were a time of marked anti-
British feelings in New Zealand, and Shadbolt's is one of the plays which
'explored the new and changing pattern of New Zealand identity'. *Shuriken*, by
Vincent O'Sullivan, is also set during the Second World War, but in the Pacific.
Here Mann examines the camaraderie among males during the difficult times
when New Zealand was fighting for the home country and receiving relatively
little thanks. The play includes passages written in both Japanese and Maori, but
skilful management shows that English audiences can be led to comprehension.
The purpose, then, is a plea for a wider appreciation of the different cultural
values in New Zealand, without which the country will not be able to shape a new
independent society. According to Philip Mann, local theatre is opening a way
towards this new ideal by revealing what are, at times, unpleasant truths to the
country.

Christopher Balme examines the recent development of Maori theatre forms
in 'Between Separation and Integration: Contemporary Maori Theatre' (*CRNLE*
1.41–8). In spite of underfunding and indifference, Maori theatre is developing a
strategy of intercultural plays which exploit traditional Maori performance forms
of *wero, karaga, powhiri, whaikorero* and *waiata*, and yet attract both Pakeha and
Maori audiences. The Marae-theatre is distinct in that it involves genuine Maori
celebration rather than the mere representation of this. Roma Potiki has been
greatly involved in the development of what she calls an integrated theatre, which
brings together traditional performance, folkloristic representations and Western
theatre. Balme concludes that intercultural theatre will come of age when the
signs of theatre language forfeit neither artistic nor cultural integrity. In '"It is
Political if it can be Passed on": An Interview with Roma Potiki' (*CRNLE* 1.35–
40) Balme explores the origins of the 'recent' increased popularity of Maori
theatre. For Roma Potiki the promotion of this theatre must take the form of
education, in order to accustom people to it. She also believes that, after such a
long period of Pakeha domination, bicultural enterprises will have to be undertaken by the Maori in order to appropriate such a theatre. In the meantime,
Marae-theatre will encourage Maori participation because the Marae has remained a place of community activity.

2.   The South Pacific

Paul Sharrad is the editor of *Readings in Pacific Literature* (New Literatures
Research Centre, University of Wollongong) in which he has collected the
essential early articles on Pacific literature that were published in various journals between 1946 and 1985, with the exception of his own article on Epeli
Hau'ofa written especially to complete this collection. In 'Telling Tales on Tiko:

Hau'ofa's Satirical Art' (128–35), Sharrad parallels the satirical trend in Hau'ofa with Albert Wendt's wry self-deprecating humour, as they consider the conflictual environment of indigenous traditions and western involvement that surrounds them; both are 'suspended between opposing worlds, belonging to both and neither at the same time'. It is but one short step to be able to bring to light the shortcomings of each society, and this Hau'ofa does with burlesque and great finesse. By lifting images from across the Pacific islands, Hau'ofa constructs an allegory which cuts across Pacific society and simultaneously represents each constituent of that society. The names used in the novels often have double meanings which embellish the satire: Sharrad points out that the butt of Hau'ofa's satire is not the church itself but rather the travesty of religion that has insidiously slid into place. Similarly, he reveals that the traditional taboo on washing one's dirty laundry in public in order to maintain the myth of idyllic peace can deteriorate into complacent dissembling. Hau'ofa, however, does not lack affection for his world, and constantly highlights the social problems of overpopulation, economic dependency and the remains of colonial domination. According to Sharrad, any attempt for the Pacific communities to unite as the political and economic force that Hau'ofa envisages will have 'to be accompanied by realistic self-appraisal, or the old outside myths of the Pacific will merely be replaced by equally delusory and damaging inside ones'.

Each article of *Readings in Pacific Literature* is preceded by its publication history and a brief introduction to the author. Included in this book are topics on Polynesian literature by Robert Dean Frisbie, Albert Wendt and Ken Arvidson. Chris Tiffin puts forward a comparative study of Stow, Ihimaera and Wendt. Besides an assessment of Albert Wendt by Roger Robinson, a paper by Bernard Gadd on Hone Tuwhare, and another by Nigel Krauth on Papua New Guinea poetry, there are also essays by Bill McGaw on Russell Soaba, by Rachel Nunns on Patricia Grace, by Francis Devlin-Glass on Vincent Eri, by Carmel Gaffney on Keri Hulme and by Richard Corballis on Witi Ihimaera. Peggy Fairbairn-Dunlop explores the close connections between Samoan story-telling and written fiction. Julian Maka'a and Stephen Oxenham also examine writing in the Solomons. Richard Hamasaki discusses the emergence of Hawaiian poetry. Vijay Mishra traces the influence of the Girmit ideology on Indo-Fijian writing and Ron Crocombe gives a detailed analysis of book distribution in the Pacific. This is a very welcome re-edition and will form a solid basis for any who wish to be informed about Pacific studies.

In 'A History of Ignorance' (*NLitsR* 20.(Winter South 1990).19–31), Ken Goodwin first looks at the various definitions that have been attributed to 'history'. He then goes on to examine the effects of colonial history and decolonization in the South Pacific. Taking literary examples from Ihimaera, Wendt, the Djanggawul Song Cycle, Soaba and Subramani, to mention but a few, Goodwin traces history through the myths of origin, the disruption of colonization (which has at times been overestimated), to the aftermath of decolonization when the initial dream of freedom is betrayed by in-fighting for the reins of power. Gilian Gorle, in 'Writing in English: Freedom or Frustration? Some Views from Papua New Guinea' (*Kunapipi* 15.ii.126–32), after a general overview of the politics of the three official languages in the country, gives the points of view of seven local writers whom she has interviewed. The older writers such as John Kasaipwalova, Russell Soaba and William Takaku consider the choice of language as a continuation of colonialism, whereas the younger Adam Delaney,

Louiaya Kouza or Steven Winduo feel that English is their natural language, while still believing in the importance of vernaculars. John Kasaipwalova and Nora Brash have both experimented with the combination of vernacular and English in their works. Gorle believes these new resonances forecast new directions in the literature of Papua New Guinea.

In a fairly descriptive and introductory essay, 'Epeli Hau'ofa's Polynesian Human Comedy' (*NLitsR* 20.(Winter South 1990).32–40) J. S. Ryan analyses *Tales of the Tikongs* and *Kisses in the Nederends* to illustrate the author's happy use of satire and irony to challenge the pretences and corruption present in well-meaning development aids. The anger behind such an outburst does not, however, detract from the infinitely compassionate prose of Hau'ofa, which seeks to 'revolutionize human relations the world over'. Hau'ofa himself, in 'The Writer as Outsider' (*NLitsR* 20.(Winter South 1990).41–52), attempts to give a very personal account of his own life, explaining that he was the eternal adolescent until the age of 40, when he decided to conform to the Establishment. This turned out to be impossible because of his innate rootlessness, his distaste for power politics, his 'knack for detecting absurdity in (serious) situations', and a self-declared agnosticism. In view of his education he is respected and even considered an expert in all fields, but he prefers to remain an outsider in order to be free to protest. With regard to colonialism he says: 'To me the most unfortunate things that colonialism, Christianity and international capitalism have done to the Pacific islands have been, first, the transformation of hitherto self-sufficient, proudly independent people into wards of rich and powerful countries; and, secondly, as a consequence of forced dependence, the forcing of people to compromise their integrity and to use all manner of trickery in order to survive in an economic and political world over which they have no meaningful control.' Finally, he admits that he prefers writing fiction because it affords him freedom and enjoyment to play with situations and words without the straitjacket of having to adhere to a certain truth, and states that this freedom has enabled him to translate oral cadences into his works of fiction.

Books Reviewed

Ackland, Michael, ed. *The Penguin Book of 19th Century Australian Literature*. PenguinA. pp. 369. pb A$19.95. ISBN 0 140 15703 4.

——, ed. *Henry Kendall: Poetry, Prose and Selected Correspondence*. UQP Australian Authors. pp. 243. pb A$19.95. ISBN 0 702 22308 5.

——, ed. *A Sydney Sovereign*. A&R Imprint Classics. pp. 146. pb A$16.95. ISBN 0 207 18121 7.

Ballstadt, Carl, Elizabeth Hopkins, and Michael Peterman, eds. *Letters of Love and Duty*. UTorP. pp. 360. hb $35. ISBN 0 802 05708 X.

Barbour, Douglas. *Michael Ondaatje*. TWAS. Macmillan. pp. 170. $22.95. ISBN 0 805 78290 7.

Bayard, Caroline, ed. *100 Years of Critical Solitudes: Canadian and Québécois Criticism from the 1880s to the 1980s*. ECW. pp. 356. $25. ISBN 1 550 22117 5.

Beasley, Jack. *A Gallop of Fire: Katherine Susannah Prichard: On Guard for Humanity: A Study of Creative Personality*. Wedgetail. pp. 187. pb A$19.95. ISBN 0 958 91382 X.

Bedson, Jack, and Julian Croft, eds. *The Campbell Howard Annotated Index of Australian Plays* 1920–1955. CALLS. pp. 425. pb A$20. ISBN 1 863 89055 6.

Benitez-Rojo, Antonio. *The Repeating Island: The Caribbean and the Postmodern Perspective*. DukeUP (1992). pp. 328. £15.95. ISBN 0 822 31221 2.

Bennett, Bruce, Peter Cowan, Denis Haskell, and Susan Miller, eds. *Westerly Looks to Asia: A Selection from* Westerly *1956–1992*. The Indian Ocean Centre for Peace Studies Monograph No. 6. pp. 248. pb A$25. ISBN 1 863 42193 9.

Bevan, Ian [Ian Archibald Winchcombe]. *The Story of the Theatre Royal*. Currency. pp. 266. A$45. ISBN 0 868 19375 5.

Bharucha, Rustom. *Theatre and the World: Performance and the Politics of Culture*. Routledge. pp. 272. hb £35.00, pb £12.99. ISBN 0 415 09215 9, 0 415 09216 7.

Branch, William, ed. *Crosswinds: An Anthology of Black Dramatists in the Diaspora*. Blacks in the Diaspora. IndUP. pp. 384. $39.95. ISBN 0 253 20778 9.

Brathwaite, Kamau. *Roots*. UMichP. pp. 300. hb $34.50, pb $14.95. ISBN 0 472 09544 7, 0 472 06544 0.

Brooks Bouson, J. *Brutal Choreographies: Oppositional Strategies and Narrative Design in the Novels of Margaret Atwood*. UMassP. pp. 316. hb $27.50. ISBN 0 870 23845 0.

Brown, Stewart, and Ian McDonald, eds. *Caribbean Poetry*. Caribbean Writers. Heinemann (1992). pp. 236. £6.99. ISBN 0 435 98817 4.

Brydon, Diana, and Helen Tiffin, *Decolonising Fictions*. Dangaroo. pp. 200. £14.95, A$29.95. ISBN 1 871 04985 7.

Buhle, Paul, and Paget Henry, eds. *C. L. R. James's Caribbean*. DukeUP (1992). pp. 304. hb $48, pb $18.95. ISBN 0 822 31231 X, 0 822 31244 1.

Butterss, Philip, and Elizabeth Webby, eds. *The Penguin Book of Australian Ballads*. PenguinA. pp. 306. pb A$17.95. ISBN 0 140 42371 0.

Canadian Writers and Their Works. Vol. 8: Poetry. ECW. pp. 412. $45. ISBN 1 550 22063 2.

Canadian Writers and Their Works. Vol. 10: Poetry. ECW. pp. 395. $45. ISBN 0 550 22069 1.

Capp, Fiona. *Writers Defiled*. PenguinA/McPheeG. pp. 239. pb A$19.95. ISBN 0 869 14338 7.

Chamberlin, J. Edward. *Come Back To Me My Language: Poetry and the West Indies*. UIllP. pp. 328. hb $44.95, pb $15.95. ISBN 0 252 01973 3, 0 252 06297 3.

Coldwall, Joan, ed. *The Tightrope Walker: Autobiographic Writings of Anne Wilkinson*. UTorP. pp. 288. $35. ISBN 0 802 05745 4.

Dance, Daryl Cumber. *New World Adams: Conversations with Contemporary West Indian Writers*. Peepal Tree (1992). pp. 260. £12.95. ISBN 0 948 83308 4.

Davey, Gwenda, and Graham Seal, eds. *The Oxford Companion to Australian Folklore*. OUPAus. pp. 381. A$49.95. ISBN 0 19 553857 8.

Davitt, Ellen. *Force and Fraud: A Tale of the Bush* (1865). Mulini Press. pp. 143. pb A$29.95. ISBN 0 094 991036 8.

Dessaix, Robert, ed. *Australian Gay and Lesbian Writing: An Anthology*. OUPAus. pp. 383. A$39.93. ISBN 0 19 553457 3.

Douglas, Stan, ed. *Vancouver Anthology: The Institutional Politics of Art*. Talonbooks. pp. 299. pb $25.95. ISBN 0 889 22293 2.

Drayton, Richard, and Andaiye, eds. *Conversations: George Lamming; Essays, Addresses and Interviews 1953–1990*. Karia (1992). pp. 304. hb £28.95, pb £15.95. ISBN 1 854 65012 2, 0 946 91888 0.

Durix, Jean-Pierre and Carole. *An Introduction to the New Literatures in English.* Longman. pp. 205. pb. FF100. ISBN 2 866 44210 5.

Emberley, Julia V. *Thresholds of Difference: Feminist Critique, Native Women's Writings, Postcolonial Theory.* UTorP. pp. 202. pb $18.95. ISBN 0 802 07729 3.

Epperley, Elizabeth Rollins. *The Fragrance of Sweet-grass: L. M. Montgomery's Heroines and the Pursuit of Romance.* UTorP. pp. 336. $35.00. ISBN 0 802 05999 6.

Fee, Margery, ed. *Silence Made Visible: Howard O'Hagan and Tay John.* ECW. pp. 160. $25. ISBN 1 550 22167 1.

Ferguson, Moira. *Colonialism and Gender Relations from Mary Wollstonecraft to Jamaica Kincaid: East Caribbean Connections.* ColUP. £11. ISBN 0 231 08223 1.

Ferres, Kay, ed. *The Time to Write: Australian Women Writers 1890–1930.* PenguinA. pp. 280. pb A$17.95. ISBN 0 140 13917 6.

Fischer, Gerhard, ed. *The Mudrooroo/Müller Project: A Theatrical Casebook.* UNSW Press. pp. 186. pb A$24.95. ISBN 0 868 40237 0.

Gelder, Ken. *Atomic Fiction: The Novels of David Ireland.* UQP Studies in Australian Literature. pp. 125. pb A$19.95. ISBN 0 702 22507 X.

George, Kadija, ed. *Six Plays by Black and Asian Women Writers.* Plays by Women. AMP. pp. 227. pb £7.50. ISBN 0 231 08223 1.

Gikandi, Simon. *Writing in Limbo: Modernism and Caribbean Literature.* CornUP (1992). pp. 272. $38.95. ISBN 0 8014 2575 1.

Gleeson, James. *Selected Poems: Poems 1938–42.* A&R. pp. 75. A$14.95. ISBN 0 207 17975 1.

Grace, Sherrill, ed. *Swinging in the Maelstrom: New Perspectives on Malcolm Lowry.* McG-QUP. $55. ISBN 0 773 50862 7.

Greet, Annie, Syd Harrex, and Susan Hosking, eds. *Raj Nostalgia: Some Literary and Critical Implications.* CRNLE (1992). pp. 153. pb A$15. ISBN 0 725 80523 4.

Griffiths, Gareth. *John Romeril.* Rodopi Australian Playwrights. pp. 228. pb Hfl.75; US$44. ISBN 905 183524 8.

Groeden, Michael, and Martin Kreiswirth, eds. *The Johns Hopkins Guide to Literary Theory and Criticism.* JHUP. $65. ISBN 0 801 84560 2.

Hall, Richard, ed. *Banjo Paterson: His Poetry and Prose.* A&UA. pp. 288. pb A$14.95. ISBN 1 863 73369 8.

Hamner, Robert, ed. *Critical Perspectives on Derek Walcott.* TWAS. Macmillan. pp. 224. $22.95.

Heyward, Michael. *The Ern Malley Affair.* UQP. pp. 284. A$32.95. ISBN 0 702 22562 2.

Hutcheon, Linda, ed. *Double-Talking: Essays on Verbal and Visual Ironies in Contemporary Canadian Art and Literature.* ECW. pp. 160. hb $25.00. ISBN 1 550 22139 6.

Indyk, Ivor. *David Malouf.* OUP Australian Writers. pp. 115. pb A$17.95. ISBN 0 19 553321 6.

Joseph, Margaret Paul. *Caliban in Exile: The Outsider in Caribbean Fiction.* Greenwood (1992). pp. 160. £38.75. ISBN 0 313 28107 6.

Julien, Eileen. *African Novels and the Question of Orality.* IndUP (1992). pp. 180. A$20.00. ISBN 0 253 33101 3.

Jurgensen, Manfred, ed. *Queensland: Words and All.* Outrider/Phoenix Publications. pp. 430. pb A$20. ISBN 0 949 78020 0.

Kadar, Marlene, ed. *Essays on Life Writing: From Genre to Critical Practice.* UTorP Theory/Culture. pp. 288. $50. ISBN 0 802 02741 5.

Keith, W. F. *Literary Images of Ontario.* UTorP Ontario Historical Studies. pp. 288. $45. ISBN 0 802 03470 5.

Kellman, Anthony, ed. *Crossing Water: Contemporary Poetry of the English-Speaking Caribbean.* Greenfield Review Press (1992). pb 10.99. ISBN 0 912 67885 2.

King, Bruce. *V. S. Naipaul.* Modern Novelists Series. Macmillan. pp. 192. £35. ISBN 0 333 51700 8.

——, ed. *Post-Colonial English Drama: Commonwealth Drama Since 1960.* Macmillan. pp. 284. £47.50. ISBN 0 333 53417 4.

Kingsley, Henry. *The Recollections of Geoffry Hamlyn* (1859). A&R Imprint Classics. pp. 474. pb A$17.95. ISBN 0 207 17953 0.

Kostash, Myrna. *Bloodlines: A Journey into Eastern Europe.* D&M. pp. 256. $26.95. ISBN 1 550 54110 2.

Kröller, Eva-Marie. *George Bowering: Bright Circles of Colour.* Talonbooks. pp. 144. pb $11.95. ISBN 0 889 22306 8.

Kuester, Martin. *Framing Truths: Parodic Structures in Contemporary English-Canadian Historical Novels.* UTP Theory/Culture. pp. 256. $50. ISBN 0 802 02818 7.

Lang, John. *Lucy Cooper: An Australian Tale,* ed. Victor Crittenden. Mulini. pp. 65. A$60. ISBN 0 949 91023 6.

Laurence, Margaret. *A Tree for Poverty: Somali Poetry and Prose.* ECW and McMaster University Library Press. pp.145. np. ISBN 1 550 022177 5.

Lees, Stella, and Pam Macintyre, eds. *The Oxford Companion to Australian Children's Literature.* OUP. pp. 485. A$49.95. ISBN 0 19 553284 8.

Lennox, John, and Janet M. Paterson, eds. *Challenges, Projects, Texts: Canadian Editing.* AMS Conference on Editorial Problems. pp. 120. $29.50. ISBN 0 404 63675 6.

Lindfors, Bernth, and Sander, Reinhard, eds. *Twentieth Century Caribbean and Black African Writers* vol. 117 (1992), vol. 125 (1993). Bruccoli Clark Layman/Gale. pp. 406. $128. ISBN 0 810 37594 X.

Litt, Paul. *The Muses, the Masses and the Massey Commission.* UTorP. pp. 336. pb $19.95. ISBN 0 802 06932 0.

Lord, Mary. *Hal Porter: Man of Many Parts.* RandomH Australia. pp. 330. A$39.95. ISBN 0 091 82794 9.

McDougall, Russell. *Henry Kendall: The Muse of Australia.* CALLS. pp. 443. pb A$29.50. ISBN 1 863 89005 X.

McLaren, John. *New Pacific Literatures: Culture and Environment in the European Pacific.* Garland. pp. 384. US$62. ISBN 0 815 30496 X.

McLeod, A. L., ed. *Claude McKay: Centennial Studies.* Sterling (1992). pp.192. £17.95. ISBN 81 207 1403 2.

Mack, Louise. *The World Is Round* (1896). A&R Imprint Classics. pp. 93. A$14.95. ISBN 0 207 18016 4.

Magarey, Susan, Sue Rowley, and Susan Sheridan, eds. *Debutante Nation: Feminism Contests the 1890s.* A&UA. pp. 267. pb A$22.95. ISBN 1 863 73296 9.

Makaryk, Irena R., ed. *The Encyclopedia of Contemporary Literary Theory.* UTorP. pp. 576. $150. ISBN 0 802 05914 7.

'Malley, Ern'. *Collected Poems*. intro. Albert Tucker. A&R. pp. 68. pb A$14.95. ISBN 0 207 17977 8.

Marathe, Sudhakar, Mohan Ramanan, and Robert Bellarmine, eds. *Provocations: The Teaching of English Literature in India*. Sangam. pp. 246. pb £15.95. ISBN 0 863 11445 8.

Marshall, Tom. *Multiple Exposures, Promised Lands: Essays on Canadian Poetry and Fiction*. Quarry. pp. 197. pb $18.95. ISBN 1 550 82047 8.

Mead, Philip, and Marion Campbell, *Shakespeare's Books: Contemporary Cultural Politics and the Persistence of Empire*. Department of English, UMel. pp. 221. pb A$10. ISBN 0 732 50514 3.

Mills, Carol, and June Dietrich, eds. *Melbourne Review Index: 1876–1885*. Centre for Information Studies, Charles Sturt University. pp. 37. pb A$25. ISBN 0 949 06021 6.

Murray, John. *The Islands and the Sea. Five Hundred Years of Nature Writing From the Caribbean*. OUP (1992). pp. 329. £15. ISBN 0 19 506677 4.

Nelson, Emmanuel S., ed. *Reworlding: The Literature of the Indian Diaspora*. Greenwood (1992). pp. 184. hb $45. ISBN 0 313 27794 X.

New, William H., ed. *Inside the Poem*. OUP. pp. 288. pb $22. ISBN 0 19 540925 6.

Niechoda, Irene. *A Sourcery for Books 1 and 2 of bp nichol's The Martyrology*. ECW. pp. 214. pb $25. ISBN 1 550 22102 7.

Nixon, Rob. *London Calling: V. S. Naipaul, Postcolonial Mandarin*. OUP (1992). pp. 256. £27.50. ISBN 0 19 506717 7.

Nourbese Philips, M. *Frontiers: Essays and Writings on Racism and Culture 1984–1992*. Mercury. pp. 286. ISBN 0 920 54490 8.

O'Callaghan, Evelyn. *Woman Version: Theoretical Approaches to West Indian Fiction By Women*. Macmillan. pp. 144. £13.95. ISBN 0 333 57837 6.

Ojinmah, Umelo. *Witi Ihimaera: A Changing Vision*. UOtagoP Te Whenua. pp. 145. pb. ISBN 0 908 56957 2.

Okpewho, Isidore. *African Oral Literature: Backgrounds, Character, and Continuity*. IndUP (1992). pp. 392. hb $37.99, pb $16.50. ISBN 0 253 34167 1, 0 253 20710 X.

Ommundsen, Wenche. *Metafictions?* UMelb Interpretations series. pp. 117. pb A$19.95. ISBN 0 522 84524 X.

Ottley, Rudolph. *Women in Calypso*, Part I. Arima (1992). np. ISBN 976 8136 24 3.

Owomoyela, Oyekan, ed. *A History of Twentieth-Century African Literatures*. UNebP. pp. 411. hb $52.50, pb $21. ISBN 0 803 28604 X.

Paravisini-Gebert, Lizabeth, and Olga Torres-Seda. *Caribbean Women Novelists: An Annotated Critical Bibliography*. Bibliographies and Indexes in World Literature. Greenwood. pp. 442. £62.95. ISBN 0 313 28342 7.

Pierce, Peter, eds. *The Oxford Literary Guide to Australia* (2nd edn). OUPAus. pp. 501. pb A$29.95. ISBN 0 19 553447 6.

Praed, Rosa. *The Bond of Wedlock* (1889). Mulini. pp. 114. pb A$29.95. ISBN 0 949 91038 4.

Reckwitz, Erhard, Lucia Vennarini, and Cornelia Wegener, eds. *The African Past and Contemporary Culture*. Blaue Eule. pp. 237. pb DM35. ISBN 3 892 06489 X.

Riach, Alan, and Mark Williams, eds. *The Radical Imagination: Lectures and Talks by Wilson Harris*. ULiège (1992). np. ISBN 2 872 33005 4.

Roderick, Colin. *Banjo Paterson: Poet by Accident*. A&UA. pp. 263. A$39.95. ISBN 1 863 73292 6.

Roe, Jill, ed. *My Congenials: Miles Franklin and Friends in Letters: Vol. I: 1879–1938*. A&R in association with the State Library of NSW. pp. 384. pb A$19.95. ISBN 0 207 16925 X.

——, ed. *My Congenials: Miles Franklin and Friends in Letters: Vol. II: 1939–1954*. A&R in association with the State Library of NSW. pp. 396. pb A$19.95. ISBN 0 207 17860 7.

Rohlehr, Gordon. *My Strangled City, and Other Essays*. Longman Caribbean (1992). np. ISBN 9 766 31018.

——. *The Shape of That Hurt, and Other Essays*. Longman Caribbean (1992). ISBN 9 766 3101 9.

Rossiter, Richard, and Lyn Jacobs, eds. *Reading Tim Winton*. A&R Imprint. pp. 97. pb A$14.95. ISBN 0 207 182191.

Rowley, Hazel. *Christina Stead: A Biography*. WHA. pp. 646. A$49.95. ISBN 0 855 61384 X.

Rutherford, Anna, ed. *From Commonwealth to Post-Colonial*. Dangaroo (1992). pp. 472. £14.95. ISBN 1 871 04942 3.

Said, Edward W. *Culture and Imperialism*. C&W. pp. 444. £20.00. ISBN 0 701 1 3808 4.

Salusinszky, Imre. *Gerald Murnane*. OUPAus Australian Writers. pp. 109. pb A$18.95. ISBN 0 19 553422 0.

——. *Gerald Murnane: An Annotated Bibliography*. Footprint. pp. 52. A$10.50. ISBN 1 862 72419 9.

Salzman, Paul. *Helplessly Tangled in Female Arms and Legs: Elizabeth Jolley's Fiction*. UQP Studies in Australian Literature. pp. 99. pb A$12.95. ISBN 0 702 22498 7.

Sankaran, Chitra. *The Myth Connection: The Use of Hindu Mythology in Some Novels of Raja Rao and R. K. Narayan*. Allied Publishers. pp. 260. Rs. 200. No ISBN.

Saunders, Ian. *Open Texts, Partial Maps: A Literary Theory Handbook*. CSAL. pp. 114. pb A$10. ISBN 0 864 22238 6.

Saxby, H. M. *The Proof of the Puddin': Australian Children's Literature 1970–1990*. Ashton Scholastic. pp. 769. pb A$29.95. ISBN 0 868 96605 3.

Scherf, Kathleen, ed. *The Collected Poetry of Malcolm Lowry*. UBCP. pp. 418. $60. ISBN 0774 80362 2.

Schulz, Gerhard. *The Languages of Australia*. Australian Academy of the Humanities. Occasional Papers No 14. pp. 166. A$9.95. ISBN 0 909 89727 1.

Sharrad, Paul, ed. *Readings in Pacific Literature*. New Literatures Research Centre, University of Wollongong. pp. 210. pb. ISBN 0 86418270 8.

Shevtsova, Maria. *Theatre and Cultural Interaction*. SASSC. pp. 221. pb A$25. ISBN 0 949 40508 6.

Shoemaker, Adam. *Mudrooroo: A Critical Study*. A&R Imprint Critical Studies. pp. 181. pb A$12.95. ISBN 0 207 17976 X.

Simes, Gary. *A Dictionary of Australian Underworld Slang*. OUPAus. pp. 225. A$39.95. ISBN 0 19 553499 9.

Simpson-Housley, Paul, and Glen Norcliff. *A Few Acres of Snow: Literary and Artistic Images of Canada*. pp. 277. hb $29.95. ISBN 1 550 02157 5.

Smith, Bernard. *Noel Counihan: Artist and Revolutionary*. OUPAus. pp. 568. A$59.95. ISBN 0 19 553538 1.

Smythe, Karen. *Figuring Grief: Gallant, Munro, and the Poetics of Elegy*. McG-QUP/UTorP. pp. 216. hb $39.95. ISBN 0 773 50939 9.

Spivak, Gayatri Chakravorty. *Outside in the Teaching Machine.* Routledge. pp. 335. hb £35, pb £12.99. ISBN 0 415 90488 9, 0 415 90489 7.

Strauss, Jennifer, ed. *The Oxford Book of Australian Love Poems.* OUPAus. pp. 294. A$39.95. ISBN 0 19 553297 X.

Stubbs, Andrew. *Myth Origins Magic: The Story of Form in Eli Mandel's Writing.* Turnstone. pp. 228. $16.95. ISBN 0 888 01170 9.

Sugars, Cynthia. *The Letters of Conrad Aiken and Malcolm Lowry 1929–1954.* ECW. pp. 350. $25. ISBN 1 550 22168 X.

Suleri, Sara. *The Rhetoric of English India.* UChicP (1992). pp. 230. $8.75. ISBN 0 226 77983 1.

Sumner, John. *Recollections at Play: A Life in Australian Theatre.* UMel. pp. 398. pb A$29.95. ISBN 0 522 84494 4.

Sunder Rajan, Rajeswari. *Real and Imagined Women: Gender, Culture and Postcolonialism.* Routledge. pp. 153. hb £35, pb £10.99. ISBN 0 415 08503 9, 0 415 08504 7.

Tait, Peta. *Original Women's Theatre: The Melbourne Women's Theatre Group 1974–77.* Artmoves. pp. 94. pb A$15. ISBN 0 646 13242 3.

Tallman, Warren. *In the Midst: Writings 1962–1992.* Talonbooks. pp. 320. $10.95. ISBN 0 889 22308 4.

Terada, Rei. *Derek Walcott's Poetry: American Mimicry.* NortheasternU (1992). pp. 224. $35. ISBN 1 55553 126 1.

Tharu, Susie, and K. Lalita, eds. *Women Writing in India: 600 B.C. to the Present: Volume II: The Twentieth Century.* Pandora. pp. 641. pb £16.99. ISBN 0 044 40874 9.

Tillery, Tyrone. *Claude McKay: A Black Poet's Struggle for Identity.* UMassP (1991). pp. 224. hb £22.95, pb £13.50. ISBN 0 870 23762 4, 0 870 23924 4.

Todd, Loreto. *Derek Walcott: Selected Poems.* Longman. np. ISBN 0 582 21536 6.

Tötösy de Zepetnek, Steven. *The Social Dimensions of Fiction: On the Rhetoric and Function of Prefacing Novels in the Nineteenth-Century Canadas.* Vieweg. pp. 188. ISBN 3 528 07335 7.

Tranter, John, ed. *Martin Johnston: Selected Poems and Prose.* UQP Australian Authors. pp. 320. pb A$22.95. ISBN 0 702 22521 5.

Walcott, Derek. *The Antilles: Fragments of Epic Memory.* Faber. $7. ISBN 0 571 17080 3.

Walmsley, Anne. *The Caribbean Artists Movement 1966–1972.* NBB (1992). pp. 376. hb £35, pb £15.95. ISBN 1 873 20101 X, 0 873 20206 0.

Walsh, Kay, and Hooton, Joy. *Australian Autobiographical Narratives: An Annotated Bibliography: Volume 1: to 1850.* Australian Scholarly Editions Centre ADFA and National Library of Australia. pp. 178. pb A$29.95. ISBN 0 642 10599 5.

Webb, Barbara. *Myth and History in Caribbean Fiction.* UMassP (1992). pp. 200. £22.50. ISBN 0 870 23784 5.

Webby, Elizabeth. *Modern Australian Plays,* 2nd edn. OUPAus Horizon Studies in Literature. pp. 85. pb A$9.95. ISBN 0 424 00199 3.

Wilding, Michael. *The Radical Tradition: Lawson, Furphy, Stead.* James CookU Foundation for Australian Literary Studies. pp. 82. pb A$10.50. ISBN 0 864 43459 6.

Williams, Mark. *Patrick White.* Macmillan Modern Novelists. pp. 185. pb £9.50. ISBN 0 333 51715 6.

Williams, Patrick, and Laura Chrisman, eds. *Colonial Discourse and Post-Colonial Theory: A Reader*. HW. pp. 570. hb £50, pb £13.95. ISBN 0 745 01490 9, 0 745 01491 7.

Woodcock, George. *Introduction to Canadian Poetry*. ECW. pp. 174. ISBN 1 550 22140 X.

Woolfe, Sue, and Kate Grenville. *Making Stories: How Ten Australian Novels Were Written*. A&UAus. pp. 293. pb A$19.95. ISBN 1 863 73316 7.

Wright, Derek. *Wole Soyinka Revisited*. TWAS. Twayne. pp. 220. $35. ISBN 0 805 78279 6.

Wyman, Max, ed. *Vancouver Forum I: Old Powers–New Forces*. D&M. pp. 207. pb $18.95. ISBN 1 550 54033 5.

Wynn, Graeme, and Timothy Oke, eds. *Vancouver and Its Regions*. UBCP. pp. 332. $45.00. ISBN 0 774 80407 6.

Index I. Critics

Authors such as Salman Rushdie and David Lodge, who are both authors of criticism and subjects of discussion, are listed in whichever index is appropriate for each reference.

Index II. Authors and Subjects Treated

Notes

1. Material which has not been seen by contributors is not indexed.

2. Authors such as Salman Rushdie and David Lodge, who are both authors of criticism and subjects of discussion, are listed in whichever index is appropriate for each reference.

3. Author entries have subdivisions listed in the following order:

   (a) author's relationship with other authors;
   (b) author's relationship with other subjects;
   (c) author's characteristics;
   (d) author's works (listed alphabetically).

4. A page reference in **bold** represents the main entry for that particular subject.